ATHLE 2021

THE INTERNATIONAL TRACK AND FIELD ANNUAL

BY PETER MATTHEWS

ASSOCIATION OF TRACK & FIELD STATISTICIANS

Published by the Association of Track and Field Statisticians (ATFS)

Copyright: ATFS 2021

ATFS
PO Box 4288
Napa CA 94558 USA

e-mail: publications@atfs.org
Website: www.atfs.org/

All rights reserved. No part of this publication may be reproduced or transmitted in any form or by any means, including photocopying and recording, without written permission of the publisher. Such written permission must also be obtained before any part of the publication is stored in any retrieval system of any nature.

This publication incorporates the 2021 ATFS Annual.

ISBN 978-1-7350028-1-1

Cover photograph: Armand Duplantis (SWE) on his actual 6.18 world record vault, at Glasgow on 15 February 2020, provided by World Athletics/Ian MacNicol, Getty Images

Cover design: Stuart Mazdon, ATFS

CONTENTS

Introduction	4
Abbreviations	5
ATFS & Web Sites	8

Review of 2020 by Peter Matthews

2020 the Coronavirus Year, Shoes and Wavelight technology	10
Diary of the Year	11
Athletes of the year – Men (20), Women (27), Juniors (33)	20
Cross-country	34
Road race review by Ken Nakamura	35
Marathon review by Ken Nakamura	36
Ultramarathon review by Andy Milroy	38

Major Championships 2020	39
Diamond League	40

Major international events 2021-2025	41
Rule Changes	42
Drugs bans	43
Corrections to Athletics 2020 (year lists 2019) - and earlier years	44
Obituary	46
Reference Books	66

National champions 2020 and biographies of leading athletes	69

Introduction to World lists and indexes	169
Records	
World and Continental records – men (women 174)	171
World bests - non-standard events	182
World long distance bests	183
World Indoor Records	184
World Veterans/Masters records	186
World and Continental Records set in 2020 & Jan-Mar 2021	189

European Indoor Championships 2021	191

All-time Lists

Men	192
Women	229
Junior men	264
Junior women	270

2020 World Lists

Men	276
Women	326
Men's Index	374
Women's Index	397

2021 World Indoor lists	416

Miscellany

Retirements announced & Transfer of national allegiance	19
Athletics International	19
Tokyo Olympic Qualification	35
Women's name changes & Marriages of athletes in 2020	45
Late amendments	373

INTRODUCTION

THE PAST YEAR has been like no other. I wrote in my Introduction to last year's Annual that the spread of the coronavirus Covid-19 had already meant that many major events had been cancelled or postponed and "it is likely that for at least some months to come the immediate prospects are for considerable further disruption to sporting events". So it proved and indeed few could have predicted just how much the world of sport would he affected and indeed continues to be. Nonetheless, although many, if not most, athletes were affected by the closing of facilities for training, regulations against handling equipment and difficulties with travel, from late summer there was a surprising amount of competition, especially in Central Europe and Japan and we even had a World Championships – that of the Half Marathon in Poland. Athletics fans have, of course, had to settle for limited permitted spectator numbers and most events going without the opportunity to watch competitions.

So this Annual includes most of the usual features. The Major Championships section was reduced from 31 pages in ATHLETICS 2020 to 2 this time, and the year lists and indexes of these are substantially reduced, but while I maintained the same cut-off levels as in 2018-19, there was still enough for 99 pages of 2020 Lists (170 for 2019) and 42 pages for the index (69 previously). Although many athletes did not compete at all in the outdoor season (most notably the loss of the usual powerhouse US Collegiate campaign), others, while having fewer competitions than usual, still posted a qualifying performance. We even had one event that had record standards in depth as 230 men beat 28:30 for 10,000m on the track (over half of them from Japan!). I write on page 10 about the new generation of shoes that have had considerable effect on distance running standards – as is already clear and as we will no doubt see in years to come.

Many nations cancelled their national championships and this has meant that my National Championships and Biographies section is reduced from 130 to 110 pages. I should note here that it was even more difficult than usual to select the some 765 athletes that I include here. While I have added up-and-coming stars of 2020 and 2021, there must be some uncertainty of some who have not competed since 2019. My annual event-by-event review of Athletes of the Year is maintained in the usual format, although I have in several cases ranked fewer than ten athletes pre event.

I am delighted to have completed this, my 37th edition of the International Annual as editor, and would like to give full appreciation to the ATFS for having taken on the role of publisher as they did in 2020. It is also a fitting time to give sincere thanks to Randall Northam who published the Annual through his company SportsBooks from 1995 to 2019 and also handled the production when Burlington Publishing/Harmsworth Active were the publishers 1991-4.

Throughout my time as Editor I have had assistance of the annual lists from many people, and that list is headed by Richard Hymans whose work in this respect dates back to 1979. As well as men's lists he does astonishing work in working out heights and weights of athletes. Major resources on the Internet are provided by World Athletics, by Mirko Jalava's *Tilastopaja*, *Track & Field News* (USA) with its email results spin-off *Track Newsletter* and Carles Baronet's *Track in Sun* and many national federations with Alfons Juck's *EME News* providing marvellous up-to-date daily coverage of the happenings of our sport. Both for this Annual and for *Athletics International* (AI) that I publish with Mel Watman (c. 36 issues per year) I am most grateful to the continued support of correspondents throughout the world. Some send regular details, many national lists and others are able to deal with specific queries.

György Csiki does extensive checking for AI and provides annual updates for the Records section here. Winfried Kramer helps with widespread probing for results, as do the area experts: *Africa*: Carole Fuchs, *Asia*: Heinrich Hubbeling, *Central and South America*: Eduardo Biscayart and Luis Vinker. Andy Milroy handles the Ultrarunning review as he has since 1985, and Ken Nakamura has added the road running reviews to his regular contribution of results from Japan. Børre Lilloe provided much index data and of the great Spanish group Juan Mari Iriondo and Miguel Villaseñor checked the biographies as usual. Finally Stuart Mazdon proof-read much of the contents with great skill and organised the production I have not listed all the national or other correspondents this year but many have been with this Annual for many years – sincere thanks to you all.

We await return to some form of normality as this year progresses and above all to the Tokyo Olympic Games. We know that there will have to be tight protocols, but trust that athletes will be able to prepare and compete as they would wish and that we enthusiasts can, if not there in person, be able to follow all the action through the miracles of modern technology.

Peter Matthews, 2 April 2021

ABBREVIATIONS

Abbreviations have been used for meetings with, in parentheses, the first year that they were held.

AAU	(USA) Amateur Athletic Union Championships (1888) (later TAC)
Af-AsG	Afro-Asian Games (2003)
AfCh	African Championships (1979)
AfG	African Games (1965)
Af-J	African Junior Championships (1994)
APM	Adriaan Paulen Memorial, Hengelo
AsiC	Asian Championships (1973)
AsiG	Asian Games (1951)
Asi-J	Asian Junior Championships (1990)
ASV	Weltklasse in Köln, ASV club meeting (1934)
Athl	Athletissima, Lausanne (1976)
Balk	Balkan Games (1929), C - Championships
Barr	(Cuba) Barrientos Memorial (1946)
BGP	Budapest Grand Prix (1978)
Bisl	Bislett Games, Oslo (1965) (Bergen 2004)
Bol G	Bolivar Games (1938)
BrGP	British Grand Prix
CAC	Central American and Caribbean Championships (1967)
CAG	Central American and Caribbean Games (1926)
C.Asian	Central Asian Championships
CAU	Inter-counties, GBR (1934)
CG	Commonwealth Games (1930)
C.Cup	Continental Cup (2010)
Déca	Décanation, Paris (C) (2005)
DL	Diamond League (2010)
DNG	DN Galan, Stockholm (1967)
Drake	Drake Relays (1910)
EAF	European Athletics Festival, Bydgoszcz (2001)
EAsG	East Asian Games (1993)
EC	European Championships (1934)
ECCp	European Clubs Cup (1975)
EChall	European Challenge (10,000m 1997, Throws 2001); see ET
ECp	European Cup - track & field (1965), multi-events (1973)
EI	European Indoor Championships (1970, Games 1966-9)
EJ	European Junior Championships (1970)
ET	European Team Championships (replaced European Cup, 2009)
EU23	European Under-23 Championships (1997) and European Under-23 Cup (1992-4)
EY	European Under-18 (Youth) Championships (2016)
FBK	Fanny Blankers-Koen Games, Hengelo (formerly APM) (1981)
FlaR	Florida Relays (1939)
FOT	(USA) Final Olympic Trials (1920)
Franc	Francophone Games (1989)
GGala	Golden Gala, Roma (from 1980), Verona (1988), Pescara (1990), Bologna (1990)
GL	Golden League (1998-2009)
GNR	Great North Run – Newcastle to South Shields, GBR (1981)
GP	Grand Prix
GPF	IAAF Grand Prix Final (1985)
GS	Golden Spike, Ostrava (1969)
Gugl	Zipfer Gugl Grand Prix, Linz (1988)
GWG	Goodwill Games (1986)
Gyulai	István Gyulai Memorial, Budapest (2011-13), Székesfehérvár (2014-20
Hanz	Hanzekovic Memorial, Zagreb (1958)
Herc	Herculis, Monte Carlo, Monaco (1987)
IAAF	International Association of Athletics Federations
IAC	IAC meeting (1968), formerly Coca-Cola
IAU	International Association of Ultrarunners
IbAm	Ibero-American Championships (1983)
Is.Sol	Islamic Solidarity Games (2005)
ISTAF	Internationales Stadionfest, Berlin (1921)
Jenner	Bruce Jenner Classic, San Jose (1979)
Jerome	Harry Jerome Track Classic (1984)
Jordan	Payton Jordan U.S. Track & Field Open, Stanford (2004)
JUCO	Junior Colleges Championships, USA
KansR	Kansas Relays, Lawrence (1923)
Kuso	Janusz Kusocinski Memorial (1954)
Kuts	Vladimir Kuts Memorial (1978)
LGP	London Grand Prix, Crystal Palace
LI	Loughborough International (1958)
MAI	Malmö Al Galan, Sweden (formerly Idag) (1958)
Mast	Masters pole vault, Grenoble (1987), Donetsk
MedG	Mediterranean Games (1951)
Mill	Millrose Games, New York indoors (1908)
ModR	Modesto Relays (1942)
MSR	Mt. San Antonio College Relays (1959)
NA	Night of Athletics, Heusden (2000) formerly Hechtel
NACAC	North American, Central American & Caribbean Championships (2003)
NC	National Championships
NC-w	National Winter Championships
NCAA	National Collegiate Athletic Association Championships, USA (1921)
NCAA-r	NCAA Regional Championships (2003)
NCp	National Cup
Nebiolo	Memorial Primo Nebiolo, Torino (2000, originally 1963)
NG	National Games
Nik	Nikaïa, Nice (1976)
NM	Narodna Mladezhe, Sofia (1955)
N.Sch	National Schools
Nurmi	Paavo Nurmi Games (1957)
NYG	New York Games (1989)
OD	Olympischer Tag (Olympic Day) (1963)
Oda	Mikio Oda Memorial Meeting, Hiroshima (1967)
Odlozil	Josef Odlozil Memorial, Prague (1994)
OG	Olympic Games (1896)
OT	Olympic Trials
Owens	Jesse Owens Memorial (1981)
PAm	Pan American Games (1951)
PArab	Pan Arab Championships (1977) (G- Games 1953)
Pedro	Pedro's Cup, Poland (2005)
PennR	Pennsylvania Relays (1895)
PTS	Pravda Televízia Slovnaft, Bratislava (1957) (later GPB)
Pre	Steve Prefontaine Memorial (1976)
RomIC	Romanian International Championships (1948)
Ros	Evzen Rosicky Memorial, Praha (1947)
RWC	Race Walking Challenge Final (2007)
SACh	South American Championships (1919)
SAsG	South Asian Games (1984)
SEAG	South East Asia Games (1959)
SEC	Southeastern Conference Championships

SGP	IAAF Super Grand Prix		WCT	World Championships Trial
Skol	Skolimowska Memorial (2010)		WG	World Games, Helsinki (1961)
Slovn	Slovnaft, Bratislava (formerly PTS) (1990)		WI	World Indoor Championships (1987), World Indoor Games (1985)
Spark	Sparkassen Cup, Stuttgart (indoor) (1987)			
Spart	(URS) Spartakiad (1956)		WIT	World Indoor Tour (2016)
Spitzen	Spitzen Leichtathletik Luzern (1987)		WJ	World Junior Championships (1986)
Stra	Stramilano Half marathon, Milan (1972)		WK	Weltklasse, Zürich (1962)
Super	Super Meet, Japan (Tokyo, Shizuoka, Yokohama, Kawasaki)		WMilG	World Military Games
			WRly	World Relays (2014)
Szew	Irena Szewinska Memorial, Bygoszcz (2019)		WTC	World Team Championships
TexR	Texas Relays (1925)		WUG	World University Games (1923)
USOF	US Olympic Festival (1978)		WY	World Youth Championships (1999)
VD	Ivo Van Damme Memorial, Brussels (1977)		Zat	Emil Zátopek Classic, Melbourne
Veniz	Venizélia, Haniá, Crete (1936)		Znam	Znamenskiy Brothers Memorial (1958)
WAC	Western Athletic Conference Championships (1962)		-j, -y, -23	Junior, Youth or under-23
WAF	World Athletics Finals (2003)		Dual and triangular matches are indicated by "v" (versus) followed by the name(s) of the opposition. Quadrangular and larger inter-nation matches are denoted by the number of nations and -N; viz 8-N designates an 8-nation meeting.	
WCh	World Championships (1983)			
WCM	World Challenge Meeting (2010)			
WCp	World Cup (1977), marathon (1985) Walking – Lugano Trophy – men (1961), Eschborn Cup – women (1979)			

Events

CC	cross-country	Hep	heptathlon	LJ	long jump	SP	shot
Dec	decathlon	HJ	high jump	Mar	marathon	St	steeplechase
DT	discus	HMar	half marathon	Pen	pentathlon	TJ	triple jump
h	hurdles	HT	hammer	PV	pole vault	W	walk
		JT	javelin	R	relay	Wt	weight

Miscellaneous abbreviations

+	Intermediate time in longer race	M/S	metres per second
=	Tie (ex-aequo)	mx	Made in mixed men's and women's race
A	Made at an altitude of 1000m or higher	nh	no height
b	date of birth	O	Made in octathlon competition
D	Made in decathlon competition	P	Made in pentathlon competition
dnf	did not finish	pb	personal best
dnq	did not qualify	Q	Made in qualifying round
dns	did not start	qf	quarter final (or q in lists)
exh	exhibition	r	Race number in a series of races
h	heat	sf	semi final (or s in lists)
H	Made in heptathlon competition	w	wind assisted
hr	hour	WIR	world indoor record
i	indoors	WR	world record or best
kg	kilograms	y	yards
km	kilometres	*	Converted time from yards to metres: For 200m: 220 yards less 0.11 second For 400m: 440 yards less 0.26 second For 110mh: 120yh plus 0.03 second
m	metres		
M	mile		

Countries

(From a founding membership of 17 nations in 1912, IAAF membership now stands at 214)

AFG	Afghanistan	BDI	Burundi	CHN	People's Republic of China
AHO	Netherlands Antilles #	BEL	Belgium	CIV	Côte d'Ivoire (Ivory Coast)
AIA	Anguilla	BEN	Benin	CMR	Cameroon
ALB	Albania	BER	Bermuda	COD	Democratic Republic of Congo
ALG	Algeria	BHU	Bhutan		
ANA	Authorised Neutral Athlete	BIH	Bosnia Herzegovina	COK	Cook Islands
AND	Andorra	BIZ	Belize	COL	Colombia
ANG	Angola	BLR	Belarus	COM	Comoros
ANT	Antigua & Barbuda	BOL	Bolivia	CPV	Cape Verde Islands
ARG	Argentina	BOT	Botswana	CRC	Costa Rica
ARM	Armenia	BRA	Brazil	CRO	Croatia
ARU	Aruba	BRN	Bahrain	CUB	Cuba
ASA	American Samoa	BRU	Brunei	CUR	Curaçao
AUS	Australia	BUL	Bulgaria	CYP	Cyprus
AUT	Austria	BUR	Burkina Faso	CZE	Czech Republic
AZE	Azerbaijan	CAF	Central African Republic	DEN	Denmark
BAH	Bahamas	CAM	Cambodia	DJI	Djibouti
BAN	Bangladesh	CAN	Canada	DMA	Dominica
BAR	Barbados	CAY	Cayman Islands	DOM	Dominican Republic
		CGO	Congo	ECU	Ecuador
		CHA	Chad	EGY	Egypt
		CHI	Chile	ENG	England

Code	Country	Code	Country	Code	Country
ERI	Eritrea	LBN	Lebanon (LIB up to 2016)	SAM	Samoa
ESA	El Salvador	LBR	Liberia	SCG	Serbia & Montenegro (to 2006)
ESP	Spain	LCA	St Lucia		
EST	Estonia	LES	Lesotho	SCO	Scotland
ETH	Ethiopia	LIE	Liechtenstein	SEN	Sénégal
FIJ	Fiji	LTU	Lithuania	SEY	Seychelles
FIN	Finland	LUX	Luxembourg	SGP	Singapore (SIN up to 2016)
FRA	France	MAC	Macao	SKN	St Kitts & Nevis
FRG	Federal Republic of Germany (1948-90)	MAD	Madagascar	SLE	Sierra Leone
		MAR	Morocco	SLO	Slovenia
FSM	Micronesia	MAS	Malaysia	SMR	San Marino
GAB	Gabon	MAW	Malawi	SOL	Solomon Islands
GAM	The Gambia	MDA	Moldova	SOM	Somalia
GBR	United Kingdom of Great Britain & Northern Ireland	MDV	Maldives	SRB	Serbia
		MEX	Mexico	SRI	Sri Lanka
GBS	Guinea-Bissau	MGL	Mongolia	SSD	South Sudan
GDR	German Democratic Republic (1948-90)	MKD	North Macedonia	STP	São Tomé & Príncipe
		MLI	Mali	SUD	Sudan
GEO	Georgia	MLT	Malta	SUI	Switzerland
GEQ	Equatorial Guinea	MNE	Montenegro	SUR	Surinam
GER	Germany (pre 1948 and from 1991)	MNT	Montserrat	SVK	Slovakia
		MON	Monaco	SWE	Sweden
GHA	Ghana	MOZ	Mozambique	SWZ	Swaziland (Eswatini)
GIB	Gibraltar	MRI	Mauritius	SYR	Syria
GRE	Greece	MSH	Marshall Islands	TAN	Tanzania
GRN	Grenada	MTN	Mauritania	TCH	Czechoslovakia (to 1991)
GUA	Guatemala	MYA	Myanmar	TGA	Tonga
GUI	Guinea	NAM	Namibia	THA	Thailand
GUM	Guam	NCA	Nicaragua	TJK	Tadjikistan
GUY	Guyana	NED	Netherlands	TKM	Turkmenistan
HAI	Haiti	NEP	Nepal	TKS	Turks & Caicos Islands
HKG	Hong Kong, China	NFI	Norfolk Islands	TLS	East Timor
HON	Honduras	NGR	Nigeria	TOG	Togo
HUN	Hungary	NI	Northern Ireland	TPE	Taiwan (Chinese Taipei)
INA	Indonesia	NIG	Niger	TTO	Trinidad & Tobago
IND	India	NMI	Northern Marianas Islands	TUN	Tunisia
IRI	Iran	NOR	Norway	TUR	Turkey
IRL	Ireland	NRU	Nauru	TUV	Tuvalu
IRQ	Iraq	NZL	New Zealand	UAE	United Arab Emirates
ISL	Iceland	OMA	Oman	UGA	Uganda
ISR	Israel	PAK	Pakistan	UKR	Ukraine
ISV	US Virgin Islands	PAN	Panama	URS	Soviet Union (to 1991)
ITA	Italy	PAR	Paraguay	URU	Uruguay
IVB	British Virgin Islands	PER	Peru	USA	United States
JAM	Jamaica	PHI	Philippines	UZB	Uzbekistan
JOR	Jordan	PLE	Palestine	VAN	Vanuatu
JPN	Japan	PLW	Palau	VEN	Venezuela
KAZ	Kazakhstan	PNG	Papua New Guinea	VIE	Vietnam
KEN	Kenya	POL	Poland	VIN	St Vincent & the Grenadines
KGZ	Kyrgyzstan	POR	Portugal		
KIR	Kiribati	PRK	North Korea (DPR Korea)	WAL	Wales
KOR	Korea	PUR	Puerto Rico	YEM	Republic of Yemen
KOS	Kosovo	PYF	French Polynesia	YUG	Yugoslavia (to 2002)
KSA	Saudi Arabia	QAT	Qatar	ZAM	Zambia
KUW	Kuwait	ROU	Romania	ZIM	Zimbabwe
LAO	Laos	RSA	South Africa		# ceased to exist as a separate territory in 2010, and absorbed into the Netherlands.
LAT	Latvia	RUS	Russia		
LBA	Libya	RWA	Rwanda		

THE ASSOCIATION OF TRACK & FIELD STATISTICIANS

The ATFS was founded in Brussels (at the European Championships) in 1950 and ever since has built upon the work of such key founding members as Roberto Quercetani, Don Potts and Fulvio Regli to produce authoritative ranking lists in the International Athletics Annual and elsewhere.

Current Executive Committee
President: Paul Jenes AUS; Vice-President: Andrew Pirie AUS; Treasurer: Tom Casacky USA; Secretary: Michael J McLaughlin AUS; Past President: Rooney Magnusson SWE; Committee: José María Lombardo URU, Giuseppe Mappa ITA, Mark Wall AUS, three vacancies.
Website: www.afts.org

Internet – Websites

World Athletics	worldathletics.org
IAU	iau-ultramarathon.org
Asian AA	athleticsasia.org
European AA	european-athletics.org
NACAC	athleticsnacac.org
Oceania AA	athletics-oceania.com
South American Fed.	atletismosudamericano.org
WMRA	wmra.info
World Masters	world-masters-athletics.com
Marathon Majors	worldmarathonmajors.com
Africa	africathle.com
Algeria	faa.dz
Andorra	faa.ad
Argentina	cada-atletismo.org
Australia	athletics.com.au
Austria	oelv.at
Bahamas	bahamasathletics.com
Belarus	bfla.eu
Belgium	val.be
Bermuda	athleticsbda.com
Brazil	cbat.org.br
Bulgaria	bfla.org
Canada	athletics.ca
Chile	fedachi.cl
China	athletics.org.cn
Costa Rica	fecoa.org
Croatia	has.hr
Cyprus	koeas.org.cy
Czech Republic	atletika.cz
Denmark	dansk-atletik.dk
Dominican Republic	fedomatle.org
Ecuador	featle.org.ec
England	englandathletics.org
Estonia	ekjl.ee
Ethiopia	eaf.org.et
Finland	yleisurheilu.fi
France	www.athle.fr
Germany	leichtathletik.de
Ghana	ghaathletics.com
Great Britain	britishathletics.org.uk
deep statistics	topsinathletics.info
	thepowerof10.info
Greece	segas.gr
Guyana	aaguyana.com
Hungary	atletika.hu
Iceland	fri.is
India	indianathletics.in
Indonesia	indonesia-athletics.org
Ireland	athleticsireland.ie
Israel	iaa.co.il
Italy	fidal.it
Jamaica	trackandfieldjm.com
Japan	jaaf.or.jp
running news	unningnews.blogspot.co.uk
Kazakhstan	kazathletics.kz
Kenya	athleticskenya.or.ke
Latvia	athletics.lv
Lithuania	lengvoji.lt
Luxembourg	fla.lu
Macedonia	afm.org.mk
Mexico	fmaa.mx
Moldova	fam.com.md
Monaco	fma.mc
Montenegro	ascg.co.me
Morocco	www.frma.ma
Netherlands	atletiekunie.nl
New Zealand	athletics.org.nz
Northern Ireland	athleticsni.org
Norway	friidrett.no
Peru	fedepeatle.org
Poland	pzla.pl
Portugal	fpatletismo.pt
	atletismo-estatistica.pt
Puerto Rico	atletismofapur.com
	pedroanibaldiaz.com
Romania	fra.ro
Russia	rusathletics.com
Scotland	scottishathletics.org.uk
	scotstats.net
Serbia	sas.org.rs
Singapore	singaporeathletics.org.sg
Slovakia	atletika.sk
Slovenia	slovenska-atletika.si
South Africa	athletics.org.za
Spain	rfea.es
Sweden	friidrott.se
Switzerland	swiss-athletics.ch
Taiwan	athletics.org.tw
Thailand	aat.or.th
Trinidad & Tobago	ttnaaa.org
Turkey	taf.org.tr
Ukraine	uaf.org.ua
Uruguay	confederacionatletica.org
USA	usatf.org
collegiate results	ustfccca.org
Uzbekistan	uzathletics.uz
Wales	welshathletics.org
	athleticsstatswales.webeden.co.uk

Other recommended sites for statistics and results

AEEA (Spain)	rfea.es/aeea
AIMS	aimsworldrunning.org
ARRS	https://arrs.run
Athletics Weekly	athleticsweekly.com
British historical	gbrathletics.com
	athlos.co.uk
Decathlon 2000	decathlon2000.com
DGLD (German stats)	ladgld.de
French history etc.	http://cdm.athle.com
Lets Run	letsrun.com
Marathons	marathonguide.com
Mirko Jalava	tilastopaja.org
NUTS/Track Stats	nuts.org.uk
Runners World	runnersworld.com
Tracklion (NED/BEL)	sportslion.net/tracklion.html
Track & Field News	trackandfieldnews.com
Track in Sun results	trackinsun.blogspot.com
Ultra marathon stats	statistik.d-u-v.org
World juniors	worldjuniorathleticsnewsnzl.co.nz
Olympic Games	olympedia.org

2020 – THE CORONAVIRUS YEAR

FOR THE FIRST ten weeks of 2020 athletics went on much as usual – with the usual intense indoor season, especially in Europe and with Collegiate action in the USA. There were major cross-country races and as usual various important road races. Indeed in the latter there were some prodigious sets of times, aided materially by the new generation of running shoes, of which more later. Substantially due to this there were a surprising number of world records set in the year on road and track.

Quite abruptly, in early to mid March the rapid spread of the Coronavirus Covid-19, declared as a pandemic, started a wholesale cancellation or postponement of events. In several major nations there were complete bans on all competitions, most of which were lifted later in the year. The first major events to be cancelled included the NCAA Indoor Championships in the USA and the World Indoor Championships in Nanjing, China, as well as the major spring marathons. On March 24 the postponement of the Olympic Games in Tokyo for a year was announced and a month later the scheduled European Championships in Paris were cancelled. Although it was to be held later in the year the World Half Marathon Championships in Gdynia, Poland, scheduled for 20 March was postponed and the World Walking Team Championships, due to be held in Minsk, Belarus in May was another casualty. On the track the US Collegiate season was abandoned and steadily meetings were cancelled all around the world.

For some the lack of competition enabled athletes to have more time to recover from injury and indeed to look ahead to the Olympic Games, which were to be held as the 2020 Games in Tokyo on the originally scheduled dates, but in 2021. However, for many the year was a write-off, not least because they were unable to access training facilities. Nonetheless, many did find a way to keep going at least in those parts of the world where restrictions were eased somewhat, and competitions were held, although mostly without spectators.

The first event to attract worldwide attention was the 'Ultimate Garden Clash' in which the three greatest male pole vaulters of the current age – Mondo Duplantis, Sam Kendricks and Renaud Lavillenie engaged in a televised event on May 3 by vaulting in their gardens. This was followed two weeks later by a similar women's event with Ekateríni Stefanídi, Katie Nageotte and Alysha Newman, and a Combined Events challenge featured Kevin Mayer, Niklas Kaul and Maicel Uibo at pole vault, shot and shuttle run in their homes.

From late May some European nations allowed limited competitions to be held under carefully controlled conditions and the first important event since the start of the Covid-19 outbreak was the Josef Odlozil Meeting in Prague with a sprinkling of spectators. For the rest of the summer central Europe was the main area for track and field activity and some athletes from further afield managed to get to compete there. At the highest level, half the Diamond League events were cancelled, but after initial initiatives by the organisers of the Bislett Games in Oslo with their 'Impossible Games' and by those of Zürich with their 'Inspiration Games', the first full-scale meeting was the Herculis in Monaco, and this was followed by DL meetings in Stockholm, Lausanne (just pole vaults), Brussels, Rome and Doha. A second wave of the virus caused shut-downs to be extended in many nations, but a notable exception was Japan where there was an extensive programme of events from July to the end of the year.

All major mass-participation road races were cancelled, but some limited elite races were held, including one of the Marathon Majors – London, when instead of the usual folk festival of tens of thousands of runners racing through the streets of the city in April a small top-quality field raced a loop course around St. James's Park closed to the public.

So overall the depth and quality of world lists were severely affected, athough in some disciplines, such as the discus, a fair proportion of the world's best had reasonably extensive seasons. In many events our lists are perhaps more extensive than might be expected, but it should be realised that even if qualifying for a list many, if not most, athletes will have had very limited competition and in a normal year could have expected to have achieved better performances.

The Shoes

After some years of experimentation by such major brands as Nike and adidas, the breakthrough of the new generation of shoes came perhaps with the development by Nike of the neon Vaporfly shoes with thick foam soles embedded with carbon fibre plates. There was especial interest for these in the 2018 attempt by Eliud Kipchoge to break the 2-hour marathon barrier. It was claimed that these shoes would save a marathon runner up to 4% in energy expenditure. A year later, for Kipchoge's second, and successful attempt, Nike had introduced their Alphafly Next% shoes. These caught on quickly as athletes rushed to obtain them, selling out, for instance in Britain, where they retailed at £260 per pair.

THE SHOES

So many marathons were cancelled in 2020 that the effect of the new shoes has to some extent been muted, but note what happened in the three most important marathons in the early months: First an all-time record of 14 men ran under 2:08 in Dubai in January. That record was equalled when there was great depth of times in the 36th Zürich Seville Marathon (a WA Gold Label race). Winner Gebre Mekuant Ayenew in his 22nd marathon improved his pb massively from 2:09:00 in 2017 to 2:04:46, Juliet Chekwel made a splendid marathon debut to win the women's race in 2:23:13, a Ugandan record. 42 of the top 48 men (under 2:20) and 25 of the top 29 women (under 2:53) finishers set pbs.

Then there was the Tokyo Marathon on March 1. Lonah Chemtai Salpeter won the women's race in an Israeli record 2:17:45 from Birhane Dibaba who set a pb with 2:18:35. Men's winner was Berhanu Legese 2:04:15 from Bashir Abdi, Belgian record 2:04:48, Sisay Lemma 2:04:55 and Suguro Osako, Japanese record 2:05:29. The use of Nike's Alphafly shoes showed in the men's race with new records set in depth. 17 men under 2:08 beat the record of 14 set in Dubai in January and in Seville just a week earlier, and there were 28 under 2:10, compared to the previous best ever of 19 in Seville. There were thus the best ever times for places 14 to 50 and beyond, those in the 20s were minutes ahead of anything ever seen before. 33 of the top 50 set pbs. Further numbers under 2:12- 35, 2:13- 47, 2:14- 53, 2:15- 57, 2:20- 86. The most previously under 2:15 was 46 for London 1991 and that race surely had significantly better participants.

After the cancellation of many races due to the pandemic, there were more amazing sets of performances in late season races. First on the track with world records from Letesenbet Gidey and Joseph Cheptegei, and on the road at half marathon. In the Valencia Marathon records went again with 30 men under 2:10 and best ever times for places 3 (=), 4, 8-17, 29- 50+.

It is clear that the new shoes with their very responsive foam midsoles working in concert with carbon rods or plates has changed the relative worth of times so that comparisons with previous years have to be looked at differently.

Reacting quickly to what had happened, World Athletics announced in February amended rules governing competition shoes to provide greater clarity to athletes and shoe manufacturers around the world and to protect the integrity of the sport. They announced that from April 30, any shoe must have been available for purchase by any athlete on the open retail market (online or in store) for a period of four months before it can be used in competition. If a shoe is not openly available to all then it will be deemed a prototype and use of it in competition will not be permitted. Subject to compliance with the rules, any shoe that is available to all, but is customised for aesthetic reasons, or for medical reasons to suit the characteristics of a particular athlete's foot, will be allowed.

Where World Athletics has reason to believe that a type of shoe or specific technology may not be compliant with the rules or the spirit of the rules, it may submit the shoe or technology for study and may prohibit the use of the shoe or technology while it is under examination.

Further, with immediate effect there will be an indefinite moratorium on any shoe (whether with or without spikes) that does not meet the following requirements: (a) The sole must be no thicker than 40mm. (b) The shoe must not contain more than one rigid embedded plate or blade (of any material) that runs either the full length or only part of the length of the shoe. The plate may be in more than one part but those parts must be located sequentially in one plane (not stacked or in parallel) and must not overlap. (c) For a shoe with spikes, an additional plate (to the plate mentioned above) or other mechanism is permitted, but only for the purpose of attaching the spikes to the sole, and the sole must be no thicker than 30mm.

The competition referee will have the power to request that an athlete immediately provide their shoes for inspection at the conclusion of a race if the referee has a reasonable suspicion that the shoes worn by an athlete do not comply with the rules.

Independent research indicates that the new technology incorporated in the soles of road and spiked shoes may provide a performance advantage and there is sufficient evidence to raise concerns that the integrity of the sport might be threatened by the recent developments in shoe technology. The World Athletics Council's Assistance Review Group therefore recommended that further research be undertaken to establish the true impact of this technology and that a new working group, comprising biomechanics specialists and other qualified experts, be formed to oversee this research, and to assess any new shoes that enter the market, where required. Shoe manufacturers will be invited to be part of this assessment process.

As a consequence of the new regulations, the Nike 'Alphafly' prototype shoes worn by Eliud Kipchoge when he covered the marathon distance in October 2019 in 1:59:41 will be banned (of course that time could never be considered as an official world record). Brigid Kosgei wore a Nike Vaporfly prototype when she broke Paula Radcliffe's world record with 2:14:04 in Chicago 2019, a mark that has been ratified, as was Kipchoge's 2:01:39 in Berlin in 2018. Similar shoes, currently on the market and conforming to the new specifications, such as the adidas Adizero Pro launched in May 2020 are allowed, as are new shoes from most of the other major manufacturers.

The most crucial factor is sole height – that varies depending on the event. By event grouping the maximum permitted is: Track events (including hurdles) shorter than the 800m – 20mm; Track events from the 800m and above – 25m; Road events (including walks) – 40m; Cross country – 25m; All field events except the TJ – 20mm, Triple jump – 25mm. There was some cynicism from athletics enthusiasts that WA had chosen 40cm as allowable for road shoes, as this was the precise sole depth of the latest Nike shoes. However, the issue was hidden somewhat for the rest of the year with lack of top races, and that times at the London Marathon were unexceptional due to poor conditions, but the terrific world records on the track by Joshua Cheptegei and Letesenbet Gidey at Valencia in October brought it back into sharp focus. Mel Watman wrote in *Athletivs Interabtional* "Watching those two stupendous world records on my computer was an exhilarating experience and I marvelled at the athletes' speed and pace judgement, although I'm not in favour of the wavelight pacing which somewhat dehumanises the physical and mental effort involved. I am more concerned about the effect of the new generation of racing shoes. Has World Athletics been too lenient in the specifications they have permitted for track and road shoes?"

The top end of marathon running has undergone a revolution since those shoes, pioneered by Nike and subsequently developed by other manufacturers, became available to elite runners. In 2017 four men broke 2:05, the 50th fastest performer in the world that year ran 2:07:39, the 100th 2:09:10. The corresponding figures for 2018 were 14 under 2:05, 2:07:09 and 2:08:47. As the 'miracle' shoes became more widespread in 2019 the statistics reflected the unprecedented upsurge: 17 under 2:05, 2:06:22 and 2:07:58. The world record during this period progressed from 2:02:57 to 2:01:39 (plus those 2:00:25 and 1:59:41 assisted time trials). In depth figures in 2020 are not too significant, with so many races cancelled, but four of the top six fastest men improved their pbs, one by 4 min 14 sec.

The women's situation is similar. The world record went from Paula Radcliffe's hitherto unapproached 2:15:25 to 2:14:04. In 2017 three women broke 2:20 with 50th at 2:25:52 and 100th at 2:28:15. The figures for 2018 were 11, 2:24:08 and 2:26:58. In 2019 they were 12, 2:23:19 and 2:25:39. In 2020 six of the top nine clocked pbs, three of them by over 3 minutes.

It is much the same story on the track. No one broke 27 minutes in 2018 but 10 did in 2019, the 50th best ran 27:56.11, a time bettered by 67 the following year, while the 100th at 28:17.63 was beaten by 136 runners last year. In the women's 10,000m there were five inside 31 min in 2017, just one in 2018 but 16 in 2019. This year seven of the ten fastest men at 10,000m to date have posted pbs, as have six of the top ten women at 5000m. These are not natural progressions; the footwear has surely been the reason and understandably it's a controversial topic. Are the shoes, some retailing at around the £250 mark, devaluing past performances?"

Tim Hutchings, former world class distance runner and a much respected voice within our sport, followed that. He said that he believes "a gross injustice" is unfolding, as record books and rankings are re-written on a weekly basis. He estimates the shoes in question are helping some athletes, the 'super responders' to the tune of between 0.7 and 1.0 sec per lap, while others may benefit to varied lesser degrees. "My own feeling is that while I retain my love for distance racing and respect all athletes who train hard without short cuts, there should be a separate set of record lists for performances achieved in the shoes. That would not be hard to police and would acknowledge what is plain for all to see. This problem, like the 'shark-skin suits' in swimming a few years back, demands attention from the authorities, who I believe have a moral obligation to step in."

Lord Coe, President of World Athletics, said in January 2021 that: "At the moment I'm pretty calm about this. And the balance of judgment here is always – and I guess this is a personal instinct of mine as well – that we shouldn't be in the business of trying to suffocate innovation."

Wavelight Technology

It is not a new idea, but another technological development was that of the Wavelight System of light emitters positioned along the track curb. These can be programmed for a desired pace and were used for world record pace in the successful record attempts by Letesenbet Gidey at 5000m and Joshua Cheptegei at 10000m. Just how much difference these pacing lights can make may be argued, but both these records were achieved from remarkably level pace, metronomic even. In Cheptegei's case, this was easily the most level paced world record at 10,000m as, apart from his first and last laps, he covered each 400m between 62.4 and 63.3 secs. Gidey started a little slower with six laps between an opening 69.0 and 67.9 – and the pacing lights were set for this at her request, but then for the rest of the way she ran between 66.5 and 67.2. Pacing light assistance was only permitted by World Athletics in 2019, and Lord Coe, President of WA expressed the view that this was a new information tool to help spectators better understand and appreciate the efforts of the athletes. This system is, however, set up for a single athlete's attempt to run a specific time, and this is quite different from the true nature of the sport that spectators love – which is racing in head-to-head competition.

DIARY OF 2020

January

11 **Valencia**, Spain. Rhonex Kipruto ran a world road record 26:24 (5k in 13:23) to win the Valencia Ibercaja 10k from Nicholas Kimeli 27:13 and Julian Wanders 27:13 European record. Sheila Kiprotich missed the women's record by just 3 seconds with 29:46. She was followed by her Kenyan compatriots Rosemary Wanjiru and Norah Jeruto Tanui, both 29:51.
18 **Lvov**, Ukraine. Yaroslava Mahuchikh set a world U20 indoor high jump record with 2.01.
19 **Houston**, USA. Despite tough conditions in the half marathon nine men bettered 1 hour, headed by Jemal Yimer 59:25, and Hitomi Niiya won in a Japanese record 66:38 with 19 women beating 70 mins (previous best 17) and best ever times from 17th onwards. There were 29 men under 62 mins and 27 women under 71 mins.
24 **Dubai**, United Arab Emirates. 21st Standard Chartered Marathon. Ethiopians dominated with 19 of the top 20 men (including Zelalem Bacha who switched to Bahrain) and 11 of the first 12 women. Worknesh Degefa was women's winner in 2:19:38 and Olika Adugna the men's in 2:06:15 on his marathon debut.
24-25 **Albuquerque (A)**, USA. Kendra Harrison started 2020 with 7.81 for 60m hurdles.
25 **Hastings**, New Zealand. Valerie Adams returned for her first competition since 19 July 2018 and won the shot with 18.65.
25 **Boston (Roxbury)**, USA (WIT). Donavan Brazier starred at the New Balance Indoor Grand Prix with 1:14.39 for 600m. Other winners included Derrick Kemp, 6.50 for 60m, Elinor Purrier, 9:29.17 for 2 miles, and Jessica Hull who set an Oceania indoor 1500m record 4:04.14 in outkicking Konstanze Klosterhalfen 4:04.38.
26 **Osaka**, Japan. 39th Women's Marathon. The 2018 winner Mizuki Matsuda won again – in 2:21:47.
26 **Grosseto**, Italy. Eleonora Giorgi recorded the second fastest ever women's 35k walk time, 2:43:43 to win the Italian title.
31 **Karlsruhe**, Germany (WIT). For the second time in three competitions this year, Yaroslava Mahuchikh (18) broke the world U20 indoor high jump record with a 2.02 leap.

February

1 **Moscow**, Russia. Mariya Lasitskene made a brilliant start to her 2020 high jump campaign with a first-time clearance at 2.04.
2 **Marugame**, Japan. The depth of Japanese distance running was shown, with 62 men under 63 mins and 102 men under 65 mins in the annual half marathon, but there were overseas winners: Brett Robinson AUS 59:57 Oceania record and Helena Johannes, Namibia women's record 68:10.
2 **Glasgow**, UK. From an 800m best of 2:01.19 outdoors Jemma Reekie ran a UK indoor record 1:57.91 from Laura Muir 1:58.44.
2 **Paris**, France. Fabrice Zango triple jumped 17.77 to add added 19cm to his African indoor record.
4 **Düsseldorf**, Germany. 14th PSD Bank meeting (WIT). After winning the pole vault at 6.00 Armand Duplantis had a very close failure with his second attempt at the world record height of 6.17. With 1500m in 4:02.09 Beatrice Chepkoech took 0.12 off her 2018 Kenyan indoor record.
8 **Hustopece**, Czech Republic. Tom Gale won the high jump with a pb 2.33.
8 **Rouen**, France. Sam Kendricks became the year's second 6m pole vaulter by clearing 6.01 on his final attempt,
8 **Torun**, Poland (WIT). Orlen Copernicus Cup. Armand Duplantis broke the world pole vault record, adding 1cm to the mark set by Renaud Lavillenie in Donetsk in 2014 by clearing 6.17 on his second attempt, just his sixth jump of the competition. Gudaf Tsegay moved up to seventh on the world all-time indoor 1500m with 4:00.09 and 2nd was Hailu Lemlem in a world U20 record 4:01.79.
8 **New York (Armory)**, USA. 113th Millrose Games. Elinor Purrier won the women's Wanamaker Mile in a North American indoor record of 4:16.85, the second fastest indoor performance ever (4:00.20 at 1500m) as Konstanze Klosterhalfen GER and Jemma Reekie GBR also moved into the top five on the world indoor all-time list, clocking indoor records of 4:17.26 and 4:17.88 (also Commonwealth record) respectively with 3:58.87 and 4:00.52 en route at 1500m. Fourth Gabriela DeBues-Stafford set Canadian records of 4:00.80 and 4:19.73. There were North American indoor records at 800m from Donavan Brazier 1:44.22 and Ajee' Wilson 1:58.29. Top field marks were Sandi Morris 4.91 pole vault and Ryan Crouser 22.19 shot.
9 **Metz**, France, Yulimar Rojas triple jumped 15.03.
9 **Moscow**, Russia. Russian Winter. Mariya Lasitskene high jumped 2.05, a mark that was to remain the best of 2020.
11 **Banská Bystrica**, Slovakia. Luis Zayas tied the world-leading high jump mark of 2.33 at the 24th edition of this high jump meeting.
14 **Berlin**, Germany, ISTAF Meeting. 12,500 spectators saw 2020 world-leading long jump of 7.07 by Malaika Mihambo. The 64.03 discus by Shanice Craft was the world best ever indoors.
14-15 **US Indoor Championships**, Albuquerque. Taking advantage of 1513m altitude

Christian Coleman ran 6.37 for 60m, a time bettered only by his 6.34 here in 2018. Adding 27cm to his previous best, Ryan Crouser jumped from fourth to second with 22.60 on the world indoor all-time shot list. World-leading times for the women's 60m were run by Javianne Oliver in her heat and by Mikiah Brisco in the final (with Oliver 2nd in 7.08). Fifth successive titles were won by Vashti Cunningham, 1.97 high jump, and Ajee' Wilson, 2:01.98 800m, while Shelby Houlihan completed a 1500m/3000m double for the third time. The North American record was broken twice in women's triple jump as Keturah Orji reached 14.60 in the second round, only for Tori Franklin to snatch it back with a sixth round 14.64.
15   **Glasgow**, UK (WIT). Müller Indoor Grand Prix, Armand Duplantis added 1cm to his world pole vault record by clearing 6.18 on his first attempt. In her first indoor race for six years, Shelly-Ann Fraser-Pryce won the 60m in a modest 7.16.
15   **Clemson**, USA. Tiger Paw Invitational. Grant Holloway ran 7.38 for 60m hurdles, easily the world's best of 2020 and Kendra Harrison improved her world-leading mark to 7.80.
16   **Kobe**, Japan. As usual the Japanese Championship at 20k walk had a terrific depth of performance, but the clear winner was Toshihazu Yamanishi 1:17:36.
16   **Monaco**: Joshua Cheptegei took the world 5k road record to respectability with 12:51.
15   **Russian Winter Walks Championships**, Sochi. 20k winners were Sergey Shirobokov 1:19:34 and Elvira Khasanova 1:26:43.
19   **Liévin**, France (WIT). After a winning 6.07 clearance, Armand Duplantis missed a third consecutive world pole vault record in the space of 12 days as he came tantalisingly close to clearing 6.19 at the Meeting Hauts-de-France Pas-de-Calais. Fabrice Zango was again in prime form as he triple jumped 17.51 and Ronnie Baker ran 6.44 for 60m, after 6.49 in his heat. Lemlen Hailu improved her world U20 indoor 1500m record to 4:01.57, 2nd to Gudaf Tsegay 4:00.60. The five fastest 3000m indoor times for 2020 were run with Getnet Wale winning in 7:32.80, the fastest indoors for seven years holding off Selemon Barega 7:33.19 and there was the fastest ever women's time for the rarely run 2000m indoor steeplechase (no water jump) – by Marusa Mismas 5:47.79.
21   **Madrid**, Spain (WIT). With her final attempt of the evening, Yulimar Rojas bounded out to a world indoor triple jump record of 15.43, a mark bettered only by the world outdoor record of 15.50 by Inessa Kravets in 1995. Another world-leading mark was 8.41 long jump by Juan Miguel Echevarría. .
21   **Ras Al Khaimah**, United Arab Emirates. The first two in the women's race at the RAK Half Marathon, Ababel Yeshaneh 64:31 and Brigid Kosgei 64:49, bettered the world record. Both were wearing variants of the controversial Nike Vaporfly shoe and had the benefit of male pacemaking. Men's winner Kibiwott Kandie improved his best from 59:31 to 58:38.
21   **Lincoln**, Nebraska, USA. Chris Nilsen added 1cm to Mondo Duplantis's US collegiate pole vault record with 5.93.
22   **Sydney**, Australia (WACT B). The first World Continental Tour meeting.
22-23 **British Indoor Championships**, Glasgow. Tom Bosworth won his sixth successive title and broke his UK record for 5000m with 18:20.97, the world's quickest for six years.
23   **Seville**, Spain. There was great depth of times in the 36th Zürich Seville Marathon (a WA Gold Label race), with 14 men under 2:08 to equal the all-time record set in Dubai in January. The winner Gebre Mekuant Ayenew in his 22nd marathon improved his pb massively from 2:09:00 in 2017 to 2:04:46, Juliet Chekwel made a splendid marathon debut to win the women's race in 2:23:13, a Ugandan record. 42 of the top 48 men (under 2:20) and 25 of the top 29 women (under 2:53) finishers set pbs (those new shoes surely had a major effect!).
25-27 **Russian Indoor Championships**, Moscow. Ilya Ivanyuk tied the world best of 2020 with a 2.33 high jump and Anzhelika Sidorova added 1cm to the pole vault best with 4.92 – a mark she improved the following day to 4.95.
27-28 **Boston (Allston)**, USA. Karissa Schweizer 8:25.70 beat Shelby Houlihan 8:26.66 in setting a North American record at 3000m, and Konstanze Klosterhalfen set a European indoor 5000m record of 14:30.78, while Josh Thompson ran the fastest indoor 1500m, 3:34.77, by an American–born athlete. On the second day Shadrack Kipchirchir won the 5000m from Marc Scott, whose 13:08.87 was a British and European record. Also this weekend many of the major US Collegiate Conference meetings were staged.
28- Mar 1 **French Indoor Championships**, Liévin. Clearing 5.80 Renaud Lavillenie won his ninth French indoor title and, competing as a guest, Nafi Thiam set a Belgian long jump record at 6.79.

March

1   **Tokyo Marathon**, Japan. Lonah Chemtai Salpeter won the women's race in an Israeli record 2:17:45 from Birhane Dibaba, second for the third time in her six Tokyo Marathon runs and in a pb 2:18:35. Men's winner was Berhanu Legese 2:04:15 from Bashir Abdi, Belgian record 2:04:48, Sisay Lemma 2:04:55 and Suguro Osako, Japanese record 2:05:29. The use of Nike's Alphafly shoes showed in the men's race in which new records were set in depth. 17 men under 2:08 beat the record of 14 set in Dubai in January and in Seville just a week

earlier, and there were 28 under 2:10, compared to the previous best ever of 19 in Seville. There were thus the best ever times for places 14 to 50 and beyond, those in the 20s minutes ahead of anything ever seen before. 33 of the top 50 set pbs. 57 under 2:15 beat the previous high of 46 for London 1991.

6-8 **New Zealand Championships**, Christchurch. Tom Walsh won his 11th successive national shot title with 21.70, and Valerie Adams, although beaten by guesting Brittany Crew 18.88 to 18.73, took her 16th title.

8 **Nagoya Women's Marathon**, Japan. Winner was Mao Ichiyama 2:20:29.

In early to mid March the rapid spread of the Coronavirus Covid-19, declared as a pandemic, meant the start of wholesale cancellation or postponement of events.

April
24 **Beijing**, China. Lu Huihui recorded a world best for the women's javelin indoors with 64.21 (previous best 61.29 by Taina Uppa of Finland in 1999). From this time competitions began to be staged in China where athletes had gathered at training centres.

May
3 "**Ultimate Garden Clash**". With pole vaults in their home gardens, Mondo Duplantis, Renaud Lavillenie and Sam Kendricks engaged in a televised competition to see who could achieve the most 5.00m clearances in 30 minutes (two 15-minute blocks). Duplantis in Lafayette and Lavillenie in Clermont-Ferrand each made 36 with one miss while Kendricks in Oxford, Mississippi did 26 with no misses. Two weeks later there was a women's competition won by Ekateríni Stefanídi in Athens with 34 times over 4.00m to 30 by Katie Nageotte in Marietta and 21 by Alysha Newman in Bolton, Ontario.

June
7 **Ultimate Garden Clash – Combined Events**. Three top multi-eventers competed at three events – pole vault, shot and shuttle run in their home environments. Kevin Mayer in Montpelier, France won with 71 points from Niklas Kaul 63 in Mainz, Germany, and Maicel Uibo 61 in Clermont, USA.

8 **Prague**, Czech Republic (WACT B). The Josef Odlozil Memorial Meeting in the Juliska Stadium was the first important athletics event to be staged since the start of the Covid-19 outbreak. Top performance was Nikola Ogrodníková's javelin throw of 64.22 in front of a maximum of 500 spectators.

11 **Oslo**, Norway (DL). The "Impossible Games" were staged as a Diamond League meeting in the Bislett Stadium. Karsten Warholm, running solo in lane seven, clocked 33.78 to shatter the world best for 300m hurdles (over seven hurdles) of 34.48 set by Chris Rawlinson in 2002. Filip Ingebrigtsen started the track programme with a Norwegian 1000m record of 2:16.46, the only man to finish the race, and less than 45 minutes later he ran 4:56.91 in a 2000m challenge event between Norway and Kenya (runners in Nairobi). He finished third behind brothers Jakob, who ran a European record 4:50.01 and Henrik 4:53.72. There was also a European record by Sondre Moen 1:12:46.5 for the rarely run 25,000 metres. Mondo Duplantis won the pole vault with 5.86 as Renaud Lavillenie, vaulting on his short runway at home, was 2nd with 5.81.

20 The death was reported of **Svein Arne Hansen**, the respected and popular President of European Athletics.

July
4 **Montverde**, USA. Shaunae Miller-Uibo won a 200m/400m double in 22.51/50.52.

9 **Inspiration Games**. The Zürich Diamond League organisers had an entertaining and innovative answer to the global coronavirus pandemic as they brought together 30 athletes competing in seven venues across two continents. Pedro Paulo Pichardo, competing in Lisbon, triple jumped 17.40w to defeat Christian Taylor, 17.27w in Bradenton, Florida. At the latter venue Noah Lyles ran 18.90 for his "200m", but the distance turned out to be 185m.

10 **Portland**, USA. North American records were set for both men's and women's 5000m. Mohammed Ahmed ran 12:47.20, improving his own record by 10.96 secs, going to 10th on the world all-time list, and Shelby Houlihan 14:23.92, 10.53 secs off the women's record and 12th on the all-time list, from Karissa Schweizer 14:26.34.

11 **Kingston**, Jamaica. At the first meeting in Jamaica for four months Shelly-Ann Fraser-Pryce ran 11.00 for 100m.

16 The **Athletics Association**, an independent organisation established for athletes, by athletes, was formally launched with Christian Taylor as President.

20 **Fort Worth**, USA. Michael Norman, having concentrated on 200m and 400m, ran his first 100m for four years and recorded a startling 9.86.

22 **Lovelhe**, Portugal, Benefitting from favourable wind, Colombian Mauricio Ortega improved his South American discus record from 67.03 (also at Lovelhe) to 70.29 – and Juan José Caicedo of Ecuador was not far behind with 69.60 from a previous best of 63.31.

23 **Amstetten**, Austria. Ivona Dadic totalled 6235 points for a women's 1-hour heptathlon, a total bettered only by Chantal Beaugéant 6242w in 1988.

24-25 **Clermont**, USA. Sprinters shone with Noah Lyles recording 9.93w for 100m and 19.94 for 200m and Shaunae Miller-Uibo 10.98 pb

and 21.98. In a separate race Trayvon Bromell returned to top form with 9.90 100m.
31   **Portland**, USA. A Nike Bowerman TC team of Colleen Quigley 4:08, Elise Cranny 4:09, Karissa Schweizer 4:06 and Shelby Houlihan 4:04 set a world record 16:27.02 for 4x1500m. A men's team recorded the second fastest ever with 14:34.97.

August
1   **Rathdrum**, USA. Valarie Allman added 98cm to the North American discus record with 70.15.
7   **Kristiansund**, Norway. Sondre Nordstad Moen achieved his aim of setting a European record for 1 hour on the track in great style. His 21,131m added 187m to the previous record set by Jos Hermens in 1976 and was just 154m short of the world record set by Haile Gebrselassie in 2007. It later transpired that he ran with what are now illegal shoes.
8   **Kingston**, Jamaica. In separate 100m races Shelly-Ann Fraser-Pryce ran 10.87 and Elaine Thompson-Herah 10.88.
8-9   **German Championships**, Braunschweig. One of the first national championships to be held since the lockdowns.
10   **Sollentuna**, Sweden. Folksam GP (WACT B). Daniel Ståhl had been in great form and here improved his season's best from 70.25 to a world-leading 71.37.
10   **Montevede**, USA, There was some sharp sprinting: Sha'Carri Richardson had a 10.83w/22.00 double, Trayvon Bromell ran 9.87w and Kenny Bednarek 19.80.
11   **Turku**, Finland, Paavo Nurmi Games (WACT G). In ideal weather and with a crowd of c.6000, there were world leads from Johannes Vetter, javelin 91.49, Andy Pozzi, 110m hurdles 13.17, and Nadine Visser, 100m hurdles 12.68.
14   **Herculis, Monaco** (DL). We were back with a full-scale Diamond League meeting that lived up to the great standards always set at Monaco. Joshua Cheptegei ran a phenomenal world 5000m record of 12:35.36, breaking the 16 year-old mark by Kenenisa Bekele. After 3000m in 7:35.14, he ran the last five laps in 60.10, 60.18, 60.33, 59.97 and 59.64 to finish well ahead of 2nd Nicholas Kimeli 12:51.78. Also great was the women's 5000m won by Hellen Obiri in 14:22.12 from Letesenbet Gidey 14:26.67, although Sifan Hassan dropped out before 4k. Further world-leading marks were recorded by Noah Lyles, 200m 19.76, Donavan Brazier, 800m 1:43.15 from Bryce Hoppel 1:43.15, Timothy Cheruiyot, 1500m 3:28.45 (despite a crazy pace by Timothy Sein of 52.59 at 400m and 1:51.24 at 800m) from Jakob Ingebrigtsen 3:28.68 European record and Jake Wightman 3:29.47, Soufiane El Bakkali, 3000mSt 8:08.04, Orlando Ortega, 110mh 13.11, Karsten Warholm, 400mh 47.10 and Faith Kipyegon, 1000m 2:29.15 second best ever and African and Commonwealth record. Behind her Laura Muir 2:30.82 and Jemma Reekie 2:31.11 both bettered the previous UK record, and between them Ciara Mageean set an Irish record of 2:31.06, and there were best ever times for places 3-5 and 9.
19   **Székesfehérvár**, Hungary. 10th István Gyulai Memorial Meeting (WACT G). Noah Lyles closed his abbreviated 2020 season with an impressive double, 100m in 10.05 and 200m 20.13. In clashes of the world's best Orlando Ortega beat Grant Holloway 13.21 to 13.22 at 110m hurdles, and Fabrice Zango won the triple jump with 17.43 from Christian Taylor 17.34 and Pedro Pablo Pichardo 17.28.
19   **Bydgoszcz**, Poland. Irina Szewinska Memorial (WACT S). After being beaten on count-back in the high jump in Monaco, Yuliya Levchenko beat Yaroslava Mahuchikh 2.00 to 1.97 and Michal Haratyk maintained his unbeaten season's record with a 21.61 shot win.
23   **Tokyo**, Japan (WACT G). Seiko Golden Grand Prix. Due to Covid-19 restrictions this was an all-Japanese affair. 20 year-old Nozomi Tanaka set a Japanese 1500m record at 4:05.27.
23   **Stockholm**, Sweden. Bauhaus Galan meeting (DL). Karsten Warholm ran the second fastest ever 400m hurdles, a European record 46.78; clipping the final barrier may have cost him the world record 46.87. 94 minutes later he returned to win the 400m in 45.05, for the best ever one-day double at these events. Laura Muir had a brilliant win at 1500m, her 3:57.86 with a 59.86 final lap taking her well clear of compatriots Laura Weightman 4:01.62 and Melissa Courtney-Bryant 4:01.81, and Timothy Cheruiyot was men's winner in 3:30.25 from Jakob Ingebrigtsen 3:30.74. As expected top home successes came from Armand Duplantis clearing 6.01 in the pole vault and Daniel Ståhl with 69.17 for his 13th successive discus win.
25   **Chorzów**, Poland. 66th Kusocinski Memorial (WACT S). Continuing his fine form, Johannes Vetter won the javelin with 90.08 and Jemma Reekie the 800m in 1:58.63. Wojciech Nowicki maintained an unbeaten hammer run with his first 80m throw of the year, 80.09. There were 5000 spectators allowed at the Slaski Stadium.
25 & 29   **Des Moines**, USA. Ryan Crouser produced ten 22m plus shot puts – four in the first meeting and all six over 22.25 in the second, winning with 22.56 and 22.72 respectively.
28-30   **Italian Championships**, Padua. Leonardo Fabbri, who started the year with a shot best of 20.99, improved from 21.57 to 21.99 here. Chiara Rosa won her 16th successive shot title.
29-30   **Pabianice**, Poland. Women's European records were set at the Polish ultras championships: 100k Dominika Stalmach 7:04:36 and 24 hours Malgorzata Pazda-Pozorska 260,679k.

September

2   Lausanne, Switzerland. Athletissima (DL). For the first time two men pole vaulted 6.02 in the same competition – Sam Kendricks (with one failure at 5.62) and Armand Duplantis (clean card). But Duplantis went over 6.07 on his first attempt before failing at 6.15 to clinch the victory. This and the women's event, won by Angelica Bengtsson with 4.72, were staged in the city centre.

3   Marseille, France (WACT B). Orlando Ortega maintained his unbeaten run in four 110m hurdles races this year with a meeting record 13.15 and the Scottish pair of Laura Muir, 800m 2:00.16, and Jemma Reekie, 1500m 4:02.20, won again.

4   Brussels, Belgium (DL). 44th Van Damme Memorial. Sir Mo Farah and Sifan Hassan set men's and women's world one hour records with 21,330m and 18,930m respectively. Farah, in his first track race for three years, ran throughout with training companion Bashir Abdi. They went through 5000m in 14:06.19, 10000m 28:12.73 and 15,000m 42:17.95 and Abdi set a world record at 20,000m in 56:00.02, 0.28 ahead of Farah. They were helped (presumably) by differently coloured LED lights installed on the inside edge of the track, getting clear of the indicated WR pace in the closing minutes. Farah made the significant break with 1 minute to go. Brigid Kosgei ran with Hassan until 300m to go and recorded 18,904m although she was ridiculously disqualified for a step on the kerb at 53 mins. The pair went through 10,000m in c.31:53 behind pacemaker Sheila Chelangat 31:52.45. Faith Kipyegon had her second near miss of the year at the 1000m world record, winning in 2:29.92 and Jakob Ingebrigtsen won the 1500m in 3:30.60 by nearly four seconds.

4-5   UK Championships, Manchester. Harry Coppell set a UK pole vault record at 5.85.

5   Prague, Czech Republic. Peres Jepchirchir set a women's only world record of 65:34 for the half marathon running on a 1280m loop, in Letna Park, Prague. She slowed a little after 5k in 15:20 and 10k in 30:32. The men's winner from a small field was Kibiwott Kandie 58:58.

5-6   Finnkampen, Tampere, Finland. Sweden beat Finland 206-201 for men and 221-186 for women in the annual clash. Best performance was 69.20 discus by the prolific Daniel Ståhl.

6   Chorzów, Poland (WACT G). Kamila Skolimowska Memorial meeting. Johannes Vetter produced a mighty javelin throw of 97.76, the second longest throw of all-time, 72cm short of Jan Zelezny's 24 year-old world record. This came in the third round and he followed with 94.84. More mighty throwing came from Ryan Crouser whose 22.70 shot put was one of five 22.40 plus throws, with Michal Haratyk 2nd with 21.79, and at hammer Pawel Fajdek producing a season's best 79.81 ahead of his great rival Wojciech Nowicki 78.88, and Alexandra Tavernier, women's winner with 74.12. Best on the track was Laura Muir with 3:58.24 for 1500m.

6   Russian Walks Championships, Voronovskoye. Yelena Lashmanova has been one of the top two women walkers in the world for several years, but has not been able to compete internationally. Here she made a sensational debut at 50km, setting what would be a world record at 3:50:42, although the Russian ban and lack of international officials would rule that out. Both she and 2nd placed Margarita Nikiforova 3:59:56 would rank high up in men's world lists, something that very few women at any event have been able to match. There was also a world-leading mark of 3:43:29 by men's winner Dementiy Cheparev.

8   Dessau. Germany (WACT B). Malaika Mihambo long jumped 7.03, the world's best outdoors for the year, to win from Maryna Bekh-Romanchuk 6.85 and Anastasiya Mironchik-Ivanova 6.72 at the Internationales LA Meeting Anhalt.

8   Ostrava, Czech Republic. 58th Golden Spike (WACT G). 3000 spectators were allowed to watch and they saw seven new meeting records. These were headed by a brilliant run by 19 year-old Jacob Kiplimo who won the 5000m in 12:48.63 narrowly from Selemon Barega 12:49.08. In third place Yemaneberhan Crippa took the Italian record down to 13:02.26. In the women's race Sifan Hassan bided her time before sprinting clear to win in 14:37.85 from Sheila Chelangat 14:40.51. Ryan Crouser continued his amazing season to win the shot with 22.43 and Faith Kipyegon was again supreme with 3:59.05 for 1500m. Previously unbeaten in 2020 Fabrice Zango 17.42 had to yield to Christian Taylor 17.46 in the triple jump, but Karsten Warholm extended his unbeaten run to ten with 400m hurdles in 47.62.

8   Rovereto, Italy. 56th Palio Città della Quercia meeting (WACT S). Hedda Hynne ran 800m in 1:59.15 to break the 10 year-old Norwegian record.

8-11   Russian Championships, Chelyabinsk. Top marks came from Yekaterina Ivonina. 3000m steeplechase 9:16.84, and Yekaterina Konova, triple jump 14.73w.

12-13   French Championships, Albi. Renaud Lavillenie won his tenth French outdoor pole vault title with 5.80 and top track performances came in the sprint hurdles – Wilhem Bélocian the men's 110mh in 13.20 and 19 year-old Cyrena Samba-Mayala the women's 100m in 12.73.

13   Berlin, Germany. 79th ISTAF (WACT S). With 47.08 for 400m hurdles Karsten Warholm broke the 40 year-old meeting record of 47.17 set by Edwin Moses. With social distancing regulations in place, 3500 spectators were

allowed to enter the stadium and they saw world-leading performances by Laura Muir, 1500m 3:57.40 (from Laura Weightman 4:00.29 and Jessica Hull 4:00.42 Oceania record), Christian Taylor, TJ 17.57, and Hyvin Jepkemoi, 9:06.14 3000m steeplechase. Andrius Gudzius won the discus with 66.72, handing Daniel Ståhl 65.89 his first defeat after 15 straight victories.
14-15 **Zagreb**, Croatia. 71st Boris Hanzekovic Memorial (WACT G). There was more top shot putting from Ryan Crouser, whose four throws over 22m were headed by 22.74 in the city park on the eve of the main meeting. There Daniel Ståhl gained revenge in the discus, beating Andrius Gudzius 68.87 to 68.22, and another Swede Khaddi Sagnia matched the long jump best she had recorded indoors with 6.92. Outstanding on the track were middle distance winners Stewart McSweyn, 1500m 3:32.17, and Daniel Rowden, 800m 1:44.09.
15 **Bellinzona**, Switzerland (WACT B). Hedda Hynne improved the Norwegian 800m record – this time to 1:58.10.
15-18 **Chinese Championships**, Shaoxing. Wang Jianan long jumped 8.36 for an outdoor world lead from Huang Changzhou 8.33 and Lu Shiying had an upset win in the javelin with a pb 67.29 over world leader Lu Huihui 65.70.
16 **Kladno**, Czech Republic (WACT B). Alexandra Tavernier improved her French hammer record to 75.23.
16 **Paris**, France. Pending appeal Lamine Diack, former president of the IAAF, was sentenced to prison for 2 years and fined €500,000 when found guilty of multiple corruption changes and breach of trust by the Paris Criminal Court with sentences handed also to five others including Diack's son Papa Massata (5 years).
17 **Rome**, Italy. 40th Golden Gala (DL). Following his two world records indoors, Armand Duplantis exceeded Sergey Bubka's outdoor world record 6.14 in 1994 by clearing 6.15 on his second attempt. The first three men in the 3000m set national records as Jacob Kiplimo won the battle of the teenagers over Jakob Ingebrigtsen 7:26.64 to 7:27.05, which was a European U23 record. 3rd-placed Stewart McSweyn set an Oceania record 7:28.02. Karsten Warholm recorded his third best ever time, with 47.08 in the 400m hurdles and Femke Bol also extended her season's unbeaten run at 400mh with 53.90. A class apart was Elaine Thompson-Herah who won the 100m in 10.85 to runner-up Aleia Hobbs 11.12 and Akani Simbine won the men's race in 9.96.
18-20 **Kumagaya**, Japan. Team Championships. The continuing strength of distance running in Japan was demonstrated by the men's 10,000m in which the first six were Kenyans headed by Richard Yator 27:01.42, Benard Koech 27:02.39 and Bedan Karoki 27:02.89, but also 26 Japanese men broke 29 mins.
19 **Leiden**, Netherlands. After excelling at 5000m, Nicholas Kimeli ran 26:58.97 for 10,000m from a previous best of 29:52.15A in 2017.
19-20 **Chinese Walks Championships**, Taian. In her first competition of the year Liu Hong won the 20k title in 1:27:48.
19-20 **Balkan Championships**, Cluj-Napoca, Romania.
25 **Doha**, Qatar (DL). Although numbers of top athletes were down this was as usual a meeting of high standard. In 32°C heat Hellen Obiri starred with a 3000m victory in a world-leading 8:22.54; her finish being too strong for those who had run with her for most of the way. Agnes Tirop and Beatrice Chepkoech came second and third, both timed at 8:22.92, while Margaret Kipkemboi 8:24.76 and Hyvin Jepkemoi 8:25.13 were fourth and fifth. Gudaf Tsegay 8:25.23 and Laura Weightman 8:26.31 set best ever times for sixth and seventh places. Another world leading mark was by Faith Kipyegon, who produced a dominant run to maintain her unbeaten streak this year with a pb 1:57.68 in her first race at 800m for five years. Stewart McSweyn capped his Diamond League season by breaking the Australian record for 1500m with 3:30.51 as the first five set pbs including Selemon Barega 2nd 3:32.97 and Soufiane El Bakkali 3rd 3:33.45. Elaine Thompson-Herah was again dominant, winning the 100m in 10.87, and after a couple of false start disqualifications, Aaron Mallett won the 110mh hurdles in a pb 13.15. The wretched 'last round counts' format was again used for the women's long jump, but Maryna Bekh-Romanchuk was a worthy winner either way with her final 6.91.

October

3 **Nairobi**, Kenya. Kip Keino Classic (WACT G). In the first-ever global one-day meeting in Kenya, three men ran the fastest ever times for 5000m at high altitude: Nicholas Kimeli 13:08.32, Berihu Aregawi 13:08.91 and Jacob Krop 13:11.88. The three Kenyan world champions won in impressive style: Timothy Cheruiyot, 1500m 3:34.31, Hellen Obiri, 5000m 15:06.36, and Beatrice Chepkoech, 3000m steeplechase 9:29.05.
6 Virgin **London Marathon**, GBR. Staged as an elite-only race on 19 laps of a loop course around St. James's Park in central London, the race was of the highest standard although times were affected by cold (10°C) and wet weather. Brigid Kosgei finished well clear in the women's race in 2:18:58 accompanied for much of the way by Ruth Chepngetich, through halfway in 68:13. Chepngetich faded and the 37 year-old Sara Hall, 2:14 behind at halfway, first passed Ashete Belere and then, with a storming finish, Chepngetich just metres from the finish line for a pb 2:22.01. Then came the astonishing men's race in which

Eliud Kipchoge succumbed to a blocked ear and sore hip to finish 8th in 2:06:49, the end of seven years of invincibility at the marathon. A minute ahead of him there was a three-man sprint for the line, won by Shura Kitata in 2:05:41, a second ahead of Vincent Kipchumba with Sisay Lemma third in 2:05:45.

7 **Valencia**, Spain. Attempts at world records were marvellously successful. First Letesenbet Gidey ran 5000m in 14:06.62 to take 4.53 secs off Tirunesh Dibaba's 2008 record, and then Joshua Cheptegei reeled off 25 laps in an average of less than 63 sec apiece for 10,000m in 26:11.00, taking 6.53 secs off Kenenisa Bekele's 2005 mark, just 54 days after he had improved on Bekele's 5000m WR. Perhaps aided by the trackside pacing lights, Cheptegei's run was a marvel of metronomic precision. After 63.6 for his first 400m, he ran every lap between 62.4 and 63.2 before his closing 60.08. Roy Hoornweg set the pace for the first kilometre (2:37.9) before Matthew Ramsden led through 2000m in 5:15.05 and 3000m in 7:52.79. handing over to Nicholas Kimeli, who stayed with Cheptegei to 5000m and came 2nd in 27:12.98. Gidey used a slightly different method as after kilometres in 2:51.10 and 2:51.63 Beatrice Chepkoech stepped up the tempo with 2:49.12 to 3000m in 8:31.85. Then Gidey took over with relentless 67 second laps and kms of 2:47.32 and 2:47.46. The only other finisher was Winnie Nanyondo 15:57.16.

10 **Hengelo, Netherlands.** Sifan Hassan smashed the European 10,000m record at the FBK After Summer Competition. Her 29:36.67 was the fourth fastest of all-time and took 24.42 secs off Paula Radcliffe's 30:01.09. Hassan was led at world record pace by Laura Weightman to 3000m in c.8:48. Hassan passed 5000m in about 14:38 but conditions were against a world record (29:17.45) as the rain got heavier and the temperature fell to 8°C.

17 **World Half Marathon Championships**, Gdynia, Poland. On a cold, breezy morning Peres Jepchirchir ran 56:16, a world record in a women-only race to regain the title that she won in 2016. Melat Kejeta smashed the European women-only record to take silver in 65:18, with Yalemzerf Yehualaw a close third in 65:19. Defending champion Netsanet Gudeta was one of several top women who fell, in her case at a sharp 90° turn while with the leaders and she fell back to finish 8th in 66:46. Ethiopia were the team winners as their three scorers totalled a championship record 3:16:39. In a race of unprecedented depth, the first three women finished inside the previous women-only world record, six broke 66 minutes, nine inside 67 min and 65 of the 101 finishers set pbs! The men's winner was 19 year-old Jacob Kiplimo in a championship record 58:48 with his Ugandan compatriot Joshua Cheptegei, just ten days after his world record in Valencia, 4th in 59:21 on his debut at the distance. The first 10 runners broke 60 minutes, the first time that ever happened at the World Champs and just the second time ever, and a record 28 men were inside 61 min. There was an East African sweep of the team medals as Uganda were 3rd behind Kenya and Ethiopia.

17 **Tachikawa**, Japan. The qualifying race for the Hakone Ekiden was a half marathon headed by four Kenyans running for Japanese corporate teams. Behind them came hundreds of Japanese runners from 46 university teams with 60 men under 63 mins, 173 under 64 mins; 246 under 65 mins, 308 under 66 mins, 360 under 67 mins and 421 under 70 minutes (all but 8 Japanese college students) with masses of pbs.

24 **Dudince**, Slovakia. The first international race of 2020 at 50k for top walkers was won by Matej Tóth in 3:41:15 for his fifth success in the annual race.

November

14 **Inzai**, Japan. Three Japanese men went well under the previous world best for 10,000m track walk of 38:01.49, Eiki Takahashi winning in 37:25.21 from Koki Ikeda 37:25.90 and Yuta Koga 37:35.00.

29 **New Delhi**, India. The 16th Airtel Delhi Half Marathon continues to grow in importance. Yalemzerf Yehualaw produced a stunning 64:46 victory, the second fastest women's time ever. A fierce pace was set as six women followed male pacemaker Alex Kibarus (who ran until 2k to go) through 5k in 15:27, Yehualew, Ababel Yeshaneh, Ruth Chepngetich and Irene Cheptai reached 10k in 30:40 and the first three 15k in 46:15. Yehualew went clear and won by 20 secs from Chepngetich with Yeshaneh 3rd in 65:31. Amdework Walelegn outsprinted compatriot and double winner Andamlak Belihu to win the men's race in 58:53 from 58:54 with Stephen Kisssa 3rd in 58:56 and, with the second best half marathon debut, Muktar Edris 4th in 59:05.

December

4 **Japanese distance championships**, Osaka. National records were set at 10,000m by Akira Aizawa 27:18.75 and by the resurgent Hitomi Niiya 30:20.44, an amazing 36.26 secs off her previous best, set when 5th at the 2013 World Champs.

6 **Fukuoka**, Japan. 74th edition of famous marathon won by Yuya Yoshida in 2:07:05.

6 **Valencia**, Spain. Four men ran inside the old world record of 58:01 at the Valencia Trinidad Alsonso EDP Half Marathon. In near ideal conditions they finished: Kibowott Kandie 57:32, Jacob Kiplimo 57:37, Rhonex Kipruto 57:49 (fastest ever debut) and Alexander Mutiso 57:59, with Kiplimo setting a world record 54:42 for 20k. There were also the best ever times for 5th Philemon Kiplimo 58:11 and 6th

Kelvin Kiptum 58:42. Genzebe Dibaba made the fastest ever women's debut at the distance as she won in 65:18 from Sheila Chepkirui 65:39. Evans Chebet and Peres Jepchirchir secured a Kenyan double in the marathon. Jepchirchir moved up to No 5 on the all-time world list with 2:17:16 and Chebet ran 2:03:00 to improve on his previous best by exactly two minutes and rank sixth fastest all-time. Second woman was Joyciline Jepkosgei 2:18:40 and third Helaria Johannes improved the women's age-40 record to 2:19:52 with a record six women under 2:20 and best ever times for places 6-8. The men's podium was completed by Lawrence Cherono 2:03:04 and Birhanu Legese 2:03:16. There were best ever times for places 3 (=), 4, 8-17, 29- 50+. 30 men under 2:10 beat the record of 28 set in Tokyo on 1 Mar 2020, 51 under 2:13. A big majority of the finishers in all the races ran pbs.
10-13 Troféu Brasil, Bragança Paulista. Top mark at the Brazilian Championships was 8364 decathlon by Felipe dos Santos, adding 335 to his pb. Darian Romani won his ninth successive shot title with 21.11.

18-19 Saint Paul, Réunion, France. Kevin Mayer achieved his goal of the Olympic qualifying standard and his 8552 decathlon was the world's best for 2020. This included a pb 110m hurdles in 13.54.
19-20 Brisbane (Nathan), Australia. Ashley Moloney added 389 points to his pb and 2 to the Oceania record as he scored 8492, including a first-day score, 12th best ever, of 4613 culminating in the third best ever 400m in a decathlon of 45.82. This, from a previous best of 46.74 was one of seven event pbs by Moloney. Second was Cedric Dubler with 8367, the third best score of 2020.
20 Hofu, Japan. With 2nd place here in 2:10:26 Yuki Kawauchi ran his 100th sub-2:20 time in 107 marathons.
27 Saransk, Russia. Yukita Lashmanova recorded a world indoor best for 5000m walk with 20:04.4, a time bettered by only three outdoor times.
29 Penguin, Tasmania, Australia. Stewart McSweyn ran the fastest mile of 2020 and an Australian all-comers record with 3:50.61.

Retired in 2020/21
Men: Andrew Bumbalough USA, Michael Butter NED, Garfield Darien FRA, Eirik Greibrokk Dolve NOR, Rico Freimith GER, Marshall Hall NZL, Mateusz Jerzy POL, Riley Masters USA, Kyle Merber USA, Florian Obst GER, Dathan Ritzenhein USA, Karl Robert Saluri EST, Michael Schrader GER, Duane Solomon USA, Zhang Guowei CHN. **Women**: Kelsie Ahbe CAN, Sharrika Barnett USA/JAM, Jackie Baumann GER, Cindy Billaud FRA, Melissa Breen AUS, Lucy Bryan GBR, Nicole Büchler SUI, Nenah De Coninck BEL, Aurélie De Ryck BEL, Tori Hoggard USA, Lexi Jacobus USA, Anne-Mari Kiekara (née Sandell, then Hyryläinen FIN), Isabel Macias ESP, Sarah MacPherson CAN, Keiko Nogami JPN, Marilyn Okoro GBR, Jelena Prokopcuka LAT, Irene Pusterla SUI, Stine Seidler GER, Hanami Sekine JPN, Jasmin Stowers USA, Diana Sujew GER, Anju Takimizawa JPN, Zivile Vaiciukeviciute LTU, Sanne Wolters-Verstagen NED

Transfer of Nationality/Allegiance 2020-21
Of athletes who have made world lists

	Name	From	To	Noted	Eligible
Men	Niklas Arrhenius	SWE	USA	20.3.20	26.8.22
	Robert Grant	USA	ITA	21.7.20	
	Eric Harrison	USA	TTO	7.5.20	15.7.21
	Ridouane Haroufi	MAR	USA	20.2.20	
	João de Oliveira	BRA	POR	.20	
	Felix Svensson	SWE	SUI	2.2.21	25.8.22
	Hilary Kipsang Yego	KEN	TUR	3.2.20	
	Zane Weir	RSA	ITA	23.2.21	25.2.21
Women	Auriel Dongmo	CMR	POR	24.3.20	26.7.20
	Edna Chepkorir Kurgat	KEN	USA	19.2.21	
	Sofia Yaremchuk	UKR	ITA	12.2.21	17.10.23

ATHLETICS INTERNATIONAL
Edited by Peter Matthews & Mel Watman

The newsletter has, since 1993, provided definite details of athletics, keeping readers in over 60 countries informed of very detailed results (to at least world top 150-200 standards) of track and field, road and cross-country, Also features and news items from around the world.
It is obtainable by email, with at least 35 issues published annually (weekly in peak season).
 Annual subscription 2021: £75 or US $105 or 95 euros. Cash or cheques drawn on a UK bank,
  payable to Athletics International or by bank transfer (details from Mel) at:
 Athletics International, 13 Garden Court, Marsh Lane, Stanmore HA7 4TE, UK
  Email: melvynwatman@gmail.com

ATHLETES OF 2020

2020 was a year unlike any other as described in the previous section. Wanting to recognise the achievements of those who did compete, I have compiled world rankings as usual, but not necessarily to the usual ten-deep per event, preferring to restrict the rankings to those who achieved levels that might normally warrant consideration – but I have been a little generous in this respect. Many athletes with very thin seasons, something that might usually have militated against their inclusion, are ranked.

Three athletes stood out in the summer months for consideration as world athletes of the year – and indeed, even without major championships, compiled season's records to compare with any in history. These were Karsten Warholm at 400m hurdles (plus a world best for 300m hurdles and some 400m flat races), Ryan Crouser with the best ever series of throws at shot and above all the charismatic Armand Duplantis. He took Sergey Bubka's long-standing pole vault world records – indoors (6.17 and 6.18) and outdoors (6.15) and matched Bubka's record of ten 6m competitions in one year. The camaraderie between Duplantis and the men who preceded him as the world's best Sam Kendricks and Renaud Lavillenie was wondrous to behold. Not far behind this trio was Johannes Vetter, with a javelin throw exceeded only by the great Jan Zelezny.

And then there was Joshua Cheptegei who set world records in his first three races of the year, at 5k on the road and then smashing the long-standing track records at 5000m and 10,000m. Only ten days after the last he ran in the World Half Marathon Championships and could not maintain his unbroken winning run as he said "I discovered I still had some fatigue in the legs" but still came in a creditable fourth in 59:21 in his debut at the distance in a very high quality race. There were also long distance world records by Mo Farah, back on the track at the 1 hour event at Brussels, where Bashir Abdi edged ahead for the WR at 20,000m, and in December at Valencia no less than four men broke the world record at half marathon as Kibiwott Kandie improved the mark by 20 seconds.

My rankings are shown for each event – notably including indoor form this year – and for some events more athletes took a full part in world events then than in the outdoor season, several competing only indoors.

100 Metres

There was very little significant competition in the sprints, but nonetheless some sharp times were produced, although just four men under 10 seconds was the least since three in 1995. Michael Norman has starred at 200m and 400m in recent years and competed just once in 2020 – and that was his first race at 100m since high school in 1996, as he ran a startling 9.86 at Fort Worth in July. That, with his bests at 200m 19.70 and 400m 43.45 in 2019, took Norman to third on the world all-time top combination sprinters behind Usain Bolt and Michael Johnson.

Further wind-legal sub-10 second times were run twice each by Trayvon Bromell in Florida and by Akani Simbine, in Pretoria and Rome, and once by Andre De Grasse, and wind-assisted marks were headed by Bromell 9.87w and Noah Lyles 9.93w twice. Bromell and Lyles each won four 100m races, including heats, and Simbine had the best depth, winning in five finals, four in Europe, with five times at 10.03 or better. Bromell and Lyles each had a win over De Grasse, but ranking is difficult as my top four were undefeated but did not meet. Yoshihide Kiryu and Asaka Cambridge went 1-2 at the Japanese Championships where the times were slowed by poor weather. Kirui had a best of 10.04 and lost just once, 10.06 to 10.04 to Cambridge at Fukui. Second best in European meetings was the consistent Arthur Gue Cissé, with a best of 10.04, behind Simbine 9.96 in Rome, with Filippo Tortu third in 10.09.

Most times at 10.00/10.05 or faster: Simbine 2/5, Bromell 2+1w/2+1w, De Grasse 1+1w/1+1w; Lyles 2w/2w, Justin Gatlin 1w/2w, Cambridge 0/2

1. Simbine, 2. Bromell, 3. Lyles, 4. Norman, 5. Cissé, 6. De Grasse, 7. Kiryu, 8. Cambridge, 9. Tortu, 10. Gatlin.

Indoors at **60 Metres** Christian Coleman won the US title at high-altitude Albuquerque in

Selections for World Top Ten

	PJM	AI
* Armand Duplantis	1	1
* Joshua Cheptegei	2	2
* Karsten Warholm	3	3
* Ryan Crouser	4	4
* Johannes Vetter	5	5
Jacob Kiplimo	6	7
Kibiwott Kandie	7	-
Timothy Cheruiyot	8	9
Daniel Ståhl	9	6
Donavan Brazier	10	8
Noah Lyles	11	10

Athletics International poll was before Kandie's world half marathon record.

Duplantis was WA athlete of the year and * indicates their five finalists.

6.37, a time bettered only by his own 6.34 at this meeting in 2018. Marvin Bracy was 2nd in the US Champs at 6.49 while the other top 12 times of the season (6.51 or better) were shared by Ronnie Baker 5, and Coleman and Demek Kemp 3 each. Baker's undefeated season took him to victory on the World Indoor tour with his best 6.44 at Liévin and Madrid with Kemp (4th US) 2nd in both those races.

200 Metres

Noah Lyles retained his supremacy, winning his three 200m races: 19.94 at Clermont, 19.76 Monaco and 20.13 Székesfehérvár (as well as 18.90 for 185m at Bradenton!). Kenny Bednarek with three and a best of 19.80 and Steven Gardiner, wins in 19.96 and 20.19. also had sub-20.20 times. Bednarek, who also ran 100m in 10.09/10.02w, was 2nd to Lyles at Clermont. Next best for depth of times was Lyles's brother Josephus with three at 20.32 or better. Eseosa Desalu ran three 20.3x times.

Most times at 20.10/20.30 or better: Bednarek 2/4, N Lyles 2/3, Gardiner 1/2, J Lyles 0/2
1. N Lyles, 2. Bednarek, 3. Gardiner, 4. J Lyles, 5. De Grasse, 6. Desalu

400 Metres

This was surely the men's track event most affected by the lack of competition, especially in the USA. Only two of the 2019 top ten raced at all at the event in 2020 and there were only two sub-45 second times this year: by US athletes Justin Robinson 44.91 and Michael Cherry 44.98 at Marietta in August. The 18 year-old Robinson had no other races and Cherry one. Next fastest were Karsten Warholm, who as well as his brilliant hurdling, had three very easy wins on the flat with a best of 45.05 at the Bauhaus Galan in Stockholm, and Akeem Bloomfield who won his two races, 46.20 indoors in Glasgow and 45.07 at Clermont. The 20 year-old Italian Eduardo Scotti showed promise with four wins and a 3rd ending with a 45.20 win in the Rome Golden Gala from Youssef Karam 45.25. Wayde van Niekerk made a nice return with wins at 100m, 200m and 400m in Bloemfontein, then a 45.48 win at Bellinzona.
1. Warholm, 2. Robinson, 3. Cherry, 4. Bloomfield, 5. Scotti

800 Metres

Donavan Brazier was dominant. Indoors he had two races, heading the world lists at 600m 1:14.39 and 800m 1:44.22. Outdoors he won three 800m races – 1:43.84 at Newberg, 1:43.15 at Monaco and 1:43.76 at Stockholm and he also won a 1500m in a pb 3:35.85. The only other man to break 1:44 was Bryce Hoppel, close with 1:43.23 at Monaco. He had won the US indoor title after 2nd to Brazier in New York, but after Monaco was 4th in Zagreb and 5th in Doha in two of the most important races.

Ferguson Cheruiyot was 8th in Monaco and 4th in Stockholm, but then had a sequence of seven wins, including in Doha, where he was followed by Elliot Giles, Wycliffe Kinyamal and Peter Bol. It was a fine year for British 800m runners with Daniel Rowden beating Jake Wightman for the UK title and Rowden (1:44.09), Giles and Wightman 1-2-3 at Zagreb. Wightman ran his best 1:44.18 to win at Ostrava from Andreas Kramer (Swedish record 1:44.47) and Amel Tuka. Kramer, 3rd at Stockholm and 6th at Zagreb, was the most prolific racer. Marco Arop was 3rd in Monaco 1:44.14 and 2nd Stockholm 1:44.67 plus 2nd to Giles in Bydgoszcz. Wesley Vázquez had five times under 1:46 but was well beaten in the biggest races although he was 2-1 v Bol, who beat his compatriot Joseph Deng 6-1. Collins Kipruto won all his six indoor races and ran 1:45s in his four outdoor races, including 5th at Zagreb with Vázquez 8th,

Most times sub-1:45.0: F Cheruiyot 5, Brazier 3+1i, Giles 3, Arop, Rowden, Wightman 2
1. Brazier, 2. F Cheruiyot 3. Rowden, 4. Giles, 5. Hoppel, 6. Arop, 7. Wightman, 8. Kramer, 9. C Kipruot, 10. Vázquez

1500 Metres

Although he only ran three 1500m races, his wins in those showed that Timothy Cheruiyot remained clearly the world's best. He beat Jakob Ingebrigtsen with 3:28.46 to 3:28.68 in Monaco and 3:30.25 to 3:30.74 in Stockholm and also won in Nairobi. Jake Wightman, 3:29.47 in his only 1500m of the year, and Filip Ingebrigtsen (who had two wins indoors) 3:30.35 rounded off the year's top four on times in Monaco, where Yomif Kejelcha, Jesús Gómez and Marcin Lewandowski also beat 3:34. Jakob Ingebrigtsen also had three wins, including 3:30.68 in Brussels and at Ostrava and in the Norwegian Champs. Stewart McSweyn was 3rd in Stockholm in 3:31.47, won in Zagreb and in Doha where he improved the Australian record to 3:30.51 with Selemon Barega, Soufiane El Bakkali and Lemecha Girma setting pbs behind him. Ignacio Fontes improved from 3:39.11 in 2019 to 3:33.72 and was 2-2 v compatriot Gómez.

After modest results indoors, Kumai Taki ended well with 2nd in Ostrava and Nairobi. McSweyn ran the year's fastest mile with 3:50.61 on December 27 after the previous bests came at San Donato Milanese, with Matthew Ramsden winning in 3:51.23 from Yemaneberhan Crippa and Ryan Gregson. Indoors the fastest 1500m was 3:34.77 by Josh Thompson.

Most times sub-3:35.0 or 3:52.0M: J Ingebrigtsen, McSweyn 5, Cheruiyot, Gómez 3, El Bakkali, Fontes 2
1. Cheruiyot, 2. J Ingebrigtsen, 3. McSweyn, 4. Wightman, 5. F Ingebrigtsen, 6. Baraga, 7. El Bakkali, 8. Kejelcha, 9. Taki, 10. Gómez

3000 Metres/2 Miles

The first three men at the Golden Gala in Rome set national records as Jacob Kiplimo won the battle of the teenagers over Jakob Ingebrigtsen 7:26.64 to 7:27.05, which was a European U23 record. 3rd-placed Stewart McSweyn set an Oceania record with 7:28.02. The next fastest times were run indoors at Liévin, when Getnet Wale won in 7:32.80 from Selemon Barega, Birhanu Yemataw and Lemecha Girma, all under 7:35. Two weeks earlier Barega had beaten Wale in Düsseldorf (Bethwel Birgen 3rd) and later Wale won from Birgen and Barega at Madrid.

Jakob Ingebrigtsen also set a European record 4:50.01 for **2000 Metres** at Oslo, when his brother Henrik was 2nd in 4:53.72.

5000 Metres

Although there were few top class races at the distance, there were still three won in under 12:50. Pride of place goes to Joshua Cheptegei's world record in Monaco on August 14 when his 12:35.36 improved Kenenisa Bekele's 2004 mark by 1.99 secs. Second to him in 12:51.78 was Nicholas Kimeli, who later won in Nairobi in 13:08.32, the fastest ever at high altitude, and who also paced Cheptegei to 5000m in 13:07.73 in his world 10,000m record. Mohammed Ahmed improved by over 10 seconds with a North American record 12:48.63 in Portland, 10.15 ahead of Lopez Lomong, and at the Golden Spike meeting in Ostrava 19 year-old Jacob Kiplimo won in 12:48.63 from 20 year-old Selemon Barega 12:49.08, with Yemaneberhan Crippa setting an Italian record 13:02.26 in third. Berihu Aregawi 13:08.91 and Jacob Krop 13:11.98 were 2-3 in Nairobi, also under the previous altitude best, and Krop was also 3rd in Monaco. Stewart McSweyn had three good times – 13:09.83 win in Gothenburg, 6th in Monaco 13:13.22 and 2nd to Yomif Kejelcha in Hengelo in 13:16.02.

Most times under 13:15: Kimeli 3, B Koech, Krop, McSweyn 2.
1. Cheptegei. 2. Kimeli, 3. Kiplimo, 4. Ahmed, 5. Barega, 6. Lomong, 7. Crippa, 8. McSweyn, 9. Aregawi, 10. Kejelcha

10,000 Metres

As with the women, the world lists are dominated by performances in Japanese races – particularly by Kenyans. But the top two times were set in Europe. At Leiden in September Nicholas Kimeli took nearly three minutes off his best with 26:58.97, winning by a big margin from Solomon Boit. Then a month later in Valencia came a marvellous display of metronomic running from Joshua Cheptegei whose 26:11.00 took 6.53 secs off Kenenisa Bekele's 2005 world record. Yes, he had the benefit of Kimeli, who hung on for 2nd with Shadrack Kipchirchir 3rd, as pacemaker and the pacing lights and no doubt the new generation of shoes made a difference, but he still showed that he is a very special athlete. The fastest races for those Japanese-based Kenyans came from wins by Richard Yator at Kumagaya in 27:01.42, closely followed by Benard Koech and Bedan Karoki, with Cleophas Kandie and Alexander Mutiso also getting into the world top ten and nine men inside 28 minutes, and at Yokohama in 27:01.74, 0.21 ahead of Jonathan Ndiku, who also won at Hatano in 27:07.20 and had won at Abashiri from Mutiso and Yator. Koech 27:14.84 and Karoki 27:15.97 featured in a fast race at Fukagawa and Koech also had a win at Isahaya in 27:31.13. There were an astonishing 105 Japanese men in the top 200 (under 28:24).
1. Cheptegei, 2. Kimeli, 3. Yator, 4. Ndiku, 5. Koech, 6. Karoki, 7. Kandie, 8. Mutiso, 9. Kipchirchir, 10. Joseph Ndirangu

Half Marathon

Jacob Kiplimo was an outstanding world champion, the 19 year-old running a championship record 58:49 in Gdynia; his only previous race at the distance was a high altitude 61:53 win in 2019. The Worlds runner-up Kibiwott Kandie, however, went on to beat Kiplimo in Valencia where the first four men beat the previous world record as these two were followed by Rhonex Kipruto (fastest ever debut) and Alexander Mutiso. Kandie became the first man ever to run three sub-59 sec times and then made it four with his world record 57:32 after his wins at Ras Al Khaimah in 58:58 and in Prague in 58:38 and 58:54 in Gdynia. Mutiso had won at Santa Pola in 59:09 and was 2nd at RAK in 59:16. Philemon Kiplimo 58:11 and Kelvin Kiptum 58:42 ran the fastest ever for 5th and 6th places in Valencia with the best ever times for 8th to 10th, and after Amedework Walelegn, Joshua Cheptegei (on debut), Andamlak Belihu and Leonard Barsoton (6th RAK) had been 3rd to 6th at the World Champs, ten men had bettered 1 hour and there were best ever times for places 13 to 38th (61:42). For further places extraordinary new peaks were achieved in the Japanese races at Yamaguchi in February and Tachikawa in October. Another top race was in New Delhi, where Walelgn won in 58:51 from Belihu 58:54, Stephen Kissa, Muktar Edris, Barsoton and Tesfahun Akinew 59:22. Jemal Yimer won at Houston in 59:22 leading nine men under an hour, with Philemon Kiplimo 4th and Belihu 9th.
1. Kandie, 2. J Kiplimo, 3. Mutiso, 4. Walelegn, 5. R Kipruto, 6. Belihu, 7. P Kiplimo, 8. Cheptegei, 9. Barsoton, 10. Kiptum

Marathon

The top early marathons of the year set new records and this was before any of the majors were scheduled to take place. With the pandemic declared in March these were postponed or cancelled, to the full impact of what many regarded as the impact of the new generation of shoes was yet to be seen. In Dubai in January a record eleven men broke 2:07 with the best ever times for places 11-14 and 16 and 14 men under 2:08 was equalled at the Seville Marathon in February. The winner Gebre Mekuant Ayenew in his 22nd marathon improved his pb massively from 2:09:00 in 2017 to 2:04:46 with Barnabas Kiptum 2nd. 42 of the top 48 men (under 2:20) and 25 of the top 29 women (under 2:53) finishers set pbs. Then there was the Tokyo Marathon on March 1. Lonah Chemtai Salpeter won the women's race in an Israeli record 2:17:45 from Birhane Dibaba who set a pb with 2:18:35. Men's winner was Berhanu Legese 2:04:15 from Bashir Abdi, Belgian record 2:04:48, Sisay Lemma 2:04:55 and Suguro Osako, Japanese record 2:05:29. The use of Nike's Alphafly shoes showed in the men's race in which new records were set in depth; 17 men under 2:08 was another record and there were 28 under 2:10, compared to the previous best ever of 19 in Seville. There were thus the best ever times for places 14 to 50 and beyond, those in the 20s minutes ahead of anything ever seen before. 33 of the top 50 set pbs. Further numbers under 2:12- 35, 2:13- 47, 2:14- 53, 2:15- 57, 2:20- 86. The most previously under 2:15 was 46 for London 1991 and that race surely had significantly better participants.

There were then no big marathons until London in October, for elite runners only over 19 laps of a loop course around St. James's Park. Conditions were not suitable for extra-special times, but there was a big shock as Eliud Kipchoge suffering from ear and hip problems, came only 8th in a race won in a close finish by Tola Shura Kitata in 2:05:41 from Vincent Kipchumba Toroitich and Sisay Lemma with the 2019 2-3 Mosinet Geremew and Mule Wasihun 4th and 5th. Finally in December at Valencia many records were left behind as Evans Chebet (who had earlier won at Lake Biwa) won in 2:03:00 from Lawrence Cherono 2:03:06, Legese 2:03:15 and Amos Kipruto (only 18th Tokyo). The record number under 2:10 was increased to 30 and there were best ever times for places 3-4, 8-17 and 29-50+.
1. Chebet, 2. Legese, 3. Shura Kitata, 4. Lemma, 5. Kipchumba Toroitich, 6. Cherono, 7. Abdi, 8. Ayenew, 9. B Kiptum, 10. Osako

3000 Metres Steeplechase

This event was highly affected by the shutdown of the sport and it was staged at just one DL meeting – in Monaco, and the best six times of 2020 came there. Soufiane El Bakkali won in 8:08.04 from Leonard Bett, Djilali Bedrani, Fernando Carro, Matt Hughes and Topi Raitanen. Then there were excellent high altitude times at Nairobi where Abraham Kibiwot ran 8:17.60 and Bett. 8:17.63. Raitanen also had two wins in Finland.
1. El Bakkali, 2. Bett, 3. Kibiwot, 4. Bedrani, 5. Carro, 6. Hughes, 7. Raitanen

110 Metres Hurdles

In 2019 Grant Holloway and Orlando Ortega were the world top two. This year Holloway had four wins in the USA but when he came to Europe was 4th in Monaco in 13.19 behind Ortega 13.11, Andrew Pozzi 13.14 and Wilhem Bélocian 13.18 and 2nd in Székesfehérvár behind Ortega, although with many of the top men behind him: 3 Freddie Crittenden, 4 Bélocian, 5 Aaron Mallett and 6 Pozzi. Other than that Pozzi had six wins and two 2nds as he was back in top form, while Mallett (pre-season best of 13.37 in 2017) improved his time in each of his seven races, ending with 2nd in Rome 13.23 behind Pozzi 13.15 and 1st in Doha in 13.15. That Monaco race provided 1-2-4 and 5 on the world list and Ortega won all his four races to be a clear number one. Crittenden had four times in 13.30-13.34 range and Jason Joseph improved his Swiss record from 13.39 to 13.29. Three men who had unbeaten records, but did not meet the world's best complete the rankings: the national champions of Japan – Taio Kanai, China – Xie Wenjun, and Russia – Sergey Shubenkov.

Most times under 13.30: Pozzi 5, Ortega, Bélocian 4, Holloway, Mallett 2, Xie 1+1w.
1. Ortega, 2. Pozzi, 3. Mallett, 4. Bélocian, 5. Holloway, 6. Crittenden, 7. Kanai, 8. Joseph, 9. Xie Wenjun, 10. Shubenkov

Holloway with 7.38 was clearly the fastest at **60 metres hurdles** with Pascal Martinot-Lagarde 7.47 and Pozzi 7.48 next. Pozzi won all his four finals.

400 Metres Hurdles

Karsten Warholm had a marvellous season. He started the summer with 33.78 for 300m hurdles in a solo run in Oslo to shatter the world best of 34.48 set by Chris Rawlinson in 2002. Then he had six races at 400mh, easily the six fastest in the world, five at 47.62 or better headed by a narrow miss at the world record when he recorded 46.87 in Stockholm. He took the average of his all-time top ten times to 47.160, passing Edwin Moses (47.254) as the world's best. He had an unprecedented margin of 1.82 secs over the second on the world list, Ludvy Vaillant, who ran 48.69 in Rome behind Warholm's 47.07, with Rasmus Mägi 3rd in 48.72 running the only other sub-49 sec. time. Of Warholm's great rivals Abderrahman Samba did not compete at all while Rai Benjamin ran pbs at 100m 10.03 and 300m 32.35i, but no hurdling, and Kyron McMaster just had a couple of indoor sprints. Mägi beat Vaillant to claim 2nd ranking, while the next two in Rome

also take their place: 4th David Kendziera and 5th Wilfried Happio, with the latter having a much better set of times. Yasmani Copello was fourth fastest with 49.04 for 2nd in Monaco and Takatoshi Abe was undefeated in Japan, Most times to 49.00: Warholm 6, Vaillant, Mägi 1
1. Warholm, 2. Mägi, 3. Vaillant, 4. Happio, 5. Copello, 6. Kendziera, 7. Abe

High Jump

As noted before there has been a sharp decline in world men's high jump standards since the peak year of 2014, when six men cleared 2.40. Even given the unusual circumstances that was the case again in 2020, with 12 performances by 9 men at 2.30 or higher after 16 by 11 men indoors. Five men indoors and one outdoors tied the world bests for the year of 2.33. Mikhail Akimenko, competing only indoors in Russia won five times and was 3rd in the Russian indoor championships; he did 2.31 twice and 2.30 once. Another Russian Ilya Ivanyuk won four times, including both national titles, 2.33 indoors and 2.24 outdoors, and was 2nd once (2.28i to Akimenko's 2.31i). The classiest competitions came with three men over 2.30+ indoors at both Banská Bystrica and Hustopece. At Banská Luis Zayas and Jamal Wilson were 1-2 with 2.33 and Tom Gale 3rd with 2.30. Gale won his other four indoor competitions including at Hustopece with 2.33 from Sylwester Bednarek and Wilson 2-3 at 2.30 and Zayas 5th 2.27. Maksim Nedosekov was only 7= and 10=at those events, but came into his own outdoors, winning his four competitions including a world-leading 2.33 at Minsk. Gianmarco Tamberi had the busiest season, with 10 wins in 13 competitions, headed by 2.31i and 2.30, and Andrey Protsenko won his five, including with 2.30 over Tamberi 2.27 in Rome. Tomohiro Shinno had 2.31 and 2.30 in Japan. The world's best for nearly a decade, Mutaz Essa Barshim, did not compete in 2020.

Most competitions over 2.30m (out + in): Akimenko, Gale 3i; Wilson 2+1i; Nedosekov, Protsenko, Shinno 2, Tamberi 1+1i
1. Gale, 2. Wilson, 3. Ivanyuk, 4. Akimenko, 5. Tamberi, 6. Nedosekov, 7. Protsenko, 8. Zayas, 9. Shinno, 10. Bednarek

Pole Vault

Armand 'Mondo' Duplantis is a super star and he had a wonderful year. Indoors he took Renaud Lavillenie's 2014 world record with 6.17 in Torun and 6.18 in Glasgow and outdoors he added 1cm to Sergey Bubka's 1991 record with 6.15 at Rome. He won all his 13 competitions, including at our World Indoor Tour meetings and all six Diamond League meetings that staged the event, clearing 6m or higher at ten meetings to equal the record that Bubka set in 1991. The erstwhile world number one Sam Kendricks was the only other man to exceed 6m, with 6.01 indoors and 6.02 outdoors. He, also, was busy with 18 competitions, of which he won eight, competing against his friend Duplantis seven times. Piotr Lisek, although he travelled less than the other top men, again ranks 3rd with a best of 5.90, beating Renaud Lavillenie on the one occasion that they met, But Lavillenie 5.94 and Chris Nilsen 5.93 went higher indoors. Some new men made the rankings for the first time, headed by Ben Broeders, who was the most prolific competitor and who set five Belgian records indoors to 5.80 and one out, also 5.80. Jacob Wooten and Matt Ludwig cleared 5.90 at high altitude Mexico City, while Harry Coppell set a British record at 5.85, but did not have as good a competitive records as some of the other 5.80+ men. Of the Americans K.C.Lightfoot (unbeaten, including a win over Nilsen) had four 5.80+ competitions to 3 by Ludwig (US indoor champion) and Nilsen, and 2 by Wooten. Of other contenders Ernest John Obiena and Thiago Braz da Silva were 2-2 and Bo Kanda Lita Baehre won German titles indoors and out. In Russia Timur Morgunov won 4/4 indoors and cleared 5.86. Overall 22 men cleared 5.80 or higher.

Most competitions over 5.75m (outdoors + in): Duplantis 9+5i, Kendricks 7+7i, Lisek 5, Lavillenie 2+3i, Broeders, Lightfoot 1+4i, Ludwig, Coppell 1+2i, Nilsen 3i, Wooten 1+1i, Zach Bradford 2i
1. Duplantis, 2. Kendricks, 3. Lisek, 4. R Lavillenie, 5. Broeders, 6. Lightfoot, 7. Ludwig, 8. Nilsen, 9. Obiena, 10. Braz da Silva

Long Jump

Competition was thin in 2020. For instance the event was only included once in the Diamond League – at Stockholm where Thobias Montler jumped 8.13, Ruswahl Samaai 8.09 in Stockholm – and only once on the World Indoor Tour, although then, in Madrid, Juan Miguel Echevarría jumped 8.41, the world's best wind-legal of the year. Echevarría jumped twice outdoors, 8.08w and 8.25 to win the Cuban title from Maykel Massó. Tajay Gayle had four wins at Kingston, including 8.52w on Jul 11, but in his only overseas competition he was 3rd with 7.99 in Bellinzona. Militiádis Tentóglou had a good indoor season with five 8m plus competitions, four wins headed by 8.26 at the Greek Champs and 2nd at Madrid. The best outdoor wind-legal jumps were by Wang Jianan 8.36 and Huang Changzhou 8.33 at the Chinese Champs, but before then Huang had three wins over Wang. Then came Yuki Hashioka with 8.29 in Niigata. Montler was the busiest jumper and had nine wins, two seconds and a third. He lost to Pulli in the Finnkampen but beat him in Stockholm, where Pulli was 3rd. Pulli had a best of 8.27 and won in Bellinzona from Samaii, whose best was only 8.09 but had wins with 8.03 and 8.00. Lester Lescay had wins at 8.28 and 8.21 in Cuba and beat Massó 8.28 to 8.26. Ranking is nearly impossible and the US outdoor best of the year was a mere 7.78!

Most competitions over 8.10m: Montler 3+1w+2i, Gayle 2+1w, Echevarría, Huang, Wang, Lescay, Cheswel Johnson, Simon Ehammer 2, Carey McLeod 2i
1. Echevarría, 2. Gayle, 3. Tentóglou, 4. Montler, 5. Huang Changzhou, 6. Wang Jianan, 7. Hashioka, 8. Pulli, 9. Lescay, 10. Samaii.

Triple Jump

Fabrice Zango takes top ranking from Christian Taylor. They met twice, Zango winning in Székesfehérvár 17.43 to 17.34 (Pedro Paulo Pichardo 3rd 17.28) and Taylor in Ostrava 17.46 to 17.41 with Max Hess 3rd and Pichardo 4th. Zango had the year's best jump, an African indoor record 17.77 in Paris and went on to three more wins indoors and three outdoors. Taylor competed only outdoors with five wins, headed by 17.57 in Berlin, and two seconds – also to Tomás Veszelka in Samorín. Cuban champion Andy Díaz competed only at home with four wins, all over 17.10, beating Cristian Nápoles for the Cuban title. Hess had three wins in Germany, and then was 3rd in Ostrava and Samorín and 2nd in Berlin with 17.17. Donald Scott beat Omar Craddock and Chris Benard for the US Indoor title, but Scott was only 11th at Liévin and 6th at Madrid, behind, for instance, Melvin Raffin, 5th and 2nd, Pablo Torrijos (who had eight wins) 7th and 4th and Benard 6th and 5th.

Most competitions over 17.00: Zango 3+1w+4i, Taylor 4+1w, A Díaz 4, Hess, Cristian Nápoles 2, Pichardo 1+1w+1i, Craddock, Torrijos 1 +1i
1. Zango. 2.Taylor, 3. A Díaz, 4. Pichardo, 5. Hess, 6. Raffin. 7. Torrijos, 8. Nápoles, 9. Craddock, 10. Benard

Shot

Ryan Crouser had the greatest series of throws in one year in the history of the event. He competed eleven times – was over 22.50 eight times topped by 22.91 for equal third on the world-all time list and other wins at 22.43, 22.19i and 21.87. In all, including all marks in a series he had 30 throws at 22.20 or better (37 over 22m), including all six at Des Moines on August 29 and five at Chorzów and Belgrade. In his career his totals to end 2020 are: competitions at 22.50+- 16, 22.20+- 31, 22.00+- 44, all throws at 22.20+- 66. These numbers compare with the next best Ulf Timmermann 7, 11, 22 and 15. The next best on the world lists were Leonardo Fabbri (who improved from a 20.99 best in 2019) 21.99, Michal Haratyk 21.88, Konrad Bukowiecki 21.88i and Tomás Stanek 21.86i. Haratyk had seven competitions at 21.50 or better with nine wins and six 2nd places, and Filip Mihaljevic had six over 21.50 with seven wins, two seconds and a third. He was 2-0 v Fabbri. Tom Walsh competed only in New Zealand, winning eight times over 21m, while Joe Kovacs competed just three times. While best indoors, Stanek was unbeaten outdoors, but did not contest the major meetings and had a best of 21.24, while Bukowiecki was well below his indoor form in a busy outdoor season. Nick Ponzio, 2nd at the US Indoor Champs to Crouser with Payton Otterdahl 3rd, was another to make notable progress from 20.73 to 21.72 in the year. While consistent David Storl struggled to regain past form, although he went over 21m in his last meeting of the year, 21.20 for 3rd at Zagreb behind Crouser and Kovacs.

Most competitions over 21.00: Ponzio 10+1i, Crouser, Haratyk 8+2i, Walsh 7, Fabbri 6+4i, Mihaljevic 4+4i, Stanek 3+4i, Otterdahl 3+2i Kovacs 1+1i, Bukowiecki 0+5i
1. Crouser, 2. Haratyk, 3. Mihaljevic, 4. Fabbri, 5. Walsh, 6. Stanek, 7. Ponzio, 8. Bukowiecki, 9. Kovacs, 10. Otterdahl.

Discus

Daniel Ståhl was again the top ranked man with two 70m performances, 71.37 and 70.25, 7 of the top 13 and 12 performances over 67m. As with compatriot Simon Pettersson, who had ten over 66m, he benefitted from Sweden's lack of a Covid-19 lockdown. The world lists were dominated by central Europeans who were able to compete regularly. There was also the benefit of many small events staged in open, wind-friendly locations. Lovelhe in Portugal was one such, and there Mauricio Ortega improved the South American record to 67.03 in February and to 70.29 in July and Juan José Caicedo took his Ecuador record to 63.31 and 69.60. Also Gudni Gudnason set an Iceland record with 69.35 in Reykjavik. Fedrick Dacres, competing only in Jamaica, had a big throw at 69.67 and was unbeaten but obviously lacked the stimulus of major opposition. Lukas Weisshaidinger was the first to show top form with six wins at Schwechat, three over 68m and the others over 65m, but he did not throw so far after that and was then beaten in his only competition against top men at St. Pölten by Kristian Ceh, who improved during the year from 63.82 to 68.75 and was 2-2 v Pettersson. Ståhl was unbeaten (18 wins) except for no throws at Södertalje and to Andrius Gudzius in Berlin, but he beat Gudzius on the other six times they met, while Gudzius was 4-2 v Pettersson. That Berlin meeting brought together many of the top men: 3 Ceh, 4 Pettersson, 5 Robert Urbanek 6 Ortega, 7 Alin Firfirica, the Balkan champion. The Skolimowska Memorial also had a top field: 1 Ståhl, 2 Ceh, 3 Gudzius, 4 Bartlomiej Stój, 5 Urbanek, 6 Malachowski. Urbanek beat his compatriot Piotr Malachowski 3-1.

Most competitions over 65m: Ståhl 18, Pettersson 14, Gudzius 12, Ceh 9, Weisshaidinger 6, Dacres 3, Urbanek 2
1. Ståhl, 2. Gudzius, 3. Pettersson, 4. Ceh, 5.Weisshaidinger, 6. Dacres, 7. Urbanek, 8. Malachowski, 9. Ortega, 10. Firfirica

Hammer

The rivalry between Wojciech Nowicki and Pawel Fajdek continued, but this year Nowicki, over 78m in all his six outings, had a 4-1 advantage, losing just their final clash at the Skolimowska Memorial, where Fajdek produced his best of the year 79.81 to Nowicki's 78.88. Bence Halász splits them in the rankings; he had 12 wins and two second places both to Nowicki. These three men had 21 of the 24 best performances (to 77.83): Halász 9, Nowicki & Fajdek 6. Rudy Winkler contested three minor meetings in the USA and recorded 77.47, 80.70 and 80.72 downhill, while Artur Kangas, from 74.40 in 2019 improved to 74.59, 75.30, 77.09, 77.82 and 79.05; he was unbeaten in 11 meetings but did not meet the top men. Myhaylo Kokhan, still a U20, was consistent, placing 3rd in the Gyulai Memorial behind the two Poles, 4th in both the Chorzów meetings and winning the Balkan title from Özkan Baltaci. The 20 year-old Hrístos Frantzeskákis was 3rd at the Skolimowska.

Most competitions over 79m/76m: Nowicki 2/6, Halász 1/12, Fajdek 1/8, Kangas 6, Kokhan, Baltaci, Pavel Boreysha 3, Winkler 2+1dh, Javier Cienfuegos, Frantzeskákis, Valeriy Pronkin, Elvind Henriksen 2
1. Nowicki, 2. Halász, 3. Fajdek, 4. Winkler, 5. Kangas, 6. Kokhan, 7. Baltaci, 8. Frantzeskákis, 9. Henriksen, 10. Cienfuegos

Javelin

Johannes Vetter had a stellar season with seven of the world's top ten performances, including three over 90m within a month: 91.49 at Turku and then at the two Chorzów meetings, 90.86 at the Kusocinski Memorial and a mighty 97.76 at the Skolimowska Memorial. That was the second best ever throw with the current specification javelin, second only to Jan Zelezny's 1996 world record of 98.48. Vetter followed that with a 94.84 throw at Chorzów. He had three no throws in his opening competition but then won all nine. Second on the world list was 87.86 by Neeraj Chopra at Potchefstroom in January but he did not compete thereafter and at the end of the year Rocco van Rooyen threw 87.86 in South Africa, They were followed by Marcin Krukowski 87.07 (8 wins from 12) and Kim Amb 86.49 (7 wins from 10, last world ranked in 2013), both consistently over 80m. Gatis Cakss was 1-1 v Amb and Krukowski. The competition that featured the most top men was the ISTAF meeting in Berlin won by Vetter from Andrian Mardare, Krukowski and Cakss.

Jakub Vadljech had only two outings but won them both – Kladno and Prague (Mardare 3rd). Spanish champion Odel Jainaga did not meet the top men but after two early losses had seven successive wins. The 2019 top ranked thrower Magnus Kirt did not compete in 2020 and the world champion Anderson Peters only once.

Most competitions over 85m/83m: Vetter 7/9, Amb 2/4, Krukowski 1/5, Cakss 0/4, Vadljech, Mardare, Jainaga 0/2
1. Vetter, 2. Amb, 3. Krukowski, 4. Cakss, 5. Vadljech, 6. Mardare, 7. Jainaga, 8. Vitezslav Vesely

Decathlon

No Götzis, no Ratingen, no Talence, no major international championships, so this was a limited year for combined events, But there were various national championships and before December the five best scores of the year, 8100 plus were at these and all by men aged 24 or less. The top mark was 8260 by Axel Hubert of France, who improved from 7810 (2019) with pbs in six individual events and tying another. Then the very promising 20 year-old Simon Ehammer, the 2018 World Junior bronze medallist and 2019 European Junior champion, took his best from 7735 to first 8028 and then 8231 at the Swiss Champs; he also had a long jump best of 8.15. Third best was 8202 for the BLR title by Vitaliy Zhuk ahead of Maksim Andraloits 8100 and Risto Lillemets won the Estonian title with 8133. The only one of the 2019 top ten to do a decathlon in 2020 was Ilya Shkurenyov, Russian champion with 8086. In December, with Olympic qualifying (8350 points) now open again, Felipe dos Santos, who had earlier won decathlons with 7932 and 8104w scores, won the Brazilian title with 8364, Kevin Mayer returned to the top with 8552 at Réunion, and Ashley Moloney set a new Oceania record with 8492 from Cedric Dubler 8367.
1. Mayer, 2. Moloney, 3. dos Santos, 4. Dubler, 5. Ehammer, 6. Hubert, 7. Zhuk

The best indoor **Heptathlon** scores were 6320 Artem Makarenko, 6209 Garrett Scantling and 6143 Jorge Ureña for the national titles of Russia, USA and Spain respectively.

20 Kilometres Walk

The 2019 number one Toshikazu Yamanishi recorded easily the year's fastest time of 1:17:36 to win the Japanese title from Koki Ikeda with guesting Perseus Karlström 3rd – then Eiki Takahashi. Isamu Fujisawa, Tomohiro Noda, Hiroki Arai, Satoshi Maruo and Yuta Koga 4th to 9th under 1:20:50. A month later there was even better marks at Kobe as Ikeda, Takahashi, Yusuke Suzuki and Koga broke 1:19 to rank 2-5 on the world list. Wang Kaihua had 1:19:46 at Jinzhou and won the Chinese title in 1:20:49 while four more men broke 1:20: the Russian champions Vasiliy Mizinov,

summer, and Sergey Shiroborokov, winter, Salih Korkmaz at Antalya and Mateo Giupponi 2nd at Podebrady. While the other had one or two 20k races, Karlström managed four, winning at Adelaide, Alytus and Podebrady.
1. Yamanishi, 2. Ikeda, 3. Karlström, 4. Takahashi, 5. Suzuki, 6. Wang Kaihua, 7. Mizinov, 8. Korkmaz, 9. Shiroborokov, 10. Koga

Yamanishi set an Asian record for a track 5000m with 18:34.88 that was improved to 18:20.14 by Ikeda. Takahashi 37:25.21, Ikeda 37:25.90 and Koga 37:35.00 recorded the three fastest ever times at 10,000m.

50 Kilometres Walk

With very limited competition until October the fastest times were by Dementiy Cheparev 3:43:29 and Sergey Sharipov 3:43:46 in the Russian Championships. Returning from a drugs ban, Ivan Hlavan won the Ukrainian title in 3:47:31. Then in October there was the first international race, the annual 50k at Dudince, that had been delayed from its usual March date. Matej Tóth won here for the fifth time as, in his first race since the European Champs of August 2019, he won in 3:41:15. He was followed under the 3:50 Olympic standard by Rafal Augustyn, Andrés Chocho and Karl Junghannss.
1. Tóth, 2. Cheparev, 3. Sharipov, 4. Augustyn, 5. Hlavan, 6. Chocho, 7. Sergey Rakov, 8. Junghannss

WOMEN

World records were set in 2020 at three distance events. Letesenbet Gidey improved her best time at 5000m from 14:23.14 to 14:06.62, a time that took 4.57 secs off Tirunesh Dibaba's 12 year-old mark. Earlier Ababel Yeshaneh had run the half marathon in 64:31 in February and Sifan Hassan took the record for the rarely run 1 hour distance to 18,930m. Gidey was second to Hellen Obiri at 5000m in Monaco in her only other race, Yeshaneh fell at the World Half Marathon and came in fifth, but Hassan won her other two races: a 14:37.85 in Ostrava just four days after her 1 hour in Brussels and a European record 29:36.67 in Hengelo for fourth on the world all-time list. But perhaps best of all, even with the suspicion that for too long has pertained to the Russian walkers, was the 3:50:42 walk by Yelena Lashmanova, a performance that would rate her highly on men's lists. She also ended the year with a world indoor best of 20:04.4 for 5000m walk. Yulimar Rojas set a world indoor record at 15.41, a mark bettered only by the world outdoor record from 1995 of Inessa Kravets, and she was the World Female Athlete of the Year for WA, but, outstanding as her 15.43i was, for me her season was too thin for that accolade.

Also worthy of high places in World Athlete of the Year consideration were Faith Kipyegon, who headed the world list at 800m, won her only 1500m and had three runs at 1000m, narrowly missing the world record twice, and Hellen Obiri who followed that 5000 with a world leading 8:22.54 for 3000m in Doha. Laura Muir had the three fastest times at 1500m, ran a UK record at 1000m and also raced strongly at 800m. Brigid Kosgei was second to Yeshaneh and (leaving aside her disqualification) to Hassan in their world records and also won the London Marathon.

Selections for World Top Ten

	PJM	AI
Yelena Lashmanova	1	-
* Sifan Hassan	2	1
* Letesenbet Gidey	3	2
* Peres Jepchirchir	4	5
* Yulimar Rojas	5	4
Brigid Kosgei	6	9
Faith Kipyegon	7	3
Hellen Obiri	8	6
Laura Muir	9	7
* Elaine Thompson-Herah	10	8
Mariya Lasitskene	-	10

Rojas was WA athlete of the year and * indicates their five finalists.

100 Metres

The great Jamaican sprinters Shelly-Ann Fraser-Pryce and Elaine Thompson-Herah shared the world's six fastest wind-legal times and both were undefeated, winning their races by clear margins. Fraser-Pryce led the way with a world-leading 10.86 at Kingston on 8 August to which Thompson-Herah responded with 10.88 in the very next race, having run 10.73w on 25 July. Two weeks later F-P improved to 10.86 with T-H 10.92 in her race, but T-H had the last word in superb style at two DL races, 10.85 at the Golden Gala in Rome and 10.87 in Doha. Two other women beat 11 seconds and were unbeaten: Shaunae Miller-Uibo ran a pb 10.98 in Clermont and Sha'Carri Richardson who had four such wind-assisted times headed by 10.79w; her legal best was 11.05. Ajla Del Ponte had a breakthrough season with eight wins in European races and a best of 11.08, but was 3rd in Chorzów in 11.35 and tailed off in her last race to 4th in Rome, behind Aleia Hobbs 11.12 and Marie-Josée Ta Lou, who had started her season slowly, 11.14.

Most times under 11.00/11.10: Thompson-Herah 4+1w/4+1w, Fraser-Pryce 2/3, Richardson 4w/1+4w.
1. Thompson-Herah, 2. Fraser-Pryce, 3. Richardson, 4. Miller-Uibo, 5. Dei Ponte, 6. Hobbs

The best times at **60 Metres** indoors were run at high-altitude Albuquerque: Mikiah Brisco 7.04 to win the US Champs final (7.08A there three weeks earlier) and Javianne Oliver 7.04A heat and 7.08A 2nd final. Top competitor, however, was Gina Bass, unbeaten in six finals in Europe with three Gambian records to 7.11.

200 Metres

Shaunae Miller-Uibo ranks top for the fourth successive year, although she only had two 200m races: 22.61 at Montverde and the year's fastest 21.89 at Clermont. In the first Lynna Irby was 2nd and Sha'Carri Richardson 3rd and in the second Jasmine Camacho-Quinn (her only 200m) was 2nd and Irby 3rd. Richardson ran the year's second fastest time of 22.00 and next was Elaine Thompson-Herah who had three races in Kingston headed by 22.19, trading wins with Shericka Jackson, while Shelly-Ann Fraser-Pryce also had wins there in 22.25 and 22.74. Irby went on to fast wins in 22.55 and 22.52w, but there was all too little competition between the best women and ranking is near impossible.

Indoors the fastest were Abby Steiner 22.57 with two wins and two 2nd places. and Anavia Battle 22.68 with wins in her three competitions including over Steiner at Clemson.

Most times under 22.70: Irby 2+1w, Miller-Uibo 2.

1. Miller-Uibo, 2. Thompson-Herah, 3. Irby,
4. Richardson, 5. Battle, 6. Fraser-Pryce, 7. Steiner,
8. Jackson, 9. Camacho-Quinn, 10. Anthonique Strachan

Dina Asher-Smith sat out the year apart from three local 150m races – in 17.20, 17.12 and 17.00, while Allyson Felix's only outdoor race was also at 150m – 16.81 into a 2.6m/s wind in her 'Impossible Games' race. At that event the year's fastest times were 16.41 by Brianna McNeil and 16.56 by Dafne Schippers.

400 Metres

At the end of the year 17 year-old Beatrice Masilingi had terrific Namibian records at high altitude times – first 50.99 in the Keino Classic in Nairobi and in December world-leading 50.44 and 50.42 in Pretoria. Then the fastest times came from two women who raced 400m just once: Lynna Irby 50.50 in Monaco and Shaunae Miller-Uibo 50.52 in Montverde. Although she did not run as fast as she had in 2019, when she improved her pb nine times, Wadeline Jonathas was the busiest of the Americans as after a couple of indoor wins, including the US title, she had three good wins in Europe with a best of 51.23, but she was well beaten with 51.40 behind Irby in Monaco. It was close for top ranking amongst the Europeans as Justyna Swiety-Ersetic beat Lieke Klaver 2-1, but Klaver came to the top as she improved her 2019 bests for 200m from 23.35 to 22.66 and 400m from 53.18 to 50.98 to win in Rome, with S-E 3rd in 51.94.

1. Masilingi, 2. Irby, 3. Miller-Uibo, 4. Jonathas,
5. Klaver, 6 Swiety-Ersetic

800 Metres

She only had one race at 800m (her first at the distance for five years) but Faith Kipyegon had a win in Doha in the year's fastest time 1:57.68 and when she won three times at 1000m she was under 2 mins twice at 800m. Jemma Reekie, with bests of 1:57.91 indoors and 1:58.63 outdoors, had six wins in her seven races. She was 4th in Bellinzona in 1:58.87 with the three ahead of her running 1:58s: Hedda Hynne, Selina Büchel and Lore Hoffmann. However, Reekie was 3-1 v Hynne, who set Norwegian records a week apart with 1:59.10 and 1:58.10. Laura Muir won in Marseille and Ostrava, was 2nd to Reekie in Glasgow (indoors) and Trieste (Hynne 3rd), and 3rd in Bydgoszcz and in Rome, behind Reekie and Hynne. Büchel had a consistent, though not outstanding, record during the year and broke 2 minutes when 4th in Trieste before 1:58.37 in Bellinzona. Hoffmann improved from 2:01.99 in 2019 to 2:01.48 in Marseille and 2:00.51 in Rovereto, both 2nd places, and ended with 7th in Rome; she was beaten 6-1 by Büchel. Rose Mary Almanza had three sub-2 times in Cuba, while Ajee' Wilson competed only indoors, winning her three races including 1:58.29 at the Millrose Games.

Most times to 1:59.50: Reekie 3, Kipyegon, Hynne, Muir 2.

1. Kipyegon, 2. Reekie, 3. Hynne, 4. Muir,
5. Wilson, 6. Büchel, 7. Almanza, 8. Hoffmann,
9. Sofia Ennaoui

1500 Metres

Laura Muir had a brief but outstanding season, running the year's three fastest 1500m times: 3:57.40 at Berlin, 3:57.86 at Stockholm and 3:58.24 at Chorzów. Then came Faith Kipyegon, who won in Ostrava in 3:59.05 in her only 1500m of the year, but note should be made of her close attempts at the 1000m world record, 2:29.15 in Monaco (Muir 2nd 2:30.82) and 2:29.92 in Brussels. Sofia Ennaoui was 2nd to Muir in Chorzów in 3:59.70, but her next was 8th in Berlin at 4:06.05. Konstanze Klosterhalfen recorded 3:59.87 en route to her second place at 1 mile indoors in New York, where her 4:17.26 was not enough to hold off Elle Purrier who won in 4:16.85 (after 4:00.20 at 1500m). Purrier's one outdoor race at this event was a 4:00.77 win, while 3rd in the New York mile was Jemma Reekie in 4:17.88 (4:00.52). Reekie had a win indoors and two outdoors before 3rd at Ostrava, a place behind Laura Weightman, who beat 4:02 three times, including when 2nd at Stockholm and at Berlin ahead of Jessica Hull, who ran an Oceania record 4:00.42, with Melissa Courtney-Bryant 3rd and 4th in these races. Gudaf Tsegay did not run the event outdoors, but won her three 1500m races indoors, twice just over 4 mins. Lemlem Hailu broke 4:02 in setting world U20 records indoors when 2nd to Tsegay in Torun and Liévin but had an outdoor best of 4:04.75.

Most times under 4:04.0 (or 4:23.6M): Muir,

Weightman 3, Hull, Reekie 2, Tsegay 2i
1. Muir, 2. Kipyegon, 3. Weightman, 4. Tsegay,
5. Purrier, 6. Klosterhalfen, 7. Reekie,
8. Courtney-Bryant, 9. Hailu, 10. Hull

3000 Metres

The seven fastest outdoor times of the year came at Doha, with a Kenyan top five, Hellen Obiri winning in 8:22.54 from Agnes Tirop, Beatrice Chepkoech, Margaret Kipkemboi and Hyvin Jepkemoi with the best ever place times for 6th Gudaf Tsegay 8:25.23 and 7th Laura Weightman 8:26.31. Indoors Karissa Schweizer ran 8:25.70 and Shelby Houlihan 8:26.66 in Boston; they finished in reverse order at the US indoor champs with Colleen Quigley 3rd in both races.

5000 Metres

Hellen Obiri had two important wins, 14:22.12 in Monaco and 15:07.36A in Nairobi. Letesenbet Gidey was 2nd to her in Monaco in 14:26.67 but two months later smashed the world record with 14:06.62 in Valencia; she was the only woman to run under 15 minutes twice. Laura Weightman was 3rd in 14:35.44 in Monaco, where 4th placed Jessica Hull set an Oceania record with 14:43.80. The year's third and fourth times came from Shelby Houlihan 14:23.92 and Karissa Schweizer 14:26.34 in Portland and the first four in Ostrava beat 14:47, Sifan Hassan winning in 14:37.85. Agnes Tirop was 2nd to Obiri in Nairobi. Konstanze Klosterhalfen ran the fastest indoor time with 14:30.79 in Boston.
1. Obiri, 2. Gidey, 3. Houlihan, 4. Schweizer, 5, Klosterhalfen, 6. Hassan, 7. Weightman,
8. Sheila Chelangat, 9. Yasemin Can, 10. Hull

10,000 Metres

Sifan Hassan ran magnificently in cold and wet conditions to become the fourth fastest of all-time with 29:36.67 in Hengelo, the only significant race in Europe. Four more East Africans followed: Tsehay Gemechu 30:57.73, then Sarah Chelangat, Evaline Chirchir and Gloria Kite, all under 31:26. Therese Johaug, with an Olympic and ten World gold medals at cross-country skiing, ran 31:40.76 in Oslo, but otherwise the world list was dominated by Japanese races, with Rosemary Wanjiru 30:38.18 and Mao Ichiyama 31:23.30 at Abashiri having the best times. Then came Honami Maeda with 31:34.94 in Fukagawa, beating Ichiyama. Then came two remarkable races in December, the Japanese Championships won by Hitomi Niiya in a national record 30:20.44 with Ichiyama improving in 2nd to 31:11.56. The following day came a remarkable race in California with 12 under 32 mins won by Rachel Schneider in 31:09.79 from Weimi Kelati and Alicia Monson.
1. Hassan, 2. Niiya, 3. Wanjiru, 4. Gemechu,
5. Ichiyama, 6. Chelangat, 7. Chirchir,
8. Schneider, 9. Kelati, 10. Monson

Half Marathon

Ababel Yeshaneh ran a world record time of 64:31 at Ras Al Khaimah in February after a first 10k in 30:18. In October she was 5th in the World Champs after falling when among the leaders and in November was 3rd in Delhi. There Yalemzerf Yehualaw, 6th at RAK and 3rd Worlds, won in 64:46 with Ruth Chepngetich 2nd. Brigid Kosgei was 2nd at RAK in 64:49, also inside the previous world record, and ran 18,904m (harshly disqualified for once stepping on the kerb) when Sifan Hassan set a world record on the track for 1 hour with 18,930m. After being a non-finisher at RAK, Peres Jepchirchir won both her half marathons 65:34 in Prague and 65:16, a women's only world record, for the World title. In a year in which 12 women broke 66 mins, 23 67 mins and 33 68 mins, the best times for place were nearly all set in 2020: 1-2 and 8 at RAK, 5-7, 9-16 and many from 29th at the World Champs, and 17th-27th (70:45) at Houston in January. There Hitomi Niiya won in a Japanese record 66:38 from Brillian Kipkoech (9th Worlds). Melat Kejeta was 2nd at the Worlds, improving her best from 68:41 (2018), and further top World placings were: 4 Zeineba Yimer, 6 Joycline Jepkosgei, 7 Yasemin Can, all in their only half marathon of the year. Then came defending champion Netsanet Gudeta, who had fallen before halfway. Kejeta had been 11th at RAK and won at Frankfurt. At RAK 3rd to 5th were Rosemary Wanjiru (10th Worlds), Evaline Chirchir and Joan Chelimo, but faster then all these was Genzebe Dibaba, who made a superb debut to win at Valencia in 65:18 from Sheila Chepkirui and Senbere Teferi.
1. Jepchirchir, 2. Yehualaw, 3. Yeshaneh,
4. Kosgei, 5. Chepngetich, 6. Kejeta, 7. Dibaba,
8. Wanjiru, 9. Yimer, 10. Jepkosgei.

Marathon

Brigid Kosgei repeated her London Marathon win with 2:18:58 despite poor conditions, winning well clear of Sara Hall, who, at the age of 37, achieved a remarkable pb 2:22:01, to some extent making up for her failure to finish at the USA Trials, with Ruth Chepngetich third. The year's fastest time came at Valencia from Peres Jepchirchir 2:17:16 followed by Joycline Jepkosgei, Helaria Johannes (world W40 record 2:19:52), Zeinaba Yimer, Tigist Girma, Degitu Azimeraw and Ruti Aga, all under 2:20, with Joan Chelimo 8th and best ever times for 6th to 8th. Earlier the best times came in the early months. First in Dubai Worknesh Degefa won in 2:19:38 from Guteni Shone 2:20:11, and then in March Lonah Chemtai Salpeter took her Israeli record of 2:19:46 down to 2:17:45 in Tokyo from Birhane Dibaba (9th Valencia) 2:18:35. Other winners in Japan were Mao Ichiyama 2:20:29 in Nagoya and Mizuki Matsuda 2:21:47 in Osaka.

Hall improved her best to 2:20:32 at Chandler in December.
1. Jepchirchir, 2. Kosgei, 3, Salpeter, 4. Jepkosgei, 5. Hall, 6. B Dibaba, 7. Degefa, 8. Johannes, 9. Yimer, 10. Girma

3000 Metres Steeplechase

The paucity of top-class action was shown as Aimee Pratt ran world-leading times at 9:35.11 and 9:30.73 in August-September. But then there were four women under 9:30 at the Russian Championships with Yekaterina Ivonina the clear winner in 9:16.84 from Olga Vovk. Four days later Hyvin Jepkemoi won in 9:06.14 at the ISTAF meeting in Berlin from Beatrice Chepkoech 9:10.07 and Marusa Mismas 3rd in a Slovenian record 9:20.68 (Pratt was 4th in 9:32.50).
1. Jepkemoi, 2. Chepkoech, 3. Ivonina, 4. Mismas, 5. Vovk

Mismas went to third on the world all-time list at **2000m steeplechase** with 5:56.28, having run a world indoor best (with no water jump) of 5:47.79 from Winfred Yavi 5:48.68 in Liévin.

100 Metres Hurdles

None of the 2019 top ten women raced significantly outdoors in 2020 and whereas in 2019 there were 70 +8w performances under 12.70, in 2020 there were just 2! Both of these were 12.68 by Nadine Visser. Three years after abandoning the heptathlon the Dutch athlete was clearly the world number one winning 8 of her 9 finals (plus five heats). Her one loss was to Elvira German at the Skolimowska Memorial. Next best on times was Luca Kozák with a Hungarian record 12.71 but her second best was 12.83 in Turku, where she was third behind Visser and Luminosa Bogliolo, who won six times and had three seconds, all to Visser. German had five wins, two seconds and a third and the top American was Payton Chadwick, who ended with a fine win in Doha in 12.78. Annimari Korte was the best of a quartet of good Finnish women with 7+1w times of 12.84 or better but ran poorly in the big races at the end of her season. 19 year-old Cyrene Samba-Mayela excelled to win the French title though she was only 7th in Rome, where Visser won from Bogliolo and Chadwick.
1. Visser, 2. Bogliolo, 3. German, 4. Kozák, 5. Chadwick, 6. Korte, 7. Samba-Mayela

Kendra Harrison was unbeaten and had the year's two fastest times at **indoor 60m hurdles** with 7.80 and 7.81A. Next in close contention were Christina Clemons 7.82 (WIT winner), Tobi Amusan 7.84 and Brianna McNeal 7.85.

400 Metres Hurdles

None of the top Americans attempted the event, but 20 year-old Femke Bol made a fine breakthrough from 55.32 in 2019 (her first year at the event) to run much faster than that in all her six races, ranging from 53.79 to 54.68. Three other women broke 55 seconds (once each): Anna Ryzhykova 54.54 and Viktoriya Tkachuk 54.93 at Rome's Golden Gala behind Bol 53.90, and Léa Sprunger 54.98 in Bellinzona behind Bol 54.33. Another to break into international class was Jessie Knight, indoors with 51.57 at 400m and then over the hurdles outdoors where she ran five times under her 2019 best of 56.04.
1. Bol, 2. Ryzhykova, 3. Tkachuk, 4. Knight

High Jump

Mariya Lasitskene remained supreme, top ranked for the fifth time, but competed only in Russia and she was one of the previously accepted Authorised Neutral Athletes who were no longer permitted to compete internationally by World Athletics. Her bests were 2.05 and 2.04 indoors. In all there were seven indoor and two outdoor performances at 2.00 or higher. Lasitskene had three indoors and a highlight of the year was the rivalry between the Ukrainians, 19 year-old Yaroslava Mahuchikh and the four years older Yuliya Levchenko. Each cleared 2.00m once outdoors and Mahuchikh had three indoors, including world U20 records at 2.01 and 2.02 and Levchenko one. On winloss Mahuchikh was ahead 3-0 indoors and Levchenko led outdoors 3-2. Two Australians come next, Eleanor Patterson cleared 1.99 and was 1st and Nicola McDermott 2nd in three competitions in Australia and New Zealand, but only McDermott came to Europe, where she improved her best to 1.98. Vashti Cunningham had two indoor competitions, 1.96 and 1.97A to win the US title. Although she did not match her indoor form Anna Chicherova ranks next.

Most competitions over 1.95m in + out: Mahuchikh 7i+5, Levchenko 3i+6, Lasitskene 4i+1, McDermott 5, Patterson 3, Cunningham 2, Chicherova 2i
1. Lasitskene, 2. Mahuchikh, 3. Levchenko, 4. Patterson, 5. McDermott, 6. Cunningham, 7. Chicherova, 8. Iryna Herashchenko, 9. Erika Kinsey

Pole Vault

It was a close call between the top two. Although only able to compete in Russia Anzhelika Sidorova won all her competitions, four indoors, including the year's best marks of 4.95 and 4.92, and four outdoors. Sandi Morris was also unbeaten, in five indoor and five outdoor competitions, with 4.91A and 4.90 indoors and an outdoor best of 4.82. She beat Katie Nageotte, who had the top outdoor mark of 4.92, on the one occasion they met. Jenn Suhr set a world W35 record with 4.85A when second to Morris 4.90 at the US indoor championships and also had 4.75 and 4.71 wins indoors. Michaela Meijer (4.83 Swedish record) was the only other women over 4.80 but was beaten 7-5 by Angelica Bengtsson, including at both Swedish championships. Holly Bradshaw beat Bengtsson 3-2 and Meijer 4-0. Yarisley Silva competed only twice (indoors) but did well with 3= 4.73 with Bengtsson at Liévin behind Morris and Robeilys Peinado (who fared poorly outdoors) and 2nd at Clermont-Ferrand 4.74 behind Morris. Tina Sutej was 3rd with 4.74 there and did 4.75 outdoors.

Most competitions over 4.70m: Sidorova 4+ 4i, Morris 3+4i, Bengtsson 4+2i, Nageotte, Meijer 3, Suhr 3i, Bradshaw 2, Silva 2i, Sutej 1+1i,
1. Sidorova, 2. Morris, 3. Nageotte, 4. Suhr,
5. Bradshaw, 6. Bengtsson, 7. Silva, 8. Meijer,
9. Sutej, 10. Peinado

Long Jump

Maryna Bekh-Romanchuk had a brilliant indoor season with four wins, all at World Indoor Tour events, from 6.90 to 6.96, and outdoors won both the DL long jump competitions, with 6.95 in Stockholm and 6.91 in Doha; she beat her great rival Anastasiya Mironchik-Ivanova 3-2. They had 10 and 3 competitions over 6.80 respectively. Malaika Mihambo had the best jumps, 7.07 indoors at Berlin and 7.03 outdoors at Dessau (2 B-R 6.85, 3 M-I 6.72), and was German champion indoors and out. But Bekh-Romanchuk (nine wins, two 2nds) beat her indoors at Karlsruhe and outdoors at Berlin and heads Mihambo for top ranking, with Mironchik-Ivanova (nine wins, two 3rd, one 5th) next. Khaddi Sagnia (12 wins two 2nds, two 3rds) made a welcome return to form, matching her all-time best of 6.92 and these four dominated the world lists with 19 of the 22 6.80+ performances. Esa Brume jumped 6.82 and 6.79 indoors as well as 3rd in the Doha DL behind Bekh-Romanchuk and Sagnia, and 6.80 was also achieved by Irina Spanovic, in her only competition, and by Larissa Iapichino, two days before her 18th birthday. Quenisha Burks competed only indoors where she won her four events, including the US title, and Alina Rotaru had a solid season, three times over 6.60, but was beaten 2-1 by UK champion Jazmin Sawyers.

Most competitions over 6.70m: Bekh-Romanchuk 8+4i, Sagnia 7+1w+1i, Mironchik-Ivanova 6+3i, Mihambo 3+3i, Brume 1+2i, Burks 2i, Brooke Stratton 1+1w.
1. Bekh-Romanchuk, 2. Mihambo, 3. Mironchik-Ivanova, 4. Sagnia, 5. Brume, 6. Burks, 7. Sawyers, 8. Rotaru , 9. Stratton

Triple Jump

Yulimar Rojas improved the South American indoor record to 15.03 in Metz and then set a world indoor record in Madrid in February of 15.43, a mark bettered only by the world outdoor record of 15.50 by Inessa Kravets in 1995. Rojas was unbeaten in two indoor and two outdoor competitions apart from no jumps in Ibiza, with an outdoor best of 14.71. Yekaterina Koneva was 2nd twice indoors but had outdoor wins at 14.75w, 14.74w to win the Russian title and 14.56, while Liadagmis Povea went even further with 14.78w in Havana; she was 2nd indoors in Madrid and had other wins in Cuba at 14.49 and 14.45. Shanieka Ricketts had five wins, all at home in Kingston, Jamaica with a best of 14.43, and the most active competitor was Patricia Mamona, 3rd in Madrid and also outdoors in Monaco behind Rojas and Gabriela Petrova, who had a best of 14.38. Kristiina Mäkelä had a consistent year to also warrant a ranking place.

Most competitions over 14.30m (out + in): Povea 3+1i, Rojas 1+2i, Ricketts 2, Mamona 2i, Koneva 1+2w
1. Rojas, 2. Koneva, 3. Povea, 4. Ricketts,
5. Mamona, 6. Petrova, 7. Tori Franklin,
8. Keturah Orji, 9. Mäkelä

Shot

Gong Lijiao only competed twice, but her 19.70 indoors and 19.53 outdoors were superior to all but Auriol Dongmo 19.53, the fourth of her Portuguese records this year (also two indoors) after a pre-2020 best of 18.37 in 2017. Dongmo, who competed often with 16 wins and one second, and Alyona Dubitskaya were the only women to have two competitions over 19m outdoors. Chase Ealey won the US indoor title and outdoors did 19.41 for third on the world list. Danniel Thomas-Dodd won her one indoor competition and then four outdoors, all at Marietta. Competing only at home Valerie Adams, ranked for the 16th year, was consistent; she had three wins and lost once each to the Canadians Brittany Crew and Sarah Mitton (who had four 18m competitions, but was usually in the 17s). Jessica Ramsey had two events over 18.90 indoors and Fanny Roos had a busy schedule with three 18.70s and 21 wins to just one loss (to Dongmo). 29 women beat 18m after 42 in 2018 and 2019.

Most competitions over 18.70m: Dongmo 5, Adams, Roos 3; Ealey, Dubitskaya 2+1i; Thomas-Dodd 2, Gong 1+1i, Ramsey 2i, Crew 1+1i.
1. Gong, 2. Dongmo, 3. Dubitskaya, 4. Ealey,
5. Thomas-Dodd, 6. Adams, 7. Ramsey, 8. Roos,
9. Crew

Discus

Valarie Allman had just one competition, but in that, at Rathdrum, she improved the American record by 98cm to 70.15; she became the 26th woman ever to exceed 70m, but only the third from 2000. Sandra Perkovic, the only woman to have thrown further in recent years, had just two competitions, winning with 65.93 and 64.67. Two more women bettered 65m, German champion Kristin Pudenz, unbeaten in seven outdoor competitions after 4th in the indoor discus in Berlin won by Shanice Craft (world indoor best 64.03), and Chen Yang, who won her three events in China. Yaimé Pérez and Denia Caballero only competed in Cuba, with Pérez having a 2-1 advantage. 41 year-old Mélina Robert-Michon was sixth on the world list with 64.14 followed by Feng Bin, 64.09 in her only competition, and only Pudenz with six had more events over 62m than the unbeaten Russian champion Yekaterina Strokova, who had four. Also on four was Irina Rodrigues, who was surprisingly beaten by Liliana Cá for the Portuguese title but won all her other nine events.

Most competitions over 63m: Pudenz 6, Pérez, Strokova, Rodrigues 4, Perkovic, Caballero 2
1. Allman, 2. Pudenz, 3. Perkovic, 4. Chen Yang, 5. Pérez, 6. Strokova, 7. Caballero, 8. Robert-Michon, 9. Rodrigues, 10. Feng Bin

Hammer

While Hanna Malyshik headed the world list with 75.45, top ranking clearly goes to Alexandra Tavernier, who improved her French record to 74.94 and 75.23 and won all six times she competed. Fittingly the Skolimowska Memorial featured three top women: Tavernier winning from Malwina Kopron and Katarzyna Furmanek. Kopron had three of the top eight performances and won six times with three second places, twice beaten by Tavernier and once by Furmanek for the Polish title, but 6-1 against Furmanek. The former prodigy Bianca Ghelber had her best throw since 2010 and her unbeaten season culminated in winning both Romanian and the Balkan titles. Second in the last was Ukrainian champion Iryna Klymets with Zalina Petrivskaya third. Julia Ratcliffe set two Oceania records to 72.35 in February and won all her six competitions, but that record was taken away by another New Zealander Lauren Bruce who made a startling improvement from 68.14 to 73.47 in September. Also unbeaten was Russian champion Sofiya Palkina. Krista Tervo set Finnish records with 71.93 and 72.12 but fell away to defeats in three late season events. With another year in junior ranks 17 year-old Silja Kosonen went to third on the world all-time U20 list with 71.34. Neither world record holder Anita Wlodarczyk nor the World champion DeAnna Price competed in 2020.

Most competitions over 72m: Kopron 7, Tavernier 6, Malyshik, Furmanek, Ghelber 2
1. Tavernier, 2. Kopron, 3. Malyshik, 4 Furmanek, 5. Ghelber, 6. Klymets, 7. Palkina, 8. Ratcliffe, 9. Bruce, 10. Tervo

Javelin

Lu Huihui started the year with two wins at Beijing (64.21 and 64.34) and three world bests indoors. Outdoors she topped the world list with 67.61 and had another win in Beijing with 66.27 but was beaten at the Chinese Championships where Liu Shiying threw 67.29 to Lu's 65.70 and Liu won her only other competition with 66.14. These performances were challenged by Tatyana Kholodovich who won her five events topped by 67.17 and 66.85. Nikola Ogrodníková beat Barbora Spotáková at the Czech Champs, but the latter won her other four competitions including three over Ogrodníková. The Golden Spike at Ostrava was the most significant as Spotáková won with 65.19 from Maria Andrejczyk, (won 6/8), Ogrodníková, Lina Muze and Sara Kolak. German champion Christin Hussong won 6/7, her only loss being when 2nd at Offenburg (1 Kolak, 3 Ogrodníková, 4 Muze). A month before her 18th birthday Elína Tzénggo set a world junior record of 63.96, although this could not be ratified as there was no drug testing immediately available.

Most competitions over 62m: Kholodovich, Andrejczyk 5, Ogrodníková 4, Lu Huihui 3+2i, Spotáková, Muze 3, Liu Shiying, Hussong, Tzénggo, Kolak 2.
1. Lu Huihui, 2. Kholodovich, 3. Liu Shiying, 4. Spotáková, 5. Andrejczyk, 6. Hussong, 7. Ogrodníková, 8. Tzénggo, 9. Muze, 10. Kolak

Heptathlon

Ivona Dadic scored 6235 for a women's 1-hour heptathlon, a total bettered only by Chantal Beaugéant 6242w in 1988, and confirmed her fine form with 6415 in poor weather at the Austrian Champs. The busiest at the event was Alina Shukh who managed three heptathlons: 6386 at Lutsk, 6235 for the Ukrainian and 5920 for the Balkan title, and four more national champions exceeded 6200 points: Carolin Schäfer 6319, Adriana Rodríguez 6304, Xénia Krizsán 6263 and Evelyn Aguilar 6254 when guesting at the Spanish Champs. The 20 year-old Swiss champion Annik Kälin had two good wins: 6170 and 6167. Just 17 women bettered 6000 points compared to 46 in 2019.
1. Dadic, 2. Shukh, 3. Schäfer, 4. Rodríguez, 5. Krizsán, 6. Aguilar, 7. Kälin

At the indoor **Pentathlon** the top three were closely matched: 4639 Noor Vidts, 4610 Annie Kunz and 4602 Alina Shukh, with two more 4500+ scores.

20 Kilometres Walk

The three fastest times of the year (1:26:43, 1:26:50 and 1:27:25) were set at the Russian Winter Championships and the next fastest at their summer champs, with Elvira Khasanova and Reykhan Kagramova 1st and 2nd in both with Marina Novikova 3rd and 6th, Yuliya Turova 4th and 3rd and U23 champion Darya Golubechkova 5th and 3rd. Next on the world lists came the first three at the Chinese Championship won by Liu Hong in 1:27:48 from Yang Jiayu and Qieyang Shenjie. The fastest outside those races was 1:28:40 by Antonella Palmisano when she won at

Podebrady from Erica de Sena, and the best depth of times was seven women under 1:30 at Antalya, won by Olena Sobchuk 1:29:12 from Meryem Bekmez with 5th Lyudmyla Olyanovska was under 1:30 three times and was UKR champion plus beating Sobchuk at the Ukrainian winter champs.
1. Khasanova, 2. Kagramova, 3. Liu Hong, 4. Novikova, 5. Yang Jiayu, 6. Qieyang Shenjie, 7. Palmisano, 8. Olyanovska, 9. Turova, 10. Golubechkova

50 Kilometres Walk

Yelena Lashmanova, in her debut at the distance, set a fantastic world record when she won the Russian title in 3:50:42, a time that would mean a high placing in the men's list,. This race dominated the world list with Margarita Nikiforova 2nd in 3:59:56. The only other fast race was the Spanish championship in which Mar Juárez recorded 4:15:46..
1. Lashmanova, 2. Nikiforova, 3. Juarez, 4. Anastasiya Kalashnikova, 5. Kristina Lyubushkina, 6. Aleksandra Bushkova.

Eleonora Giorgi recorded the second fastest time ever by a woman with 2:43:43 at 35k in January.

TOP JUNIORS 2020

There was even less opportunity for top young athletes in 2020 than there was for senior élite men and women. Nonetheless there was one world U20 record, although that, the 63.96 javelin throw by Elína Tzénggo, cannot be ratified (as above). There was also a world U20 best for men's 300m 32.10A by Sineshipo Dambile. Under-20 athletes topped the world lists and rankings in the 400m, although that was the event with least top-class competition. Justin Robinson ran 44.91 in his only race, but the 18 year-old had run faster in 2019 with 44.84A, and Beatrice Masilingi, still a youth at 17, ran the fastest women's times of 50.42A, second best ever by a U18, and 50.44A (plus 200m 22.94A and 22.71Aw), but all her times were at high altitude and she did not meet other top women.

The top athlete in this age group, however, is surely Yaroslava Mahuchikh, ranked second in the world at high jump with five competitions at 2m or above, although her best of 2.02 was less than the WJR 2.04 she had set in 2019. Three other women made my world rankings for the year: Lemlem Hailu, 9th at 1500m with bests of 4:01.57i and 4:04.75, and 8:35.78 for 3000m, close to her 2019 8:34.03 that ranks third on the world U20 all-time list, Sarah Chelangat, 6th at 10,000m with 31:06.46, and Tzénggo, 9th at javelin with marks of 62.21, 61.76, 61.50 and 60.80 to back up her 63.96. There are also three more men in the rankings: Myhaylo Kokhan followed his 8th in 2019 with 6th at the hammer – he had seven performances over 75m topped by 77.75 for 4th on the world all-time U20 lists, Lester Lescay was 9th at long jump with jumps of 8.28 (6= world U20 AT) and 8.21, and Berihu Aregawi ran 7:35.78i and 7:36.85i for 3000m and ranked 9th at 5000m with his 13:08.91 in Nairobi the best ever by a junior at high altitude.

Others to move to high positions on world U20 all-time lists were Connor Bell, 5th with 63.25 for the 2kg discus and 4th with 67.40 for the 1.75kg and Bravin Kiplagat, 6th at half marathon with 59:37 (27:25 at 10k en route). Then there was Silja Kosonen in the women's hammer, whose best of 71.34 took her to 3rd on the all-time list. She had easily the greatest domination in junior lists, as she had 11 competitions over 67m compared to 66.54 by the next best in the world. Top domination of men's lists was by the pole vaulter Pal Haugen Lillefosse with seven performances at 5.60 or better, topped by 5.70i.

Although she only contested one meeting at her main event of 100m hurdles Britany Anderson, who set the word U20 record at 12.71 in 2019, ran 12.81 and 12.71w at Clermont. Others to note who showed great promise included Larissa Iapichino (daughter of Fiona May) with 6.80 long jump, two days before her 18th birthday, Max Burgin, also still a junior in 2021, 1:44.75 at 800m, Markus Rooth, who topped the junior specification decathlon list with 8238 points, and youngest of all, Erriyon Knighton, who at 16 ran 20.33 for 200m. Only one youth has ever run faster, one Usain Bolt, 20.10 in 2003, and Knighton remains in that age group in 2021.

OLYMPIC QUALIFICATION CRITERIA

Athletes eligible to compete in the Tokyo Olympics will be determined in two ways: via IAAF entry standards and/or the new IAAF world ranking system.

Entry standards: 100- 10.05/11.15; 200- 20.24/22.80; 400- 44.90/51.35; 800- 1:45.20/1:59.50; 1500- 3:35.00/4:04.20; 5000- 13:13.50/15:10.00; 10,000- 27:28.00/31:25.00; Mar- 2:11:30/2:29:30; 3000SC- 8:22.00/9:30.00; 110/100H- 13.32/12.84; 400H- 48.90/55.40; HJ- 2.33/1.96; PV- 5.80/4.70; LJ- 8.22/6.82; TJ- 17.14/14.32; SP- 21.10/18.50; DT- 66.00/63.50; HT- 77.50/72.50; JT- 85.00/64.00; Dec/Hep: 8350/6420; 20kW- 1:21:00/1:31:00; 50k (men only)- 3:50:00. Indoor performances for all field events and track events of 400m and longer (except on oversized tracks) will be accepted. Performances at altitudes of above 950m in the 100, 200, 400, 110/100H and 400H will not be accepted. Qualification period after adjustments: Mar & 50kW: 1.1.19-5.4.20 and 1.9.20-31.5.21; 10,000, 20kW, Dec & Hep: 1.1.19-5.4.20 & 1.12.20-29.6.21; all other events: 1.5.19-5.4.20 and 1.12.20-29.6.21.

CROSS-COUNTRY 2020

Some of the major international races were held in January and February, but then came the shut down and the cancellations of international and some national championships. In the closing months of the year various national championships were held, but not the most important event – the European Championships, scheduled to be held in Dublin on December 13.

National Champions 2020

Algeria	Hamza Hadjlaoui	Amine Bettiche
Belarus (Oct)	Sergey Platonov	Inna Savina
Brazil	Daniel do Nascimento	Tatiane da Silva
Bulgaria (Oct)	Mitko Tsenov	Marinela Nineva
Chile	Ignacio Andrés Velásquez	Johanna Cecilia Rivas
Colombia	Diego Armando Vera	Laura Cusaría
Czech Republic (Dec)	Jirí Homolac	Tereza Hrochová
Denmark	Mikkel Dahl-Jessen	Anna Emilie Møller
England	Callum Johnson	Anna Emilie Møller DEN
Eritrea	Yemane Hayleslassie	Dolshi Tesfu
Estonia (Oct)	Karel Hussar	Laura Maasik
Ethiopia	Nibret Melak	Tsige Gebreselama
Finland (Sep)	Antti Ihamäki	Johanna Peiponen
Germany	Samuel Fitwi Sibhati	Dominika Mayer
Greece	Mários Anagnóstou	Anasatasía Karakatsáni
Hungary (Oct)	Bence Bicsál	Lilla Böhm
India	Abhishek Pal	Kavita Yadav
Japan	Yuhei Urano	Yukari Ishizawa
Kenya	Kibiwot Kandie	Sheila Chelangat
Luxembourg	Max Lallemang	Anny Wolter
Morocco	Hassan Toriss	Kaitoum Bouaasayriya
Netherlands	Noah Schutte	Diane van Es
Northern Ireland	Neil Johnston	Emma Mitchell
Norway (Oct)	Filip Ingebritsen	Karolina Grøvdal
Poland (Nov)	Tomasz Grycko	Ieksandra Brzezinska
Romania (Oct)	Elie Corneschi	Ancuta Bobocel
Scotland	Jamie Crowe	Mhairi Maclennan
Serbia (Oct)	Ognjen Stojanovic	Olivera Jevtic
Slovakia (Dec)	Marek Hladik	Kristina Nec-Lapinova
Spain	Carlos Mayo	Irene Sánchez-Escribano
Sweden (Oct)	Samuel Tsegay ERI	Meraf Bahta
Turkey (Oct)	Huseiyn Özturk	Burcu Sabatan
UK	Mahamed Mahamed	Charlotte Dannatt
USA	Anthony Rotich	Natosha Rogers
Wales	James Hunt	Melanie Wilkins
Pan-American Cup	Jhonatas de Oliveira Cruz BRA	Geneviève Lalonde CAN
Short Course		
Finland (Sep)	Hannu Granberg	Sara Kuivisto
Germany	Simon Boch	
Poland (Nov)	Marcin Lewandowski	Paulina Kaczynska
Portugal	Paulo Barbosa	Mariana Machado
Slovenia (Oct)	Jan Kokalj	Karin Gosek
Sweden (Oct)	Mohammad Reza	Meraf Bahta

Winners Major Cross-Country Races 2020

5 Jan	Amorebieta (EA)	Enyew Mekonnen ETH	Abreha Tsige ETH
6 Jan	San Georgio su Legnano (WA)	Mogos Tuemay ETH	Fotyen Tesfay ETH
11 Jan	Stirling	Kristian Jones GBR	Kate Avery GBR
12 Jan	Elgóibar (IAAF)	Tadese Worku ETH	Hellen Obiri KEN
19 Jan	Hannut (EA)	Samuel Fitwi GER	Anna Gosk POL
19 Jan	Kerkrade (EA)	Mahamed Mahamed GBR	Bo Ummels NED
19 Jan	Della Lagarina, Rovereto (EA)	Cesare Maestri	Moira Stewartová CZE

19 Jan	Santiponce, Seville (IAAF)	Tadese Worku ETH	Margaret Chelimo KEN
26 Jan	San Vittore Olana (Cinque Mulini) (WA)		
		Leonard Bett KEN	Winfred Yavi BRN
2 Feb	Albufeira (WA)	David Kiplangat KEN	Lydia Lagat KEN
26 Sep	Lidingöloppet (EA) 15k	Samuel Russom ERI	Charlotta Fougberg SWE

WA - World Athletics permit races, EA - European Athletics permit races

WORLD ROAD RACE REVIEW 2020
By K Ken Nakamura

THE WORLD RECORDS at the men's 5km, 10km and the half marathon as well as the women's half marathon were established in 2020. First on January 12 in Valencia, Rhonex Kipruto, the 2019 World Championships bronze medallist at 10000m, improved the world 10km road record to 26:24. The previous record was 26:38 by Joshua Cheptegei, defending World Championships gold medallist at 10000m, recorded in December of 2019 in Valencia.

On February 16 in Monaco, Cheptegei who just lost the 10km road record gained the world 5km road record with 12:51, faster than Sammy Kipketer mark of 13:00 from 2000. Next on February 21 in the RAK Half Marathon, the world half marathon record over the standard course of 64:31 was established by Ababel Yeshaneh eclipsing Joyciline Jepkosgei's world record of 64:51 from 2017. The time is still slower than 64:28 by Brigid Kosgei over the downhill course in the Great North Run, however. Kosgei also ran the RAK Half Marathon and finished under the Jepkosgei's world record but Ababel Yeshaneh finished ahead of her.

Finally, in December at Valencia, Kibiwott Kandie set the world half marathon record of 57:32. But that is not all. First four finishers of the race run under 58 minutes and thus faster than the previous world record (58:01) by Geoffrey Kamworor from 2019.

It was a great year for Kibiwott Kandie. He recorded four straight sub-59 minutes half marathons. Even Zersenay Tadese, four-time World Half Marathon Champion (plus World 20km championships) only has three sub-59 minutes times to his credit, which were recorded in three separate years. Earlier in the year Kandie won RAK and Praha and thus was one of the favourites in the 2020 World Half Marathon Championships, where 5000m, 10000m world record holder and the defending world cross country champion Joshua Cheptegei was making a highly anticipated half marathon debut. But late in the race the man who was leading the race was another Ugandan Jacob Kiplimo, running his second half marathon. At the end Kiplimo was crowned the champion five second ahead of Kandie, while Cheptegei was only fourth.

Seven weeks later Kiplimo and Kandie clashed again at half marathon and this time Kandie came on top with the world record. In the same race Rhonex Kipruto, world 10km road record holder, was third with the half marathon debut record of 57:49, first sub-59 (and first sub-58) half marathon debut. The best marks for place for the top six places for men were improved in Valencia. Genzebe Dibaba also recorded the fastest half marathon debut by a woman with her winning 1:05:18.

The World Half Marathon Championships for women was won by one time world record holder Peres Jepchirchir with the championships record of 1:05:16. The current world record holder Ababel Yeshaneh was only fifth, 25 seconds behind the winner. However, Yeshaneh recorded three sub-66 minutes half marathons in a season, the first to do so in history. In 2019 Kosgei recorded three sub-66 minutes half marathon, but one of them was on the slightly downhill course in the Great North Run. In Gdynia, the best marks for place for fifth to seventh, as well as ninth to 16th were recorded.

As for the 10km by women, although the world record of 29:43 by Jepkosgei was not threatened, Sheila Kiprotich recorded 29:46 in Valencia, and thus became the first to run sub-30 minutes 10km twice in a career. Furthermore, two other runners – Rosemary Wanjiru and Norah Tanui also ran under 30 minutes in Valencia for a record three runners ran in a single race. Last year in Praha, for the first time in history two runners led by Kiprotich ran sub-30 minutes 10km on the road.

Even in the shortened season, 33 runners cracked 60 minutes for the half marathon, third highest in history behind 2019 and 2018. On the women's side 23 runners were under 67 minutes, the second highest in history behind 2019.

In 2020, sub-60 minutes half marathons were recorded in ten races: Santa Pola, Houston, Marugame, Barcelona, RAK, Den Haag, Praha, New Delhi, Valencia and the World Half Marathon Championships. It should be noted that nine races that produced sub-60 minutes clocking in 2019 were not held in 2020. Sub-66 minutes half marathons were recorded by women in five races: RAK, Praha, New Delhi, Valencia and the World Half Marathon Championships and five races that produced sub-66 minutes clocking in 2019 were not held in 2020.

WINNERS OF LEADING 2020 ROAD RACES

Date	Race	Men	Women
5 Jan	Adana HMar	Joseph Nganga KEN 61:14	Irine Kimais KEN 69:01
12 Jan	Valencia 10k	Rhonex Kipruto KEN 26:24#	Sheila Kiprotich KEN 29:46*
13 Jan	Egmond van Zee HMar	Bashir Abdi BEL 68:23	Tsehay Gemechu ETH 1:20:29
19 Jan	Santa Pola HMar	Alexander Mutiso KEN 59:09	Vivian Chepkirui KEN 69:28
19 Jan	Houston HMar	Jemal Yimer ETH 59:25	Hitomi Niiya JPN 66:38
19 Jan	Okukuma HMar	Joel Mwaura KEN 60:44*	Mao Ichiyama JPN 70:25*
26 Jan	Marrakech HMar	Mohamed El Aaraby MAR 61:25	Oumaima Saoud MAR 71:20
26 Jan	Sevilla HMar	Eyob Ghebrehiwei Faniel ITA 60:44	Izabela Trzaskalska POL 71:09
2 Feb	Marugame HMar	Brett Robinson AUS 59:57	Helalia Johannes NAM 68:10
2 Feb	Granollers HMar	Stephen Mokoka RSA 61:28	Darya Mykhaylova UKR 72:39
9 Feb	Yamaguchi HMar	James Rungaru KEN 60:27	Kaena Takeyama JPN 69:12
16 Feb	Guadalajara HMar	Benson Kipruto KEN 62:13	Lucy Cheruiyot KEN 70:52
16 Feb	Barcelona HMar	Victor Chumo KEN 59:58	Ashete Bekere ETH 66:37
16 Feb	Monaco 5k	Joshua Cheptegei UGA 12:51#	Liv Westphal FRA 15:31
16 Feb	Verona HMar	Joel Maina Mwangi KEN 60:40	Valeria Straneo ITA 71:34
21 Feb	Ras Al Khaimah HMar	Kibiwott Kandie KEN 58:58	Ababel Yeshaneh ETH 64:31#
23 Feb	Napoli HMar	Henry Rono KEN 60:04	Viola Lagat KEN 66:47
1 Mar	London (Greenwich) HMar	Kenenisa Bekele ETH 60:22	Lily Partridge GBR 70:50
7 Mar	Jacksonville 15k US Ch	Frank Lara USA 44:44	Marielle Hall USA 48:52
8 Mar	Den Haag HMar	Dawit Wolde ETH 59:58	Joyline Chemutai KEN 69:44
7 Aug	Eugene HMar	Eric Finan USA 68:24	Sara Hall USA 68:18
5 Sep	Prague HMar	Kibiwott Kandie KEN 58:38	Peres Jepchirchir KEN 65:34*
12 Sep	Larne HMar	Mo Farah GBR 60:27	Lily Partridge GBR 71:36
13 Sep	Frankfurt HMar	Amanal Petros GER 63:31	Melat Kejeta GER 69:04
19 Sep	Ústí nad Labem HMar	Bohdan Horodyskyy UKR 63:54	Kristina Hendel CRO 73:29
20 Sep	Istanbul HMar	Sezgin Atac TUR 63:16	Fatma Demir TUR 73:17
26 Sep	Berlin 10k	Daniel Simiyu KEN 27:18	Helen Tola ETH 30:59
17 Oct	Gdynia World Half	Jacob Kiplimo UGA 58:49	Peres Jepchirchir KEN 65:16
17 Oct	Tachikawa HMar	Joseph Lemeteki KEN 60:13	Men only
28 Oct	Shelby Township HMar	Morgan Pearson USA 62:15	Keira D'Amato USA 68:57
30 Oct	Dorena HMar	Galen Rupp USA 60:22	Men only
22 Nov	Alcobendas 10k dh8 6m	Fernando Carro ESP 27:46	Marta García ESP 32:38
29 Nov	New Delhi HMar	Amdework Walelegn ETH 58:53*	Yalemzerf Yehualaw ETH 64:46*
6 Dec	Valencia HMar	Kibiwott Kandie KEN 57:32#	Genzebe Dibaba ETH 65:18
13 Dec	Launceston HMar	Brett Robinson AUS 61:38	Andrea Seccafien CAN 71:39
20 Dec	Okayama HMar	Women only	Husan Zeyituna ETH 69:24
31 Dec	Madrid 10k	Daniel Simiyu KEN 27:41	Yalemzerf Yehualaw ETH 31:17
31 Dec	Barcelona 5k	Jimmy Gressier FRA 13:39	Genzebe Dibaba ETH 15:00
31 Dec	Barcelona 10k	Morhad Amdouni FRA 27:42	Hellen Obiri KEN 30:53
31 Dec	Bolzano 5k/10k	Oscar Chelimo UGA 13:17*	Margaret Kipkemboi KEN 30:43*

* = course record; # = World Record;

WORLD MARATHON REVIEW 2020
By K Ken Nakamura

LIKE ALL sports events, the effect of COVID-19 was devastating to the Marathon season. Only two Abbott Marathon Major races – Tokyo Marathon in March, and delayed London Marathon in October – were held in 2020. Even in these two marathons, only elite division of the races were held, however. After Lake Biwa, Nagoya Women and Los Angeles Marathons on March 8, most of the marathons were cancelled until October when the delayed London Marathon was held on a multiple loop course.

One of the most talked about topics on the road race scene is a new shoe technology. Its effect may be most striking in an improvement of middle elite level (2:07 to 2:08) runners as opposed to truly elite (2:02 to 2:04) runners. First, the best marks for places for 11th to 13th places were set in Dubai in January, but truly spectacular depth results were witnessed in the Tokyo Marathon in March. Ryu Takaku improved his marathon best from 2:10:02 to 2:06:45, Daisuke Uekado improved from 2:09:27 to to 2:06:57, and Toshiki Sadakata improved from 2:15:53 (in Tokyo 2019) to 2:07:05. The list of dramatic improvement in personal bests were truly astounding. In the Tokyo Marathon record 24 runners cracked 2:09 and 17 runners bettered 2:08 for the marathon, also a record. Previously, before 2020, the record was 13 runners under 2:08 and 15 runners under 2:09 in a single race. The assault on the best-marks for places continued. In the Valencia Marathon in early December, where both the fastest men's time (2:03:00) of the year, as well as the fastest women's time (2:17:16) of the year were recorded, the records for best marks for places were further improved. Record eleven runners cracked 2:06 for the marathon and 13 runners broke 2:07 for the marathon, also a record. Furthermore, in addition to the best marks for eighth to 13th place, the best marks for place 14 to 17 were recorded in Valencia. The depth in the women's side was not as impressive as the men's side, but in Valencia, not only record six runners broke 2:20 for the marathon, but the best sixth, seventh and eighth place time were also recorded.

The Valencia Marathon was the fastest marathon of the year. In Valencia, six fastest times of the year for men were recorded, while for women there were seven of the eleven fastest times of the year. Beside Valencia, top ten times of the year were recorded in Tokyo and Sevilla for men and Tokyo, London and Dubai for women. Fast course records were set by both men and women in Valencia as well as Sevilla. The combined men's and women's time for the Valencia Marathon is third fastest in history behind 2019 Chicago Marathon and 2018 Berlin Marathon where the world record for women and men, respectively were set.

The most shocking event of the year in the marathon took place in October. Eliud Kipchoge's ten marathon winning streak came to an abrupt end in the London Marathon. He only finished eighth with 2:06:49, the slowest time of his career except for his Olympic victory in 2016. Are his days of marathon supremacy over? The women's world record holder Brigid Kosgei also ran the London Marathon. Unlike Kipchoge, the men's world record holder, Kosgei fared much better. She won with 2:18:58; it was her fourth straight victory with fourth straight sub-2:20 of her career, thus tying Paula Radcliffe with the number of sub-2:20 (or for that matter number of sub-2:19) in her career.

Despite being a short season, depth at the highest level was quite impressive. For example, ten women cracked the 2:20 barrier, 16 women 2:21 and 19 women 2:22 in 2020. For comparison, 12 women cracked 2:20 in 2019 and 11 women 2:20 in 2018, but the number of sub-2:20 runners were less than ten in all previous years. Furthermore, the numbers of runners cracking 2:21 and 2:22 in 2020 are higher than all previous years before 2018. The number is similar on the men's side. Four runners cracked 2:04, ten runners 2:05, and 19 runners 2:06 in 2020. Only 2019 had more sub-2:04 performers, while only 2019, 2018 and 2012 had more sub-2:05 as well as sub-2:06 runners.

As COVID-19 continued to trouble the marathon season in 2021, the Dubai Marathon was cancelled and all of the spring Abbott World Marathon Majors races were rescheduled to the fall of 2021.

WINNERS OF 2020 INTERNATIONAL MARATHONS

Date	Location	Winner	Time	Winner	Time
3 Jan	Tiberias	Takhluini Malaka ERI	2:14:57	Beatie Deutsch ISR	2:32:25
5 Jan	Xiamen	Birhan Nenmebew ETH	2:08:16	Medina Armino ETH	2:26:12
19 Jan	Houston	Kelkile Gezahegn ETH	2:08:36	Askale Merachi ETH	2:23:29
19 Jan	Mumbai	Derara Hurisa ETH	2:08:09*	Amane Beriso ETH	2:24:51
24 Jan	Dubai	Olika Adugna ETH	2:06:15	Worknesh Degefa ETH	2:19:38
26 Jan	Marrakech	Hicham Laquoahi	2:06:32*	Hawi Alemu ETH	2:27:56
26 Jan	Osaka	women only		Mizuki Matsuda JPN	2:21:47
26 Jan	Hitachinaka	Toshinori Watanabe JPN	2:11:17	Chiharu Suzuki JPN	2:37:32
2 Feb	Oita	Hamza Sahli MAR	2:08:01*	Rochelle Rodgers AUS	2:40:02
8 Feb	Lagos	David Barmasai KEN	2:10:23*	Sharon Cherop KEN	2:31:40
9 Feb	Buriram	Conelius Chepkok KEN	2:11:46	Immaculate Chemutai UGA	2:32:41
16 Feb	Castellón	Lemi Dulecha ETH	2:07:43*	Webalem Ayele ETH	2:27:39*
23 Feb	Sevilla	Mekuant Ayenew ETH	2:04:46*	Juliet Chekwel UGA	2:23:13*
29 Feb	Atlanta (US OT)	Galen Rupp USA	2:09:20	Aliphine Tuliamuk USA	2:27:23
1 Mar	Tokyo	Birhanu Legese ETH	2:04:15	Lornah Chemtai Salpeter ISR	2:17:45
8 Mar	Otsu	Evans Chebet KEN	2:07:29	men only	
8 Mar	Nagoya	women only		Mao Ichiyama JPN	2:20:29*
8 Mar	Santa Monica (dh)	Bayelign Teshager ETH	2:08:27	Margaret Muriuki KEN	2:29:29
4 Oct	London	Tola Shura Kitata ETH	2:05:41	Brigid Kosgei KEN	2:18:58
4 Oct	Kosice	Marek Hladik SVK	2:26:08	Petra Pastorova CZE	2:52:11
11 Oct	Sofia	Youssef Sbaai MAR	2:13:03	Viktoriya Khapilina UKR	2:27:57*
1 Nov	Wuxi	Li Zicheng CHN	2:14:52	Li Dan CHN	2:33:16
8 Nov	Istanbul	Benard Sang KEN	2:11:49	Diana Kipyogei KEN	2:22:06
22 Nov	Changzhou	Su Guoxiong CHN	2:13:23	Wang Min CHN	2:38:18
29 Nov	Shanghai	Jia'a Renjia CHN	2:12:44	Li Zhixuan CHN	2:26:39
29 Nov	Nanjing	Penng Jianhua CHN	2:08:50	Li Dan CHN	2:26:59
6 Dec	Fukuoka	Yuya Yoshida JPN	2:07:05	men only	
6 Dec	Valencia	Evans Chebet KEN	2:03:00*	Peres Jepchirchir KEN	2:17:16*
13 Dec	Vienna	Björn Koreman NED	2:11"07	Eva Wutti AUT	2:30:43
20 Dec	Chandler	Martin Hehir USA	2:08:59*	Sara Hall USA	2:20:32*
20 Dec	Taipei	Paul Lonyangata KEN	2:09:18*	Askale Merachi ETH	2:28:31
20 Dec	Hofu	Tatsuya Maruyama JPN	2:09:36	Yomogi Akasaka JPN	2:29:21

* course record; um = uncertain measurement; A = altitude over 1000m; dh = downhill course (Santa Monica 122.2m).

REVIEW OF ULTRAMARATHONING 2020
By Andy Milroy

2020 was an interesting year. The Covid-19 virus meant no international championships, and in numerous countries the sport shut down almost entirely. Eastern Europe was less affected during the first half of 2020, and some races were held, including national championships. There were over 3000 ultra events held globally, 233 100k races, 125 24 hours, but just over twenty 48 hour races and ten 6 Day events. Overall this was half the number of ultra events held in 2019.

The slower paced, less intensely competitive 24 hour events were more popular. The 100k, with the prospect of athletes running together, as in shorter road races, were either cancelled or attracted small numbers. In the United States where the big cities were badly hit with infection, runners went for widely dispersed trail races. Standards in the 100k event were depressed but less affected were the 24 hours that became less competitive time trials, with runners able to run almost in isolation, focussed on their own pace. Still in the race situation, but able to space themselves out.

Zoltán Csécsei covered 277.484k at Balatonalmádi in the Hungarian national championships despite very little opposition. It was a big step up for him; he ran 264.949k in the Albi World event in 2019. There were multiple Polish Ultra championships in Pabianice - with both 100k and 24 hour events. This took place before the pandemic hit, so the Polish runners could prepare and run normally. The championships featured remarkable performances by women. Dominika Stelmach ran 7:04:36 in the 100k. (The men's race was won by Aleksandr Sorokin LTU who produced what turned out to be the best male mark of 2020, 6:43:13). In recent years Polish women have been very strong in the 24 hour event but Malgorzata Pazda-Pozorska was an emerging figure. She finished well clear of the second runner with 260.679k. That mark was set on the road, but the best track mark was set under peculiarly Covid circumstances. British international Joasia Zakrzeski was undertaking winter training in Australia but the onset of the virus left her stranded. She entered a 24 hours race in Bruce ACT, and covered 236.561k, tracked by British enthusiasts online.

The geographical twist of the virus removed normally dominant nations. For 6 day the best distance of the year 787.017k was set by a Mongolian runner, Bymbaa Budyargal at Fort Lauderdale in Florida. The top woman was more traditional, American Amy Mower running 619.597k at Augusta, New Jersey.

At 48 hours, with a reduced number of events, the best male mark was 386.810k, but Bob Hearn did not win the race in Augusta, New Jersey, he was beaten by a fellow American, with the best female mark of the year, 391.963k by Marisa Lizak. This was a US record and the third best mark of all-time. The best 1000 mile mark of the year was by Italian Andreas Marcato, with 14 days 5 hours 20:20; this was his split in the 3100 mile race, normally held in New York, transplanted across the Atlantic because of Covid, to a park in Salzburg, Austria. Marcato ran 43 days 12:25 for 5000k.

Typically creative Ultra directors came up with a new international race format, or perhaps more correctly reached back to a format popular two hundred years ago. The so-called Barclay feat involved covering a mile each and every hour for a 1000 hours. The test was more coping with lack of sleep than speed or endurance. American race director Gary Cantrell came up with a version which was more competitive using a 6706m circuit, the so-called Back Yard Ultra, ideally suited to the pandemic, using a short local loop. The winner was the last person still wanting to carry on! (The Japanese version was the Last Samurai Standing!). This developed into a virtual "World Championships" of 21 countries, so each country would have its own national champion and there would be an overall winner. Mexico was represented by a team of the legendary Tarahumaras. With 75 hours, covering 6706m each and every hour, with the only rest/sleep grabbed after each loop, before going out again for the next, Karel Sabbe of Belgium was the final competitor left having covered 312.5 miles/502.92k. The first woman was Courtney Dauwalter USA 68 hours who covered 283.3 miles/455.592k. Dauwalter is a former world record holder and US 24 Hour national team member.

So it was a tough year, but the sport adapted and produced some exceptional performances. The slowdown in results have given ultra statisticians that chance to study the overall development in the sport, particularly in South America and Asia which have grown markedly in the 21st century.

CHAMPIONSHIPS 2020

The effects of the coronavirus pandemic meant that most of the important international championships scheduled to be held in 2020 were cancelled or postponed. These included:
Olympic Games – Tokyo, Japan Jul 31- Aug 9 (re scheduled for same dates in 2021)
World Indoor Championships – Nanjing, China Mar 13-15 (re-scheduled for 19-21 Mar 2012 in Nanjing)
World U20 Championships – Nairobi, Kenya Jul 7-12 (re-scheduled for 17-22 Aug 2021)
World Walking Team Championships – Minsk, Belarus May 2-3 (next in Minsk 23-24 Apr 2022)
World Masters Championships – Toronto, Canada Jul 20-Aug 1 (cancelled)
World Mountain Running Championships – Stubaital, Tirol, Austria 4-6 Sep (cancelled)
European Championships – Paris (Charléty), France Aug 25-30 (cancelled)
European Mountain Running Championships – Cinfaes, Portugal Jul 4 (re-scheduled for 3 Jul 2021)
European 10,000m Cup – London (PH) June 6 (cancelled)
European Throwing Cup –Leiria, Portugal Mar 21-22 (cancelled)
IAU 50k World Championships – Aqaba, Jordan Nov 28-29
IAU 100k World Championships – Winschoten, Netherlands Sep 12 (cancelled)
Ibero-American Championships – Santa Cruz de Tenerife, Spain May 22-24

WA World Half Marathon Championships 2020

At Gdynia, Poland 17 October
1. Jacob Kiplimo UGA 58:49
2. Kibiwott Kandie KEN 58:54
3. Amadework Walelegn ETH 59:08
4. Joshua Cheptegei UGA 59:21
5. Andamlak Belihu ETH 59:32
6. Leonard Barsoton KEN 59:34
7. Stephen Mokoka RSA 59:36
8. Morhad Amdouni FRA 59:40
9. Benard Kimeli KEN 59:42
10. Leul Gebrselassie ETH 59:45
11. Hailemariyam Kiros ETH 60:01
12. Hamza Sahili MAR 60:04
13. Mohamed Réda El Aaraby MAR 60:17
14. Precious Mashele RSA 60:24
15. Mouhcine Outalha MAR 60:26
16. Victor Kiplangat UGA 60:29
17. Othmane El Goumri MAR 60:30
18. Jake Smith GBR 60:31
19. Stephen Kissa UGA 60:34
20. Bohdan-Ivan Horodyskyy UKR 60:40
Teams: (3 to score) 1. KEN 2:58:10, 2. ETH 2:58:25, 3. UGA 2:58:39, 4. MAR 3:00:47, 5. RSA 3:00:51, 6. FRA 3:02:10, 7. ISR 3:03:53, 8. ESP 3:05:30, 9. ITA 3:05:49, 10. GBR 3:06:17, 11. TUR 3:06:54, 12. MEX 3:07:06, 13. SWE 3:07:21, 14. UKR 3:07:47, 15. POL 3:11:29, 16. GER 3:11:43, 17. DEN 3:12:26, 18. BRA 3:12:37, 19. POR 3:12:45, 20. LTU 3:13:37, 21. ECU 3:14:31
Women
1. Peres Jepchirchir KEN 65:16
2. Melat Kejeta GER 65:18
3. Yalemzerf Yehualaw ETH 65:19
4. Zeineba Yimer ETH 65:39
5. Yeshaneh Ababel ETH 65:41
6. Joyciline Jepkosgei KEN 65:58
7. Yasemin Can TUR 66:20
8. Netsanet Gudeta ETH 66:46
9. Brillian Kipkoech KEN 66:56
10. Rosemary Wanjiru KEN 67:10
11. Dorcas Kimeli KEN 67:55
12. Lonah Chemtai Salpeter ISR 68:31
13. Fabienne Schlumpf SUI 68:38
14. Juliet Chekwel UGA 68:44
15. Meseret Gola ETH 69:02
16. Glenrose Xaba RSA 69:26
17. Doreen Chemutai UGA 70:18
18. Charlotta Fougberg SWE 70:19
19. Ursula Sánchez MEX 70:19
20. Andrea Soraya Limon MEX 70:20
Teams: 1. ETH 3:16:39, 2. KEN 3:18:10, 3. GER 3:28:42, 4. UGA 3:30:06, 5. MEX 3:31:01, 6. TUR 3:31:39, 7. POL 3:33:01, 8. SWE 3:33:37, 9. UKR 3:34:12, 10. FRA 3:35:37, 11. ITA 3:35:54, 12. CZE 3:36:37, 13. ARG 3:36:38, 14. ESP 3:36:50, 15. GBR 3:38:12, 16. ECU 3:42:14, 17. ROU 3:43:20, 18. LTU 3:47:36.

Balkan Championships 2020

At Cluj-Napoca, Romania 19-20 September
Men: **100m/200m:** Jak Ali Harvey TUR 10.30/20.77, **400m:** Bosko Kijanovic SRB 46.56, **800m:** Oleh Myronets UKR 1:49.60, **1500m/3000m:** Yervand Mkrtchyan ARM 3:47.60/8:12.02, **5000m:** Maxim Raileanu MDA 14:09.23, **3000mSt:** Turgay Bayram TUR 8:54.92, **110mh:** Mikdat Sevler TUR 14.07, **400mh:** Berke Akçam TUR-J 50.60, **HJ:** Andriy Protsenko UKR 2.25, **PV:** Illya Kravchenko UKR 5.20, **LJ:** Marko Ceko CRO 7.88, **TJ:** Levon Aghasyan ARM 16.53, **SP:** Andrei Toader ROU 19.44, **DT:** Alin Firfirica ROU 64.72, **HT:** Myhaylo Kokhan UKR-J 75.43, **JT:** Andrian Mardare MDA 83.60, **Dec:** Aleksander Grnovic SRB 7179, **4x100m/4x400m:** TUR 39.63/3:06.35; **Women:** 100m: Milana Tirnanic SRB 11.67, **200m:** Irina Eftimova BRL 23.81, **400m:** Anna Ryzhykova UKR 51.74, **800m/1500m:** Claudia Bobocea ROU 2:03.32/4:12.95, **3000m:** Burcu Sabatan TUR 9:24.89, **5000m:** Yuliya Shmatenko UKR 15:41.17, **3000mSt:** Nataliya Strebkova UKR 9:41.38, **100mh:** Hanna Plotitsyna UKR 13.21, **400mh:** Viktoriya Tkachuk UKR 55.58, **HJ:** Daniela Stanciu ROU 1.88, **PV:** Yana Hladychuk UKR 4.40, **LJ/TJ:** Gabriela Petrova BUL 6.41/14.19, **SP:** Andreea Huzum-Vitan ROU 14.56, **DT:** Özlem Becerek TUR-J 53.41, **HT:** Bianca Ghelber ROU 72.18, **JT:** Vanja Spaic ROU 53.31, **Hep:** Alina Shukh UKR 5940, **4x100m:** ROU 46.11 **4x400m:** UKR 3:34.21
Medal table leaders: UKR 12G-13S-7B, TUR 10-3-11, ROU 8-14-7, BUL 3-6-6, SRB 3-1-4, ARM 3-0-0, MDA 2-0-3, CRO 1;5-2; BIH 1-1-3

Walks: *At Ivano-Frankivsk, Ukraine March 14*
Men 20k: Eduardo Zabuzhenko UKR 1:20:46;
Women 20k: Maria Sakharuk 1:30:22
Half Marathon: *At Zagreb, Croatia August 23*
Men: Maxim Raileanu MDA 65:58
Women: Fatma Demir TUR 73:48.
Marathon: *At Kyustendil, Bulgaria September 13*
Men: Artyom Kazban UKR 2:28:17
Women: Marinela Nineva BUL 2:57:53.

Central American Championships
December 28-29, San José, Costa Rica
Men: 100m: Emmanuel Niño CRC 10.75, **200m:** Jeikob Monge CRC 21.58, **400m:** José Humberto Bermúdez GUA 46.99, **800m/1500m:** Josué Canales HON 2:01.30/ 4:05.46, **5000m:** Mario Pacay 14:33.58, **10000m:** Danile Johanning CRC 30:43.96, **3000mSt:** Daniel González PAN 9:52.69, **110mh:** Wienstan Mena GUA 14.32, **400mh:** Pablo Ibáñez ESA 50.58, **HJ** exh: Byron Villalobos CRC 1.88, **PV:** Christian Higueros GUA 4.81*, **LJ:** Rasheed Miller CRC 7.44, **TJ:** Brandon Jones BIZ 15.86, **SP/DT:** Zack Short HON 18.08*/ 51.52*, **HT:** Dylan Suárez CRC 57.38, **JT:** Luis Mario Taracena GUA 69.65, **Dec:** Estevan Ibáñez ESA 6179, **10000mW:** José Eduardo Ortiz GUA 43:00.82* **4x100m:** HON 40.55. **Women: 100m:** María Andrée Chacón GUA 12.18, **200m:** Samantha Dirks BIZ 24.72, **400m:** Daniela Rojas CRC 56.34, **800m/1500m** exh: Mónica Vargas CRC 2:21.21/5:04.20, **5000m:** María Del Carmen Osorio VEN 17:23.34, **10000m:** Viviana Aroche GUA 39:08.50, **3000mSt** Exh: Chrisdyala Moraga CRC 11:46.07, **100mh:** Denisse Reyes HON 15.30, **400mh:** Daniela Rojas CRC 60.02, **HJ:** Abigail Obando CRC 1.70, **PV** exh: Rebeca Jara CRC 2.70, **LJ:** Nathalee Aranda PAN 6.25, **TJ:** Thelma Fuentes 13.56w, **SP:** Deisheline Mayers CRC 12.06, **HT:** Gabrielle Figueroa HON 56.59, **JT** exh: Génova Arias CRC 42.94, **Hep:** Mariel Brokke CRC 4163, **10000mW** exh: Alegna González MEX 45:27.26, **4x100m:** CRC 48.22. Exh – only one or two contestants, rated as 'exhibitions'.

Central American Championships Walks
At San José, Costa Rica March 1
Men 20k: José Ortiz GUA 1:24:22.9; **Women 20k:** Noelia Vargas CRC 1:37:27.8.

Oceania Road Walk Championships
At Adelaide, Australia February 9 (Combined with IAAF Walks Challenge)
Men 20k: 1. Dane Bird-Smith AUS 1:23:01, 2. Rhydian Cowley AUS 1:24:40, 3. Kyle Swan AUS 1:27:41;
Women 20k: 1. Jemima Montag AUS 1:33:15, 2. Katie Hayward AUS 1:34:00, 3. Beki Smith AUS 1:35:06.

South American Championships Walks.
At Lima, Peru March 8
Men 20k: 1. Caio Bonfim BRA 1:24:33, 2. Brian Pintado ECU 1:25:32, 3. Mauricio Arteaga ECU 1:26:16; **50k:** 1. Claudio Villenueva ECU 4:14:11, 2. Jonathan Cáceres ECU 4:20:17, 3. Pablo Rodríguez BOL 4:29:24; **Women 20k:** 1. Karla Jaramillo ECU 1:34:59, 2. Paola Pérez ECU 1:35:57, 3. Mary Luz Andia PER 1:36:11; **50k:** 1. Viviane Lyra BRA 4:41:07, 2. Mayara Vicentainer BRA 5:00:29, 3. Yoci Caballero PER 5:10:00.

U20: 10k: Men: Oscar Patín ECU 43:20; **Women:** Paula Doménica Valdez ECU 51:14; **U18: 10k:** Mateo Romero COL 46:29; **Women 5k:** Natalia Pulido COL 24:54

Wanda Diamond League 2020
The following scheduled Diamond League meetings were cancelled in 2020:
Shanghai (16 May), Rabat (31 May), Eugene (7 Jun), Paris (13 Jun), London (4-5 Jul), Gateshead (16 Aug). A coherent series with finals was not possible, but after Oslo (11 Jun, "Impossible Games") and Zürich (9 Jul, "Inspiration Games" at seven venues), seven DL meetings were held: **M-** Monaco (14 Aug), **S-** Stockholm (23 Aug), **L-** Lausanne (2 Sep, only PV), **B-** Brussels (4 Sep), **R-** Rome (17 Sep), **D-** Doha (25 Sep). Individual event winners at these meetings:
Men
100m: Akani Simbine R 9.96
200m: Noah Lyles M 19.76, Adam Gemili S 20.61w, Eseosa Dasalu B 20.39, Arthur Gue Cissé D 20.23
400m: Karsten Warholm S 45.05, Edoardo Scotti R 45.21, Kahmari Montgomery D 45.55
800m: Donavan Brazier M 1:43.15, S 1:43.76; Ferguson Cheruiyot D 1:44.16
1500m: Timothy Cheruiyot M 3:28.45, S 3:31.25; Jakob Ingebrigtsen B 3:30.69, Stewart McSweyn D 3:30.51
3000m: Jacob Kiplimo R 7:26.64, **5000m:** Joshua Cheptegei M 12:35.36; **1 Hour:** Mo Farah B 21.330m
3000mSt: Soufiane El Bakkali M 8:08.04
110mh: Orlando Ortega M 13.11, Andy Pozzi R 13.15, Aaron Mallett 13.15
400mh: Karsten Warholm M 47.10, S 46.87, R 47.07
HJ: Andriy Protsenko R 2.30
PV: Armand Duplantis M 6.00, S 6.01, L 6.07, B 6.00, R 6.15, D 5.82
LJ: Thobias Montler S 8.13 (Ruswahl Samaai 8.09 on WA gimmick rules)
SP: Nick Ponzio R 21.09
DT: Daniel Ståhl S 69.17
Women
100m: Ajla Del Ponte M 11.16, S 11.20; Rani Rosius B 11.43, Elaine Thompson-Herah R 10.85, D 10.87
400m: Lynn Irby M 50.50, Wadeline Jonathas S 51.94, Iga Baumgart-Witan B 52.13, Lieke Klaver R 50.98
800m: Jemma Reekie S 1:59.68, R 1:59.76; Faith Kipyegon D 1:57.68
1000m: Faith Kipyegon M 2:29.15, B 2:29.92
1500m: Laura Muir S 3:57.86
3000m: Hellen Obiri D 8:22.54;**5000m:** Helen Obiri M 14:22.12; **1 Hour:** Sifan Hassan B 18.930m
100mh: Luminosa Bogliolo S 12.88, Anne Zagré B 13.21, Nadine Visser R 12.72, Payton Chadwick D 12.78
400mh: Femke Bol S 54.68, R 53.90
HJ: Yaroslava Mahuchikh M 1.98, S 2.00; Nicola McDermott B 1.91, Yuliya Levchenko R 1.98
PV: Holly Bradshaw S 4.69, Angelica Bengtsson S 4.72
LJ: Maryna Bekh-Romanchuk S 6.85, D 6.91
TJ: Yulimar Rojas M 14.27

* Indicates Championships or Games record

INTERNATIONAL EVENTS 2021-25   41

MAJOR INTERNATIONAL CHAMPIONSHIPS & GAMES 2021-24

This list is of necessity provisional, with restrictions and possible changes due to the pandemic

2021
World Relays- Chorzów (POL) (1-2 May)
European Throwing Cup Split (CRO) (8-9 May)
European Race Walking Cup- Podebrady (CZE)
South American Ch- Buenos Aires (ARG) (14-16 May)
European Mountain Running Champs- Cinfaes (POR)
African Champs- Algiers, Algeria (May/June)
European Cup 10,000m- Birmingham (Un) (5 June)
Junior Pan-American Games- Cali (COL) (5-20 June)
European Team Champs Super League- Chorzów (POL) (19-20 June); First League- Cluj-Napoca, (ROU)Second League- Stara Zagora (BUL) Third League- Nicosia, Cyprus
Mediterranean Games- Oran, Algeria (June)
European Mountain Running Ch- Cinfaes (POR) (3 Jul)
European U23 Champs- Bergen (Fana (NOR) (8-11 Jul)
European U20 Champs- Tallinn (EST) (15-18 Jul)
World U20 Champs- Nairobi (KEN) (17-22 Aug)
World Masters Champs- Göteborg (SWE) (17-27 Aug)
Francophone Games- Moncton (CAN) (23 Jul-1 Aug)
Olympic Games- Tokyo, Japan (30 July-8 Aug)
Diamond League Final- Zürich, Switzerland
Junior Pan-American Games- Cali, Colombia (Sep)
World Mountain & Trail Champs- Chiang Mtembera (THA) (11-14 Nov)
European Cross Country Champs- Fingal, Dublin (IRL) (12 Dec)

2022
World Cross Country Ch– Bathurst (AUS) (19 Feb)
World Indoor Champs- Belgrade (SRB) (18-20 Mar)
World Half Marathon Ch- Yangzhou, China (27 Mar)
European Throwing Cup Leiria (POR)
World Race Walking Team Ch- Minsk (BLR) (23-24 Apr)
European Cup 10,000m- Pace, Rennes, France
European U18 Champs- Jerusalem, Israel (4-7 July)
World Champs- Eugene, USA (15-24 July)
World U20 Champs- Cali, COL (2-7 Aug)
Commonwealth Games- Birmingham, GBR (2-7 Aug)
European Champs- Munich, Germany (15-21 Aug)
World University Games- Chengdu, China
Asian Games- Hangzhou, China (10—25 Sept)
Youth Olympic Games- Dakar, Sénégal
South American Games- Asunción (PAR) (1-15 Oct
European Cross Country Champs- Turin (ITA) (Dec)

2023
European Indoor Champs- Istanbul (TUR) (March)
World Indoor Champs- Nanjing, China (17-19 March)
European Race Walking Cup- Podébrady (CZE)
European Cup 10,000m- Pace, Rennes, France
African Games- Accra, Ghana (Aug)
Asian Champs- Pattaya, Thailand
World University Games- Yekaterinburg, Russia
Pan-American Games, Santiago, Chile
IAAF World Champs- Budapest, Hungary (19-27 Aug)
Europe v USA- in USA

2024
European Cup 10,000m- Pace, Rennes, France
Olympic Games- Paris (Aug)
European Champs- Rome, Italy (Aug)

WANDA DIAMOND LEAGUE 2021

In 2021 there will be 13 meetings in 12 countries leading up to a two-day final in Zürich in September. Athletes will compete in 32 disciplines for the prestigious Diamond Trophy, there will be a two-hour world broadcast feed and a new prize money structure will total $7 million. Changes to the competition in 2021 include the introduction of a new award for the "Best Performing Athletes" across five discipline groups.

23 May	Meeting International Mohammed VI d'Athlétisme	Complexe Sportif Prince Moulay Abdellah, Rabat
28 May	Diamond League Meeting	Khalifa International Stadium, Doha
4 Jun	Golden Gala Pietro Mennea	Stadio Olimpico, Roma
10 Jun	Bislett Games	Bislett Stadion, Oslo
4 Jul	Bauhaus-Galan	Olympiastadion, Stockholm
9 Jul	Herculis EBS	Stade Louis II, Monaco
13 Jul	Müller Anniversary Games	Olympic Stadium, London
14 Aug	Diamond League Meeting	Shanghai Stadium, Shanghai
21 Aug	Prefontaine Classic	Hayward Field, Eugene, OR
22 Aug	China 2 DL	TBC
26 Aug	Athletissima	Stade Olympique de la Pontaise, Lausanne
28 Aug	Meeting de Paris	Stade Charléty, Paris
3 Sep	Allianz Memorial Van Damme	Boudewijnstadion, Bruxelles
8-9 Sep	Weltklasse	Letzigrund, Zürich

2021 Continental Tour Gold

9 May	Continental Tour Meeting	Tokyo (JPN)
11 May	Continental Tour Meeting	Nanjing (CHN)
19 May	Golden Spike	Ostrava (CZE)
5 Jun	Racers Adidas Grand Prix	Kingston (JAM)
6 Jun	FBK Games	Hengelo (NED)
8 Jun	Paavo Nurmi Games	Turku (FIN)
30 Jun	Irena Szewinska Memorial/Bydgoszcz Cup	Bydgoszcz (POL)
6 Jul	István Gyulai Memorial	Székesfehérvár (HUN)
5 Sep	Kamila Skolimowska Memorial	Chorzów (Silesia) (POL)
14 Sep	Boris Hanzekovic Memorial	Zagreb (CRO)
18 Sep	Kip Keino Classic	Nairobi (KEN)

In addition to the above schduled are 12 Silver Tour meetings and 54 Bronze Tour meetings
The pilot year of the Tour was in 2020, when It is divided into three levels – Gold (offering $200,000 in prize money), Silver ($75,000) and Bronze ($25,000).

WORLD ATHLETICS RULE CHANGES

CHANGE TO LONG JUMP TAKE-OFF RULE
A significant change to the way take-off fouls are judged in long and triple jumps is to start on 1 November 2021. Currently, a no-jump is called if an athlete is judged, while taking off, to have touched the ground beyond the take-off line. A plasticine board set at an angle of 45° has been long used to assist with such decisions. Under the new Technical Rule (30.1.1), it will be a failure on take-off if any part of the take-off shoe or foot breaks the vertical plane of the take-off line. It was felt that this would be more understandable and simpler to judge. The old rule occasionally allowed toecaps to visibly broach the line without marking plasticine. In the future, such moments are to be fouls and the plasticine board, if used, is to be set at 90°. In view of the exceptional circumstances – and particularly because of the postponement of the Olympic Games to 2021 – it was delayed for one year.

Summary of recent rule modifications
That is one of a number of rule changes passed in the last year or so which are all now detailed in the World Athletics Competition & Technical Rules 2020 Edition, which can be found in World Athletics' Library section, whose tab is located in the top right corner of the website. From there, navigate to Technical Information, then Manuals & Guidelines, then to Competition & Technical Rules 2020 Edition. A summary of the more significant rule changes is listed below. These are in addition to the recent rule amendments regarding shoe technology.

* Technical Rule 1 (was IAAF rule 100) – World Championships and Olympic Games no longer excluded from competitions where events may be held in an alternative format
* TR 3.1 (was 141.1) – Under-18 category descriptors boys and girls are replaced with men and women
* TR 3.3-4 (was 141.4-6) – Eligibility for men's, women's and universal categories is elaborated with further references to the terms transgender and differences in sex development
* TR 5.1 (was 143.1) – It is no longer required that vests should have the same colour on the front and back; It is noted that the way hair is worn may be regarded as impeding the judge's view
* TR 6.4.7-8 (was 144.4) – Physical support by designated individuals and pacing by lights or similar added to list of allowable assistances
* TR 8.4.4 (was 146.4.d) – Any protest of a non-finishing athlete or relay team is to be dismissed if they commit a rule breach unrelated to that protest
* TR 9.2 (was 147.2) – The acceptable conduct of mixed competition in field events and stadium races of 5000m or longer is elaborated
* TR 17.6 (was 163.6) – It is clarified that relay runners who correctly leave and return to the track while retrieving a baton (under TR 24.6.3) are not to be disqualified
* TR 17.15.3 (was 163.15.c) – Athletes in track races may carry water or refreshment providing it was there from the start or supplied at an official station
* TR 19.18 (was 165.18) – Timing systems operating automatically at the start but not the finish are prohibited
* TR 20.8 (was 166.8) – It is recommended that in races longer than 800m where rounds are conducted, the number of athletes qualifying by time (as opposed to place) should be minimised
* TR 23.5 (was 169.5) – Steeplechase barrier height for under-18 men is lowered from 0.914m to 0.838m
* TR 25.17 (was 180.17) – The time allowed for trials across all field events, with more than three athletes competing (or for their very first trial), is again one minute (as was the case prior to 2017)
* TR 30.1.1 (was 185.1) – (From 1 Nov 2021) – Horizontal jump take-off failures shall be re-defined to include any breaking of the vertical plane of the take-off line. Rule 29.5 (was 184.5) strongly encourages the use of video or technology to assist with such judgements. It further specifies that a plasticine indicator board may be used, and that this should be set at an angle of 90° rather than the previous 45°
* TR 32.2 (was 187.2) – Number of implements submitted by an athlete in a throwing event is limited to two, unless the Technical Delegate decides otherwise
* TR 39 (was 200) – It is clarified that heptathlons and decathlons may be held on two consecutive 24-hour periods rather than two consecutive days. Therefore allowing for situations where a contest may continue after midnight. The same applies to indoor Heptathlons under TR 53.2 (was 223.2)
* TR 54.7 (was 230.7) – In walks, the term "Pit Lane" is renamed "Penalty Zone"
* TR 56.3.2 (was 250.3.b) – The required length of the "unhampered" run at the start of cross country races is reduced from 1500m to 300m
* TR 57 (was 251 & 252) – The previous rules are replaced with a new and single one covering both Mountain and Trail running
* Competition Rule 32 (was 261) – The 20,000m, 25,000m and 30,000m are deleted from the list of events for which world records are recognised.

Vitaliy Shafar UKR   31 Jan   3m 7m
(results annulled from 17 Apr 2014)
Women
Jessica Peris AUS   18 Nov   4y
Vikoriya Pohoryelska UKR   7 Jun   4y
4y+8y: Francesco Barrano ITA (18 Mar); **4y**: Virjilio Griggs PAN (20 Jul), Andrey Yeremenko RUS (2 Sep); **3y**: Gabriella Fella CYP (1 May), **2y+2y**: Irene Kipchumba KEN (19 Mar); **2y**: Henry Sang KEN (3 Dec)

Earlier – Men
Sadik Mikhou BRN   3 Jun 16   2y 3m
4y: Mathew Kosgei KEN (25 Dec 16), Sorin Mineran ROU (9 Oct 16); **2y+2m**: Lazarus Too KEN (4 Dec 16)
Vitaliy Shafar UKR   6 Jul 12   3y 7m
Aleksandr Shustov RUS   6 Jul 13   4y
(results annulled 8 Jul 2013 to 7 Jul 2017)
Stanislav Tivonchik BLR   7 Aug 12   2y
Women: 2015: 4y: Anna Gladkikh RUS (2 Jun, results annulled 2 Jun 15 – 1 Jun 19), Cornelia Klöpper AUT (12 Oct), Marina Panteleyeva RUS (20 Jun); Olesya Sviridova 4y ban from 27 May 2016 extended back to 27 Oct 2015
Nastalya Ivoninskaya KAZ   6 Aug 12   2y
Gulcan Mingir TUR   4 Aug 12   2y

See also additions on page 45

DRUGS BANS 2020/21

Drugs bans in 2021
As announced by Athletics Integrity Unit or national governing bodies. Suspension: L - life ban, y = years, m = months, W = warning and disqualification, P = pending hearing

Sergey Shubenkov RUS   P

Drugs bans in 2020
Leading athletes – Men

Dmitriy Bobkov RUS	18 Jan	2y
Christian Coleman USA	14 May	2y
Ridouane Haroufi MAR	7 Mar	8y
Maksim Krasnov RUS	5 Sep	4y
Luvo Manyonga RSA	Dec	P
Mohamed Tindouft MAR	23 Feb	3m
Cole Walsh USA	29 Jan	3m

Women

Viktoriya Khapilina UKR	11 Oct	4y
Viktoriya Kolb BLR	21 Feb	4y
Nataliya Krol UKR	16 Jan	20m
Tebogo Mamathu RSA	23 Feb	4y
Marina Panteleyeva RUS results cancelled from 2015	May	4y
Nataliya Pryshchepa/Krol UKR	16 Jan	18m
Mariya Telushkina KAZ	24 May	2y

Olesya Sviridova received an additional 4y ban as she participated as a judge and official during her ban 2016-20.

8y: Eondwosen Ketema ETH (4 Mar) **4y**: Olga Grigoryeva RUS (12 Jan), Eyob Habtesilasse ETH (2 Feb), Marzhanat Ibayeva RUS (19 Sep), Takhir Kadyrkulov KAZ (18 Jan), Ben Matiso RSA (16 Feb), Vadim Ulizhov RUS (7 Jan), Lubov Ushakova KAZ (17 Jan); **2y**: Aleksandr Bezrukov KAZ (17 Jan), Nicola Forcchia ITA (2 Feb); Olesya Zadorozhnaya KAZ (18 Jan)

Add to Drugs Bans 2019
Men

Samir Dahmani FRA	27 Mar	4y
El Mahjoub Dazza MAR	4 May	4y
Robel Fsiha SWE	25 Nov	4y
Noel Hitimana RWA	20 Aug	4y
Philip Kangogo KEN	28 Apr	2y
James Kibet KEN	1 Nov	4y
Kenneth Kipkemoi KEN	12 Sep	4y
Japhet Kipkorir KEN	10 Nov	4y
Alfred Kipketer KEN	18 Nov	2y
Wilson Kipsang KEN	12 Apr	4y
Ioánnis Kiriazis GRE	18 Apr	4y
Mehbood Ali PAK	Dec	4y
Peter Ndorobo Kwemoi KEN	3 Nov	4y
Artyom Leonenko RUS		4y
Elijah Manangoi KEN	22 Dec	2y
Boniface Mbuvi Muema KEN	27 Oct	4y
Mikel Mutai KEN	15 Dec	4y
Dmitriy Nabokov BLR	9 Sep	2y
Alex Oliotiptip KEN	19 Jul	2y
Mouname Sassioui MAR	13 Jun	4y
Lebogang Shange RSA		4y
Patrick Siele KEN	18 Dec	3y 6m
Bralon Taplin GNR	13 Apr	4y + 3y
Luke Traynor GBR	27 May	2y
Daniel Wanjiru KEN	9 Mar	4y
Vincent Yator KEN	10 Apr	4y

Women

Marina Arzamasova BLR	29 Jul	4y
Joyce Chepkirui KEN		P
Marimuthu Gomathi IND	18 Mar	4y
María Guadelipe González MEX	May	4y
Mercy Kibarus KEN	13 Sep	8y
Hanna Krasutska UKR	20 Feb	4y
Andressa de Morais BRA	6 Aug	1y 4m
Beatrice Rutto KEN	21 Apr	6y
Deajah Stevens USA	25 Nov	18m
Etaferahu Temesgen ETH	20 Oct	12y
Lyudmila Yeryomina RUS	20 Nov	2y

8y: Zenia Hamid IRQ (7 Mar), Yelena Ikonnikova RUS (17 May); **6y**: Yelena Orlova RUS (17 May) **4y 2m+4y**: Christian Barchi ITA (3 Mar); **4y**: Maksim Aleksandrov RUS (27 Jul), Idriss Barud MAR (30 Jun), Rachid Benissa MAR (15 Dec), Andreas Beraz GER (29 Mar), Kevin Castille USA (28 Apr), Amit Dahita IND (16 Apr), Urmila Devi IND (21 Jul), Davide Di Folco ITA (1 Dec), Marcelo Diniz BRA (27 Jul), Valentina Galimova RUS (27 Jul) Mauro Guicciardi ITA (15 Jan), Ashish Jakhar IND (21 Oct), Kiranjeet Kaur IND (15 Dec), Eondwosen Ketema ETH (1 Dec), Shyam Lal IND (10 Apr), Raul Machacuay PER (19 May), Nourdine Mansouri MAR (13 Oct), Joseph Mbatha KEN (29 Sep), Ali Mehboob PAK (6 Dec), Talimo Monesa LES (30 Mar), Muhammad Naeem PAK (5 Dec), Kadali Sathya Narayana IND (9 Jun), Gabriel Pedroso CUB/ESP (29 Jun), Ilaria Pizzulli ITA (1 Sep), K Priya IND (19 May), Rohit IND (17 Aug), Muh. Syazrul Adli Saiful MAS (18 Aug), Haidar Abdul Shahid (Nasera) IRQ (8.Mar), Vikos Sheokand IND (13 Oct), Anmol Singh IND (13 Jan), Rakhi Singh IND (4 Nov), Libonto Tootse LES (30 Mar), Sami Ullah PAK (3 Dec), Xue Dong CHN (25 Aug), Zhou Yu CHN 26.8.99 (24 May); **3y 9m**: Melissa van Vuuren RSA (7 Apr); **3y**: Martha Ccorahua ESP (13 Jul); **2y**: Hazril Bin Hassan MAS (18 Aug), Alex Chesakit UGA (14 Apr), Jaykumat Gavade IND (25 Jun), Zach Gehm USA (22 Jun), Geoffrey Kipsang UGA (1 Jun), Mandeep IND (21 Jul), Park Hyun-ji KOR (26 Jul), Graeme Thompson CAN (27 Jul); **18m**: Carolin Gottschalk GER (8 Jun), Max Belisario Sucapoca PER 7 Apr); **1y**: Matti Herrman GER (14 Sep), Kong Xianglong CHN (21 Dec), Loïc Thevin FRA (15 Aug); **9m**: Benjamin Duicu ROU (9 Mar), **6m**: Liu Fang CHN (24 Jul), Dominik Mieczkowski POL (9 Feb); **1m**: Hayat Ahammiche MAR (12 Jan).

2018 – Men:

Mark Dry GBR	18 Oct	4y
Dmuytro Kosynskyy UKR	20 Apr	8y
Vladyslav Malykhin UKR	1 Nov	19m
Rudolf Verkovykh RUS	15 Nov	1y

Women

María Guadelupe González MEX	17 Oct	4y
Jhuma Khatun IND	29 Jun	4y
Sandeep Kumari IND	26 Jun	4y
Joy Loyce KEN	13 Oct	4y
Marina Pospelova RUS	30 Jun	2y

8y: Anastasiya Bazdyrave RUS (29 Jan). Sébastien Palau Garcia FRA; **4y + 4y**: Gilles Zozzoli FRA (7 Apr); **4y + 2y**: Veronika Broslavskaya KAZ (29 Jun); 4y: Wallace Caldas BRA (9 Oct), Reda Jaafar MAR (8 Nov), Henry Kosgei KEN (16 Dec), Recho Jerubet Kosgei KEN (17 Nov), Lucas Longen BRA (27 Jul), Tomás Vilikek CZE (9 Aug); **2y + 2m**: Alessio Guidi ITA (1 Nov); **2y**: Rholex Jelimo KEN (28 Oct), Khadija Ouardi MAR (21 Jun); **1y**: Andrey Isaychev RUS (16 Dec), Anna Kyazeva RUS (16 Dec); **6m**: Berth Muthoni KEN (10 Jun).

2017 – Men

Hassan Chani BRN	3 Aug	4y
Asbel Kiprop KEN	27 Nov	4y

Continued opposite

AMENDMENTS TO ATHLETICS 2020

p.18 Kevin Young (not Andre Phillips) holds WR at 400mh
p.20 Shot: Most over 22m/21m: Bukowiecki 1/17, Bertemes 2/10+1i
p.33 European CC Men's Champs. Robel Fisha stripped of title after receiving a 4-year drugs ban. Move the rest up a place.
p.40-41 Marathon winners: Dazza dq so 5 May Praha- Dawit Wolde ETH 2:06:18, 1 Dec Fukuoka- Takuya Fujimoto JPN 2:09:36
p.47 World Champs 10,000m dr dq (11) Oloitiptip
p.51 World Champs 4x400m h 5th, F 6th
p.63 Asian Champs 10000m: drugs dq (2) Chani, add 3. Tetsuya Yoroizawa JPN 28:44.86
p.71 Pan-American Games: Women DT: drugs dq 2. de Morais, so: 2. Borges, 3. Denia Caballero CUB 60.46
p.74 South Asian Games: drugs dq: 110mh: Muhammad Naeem PAK 14.30, 400mh: Mehboob Ali PAK 50.71; replace by: 110mh: Jayakumar Surendral IND 14.37, 400mh: M.P.Jabir IND 51.42.
p.93 Roman Virastyuk b. 20 Apr 1968
p.98 Drugs bans: Vincent Yator 10 Apr 4y
p.114 Brazil: Champs W DT: de Morais dq – to Fernanda Borges 60.54
p.139 German SP: Bayer
p.164 Lithuania. JT: Matusevicius 89.17
p.184 Spain. 3000mSt: Fernando Carro
p.207-211 Biographies: USA. Emma Coburn also US champ in 2018. Tonia Marshall b. 17 Oct 98
p.237 Records: W DT: 65.98 dq de Morais
p.239 Harroufi transfer to USA
p.241 Trends: Men: SP: 2019 202 not 199 over 18.70. Women 10th best Marathon: 2019- 2:19:28
p.319 U20 All-time: 84.73 Kokhan and 84.22 Frantzeskákis should be in 6kg HT lists not in JT
p.332 Delete last five lines (10 athletes left over from 2018 lists!)

2019 Lists

200m: 20.68 Takordmioui 3.8.95
400m: 44.90 Abubaker 25 Aug, 45.28 Mazen Al-Yassin, drugs dq: 44.92 Taplin (best pre ban 45.26i 1 College Station 2 Feb), 45.67 Thompson; Jnr: 46.21 Moussa Ali Isah, 46.29 Terrance Jones 8.2.02
800m: delete 1:46.63 Arima
1 Mile indoors: 3:48.46i Kejelcha 9 Feb
5000m: 13:28.94 Anthony Maina 27.3.03, 13:29.26 Omwamba, 13:30.38 Kandie – move up four places, 13:33.06 Kuira 25.1.90 (& 10000m 28:12.98, HMar 61:32); 13:33.74 Kimutai 28.12.95, 13:37.31 Meshack Kumungetei –J .00, 13:37.00 Muluwa –J 3.3.02
10000m: 27:28.74 drugs dq Oloitiotip ¶ (best pre-ban 28:19.0A 2 Jul); 27:21.76 Tilahun 7.1.95, 27:51.72 Saidimu 2 Nagoya 13 Oct (from 28:03.53), 28:21.08 Rop; Numbering 1 out from 60 - 100th 28:09.21 Lorenzo Dini 6 ECp London (PH) 6 Jul; Juniors: 28:32.33 Hiroki Kishimoto JPN .00 2B Yokohama 23 Nov; drugs dq 28:11.84 Hitimana
15k: 42:28 Keter 26.12.89
HMar: 61:22 Mmone & 61:31 Mathanga 27 Jul; drugs dq: 60:37 Hitimana, 61:17 Wanjiru, 61:22 P Mwangi
30k: 1:29:36 Paul Maina 26.8.82
Mar: 2:05:18 Tamru 1.10.98; drugs dq 2:05:58 El Mahjoub Dazza, 2:08:40 Daniel Wanjiru, 2:09:18 Wilson Kipsang; **100km**: 6:19:54 Yamauchi
3000mSt: 8:21.94A Kiplimo 21.5.91, 8:22.66 drugs dq Sassioui
110mh: 13.78/13.76w Kashima; wa: 13.82w 2.7 Ryo Tokuoka JPN .99 6 Jul; Junior: 13.91 -0.1 Rashid Muratake JPN-Y 6.2.02 1 Hitachinaka 17 Jun, 13.94 2.0 Hiromasa Yokochi JPN 1.10.00 1 Sagamihara 21 Sep (& at 13.89w), delete 13.96 Shimizu (see 13.81); wa: 13.93 2.5 Mizuki Kondo JPN-Y .03 2 Niigata 14 Jul, 13.97w Yasue Suzuki 12.1.00; Jnr 99cm: 13.47 Faircloth 29.3.00, 13.54 -0.6 Rashid Muratake JPN-Y 6.5.02 1 Hiroshima 18 Oct; wa: 13.3w 3.6 Pedro P. Gutiérrez CUB 25.4.00 1 La Habana 8 Mar
400mh: 50.55 Takahiro Matsumoto JPN 19.9.94 11 Aug; Jnr: 50.78 Taiyo Yoneda
HJ: 2.28i Asanov 30.3.95; 2.25 Hasegawa at Niigata; Jnr: 2.18 Rypo Eto 12.10.01 (not Y) 1 Higashiosaka 26 Jul; **PV**: 5.55 Scerba at Praha (Strahov), 5.53Ai Ruiz on 8 Feb
LJ: 8.05 Mitrevski, 7.92/8.09w Maikel Yorges Vida, 7.82 Tsudo, 7.88w Yasunari Obata J
TJ: 16.85 Yamamoto & 16.55w Yamashita at Hitachinake, 16.35 Tonai, 16.26w Ryoseoi Kakino
SP: 19.27 Johnson 18.10.99, 19.11i M Otterdahl 31.5.01; (185) to 18.80
DT: 63.82 Ceh EU23 (not EJ)
HT: 68.19 Huckaby 16 Jun (from 68.04); Jnr 6kg: delete 74.04 Damneet Singh (2018 mark)
JT: 79.05 Kaul 3 Oct, 78.78 Sasimovich BLR, 75.25 Mori 20.10.99, 74.46 Nakajima
Dec: 7679 Kawasaki; Jnr Dec: 7439 Yancarlos Hernández; **5000mW**: 19:35.57 Takahashi b.17.6.96, 19:36.54 Yamamoto
10000mW: marks on 8 Dec at Sasebo not Nagasaki, 40:20.91 Toyama .98 so not –J; Juniors: 40:49.98 Hayato Yamahara JPN .00 1 Otsu 8 Dec
20kW: 1:21:28 Sun Song 27 La Coruña 8 Jun, 1:22:30 Suwa 22.10.99; **35kW**: 2:35:59 Rakov not J
50kW: 3:53:23 (not 3:55:23) Ojala.

Women
100m: hand 11.1w 3.2 Yunisleidy de la C García CUB 11.8.99 1r2 La Habana 17 May
300m: delete 37.34i Holmes (2018 mark)
400m: 51.47A Leni Shida, 51.56 Price repeated, 52.43 Surin 15.2.96; **600m**: 1:27.82 drugs dq Arzamasova
800m: 1 down for (80) and (90)
1500m: Jnr: 4:14.46 Muita KEN-Y
3000m: 8:51.77 Teresa Musso 5.1.02, 8:55.69 Naomi Mussoni 6.12.98, 8:57.56 Esther Wambui 8.5.00, 9:02.26 Njeri 19.1.99 (not -Y) and delete 9:03.66 Njueri; Jnr: 9:05.32 Margaret Ekidor KEN-Y 26.6.02 4 Yokohama 30 Nov, 9:05.72 Hagitani at Kitami
5000m: 15:12.72 Mussoni 6.12.98, 15:29.91 Jerotich 27.11.99' **10000m**: 32:02.36 Tsutsui, 32:20.97A Korokwiang, 32:59.0A Cherono 29.11.94
10kRd: 32:05 Burka J 17.4.01, 31:39 drugs dq Loyce (& 70:20 HMar), 31:42 Temesgen
Mar: Drugs dq: 2:25:35 Loyce, 2:27:21 Temesgen **100km**: 7:52.22 Nakata' **3000mSt**: 9:31.68 Rosie Clarke, delete 9:52.40 Aich (was flat 3000m)
400mh: 55.91 Andreyeva 13.8.92, 56.04 Knight BEL Ch' **4x100m**: 1.94 Orcel FRA Ch
PV: 4.39i Campbell 2, 4.30i Marty 1 Feb
LJ: 7.02w Rodríguez – series: 6.72w, 7.02w, 6.69w
TJ: numbering 1 out from 70 to 100, move 13.44

AMENDMENTS   45

Korsun from Best out to main list; 14.24w Panturoiu 24.2.95; drugs dq: 14.15 Krasutska, best pre ban 14.01i 1 Sumy 26 Jan
DT: 65.98 drugs dq de Morais – best pre ban 65.34 1 Leiria 26 Jun; HT: 63.89 Rachel Lee Wilson 4.1.97, 63.75 Pronkina (not 64.75)
JT: 56.52 Yiselena Ballar, 54.66 Nakata
Hep: 5907 Gerevini NC – 13.87/0.4, 5847A Hall + LJ 5.49/-1.6, 5718w Winters + LJ 6.09w/3.4. 5694 Lavin 18 Apr; 5528 Otama
4x400m: 8 nations to ITA 3:27.32. move up (20) and (30)
10kW: 45:45 Jiang Jinyan 27.4.03
20kW: 1:29:94 Sergeyeva 12.3.94, 1:35:04 Marie Quennehen
35kW: 2:34:24 Afanasyeva, 2:45:23 Sobchuk
50kW: 4:40:40: Kusahara, 4:44:55 Casale 27 Oct; 80 in list; Note Alytus on 19 May, Huangshan on 9 Mar (final letter cut off in some cases)

World Indoor Lists 2020
Men: **PV**: 5.80 drugs dq Walsh (best pre ban 5.60A 16 Jan), 5.75 Reese Watson 1 Navasota 7 Mar (from 5.65A). 5.65 Drew Volz USA 20.11.92 3 Navasota 7 Mar; **Dec**: 5939 Cairoli b. 13.1.90

Drugs disqualifications & annulled marks
Men
Hassan Chani MAR (3 Aug 17-16 Mar 20) 2017- HMar 60:23 short?; 2018- 10000m 27:38.16
Dmytro Kosynskyy UKR JT: 2017- 80.37
Sadik Mikhou BRN (3 Jun 2016 – 4 Dec 2020) 2016- 1500m 3:32.30 & 3:32.85, 3000m 7:39.02; 2017- 1500m 3:31.34, 3:31.49 & 3:32.32; 3000m 7:44.36, 10kRd 28:05; 2018- 1000m 2:16.09, 1500m 3:34.55 & indoor 3:48.48; 1M 3:57.10, 3000m 7:41.39i
Dilshot Nazarov TJK 2011- 80.71 (best pre-ban 77.91); 2012- 77.70; 2013- 80.71
Aleksandr Shustov RUS (8 Jul 13-7 Jul 17) HJ: 2013- 2.32 (best pre ban 2.31 2 Beijing 21 May), 2014- 2.26i/2.25, 2015- 2.30
Stanislav Tivonchik BLR PV: 2013- 5.40, 2014- 5.52
Women
Meraf Bahta SWE (24 May-31 Aug 2018): 2018: 800m 2:02.45, 1500m: 4:02.31, 1M 4:27.03, 2000m 5:37.12, 3000m 8:57.61, 5000m 15:08.17, 10000m 32:19.34 (pre/after ban 1500m 4:04.89i 2 Torun 15 Feb, 1M 4:32.82 2 Sep, 5000m 15:15.33 1 Jordan Stanford 3 May)
Yuliya Gushchina RUS (1 Sep 11 -31 Dec 14) 200m/400m: 2012- 22.95, 49.28; 2013- 23.32, 51.06
Natalya Ivoninskaya KAZ (6 Aug 12-5 Aug 14) 2013- 100mh 13.24, 2014- 60mh 8.13i
Gülcan Mingir TUR (4 Aug 2012-3 Aug 2014) 3000mSt 2013- 9:45.80
Olesya Sviridova RUS (4y from 16.6.16 extended back to 23.10.15) 2016- also loses her 17.87i & 17.73

International Championships Changes
Drugs dqs – move rest up accordingly, Additions to those shown in previous Annuals
2019 European Indoors: W TJ: (8) Hanna Krasutska
2018 Asian Games: 10000m: (1) Hassan Chani (3rd to Kieran Tuntivate THA 30:27.49)
2018 European Champs: W 10000m: (3) Bahta
2018 West Asian Championships: 1500m: Mikhou
2017 World Champs: 1500m: (6) Mikhou; HJ: (7) Shustov
2017 Islamic Solidarity Games: 1500m: Mikhou (winner becomes Fouad El Kaam MAR 3:37,81)
2015 European Team Champs: W 4x100m: 2 RUS 42.99 – Panteleyeva drugs dq
2015 World University Games: W 3000mSt: (3) Mingir (with original 1st 3 all disqualified result becomes: 1. Chantelle Groenewoud CAN 9:51.17, 2. Jessica Furlan CAN 9:51.23, 3. Sandra Eriksson FIN 9:55.11)
2015 European Race Walking Cup: 50k: (1) Ivan Noskov

Corrections to previous World lists
2018: 200m: Drugs dq: 20.58/20.38w Virjilio Griggs
W DT: 58.41 Kumari confirmed as drugs dq
10k Road: drugs dq: 27:36 Berhanu Wendim Tsegu 30 Dec
2017: Drugs dq W 5000m 15:34.60 Porhoryelska
2014: Drugs dq: 2:09:53 & 2:09:38dh Vitaliy Shafar
2005: HT: 73.95 Sergey Litvinov with 6kg hammer

Thanks to Knut Gilbrandsen, Norbert Heinrich, Juan Mari Iriondo, Yoshimasa Noguchi, Zdenek Procházka, Alberto Sánchez Traver

---

Married in 2019-20
Female	Male
Tetyana Fetiskina UKR	Oleksandr Nychyporchuk
Maja Mihalinec SLO	Luka Zidar	17.9.20
Marusa Mismas SLO	Zrimsek	12.7.20
Kortney Ross USA	Tray Oates USA	
Ruth Spelmeyer GER	Tobias Preuss (water polo)	.12.20
Amela Terzic SRB	Jasmin Ljajic	1.1.20
Elaine Thompson JAM	Derron Herah	2.11.19
Martin Wierig GER	Anna Rüh	

Add to Drugs Bans
2019
Roman Georgiyev RUS   20 Jun   2y
Gilbert Kwemoi KEN   9 Nov   4y
Paul Mwangi KEN   12 May   2y
4y: Hassan Narzouk Eisa EGY (26 Jul); 2y: Fatma Mohamed EGY (26 Jul), Jane Wanjiru KEN (1 Dec); Chen Mei-Wen TPE (8 Dec); 6m: Shehab Abdelaziz EGY (26 Jul), Rehab Youssef Mohamed EGY (26 Jul);
2018: Jacob Kendagor KEN   21 Nov   4y
2012: Klodiana Shala ALB   31 Jul   2y
2011: Dilshod Nazarov TJK   29 Aug   2y

Women's name changes
Sabine Büchel SUI	Rutz-Büchel
Zinzi Chabanga RSA	Zulu
Pamela Dutkiewicz GER	Emmerich
Mariya Filyuk UKR	Sakharuk
Aliyah Johnson AUS	Parker
Kellyn Johnson USA	Taylor
Anastasiya Kalina RUS	Aleksandrova
Svetlana Lajcáková SVK	Skvarková
Lenka Ledvinová CZE	Valesová
Brittany McGowan AUS	Kaan
Klaudia Maruszewska POL	Regin
Olena Mizurnyuk UKR	Sobchuk
Amy-Eloise Neale GBR	Markovc
Lead O'Connor USA	Falland
Cindy Ofili GBR	Sember
Jirina Ptácníková CZE	Kudlicková
Vera Rudakova RUS	Chalaya
Irena Sedivá CZE	Gillarová
Jessica Trengrove AUS	Stenson
Izabela Trzaskalska POL	Paszkiewicz
Viktoriya Zyabkina KAZ	An

OBITUARY 2020

Obituaries of the following who died in early 2020 were included in ATHLETICS 2020: Igor Avrunin, Dick Bank, Tetyana Burakova, Jean Clausse, Simone Créantor, Jacques Delelienne, Abadi Hadis, Volodomyr Inozemtsev, Nick Jones, Aare Kainlauri, Santiago Llorente, Dezó Lombos, Orlando McDaniel, Bruce MacDonald, Teresa Machado, Kennedy Nijiri, Philip Olsen, Maurie Plant, Bill Roe, Tomás Salinger, Robert Shavlakadze, Henry Smith, Guillermo Solá, Juan Taylor, Braian Toledo, Mike Wheeler, Malcolm Yardley, Dana Zatopková.

Marlene AHRENS Osterdag (Chile) (b. 27 Jul 1933 Concepción) on 17 June in Santiago. The daughter of German immigrants, she became the first Chilean woman to win an Olympic medal with silver at javelin in 1956 (12th 1960). She set South American records with 47.64 in 1955 and 48.73 and 50.38 in 1956 and won at the Pan-American Games in 1959 and 1963, the South American Championships in 1956, 1958, 1961 and 1964 and Ibero-American in 1964. She won the Chilean mixed doubles tennis title in 1967 and was also an equestrienne, who at the age of 62 competed at team dressage at the 1995 Pan-American Games.

Aleksandr Timofeyevich **AKSININ** (Russia) (b. 4 Nov 1954 St. Petersburg) on 28 July in St. Petersburg. On USSR 4x100m teams he won Olympic gold in 1980 (also 4th 100m) and bronze in 1976 (sf 100m), after 4R in 1974 and 3R and 7th 200m in 1978, European gold in 1982 after 4R in 1974 and 3R and 7th 200m in 1978, and World University Games gold in 1977 and silver in 1981. World Cup: 1972- 4R, 1979- 6R, 1981- 4R; European Cup: 1979- 1R, 1981- 2R. He won three European Indoor 60m medals: 2nd 1975 and 3rd 1978 & 1980. USSR 200m champion 1976, 2nd 100m 1977-78, 3rd 1976. Pbs: 60m 6.56i (1980), 100m 10.19/9.9h (1980), 200m 20.80 (1980).

Arvid Folke ALNEVIK (Andersson) (Sweden) (b. 31 Dec 1919 Ardrå, Bollnäs) in Gävle on 8 August at the age of 100, when he was the oldest living athletics Olympic medallist – the bronze at 4x400m in 1948 (qf 400m). World War II delayed his international career, but he won a bronze at 4x400m at the 1946 Europeans. At Swedish 400m Champs he was 2nd in 1947-8 and 3rd in 1945-6 and 1949. Pb 48.1 (1947).

Gudrun Eivor Elisabeth **ARENANDER** (Sweden) (née Eklund, married in 1947) (b. 25 Mar 1921 Lovö) on 20 August in Bromma. At the discus she was 4th at the 1946 Europeans, 12th at the 1948 Olympic Games and Swedish champion in 1942-3 and 1945-7. Pb 40.37 (1943).

Francisco ARITMENDI Criado (Spain) (b. 17 Sep 1938 Málaga del Fresno) died on 12 April in Guadalajara. Just 1.57m tall, his greatest achievement was his win in the International Cross-country in 1964 (but outside the top 20 in his five other appearances in this race). He was Spanish champion at 10,000m in 1966 and cross-country in 1964-5, and competed in the 1964 Olympic Games at 5000m (4th in heat). He set Spanish records at 5000m 13:53.4 in 1964 and indoor 3000m 8:22.2 in 1965 with other pbs: 1500m 3:58.8 (1964), 3000m 8:12.2 (1965) and 10,000m 29:52.0 (1965); 14 internationals 1962-8.

Mykola BAGACH (Ukraine) (b. 24 Jun 1993) in November. The son of 1998 European shot champion Oleksandr Bagach, he competed at the shot at the 2011 European Junior and 2012 World Junior Championships. Pb 19.19 (2019).

James John **'Jim' BAILEY** (Australia) (b. 21 Jul 1929 Sydney) on 31 March in Bellingham, Washington, USA. At 880y he was Australian champion in 1951 and 1954 and 9th at the 1954 British Empire & Commonwealth Games before going to the University of Oregon in the USA. There he won the NCAA 1 mile in 1955 and was 2nd at 1500m in 1956. In May 1956 he ran the first sub-4 minute mile in the USA, but ran the 800m at the Olympic Games (semi). He returned to Australia and played professional rugby league, but then settled for the rest of his life in the Pacific Northwest in the USA. Pbs: 880y 1:49.4 (1957), 1500m 3:43.3 (1956), 1M 3:58.6 (1956).

Vesmonis Vitatus **'Wes' BALODIS** (Australia) (b. 24 Oct 1933 Auce, Latvia) on 29 October. He competed at the 1956 Olympic Games (dnq 20th) and was Australian champion 1957-9 at discus – also third six times at shot. Pbs: SP 15.68 (1959), DT 49.77 (AUS record, 1960), JT 61.07 (1959). He had emigrated from Latvia to Australia in 1950.

Witold BARAN (Poland) (b. 29 Jul 1939 Chmielów) on 22 June in Bydgoszcz. A world-ranked 1500m runner in the early 1960s, he set three Polish records: 3:40.90 in 1961 and 3:39.81 and 3:38.9 in 1964. The last came in his semi-final before 6th in the final at the Tokyo Olympics. He was also 2nd at the 1962 Europeans and Polish champion at 800m 1961, 1500m 1962-4 and 1966-7 and 5000m 1968. 2nd European Cup

5000m 1965. He set a European 1 mile record at 3:56.0 (1964) and another Polish record 2000m 5:03.6 (1962). His other pbs were: 800m 1:48.1 (1966), 1000m 2:21.2 (1962), 3000m 7:55.4 (1963), 5000m 13:41.6 (1969).
Annual progression at 1500m: 1956- 4:10.8, 1957- 4:03.7, 1958- 3:48.8, 1959- 3:46.23, 1960- 3:47.2, 1961- 3:40.0, 1962- 3:40.8, 1963- 3:40.5, 1964- 3:38.9, 1965- 3:41.2, 1966- 3:39.5, 1967- 3:41.6, 1968- 3:40.8, 1969- 3:40.6, 1970- 3:40.8, 1971- 3:44.1, 1972- 3:42.5.

Matthew '**Matt**' **BARBER** (Australia) (b. 26 Feb 1956) on 12 October. At shot, was 5th at the 1982 Commonwealth Games and Australian champion in 1980 and 1982. Pb 18.40 (1981)

Madeline Christina **BARRINGTON** (GBR) (b. 31 Dec 1935 Twickenham) (née Wooller, she married Derek **IBBOTSON** in 1957, and after their divorce squash champion Jonah Barrington) on 23 September. She competed in four internationals for Britain 1955-63 at 800m, including heats at the 1962 European Championships. She was also 6th in 1955 and 5th in 1956 at the International Cross-country. She won the National CC in 1963 and 1964 (2nd 1959, 3rd 1962 and 1966) and at the WAAAs was 2nd at 1 mile 1962-63, 3rd at 440y 1954, 880y 1955-56 and 1M 1958. She ran on the Spartan Ladies team that set a world best for 4x440y in 1954 and on national teams that set British records at 3x800m and 3x880y in 1956, 880m 2:09.7 (1962), 1500m 4:43.6 (1958), 1M 4:57.8 (1962), 3000m 10:10.8 (1969).

Gábor **BÁTHORY** (Hungary) (b. 15 Sep 1950 Budapest) in June. Competed in 3 internationals 1973-4 and in 1973 was Hungarian champion at 5000m and 15th at 5000m and 22nd at 10000m at the World University Games. Pbs: 800m 1:55.7 (1968), 1500m 3:48.4 (1975), 3000m 8:06.0, 5000m 13:44.6 and 10,000m 29:01.0 (all 1973).

Vera **BERNARDOVÁ** (Czech Republic) (b. 18 Feb 1947 Mlada Bleslav) (later Lisková then Cervena) on 26 February. She set a Czechoslovak high jump record at 1.69 in 1963 and was 11th at the European Champs in 1966, with 9 internationals. Pb 1.70 (1966).

Dr. Clifton '**Cliff**' **BERTRAND** (Trinidad & Tobago) (b. 2 Mar 1936 Arima) on 28 November in Long Island City, New York. Represented the West Indies Federation when he won a 4x100m bronze in the 1959 Pan-American Games and in the 200m heats at the 1960 Olympic Games. Then for Trinidad & Tobago he won another Pan-American 4x100m bronze in 1963 and ran in the 200m heats at the 1964 Olympics. At the Commonwealth Games he ran (heats) at 220y, 440y and both relays in 1958 and 220y in 1966 with 8th at 4x110y. Pbs: 100m 10.4 (1962), 10.3w (1966); 200m 20.7 (1965), 400m 46.6 (1960). He graduated from New York University, where he was later head coach, and with a doctorate from Columbia University, New York.

Heinfried **BIRLENBACH** (FRG/Germany) (b. 7 Dec 1940 Siegen) on 11 November in Siegen. Ranked in the world top ten at the shot each year 1967-70, he competed at three Olympic Games: 1964- dnq 14, 1968- 8, 1972- 7, and at European Championships: 1966- 5th, 1971- dns final (injured after 3rd best in qualifying). He won the European Indoor title in 1966 and 1969, 2nd in the European Cup 1967 and 1970, and was FRG champion 1966-71 (2nd 1963-5 and 1972) and indoors 1965-72. Set seven FRG records 18.70 (1964) to 20.35 (1970) and had pbs: SP 20.37 (1972 in qualifying at the Olympics), DT 50.64 (1963). 46 internationals 1963-72.
Annual progression at SP: 1961- 14.26, 1962- 16.06, 1963- 18.25, 1964- 18.70, 1965- 18.59, 1966- 19.06, 1967- 19.20, 1968- 20.18, 1969- 20.19, 1970- 20.35, 1971- 19.59, 1972- 20.37, 1973- 19.46, 1974- 16.80.

Neil **BLACK** (GBR) (b. 23 May 1959) on 18/19 April. A highly-regarded physiotherapist, who had worked for many years with leading British athletes, he was appointed performance director for UK Athletics in 2012. However, after seven years he left in the Autumn in a fall-out from the Salazar affair. As a promising young athlete for Morpeth H, he was 2nd at 1500m and 3rd at 3000m at the 1978 AAA Junior Championships and set all his pbs that year at the age of 19: 800m 1:52.7, 1500m 3:44.40, 1M 4:02.28 and 3000m 8:11.9. Also 10M Rd 29:04 (1983).

Dr. Anthony Arthur Crampton '**Tony**' **BLUE** (Australia) (b. 4 February 1936 Dubbo, New South Wales) on 1 October in Brisbane. He was an 800m semi-finalist at the 1960 and 1964 Olympic Games, and was 3rd at 880y and 4th at 1 mile at the 1962 Commonwealth Games. Australian 880y champion 1959 & 1962-3. Pbs: 440y 48.1 (1959), 880y 1:47.8 (1963), 1000m 2:20.5 (1960), 1500m 3:46.3 (1960), 1M 4:04.0 (1960).

Virginia **BONCI/IOAN** (Romania) (b. 5 Jan 1949 Pielesti) on 9 November in Bucharest. A high jumper, in 1968 she was 2nd at the European Indoors and dnq 21st at the Olympics, and in 1973 won the World University Games title. Also dnq 1969 and 12th 1974 at European Champs. Romanian champion 1973, 1975 and 1977, she set a Romanian record with 1.91 (1974) and had a best of 1.92 later that year. Married Serban Ioan, 1972 Olympian, who set five ROU records and had a best of 2.18i (1974).

Jeff **BRAUN** (USA) (b. 2 June 1957) on October 18. At the shot he won the US Indoor title in 1982 and was 3rd for Wisconsin in the 1979 NCAA Indoors. PB 20.12 (1982).

Richard '**Dick**' **BUERKLE** (USA) (b. 3 Sep 1947 Rochester, New York) on 22 June in Atlanta. After university at Villanova (3rd NCAA 3M

48 OBITUARY

1970), he moved with his family to Atlanta in 1979 and stayed there for the rest of his life. He was 8th at 10,000m at the 1970 World University Games and AAU champion at 5000m in 1974 and in 1976 when he also won at the US Olympic Trials, before a non-qualifying 9th in his Olympic heat. In 1978 he set a world indoor record for 1 mile with 3:54.93 and also won the Wanamaker Mile at the Millrose Games. He was 2nd in the US Olympic Trials in 1980 but was denied his opportunity by the US boycott of the Moscow Games. Other pbs: 1500m 3:39.8i (1978), 3:41.9 (1975); 1M 3:57.8 (1974), 3000m 7:43.2 (1974), 2M 8:21.8 (1976), 3M 12:58.00i (1982), 5000m 13:23.20 (1980), 6M 27:36.2 (1974), 10,000m 28:25.0 (1974). After a variety of jobs he taught Spanish and coached.

Stefan BURKART (Switzerland) (b. 9 Dec 1957) on 3 May. He set a Swiss 100m record of 10.32 in 1992, going on to run at the Olympic Games in the 100m and 200m (heats) that year and at 100m (heat) in 1996, when at 38y 230d he was the oldest ever Olympic 100m competitor. European Champs 100m: sf 1982, ht 1990, qf 1994; European Indoor 60m: ht 1985 & 1990, sf 1986. Also set Swiss indoor 50m records at 5.84 in 1990 and 5.82 in 1991 and at 60m with 6.66 in 1985 and 6.61 in 1986. Pb 200m 20.76 (1992). Swiss champion at 100m 1982 (& 1988 tie), 1985-7, 1989-90 and 1995-6 and at 60m indoors 1985-92 and 1995-6 (2nd 1982-4 and 1994). In 1986 he married British international sprinter Helen Barnett, who, after competing for Britain at the 1984 Olympics, ran for Switzerland in 1992.

Ernesto CANTO Gudiño (Mexico) (b. 18 Oct 1959 Mexico City) on 20 November. He was the best 20km walker of the mid-1980s, when he won the World title in 1983 and Olympic in 1984 (also 10th 50k). He was also the Pan-American Games champion in 1983 (dq 1987, 5th 1991), Central American in 1982, 1986 and 1990, Goodwill Games 1990, and at the World Cup he won in 1981 and was 2nd in 1983 and 1991, 5th 1987, 6th 1979. At subsequent Olympics: disqualified in 1988, and only 29th in 1992; also dq at 1987 Worlds. He was 3rd in the World Indoor 5000m walk in 1987. He set world walking records at 20km 1:18:40.0 and 1 hour 15,253m in 1984. Other best times: Track 3000m 11:50.0 (1983), 5000m 18:38.71i (1987), 10,000m 39:29.2 (1984). Road 30km 2:08:49 (1990), 50km 3:51:10 (1982).

Llorenç CASSI (Spain) (b. 14 May 1940 Barcelona) on 23 March in Barcelona. Twice 2nd and four times 3rd at hammer at Spanish Championships, 6 internationals 1964-75. Pbs: SP 14.13 (1969), DT 47.04 (1972), HT 60.22 (1975 ESP M35 record).

Murray Spencer **CHEATER** (New Zealand) (b. 26 Jan 1947 Auckland) on 4 August in Rotorua. He set 16 NZ hammer records from 54.38 (1968) to 71.20 in 1976, six of them in Britain where he spent several years, competing for Woodford Green. He was 5th at the 1974 Commonwealth Games and dnq 16 at the 1976 Olympics; NZ champion 1974-9 and 1981-4.

CHOI Yun-chil (Korea) (b. 19 Jul 1928 Tanchon) on 8 October in Seoul. At the marathon, after not finishing in 1948 (3rd at 30k point) he was 4th at the 1952 Olympic Games and 3rd at Boston in 1950. At the 1954 Asian Games he won the 1500m and 2nd at 5000m. Pbs: 1500m 3:56.2 (1954), Mar 2:26:07 (Asian record 1952), 2:25:16 short (1951).

Alan COCKING (GBR) (b. 12 Oct 1936) on 31 October. A lifelong member of Pudsey & Bramley H, he had a splendid record in the National cross-country championships, winning the Youth race in 1954 and 1955, and 2nd in the Junior in 1956 and 1st in 1958. when he was also 2nd in the CAU and 10th in the senior International CC. His best placing in the senior National was a more modest 30th in 1962. His track pbs: 1M 4:08.5 (1960), 2M 8:56.6 (1958), 3M 14:01.8 (1960), 3000SC 9:19.6 (1962).

János DALMATI (Hungary) (b. 26 Feb 1942 Szabadhídvég) on 29 September in Budapest. A race walker, he was 22nd in the 1972 Olympic Games 50k and at the Europeans was 10th at 20k in 1966, 15th at 20k and 10th at 50k in 1969, and 11th at 50k in 1971. He was Hungarian champion at 20k in 1965 and 1969-70 and at 50k in 1970-72, He set Hungarian walks records for 10,000m 43:12.0 (1965), and for 3000m 12:16.4, 15,000m 1:06:33.2, 25k 1:56:51.2 and 2Hr 25,662k (all 1970), with pbs 20k 1:27:39 (1977) and 50k 4:08:42 (1979). 18 internationals 1965-81.

Walter Francis **'Buddy' DAVIS** (USA) (b. 5 Jan 1931 Beaumont, Texas) on 17 November at Port Arthur, Texas. Crippled by polio as a boy he became an All-American in basketball (he was 2.04/6'8½" tall) at Texas A&M University. He made rapid progress as a high jumper from 1.87 in 1949, 1.94 in 1950, to 2nd in the world with 2.057 (6'9") in 1951. He tied for the NCAA title in 1952 after 2= in 1951. He changed to Western Roll in 1952, cleared 2.095 twice including at the AAU, just half an inch behind the world record set by Les Steers in 1941, and won the Olympic title at 2.04 in cold weather. In his final year of competition, 1953, he took that world record with 2.12 (6'11⅝") at Dayton, Ohio for his second AAU title. He then played NBA basketball for five years for the Philadelphia Warriors and St. Louis Hawks, and after that worked in banking for most of his career.

Luigi DE ROSSI (Italy) (b. 5 May 1935 Velo d'Astico, Vicenza) on 28 April. He was 22nd in the 1960 Olympic 20k walk and set a a pb of 1:32:19 in 1967; 10 internationals 1960-67.

Fred DeBERNARDI (USA) (b. 2 Mar 1949) on

OBITUARY

3 December in Las Vegas. In 1972 he won the AAU indoor shot and both shot and discus at the 1972 NCAAs for UTEP (University of Texas at El Paso) after 2nd in the discus in 1970-1 and 3rd in the shot in 1971. He was 6th at discus and 7th at shot at the 1970 World University Games and had a discus pb in 61.47 1971, He had a shot best of 21.42i/21.41 in 1974 (4th in the world that year) while competing for the ITA.

Jacques DÉPREZ (France) (b. 3 Mar 1938) on 20 November. At 110m hurdles: heat at the Olympic Games and French champion in 1960. Pbs: 110m 14.4 (1960), PV 4.45 (1959), Dec 6130 (1958). He became a leading coach.

Gustav DISSE (Germany (b. 28 Sep 1933 Wattenscheid) on 11 November in Bochum. He won the FRG marathon title in 1956-7 and 1959, 2nd 10,000m 1961-2. Set German records at 10,000m 1:01:41.8 & 1 Hour 19.441m in 1962, with other pbs: 1500m 3:53.4 (1961), 3000m 8:13.4 (1961), 5000m 14:07.4 (1961), 10,000m 29:24.4 (1962), Mar 2:24:51 (1963), 15 internationals 1956-62.

Clement George **EISCHEN** (USA) (b. 24 Dec 1926 Holstein, Nebraska) on 7 December. After 2nd at the Olympic Trials he ran the 1500m (6th heat) at the 1948 Olympic Games. For Washington State University he was 2nd in the NCAA 880y in 1951. Pbs: 880y 1:51.3 (1951), 1500m 3:52.5 (1948), 1M 4:13.5 (1948). He became a notable physical therapist.

Georges ELLOY (France) (b. 13 May 1930 Paris) on 5 June in Jullouville. French champion at 400m hurdles in 1950-1, he was 6th at the 1950 Europeans and won the 1949 World University Games title in 53.0, his third world junior record that year and his pb. Other pbs: 400m 49.6 (1950), 110mh 15.1 (1949), 200mh 24.9 (1949). 13 Internationals 1949-55. His daughter Laurence (b. 3 Dec 1959) set four French records at 100m hurdles from 1982 to 12.69 in 1986; 6th Europeans 1986 and Worlds 1987, 2nd World Indoor 60mh in 1985.

Per Olov ENQUIST (Sweden) (b. 23 Sep 1934 Hjoggböle, Västerbotten) on 25 April in Vaxholm. He was the best-known Swedish author still living; his most famous book "A Royal Affair". He was also a notable playwright and won many awards. At high jump he had a pb of 1.97 in 1959, in which year he was 5th at the World Student Games.

Ingvar Axel Harald **ERICSSON** (Sweden) (b. 31 Aug 1927 Rinna) on 14 May in Stockholm. A world-ranked 1500m runner in the 1950s, he was 7th in 1950 and 4th in 1954 (heat 1958) at the European Championships and 8th at the 1952 Olympics; Swedish champion 1952 and 1954-5 (2nd 1950 and 1956-8, 3rd 1948, 1951 and 1953). 22 internationals 1950-8. Swedish records at 1500m 3:41.2 in 1956 (2nd in world that year) and 2000m 5:11.4 & 5:09.6 (1955). Other pbs: 800m 1:52.6 (1953), 1000m 2:22.7 (1952), 1M 4:00.4 (1957), 3000m 8:15.8 (1958), 5000m 14:27.0 (1958).

Ary FAÇANHA de SÁ (Brazil) (b. 1 Apr 1928 Guimarães) on Aug 16 in Brasilia. At long jump he was 4th in 1952 and dnq 20th in 1956 (also 4x100m ht) at the Olympic Games. Winner at the World University Games and 3rd Pan-American Games 1955. South American champion 1952 (3rd 1954, 2nd 1956 & 1958. Brazilian records 7.57 (1952), 7.72A & 7.84A, South American record, (1955). Pb 100m 10.6 (1952).

Ödön FÖLDESSY (Hungary) (b. 1 Jul 1929 Békés) on 9 June in Budapest. At long jump he was the Olympic bronze medallist in 1952 (dnq 21st 1956), European champion in 1954 (10th 1958) and 2nd in 1951 and winner in 1954 at the World University Games. Hungarian champion LJ 1950-5 & 1957-9. Set three Hungarian records in 1953 – 7.63, 7.66 and 7.76 (the second best in the world that year) and he was successively 5th, 3rd, 2nd and 8th in the *Track & Field News* world rankings 1951-5. 40 internationals 1949-60. Other pbs: HJ 1.90 (1953), TJ 13.37 (1952). His wife Paula Marosi won Olympic gold in 1964 and silver in 1968 at team foil fencing. Annual progression: 1950- 7.34, 1951- 7.41, 1952- 7.42, 1953- 7.76, 1954- 7.70, 1955- 7.56, 1956- 7.41, 1957- 7.41, 1958- 7.43, 1959- 7.44, 1960- 7.38.

Paul Leighton **FOREMAN** (Jamaica) (b. 25 Jan 1939 Kingston) on 15 December. At long jump he won the Empire Games title in 1958, was 12th at the 1960 Olympic Games (for the British West Indies) and set Jamaican records at 7.58 (1958) and 7.62 (1960).

Peter Edward **FULLAGER** (GBR) (b. 19 Sep 1943 Chatham) on 20 December in Adelaide, Australia. As a race walker he had nine internationals for Britain 1965-9 before emigrating to Australia in 1970. At 20k he was 7th in 1966 and 13th in 1969 at the European Championships and was 4th in 1965 and 6th in 1967 at the Lugano Trophy (later World Cup), 2nd in the RWA Champs in 1965 and 1969 (3rd 1968 and 1970). For Australia he won the bronze medal at 20 miles at the 1974 Commonwealth Games and competed at the 1979 and 1981 World Cups and was Australian 20k champion in 1972, 1974 and 1980. Walks pbs: 3000m 12:39.6 (1979), 2M 13:34.0 (1968) (3200m + 5 secs), 10000m 45:07.0 (1967), 43:40 Rd (1966); 7M 50:16.2 (1966), 1Hr 13,166m (1968), 20k 1:30:35 (1970), 1:28:26sh (1968; 2Hr 25,318m (1967), 30k 2:24:32.8 (1967), 20M 2:36:10.0 (1967), 50k 4:20:38 (1971).

Bruno GALLIKER (Switzerland) (b. 29 Dec 1931 Ennembrücke) in a car accident in Zürich on 27 May. He set eight Swiss records at 400m hurdles from 52.5 in 1957 to 51.0 twice in 1960. Those two came in heat and final when he was 6th (50.11 auto time) at the Rome Olympic Games. He won European bronze medals at

400mh in 1958 and 4x400m in 1962 (sf 400mh). 35 internationals 1955-64. Swiss champion at 400mh 1960 and 1962-4 and 200mh 1963. Pbs: 400m 47.7 (1957), 200mh 23.9 (1962, Swiss record). He became a sports reporter for Swiss radio.

George GANDY (GBR) (b. 10 May 1940 Newcastle) on 8 October. Previously Administrator for South of England Athletics, he worked at Loughborough University where he was a member of the School of Sport, Exercise and Health Sciences 1971-2009 and was director of athletics for many years. As well as overseeing a massive improvement in the facilities for the sport, he developed the talents of scores of top-class runners, playing an important role in their development of such Loughborough athletes as Seb Coe, David Moorcroft, Jack Buckner, Paula Radcliffe and Lisa Dobriskey. He was national endurance coach in 1990-97 and 2009-13 and coached more than 80 international athletes. He competed for Gosforth Harriers as an 880y/1 mile runner and went to St. Mary's College.

Sidney GARTON (USA) (b. 24 Mar 1959 New Boston, Texas) on October 28 in Tyler, Texas. In 1959 at 220y he won the NAIA 220y title and ran pbs of 100y 9.4/9.3w and 220y 20.9t and 20.5wSt. Other pbs: 100m 10.3 (1960), 220yST 20.8 (1958).

Hartwig GAUDER (Germany/GDR) (b. 10 Nov 1954 Vaihingen, Württemberg) on 22 April in Erfurt. An outstanding walker for two decades, he is one of the élite few to have won European junior (10km 1973), European (50km 1986), Olympic (50km 1980) and World (50km 1987) outdoor titles. At 50k walk he also won bronze medals at the 1988 Olympics (in his best ever time of 3:39:45), 1990 Europeans and 1991 Worlds, and was 4th in the 1982 Europeans and 6th at the 1992 Olympics, prevented by the boycott of 1984 from competing at a fourth Olympics. At the World Cup he won in 1985 and was second in 1981 and 1987. He concentrated on the 50k, but at 20k he had a best of 1:20:51 in 1987 and was 7th in the 1978 Europeans, and he set a world indoor 1 hour best with 14,906m in 1986. He won GDR titles at 20k 1975-6, 1985-6; 50k 1979, 1982, 1986; and the German 50k in 1993 and also set GDR walk records at 20k in 1979 and four at 30k to 2:12:11 in 1984. Track pbs: 3000mW 11:20.0 (1984), 5000mW 18:59.67i (1988), 19:31.62 (1984); 10000mW 39:13.15i (1988), 40:13.36 (1990); 20000mW 1:22:47.47 (1990).

He trained as an architect and competed for TSV Erfurt; coached by Siegfried Herrmann, the stylish runner who set a world record for 3000m at 7:46.0 in 1965. Gauder's family moved from West Germany when he was five. Gauder had a heart transplant in January 1997, but made such an excellent recovery that he competed in the New York Marathon several times.

Hartwig Gauder – progression at 50k walk
Gauder had 12 years ranked in the world top ten at 50k, second only to Jésus Ángel García 15 (followed by Robert Korzeniowski with 11), although four years at no. 1 to García's one with Korzeniowski the leader at seven and Raúl González with five.

Year	Best	WL	WR	Year	Best	WL	WR
1979	4:01:20	58	-	1987	3:40:53	2	1
1980	3:48:15	7	1	1988	3:39:45	3	3
1981	3:46:57	2	2	1989	retired		
1982	3:49:44	12	7	1990	3:47:08	9	4 (3)
1983	3:43:23	3	5	1991	3:49:10	12	4 (4)
1984	3:41:24	2	2	1992	3:56:47	30	6 (7)
1985	3:43:33	5	1	1993	3:52:46	17	–
1986	3:40:55	2	1				

WL = position on annual world list, WR – Track & Field News world ranking position (PJM)

David GIRALT Agramonte Sr (Cuba) (b. 28 Jun 1959 Dos Caminos/San Luis, Santiago de Cuba) on 13 April in Havana.He was the first Cuban to long jump over 8 metres with 8.00 in 1977, the first of five Cuban records he set to 8.22 when 3rd in the 1979 World Cup in Montreal. That year he was also 2nd at the Pan-American Games, was 3rd at the World University Games in 1977 and won the CAG title in 1978. Dnq 22nd at 1980 Olympics. Pb TJ 16.25 (1976), LJ also 8.32w (1979). His son Arnie David Girat was a top triple jumper, pb 17.62 '09; junior champion in 2002; 4th OG 2008, 14th-8th-7th-5th at World Champs 2003-09; 2nd WY 2001, 2nd 2008, 3rd 2010 World Indoors.

Paula Darcel GIRVEN (USA) (later Pittman) (b. 12 Jan 1958) on 17 October at Asheville, NC. As a high jumper for the University of Maryland and the Houston Track Club she was 18th at the 1976 Olympic Games at the age of 18 after winning the US Olympic Trials. She also made the 1980 team that did not go to Moscow as she was 2nd at the Trials. She did not win a national title although she had several 2nd and 3rd places. Pb 1.88 (6' 2¹⁄₄) in 1981.

David Keir GRACIE (GBR) (b. 26 Jan 1927 Stirling) on 26 October in Edinburgh. His four internationals for Britain at 400m hurdles 1952-3 included the 1952 Olympic Games, when he was 4th in his semi final. The next year he won the World Student Games title (plus 2nd at medley relay). He was 3rd in the AAA 440yh in 1952 and 1954 and Scottish champion at 440y 1949 and 1951-2 and 440yh 1951-4. He set five Scottish records at 440yh from 54.7 to 52.7 (also UK record) and four at 400mh from 53.6 to 52.65 and 52.3 in 1952. Pb 440y 48.7 (1952). Having been to Glasgow University, he became a veterinary surgeon. Larkhall YMCA and Atalanta.

Andrew Richard 'Andy' GREEN (GBR) (b.26 Nov 1942 Hillingdon, Middlesex) on 18 April in Leigh-on-Sea. He had seven GB internationals

OBITUARY

1963-7 and was 2nd in the 1965 World University Games. After 2nd in 1965 he won the 1967 AAA 1 mile title and indoors was 2nd at 1000y in 1963 and 3rd at 1M in 1965, and won Southern 880y titles in 1965 and 1967. He was a schoolteacher and member of Salford H and Hadleigh Olympiads. He set a UK indoor 800m record with 1:52.6 in 1963 and had pbs: 880y 1:49.5 (1964), 1000y 2:08.7 (1969), 1000m 2:21.6 (1968), 1500m 3:42.2 (1965), 1M 3:57.74 (1965), 2000m 5:19.0 (1968), 3000m 8:06.2 (1969), 2M 8:47.0 (1965), 3M 13:48.6 (1968), 5000m 14:19.6 (1969). He married Mary Tagg (sister of Mike), who ran the 400m at the 1968 Olympic Games.

James Edward 'Jim' GRELLE (USA) (b. 30 Sep 1936 Portland) on 13 June. World ranked in the 1960s, he was 8th at the 1960 Olympic Games and 2nd in 1959 and 1st in 1963 at the Pan-American Games at 1500m. AAU champion 1960 (2nd 1959, 1962, 1967; 3rd 1961, 1964-6) and indoor 1 mile 1965-6. He was 2nd at the US Olympic Trials in 1960 and 4th in 1964 when he was edged out of an Olympic place by 17 year-old Jim Ryun, both in 3:46.1. At the University of Oregon he was coached by Bill Bowerman and won the NCAA 1 mile title in 1959, after 2nd in 1957-8. He set a US record for 1 mile with 3:55.4 in 1965 that lasted for 9 days until beaten by Ryun and for 2 miles 8:25.2 in 1966. Other pbs: 800m 1:48.4 (1958), 1500m 3:38.9 (1964), 2000m 5:07.4 (1966), 3000m 8:01.8 (1962), 5000m 14:10.8 (1966), 3000mSt 9:00.8 (1968).

Annual progression at 1500m, 1 mile (M): 1955- 4:35.0M, 1956- 4:19.8M, 1957- 4:07.1M, 1958- 3:43.4, 4:01.7M; 1959- 3:44.1, 4:01.0M; 1960- 3:42.7, 4:00.1M; 1961- 4:01.3M, 1962- 3:40.2, 3:56.7M; 1963- 3:56.1M, 1964- 3:38.97, 3:58.5M; 1965- 3:39.0, 3:55.4M; 1966- 3:44.3, 3:55.4M; 1967- 3:56.1M.

Roger William Henry GYNN (GBR) (b. 19 Sep 1935 Launceston, Cornwall) on 8 November in Derby. He worked as a police sergeant in London prior to his retirement and was a great athletics enthusiast. Concentrating on the marathon, he co-authored with Dr. David Martin the definitive work *The Marathon Footrace* (Charles C. Thomas, 1979) and also *The Olympic Marathon* (Human Kinetics 2000). He wrote *The Guinness Book of the Marathon* (Guinness, 1984). For many years he contributed road race and marathon reviews for the International Athletics Annual, having earlier helped with producing the ATFS Annual when it was published by World Sports, for whom he helped with the Scoreboard section. He became a member of the NUTS and ATFS. In his last year he was much enthused by working on a marathon analysis 1920-45. Andy Milroy writes that "The Historic Marathon Ranking from 1906-2017 on the ARRS website was based initially on his remarkable archives".

Svein Arne HANSEN (Norway (b. 6 May 1946) on 20 June in Oslo. He grew up in Bygdøy to the west of Oslo. He took part in many sports during his youth and at the age of 17 formed an ice hockey club. After graduating from university with a degree in mathematics, he qualified as a track and field referee and later became host of a sports programme at a local radio station. He also embarked on his sports administration career as a member of the Norwegian Athletics Federation Junior Committee 1968-72. On the eve of the 1972 Bislett Games, the meeting organiser was injured by a stray javelin. Hansen was asked to stand in, and he continued to work as an assistant to the organiser for several years. Around this time he turned to his other passion, stamp collecting, and started his own stamp shop, which he sold in the early 1990s but retained an office in a stamp shop until 2012. In 1985 he was promoted to the role of meeting director for the Bislett Games, a position he held for 24 years. During his time there the Bislett Games was part of the IAAF Grand Prix, Golden Four and the Golden League. He was also a member of the IAAF Grand Prix Commission 1985-98 and the IAAF Golden League working group 1997-2009, and president of the Norwegian Athletics Federation 2003-15. After serving as president of Euro-Meetings 1998-2006, Hansen was vice president of European Athletics 2007-11 and then elected president in 2015 and re-elected in 2019. A World Athletics Council Member since 2015.

Anders HANSSON (Sweden) (b. 10 Mar 1992 Borås) on 30 October. At 50k walk he was 28th at the 2017 World Champs in a pb 3:58:00 (after dnf in 2015), and was 23rd at the 2018 European Champs. Swedish walks champion 10,000m 2017, 50k 2014 & 2018, 5000m indoors 2014, 2017 & 2020. Other pbs: 10,000mW 41:52.6 (2017), 20kW 1:25:51 (2018).

Mohamad 'Bob' HASAN (Indonesia) (b. 24 Feb 1931 The Kian Seng, Semarang) on 31 March in Jakarta. He was a businessman, briefly Minister of Trade and Industry in 1998, and served a prison term for corruption. Chairman of the Indonesian Athletics Association from 1984 until his death, the fourth President of the Asian Athletics Association from 1991-2000, IAAF Council Member 1995-9 and member of the IOC 1994-2004.

Beverly HAYMAN/Wilkins (Australia) (b. 9 May 1961) on 19 August. She was 6th at 10k walk at the 1990 Commonwealth Games and won the Australian 20k title in 1988. Walks pbs: 3000m 12:59.4 (1989), 5000m 22:37.8 (1988), 10k 46:50 (1986), 20k 1:37:59 (1989).

Alfred HEBAUF (FRG/Germany) (b. 5 Jan 1940 Frankfurt am Main) on 14 July in Kornwestheim. He had 24 internationals 1960-4 and at 100m he was 4= at the 1962 Europeans. FRG champion at 100m 1963 (2nd 1962, 3rd 1961), and 2nd 200m 1964. He ran on three German teams that set national 4x100m records. Pbs: 60y 6.1i (1963), 60m 6.7i (1963). 100m 10.3 (1960), 10.2w (1963); 200m 20.7 (1963), 400m 49.3 (1965), LJ 6.76 (1958).

Melvin HEIN Jr (USA) (b. 10 Jan 1941 Los Angeles) on 8 July in Reno, Nevada. A pole vaulter who went to the University of South California, he had a best of 5.03 in 1966. He was AAU 4th in 1966 and 5th in 1962 and 6th in 1963 at the NCAAs. His father, also Mel, was a famous American footballer.

Frank HENSEL (Germany) (b. 3 Sep 1950 Grambin) on 29 November in Frankfurt am Main. Decathlon pb 7441 (1975), competed once for FRG (1973) and also internationally at bobsleigh. Other pbs included: 100m 10.5 (1974), HJ 2.01i, PV 4.30 (1975), LJ 7.28, SP 14.96. He became a coach, and was head coach and high performance director of the German Athletics Federation (DLV) 1994-8. In 2004 he was appointed general secretary and director general of the DLV, serving until 2016, and was CEO of the 2009 Berlin World Championships. He was first elected to the European Athletics Council in 2007, was chair of the EA Development Commission and was European Athletics vice president 2015-19, when he was elected onto the executive board.

Jerry Lyn **HERNDON** (USA) (b. 12 March 1955 Ada, Oklahoma) on 14 June in San Bernardino, California. In 1974 he had a long jump best of 8.11i (ranked 9th in the world that year) and won the NCAA title for UCLA. He was a cousin of the acclaimed writer and civil rights activist Maya Angelou, and his granddaughter Kyrah Johnson is a 400m runner for UCLA.

Heidi HERTZ (later SWEET) (USA) (b. 1956) on 28 November in Tampa, Florida. AIAW indoor pentathlon champion for Florida in 1976 with 3805 points and 3rd in the 1977 AAU Champs outdoors.

Ondrej HODBOD (Czech Republic) (b. 1 Jun 2001) on 24 September. His international results: EU18: 2018- 4; YOG: 2018- 12; EJ: 2019- ht. Pbs: 1500 3:53.94 and 3000SC 9:05.41 in 2020. His older brother is international 800m runner Lukáš Hodbod.

Willi HOLDORF (Germany/FRG) (b. 17 Feb 1940 Blomesche Wildnis) on 5 July at Achterwehr near Kiel. He was Olympic champion at decathlon in 1964 after 5th at the 1962 European Championships; FRG champion 1961 and 1963 (and at 200mh 1962), 19 internationals 1959-65. He set a German record with 8085 points (1952 tables, 7845 on current tables) in 1963 and a pb of 8119 (7887) to win the Olympic title. Event pbs: 100m 10.4 (1964), 200m 21.6 (1968), 400m 47.8 (1964), 1500m 4:29.7 (1962), 110mh 14.5 (1963), 200mh 23.6 (1963), 400mh 54.5, HJ 1.85 (1965), PV 4.30 (1964), LJ 7.37 (1964) SP 15.07 (1963), DT 46.86 (1961), JT 60.53 (1961), Pen 3764 (1963). He was 2nd in the European 2-man bobsleigh in 1973.

Annual progression at Dec on current tables: 1959- 6675, 1960- 6936, 1961- 7331, 1962- 7597, 1963- 7845, 1964- 7887, 1969- 7170 (162 tables).

Patrick HOOPER (Ireland) (b. 12 May 1952) on 9 October. He was 42nd in the 1980 Olympic Games marathon and 27th in the Europeans in 1978. Pb 2:17:46 to win the Irish title in 1979. He was a driving force in his club Raheny Shamrock. His brother Dick was Irish champion five times as well as running in the Olympic marathon in 1980 (38th), 1984 (51st) and 1988 (24th).

Attila HORVÁTH (Hungary) (b. 28 July 1967 Kőszeg) on 13 November in Szombathely. Had consistent record in major championships at discus: Olympics 1992 5th, 1996 10th; Worlds 1991 3rd, 1995 4th, 1997 & 1999 dnq; Europeans 1990 8th, 1994 5th. World Juniors 1986 5th, European Juniors 1985 1st. 1st European Cup 1991, HUN champion 1987 & 1990-7. Hungarian record with 68.58 in 1994 and from a world age-17 best of 61.85 in 1985 was over 60m every year to 2001 (8 years over 65m). Pbs: SP 17.55 (1992), HT 65.64 (1985). 33 Internationals 1985-96.

Annual progression at DT: 1981- 31.30, 1982- 44.56, 1983- 52.44, 1984- 56.28, 1985- 61.84, 1986- 60.76, 1987- 62.94, 1988- 64.18, 1989- 63.44, 1990- 65.46, 1991- 67.06, 1992- 65.24, 1993- 64.52, 1994- 68.58, 1995- 65.72, 1996- 65.02, 1997- 64.56, 1998- 66.56, 1999- 65.13. 2000- 60.12, 2001- 60.79.

Christine HUNT (later Thompson, Clifford) (Australia) (b. 15 Jun 1950 Sydney) in Lakeland, Florida on 25 September. With a pb of 57.84 (1976) she was Australian javelin champion in 1975-6, and competed (dnq) at the 1976 Olympic Games. She went to the University of Florida and settled in the USA, where she became a real estate agent.

Sheila Rena **INGRAM** (USA) (b. 23 Mar 1957 Washington DC) on 1 September. She set a US junior record of 53.0 as a 17 year-old in 1974. and while at Coolidge HS , Washington in 1976 won 4x400m silver a the Olympic Games after 6th in the individual 400m in 50.90, having set pb at 51.81 and US record 51.31 in the preliminary rounds. Earlier she was 2nd at the AAU Champs and won at the US Olympic Trials, with other pbs: 100y 10.7/10.6w and 200m 23.9. She did not compete thereafter except when she went to St. Augustine College, NC in 1982.

Volodymr INOZEMTSEV (Ukraine) died on February 5.

Mariya Leontyevna **ITKINA** (USSR/Belarus) (b. Roslavl, Smolensk) on 1 December in Minsk. A pioneer of women's 400m running, she won the first two European titles, in 1958 and 1962, following her 200m victory in 1954, and ran a world best 53.9 in 1955. After the IAAF accepted the event she ran four official world records from 54.0 in 1957 to 53.4 in 1962. She had been 4th at the 1960 Olympics at both 100m and 200m, but when the 400m was added to the Olympics in 1964 she was no longer supreme and placed fifth, although she ran her fastest ever time of 52.9 in 1965. She won 14 Soviet titles, four each at 100m (1960-3), five at 400m (1959-60, 1963-5), six at 200m (1954, 1956-7, 1960-2). European Cup 400m winner 1965, World Universities 200m 1957 (& 1st UIE 1954, 2nd 1955 & 1957). Other pbs: 100m 11.4 (1960), 200m eight USSR records to 23.4 in 1956 and 1961.

Annual progression at 200m, 400m (position on world list): 1952- 26.3, 58.4 (11=); 1953- 24.7 (7=), 55.8 (2); 1954- 23.8 (2), 58.6 (53=); 1955- 23.8 (3), 53.9 (1); 1956- 23.4 (2), 55.9 (7=); 1957- 23.8 (1=), 53.6 (1); 1958- 23.7 (3=), 53.6 (1); 1959- 23.4 (5=), 53.4 (1); 1960- 23.6 (4=), 53.8 (2); 1961- 23.4 (1), 53.8 (2); 1962- 23.6 (3=), 53.4(2); 1963- 23.5 (5=), 53.2 (4=); 1964- 24.0 (25=), 53.0 (4); 1965- 24.0 (18=), 52.9 (2); 1966- 24.1 (40=), 54.0 (121).

Vladimir **IVANOV** (Bulgaria) (b. 23 Apr 1955 Sofia) on 26 November in Sofia. At 200m he was 8th at the 1978 Europeans and ran (ht) at the 1980 Olympic Games; he set three Bulgarian records from 20.86 (1976) to 20.74 (1978). BUL champion at 100m 1976, 200m 1979-80. Pb 100m 10.40 (1979).

Mirja JÄMES/SALMINEN (Finland) (b. 13 Oct 1924 Jyväskylä) on 20 July in Espoo, the last surviving Finnish athletics Olympian from 1948, when she ran in the heats of the 80m hurdles. At that event she won the International University title in 1947. Finnish champion at 100m 1945 and 1947, 80mh 1945 and 1947-8, and long jump 1945. Pbs: 100m 12.6 (1948), 80mh 11.9 (1947), 11.8w (1948); HJ 1.48 (1948), LJ 5.21.

Benjamin Wabura **JIPCHO** (Kenya) (b. 1 Mar 1943 Chepchabai) on 24 July in Eldoret. After helping Kip Keino win the Olympic 1500m title in 1968, running the first lap in 56 seconds at the high altitude of Mexico City, Jipcho faded back to 10th place. He emerged as a top-class runner with silver medals at steeplechase at the 1970 Commonwealth Games and 1972 Olympics, and in 1973 set three world records for the 3000m steeplechase, despite very rudimentary hurdling technique, from 8:20.69 at the All-Africa Games (when he also won the 5000m) to two records in June at Helsinki, 8:19.8 and 8:13.91. In 1974 he had a great Commonwealth Games, winning 5000m (13:14.3) and steeplechase with bronze at 1500m. Turned professional and was the leading money winner on the ITA circuit in 1974 and 1975. Other bests: 880y 1:47.7 (1975), 1500m 3:33.16 (1974), 1 mile 3:52.17 (1973), 3000m 7:44.4 (1973), 2 miles 8:16.38 (1973),

Annual progression at 1500m/1M, 5000m, 3000mSt: 1968- 3:43.4/3:59.8M, 1969- 3:43.3/4:00.4M, 8:48.8; 1970- 3:43.2/4:00.6M, 14:09.2, 8:29.6; 1971- 3:41.2/3:56.4M, 13:40.8, 8:29.6; 1972- 3:42.5, 13:46.2, 8:24.6; 1973- 3:36.6/3:52.17, 13:30.0, 8:13.91; 1974- 3:33.16, 13:14.4, 8:20.8; 1975- 3:39.9i/3:57.6M

Marian Gerard **JOCHMAN** (Poland) (b. 2 Feb 1935 Torun) on 27 December in Bydgoszcz. At 5000m he had a best of 13:54.8 (1958) and ran (heat) at the 1960 Olympic Games.

Rafer Lewis **JOHNSON** (USA) (b.18 Aug 1934 Hillsboro, Texas) on 2 December at his home in Sherman Oaks, Los Angeles. A brilliant all-rounder, he set a world record for the decathlon at his fourth attempt at the event with 7985 points (7608 on current tables) in 1955 while a student at UCLA. He was second at the 1956 Olympics and after setting a new world record at 8302 points (7789) in 1958 for USA v USSR, he won the Olympic gold, having set a third record 8683 points (7982) to win the AAU title in 1960. In his career he won nine of eleven decathlons contested, with other titles including the 1955 Pan-Americans (also 8th javelin) and the AAU of 1956, 1958 and 1960. He was also 3rd in the long jump at the 1956 Olympic Trials, but injury prevented him from competing at that event. He was 2nd at LJ and 110mh at the 1956 NCAAs. The US flag bearer at the 1960 Games, he subsequently became a film star, and lit the Olympic flame as the last torchbearer in Los Angeles in 1984. His outstanding individual bests included: 100m 10.3 (1957), 220ySt 21.0 (1956), 400m 47.9 (1956), 1500m 4:49.7 (1960), 110mh 13.8 (1956), 220yh St 22.7 (19567), HJ 1.89 (1955), PV 4.10 (1960), LJ 7.76 (1956), SP 16.75 (1958), DT 52.50 (1960), JT 76.75 (1960).

His brother Jimmy (b. 31 Mar 1938 Dallas) had bests of 13.9 for 120y hurdles (1960) and 7.56m long jump (1959), and spent 16 seasons with the San Francisco 49ers 1961-76; elected to the Pro Football Hall of Fame in 1994. Rafer's son Josh was at UCLA and threw the javelin 76.16 in 2003, while his daughter Jennifer competed in beach volleyball at the 2000 Olympics.

Ron JONES (USA) (b. 1 Jan 1962) on October 21 in Evansville. He set his high jump best of 2.24i in 1984 and this remained the Indiana University record for 26 years. Just 1.78m tall, he had been rated the top US high school jumper with 2.18 in 1960.

Aarne KAINLAURI (Finland) died on March 11 in Kouvola.

Vitold Anatolyevich **KREYER** (USSR/Russia) (b. 12 Nov 1932 Krasnodar) on 1 August. At the triple jump he ranked in the world top five for eight successive years 1956-63, including top ranked in 1961 when he recorded the top four performances of the year headed by his pb of

16.71, then second on the world all-time list. He was also ranked 10th in 1964 and over 16m each year 1956-65. He won Olympic bronze medals in 1956 and 1960, but did not qualify for the 1964 final or for the European finals of 1958 and 1962. USSR champion in 1960-1 (2nd 1958, 1962, 3rd 1957, 1963). Pb LJ 7.17. He was senior coach of the USSR team from 1967 including at the four Olympic Games 1968-80 and of the Russian team at the 2000 Olympic Games.
Annual progression: 1951- 13.65, 1952- 14.66, 1953- 14.70, 1954- 14.86, 1955- 15.53, 1956- 16.02, 1957- 16.00, 1958- 16.43, 1959- 16.46, 1960- 16.49, 1961- 16.71, 1962- 16.38, 1963- 16.45, 1964- 16.27, 1965- 16.03.

Jürgen KÜHL (Germany) (b. 30 Nov 1934 Hamburg) on 3 August. FRG 400m champion in 1957 and indoors 1956-7, after running in the 400m heats he was on the team that was 4th at 4x400m at the 1956 Olympic Games. 16 internationals 1955-8. Pbs: 400m 47.4 (1956), 600y 1:13.8 (European record 1958).

Gergely KULCSÁR (Hungary) (b. 10 Mar 1934 Nagyhalász) on 12 August in Vác. He was ranked in the world's top ten 11 times from 1958 to 1971 and compiled a brilliant competitive record. At the Olympic Games he was 3rd in 1960, 2nd in 1964, 3rd in 1968 (pb 87.06A) and dnq 14th 1972, being the flag bearer for the HUN team at his last three Games. At his five European Championships he was 3rd in 1958 and 1966, 4th 1969, 5th 1962, and dnq 15th 1971, and at World University Games he won in 1961, with 2nd 1959, 3rd 1963 and 5th 1957. He was Hungarian champion in 1958-60, 1962-9 and 1971 and set nine HUN records from 78.54 (1959) to 85.38 (1966), including being the first Hungarian over 80m (80.29, 1963) 56 internationals 1955-72.. Later he coached Miklós Németh who won the Olympic title in 1976.
Annual progression: 1953- 56.59, 1954- 63.18, 1955- 69.51, 1956- 72.00, 1957- 73.97, 1958- 76.36, 1959- 78.54, 1960- 79.30, 1961- 78.48, 1962- 78.80, 1963- 80.29, 1964- 82.32, 1965- 84.18, 1966- 85.38, 1967- 85.74, 1968- 87.06A, 1969- 83.30, 1970-80-.04, 1971- 85.14, 1972- 79.82. 1973- 75.50, 1974- 76.12, 1975- 73.40, 1976- 75.74.

Galina Vasilyevna **KULIKOVA** (USSR/Russia) (b. 23 Jan 1955) (née Odnodvorkina) on 30 January in Kostroma. She had a best heptathlon score of 5876 points when 3rd in the USSR Cup in 1981, with other pbs: Pen 4312 (1980), HJ 1.77 (1981), LJ 6.25 (1981). She worked as a children's coach from 1976 to 2019.

David 'Doodik' KUSHNIR (Israel) (b. 21 Jun 1931 Afuia) on 18 October. He was 25th in the qualifying round at long jump in the Olympic Games in both 1956 and 1960. Israel champion at 100m 1955-6, PV 1952-3, LJ (6) 1955-61. Israeli records LJ from 6.93 to 7.43 (1961), also 7.47w

(1961); TJ 14.05 (1953), Dec four to 4650 (1954, 1952 tables). He became a leading coach.

Raymond Charles **LAND** (Australia) (b. 14 Nov 1930) on 14 May. He ran in the heats of the 100m and 4x100m at the 1956 Olympic Games in Melbourne. Pbs 100y 9.8/9.6w (1957), 100m 10.5/10.3w (1956), 200m 21.7 (1956)

Gilbert **Ron**ald **LARRIEU** (USA) (b. 29 May 1937 San Francisco) on 1 June. He was 24th in the 1964 Olympic 10,000m, and AAU cross-country champion in 1965-6. He did not win an AAU track title but was 3rd at 5000m in 1965 and at 10,000m in 1967. He went to Cal State Pomona and ran for Los Angeles TC, Santa Monica TC, SC Striders and Culver City AC. Pbs: 1500m 3:49.2 (1960), 1M 4:03.6 (1966), 2M 8:32.0 (1967), 3M 13:11.4 (US record 1965), 5000m 13:43.0 (1964), 6M 28:03.0 (1966), 10000m 28:54.2 (1966). His sister Francie Larrieu-Smith (b. 23 Nov 1952) had a long and distinguished career, competing at four Olympic Games 1972-92 and making the team in 1980, and winning a total of 18 US titles from 1500m to 10000m and cross-country.

Endre LÉPOLD (Hungary) (b. 27 Oct 1955 Lánycsók) on 18 June. He set Hungarian records with 10.2 for 100m in 1973 and 20.6 for 200m in 1975; auto timed best 100m 10.41 (1977). After 7th at both 100m and 200m at the 1973 European Juniors, he ran in the heats of both sprints at the 1976 Olympics and at 60m in the European Indoors and at 100m in the Europeans in 1974. He was HUN 100m champion in 1975 and at 60m indoors in 1974 and 1977.

Kriemhild LIMBERG-HAUSMANN (Germany/FRG) (b. 8 Sep 1934 Rheinausen) on 24 August in Neuss. At discus she was 4th in 1960 and 7th in 1964 at the Olympic Games, 3rd in 1958, 7th in 1962 and 11th in 1966 at European Championships and FRG champion 1958-65. 32 internationals 1955-66. She set five FRG records from 51.22 (1958) to 55.86 (1964). Other pbs: 80mh 11.6 (1966), HJ 1.56 (1966), LJ 5.83 (1960), SP 13.86 (1966), JT 39.92 (1959), Pen 4506 (1966).

Ronald William **LIVERS** (USA) (b. 20 Jul 1955 Norristown, PA) on 19 December at Collegeville, PA. One of the greatest doublers with pbs of HJ 2.24 (1975, a world best differential of 51cm as he was only 1.73m tall) and TJ 17.19 (1977). At TJ he was US champion in 1979 with 17.56w, for San Jose State NCAA champion 1975 and 1977-8 and 2nd at the 1975 World University Games. His older brother Larry was 7th at 110mh at the 1968 US Olympic Trials and his twin Dan ran 100y in 9.4 (1975).

Jorge **'Jordi' LLOPART** Ribas (Spain) (b. 5 May 1952 El Prat de Llobregat, Barcelona) on 11 November in Badalona. At 50k walk he was the 1978 European champion (6th 1982, 9th 1986, dnf 1990) and 1980 Olympic silver medallist (7th

OBITUARY

1984, 13th 1988) – the first ever Olympic medal by a Spanish athlete. World Cup winner 1987, Spanish champion 1978-9, 1981, 1985-6 and 1989-91. Spanish walks records: track: 3000m 12:13.5 (1978), 5000m (3) to 20:15.9 (1979), 10,000m (3) to 41:30;4 (1980), 1Hr 13.981m (1979), 50,000m 3:52:15.0 (1981); road: 30k 2:20:17, 35k (5) to 2:36:50, 50k (4) 4:01:37 & 3:53:30 (1978) & European 3:50:03 & 3:44:33 (1979). Other walks pbs: 5000m 19:51.1 (1985), 10000m 41:17.8 (1985), 10k Rd 41:13 (1987), 30000m 2:08:39 '79, 1Hr 14285m (1986), 2Hr 27986m (1979), 20k 1:24:54 '86. 50k sub 4 hours in 1978-83, 1985-8 and 1990-2. 46 internationals. Annual progression at 50k walk: Progress at 50kW: 1975- 4:30:11, 1976- 4:22:43, 1978- 3:53:30, 1979- 3:44:33, 1980- 3:45:55, 1981- 3:48:17, 1982- 3:51:12, 1983- 3:47:48, 1984- 4:03:09, 1985- 3:52:28, 1986- 3:50:26, 1987- 3:55:35, 1988- 3:48:09, 1989- 4:06:18, 1990- 3:50:05, 1991- 3:54:00, 1992- 3:49:31.

Maj-Lena LUNDSTRÖM (Sweden) (b. 29 Dec 1941) on April 6. (later **Andersen** NOR). 6th European high jump 1958 (ht 4x100m). Swedish champion 100m 1962, 80mh 1959 & 1962, HJ 1958, Pen 1959; Norway 100m 1966. Represented Norway after marriage in 1963. Swedish records 80mh 11.5 (1959), Pen 4169 (1959); Norway records 100m 11.8 (= 1963), 80mh 11.2 (1963), HJ 1.63 (1963). Other pbs: HJ 1.66 (1959), LJ 5.69 (1958).

Janis Voldemarovits **LUSIS** (USSR/Latvia) (b. 19 May 1939 Jelgava, Latvia) on 29 April in Riga. He was generally acknowledged as the greatest ever javelin thrower until Jan Zelezny took that accolade for many and ranked number one in the world nine times, won four European titles between 1962 and 1971 (and sixth in 1974) and won a complete set of Olympic medals – gold 1968, silver 1972, bronze 1964, before placing eighth in 1976. He won 12 USSR titles (1962-6, 1968-73 and 1976), the World University Games title in 1963, and in four European Cup Finals was first twice (1965 and 1967) and second twice (1970 and 1973), for an outstandingly consistent record. He married the 1960 Olympic javelin champion, Elvira Ozolina. He set his first Latvian record with 77.48m in 1961 and set six USSR records from 86.04 in 1962 to world records of 91.98 in 1968 and 93.80 in 1972. A fine all-rounder, he was also fifth on the world list in 1962 for the decathlon with 7764 points (7483 on 1962 tables, 7496 on 1984 tables). He coached javelin in Latvia and the USSR, and with Elvira spent three years in Madagascar 1987-90. He was Olympic team coach in 1980, 1992 and 2000, when his son Voldemars (b. 7 Dec 1974), pb 84.19 with new javelin in 2003, competed in the javelin for Latvia (dnq 18th).

He had 13 years ranked in the world top ten by *Track & Field News*, behind Jan Zelezny 19, Janusz Sidlo 18, Steve Backley 15 and Sergey Makarov 14. But his 9 years at no. 1 is the most for the javelin as he is followed by 7 Zelezny and 5 Sidlo and Andreas Thorkildsen.

Progression at javelin (old specification)

Year	Best	WL	WR	Year	Best	WL	WR
1957	53.37			1967	90.98	1	1
1958	63.31			1968	91.98	1	1
1959	72.63	77	-	1969	91.52	2	1
1960	74.89	55	-	1970	88.02	6	6
1961	81.01	9=	-	1971	90.68	1	1
1962	86.04	1	1	1972	93.80	1	1
1963	83.65	4	1	1973	91.32	1	2
1964	82.59	8	5	1974	84.08	18	7
1965	86.56	2	1	1975	79.82	76	
1966	85.70	2	1	1976	86.32	15	(13)

WL = position on annual world list, WR – *Track & Field News* world ranking position.

Donald Forbes **MACGREGOR** (GBR) (b. 23 Jul 1939 Prestonpans, East Lothian) on 3 June in St. Andrews. A tough and consistent marathon runner, he was 7th at the 1972 Olympic Games and was 8th in 1970 and 6th in 1974 (pb 2:14:15.4) for Scotland at the Commonwealth Games with 3rd in 1967 and 2nd in 1973 in the AAA Champs. He won Scottish titles at 6 miles 1966, 10 miles 1965, marathon 1973-4 and 1976. A language graduate of St. Andrews University and running for Edinburgh Southern H and Fife AC, he had pbs of: 1M 4:19.0 (1963), 2M 8:58.0 (1967), 3M 13:50.0 (1964), 5000m 14:09.0 (1972), 6M 28:42.0 (1964), 10000m 29:53.8 (1973), 10M 49:41.0 (1967), 1Hr 18,932m (1970), 20000m/15M 1:03:24.0/1:16:31.8(1970), 25000m/30000m/2Hr/ 20M 1:19:16.6/1:35:13.8/37,529m/1:42:06.8 (1970). His 24 sub-2:20 marathons from 1967 to 1983 (2:17:24 at age 43) was the most by a Scot. He published his autobiography *Running My Life* in 2010 and co-authored with Tim Johnston a biography *His Own Man* of Otto Peltzer.

Elaine McLEOD (née **FRAWLEY**) (Australia) (b. 15 Apr 1943) on April 17. Australian 400m champion 1969. Pbs 100y 10.7 (1966), 100m 11.6 (1971), 200m 23.9 (1967), 400m 54.2 (1972). Married 1969 Stawell Gift winner Barry McLeod.

Jean MAISSANT (France) (b. 23 Jan 1926 Gennevilliers) on 7 November at Le Chesnay, near Paris. He competed for Stade Français and was French discus champion in 1951-2 with 21 internationals 1951-61, including placing 17th at the 1952 Olympic Games. Pbs: SP 14.72 (1952), DT 49.84 (1951).

Leopold MILEK (Slovenia) (b. 4 Nov 1948 Ljubljana) on 24 December in Kranj. At high jump he set Yugoslav record of 2.13 (1968) and that year was dnq 33rd at the Olympic Games. Yugoslav champion 1967-8; 10 internationals 1967-72. Slovenian champion indoors and out in 1967-8 and won the indoor 60m and LJ titles in 1972. He set SLO records at HJ (also 2.10 in 1967), LJ (7.49 in 1971) and TJ (15.03 in 1967). Other pbs: 100m 10.7 (1971), 200m 22.1 (1972).

Lutvian Ahmedova **MOLLOVA** (Bulgaria) (b. 18 Dec 1947 Kazanlak) on 19 August in Istanbul. At the javelin she was 4th at the 1972 Olympic Games and at the 1974 European Champs (13th 1971); also 3rd at the 1973 World University Games, and 2nd in 1973 and 2nd in 1975 at the European Cup, Balkan champion 1972 and 1974-5 and Bulgarian 1969 and 1972-4, she set 11 national records from 53.86 to 62.60 in 1964.

Charles Hewes **'Charlie' MOORE** Jr (USA) (b. 12 Aug 1929 Coatesville PA) on 8 October in Laporte, Pennsylvania. An all-time great at the 400m hurdles, he was unbeaten in his 23 races at the event. He was Olympic champion in 1952 (and silver medallist at 4x400m having run in the heat), AAU champion each year 1949-52 (2nd 200mh 1948 & 1952) and while at Cornell University won NCAA titles at 440y in 1949 and 220yh in 1951. He also won the AAU indoor 600y in 1952. Pbs: 440y 47.0 (1949), 220yhSt 22.7 (1951), 400mh 50.7 (1952, missing the world record by 0.1, but auto best of 50.98). He also set world records for 440yh at 51.9 and 51.6 at the White City in London in August 1952.

He became managing director of investment bankers Peers & Co., and then CEO of Peers Management Resources and later vice-president of Advisory Capital Partners, an investment advising company. He was athletic director at Cornell 1994-9 and was president of the IC4A from 1999. He was later Chairman of the Institute for Sustainable Value Creation and executive director of the Committee Encouraging Corporate Philanthropy (CECP) from the organisation's founding in 1999 to 2013.

Annual progression at 400mh (position on world list): 1949- 51.1 (1), 1950- 51.5 (1), 1951- 51.4 (1), 1952- 50.7/50.98 (1).

His father Charles 'Crip' Moore was reserve for the 1924 Olympic team after 5th at 110m hurdles at the US Olympic Trials. Pb 14.8y (1928).

Nicholas **'Nick' MORGAN** (GBR) (b. 6 Feb 1939 Croydon) on 1 November in Bromley. Competing for Queens Park H, Croydon H and the RAF, he had two international appearances at the shot for Britain in 1961-2, after placing 5th at the 1958 Commonwealth Games, 2nd AAA indoor 1962. Pbs: SP 16.95 (1961), DT 41.31 (1959).

Bobby Joe MORROW (USA) (b. 15 Oct 1935 Harlingen, Texas) on 30 May in San Benito, Texas. He was a most impressive Olympic triple gold medallist at the 100m, 200m and relay at the Melbourne Games in 1956. His time at 200m was a world record 20.6 (20.75 on automatic timing) but, running into a cold and strong adverse wind of 5m/s in the final his time was slowed to 10.62 in the 100m final. He had run 20.6 twice earlier in 1956, to win the NCAA and US Olympic Trials races, but neither was ratified. At 100m he tied the world record of 10.2 three times in 1956 and at 100 yards equalled the record with 9.3 in 1957, having run a wind-assisted 9.1 in 1955. He also set six relay world records, two on US teams and four for Abilene Christian College, for whom he completed the NCAA sprint double in 1956 and 1957. AAU champion at 100y/100m in 1955-6 and 1958 and at 220y 1958. After injury in 1959, in 1960 he failed to make a second Olympics as he was 4th at 200m in the US Trials and then retired. He had been unbeaten as a high school senior in 1954 and in his freshman year at Abilene Christian, winning 30 successive 100 races until Dave Sime beat him at the 1956 Drake Relays. In the annual *Track & Field News* world rankings he was no. 1 at 100m in 1956-8 (3rd 1955 and 6th 1959) and at 200m in 1956-7 (4th 1955, 2nd 1958, 9th 1959). Other pbs: 220y turn: 20.6 (1955), 220y straight 20.4 (1958), 20.0w (1957), 440y 48.0 (1959). *Sports Illustrated* Sportsman of the Year 1956 and winner of the Sullivan Award in 1957.

Annual progress at 100y/100m, 220ySt/200mt: 1950- 11.1y, 1951- 10.5y, 1952- 9.9y, 1953- 9.7y, 1954- 9.6wy, 21.1yStw; 1955- 9.4/9.1wy, 20.7ySt/ 20.5*w; 1956- 9.4y/10.2, 20.6/20.75; 1957- 9.3y/ 10.4w, 20.6ySt/20.9*; 1958- 9.4/9.3wy, 20.4ySt/ 20.8*; 1959- 9.4y/10.2, 20.5yS/20.9*; 1960- 9.5y/ 10.2, 20.8.

Roberto Saturnino **MOYA** Sandoval (Cuba) (b. 11 Feb 1965 Havana) on 21 May in Valencia, Spain. At the discus for Cuba he won the 1992 Olympic bronze medal (dnq 22 in 1996), won at the Pan American Games in 1995 after silver in 1991 and was 2nd at the 1992 World Cup. He was Ibero-American champion in 1986, won the Central American and Caribbean Champs in 1987 and 1989-90 and was 3rd at the 1989 World University Championships. At World Championships he was 8th 1991, dnq 17th 1993 and dnq 31st 1995. He retired in 1998 and became a coach, moving to Spain and gaining Spanish citizenship on 31 July 2001. Pb 65.68 (1990).

Peter NEMSOVSKY (Czech Republic) (b. 6 Jan 1943 Bratislava) on 11 May in Prague. At triple jump he set four TCH records from 16.04 (1965) to 16.34 (1967) and indoors with 16.57 when he won at the 1967 European Indoor Games in Prague (3rd in 1966 and 6th in 1968). He was 10th at the 1966 Europeans, national champion in 1965-7 and 1969, 17 internationals 1964-70. Sparta Praha 1959-60, Dukla Praha 1961-8 and Slavia Praha 1969-72, with whom he became a coach. Pb LJ 7.56 (1967), 7.62w (1970).

Paul NIHILL (GBR) (b. 5 Sep 1939 Colchester) on 15 December in Gillingham, Kent. He won a record 27 UK national walking titles between 1963 and 1975: on the track, he was AAA champion at 2 miles 1965, 3000m 1970-1 and 1975, 7 miles 1965-6 and 1968, 10,000m 1969; and on the roads he won RWA 10 miles 1965, 1968-9, 1972; 20km 1965-6, 1968-9, 1971-2; 20 miles 1963-5 1968-9, 1971; 50k 1964, 1968, 1971; not only was he the only man to win at all the four road distances, he won them all in one year, 1968. He also won the Irish 1M title in 1962 and 1964 (in an Irish record 6:31.4). A member of Surrey Walking Club, he won the 50km silver medal at his first Olympics in 1964 and he won 35 successive walks races from December 1967 to his failure to finish the Olympic 50km in 1968 in the heat and high altitude of Mexico City, but then won a further 51 consecutive races to June 1970, including the European 20km in 1969. He took the European 20km bronze medal in 1971 and was 6th at 20km and 9th at 50km at the 1972 Olympics and was 30th in the 1976 20k. 2nd Lugano Cup 20k 1963. 15 GB internationals 1963-76. In his career 1960-77 he won 355 races. He was awarded MBE in 1976.

He set world track bests for 3000m 11:51.1 (1971) and 5000m 20:14.2 (1972), and road 20k 1:24:50 (1972). His numerous other British records and bests included track: 1M 6:17.0 (1970), 30k 2:28:44.0 (1972), 20 miles 2:40:42.6 (1972), and road: 10M 1:08:18 (1972), 20k 1:24:50 (1972), 20 miles 2:30:35 (1971), 50k 4:11:31.2 (1964). Other pbs: track 2M 13:16.0 (1969), 5M 34:25.0 (1969), 7M 49:03.0 (1969), 10,000m 42:34.6 (1972), 1 hour 13.671. (1969); road 10k 42:17 (1972), 30k/35k 2:23:54/2:49:53 (1972).

Vladimir NJARADI (Serbia) (b. 16 Mar 1939) on 17 November 17 in his hometown of Vrbas. He was Yugoslav triple jump champion in 1963 and 1965-8, pb 15.73 (1963). 14 Internationals 1963-8. His son Nenad had a TJ pb 16.26 (1998).

Seppo NUUTTILA (Finland) (b. 9 Oct 1939 Kangasala) on 1 October in Mäntsälä. A young half-miler with 800m pb 1:55.5, his long career at Finnish Athletics Federation (SUL) started as a youth coach in 1965, then head coach in 1971-4 and again in 1985-8. He was the initiator behind Juha Väätäinen´s training winters in Spain and Brazil, resulting in 5000 and 10,000m European titles in Helsinki 1971. In 1981-4 Nuuttila worked for the Rowing Federation, his leading pupil being three-time Olympic Champion Pertti Karppinen.

Keiji OGUSHI (Japan) (b. 3 Apr 1934 Shiroishi) on 17 March in Kawasaki. He competed at 400mh (heats) at the Olympic Games of 1956, 1960 and 1964 as well as at relays. At the Asian Games he won gold medals at 4x400m in 1958 (3rd 1962) and 400mh in 1962 (2nd 1958). Pbs 400m 48.2 (1962), 400mh 51.2 (1964).

Benedicta Souza de OLIVEIRA (Brazil) (b.10 Oct 1927 Jundiai, São Paulo) on 14 September in Santos. She ran at 100m and 4x100m at the 1948 Olympic Games and at South American Championships was 3rd at 100m and 200m in 1949 and 1st at 100m and 3rd at 200m in 1954, while at 4x100m she ran on the Brazilian teams that were 1st in 1949 and 2nd in 1952 and 1954. She set BRA records for 200m with 25.7 (1948) and 25.6 (1949) and her 100m pb was 12.3 (1953).

William Barclay Livingstone PALMER (GBR) (b. 2 Mar 1932 Toronto, Canada) on 27 September in Brunswick, Maine, USA. At the shot he was the first British shot putter to use the O'Brien technique. He competed in nine internationals 1955-8, was 12th at the 1956 Olympics and AAA champion 1955-6. After Army service he went to Oxford University and set a British record with 16.92 in 1956 (when he also had a downhill 17.17) and had other pbs: DT 45.85 (1956), JT 58.02 (1954). He taught in the USA into his 80s and was described as "a passionate humanities teacher and administrator, education reformer, and pianist". He was a great-grandson of William Booth, founder of the Salvation Army and a first cousin to opera singer Dame Felicity Palmer.

Georgios PAPAVASILEIOU (Greece) (b. 10 Dec 1930 Arethousa) on March 12 in Athens. At 3000m steeplechase he ran in the heats in 1956 (also 1500m) and 1960 at the Olympic Games, and at the Europeans he was 8th in 1958 and heats 1962. Mediterranean Games champion 1955 and 1959 and Balkan 1955-61. Ten Greek records from 9:20.8 (1954) to 8:45.8 (1960). Pb 1500m 3:51.4 (1958).

June Florence **PAUL** (née Foulds, later Carroll and Reynolds) (GBR) (b. 13 June 1934 London) on 6 November. She competed in 15 internationals for Britain in 1950-8 starting, at the age of 16, with 3rd at 100m and 1st at 4x100m at the European Championships, at which she also competed in 1958. She won Olympic medals at 4x100m: silver 1952 (also ht 100m) and bronze 1956 (sf 100m, 5th 200m), At the 1958 Commonwealth Games she was 5th at 100y, 4th 220y and 1st 4x100m, WAAA champion at 100 1950-1 and 1958, 220y 1956. She was on teams that set six world relay records: 4x100m (2) 1956, 4x 110y 1958, 4x200m 1952 and, for Spartan Ladies, 4x220y 1951. After junior records in 1950-2 she set UK records: 100y (5) 11.0 '50 to 10.7 '58, 100m 11.9 '52 & 11.6 '56, 200m (3) 24.1 '56 to 23.8/24.00 '56, and half turn 23.7 '56, 220y 24.1 '58; 4x100m (6) 1950-6, 4x110y (5) 1951-8, 4x220y (3) 1951-2. Other pbs: 60m 7.7i (1958), 100y 10.93 (1958), 10.6w (1956); 100m 11.5w (1956). In 1953 she married Raymond Paul, who competed at the 1952 and 1956 Olympics as a fencer, and later married to singer Ronnie Carroll 1970-9, and briefly to Eric Reynolds.

Francesco PERRONE (Italy) (b. 3 Dec 1930 Cellino San Marco, Brindisi) died of Covid-19 in Bari in April. He was 37th in the 1960 Olympic marathon and ran a pb of 2:27:23 in 1961. He was Italian champion at 5000m 1955-6, 10,000m 1957, Marathon 1958 & 1961, and cross-country 1961, and won the Cinque Mulini CC in 1959, set an Italian record at 5000m 14:31.0 (1957) and had a 10,000m pb of 30:44.6 (1960); 7 internationals 1955-61.

Mark PHARAOH (GBR) (b. 18 Jul 1931 Streatham, London) on 27 April in Malvern, Worcestershire. His 4th at the 1956 Olympic Games remains the only top eight discus finish at the Games by a British man apart from George Robertson's 6th in 1896. At discus he set ten British records from 47.51 in 1953 to 53.26 and 54.27 at the 1956 Olympics (48.68 and 50.51 in 1951 were also Commonwealth records). UK junior records 39.35 and 42.23 (1950) and three at shot to 13.28 (1950). 19 internationals for Britain 1951-6 and was also dnq 19 at the 1952 Olympics, 10th 1964 Europeans (& 16th shot), 3rd 1954 Commonwealth Games (6th shot, dnq 10 hammer), and 1st 1953 World Student Games (2nd shot and hammer). AAA champion 1952-4 and 1955-6 after junior champion 1949. 2nd AAA shot 1954-5. Other pbs: 120yh 15.3 (1956), PV 3.20 (1951), SP 15.09 (1954) HT 49.40 (1956), Dec 4860 (1952 tables) (1956). He competed for Walton AC and went to Manchester University with service in the RAF, after which he worked as a civil engineer.

Maria PIATKOWSKA (ILWICKA-CHOJNACKA) (Poland) (b. 24 Jan 1931 Goleni MDA) on 19 December in Warsaw. She competed at three Olympic Games: 1952- dnq 32 LJ, ht 4x100m; 1956- 11th LJ; 1964- 6th 80mh 10.76w (10.6/10.75 OR/POL record in heat); and three European Champs: 1954- 6th LJ, 5th 4x100m, 1958- 6th LJ, 3rd 4x100m; 1962- 3= 80mh (10.6 POL rec), 1st 4x100m. Also POL record 80mh 10.7 '16, Other pbs: 100m 11.7 (1962), 6.10 (1959). Polish champion 80mh 1963, LJ 1958. Married world discus record setter Edmund Piatkowska (1963-2016).

Irene Maria **PIOTROWSKI** (Canada) (b. 9 Jul 1941 Skaudvile, Lithuania, née Macijauskas) on 13 August in Los Angeles. A top sprinter in the 1960s, she had this record at major championships: Olympics: 1964- sf 100m, ht 200m; 1968- h 100m, 200 & 4x100m; Commonwealth Games: 1966- 2nd 100y, 3rd 220y, 4th 4x110y; 1970- h 100m Pan-Am Games: 1967- 2nd 4x100m, 3rd 100m, 4th 200m. She was Canadian champion at 100m 1964 and 1967-9 and 200m 1967 and 1969. Her Canadian records included 3 at 100y from 10.7 (1963) to 10.4 (1968), 6 at 100m from 11.8 (1964) to 11.3A/11.40A 1968), and 3 at 200m/220y from 24.0 (1964) to 23.5 (1967). Pb 440y 56.3 (1964).

Charles Michael **'Chilla' PORTER** (Australia) (b. 11 Jan 1936 Brisbane) on 16 August in Innaloo, Western Australia. The bespectacled Porter had his greatest moment when he added 5cm to his pb in setting successive Commonwealth records at 2.06, 2.08 and 2.10 to take the silver medal behind Charles Dumas 2.12 at the Olympic Games in Melbourne in 1956. He also won silver medals at the Commonwealth Games in 1958 and 1962 and was dnq 27th at the 1960 Olympics. He was seven times Australian champion 1955-61. His father Charles had been a Queensland MP and his son Christian is the Australian Attorney-General

Tatyana Vasilyevna **PROROCHENKO** (USSR/Ukraine) (b. 15 Mar 1952 Berdyansk, Ukraine). on March 11 in Kiev. A former gymnast, at the Olympic Games she was 6th at 200m and 3rd at 4x100m in 1976 and won 4x400m gold in 1980. At the 1978 Europeans she was 2nd at 4x400m with semis 200m, and was 3rd at 200m at the 1977 World Cup. USSR champion at 200m 1976 and 400m 1980, and UKR champion 100m 1974-7 and 200m 1977. World record with USSR 4x300m team 1979. Pbs: 100m 11.2/11.1w (1976), 200m 22.98 (12976), 400m 50.6 (1977). She married 1980 Olympian (400m) Viktor Burakov, and was a team manager of the UKR team from 1993.

Lawrence Ronald **'Larry' QUESTAD** (USA) (b. 10 Jul 1943 Livingston, Montana) on 29 October in Boise, Idaho. He was 6th in the 200m at the 1968 Olympic Games after 3rd at the US Olympic Trials. While at Stanford University he won the 1963 NCAA 100y and was 2nd at 220, and he later earned an MBA from USC. Pbs: 100y 9.3 (1965), 100m 10.0/10.18 (1968), 200m 20.1A/20.28A (1968), 400m 48.7 (1963). He became a mechanical engineer with IBM and later bought Superior Steel Products in Idaho.

Ian Manley **REED** (Australia) (b. 13 Jul 1927 Footscray, Victoria) on 7 August in the USA. He won the discus at the 1950 British Empire Games and competed (dnq 21) at the 1952 Olympic Games; Australian champion 1948-50 and 1954. Pb 49.55 (1952). He moved to the USA for his education in the early 1950s and stayed there, becoming a naturalized US citizen in 1965. He set Masters' world records, competing into his 90s.

Tomás RINCÓN (Spain) (b. 18 Sep 1952) on 9 October. He held the current Basque 800m record with 1:47.2 (1977) in his one international. Other pbs: 400m 48.22 (1978), 1500m 3:59.6 (1975).

Neil James **ROBBINS** (Australia) (b. 8 Sep 1920) on 6 December. Australian cross-country champion 1952. He did not finish in the 6 miles at the 1954 Empire Games, but was 7th in the 3000m steeplechase at the 1956 Olympic Games in an Australian record 8:50.36. Other pbs: 1M 4:21.2 (1954), 2M 9:13.0 (1954), 3M 14:04.8 (1955), 5000m 14:57.4 (1954), 6M 29:26.2 (1954), 10000m 30:28.4 (1954).

Clarence `Earl **'Arnie' ROBINSON** (USA) (b. 7 Apr 1948 San Diego) on 1 December in San

OBITUARY

Diego. At the long jump he won Olympic bronze in 1972 and gold in 1976 with his lifetime best of 8.35 (then 3= world all-time), having won at the US Trials in both years (8.37w in 1976 and 6th in 1980). He won the NCAA title for San Diego State in 1970, and at the Pan-American Games 1971 (2nd 1975) and World Cup 1977; 2nd World University Games 1970 US champion outdoors in 1971-2 and 1975-8 (2nd 1974, 3rd 1980) and Indoors in 1975. He was ranked as world no. 1 in 1971 and 1976-8. Other pbs: HJ 2.08 (1971), TJ 15.54 (1971).
Annual progression at LJ: 1969- 7.77, 1970- 7.87, 1971- 8.04/8.17w, 1972- 8.14, 1973- 7.78/7.84w, 1974- 8.30, 1975- 8.29, 1976- 8.35/8.37w, 1977- 8.24, 1978- 8.21/8.33w, 1979- 8.07, 1980- 8.03/ 8.08w, 1981- 7.82, 1984- 7.67w.

George **Kiprotich RONO** (Kenya) (b. 4 Jan 1958) on 13 October. At 3000m steeplechase he was 3rd at the 1978 Commonwealth Games and African Champs, was ranked 3rd in the world in 1979, when he won at the African Championships (and 3rd 5000m) and at the World Cup, and 2nd in 1980. He went out in the World semis in 1983 and was 9th in his steeple heat at the 1984 Olympics. Pbs: 3000mSt 8:12.0 (1980), 1500m 3:42.6 (1980), 3000m 8:02.65, 5000m 13:19.24 (1980), 10.000m 28:49.1 (1980).

Kevin W **ROSS** (New Zealand) on 9 July aged 73. A small and tough competitor, he ran the first leg (4:01.2) on the New Zealand team that set a world record of 16:04.8 for 4x 1 mile at Auckland on 3 Feb 1972. NZ champion 880y 1967-9, 1500m 1971. Pbs: 800m 1:48.6 (1972), 1500m 3:42.05 (1971), 1M 3:59.9? (1972).

Ary Façanha da SA (Brazil) (b. 1 Apr 1928 Guimarães) on 16 August in Brasilia. At the long jump he was 4th at the 1952 Olympics (dnq 20th & ht 4x100m 1956)., 3rd 1955 Pan-American Games and South American champion in 1952 and 2nd 1956. He set three South American records 7.57 (1952) and 7.72A and 7.84A at the 1955 Pan-Ams. Pb 100m 10.6 (1952).

Donato SABIA (Italy) (b. 11 Sep 1963 Potenza) of Covid-19 on 7 April in Potenza. At 800m he was 5th in 1984 and, after returning from an Achilles operation, 7th in 1988 at the Olympic Games. He was European Indoor champion in 1984, and 5th in 1984 and 2nd in 1987 at European Cup final plus heats at the 1982 Europeans and 1983 Worlds; 17 internationals 1982-8. Italian champion at 400m 1984 and 800m 1983-4 and 1988. World bests at 500m (1:00.08) and for indoor 600m (1:15.77) in 1984. Pbs: 400m 45.73, 600m 1:15.33, 800m 1:43.88 (all 1984).

KURT SAKOWSKI (Germany/GDR) (b. 23 Dec 1930 Berlin) on 25 February. He was 8th at 50k walk at the 1964 Olympic Games after being disqualified in 1960 and was 4th at the 1966 European Champs. 10 GDR internationals 1965-9, he was GDR 50k champion in 1953 and at 20k in 1957, with GDR track records at 3000m 12:26.8u (1956) and 20,000m 1:37:23.6 (1955) and road 20k 1:39:19.4 (1955). Walks pbs: track: 3000m 12:05.0 (1956), 5000m 21:33.0 (1956), 10000m 43:37.4 (1956), 1Hr 13,264m (1967), 20000m 1:32:21.0 (1956), 2Hr 23,671m (1963), 30000m 2:28:51.0 (1970), 50000m 4:19:53.4 (1969); road: 20k 1:32:11.8 (1968), 30k 2:26:11 (1969), 35k 2:43:14 (1969), 50k 4:10:33.2 (1969), 100k 9:29:48.6 (1967).

Hermann SALOMON (Germany) (b. 13 Apr 1938 Danzig (now Gdansk POL) on 11 June in Mainz. At the javelin he set a German record of 83.48 in 1968, having ranked in the world top ten in 1962-3. He was 12th at the Europeans in 1962 (dnq 16 1966) and at the Olympic Games in 1960 and 1968 (dnq 14th 1964). He was 5th at the 1977 European Cup and at the World University Games: 1959- 1 (& 2nd Pen), 1961- 8 (& 4 Dec), 1963- 2, 1965- 5. FRG champion JT 1960, 1962-4 and 1967-8, Pen 1959-62. Pbs: DT 50.79 (1960), Dec 6443 (1961), Pen 3702 (1961 FRG record, 1952 tables). He competed from 1961 for USC Mainz and became a professor at the Johannes Gutenberg University.

Ann Rosemary **SAYER** (GBR) (b. 16 Oct 1936 Whitstable, Kent), a legend in long distance walking, died of Covid-19 and complications from a fall in 2018 on 15 April. She was the first woman to join the Centurions (for those who have completed a 100 mile race) and their first President and the first female President of the Long Distance Walkers Association. Amongst numerous records, she set women's world bests for 24 hours with 187.7k on the roads in Rouen in 1979 and 186.72k on the track at Altrincham (also bests of 12:34:21 for 100k and 20:37:25 for 100 miles) in 1982; and 48 hours 294.114k at Nottingham in 1982. She improved her road 100 miles with a British best of 19:32:37 in 1980, and that year set the women's record for the length of Britain from Land's End to John O'Groats (1351.9k) with 13 days 17:42 (walking, but beating the previous running record). 6-foot tall, she started rowing in 1955 while at Bedford College, University of London and competed for Britain in the eights (placing fifth) at the 1962 European Rowing Championships. She worked as a geologist with BP and was awarded the MBE for services to sport in 2005.

Gale Eugene **SAYERS** (USA) (b. 30 May 1943 Wichita, Kansas) on 23 September in Wakarusa, Indiana. A Hall of Fame American Footballer, he had a short career but he was for a while one of the greatest ever running backs. After the University of Kansas he was the first-round draft choice of the Chicago Bears in 1965 and was stunning in his rookie season, breaking or tying eight NFL records, including one for most touch–downs (22) in a season and he also tied an NFL record by scoring six touchdowns in one game. He led the NFL in rushing in 1966 and 1969 and led the league in kick-off returns in 1966 (with an NFL record average of 30.6). He was fast, quick, and electrifying before he succumbed to knee injuries. He was ranked third on the world junior long jump list in 1961 at 7.58m (indoors) and his older brother Roger (pbs 9.4y, 10.2, 20.6* in 1962) was one of only two men ever to beat Bob Hayes at 100 yards.

Edward Seldon **SEARS** (USA) on 1 September in Shawsville, Virginia. A dedicated runner, he wrote two outstanding books: *Running Through The Ages* (McFarland 2008 and 2015) and *George Seward: America's First Great Runner*. He graduated in physics and took a Master's Degree in Aerospace Engineering from Notre Dame, working in defence intelligence at the Pentagon.

Anneliese SEONBUCHNER (FRG/Germany) (b. 13 Sep 1929 Nürnberg) on 20 November. in Nürnberg. 18 internationals for FRG 1951-8 and at 80m hurdles was 4th at 1952 Olympic Games and 2nd at 1954 Europeans., setting a German record of 11.1 in 1954. FRG champion 80mh 1950 (2nd 1951-3, 3rd 1954. and 1958); LJ 1953 (2nd 1955 and 1957), 2nd pentathlon 1952, 1956 and 1958. Pbs: 100m 12.0 (1956), 200m 25.2 (1967), 80mh 11.0 (1959), HJ 1.52 (1958), LJ 6.15 (1957), Pen 4480 (1954 tables) (1958).

Hugh Joseph **SHORT** (USA) (b. 3 Mar 1922 Newark NJ) on 4 November. He won the 1942 ICAAAA 440y title in 47.2 (= 46.9 400m) to rank third in the world that year. At the 1943 Millrose Games he equalled the world indoor 600y best of 1:10.2. His track career ended when he joined the US Army, serving in Italy and awarded the Bronze Star for meritorious service. Later he returned to running; 2:54 in the 1979 Boston Marathon aged 57 and competing until he was 80. His proudest record was his marriage for nearly 75 years, the longest in Vermont.

Petras SIMONELIS (Lithuania) (b. 17 Jan 1947 Nolénuose) on 21 June. At 5000m he was 10th for the USSR at the 1971 European Championships and won a total of ten LTU titles – at 5000m, 10,000m, 30k, marathon and cross-country. He set LTU records at 5000m 13:40.0 and 13:36.8 (1971)and 10,000m 28:41.8 (1971) and 28:15.8 (1973).

Linda **Janell SMITH** (- CARSON) (USA) (b. 3 May 1947 Killeen, Texas) on 25 July in Parsons, Kansas. At 400m she won AAU titles in 1964-5 and at the US Olympic Trials in 1964, going on to run (heat) at the Games. She set four US records from 54.8 for 440y in 1964 to 53.7 for 400m in 1965 (at age 18). She went to Emporia State University and then Pittsburg Sate University, becoming a teacher. Pb 220y 24.4 (1965).

Stephen Norwood **'Steve' SMITH** (USA) (b. 24 Nov 1951 Long Beach) on 23 September. After 2nd in the US Trials pole vault he did not qualify for the final at the 1972 Olympic Games, but was ranked 6th in the world that year. He was AAU indoor champion in 1972 and in 1973 when he was ranked as world number one and set world indoor records at 5.46 and 5.49 (the first indoor 18ft vault). He improved that WIR to 5.51A and 5.53A in 1974 and 5.55, 5.59 and 5.61 in 1975 when he was an ITA pro (1974-6). He was at Cal State Long Beach and after not competing in 1978-9 returned for the next four years and was 2nd in the 1981 US Champs.

Willie James **SMITH** III (USA) (b. 28 Feb 1956 Rochester, PA) on 7 November at Sylacauga, Alabama. He won an Olympic gold medal at 4x400m in 1984 having run for the US team in their heat and semi. He had been 6th in the US Olympic Trials, having been 2nd in the boycott year of 1980. In 1974 he set US high school records indoors with 31.0 for 300y and outdoors 9.3 for 100y and 20.6 for 220y. While at Auburn University he won the NCAA 440y in 1977 and 1978, going on to be US 400m champion in 1979 and 1980 (3rd 1981). World University Games 1977: 2nd 400m, 1st 4x400m; Pan-Am Games 1979: 3rd 4x400m; World Cup 1979 and 1981 1st 4x400m. Other pbs: 100m 10.26 (1976), 200m 20.76 (1978), 400m 44.73 (1978). He became a television news director.

Annual progression at 400m: 1975- 45.9*, 1976- 45.4*, 1977- 45.31, 1978- 44.73, 1979- 45.10, 1980- 45.33, 1981- 45.05, 1983- 45.19, 1984- 45.07, 1985- 45.04, 1986- 46.41, 1987- 45.66, 1988- 44.92.

Gennadiy Stepanovich **SOLODOV** (USSR/ Russia) (b. 6 Oct 1934 Kurgan) on 2 May. At 20k walk he was disqualified in 1960 and was 5th in 1964 at the Olympic Games. Pbs: 10,000mW 44:27.6 (1961), 20kW 1:28:23.8 (1963), 50kW 4:11:32 (1965)

Andrzej STALMACH (Poland) (b. 1 May 1942 Jaworzno) on 14 September. At the long jump he was 8th at the Olympic Games in both 1964 and 1968, 10th at the 1966 Europeans, and won the European Indoor bronze medal and was 2nd at the European Cup in 1967. He was Polish champion in 1963-4 and 1966-68 and set Polish records with 7.96 in 1964 and 8.11 in 1968 with a pb TJ 15.33 (1966).

Neil Claud **STEINHAUER** (USA) (b. 18 Aug 1944) on 7 September in Modesto. World ranked for five years at the shot from 1965 to 1969, his 21.01 in 1967 was then 2nd all-time to Randy Matson. In that year he won the World University Games title (and 3rd discus) and was 2nd at the Pan-American Games. A back injury in April 1968 meant that he had not fully recovered by the US Olympic Trials, where he was 5th. After 2nd in 1966 and 1967, he finally won the AAU title in 1969. He went to University of Oregon and won the NCAA title in 1965 and was 2nd in 1966-67. Pb DT 57.07 (1967).

OBITUARY

Annual progression (position on world list): 1963- 16.00, 1964- 17.59 (69=), 1965- 19.34 (2), 1966- 20.37 (2), 1967- 20.01 (2), 1968- 19.90 (10), 1969- 20.64 (1), 1970- 19.57 (19).

Strecko STIGLIC (Croatia/Yugoslavia) (b. 11 June 1943 Zagreb) on 10 September in Zagreb. At the hammer he was 14th at the 1972 Olympic Games and dnq 17th at the 1971 Europeans. He won the Balkan Games title in 1971 and Mediterranean Games in 1975, with 22 (21 successive) Yugoslav titles 1966-86 and 1988, and set seven YUG records from 65.52 (1971) to pb 71.36 (1984); 67 internationals.

Mikhail Mikhaylovich **STOROZHENKO** (USSR/Ukraine) (b. 12 Nov 1937 St. Petersburg) on March 30. At the decathlon he was 8th at the 1964 Olympic Games, 7th at the 1966 Europeans and USSR champion 1964. Pb 7759 (current Tables) (1965). UKR champion at 110mh 1961.

Reinhard THEIMER (GDR) (b. 28 Feb 1948 Berlin) on 3 September in Hohen Neuendorf, Brandenburg. World ranked each year 1968-74 for hammer, six times in the top four, he set six GDR records from 68.82 in 1968 to world record 76.60 at Leipzig on 4 Jul 1974. At European Champs he was 2nd in 1971 and 3rd in 1969 and 1974 and had been 2nd at the 1966 European Juniors, but fared less well at the Olympic Games: 7th in 1968 and 13th in 1972. He was 3rd in 1970 and 2nd in 1973 at the European Cup and GDR champion in 1968-70 and 1973-4 (2nd 1967, 1971-2). 26 internationals 1968-74.
Annual progression (position on world list): 1965- 48.86, 1966- 60.26, 1967- 64.13 (45), 1968- 71.26 (4), 1969- 72.90 (4), 1970- 71.56 (5), 1971- 74.02 (5), 1972- 72.80 (13), 1973- 73.44 (5), 1974- 76.60 (2), 1975- 68.02 (88?), 1976- 73.30 (29), 1977- 60.24, 1978- 60.28, 1979- 59.14, 1980- 58.80.

Tor Olav **TORGERSEN** (Norway) (b. 20 Mar 1928 Drammen) on 25 October in Tønsberg. In 1960 he was 26th in the Olympic marathon in his pb of 2:27:30 and won NOR title in 2:28:00. 11th European 10,000m 1958. NOR champion at 5000m & 10,000m 1959. Other pbs: 1500m 3:56.5 (1958), 1M 4:19.8 (1955), 3000m 8:13.0 (1959), 2M 8:58.0 (1958), 3M 13:40.6 (1959), 5000m 14:13.8 (1959), 10.000m 29:30.8 (NOR record, 1959), 1Hr 19,011m (1960). 16 internationals 1955-60.

Béla TÓTH (Hungary) (b. 13 Jul 1945 Budapest) on 17 November in Budapest. He was Hungarian champion at 10,000m 1972-73 and cross-country 1972. 8 Internationals 1969-74. Pbs: 1500m 3:48.6 (1967), 3000m 8:10.4 (1970), 5000m 13:45.8 (1973), 10,000m 29:05.4 (1972), Marathon 2:33:06 (1972).

Jeanine TOULOUSE (France) (b. 16 May 1923 Lesparre-Médoc) on 29 December in Cambo-les-Bains, Pyrénées-Atlantique. She ran in the heats of the 80m hurdles and 4x100m at the 1948 Olympic Games, set French 100m records at 12.1 (1948) and 12.0 (1949), and also had pbs 200m 26.2 (1941) and 80mh 12.0 (1948). French champion 60m 1939, 1946 and 1949; 100m 1941-2, 1945 and 1949; 200m 1941-2 and 1945. 6 internationals 1939-49.

Ursula 'Ulla TRUMPF (Germany) (née Wittmann, later Künzel) (b. 22 Feb 1944) on 2 November. At the long jump she was FRG champion in 1965 and competed at the 1966 Europeans (dnq). Pbs: 100m 11.9 (1968), 200m 25.3 (1966), LJ 6.32 (1968), 6.36w (1965).

John Martin **TUSHAUS** (USA) (b. 6 Jan 1944 Lake City, Minnesota) in Rochester, Minnesota on 23 December, He set an American javelin (old model) record of 86.58 in 1966, won the 1966 American AAU title and ranked no 7 in the world that year, and was NCAA champion in 1965 for the University of Arizona (2nd 1966).

Gilbert VAN MANSHOVEN (Belgium) (b. 26 Mar 1946 Rijkel) on 10 March in Tongeren. A member of RFS Liége, he was Belgian champion at 800m, ran at the Olympic Games and set a pb of 1:47.7 in 1968. In 1971 he ran his 1500m best of 3:40.8 and ran at the European Champs (heat).

Ivanka Borisova **VANCHEVA** (Bulgaria) (b. 31 Oct 1953 Plovdiv) on 5 August in Plovdiv. At the javelin (old specification) she set BUL records at 62.98 and 63.04 in 1979 and improved to a pb of 65.38 (then 14th on the world all-time list) when 5th at the 1980 Olympic Games. She was also 2nd at the World University Games in 1977 and 1979, and at the European Cup: 5th 1977, 6th 1979 and 7th 1985. Bulgarian champion 1977 and 1980, Balkan 1977 & 1978.

Vasiliy Ivanovich **VLASENKO** (USSR/Ukraine) (b. 10 Jan 1928 Kharkiv) on 5 August probably in Volgograd. He competed (heat) at steeplechase at the 1956 Olympic Games after 3rd in the USSR Championships that year. Pbs: 5000m 14:04.6 (1958), 3000mSt 8:43.2 (1958).

Yuriy VOLKOV (Russia) (b. 1 Feb 1940 Irkutsk) on 23 October. He had a pole vault best of 5.16i/5.00 (1970) and became a renowned coach of many top Soviet vaulters. These included his son Konstantin, silver medallist at the 1980 Olympics and 1983 Worlds with a best of 5.85 in 1984, having set two world junior records in 1979. His grandson Matvey (who is looking to compete for Belarus) jumped 5.50 indoors in 2020 at the age of 16.

Robert 'Rob' WALLACE (Australia) (b. 21 Jun 1951) on 21 July. At the marathon he was Australian champion in 1977 and in 1982, when he was also 10th at the Commonwealth Games. Pb 2:13:15 (3rd Duluth 1981).

Robert Oscar **WALTERS** (USA) (b. 4 October 1927 Wiergate, Texas) on 21 December in San Antonio, Texas. He topped the world high jump list with 2.036 in 1949 and 2.048 in 1950 while at

OBITUARY

the University of Texas, after which he had a distinguished career in the US Air Force, reaching the rank of Colonel.

John James **'J.J' WILLIAMS** (GBR) (b. 1 Apr 1948 Nantyffyllon, Bridgend) on 29 October. A legendary rugby union player, he scored 12 tries in 30 internationals for Wales 1973-9, plus 7 Tests for British Lions 1974-7. Earlier he had starred as a sprinter, competing for Wales at the 1970 Commonwealth Games (heat 100m, qf 200, 5th 4x100m) and Welsh champion at 100m 1971 and 200m 1968-69 and 1971. Pbs: 60y 6.4i (1969), 60m 6.9i (1968), 100y 9.8 (1967), 9.6w (1968); 100m 10.5/10.4w/10.67w (1970), 200m 21.2 (1971), 400m 47.4 (1971). Awarded MBE 2013. He was the father of Rhys (400mh 48.84 in 2013, European champion – Junior 2003, U23 2005, senior 2012, 2nd 2010 and 3rd 2006), James (1500m 3:49.11 in 2007, Welsh indoor champion 2006-07, now CEO of Welsh Athletics) and Kathryn (400mh Welsh champion 2000, UK U20 inter-national, pb 59.56 (2005)

Liane WINTER (Germany) (b. 24 Jun 1942) on 17 January. She was one of the earliest women's winners at the Boston Marathon, when she ran 2:42:24 in 1975, then a world women's best. She had set a European best of 2:50:31.4 at Waldniel in 1974 and was FRG champion in 1979.

Keizo YAMADA (Japan) (b. 30 Nov 1927 Odate, Akita) on 2 April in Kawasaki, Kanagawa. Having served with the Japanese army in Manchuria in WWII, he ran his first marathon in 1949 and was 26th at the 1952 Olympic Games. He then won at Beppu and at Boston in 1953. There he ran 2:18:51, originally thought to be the world's fastest ever time, but the course was short in those days at 25 miles 938 yards. He continued to place well in major Japanese races and at the end of 1956 had two wins – taking the national title in Sendai and then when setting a pb of 2:25:15 at Nagoya. He was reported to have run c.340 marathons in all, the last at Boston in 2009.

John Robert Chester **YOUNG** (GBR) (b. 6 Sep 1937 Upton, Chester) on 19 March. He was one of the rare people in the modern era to reach the top in two sports, despite a limited career cut short by injuries. At rugby union he played nine times for England (2 tries) 1958-61 and once for the British Lions (1 try) on tour in New Zealand in 1959 on the wing. In athletics he competed in two internationals for England in 1956 when he was AAA Junior champion at 100y and 220y and AAA champion at 100y. He won English Schools titles at 220y – intermediates in 1954 and seniors in 1954 & 1955 and set six British junior records at 100y from 9.9 in 1955 to 9.8 in 1956, with other pbs of 100y 9.6w (1958), 220y 21.4 (1958), LJ 7.01 (1959) and he ran on the England team that set a national record for 4x110y at the Trials for the Commonwealth Games in 1958, but injuries prevented him from competing at the Games as they had the 1956 Olympic Games. A blue at both sports at Oxford University where he read law, he was called to the Bar in 1961, but immediately switched from law to become a stockbroker. He was director of policy and planning at the London Stock Exchange 1982-7, and chairman of Lloyd's Regulatory Board. Awarded OBE in 1992.

Ioan ZAMFIRACHE (Romania) (b. 23 Aug 1953) on 19 December. At discus he was 7th at the 1982 Europeans, 21st at the 1983 Worlds and 3rd at the 1981 World University Games; Balkan champion 1977 and 1982 and Romanian 1977-8, 1983-5 and 1987. Pb 67.30 (1985).

Bohumír ZHÁNAL (Czech Republic) (b. 17 Oct 1931 Moravsky Zizkov) on 16 April in Zlin. He was ranked 4th in the world at 3000m steeplechase in 1957 and 1959 and set Czechoslovak records at 8:42.2 and 8:39.8 in 1963. He was national champion at 3000mSt in 1957-8 and 1961-4 and 4k cross-country in 1959 and 1961. He made 26 international appearances 1956-65 including at European Champs in 1958 (12th) and 1962 (heat) and Olympic Games in 1960 (heat). Other pbs: 1500m 3:51.4 (1964), 3000m 8:09.4 (1964), 5000m 14:11.2 (1962).

Died in 2021

Lloyd COWAN (GBR) (b. 8 Jul 1962 Hackney, London) on 11 January. He competed in two internationals for Britain –12 years apart, in 1983 at 110mh v USSR and in 1995 at 400mh v USA. He also ran for England at the 1994 Commonwealth Games at 110mh, at which he was UK 2nd in 1983 and AAA 3rd in 1994-95 and 1999. He competed for three London clubs: North London, Shaftesbury Barnet H and Woodford Green and had pbs: 100m 10.8w (1986), 200m 21.7/21.48w (1986), 21.71/21.3w (1993); 300m 33.92 (1986), 400m 47.42 (1986, 60m 8.10i (1999), 110mh 13.75 (1994),13.7w (1995); 400mh 50.99 (1995). He became a popular and highly respected coach and mentor, most notably of Christine Ohuruogu and Andy Turner, and was awarded MBE in 2015. His son Dwayne is a UK 400m international (pb 45.34 and World 4x400m bronze in 2017).

Steven Charles **'Steve' DeAUTREMONT** (USA) (b. 17 Nov 1947) on 2 January. At the hammer he was NCAA champion for Oregon State in 1969 and 1970 and was US champion in 1974 (3rd 1973 & 1975). Pb 70.14 (1974).

Alejandro GÓMEZ Cabral (Spain) (b. 11 Apr 1967 Vigo) on 31 January in Zamáns, Vigo. 2nd at 5000m at the 1986 World Juniors and in the 1995 European Cr0ss-Country. At the Olympic Games: 1988- sf 5000m, 1992- dnf ht and 1996- 15th at 10,000m; 10th European 10,000m 1990.

OBITUARY 63

36 Internationals 1987-2002 and ran for Spain at the World Cross at juniors 1985-6 and seniors 1987-91, 1993-8 and 2000-01, with a best of 6th 1989. Track pbs: 1500m 3:39.18 (1991), 3000 7:47.7 (1989), 5000 13:20.91 (1989), 10,000 27:39.38 (1993), 3000SC 8:33.6 (1989). Turning to the marathon, he was 2nd at Rotterdam in 1997 in a Spanish record 2:07:54 and was 5th in 1998 and 6th in 1992 at the Europeans, dnf 2001 Worlds. Pb HMar 61:20 (1992 ESP record). Spanish champion 10,000m 1989, 1991, 1993, 1995-6, half mar 1992 and 2003, CC 1989 and 1995.

Margitta HELMBOLD-GUMMEL (Germany/GDR) (b. 29 Jun 1941 Magdeburg) on 26 January in Wietmarschen, Niedersachsen. At the shot she ranked in the world top three each year 1966-72 after being in the top-ten 1962-5. She was 5th in 1964, 1st in 1968 and 2nd in 1972 at the Olympic Games, 2nd in 1966 and 1969 and 3rd in 1971 at the Europeans, won in 1966 and was 2nd in 1968 and 1971 at the European Indoors and 2nd in the 1967 European Cup. Also GDR champion 1966, 1968-9 and 1971-2 and indoors 1966, 1968 and 1971. After six GDR records from 17.54 (1964) to 19.43 (1968), she set four world records: first 18.87 in September 1968, then improving to 19.07 and 19.61 at the Olympic Games a month later (she won by 83 cm from compatriot Maritta Lange) and 20.10 in 1969, swapping the record with another all-time great Nadezhda Chizhova, and an 11th GDR record and final pb of 20.22 (1972). She also set five world indoor records, all in 1971, from 18.66 to 19.54. She married Jens Gummel in January 1966.
Annual progression (position on world list): 1956- 10.70, 1957- 11.99, 1958- 13.32 (98), 1959- 14.85 (22), 1960- 15.38 (17), 1961- 15.74 (13), 1962- 16.10 (10), 1963- 17.30 (3), 1964- 17.54 (3), 1965- 17.09 (5), 1966- 17.45 (2), 1967- 17.69 (2), 1968- 19.61 (1), 1969- 20.10 (2), 1970- 18.74 (3), 1971- 20.03 (2), 1972- 20.22 (2).

Raymund Karl **HERDT** (Hungary) (b. 26 Dec 1932 Kalusenburg, ROU) on 19 January. A distinguished race walking statistician, member of the DGLD and ATFS, and a great help for both *Athletics International* and the International Athletics Annual. Lived in Cluj-Napoca, Romania before moving to Frankfurt in Germany in 1980.

Andrew HUXTABLE (GBR) (b. 29 Nov 1938 Wimbledon) in January. For many years a top athletics statistician, He was one of the earliest NUTS members (November 1958) and served as NUTS secretary 1968-78 and editor of NUTS Notes 1965-78. He became an ATFS member in 1962, was its secretary general 1980-8 and edited the ATFS Bulletin for several years from 1968. He compiled or edited numerous statistical booklets between 1961 and 1990, including British Best Performers of All Time, UK Indoor Track & Field Handbook, UK Junior All-Time Handbook and Statistical History of UK Track & Field Athletics. In 2001 he collaborated with Tom McNab and Peter Lovesey to produce *An Athletics Compendium* – a guide to UK track & field literature published by the British Library.

Danial JAHIC (Serbia) (b. 1 Jul 1979) on 19 January in Celije, Croatia At long jump he was 5th at the 1998 World Juniors, 8th 2000 European Indoors and dnq 21 at the 2000 Olympic Games. Yugoslav champion 1999-2001, Serbian 2003 & 2005, Balkan indoors and out 1998. Pbs: LJ 8.18/8.27w (1999) with Serbian indoor record 8.02 (1999), TJ 15.95 (1997). 18 internationals for YUG 1997-2005. His mother was a European karate medallist and his father Fahrudin a Yugoslav athletics international.

Erik **Thorsten JOHANSSON** (Sweden) (b. 9 Oct 1950 Bärbo) on 18 January in Sölbesirg. Swedish champion at 100m 1971 and 1973, and 200m 1973-8. He competed at Europeans in 1971 (ht 100m) and 1974 (sf 200m), Olympic Games 1976 (ht 200m). and was 3rd at 200m at the 1975 World University Games. 27 internationals 1970-8. He set Swedish records for 100m 10.3 (1972) and 200m 20.7 (1972) and 20.61 (1976). Pbs: 100m 10.61 (1973), 400m 47.28 (1976).

Bernhard **'Bernd' KANNENBERG** (Germany) (b. 20 Aug 1942 Königsberg) on 13 January at Münster. Olympic champion at 50k walk in 1972 (dnf 20k), he was also dnf 20k in 1976. At the Europeans he was 9th at 20k in 1991, 2nd at 20k and 9th at 50k in 1974 and also won the Lugano Trophy 50k in 1973 with 2nd at 20k in 1975, and was FRG champion at 20k in 1972 and 1974-5 and at 50k 1972-3 and 1975. He set six world records: track 20,000m 1:24:45.0, 30,000m 2:12:58.0 and 2 hours 27,153m in 1974, and 30M 3:48:23.4 and 50,000m 3:56:51.4 in 1975; road 3:52:45 in 1972. Further FRG records included 5000m 20:51.0 and 10,000m 41:36.2 in 1972, 1 hour 13,635m & 14,241m in 1974, and 20M 2:30:37.4 in 1975. 26 internationals 1970-6. He became the German walks team coach.

Jeremiah **'Jerry' KIERNAN** (Ireland) (b. 31 May 1953 Listowel, Kerry) on 20 January in Dublin. A member of Clonliffe Harriers, he was 9th in the 1984 Olympic Marathon in his pb 2:12:20. He ran seven times in the World Cross-country Championships plus once as a junior 1973-93, with a best of 26th in 1982. Other pbs: 1500m 3:41.9 (1976), 1M 3:59.1 (1976), 3000m 7:54.70 (1987), 5000m 13:32.71 (1981), 10,000m 28:55.9 (1981). Irish champion 1500m 1975, 10,000m 1981, Marathon 1992, CC 1984. He became a leading coach and worked for RTE as an athletics pundit.

Volodomyr Viktorovych **KISELYOV** (USSR/Ukraine) (b. 1 Jan 1957 Myski, Kemerovo) on 7 January at Kremenchuk. He was the surprise Olympic shot put champion in 1980 with an

Olympic record 21.35. European Junior champion in 1975, and in 1979 was 3rd at the European Indoors and 4th World Student Games. In 1982 he was USSR champion and 7th Europeans. Pb 21.58 (1984). He revealed in 1991 that steroid abuse nearly killed him, when in 1985 he suffered from high blood pressure and lost almost four stone in weight. After recovering his health he took up gold prospecting in Siberia before working as a coach.

Helga KLEIN (Germany) (later ERNY) (b. 15 Aug 1931 Mannheim) on 27 January. She won an Olympic silver medal in 1952 running the third leg on the German team that, along with the US winners, set a world record of 45.9; she was also 5th at 200m and ran in a heat at 100m. A semi-finalist at the 1954 Europeans, with 7 internationals 1952-4, she was FRG champion at 200m in 1952-3. She set German records at 100m 11.8 and 200m 24.4 in 1952.

Leslie Alphonso **LAING** (Jamaica) (b. 19 Feb 1925 Linstead) on 7 February. He ran the second leg (in 47.0) on the Jamaican team that won Olympic gold at 4x400m in 1952 in a world record 3:03.9. He was also 5th at 200m at the Games after 6th in 1948. Gold medallist at both relays with 2nd 100m and 1st 200m at the Central American & Caribbean Games in 1954, and 5th 100m, 4th 200m and 3rd 4x400m 1950. Pbs: 100y 9.7 (1949, 9.5w (1953); 100m 10.5 (1949), 10.66 (1954); 200m21.2 (1952), 21.0*w (1948), 220ySt 20.9 (1953), 440y 47.8 (1952).

Alan Leslie **LERWILL** (GBR) (b. 15 Nov 1948 Portsmouth) on 6 February. A multi-talented jumper, he competed in 42 UK internationals 1967-76. At long jump he was Commonwealth champion in 1974 after 3rd in 1970 (10th TJ at both). World University Games champion in 1970 and his other major championships record: Olympics: 1968- dnq 19, 1972- 7; Europeans: 1969 & 1971- dnq, 1974-9 (ht 4x100m); European Indoors: 1970- 10, 1971- 9, 1974- 6; European Cup: 1973- 4, 1975- 8. AAA champion 1970, 1972, 1974-5, indoor 1970-71 & 1973. He set a UK high jump record 2.10 (1973) and had pbs: LJ 7.98 (1974), 8.15w (1973); TJ 16.10/16.21w (1971), Dec 6186 (1970), 100m 10.8 (1974), 10.97 (1975); 400m 49.9 (1976), 110mh 15.9 (1971), 200m 25.2 '72, 400mh 55.0 (1973). He went to Borough Road College and competed for Queens Park H and Borough of Enfield AC. His son Tom was 2nd at 800m and 3rd at 4x400m at the 1996 World Juniors and won 4x400m gold at the 1975 European Juniors; pb 800m 1:47.27 (1996).

Gabriele MANFREDINI (Italy) (b. 19 Dec 1953) on 13 January. Decathlon expert and the statistician of the annual Multistars combined events meeting.

Robert Norman **'Bob' MAPLESTONE** (b. 15 Jul 1946 Cardiff) on 2 January in Seattle, USA. A founder member of Cardiff AAC, he was the first British athlete to run a mile indoors in under 4 minutes with 3:59.5 at San Diego in 1972. He had six internationals for Britain 1973-6 and ran for Wales at 1500m at the 1970 Commonwealth Games. He set Welsh records: 1500m 3:42.6 & 3:39.7 (1972), the last when 3rd in the US Championships, 1M 3:58.5 (1973), with other pbs: 800m 1:48.3 (1977), 3000m 8:16.2i (1977), 2M 8:52.4i (1977), 8:53.2 (1974), 3M 13:48.8 (1971), 5000m 14:09.0 (1972), Mar 2:31?? (1979), 2kSt (21 barriers) 6:00.6 (1969), 3kSt 9:19.8 (1973). He went to university, in the USA, first at Eastern Washington State and then Oregon State and become a US citizen. He retired as professor of Mechanical Engineering at Highline College in 2008.

Alberto Jorge Rodrigues **MATOS** (Portugal) (b. 6 Jun 1944 Lisbon) on 28 January. Portuguese champion at 200m 1970, 400m 1971, 110mh 1967-68, 1970 and 1972; 200mh 1968-70. He ran in the heats of the Olympic 110mh in 1972, Europeans 110mh & 400mh 1969, 110mh 1971. Portuguese records at 110mh from 14.6 (1968) to 14.2 (1972), 400mh 52.5 (1969) to 51.2 (1972). Pb 400m 47.5 (1972).

Álvaro MEJIA (Colombia) (b. 15 May 1940 Medellín) on 12 January in Bogotá. His top performances came at the 1971 Pan-American Games: 3rd 10,000m and 4th Marathon, and at the CAC Games he won the 1500m in 1962 and a treble of 1500m, 5000m and 10,000m in 1966. Competing at three Olympic Games: he ran in the 5000m heats in 1964 and at 10,000m was 19th in 1968 and 48th in 1972. South American records 5000m 13:53.4 (1964), 10,000m 29:10.4 (1966) and marathon 2:17:23 (1971); pb 1500m 3:48.9 (1964).

George William **'Bill' NANKEVILLE** (b. 24 Mar 1925 Guildford) on 8 January in Laleham, Surrey. Britain's premier miler in the immediate post-war years, he was 6th in 1948 and a semi-finalist in 1952 at 1500m at the Olympic Games and 3rd at the 1950 European Championships; 9 Internationals 1947-53. AAA 1 mile champion 1948-50 and 1952 (2nd 1951, 3rd 1947 and 1953), he ran on two British world record relay teams: 4x880y 7:30.6 (1951) and 4x1500m 15:27.2 (1953), both at White City, London, and he also set British records at 1000y 2:11.1 (1952), 1000m 2:24.6 (1949), ³4M 3:00.4 (1952), 1500m 3:48.0 (1950), Other pbs: 800m 1:52.6 (1953), 1000y 2:10.9 (1954), 1500m 3:46.6 (1953), 1M 4:07.4 (1953). His Autobiography 'Miracle of the Mile' was published in 1956. His son is the comedian Bobby Davro.

Richard NEWBLE (GBR) (b. 21 April 1946) on 2 January. He set UK junior records in 1965 at 3 miles 13:57.0 amd 10,000m 31:02.0 and had two internationals for Britain at 5000m in 1972, also winning the CAU 10,000m that year. He ran for Maidstone, Medway, and Sheffield University, Pbs: 880y 1:54.1 (1966), 1500m 3:44.4 (1974), 1M 4:05.5 (1974), 3000m 7:57.6 (1971), 2M 8:39.42 (1973), 5000m 13:45.8 (1974), 10000m 28:53.84 (1973), 10M Rd 49:33 (1975).

Marius van HEERDEN (South Africa) (b. 8 Sep 1974 Clanwilliam, Western Cape) on 21 January in Cape Town. In 1996 he ran an 800m South African record 1:44.57 before a heat at the Olympic Games. 6th at World Juniors 1993, qf Worlds 1997. RSA champion 1500m 1997. Other pbs: 600m 1:18.94 (2000), 1000m 2:17.64 (RSA record), 1500m 3:40.51, 1M 3:57.49 (all 1996).

Elisabeth Cornelia 'Els' VADER (-SCHARN) (Netherlands) (b. 24 Sep 1959 Vlissingen) on 8 February. She set Dutch records at 100m: 11.28 and 11.25 (1981) and 200m: 23.08 (1980), 22.99 & 22.81 (1981). Pbs; 50m 6.21i (1985, NED rec), 60m 7.1i (1987), 100m 11.17 (1986), 400m 51.92 (1986). Champs record: Olympics: 1980 & 1984- hts 100m & 200m, 1988- hts 100m & 4x100m; Europeans: 1986- sf 100m; EJ: 1977- 6 200m; EI: 1985- 3 200m. NED champion 100m & 200m 1979-82, 1984; Indoor 60m 1979-82, 1984-5.; 200m 1984-5, 1987-8.

Stanislaw WOLODKO (Poland) (b. 20 Mar 1950 Vilnius, Lithuania) on 4 February. At the discus he set three Polish records: 64.30 in 1976 and 64.46 and 64.80 in 1978, all at Bydgoszcz. He competed at the 1974 Europeans and 1976 Olympics, not qualifying for the finals, and at the European Cup was 6th 1975, 4th 1977, 5th 1979 and 4th 1981. Polish champion 1975-6 and 1980-1.

Mikhail Stoykov **ZHELEV** (Bulgaria) (b. 15 Jul 1943 Sliven) on 5 January. At 3000m steeplechase he was European champion in 1969 in his fourth BUL record (after 8:37.8 in 1967, 8:36.8 in 1968 and 8:33.2 in 1960). At Olympic Games he was 6th in 1968 and 12th in 1972, ran in the heats at the 1966 and 1971 Europeans and was World Student Games champion in 1970. Balkan champion five times 1967-71 and BUL 1968-70 and 1974 (also 5000m 1969-70, 10,000m 1986, 3000m indoor 1973 and CC 1967-68 and 1972). He also set BUL records at 2000m 5:18.0 (1967), 5000m 13:49.6 (1969), 10,000m 29:28.4 (1967) and 29:14.4 (1968), and indoor 3000m 7:59.8 (1973). Other pbs: 800m 1:52.1 (1968), 1500m 3:43.2 (1970), 3000m 7:57.0 (1972), 5000m 13:42.6 (1972),, He married Rayna Zheleva (800m 2:11.7); their son Zhelyazko 1500m 3:44.10 & 5000m 14:22.01, daughter Olga 800m 2:04.17, 1500m 4:12.02; and grandson Mihail, a national U23 volleyball player.

Add to 2019 Deaths

Günther Gerhard **LOHRE** (Germany) *add* Pbs: HJ 2.00 (1973), LJ 7.32/7.36w (1970). Married on 15 Sep 1969 Dagmar Schenten (pbs 100m 11.61 and 200m 23.19 in 1977). Their son Leo Lohre had PV pb 5.41 (2013).

Uwe MARTIN (Germany/FRG) (b. 14 Aug 1962 Wiesbaden) on 31 May in Mainz. HJ pb 2.25 (1987).

Anita OTTO (née **HENTSCHEL**) (Germany/GDR) (b. 12 Dec 1942 Löbnitz) on 16 April (unconfirmed). At discus she was 3rd at the 1966 Europeans and 4th at the 1968 Olympics. GDR champion 1965-6 (2nd 1964, 1967, 3rd 1963 & 1968-9) with 13 Internationals 1961-9. Pbs: SP 13.84 (19), DT 59.40 (1968).

Annual progression: 1962- 51.14, 1963- 51.72, 1964- 54,73, 1965- 56.20, 1966- 59.02, 1967- 57.13, 1968- 59.40, 1969- 57.88, 1975- 47.38, 1977- 48.48, 1983- 42.54.

Liliane SPRECHER (France) (b. 20 Jun 1926, née Miannay, later Lazare) on 2 April. 6 internationals 1946-54, 2nd 4x100m 1946 Europeans. French champion 60m 1945 & 1952, 200m 1948, Pbs: 100m 12.4 (1948), 200m 26.0 (1948), DT 36.68 (1946).

Maria STURM (Germany/FRG) (b. 30 Jan 1935 Nürnberg) on 10 February in Nürnberg. She had 7 Internationals 1954-64 and won the bronze medal for pentathlon at the 1954 Europeans. German champion at pentathlon 1955-6 and indoors at high jump 1954-5 and long jump 1956. Pbs: 80mh 11.2 (1956), HJ 1.61 (1956), LJ 5.98 (1965), SP 13.25 (1955), Pen 4579 (1965, on 1954 tables, 4072 on 1971 tables). She married Karl-Friedrich Haas (4/2 Olympics 1952-56, 4/3 European 1954/58 at 400m).

Herbert SWOBODA (Germany/FRG) (b. 19 Sep 1945 Kempten) on 28 February in Mainz. German champion: pentathlon 1967, decathlon 1973. Pbs: 100m 10.4 1968), 400m 49.3 (1971), 1500m 4:13.7 (1966), 110mh 15.3 (1971), HJ 1.92 (1972), PV 4.50 (1971), LJ 7.38 (1971), SP 13.90 (1971), DT 43.08 (1972), JT 71.40 (1974), Pen 3804 (1969), Hep 5563 (1971, world indoor best), Dec 8008 (1971 on 1964 tables, 7856 on current tables).

Kenneth George **WIESNER** (USA) (b. 17 Feb 1925 Milwaukee) on 20 March on Minocqua, Wisconsin. US Navy. At the high jump he won the silver medal at the 1952 Olympic Games after 2nd at the Olympic Trials, on both occasions behind Walter Davis. In March 1953 he set world indoor bests at 2.08 and 2.10. While at Marquette University he won the NCAA title in 1946 and 1948 and tied for first in 1947 and also tied for first in the AAU Indoors in 1945.

Karl Erik Gunnar **WREDLING** (Sweden) (b. 8 Oct 1920 Yttergdal) on 2 November. Two internationals 1947-9. Pbs: 3000m: 8:25.4 (1949), 5000m: 14:35.2 (1949), 10,000m: 30:23.4 (9th on world list 1949)

REFERENCE BOOKS 2020-21

PROGRESSION OF IAAF WORLD RECORDS (2020 edition). A5 674 pages. Edited by Richard Hymans and published by World Athletics Heritage. This is the ninth edition of this invaluable work initiated in 1987 by the late Ekkehard zur Megede. As with previous editions the work has not only been updated with new records but there has also been much work on previous marks, most notably for women thanks to the great work of John Brant, Janusz Wasko and Steponas Misiunas with the latest edition of their *World Women's Athletics 100 Best Performer lists 1911-62* with John Brant adding much information on women's details from 1870 to 1905. For this edition András Szabó produced many adjustments and Pierre-Jean Vazel many new race splits. The records (and bests) are fleshed out with such additional information as intermediate times, field event series and the complete result for track and field events, walks and road events. Indoor and junior (U20) world records are also included. There is a 159 page index of all the record breakers with dates of birth and height and weight where available. Also tables of the places and stadia where most records have been set and of the youngest and oldest record setters. Price $28 including postage and packaging from World Athletics, 6-8 Quai Antoine 1er, BP 359, MC 98007 MONACO cedex. An e-book version was expected later.

2020 COMBINED EVENTS ANNUAL. 98 pp pdf by Hans van Kuijen, who has maintained his sequence of publications, so while this is a smaller book than usual it provides very comprehensive coverage. He writes that: "In the all-time chapters and national records chapter I have only mentioned the changes in 2020 and also the content of the Who's Who section is limited as many athletes did not have any competition during 2020 and therefore for them their published results in the 2019 version are still the same." He generously determined to make this Annual freely available for his regular customers. Others can contact him for this or past numbers: Hans van Kuijen, de Bergen 66, 5706 RZ Helmond, Netherlands. email <j.kuijen4@upcmail.nl>

ANNUAIRE FLA 2020. A4 312pp. Once again the Luxembourg Annual, edited by Georges Klepper, is the most magnificent national annual. It is an extraordinarily comprehensive volume, with reviews, results, 2020 and all-time lists for Luxembourg with hundreds of colour photographs as well as some historical features. 25 euros locally, €31 elsewhere to account no. LU32 1111 0200 0321 0000. See www.fla.lu

ASIAN ATHLETICS 2019 Rankings. A5 111 pages. Heinrich Hubbeling has produced the 31st edition of his invaluable annual rankings for Asia as an e-book. There are top 30 lists for 2019 for athletes from Asian nations, with continuation lists for countries other than China and Japan (up to 4 best per country), national records set in 2019, and full lists of Asian records. Euro 15 from the author, Haaksbergener Str 25, 48691 Vreden, Germany. email hhubbeling@t-online.de.

ATHLÉRAMA 2019. A5 816pp. The magnificent French Annual is again a massive tome with Thierry Wangermez leading the strong team of compilers. Packed with information on French athletics, there are records, profiles of top athletes, results, deep year lists for 2019 for all age groups plus lists of all those who have had 20 or more internationals for France, all-time lists and indexes. Maintaining the sequence, there are French top ten lists and reviews for 1919 and 1969. 28 euros from the FFA, 33 avenue Pierre de Coubertin, 7540 Paris Cedex 13, France. www.athle.fr

ISRAEL ATHLETICS ANNUAL 2020/21. 240 x 170mm, 58pp, illustrated. By David Eiger and Arit Cooks for the Israeli Athletic Association. Records, championship results, 2020 top 20s and all-time lists, with profiles of leading Israeli athletes. 8 euro or US $9 from David Eiger, 10 Ezra Hozsofer Str, Herzliya 46 371, Israel. Past editions from 1986 onwards also available.

LATVIJAS VIEGLATLETIKAS GADAGRAMATA 2020. A5 296 pp. Andris Stagis has again produced an exemplary example of a national annual with its most comprehensive coverage of Latvian athletics, including an extensive chronology of the year, records, results, athlete profiles and year and all-time lists. From the Latvian Athletic Association, Augsiela 1, Riga LV-1009, Latvia. email: lvs@latathletics.lv. Or contact Andris at andris.stagis@athletics.lv for further details of his splendid histories of Latvian athletics.

SVERIGE-BÄSTA 2019. A5 296 pages. Edited by Jonas Hedman. Detailed 2019 Swedish lists for seniors (100 deep) and younger age groups (20 deep). 299 Swedish crowns, 29 euros or $35 (plus postage and shipping) from TextoGraf Publishing: Jonas Hedman, Springarvägen 14, 142 61 Trångsund, Sweden. www.textograf.com. Email: jonas.hedman@textograf.com. Jonas writes that the Swedish Federation will not publish this annual as a printed book in future, so just available as a pdf (another nail in the coffin for books? **PJM**).

On the Irish Athletics History Facebook page is

BOOKS 67

a 444 page pdf of the **Irish outdoor champions 1861-2020** by Pierce O'Callaghan. https://www.facebook.com/groups/726449857879510/
This compilation includes all the champions (seniors and younger age groups) for the various governing bodies that have staged national championships, and also has analyses for each event such as those to have won most titles and some fascinating lists of relatives to have won titles.

ENCIKLOPEDIJA JUGOSLOVENSKE ATHLETIKe. Ljubisa Gajic has announced the publication of his Encyclopedia of Yugoslav Athletics – 528 A4 pages with about 2500 photos, many in colour, Price about 60 Euros including postage and packaging. <akvozd57@gmail.com>

ISRAEL ATHLETICS ANNUAL 2020/21, 240 x 170mm, 58pp, illustrated, By David Eiger and Arit Cooks for the Israeli Athletic Association, Records, championship results, 2020 top 20s and all-time lists, with profiles of leading Israeli athletes, 8 euro or US $9 from David Eiger, 10 Ezra Hozsofer Str, Herzliya 46 371, Israel, Past editions from 1986 onwards also available at a reduced price.

David Eiger and Prof. Uri Goldbourt have compiled a comprehensive progression list of the **Israeli national athletic records** during the last 90 years. This booklet is in Hebrew, 185x150mm, 88 illustrated pages at postal cost. eigerdavid@gmail.com". Past editions of the Israeli Athletics Annual (in English) from 1986 onwards are also available at a reduced price.

ANUÁRIO ESTATÍSTICO 2020. Pdf 302 pages. The Portuguese Annual edited by António Fernandes for the Federação Portuguesa de Atletismo, which celebrates its centenary 1921-2021. Records, results, 2020 and deep all-time lists. www.fpatletismo.pt

DECATHLON EN SUDAMERICA – "El Mundo de los Super Atletas" by Eduardo Biscayart, Nestor Calixto and Luis Vinker. 285 pages digital production. In Spanish, this is a most comprehensive review of the decathlon in South America and by their athletes. Sections include:Details of Argentinian champions and all-time lists to 5000 with all 7000+ scores plus U20 lists; Detailed profiles of top men; Complete results of senior and U20s South American, Pan-American and Odesur Championships, Bolivar Games; South American all-time lists (210 to 6400 in seniors).; South Americans at Olympic Games, World Champs, World U20 & U18s. National records. Available on the consudatle website, where there is also a new book about Gerrado Bönnhof and Eduardo Balducci.

EL LIBRO DE LA PISTA COUBERTA – ARGETINA Y SUDAMÉRICA. 198-page pdf by Luis Vinker Includes records and all-time indoor lists for Argentina and South America.

Also interviews and profiles of Germán Lauro and Yulimar Rojas, results from the inaugural South American Indoor Championships 2020, medalists from all World Indoor Championships with all results by South American athletes. Contact Luis at Lvinker@agea.com.ar

Ed*uado Biscayart* has updated his **Ranking Sudamericano de Todos los Tiempos** to include 2020. Deep (up to c.200) performer and performance lists. Contact him at edubisca@yahoo.com

PRODIGIOS SOBRE LAS VALLAS (Prodigies of the Hurdles) by Luis Vinker. 293 pages in pdf format. This book (in Spanish) presents profiles of the best South American hurdlers of all-time with extensive statistics for them and with details of South American athletes at major championships and all-time lists for men's hurdles plus profiles of some of all-time greats.

NURMI – Athletics in the 19th Century, A Statistical Review Volume V 1801-1848 by Ari Törmä. A4 100 pages. Published by the Finnish Athletics Archive Association, the latest part of this remarkable work has unique lists by event for each year in this period. The author, who has done prodigious research in newspapers and magazines, has thus followed his volumes dealing with 1849-64, 1857-64 and 1881-88. He draws attention to the way he has presented the data, mostly drawn from digital newspaper archives as well as from many experts. He uses mathematical rules to convert performances at a variety of distances as well as different weights in the throwing events so as to produce lists for today's standard events. See www.aritorma.net. Order to mikko.nieminen@dic.fi

The **DGLD** – the **German** statistical group, Deutsche Gesellschaft für Leichtathletik-Dokumentation produces three annual bulletins plus an annual German lists book. The annual subscription is 55 euro. Contact Manfred Holzhausen, Bergheimer Str.33, 41515 Grevenbroich, Germany; manfred.holzhausen@gmx.de. Website: www.ladgld.de

Bulletin No. 85 dated 1 March 2020 had 128 A5 pages. The first half of this issue is occupied by the usual athlete profiles for German athletes celebrating 70th, 80th and 90th birthdays in 2020, together with details for athletes who died in 2019 (and some from 2018). These are followed by full results from FRG v France Junior Internationals 1955-8, key dates in German seniors (masters) Athletics, corrections to the details for Internationals from recent bulletins, and then updates to the volumes of the Biographical Handbook 1898-2005.

Bulletin No. 86; 284 A5 pages is entitled "Leichtathletik in Deutschland teil 2: 1910 bis 1918. There are comprehensive year lists with national and regional championship results for each year and statistical profiles of top athletes. Also an athlete index and chronology 1895-1918.

Bulletin No. 87 of 268 A5 pages is the "Jahrbuch der Leichtathletik 1951" with comprehensive reviews, results and year lists for East and West Germany in 1951. Special athlete features and 1951 top tens for Europe and the World.

Bulletin No. 88 1 November 2020, 238 A5 pages starts with five pages of statistical profiles of athletes born 125 (1896) or 100 (1921) years ago. Then a 54-page section listing all the German athletes who placed in the first three of the English AAA or WAAA Championships 1909-80. Dieter Noack contributes a 128-page 'Book 7' of German Championships results, first 8s at all events 2016-20. Finally there are further updates to the Biographical Handbooks 1898-2019.

DEUTSCHEN BESTENLISTE 2019. A4 180pp. The annual deep German ranking lists for the 2019 outdoor season – up to 100 deep with top performances – and 2018-19 indoors.

The Spanish statisticians' group continues to produce magnificent publications. Membership (4 bulletins per year) is 55 euros (€61 outside Europe) from AEEA secretary Ignacio Mansilla, C/Encinar del Rey, 18 - 28450 Collado Mediano, Madrid, Spain. email: imansilla@rfea.es

AEEA Bulletin No. 105, June 2020. has 352 A5 pages. After detailed profiles of Spanish athletes to have died recently, there is the 183-page Spanish Annual 2018-19 by José Luis Hernández, Ignacio Mansilla and Miguel Villaseñor – deep rankings for 2019 (and late 2018), chronology, trends and top performances. Then a 42-page listing of Progressive Spanish U16 records by José María García and finally 84 pages of All-time Ibero-American lists with about 40 performers per event.

No. 106, October 2020 A5 222 pages, has details of the career of one of the greatest Spanish athletes of all time: Mariano Haro. With text in Spanish and hundreds of photographs, some in colour, it starts with 17 pages relating his career, then a very detailed 77-page statistical section, cataloguing and analysing all his races with progressive Spanish all-time lists to set his times in perspective. Pages 105-206 are totally given over to photographs and at the end various leading Spanish athletes pay tribute.

The AEEEA also produced deep Spanish indoor all-time lists, **Pista Cubierta – Lista Española de todos los tiempo** to 21 Mar 2020. A pdf of 231 pages at https://www.rfea.es/ranking/pctt/pc_alltimeESP2020.pdf

Ránking de España de todos los tiempos al aire libre, For deep Spanish all-time lists to 31 Dec 2020 see the notice of publication on the RFEA web-site.

Spanish all-time indoor lists (386 pages) by Miguel Villasñor are at https://www.rfea.es/ranking/altt/alltimeESP_2020.pdf.

Cronolgogía de los Records y Mejores Marcas Españolas de Atletismo en Pista Cuberta. A most attractively produced book of 260 pages, 240mm x 170 mm. The AEEA have compiled and the Spanish Federation published details of the chronology of Spanish indoor records for all events, men and women, giving full details of each race and competition. There is also an index of all the record setters together with analysis such as tables of youngest and oldest and 'mosts'. Illustrated with hundreds of black and white and colour photographs, 20 euros. See 'Publicaciones' on <www.rfea.es>.

TRACK STATS, the NUTS' quarterly (each of 64 pages) edited by Bob Phillips continues contain the usual eclecticand fascinating mix of historical and statistical features. For instance **August 2020** included an investigation by Stuart Mazdon into the estimated place times in the 1920 Olympic 400m and 4x400m; a profile by Neil Shuttleworth of 1936 Olympic runner-up Ernie Harper; a review by Colm Murphy of a lengthy biography of Irish-American discus legend Martin Sheridan; European road 10k all-time list (164 men down to 28:30) compiled by Giuseppe Mappa; and reflections on his writing career by Peter Lovesey. For subscription details contact Liz Sissons at lizsissons9@gmail.com

HAMMER THROW BULLETIN No. 24 by Zdenek Procházka is a 124-page pdf. This features the men's hammer world lists for 2019 (1083 men to 54.74, 184 Juniors to 60.07, 157 Youths to 60.01 and Masters lists) and the deep performances show 1037 by 143 men to 68.87. There are updates to national records and all-time lists for senior, 6kg and 5kg weights, with an index of all the men over 60m. He includes the complete list of men to have exceeded 70m – now numbering 925 with 15 added to the list in 2019, withs annual progressions. He publishes three bulletins per year, price 20 euro or $30.

No. 25 is a 109-page pdf with men's hammer world lists for each year 1991 to 2000 with all performers over 60m plus the bests by men from other nations. tables of numbers for each country year by year and of annual progression 1948-2019 and an index of all the 60m men of the 1991-2000 era.

No. 26 is a 94-page pdf. This features a weight throw history – For 35lbs: 222 performances by 51 men over 77ft/23.47m with national bests and champions and world record progression. Also bests with other weights. Then follow men's hammer world lists for 2020 as for No. 24 above, national champions and an index of all the men over 70m.

Zdenek Procházka, Rychtáre Petríka 1629/1, 10200 Praha - Hostivar, Czech Republic. email: zpht@seznam.cz

NATIONAL CHAMPIONS 2020
and BIOGRAPHIES OF LEADING ATHLETES
By Peter Matthews

THIS SECTION incorporates biographical profiles of 769 of the world's top athletes this year – 390 men and 379 women, listed by nation. Also listed are national champions at standard events in 2020 for the leading countries prominent in athletics (many not held in 2020).

The athletes profiled have, as usual, changed quite considerably from the previous year. But the choice has been very difficult this year as so many missed the 2020 season due to the COVID-19 oubreak. As usual I have concentrated on those who are currently in the world's top 10-15 per event, those who have the best championship records and some up-and-coming athletes who I consider may make notable impact during the coming year.

Since this section was introduced in the 1985 Annual, biographies have been given for a total of 5286 different athletes (2977 men and 2309 women).

There are usually many newcomers to this section although lees so this year due to the reduction of competition – 85 in all, (46 men, 39 women), as well as 12 athletes (3 men, 9 women) reinstated from previous Annuals. The athletes who now have the longest continuous stretch herein are now Eliud Kipchoge on 19 years, with Valerie Adams, Tirunesh Dibaba, Allyson Felix and Justin Gatlin on 18 years. Athletes who have retired or who have been given drugs bans have generally been omitted.

No doubt some of those dropped from this compilation will also again make their presence felt; the keen reader can look up their credentials in previous Annuals, and, of course, basic details may be in the athletes' index at the end of this book.

Athletes included in these biographies are identified in the index at the end of this Annual by * for those profiled in this section and by ^ for those who were included in previous Annuals.

The biographical information includes:
a) Name, date and place of birth, height (in metres), weight (in kilograms).
b) Previous name(s) for married women; club or university; occupation.
c) Major championships record – all placings in such events as the Olympic Games, World Championships, European Championships, Commonwealth Games, World Cup and Continental Cup; leading placings in finals of the World Indoor Championships, European or World Junior/U20 or Youth/U18 Championships, European Under-23 Championships and other Continental Championships; and first three to six in European Indoors or World University Games.
European Cup/Team Champs and IAAF Grand Prix first three at each event or overall. World Athletics Final (WAF), Diamond League series (DL) and World Indoor Tour (WIT) winners.
d) National (outdoor) titles won or successes in other major events.
e) Records set: world, continental and national; indoor world records/bests (WIR/WIB).
f) Progression of best marks over the years at each athlete's main event(s).
g) Personal best performances at other events.
h) Other comments.
See Introduction to this Annual for lists of abbreviations used for events and championships.

Information given is as known at 2 April 2021 with some early indoor and outdoor events of 2021. I am most grateful to various ATFS members who have helped check these details. Additional information or corrections would be welcomed for next year's Annual.
Peter Matthews

ALBANIA
Governing body: Federata Shqiptare e Atletikes. **National Championships** first held in 1945 (women 1946).
Luiza GEGA b. 5 Nov 1988 Dibër 1.66m 56kg.
At 800m: WCh: '11- h. At 1500m: WCh: '13- sf, '15- h; EC: '12- sf, '14- h; WI: '14- 6; EI: '17- 5; WUG: '13- 2. At 3000mSt: OG: '16- h; WCh: '19- 9; EC: '16- 2, '18- 4. Won Balkan 1500m 2011, 2015, Med G 3000mSt 2018.
Albanian records: 800m (3) 2011-14, 1500m (4) 2013-15, 3000m (2) 2012-16, 5000m 2014, 10000m & Mar 2020, 2000mSt 2019, 3000mSt (7) 2011-19. Progress at 1500m, 3000mSt: 2006- 4:38.0, 2010- 4:23.20, 2011- 4:14.22, 9:54.72; 2012- 4:08.65mx/ 4:09.76. 2013- 4:05.11, 2014- 4:03.12, 2015- 4:02.63, 2016- 4:06.89i, 9:28.52; 2017- 4:06.66i/4:09.76, 9:26.05; 2018- 4:10.36i, 9:22.00; 2019- 4:09.58i, 9:19.93; 2020- 4:13.06i. pbs: 800m 2:01.31 '14, 3000m 8:44.46i '20, 8:53.78 '16; 5000m 15:46.89 '14, 10000m 32:31.69 '20, Mar 2:35:34 '20, 2000mSt 6:00.07 '19.

ALGERIA
Governing body: Fédération Algerienne d'Athlétisme. Founded 1963.
National Champions 2020: Men: HMar: Maamer Bengriba 65:31. **Women**: HMar: Riham Senani 74:33.
Abdelmalik LAHOULOU b. 7 May 1992 Jijel 1.80m 70kg.
At 400mh: OG: '16- sf; WCh: '15/17- sf; 19- 8; WJ: '10- h; WY: '09- h; AfG: '15- 1/3R, '19- 1; AfCh: '14- h, '18- 1; Af-J: '11- 1; WUG: '15- 2, '17- 3; CCp: '18- 5. Won W.Mil 2015, Arab 2019, ALG 2013-19.
Six Algerian 400mh records 2015-19.
Progress at 400mh: 2010- 53.00, 2011- 51.68, 2013- 50.71, 2014- 50.15, 2015- 48.67, 2016- 48.62, 2017- 49.05, 2018- 48.57; 2019- 48.39; pbs: 200m 22.13 '19, 400m 46.75 '18, 300mh 35.52 '17.
Taoufik MAKHLOUFI b. 29 Apr 1988 Souk Ahras 1.81m 66kg.
At (800m)/1500m: OG: '12- h/1, '16- 2/2; WCh: '09/11- sf, '15- 4, '19- 2; AfG: '11- 1/3, '15- (2); AfCh: '10- h, '12- (1), '14- (3).
Algerian records 800m 2016, 1000m 2015.
Progress at 800m, 1500m: 2008- 3:43.4, 2009- 1:49.40, 3:34.34; 2010- 1:48.39, 3:32.94; 2011- 1:46.32, 3:34.4; 2012- 1:43.71, 3:30.80; 2013- 3:36.30, 2014- 1:43.53, 3:30.40; 2015- 1:44.24, 3:28.75; 2016- 1:42.61, 3:31.35; 2019- 1:45.33, 3:31.38. pbs: 600m 1:16.5+ '16, 1000m 2:13.08 '15, 1M 3:52.16 '14.

ARGENTINA
Governing body: Confederación Argentina de Atletismo (CADA). Founded 1954 (original governing body founded 1919). **National Championships** first held in 1920 (men), 1939 (women).

2020 Champions: Men: 100m: Franco Florio 10.24, 200m: Daniel Londero 21.70, 400m: Elián Larregina 47.67, 800m: Julián Gaviola 1:57.88, 1500m: Diego Lacamoire 3:46.78, 5000m: Bernardo Maldonadeo 14:16.38, 10000m/3000mSt: Marcos Molina 28:59.12/9:05.27, HMar: Miguel Ángel Bárzola 65:36, 110mh: Renzo Cremaschi 15.10, 400mh: Guillermo Ruggeri 52.20, HJ: Carlos Layoy 2.16, PV: Germán Chiaraviglio 5.50, LJ: Luciano Ferrari 7.53w, TJ: Maximiliano Díaz 16.44w, SP/DT: Nazareno Sasia 19.67/53.48, HT: Joaquín Gómez 70.92, JT: Gustavo Osorio 63.43, Dec: Ignacio Fontana 5934, 20000mW: Juan Manuel Cano 1:29:40.2. **Women**: 100m/200m: Florencia Lamboglia 11.91/24.77, 400m/800m: Martina Escudero 55.91/2:09.37, 1500m: Mariana Borelli 4:21.82, 5000m: Marcela Cristina Gómez 16:14.91, 10000m: Chiara Mainett 35:12.96, 3000mSt: Carolina Lozano 10:11.54, 100mh: M.Florencia Lamboglia 14.88, HJ: Celina Harte 1.65, PV: Luciana Gómez Iriondo 3.85, LJ: Andrea Ubiedo 6.00, TJ: Silvina Ocampos 12.80w, SP/DT: Ailén Armada 15.31/51.35, HT: Jennifer Dahlgren 62.76, JT: Yohana Arias 47.14, Hep: Mariam Buenanueva 4194, 20000mW: Sofía Kloster 1:52:52.4.

AUSTRALIA
Governing body: Athletics Australia. Fd 1897.
National Championships first held in 1893 (men) (Australasian until 1927), 1930 (women).
2020 Champions: Men: 5000m: Stewart McSweyn 13:37.77, 20kW: Dane Bird-Smith 1:23:01. **Women**: 5000m: Jessica Hull 15:06.12. 20kW: Jemima Montag 1:33:15.
Dane BIRD-SMITH b. 15 Jul 1992 Kippa-Ring 1.78m 66kg. Racewalking Queensland. University of Queensland.
At 20kW: OG: '16- 3; WCh: '13-15-17-19: 10/8/6/15; CG: '18- 1; WCp: '14- 13, '16- 4; WUG: '15- 1; OCE Champion 2014, 2016-17, 2019; At 10000mW: WJ: '10- 5; WY: '09- 8. Won AUS 5000mW 2013, 10000mW 2014-17, 2019; 20kW 2013-14, 2017-19. OCE 5000m walk record 2016.
Progress at 20kW: 2011- 1:26:38, 2012- 1:23:15, 2013- 1:22:03, 2014- 1:20:27, 2015- 1:20:05, 2016- 1:19:37, 2017- 1:19:28, 2018- 1:19:34, 2019- 1:20:52, 2020- 1:23:01. pbs: 3000mW 10:56.23 '14, 5000mW 18:38.97 '16, 10000mW 38:34.23 '17.
Matthew DENNY b. 2 Jun 1996 Toowoomba, Queensland 1.95m 115kg.
At DT (HT): OG: '16- dnq 19; WCh: '19- 6; CG: '18- 4 (2); WJ: '14- 4 (dnq 23); WY: '13- 1 (3); CCp: '18- 2; WUG: '15- 2, '19- 1. Won AUS DT 2016, 2018-19, HT 2015-18.
Two Oceania junior discus records 2015.
Progress at DT: 2012- 51.77, 2013- 56.91, 2014- 59.04, 2015- 62.58, 2016- 65.37, 2017- 63.15, 2018- 64.67, 2019- 65.43, 2020- 65.47. pbs: SP 16.63 '15, HT 74.88 '18.

Cedric DUBLER b. 13 Jan 1995 Brisbane 1.90m 82kg.
At Dec: OG: '16- 14; WCh: '17- 18, '19- 11; CG: '18- 3; WJ: '12- 4, '14- 2. Won AUS 2016-18, 2020.
Progress at Dec: 2015- 7197, 2016- 8114, 2017- 7779, 2018- 8229, 2019- 8185, 2020- 8367. pbs: 100m 10.63 '18, 200m 21.71 '15, 400m 47.84 '20, 1500m 4:29.69 '19, 110mh 13.86 '19, HJ 2.15 '16, PV 5.20 '18, LJ 7.74 '14, 7/7.90w '21; SP 13.24 '20, DT 44.30 19, JT 62.48 '20.

Oliver HOARE b. 29 Jan 1997 Caringbah, Sudney 1.88m 73kg. Was at University of Wisconsin, USA.
At 1500m: won NCAA 1500m 2018.
Oceania indoor 1500m record 2012.
Progress at 1500m: 2015- 3:52.74, 2016- 3:46.69, 2017- 3:43.48, 2018- 3:37.84, 2019- 3:37.20, 2020- 3:34.53, 2021- 3:32.35i. pbs: 800m 1:49.96i '20, 1000m 2:23.84 '20, 1M 3:53.35 '20, 3000m 7:48.81i '19, 5000m 13:22.16 '21.

Stewart McSWEYN b. 1 Jun 1995 Launceston, Tasmania 1.88m 68kg. Melbourne TC. Was at La Trobe University & University of Southern Queensland.
At 1500m/5000m: WCh: '19- sf/12. At 5000m/10000m: CG: '18- 5/11. At 3000mSt: WCh: '17- h. 3000m: CCp: '18- 4. Won AUS 5000m 2020, 10000m 2017-19. Oceania records 10000m 2019, 3000m 2020; AUS 1500m 2020
Progress at 1500m, 5000m, 10000m: 2013- 14:57.95, 2014- 14:34.60, 2015- 13:55.73, 2016- 13:41.74, 28:29.65; 2017- 3:41.31, 13:19.98, 28:37.28; 2018- 3:34.32, 13:05.23, 27:50.89; 2019- 3:31.81, 13:05.63, 27:23.80; 2020- 3:30.51, 13:09.83; 2021- 13:05.87. pbs: 1M 3:50.61 '20, 2000m 4:59.47+ '20, 3000m 7:28.02 '20, 2M 8:16.28 '19, 3000mSt 8:34.25 '17.

Kurtis MARSCHALL b. 25 Apr 1997 North Adelaide 1.88m 78kg. Western District, Adelaide. Student at the University of South Australia.
At PV: OG: '16- dnq 15; WCh: '17- 7; CG: '18- 1; WJ: '14- dnq 20=, '16- 2; WI: '18- 4. Won AUS 2016-18.
Progress at PV: 2013- 4.90, 2014- 5.35, 2015- 5.42, 2016- 5.70, 2017- 5.73, 2018- 5.86i/5.80, 2019- 5.87i/5.81, 2020- 5.80, 2021- 5.80.

Ashley MOLONEY b. 13 Mar 2000 Brisbane 1.87m 79kg. Jimboomba.
At Dec: WJ: '18- 1. OCE champon 2019.
Oceania decathlon record 2020.
Progress at Dec: 2017- 7438, 2018- (8190J), 2019- 8103, 2020- 8492. pbs: 100m 10.36 '20, 200m 21.62 '20, 400m 45.82 '20, 1500m 4:42.65 '20, 110mh 14.09 '21, HJ 2.11 '20, PV 5.00 '19, LJ 7.67 '20, SP 13.69 '19, DT 43.93 20, JT 57.77 '20.
In 2018 he set pbs in eight of the ten events to win the world U20 title and in 2020 he set pbs in 7/10 to take the Oceania record, adding 389 points to his pb. This included a brilliant 45.82,

the third best 400m ever in a decathlon.

Brandon STARC b. 24 Nov 1993 Baulkham Hills, New South Wales 1.88m 73kg. Parramatta.
At HJ: OG: '16- 15; WCh: '13- dnq 25, '15- 12, '19- 6; CG: '18- 1; WJ: '12- 6; YOG: '10- 2; CCp: '18- 2. AUS champion 2013, 2015, 2018; DL 2018. Equalled Oceania high jump record 2018.
Progress at HJ: 2009- 1.96, 2010- 2.19, 2011- 2.20, 2012- 2.18, 2013- 2.28, 2014- 2.25, 2015- 2.31, 2016- 2.29, 2017- 2.25, 2018- 2.36, 2019- 2.30, 2020- 2.30.
Brother of Australian cricketer Mitchell Starc.

Women

Kelsey BARBER b. 21 Sep 1991 East London, South Africa 1.75m 70kg. née Kelsey-Lee Roberts. South Canberra Tuggeranong.
At JT: OG: '16- dnq 28; WCh: '15- dnq 20, '17- 10, '19- 1; CG: '14- 3, '18- 2; CCp: '18- 5; AUS champion 2017, 2019; OCE 2019.
Progress at JT: 2009- 46.10, 2010- 49.29, 2011- 52.01, 2013- 58.58, 2014- 63.92, 2015- 63.78, 2016- 59.02, 2017- 64.53, 2018- 64.57, 2019- 67.70.

Linden HALL b. 29 Jun 1991 Sunbury, Victoria 1.67m 51kg. Essendon.
At 1500m: OG: '16- sf; WCh: '17- h, 19- sf; CG: '18- 4; CCp: '18- 5; won AUS 2018/
Oceania 1000m & 1500m records 2021. AUS records 1500m & 1M 2018.
Progress at 1500m: 2006- 4:27.56, 2007- 4:29.86, 2008- 4:34.38, 2009- 4:29.94, 2010- 4:23.41, 2011- 4:23.37, 2012- 4:22.84, 2013- 4:15.51, 2014- 4:16.42, 2015- 4:10.41, 2016- 4:01.78, 2017- 4:04.37, 2018- 4:00.64, 2019- 4:04.22, 15:00.32; 2020- 4:05.16, 2021- 3:59.67. pbs: 800m 1:59.22 '21, 1000m 2:35.90 '21, 1M 4:21.40 '18, 3000m 8:51.20 '20, 5000m 15:18.77.

Jessica HULL b. 22 Oct 1996 Albion Park, NSW 1.67m 50kg. Bankstown, was at University of Oregon, USA.
At 1500m: WCh: '19- sf. At 3000m: WJ: '14- 7. won AUS 5000m 2020, NCAA 1500m 2018, indoor 3000m 2019.
Oceania records 1500m (indoors & out) & 5000m, AUS 1000m 2020.
Progress at 1500m, 5000m: 2012- 4:28.11, 2013- 4:27.60, 2014- 4:20.66, 2015- 4:20.49, 2017- 4:13.48, 16:29.14; 2018- 4:08.75, 16:34.96; 2019- 4:01.80, 15:00.32; 2020- 4:00.42, 14:43.80. pbs: 800m 2:03.78 '19, 1M 4:24.93 '19, 2000m 5:40.5+ '20, 3000m 8:36.03 '20.

Nicola McDERMOTT b. 28 Dec 1996 Tascott, NSW 1.86m 63kg. Biochemistry graduate of University of Sydney.
At HJ: WCh: 17/19; dnq- nh/15; CG: '18- 3; WJ: '14- dnq 16=; CCp: '18- 5. Won AUS 2019.
Progress at HJ: 2010- 1.73, 2011- 1.76, 2012- 1.78, 2013- 1.83, 2014- 1.86, 2015- 1.88, 2016- 1.88, 2017- 1.90, 2018- 1.91, 2019- 1.96, 2020- 1.98, 2021- 1.96.

Kathryn MITCHELL b. 10 Jul 1982 Hamilton, Victoria 1.68m 72kg. Eureka AC.

AUSTRALIA – AUSTRIA

At JT: OG: '12- 9, '16- 6; WCh: '13- 5, '15/17- dnq 17/25; CG: '06-10-14-18: 6/5/4/1; AUS champion 2008, 2018.. Three Oceania javelin records 2018. Progress at JT: 1999- 43.17, 2000- 51.44, 2001- 54.98, 2002- 54.72, 2003- 57.11, 2004- 48.10, 2005- 54.87, 2006- 58.81, 2007- 58.61, 2008- 58.77, 2010- 59.68, 2011- 59.47, 2012- 64.34, 2013- 63.77, 2014- 66.10, 2015- 63.70, 2016- 64.37, 2017- 66.12, 2018- 68.92, 2019- 62.78, 2020- 59.82.

Eleanor PATTERSON b. 22 May 1996 Leongatha, Victoria 1.82m 66kg. South Coast Athletics.
At HJ: OG: '16- dnq 22=; WCh: '15- 8; CG: '14- 1; WY: '13- 1. Won AUS 2014-15, 2017.
High jump records: World youth and Oceania junior 2013, Australian & Oceania 2020.
Progress at HJ: 2010- 1.73, 2011- 1.82, 2012- 1.87, 2013- 1.96, 2014- 1.94, 2015- 1.96, 2016- 1.93, 2017- 1.90, 2018- 1.88, 2019- 1.90, 2020- 1.99.

Dani STEVENS b. 26 May 1988 Fairfield, Sydney 1.82m 82kg. née Samuels. Westfields, University of Western Sydney.
At DT/(SP): OG: '08- 8, '12- 11, '16- 4; WCh: '07-09-11-13-15-17: dnq 13/1/10/10/6/2; CG: '06-3/12, '14- 1, '18- 1; WJ: '06- 1/7; WY: '05- 1/3; WCp: '06- 6; WUG: '07- 2, '09- 1; CCp: '10- 14-18: 4/2/4. AUS champion SP 2006-07, 2009, 2012; DT 2005-12, 2014-15, 2017-18.
Commonwealth & Oceania discus record 2017.
Progress at DT: 2001- 39.17, 2002- 45.52, 2003- 47.29, 2004- 52.21, 2005- 58.52, 2006- 60.63, 2007- 60.47, 2008- 62.95, 2009- 65.44, 2010- 65.84, 2011- 62.33, 2012- 63.97, 2013- 64.46, 2014- 67.99, 2015- 66.21, 2016- 67.77, 2017- 69.64, 2018- 68.26, 2019- 65.93, 2021- 63.36. pbs: SP 17.05 '14, HT 45.39 '05.
Sisters Jamie and Casey played basketball for Australia. Married Joe Stevens (SP: pb 17.34 '88; 11 WJ '06).

Brooke STRATTON b. 12 Jul 1993 Box Hill, Melbourne 1.68m 58kg. Nunawading. Was at Deakin University, Melbourne.
At LJ: OG: '16- 7; WCh: '15- dnq 14, '17- 7, '19- 10; CG: '18- 2; WJ: '10- 6, '12- 7; WY: '09- 10; CCp: '18- 3; WI: '16- 5. AUS champion 2014, 2018. Oceania long jump record 2016.
Progress at LJ: 2004- 5.38, 2005- 5.40, 2006- 5.52, 2007- 5.90, 2008- 6.06, 2009- 6.13, 2010- 6.30, 2011- 6.60, 2012- 6.56, 2013- 6.53, 2014- 6.70, 2015- 6.73, 2016- 7.05, 2017- 6.79, 2018- 6.88, 2019- 6.74, 2020- 6.67/6.78w. Pbs: 100m 11.98 '13, 11.91w '18; 200m 24.79 '16, 100mh 14.18 '10, TJ 13.34 '12.

AUSTRIA

Governing body: Österreichischer Leichtathletik Verband (OLV). Founded 1902.
National Championships first held in 1911 (men), 1918 (women). **2020 Champions: Men**: 100m: Markus Fuchs 10.45, 200m: Samuel Reindl 21.68, 400m: Markus Kornfeld 48.73, 800m/1500m: Andreas Vojta 1:52.43/3:48.25, 5000m: Peter Herzog 13:54.25, 10000m: Timon Theuer 29:53.78, HMar: Manuel Innerhofer 65:06, Mar: Isaac Kosgei KEN 2:26:35, 3000mSt: Jürgen Aigner 9:25.59, 110mh: Lorenz Urspringer 14.38, 400mh: Leo Köhldorfer 51.95, HJ: Andreas Steinmetz 2.17, PV: Herbert Winkler 4.75, LJ: Samuel Szihn 7.24, TJ: Philipp Kronsteiner 16.37, SP: Will Dibo 14.96, DT: Lukas Weisshaidinger 64.81, HT: Marco Cozzoli 62.27, JT: Matthias Kaserer 66.99, Dec: Stanislav Vala 6361, 20kW/50kW: Roman Brzekowsky 1:50:44/5:13:32. **Women**: 100m: Alexandra Toth 11.53, 200m: Julia Schwarzinger 23.78, 400m: Susanne Walli 54.37, 800m: Carina Schrempf 2:13.43, 1500m: Lotte Seiler 4:34.69, 5000m: Julia Hauser 16:16.67, 10000m/HMar: Julia Mayer 34:04.77/76:03, Mar: Eva Wutti 2:30:43, 3000mSt: Jasmin Zweimüller 11:00.94, 100mh: Beate Schrott 13.27, 400mh: Lena Pressler 59.71, HJ: Ekaterina Krasovskiy 1.77, PV: Agnes Hodi 3.80, LJ: Ivona Dadic 6.09, TJ: Michaela Egger 12.46w, SP: Verena Preiner 15.07, DT: Djeneba Touré 52.70, HT: Bettina Weber 57.68, JT: Patricia Madl 49.31, Hep: Ivona Dacic 6419, 20kW: Barbara Hollinger 2:06:31.

Lukas WEISSHAIDINGER b. 20 Feb 1992 Schärding 1.96m 136kg. ÖTB OÖ Leichtathletik.
At DT (SP): OG: '16- 6; WCh: '15- dnq 20, '17- 9, '19- 3; EC: '18- 3; WJ: '10- dnq 16 (6); WY: '09-dnq 36 (4); EU23: '13- 7; EJ '11- 1 (5 SP). Won AUT SP 2012-15, DT 2015-16, 2018-20.
Three Austrian discus records 2015-18.
Progress at DT: 2008- 43.47, 2009- 45.98, 2010- 54.21, 2011- 54.85, 2012- 58.00, 2013- 59.13, 2014- 60.68, 2015- 67.24, 2016- 66.00, 2017- 66.52, 2018- 68.98, 2019- 68.14, 2020- 68.63. pb SP 18.90 '13.

Women

Ivona DADIC b. 29 Dec 1993 Weis 1.79m 65kg. PSV Hornbach Weiss.
At Hep: OG: '12- 23, '16- 21; W Ch: '17- 6, '19- dnf; EC: '16- 3, '18- 4; WJ: '12- dnf; WY: '09- 10; EU23: '13- 5, '15- 3; EJ: '11- 10. At Pen: WI: '18- 2; EI: '17-19-21: 2/4/4. Won AUT LJ 2018, 2020; SP 2017, Hep 2012.
7 Austrian heptathlon records 2012-18.
Progress at Hep: 2011- 5455, 2012- 5959, 2013- 5874, 2015- 6151, 2016- 6408, 2017- 6417, 2018- 6552, 2019- 6461, 2020- 6419. pbs: 60m 7.78i '12, 100m 11.74 '20, 200m 23.61 '18, 300m 38.68 '20, 400m 56.27 '11, 800m 2:10.67 '12, 60mh 8.32i '18, 100mh 13.36 '19, HJ 1.87i/1.83 '17, LJ 6.49 '16, SP 14.97 '20, JT 52.48 '15, Pen 4767i '17.
Improved heptathlon pb by 212 points for 3rd EC '16 and pentathlon best by 247 for 2nd EI '17. 6235 points 1-hour heptathlon 2020.

Verena PREINER b. 1 Feb 1995 Ebensee 1.77m 64kg. UNION Ebensee.
At Hep: W Ch: '17-dnf, '19- 3; EC: '16- 7, '18- 8; WJ: '14- 9; WY: '11- 23; EU23: '15- 4, '17- 2; WUG: '17- 1; At Pen: EI: '17- 6, '19- 6. Won AUT 400mh 2016, SP 2020, Hep 2014-16.

AUSTRIA – AZERBAIJAN – BAHAMAS – BAHRAIN 73

Austrian heptathlon record 2019.
Progress at Hep: 2013- 5095, 2014- 5530, 2015- 5840, 2016- 6050, 2017- 6232, 2018- 6337, 2019- 6591. pbs: 60m 7.75i '18, 100m 12.14 '18, 200m 23.96 '19, 300m 39.14 '20, 400m 55.76 '16, 800m 2:07.74 '19, 60mh 8.38i '19, 100mh 13.25 '19, 400mh 60.31 '16, HJ 1.80 '19, LJ 6.36 '19, SP 15.07 '20, DT 39.06 '14, JT 49.58 '19, Pen 4637i '19. Won WA CE Challenge 2019.

AZERBAIJAN

Governing body: Azerbaijan Athletics Association. Founded 1923, reorganised 1992.

Nazim BABAYEV b. 8 Oct 1997 Baku 1.85m 70kg.
At TJ: OG: '16- dnq 25; WCh: '17/19- dnq 14/19; EC: '16: dnq 23=, '18- 4; WJ: '16- dnq 15; EU23: '17- 1, '19- 2; EJ: '15- 1; YOG: '14- 3; WI: '16- 8; EI: '19- 1; WUG: '17- 1, '19- 1. Won Is.Sol 2017.
Progress at TJ: 2013- 15.53, 2014- 16.18, 2015- 17.04, 2016- 16.83, 2017- 17.18, 2018- 16.89, 2019- 17.29i/17.06, 2020- 17.15i. pbs: 60m 7.05i '17, LJ 7.49 '16.

Alexis COPELLO Sánchez b. 12 Aug 1985 Santiago de Cuba 1.85m 80kg. F/C: Barcelona.
At TJ: OG: '08- dnq 13, '12- 8; WCh: '09-11-17-19: 3/4/5/7; EC: '18- 2; WI: '12- 7, '18- 4; EI: '21- 2; PAmG: '11- 1; CAG: '06- 2; CCp: '10- 2. Won IbAm 2010, CAC 2009, Cuban 2009, 2011.
Progress at TJ: 2002- 15.38, 2003- 16.34, 2004- 16.90, 2005- 16.95/17.09w, 2006- 17.38, 2007- 16.87/17.15w, 2008- 17.50, 2009- 17.65/17.69w, 2010- 17.55, 2011- 17.68A/17.47, 2012- 17.17, 2014- 17.05, 2015- 17.15/17.24w, 2016- 16.99i/16.98, 2017- 17.16/17.17w, 2018- 17.24, 2019- 17.10, 2020- 16.92, 2021- 17.04i. pb LJ 7.35 '04.
Former Cuban, Azeri citizenship 26 Apr 2016, cleared to compete for them from 24 Apr 2017. Brother Alexander (b. 19 Feb 1978) Dec 7359 '02.

Women

Hanna SKYDAN b. 14 May 1992 Krasnyi Luch, UKR 1.83m 114kg.
At HT: OG: '12/16- dnq 14/13; WCh: '15- dnq 23, '17- 5, '19- 7; EC: '16- 3, '18- 5; WJ: '10- dnq 27; WY: '09- 12; EJ: 11- dnq; WUG: '15- 1; UKR champion 2012, Is.Sol 2017.
Eight AZE hammer records 2015-17.
Progress at HT: 2009- 56.90, 2010- 56.76, 2011- 67.56, 2012- 74.21, 2013- 68.44, 2014- 71.14, 2015- 72.31, 2016- 73.87, 2017- 75.29., 2018- 74.02, 2019- 73.32. pbs: SP 13.98 '17, DT 49.50 '15.
Competed for Ukraine to 2012, AZE citizenship 15 Jan 2015 and cleared to compete for them from 1 Jun 2015.

BAHAMAS

Governing body: Bahamas Association of Athletics Associations. Founded 1952.

Steven GARDINER b. 12 Sep 1995 Moore's Island 1.95m 82kg.
At 400m: OG: '16- sf/3R; WCh: '15-17-19: sf/2/1; WJ: '14- 6R (sf 200m); Won BAH 2015-17, 2019. CAC 400m record 2019, Bahamas records: 200m 2018, 300m (2) 2020, 400m (5) 2015-19.
Progress at 200m, 400m: 2013- 47.78, 2014- 20.66, 2015- 20.69/20.51w, 44.27; 2016- 20.63/20.53w, 44.46; 2017- 43.89; 2018- 19.75, 43.87; 2019- 20.04, 43.48; 2020- 19.96, 2021- 20.24. pbs: 100m 10.35 '20, 150m 15.07 '20, 300m 31.83 '20, St 31.28 '17.

Jamal WILSON b. 1 Sep 1988 Nassau 1.88m 68kg. Was at University of Texas, USA.
At HJ: OG: '16- dnq 25; WJ: '06- dnq 25; WY: '05- dnq; CG: '14- dnq 14=, '18- 2; PAm: '19- nh; PAm-J: '07- 1. BAH champion 2017.
Progress at HJ: 2005- 2.08, 2006- 2.11, 2007- 2.11m 2008- 2.23A, 2009- 2.10, 2010- 2.16, 2011- 2.24Ai/2.21, 2012- 2.15i/2.10, 2013- 2.28, 2014- 2.26A, 2015- 2.22, 2016- 2.31i/2.30, 2017- 2.27, 2018- 2.31i/2.30, 2019- 2.25, 2020- 2.33i/2.30. pb TJ 16.23 '11.

Women

Shaunae MILLER-UIBO b. 15 Apr 1994 Nassau 1.85m 69kg. University of Georgia, USA.
At (200m)/400m: OG: '16- ht, '16- 1; WCh: '13- (4), '15- 2, '17- 3/4, '19- 2; CG: '14- 6, '18- (1); WJ: '10- 1, '12- 4; WY: '11- 1; CCp: '18- (1)/1R/1mxR; WI: '14- 3. Won DL 200m 2017-19, 400m 2017, BAH 200m 2017, 400m 2010-11, 2014-16, 2019; HJ 2018 NCAA indoor 400m 2013.
Records: Tied world indoor 300m 2018, world best 150m straight 2018, 300m 2019, Commonwealth & CAC 400m 2019, BAH 200m (5) 2015-19, 400m 2018 & 2019. CAC indoor 400m 2021, junior 200m 2013, 400m 2013.
Progress at 200m, 400m: 2009- 55.52, 2010- 24.09, 52.45; 2011- 23.70, 51.84; 2012- 22.70, 51.25; 2013- 22.45/22.41w, 50.70; 2014- 22.87, 51.63i/51.86; 2015- 22.14, 49.67; 2016- 22.05, 49.44; 2017- 21.88, 49.46; 2018- 22.06, 48.97; 2019- 21.74, 48.37; 2020- 21.98, 50.52; 2021- 50.21i. Pbs: 60m 7.59i '13, 100m 10.98 '20, 150m 16.23 St '18, 300m 34.41 '19, HJ 1.70 '18, LJ 6.29 '17, SP 11.48 '18.
Married Estonian decathlete Maicel Uibo (qv) on 4 Feb 2017. Great-uncle Leslie Miller set BAH 400m record of 46.99 at 1968 Olympics.

BAHRAIN

Governing body: Bahrain Athletics Association. Founded 1974.

Abraham Naibei **CHEROBEN** b. 11 Oct 1992 1.76m 60kg.
At 10000m: OG: '16- 10; WCh: 17- 12; AsiG: '18- 1; won Is.Sol 2017. At HMar: WCh: '18- 2.
BRN records 10000m 2017, HMar (61:00) 2016.
Progress at 10000m, HMar: 2012- 63:53, 2013- 60:38, 2014- 58:48, 2015- 59:10, 2016- 27:31.86, 60:35; 2017- 27:11.08, 58:40; 2018- 60:22, 2019- 59:42. Road pbs: 15k 41:55 '14, 20k 55:50 '14, 25k 1:11:47 '14. Transferred from Kenya to Bahrain on 19 Aug 2015, with eligibility to compete for them from 1 Aug 2016.

BAHRAIN – BELARUS

Birhanu YEMATAW Balew b. 27 Feb 1996 Ethiopia 1.67m 54kg.
At 5000m: OG: '16- 9; WCh: '17- 12, '19- 9; AsiG: '18- 1; AsiC: '19- 1; Won Arab & W.Mil 2019. At 3000m: CCp: '18- fa; WI: '18- 10; World CC: '19- 19.
Asian indoor records 2000m 2019, 3000m 7:38.67 & 7:34.58 2020.
Progress at 5000m: 2015- 13:39.65, 2016- 13:09.26, 2017- 13:09.93, 2018- 13:01.09, 2019- 12:56.26. Pbs: 2000m 5:00.34i '19, 3000m 7:34.26 '18, 2M 8:20.56 '19, 10000m 31:16.51 '17, Road: 10k 29:01 '18, 15k 43:19 '16, HMar 61:45 '17.
BRN citizen 8 Oct 2014, eligible 8 Oct 2015.

Women

Mimi BELETE b. 9 Jun 1988 Addis Ababa, Ethiopia 1.69m 55kg.
At 1500m/(5000m): OG: '12- sf, '16- (h); WCh: '09-11-13-15: sf/7/sf/(11); AsiG: '10- 3/1, '14- 2/2; AsiC: '09- 6, '13- 2; CCp: '10- 4, '14- 6 (5 3000m); Asi CC: '09-14-16: 2/3/3. won W.Asian 2010, Arab 5000m 2015. Asian 2M record 2014.
Progress at 1500m, 5000m: 2007- 4:13.55, 2008- 4:06.84, 15:44.20; 2009- 4:04.36, 2010- 4:00.25, 15:15.59; 2011- 4:03.13, 2012- 4:01.72, 2013- 4:03.63, 2014- 4:00.08, 15:00.87; 2015- 4:05.37, 14:54.71; 2016- 4:12.84, 15:29.72; 2017- 15:26.49. At Mar: 2018- 2:22:29, 2019- 2:21:22, 2020- 2:22:40. pbs: 800m 2:04.63 '10, 2000m 5:38.0+ '14, 3000m 8:30.00 '14, 2M 9:13.85 '14, 10000m 32:46.74 '16, 10MRd 53:33 '17, HMar 68:16 '19.
From Ethiopia, has lived in Belgium from 2005; BRN from 2009. Made marathon debut with 3rd in Hamburg, then 1st in Toronto 2018. Younger sister Almensch Belete BEL pbs 1500m 4:06.87 '10, 5000m 15:03.63 '11; 5 EI 3000m 2013.

Rose CHELIMO b. 12 Jul 1989 Kenya 1.62m 45kg.
At Mar: OG: '16- 8; WCh: 17- 1, '19- 2; AsiG: 18- 1. World CC: '17- 9. At HMar: WCh: '18- 14.
Progress at HMar, Mar: 2010- 72:48, 2011- 69:45, 2012- 70:50, 2014- 68:40, 2015- 68:22 , 2016- 68:08, 2:24:14; 2017- 68:37, 2:22:51; 2018- 70:07, 2:26:03; 2019- 2:30:35. Pbs: 10000m 31:37.81 '17, Road: 15k 49:08 '17, 20k 64:47 '15.
Transferred from Kenya to Bahrain on 19 Aug 2015, eligible to compete for them from 1 Aug 2016. Won in Seoul on marathon debut in 2016, 2nd Boston 2017.

Salwa Eid NASER (Ebelechukwu Agbapuonwu) b. 23 May 1998 Anambra, Nigeria 1.67m 50kg.
At 400m: OG: '16- sf; WCh: '17- 2, '19- 1/3MxR; WY: '15- 1; Yth OG: '14- 2; AsiG: '18- 1 (1 4x400), 2 4x400); AsiC: '19- 1 (1 200m, 4x100, Mx 4x400, 3 4x400); CCp: '18- 1. Won Arab Jnr 200m & 400m 2014, Asi-Y 2015, W.MilG 2015 & 2019, Gulf & Isl Sol 2017, W.Asian 2018, Arab 2019 (& 200m), DL 2018-19.
400m records: 3 Asian 2018-19 (2 at Mx4x400m), 8 Bahrain 2017-19 (& two 200m 2019).

Progress at 400m: 2014- 52.74, 2015- 51.39, 2016- 50.88, 2017- 49.88, 2018- 49.08, 2019- 48.14. pbs: 100m 11.24 '19, 200m 22.51 '19.
Improved from 49.08 to 48.14 (3rd world all-time) to win 2019 World gold. Nigerian parents; her mother married a Bahraini father c. 2013, moving to Bahrain when Naser was 15. Provisional 2-year suspension for missing three drugs tests, but charges cleared when ruled that these were not within 12 months.

Winfred Mutile **YAVI** b. 31 Dec 1999 Kenya 1.57m 48kg.
At 3000mSt: WCh: '17- 8, '19- 4; WJ: 18- 3; AsiG: '18- 1; AsiC: '19- 1 (1 5000m, 3 1500m); CCp: '18- 3. Won Arab 5000m & 3000mSt 2019, W.MilG 3000mSt 2019.
Asian 2000m steeple record 2019. World indoor 2000mSt best 2021.
Progress at 3000mSt: 2015- 10:21.4A, 2016- 10:07.2A, 2017- 9:22.67, 2018- 9:10.74, 2019- 9:05.68, 2020- 9:52.99A. pbs: 1500m 4:20.7A '17, 3000m 8:39.64i '20, 9:10.5A '16; 5000m 15:15.93 '19, 2000mSt 5:56.83 '19., no WJ: 5:45.09i '21
Switched from Kenya to acquire BRN citizenship on 19 Aug 2015, and able to compete for them from 19 Aug 2016.

BELARUS

Governing body: Belarus Athletic Federation. Founded 1991.
National Champions 2020: Men: 100m: Yuriy Zabolotniy 10.32, 200m: Sergey Pustadeyev 21.58, 400m: Aleksandr Vasilevskiy 46.48, 800m/1500m: Ilya Karnaukhov 1:48.79/3:44.06, 5000m/3000mSt: Vyacheslav Skudniy 14:09.01/ 8:42.98, 10000m: Sergey Kravchenya 29:20.86, 110mh: Vitaliy Parakhonko 13.72, 400mh: Igor Khovratovich 51.59, HJ: Maksim Nedosekov 2.29 PV: Vladislav Chemarmasovich 5.20, LJ: Vladislav Bulakov 8.10, TJ: Maksim Nesterenko 16.27, SP: Aleksey Nichipor 20.42, DT: Viktor Trus 56.71, HT: Pavel Boreyssha 76.23, JT: Aleksey Kotkovets 86.05, Dec: Vitaliy Zhuk 8202, 5000mW/10000m/20kW: Aleksandr Lyakhovich 18:53.19/39:41.07/1:24:26, 35kW: Dmitriy Dyubkin 2:41:07. Women: 100m/200m: Kristina Timanov-skaya 11.51/23.44, 400m: Alina Lushcheva 52.15, 800m/1500m: Darya Borisevich 2:04.15/ 4:28.45, 5000m: Yekaterina Korneyenko 15:51.39, 10000m: Nina Savina 33:17.53, 3000mSt: Tatyana Shabanova 10:19.76, 100mh: Elvira German 12.78, 400mh: Hanna Mikhaylova 57.75, HJ: Mariya Zhodzik 1.830, PV: Irina Zhuk 4.72, LJ: Anastasiya Mirochik-Ivanova 6.81 TJ: Irina Vaskovskaya 14.24, SP: Alyona Dubitskaya 19.14, DT: Svetlana Serova 52.60, HT: Alena Soboleva 69.61, JT: Tatyana Kolodovich 66.85, Hep: Diana Rabkova 5937, 5000mW/10000mW: Anna Terlyukevich 21:45.84/44:43.31, 20kW: Viktoriya Roshchupkina 1:34:42, 35kW: Nadezhda Dorozhuk 3:05:39.

Pavel BOREYSHA b. 16 Feb 1991 Grodno 1.93m 120kg. Grodno State University.
At HT: OG: '16- dnq 13; WCh: '15- dnq 25, '17- 9; EC: '14-16-18: 10/dnq 14/4; WJ: '10- 6; EU23: '11- dnq 17; WUG: '15- 2, '17- 2; ET: '17- 2. Won BLR 2014, 2020.
Progress at HT: 2011- 69.62, 2012- 72.25, 2013- 75.62, 2014- 76.86, 2015- 77.03, 2016- 78.60, 2017- 78.04, 2018- 77.37, 2019- 75.62, 2020- 76.41.

Gleb DUDAREV b. 17 Oct 1996 Vitebsk 1.96m 109kg. University of Kansas, USA.
At WCh: '19- 8; EC: '18- dnq 18; EJ: '15- 9; WUG: '19- 4. Won BLR 2019.
Progress at HT: 2016- 72.86, 2017- 74.20, 2018- 78.04, 2019- 78.29. Pb Wt 24.82i '21 (BLR rec).
Mother (HT) and grandmother (DT) were BLR record hoders.

Maksim NEDOSEKOV b. 21 Jan 1998 Vitebsk 1.88m 70kg.
At HJ: WCh: '19- 4; EC: '18- 2; WJ: '16- 8; E23: '19- 1; EJ: '17- 1; CCp: '18- 3; WI: '18- 6; EI: '21- 1. Won BLR 2017, 2020.
Progress at HJ: 2015- 2.10, 2016- 2.20, 2017- 2.33, 2018- 2.33, 2019- 2.35, 2020- 2.33, 2021- 2.37i.

Women

Karyna DEMIDIK b. 10 Feb 1999 Baranavichy 1.81m 60kg. née Taranda.
At HJ: WCh: '19- 6; EC: '18- 12; WJ: '18- 1; E23: '19- 4; EJ: '17- 2. Won BLR 2017-19.
Belarus high jump record 2019.
Progress at HJ: 2015- 1.70, 2016- 1.78, 2017- 1.89, 2018- 1.92, 2019- 2.00.

Alyona DUBITSKAYA b. 25 Jan 1990 Grodno 1.82m 77k. née Hryshko. Grodnenskaya.
At SP: OG: '16- 8; WCh: '13- dnq 27, '15- 6, '17- dnq 14, '19- 6; EC: '14-16-18: 7/6/3; WJ: '08- 4; WY: '07- 1; EJ: '09- 1; WI: '16- 9, '18- 6; EI: '17-19-21: 7/4/4; ET: '15- 3, '17- 1. BLR champion 2009, 2014-15, 2018-20.
Progress at SP: 2007- 15.91, 2008- 16.55, 2009- 17.95, 2010- 18.12i/17.75, 2012- 16.63, 2013- 17.88, 2014- 19.03, 2015- 18.88, 2016- 18.78, 2017- 19.01, 2018- 19.21, 2019- 19.21, 2020- 19.27. pb DT 46.30 '14. 6-month drugs ban 2014-15.

Elvira GERMAN b. 9 Jan 1997 Pinsk 1.68m 54kg.
At 100mh: WCh: '17/19: sf; EC: '16- sf, '18- 1; WJ: '16- 1; EU23: '17- 2, '19- 1; EJ: '15- 1; CCp: '18- 4; WUG: '17- 2; Yth OG: '14- 2; won BLR 2017, 2019-20. At 60mh: EI: '19- 3.
European junior 100m hurdles record 2016.
Progress at 100mh: 2014- 13.50, 2015- 13.20/13.15w, 2016- 12.85, 2017- 12.96/12.95w, 2018- 12.64, 2019- 12.70, 2020- 12.73. pbs: 60m 7.57i '18, 200m 23.33 '20, 300m 38.99i '18, 50mh 7.18i '14, 60mh 7.97i '19.

Tatyana KHOLODOVICH b. 21 Jun 1991 Brest 1.81m 83kg.
At JT: OG: '16- 5; WCh: '15- dnq 21, '17- 6, '19- 6; EC: '14-16-18: 5/1/5; WJ: '08/10- dnq 16/21; EU23: '13- dnq; WUG: '15- 1; ET: '15- 2, '17- 2. BLR champion 2012-16, 2018-20, DL 2018.
Three Belarus javelin records 2014-16.
Progress at JT: 2007- 46.12, 2008- 53.51, 2009- 46.80, 2010- 51.17, 2011- 55.94, 2012- 59.15, 2013- 59.37, 2014- 63.61, 2015- 62.00, 2016- 66.34, 2017- 66.30, 2018- 67.47, 2019- 67.22, 2020- 67.17.

Hanna MALYSHIK b. 4 Feb 1994 Drachichyn 1.75m 90kg. née Zinchuk.
At HT: OG: '16- 7; WCh: '17- 10, '19- 10; EC: '16- dnq 26, '18- nt; WJ: '12- dnq; WY: '11- dnq 15, EJ: '13- 1; WUG: '17- 2; ET: '17- 1. Won EY Oly 2011, BLR 2016, 2018.
Progress at HT: 2009- 50.70, 2010- 57.38, 2011- 60.11, 2012- 63.41, 2013- 66.36, 2014- 67.53, 2015- 66.50, 2016- 72.78, 2017- 74.94, 2018- 76.26, 2019- 74.95, 2020- 75.45.

Anastasiya MIRONCHIK-IVANOVA b. 13 Apr 1989 Slutsk 1.71m 54kg. Minsk.
At LJ: OG: '12- dq7; WCh: '09-11-15-19: 10/3/9/5; EC: '10- 6, '18- 5; WJ: '08- 2; WY: '05- 8; EU23: '09- 2, '11- 6; WI: '12- 5; EI: '11-19-21: 6/2/4. BLR champion 2007, 2010-12, 2015, 2019.
Progress at LJ: 2004- 5.90, 2005- 6.10/6.13w, 2007- 6.03i/5.89, 2008- 6.71, 2009- 6.65/6.76w, 2010- 6.84, 2011- 6.85/6.92w, 2012- 7.08/7.22w, 2013- 6.60, 2015- 6.82, 2016- 6.84i, 2018- 6.77, 2019- 6.93i/6.76, 2020- 6.93. pb TJ 14.29 '11.
Son born June 2014. Disqualified after positive re-test of sample from 2012 Olympics.

Violetta SKVORTSOVA b. 15 Apr 1998 1.78m 58kg. Vitebsk
At TJ (LJ): EC: '18: dnq 21; WJ: '16- (dnq 14); WY: '15- (3); EU23: '19- 3; EJ: '17- 1 (12); EI: '21- 4.
Progress at TJ: 2015- 12.80, 2016- 13.45, 2017- 13.94/14.21w, 2018- 13.95, 2019- 13.79, 2020- 14.17, 2021- 14.39i. pb LJ 66.56i '20, 6.45 '15.

Alina TALAY b. 14 May 1989 Orsha, Vitebsk 1.64m 54kg.
At 100mh: OG: '12/16- sf; WCh: '13-15-17: sf/3/6; EC: '10-12-14-16-18: sf/1/5/2/dq (fell); WJ: '08- 4; EU23: '09- 3, '11- 1; WUG: '13- 2; ET: '11-15-17: 2/1/2; won W.MilG 2011, BLR 2009-10, 2013-17 (200m 2015). At 60mh: WI: '12- 3, '16- 6; EI: '11-13-15-17: 5/1/1/2.
Four BLR 100m hurdles records 2015-18.
Progress at 100mh: 2007- 14.38/14.01w, 2008- 13.31, 2009- 13.07, 2010- 12.87, 2011- 12.91, 2012- 12.71, 2013- 12.78, 2014- 12.89, 2015- 12.66, 2016- 12.63, 2017- 12.72, 2018- 12.41, 2019- 12.84. pbs: 60m 7.31i '15, 100m 11.48 '11, 200m 23.59 '11, 50mh 6.89i '11, 60mh 7.85i '15.

BELGIUM

Governing bodies: Ligue Royale Belge d'Athlétisme (KBAB/LRBA). Vlaamse Atletiekliga (VAL); Ligue Belge Francophone d'Athlétisme (LBFA). Original governing body founded 1889.
National Championships first held in 1889

(women 1921). **2020 Champions: Men**: 100m: Kobe Vleminckx 10.43, 200m: Julien Watrin 21.15, 400m: Christian Iguacel 46.80, 800m: Elliott Crestan 1:49.8, 1500m: Ismael Debjani 3:47.47, 5000m: Ward D'Hoore 14:08.92, 10000m: Valentin Poncelet 29:47.08, 3000mSt: Clement Deflandre 9:08.61, 110mh: Michael Obasuyi 13.82, 400mh: Tuur Bras 50.69, HJ: Thomas Carmoy 2,25, PV: Ben Broeders 5.60, LJ: Daniel Segers 7.89, TJ: Bjorn De Decker 14.67, SP/DT: Philip Milanov 16.65/60.16, HT: Remi Malengreaux 63.19, JT: Timothy Herman 77.53, Dec: Niels Pittomvils 7516, 20000mW: Peter Van Hove 1:56:09.7.
Women: 100m: Rani Rosius 11.39, 200m: Imke Vervaet 23.85; 400m: Camille Laus 53.13, 800m: Renée Eykens 2:03.90, 1500m: Elise Vanderelst 4:18.69, 5000m: Nina Lauwaert 16:31.36, 10000m: Hanna Verbruggen 33:30.67, 3000mSt: Eline Dalemans 10:05.02, 100mh: Anne Zagré 13.07w, 400mh: Paulien Couckuyt 56.14, HJ: Merel Naes 1.84, PV: Ellen Vekemans 4.20, LJ: Bo Brasseur 5.98, TJ: Elsa Loureiro 12.79, SP: Myrthe Van Der Borght 14.28, DT: Katelijne Lyssens 51.48, HT: Vanessa Sterckendries 67.62, JT: Cassandre Evans 44.24, Hep: Hanne Maudens 6167, 10000mW: Annelies Sarrazin 55:09.42.

Bashir ABDI b. 10 Feb 1989 Mogadishu, Somalia 1.68m 59kg. NN Running Team.
At 5000m: OG: '16- h; WCh: '17- h; EC: '12- 8, '14- 16; E23: '11- 15. At 10000m: OG: '16- 20; WCh: '13- 23, '15- dnf; EC: '12- 4, '14- 5, '18- 2; Eur CC: '12-13: 9/8.
World record 20,000m 2020, Belgian marathon records 2018 & 2019, 1 hour 2020.
Progress at 10000m, Mar: 2012- 28:18.50, 2013- 27:43.99, 2014- 27:36.40, 2015-27:47.55, 2016- 28:01.49, 2017- 28:15.58, 2018- 28:11.76, 2:10:46; 2019- 2:06:14, 2020- 2:04:49. Pbs: 1500m 3:36.55 '14, 3000m 7:40.44 '15, 5000m 13:04.91 '18, 15000m c.42:18 '20, 20000m 56:20.02 '20. 1 Hr 21,332m '20, Road: 10M 46:08 '18, 15k 42:29 '19, HMar 60:42dh '18, 25k 1:13:25 '20, 30k 1:28:28 '20. 2nd Tokyo marathon 2020. Came to Belgium in 2002.

Ben BROEDERS b. 21 Jun 1995 Leuven 1.78m 75kg. DC Leuven.
At PV: WCh: '19- 12; EC: '16- 4, '18- dnq nh; WJ: '14- dnq 20=; EU23: '15- 9, '17- 1; WUG: '19- 3; Won BEL 2019-20.
BEL pole vault records 2019 & 2020.
Progress at PV: 2013- 4.90, 2014- 5.15, 2015- 5.35, 2016- 5.61, 2017- 5.60, 2018- 5.65i/5.60, 2019- 5.76, 2020- 5.80.

Philip MILANOV b. 6 Jul 1991 Bruges 1.91m 118kg. Vilvoorde AC, Lille Metropole, FRA.
At DT: OG: '16- 9; WCh: '15- 2, '17/19- dnq 14/29; EC: '14- dnq 20, '16- 2; EU23: '13- 5; WUG: '15- 1. Won BEL DT 2011-20, SP 2016-18, 2020.
Six Belgian discus records 2014-16.
Progress at DT: 2011- 56.00, 2012- 57.66, 2013- 61.81, 2014- 66.02, 2015- 66.90, 2016- 67.26, 2017- 67.05, 2018- 66.51, 2019- 64.73, 2020- 63.51. pb SP 18.63 '18. His father Emil Milanov had DT pb 58.28 '82, moved Bulgaria to Belgium in 1989.

Women

Nafissatou THIAM b. 19 Aug 1994 Namur 1.84m 69kg. RFCL. Student of geographical science at University of Liège.
At Hep: OG: '16- 1; WCh: '13-15-17-19: 14/11/1/2; EC: '14- 3, '18- 1; WJ: '12- 14; WY: '11- 4; EJ: '13- 1. At Pen: EI: '13-15-17-21: 6/2/1/1. At HJ: EC: '16- 4; EU23: '15- 2; WI: '14- 8=. Won BEL Hep 2012, LJ 2015, 2018.
Belgian records: heptathlon (4) 2013-17, javelin 2017, long jump (3) 2019. World junior heptathlon best 2013.
Progress at HJ, Hep: 2010- 1.74, 2011- 1.81, 2012- 1.88, 5916; 2013- 1.92, 6298, 2014- 1.97, 6508; 2015- 1.92, 6412; 2016- 1.98, 6810; 2017- 1.98, 7013; 2018- 2.01, 6816; 2019- 2.02, 6819. pbs: 60m 7.81i '13, 200m 24.37 '19, 800m 2:15.24 '17, 60mh 8.23i '17, 100mh 13.34 '17, LJ 6.79i '20, 6.67 '19; TJ 12.82 '14, SP 15.52i '18, 15.41 '19; JT 59.32 '17, Pen 4904i '21.
Tied high jump world best in a heptathlon with 1.97 at EC 2014 and improved that to 1.98 at the Olympic Games, when she set five events pbs en route to the gold medal and adding 319 points to her pb. IAAF female Rising Star award 2016, Female Athlete of the Year 2017. Won at Götzis 2017 and in 2018, with world heptathlon high jump bests of 2.01 there, and at 2.02 when she won at Talence in 2019.

Noor VIDTS b. 30 May 1996 1.77m 70kg. Vilvoorde AC, Catholic University of Leuven.
At Hep: WCh: '19: 15; EC: '18- 20; WJ: '14- 16; WY: '13- 15; E23: '17- 5; EJ: '15- 4; WUG: '17- 3; won BEL 2019. At Pen: EI: '21- 2.
Progress at Hep: 2014- 5439, 2015- 5652, 2016- 5851, 2017- 6024, 2018- 5598, 2019- 6194, 2020- 5837. pbs: 60m 7.82i '18, 100m 12.14 '17, 200m 24.11 '19, 800m 2:10.96 '17, 60mh 8.27i '21, 100mh 13.51 '19, HJ: 1.84 '19, LJ 6.47i '21, 6.39 '19; SP 14.08 '19, JT 36.44 '17, Pen 4791i '21.

BOSNIA & HERZEGOVINA

Governing body: Atletski savez Bosne i Hercegovine (AsBIH). Founded 1948.

Amel TUKA b. 9 Jan 1991 Kakanj 1.87m 77kg. AK Zenica. Mechanical engineering graduate.
At 800m: OG: '16- sf; WCh: '15- 3, '17- h, '19- 2; EC: 12-14-16-18: sf/6/4/sf; EU23: '13- 3; EI: '19- 6, '21- 5. Won BIH 400m & 800m 2010, 2012-13, 2015; 400m 2017, 2019.
BIH records: 400m (6) 2012-19, 800m (5) 2013-15.
Progress at 800m: 2010- 1:51.04, 2011- 1:51.09, 2012- 1:48.31, 2013- 1:46.29, 2014- 1:46.12, 2015- 1:42.51, 2016- 1:44.54, 2017- 1:44.62, 2018- 1:45.68, 2019- 1:43.47, 2020- 1:44.51. pbs: 100m 10.93w '18, 300m 34.46 '16, 400m 46.15 '19, 600m 1:15.21 '16,

BOTSWANA

Governing body: Botswana Athletics Association.

Nijel AMOS b. 15 Mar 1994 Marobela 1.79m 60kg.
At 800m: OG: '12- 2, '16- h; WCh: '15- sf, '17- 5; CG: '14- 1, '18- 8; WJ: '12- 1, WY: '11- 5; AfG: '15- 1/2R; AfCh: '14- 1/1R, '16- 1, '18- 1; CCp: '14- 1, '18- 3; WUG: '13- 1. Won DL 2014-15, 2017.
World junior 800m and two Botswana 800m records 2012.
Progress at 800m: 2011- 1:47.28, 2012- 1:41.73, 2013- 1:44.71, 2014- 1:42.45, 2015- 1:42.66, 2016- 1:44.66, 2017- 1:43.18, 2018- 1:42.14, 2019- 1:41.89, 2020- 1:49.23. pbs: 200m 21.34 '15, 400m 44.99 '19, 600m 1:15.0+ 12.
In 2019 he ran world's fastest 800m for seven years and became the first ever to run sub 45 sec for 400m and 1:42 for 800m.

Isaac MAKWALA b. 24 Sep 1985 Tutume 1.83m 79kg.
At (200m)/400m: OG: '12- h, '16- sf; WCh: '09- h, '13- (h), '15- 5, '17- 6/dns; CG: '10- sf, '14- sf, '18- 1/1R; AfG: '07- sf/1R, '11- 7, '15- 1/2R, '19- sf; AfCh: '08-10-12-14-16: 2/sf/1/1 & (2),1R/4; CCp: '14- 6/2/1R. Won DL 2017.
Records: Commonwealth 400m 2015, African 400m (2) 2014-15, Botswana 100m (2) 2013-14, 200m 2013-14, 300m 2017, 400m (4) 2014-15.
Progress at 200m, 400m: 2007- 46.48, 2008- 21.20, 45.64A; 2009- 20.73, 45.56; 2010- 21.33, 46.07; 2011- 21.17, 46.27; 2012- 20.87, 45.25; 2013- 20.21, 45.86; 2014- 19.96/19.7A, 44.01; 2015- 20.44A/20.77, 43.72; 2016- 20.42A, 44.85; 2017- 19.77, 43.84; 2018- 19.96, 44.23; 2019- 45.43A/45.74, 2020- 20.69w, 46.14A. Pbs: 100m 10.20A/10.14wA '14; 300m 31.44 '17.
Ran 43.92 & 19.77 double within two hours at Madrid 2017.

BRAZIL

Governing body: Confederação Brasileira de Atletismo (CBAt). Fd 1914 (Confederação 1977).
National Championships first held in 1925.
2020 Champions: **Men**: 100m: Paulo André de Oliveira 10.13, 200m/400m: Lucas Carvalho 20.40/45.68, 800m/1500m: Thiago André 1:46.33/3:39.24, 5000m/3000mSt: Altobeli da Silva 14:03.18/8:34.32, 10000m: Daniel do Nascimento 29:32.61, 110mh: Jonitas Brito 13.57, 400mh: Arthur Terezan 50.23, HJ: Thiago Moura 2.27, PV: Abel Curtinove 5.20, LJ/TJ: Alexsandro de Melo 8.16/16.48, SP: Darlan Romani 21.11, DT: Douglas dos Reis 58.19, HT: Allan Wolski 66.01, JT: Luiz da Silva 67.10, Dec: Felipe dos Santos 8364, 20kW: Caio Bonfim 1:25:43/1:23:05.45, 35000mW: Rudney Nogueira 3:00:33.7. **Women**: 100m: Vitória Rosa 11.41, 200m: Ana Carolina Azevedo 23.01, 400m: Tiffani do Nascimento 52.95, 800m: Mayara Leite 2:07.29, 1500m/3000mSt: Tatiane da Silva 4:22.83/9:59.72, 5000m/10000m: Jenifer Silva 16:16.78/34:20.64, 100mh: Ketiley Batista 13.21, 400mh: Bianca dos Santos 57.44, HJ: Sara Freitas 1.78, PV: Juliana Campos 4.20, LJ: Eliane Martins 6.42, TJ: Gabriele dos Santos 14.17, SP: Geisa Arcanjo 17.22, DT: Fernanda Borges 61.83, HT: Mariana Marcelino 63.73, JT: Laila Ferrer e Silva 61.76, Hep: Raiane Procópio 5759, 20kW: Erica de Sena 1:37:06/1:36:39.94, 35000mW: Viviane Lyra 3:15:35.7.

Gabriel de Oliveira **CONSTANTINO** b. 9 Feb 1995 Rio de Janeiro 1.86m 77kg. E.C.Pinheiros.
Was at Salgado de Oliveira University.
At 110mh: WCh: '19- h; WJ: '14- sf (h 200m); PAm: '19- dnf; SACh: '19- 1; WUG: '19- 1; won S.Am U23 2016, IbAm 2018. At 60mh: WI: '18- 6; SAmI: '20- 1. Won S.Am-Y LJ 2012.
South American records: 60m hurdles indoor 2018 and two 110m hurdles 2018-19.
Progress at 110mh: 2014- 13.92, 2015- 13.75, 2016- 13.50, 2017- 13.52, 2018- 13.23, 2019- 13.18, 2020- 13.60. Pbs: 100m 10.28 '18, 200m 20.21 '19, 400m 50.42 '12, 60mh: 7.60i '18, HJ 2.01 '12, LJ 6.97 '12.

Darlan ROMANI b. 9 Apr 1991 Concórdia 1.88m 140kg. E.C.Pinheiros.
At SP: OG: '16- 5; WCh: '15-17: dnq 15/dnq 15, '19- 4; WJ: '10- 7; PAm: '15- 6, '19- 1; SAG: '18- 1; SACh: '13-15-17-19: 2/2/1/1; CCp: '18- 1; WI: '18- 4; won IbAm 2018, W.MilG 2019, BRA 2012-20.
Eight South American shot records 2017-19 and 17 Brazilian records 2012-19. Two South American indoor shot records 2018.
Progress at SP: 2009- 4.60, 2010- 17.66, 2011- 18.46, 2012- 20.48, 2013- 20.08, 2014- 20.84, 2015- 20.90, 2016- 21.02, 2017- 21.82, 2018- 22.00, 2019- 22.61, 2020- 21.52.

Alison Brendom Alves **dos SANTOS** b. 3 Jun 2000 São Joaquim da Barra, São Paulo 1.93m 79kg. E.C.Pinheiros.
At 400mh: WCh: '19- 7; WJ: '18- 3, WY: '17- 5 (1 mxR); PAm: '19- 1; WUG: '19- 1; SACh: '19- 1; won S.Am-U23 2018, PAm-J 2019, S.Am U20 400m 2019. 7 South American U20 400mh records 2018-19.
Progress at 400mh: 2017- 53.82, 2018- 49.78, 2019- 48.28. Pbs: 200m 21.96 '18, 400m 45.78A, 46.09 '19.

Almir Cunha **dos SANTOS** b. 4 Sep 1993 Matupá 1.91m 80kg. Orcampi.
At TJ: WCh: '19- 12; PAm: '19- 4; WI: '18- 2. HJ: WJ: '12; dnq 26=; won S.Am-Y 2010, BRA 2019.
Progress in TJ: 2016- 15.89, 2017- 16.86, 2018- 17.53, 2019- 17.23, 2020- 16.65. Pbs: HJ 2.18 '14, LJ 7.96 '17. Formerly a high/long jumper, he took up triple jumping in late 2016.

Felipe Vinícius **dos SANTOS** b. 30 Jul 1994 São Paulo 1.81m 80kg. AABLU – SC FCA.
At Dec: WCh: '15- dnf; WJ: '12- 11; PAm: '15- 4; Won Ibero-American 2014, 2018; PAm-J 2013, BRA 2014, 2020. WY Oct: '11- 3.

BRAZIL – BRITISH VIRGIN ISLANDS – BULGARIA

S.American U20 decathlon record 7762A 2013
Progress at Dec: 2014- 7952, 2015- 8019, 2016- 7859, 2018- 7886, 2019- 7856, 2020- 8364. pbs: 60m 6.85i '14, 100m 10.37 '15, 200m 21.57 '18, 400m 47.73 '14, 1000m 2:44.38 '11, 1500m 4:39.82 '13, 60mh 8.00i '14, 110mh 13.74 '15, HJ 2.07 '20, PV 4.90 '20, LJ 7.80 '13; SP 14.22 '15, DT 42.46 '20, JT 58.82 '20, Hep 5765i '14.

Thiago Braz da SILVA b. 16 Dec 1993 Marília 1.93m 84kg. E.C.Pinheiros.
At PV: OG: '16- 1; WCh: '13-15: dnq 14=/1, '19- 5; WJ: '12- 1; WI: '14- 4; PAm: '15- nh, '19- 4; SACh: '13- 1, '19- 2; Yth Oly: '10- 2, won BRA 2015-16, 2017 (=), 2018, PAm-J 2011.
Six South American pole vault records 2013-16, indoors (5) 2014-16.
Progress at PV: 2009- 4.60, 2010- 5.10, 2011- 5.31, 2012- 5.55, 2013- 5.83, 2014- 5.76i/5.73, 2015- 5.92, 2016- 6.03, 2017- 5.86i/5.60, 2018- 5.90i/5.70, 2019- 5.92, 2020- 5.82.
Married Ana Paula de Oliveira (HJ 1.86 '15) on 13 Dec 2014.

Women

Fernanda Raquel **BORGES** Martins b. 26 Jul 1988 Santa Cruz do Sul 1.75m 85kg. IEMA.
At DT: OG: '16- dnq 31; WCh: '13/15/17: dnq nt/26/16, '19- 6; PAm: '11/15/19: 7/4/2; SACh: 11-13-15-17-19: 3/1/2/2/2. Won SAm-J 2007, BRA 2011, 2014, 2020.
Progress at DT: 2006- 45.35, 2007- 44.44, 2008- 50.46, 2009- 53.71, 2010- 57.56, 2011- 60.91, 2012- 58.92, 2013- 60.79, 2014- 64.01, 2015- 62.80, 2016- 62.74, 2017- 62.30, 2018- 64.66, 2019- 64.16, 2020- 62.37. pb SP 13.47 17.

Andressa Oliveira **de MORAIS** b. 21 Dec 1990 João Pessoa, Paraíba 1.78m 100kg. EC Pinheiros.
At DT: OG: '12/16- dnq 15/21; WCh: '11/15- dnq 17/19, '17- 11; WJ: '08- dnq 20; PAm: '15- 6. '19-2dq; SACh: '09-11-13-15-17-19: 5/1/5/1/1/1; CCp: '18- 5. Won IbAm 2012, 2018; SAm U23 2012, SAmG 2018; BRA 2012-13, 2015, 2017-19. At HT: SAm-J: '09- 6.
Five South American discus records 2012-19.
Progress at DT: 2007- 42.84, 2008- 54.35, 2009- 55.52, 2010- 58.06, 2011- 59.56, 2012- 64.21, 2013- 61.04, 2014- 59.65, 2015- 64.15, 2016- 59.64, 2017- 64.68, 2018- 65.10, 2019- 65.74, 65.98dq, 2020- 60.84. pbs: SP 13.87 '08, HT 58.89 '12.
1-year 4 month drugs ban with results dq from 6 Aug 2019, losing Pan-Am silver.

Érica Rocha **de SENA** b. 3 May 1985 Camaragibe, Pernambuco 1.68m 55kg. Orcampi Unimed.
At 20kW: OG: '16- 7; WCh: '15-17-19: 6/4/4; WCp: '16- 3, '18- 4; PAm: 15- 2, '19- 3; SACh: '16/18- 1; BRA champion 2011-18, 2020. Won IbAm 10000mW 2016.
Walk records: S.American 10k 2017. 20k (6) 2014-17, 35k 2021; BRA: 10000mW 2014, 20kW (5) 2012-16.
Progress at 20kW: 2006- 1:51:45.5t, 2007- 1:44:52.96t, 2008- 1:44:14.6t, 2009- 1:44:27, 2010- 1:38:59, 2011- 1:35:29.6t, 2012- 1:31:53, 2013- 1:32:59, 2014- 1:30:43, 2015- 1:29:37, 2016- 1:27:18, 2017- 1:26:59, 2018- 1:28:40, 2019- 1:27:38, 2020- 1:29:14. Pbs: 5000mW 23:10.59 '11, 10000mW 43:31.30 '14, 43:03 '17, 35kW 2:51:11A '21.
Won IAAF Walks Challenge 2017. Married to and coached by Andrés Chocho ECU (20kW 1:20:07 '16, 50kW 4 S.Am records to 3:42:57A '16, 8 WCh '15). Lives in Cuenca, Ecuador.

BRITISH VIRGIN ISLANDS

Governing body: BVI Athletics Association. Founded 1970.

Kyron McMASTER b. 3 Jan 1997 Road Town 1.87m 79kg. Central Arizona University, USA.
At 400mh: WCh: '17- dq h, '19- 4; CG: '18- 1; CAG: '18- 1; WJ: '16- 3; CCp: '18- 8; won DL 2017-18, NACAC 2018. At 400m: WY: '13- h (h 200m).
Six IVB 400mh records 2015-18.
Progress at 400mh: 2014- 53.26, 2015- 50.16, 2016- 49.56, 2017- 47.80, 2018- 47.54, 2019- 48.10. pbs: 200m 21.24 '17, 21.14w '15; 300m 32.91i '20, 400m 45.84i '20, HJ 1.86.

BULGARIA

Governing body: Bulgarian Athletics Federation. Founded 1924.
National Championships first held in 1926 (men), 1938 (women). **2020 Champions**: **Men**: 100m/200m: Peter Peev 10.32w/20.98, 400m: Mikhail Gargov 48.74, 800m: Aleks Vasilev 1:52.40, 1500m: Hristan Stoyanov 3:56.34, 5000m: Yolo Nikolov 14:38.30, HMar/Mar: Ismail Senandji 66:57/2:23:12, 3000mSt: Mitko Tsenov 8:58.45, 110mh/400mh: Stanislav Stankov 13.93/52.93, HJ: Tihomir Ivanov 2.20, PV: Aleks Lyubenov 4.86, LJ: Boris Linkov 7.93w, TJ: Georgi Tsonov 15.70w, SP: Khristo Bankov 16.59, DT: Deyan Gemizhev 54.67, HT: Valentin Andreev 67.52, JT: Mark Slavov 73.38, Dec: Vasil Vlasov 6317. **Women**: 100m/200m: Inna Eftimova 11.43w/23.50, 400m Kristina Borukova 56.28, 800m/1500m: Lilyana Georgieva 2:08.08/4:41.04, 5000m: Militsa Mircheva 16:34.31, HMar/Mar: Marinela Nineva 77:33/2:57:53, 3000mSt: Silvia Georgieva 10:53.04, 100mh/Hep: Elena Miteva 13.30/4793, 400mh: Kristina Borukova 58.91; HJ: Galina Nikolova 1.74, PV: Maria Kapusheva 3.36, LJ: Milena Mitkova 6.06, TJ: Dimana Yordanova 12.18, SP: Yana Kopcheva 13.35, DT: Renata Petkova 45.83, HT: Ekaterina Dimova 47.27, JT: Mihaela Petkova 51.60.

Women

Mirela DEMIREVA b. 28 Sep 1989 Sofia 1.80m 58kg. Beroe Stara Zagora
At HJ: OG: '16- 2; WCh: '13-15-17-19: dnq 26/9=/7=/10; EC: '12-14-16-18: 8/dnq 17/2=/2; WJ: '06- dnq 16, '08- 2; EU23: '09- 7, '11- dnq 17; EJ: '07- 3; WI: '18- 6 EI: '13- 7. BUL champion 2007-08, 2011, 2013-14; Balkan 2015-16, 2018-19.

BULGARIA – BURKINA FASO – CANADA

Progress at HJ: 2005- 1.76, 2006- 1.86, 2007- 1.88, 2008- 1.86, 2009- 1.86, 2011- 1.85i/1.84, 2012- 1.95, 2013- 1.92, 2014- 1.94, 2015- 1.94, 2016- 1.97, 2017- 1.92, 2018- 2.00, 2019- 1.97.
Her mother Valia Demireva (100m 11.34) was at 4x100m 4th at the 1987 Worlds and 5th at the 1998 Olympics and father Krasimir Demirev won the EJ 400m hurdles in 1981; pb 49.48 '88, also Bulgarian 400m record with 46.34 '83.

Gabriela PETROVA b. 29 Jun 1992 Haskovo 1.67m 61kg. Lokomtiv Plovdiv.
At TJ: OG: '16- dnq 22; WCh: '15- 4, '17/19- dnq 17/16; EC: '14-16-18: 5/dnq 20/6; WJ: '10- dnq 17; WY: '09- dnq 18; EU23: '13- 1; EJ: '11- 5; EI: '15- 2; Won Balkan LJ & TJ 2020. BUL LJ 2017, TJ 2010, 2013, 2016-17.
Progress at TJ: 2007- 12.43, 2008- 12.72i, 2009- 12.64, 2010- 13.35, 2011- 13.27/13.44w, 2012- 13.45, 2013- 14.14i/13.92/13.96w, 2014- 14.13, 2015- 14.66/14.85w, 2016- 14.32i/13.92, 2017- 14.19, 2018- 14.40/14.48w, 2019- 14.22/14.29w, 2020- 14.38. pbs: 100m 11.85 '18, LJ 6.62 '19.

BURKINA FASO

Governing body: Fédération Burkinabe d'Athlétisme.

Hugues Fabrice ZANGO b. 25 Jun 1993 Ouagadougou 1.80m 75kg. Artois Athlétisme, France. Studied at Artios University
At TJ: OG: '16- dnq 34; WCh: '15- dnq, '19- 3; AfG: '15- 5, '19- 1; AfCh: '16- 2, '18- 1; CCp: '18- 3; WUG: '15- 2, 17- 2; WI: '18- 6. Won WIT 2020. TJ records: World indoor 2021, African indoor (4) 2018-21, outdoor (3) 2019, 8 BUR 2017-19.
Progress at TJ: 2011- 14.88, 2012- 15.89, 2013- 15.97, 2014- 15.83, 2015- 16.76, 2016- 16.81/16.84w, 2017- 16.79, 2018- 16.97, 2018- 17.11, 2019- 17.66. 2020- 17.77i/17.43; 2021- 18.07i. pbs: 60m 6.81i'18, 100m 10.72/10.71w '17, LJ 7.71 '20.
Set five national indoor records in one competition – at Val-de-Reuil in 2018.

CANADA

Governing body: Athletics Canada. Formed as Canadian AAU in 1884.

Mohammed AHMED b. 5 Jan 1991 Mogadishu, Somalia 1.80m 56kg. Nike Bowerman TC.
At (5000m)/10000m: OG: '12- 18, '16- 4/32; WCh: '13- 9, '15- (12), 17- 6/8, '19- 3/6; CG: '14- 5/6, '18- 2/2; PAm: '15- 1; WJ: '08- 9, '10- 4; PAm-J: '09- (1). At 3000m: CCp: '18- 2; WI: '16- 9. Won CAN 5000m 2016-19, 10000m 2012.
North American 5000m record 2020, CAN records 3000m 2017, 5000m 2019 & 2020, 10000m (4) 2015-19.
Progress at 5000m, 10000m: 2008- 14:26.71, 30:03.53; 2009- 14:11.84, 2010- 14:02.04, 28:57.44; 2011- 13:34.23, 29:08.29; 2012- 13:41.06, 27:34.64, 2013- 13:40.43i, 27:35.76; 2014- 13:18.88, 28:02.96; 2015- 13:10.00, 27:46.90; 2016- 13:01.74, 29:32.84; 2017- 13:04.60i/13:08.16, 27:02.35; 2018- 13:03.08, 27:20.56; 2019- 12:58.16, 26:59.35; 2020- 12:47.20. pbs: 1500m 3:34.89 '20, 1M 3:56.60 '17, 2000m 5:00.72 '20, 3000m 7:40.11i '16, 7:40.49 '17; 2M 8:13.16i '17, 8:15.76 '19.
Moved to Canada at age 11. Younger twin brother Ibrahim 25 WJ 10000m 2012.

Marco AROP b. 20 Sep 1998 Khartoum, Sudan 1.94m 82kg. adidas. Computer science student at Mississippi State University, USA.
At 800m: WCh: '19- 7; PAm: '19- 1; PAm-J: '17- 2; Canadian champion 2018.
Progress at 800m: 2016- 1:53.12A, 2017- 1:47.08, 2018- 1:45.25, 2019- 1:44.25, 2020- 1:44.14. s: 400m 47.99A '18, 600m 1:16.85+ '20, 1000m 2:17.10i '21, 1M 3:57.50i '21. Lived in Canada from 2002.

Aaron BROWN b. 27 May 1992 Toronto 1.85m 79kg. University of Toronto TC. Was at University of Southern California.
At (100m)/200m/4x100mR: OG: '12- sf, 16- h/sf/3R; WCh: '13- (sf)/3R, '15- sf/h/3R, '17- h. '19- 8/6; WJ: '10- 5/3; WY: '09- (2); CG: '14- (sf), '18- 2; PAm-J: '11- (3); Won CAN 100m 2013, 2018-19; 200m 2015, 2018-19.
Canadian 200m record 2014.
Progress at 100m, 200m: 2008- 10.73, 2009- 10.46, 21.44/21.34w; 2010- 10.47/10.37w, 21.00; 2011- 10.38/10.25w; 21.11, 2012- 10.18/10.09w, 20.42; 2013- 10.05/10.01w, 20.44/20.26w; 2014- 10.07, 20.16 20.02w; 2015- 10.10/10.03w, 20.30/20.11w; 2016- 9.96/9.95w, 20.00; 2017- 10.15/9.98w, 20.17/20.13w; 2018- 10.12, 19.98; 2019- 9.96, 19.95; 2020- 10.15, 20.24. Pbs: 60m 6.55A/6.59 '14, 400m 46.33 '19.

Andre DE GRASSE b. 10 Nov 1994 Scarborough, Ontario 1.80m 73kg. Speed Academy, University of Southern California (sociology).
At (100m)/200m: OG: '16- 3/2/3R; WCh: '15- (3=)/3R, '19- 3/2; CG: '14- sf; PAm: '15- 1/1; PAm-J: '13- 2/3. Won NCAA 100m & 200m 2015, CAN 100m 2015-17, 200m 2017.
Four Canadian 200m records 2015-16.
Progress at 100m, 200m: 2012- 10.59, 2013- 10.25/9.96w, 20.74A/20.57w; 2014- 10.15/10.03w, 20.38; 2015- 9.92/9.75w, 19.88/19.58w; 2016- 9.91, 19.80; 2017- 10.01/9.69w, 20.01/19.96w; 2018- 10.15, 20.46; 2019- 9.90, 19.87; 2020- 9.97, 20.24. pbs: 55m 6.21i '13, 60m 6.60i '15, 400m 47.93 '14.
Father came from Barbados and mother from Trinidad. IAAF male Rising Star award 2016. Partner of Nia Ali (qv).

Matthew HUGHES b. 3 Aug 1989 Oshawa, Ontario 1.80m 64kg. Was at University of Louisville, USA.
At 3000mSt: OG: '16- 10, WCh: '11-13-15-17-19: h/6/8/6/14; CG: '14- 4, '18- 4; WJ: '08- h; PAm: '15- 1; CCp: '14- 7, '18- 2; CAN champion 2013-15, 2017-19; NCAA 2010-11.
Canadian 3000m steeplechase record 2013.
Progress at 3000mSt: 2007- 9:20.61, 2008- 8:59.83,

80   CANADA

2009- 8:47.36, 2010- 8:34.18, 2011- 8:24.87, 2012- 8:31.77, 2013- 8:11.64, 2014- 8:12.81, 2015- 8:18.63, 2016- 8:20.63, 2017- 8:21.84, 2018- 8:12.33, 2019- 8:13.12, 2020- 8:16.25. pbs: 1500m 3:37.20 '20, 1M 4:01.98 '16, 2000m 5:02.31 '20, 3000m 7:51.87i '15, 8:11.64 '13; 5000m 13:13.38i '20, 13:19.56 '15.

Pierce LePAGE b. 22 Jan 1996 Whitby, Ontario 2.01m 91 kg. Studied law at York University, Toronto.
At Dec: WCh: '19- 5; CG: '18- 2; PAm: '19- 3. Won CAN 2017.
Progress at Dec: 2016- 8027, 2017- 7948, 2018- 8171, 2019- 8453. pbs: 60m 6.98i '17, 100m 10.31 '19, 200m 20.83 '16, 400m 47.35 '19, 1000m 2:50.85i '13, 1500m 4:45.09 '19, 60mh 7.83i '18, 110mh 14.07 '19, HJ 2.09 '17, PV 5.25 '19, LJ 7.80, 7.87w '19; SP 14.35 '19, DT 44.46 '19, JT 58.24 '18.

Brandon McBRIDE b. 15 Jun 1994 Windsor, Ontario 1.95m 75kg. Border City. Was at Mississippi State University, USA.
At 800m: OG: '16- sf, WCh: '17- 8, '19- sf; CG: '14- sf; WJ: '12- 6; WY: '11- h; NCAA champion 2014, NACAC 2018, CAN 2014, 2016-17, 2019. At 400m: PAm-J: 13- 1.
Canadian 800m record 2018.
Progress at 800m: 2011- 1:48.41, 2012- 1:46.07, 2013- 1:46.38, 2014- 1:45.35, 2015- 1:45.87, 2016- 1:43.95, 2017- 1:44.41, 2018- 1:43.20, 2019- 1:43.51. pbs: 100m 10.29w '11, 400m 45.89 '13, 500m 1:01.40i '14, 600m 1:15.60+ '19. 1500m 3:41.55 '16, 1M 4:11.96 '16, 3000m 8:27.13i '17.

Michael MASON b. 30 Sep 1986 New Westminster, BC 1.88m 67kg. Valley Royals.
At HJ: OG: '08- dnq 19=, '12- 8, '16- dnq 6; WCh: '13/15/17- dnq 25/18=/18, '19- 7; CG: '10- 14-18: 7/3/6; WJ: '04- 1; WY: '03- dnq 19; PAm: '15- 2, '19- 2; WUG: '09- 2; WI: '08- 8, '14- 8. Won CAN 2007-08, 2017-19.
Progress at HJ: 2002- 2.12, 2003- 1.95, 2004- 2.21, 2005- 2.20, 2006- 2.23, 2007- 2.27, 2008- 2.30i/2.27, 2009- 2.25, 2010- 2.28, 2011- 2.19A, 2012- 2.31, 2013- 2.31, 2014- 2.30i/2.28, 2015- 2.33, 2016- 2.29, 2017- 2.30, 2018- 2.32, 2019- 2.31, 2020- 2.22i.

Damian WARNER b. 4 Nov 1989 London, Ontario 1.85m 83kg.
At Dec: OG: '12- 5, '16- 3; WCh: '11-13-15-17-19: 18/3/2/5/3; CG: '14- 1, '18- dnf; PAm: '15- 1, '19- 1 Won Canadian 110mh 2014-15, 2019; LJ 2017, Dec 2011-13. At Hep: WI: '14- 7, '18- 2.
Two Canadian decathlon records 2015.
Progress at Dec: 2010- 7449, 2011- 8102A/7832, 2012- 8442, 2013- 8512, 2014- 8282, 2015- 8695, 2016- 8666, 2017- 8591, 2018- 879, 2019- 8711. pbs: 60m 6.74i '10, 100m 10.12 '19, 10.09w '16; 200m 20.96 '13, 20.90w '19; 400m 46.36i '15, 46.54 '16, 1000m 2:37.12i '18, 1500m 4:24.73 '15, 60mh 7.62i '20 110mh 13.27 '15, HJ 2.09 '13, PV 4.90 '16, LJ 8.04 '16, TJ 14.75w '08, SP 15.59i '20, 15.34 '19; DT 50.26 '16, JT 64.67 '13, Hep: 6343i '18 (CAN rec). Made 340 points improvement on pb when 5th at 2012 Olympics, setting six pbs, and 70 more at 2013 Worlds, with three pbs. Won Götzis 2013, 2016-19, Talence 2013, 2017; IAAF CE Challenge 2019. Ran fastest ever in decathlons: 110mh 13.44 '15 and 100m 10.15 '16 & 10.12 '19.

Women

Brittany CREW b. 6 Mar 1994 Mississauga, Ontario 1.76m 111kg. Sisu Throws, was at York University.
At SP: OG: '16- dnq 18; WCh: '17- 6, '19- 8; WJ: '12- dnq 17; CG: '18- 3; WI: '18- 10; PAm: '19- 2; WUG: '15- 3, '17- 1; Canadian champion 2016-19. Seven Canadian shot records 2017-19.
Progress at SP: 2013- 14.03, 2014- 16.59, 2015- 17.27, 2016- 18.06, 2017- 18.59, 2018- 18.60, 2019- 19.28, 2020- 18.88. Pb: DT 51.68 '18, HT 55.50 '20, Wt 19.90i '17.

Gabriela DeBUES-STAFFORD b. 13 Sep 1995 London, Ontario 1.65m 53kg. née Stafford. Bowerman TC/ University of Toronto TC.
At 1500m: OG: 16- h; WCh: '17- sf, '19- 6; CG: '18-h; WUG: '15- 2; CAN champion 2016-19. At 3000m: WJ: '14- 9.
Canadian records 1500m (3), 1M, 5000m (2) 2019
Progress at 1500m, 5000m: 2014- 4:17.00, 2015- 4:07.44, 2016- 4:06.53, 2017- 4:03.55, 2018- 4:05.83, 2019- 3:56.12, 14:44.12; 2020- 4:00.80i. Pbs: 400m 56.27 '10, 600m 1:31.64i '16, 800m 2:00.96i '20, 2:02.48 '17; 1000m 2:37.93 '19, 1M 4:17.87 '19, 3000m 8:38.51 '21, 5000m 14:44.12 '19.
Married Rowan DeBues on 12 Jan 2019. Her father James Stafford ran in four World CC Champs. Her sister Lucia (b. 17 Aug 1998) has pbs 800m 2:03.34 '19, 1500m 4:08.92 '18.

Alysha NEWMAN b. 29 Jun 1994 London, Ontario 1.72m 67kg. Bolton PV. Was at University of Miami.
At PV: OG: '16- dnq 17; WCh: '17- 7, '19- 5; WJ: '12- dnq 25; WY: '11- 12; CG: '14- 3, '18- 1; WI: '18- 6; PAm: '19- 3; PAm-J: 13- 1; Canadian champion 2016-17.
Eight Canadian pole vault records 2016-19.
Progress at PV: 2010- 3.91, 2011- 4.00i/3.91, 2012- 4.06, 2013- 4.40A, 2014- 4.41, 2015- 4.40, 2016- 4.61, 2017- 4.75, 2018- 4.75, 2019- 4.82, 2020- 4.63i, 2021- 4.70i. Pb 100mh 14.07 '14.

Sage WATSON b. 20 Jun 1994 Medicine Hat, Alberta 1.75m 62kg. Studied at Florida State, then University of Arizona, USA.
At 400mh: OG: '16- sf; WCh: '15- 17-19: sf/6/8; CG: '18- 5; PAm: '15- h/3R, '19- 1/2R; WJ: '12- sf; WY: '11- 8 (3 MedR). Won NCAA 2017, CAN 2011, 2017, 2019.
Canadian 400mh record 2019.
Progress at 400mh: 2011- 59.00, 2012- 58.04, 2013- 56.81A/58.20, 2015- 55.97, 2016- 54.82, 2017- 54.52, 2018- 54.55, 2019- 54.32, 2020- 56.29. pbs: 200m 23.80 '17, 300m 37.08i '18, 400m 51.42 '18, 500m 1:08.40i '17, 600m 1:28.31 '17.

CHILE

Governing body: Federación Atlética de Chile.
Founded 1914. HJ: Juan Pablo Maturana 1.90,
2020 Champions: Men: 100m/200m: Mauricio Martínez 11.06/22.86, 400m/800m: Rafael Muñoz 52.17/1:55.55, 1500m: Alfredo Toledo 3:57.99, 5000m: Gabriel Muñoz 15:15.80, 110mh: Martín Sáenz de Santa María 14.77, HJ: Juan Pablo Maturana 1.90, PV: Guillermo Correa 5.02, LJ: Daniel Pineda 7.47, TJ: Luis Reyes 15.10w, SP: José Joaquín Ballivián 16.59, DT: Claudio Romero 59.76, HT: Gabriel Kehr 76.61, JT: Francisco Muse 67.71, 20kW: Tarik Figueroa 1:49:18. **Women:** 100m/200m: María Ignacia Montt 12.32/25.01, 400m: María Pavez 59.11, 800m/1500m: Laura Acuña 2:11.22/4:30.21, 5000m: Paulina Saavedra 17:18.04, HJ: Olivia García Huidobro 1.65, LJ: Macarena Reyes 6.21, SP: Ivana Gallardo 16.40, DT: Karen Gallardo 55.18, HT: Mariana García 66.33, 20kW: Anastasia Sanzana 1:45:43.

CHINA

Governing body: Athletic Association of the People's Republic of China.
National Championships first held in 1910 (men), 1959 (women). **2020 Champions: Men:** 100m/200m: Xie Zhenye 10.31/20.72, 400m: Guo Zhongze 46.43, 800m: Xia Chenyu 1:51.75, 1500m: Kiang Qi 3:45.25, 5000m/Mar: Peng Jianhua 14:13.78/2:08:50, 10000m: Dong Guojian 29:35.46, 3000mSt: Luo Chun 8:59.53, 110mh: Xie Wenjun 13.24, 400mh: Feng Zhiqiang 50.43, HJ: Li Jialun 2.24, PV: Yao Jie 5.40, LJ: Wang Jianan 8.36, TJ: Wu Ruiting 16.90, SP: Tian Zhizhong 19.51, DT: Sun Shichen 58.40, HT: Wang Shizhu 71.89, JT: Ma Qun 81.13, Dec: Guo Qi 7405, 20kW: Wang Kaihua 1:20:49, 50kW Zhaxi Yangben 3:52:19. **Women:** 100m: Ge Manqi 11.35, 200m: Kong Lingwei 23.64, 400m: Yang Huizhen 52.67, 800m: Wang Chunyu 2:04.79, 1500m: Hu Zhiying 4:27.98, 5000m/3000mSt: Xu Shuangshuang 16:18.08/9:56.53, 10000m: Zhang Deshun 33:26.85, Mar: Li Dan 2:26:59, 100mh: Wu Yanni 13.09, 400mh: Mo Jiaxie 56.77, HJ: Huang Min 1.80, PV: Song Tingting 4.30, LJ: Xu Xiaoling 6.63, TJ: Li Ying 14.02, SP: Gao Yang 17.98, DT: Chen Yang 60.80, HT: Luo Na 69.19, JT: Liu Shiying 67.29, Hep: Ren Shimei 5746, 20kW: Liu Hong 1:27:48.

CAI Zelin b. 11 Apr 1991 Dali, Yunnan 1.72m 55kg.
At 20kW: OG: '12- 4, '16- 2; WCh: '13-15-19: 25/5/dnf; AsiG: '14- 4; WCp: '14- 2, '16- 2. At 10000mW: WJ: '10- 2; WCp: '10- 2J. Won CHN 20kW 2012.
At 20kW: 2010- 1:22:28, 2011- 1:21:07, 2012- 1:18:47, 2013- 1:18:55, 2014- 1:18:52, 2015- 1:19:45, 2016- 1:19:26, 2018- 1:20:38, 2019- 1:19:36, 2020- 1:22:03, 2021- 1:17:39. Pbs: 5000mW 19:35.00 '14, 10,000mW 38:59.08 '12, 30kW 2:45:13 '09.

HUANG Changzhou b. 20 Aug 1994 Guanghan, Sichuan Prov 1.83m 66kg.
At LJ: OG: '16- 11; WCh: '17/19- dnq 24/16; AsiC: '15-17-19: dnq/1/3; WI: '16- 3; Won CHN 2019, NG 2017.
Progress at LJ: 2012- 7.79, 2013- 7.97, 2014- 8.12, 2015- 8.17, 2016- 8.21i/8.12, 2017- 8.28, 2018- 8.19i/8.19A/8.16, 2019- 8.24, 2020- 8.33.

LUO Yadong b. 15 Jan 1992. Gansu.
At 50kW: WCh: '19- 5. Won CHN 2021.
Progress at 50kW: 2012- 4:28:12, 2014- 4:04:26, 2015- 3:48:48. 2016- 4:08:22, 2017- 3:56:22, 2018- 4:02:15, 2019- 3:41:15, 2021- 3:46:51. Pbs: 10kW 41:01 '15, 20W 1:23:20 '13.

NIU Wenbin b. 20 Jan 1991 1.73m 60kg. Yunnan.
At 50kW: WCh: '17- 29, '19- 4; At 10kW: WCp: '10- 6J.
Progress at 50kW: 2011- 3:45:19, 2012- 4:07:51, 2013- 3:56:56, 2015- 3:51:00. 2016- 3:48:32, 2017- 3:46:12, 2018- 3:59:47, 2019- 3:41:04. Pbs: 10kW 41:06 '09, 20W 1:21:41 '13.

SU Bingtian b. 29 Aug 1989 Zhongshan, Guangdong Prov. 1.85m 65kg. Guandong.
At 100m: OG: '12- sf, '16- sf/4R; WCh: '13- sf, '15- 9/2R, '17- 8, '19- sf; AsiG: '14- 2/1R, '18- 1/3R; AsiC: '11- 1, '13- 1, '15- 1R; CCp: '18- 2; WUG: '11- 3. Won Chinese 100m 2009, 2011-13; E.Asian G 2013. At 60m: WI: '14-16-18: 4/5/2; AsiG: '09- 1; WIT 2018.
Records: Asian 100m (2) 2018, 4x100m 2016, indoor 60m (4) 2016-18, Chinese 100m (5) 2011-18.
Progress at 100m: 2006- 10.59, 2007- 10.45, 2008- 10.41, 2009- 10.28, 2010- 10.32, 2011- 10.16, 2012- 10.19/10.04w, 2013- 10.06, 2014- 10.10, 2015- 9.99, 2016- 10.08/10.04w, 2017- 10.03/9.92w, 2018- 9.91/9.90w, 2019- 10.05. pbs: 60m 6.42i '18, 200m 21.15 '19.

WANG Jianan b. 27 Aug 1996 Shenyang, Liaoning prov. 1.78m 61kg.
At LJ: OG: '16- 5; WCh: '13-15-17-19: dnq 23/3/7/6; WJ: '14- 1; AsiG: '18- 1; AsiC: '13- 1; CCp: '18- 5; WI '16- 8. Won W.MilG 2019.
LJ records: Chinese 2018, Asian junior 2015.
Progress at LJ: 2012- 8.04, 2013- 7.95, 2014- 8.10, 2015- 8.25, 2016- 8.24, 2017- 8.29, 2018- 8.47A/8.24, 2019- 8.20, 2020- 8.36. pbs: 60m 6.89i '12, 100m 10.88 '12, 60mh 8.46i '12, HJ 1.94 '12, PV 5.00 '12, Dec 7063 '12.
At 18 in 2015 he became the youngest ever male World Champs medallist at a field event.

WANG Kaihua b. 16 Feb 1994 Guangdong Prov. 1.80m 65kg.
At 20kW: WCh: '17- 7, '19- 8; AsiG: '18- 1; WT: '18- 2. Won CHN NG 2017, CHN 2020-21. At 10000mW: WY: '11- 6. CHN 20kW record 2021.
At20kW: 2011- 1:26:48, 2013- 1:23:35, 2014- 1:26:54, 2015- 1:19:49, 2016- 1:19:51, 2017- 1:17:54, 2018- 1:19:45, 2019- 1:19:01, 2020- 1:19:46, 2021- 1:16:54. Pbs: 10000mW 41:50.75 '11, 38:23R '20.

CHINA

WANG Qin b. 8 May 1994 1.78m 65kg. Shaanxi.
At 50kW: WCh: '19- dnf; AsiG: '18- 2; WT: '18- 5. Won CHN & W.MilG 2019.
Progress at 50kW: 2016- 3:50:16, 2017- 3:54:46, 2018- 3:45:29, 2019- 3:38:02, 2021- 3:47:35. Pbs: 10000mW 40:00.13 '18, 20W 1:22:08 '16, 35kW: 2:33:18 '18. 6-months drugs ban 2016-17.

WU Ruiting b. 29 Nov 1995. Guangdong 1.90m 73kg.
At TJ: WCh: '17- 9, '19- 9. Won CHN 2018, 2020.
Progress at TJ: 2014- 15.48, 2015- 16.83, 2016- 16.60, 2017- 17.18, 2018- 16.89, 2019- 17.47, 2020- 16.99i/16.90, 2021- 17.20i.

XIE Wenjun b. 11 Jul 1990 Shanghai 1.88m 77kg, Shanghai.
At 110mh: OG: '12- sf, '16- h; WCh: '13-15-17-19: h/sf/sf/4; AsiG: '14- 1, '18- 1; AsiC: '15/19- 1; CCp: '14- 4; Won CHN 2012, 2015-16, 2018, 2020; NG 2013, 2017.
Progress at 110mh: 2007- 14.09, 2008- 13.47, 2009- 13.53, 2010- 13.47, 2011- 13.45, 2012- 13.34, 2013- 13.28, 2014- 13.23, 2015- 13.36, 2016- 13.34, 2017- 13.31, 2018- 13.34, 2019- 13.17, 2020- 13.24/13.20w. pbs: 100m 11.04 '06, 60mh 7.60i '13.

XIE Zhenye b. 17 Aug 1993 Zhejiang Prov. 1.85m 80kg.
At (100m)/200m: OG: '12- h, '16- (sf)/4R; WCh: '13- h, 15- h/2R, '17- (sf)/4R, '19- sf/7; WJ: '12- 8/5; AsiG: '14- sf/1R; AsiC: '13- 1/3R, '15- (4, '19- 1); Asi-J: '12- 2/1; YOG: '10- 1. Won Chinese 100m 2014, 2017, 2020; 200m 2012-15, 2020; NG 100m & 200m 2017. At 60m: WI: '16-4, '18: 4.
Records: Asian 200m 2019, Chinese 100m 2018, 200m (5) 2014-19.
Progress at 100m, 200m: 2009- 21.85, 2010- 10.59, 21.18; 2011- 10.36, 20.79; 2012- 10.45, 20.54; 2013- 10.31, 20.55; 2014- 10.34/10.24w, 20.44; 2015- 10.25, 20.60; 2016- 10.08, 20.78; 2017- 10.04/9.91w, 20.20; 2018- 9.97, 20.16; 2019- 10.01, 19.88; 2020- 10.31/10.13w, 20.72. pb 60m 6.55 '17, 6.45i '18.

Women

CHEN Yang b. 10 Jul 1991 Hebei Prov. 1.80m 97kg. Hebei.
At DT: OG: '16- 7; WCh: '17- 10, '19- 4; AsiG: '18- 1; AsiC: '17- 1, '19- 2; CCp: '18- 3. Won CHN 2020.
Progress at DT: 51.05- 53.79, 2011- 51.10, 2012- 53.10, 2013- 52.10, 2014- 58.53, 2015- 61.16, 2016- 63.61, 2017- 62.90, 2018- 67.03, 2019- 64.88, 2020- 65.24.

FENG Bin b. 3 Apr 1994 1.84m 95kg. Shandong.
At DT: OG: '16- 8; WCh: '17- 8, '19- 5; AsiG: '18- 2; AsiC: '19- 1; WY: '11- 4. Won CHN 2018-19, W.MilG 2015 & 2019.
Progress at DT: 2010- 53.77, 2011- 55.94, 2012- 55.62, 2013- 58.14, 2014- 59.73, 2015- 62.07, 2016- 65.14, 2017- 64.46, 2018- 64.58, 2019- 65.45, 2020- 64.09, 2021- 63.19.

GONG Lijiao b. 24 Jan 1989 Luquan, Hebei Prov. 1.74m 110kg. Hebei.

At SP: OG: '08- 3, '12- 2, '16- 4; WCh: '07-09-11-13-15-17-19: 6/3/3/3/2/1/1; WI: '10-14-18: 6/3/3; AsiG: '10-14-18: 2/1/1; AsiC: '09- 1, '19- 1; CCp: '10-14-18: 2/3/3. Won DL 2017-19, Chinese 2007-12, 2014, 2016-19; NG 2009, 2013, 2017; Asian indoor 2008.
Progress at SP: 2005- 15.41i, 2006- 17.92, 2007- 19.13, 2008- 19.46, 2009- 20.35, 2010- 20.13, 2011- 20.11, 2012- 20.22, 2013- 20.12, 2014- 19.65, 2015- 20.34, 2016- 20.43, 2017- 20.11, 2018- 20.38, 2019- 20.31, 2020- 19.70i/19.58. pb JT 53.94 '07.

LI Ling b. 6 Jul 1989 Zhubo, Henan Province 1.84m 65kg. Zhejiang
At PV: OG: '08/12/16- dnq 27=/30/16; WCh: '09-11-15-19: dnq 18/dnq 29/11/9/13=; WJ: '06- nh; AsiG: '10-14-18: 2/1/1; AsiC: '11-13-15-17-19: 2/1/1/2/1; CCp: '14- 1; WUG: '15- 1. Won CHN 2008-09, 2011-13, 2015-16, 2018-19; NG 2013, Asian Indoors 2009, 2012, 2016.
Asian PV records (3) 2013-19, indoor (4) 2015-16, junior 2008.
Progress at PV: 2005- 3.90i/3.70, 2006- 4.15, 2007- 4.30, 2008- 4.45, 2009- 4.40, 2010- 4.45i/4.40, 2011- 4.40, 2012- 4.50i/4.40, 2013- 4.65, 2014- 4.61, 2015- 4.66, 2016- 4.70i/4.63, 2017- 4.50, 2018- 4.60, 2019- 4.72, 2020- 4.60.

LI Maocuo b. 20 Oct 1992.
At 50kW: WCh: '19- 2; WT: '18- 7.
Progress at 20kW, 50kW: 2010- 1:42:15, 2011- 1:35:40, 2012- 1:38:13, 2013- 1:36:06, 2014- 1:31:55, 2015- 1:33:55, 2016- 1:38:01, 4:47:28; 2017- 1:31:00, 2018- 1:30:15, 4:13:04; 2019- 1:30:34, 4:03:51; 2020- 1:32:12, 2021- 1:29:53. pb 10kW 43:48R '20.

LIANG Rui b. 18 Jun 1994 Yixian, Gansu Prov. 1.59m 48kg.
At 50kW: WCh: '19- 1; WCp: '18- 1; CHN champion 2018.
World record 2018 on 50k walk debut.
Progress at 20kW, 50kW: 2012- 1:37:21, 2014- 1:37:28, 2015- 1:29:22, 2016- 1:28:43, 2017- 1:28:50, 2018- 1:35:20, 4:04:36; 2019- 1:28:49, 4:19:34; 2020- 1:33:15. pbs: 5000mW 22:33.10 '14, 10000mW 46:04.91 '14, 44:34R '20; 35kW 2:48:23 '18.

LIU Hong b. 12 May 1987 Anfu, Jiangxi Prov. 1.61m 48kg. Guangdong.
At 20kW: OG: '08- 4, '12- 3, '16- 1; WCh: '07-09-11-13-15-19: 19/2/1/2/1/1; WCp: '06-14-16: 6/2/dq1; AsiG: '06- 1, '10- 1; won CHN 2010-11, NG 2009. At 10000mW: WJ: '06- 1; won IAAF Race Walking Challenge 10k 2012, 2014 (2nd 2011). At 50kW: won CHN 2019-20.
Walk records: World 20k 2015, 50k 2019 (on debut); Asian 5000m & 20k 2012.
At 20kW, 50kW: 2004- 1:35:04, 2005- 1:29:39, 2006- 1:28:26, 2007- 1:29:41, 2008- 1:27:17, 2009- 1:28:11, 2010- 1:30:06, 2011- 1:27:17, 2012- 1:25:46, 2013- 1:27:06, 2014- 1:26:58, 2015- 1:24:38, 2016- 1:25:56, 2019- 1:25:56, 3:59:15; 2020- 1:27:48. 2021- 1:24:27. pbs: 3000mW 12:18.18 '05, 5000mW 20:34.76 '12, 10kW 42:30R '10, 43:16.68t '12. Mar 2:51:23 '15.

Won IAAF Race Walking Challenge 2011-12 and 2014-15. Failed drugs test when 'winning' the World Cup 20k race in 2016 and received a three-months ban. Baby born on 20 Nov 2017.
LIU Shiying b. 24 Sep 1993 Shandong prov. 1.79m 76kg.
At JT: OG: '16- dnq 23; WCh: '17- 8, '19- 2; WJ: '12- 2; AsiG: '18- 1; AsiC: '15- 1, Asi-J '12- 1. Won CHN 2020. Asian javelin record 2017.
Progress at JT: 2010- 50.92, 2011- 55.10, 2012- 59.20, 2013- 60.23, 2014- 62.72, 2015- 62.77, 2016- 65.64, 2017- 66.47, 2018- 67.12, 2019- 65.88, 2020- 67.29, 2021- 64.56.
LU Huihui b. 26 Jun 1989 Huwan, Henan 1.71m 68kg.
At JT: OG: '12- 5, '16- 7; WCh: '15-17-19: 2/3/3; AsiG: '18- 2; AsiC: '19- 1; CCp: '18- 1. Won DL 2019, CHN 2018-19.
Seven Asian javelin records 2012-19. World indoor bests 62.65 & 64.21 in 2020.
Progress at JT: 2005- 49.62, 2006- 49.96, 2010- 55.35, 2011- 58.72, 2012- 64.95, 2013- 64.48/65.62dq, 2015- 66.13, 2016- 64.03, 2017- 67.59, 2018- 67.69, 2019- 67.98, 2020- 67.61, 2021- 66.55.
One-year drugs ban – positive test 27 Apr 2013.
LU Xiuzhi b. 26 Oct 1993 Chuzhou 1.67m 52kg.
At 20kW: OG: '12- 4, '16- 3; WCh: '15- 2, '17- dq; AsiC: '14- 1; WCp: '12-14-16: 3/6/5, won CHN 2014, 2018; NG 2013.
Asian 20k walk record 2015, junior 2012.
Progress at 20kW: 2011- 1:29:50, 2012- 1:27:01, 2013- 1:27:53, 2014- 1:27:15, 2015- 1:29:06, 2016- 1:28:07, 2017- 1:26:28, 2018- 1:29:06, 2019- 1:30:54, 2020- 1:32:31, 2021- 1:25:51. pb 10kW 43:08R '20.
LUO Na b. 8 Oct 1993 1.73m 78kg. Heilongjiang Prov.
At HT: WCh: '17- dnq 13, '19- 8; WJ: '12- 6; AsiG: '18- 1; AsiC: '15-17-19: 2/1/2; CCp: '18- 5; won CHN 2017, 2020. World indoor HT best 2020.
Progress at HT: 2010- 60.43, 2011- 62.68, 2012- 63.61, 2013- 67.09, 2014- 69.81, 2015- 67.11, 2016- 62.65, 2017- 72.27, 2018- 75.02, 2019- 72.93, 2020- 69.44i, 2021- 71.55.
MA Faying b. 30 Aug 1993 1.61m 50kg. Qinghai.
At 50kW: WCh: '19- 5; WT: '18- 5.
Progress at 50kW: 2016- 4:49:54, 2018- 4:13:28, 2019- 4:07:30. pbs: 10000mW 47:19.07 '14, 20kW 1:31:36 '17, 30kW 2:29:11 '18, 35k 2:54:21 '18.
QIEYANG Shenjie b. 11 Nov 1990 Haiyan, Qinghai Prov. 1.60m 50kg.
At 20kW: OG: '12- 2, '16- 5; WCh: '11-13-19: 3/14/2; AsiC: '18- 2; WCp: '12-16-18: 12/2/2. CHN champion 2015. Won IAAF Race Walking Challenge 2016 (1=), 2019.
Asian 20k walk record 2012.
Progress at 20kW: 2009- 1:35:54, 2010- 1:30:33, 2011- 1:28:04, 2012- 1:25:16, 2013- 1:28:05, 2015- 1:27:44, 2016- 1:26:49, 2017- 1:28:33, 2018- 1:27:06, 2019- 1:25:37, 2020- 1:28:27., 2021- 1:24:45 pbs: 5000mW 20:42.67 '12, 10kW 42:41R '20.

First athlete from Tibet to win Olympic medal. Won IAAF Race Walking Challenge 2018.
SU Xinyue b. 8 Nov 1991 1.79m 70kg. Hebei
At DT: OG: '16- 5; WCh: '13- dnq 19, '15- 8, '17- 7; AsiC: '13- 1, '15- 1; WJ: '10- dnq 13. Won CHN NG 2017.
Progress at DT: 2007- 48.29, 2009- 52.51, 2010- 56.11, 2011- 57.57, 2012- 60.32, 2013- 61.67, 2014- 61.31, 2015- 64.27, 2016- 65.59, 2017- 64.56, 2018- 63.73, 2019- 63.74, 2020- 61.94.
WANG Zheng b. 14 Dec 1987 Xian, Shanxi Province 1.74m 108kg.
At HT: OG: '08- dnq 30, '16- nt; WCh: '13-15-17-19: 3/5/2/3; WJ: '06- 9; AsiG: '10-14-18: 2/2/2; AsiC: '13- 1, '19- 1; CCp: '14- 4; won Asi-J 2006, E.Asian 2009, W.MilG 2019, CHN 2014, 2016, 2019. Asian hammer record 2014.
Progress at HT: 2004- 54.57, 2005- 55.72, 2006- 61.43, 2007- 64.04, 2008- 70.07, 2009- 67.06, 2010- 71.19, 2011- 68.75, 2012- 69.14, 2013- 74.90, 2014- 77.68, 2015- 74.92, 2016- 74.50, 2017- 76.25, 2018- 73.73, 2019- 76.26, 2020- 71.36, 2021- 73.55.
YANG Jiayu b. 18 Feb 1996 Wuhai, Hainan 1.63m 48kg.
At 20kW: WCh: '17- 1, '19- dq; WT: '16- 7, '18- 3; AsiC: '18- 1; WUG: '15- 5, won W.MilG 2019, CHN NG 2017. At 10kW: WCp: '14- 2J.
World 20k walk record 2021.
Progress at 20kW: 2013- 1:40:27, 2015- 1:36:50, 2016- 1:28:12, 2017- 1:26:18, 2018- 1:27:22, 2019- 1:25:34, 2020- 1:28:06, 2021- 1:23:49. Pbs: 5000mW 22:22.47 '14, 10000mW 42:00.4 '20, 41:25R '20.
YANG Liujing b. 22 Aug 1998 Shaanxi Prov.
At 20kW: WCh: '19- 3.
Progress at 20kW: 2018- 1:29:31, 2019- 1:27:15, 2020- 1:31:00, 2021- 1:25:59. Pbs: 10000mW 46:25.37 '15, 43:40R '17.
YIN Hang b. 7 Feb 1997 1.61m 50kg. Army.
At 50kW: WCh: '17- 2; WT: '18- 2.
Two Asian 50kW records 2017.
Progress at 20kW, 50kW: 2016- 1:34:25, 2017- 1:31:23, 4:08:58; 2018- 1:35:27, 4:09:09; 2019- 1:33:16, 4:27:50. pb 10kW 44:52 '16.

COLOMBIA

Governing body: Federación Colombiana de Atletismo. Founded 1937.
National Games Champions 2020: Men: 20kW: Jhon Casteñeda 1:29:43. **Women**: 20kW: Laura Cristina Chalarca 1:43:58.

Mauricio ORTEGA b. 4 Aug 1994 Apartadó 1.84m 102kg.
At DT: OG: '16- dnq 18; WCh: '15- 11, '17/19- dnq 15/20; WJ: '12- 9, WY: '11- 4; PAm: '15- 7, '19- 5; PAm-J '13-2; SAG: '14/18- 1; SACh: '15/17/19- 1, CAG: '18- 1; Won SAm-J 2011, 2013, U23 2012, 2014; IbAm 2018, COL 2018-19.
South American discus records: U18 1.5kg 2011, U20 1.75kg in 2013, U23 (3) 2015-16, Senior (3)

2019-20, 12 COL 2013-20.
Progress at DT: 2012- 55.00, 2013- 59.67, 2014- 62.30, 2015- 64.47A, 2016- 65.84, 2017- 65.81, 2018- 66.30, 2019- 66.42, 2020- 70.29

Anthony ZAMBRANO b. 17 Jan 1998 Maicao, La Guajira 1.79m 68kg.
At 400m: WCh: '19- 2; WJ: '16- 6; WY: '15- 7, PAm: '19- 1/1R; SACh: '19- 1/1R; SA23: '18- 1. South American & 3 COL 400m records 2019. Progress at 400m: 2014- 48.17A, 2015- 46.27A, 2016- 45.81, 2017- 48.66, 2018- 45.19, 2019- 44.15. pb 200m 20.61 '19. In 2019 won Colombia's first track medal at a World Championships.

Women

Sandra Lorena **ARENAS** b. 17 Sep 1993 Pereira, Risaralda 1.60m 50kg.
At 20kW: OG: 12- 30, '16- 32; WCh: '13-15-17-19: 20/19/5/5; WCp: '16- 10, '18- 15; PAm: '15- 4, '19- 1; SACh: '13- 1, '15- 1; SAG: '14- 1. COL champion 2012-14, 2016, 2019; SAm-J 2011, BolG 2017. At 10000mW: WJ: '12- 3; won PAm-J & SAm-J 2011.
10kW: WCp: '12- 1J; won IbAm 2018.
Walk records: S.American track 20000m 2014, 10000m 2018. Seven COL 20k 2012-19.
Progress at 20kW: 2011- 1:48:36.0A, 2012- 1:32:36, 2013- 1:32:25, 2014- 1:30:18, 2015- 1:31:02.25t, 2016- 1:29:31, 2017- 1:28:10, 2018- 1:28:48, 2019- 1:28:03. Pbs: 5000mW 23:01.4A '15, 10000mW 42:02.99 '18.

Caterine IBARGÜEN b. 12 Feb 1984 Apartadó, Antioquia 1.81m 65kg. Studying nursing.
At TJ/(LJ): OG: '12- 2, '16- 1; WCh: '11-13-15-17-19: 3/1/1/2/3; WJ: '02: dnq 17; PAm: '11- 1/3; '15- 1. '19- /5; SACh: '03- 3/2, '05- 3/3, '06- 2/2, '07- (3), '09- 1, '11- 1/3; CAG: '02-06-10-14-18: 2/(2)/2/1/1&1; CCp: '14- 1, '18- 1/1. At HJ: OG: '04- dnq 27=; WCh: '09- dnq 25=; PAm: '07- 4; SACh: '99-05-06-07-09: 3/1/1/1/1; CAG: '02- 2, '06- 2. Won DL 2013-16, 2018 (& LJ 2018) COL HJ 1999, 2001-03, 2005-12, 2015; LJ 2003-04, 2006-08, 2011-12, 2015; TJ 2002-05, 2007-12, 2014.
Records: South American triple jump (7) 2011-14, junior HJ 2003. Colombia HJ (7) 2002-05, LJ (10) 2004-18, TJ (15) 2004-14. Two world W35 TJ records 2019.
Progress at LJ, TJ: 2001- 12.90, 2002- 6.08A, 13.38A; 2003- 6.18A, 13.23A; 2004- 6.42A, 13.64A; 2005- 6.54A, 13.66A; 2006- 6.49A/6.52Aw, 13.91A/13.98Aw; 2007- 6.22A, 12.66A; 2008- 6.54A, 13.79A; 2009- 6.41A, 13.96A/13.93; 2010- 6.29/6.34w, 14.29; 2011- 6.63A, 14.99A/14.84; 2012- 6.73A, 6.87Aw, 14.95A/14.85; 2013- 6.54, 14.85/14.93w; 2014- 15.31, 2015- 6.63/6.66w; 14.90/15.18w; 2016- 15.17, 2017- 14.89, 2018- 6.93, 14.96; 2019- 6.87, 14.89. pbs: 200m 25.34 '08, 100mh 14.09 '11, HJ 1.93A '05, SP 13.79 '10, JT 44.81 '09, Hep 5742 '09.
First Colombian woman to win a medal in world champs. 34 successive TJ wins 2012-16. She had 77 successive competitions over 14m from April 2010 to June 2017. IAAF Female athlete of the Year 2018. Lives in Puerto Rico.

COSTA RICA

Andrea Carolina **VARGAS** b. 28 May 1996 Santiago de Purisca 1.68m 60kg. Law degree from Universidad Panamericana.
At 100mh: WCh: '19- 5; WJ: '14- sf; PAm: '19- 1; CAG: '18- 1. Ib.Am champion 2018, C.Am 2016. 13 CRC 100mh records 2014-19.
Progress at 100mh: 2013- 13.92A, 2014- 13.72A, 2016- 13.60, 2017- 13.12, 2018- 12.90/12.75w, 2019- 12.64. pbs: 100m 12.12 '17, 200m 24.59A '16, 60mh 8.19i '18.
In 2019 won Costa Rica's first Pan-Am Games athletics gold medal by a female. Daughter Abril born 2015. Sister Noelia (b. 17 Apr 2000, 20kW pb 1:33:09 '19).

CROATIA

Governing body: Hrvatski Atletski Savez. Founded 1912.

National Champions 2020: Men: 100m/200m/LJ: Marko Ceko 10.45/21.18/8.04, 400m: Mateo Ruzic 47.63, 800m: Sven Cepus 1:54.55, 1500m: Daniel Ivanicic 3:54.70, 3000m/5000m/10000m: Dino Bosnjak 8:33.63/14:53.79/30:17.73, 3000mSt: Bruno Belcic 9:06.90, 110mh: Trpimic Siroki 14.48, 400mh: Mateo Parlov 52.12, HJ: Filip Mrcic 2.12, PV: Ivan Horvat 5.00, TJ: Ivan Feiss 14.71, SP: Filip Mihaljevic 21.58, DT: Marin Premeru 73.30, HT: Mirko Micuda 62.94, JT: Vitaliy Favoriov 60.11; **Women:** 100m: Margareta Risek 11.95, 200m/400m: Veronika Drljacic 24.42/54.66, 800m: Maja Pacaric 2:10.74, 1500m: Klara Andrijasevic 4:37.35, 5000m: Bojana Bjeljac 17:38.35, 10000m: Mateo Parlov 34:35.10, 3000mSt: Helena Valentic 11:21.11, 100mh: Ivana Loncarek 13.17, 400mh: Ida Simuncic 59.80, HJ: Sara Ascic 1.75, PV: Lara Jurisa 3.60, LJ/TJ: Paola Borovic 6.06/13.61, SP/DT: Marija Tolj 15.12/54.71, HT: Anamari Kozul 64.50, JT: Mirta Kulisic 50.37.

Filip MIHALJEVIC b. 31 Jul 1994 Livno, Bosnia & Herzegovina 2.01m 113kg. University of Virginia, USA.
At SP/(DT): OG: '16- dnq 21; WCh: '17- dnq 14, '19- 11; EC: '16/18: dnq 21/22; EU23: '15- 1/4; EJ: '13- 2/11; WI: '16- 3; EI: '21- 3; WIT 2020. Won CRO SP 2013, 2020; DT 2015-17, NCAA SP 2016-17, DT 2017. Croatian shot record 2019.
Progress at SP: 2012- 16.52, 2013- 17.54, 2014- 19.65, 2015- 20.16, 2016- 20.87i/20.71, 2017- 21.30, 2018- 21.33, 2019- 21.84, 2020- 21.84i/21.69, 2021- 21.31i. pb DT 63.76 '17.
Father Mirko Yugoslav CC champion 1987-8.

Women

Sara KOLAK b. 22 Jun 1995 Koprivnica 1.70m 74kg. AK Kvarner Rijeka.
At JT: OG: '16- 1; WCh: '17- 4, '19- 7; EC: '14- dnq

21, 16- 3; WJ: '12- dnq 23, '14- 3; EU23: '17- 1; EJ: '13- 3; Croatian champion 2012-14, 2016.
11 Croatian JT records 2013-17.
Progress at JT: 2008- 31.78, 2009- 43.13, 2010- 55.69, 2011- 45.94, 2012- 53.98, 2013- 57.79, 2014- 57.79, 2016- 66.18, 2017- 68.43, 2019- 66.42, 2020- 62.68. CRO javelin records 63.50 for 3rd EC, and at OG 64.30 qualifying and 66.18 gold in final.
Sandra PERKOVIC b. 21 Jun 1990 Zagreb 1.83m 80kg. Zagreb.
At DT(/SP): OG: '12- 1, '16- 1; WCh: '09-13-15-17-19: 9/1/2/1/3; EC: '10-12-14-16-18: 1/1/1/1/1; WJ: '06- dnq 21, '08- 3/dnq 13; WY: '07- 2/dnq 13; EJ: '07- 2, '09- 1/5; CCp: '10-14-18: 2/3/1. Won DL 2012-17, Med G 2013, 2018; CRO SP 2008-10, DT 2010, 2012.
9 Croatian DT records 2009-14, 2 SP 2010-11.
Progress at DT: 2004- 30.37, 2005- 36.21, 2006- 50.11, 2007- 55.42, 2008- 55.89, 2009- 62.79, 2010- 66.93, 2011- 67.96/69.99dq, 2012- 69.11, 2013- 68.96, 2014- 71.08, 2015- 70.08, 2016- 70.88, 2017- 71.41, 2018- 71.38, 2019- 68.58, 2020- 65.93. pb SP 16.99i/16.40 '11.
First woman to win European and Olympic gold for Croatia, now has record five European titles. Won 79 of 94 competitions 2012-20, inc. all seven in 2016. Ties women's record with six Diamond League titles. Her 70.51 and 71.08 to win her third European title in 2014 and her 71.41 in 2017 were the women's world's best throws since 1992. Six months drugs ban 2011. Served the Croatian Parliament 2015-16.

CUBA

Governing body: Federación Cubana de Atletismo. Founded 1922.
National Champions 2020: Men: 100m/200m Reynier Mena 10.02w/20.37, 400m: Raydel Rojas 47.75, 800m/1500m: Pedro Acuña 1:49.71/3:53.29, 5000m/10000m: Luis A Martínez 14:51.30/30:52.8, 3000mSt: Luis E Hernández 9:30.06, 110mh: Yordan O'Farrill 13.61, 400mh: Lázaro T Rodríguez 51.10, HJ: Luis Enrique Zayas 2.20, PV: Eduardo Nápoles 5.32, LJ: Juan Miguel Echevarría 8.25, TJ: Andy Díaz 17.30, SP: Bryan F Pérez 17.43, DT: Jorge Fernández 60.93, HT: Yasmani Fernández 70.75, JT: Osmany Laffita 71.44, Dec: Leonel Suárez 7790, 20kW: Ronaldo Hernández 1:38:05. **Women**: 100m/200m: Yunisleidy García 11.32/23.26, 400m: Lisneidy Veitía 53.82, 800m: Rose Mary Almanza 1:59.05, 1500m: Sahily Diago 4:21.57, 5000m/10000m: Arletis Thaureaux 17:02.61/36:13.09, 100mh: Keily Pérez 13.12, 400mh: Zurian Hechavarría 55.89, HJ: Nataly Armenteros 1.75, PV: Lisa M Salomón 4.10, LJ: Yanisley Carrión 5.76, TJ: Liadagmis Povea 14.45, SP: Yaniuvis López 16.68, DT: Yaimé Pérez 64.76, HT: Yaritza de le C Martínez 65.00, JT: Yiselena Ballar 55.60, Hep: Adriana Rodríguez 6304, 20kW: Yunialed Contreras 1:49:54/1:48.52

Andy DÍAZ b. 25 Dec 1995 Guanabacoa, La Habana 1.91m 80kg.
At TJ: WCh: '17- 7, '19- dnq 24; WJ: '14- 4; PAm: '19- 3. Won CUB 2017, 2019-20.
Progress at TJ: 2010- 13.29, 2012- 14.44, 2013- 15.70, 2014- 16.38/16.43w, 2015- 16.81, 2016- 16.80, 2017- 17.40, 2018- 16.52, 2019- 17.22/17.41w, 2020- 17.30. pb LJ 7.40 '17.
Jordan Alejandro **DÍAZ** Plaza de la Revolución b. 23 Feb 2001 La Habana 1.92m 73kg.
At TJ: WCh: '19- 8; WJ: '18- 1; WY: '17- 1; PAm: '19- 2; CAG: '18- 2; YthOG: '18- 1 Won NACAC 2018. Three world U18 TJ records 2017-18.
Progress at TJ: 2015- 15.02, 2016- 15.65, 2017- 17.30A/16.66, 2018- 17.41, 2019- 17.49, 2020- 17.07i.
Juan Miguel ECHEVARRÍA b. 11 Aug 1998 Camagüey 1.86m 76kg.
At LJ: WCh: '17- dnq 15, '19- 3; WJ: '16- 5, WY: '15- 4; PAm: '19- 1; PAm-J: '15- 1; WI: '18- 1. Won DL 2019, Cuban 2016, 2019-20; WIT 2020-21.
Progress at LJ: 2012- 5.69, 2013- 6.36, 2014- 7.47, 2015- 8.05, 2016-7.96/8.15w, 2017- 8.28/8.34w, 2018- 8.68/8.83w, 2019- 8.65/8.92w, 2020- 8.41i/8.25, 2021- 8.25i. Pb TJ 14.67 '14.
Lázaro MARTÍNEZ b. 3 Nov 1997 Guantánamo 1.92m 85kg.
At TJ: OG: '16- 8; WCh: '17- 12; WJ: '14- 1, '16- 1; WY: '13- 1; CAG: '14- 2; PAm-J: '13- 1. Won CUB 2016. World youth triple jump record 2014.
Progress at TJ: 2011- 14.62, 2012- 15.38, 2013- 16.63, 2014- 17.24, 2015- 17.02, 2016- 17.06, 2017- 17.07, 2018- 17.28, 2020- 17.08.
Maykel Demetrio **MASSÓ** b. 8 May 1999 Santiago de Cuba 1.78m 69kg.
At LJ: OG: '16- dnq 15; WCh: '15- dnq 23, '17- 5; WJ: '16- 1; WY: '15- 1; PAm: '19- 12; CUB champion 2017. CAC junior LJ record 2017.
Progress at LJ: 2013- 6.41, 2014- 7.59, 2015- 8.12, 2016- 8.28, 2017- 8.33, 2018- 7.92, 2019- 8.22/8.30w, 2020- 8.26.
Cristian Atanay **NÁPOLES** b. 27 Nov 1998 Marianao, La Habana 1.81m 80kg.
At TJ: WCh: '17- 4, '19- 5; WJ: '16- 2; WY: '15- 1; CAG: '18- 1; CCp: '18- 2. Won IbAm 2018, SAm-Y 2014.
Progress at TJ: 2013- 14.41, 2014- 15.42, 2015- 16.45, 2016- 16.92, 2017- 17.27, 2018- 17.34, 2019- 17.38/17.43w, 2020- 17.18. pb LJ 7.51 '19.
Luis Enrique ZAYAS b. 7 Jun 1997 Santiago de Cuba 1.94m 79kg.
At HJ: WCh: '19- 5; WJ: '16- 1; PAm: '19- 1. Cuban champion 2016-17, 2019-20.
Progress at HJ: 2010- 1.65, 2011- 1.85, 2012- 1.94, 2013- 2.13, 2014- 2.18, 2015- 2.16, 2017- 2.20, 2018- 2.23, 2019- 2.30, 2020- 2.33i/2.20, 2021- 2.31i.

Women

Rose Mary ALMANZA b. 13 Jul 1992 Camagüey 1.65m 55kg.

CUBA – CYPRUS

At 800m: OG: '12- sf, '16- h; WCh: '13/15/17/19- sf; WJ: '10- 4; WY: '09- 4; PAm: '11-15-19: 4/4/2 (7 1500m); CAG: '14- 1, '18- 1/1 1500m/1R; WUG: '17- 1. Won Cuban 800m 2010-11, 2014-15, 2017, 2019-20; 1500m 2013, 2015, 2017, 2019.
Two CAC junior 800m records 2010-11.
Progress at 800m: 2008- 2:11.1, 2009- 2:03.61, 2010- 2:02.04, 2011- 2:00.56, 2012- 1:59.55, 2013- 1:59.4, 2014- 1:59.48, 2015- 1:57.70, 2016- 1:58.49, 2017- 1:59.11, 2018- 2:00.15, 2019- 1:59.04, 2020- 1:58.92. pbs: 400m 53.66 '17, 600m 1:26.33mx '14, 1:26.9 '13; 1000m 2:38.1 '14, 1500m 4:14.53 '14.

Denia CABALLERO b. 13 Jan 1990 Caibarién, Villa Clara 1.75m 80kg. VCL.
At DT: OG: '12- dnq 25, '16- 3; WCh: '11-13-15-17-19: 9/8/1/5/2; PAm: '11-15-19: 3/1/3; CAG: '14- 1, '18- 2. Won CAC 2011, Cuban 2015.
Progress at DT: 2005- 36.10, 2006- 44.13, 2007- 46.08, 2008- 52.10, 2009- 57.21, 2010- 59.92, 2011- 62.94, 2012- 65.60, 2013- 63.47, 2014- 64.89, 2015- 70.65, 2016- 67.62, 2017- 67.04, 2018- 66.09, 2019- 69.20, 2020- 63.71.

Yaimé PÉREZ b. 29 May 1991 Santiago de Cuba 1.72m 780kg.
At DT: OG: '12- dnq 28, '16- nt; WCh: '13-15-17-19: 11/4/4/1; WJ: '10- 1; PAm: '15- 2, '19- 1; CAG: '14- 2, '18- 1; CCp: '14- 5, '18- 2. Won Cuban 2013-14, 2016-17, 2019-20; NACAC 2018, DL 2018-19.
Progress at DT: 2005- 36.10, 2006- 44.13, 2007- 46.29, 2008- 51.80, 2009- 55.23, 2010- 59.30, 2011- 59.26, 2012- 62.50, 2013- 66.01, 2014- 66.03, 2015- 67.13, 2016- 68.86, 2017- 69.19, 2018- 67.82, 2019- 69.39, 2020- 64.76, 2021- 67.73. pbs SP 13.88 '08.

Liadagmis POVEA b. 6 Feb 1996 Pinar del Rio 1.66m 52kg.
At TJ: OG: '16- dnq 15; WCh: '17/19- dnq 22/15; PAm: '15- 6, '19- 3; WJ: '14- 2. Won WIT 2021, CUB 2016-17, 2020.
Progress at TJ: 2010- 12.09, 2011- 11.89, 2012- 12.88, 2013- 13.54, 2014- 14.02/14.07w, 2015- 14.08, 2016- 14.56, 2017- 14.45, 2018- 14.30/14.44w, 2019- 14.77/15.05w, 2020- 14.55/14.78w, 2021- 14.54i. pb LJ 6.15 '17.

Adriana RODRÍGUEZ b. 12 Jul 1999 La Palma 1.72m 62kg.
At Hep: WJ: '16- 2; '18- 4; WY: '15- 6; PAm: '19- 1 (6 LJ); PAm-J: '17- 1; won CUB 2019-20. At LJ: WCh: '19- dnq 25.
Progress at Hep: 2016- 5925, 2017- 5733, 2018- 6094, 2019- 6293w/6113, 2020- 6304. pbs: 100m 11.39 '18, 200m 23.59 '20, 23.40w '15; 400m 54.14 '19, 800m 2:16.14 '20, 100mh 13.10 '19, 12.8w '20; HJ 1.84 '20, LJ 6.70 '19, SP 13.29 '18, JT 37.36 '16.

Yorgelis RODRÍGUEZ b. 25 Jan 1995 Guantánamo 1.71m 65kg.
At Hep: OG: '16- 7; WCh: '13- 12, '15- 21, '17- 4; WJ: '12- 1; '14- 2 (dnq 16= HJ); WY: '11- 2; PAm: '15- 1, '19- dnf; CAG: '18- 1; At Pen: WI: '18- 3; won PAmCp 2013, 2015; CAG 2014, Cuban HJ 2017, Hep 2013, 2016.

Heptathlon records: CAC 2017 & 2018, 2 Cuban 2016-17, 3 CAC junior 2012-14.
Progress at Hep: 2012- 5994, 2013- 6186, 2014- 6231, 2015- 6332, 2016- 6481, 2017- 6594, 2018- 6742. pbs: 200m 23.96 '18, 800m 2:10.48 '17, 60mh 8.57i '18, 100mh 13.48 '18, HJ 1.95 '17, LJ 6.41 '17, SP 14.64 '16, JT 48.96 '18, Pen 4637i '18.
Three HJ pbs 1.89, 1.92 & 1.95 in World heptathlon 2015.

Yarisley SILVA b. 1 Jun 1987 Pinar del Río 1.69m 68kg.
At PV: OG: '08- dnq 27=, '12- 2, '16- 7=; WCh: '11-13-15-17-19: 5/3/1/3=/11; WI: '12-14-18: 7/1/7; WJ: '06- dnq; PAm: '07-11-15-19: 3/1/1/1; CAG: '14- 1, '18- 1; CCp: 18- 4; Won CAC 2009, Cuban 2004, 2006-07, 2009, 2012-13, 2015, 2017, 2019.
Pole vault records: 19 Cuban & CAC 2007-15 (9 in 2011), 8 CAC indoor 2012 & 2013 (to 4.82).
Progress at PV: 2001- 2.50, 2002- 3.10, 2003- 3.70, 2004- 4.00, 2005- 4.10, 2006- 4.20, 2007- 4.30, 2008- 4.50, 2009- 4.50, 2010- 4.40, 2011- 4.75A/4.70, 2012- 4.75, 2013- 4.90, 2014- 4.70, 2015- 4.91, 2016- 4.84, 2017- 4.81, 2018- 4.80, 2019- 4.75, 2020- 4.74i.

CYPRUS

Governing body: Amateur Athletic Association of Cyprus. Founded 1983.
National Championships first held in 1896, 1952 (women). **2020 Champions: Men**: 100m: Emmanouil Christodoulou 10.70w, 200m/400m: Andeas Christoforou 21.69/49.21, 800m: Stavros Spyrou 1:54.37, 1500m: Andreas Michiara 4:03.62, 5000m: Fanis Pittalis 15:46.39, 10000m/ 3000mSt: Nikolaos Frangou 32:57.7/9:34.59, HMar: Marios Apostolides 73:00, 110mh/LJ: Elvis Kryoukov 14.15w/7.42w, 400mh: Anastasios Vasileiou 55.10, HJ: Ioannis Ananiadis 1.95, PV: Christos Tamanis 4.60, TJ: Grigoris Nikolaou 15.53, SP: Vasilis Mouaimis 16.27, DT: Apostolos Parellis 59.86, HT: Alexandros Poursanides 69.40, JT: Spyros Savva 69.86. **Women**: 100m: Santa Colomeiteva 11.91, 200m: Eleni Artymata 23.48w, 400m/800m: Kalliopi Kountouri 55.35/ 2:13.83, 1500m: Maria Papanastasiou 4:49.51, 5000m/HMar: Thalia Charalambous 16:58.08/ 77:22, 10000m: Dagmara Handzlik 37:23.68, 3000mSt: Charitini Pavlou 12:15.71, 100mh: Natalia Christofi 13.58w, 400mh: Michailina Retiskin 66.05, HJ: Styliana Ioannidou 1.84, PV: Andrea Vassou 3.60, LJ: Charithea Irakleous 5.93w, TJ: Christonymfi Pediou 12.19, SP: Styliana Kyriakidou 13.21, DT: Androniki Lada 52.82, HT: Chrystalla Kyriakou 58.40, JT: Christiana Ellina 47.74.

CZECH REPUBLIC

Governing body: Cesky atleticky svaz. AAU of Bohemia founded in 1897.
National Championships first held in 1907 (Bohemia), 1919 (Czechoslovakia), 1993 CZE.
2020 Champions: Men: 100m: Jan Veleba 10.28,

CZECH REPUBLIC

200m: Jirí Polák 20.63, 400m: Matej Krsek 46.25, 800m: Lukás Hodbod 1:47.98, 1500m: Filip Sasinek 3:36.72, 5000m: Viktor Sinágl 14:31.37, 10000m/HMar: Vit Pavlista 30:14.01/65:56, 3000mSt: Damián Vích 8:48.47, 110mh: Jan Kisiala 14.33, 400mh: Vit Müller 49.93, HJ: Marek Bahník 2.14, PV: Jan Kudlicka 5.51, LJ: Radek Juska 8.10, TJ: Jirí Vondrácek 16.34, SP: Martin Novák 18.27, DT: Marek Bárta 61.01, HT: Patrik Hájek 71.19, JT: Petr Frydrych 79.38, Dec: Radol Rykl 7130, 20kW: Lukás Gdula 1:27:07; 50000mW: Vit Hlavác 3:56:28.40. **Women**: 100m: Marcela Pírková 11.61, 200m: Martina Hofmanová 23.43, 400m: Barbora Malíková 51.65, 800m: Vendula Hluchá 2:09.75, 1500m/5000m: Simona Vrzalová 4:17.41/16:08.63, 10000m: Moira Stewartová 34:20.75, HMar: Marcela Joglová 73:46, 3000mSt: Tereza Novotná 10:12.94, 100mh: Katerina Cachová 13.23, 400mh: Zuzana Hejnová 55.70, HJ: Bára Sajdoková 1.90, PV: Amálie Svabíková & Romana Malácová 4.46, LJ/TJ: Linda Suchá 6.45/13.35, SP: Markéta Cervenková 18.08, DT: Eliska Stanková 56.34, HT: Lenka Valesová 65.50, JT: Nikola Ogrodníková 61.41, Hep: Jana Novotná 5878, 20kW: Teresa Durdiaková 1:33:54.

Tomás STANEK b. 13 Jun 1991 Prague 1.90m 127kg. Dukla Praha.
At SP: OG: '16- dnq 20; WCh: '15- dnq 19, '17- 4, '19- 10; EC: '14: dnq 14, '18- 4; EU23: '13- 5; WI: '18- 3; EI: '17- 2, '19- 3; CCp: '18- 5; ET: '17- 19-21: 1/2/1. CZE champion 2016-19; WIT 2018.
Two Czech records 2017.
Progress at SP: 2009- 15.01, 2010- 15.40, 2011- 17.16, 2012- 18.52, 2013- 19.50, 2014- 20.93, 2015- 20.94i/20.64, 2016- 21.30i/21.26, 2017- 22.01, 2018- 22.17i/21.87, 2019- 21.67, 2020- 21.86i/21.24, 2021- 21.62i.

Jakub VADLEJCH b. 10 Oct 1990 Praha 1.92m 93kg. Dukla Praha.
At JT: OG: '12- dnq 24, '16- 8; WCh: '11/15- dnq 16/20, '17- 2, '19- 5; EC: '10-14-16-18: dnq 16/dnq 20/9/8; WJ: '08- 10; WY: '07- 12; EJ: '09- 8; CCp: '18- 2; ET: '17- 1, '19- 2. Won DL 2016-17, Czech 2014-15, 2017, 2019.
Progress at JT: 2006- 55.24, 2007- 66.12, 2008- 76.59, 2009- 81.95, 2010- 84.47, 2011- 84.08, 2012- 80.40A, 2013- 75.85, 2014- 82.97, 2015- 86.21, 2016- 88.02, 2017- 89.73, 2018- 89.02, 2019- 85.78, 2020- 84.31. Married Lucia Slaníckova (SVK records: 400mh 56.96 '14, Hep 6103 '17, Indoor Pen 4488 '20) in October 2017.

Women

Zuzana HEJNOVÁ b. 19 Dec 1986 Liberec 1.70m 54kg. Dukla Praha.
At 400mh/4x400mR: OG: '08- 7, '12- 3, '16- 4; WCh: '05-07-09-: sf, '11-13-15-17-19: 7/1/1/4/5; EC: '06-10-12-18: sf/4/4&3R/sf; WJ: '02- 5, '04- 2; EU23: '07- 3; EJ: '03- 3; '05- 1; WY: '03- 1; WI: '10- 2R; ET: '09-11-19: 3/1/1. Won DL 2013, 2015. At 400m: EI: '13- 4/3R, '17- 2. At Pen: EI: '11- 7. Won CZE 400m 2006, 2009; 400mh 2018, 2020.
12 Czech 400mh records 2005-13. 3 world bests 300mh 2011 (38.91) and 2013 (38.75 & 38.16).
Progress at 400mh: 2002- 58.42, 2003- 57.54, 2004- 57.44, 2005- 55.89, 2006- 55.83, 2007- 55.04, 2008- 54.96, 2009- 54.90, 2010- 54.13, 2011- 53.29, 2012- 53.38, 2013- 52.83, 2014- 55.86, 2015- 53.50, 2016- 53.92, 2017- 53.93, 2018- 55.16, 2019- 54.11, 2020- 55.49. pbs: 60m 7.64i '17, 150m 17.66 '13, 200m 23.65 '13, 300m 37.49A/37.80 '13, 400m 51.90/51.27i '13, 600m 1:28.04i '15, 800m 2:03.40i '16, 60mh 8.24i '17, 100mh 13.36 '11, 13.18w '10; 200mh 26.29 '17, 300mh 38.16 '13, HJ 1.80i '11, 1.74 '04; LJ 5.96i '11, 5.76 '07, SP 12.11i '11, JT 36.11 '10, Pen 4453i '11.
Unbeaten season at hurdles in 2013. Sister of Michaela Hejnová (b. 10 Apr 1980) pb Hep 6174w/6065 '04; OG: '04- 26; EC '02- 7; EU23: '01- 5; WJ: '98- 5; EJ: '97- 6/'99- 6 (100mh); WUG: '01- 5, '03- 3.

Nikola OGRODNÍKOVÁ b. 18 Aug 1990 Ostrava 1.75m 73kg. Dukla Praha.
At JT (Hep): WCh: '17- dnq 19, '19- 11; EC: '14- dnq 20, '18- 2; WJ: '08- 8 (22); WY: '07- (7); EU23: '11- dnq 22; EJ: '07- (3), '09- dnq 17; CCp: '18- 6; CZE champion 2018, 2020.
Progress at JT: 2004- 36.49, 2005- 43.06, 2006- 42.94, 2007- 50.41, 2008- 54.48, 2009- 53.58, 2010- 53.94, 2011- 54.46, 2012- 54.07, 2013- 56.20, 2014- 60.04, 2015- 56.30, 2016- 58.18, 2017- 62.24, 2018- 65.61A, 2019- 67.40, 2020- 64.22. Pbs: 200m 25.67 '07, 800m 2:21.92 '07, 60mh 8.44i '18, 100mh 13.75 '09, HJ 1.72 '07, LJ 5.77/5.79w '07, SP 12.82 '07, Pen 4068i '08, Hep 5607 '07.

Barbora SPOTÁKOVÁ b. 30 Jun 1981 Jablonec nad Nisou 1.82m 80kg. Dukla Praha.
At JT: OG: '04- dnq 23, '08- 1, '12- 1, '16- 3; WCh: '05-07-09-11-15-17-19: dnq 13/1/2/1/9/1/9; EC: '02-06-10-14-16: dnq 17/2/3/1/5; EU23: '03- 6; WUG: '03- 4, '05- 1; CCp: '14- 1; ET: '09-11-14-17: 2/3/1;/1 won DL 2010, 2012, 2014-15, 2017; WAF 2006-09, Czech 2003, 2005-13, 2015-17, 2019. At Hep: WJ: '00- 4.
World javelin record 2008, two European records 2008, 11 Czech records 2006-08. World heptathlon javelin best (60.90) in 2012.
Progress at JT: 1996- 31.32, 1997- 37.28, 1998- 44.56, new: 1999- 41.69, 2000- 54.15, 2001- 51.97, 2002- 56.76, 2003- 56.65, 2004- 60.95, 2005- 65.74, 2006- 66.21, 2007- 67.12, 2008- 72.28, 2009- 68.23, 2010- 68.66, 2011- 71.58, 2012- 69.55, 2013- 62.33, 2014- 67.99, 2015- 65.66, 2016- 66.87, 2017- 68.26, 2019- 63.85, 2020- 65.19. pbs: 200m 25.33/25.11w '00, 800m 2:18.29 '00, 60mh 8.68i '07, 100mh 13.99 '00, 400mh 62.68 '98, HJ 1.78 '00, LJ 5.45 '00, SP 14.53 '07, DT 36.80 '02, Hep 5880 '12, Dec 6749 '04.
Sons Janek born 24 May 2013 and Darek on 14 July 2018.

DENMARK
Governing body: Dansk Athletik Forbund. Founded 1907.
National Championships first held in 1894.
2020 Champions: Men: 100m/200m: Kojo Musah 10.29/20.87w, 400m: Gustav Lundholm Nielsen 47.67, 800m/1500m: Kristian Uldbjerg Hansen 1:50.20/4:06.53, 5000m: Thijs Nijhuis 14:19.75, 10000m: Abdi Hakin Ulad 29:43.53, 3000mSt: Jakob Dybdal Abrahamsen 9:05.14, 110mh: Andreas Martinsen 14.31, 400mh: Mathias Olsen 55.21, HJ: Mads Moos Larsen 2.05, PV: Nikolaj Graves 4.80, LJ: Sebastian Ree Pedersen 7.72, TJ: Jannick Bagge 14.85, SP: Kristoffer Thomsen 18.37, DT: Emil Mikkelsen 57.63, HT: Hans Barrett 59.74, JT: Arthur Wiborg Petersen 73.89, Dec: Christian Gundersen 7179w, 5000mW: Asbjørn Birkelund 25:54.8, 30kW: Andreas Nielsen 2:42:02. **Women**: 100m: Mathilde Kramer 11.60, 200m/100mh: Mette Graversgaard 23.54/13.42, 400m: Sara Slott Petersen 53.39, 800m: Mathilde Diekema Jensen 2:07.33, 1500m: Simobne Glad 4:26.56, 5000m/10000m: Laura Valgreen Petersen 16:39.18/33:35.13, 3000mSt: Laura Astrup 11:44.38, 400mh: Martha Danneskjold 59.60, HJ: Rikke Andersen 1.79, PV: Caroline Bonde Holm 4.20, LJ/TJ: Janne Nielsen 6.05/13.82, SP: Thea Jensen 15.20, DT: Kathrine Bebe 58.24, HT: Katrine Koch Jacobsen 60.97, JT: Liv Cantby 45.29, Hep: Sandra Böll 5442.

Anna Emilie MØLLER b. 28 Jul 1997 Copenhagen 1.68m 52kg. Blovstrød Løverne.
At (5000m)/3000mSt: OG: '16- h; WCh: '17- h, '19- h/7; WJ: '16- 5; EC: '18- 7; EU23: '17- 1, '19-1/1; At 3000m: EJ: '15- 3 (2). Eur CC: '14-15-16-17-18-19: 6J/8J/2J/7 U23/1 U23/1 U23. Won DEN 800m 2016, 2018; 1500m 2015-16, 2019; 5000m 2015, 2017, 2019; 3000mSt 2018.
Records: European U20 3000mSt 2016, U23 3000mSt (3) 2019; DEN records 5000m 2019, 3000mSt (8) 2016-19.
Progress at 5000m, 3000mSt: 2014- 16:28.85, 2015- 16:07.43, 10:09.58; 2016- 9:32.68. 2017-16:06.87, 9:34.30; 2018- 15:44.95, 9:31.66; 2019-15:07.70, 9:13.46; 2020- 15:21.0mx. pbs: 800m 2:05.91 '16, 1500m 4:09.12 '19, 3000m 8:47.83 '16, 10000m 34:29.41 '15.

Sara SLOTT PETERSEN b. 9 Apr 1987 Nykøbing Falster, Sjælland 1.71m 57kg. Århus 1900 AM.
At 400mh: OG: 12- sf, '16- 2; WCh: '09/11/17- sf, '15- 4, '19- h; EC: '10-12-14-16-18: h/sf/h/1/sf; WJ: '04- h; WY: '03- 4; EU23: '07- 6, '09- 6; EJ: '05- 4; WUG: '09- 3, '11-4; Won Danish 400mh 2002-09, 2011-12, 2014-15, 2019; 100m 2007, 2009; 200m 2009, 2012, 2016-17; 400m 2008-09.
12 Danish 400mh records 2007-16.
Progress at 400mh: 2002- 60.67, 2003- 59.42, 2004- 60.60, 2005- 58.21, 2006- 57.65, 2007- 57.01, 2008- 57.06, 2009- 56.40, 2010- 57.28, 2011- 55.97, 2012- 55.68, 2014- 56.44, 2015- 53.99, 2016- 53.55, 2017-54.35, 2018- 55.48, 2019- 54.89, 2020- 55.20. pbs: 60m 7.62i '15, 100m 12.07 '07, 11.93w '09; 200m 23.59 '16. 400m 52.59i '16, 53.39 '20, 800m 2:15.70 '20, 1500m 4:27.96 '11, 60mh 8.58i '07, 100mh 14.25 '05, 300mh 39.42 '20.
Her silver was the best ever for a Danish woman at the Olympics. Partner of Thomas Cortebeeck, their son Tobias born 8 Oct 2013.

DJIBOUTI
Hassan **Ayanleh SOULEIMAN** b. 3 Dec 1992 Djibouti City 1.77m 60kg.
At (800m)/1500m: OG: '16- sf/4; WCh: '13- 3/sf, '15/17- h, '19- sf; WI: '12- 5; AfG: '11- 6, '19- 2; AfCh: '12/14/18: 2/1/4; CCp: '14- 1; WI: '14- 1, '16- 9; won DL 2013, Arab G 2011, Franc G 2013. At 3000m: WY: '09- h. Won Arab 1500m 2019, 5000m 2015.
World indoor 1000m record 2016. DJI records: 800m (5) 2012-15, 1000m (2) 2013-16, 1500m (3) 2011-14, 1M (3) 2012-14, 3000m 2012.
Progress at 800m, 1500m: 2011- 1:51.78A, 3:34.32; 2012- 1:47.45, 3:30.31; 2013- 1:43.63, 3:31.64; 2014-1:43.69, 3:29.58; 2015- 1:42.97, 3:30.17; 2016-1:43.52, 3:31.68; 2017- 1:45.01, 3:34.70; 2018-3:31.19, 2019- 1:44.38, 3:30.66. pbs: 1000m 2:13.49 '16, 1M 3:47.32 '14, 3000m 7:39.81i '13, 7:42.22 '12, 5000m 13:17.97 '15.
Djibouti's first ever world champion 2013 and first to set an official world record.

ECUADOR
Governing body: Federación Ecuatoriana de Atletismo. Founded 1925.

Alex Leonardo **QUIÑÓNEZ** b. 11 Aug 1989 Esmeraldas 1.76m 65kg. FC Barcelona.
At (100m)/200m: OG: '12- 7; WCh: '13- h/sf, '15- h, '19- 3; PAm: '11-15-19: 6/sf/1; SAG: '14- 3/2, '18- 2/1; SACh: '11- h, '13- 1/1, '15- 2/1/1R; CCp: '18- 3. Won IbAm 100m & 200m 2012, BolG 100m & 200m 2013. ECU records 100m 2013 & 2018, 200m (7) 2013-19, 400m 2019.
Progress at 200m: 2008- 21.29A, 2009- 21.81w, 2011- 20.49A/21.05/20.95w, 2012- 20.28, 2013-20.44, 2014- 20.66, 2015- 20.76/20.59w, 2016-21.05A/21.12, 2017- 20.27, 2018- 19.93A/20.03, 2019- 19.87, 2020- 21.08A. pbs: 60m 6.66i '19, 100m 10.09A '13, 10.13 '17; 400m 46.28 '19.
In 2019 won Ecuador's first track medal at a World Championships and also the country's first track gold at Pan-Am Games.

Women
Glenda Estefanía **MOREJÓN** b. 30 May 2000 Ibarra, Imbabura 1.50m 49kg.
At 5000mW: WY: '17- 1. At 10k/10000mW: WJ: '18- 3; WCp: '18- 2J; PAm-J: '19- 1; At 20kW: WCh: '19- 25.
Walks records: World junior 20k 2019, S. American U20 10k (4) 2017-19, 10000mt (2) 2018.

ERITREA – ESTONIA – ETHIOPIA

Progress at 20kW: 2019- 1:25:29, 2020- 1:29:12. pbs: 15kW 21:16 '17, 22:25.16 '17; 10kW 43:04 '19, 44:12.75 '18.

ERITREA

Governing body: Eritrean National Athletics Federation. Founded 1992.

Aron KIFLE Teklu b. 20 Feb 1998 1.67m 52kg.
At 5000m/(10000m): OG: '16- h; WCh: '15- h, 17- 7/11, '19- (14); AfG: '15- 8. '19- (2); WJ: 16- 5/2.
At HMar: WCh: '18- 3. World CC: '17- 5, '19- 4, AfCC: 16- 3J.
Progress at 5000m, 10000m: 2015- 13:17.62, 28:18.44; 2016- 13:13.39, 27:26.20; 2017- 13:13.31, 27:09.92; 2018- 13:07.59, 2019- 13:13.85, 27:27.68. pbs: 3000m 7:52.19 '17, 15k Rd 45:08 '15, HMar 59:51 '18.

ESTONIA

Governing body: Eesti Kergejõustikuliit. Founded 1920.
National Championships first held in 1917.
2020 Champions: Men: 100m/200m: Henri Sai 10.53/21.08, 400m: Rasmus Mägi 46.26, 800m: Karel-Sander Kljuzin 1:52.13, 1500m/10000m/ 3000mSt: Kaur Kivistik 3:54.56/30:19.19/9:19.12, 5000m: Tiidrek Nurme 14:36.84, HMar: Karel Hussar 68:19, Mar: Rauno Jallai 2:27:14, 110mh: Keiso Pedriks 14.12, 400mh: Jaak-Heinrich Jagor 50.76, HJ: Kristjan Kafenau 2.10, PV: Eerik Haamer 5.20, LJ: Hans-Christian Hausenberg 7.91, TJ: Jaak Joomas Uudmäe 16.36, SP: Jander Heuil 19.70, DT: Martin Kupper 61.82, HT: Adam Kelly 66.97, JT: Ranno Koorep 69.08, Dec: Risto Lillemets 8133, 10000mW/20kW: Virgo Adusoo 48:26.34/1:42:54. **Women**: 100m: Ksenija Balta 11.66, 200m: Ann Marii Kivikas 23.96, 400m: Marielle Kleemeier 54.97, 800m/1500m: Kelly Nevolihhin 2:11.54/4:34.72, 5000m/10000m: Jekaterina Patjuk 15:41.26/34:28.02, HMar: Liina Luik 76:48, Mar: Marion Tibar 2:46:59, 3000mSt: Laura Maasik 10:24.71, 100mh: Kreeta Verlin 13.47w, 400mh: Marielle Kleemeier 59.50, HJ: Lilian Turban 1.79, PV: Marleem Mülla 3.75, LJ: Tähti Alver 6.54, TJ: Merliyn Uudmäe 13.32, SP: Valeria Radajeva 13.93, DT: Kätlin Töllasson 53.37, HT: Anna Maria Orel 63.29, JT: Gerli Israel 55.81, Hep: Mari Klaup 6080, 10000mW: Jekaterina Mirotvortseva 50:11.02, 20kW Alla Subina 2:09:51.

Johannes ERM b. 26 Mar 1998 Tartu 1.98m 91kg. University of Georgia.
At Dec: WJ: '16- 3; E23: '19- 2; EJ: '17- 2 (dnq 15 LJ). Won NCAA 2019.
Progress at Dec: 2013- 4283, 2014- 6000, 2016- 5793, 2018- 8046, 2019- 8445. pbs: 60m 7.08i '17, 100m 10.73 '19, 200m 21.58 '19, 400m 47.40 '19, 800m 2:01.83 '15, 1000m 2:39.45i '18, 1500m 4:28.96 '16, 60mh 8.11i '19, 110mh 14.19/14.02w '19, 400mh 54.07 '16, HJ 2.03 '19, PV 5.05 '19,; LJ 7.98 '18, TJ 15.19i '17, 15.10 '16; SP 14.69 '18, DT 46.46 '19, JT 59.60 '19, Hep 5996i '19.

Magnus KIRT b. 10 Apr 1990 Törva 1.92m 89kg. Tallinn University of Technology. Audentes SC.
At JT: OG: '16- dnq 23; WCh: '15- dnq 22, '17- 11, '19- 2; EC: '14/16- dnq 22/26, '18- 3; EU23: '11- dnq 18; EJ: '09- dnq 22; Won DL 2019, EST 2015, 2017-19. Five Estonian javelin records 2018-19.
Progress at JT: 2008- 54.40, 2008- 59.88, 2009- 72.97, 2010- 71.41, 2011- 70.07, 2012- 76.97, 2013- 79.82, 2014- 79.70, 2015- 86.65, 2016- 84.47, 2017- 86.06, 2018- 89.75, 2019- 90.61. Pbs: HJ 2.10 '09, LJ 6.96 '09, TJ 13.68 '09, DT 38.09 '09.
Best ever javelin by a left-handed thrower.

Rasmus MÄGI b. 4 May 1992 Tartu 1.88m 74kg. Tartu University ASK.
At 400mh: OG: '12- h, '16- 6; WCh: '13/15/19- sf; EC: '12-14-16-18: 5/2/sf/6; WJ: '10- h; EU23: '13- 3; EJ: '11- 4; CCp: '14- 4. Won EST 400m 2012, 2016-18, 2020; 400mh 2009, 2014-15, 2018.
Seven Estonian 400m records 2012-16
Progress at 400mh: 2010- 52.79, 2011- 50.14, 2012- 49.54, 2013- 49.19, 2014- 48.54, 2015- 48.65, 2016- 48.40, 2017- 48.94, 2018- 48.60, 2019- 48.93, 2020- 48.72. pbs: 200m 21.90 '11, 400m 46.26 '20, 600m 1:18.48i '19, 200mh 24.01 '11, LJ 7.73 '12.
His sister Maris has won 22 Estonian titles in sprints and hurdles, pbs: 400m 52.21 '11, 400mh 56.56 '13 (EST record).

Maicel UIBO b. 27 Dec 1992 Põlva 1.88m 86kg. Põlva. Was at University of Georgia, USA.
At Dec: OG: '16- 24; WCh: '13-15-17-19: 19/10/ dnf/2; EC: '16- dnf; ET: '19- 2; Won NCAA 2014- 15. At Hep: WI: '18- 3. At HJ: WY: '09- dnq 19; EU23: '13- dnq 21. Won EST 110mh & PV 2018.
Progress at Dec: 2012- 7548, 2013- 8223, 2014- 8182, 2015- 8356, 2016- 8315, 2017- 8371, 2018- 8514, 2019- 8604. pbs: 60m 7.16Ai '14, 7.18 '15; 100m 10.99 '13, 400m 50.18 '18, 1000m 2:38.51i '18, 1500m 4:25.53 '15, 60mh 8.19i '18, 110mh 14.43 '19, HJ 2.18 '15, PV 5.40 '19, LJ 7.82 '13, SP 15.12 '19, DT 49.14 '15, JT 64.51 '15, Hep 6265i '18.
Married Shaunae Miller (qv) on 4 Feb 2017.

ETHIOPIA

Governing body: Ethiopian Athletic Federation. Founded 1961.

Guye ADOLA Idemo b. 20 Oct 1990 Adola, Oromiya region 1.74m 54kg.
At Half Marathon: WCh: '14-16-20: 3/16/22; AfG: '15- 5; ETH champion 2015.
Progress at 10000m, Mar: 2016- 27:09.78, 2017- 28:14.19, 2:03;46; 2018- 2:32:35, 2019- 27:46.65, 2:04:42. pbs: HMar 59:06 '14, 25k 1:12:50 '17, 30k 1:27:24 '17.
Ran world's fastest debut marathon when 2nd in Berlin 2017, 3rd Valencia 2019.

Mohamed AMAN Geleto b. 10 Jan 1994 Asella 1.69m 55kg.
At 800m: OG: '12- 6, '16- sf; WCh: '11-13-15-17: 8/1/dq sf/6; WY: '11- 2; WI: '12-14-16: 1/1/4; AfCh: '14- 2; CCp: '14- 2; won DL 2012-13, Afr-J

ETHIOPIA

2011, Yth OG 1000m 2010.
Records: Ethiopian 800m (6) 2011-13, 1000m 2014, world youth 800m indoors and out 2011, world junior 600m indoor 2013 (1:15.60), African indoor 800m 2014.
Progress at 800m: 2008- 1:50.29, 2009- 1:46.34, 2010- 1:48.5A, 2011- 1:43.37, 2012- 1:42.53, 2013- 1:42.37, 2014- 1:42.83, 2015- 1:43.56, 2016- 1:44.70, 2017- 1:45.40, 2018- 1:46.74, 2019- 1:48.57. pbs: 600m 1:15.0+ '12, 1000m 2:15.75 '14, 1500m 3:43.52 '11, 1M 3:57.14 '11.
Was disqualified from taking the African Junior 800m gold in 2009 for being under-age (at 15). Youngest ever World Indoor champion at 18 years 60 days in 2012. Beat David Rudisha in the latter's last races in both 2011 and 2012.

Berihu AREGAWI b. 28 Feb 2001 Atsbi Womberta, Tigray region 1.73m 55kg.
At 10000m: WJ: '18- 3; At 3000m: YOG: '18-2 (& 2 CC); Af-Y '18- 1.
Progress at 5000m, 10000m: 2018- 13:15.44, 27:48.41; 2019- 12:53.04, 26:49.46; 2020- 13:08.91A. Pbs: 3000m 7:29.24i '21, 7:42.12 '18; 15kRd 46:09 '19.

Selemon BAREGA b. 20 Jan 2000 Bitena, Gurage 1.73m 59kg.
At 5000m: WCh: '17- 5, '19- 2; WJ: '16- 1, '18- 4; AfCh: '18- 4; Af-J: '17- 1; won DL 2018. At 3000m: WY: '17- 1; WI: '18- 2. World CC: '17- 5J, '19- 5. Won ETH 10000m 2019, WIT 1500m 2021.. World junior 5000m record 2018., 2M best 2019
Progress at 5000m, 10000m: 2015- 13:58.8A, 2016- 13:21.21, 2017- 12:55.58, 2018- 12:43.02, 2019- 12:53.04, 26:49.46; 2020- 12:49.08. Pbs: 1500m 3:32.97 '20, 3000m 7:26.10i '21, 7:32.17 '19; 2M 8:08.67 '19. WA Rising Star award for 2019.

Kenenisa BEKELE b. 13 Jun 1982 near Bekoji, Arsi Province 1.62m 54kg.
At 5000m(/10000m): OG: '04- 2/1, '08- 1/1, '12- (4); WCh: '03- 3/1, '05- (1), '07- (1), '09- 1/1, '11- (dnf); WJ: '00- 2; AfGi: '03- 1; AfCh: '06- 1, '08- 1. At 3000m: WY: '99- 2; WI: '06- 1; WCp: '06- 2. World CC: '99- 9J, 4k: '01- 1J/2 4k, '02-03-04-05-06: all 1/1, '08- 1. Won WAF 3000m 2003, 2009; 5000m 2006.
World records: 5000m 2004, 10000m 2004 & 2005, indoor 5000m (12:49.60) 2004, 2000m 2007, 2M 2008; World junior record 3000m 2001. ETH marathon records 2016 & 2019. World M35 marathon record 2019.
Progress at 5000m, 10000m, Mar: 2000- 13:20.57, 2001- 13:13.33, 2002- 13:26.58, 2003- 12:52.26, 26:49.57; 2004- 12:37.35, 26:20.31; 2005- 12:40.18, 26:17.53; 2006- 12:48.09, 2007- 12:49.53, 26:46.31; 2008- 12:50.18, 26:25.97; 2009- 12:52.32, 26:46.31; 2011- 13:27e+, 26:43.16; 2012- 12:55.79, 27:02.59; 2013- 13:07.88, 27:12.08; 2014- 2:05:04, 2016- 2:03:03, 2017- 2:05:57, 2018- 2:08:53, 2019- 2:01:41. pbs: 1000m 2:21.9+ '07, 1500m 3:32.35 '07, 1M 3:56.2+ '07, 2000m 4:49.99i '07, 4:58.40 '09, 3000m 7:25.79 '07, 2M 8:04.35i '08, 8:13.51 '07; Road: 15k

42:42 '01, 10M 46:06 '13, 20k 57:19 '13, HMar 60:09 '13, 25k 1:12:30 '19, 30k 1:26:55 '19.
At cross-country has a record 16 (12 individual, 4 team) world gold medals from his record 33 secs winning margin for the World Juniors in 2001, a day after 2nd in senior 4km. The only man to win both World senior races in the same year (did so five times). Won Great North Run on half marathon debut 2013. Won in Paris on marathon debut 2014, then 4th Chicago; 3rd London and 1st Berlin 2016, 2nd London 2017 with 2nd fastest ever to win at Berlin in 2019. IAAF Athlete of the Year 2004-05.

Andamlak BELIHU b. 20 Nov 1998 1.81m 62kg.
At 10000m: WCh: '17- 10, '19- 5; AfCh: '18- 2. HMar: WCh: '20- 5. World CC: '19- 8.
Progress at 10000m, HMar: 2017- 27:08.94, 59:51; 2018- 28:29.7A, 59:18; 2019- 26:53.15, 59:10; 2020- 58:54. Pbs: 15k 42:00 '20, 20k 56:00 '20

Solomon BERIHU b. 2 Oct 1999 1.72m 55kg.
World CC: '17- 14J; Afr CC: '16- 8J, '18- 3J.
Progress at 5000m, 10000m: 2016- 13:12.67, 2017- 13:17.27, 2018- 13:16.77, 2019- 13:02.08, 27:02.26. Pbs: Road: 15k 42:46 '19, 10M 45:51 '19, HMar 59:17 '19.

Chala BEYO Techo b. 18 Jan 1996 1.74m 57kg.
At 3000mSt: OG: '16- h; WCh: '19- dnf; AfG: '15- 5; AfCh: '14- 4, '16- 1; CCp: '14- 4.
Progress at 3000mSt: 2014- 8:25.25, 2015- 8:25.82, 2016- 8:17.84, 2017- 8:13.24, 2018- 8:07.27, 2019- 8:06.48. Pbs: 2000m 5:15.38 '17, 3000m 7:47.29i '18, 7:59.67 '15, 5000m 14:05.43 '18.

Lelisa DESISA Benti b. 14 Jan 1990 Shewa 1.70m 52kg.
At 10000m: Af-J: '09- 1. At: HMar: WCh: '10- 7, AfG: '11- 1. At Mar: WCh: '13- 2, '15- 7, '19- 1.
Progress at 10000m, HMar, Mar: 2009- 28:46.74, 2010- 59:39; 2011- 59:30, 2012- 27:11.98, 62:50; 2013- 2:04:45, 2014- 59:36, 2:11:06; 2015- 2:05:52, 2016- 60:37, 2:13:32dh, 2017- 2:11:32, 2018- 59:52, 2:05:59; 2019- 2:07:59dh, 2020- 2:10:44. pbs: 5000m 13:22.91 '12, Road: 15k 42:25 '10, 10M 45:36 '11.
Brilliant marathon debut to win Dubai 2013 and then won Boston and 2nd Worlds. 1st New York 2018 (2nd 2014, 3rd 2015, 2017), 2nd Dubai 2015. Won Boston again in 2015 (2nd 2016, 2019).

Muktar EDRIS Awel b. 14 Jan 1994 Adio 1.72m 5/7kg.
At 5000m: OG: '16- dq; WCh: '13- 7, '17- 1, '19- 1; WJ: '12- 1. At 10000m: WCh: '15- 10; Af-J: '11- 4. World CC: '11-13-15-17: 7J/3J/3/6; AfCC: 12- 1J.
Progress at 5000m, 10000m: 2011- 28:44.95A, 2012- 13:04.34, 2013- 13:03.69, 2014- 12:54.83, 2015- 13:00.30, 27:17.18; 2016- 12:59.43, 2017- 12:55.23, 27:20.60; 2018- 12:55.18, 2019- 12:58.85. pbs: 3000m 7:32.31 '17, 2M 8:26.11 '18, road: 15k 42:00 '20, 20k 56:02 '20, HMar 59:04 '20.
Disqualified for stepping inside kerb after finishing 4th in 2016 Olympic 5000m final.

Second fastest ever half marathon debut when 4th New Delhi 2020.

Hagos GEBRHIWET Berhe b. 11 May 1994 Tsaedaenba, Tigray region 1.67m 55kg. Mesfen Engineering.
At 5000m: OG: '12- 11, '16- 3; WCh: '13- 2, '15- 3; AfCh: '14- dnf; won DL 2016. At 10000m: WCh: '19- 9. At 3000m: WY: '11- 5; WI: '14- 5, '18- 4. World CC: '13- 1J, '15- 4, AfCC: '12- 4J. World junior records 5000m 2012, indoor 3000m 2013.
Progress at 5000m, 10000m: 2011- 14:10.0A, 2012- 12:47.53, 2013- 12:55.73, 2014- 13:06.88, 2015- 12:54.70, 2016- 13:00.20, 2018- 12:45.82. 2019- 12:54.92, 26:48.25. pbs: 2000m 5:03.18 '19, 3000m 7:30.36 '13.

Leul GEBRSELASSIE Aleme b. 20 Sep 1993 1.70m 55kg.
At 5000m: AfG: '15- 2. At HMar: WCh: '18- 10, '20- 10.
Progress at 10000m, Mar: 2012- 28:10.49. 2013- 28:05.66, 2015- 27:22.89, 2016- 27:17.91, 2017- 28:10.15, 2018- 2:04:02, 2019- 2:07:15, 2020- 2:05:29. pbs: 3000m 7:44.50i '16, 7:53.58 '14; 5000m 13:13.88 '16, Road: 15k 42:05 '17, 10M 47:18 '14, 20k 56:17 '17, HMar 59:18 '17, 25k 1:12:57 '18, 30k 1:27:37 '18.
2nd Dubai 2018 in 2:04:02, the third fastest ever marathon debut, and 1st in Valencia in 2:04:31.

Mosinet GEREMEW Bayih b. 12 Feb 1992 1.74m 57kg.
At 10000m: WCh: '15- 11. At Mar: WCh: '19- 2. Ethiopian marathon record 2019.
Progress at HMar, Mar: 2013- 62:47, 2014- 59:11, 2015- 59:21, 2016- 60:43, 2017- 60:56, 2:06:12; 2018- 2:04:00, 2019- 59:37, 2:02:55; 2020- 2:06:04. pbs: 5000m 13:17.41 '12, 10000m 27:18.86 '15, Road: 25k 1:12:57 '18, 30k 1:27:38 '18.
Marathons: 2nd Xiamen & 3rd Berlin 2017, Won Dubai and 2nd Chicago 2018, 2nd London 2019.

Lamecha GIRMA Mamo b. 26 Nov 2000 Bekoji, Oromia region 1.87m 66kg.
At 3000mSt: WCh: '19- 2. ETH 3000mSt rec 2019.
Progress at 3000mSt: 2018- 8:46.2A (c.8:40?), 2019- 8:01.36, 2020- 8:22.57. Pbs: 1500m 3:33.77 '20, 2000m 4:57.87 '20, 3000m 7:27.98i '21, 7:42.5 '20.

Telahun HAILE Bekele b. 13 May 1999 Gurage district 1.71m 55kg.
At 5000m: WCh: '19- 4; WJ '18- 5, won ETH 2019.
Progress at 5000m: 2017- 13:44.9A, 2018- 13:04.63, 2019- 12:52.98. pbs: 3000m 7:38.55 '18.

Yomif KEJELCHA Atomsa b. 1 Aug 1997 1.86m 58kg. Nike.
At 10000m: WCh: '19- 2; At 5000m: WCh: '15- 4, '17- 4; WJ: '14- 1; Af-J: '15- 1; won DL 2015. At 3000m: WY: '13- 1; WIT 2018; Yth OG: '14- 1; WI: '16- 1, '18- 1. World CC: '17- 2 mxR.
World records: junior 3000m 2016, indoor 1M 2019.
Progress at 1500m, 5000m, 10000m: 2014- 13:25.19, 2015- 12:53.98, 2016- 13:03.29, 2017- 3:32.94; 13:01.21; 2018- 3:32.59, 12:46.79; 2019- 3:31:25i/3:39.95, 13:00.56, 26:49.34; 2020- 3:32.69, 13:12.84. pbs: 1000m 2:18.34i '19, 1M 3:47.01i '19, 2000m 4:57.74i '14, 3000m 7:28.00 '18, Road: 15k 42:08 '19, 20k 56:13 '19, HMar 59:05 '19.

Shura KITATA Tola b. 9 Jun 1996 1.65m 50kg.
At 10000m: AfCh: '16- 5. Won ETH 2016.
World junior marathon record 2015 (3rd on debut in Shanghai).
Progress at Mar: 2015- 2:08:53, 2016- 2:10:04, 2017- 2:05:50, 2018- 2:04:49, 2019- 2:05:01, 2020- 2:05:41. pbs: 10000m: 32:14.25 '16, 15k 42:42 '17, 20k 57:14 '17, HMar 59:17 '18, 25k 1:12:36 '18, 30k 1:27:24 '18. Won Rome and Frankfurt marathons 2017, London 2020 (2nd 2018), 2nd New York 2018, 4th London 2019.

Birhanu LEGESE b. 11 Sep 1994 1.68m 55kg.
At 5000m: AfCh: '14- 8.
Progress at Mar: 2018- 2:04:15, 2019- 2:02:48, 2020- 2:03:16. pbs: 1500m 3:44.07 '14, 3000m 7:51.09 '14, 5000m 13:08.88 '14, Road: 10k 27:34 '13, HMar 59:20 '15, 25k 1:12:30 '19, 30k 1:26:53 '19. Won Tokyo Marathon 2019 and 2020, 2nd Berlin 2019, 3rd Valencia 2020.

Sisay LEMMA Kasaye b. 12 Dec 1990 1.79m 57kg.
Progress at Mar: 2012- 2:11:58, 2013- 2:09:02, 2015- 2:06:26, 2016- 2:05:16, 2017- 2:08:04, 2018- 2:04:08, 2019- 2:03:36, 2020- 2:04:51. pbs: HMar 61:06 '19, 25k 1:12:31 '19, 30k 1:26:53 '19.
Marathon wins: Carpi 2012 (debut), Warsaw 2013, Vienna & Frankfurt 2015, Ljubljana 2018; 3rd Dubai 2017, 2nd Prague 2018, 3rd Berlin 2019, Tokyo & London 2020.

Asefa MENGISTU Negewo b. 18 Jan 1985 1.66m 52kg.
World HMar: '10- 15. Progress at Mar: 2014- 2:19:40, 2016- 2:08:41, 2017- 2:10:01, 2018- 2:04:06, 2019- 2:04.24, 2020- 2:06:23. pbs: 3000m 8:15.05 '09, 5000m 13:43.28 '12, 10000m 28:54.98 '12, road: HMar 59:54 '17, 25k 1:12:57 '18, 30k 1:27:37 '18. Marathons: 2nd Paris, 3rd Dubai & Chicago 2019, 1st Cape Town 2017-18, Seoul (Nov) 2018.

Getaneh MOLLA Tamire b. 10 Jan 1994 1.71m 55kg.
At 5000m: AfCh: '16- 4, '18- 2; AfG: '15- 1. At HMar: WCh: '18- 5. Afr CC: '16- 6. Won ETH 5000m 2015-16, CC 2016-17, HMar 2018.
Progress at 5000m: 2014- 13:13.04, 2015- 13:21.88, 2016- 13:05.59, 2017- 13:18.40, 2018- 12:59.58. at Mar: 2019- 2:03:34, 2020- 2:08:12. pbs: 1500m 3:44.91 '16, 3000m 7:46.06 '19, 2M 8:18.88 '19, 10k Rd 28:18A '18, HMar 60:26 '19, 3000mSt 8:41.5A '16.
Ran fastest ever debut marathon to win in Dubai in 2019.

Herpasa NEGASA b. 11 Sep 1993 1.72m 57kg.
Progress at Mar: 2013- 2:10:51, 2015- 2:10:17, 2016- 2:10:17, 2018- 2:09:14, 2019- 2:03:40. pb: 15k

ETHIOPIA

43:02 '16, HMar 60:41 '19. Improved best by 5:34 for 2nd in Dubai Marathon in 2019.

Samuel TEFERA b. 23 Oct 1999 Damu Wange, Ambo, Oromiya reg 1.71m 52kg.
At 1500m: WCh: '17- h, '19- sf; WJ: '18- 5; AfCh: '18- 10; WI: '18- 1; WIT 2020.
World indoor 1500m record 2019, junior 2018.
Progress at 1500m: 2015- 13:58.8A, 2016- 3:43.0A, 2017- 3:33.78, 2018- 3:31.63, 2019- 3:31.04i/3:31.39, 2020- 3:35.54i. Pbs: 800m 1:48.40 '19, 1M 3:49.45 '19.

Adera Tamirat TOLA b. 11 Aug 1991 1.81m 59kg.
At 10000m: OG: '16- 3. At HMar: WCh: '16- 5. At Mar: WCh: '17- 2. World CC: '15- 6.
Progress at Mar: 2014- 2:06:17, 2015- 27:22.64, 2016- 26:57.33, dnf; 2017- 2:04:11, 2018- 2:04:06. 2019- 27:18.10, 2:06:57; 2020- 2:06:41. pbs: 15k 42:26 '17, 20k 56:36 '17, HMar 59:13 dh '19, 25k 1:12:54 '17, 30k 1:27:38 '19.
Won Dubai Marathon 2017 (3rd 2018).

Getnet WALE b. 16 Jul 2000 1.78m 60kg.
At 3000mSt: WCh: '17- 9, '19- 5; WJ: '16- 3, '18- 3; AfG: 19- 2; AfCh: '18- 3. Won DL 2019, ETH 2018-19, WIT 3000m 2020. Two Ethiopian 3000mSt records 2019, indoor 3000m 2021.
Progress at 3000mSt: 2016- 8:22.83, 2017- 8:12.28, 2018- 8:22.68, 2019- 8:05.21, 2020- 8:35.85. Pbs: 1500m 3:35.54i '21, 2000m 4:58.26 '20, 3000m 7:24.98i '21, 5000m 13:13.87 '18.

Amedework WALELEGN Tadese 11 Mar 1999 1.67m 52kg.
At HMar: WCh: '20- 3. At 10000m:'16- 4. World CC: '17- 2J.
Progress at HMar: 2018- 59:22, 2019- 59:39, 2020- 58:53. pbs: 5000m 13:14.52 '17, 10000m 28:00.14 '16; Road: 10k 27:37 '18, 15k 42:00 '20, 20k 56:00 '20.

Mule WASIHUN Lakew b. 20 Oct 1993 1.66m 52kg.
At Mar: WCh: '19- dnf. At HMar: WCh: '16- 8. At 10000m: AfG: '15- 7.
Progress at Mar: 2015- 2:10:57, 2016- 2:05:44, 2017- 2:05:39, 2018- 2:04:37, 2019- 2:03:16, 2020- 2:06:08. pbs: 1500m 3:45.03 '14, 10000m 28:23.87 '15, road: 10k 27:57 '13, 15k 42:03 '19, 20k 56:26 '19, HMar 59:34 '19, 25k 1:13:49 '18, 30k 1:28:58 '18.
Marathons include 2nd Dubai 2017, Amsterdam 2018, 3rd London 2019.

Jemal YIMER Mekonnen b. 11 Sep 1996 1.63m 48kg.
At 10000m: WCh: '17- 5; AfG '19- 3; AfCh: 16- 4, '18- 1. At HMar: WCh: '18- 4. World CC: 17- 4.
Ethiopian half marathon record 2018.
Progress at 10000m, HMar: 2016- 28:08.92, 2017- 26:56.11, 2018- 28:30.3A, 58:33; 2019- 26:54.39, 59:09; 2020- 59:25. pbs: 15k 41:14 '18, 20k 55:56 '18.

Women

Ruti AGA b. 16 Jan 1994 1.59m 45kg.
At Mar: WCh: '19- dnf; At 5000m: WJ: '12- 2; Afr-J: '13- 1; World CC: '13- 5K.
Progress at Mar: 2016- 2:24:41, 2017- 2:20:41, 2018- 2:18:34, 2019- 2:20:40, 2020- 2:20:05. pbs: 3000m 8:56.73 '13, 5000m 15:13.48 '13, 10000m 33:38.4A '13; Road: 10k 31:33 '18, 15k 47:28 '18, 20k 63:13 '18, HMar 66:39 '18, 25k 1:21:48 '20, 30k 1:38:04 '18.
Won Tokyo marathon 2019, 3rd/2nd/2nd Berlin 2016-18, 2nd Vienna 2016, Tokyo 2018; 3rd New York 2019.

Habitam ALEMU b. 9 Jul 1997 Gojam, Amhara 1.71m 52kg.
At 800m: OG: '16- sf; WCh: '15- h, '17- sf; AfG: '15- 4; AfCh: '18- 3; WI: '16- 6, '18- 4; WIT 2019, 2021. Ethiopian 800m records 2017 & 2018.
Progress at 800m, 1500m: 2014- 2:09.6A, 2015- 2:01.27, 4:14.67; 2016- 1:58.99, 2017- 1:57.05, 2018- 1:56.71, 4:01.41; 2019- 1:59.25, 2020- 2:00.11, 4:08.23; 2021- 1:58.19i.

Meskerem ASSEFA b. 20 Sep 1985 1.55m 43kg.
At 800m: WY: '10- h. At 1500m: OG: '12- h; WCh: '09- sf, '11- h; AfG: '07- 4, '11- 4; AfCh: '08- 2, '10- 5.
Progress at Mar: 2013- 2:25:17, 2014- 2:25:59, 2015- 2:25:11, 2016- 2:30:13, 2017- 2:24:18, 2018- 2:20:36, 2019- 2:22:11, 2020- 2:23:31. pbs: 800m 2:02.12 '08, 1500m 4:02.12 '11, 3000m 8:46.37 '09, 5000m 15:03.49i '10, Road: 10k: 31:43 '17, 15k 47:42 '17, 20k 64:18 '17, HMar 67:42 '17, 25k 1:24:37 '18, 30k 1:41:09 '18.
Marathon wins: Houston & Rotterdam 2017, Nagoya and Frankfurt 2018.

Degitu AZIMERAW b. 24 Jan 1999 1.65m 48kg.
At HMar: AfG: '19- 2.
Progress at HMar, Mar: 2018- 66:47, 2019- 66:07, 2:19:26; 2020- 67:02, 2:19:56. pbs: 10000m 31:03:32 '19, road: 10k 31:01 '20, 15k 47:01 '20, 20k 63:26 '20, 25k 1:21:48 '20, 30k 1:38:15 '20.
Won Amsterdam Marathon 2019.

Tadelech BEKELE Alemu b. 11 Apr 1991 Debre Birhan 1.54m 40kg.
Afr CC: 14- 5. Progress at 10000m, Mar: 2014- 2:23:02, 2015- 33:30.7A, 2:22:51; 2016- 30:54.61, 2:26:31; 2017- 2:21:54, 2018- 2:21:40, 2019- 2:22:53. pbs: 5000m 15:28.27 '12, 10k 30:38 '13, HMar 68:38 '13, 25k 1:23:04 '18, 30k 1:40:02 '18.
Won Amsterdam marathon 2017-18, after 3rd Prague and 4th Dubai 2017. 3rd London 2018.

Ashete BEKERE b. 17 Apr 1988 1.69m 52kg.
Progress at Mar: 2011- 2:34:00, 2012- 2:31:23, 2013- 2:27:47, 2014- 2:24:59, 2015- 2:23:43, 2016- 2:25:50, 2017- 2:25:57, 2018- 2:21:14, 2019- 2:20:14, 2020- 2:22:51. pbs: HMar 66:37 '20, 25k 1:23:12 '16, 30k 1:39:52 '19.
Major marathon wins: Kosice 2013, Valencia 2018, Rotterdam & Berlin 2019.

Gelete BURKA Bati b. 15 Feb 1986 Kofele 1.65m 45kg.
At 1500m: OG: '08- h; WCh: '05- 8, '09- 9 (fell), '11- sf, '13- h; WI: '08- 1, '10- 3; AfG: '07- 1; AfCh: '08- 1, '10- 2; CCp: '10- 6. At 3000m: WI: '12- 3. At 5000m: OG: '12- 5; WCh: '07- 9. At 10000m: OG: '16- 8; WCh: '15- 2; AfG: '15- 3. World CC: '03-05-06-07-08-09: 3J/1J/1 4k/4/6/8. Won ETH 800m 2011, 1500m 2004-05, 2007; 5000m 2005, 4k CC 2006.
African records: 1M 2008, 2000m 2009, indoor 1500m 2008, junior 1500m 2005. World youth 1M best (4:30.81) 2003.
Progress at 1500m, 5000m, 10000m, Mar: 2003- 4:10.82, 16:23.8A, 2004- 4:06.10, 2005- 3:59.60, 14:51.47; 2006- 4:02.68, 14:40.92; 2007- 4:00.48, 14:31.20; 2008- 3:59.75i/4:00.44, 14:45.84; 2009- 3:58.79, 2010- 3:59.28, 2011- 4:03.28, 2012- 14:41.43, 2013- 4:04.36, 14:42.07, 2:30:40; 2014- 2:26:03, 2015- 14:40.50, 30:49.68; 2016- 14:52.4, 30:26.66; 2017- 15:06.01, 30:40.87; 2018- 2:20:45, 2019- 2:20:55. pbs: 800m 2:02.89 '10, 1M 4:18.23 '08, 2000m 5:30.19 '09, 3000m 8:25.92 '06; Rd: 15k 49:26 '12, HMar 66:11 '18, 25k 1:23:10 '18, 30k 1:39:42 '18.
Won Ottawa Marathon 2018, Paris 2019; 3rd Chicago 2019. Married Taddele Gebrmehden 2007.

Worknesh DEGEFA b. 28 Oct 1990 1.59m 42kg.
At HMar: AfG: '15- 2.
Ethiopian marathon record 2019.
Progress at HMar, Mar: 2012- 76:48, 2013- 67:49, 2014- 68:46, 2015- 67:14, 2016- 66:14, 2017- 68:10, 2:22:36; 2018- 68:10, 2:19:53; 2019- 69:10, 2:17:41, 2020- 2:19:38. pbs: 10k 31:53 '12, 25k 1:23:09 '18, 30k 1:37:16 '19.
Won at Dubai 2017 (on marathon debut) and 2020 (4th 2018, 2nd 2019), won Boston 2019.

Shure DEMISE Ware b. 21 Jan 1996 Bore 1.59m 45kg.
At 10000m: AfCh: '16- 5. Won ETH 2016. At Mar: WCh: '17- 5, '19- dnf. World junior marathon record 2015 (4th on debut at Dubai).
Progress at Mar: 2015- 2:20:59, 2016- 2:25:04, 2017- 2:22:57, 2018- 2:22:07, 2019- 2:21:05, 2020- 2:27:42. pbs: 10000m: 32:14.25 '16, 15k 49:22 '14, HMar 68:53 '14.
Won Toronto marathon 2015-16, 2nd Dubai 2017, 3rd Chicago 2018 & Tokyo 2019.

Roza DEREJE b. 6 May 1997 1.68m 52kg.
At Mar: WCh: '19- dnf.
Progress at Mar: 2015- 2:34:02, 2016- 2:26:18, 2017- 2:22:43, 2018- 2:19:17, 2019- 2:18:30. pbs: Road: 10k 31:43 '17, 15k 47:41 '17, 20k 63:59 '17, HMar 66:01 '19, 25k 1:23:09 '18, 30k 1:39:41 '18.
Marathon wins: Odense 2016, Shanghai 2016-17, Dubai 2018, Valencia 2019; 2nd Chicago 2018, 3rd London 2019. Married to Dereje Abera (Mar 2:10:19 '11).

Birhane DIBABA b. 11 Sep 1993 Moyagajo 1.59m 44kg.
At Mar: WCh: '17- 10. Progress at Mar: 2012- 2:29:22, 2013- 2:23:01, 2014- 2:22:30, 2015- 2:23:15, 2016- 2:23:16, 2017- 2:21:19, 2018- 2:19:51, 2019- 2:18:46, 2020- 2:20:30. pbs: HMar 65:57 '19.
Won Valencia marathon 2012, Tokyo 2015 & 2018; 2nd São Paulo 2012, Nagoya 2013, Tokyo 2014, 2017 & 2020, Berlin 2016; 3rd Frankfurt 2013, Chicago 2014-15.

Genzebe DIBABA b. 8 Feb 1991 Bekoji. Muger Cement. 1.68m 52kg.
At 1500m: OG: '12- h, '16- 2; WCh: '13- 7, '15- 1, '17- 12; WI: '12- 1, '18- 1. At 3000m: CCp: '14- 1; WI: '14-16-18: 1/1/1. At 5000m: WCh: '09 -8, '11- 8, '15- 3; AfCh: '14- 2; WJ: '08- 2, '10- 1; Af-J: '09- 1. World CC: '07-08-09-10-11-17: 5J/1J/1J/1J/9/2 mxR. Won DL 5000m 2015, ETH 1500m 2010. Records: World 1500m 2015, indoor 1500m, 3000m & 2M 2014, 5000m 2015, 1M 2016, 2000m 2017. Two African 1500m 2015. Ethiopian 1500m (3) 2012-15, 2000m 2014.
Progress at 1500m, 5000m: 2007- 15:53.46, 2008- 15:02.41, 2009- 14:55.52, 2010- 4:04.80i/4:06.10, 15:08.06; 2011- 4:05.90, 14:37.56; 2012- 3:57.77, 2013- 3:57.54, 14:37.68; 2014- 3:55.17i/4:01.00, 14:28.88; 2015- 3:50.07, 14:15.41; 2016- 3:56.46i+/3:57.31, 2017- 3:57.82, 14:25.22; 2018- 3:54.60, 14:26.89; 2019- 3:55.47. pbs: 800m 1:59.37 '17, 1000m 2:33.06i '17, 2:35.6+ '15; 1M 4:13.31i/4:14.30 '16, 2000m 5:23.75i '17, 5:27.50 '14; 3000m 8:16.60i '14, 8:21.29 '19; 2M 9:00.48i/9:14.28 '14, 10k 31:00 '20, 15k 46:34 '20, 20k 62:00 '20, HMar 65:18 '20
Laureus World Sportswomen of the Year 2014, IAAF Woman Athlete of the Year 2015. Ran fastest ever debut for half marathon with win at Valencia in 2020. Younger sister of Ejegayehu (2 OG 10000m 2004, 3 WCh 5000 & 10000m 2005) and Tirunesh Dibaba.

Mare DIBABA Hurssa b. 20 Oct 1989 Sululta, Oromia 1.52m 40kg.
At Mar: OG: '12- 22, '16- 3; WCh: '15- 1, '17- 8. At HMar: AfG: '11- 1. Won AZE 3000m and 5000m 2009. AZE records (as Mare Ibrahimova) at 3000m, 5000m and HMar 2009.
Progress at HMar, Mar: 2008- 70:28, 2009- 68:45, 2010- 67:13, 2:25:27, 2011- 68:39, 2:23:25; 2012- 67:44, 2:19:52; 2014- 68:56, 2:21:36/2:20:35dh; 2015- 2:19:52, 2016- 67:55, 2:24:09; 2017- 69:43, 2:28:49; 2018- 69:15, 2:25:24; 2019- 2:20:21. pbs: 3000m 9:16.94 '09, 5000m 15:42.83 '09, Road: 10k 31:55 '10, 15k 48:04 '10, 10M 51:29 '10, 20k 63:47 '10, 30k 1:39:19 '14.
Switched to Azerbaijan in December 2008 but back to Ethiopia from 1 Feb 2010. Marathons: won at Xiamen 2014 and 2015, Chicago 2014; 2nd Boston 2014-15, Berlin 2019; 3rd Dubai 2012.

Tirunesh DIBABA Kenene b. 1 Oct 1985 Chefa near Bekoji, Arsi region 1.60m 47kg.
At 5000m(/10000m): OG: '04- 3, '08- 1/1, '12- 3/1, '16- (3); WCh: '03- 1, '05- 1/1, '07- (1), '13- (1), '17- (2); WJ: '02- 2; AfG: '03- 4; AfCh: '06- 2, '08- (1), '10- (1). At 3000m: WCp: '06- 1. World CC: '01-02-03-05-06-07-08-10: 5J/2J/1J/1/1/2/1/4;

ETHIOPIA

4k: '03-04-05: 7/2/1. Won WAF 5000m 2006, ETH 4k CC & 5000m 2003. 8k CC 2005.
Records: World 5000m 2008, indoor 5000m 2005 (14:32.93) & 2007, junior 5000m 2003-04, indoor 3000m & 5000m 2004, world road 5k best 14:51 2005, 15k 2009. African 10000m 2008, Ethiopian Mar 2017.
Progress at 5000m, 10000m, Mar: 2002- 14:49.90, 2003- 14:39.94, 2004- 14:30.88, 2005- 14:32.42, 30:15.67; 2006- 14:30.40, 2007- 14:27.42i/14:35.67, 31:55.41; 2008- 14:11.15, 29:54.66; 2009- 14:33.65, 2010- 14:34.07, 31:51.39A; 2012- 14:50.80, 30:20.75; 2013- 14:23.68, 30:26.67; 2014- 2:20:35, 2016- 14:41.73, 29:42.56; 2017- 31:02.69, 2:17:56; 2018- 2:18:55. pbs: 2000m 5:42.7 '05, 3000m 8:29.55 '06, 2M 9:12.23i '10, road 15k 46:28 '09, 10M 51:49 '16, HMar 66:50 '17, 25k 1:20:51 '17, 30k 1:37:23 '17.
At 17 years 333 days in 2003, the youngest ever world champion at an individual event and in 2005 the first woman to win the 5000m/10000m double. Women's record 21 World CC medals. Married Sileshi Sihine on 26 Oct 2008; sons Natan Seleshi born 26 Mar 2015, Allon Dec 2019. Won all her eleven 10,000m track races from 2005 until 3rd in the 2016 Ethiopian Trial.

Dera DIDA b. 26 Oct 1996 1.55m 42kg.
At 5000m: AfCh: '16- 3. At 10000m: WCh: '17- 14; AfG: '19- 3. World CC: 15- 2J, '19- 2; AfCC: '16- 4. Won ETH 5000m 2016, 10000m 2017, CC 2017, 2019.
Progress at 5000m, 10000m: 2014- 16:26.2A, 2015- 15:28.81, 2016- 14:42.84, 2017- 15:07.27, 30:56.48; 2019- 30:51.86. At Mar: 2018- 2:21:45, 2020- 2:22:52. pbs: 1500m 4:15.41 '15, 3000m 8:48.31 '16, Road: 20k 66:19 '18, HMar 68:06 '17, 25k 1:22:54 '18, 30k 1:39:30 '18.

Axumawit EMBAYE Abraya b. 18 Oct 1994 1.60m 50kg.
At 1500m: WCh: '19- h; WJ: '12- 7; AfCh: '14- 4; WI: '14- 2, '16- 4; WIT 2016.
Progress at 1500m: 2012- 4:12.92, 2013- 4:05.16, 2014- 4:02.35, 2015- 4:02.92i/4:03.00, 2016- 4:03.05, 2017- 4:04.95i/4:09.17, 2018- 4:02.44, 2019- 3:59.02, 2020- 4:02.96i. pbs: 800m 2:02.77 '19, 1000m 2:37.43 '15, 1M 4:18.58 '19, 3000m 8:43.83 '18.

Hawi FEYSA b. 1 Feb 1999 1.62m 50kg.
At 5000m: WCh: '19- 8; AfG: '19- 2; AfCh: '18- 4; World CC: '17- 2J.
Progress at 5000m: 2017- 15:39.8A, 2018- 15:31.5A, 2019- 14:38.76. pbs: 1500m 4:04.13 '19, 2000m 5:38.66 '19, 3000m 8:40.79 '19, 15k Rd 50:09 '17, Mar 2:23:36 '20.

Tsehay GEMECHU Beyan b. 20 May 1998 1.60m 52kg.
At 5000m: WCh: '19- 4; At 10000m: AfG: '19- 1; World CC: '19- 6.
Progress at 5000m, 10000m: 2019- 14:29.60, 30:53.11; 2020- 14:54.03, 30:57.73. pbs: 2000m 5:41.0+ '20, 3000m 8:33.42 '20, 20k 63:55 '20, HMar: 66:50 '18.

Letesenbet GIDEY b. 20 Mar 1998 Endameskel, Tigray region 1.63m 48kg.
At 10000m: WCh: '19- 2, won ETH 2019; At 5000m: WCh: '17- 11; At 3000m: WY: '15- 4. World CC: '15-17-19: 1J/1J/3.
Records: World 5000m 2020, 15k best 2019, African 3000m 2019, junior 5000m 2016.
Progress at 5000m, 10000m: 2014- 16:19.3A, 2015- 15:39.83, 2016- 14:45.63, 2017- 14:33.32, 2018- 14:23.14, 2019- 14:29.54, 30:21.23; 2020- 14:06.62. pbs: 1500m 4:11.11 '17, 2000m 5:43.0 '18, 3000m 8:20.27 '19; Rd: 10k 29:43 '19, 15k 44:20 '19.

Tigist GIRMA Getachew b. 12 Jul 1993 1.68m 52kg.
Progress at Mar: 2016- 2:32:48, 2017- 2:29:05, 2018- 2:26:44, 2019- 2:19:52, 2020- 2:19:56. pbs: 3000m 8:56.73 '13, 5000m 15:13.48 '13, 10000m 33:38.4A '13; Road: 10k 31:33 '18, 15k 47:28 '18, 20k 63:13 '18, HMar 66:39 '18, 25k 1:21:48 '20, 30k 1:38:04 '18. 2nd Amsterdam Marathon 2019,

Netsanet GUDETA Kebede b. 12 Feb 1991 Bekoji 1.56m 42kg.
At 10000m: WCh: '19- dnf; AfG: '15- dnf. At HMar: WCh: '14-16-18-20: 6/4/1/8. World CC: '15- 3. ETH half marathon record 2015, world women-only best 2018.
Progress at 10000m, HMar: 2014- 68:46, 2015- 31:06.53, 67:31; 2016- 30:36.75, 68:01; 2017- 67:26, 2018- 66:11, 2019- 30:40.85, 65:45; 2020- 66:46. pbs: 5000m 15:25.0A '17, Rd: 5k 15:22 '15, 10k 31:03 '19, 15k 46:43 '19, 20k 62:26 '19, Mar 2:29:15 '17.

Lemlem HAILU b. 21 May 2001 Keyoh Tekill, Alage 1.62m 52kg.
At 1500m: WCh: '19- sf; WY: '17- 1; AfG: '19- 3. Af-Y: '17- 1; won ETH 2019; YOG: '18- 5 (5 CC). Won WIT 3000m 2021.
Two world U20 indoor 1500m records 2020.
Progress at 1500m: 2015- 4:17.7A, 2017- 4:17.0A, 2018- 4:25.03, 2019- 4:02.97, 2020- 4:01.57i/4:04.75. pbs: 1000m 2:39.2+ '19, 2000m 5:37.5+i '21, 5:40.1+ '20; 3000m 8:29.28i '21, 8:34.03 '19.

Besu SADO Beko b. 12 Jun 1996 1.72m 56kg.
At 1500m: OG: '16- 9; WCh: '15/17- sf; AfG: '15- 2; AfCh: '14- 7, '18- 4; Af-J: '15- 2; won ETH 2014, 2018. At 800m: CCp: '18- 7.
Progress at 1500m: 2014- 4:07.59, 2015- 4:00.65, 2016- 3:59.47, 2017- 4:00.98, 2018- 4:01.75. pbs: 800m 2:02.6A '14, 1000m 2:37.73 '15, 1M 4:25.99 '18, road: 10k 31:58 '19, HMar 70:34 '19, Mar 2:21:03 '19.

Dawit SEYAUM Biratu b. 27 Jul 1996 Tumano 1.61m 49kg.
At 1500m: OG: '16- 8; WCh: '15- 4; WJ: '14- 1; WY: '13- 2; AfG: '15- 1; AfCh: '14- 2; Af-J: '13/15- 1; CCp: '14- 3; WI: '16- 2.
Progress at 1500m: 2013- 4:09.00, 2014- 3:59.53, 2015- 3:59.76, 2016- 3:58.09, 2017- 4:00.52, 2018- 4:02.81, 2019- 4:01.40, 2020- 4:04.24i. pbs: 1M 4:26.84i '19, 2000m 5:35.46i '15, 3000m 8:37.65i '17.

Senbere TEFERI Sora b. 3 May 1995 1.59m 45kg. Oromiya.
At 1500m: WCh: '13- h; WJ: '12- 3; WY: '11- 2. At 3000m: CCp: '18- 2. At 5000m: OG: '16- 5; WCh: '15- 2, '17- 4; AfCh; '18- 2; ETH champion 2017; At 10000m: WCh: '19- 6. World CC: '15- 2, '17- 10. Two Ethiopian half marathon records 2019.
Progress at 1500m, 5000m, 10000m: 2011- 16:09.0A, 2012- 15:36.74, 2013- 4:04.55, 16:21.0A, 2014- 4:08.49, 2015- 4:01.86, 14:36:44; 2016- 14:29.82, 30:40.59; 2017- 14:31.76, 30:41.68; 2018- 14:23.33, 2019- 15:33.12, 30:44.23. pbs: 2000m 5:34.27 '14, 3000m 8:32.49 '18, Road: 10k 30:38 '17, 15k 46:15 '19, 10M 52:51 '16, 20k 62:00 '19, HMar 65:32 '19, Mar 2:24:11 '18.
Ran fastest ever debut half marathon to win at Ras Al Khaimah in 2019.

Gudaf TSEGAY Desta b. 23 Jan 1997 Bora, Alege 1.59m 45kg.
At 1500m: WCh: '17- sf, '19- 3; WJ: '14- 2; WI: '16- 3; WIT 2020. At 800m: OG: '16- h.
Records: World indoor 1500m 2021, World junior indoor 1500m 2016.
Progress at 1500m, 5000m: 2013- 4:07.27, 2014- 4:02.83, 2015- 4:03.09, 2016- 4:00.18, 2017- 3:59.55, 2018- 3:59.09, 14:51.30; 2019- 3:54.38, 2020- 4:00.09i, 14:46.22; 2021- 3:53.09i. pbs: 800m 1:59.52 '19, 1000m 2:36.9 '18, 1M 4:16.14 '18, 2000m 5:37.2+i '21, 3000m 8:22.65i '21, 8:25.13 '20; 15k Rd 15:37 '15.

Fantu WORKU Taye b. 29 Mar 1999 1.62m 46kg.
At 1500m: WCh: '17- h; WJ '16- 2; AfCh: '16- 4, Af-J: '17- 2. At 3000m: WI: '18- 6. At 5000m: WCh: '19- 6. World CC: '19- 1mxR; Won ETH 1500m 2017, 5000m 2019.
Progress at 1500m. 5000m: 2016- 4:05.84, 2017- 4:05.81, 2018- 4:06.01, 15:30.39; 2019- 4:06.27, 14:40.47; 2020- 4:06.39i. pbs: 3000m 8:32.10 '19, HMar: 66:50 '18.

Yalemzerf YEHUALAW b. 3 Aug 99 1.58m 45kg.
World HMar: '20- 3; AfG: '19- 1.
Progress at HMar 2019- 66:90, 2020- 64:46. pbs: 10000m 32:03.0A '21, Road: 5k 15:27A '20, 15k 46:15 '20, 20k 61:32 '20.

Ababel YESHANEH Birhane b. 22 Jul 1991 1.58m 42kg.
At 5000m: OG: '16- 14; at 10000m: WCh: '13- 9; AfrCC: '14- 6; at HMar: WCh: '20- 5.
World half marathon record 2020.
Progress at 10,000, HMar, Mar: 2011- 34:10.0A, 69:00, 2:34:36; 2013- 30:35.91, 2:33:10; 2014- 72:11, 2015- 31:23.60, 71:11; 2016- 30:54.12, 67:52; 2017- 67:21, 2018- 65:46, 2019- 67:43, 2:20:51; 2020- 64:31. pbs: 3000m 8:49.45 '14, 5000m 14:41.58 '16, 10000m: 30:35.91 '13, Road: 10k 30:18 '20, 15k 45:41 '20, 20k 61:11 '20. 2nd Chicago Mar 2019.

Zeineba YIMER Worku b. 17 Jun 1998 1.62m 48kg.
At 10000m: AfG: '19- 2; At HMar: WCh: '18- 5, '20- 4. World CC: 17- 10J.
Progress at 10000m, HMar, Mar: 2016- 73:17, 2017- 71:31, 2018- 66:21, 2019- 30:46.24, 65:46, 2:19:28; 2020- 65:39, 2:19:54. pbs: Road: 5k 15:26 '19, 15k 46:24 '24, 20k 62:17 '20, 30k 1:38:07 '20.

FINLAND

Governing body: Suomen Urheiluliitto. Founded 1906.
National Championships first held in 1907 (men), 1913 (women). **2020 Champions: Men**: 100m: Viljami Kaasalainen 10.35, 200m: Samuli Samuelsson 21.15, 400m: Tommi Mäkinen 47.85, 800m/1500m: Joonas Rinne 1:50.14/3:49.84, 5000m: Konsta Hämäläinen 14:28.54, 10000m: Eero Saleva 29:52.65, HMar: Jarkko Järvenpää 66:10, Mar: Jaakko Nieminen 2:19:49, 3000mSt: Hannu Granberg 8:56.07, 110mh: Elmo Lakka 13.70, 400mh: Tuomas Lehtonen 50.53, HJ: Arttu Mattila 2.17, PV: Mikko Paavola 5.31, LJ: Kristian Pulli 7.83, TJ: Simo Lipsanen 16.30, SP: Eero Ahola 18.30, DT: Frantz Kruger 58.38, HT: Aaron Kangas 76.94, JT: Lassi Etelätalo 82.20, Dec: Juuso Hassi 7379, 20,000mW: Aleksi Ojala 1:23:49.7. **Women**: 100m: Lotta Kemppinen 11.62, 200m: Anniina Kortetmaa 23.74, 400m: Mette Baas 54.29, 800m/1500m: Sara Kuivisto 2:03.24/4:18.00, 5000m/10000m/HMar: Annemari Kiekara 16:21.69/34:12.33/74:01, Mar: Laura Manninen 2:42:43, 3000mSt: Janica Rauma 10:17.26, 100mh: Annimari Korte 12.79, 400mh: Viivi Lehikoinen 58.58, HJ: Heta Tuuri 1.86, PV: Wilma Murto 4.32, LJ: Senni Salminen 6.56, TJ: Kristiina Mäkelä 13.61, SP: Senja Mäkitörmä 16.35, DT: Salla Sipponen 58.19, HT: Silja Kosonen 68.40, JT: Sanne Erkkola 57.04, Hep: Maria Huntington 6074, 10,000mW: Anniina Kivimäki 47:11.84, 20kW: Elisa Neuvonen 1:39:18

Lassi ETELÄTALO b. 30 Apr 1988 Helsinki 1.93m 90kg. Joemsuun Kataja.
At JT: WCh: '19- 4; EC: '14- 4; EU23: '09- 9; EJ: '07- dnq 15. Won FIN 2019-20.
Progress at JT: 2006- 66.70, 2007- 68.81, 2008- 76.07, 2009-79.70, 2010- 77.58, 2011- 84.41, 2012- 84.06, 2013- 80.39, 2014- 84.98, 2016- 74.33, 2017- 77.80, 2018- 78.38, 2019- 84.11, 2020- 82.20.

Aaron KANGAS b. 3 Jul 1997 Kankaanpää 1.84m 115kg. Kankaanpään seudun Leisku,.
At HT: WJ: '16- 9; EU23: '17- 11, '19- 5; EJ: '15- 12. Won FIN 2020.
Progress at HT: 2015- 63.37, 2017- 70.30, 2018- 72.09, 2019- 74.40, 2020- 79.05.
His elder brother **Arttu** (b. 13 Jul 1993) has shot pb 20.30 '16, 4 WJ 2012.

Antti RUUSKANEN b. 21 Feb 1984 Kokkola 1.89m 86kg. Pielaveden Sampo.
At JT: OG: '12- 2, '16- 6; WCh: '09-11-13-15-19: 6/9/5/5/dnq 28; EC: '14- 16-18-1: 1/3/6; EU23: '05- 2; EJ: '03- 3; CCp: '14- 8. Won FIN 2012, 2014-15.
Progress at JT: 2002- 66.08, 2003- 72.87, 2004- 75.84, 2005- 79.75, 2006- 84.10, 2007- 82.71/87.88dh, 2008- 87.33, 2009- 85.39, 2010- 83.45, 2011- 82.29,

96   ETHIOPIA

2012- 87.79, 2013- 85.70, 2014- 88.01, 2015- 88.98, 2016- 88.23, 2018- 82.59, 2019- 85.15, 2020- 79.22.
Women
Ella JUNNILA b. 6 Dec 1998 Espoo 1.83m 60kg. Tampereen Pyrintö.
At HJ: WCh: '19- dnq 28; EC: '18- dnq 17; EU23: '19- 3; EI: '21- 3. FIN champion 2019. Two Finnish HJ records 2019, and indoors 2021.
Progress at HJ: 2012- 1.65, 2013- 1.68, 2014- 1.72, 2015- 1.72, 2017- 1,83, 2018- 1.92, 2019- 1.95, 2020- 1.90, 2021- 1.96i.
Her mother Ringa Ropo holds FIN LJ record 6.85 '90, 3 EI 1989, 4 WI 1994, also FIN HJ champion 1987, pb 1.88i/1.86 '87; formerly married to Juha Junnila, LJ 7.44 '87.

FRANCE
Governing body: Fédération Française d'Athlétisme. Founded 1920.
National Championships first held in 1888 (men), 1918 (women). **2020 Champions: Men**: 100m: Mouhamadou Fall 10.16, 200m: Amaury Golitin 20.67, 400m: Ludvy Vaillant 45.46, 800m: Benjamin Robert 1:48.26, 1500m: Alexis Miellet 3:40.92, 5000m: Jimmy Gressier 13:33.08, 10000m: Florian Carvalho 28:04.05, 3000mSt: Djilali Bedrani 8:35.39, 110mh: Wilhem Bélocian 13.20, 400mh: Wilfried Happio 49.97, HJ: Sébastien Micheau 2.18, PV: Renaud Lavillenie 5.80, LJ: Yann Randrianasolo 7.91w, TJ: Jean-Marc Pontvianne 16.85w, SP: Fréderíc Dagée 19.74, DT: Lolassonn Djouhan 60.07, HT: Quentin Bigot 76.42, JT: Lukas Moutarde 75.71, Dec: Axel Hubert 8260, 10kW: Gabriel Bordier 39:17. **Women**: 100m/200m: Carolle Zahi 11.28/22.98, 400m: Sokhna Lacoste 52.48 , 800m: Cynthia Anais 2:05.28, 1500m: Berénice Fulchiron 4:23.66, 5000m: Alessia Zarbo 15:56.46, 10000m: Samira Mezeghrane-Saad 32:37.35, 3000mSt: Alice Finot 10:10.58, 100mh: Cyrène Samba-Mayela 12.73, 400mh: Farah Clerc 57.91, HJ: Solène Gicquel 1.87, PV: Marion Lotout 4.55, LJ: Éloyse Lesueur-Aymorin 6.44, TJ: Jeanine Assani Issouf 13.59, SP: Amanda Ngandu-Ntumba 16.01, DT: Mélina Robert-Michon 60.06, HT: Alexandra Tavernier 72.76, JT: Alexie Alais 58.11, Hep: Cassandre Aguessy Thomas 5542, 10kW: Eloise Terrec 45:35.
Morhad AMDOUNI b. 21 Jun 1988 Porto-Vecchio, Corsica 1.75m 60kg. Val d'Europe Atlétisme.
At 5000m/(10000m): WCh: '09- h; EC: '16- 5, '18- 3/1; EJ: '07- 1; ET: '15- 1; ECp: '18- (2); At 1500m: WCh: '15- sf; EC: '16- 13; WJ: '06- h; At HMar: WCh: '20- 8. Eur CC: '06-07-08-10-11-15: 12J/1J/8U23/5/6/9. Won FRA 1500m 2016 ,5000m 2016. European U23 3000m record 2009, French records 1 hour record, 20000m & HMar 2020.
Progress at 5000m, 10000m: 2006- 14:16.55, 2007- 13:56.03, 2008- 14:04.16, 2009- 13:14.19, 2010- 13:45.49, 2015- 14:04.63, 2016- 13:22.64,
2017- 13:11.18i, 2018- 13:19.14, 27:36.80. pbs: 800m 1:47.20 '15, 1500m 3:34.05 '15, 3000m 7:37.50 '09, 20000m 57:50.25 '20, 1Hr 20.772m '20, Rd: 15k 42:19 '20, 20k 56:39 '20, HMar 59:40 '20, Mar 2:09:14 '19.

Djilali BEDRANI b. 1 Oct 1993 Toulouse 1.79m 59kg. SA Toulouse UC.
At 3000mSt: WCh: '19- 5; EC: '16- h, '18- 10; EU23: '13/15- 8; At 3000m: EI: '19- 4; Eur CC: '12- 5J, '15; 5 U23; Won FRA 3000mSt 2019-20.
Progress at 3000mSt: 2011- 9:04.66, 2012- 8:42.67, 2013- 8:46.06, 2014- 8:46.98, 2015- 8:40.6, 2016- 8:28.34, 2017- 8:33.02, 2018- 8:20.55, 2019- 8:05.23, 2020- 8:13.43. pbs: 800m 1:47.46 '20, 1500m 3:37.71 '19, 3000m 7:41.40i '20, 8:15.96 '18; 5000m 14:21.18 '14, road: 5k 13:45 '20, 10k 27:50 '20, HMar 64:57 '17.

Wilhem BÉLOCIAN b. 22 Jun 1995 les Abymes, Guadeloupe 1.78m 78kg. Stade Lamertin.
At 110mh: WCh: '19- sf; OG: '16- h; EC: '16- 3; WJ: '12- 3, '14- 1; WY: '11- 3 (3 Med R); EJ: '13- 1; WUG: '19- 2; FRA champion 2019-20. At 60mh: EI: '15-19-21: 3/7/1.
World junior record 99cm 110mh 12.99 in 2014, three European JR 2013-14.
Progress at 110mh: 2014- 13.54, 2015- 13.28, 2016- 13.25/13.15w, 2017- 13.89, 2018- 13.91, 2019- 13.28/13.14w, 2020- 13.18. pbs: 60m 6.82i '12, 100m 10.61 '16, 60mh 7.43i '21.

Quentin BIGOT b. 1 Dec 1992 Hayange 1.77m 105kg. Athlétisme Metz Metropole.
At HT: OG: '12- dnq 22; WCh: '13- dnq 12, '17- 4, '19- 2; EC: '12- dnq 24, '18- dnq 15; WJ: '10- 7; WY: '09- dnq 13; EU23: '13- 3; EJ: '11- 1; ET: '13- 3, '19- 2. FRA champion 2017-20.
Progress at HT: 2010- 64.81, 2011- 72.71, 2012- 78.28, 2013- 76.97, 2014- 78.58, 2016- 76.10, 2017- 77.87, 2018- 76.98, 2019- 78.19, 2020- 76.42.
2-years drugs ban 2014-16.

Pierre-Ambroise BOSSE b. 11 May 1992 Nantes 1.85m 68kg. UA Gujan Mestras.
At 800m: OG: '12- sf, '16- 4; WCh: '13-15-17-19: 7/5/1/sf; EC: '12-14-16-18: 3/8/5/3; WJ: '10- 8; EU23: '13- 1; EJ: '11- 1; ET: 15- 2; EI: '21- 6. French champion 2012, 2014-15, 2018-19.
French 800m and European U23 1000m records 2014; European 600m record 2016.
Progress at 800m: 2007- 2:02.81, 2008- 1:56.05, 2010- 1:48.38, 2011- 1:46.18, 2012- 1:44.97, 2013- 1:43.76, 2014- 1:42.53, 2015- 1:43.88, 2016- 1:43.41, 2017- 1:44.67, 2018- 1:44.20, 2019- 1:45.07, 2020- 1:47.52i. pbs: 400m 47.54 '16, 600m 1:13.21 '16, 1000m 2:15.31 '14, 1500m 3:54.81 '09.
Real name Bossé, but he dropped the accent.

Yohann DINIZ b. 1 Jan 1978 Epernay 1.85m 69kg. EFS Reims Athlétisme.
At 20kW: ECp: '07- 1, '15- 3; At 50kW: OG: '08- dnf, '12- dq, '16- 8; WCh: '05-07-09-11-13-17-19: dq/2/11/dq/9/1/dnf; EC: '06-10-14: 1/1/1; ECp: '05-13-19: 4/1/1. Won French 10000mW 2010,

2012, 2014; 20kW 2007-09, 2015; 35kW 2019; 50kW 2005, 2016.
Walks records: world track 50,000m 2011, road 50k 2014, 20k 2015; M40 50k 2019. French 5000mW (3) 2006-08, 10000mW 2014, 20000mW 2014, 20kW (4) 2005-15, 35kW 2019, 50kW 2006 & 2009, 1 Hr 2010.
Progress at 20kW, 50kW: 2001- 1:35:05.0t, 2002- 1:30:40, 2003- 1:26:54.99t, 2004- 1:24:25, 3:52:11.0t; 2005- 1:20:20, 3:45:17; 2006- 1:23:19, 3:41:39; 2007- 1:18:58, 3:44:22; 2008- 1:22:31, 2009- 1:22:50, 3:38:45; 2010- 1:20:23, 3:40:37; 2011- 3:35:27.2t, 2012- 1:17:43, 2013- 1:23:17, 3:41:07; 2014- 1:19:42.1t, 3:32:33; 2015- 1:17:02, 2016- 3:37:48, 2017- 1:27:19, 3:33:12; 2019- 3:37:43. pbs: 3000mW 10:52.44 '08, 5000mW 18:16.76i '14, 18:18.01 '08; 10000mW 38:08.13 '14, 20000mW 1:19:42.1 '14, 1HrW 15,395m '10, 35kW 2:29:28 '19.

Renaud LAVILLENIE b. 18 Sep 1986 Barbezieux-Saint-Hilaire 1.77m 71kg. Clermont Athl. Auvergne.
At PV: OG: '12- 1, '16- 2; WCh: '09-11-13-15-17-19: 3/3/2/3=/3/dnq 15=; WI: '12-16-18- 1/1/1; EC: '10-12-14-16-18: 1/1/1/nh/3; EU23: '07- 10; EI: '09-11-13-15: 1/1/1/1; CCp: '10- 2, '14- 1, '18- 2; ET: '09-10-13-14-15-17-19: 1/1/1/1/1/3. Won DL 2010-16, French 2010, 2012-15, 2017-20.
World indoor pole vault record 2014. French record (indoors) 2011 and outdoors 2013.
Progress at PV: 2002- 3.40, 2003- 4.30, 2004- 4.60, 2005- 4.81i/4.70, 2006- 5.25i/5.22, 2007- 5.58i/5.45, 2008- 5.81i/5.65, 2009- 6.01, 2010- 5.94, 2011- 6.03i/5.90, 2012- 5.97, 2013- 6.02, 2014- 6.16i/5.93, 2015- 6.05, 2016- 6.03i/5.98, 2017- 5.91, 2018- 5.95, 2019- 5.85, 2020- 5.94i/5.82, 2021- 6.06i. pbs: 60m 7.23i '08, 100m 11.04 '11, 60mh 8.41i '08, 1 110mh 14.51 '10, HJ 1.89i '08, 1.87 '07; LJ 7.31 '10, Hep 5363i '08, Dec 6676 '13.
Broke Sergey Bubka's 21 year-old absolute world pole vault record indoors in 2014. 23 successive wins 31 Aug 2013 to EC 2014, only man to win all seven Diamond League titles from 2010. IAAF Male Athlete of the Year 2014. Married Anais Poumarat (PV 4.26i/4.20 '14) in September 2018.

Valentin LAVILLENIE b. 16 Jul 1991 Barbezieux-Saint-Hilaire 1.71m 66kg. Clermont Athl. Auvergne.
At PV: WCh: '13- nh, '17- dnq 14, '19- 6=; EU23: '13- 3; EI: '15- 6, '21- 2.
Progress at PV: 2006- 3.30, 2007- 3.70, 2008- 4.31i/4.15, 2009- 4.70, 2010- 5.00i/4.80, 2011- 5,31i/5.21, 2012- 5.52, 2013- 5.70i/5.65, 2014- 5.66i/5.50, 2015- 5.80i/5.70, 2016- 5.71, 2017- 5.70, 2018- 5.72i/5.32, 2019- 5.82, 2020- 5.74i/5.70, 2021- 5.80i. pbs: 60m 7.03i '1, 100m 11.34 '18. 110mh 15.81 '11. Brother of Renaud.

Pascal MARTINOT-LAGARDE b. 22 Sep 1991 St Maur-des-Fossés 1.90m 80kg. Neuilly Plaisance Sport.
At 110mh: OG: '16- 4; WCh: '13- h, '15- 4, '19- 3;

EC: '14- 3, '18- 1; WJ: '10- 1; EU23: '11- h; EJ: '09- 4; CCp: '18- 3; ET: '13-14-15-19: 2/3/2/2; won DL 2014, FRA 2014, 2018. At 60mh: WI: '12-14-16-18: 3/2/2/5; EI: '13-15-17-19: 3/1/2/2.
French 110m hurdles record 2014.
Progress at 110mh: 2008- 15.03, 2009- 14.13, 2010- 13.74, 2011- 13.94, 2012- 13.41/13.30w, 2013- 13.12, 2014- 12.95, 2015- 13.06, 2016- 13.12, 2018- 13.17, 2019- 13.12, 2020- 13.63. pbs: 60m 7.07i '10, 100m 10.94 '13, 60mh 7.45i '14.
His brother **Thomas** (b. 7 Feb 1988) has 110mh pb 13.26, 7 WCh and French champion in 2013.

Kevin MAYER b. 10 Feb 1992 Argenteuil 1.86m 82kg. EA Tain-Tournon.
At Dec: OG: '12- 15, '16- 2; WCh: '13- 4, '17- 1, '19- dnf; EC: '12-14-18: dnf/2/dnf; WJ: '10- 1; EJ: '11- 1; ECp: '13- 1. At Oct: WY: '09- 1. At Hep: WI: '18- 1; EI: '13-17-21: 2/1/1.
Records: World decathlon 2018, European indoor heptathlon 2017, French Dec 2016 & 2018.
Progress at Dec: 2011- 7992, 2012- 8447w/8415, 2013- 8446, 2014- 8521, 2015- 8469, 2016- 8834, 2017- 8768, 2018- 9126, 2020- 8552. pbs: 60m 6.85i '18, 100m 10.55 '18, 200m 21.76 '17, 400m 48.26 '17, 1000m 2:37.30i '13, 1500m 4:18.04 '12, 60mh 7.68i '21, 110mh 13.54 '20. 13.49w '19, 400mh 54.57 '17, HJ 2.10i '10, 2.09 '12; PV 5.60i/5.45 '18; LJ 7.80 '18, SP 17.08 '19, DT 52.38 '18, JT 71.90 '87, Hep 6479i '17.
Four individual event pbs when adding 313 points to his decathlon best for 2016 OG silver and also in WR at Talence 2018. Three no jumps in European Champs decathlon 2018.

Mahiédine MEKHISSI-BENABBAD b. 15 Mar 1985 Reims 1.90m 75kg. Paris Racing.
At 3000mSt: OG: '08- 2, '12- 2, '16- 3; WCh: '07/09- h, '11- 3, '13- 3, '17- 4 (h 1500m); EC: '10-12-14-16-18: 1/1,dq (1 1500m)/1/1; WJ: '04- h; EU23: '05- h, '07- 1; CCp: '10- 3; ET: '07-08-17: 2/1/1. At 1500m: WI: '10- 8; EI: '13- 1; WCp: '06- 7, '14- 3. Eur CC: '18- 2 mxR. Won FRA 1500m 2014, 3000mSt 2008, 2012-13, 2016, 2018.
Records: World best 2000m steeplechase 2010. European 3000mSt 2013, French 1M 2014.
Progress at 3000mSt: 2003- 9:52.07, 2004- 9:01.01, 2005- 8:34.45, 2006- 8:28.25, 2007- 8:14.22, 2008- 8:08.95, 2009- 8:06.98, 2010- 8:02.52, 2011- 8:02.09, 2012- 8:10.90, 2013- 8:00.09, 2014- 8:03.23, 2016- 8:08.15, 2017- 8:14.67, 2018- 8:16.97. pbs: 800m 1:53.61 '04, 1000m 2:17.14 '09, 1500m 3:33.12 '13, 1M 3:51.55 '14, 2000m 4:56.85 '13, 3000m 7:43.72i '13, 7:44.98 '10; 5000m 13:20.53 '18, HMar 66:52 '19, 2000mSt 5:10.68 '10.
Disqualified after he took his vest off in the finishing straight when finishing well clear in 2014 EC steeplechase.

Melvin RAFFIN b. 9 Aug 1998 Bourg-la-Reine 1.86m 66kg. Savigny SA.
At TJ: WCh: '17- dnq 24; WJ: '16- 3; WY: '15- 11; EJ: '17- 3; EI: '17- 5.
Progress at TJ: 2014- 15.39/15.66w, 2015- 15.81i/

98   FRANCE – GAMBIA – GERMANY

15.62, 2016- 16.47/16.93w, 2017- 17.20i/16.85, 2018- 16.21i, 2020- 17.07i, 2021- 17.09i. pbs: 60m 6.75i '17, 100m 10.67 '17, 200m 21.72 '17.

Ludvy VAILLANT b. 15 Mar 1995 Fort-de-France, Martinique 1.80m 64kg. AC Saleen.
At 400mh: WCh: '17/19- sf; EC: '18- 4; E23: '15- 1R, 17- 3/3R; EJ: '13- 8; ET: '19- 2; won MedG 2018. At 400m: E23: '15- 7. Won FRA 400m 2020, 400mh 2018..
Progress at 110mh: 2013- 51.81, 2014- 51.68, 2015- 50.53, 2016- 50.32, 2017- 49.31, 2018- 48.42, 2019- 48.30, 2020- 48.69. pbs: 60m 6.79i '17, 100m 10.80 '16, 200m 20.97 '17, 400m 45.25 '18, 60mh 7.52i '15.

Jimmy VICAUT b. 27 Feb 1992 Bondy 1.88m 83kg. SCO Sainte-Marguerite de Marseille.
At 100m/(200m)/4x100mR: OG: '12- sf/3R, '16- 7; WCh: '11- 6/2R, '13- sf/sf, '15- 8, '17- 6, '19- sf; EC: '10- 1R, '12- 2/3R (res), '14- sf, '16- 3/2R, '18- dns; WJ: '10- 3; WY: '09- 7; EJ: '11- 1/1R; ET: '13- 14-19: 1/1/1/1. At 60m: EI: '13- 1. Won French 100m 2013, 2015-16; 200m 2016.
Equalled European 100m record 2015 & 2016. Progress at 100m: 2005- 13.0, 2006- 12.50, 2007- 11.0, 2008- 10.75/10.69w, 2009- 10.56, 2010- 10.16, 2011- 10.07, 2012- 10.02, 2013- 9.95, 2014- 9.95/9.89w, 2015- 9.86, 2016- 9.86, 2017- 9.97, 2018- 9.91, 2019- 10.02. pbs: 60m 6.48i '13, 200m 20.30 '13.
His brother Willi was French U17 shot champion in 2012 and has senior pb of 17.33 '14.

Women

Mélina ROBERT-MICHON b. 18 Jul 1979 Voiron 1.80m 85kg. Lyon Athlétisme
At DT: OG: '00/04- dnq 29/30, '08- 7, '12- 5, '16- 2; WCh: '01-03-07-09-13-15-17-19: dnq 20/11/12/2/10/3/10; EC: '98-02-06-12-14-16: dnq 29/12/dnq 16/6/2/5; WJ: '98- 2; EU23: '99-12, '01- 1; WUG: '01- 3; CCp: '14- 4; ECp: '00-01-02-03-04-06-07-08-09-13-14-15-17-19: 5/6/8/2/4/7/5/4/2/1/1/1/1/2. Won French 2000-09, 2011-17, 2019-20; MedG 2009.
Six French discus records 2000-16.
Progress at DT: 1997- 49.10, 1998- 59.27, 1999- 60.17, 2000- 63.19/63.61dh, 2001- 63.87, 2002- 65.78, 2003- 64.27, 2004- 64.54, 2005- 58.01, 2006- 59.89, 2007- 63.48, 2008- 62.21, 2009- 63.04, 2010- 56.52, 2011- 61.07, 2012- 63.98, 2013- 66.28, 2014- 65.51, 2015- 65.04, 2016- 66.73, 2017- 66.21, 2019- 64.02, 2020- 64.14. pbs: SP 15.23 '07, HT 47.92 '02.
Daughters Elyssa born in 2010 and Enora in June 2018. Broke her 11 year-old French record in winning 2013 World silver.

Alexandra TAVERNIER b. 13 Dec 1993 Annecy 1.70m 82kg. Annecy Haute Savoie.
At HT: OG: '16- 11; WCh: '15- 3, '17- 12, '19- 6; EC: '14-16-18: 6/dnq/2; WJ: '12- 1; EU23: '15- 1; EJ: '11- 6; CCp: '18- 3; ET: '15- 3, '19- 1. Won MedG 2018, French 2014, 2016-17, 2019-20.
Five French hammer records 2018-21.
Progress at HT: 2009- 44.96, 2010- 58.44, 2011-

62.13, 2012- 70.62, 2013- 70.79, 2014- 71.17, 2015- 74.39, 2016- 72.16, 2017- 72.69, 2018- 74.78, 2019- 74.84, 2020- 75.23, 2021- 75.38. Pbs: SP 11.81 '14, DT 41.58 '10.
Her brother **Hugo** (b. 12 Dec 1999) was 5th in the 2018 World Junior hammer with a 6kg pb of 75.99; pb senior hammer 72.45 '21.

GAMBIA

Gina BASS b. 3 May 1995 Toubacouta, Sénégal 1.64m 62kg. Police officer in Dakar, Sénégal.
At (100m)/200m: OG: '16- h; WCh: '17- h, '19- sf/6; WY: '11- (h); CG: '18- sf/sf; AfG: '15- sf/sf, '19- 2/1; AfCh: '16- sf/3, '18- 8/4.
Gambian records: 100m (6), 200m (8) 2015-19.
Progress at 200m: 2014- 24.53w, 2015- 24.13/24.0, 2016- 22.92, 2017- 22.97, 2018- 23.24/23.10w, 2019- 22.58. pbs: 60m 7.11i '20, 100m 11.13 '19.

GERMANY

Governing body: Deutscher Leichtathletik Verband (DLV). Founded 1898.
National Championships first held in 1891.
2020 Champions: Men: 100m: Deniz Almas 10.09, 200m: Steven Müller 20.79, 400m: Marvin Schlegel 45.80, 800m: Marc Reuther 1:46.97, 1500m: Marius Probst 3:52.48, 5000m: Mohamed Mohumed 14:02.75, 3000mSt: Karel Bebendorf 8:42.43, 110mh: Matthias Bühler 13.62, 400mh: Constantin Preis 49.58, HJ: Mateusz Przybylko 2.28, PV: Bo Kanda Lita Baehre 5.70, LJ: Maximilian Entholzner 7.96, TJ: Max Hess 16.58, SP: David Storl 20.17, DT: Clemens Prüfer 62.97, HT: Tristan Schwandke 70.85, JT: Johannes Vetter 87.36, Dec: Jannis Wolff 7690. **Women**: 100m: Lisa Marie Kwayie 11.30, 200m: Jessica-Bianca Wessoly 23.07, 400m: Corinna Schwab 51.73, 800m: Christina Hering 2:01.62, 1500m: Hanna Klein 4:13.71, 5000m: Alina Reh 16:08.33, 3000mSt: Elena Burkard 9:50.31, 100mh: Ricarda Lobe 13.24, 400mh: Carolina Krafzik 55.90, HJ: Christina Honsel 1.90, PV: Stefanie Dauber & Ria Möllers 4.40, LJ: Malaika Mihambo 6.71, TJ: Maria Purtsa 13.65, SP: Alina Kenzel 17.96, DT: Kristin Pudenz 62.30, HT: Carolin Paesler 70.99, JT: Christin Hussong 63.93, Hep: Carolin Schäfer 6319.

Arthur ABELE b. 30 Jul 1986 Mutlangen, Baden-Württemberg 1.84m 80kg. SSV Ulm 1846.
At Dec: OG: '08- dnf, '16- 15; WCh: '07- 9; EC: '14- 5, '18- 1; WJ: '04- 7; EJ: '05- 2; ECp: '04- 4. German champion 2013. At Hep: EI: '15- 2.
Progress at Dec: 2006- 8012, 2007- 8269, 2008- 8372, 2013- 8251, 2014- 8477, 2016- 8605, 2017- dnf, 2018- 8481. pbs: 60m 6.93i '15, 100m 10.67 '14, 200m 22.41 '14, 400m 47.98 '08, 1000m 2:35.64i '15, 1500m 4:15.35 '08, 60mh 7.67i '15, 110mh 13.55 '14, 400mh 51.71 '04, HJ 2.04 '07, PV 5.01 '14, LJ 7.57 '16. SP 15.93 '18, DT 46.20 '16, JT 71.89 '16, Hep 6279i '15.
Five individual event absolute bests in 2015

GERMANY 99

European Indoor heptathlon, but Achilles injury cost him the summer season. Won at Ratingen 2007, 2016, 2018, IAAF Challenge 2018.
Torben BLECH b. 12 Feb 1995 Siegen 1.92m 87kg. TSV Bayer 04 Leverkusen, was at University of Köln.
At PV: WCh: '19- dnq 23=; WUG: '19- 2. At Dec: EU23: '17- 9.
Progress at PV: 2014- 4.70, 2016- 5.10, 2017- 5.30, 2018- 5.42, 2019- 5.80, 2020- 5.70i/5.62, 2021- 5.86i. Pbs: 100m 10.84 '16, 400m 50.58 '17, 1500m 4:59.83 '17, 60mH 8.18i '16, 110mH 14.40 '17, HJ 1.97 '16. LJ 7.39 '17, SP 14.94 '17, DT 43.26 '17, JT 58.18 '17, Dec 7872 '17

Christoph HARTING b. 10 Apr 1990 Cottbus 2.07m 120kg. SCC Berlin. Police officer.
At DT: OG: '16- 1; WCh: '13- dnq 13, '15- 8, '19- dnq 14; EC: '16- 4, '18- dnq; EU23: '11- 5. German champion 2015, 2018.
Progress at DT: 2008- 52.00, 2009- 50.19, 2010- 61.19, 2011- 62.12, 2012- 61.22, 2013- 64.99, 2014- 63.78, 2015- 67.93, 2016- 68.37, 2017- 64.55, 2018- 67.59, 2019- 66.01, 2020- 61.28i. pb SP 17.75 '12.
Robert (2012) and Christoph Harting are the first siblings to win the same individual event in the history of the Summer Olympics.

Max HESS b. 13 Jul 1996 Chemnitz 1.86m 79kg. LAC Erdgas Chemnitz.
At TJ: OG: '16- dnq 15; EC: '16- 1, '18- dnq 15; WJ: '14- 2; WY: '13- 8; EU23: '17- 3; WI: '16- 2; EI: '17-19-21: 3/3/3; ET: 17- 1. GER champion 2016-17, 2019-20.
Progress at TJ: 2012- 14.58, 2013- 15.52, 2014- 16.55, 2015- 16.34i/16.07, 2016- 17.20, 2017- 17.52i/17.13/17.24w, 2018- 16.95, 2019- 17.10i/16.50, 2020- 17.17. pbs: 60m 6.93i '18, LJ 8.03i '16.

Andreas HOFMANN b. 16 Dec 1991 Heidelberg 1.95m 108kg. MTG Mannheim. Sports student.
At JT: WCh: '15- 6, '17- 8, '19- dnq 20; EC: '14- 9, '18- 2; EJ: '09- 1; WUG: '17- 2; ET: '14- 1. German champion 2018-19, DL 2018.
Progress at JT: 2008- 65.03, 2009- 77.84, 2010- 66.75, 2011- 73.98, 2012- 80.81, 2013- 75.56, 2014- 86.13, 2015- 86.14, 2016- 85.42, 2017- 91.07, 2018- 92.06, 2019- 89.65, 2020- 85.24. pb SP 18.59i '17.

Niklas KAUL b. 11 Feb 1998 Mayence 1.92m 84kg. USC Mainz.
At Dec: WCh: '19- 1; EC: '18- 4; WJ: '16- 1; WY: '15- 1 (2 JT); EJ23: '19- 1; EJ: '17- 1.
World junior record 8435 for U20 spec 2017.
Progress at Dec: 2018- 8220, 2019- 8691. pbs: 100m 11.17 '19, 400m 48.09 '18, 1500m 4:15.52 '17, 60mH 8.24i '19, 110mH 14.55 '18, HJ 2.10 '16, PV 5.00 '19, LJ 7.29 '18. SP 15.19 '19, DT 49.20 '19, JT 79.05 '19. Pbs at DT and JT (best ever in an 8000+ decathlon) when won 2019 world title. His father Michael had 400mH pb 49.55 and his Austrian mother Stefanie Zotter 400mH pb 57.27, both in 1994.

Kai KAZMIREK b. 28 Jan 1991 Torgau 1.89m

91kg. LG Rhein-Wied.
At Dec: OG: '16- 4; WCh: '15-17-19: 6/3/17; EC: '14- 6; WJ: '10- 6; EU23: '11- 6, '13- 1; EJ: '09- 3. GER champion 2012. At Hep: WI: '14- 6, '18- 4.
Progress at Dec: 2011- 7802, 2012- 8130, 2013- 8366, 2014- 8471, 2015- 8462, 2016- 8580, 2017- 8488, 2018- 8329, 2019- 8444. pbs: 60m 7.01i '15, 100m 10.62 '16, 10.61w '13; 200m 21.40 '12, 400m 46.75 '11, 1000m 2:39.51i '14, 1500m 4:30.75 '18, 60mH 7.95i '18, 110mH 14.05 '14, HJ 2.15 '14, PV 5.20 '13, LJ 7.69 '16, SP 14.94 '19, DT 45.83 '15, JT 64.60 '16, Hep 6238i '18.
Won Götzis decathlon 2015, Ratingen 2019, IAAF Combined Events Challenge 2016.

Christopher LINKE b. 24 Oct 1988 Potsdam 1.90m 65kg. SC Potsdam
At 20kW/(50kW): OG: '12- (21), '16- 5; WCh: '11-13-15-17-19: 16/8/38/5/4; EC: '10-14-18: (dnf)/4/13; EU23: '09- 4; WCp: '12- (3), '16- 10; ECp: '11-13-15-17: (3)/9/7/1. At 10000mW: EJ: '07- 6. Won GER 10000W 2011, 2014-16, 2019; 20kW 2012, 2014, 2016-18; 50kW 2008.
German 20k walk record 2019.
Progress at 20kW, 50kW: 2008- 1:25:25, 4:03:59; 2009- 1:24:29, 2010- 1:27:25, 3:53:24; 2011- 1:20:51, 3:52:56; 2012- 1:20:41, 3:47:33; 2013- 1:22:36, 2014- 1:21:00, 2015- 1:20:37, 2016- 1:19:19, 2017- 1:18:59, 2018- 1:20:40, 2019- 1:18:42. pbs: 3000mW 10:49.33i '18, 11:49.10A '10, 5000mW 18:33.86i '19, 20:37.47 '08; 10000W 38:40.25 '16.

Bo Kanda LITA BAEHRE b. 29 Apr 1999 Düsseldorf 1.93m 87kg. TSV Bayer 04 Leverkusen.
At PV: WCh: '19- 4; EC: '18- dnq 19; WJ: '18- 4; EU23: '19- 1; EJ: '17- 2; EY: '16- 1; EI: '19- 7. German champion 2020.
Progress at PV: 2011- 2.71, 2012- 3.50i/3.30, 2013- 3.72, 2014- 4.60, 2015- 4.92, 2016- 5.30, 2017- 5.61, 2018- 5.60, 2019- 5.72, 2020- 5.81.

Mateusz PRZYBYLKO b. 9 Mar 1992 Bielefeld 1.95m 79kg. TSV Bayer 04 Leverkusen.
At HJ: OG: '16- dnq 28; WCh: '15- dnq 28=, '17- 5, '19- dnq 30; EC: '18- 1; WJ: '10- dnq; WY: '09- 11; EU23: '13- 5; EJ: '11- 7; WI: '18- 3; EI: '17-19-21: 7/8/7; ET: '15- 3. GER champion 2017-20.
Progress at HJ: 2009- 2.14i/2.10, 2010- 2.16, 2011- 2.20, 2012- 2.20, 2013- 2.24, 2014- 2.24i/2.22, 2015- 2.30, 2016- 2.29, 2017- 2.35, 2018- 2.35, 2019- 2.30, 2020- 2.28.
Clear at six heights to 2.35 for 2018 EC gold.

Thomas RÖHLER b. 30 Sep 1991 Jena 1.92m 92kg. LC Jena. Sports student.
At JT: OG: '16- 1; WCh: '13-15-17-19: dnq 29/4/1/dnq 23; EC: '12-14-16-18: dnq 13/12/5/1; WJ: '10- 9; EU23: '11- 7, '13- 3; CCp: '18- 1; ET: '13- 2, '17- 3. Won DL 2014, German champion 2012-16. German javelin record 2017.
Progress at JT: 2009- 61.26, 2010- 76.37, 2011- 78.20, 2012- 80.79, 2013- 83.95, 2014- 87.63, 2015- 89.27, 2016- 91.28, 2017- 93.90, 2018- 91.78, 2019- 86.99.

GERMANY

David STORL b. 21 Jul 1990 Rochlitz 1.98m 125kg. Leipzig SC DHfK. Federal police officer.
At SP: OG: '12- 2, '16- 7; WCh: '09-11-13-15-17: dnq 26/1/1/2/10; EC: '10-12-14-16-18: 4/1/1/1/3; WJ: '08- 1; WY: '07- 1; EU23: '11- 1; EJ: '09- 1; WI: '10-12-14-18: 5/2/2/2; EI: '11-15-17-19: 2/1/3/2; WCp: '14- 1; ET: '11-13-14-15-17: 1/1/1/1/2. GER champion 2011-12, 2014-18, 2020.
World junior shot record and three with 6kg (to 22.73) 2009.
Progress at SP: 2008- 18.46, 2009- 20.43, 2010- 20.77, 2011- 21.78, 2012- 21.88i/21.86, 2013- 21.73, 2014- 21.97, 2015- 22.20, 2016- 21.31, 2017- 21.87, 2018- 21.62, 2019- 21.54i/19.77, 2020- 21.20.
10 major international titles & 7 second places.

Johannes VETTER b. 26 Mar 1993 Dresden 1.88m 105kg. LG Offenburg.
At JT: OG: '16- 4; WCh: '15- 7, '17- 1, '19- 3; EC: '16- dnq 16, '18- 5; EU23: '15- 4; EJ: '11- 12; ET: '15- 2. GER champion 2017, 2020.
German javelin records 2017 & 2020.
Progress at JT: 2010- 63.60, 2011- 71.60, 2012- 60.19, 2013- 76.58, 2014- 79.75, 2015- 85.40, 2016- 89.57, 2017- 94.44, 2018- 92.70, 2019- 90.03, 2020- 97.76. Best ever throw in a qualifying round with 90.26 at 2017 Worlds, then 89.89 to win final. His 97.76 in 2020 is second best ever.

Julian WEBER b. 29 Aug 1994 Mainz 1.90m 94kg. USC Mainz.
At JT: OG: '16- 9; WCh: '19- 6; EU23: '15- 5; EJ: '13- 1; ET: '19- 1.
Progress at JT: 2012- 71.12, 2013- 79.68, 2014- 80.72, 2015- 81.15, 2016- 88.29, 2017- 85.85, 2018- 86.63, 2019- 86.86.

Martin WIERIG b. 10 Jun 1987 Neindorf 2.02m 127kg. SC Magdeburg. Federal police officer.
At DT: OG: '12- 6; WCh: '11/15/17: dnq 18/19/nt, '13- 4, '19- 8; EC: '10-12-14-16: 7/dnq 14/11/dnq 14; WJ: '04- 8, '06- 3; EU23: '10- 1, '09- 3; EJ: '05- 3 (dnq SP); ET: '15- 2, '19- 2. Won GER 2019.
Progress at DT: 2005- 57.44, 2006- 57.37, 2007- 61.10, 2008- 63.09, 2009- 63.90, 2010- 64.93, 2011- 67.21, 2012- 68.33, 2013- 67.46, 2014- 66.59, 2015- 65.94, 2016- 67.16, 2017- 69.1, '09- 3; EJ: 65.98, 2019- 66.04, 2020- 62.07i. pb SP 17.30 '11.
Married Anna Rüh (b. 17 Jun 1993) DT 66.14 '15, 4 EC '12 & '16; 1/2 EU23 '13/15, 2 EJ '11.

Women

Shanice CRAFT b. 15 May 1993 Mannheim 1.85m 89kg. Halle. Police officer.
At (SP)/DT: OG: '16- 11; WCh: '15- 7; EC: '14-16- 18: 3/3/3; WJ: '12- 1/2; WY: '09- 3; EU23: '13- 2/2, '15- 2/1; EJ: '11- 1; ET: '14- 2. Won GER 2014, 2018; Yth Oly 2010.
World indoor discus best 2020.
Progress at DT: 2007- 44.86, 2008- 48.14, 2009- 50.57, 2010- 55.49, 2011- 58.65, 2012- 62.92, 2013- 60.77, 2014- 65.88, 2015- 64.79, 2016- 64.82, 2017- 63.18, 2018- 62.91, 2019- 63.22, 2020- 64.03i. Pb SP 17.75 '14. US father.

Neele ECKHARDT b. 2 Jul 1992 Ostercappeln 1.68m 52kg. LG Göttingen
At TJ: WCh: '17- 12; EC: '18: 10; WJ: '10- 8; WY: '09- 10 (11 LJ); EU23: '13- 8; EI: '21- 3; WUG: '17- 1 German champion 2018.
Progress at TJ: 2008- 12.08, 2009- 13.13, 2010- 13.16, 2012- 13.25, 2013- 13.23, 2014- 13.67/13.98w, 2015- 13.34i, 2016- 13.93, 2017- 14.35, 2018- 14.33, 2019- 14.16, 2020- 14.17i/13.73/13.80w, 2021- 14.52i. pbs: 60m 7.41i '20, LJ 6.29 '19.

Kristin GIERISCH b. 20 Aug 1990 Zwickau 1.78m 59kg. TSV Bayer 04 Leverkusen. Police.
At TJ: OG: '16- 11; WCh: '15- 8, '17- 5; EC: '14-16- 18: 9/8/2; WY: '07- 6; EU23: '11- dns; EJ: '09- 5; EI: '15- 4, '17- 1; CCp: '18- 5; ET: '15- 2, '17- 2; WI: '16- 2. German champion 2014-15, 2017, 2019.
German triple jump record 2019,
Progress at TJ: 2006- 12.09, 2007- 13.00, 2008- 12.22, 2009- 14.02, 2010- 13.84, 2011- 14.10i/13.47, 2012- 14.19i/13.94, 2013- 13.91i/13.67, 2014- 14.31/ 14.34w, 2015- 14.46i/14.38/14.46w, 2016- 14.31, 2017- 14.40, 2018- 14.45, 2019- 14.61, 2020- 14.03i. pbs: 60m 7.59i '12, LJ 6.46i '15, 6.21 '14.

Christin HUSSONG b. 17 Apr 1994 Zweibrücken 1.87m 82kg. LAZ Zweibrücken. Sports student.
At JT: OG: '16- 12; WCh: '15- 6, 17- dnq 17, '19- 4; EC: '14-16-18: 7/dnq 17/1; WJ: '12- 7; WY: '11- 1; EU23: '15- 1; EJ: '13- 2, YthOG: '10- 4; CCp: '18- 2. GER champion 2016, 2018-20.
Progress at JT: 2009- 49.93, 2010- 55.35, 2011- 59.74, 2012- 55.74, 2013- 58.55, 2014- 63.34, 2015- 65.92, 2016- 66.41, 2017- 64.18, 2018- 67.90, 2019- 66.59, 2020- 64.10. Pbs: SP 15.02i '14, 14.02 '11.

Marie-Laurence JUNGFLEISCH b. 7 Oct 1990 Paris, France 1.81m 68kg. VfB Stuttgart. Soldier.
At HJ: OG: '16- 7=; WCh: '13- nh, '15- 6, '17- 4; EC: '12-14-16-18: dnq 13=/5/5/3; EU23: '11- 8; EJ: '09- 6; CCp: '18- 4; ET: '17- 2; WI: '14- 8. Won GER 2013-19; WIT 2016.
Progress at HJ: 2006- 1.70, 2007- 1.75, 2008- 1.78, 2009- 1.86, 2010- 1.90, 2011- 1.93, 2012- 1.95, 2013- 1.95, 2014- 1.97, 2015- 1.99, 2016- 2.00, 2017- 2.00, 2018- 1.96, 2019- 1.96.
Father from Martinique, mother German.

Melat Yisak **KEJETA** b. 27 Sep 1992 Ethiopia 1.58m 45kg. World HMar: '20- 12. European women only half marathon best 2020.
Progress at HMar, Mar: 2011- 70:43, 2012- 70:27, 2014- 75:06, 2015- 75:18, 2016- 74:00, 2017- 71:00, 2018- 68:41, 2019- 69, 2:23:57; 2020- 65:18. pbs: 3000m 9:38.17 '17, 5000m 16:06.43 '16, Road: 10k 30:47 '20, 15k 46:25 '20, 20k 62:04 '20.
Moved to Germany in 2013, citizenship in 2019 and able to compete for Germany from 20 Mar 2019.

Konstanze KLOSTERHALFEN b. 18 Feb 1997 Königswinter 1.74m 48kg. TSV Bayer 04 Leverkusen.
At 1500m: OG: '16- sf; WCh: '17- sf; EU23: '17- 1;

EJ: '15- 3, EI: '17- 2; YthOG: '14- 4, ET: '17- 1. At 3000m: WJ: '16- 3; CCp: '18- 4; WI: '18- 7; EI: '19- 2. At 5000m: WCh: '19- 3; EC: '18- 4. Eur CC: 14-15-16-17: 28J/1J/1J/2U23. Won GER 1500m 2016-18.
European indoor 5000m record 2020, German records 3000m 2017, 1M 2019, 3000m, 5000m 2019; 10000m 2021.
Progress at 1500m, 5000m: 2012- 55.74, 2013- 4:26.58, 2014- 4:19.97, 2015- 4:09.58, 2016- 4:06.91, 15:16.98; 2017- 3:58.92, 14:51.38; 2018- 4:04.00i/ 4:06.34, 15:03.73; 2019- 3:59.02, 14:26.76; 2020- 3:59.87, 14:30.79i. Pbs: 800m 1:59.65 '17, 1000m 2:37.05 '20, 1M 4:17.26i '20, 4:21.11 '19; 3000m 8:20.07 '19, 10000m 31:01.71 '21.

Gesa Felicitas KRAUSE b. 3 Aug 1992 Ehringshausen 1.67m 55kg. LG Eintracht Frankfurt. Student.
At 3000mSt: OG: '12- 7, '16- 6; WCh: '11-13-15-17- 19: 6/9/3/9/3; EC: '12-14-16-18: 3/5/1/1; WJ: '10- 4; EU23: '13- 1; EJ: '11- 1; ET: 15-17-19: 1/1/1; GER champion 2015-19 (& 5000m 2017). At 2000mSt: WY: '09- 7. At 1500m: EI: '15- 5, '21- 8.
Records: World best 2000mSt 2019, European junior 3000mSt 2011, German 2000mSt (3) 2015- 19, 3000mSt (5) 2016-19.
Progress at 3000mSt: 2010- 9:47.78, 2011- 9:32.74, 2012- 9:23.52, 2013- 9:37.11, 2014- 9:35.46, 2015- 9:19.25, 2016- 9:18.41, 2017- 9:11.85, 2018- 9:19.80, 2019- 9:03.30. pbs: 800m 2:03.09mx '17, 1000m 2:44.68 '10, 1500m 4:06.99 '16, 1M 4:29.58 '16, 3000m 8:49.43i '16, 9:02.04 '15; 5000m 15:24.53 '17; 10k Rd 33:26 '15, HMar 72:16 '18, 2000mSt 5:52.80 '19.

Gina LÜCKENKEMPER b. 21 Nov 1996 Hamm 1.70m 57kg. SCC Berlin.
At 100m/(200m)/4x100mR: OG: '16- (sf); WCh: '15- h, '17/19- sf; EC: '16- (3)/3R, '18- 2/3R; WJ: '12- (sf), 14- (8)/3R; WY: '13- (5); EJ: '15- (1); ET: '17- 2/1R. Won GER 100m 2018.
Progress at 100m, 200m: 2012- 11.89, 23.98; 2013- 11.61, 23.35; 2014- 11.54/11.34w, 23.26; 2015- 11.25, 23.04/22.41w; 2016- 11.04, 22.67; 2017- 10.95, 23.04; 2018- 10.98, 2019- 11.14, 2020- 11.31. pbs: 60m 7.11i '18, 300m 37.11 '15.

Malaika MIHAMBO b. 3 Feb 1994 Heidelberg 1.70m 55kg. LG Kurpfalz. Studied political science at Mannheim University.
At LJ: OG: '16- 4; WCh: '13- dnq 13, '15- 6, '19- 1; EC: '14-16-18: 4/3/1; WJ: '12- dnq 14; WY: '11- 9; EU23: '15- 1; EJ: '13- 1; WI: '18- 5; EI: '19- 4, '21- 2; CCp: '18- 2; ET: '14- 1, '19- 1. Won DL 2019, GER 2016, 2018-20.
Progress at LJ: 2008- 5.55, 2009- 5.81, 2010- 5.96, 2011- 6.40, 2012- 6.45i/6.32/6.50w, 2013- 6.70/6.80w, 2014- 6.90, 2015- 6.84, 2016- 6.95, 2017- 6.62, 2018- 6.99, 2019- 7.30, 2020- 7.07i/7.03. pbs: 60m 7.22i '20, 100m 11.21/11.13w '19, 200m 23.90 '18, HJ 1.78i/1.75 '10.
Tanzanian father, German mother.

Nadine MÜLLER b. 21 Nov 1985 Leipzig 1.93m 90kg. Hallesche LA-Freunde. Federal police officer.
At DT: OG: '12- 4, '16- 6; WCh: '07-09-11-13-15-17- 19: dnq 23/6/2/4/3/6/8; EC: '10-12-16-18: 8/2/4/2; WJ: '04- 3; EU23: '05- 10, '07- 8; EJ: '03- 2; CCp: '18- 6; ET: '10-11-17: 1/3/2. German champion 2010-13, 2016.
World indoor discus best 63.89 in 2019.
Progress at DT: 2000- 36.10, 2001- 46.27, 2002- 48.90, 2003- 53.44, 2004- 57.85, 2005- 59.35, 2006- 58.46, 2007- 62.93, 2008- 61.36, 2009- 63.46, 2010- 67.78, 2011- 66.99, 2012- 68.89, 2013- 66.89, 2014- 67.30, 2015- 65.72, 2016- 66.84, 2017- 65.76, 2018- 63.00, 2019- 64.52, 2020- 60.44i.
Father Hans-Joachim Muller was a 55m discus thrower.

Kristin PUDENZ b. 9 Feb 1993 Herford 1.80m 92kg. SC Potsdam
At DT: WCh:'19- 11; EU23: '13- 4, '15- 3; WUG: '17- 1. German champion 2019-20.
Progress at DT: 2008- 41.76, 2009- 46.79, 2010- 54.07, 2011- 54.15, 2012- 57.74, 2013- 59.74, 2014- 60.89, 2015- 62.61, 2016- 61.01, 2017- 62.89, 2018- 61.11, 2019- 64.37, 2020- 65.58.

Carolin SCHÄFER b. 5 Dec 1991 Bad Wildungen 1.78m 64kg. TV Friedrichstein.
At Hep: OG: '16- 5; WCh: '15- dnf, '17- 2; EC: '12-14-18: 10/4/3; WJ: '08- 1; EU23: '11- 5, '13- 6; EJ: '09- 1. German champion 2013, 2020.
Progress at Hep: 2007- 5545, 2008- 5833, 2009- 5697, 2010- 5333, 2011- 5941, 2012- 6072, 2013- 5972, 2014- 6395, 2015- 6547, 2016- 6557, 2017- 6836, 2018- 6549, 2019- 6426, 2020- 6319. pbs: 60m 7.86i '07, 200m 23.27 '17, 800m 2:14.10 '15, 60mh 8.45i '16, 100mh 13.07 '17, HJ 1.86 '17, LJ 6.57 '17, SP 14.84 '17, JT 53.73 '18, Pen 4098i '09. Won IAAF Combined Events Challenge 2016- 18. Won Ratingen 2017-18, Talence 2018. Her elder brother Sebastian had 400m best 47.10 '08 and ran at 4x100m in EJ 2005 & 2007.

Christina SCHWANITZ b. 24 Dec 1985 Dresden 1.80m 103kg. LV 90 Erzebirge. Soldier.
At SP: OG: '08- 9, '12- 9, '16- 6; WCh: '05-09-11- 13-15-19: 7/11/10/2/1/3; EC: '12-14-16-18: 5/1/1/2; WJ: '04- 3; EU23: '05- 2; WI: '08- 5, '14- 2; EI: '11-13-19-21: 2/1/2/3; CCp: '14- 1, '18- 2; ET: '08-13-14-15-19: 1/1/1/1/1. Won DL 2015, WIT 2019, German 2011, 2013-16, 2018-19.
Progress at SP: 2001- 13.57, 2002- 14.26, 2003- 15.25, 2004- 16.98, 2005- 18.84, 2007- 17.06, 2008- 19.68i/19.31, 2009- 19.06, 2010- 18.28, 2011- 19.20, 2012- 19.15i/19.05, 2013- 20.41, 2014- 20.22, 2015- 20.77, 2016- 20.17, 2018- 20.06, 2019- 19.54i/19.37. pb DT 47.27 '03. Gave birth to twins in 2017.

Claudine VITA b. 18 Sep 1996 Frankurt/Oder 1.79m 80kg. SC Neubrandenburg.
At (SP)/DT: WCh: '19- 9; EC: '18- 4; WJ: '14- 5; WY: '13- 2; EU23: '17-5/1; EJ: '15- 2/1; EI: '17- (5); ET: '19- 1; WUG: '19- 2.

Progress at DT: 2012- 47.44, 2013- 52.59, 2014- 56.98, 2015- 62.31, 2016- 62.77, 2017- 64.45, 2018- 65.15, 2019- 66.64, 2020- 63.21. Pbs: LJ 5.79 '13, SP 18.09i '17, 17.90 '16.

GREECE

Governing body: Hellenic Amateur Athletic Association (SEGAS). Founded 1897.
National Championships first held in 1896 (men), 1930 (women). **2020 Champions**: 100m: Ioánnis Nifadópoulos 10.52, 200m: Panayiótis Trivizás 20.92, 400m: Petros Kiriakídis 47.73, 800m: Harálabos Lagós 1:51.33, 1500m/5000m: Andréas Dimitrákis 3:45.67/14:13.99, 10000m: Mários Anagnóstou 29:53.93, HMar: Panayiótis Karaískos 69:33, 3000mSt: Yeóryios Minos 8:56.26, 110mh: Konstantínos Douvalídis 13.49, 400mh: Konstadínos Nákos 51.55, HJ: Antónios Mérlos 2.13, PV: Konstadínos Filippídis 5.50, LJ: Aléxandros-Víktor Peristéris 7.79, TJ: Pávlos Bóftsis 16.21, SP: Kiriákos Zótos 19.19, DT: Iáson Thanópoulos 59.09, HT: Hrístos Frantzeskákis 76.64, JT: Yeóryios Hristakákos 70.31, Dec: Ággelos-Tzanís Andréoglou 7385, 20kW: Aléxandros Papamihaíl 1:28:36, 50kW: Dimítrios Tsordiás 4:41:33. **Women**: 100m/200m: Rafailía Spanoudáki-Hatziríga 11.43/23.20, 400m: Korína Políti 53.84, 800m: Konstantína Yiannopoúlou 2:05.41, 1500m: Anastasía-Panayióta Marinákou 4:28.27, 5000m/10000m: Glória-Tziovánna Privilétzio 16:41.07/35:11.94, HMar: Ekateríni Asimakopoúlou 79:20, 3000mSt: Isavélla Kotsahíli 10:25.87, 100mh: Anaís Karayiánni 13.31, 400mh: Dímitra Gnafáki 58.17, HJ: Panayióta Dósi 1.85, PV: Eléni-Klaoúdia Pólak 4.50, LJ: Eléni Koutsaliári 6.42w, TJ: Spiridoúla Karídi 13.91, SP: Sofía Kaisídou 14.85, DT: Hrisoúla Anagnostopoúlou 57.98, HT: Iliána Korosídou 63.94, JT: Elína Tzénggo 61.76, Hep: Sofía Ifantídou 5376, 20kW: Antigóni Drisbióti 1:34:00, 50kW: Nikolítsa Andreopoúlou 5:06:32.

Hrístos FRANTZESKÁKIS b. 26 Apr 2000 Haniá 1.86m 88kg. Venizélos (Haniá)
At HT: WJ: '18- dnq nt; EJ: '17- dnq nt, '19- 2. GRE champion 2020, Balkan 2019.
Progress at HT: 2018- 68.76, 2019- 76.67, 2020- 76.78

Emmanouíl KARALÍS b. 20 Oct 1999 Athens 1.86m 82kg. YS Apóllon Pírgou.
At PV: WCh: '17-19: dnq 21/15=; WJ: '16- 4; WY: '15- 3; EU23: '19- 2; EJ: '17- dnq; WI: '18- 5; EI: '19- 4=. Won Balkan 2019. World junior indoor pole vault record (5.78) 2018, world youth records (2 indoor, 1 outdoor) 2016.
Progress at PV: 2014- 4.65, 2015- 5.25, 2016- 5.55, 2017- 5.70i/5.63, 2018- 5.80i, 2019- 5.75i/5.71, 2020- 5.50.
His father Charis decathlon pb 7392 in 1987.

Miltiádis TENTÓGLOU b. 18 Mar 1998 Grevena 1.87m 70kg. YS Kificiás.
At LJ: OG: '16- dnq 27; WCh: '17- dnq 19, '19-10; EC: '18- 1; WJ: '16- 2; WY: '15- 5; EU23: '19- 1; EJ:

'17- 1; CCp: '18- 2; ET: '19- 1; WI: '18- 9; EI: '19- 1, '21- 1. Greek champion 2017-19, Balkan 2018.
Progress at LJ: 2013- 6.40, 2014- 7.13, 2015- 7.73, 2016- 8.19, 2017- 8.30, 2018- 8.25, 2019- 8.38i/8.32, 2020- 8.26i, 2021- 8.35i. Pb TJ 15.61 '16, 16.04w '19.

Women

Nikoléta KIRIAKOPOÚLOU b. 21 Mar 1986 Athens 1.67m 56kg. AYES Kámiros Rhodes.
At PV: OG: '08/12- dnq 27=/19=; WCh: '09-11-13-15-19: dnq 19/8/dnq 13=/3/13=; EC: '10-12-14-16-18: dnq 13/3/7=/4/2; WJ: '04- 6; EJ: '05- 7; WI: '16- 6=; EI: '11-15-19: 9/5=/3. Won DL 2015, Balkan 2008, Med G 2009, G
RE 2009, 2011-14, 2018. Nine Greek pole vault records 2010-15.
Progress at PV: 2001- 2.90, 2002- 3.10, 2003- 3.70, 2004- 4.00, 2005- 4.10, 2006- 3.60, 2007- 4.00i/3.90, 2008- 4.45, 2009- 4.50, 2010- 4.55, 2011- 4.71, 2012- 4.60, 2013- 4.65, 2014- 4.72i/4.67, 2015- 4.83, 2016- 4.81i/4.75, 2018- 4.80, 2019- 4.81i/4.72, 2020- 4.63. Married to Andreas Linardátos (400m pb 47.27 '90). Gave birth to daughter on 23 May 2017.

Paraskeví 'Voula' PAPAHRÍSTOU b. 17 Apr 1989 Athens 1.70m 53kg. AO Kállistos (Athens).
At TJ: OG: '16- 8; WCh: '09/11/17- dnq 27/16/20; EC: '12-16-18: 11/3/1; WJ: '08- 3; EU23: '09/11- 1/1; WI: '16- 3, '18- 6; EI: '17-19-21: 3/2/5; CCp: '18- 4; ET: '17- 1, '19- 1. Won Balkan TJ 2018-19; Greek LJ 2011-12, 2016, 2018; TJ 2009, 2011, 2015, 2017-19.
Progress at TJ: 2005- 12.75, 2006- 12.81/13.13w, 2007- 12.98i/12.92, 2008- 13.86i/13.79/13.94w, 2009- 14.47i/14.35, 2010- 13.94i/13.85, 2011- 14.72, 2012- 14.58/14.77w, 2013- 14.21, 2015- 13.99/14.20w, 2016- 14.73, 2017- 14.24, 2018- 14.60/14.74w, 2019- 14.5, 2020- 13.85i, 2021- 14.60i. pb LJ 6.60 '12, 6.65w '19. Daughter Konstantína born Nov 2014.

Ekateríni STEFANÍDI b. 4 Feb 1990 Athens 1.72m 63kg. AO Filothéis. Was at Stanford University, USA and then MSc in cognitive psychology at Arizona State University.
At PV: OG: '12- dnq 24, '16- 1; WCh: '15- dnq 15, '17- 1, '19- 3; EC: '12-14-16-18: nh/2/1/1; WJ: '08- 3; WY: '05- 1, '07- 2; EU23: '11- 2; EJ: '07- 10; WI: '16- 3, '18- 3; EI: '15-17-19: 2/1/4; WUG: '11- 3; CCp: 18- 2; ET: '17- 1, '19- 1. Greek champion 2015-16, 2019; NCAA 2012, DL 2016-19.
World youth pole vault best 2005. Two Greek PV records 2016-17 and indoors 2016
Progress at PV: 2001- 2.30, 2002- 3.50, 2003- 3.90, 2004- 4.14, 2005- 4.37i/4.30, 2006- 4.10, 2007- 4.25, 2008- 4.25, 2009- 4.13, 2010- 4.30, 2011- 4.45, 2012- 4.51, 2013- 4.45Ai/4.40, 2014- 4.71, 2015- 4.77Ai/ 4.71, 2016- 4.90i/4.86, 2017- 4.91, 2018- 4.87, 2019- 4.85.
Married to Mitchell Krier (USA, PV 4.95i '16).

Elína TZÉNGGO b. 2 Sep 2002 Thessaloníki 1.72m 72kg. AS Kéntavros Néas Kalliktraátias'
At JT: EJ: '19- 4; YOG: '18- 1. Won GRE 2020.

Javelin records: World U20 2020, European U18 2019, World U18 with 500g JT 65.80 '19. Progress at JT: 2019- 61/48, 2020- 63.96. Pb SP 13.33i '19, 13.22 '20.

GRENADA

Governing body: Grenada Athletic Assocation. Founded 1924.

Kirani JAMES b. 1 Sep 1992 St George's 1.85m 74kg. Student at University of Alabama, USA
At (200m)/400m: OG: '12- 1, '16- 2; WCh: '11-13-15-19: 1/7/3/5; CG: '14- 1; WJ: '08- 2, '10- 1; WY: '07- 2, '09- 1/1; WI: '12- 6. Won DL 2011, 2015; PAm-J 400m 2009, 200m 2011; NCAA 2010-11. Records: CAC & Commonwealth 400m 2012 & 2014, GRN 200m 2011, 400m (3) 2011-14; Indoor 400m: CAC & Commonwealth 2010 (45.24) &. 2011, World Junior (44.80) 2011.
Progress at 400m: 2007- 46.96, 2008- 45.70, 2009- 45.24, 2010- 45.01, 2011- 44.36, 2012- 43.94, 2013- 43.96, 2014- 43.74, 2015- 43.78, 2016- 43.76, 2017- 45.44, 2018- 44.35. 2019- 44.23. pbs: 200m 20.41A/20.53w '11, 20.76 '10; 300m: 31.3+ '16.
World age bests at 14 and 15 and in 2011 became the youngest ever World or Olympic champion at 400m and in 2012 the first Olympic medallist for Grenada at any sport. In January 2012 the 'Kirani James Boulevard' was opened in the Grenadan capital St. George. IAAF Rising Star award 2011.

Anderson PETERS b. 21 Oct 1997 Saint Andrew, Grenada 1.87m 84kg. Mississippi State University, USA.
At JT: WCh: '17- dnq 20, '19- 1; CG: '18- 4; WJ: '16- 3; WY: '13- 9; PAm: '19- 1; CAG: '18- 2; CCp: '18- 3. Won CAC-Y 2015, NCAA 2018-19, NACAC 2018 & U23 2019.
Nine GRN javelin records 2015-19.
Progress at JT: 2015- 74.20, 2016- 79.65, 2017- 84.81, 2018- 82.82, 2019- 87.31, 2020- 80.50. pbs: 60m 7.11i '19, 100m 11.15 '13, 10.89w '16.

Lindon VICTOR b. 28 Feb 1993 St. George's 1.91m 90kg. Was at Texas A&M University, USA.
At Dec: OG: '16- 16; WCh: '17/19- dnf; CG: '14- 9, '18- 1; PAm: '15- 7, '19- 2. Won NCAA 2016-17. Grenada records: decathlon 2016 & 2017, pole vault (2) 2017.
Progress at Dec: 2014- 7429, 2015- 7453, 2016- 8446, 2017- 8539, 2018- 8303, 2019- 8473. pbs: 60m 6.94i '17, 100m 10.56 '19, 400m 48.24 '17, 1000m 2:51.14i '17, 1500m 4:43.81 '16, 60mh 8.24i '16, 110mh 14.45 '17, HJ 2.09 '17, PV 4.90 '19, LJ 7.51 '19, SP 16.55i/16.52 '17, DT 55.22 '17, JT 71.23 '14, Hep: 5976i '17. Half brother of Kurt Felix (Dec 8509 '17, 3/4 CG '14/18.)

HUNGARY

Governing body: Magyar Atlétikai Szövetség. Founded 1897.

National Championships first held in 1896

GREECE –GRENADA – HUNGARY   103

(men), 1932 (women). **2020 Champions**. Men: 100m/200m: Tamás Máté 10.54/21.03, 400m: Dániel Ajide 47.55, 800m: Balázs Vindics 1:46.50, 1500m/5000m: István Szögi 3:54.67/14:40.69, 10000m: Levente Szemerei 30:12.40, HMar: Gáspár Csere 66:30; Mar: Gáspár Csere 2:17:43, 3000mSt: István Palkovits 8:54.77, 110mh: Valdó Szücs 13.66, 400mh: Máté Koroknai 50.56, HJ: Dániel Jankovics 2.20, PV: Marcell Nagy 5.10, LJ/TJ/Dec: Tibor Galambos 7.29/15.62/6759, SP: Balázs Tóth 17.18, DT: János Huszák 61.58, HT: Bence Halász 79.88, JT: Norbert Rivasz-Tóth 79.83, 5000mW/20kW: Máté Helebrandt 20:26.41/1:23:22, 35kW: Bence Venyercsán 2:40:34. **Women**: 100m/100mh: Luca Kozák 11.64/12.97, 200m: Vanessza Nagy 24.34, 400m/400mh: Janka Molnár 53.25/56.94, 800m: Bianka Bartha-Kéri 2:05.08, 1500m/5000m: Viktória Wagner-Gyürkés 4:15.92/16:17.51, 10000m: Lilla Böhm 34:53.42, HMar: Katalin Garami 78:53, Mar: Tünde Szabó 2:43:39, 3000mSt: Lili Tóth 10:10.22, HJ: Barbara Szabó 1.84, PV: Hanga Klekner 4.00, LJ: Anasztázia Nguyen 6.42, TJ: Szabina Szücs 12.98, SP: Violetta Veiland 15.50, DT: Dóra Kerekes 54.74, HT: Réka Gyurátz 69.31, JT: Réka Szilágyi 59.04, Hep: Xénia Krizsán 6263, 5000mW/20kW: Barbara Kovács 23:42.85/1:34:20, 35kW: Rita Recsei 3:08:24.

Bence HALÁSZ b. 4 Aug 1997 Kiskunhalas 1.88m 93kg. Dobó SE.
At HT: WCh: '17- 11, '19- 3; EC: '18- 3; WJ: '14- dnq 14, '16- 1 (dnq 35 DT); WY: '13- 7; EJ: '15- 1 (dnq 15 DT); EU23: '17- 1, '19- 2; CCp: '18- 3; YthOG: '14- 2. Won HUN 2017-20.
Progress at HT: 2012- 51.56, 2013- 62.33, 2014- 68.55, 2015- 69.80, 2016- 73.97, 2017- 78.85, 2018- 79.57, 2019- 78.54, 2020- 79.88. pbs: SP 16.32 '20, DT 57.89 '20. World youth record 87.16 with 5kg hammer in 2014.

Women

Luca KOZÁK b. 1 Jun 1996 1.66m 55kg. Debreceni SC.
At 100mh: WCh: '17- h. '19- sf; EC: '18- sf; E23: '17- 3; EJ: '15- 2; WUG: '17 ·3. At 60mh: EI: '21- 8. Won HUN 100m 2020, 100mh 2018-20.
HUN 100m record 2020, 60mh indoors 2019-20.
Progress at 100mh: 2013- 14.28, 2014- 13.72/13.58w, 2015- 13.46/13.20w, 2016- 13.20, 2017- 13.10/12.99w, 2018- 12.86, 2019- 12.87, 2020- 12.71. Pbs: 60m 7.52i '17, 100m 11.49 '18, 200m 23.92 '18, 60mh 7.97i '19.

Xénia KRIZSÁN b. 13 Jan 1993 Budapest 1.71m 62kg. MTK Budapest.
At Hep: OG: '16- 16; WCh: '15- 9, '17- 9; EC: '14- 16-18: 9/4/7; WJ: '10- 7, '12- 2; WY: '09- 4; EU23: '13- 7, '15- 1; EJ: '11- 7. At Pen: WI: '18- 6; EI: '17- 19-21: 4/7/3. Won HUN 100mh 2013, 2015; LJ 2011-12, Hep 2013, 2020.
HUN heptathlon record 2019.
Progress at Hep: 2010- 5594, 2011- 5794, 2012-

104   HUNGARY – ICELAND – INDIA – IRAN – IRELAND

5957, 2013- 5896, 2014- 6317, 2015- 6322, 2016- 6266, 2017- 6390, 2018- 6367, 2019- 6619, 2020- 6263. pbs: 200m 24.38 '19, 400m 56.48 '12, 800m 2:07.17 '17, 60mh 8.27i '21, 100mh 13.36 '19, HJ 1.82 '17, LJ 6.26 '17, TJ 11.83 '10, SP 14.48i '21, 14.34 '17; JT 53.27 '19, Pen 4644i '21.

Anita MÁRTON b. 15 Jan 1989 Szeged 1.71m 84kg. Békéscsabai AC.
At SP (DT): OG: '12- dnq 22, '16- 3; WCh: '09-11-13: dnq 23/20/19, '15- 4, '17- 2 (dnq 24), '19- 5; EC: '10-12-14-16: 9/7/3/2; WJ: '06- dnq 15 (12), '08- 7 (6); WY: '05- 11 (dnq); EU23: '09- 5, (11) '11- 5 (3); EJ: '07- 7 (6); WUG: '13- 4; WI: '14-16-18: 5/2/1; EI: '11-15-17-19: 5/1/1/3; won WIT 2017; HUN SP 2006-19, DT 2008-19.
Three Hungarian shot records 2014-16.
Progress at SP: 2004- 13.88, 2005- 14.12i/13.90, 2006- 15.57, 2007- 15.68, 2008- 16.90, 2009- 17.27, 2010- 18.20, 2011- 18.15, 2012- 18.48, 2013- 18.18, 2014- 19.04, 2015- 19.48, 2016- 19.87, 2017- 19.63, 2018- 19.62i/19.12, 2019- 19.00i/18.95, 2020- 18.77i/17.40. pbs: DT 60.94 '16, HT 51.12 '17.
In 2018 became the first Hungarian to win a World title. Daughter Luca born 31 Jan 2021.

ICELAND
Governing body: Frjálsíthróttasamband Islands. Founded 1947.
National Championships first held in 1927.
2020 Champions: Men: 100m/200m/400m: Kolbeinn Höður Gunnarsson 10.68w/21.57w/49.92, 800m: Sæmundur Ólafsson 1:57.53, 1500m: Hylnur Ólason 4:13.15. 5000m/3000mSt: Arnar Pétursson 15:31.99/10:51.97, 110mh: Arni Björn Höskoldsson 15.14, 400mh: Dagur Fannar Einarsson 55.69, HJ: Kristján Viggó Sigfinnsson 2.02, PV: Ingi Rúnar Kristinsson 4.20, LJ: Gylfi Ingvar Gylfason 6.82w, TJ: Kristinn Torfason 14.22w, SP/DT: Gudni Valur Gudnason 16.37/59.13, HT: Hilmar Örn Jónsson 73.84, JT: Dagbjartur Dadi Jónsson 76.33. **Women**: 100m/200m: Gudbjörg Jóna Bjarnadóttir 11/70/24.04w, 400m: Thórdis Eva Steinsdóttir 57.38, 800m/400mh: Ingbjörg Sigurdardóttir 2:22.11/63.86, 1500m: Anna Karen Jónsdóttir 4:59.56, 3000m: Sigbóra Brynja Kristjánsdóttir 10:30.10, 100mh: Glódis Edda Thurídardóttir 14.12w, HJ: Birta María Haraldsdóttir 1.75, PV: Katie Sif Ársælsdóttir 3.32, LJ: Hafdís Sigurdardóttir 6.25w, TJ: Hekla Sif Magnúsdóttir 11.95w, SP: Erna Sóley Gunnarsdóttir 15.40, DT: Kristín Karlsdóttir 48.40, HT: Vigdis Jónsdóttir 60.82, JT: María Rún Gunnlaugsdóttir 39.97.

INDIA
Governing body: Athletics Federation of India. Founded 1946.
National Championships first held as Indian Games in 1924. **2020 Champions: Men**: 20kW: Sandeep Kumar 1:21:34, 50kW: Sanabam Singh 4:08:10. **Women**: 20kW: Bhawana Jat 1:2924.

Neeraj CHOPRA b. 24 Dec 1997 Khandra Panipat, Haryana 1.84m 80kg.
At JT: WCh: '17- dnq 15; CG: '18- 1; WJ: '16- 1; WY: '13- dnq 17, AsiG: '18- 1; AsiC: '15- 9, '17- 1; AsiJ: '16- 2; CCp: '18- 5. Won S.Asian 2016.
Javelin records: World junior 2016, two Asian junior 2016, five Indian 2016-21.
Progress at JT: 2014- 70.19, 2015- 81.04, 2016- 86.48, 2017- 85.63, 2018- 88.06, 2020- 87.86A, 2021- 87.87.

IRAN
Governing body: Amateur Athletic Federation of Islamic Republic of Iran. Founded 1936.

Ehsan HADADI b. 21 Jan 1985 Ahvaz 1.93m 125kg.
At DT: OG: '08- dnq 17, '12- 2, '16- dnq 24; WCh: '07-11-15-17-19: 7/3/dnq 24/dnq 15/7; WJ: '04- 1; AsiG: '06-10-14-18: 1/1/1/1; AsiC: '03-05-07-09-11-17-19: 8/1/1/1/1/1; AsiJ: '04- 1; WCp: '06- 2, '10- 3. Won W.Asian 2005.
Eight Asian discus records 2005-08.
Progress at DT: 2002- 53.66, 2003- 54.40, 2004- 54.96, 2005- 65.25, 2006- 63.79, 2007- 67.95, 2008- 69.32, 2009- 66.19, 2010- 68.45, 2011- 66.08, 2012- 68.20, 2013- 66.98, 2014- 65.24, 2015- 65.22, 2016- 63.61, 2017- 65.66, 2018- 68.85, 2019- 67.19. pb SP 17.82i '08, 16.00 '06.
First Iranian athlete to win an Olympic medal.

IRELAND
Governing Body: The Athletic Association of Ireland (AAI). Founded in 1999. Original Irish federation (Irish Champions AC) founded 1873.
National Championships first held in 1873.
2020 Champions: Men: 100m: Stephen Gaffney 10.63, 200m: Marcus Lawler 20.95, 400m: Christopher O'Donnell 47.12, 800m: Harry Purcell 1:52.49, 1500m: Paul Robinson 3:43.90, 5000m: Darragh McElhinney 13:56.00, 10000m: Sean Tobin 29:35.14, 3000mSt: Rory Chesser 9:39.62, 110mh: Gerard O'Donnell 13.96, 400mh: Matthew Behan 52.47, HJ: David Cussen 2.17, PV: Yuri Kanash 4.50, LJ: Shane Howard 7.44w, TJ: Jai Benson 14.53w, SP: John Kelly 18.40, DT: Colin Quirke 55.50, HT: Brendan O'Donnell 64.62, JT: Stephen Rice 72.73, Dec: Rolus Olusa 6400, 10000mW: Callum Wilkinson GBR 39:52.05, 20kW/30kW: David Kenny 1:23:07/2:10:40. **Women**: 100m/200m: Phil Healy 11.71/23.57, 400m: Sophie Becker 54.06, 800m: Iseult O'Donnell 2:09.13, 1500m: Amy O'Donoghue 4:21.51, 5000m/3000mSt: Michele Finn 16:37.49/9:59.72, 100mh: Sarah Quinn 13.67, 400mh: Nessa Millet 59.52, HJ: Pippa Rogan 1.85, PV: Orla Coffey 3.50, LJ/TJ: Saragh Buggy 6.09/12.97, SP: Michaela Walsh 14.27, DT: Niamh Fogarty 49.46, HT: Nicola Tuthill 60.04, JT: Kate O'Connor 49.24, Hep: Anna McCauley 5051, 5000mW/20kW: Kate Veale 24:51.49/1:56:06.

Women

Ciara MAGEEAN b. 12 Mar 1992 Portaferry, Co. Down, Northern Ireland 1.68m 56kg. University College Dublin.
At 1500m (800m): OG: '16- sf; WCh: '17- h, '19- 10; EC: '16- 3, '18- 4; CG (N.Ireland): '10- 10, '18- 13 (h); WJ: '08- 10, '10- 2; WY: '09- (2); EJ: '11- 2; EI: '19- 3; Comm-Y: '08- 3 (5). Won IRL 800m 2015, 2017-19; 1500m 2011, 2014, 2016, 2018. Eur-J CC: '09- 9, '10- 7. Irish records 800m & 1000m 2020, Northern Ireland 800m & 1500m.
Progress at 1500m: 2007- 4:32.18, 2008- 4:21.2, 2009- 4:15.46, 2010- 4:09.51, 2011- 4:07.45, 2012- 4:10.74, 2014- 4:15.35, 2015- 4:06.49, 2016- 4:01.46, 2017- 4:03.57, 2018- 4:04.13, 2019- 4:00.15, 2020- 4:06.42i/4:10.99. pbs: 800m 1:59.69 '20, 1000m 2:31.06 '20, 1M 4:19.03 '19, 3000m 8:48.27i '20, 9:07.47mx '16; 5kRd 15:44 '19.

ISRAEL

Governing body: Israeli Athletic Association. Founded as Federation for Amateur Sport in Palestine 1931.
National Championships first held in 1935. **2020 Champions: Men**: 100m/200m: Blessing Afrifa 10.49/21.17, 400m: Mohamed Abu-Anza 48.17, 800m/1500m: Necho Tayachew 1:54.17/3:51.83, 5000m: Girmaw Amare 13:54.38, HMar (6 Dec 2019): Maru Teferi 63:19, Mar: Amir Ramon 2:25:40, 3000mSt: Zemenu Muchie 9:14.48, 110mh: Dor Khayoun 14.36, 400mh: Adam Yaaccci 52.89, HJ: Yonatan Kapitolnik 2.15, PV: Lev Skorish 5.50, LJ: Gilron Tsabkevich 7.53w, TJ: Ilai Foorman 14.94, SP: Itamir Levi 18.45, DT: Dennis Valliulin 51.52, HT: Viktor Zaginaiko 57.08, JT: Orr Katav 61.90, Dec: Ariel Attias 7136. **Women**: 100m: Nitzan Levi 12.03, 200m: Gal Kadmon 24.81, 400m: Jouman Joubran 56.76, 800m/1500m/5000m/HMar (6 Dec 2019): Chemtai Salpeter 2:06.63/4:17.96/15:29.43/70:05, Mar: Beatie Deutsch 2:32:35, 3000mSt: Adva Cohen 10:10.62, 100mh: Aleksandra Lokshin 13.96, 400mh: Linoy Levy 61.57, HJ: Danielle Frenkel 1.75, PV: Na'ama Bernstein 4.00, LJ/TJ: Marina Rayber 6.02/12.54, SP/DT: Estelle Valeanu 13.01/51.90, HT: Yevgeniya Zabolotniy 55.24, JT: Bareket Derhi 41.21, Hep: Danielle Polster 4597.

Women
Lonah Chemtai SALPETER b. 12 Dec 1988 Kapkanyar, Kenya 1.65m 52kg. née Korlima. Maccabi Tel Aviv.
At (5000m)/10000m EC: '18- dq (4)/1; ET: '18- 1, '19- 1. At Mar: OG: '16- dnf. WCh: '17- 41, '19- dnf. At HMar: WCh: '18- 12., '20- 12 Won ISR 800m 2020, 1500m 2018, 2020; 5000m 2016, 2020; 10000m 2016-18, HMar 2018, 2020-21.
European 10k road best 2019, Israeli records: 1500m 2018, 2000m 2019, 3000m (2) 2018, 5000m (2) 2018-19, 10000m (6) 2018-19, 15k 2019, HMar (4) 2017-19, Mar (3) 2018-20, 1Hr 2020.
Progress at 5000m, 10000m, Mar: 2011- 17:51.76, 38:16.68; 2012- 16:32.98, 35:37.59; 2013- 16:23.64, 2014- 17:00.69, 35:12.99; 2015- 16:41.30, 36:05.01; 2016- 16:27.20, 35:01.33, 2:40:16; 2017- 16:12.51, 32:43.89, 2:40:22; 2018- 15:17.81, 31:33.03. 2:24:17; 2019- 14:59.02, 31:15.78, 2:19:46; 2020- 15:29.43, 2:17:45; 2021- 2:22:37. pb: 800m 2:06.63 '20, 1500m 4:11.69 '18, 1M 4:47.50 '17, 2000m 5:52.3 '19, 3000m 8:42.88 '18, 1 hour 18,571m '20; road: 5k: 15:15 '19, 10k 30:05 '19, 15k 46:43 '19, 10M 50:45 '18, 20k 62:43 '19, HMar 66:09 '19, 25k 1:22:00 '20.
Moved from Kenya in 2008, married her coach Dan Salpeter and became an Israeli citizen in 2016; their son Roy born 2015. Won Florence Marathon 2018, Prague 2019, Tokyo 2020.

ITALY

Governing Body: Federazione Italiana di Atletica Leggera (FIDA. First governing body formed 1896.
National Championships first held in 1897 (one event)/1906 (men), 1927 (women). **2020 Champions: Men**: 100m: Lamont Marcell Jacobs 10.10w, 200m: Antonio Infantino 20.71, 400m: Edoardo Scotti 45.77, 800m: Simone Barontini 1:48.16, 1500m: Neves Junior Bussotti 3:47.51, 5000m/3000mSt: Ala Zoghlami 14:04.44/8:26.22, 10000m: Osama Zoghlami 29:07.27, HMar: Daniele D'Onofrio 63:15, Mar: Giovanni Grano 2:14:31, 110mh: Lorenzo Perini 13.53, 400mh: Mario Lambrughi 49.84, HJ: Gianmarco Tamberi 2.28, PV: Max Mandusic 5.40, LJ: Filippo Randazzo 7.77w, TJ: Andrea Dallavalle 16.79, SP: Leonardo Fabbri 21.99, DT: Giovanni Faloci 61.87, HT: Marco Lingua 71.98, JT: Norbert Bonvecchio 74.64, Dec: Dario Dester 7652; **Women**: 100m: Zaynab Dosso 11.35w, 200m: Dalia Kaddari 23.30, 400m: Alice Mangione 52.70, 800m: Elena Bellò 2:04.01, 1500m: Eleonora Vandi 4:18.39, 5000m: Nadia Battocletti 15:46.26, 10000m/HMar: Valeria Straneo 32:55.25/71:34, Mar: Giovanna Epis 2:28:03, 3000mSt: Martina Merlo 9:59.54, 100mh: Luminosa Bogliolo 13.02, 400mh: Ayomide Folorunso 56.47, HJ: Elena Vallortigara 1.88, PV: Roberta Bruni 4.30, LJ: Larissa Iapichino 6.32, TJ: Dariya Derkach 13.56, SP: Chiara Rosa 16.55, DT: Daisy Osakue 58.26, HT: Sara Fantini 68.50, JT: Carolina Visca 55.57, Hep: Sveva Gerevini 5741, 10kW: Antonella Palmisano 41:28.

Yemaneberhan CRIPPA b. 15 Oct 1996 Dessie, Wollo, Ethiopia 1.79m 62kg. GS Fiamme Oro Padova.
At 1500m: WJ: '14- 10; WY: '13- 6; At 5000m/(10000m): WCh: '19- h/8; EC: '16- 8, '18- 4/3; EU23: '17- 1; EJ: '15- 3; ET: '18 (3), '19- 1. Eur CC: '14-15-16-17: 1J/1J/3 U23/3 U23, '18/19- 6/2. Won ITA 1500m 2016.
Italian 3000m & 5000m records 2020
Progress at 5000m, 10000m: 2015- 13:58.31, 2016- 13:36.65, 2017- 14:14.28, 2018- 13:18.83, 2017- 13:07.84, 27:10.76; 2020- 13:02.26. Pbs: 800m 1:50.16 '16, 1500m 3:35.26 '20, 1M

3:52.08 '20. 2000m 5:02.0+e '20, 3000m 7:38.27 '20. Adopted by an Italian couple in 2001. Brother Nekagenet (b. 16 Sep 1994) pbs: 1500m 14:00.87 '19, 10000m 29:24.47 '19, HMar 63:23 '20, Mar 2:21:17 '16, won ITA HMar 2019.

Leonardo FABBRI b. 15 Apr 1997 Bagno a Ripoli 2.00m 120kg. CS Aeronautica Militare.
At SP: WCh: '19- dnq 13; EC: '18- dnq 29; EU23: '17- 17, '19- 2; WJ: '16- dnq 26; WY: '13- dnq 15. Won ITA 2019-20.
Progress at SP: 2015- 15.95, 2016- 17.12, 2017- 19.33, 2018- 20.07, 2019- 20.99, 2020- 21.99. Pbs: DT 53.02 '19.

Lamont Marcell JACOBS b. 26 Sep 1994 El Paso, USA1.88m 79kg. GS Fiamme Oro Padova.
At 100m: WCh: '19- sf; EC: '18- sf; ET: '19- 2. At LJ: EC: '16- 11; EJ: '13- 9. At 60m: EI: '21- 1.. Won ITA 100m 2018-20. LJ 2016.
Progress at LJ, 100m: 2012- 7.29, 2013- 7.75i/7.69, 2014- 10.53, 7.32i; 2015- 8.03i, 2016- 10.23, 7.95/ 8.48w; 2017- 10.82, 8.07i; 2018- 10.08/10.04w, 2019- 10.03, 8.05i; 2020- 10.10. Pbs: 60m 6.47i '21, 200m 20.61 '18.
Became Italian citizen on 14 Jan 2010, able to compete for Italy 2012.

Massimo STANO b. 27 Feb 1992 Grumo Appula, Puglia 1.79m 63kg. GS Fiamme Oro.
At 20kW: WCh: '15- 19, '19- 14; EC: '14- 24, '18- 4; EU23: '13- 2; WT: '18- 3; ECp: '19- 7. At 10000mW: WJ: '10- 13; WY: '09- 14; EJ: '11- 5; WCp: '10- 11J; ECp: '11- 14J. Won ITA 10kW 2018, 20kW 2015, 2018. Italian 20k walk record 2019.
Progress at 20kW: 2011- 1:31:00, 2013- 1:25:25, 2014- 1:23:01, 2015- 1:22:16, 2016- 1:25:16, 2017- 1:22:30, 2018- 1:20:51, 2019- 1:17:45. pbs: 5000mW 19:22.62i '15, 19:52.74 '13; 10000mW 38:28.05 '19.

Gianmarco TAMBERI b. 1 Jun 1992 Civitanove Marche 1.89m 71kg. Fiamme Gialle.
At HJ: OG: '12- dnq 21=; WCh: '15- 8=, '17- dnq 13=, '19- 8=; EC: '12-14-16-18: 5/7=/1/4; WY: '09- dnq 18; EU23: '13- dnq 13=; EJ: '11- 3; WI: '16- 1; EI: '13-17-19-21: 5/6/1/2; won WIT 2021, ITA 2012, 2014, 2016, 2018, 2020.
Four Italian high jump records 2015-16 & three indoor 2016.
Progress at HJ: 2005- 1.52, 2006- 1.62i, 2007- 1.80, 2008- 2.01, 2009- 2.07, 2010- 2.14, 2011-2.25, 2012- 2.31, 2013- 2.30i/2.25, 2014- 2.29, 2015- 2.37, 2016- 2.39, 2017- 2.29, 2018- 2.33, 2019- 2.32i/2.29, 2020- 2.31i/2.30, 2021- 2.35i.
Suffered serious injury, costing him Olympic chance, just after setting Italian records at 2.37 and 2.39 in Monaco 2016. His father Marco had pb 2.28i (Italian indoor record)/2.27 '83, elder brother Gianluca 4th EJ JT 2009, pb 78.61 '10.

Women

Luminosa BOGLIOLO b. 3 Jul 1995 Albenga 1.70m 60kg. GS Fiamme Oro.
At 100mh: WCh: '19- sf; EC: '18- sf; EU23: '17- sf; WUG: '19 ·1, ET: '19- 1. Won ITA 2020. At 60mh: EI: '21- 6.
Progress at 100mh: 2015- 14.18, 2016- 13.85, 2017- 13.44, 2018- 12.99, 2019- 12.78/12.74w, 2020- 12.79. Pbs: 60m 7.54i '20, 100m 11.74 '20, 60mh 7.99i '21.

Eleonora GIORGI b. 14 Sep 1989 Cuneo 1.63m 52kg. Fiamme Azzurre. Social-economic law graduate of University 'Bocconi' of Milan.
At 20kW: OG: '12- 12, '16- dq; WCh: '13-15-17: 9/dq/14; EC: '14- 5, '18- dq; EU23: '09- 11, '11- 3; WCp: '12-14-18: 11/5/5; ECp: '13- 5, '15- 2; won MedG 2013. At 50kW: WCh: '19- 3; ECp: '19- 1. At 10000mW: WJ: '08- 18; Won ITA 10kW 2019, 20kW & 35kW 2021.
Walk records: World best 5000m 2014, 25k & 30k 2016, 35k 2019; European 50k 2019. Italian 20k (3) 2014-15, 35k (2) 2019- 20.
Progress at 20kW. 50kW: 2009- 1:34:27, 2010- 1:34:00, 2011- 1:33:46, 2012- 1:29:48, 2013- 1:30:01, 2014- 1:27:05, 2015- 1:26:17, 2016- 1:28:05, 2017- 1:30:34, 2018- 1:28:31, 2019- 1:27:46, 4:04:50; 2021- 1:28:39. pbs: 3000mW 11:50.08i/12:05.83 '13, 5000mW 20:01.80 '14, 10kW 44:33.56t '13, 43:27R '19; 25kW 1:56:12 '16, 30kW 2:19:43 '16, 35k: 2:43:43 '20.

Larissa IAPICHINO b. 18 Jul 2002 1.71m 56kg. Atletica Firenze Marathon S.S.
At LJ: EJ: '19- 1, EY: '18- 7; EI: '21- 5. Won ITA 2020.. World indoor U20 LJ record 2021.
Progress at LJ: 2018- 6.38, 2019- 6.64, 2020- 6.80, 2021- 6.91i. Pbs: 100m 12.26 '18, 200m 24.71 '19, 60mh 8.66i '20, 100mh 13.63 '19, 400mh 62.48 19.
Her mother Fiona May distinguished LJ record for GBR and ITA (from 1994): ITA rec 7.11 '98; 2 OG 1996 & 2002, 1 WCh 1995 & 2001 (2- 1999, 3 1997); 2 EC 1998, 3 CG 1990, 1 WJ 1988, 1 WI 1997, 1 EI 1998; married Gianni Iapichino (PV 5.70 ITA record '94).

Antonella PALMISANO b. 6 Aug 1991 Mottola, Taranto 1.66m 49kg. Fiamme Galle.
At 20kW: OG: '16- 4; WCh: '13-15-17-19: 12/5/3/13; EC: '14- 7, '18- 3; EU23: '11- 2, '13- 2; WCp: '14- 9; ECp: 17- 1. At 10000mW: WJ: '08- 9, '10- 4; EJ: '09- 2; WCp: '10- 1J; ECp: '09- 3J. At 5000mW: WY: '07- 5. Won ITA 10kW 2018.
Italian 5000m walk record 2017.
Progress at 20kW: 2009- 1:38:47, 2010- 1:36:21, 2011- 1:34:31, 2012- 1:34:27, 2013- 1:30:50, 2014- 1:27:51, 2015- 1:28:40, 2016- 1:29:03, 2017- 1:26:36, 2018- 1:27:30, 2019- 1:37:36, 2020- 1:28:40. pbs: 3000mW 11:55.30i '18, 5000mW 21:00.0 '20, 10kW 41:57.29t '17.
Married Lorenzo Dessi (pbs 20kW 1:26:17 '16, 50kW 3:57:32 '11) on 22 September 2018.

Alessia TROST b. 8 Mar 1993 Pordenone 1.88m 68kg. Fiamme Gialle.
At HJ: OG: '16- 5; WCh: '13- 7=, '17/19- dnq 19/14; EC: '14-16-18: 9=/6=/8; WJ: '12- 1; WY: '09- 1; EU23: '13- 1, '15- 1; EJ: '11- 4; WI: '16- 7, '18- 3; EI: '13-15-21: 4=/2/6; ET: '13-17-19: 2/3=/3; YthOly:

'10- 2. ITA champion 2013-14, 2016, 2019.
Progress at HJ: 2003- 1.37, 2004- 1.55, 2005- 1.62, 2006- 1.68, 2008- 1.81, 2009- 1.89, 2010- 1.90, 2011- 1.87, 2012- 1.92, 2013- 2.00i/1.98, 2014- 1.96i/1.91, 2015- 1.97i/1.94, 2016- 1.95i/1.94, 2017- 1.93i/1.94, 2018- 1.93i/1.91, 2019- 1.94, 2020- 1.90i/1.84. pbs: 100mh 15.5 '11, LJ 6.01 '14, SP 10.76i '14, Pen 4035i '14.

Elena VALLORTIGARA b. 21 Sep 1991 Schio 1.84m 66kg. Carabinieri Bologna.
At HJ: WCh: '19- dnq 17; EC: '18- dnq 15; WJ: '08- dnq 30=, '10- 3; WY: '07- 3; EJ: '09- 4; EYOF: '07- 1. Won ITA 2018, 2020.
Progress at HJ: 2006- 1.75, 2007- 1.86, 2008- 1.85i/1.82, 2009- 1.87, 2010- 1.91, 2011- 1.90i, 2012- 1.86, 2013- 1.85, 2014- 1.84, 2015- 1.86i/1.84, 2016- 1.82, 2017- 1.87i/1.86, 2018- 2.02, 2019- 1.92i/1.91, 2020- 1.96i/1.88. pbs: 100mh 15.62 '09, SP 10.66i '14, Pen 3626i '10.
Breakthrough from 1.96 to 2.02 at the London Diamond League 2018.

IVORY COAST

Governing Body: Fédération Ivoirienne d'Athlétisme, Abidjan. Founded 1960.

Women

Murielle AHOURÉ b. 23 Aug 1987 Abidjan 1.67m 57kg. Graduated in criminal law from the University of Miami, USA.
At 100m/(200m): OG: '12- 7/6, '16- sf/sf; WCh: '13- 2/2, '15- sf, '17- 4, '19- 5; AfCh: '14- 2/1, '16- 1; won DL 2018. At 60m: WI: '12-14-18: 2/2/1. Won NCAA indoor 200m 2009.
Three African 60m indoor records 2013-18. CIV records 100m (8) 2009-16, 200m (3) 2012-13.
Progress at 100m, 200m: 2005- 11.96, 2006- 11.42, 23.33; 2007- 11.41/11.28w, 23.34; 2008- 11.45, 23.50; 2009- 11.09, 22.78; 2010- 11.41, 2011- 11.06/10.86w, 2012- 10.99, 22.42; 2013- 10.91, 22.24; 2014- 10.97, 22.36; 2015- 10.81, 22.29; 2016- 10.78, 22.52; 2017- 10.83, 22.68; 2018- 10.90, 22.60; 2019- 11.02, 2020- 11.36. pbs: 60m 6.97i '18, 300m 38.09i '07, 400m 54.67 '19.
Lived in Paris from age 2, then USA from age 12. Won first Ivory Coast World medals.

Marie Josée TA LOU Gonerie b. 18 Nov 1988 Bouaflé 1.59m 57kg.
At 100m/200m: OG: '16- 4/4; WCh: '15- sf/sf, '17- 2/2, '19- 3/-; AfG: '11- 7/6, '15- 1/1/3R, '19- 1/3; AfCh: '10- sf/-, '12- 4/3/3R, '14- 3/2/2R, '16- 3/1, '18- 1/1/2R; CCp: '14- 4/5, '18- 1/3/dqR. At 60m: WI: '16- 7, '18- 2.
CIV 200m records 2016-17.
Progress at 100m, 200m: 2010- 12.10/11.6, 24.3; 2011- 11.56, 24.12; 2012- 11.53, 23.26; 2013- 11.58, 23.63; 2014- 11.20, 22.78; 2015- 11.02/10.95w, 22.56; 2016- 10.86, 22.21; 2017- 10.86, 22.08; 2018- 10.85/10.7mxw, 22.34/22.2mxw; 2019- 10.85, 22.36; 2020- 11.14, 23.33. pb 60m 6.95+ '19, 7.02i '19.

JAMAICA

Governing body: Jamaica Athletics Administrative Association. Founded 1932.

Nathon ALLEN b. 28 Oct 1995 Bethany, St.Ann 1.78m 68kg. MVP, Auburn University, USA.
At 400m/4x400mR: OG: '16- 2R; WCh: '17- 5, '19- 2R/2MxR; WJ: '14- sf/3R; WI: '16- 4R. JAM champion 2017.
Two CAC & Commonwealth records mixed 4x400m 2019.
Progress at 400m: 2014- 46.11, 2015- 45.30, 2016- 45.39, 2017- 44.19, 2018- 44.13, 2019- 44.85. 2020- 46.50 pbs: 200m 20.45 '20, 20.39w '18; 300m 31.9+ '18.

Yohan BLAKE b. 26 Dec 1989 St. James 1.81m 79kg. Racers TC.
At 100m/(200m)/4x100mR: OG: '12- 2/2/1R, '16- 4/sf/1R; WCh: '11- 1/1R, '17- 4/sf, '19- 5/sf/sf; CG: '18- 3/3R; WJ: '06- 3/1R, '08- 4/2R; WY: '05- 7; PAm-J: '07- 2 (3 4x400m); CCp: '18- 8/1R; won CAC-J 100m & 200m 2006; JAM 100m & 200m 2012, 2016-17, 100m 2019.
World record 4x100m 2012, 4x200m 2014.
Progress at 100m, 200m: 2005- 10.56, 22.10; 2006- 10.33, 20.92; 2007- 10.11, 20.62; 2008- 10.27/ 10.20w, 21.06; 2009- 10.07/9.93dq, 20.60; 2010- 9.89, 19.78; 2011- 9.82/9.80w, 19.26; 2012- 9.69, 19.44; 2013- 20.72, 2014- 10.02, 20.48; 2015- 10.12, 21.57; 2016- 9.93, 20.13; 2017- 9.90, 19.97; 2018- 9.94, 20.95; 2019- 9.96, 20.23; 2020- 10.15/10.07w, 20.62. pbs: 60m 6.75i '08, 150mSt 14.71 '14, 400m 46.32 '13.
3-month drugs ban from positive test at Jamaican Champs 25 Jun 2009. Cut 200m pb from 20.60 to 19.78 in Monaco 2010 and then to 19.26 in Brussels 2011. Youngest ever World 100m champion at 21 in 2011.

Akeem BLOOMFIELD b. 10 Nov 1997 Kingston 1.88m 77kg. MVP, was at Auburn University, USA.
At 400m: WCh: '19- 8/2R.
Progress at 200m, 400m: 2014- 21.06, 2015- 44.93, 2016- 20.66, 46.01; 2017- 20.29w, 44.74; 2018- 19.81, 43.94; 2019- 20.24, 44.40; 2020- 20.80, 45.07. pbs: 100m 10.42 '14, 300m 31.8+ '18.

Fedrick DACRES b. 28 Feb 1994 Kingston 1.93m 121kg. Irvine.
At DT: OG: '16- dnq 34; WCh: '15-17-19: 7/4/2; CG: '18- 1; PAm: '15- 1, '19- 1; WJ: '12- 1; WY '11- 1; CCp: '18- 1; won CAC-J 2012; JAM 2015-18, NACAC 2018, DL 2018.
Commonwealth discus record 2019 and four Jamaican records 2017-19.
Progress at DT: 2011- 53.05, 2012- 55.45, 2013- 59.30, 2014- 66.75, 2015- 66.40, 2016- 68.02, 2017- 68.88, 2018- 69.67/69.83 light, 2019- 70.78, 2020- 69.67. pb SP 20.46 '17.

Demish GAYE b. 20 Jan 1993 Mandeville 1.88m 77kg. Sprintec TC.
At 400m/4x400mR: WCh: '17- 6, '19- 4/2R; CG:

JAMAICA

'18- 6/3R; PAm: '19- 2; WI: '16- 4R. Won NACAC 2018, JAM 2019.
Progress at 400m: 2015- 46.15, 2016- 45.30, 2017- 44.55. 2018- 45.08, 2019- 44.46. pb 200m 20.48 '17.

Tajay GAYLE b. 2 Aug 1996 Kingston 1.83m 75kg. University of Technology.
At LJ: WCh: '19- 1; CG: '18- 4; PAm: '19- 2; NACAC: '18- 2. Won JAM 2019.
Commonwealth LJ record 2019.
Progress at LJ: 2016- 7.54, 2017- 8.00, 2018- 8.24, 2019- 8.69, 2020- 8.23/8.52w. Pbs: 60m 6.80i '17, 100m 10.42 '19, 200m 21.34 '16, 21.18w '18; HJ 2.00 '16, TJ 15.78w '16.
Improved his best from 8.32 to 8.46 and 8.69 in 2019 World final.

Ronald LEVY b. 30 Oct 1992 Westmoreland 1.84m 77kg. MVP. Kingston University of Technology.
At 110mh: WCh: '17- h, '19- sf; CG: '18- 1; CCp: '18- 2; JAM champion 2018-19.
Progress at 110mh: 2013- 14.42, 2015- 13.63, 2016- 13.50, 2017- 13.05, 2018- 13.12, 2019- 13.22. Pbs: 60m 6.62 '16, 100m 10.17 '17, 10.10w '16; 200m 20.81 '14, 800m 1:52.47 '16, 60mh 7.49i '18, 400mh 51.77 '13.

Omar McLEOD b. 25 Apr 1994 Kingston 1.80m 73kg. Studied business management at University of Arkansas, USA.
At 110mh: OG: '16- 1; WCh: '15- 6, '17- 1, '19- dq; WY: '11- 4 (8 400mh). At 60m: WI: '16- 1. Won JAM 2015-17, NCAA 110mh 2015 (& 60mh indoors 2014-15).
Commonwealth 110m hurdles record 2017.
Progress at 110mh: 2014- 13.44, 2015- 12.97, 2016- 12.98, 2017- 12.90, 2018- 13.16/13.01w, 2019- 13.07. Pbs: 60m 6.61i '17, 100m 9.99 '16, 200m 20.48i '17, 20.49 '18; 400m 47.41i '15, 60mh 7.41i '16, 400mh 49.98 '13. First man ever to run under 10 secs for 100m as well as 13 secs for 110m hurdles.

Kemar MOWATT b. 12 Mar 1995 Saint-Elizabeth 1.88m 77kg. Was at University of Arkansas, USA.
At 400mh: WCh: '17- 4, '19- sf; PAm: '19- 3. Won JAM 2019.
Progress at 400mh: 2014- 52.03, 2015- 51.13, 2016- 50.66, 2017- 48.49, 2018- 48.83, 2019- 48.70. Pbs: 200m 21.07i '17, 21.34 '15; 300m 33.57i '20, 400m 47.15i '17, 60mh 7.93i '16, 110mh 13.90 '17, 13.75w 16.

O'Dayne RICHARDS b. 14 Dec 1988 St. Andrew 1.77m 120kg. Data communications graduate. MVP TC.
At SP: OG: '16- 8; WCh: '13- 17-19: dnq 20/19/22, '15- 3; CG: '14- 1, '18- 4; PAm: '15- 1; CAG: '18- 1; WUG: '11- 1; CCp: '14- 2; won CAC 2011, 2013; JAM 2013-19.
Four CAC shot records 2014-17, indoor 2019.
Progress at SP: 2008- 16.76, 2009- 18.05, 2010- 18.74, 2011- 19.93, 2012- 20.31, 2013- 20.97, 2014- 21.61, 2015- 21.69, 2016- 20.82, 2017- 21.96, 2018-

21.02, 2019- 20.93. pb DT 58.31 '12.

Traves SMIKLE b. 7 May 1992 Kingston 1.93m 126kg. UWI Mona.
At DT: OG: '12- dnq 20; WCh: '17- 8, '19- dnq 15; CG: '18- 2; WJ: '10- 7; WY '09- 3; won PAm-J 2011, NACAC U23 2012, JAM 2011-12, 2019.
Progress at DT: 2010- 51.54, 2011- 59.83, 2012- 67.12, 2013- 63.48, 2015- 58.96, 2016- 63.42, 2017- 65.00, 2018- 67.72, 2019- 67.57, 2020- 64.66. pb SP 15.99 '17. Two-year doping ban 2013-15.

Women

Brittany ANDERSON b. 31 Jan 2001 1.65m 60kg.
At 100mh: WJ: '18- 2; WY: '17- 1.
Two world junior 100m hurdles records 2019.
Progress at 110mh: 2018- 13.01, 2019- 12.71, 2020- 12.82/12.71w. pbs: 100m 11.50 '20, 200m 23.71 '20, 60mh 8.02i '20, LJ 6.02 '16.

Janeek BROWN b. 14 May 1998 Kingston 1.65m 52kg. Puma, University of Arkansas, USA.
At 100mh: WCh: '19- 7; WY: '15- sf; YOG: '14- 6; PAm-J: '17- 8. Won NCAA 2019.
Tied CAC 100mh record 2019.
Progress at 100mh: 2014- 13.79, 2016- 14.08, 2017- 13.16, 2018- 12.80/12.73w, 2019- 12.40. pbs: 60m 7.27i '19, 100m 11.34, 11.19w '18, 200m 22.40 '19, 60mh 7.95i '19.

Rushell CLAYTON b. 18 Oct 1992 Westmoreland 1.75m 61kg. Mico University College.
At 400mh: WCh: '19- 3; PAm: '11- h, '19- 3; CAG: '18- 4. Jamaican champion 2019.
Progress at 400mh: 2011- 59.03, 2012- 56.67, 2013- 59.99, 2014- 56.41, 2015- 56.29, 2016- 56.42, 2017- 56.61, 2018- 55.08, 2019- 53.74. pbs: 200m 24.12 '20, 400m 52.55 '17, 800m 2:12.18 '16, 100mh 14.00 '15.

Shelly-Ann FRASER-PRYCE b. 27 Dec 1986 Kingston 1.60m 52kg. MVP. Graduate of the University of Technology. née Fraser. Married Jason Pryce on 7 Jan 2011.
At 100m/(200m)/4x100mR: OG: '08- 1, '12- 1/2/2R, '16- 3/2R; WCh: '07- res (2)R, '09- 1/1R, '11- 4/2R, '13- 1/1/1R, '15- 1/1R, '19- 1/1R; CG: '14- 1R; PAm: '19- (1). At 60m: WI: '14- 1. Won WAF 2008, DL 100m 2012-13, 2015; 200m 2013; JAM 100m 2009, 2012, 2015; 200m 2012-13.
CAC and Commonwealth records 100m 2009 & 2012, 4x100m (4) 2011-15; CAC 4x200m 2014.
Progress at 100m, 200m: 2002- 11.8, 2003- 11.57, 2004- 11.72, 24.08; 2005- 11.72; 2006- 11.74, 24.8; 2007- 11.31/11.21w, 23.5; 2008- 10.78, 22.15; 2009- 10.73, 22.58; 2010- 10.82dq, 22.47dq; 2011- 10.95, 22.59/22.10w; 2012- 10.70, 22.09; 2013- 10.71, 22.13; 2014- 11.01, 22.53; 2015- 10.74, 22.37; 2016- 10.86, 23.15; 2018- 10.98, 2019- 10.71, 22.22; 2020- 10.86, 22.34. pb 60m 6.81+ '19. 6.98i '14, 400m 55.34 '19.
Double World and Olympic champion with eight global gold medals (and four silver). Huge

improvement in 2008 and moved to joint third on world all-time list for 100m when winning 2009 world 100m title. 6-month ban for positive test for a non-performance enhancing drug on 23 May 2010. IAAF Athlete of the Year 2013. Son Zyon Pryce born 7 Aug 2017.

Natoya GOULE b. 30 Mar 1991 Manchester 1.60m 50kg. Was at Louisiana State University and then Clemson Univerity, USA.
At 800mh: OG: '16- h; WCh: '13-15-17: h, '19- 6; CG: '14- sf, '18- 3; PAm: '19- 1/3R; WJ: '08- h; WY: '07- sf; CCp: '18- 3; WI: '14- res2R. Won CAC 2013, JAM 2013-17, 2019; NCAA 2013.
Two Jamaican 800m records 2018, CAC indoor 800m & 1000m records 2019.
Progress at 800m: 2006- 2:08.89, 2007- 2:08.37, 2008- 2:05.90, 2009- 2:04.29, 2010- 2:03.52, 2011- 2:01.45, 2012- 2:04.76, 2013- 1:59.93, 2014- 2:00.28, 2015- 1:59.63, 2016- 1:59.38, 2017- 2:00.56, 2018- 1:56.15, 2019- 1:57.90, 2020- 1:59.35i/2:00.43. Pbs: 200m 24.30 '16, 300m 38.74i '20, 51.52A/52.23 '11, 600y 1:18.82i '11, 600m 1:25.35i '17, 1:26.33 '19; 1000m 2:37.55i '19, 2:43.03 '15; 1500m 4:17.10 '18, 1M 4:45.71i '16, 3000m 9:56.79 '06.
Won 14 gold medals at the Jamaican Schools Champs and 12 at Carifta Games.

Shericka JACKSON b. 16 Jul 1994 Saint-Anne 1.73m 60kg. UTech.
At 400m/4x400mR: OG: '16- 3/2R; WCh: '15- 3/1R, '17- 5, '19- 3/3R (1 400R); PAm: '19- 1; won JAM 2017, 2019. At 200m: CG: '18- 2; WJ: '12- 8/2R; WY: '11- 3/1 MedR; Yth OG: '10- 4; CCp: '18- 4; won NACAC 2018.
CAC & Commonwealth 4x200m record 2017
Progress at 200m, 400m: 2008- 24.56, 54.27; 2009- 23.62, 53.13; 2010- 23.94/23.64w, 53.71; 2011- 23.32, 52.94; 2012- 23.35, 53.34; 2013- 22.84, 51.60; 2014- 23.29, 51.32; 2015- 22.87, 49.99; 2016- 22.95/22.86w, 49.83; 2017- 22.46, 50.05; 2018- 22.05, 2019- 49.47, 2020- 22.70, 51.76. pbs: 60m 7.31 '18, 100m 11.13 '18, 11.03w '19.
11 wins at Carifta Games 2008-13.

Stephenie Ann McPHERSON b. 25 Nov 1988 Westmoreland 1.68m 55kg. MVP. Was at Kingston University of Technology.
At 400m/4x400mR: OG: '16- 6/2R; WCh: '13- 3, '15- 5/1R, '17- 6, '19- 6/3R; CG: 14- 1/1R, '18- 3/1R; CCp: '14- 1R, '18- 3/1mxR; WI: 14- 2R, '16- 4. Won DL 2016, NACAC 2018, JAM 2016, 2018
Progress at 400m: 2006- 56.42, 2007- 55.77, 2008- 52.80, 2009- 51.95, 2010- 51.64, 2012- 52.98, 2013- 49.92, 2014- 50.12, 2015- 50.32, 2016- 50.04, 2017- 50.56, 2018- 50.31, 2019- 50.70, 2020- 52.20. pbs: 100m 11.44 '10, 11.30w '19; 200m 22.93 '14, 800m 2:15.24 '12, 400mh 57.46 '12.

Shanieka RICKETTS b. 2 Feb 1992 Saint Andrew 1.82m 66kg. née Thomas.Was at San Diego State University, USA.
At TJ: OG: '16- dnq 14; WCh: '15- 11, '17- 8, '19- 2; CG: '14- 4, '18- 2; PAm: '15- 9, '19- 2; WI: '16- 8; Won DL 2019, NCAA 2013-14, NACAC 2015, 2018, JAM 2018-19.
Progress at TJ: 2008- 11.83, 2011- 12.98i/12.90, 2012- 13.64, 2013- 14.15, 2014- 14.00, 2015- 14.23A/14.08, 2016- 14.57, 2017- 14.45, 2018- 14.61, 2019- 14.93, 2020- 14.43, 2021- 14.63. pbs: 100m 12.24 '17, 400m 55.38 '13, HJ 1.75 '10, LJ 6.63 '15.
Married coach Kerry-Lee Ricketts in 2016.

Janieve RUSSELL b. 14 Nov 1993 Manchester 1.75m 63kg. UTech.
At 400mh/4x400mR: OG: '16- 7; WCh: '15- 5, '19- res2MxR; CG: '14- 3, '18- 1/1R; WJ: '12- 1/2R; CCp: '18- 1. At 400m: WJ: '10- sf/3R. At LJ: WY: '09- 9. Won JAM Hep 2011, 400mh 2015, 2018. CAC & Commonwealth record 4x400mMx 2019.
Progress at 400mh: 2011- 57.71, 2012- 56.62, 2013- 56.30, 2014- 54.75, 2015- 54.64, 2016- 53.96, 2017- 54.02, 2018- 53.46, 2019- 54.70. 2020- 55.40. pbs: 200m 23.43 '18, 400m 51.17 '16, 800m 2:11.5 '15, 100mh 13.80 '12, HJ 1.80 '09, LJ 6.20 '10, 6.26w '11; SP 10.86 '11, JT 26.53 '11, Hep 5361 '11.

Jonielle SMITH b. 30 Jan 1996 Kingston 1.71m 59kg. Auburn Univerity, USA.
At 100m/(200m): WCh: '19- 6/1R; WY: '13 – sf/sf; CAG: '18- 1; NACAC: '18- 2; PAm-J: '15- 4/2R. World U18 and CAC U20 100m record 2019.
Progress at 100m: 2012- 11.87, 2013- 11.58, 2014- 11.32/11.17w, 2015- 11.37, 2017- 11.13/11.08w, 2018- 11.07/11.04w, 2019- 11.04. pbs: 60m 7.15i '18, 200m 23.22 '17.

Megan TAPPER b. 18 Mar 1994 Content Gap 1.59m 48kg. née Simmonds, married to Matheu Tapper. University of Technology, Kingston.
At 100mh: OG: '16- sf; WCh: '17- sf, '19- dnf; CG: '18- 7; PAm: '19- 3; WY: '11- 6; YOG: '10- 4.
Progress at 100mh: 2010- 13.96, 2011- 14.02/13.82w, 2012- 13.79/13.53w, 2013- 13.33/13.23w, 2014- 13.07/13.06w, 2015- 12.91, 2016- 12.79, 2017- 12.63, 2018- 13.17, 2019- 12.61, 2020- 12.96. pbs: 60m 7.32i '17, 100m 11.75 '16, 60mh 8.07i '17.

Danniel THOMAS-DODD b. 11 Nov 1992 Westmoreland 1.68m 91kg. née Thomas. PE student at Kent State University, USA.
At SP: OG: '16- dnq 25; WCh: '15- dnq 22, '17- 4, '19- 2; CG: '18- 1; PAm: '15- 5, '19- 1; CCp: '18- 6; WI: '18- 2; won NCAA 2017. At DT: CG: '14- 8. Won JAM SP 2014-17, 2019; DT 2015.
Seven Jamaican shot records 2017-19.
Progress at SP: 2012- 14.58, 2013- 16.10, 2014- 16.97i/16.82, 2015- 17.76, 2016- 17.60, 2017- 19.15, 2018- 19.36, 2019- 19.55, 2020- 19.18. pbs: DT 59.38 '14. Married to Shane Dodd.

Elaine THOMPSON-HERAH b. 28 Jun 1992 Manchester 1.69m 57kg. MVP. Kingston University of Technology.
At 100m: OG: '16- 1; WCh: '17- 5, '19- 4/sf; PAm: '19- 1; At 200m/4x100mR: OG: '16- 1/2R; WCh: '15- 2/1R; CG: '14- res 1R, '18- 4/2R Won DL

JAMAICA – JAPAN

100m 2016-17, JAM 100m 2016-19, 200m 2015, 2019. At 60m: WI: '16- 3, '18- 4.
CAC and Commonwealth records 4x100m 2015, 100m 2016, 4x200m 2017.
Progress at 100m, 200m: 2008- 12.16, 25.56; 2009- 12.01, 24.35; 2010- 11.94w, 2012- 23.89, 2013- 11.41, 23.73; 2014- 11.17, 23.23; 2015- 10.84, 21.66, 2016- 10.70, 21.78; 2017- 10.71, 21.98; 2018- 10.93, 22.30; 2019- 10.73, 22.00; 2020- 10.85/10.73w, 22.19. pbs: 60m 6.98i '17, 6.96+ '19, 7.02 '17; 150mSt 15.00 '14, 400m 55.98 '17. Married Derron Herah (400mh 51.01 '03) on 2 Nov 2019.

Briana WILLIAMS b. 21 Mar 2002 Miami, Florida 1.62m 52kg. Northeast.
At 100m/200m: WJ: '18- 1/1, won PAm-J 100m 2019. World U18 and CAC U20 100m record 2019.
Progress at 100m, 200m: 2014- 13.25, 2015- 12.09, 24.79; 2016- 12.58, 26.16; 2017- 11.30, 23.57/23.53w; 2018- 11.13, 22.50; 2019- 10.94, 22.88A/22.95; 2020- 24.70. pb: 50m 6.25i '21, 60m 7.15 '20.
World age 15 record (11.13 on 16 Mar 2018), At 16, youngest to win WJ sprint double in 2018. Father from Philadelphia, mother from Jamaica.

Danielle WILLIAMS b. 14 Sep 1992 St.Andrew 1.68m 59kg. Johnson C.Smith University, USA.
At 100mh: WCh: '13-15-17-19: sf/1/sf/3; CG: '14- 4, '18- 2; WJ: '10- 4; WUG: '13- 3, '15- 1; PAm-J: '11- 2; CCp: '18- 1. Won DL 2019, JAM 2013, 2015, 2017-18. CAC and Commonwealth 4x100m record 2015, CAC 100mh 2019.
Progress at 100mh: 2010- 13.46/13.41w, 2011- 13.32/13.13w, 2012- 14.02, 2013- 12.69, 2014- 12.99, 2015- 12.57, 2016- 12.77/12.55w, 2017- 12.56, 2018- 12.48, 2019- 12.32, 2020- 13.23. pbs: 60m 7.32i '14, 100m 11.24A '13, 11.25 '17; 200m 22.62A '13, 23.12i '20, 23.48 '14; 300m 37.21i '20, 60mh 7.86i '20.
Sister **Shermaine** (b. 4 Feb 1990) at 100mh: OG: '12/16- sf; WCh: '13- sf, '15- 7; WJ: '08- 2; WY: '05- 6, '07- 2; PAm-J: '09- 1; pb 12.78/12.65w '12.

Kimberly WILLIAMS b. 3 Nov 1988 Saint Thomas 1.69m 66kg. Florida State University, USA.
At TJ: OG: '12- 6, '16- 7; WCh: '09/11 dnq 14/14, '13-15-17-19: 4/5/10/4; CG: '14- 1, '18- 1; WJ: '06- dnq 15; WY: '05- dnq; CAG: '10- 1; PAm: '19- 4; PAm-J: '07- 2; CCp: '14- 4; WI: '12-14-18: 5/3/2. Won NCAA LJ & TJ 2009, JAM TJ 2010, 2012-17.
Progress at TJ: 2004- 12.53/12.65w, 2005- 12.63/13.09w, 2006- 13.18, 2007- 13.52, 2008- 13.82i/13.69/13.83w, 2009- 14.08/14.38w, 2010- 14.23, 2011- 14.25, 2012- 14.53, 2013- 14.62/14.78w, 2014- 14.59, 2015- 14.45, 2016- 14.56/14.66w, 2017- 14.54/14.60w, 2018- 14.64, 2019- 14.64, 2020- 14.12i, 2021- 14.54w. pbs: 100m 11.76 '12, 200m 24.55 '11, LJ 6.55i 11, 6.42/6.66w '09.

JAPAN

Governing body: Nippon Rikujo-Kyogi Renmei. Founded 1911.

National Championships first held in 1913 (men), 1925 (women). **2020 Champions: Men**: 100m: Yoshihide Kiryu 10.27, 200m: Shota Iizuka 20.75, 400m: Rikiya Ito 45.94, 800m: Daichi Setoguchi 1:47.70, 1500m: Ryoji Tatezawa 3:41.32, 5000m: Yuta Bando 13:18.49, 10000m: Akira Aizawa 27:18.75, Mar: Naoya Sakuda 2:08:59, 3000mSt: Kosei Yamaguchi 8:24.19, 110mh: Taio Kanai 13.36, 400mh: Takatoshi Abe 49.73, HJ: Tomohiro Shinno 2.30, PV: Koki Kuruma 5.60, LJ: Hibiki Tsuha 7.99, TJ: Hikaru Ikehata 16.54, SP: Shin-ichi Yukinaga 17.77, DT: Yuji Tsutsumi 60.24, HT: Ryota Kashimura 71.03, JT: Ryohei Arai 81.57, Dec: Akihiko Nakamura 7739, 20kW: Toshikazu Yamanishi 1:17:36. **Women**: 100m: Mei Kodama 11.36, 200m: Remi Tsuruta 23.17, 400m: Seika Aoyama 53.55, 800m: Ayaka Kawata 2:03.54, 1500m/5000m: Nozomi Tanaka 4:10.21/15:05.65, 10000m: Hitomi Niiya 30:20.44, Mar: Mao Ichiyama 2:20:29, 3000mSt: Yukari Ishizawa 9:48.76, 100mh: Masumi Aoki 13.02, 400mh: Ayesysa Ibrahim 56.50, HJ: Shieriai Tsuda 1.78, PV: Mayu Nasu 4.20, LJ: Ayaka Kora 6.32, TJ: Mariko Morimoto 13.14, SP: Yuka Takahashi 15.26, DT: Maki Saito 55.41, HT: Akane Watanabe 64.84, JT: Yuka Sato 59.32, Hep: Yuki Yamasaki 5799, 20kW: Kumiko Okada 1:29:56.

Hirooki ARAI b. 18 May 1988 Obuse, Nagano pref. 1.80m 62kg. Fujitsu, was at Fukui University of Technology.
At 50kW: OG: '16- 3; WCh: '11-13-15-17: 9/10/4/2; WT: '18- 1; JPN champion 2015, 2017.
Progress at 50kW: 2009- 4:04:01, 2010- 3:55:56, 2011- 3:48:40, 2012- 3:47:08, 2013- 3:45:56, 2014- 3:40:34, 2015- 3:40:20, 2016- 3:41:24, 2017- 3:41:17, 2018- 3:44:25, 2019- 3:43:02. Pbs: 3000mW 12:12.73 '09, 5000mW 19:05.46 '16, 10000mW 39:17.66 '14, 20kW 1:19:00 '19, 30kW 2:12:42 '19, 35kW 2:34:23 '19.

Yuki HASHIOKA b. 23 Jan 1999 Urawa Saitama pref, 1.83m 77kg. Nihon University.
At LJ: WCh: '19- 8; WJ: '16- 10, '18- 1; AsiG: '18- 4; AsiC: '19- 1; WUG: '19- 1. JPN champion 2017-19. Japanese long jump record 2019.
Progress at LJ: 2015- 7.70, 2016-7.75, 2017- 8.05/ 8.07w, 2018- 8.09/8.30w, 2019- 8.32, 2020- 8.29. Pbs: 100m 10.53 '20, 200m 21.61 '17, HJ 2.02 '15. Both his parents set Japanese records and were Japanese champions, father Toshiyuki (PV 5.55 '86), mother Naomi (nee Jojima, 100mh 13.44 '92, LJ 6.18 '85, 6.28w '92, TJ 13.23 '93&95)

Koki IKEDA b. 3 May 1998 Hamamatsu, Shizuoka pref. 1.68m 53kg. Toyo University.
At 20kW: WCh: '19- 6; WT: '18- 1; WUG: '19- 1. Asian 5000m walk best 2020.
Progress at 20kW: 2017- 1:20:48, 2018- 1:19:13, 2019- 1:17:25, 2020- 1:18:22, 2021- 1:18:45. pbs: 5000mW 18:20.14 '20, 10kW 38:27 '19, 10000mW 37:25.90 '20.

Masatora KAWANO b. 23 Oct 1998 Hyuga, Miyazaki Pref. 1.77m 60kg. Toyo University.
At 20kW: WUG: '19- 2. At 10000mW: WJ: '16- 9. Japanese 50k walk record 2019.
Progress at 20kW, 50kW: 2016- 1:25:37, 2017- 1:23:51, 2018- 1:19:52, 3:47:30; 2019- 1:17:24, 3:36:45. Pbs: 5000mW 18:28.26 '20, 10000mW 38:23.95 '20, 30kW 2:09:17 '17, 35kW 2:30:45 '19.

Yoshihide KIRYU b. 15 Dec 1995 Hikone, Shida 1.75m 70kg. Toyo University.
At 100m/4x100mR: OG: '16- h/2R; WCh: '13- h, '17- 3R, '19- sf/3R; WJ: '14- 3/2R; AsiG: '18- 1R; AsiC: '19- 1; JPN champion 2014, 2020.
JJPN 100m record 2017, world youth record 2012.
Progress at 100m: 2011- 10.58, 2012- 10.19, 2013- 10.01, 2014- 10.05, 2015- 10.09/9.87w, 2016- 10.01, 2017- 9.98, 2018- 10.10, 2019- 10.01, 2020- 10.04A/10.06. pbs: 60m 6.56i '16, 6.60 '17; 150m 15.35 '17, 200m 20.39 '19, 300m 32.59 '17.

Kai KOBAYASHI b. 28 Feb 1993 Odate, Akita pref. 1.65m 53kg. Albirex Niigata. Was at Waseda University.
At 50kW: WCh: '17- 3.
Progress at 20kW, 50kW: 2013- 1:22:47, 2014- 1:21:13, 2015- 1:19:12, 2016-1:19:57, 3:42:08; 2017- 1:19:13, 3:41:17; 2018- 3:46:26, 2019- 1:21:33, 3:43:46; 2020- 1:22:28. Pbs: 5000mW 19:11.94 '16, 10000m 39:06.86 '17, 30kW 2:09:40 '19, 35kW 2:34:23 '19.

Yuta KOGA b. 15 Jul 1999 Itoshima, Fukuoka pref, 1.76m 57kg. Meiji University.
At 20kW: WUG: '19- 3.
Progress at 20kW: 2017- 1:26:23, 2018- 1:21:54, 2019- 1:20:24, 2020- 1:18:42. Pbs: 5000m 14:54.18 '16, 5000mW 18:26.70 '20, 10000mW 37:35.00 '20.

Satoshi MARUO b. 28 Nov 1991 Kyoto 1.75m 60kg. Aichi Steel Corporation. Was at Biwako Seikei Sport College.
At 50kW: WCh: '17- 4; AsiG: '18- 4; WT: '18- 3.
Progress at 20kW, 50kW: 2010- 1:30:56, 2011- 1:27:20, 2012- 1:25:09, 2013- 1:24:42, 2014- 1:24:57, 2015- 1:19:42, 2016-1:20:14, 4:02:36; 2017- 1:20:31, 3:43:03; 2018- 1:21:10, 3:44:52; 2019- 1:20:56, 3:37:39; 2020- 1:20:41. Pbs: 5000mW 19:11.45 '20, 10000m 39:33.30 '15, 30kW 2:09:17 '17, 35kW 2:34:21 '19. Run: 3000m 8:53.7 '06.

Daisuke MATSUNAGA b. 24 Mar 1995 Yokohama, Kanagawa pref. 1.74m 60kg. Fujitsu, was at Toyo University.
At 20kW: OG: '16- 7; WCh: '17- 38; WUG: '15- 3. At 10000mW: WJ: '14- 1; As-J 12- 2; WCp: '14-2J. 10000m walk records: JPN 2018, Asian junior 2013, Asian 2018.
Progress at 20kW: 2013- 1:23:56, 2014- 1:21:17, 2015- 1:19:08, 2016- 1:18:53, 2017- 1:19:40, 2018- 1:17:46, 2020- 1:23:59. pbs: 5000mW 19:28.91 '14, 10000mW 37:58.08 '18.

Tomohiro NODA b. 24 Jan 1996 Izumi, Osaka Pref. 1.74m 58kg. Japan Self-Defense Forces Physical Training School, was at Meiji University.
At 50kW: WCh: '19- dnf; JPN champion 2018. Japanese 50k walk record 2018.
Progress at 20kW, 50kW: 2014- 1:22:37, 2015- 1:20:08, 2016-1:22:29, 2017- 1:20:04; 2018- 1:19:49, 3:39:47; 2019- 1:19:00, 2020- 1:20:26. Pbs: 5000mW 19:09.89 '20, 10000m 39:06.86 '17, 30kW 2:11:06 '18, 35kW 2:32:31 '18.

Suguru OSAKO b. 23 May 1991 Machida, Tokyo Metropolis 1.70m 52kg. Nike Oregon Project. Was at Waseda University.
At 5000m: OG: '16- h; WCh: '15- h. At 10000m: OG: '16- 17; WCh: '13- 21; WJ: '10- 8; AsiG: '14- 2; WUG: '11- 1.
Asian records: junior half marathon 61:47 '10, marathon 2018. Japanese records: 3000m 2014, 5000m 2015, Marathon 2019 & 2020.
Progress at 5000m, 10000m, Mar: 2008- 13:58.66, 2009- 28:57.00, 2010- 13:47.29, 28:35.75; 2011- 13:31.27, 28:42.83; 2012- 13:33.84, 27:56.94; 2013- 13:20.80, 27:38.31; 2014- 13:26.15, 28:11.94; 2015- 13:08.40, 27:45.24; 2016-13:31.45, 27:50.27; 2017- 13:25.56, 27:46.64, 2:07:19; 2018- 13:29.11, 28:26.41, 2:05:50; 2019- 13:40.48, 27:57.41, 2:11:41; 2020- 13:33.83, 27:36.93, 2:05:29. Pbs: 1500m 3:40.49 '16, 3000m 7:40:09 '14, 2M 8:16.47i '15, 8:28.30 '15; HMar 61:01 '18.
Marathons: 3rd Boston and Fukuoka 2017, 3rd Chicago in 2018, when he won 100 million yen ($879,350) for setting a Japanese record.

Abdul Hakim SANI BROWN b. 6 Mar 1999 Kitakyushu, Fukuoka pref. 1.90m 83kg. Tumbleweed TC, University of Florida, USA.
At (100m)/200m: WCh: '15- sf, '17- sf/7, '19- (sf)/3R; WY: '15- 1/1. Won JPN 100m & 200m 2017, 2019. Asian 4x100m record 2019, Japanese 100m record 2019.
Progress at 100m, 200m: 2010- 12.95; 2013- 10.88, 21.85; 2014- 10.45, 21.09; 2015- 10.28, 20.34; 2016- 10.22, 20.54; 2017- 10.05, 20.32; 2018- 10.46/10.19w, 20.64; 2019- 9.97, 20.08. pb 60m: 60m 6.54i '19.
Ghanaian father, Japanese mother.

Yusuke SUZUKI b. 2 Jan 1988 Nomi, Iskikawa pref. 1.71m 58kg. Fujitsu. Juntendo University.
At 50kW: WCh: '19- 1; At 20kW: OG: '12- 35; WCh: '09-11-13-15: 39/4/11/dnf WCp: '14- 4; AsiG: '10- 5, '14- 2; WUG: '07- 4; Asian champion 2013, 2015; JPN 2011, 2013-14. At 10000mW: WJ: 04- 17, '06- 3; WY: '05- 3.
Walk records: World 20k 2015, Asian 5000m 2015, 10000m (2) 2014-15, Japanese 10k (4) 2010-15, 20k (4) 2013-15, 50k (on debut) 2019.
Progress at 20kW, 50kW: 2007- 1:24:40, 2008- 1:22:34, 2009- 1:22:05, 2010- 1:20:06, 2011- 1:21:13, 2012- 1:22:30, 2013- 1:18:34, 2014- 1:18:17, 2015- 1:16:36, 2018- 1:21:14, 2019- 1:17:47, 3:39:07; 2020- 1:18:36. pbs: 3000mW 18:37.60 '15, 5000mW 18:37.22 '15, 10kW 38:05 '15, track 38:10.23 '15; 30kW 2:12:42 '19. 35k: 2:34:20 '19.

JAPAN – KAZAKHSTAN – KENYA

Eiki TAKAHASHI b. 19 Nov 1992 Hanamaki, Iwate pref. 1.75m 56kg. Fujitsu, Iwate University.
At 20kW: OG: '16- 42; WCh: '15-17-19: 47/14/10; WCp: '14- 9, '16- 12; AsiG: '14- 7, '18- 5. Won JPN 2015-19.. Walk records: World best 10000m 2020, Asian 5000m & 10000m 2015, JPN 20k 2015.
Progress at 20kW: 2011- 1:26:16, 2012- 1:22:33, 2013- 1:20:25, 2014- 1:18:41, 2015- 1:18:03, 2016- 1:18:26, 2017- 1:18:18, 2018- 1:17:26, 2019- 1:18:00, 2020- 1:18:29, 2021- 1:18:04. pbs: 5000mW 18:37.60 '15, 10000mW 37:25.21 '20.

Naoto TOBE b. 31 Mar 1992 Noda, Chiba pref. 1.94m 74kg. Japan Airlines, graduated from University of Tsukuba.
At HJ: WCh: '15/19- dnq 25=/14=; WJ: '08- 10, '10- 3; AsiG: '14- 5, '18- 3; AsiC: '19- 3; JPN champion 2011, 2015, 2019; WIT 2019. Japanese high jump record (indoor) 2019.
Progress at HJ: 2007- 2.08, 2008- 2.16, 2009- 2.23, 2010- 2.24, 2011- 2.22, 2012- 2.22, 2013- 2.28, 2014- 2.31, 2015- 2.29, 2016- 2.25, 2017- 2.26, 2018- 2.32, 2019- 2.35i/2.28, 2020- 2.31i/2.24. pb LJ 7.52 '12.

Toshikazu YAMANISHI b. 15 Feb 1996 Nagaokakyo, Kyoto Pref. 1.64m 54kg. Aichi Steel, was at Kyoto University,
At 20kW: WCh: '19- 1; WCp: '18- 4; AsiG: '18- 2; WUG: '17- 1; Asian champion 2019, Japan 2020- 21. At 10000mW: WY: '13- 1.
Asian 5000m walk best 2020,
Progress at 20kW: 2015- 1:21:20, 2016- 1:20:50, 2017- 1:19:03, 2018- 1:17:41, 2019- 1:17:15, 2020- 1:17:36, 2021- 1:17:20. pbs: 5000mW 18:34.88 '20, 10kW 38:27 '19, 10000mW 39:24.49 '17.

Women

Mao ICHIYAMA b. 29 May 1997 Izumi, Kagoshima pref.1.58m 43kg. Wacoal
World HMar: '18- 19. Won JPN CC 2017, Mar 2020.
Progress at 10000m, Mar: 2016- 32:15.73, 2017- 31:49.01; 2018- 31:57.91, 2019- 31:34.56, 2:24:33; 2020- 31:11.56, 2:20:29; 2021- 2:21:11. pbs: 1500m 4:28.35 '15, 3000m 8:53.54 '17, 5000m 15:06.66 '20, Road: HMar 68:49 '19, 25k 1:23:30 '20, 30k 1:40:31 '20.
Won Nagoya Marathon 2020, Osaka 2021.

Haruka KITAGUCHI b. 16 Mar 1998 Asahikawa, Hokkaido 1.79m 86kg. Japan Airlines, was at Nihon University.
At JT WCh: '19- dnq 13; WJ: '16- 8; WY: '15- 1; WUG: '19- 2. JPN champion 2019.
Two Japanese javelin records 2019.
Progress at JT: 2014- 53.15, 2015- 58.90, 2016- 61.38, 2017- 61.07, 2018- 60.48, 2019- 66.00, 2020- 63.45.

Hitomi NIIYA b. 26 Feb 1988 Soja, Okayama pref. 1.66m 43kg. Nike Tokyo TC.
At (5000m)/10000m: OG: '12- h/9; WCh: '11- (13), '13- 5, '19- 11; AsiC: '11- (2), '19- 2. At 3000m: WY: '05- 3. Won JPN 5000m 2012, 10000m 2013,

2020.. Japanese 10000m & HMar records 2010. Progress at 10000m: 2012- 30:59.19, 2013- 30:56.70, 2018- 31:32.50, 2019- 31:12.99, 2020- 30:20.44. pbs: 1500m 4:20.14 '20, 3000m 9:10.34 '05, 5000m 14:55.83 '20, HMar 66:38 '20, Mar 2:30:58 '09.
Led for much of 10,000m races at OG 2012 and WCh 2013. Returned after 5-year gap in 2018.

Kumiko OKADA b. 17 Oct 1991 Ageo, Saitama pref. 1.58m 47kg. Bic Camera, was at Rikkyo University.
At 20kW: OG: '16- 16; WCh: '15-17-19: 25/18/6; AsiG: '18- 3; won JPN 2015-20. At 10000mW: WJ: '08- 8, '10- 2.
JPN walks records 5000m, 10000m & 20k 2019.
Progress at 20kW: 2011- 1:34:30, 2012- 1:34:27, 2013- 1:32:22, 2014- 1:33:25, 2015- 1:29:46, 2016- 1:29:40, 2017- 1:29:40, 2018- 1:31:29, 2019- 1:27:41, 2020- 1:29:56. Pbs: 3000mW: 12:42.96 '08, 5000mW 20:42.25 '19, 10000m: 42:51.82 '19.

KAZAKHSTAN

Governing body: Athletic Federation of the Republic of Kazakhstan. Founded 1959.

Women

Olga RYPAKOVA b. 30 Nov 1984 Kamenogorsk 1.83m 62kg. née Alekseyeva.
At TJ/(LJ): OG: '08- 2 (dnq 27), '12- 1, '16- 3; WCh: '07-09-11-15-17-19: 9/9/2/3/3/dnq 13; WJ: '00- (dnq 23); AsiG: '06- (3), '10- 1/2, '14- 1, '18- 1; AsiC: '07- 1/1, '09- 1; WI: '08-10-12: 3/1/2; WUG: '07- (1); WCp: '06- (8), '10- 1/3, '18- 3; won DL TJ 2012, 2017; C.Asian 2003, W,MilG 2019, Asian Indoor LJ 2009, 2017; TJ 2009, 2016-17; Pen 2005- 06. At Hep: WJ: '02- 2; WY: '01- 4; AsiG: '06- 1; Won KAZ LJ 2005, 2008, 2011, 2015; TJ 2008, 2011, 2015; Hep 2006.
Four Asian TJ records 2008-10, five indoors 2008-10, seven KAZ records 2007-10.
Progress at LJ, TJ: 2000- 6.23, 2001- 6.00, 2002- 6.26, 2003- 6.34i/6.14, 2004- 6.53i, 2005- 6.60, 2006- 6.63, 2007- 6.85, 14.69; 2008- 6.52/6.58w, 15.11; 2009- 6.58i/6.42, 14.53/14.69w; 2010- 6.60, 15.25; 2011- 6.56, 14.96; 2012- 14.98, 2014- 14.37, 2015- 14.77, 2016- 14.74, 2017- 14.77, 2018- 14.26, 2019- 14.37. pbs: 200m 24.83 '02, 800m 2:20.12 '02, 60mh 8.67i '06, 100mh 14.02 '06, HJ 1.92 '06, SP 13.04 '06, JT 41.60 '03, Hep 6122 '06, Pen 4582i '06 (Asian rec).
Former heptathlete, concentrated on long jump after birth of daughter. Four KAZ and three Asian TJ records with successive jumps in Olympic final 2008, three Asian indoor records when won World Indoor gold in 2010. Son Kiril born June 2013.

KENYA

Governing body: Kenya Amateur Athletic Association. Founded 1951.
2020 National Champions: **Men**: 20kW:

Samuel Gathimba 1:22:56. **Women**: Grace Wanjiru Niue 1:46:40.

Leonard Kiplimo **BARSOTON** b. 21 Oct 1994 1.66m 56kg.
At 10000m: AfG: '15- 2. At HMar: WCh: '18- 12, '20- 6. World CC: '13-15-17: 2J/5/2; AfCC: '14- 1. Won KEN CC 2017.
Progress at 10000m, HMar: 2013- 27:33.13, 2014- 27:20.74, 2015- 27:27.55, 2016- 27:31.86, 2017- 27:47.4A, 59:28; 2018- 61:14, 2019- 59:09. 2020- 59:10. pbs: 1500m 3:47.95 '16, 3000m 7:52.33 '17, 5000m 13:16.25 '15, 15k 42:00 '20, 20k 56:04 '20.

Leonard Kipkemoi **BETT** b. 3 Nov 2000 1.73m 57kg.
At 3000mSt: WCh: '19- 9; WJ: '18- 2; Af-J: '19- 1. At 2000mSt: WY: '17-1. World CC: '19- 4J.
Progress at 3000mSt: 2018- 8:16.97, 2019- 8:08.61, 2020- 8:08.78 Pbs: 1M Rd 3:55 '18, 3000m 7:47.59 '18, 5000m 13:56.8A '19, 2000mSt 5:28.52A '17.

Nicholas Kiptanui **BETT** b. 20 Dec 1996 1.72m 52kg. At 2000mSt: WY: '13- 2.
Progress at 3000mSt: 2013- 8:52.1A, 2014- 8:28.83, 2015- 8:19.26, 2016- 8:10.07, 2017- 8:12.20, 2018- 8:13.18, 2019- 8:11.47. pbs: 5000m 14:33.6A '16, 2000mSt 5:20.92 '13.

Bethwel Kiprotich **BIRGEN** b. 6 Aug 1988 Eldoret 1.78m 64kg.
At 1500m: WCh: '13- sf; WI: '14- 8, won WIT 2017. At 3000m: WI: '18- 3.
Progress at 1500m, 5000m: 2010- 3:35.60, 2011- 3:34.59, 2012- 3:31.00, 14:01.0A; 2013- 3:30.77, 13:50.6A; 2014- 3:31.22, 2015- 3:34.62i, 2016- 3:33.94, 13:04.66; 2017- 3:32.27, 13:17.80; 2018- 3:34.27, 13:20.08; 2019- 3:31.45, 13:10.21; 2020- 3:36.22i/3:36.67. pbs: 800m 1:48.32 '11, 1M 3:50.42 '13, 3000m 7:32.48 '16.

Evans Kiplagat **CHEBET** b. 10 Nov 1988 Buret 1.70m 54kg.
Progress at Mar: 2013- 2:11:26, 2014- 2:07:46, 2015- 2:08:50, 2016- 2:05:31, 2017- 2:05:30, 2019- 2:05:00, 2020- 2:03:00. pbs: 10M 45:06 '17, HMar 61:11+ '16, 25k 1:13:03 '20, 30k 1:27:42 '20.
Marathons: won Buenos Aires 2019, Lake Biwa & Valencia 2020; 2nd Prague 2014-15, Seoul Nov 2014 & Mar 2016, Valencia 2017, 3rd Berlin 2016.

Lawrence CHERONO b. 7 Aug 1988 1.78m 61kg.
Progress at Mar: 2014- 2:10:16, 2015- 2:09:39, 2016- 2:07:24, 2017- 2:05:09, 2018- 2:04:06, 2019- 2:05:45, 2020- 2:03:04. pbs: 10M 45:06 '17, HMar 61:41 '20, 25k 1:13:03 '20, 30k 1:27:43 '20.
Marathon wins: Seville 2015, Prague 2016, Honolulu 2016-17, Amsterdam 2017-18, Boston & Chicago 2019; 2nd Rotterdam 2017, Valencia 2020.

Ferguson Rotich **CHERUIYOT** b. 30 Nov 1989 Kericho 1.83m 73kg.
At 800m: OG: '16- 5; WCh: '13-15-17-19: sf/4/sf/3; CG: '14- 4; AfCh: '14- 4, '18- 5. Won DL 2016, Kenyan 2014.
Progress at 800m: 2013- 1:43.22, 2014- 1:42.84, 2015- 1:43.60A, 2016- 1:43.43, 2017- 1:44.37, 2018- 1:43.73, 2019- 1:42.54, 2020- 1:44.16. Pbs: 1000m 2:14.88 '18, 1500m 3:33.21 '18.
Changed first name from Simon to Ferguson in honour of Manchester United manager Alex Ferguson.

Timothy CHERUIYOT b. 20 Nov 1995 Bomet, Rift Valley 1.78m 64kg.
At 1500m: WCh: '15-17-19: 7/2/1; CG: '18- 2; AfCh: '16- 2, '18- 2. Won DL 2017-19, KEN 2017-18 (800m 2019).
Progress at 800m, 1500m: 2014- 1:45.92A, 2015- 1:49.3A, 3:34.86A; 2016- 3:31.34, 2017- 3:29.10, 2018- 1:44.74A, 3:28.41; 2019- 1:43.11A, 3:28.77; 2020- 1:46.78, 3:28.45. pbs: 800m '19, 1M 3:49.64 '17, 2000m 5:03.05A '20, 5000m 13:47.2A '20.

Edward CHESEREK b. 2 Feb 1994 Kenya 1.68m 57kg. Marakwet. Was at University of Oregon. Won NCAA 5000m 2015-16, 10000m 2014-16, CC 2013-15, Ind 1M 2015, 3000m & 5000m 2014, 2016-17, Dist.Med R 2015-16.
Progress at 1500m (1M), 5000m, 10000m: 2011- 4:03.29M, 14:02.33, 2012- 4:02.21iM, 13:57.04i; 2013- 3:48.89+, 2014- 3:36.50, 13:18.71, 28:30.18; 2015- 3:37.08, 13:45.25; 2016- 3:41.57 (3:57.38iM), 13:25.59; 2017- 3:37.01i (3:52.01iM), 13:24.72; 2018- 3:33.76i, 3:49.44Mi; 2019- 3:37.71i/3:37.92, 13:04.44; 2020- 13:09.05i/13:21.78, 27:23.58. pbs: 800m 1:49.98 '12, 1M 3:49.44i '18, 4:03.29 '11; 3000m 7:38.74i '18, 7:43.47 '19; 2M 8:39.15i '13, 3000mSt 9:00.11 '11.
Record 17 NCAA titles. Applying for US citizenship.

Rodgers Kwemoi **CHUMO** b. 3 Mar 1997 Mount Elgon district 1.65m 49kg.
At 10000m: WCh: '19- 4; CG: '18- 3; WJ: '16- 1. World CC: '15- 10J,
Progress at 10000m: 2013- 29:25.0A, 2015- 27:42.09, 2016- 27:25.23, 2017- 27:38.61, 2018- 27:28.66, 2019- 26:55.36. pbs: 1500m 3:50.44 '15, 5000m 13:18.98 '16, 10M Rd 45:03 '17.

Geoffrey Kipsang **KAMWOROR** b. 22 Nov 1992 Chepkorio, Keiyo district 1.68m 54kg.
At 10000m: OG: '16- 11; WCh: '15- 2, 17- 6. World CC: '11-15-17-19: 1J/1/1/3; HMar: '14-16-18: 1/1/1. Won KEN 5000m 2015, 10000m 2019, CC 2016, 2018.
Tied world 30km record 2014, world 15, 20k & HMar records 2019.
Progress at 5000m, 10000m, HMar, Mar: 2010- 13:32.01, 2011- 13:12.23, 27:06.35, 59:31; 2012- 13:28.8A, 59:26, 2:06:12; 2013- 28:17.0A, 58:54, 2:06:26; 2014- 59:08, 2:06:39; 2015- 13:13.28A, 26:52.65, 2:10:48; 2016- 12:59.98, 27:31.94, 59:10; 2017- 13:01.35, 26:57.77, 2:10:53; 2018- 60:02, 2:06:26; 2019- 27:24.76A, 58:01, 2:08:13. pbs: 1500m 3:40.7A '15, 3000m 7:51.55 '17; Road: 15k 41:05 '19 20k 55:00 '19, 30k 1:27:37 '14.

KENYA

3rd in Berlin Marathon 2012 (on debut) and 2013 (4th 2014), won New York 2017 & 2019 (2nd 2015, 3rd 2018). Won RAK half marathon 2013.
Kibiwott KANDIE 20 Jun 1996 1.72m 55kg.
At HMar: WCh: '20- 2. Won KEN CC 2020.
Progress at HMar: 2017- 63:34A, 2019- 59:31, 2020- 57:32. pbs: 5000m 14:19.2A '17, 10000m 28:28.0A '21; Road: 10k 27:25 '20, 15k 41:10 '20, 20k 54:43 '20, Mar 2:22:48 '19.
World half marathon record 2020.
In 2020 he became the first man to run first three then four sub-59 half marathons in one year., winning RAK, Prague and Valencia. Sister Dorcas pb HMar 67:10 '20, 11 WCh 2020.
Bedan KAROKI Muchiri b. 21 Aug 1990 Nyandarua 1.69m 53kg. Toyota, Japan.
At 10000m: OG: 12- 5, '16- 7; WCh: '13-15-17: 6/4/4; AfG: '11- 2. World CC: '15- 2; HMar: '16- 2. Won Kenyan CC 2012.
Progress at 10000m, HMar, Mar: 2010- 27:23.62, 2011- 27:13.67, 2012- 27:05.50; 2013- 27:13.12, 2014- 26:52.36, 59:23; 2015- 27:04.77, 59:14; 2016- 27:07.30, 59:32; 2017- 26:52.12, 59:10, 2:07:41; 2018- 58:42, 2:07:59; 2019- 59:05, 2:05:53; 2020- 27:02.80, 2:06:15. pbs: 1500m 3:50.91 '08, 3000m 7:37.68 '13, 5000m 13:15.25 '14, 15k 41:41 '16, 10M 45:02 '14, 20k 55:55 '18, 25k 1:12:37 '18, 30k 1:27:24 '18.
Went to Japan in 2007. 3rd London 2017 on marathon debut. 2nd Tokyo 2019. Won Ras Al Khaimah half marathon 2018, sixth win in eight races at the distance, seven under 1 hour.
Abraham KIBIWOT b. 6 Apr 1996 1.75m 55kg.
At 3000mSt: WCh: '19- 7; CG: '18- 2; AfCh: '16- 3; won Af-J 2015, Kenyan 2016.
Progress at 3000mSt: 2014- 8:52.36A, 2015- 8:22.10, 2016- 8:09.25, 2017- 8:10.62, 2018- 8:10.62, 2019- 8:05.72, 2020- 8:17.60A. pbs: 3000m 8:02.95 '16, 5000m 14:10.8A '15.
Benjamin KIGEN b. 5 Jul 1993 Baringo County 1.73m 57kg.
At 3000mSt: WCh: '19- 6; AfG: '19- 1; KEN & W.Military champion 2019.
Progress at 3000mSt: 2017- 8:11:38, 2018- 8:06.19, 2019- 8:05.12. 2020- 8:55.28A. pbs: 800m 1:52.0A '16, 1500m 3:36.36 '17, 3000m 7:44.77i '18, 5000m 14:06.2A '13, 2000mSt 5:18.67 '17.
Nicholas Kipkoroir **KIMELI** b. 29 Sep 1998 1.70m 55kg.
At 5000m: WCh: '19- 8; CG: '18- 9; Af-J: '17- 3 (1 10000m).
Progress at 5000m, 10000m: 2015- 13:59.34A, 2016- 13:44.4A, 2017- 13:11.58, 29:52.15A; 2018- 13:28.53A, 2019- 12:57.90, 2020- 12:51.78, 26:58.97. pbs: 3000m 7:34.25 '19.
Wycliffe KINYAMAL b. 2 Jul 1997 Trans Mara District 1.86m 75kg.
At 800m: CG: '18- 1.
Progress at 800m: 2016- 1:46.8A, 2017- 1:43.94, 2018- 1:43.12, 2019- 1:43.48, 2020- 1:45.52A.

Eliud KIPCHOGE B. 5 Nov 1984 Kapsisiywa, Nandi 1.67m 52kg.
At Mar: OG: '16- 1; At 5000m: OG: '04- 3, '08- 2; WCh: '03-05-07-09-11: 1/4/2/5/7; CG: '10- 2. At 3000m: WI: '06- 3. World CC: '02-03-04-05: 5J/1J/4/5; HMar: '12- 6. Won WAF 5000m 2003, 3000m 2004, Kenyan CC 2005.
World junior 5000m record 2003. World road best 4M 17:10 '05 and WR 30k 2016 & 2018, World marathon record 2018.
Progress at 1500m, 5000m, 10000m: 2002- 13:13.03, 2003- 3:36.17, 12:52.61; 2004- 3:33.20, 12:46.53; 2005- 3:33.80, 12:50.22; 2006- 3:36.25i, 12:54.94; 2007- 3:39.98, 12:50.38, 26:49.02; 2008- 13:02.06, 26:54.32; 2009- 12:56.46, 2010- 3:38.36, 12:51.21; 2011- 12:55.72i/12:59.01, 26:53.27; 2012- 12:55.34, 27:11.93. At HMar, Mar: 2012: 59:25, 2013- 60:04, 2:04:05, 2014- 60:52, 2:04:11; 2015- 60:50, 2:04:00; 2016- 59:44, 2:03:05; 2017- 61:29, 2:03:32/2:00:25 irreg; 2018- 2:01:39, 2019- 2:02:37/1:59:41 irreg, 2020- 2:06:49. pbs: 1M 3:50.40 '04, 2000m 4:59.?+ '04, 3000m 7:27.66 '11, 2M 8:07.39i '12, 8:07.68 '05; Road: 10k 26:55dh '06, 27:34 '05; 25k 1:12:24 '18, 30k 1:26:45 '18.
Ran 26:49.02 in 10,000m debut at Hengelo in 2007. All his seven marathons were in 2:05:30 or better until his Olympic win in 2:08:44, and now has record 11 sub 2:06 times (9 sub-2:05). He won at Hamburg on debut then 2nd Berlin in 2013, 1st Rotterdam & Chicago 2014, London 2015-16, 2018-19, Berlin 2015, 2017-18 (WR) but 8th at London 2020. IAAF/WA male athlete of the Year 2018-19. Won World Marathon Majors four times: 2015/16 to 2018/19. Ran 2:00:25 in Nike's carefully contrived 2-hour marathon bid at Monza racetrack on 6 May 2017 and a year later (10 October 2018) became the first man to run a marathon in under two hours with 1:59:41 in a similarly paced and aided effort in the INEOS Challenge in Vienna.
Vincent KIPCHUMBA Torotich b. 3 Aug 1990. 1.78m 61kg.
Progress at Mar: 2015- 2:15:22, 2016- 2:10:32, 2017- 2:12:39, 2018- 2:15:15, 2019- 2:05:09, 2020- 2:05:42. pbs: 10000m 29:43.97A '19, HMar 60:32 '17. Won Vienna & Amsterdam Marathons 2019, 2nd London 2020.
Stephen KIPROP Kiptoo 8 Sep 1999 1.73m 52kg.
Progress at HMar: 2018- 59:21, 2019- 58:42. pbs: 10000m 29:05.7A '18; Road: 10k 28:11 '19, 15k 41:49 '19, 10M 45:14 '19, 20k 55:46 '19.
Won Ras Al Khaimah half marathon in 2019.
Amos KIPRUTO b. 19 Sep 1992. 1.65m 50kg.
At Mar: WCh: '19- 3.
Progress at Mar: 2016- 2:08:12, 2017- 2:05:43, 2018- 2:06:23, 2019- 2:06:46, 2020- 2:03:30. pbs: Road: 15k 43:52 '20, HMar 60:24 '17, 25k 1:12:53 '17, 30k 1:27:39 '17.
Won first completed marathon in Rome 2016. Won Seoul 2017, 3rd Tokyo and 2nd Berlin 2018.

Conseslus KIPRUTO b. 8 Dec 1994 Eldoret 1.71m 55kg.
At 3000mSt: OG: '16- 1; WCh: '13-15-17-19: 2/2/1/1; CG: '18- 1; AfCh: '18- 1; WJ: '12- 1; CCp: 18- 1; won DL 2013, 2016-18; KEN 2018 At 2000St: WY: '11- 1. World CC: '13- 5J, '19- 3 mxR.
Progress at 3000mSt: 2011- 8:27.30, 2012- 8:03.49, 2013- 8:01.16, 2014- 8:09.81, 2015- 8:05.20, 2016- 8:00.12, 2017- 8:04.63, 2018- 8:08.40, 2019- 8:01:35. pbs: 800m 1:49.0A '15, 1000m 2:19.85 '12, 1500m 3:39.57 '13, 3000m 7:44.09 '12, 5000m 13:47.5A 16, 2000mSt 5:28.65 '11.

Rhonex KIPRUTO b. 12 Oct 1999 1.72m 57kg.
At 10000m: WCh: '19- 3; WJ: '18- 1; World CC: '19- 6; AfrCC: '18- 1J.
World road 10k best 26:24 in 2020, U20 bests 27:08 & 26:46 in 2018
Progress at 10000m: 2017- 28:56.5A, 2018- 27:21.08, 2019- 26:50.16. Pbs: 3000m 7:48.08 '18, 5000m 13:07.40 '19, 2000mSt 5:44.8A '15, road: 10k 26:24 '20, 15k 41:10 '20, 20k 54:50, HMar 57:49 '20. Fastest debut half marathon when 3rd Valencia 2020. His younger brother Bravin Kipkogei won the African U20 10,000m in 28:17.06 in 2019 and ran 59:37 in his half marathon debut at Valencia in 2020.

Abel KIRUI b. 4 Jun 1982 Bornet, Rift Valley 1.77m 62kg. Police.
At Mar: OG: '12- 2; WCh: '09- 1, '11- 1.
Progress at Mar: 2006- 2:15:22, 2007- 2:06:51, 2008- 2:07:38, 2009- 2:05:04, 2010- 2:08:04, 2011- 2:07:38, 2012- 2:07:56, 2014- 2:09:04, 2015- 2:10:55, 2016- 2:08:06, 2017- 2:07:45, 2018- 2:07:07, 2020- 2:05:05. pbs: 1500m 3:46.10 '05, 3000m 7:55.90 '06, 5000m 13:52.71 '05, 10000m 28:16.86A '08; Road: 10k 27:59 '09, 15k 42:22 '07, 10M 46:40 '11, HMar 60:11 '07, 25k: 1:13:02 '20, 30k 1:27:43 '20.
Has run 15 sub-2:10 marathons; won Vienna 2008, Chicago 2016 (2nd 2017), 2nd Berlin 2007, 3rd Rotterdam 2009. Uncle Mike Rotich had marathon pb 2:06:33 '03.

Amos KIRUI b. 9 Feb 1998 1.69m 54kg. Toyota Boshoku Corporation, Japan.
At 3000mSt: CG: '18- 3; AfCh: '18- 4; WJ: '16- 1; At 2000mSt: 2 Yth OG '14. World CC: '17- 7J.
Progress at 3000mSt: 2015- 8:51.0A, 2016- 8:20.43, 2017- 8:08.37, 2018- 8:12.24, 2019- 8:17.07. pbs: 3000m 7:51.48 '17, 5000m 13:25.91 '16, 10000m 28:08.98 '16, 10kRd 27:48 '17, 2000mSt 5:39.23A '14.

Jonathan Kiprotich KITILIT b. 24 Apr 1994 Trans-Nzoia 1.71m 61kg.
At 800m: CG: '18- 6; AfCh: '18- 6; Af-J: '13- 2; Won KEN 2018.
Progress at 800m: 2012- 1:47.8A, 2013- 1:48.03, 2015- 1:45.0A, 2016- 1:43.05, 2018- 1:43.46A, 2019- 1:44.50A. pbs: 600m 1:15.9+ '18. 2:13.95 '16, 1500m 3:39.81 '15.

Benard Kibet KOECH b. 25 Nov 1999 1.59m 42kg. Kyudenko, Japan.

KENYA 115

Progress at 5000m, 10000m: 2018- 13:27.37, 27:31.83; 2019- 13:13.48, 27:26.11; 2020- 13:11.10, 27:02.39. pbs: 800m 1:49.2A '15, 1500m 3:48.7A '16, 3000m 7:54.39 '18, HMar 64:42 '19

Emmanuel Kipkurui KORIR b. 15 Jun 1995 1.77m 64kg. University of Texas El Paso.
At 800m: WCh: '17- sf, '19- sf (6 400m); AfCh: '18- 2; CCp: '18- 1. Won DL 2018, NCAA indoors and out 2017, KEN 400m 2018.
World indoor best 600m 2017, African & Commonwealth 800m indoor record 2018.
Progress at 400m, 800m: 2016- 1:46.94A, 2017- 44.53A, 1:43.10; 2018- 44.21A/44.52, 1:42.05; 2019- 44.376, 1:43.69. Pb 600m 1:14.97Ai '17.

Jacob KROP b. 4 Jun 2001 1.69m 55kg.
At 5000m: WCh: '19- 6; Af-J: '19- 2.
Progress at 5000m: 2019- 13:03.08, 2020- 13:11.32. pbs: 10kRd 27:30 '19, 2000mSt 5:47.7A '17.

Ronald Chebolei KWEMOI b. 19 Sep 1995 Mt. Elgon 1.80m 68kg.
At 1500m: OG: '16- 13; WCh: '17- sf, '19- 7; CG: '14- 2; AfG: '15- 4; AfCh: '14- 3; Won KEN 1500m 2014. World CC: '13- 9J.
World junior 1500m record 2014.
Progress at 1500m: 2013- 3:45.39, 2014- 3:28.81, 2015- 3:30.43, 2016- 3:30.49, 2017- 3:30.89A, 2019- 3:32.72, 2020- 3:38.33. pbs: 800m 1:47.43 '19, 1M 3:49.04 '17, 3000m 7:28.73 '17, 2M 8:42.41 '19, 5000m 13:16.14 '15, 10000m 27:33.94 '16. road: 15k 42:15 '18, 10M 45:23 '18.
Younger brother Samuel Chebolei won KEN 5000m 2018.

Alexander MUTISO Munyao b. 10 Sep 1996 1.71m 52kg.
At 3000m: WY: '13- 3.
Progress at 10000m, HMar: 2015- 27:56.87, 2016- 27:39.25, 60:59; 2017- 27:41.54, 60:57; 2018- 27:42.16, 60:11; 2019- 27:44.81, 61:10;, 2020- 27:30.81, 57:59. pbs: 1500m 3:43.9A '13, 3000m 7:56.86 '13, 5000m 13:21.90 '16; Road: 10k 27:25 '20, 15k 41:11 '20, 20k 54:57 '20.

Jonathan Muia NDIKU b. 18 Sep 1991 Machakos 1.73m 60kg. Hitachi Distribution, Japan.
At 3000mSt: CG: '14- 1; AfCh: '14- 2; WJ: '08- 1, '10- 1; Af-J: '09- 1. At 2000mSt: WY: '07- 4. At 10000m: CG:'18- 8
Progress at 10,000m, 3000mSt: 2008- 28:08.28, 8:17.28; 2009- 27:37.72, 8:28.1A; 2010- 8:19.25A. 2011- 8:07.75, 2012- 8:17.88, 2013- 8:18.78, 2014- 8:10.44, 2015- 27:40.64, 8:11.64; 2016- 27:11.23, 2017- 27:39.40, 2018- 27:28.27, 8:30.75; 2019- 27:32.68, 8:27.19; 2020- 27:01.95, 8:24.38. pbs: 1500m 3:39.27 '10, 3000m 7:39.63 '14, 5000m 13:10.64 '20, HMar 61:55 '19, 2000mSt 5:37.30 '07.

David Lekuta RUDISHA b. 17 Dec 1988 Kilgoris 1.89m 73kg. Masai.
At 800m: OG: '12- 1, '16- 1; WCh: '09- sf, '11- 1, '15- 1; CG: '14- 2; WJ: '06- 1/4R; AfCh: '08- 1, '10- 1; Af-J: '07- 1; CCp: '10- 1. Won DL 2010-11,

KENYA

WAF 2009, Kenyan 2009-11.
Three world 800m records 2010-12, four African records 2009-10., Commonwealth & African 600m record 2016.
Progress at 800m: 2006- 1:46.3A, 2007- 1:44.15, 2008- 1:43.72, 2009- 1:42.01, 2010- 1:41.01, 2011- 1:41.33, 2012- 1:40.91, 2013- 1:43.87, 2014- 1:42.98, 2015- 1:43.58, 2016- 1:42.15. pbs: 400m 45.50 '10, 45.2A '13; 600m 1:13.10 '16.
IAAF Male Athlete of the Year 2010, won 26 successive 800m finals 2009-11. His father Daniel won 4x400m silver medal at 1968 Olympics with 440y pb 45.5A '67.

Michael Lotoromom **SARUNI** b. 18 Jun 1995 1.80m 68kg. University of Texas at El Paso.
At 800m: Won NCAA indoor 2018.
World best 600m indoors 2018, African & Commonwealth indoor 800m record 2019.
Progress at 800m: 2017- 1:44.61A, 2018- 1:43.25, 2019- 1:43.70, 2020- 1:46.13, 2021- 1:45.34i. pbs: 400m 45.42A '18, 600m 1:14.79Ai '18, 1500m 3:46.15A '17, 1M 4:03.32i '17.

Charles Cheboi **SIMOTWO** b. 6 May 1995 1.78m 60kg. At 1500m: AfG: '19- 3; AfCh: '18- 8.
Progress at 1500m: 2015- 3:35.86A, 2017- 3:32.59, 2018- 3:32.51, 2019- 3:33.25. pbs: 800m 1:46.20 '17, 1M 3:53.31 '19.

Kumari TAKI b. 6 May 1999 1.72m 59kg. Police.
At 1500m: WCh: '19- h; WJ: '16- 1; WY: '15- 1; CG: '18- 7; Af-Y: '15- 1.
Progress at 1500m: 2015- 3:36.38, 2016- 3:38.8A, 2017- 3:36.07, 2018- 3:35.83A, 2019- 3:34.57, 2020- 3:34.14. pbs: 800m 1:46.29 '18, 1M 3:59.20 '18.

Paul Kipngetich **TANUI** b. 22 Dec 1990 Chesubuno village, Moio district 1.72m 54kg. Kyudenko Corporation, Japan.
At 10000m: OG: '16- 2; WCh: '11-13-15-17: 9/3/3/3. World CC: '09-10-11: 4J/8/2. Won Kenyan CC 2010.
Progress at 5000m, 10000m: 2008- 13:59.2A, 2009- 13:37.15, 27:25.24; 2010- 13:14.87, 27:17.61; 2011- 13:04.65, 26:50.63; 2012- 13:19.18, 27:27.56; 2013- 13:16.57, 27:21.50; 2014- 13:00.53, 26:49.41; 2015- 12:58.69, 26:51.86; 2016- 13:15.22, 27:05.64; 2017- 13:14.09, 26:50.60; 2018- 13:36.97, 28:11.41; 2019- 13:06.10, 27:58.06A; 2020- 13:15.72i, 28:09.90A. pbs: 1500m 3:43.97 '10, 3000m 7:46.61 '16, HMar 62:48 '14.

Richard Kimunyan **YATOR** b. 6 Apr 1998 1.75m 57kg. Hitachi Distribution, Japan.
At 3000m: WY: '15- 1; Af-Y: '15- 2. At 5000m: AfG: '19- 3. World CC: '17- 3J, '19- 3.
Progress at 5000m, 10000m: 2016- 13:51.3A, 2017- 13:22.66, 27:52.10; 2018- 12:50.44, 27:14.70; 2019- 13:09.79, 27:47.86A; 2020- 13:18.76, 27:01.42. pbs: 3000m 7:45.78 '19, 2M 8:18.09 '19.

Julius Kiplangat **YEGO** b. 4 Jan 1989 Cheptonon, Nandi district 1.75m 90kg.
At JT: OG: '12- 11, '16- 2; WCh: '13- 15-17-19: 4//1/13/nt; CG: '10- 7, '14- 1, '18- dnq 13; AfG:

'11- 1, '19- 1; AfCh: '10-12-14-18: 3/1/1/1; CCp: '14- 4, '18- 6. Kenyan champion 2008-14, 2018.
Javelin records: Commonwealth & two African 2015, nine Kenyan 2011-15.
Progress at JT: 2008- 72.18A, 2009- 74.00A, 2010- 75.44, 2011- 78.34A, 2012- 81.81; 2013- 85.40, 2014- 84.72, 2015- 92.72, 2016- 88.24, 2017- 87.97, 2018- 80.91A, 2019- 87.73.
His winning throw at the 2015 Worlds was the world's best javelin throw since 2001.

Edward Pingua **ZAKAYO** b. 25 Nov 2001 1.73m 59kg.
At 5000m: CG: '18- 3; WJ: '18- 1; AfG: '19- 2; AfCh: '18- 1, Af-J: '19- 1. At 3000m: WY: '17- 2; CCp: '18- fa.
Progress at 5000m: 2017- 13:48.0A, 2018- 13:19.74A, 2019- 13:03.19. Pb 3000m 7:46.8+ '19.

Women

Valary Jemeli AIYABEI b. 8 Jun 1991 1.56m 42kg.
Progress at Mar: 2013- 2:39:47, 2014- 2:30:19, 2015- 2:31:57, 2016- 2:24:48, 2017- 2:20:53, 2018- 2:21:38, 2019- 2:19:10, 2020- 2:28:16. Road pbs: 10k 31:03 '19, 15k 46:44 '17, 20k 62:42 '19, HMar 66:14 '19, 25k 1:20:42 '17, 30k 1:36:48 '17.
Nine marathon wins including Beijing 2018 and Frankfurt 2019.

Alice APROT Nawowuna b. 2 Jan 1994 1.74m 55kg. Turkana.
At (5000m)/10000m: OG: '16- 4; WCh: '17- 4; WJ: '10- (3); AfG: '15- 3/1; AfCh: '16- 1, '18- 2. World CC: '10- 9J, '17- 2; AfCC: 14- 3. Won African & Kenyan CC 2016, KEN 10000m 2016-17.
Progress at 5000m, 10000m: 2010- 15:16.74, 2011- 16:36.8A, 2014- 16:22.8A, 2015- 15:31.82, 31:24.18; 2016- 14:39.56, 29:53.51; 2017- 31:11.86, 2018- 15:11.00, 31:36.12; 2019- 32:10.94A. pbs: 1500m 4:23.92 '14, 3000m 8:44.7 '16, 10M 51:59 '16.
Elder brother Joseph Ebuya won World CC in 2010, pb 5000m 12:51.00 '07.

Winny CHEBET b. 20 Dec 1990 1.65m 50kg.
At 800m: OG: '16- sf; WCh: '13- sf; CG: '10- 7, '18- h (fell); AfG: '15- 5 (2- 4x400m); AfCh: '10- 5; WJ: '06- 2, '08- 5; WY: '05- 2, '07- dq (for obstruction after 2nd); Af-J: '09- 2. At 1500m: WCh: '17- sf, '19- 7; AfCh: '18- 1; WI: '18- 5; CCp: '18- 1; won KEN 1500m 2018, W.MilG 2019.
Progress at 800m, 1500m: 2005- 2:08.15, 2006- 2:04.59, 2007- 2:04.10, 2008- 2:04.13, 2009- 2:01.36, 2010- 2:00.88A, 2011- 2:03.80A, 2012- 1:59.37, 4:16.0A; 2013- 1:59.30, 2015- 2:02.38A, 2016- 1:59.88, 4:02.66; 2017- 1:58.13, 3:59.16; 2018- 4:00.60, 2019- 3:58.20, 2020- 4:02.58. pbs: 1000m 2:35.73 '13, 1M 4:19.55 '17.

Fancy CHEMUTAI b. 20 Mar 1994 1.63m 52kg.
Progress at HMar: 2017- 65:36, 2018- 64:52, 2019- 66:48, 2020- 68:02. Road pbs: 5k 15:26 '19, 10k 30:09 '17, 15k 45:59 '17, 10M 49:30 '18, 20k 61:35 '18, HMar 64:52 '18, Mar 2:24:37 '20.
Won Ras Al Khaimah half marathon 2018.

Sheila CHEPKIRUI Kiprotich b. 27 Dec 1990 1.72m 52kg.
At 800m: Af-J: '09- 8; At 1500m: WJ: '08- h; WY: '05- 1, '07-31. At 5000m: WCh: '17- 7; AfCh '16- 1. AfCC: '16- 2.
Progress at 5000m: 2016- 15:05.45, 2017- 14:54.05, 2018- 15:23.69A, 2019- 15:23.69A, 2020- 16:14.36A. pbs: 800m 2:06.2A '15, 1500m 4:12.29 '05, 3000m 8:45.94 '17, 10000m 32:35.0A '17, road; 10k 29:46 '20, 15k 46:34 '20, 20k 62:15 '20, HMar 65:39 '20.

Beatrice CHEPKOECH Sitonik b. 6 Jul 1991 Bornet 1.71m 57kg.
At 3000mSt: OG: '16- 4; WCh: '17- 4, '19- 1; AfCh: '18- 1; CCp: '18- 1; won DL 2018-19 At 1500m: CG: '18- 2; AfG: '15- 3; WI: '18- 7. World CC: '17- 1 mxR, '19- 7. Won KEN 1500m 2017, 3000mSt 2018; WIT 1500m 2018.
World records 3000mSt 2018, 5k road 14:43 2021.
Progress at 1500m, 3000mSt: 2011- 10:41.3A, 2013- 4:16.6A, 2014- 4:12.37A, 2015- 4:03.28, 2016- 4:18.0A, 9:10.86; 2017- 8:59.84, 2018- 8:44.32, 2019- 4:07.82A, 8:55.58; 2020- 9:10.07. pbs: 800m 2:05.73 '15, 1000m 2:44.44 '20, 1500m 4:02.09i '20, 4:03.09 '18; 3000m 8:22.92 '20, 5000m 14:39.33 '17, 10000m 33:15.72A '19, 2000mSt 6:02.47 '15.
4th in 2017 Worlds despite missing the water jump after the first lap and having to run back to clear it and also later falling. Took 8.46 recs off the world record for the steeplechase in an astonishing run at Monaco 2018.

Ruth CHEPNGETICH b. 8 Aug 1994 West Pokot 1.68m 49kg.
At Mar: WCh: '19- 1; World HMar: '18- 13.
Progress at HMar, Mar: 2016- 64:13A, 2017- 66:19, 2:22:36; 2018- 67:02, 2:18:35; 2019- 65:29, 2:17:08; 2020- 65:06, 2:22:05. pbs: 10k 30:33 '19, 15k 46:15 '20, 20k 61:44 '20, 30k 1:37:16 '19.
Marathon wins: Istanbul 2017 & 2018, Dubai 2019, 2nd Paris 2018, 3rd London 2020.

Gladys Kiprono **CHERONO** b. 12 May 1983 Kericho 1.66m 50kg.
At 10000m: WCh: '13- 2; AfCh: '12- 1 (1 5000m). World HMar: '14- 1. Won Kenyan 5000m 2012.
Progress at 5000m, 10000m, Mar: 2005- 16:16.8A, 2007- 16:03.8A, 2008- 15:56.0A, 2012- 15:39.5A, 32:41.40; 2013- 14:47.12, 30:29.23; 2014- 16:49.8A, 34:13.0A; 2015- 15:50.3A, 32:24.10A, 2:19:25; 2017- 2:20:23, 2018- 2:18:11, 2019- 2:20:52; pbs: 1500m 4:25.13 '04, 3000m 8:34.05 '13, Road: 15k 47:43 '13, 20k 63:26 '13, HMar 66:07 '16, 25k 1:21:52 '18, 30k 1:38:04 '18.
Second Dubai Marathon (2:20:03, third fastest ever debut) and won Berlin in 2015, 2017-18. Married to Joseph Bwambok (62:25 HMar 2010).

Vivian Jepkemoi **CHERUIYOT** b. 11 Sep 1983 Keiyo district 1.55m 38kg. Police.
At 5000m (/10000m): OG: '04- 14, '08- 4, '12- 2/3, '16- 1/2; WCh: '07- 2, '09- 1, '11- 1/1, '15- (1); CG: '10- 1; WJ: '02- 3; AfG '99- 3; AfCh: '10- 1; Af-J: '01- 1; CCp: '10- 1; won DL 2010-12. At 3000m:

KENYA 117

WY: '99- 3; WI: '10- 2. World CC: '98-9-00-01-02-04-06-07-11: 5J/2J/1J/4J/3J/8 4k/8 4k/8/1. Won KEN 1500m 2009, 5000m 2010-11, 10000m 2011-12. Records: African 2000m 2009, Commonwealth 5000m 2009 & 2011, 10000m 2016, indoor 3000m (8:30.53) 2009; Kenyan 5000m 2007 & 2011, 10000m 2016.
Progress at 5000m, 10000m: 1999- 15:42.79A, 2000- 15:11.11, 2001- 15:59.4A, 2002- 15:49.7A, 2003- 15:44.8A, 2004- 15:13.26, 2006- 14:47.43, 2007- 14:22.51, 2008- 14:25.43, 2009- 14:37.01, 2010- 14:27.41, 2011- 14:20.87, 10:30:48.98; 2012- 14:35.62, 30:30.44; 2015- 14:46.69, 31:13.29; 2016- 14:26.17, 29:32.53. At Mar: 2017- 2:23:35, 2018- 2:18:31, 2019- 2:18:52. pbs: 1500m 4:06.6A '12, 4:06.65 '07; 2000m 5:31.52 '09, 3000m 8:28.66 '07, 2M 9:12.35i '10, 10M Rd 51:17 '15, HMar 66:34 '19, 25k 1:21:56 '18, 30k 1:38:19 '18.
Laureus Sportswomen of the Year for 2011. Married Moses Kiplagat on 14 Apr 2012; son Allan Kiprono Kiplagat born 19 Oct 2013. Won Great North Run on half marathon debut 2016 and again in 2018, and 4th London on marathon debut 2017, then 1st Frankfurt, 1st London & 2nd New York 2018, 2nd London 2019.

Celliphine Chepteek **CHESPOL** b. 23 Mar 1999 Bungoma 1.65m 49kg.
At 3000mSt: WCh: '17- 6, '19- dnf; CG: '18- 2; AfCh: '18- 2; WJ: '16- 1, '18- 1; At 2000mSt: WY: '15- 1, World CC: 17- 3J, AfCC: '18- 1.
Two World junior records 3000mSt 2017.
Progress at 3000mSt: 2015- 10:18.3A, 2016- 9:24.73, 2017- 8:58.78, 2018- 9:01.82, 2019- 9:06.76. pbs: 800m 2:06.48A '17, 1500m 4:11.1A '17, 10kRd 31:42 '19, 2000mSt 6:17.15 '15.

Evaline CHIRCHIR b. 10 May 1998 1.66m 48kg.
Progress at 10000m: 2016- 34:31.7A, 2018- 72:26, 2019- 32:06.74A, 66:22; 2020- 31:08.09, 66:01. pbs: Road: 10k 30:43 '19, 15k 46:13 '20, 10M 50:32 '19, 20k 62:34 '20.

Peres JEPCHIRCHIR b. 27 Sep 1993 Usain Gishu 1.53m 40kg.
World HMar: '16- 1, '20- 1. World records 20k and HMar 2017, two women only HMar 2020.
Progress at HMar, Mar: 2014- 69:12, 2015- 67:17, 2016- 66:39, 2017- 65:06, 2018- 2:46:15A, 2019- 66:54, 2:23:50; 2020- 65:16, 2:17:16. pbs: Road: 10k 30:47 '20, 15k 46:24 '20, 20k 61:40 '17, 25k 1:21:47 '20, 30k 1:38:07 '20.
10 wins in 13 half marathons 2014-20, inc. RAK 2017. Won Valencia Marathon 2020. Married to David Ngeno. Baby born 2018.

Daisy JEPKEMEI b. 13 Feb 1996 1.67m 50kg.
At 3000mSt: WJ: '12- 1, '14 - 3. At 2000mSt: WY: '13- 2, Af-Y: '13- 1 (2 3000m); World CC: '15- 4J, '16- 5.
Progress at 3000mSt: 2012- 9:47.22, 2014- 9:47.65, 2015- 9:38.16, 2016- 10:02.04A, 2017- 9:19.68, 2018- 9:10.71, 2019- 9:06.66. pbs: 1500m 4:26.96i '19, 3000m 8:52.16 '19, 5000m 14:51.72 '19, 10k Rd

118 KENYA

32:05 '18, 31:01dh '19. Sister of Norah Tanui.
Hyvin Kiyeng **JEPKEMOI** b. 13 Jan 1992 1.56m 45kg.
At 3000mSt: OG: '16- 2; WCh: '13-15-17-19: 6/1/3/8; AfG: '11- 1 (4 5000m); AfCh: '12- 3. Kenyan champion 2015. World CC: '17- 4.
African and Commonwealth 3000m steeplechase record 2016.
Progress at 3000mSt: 2011- 10:00.50, 2012- 9:23.53, 2013- 9:22.05, 2014- 9:22.58, 2015- 9:10.15, 2016- 9:00.01, 2017- 9:00.12, 2018- 9:01.60, 2019- 9:03.83, 2020- 9:06.14. pbs: 1500m 4:19.4A '17, 4:19.44 '11; 2000m 5:40.3+ '20, 3000m 8:25.13 '20, 5000m 15:35.40A '19, 10000m 35:14.0A '14.
Joyciline JEPKOSGEI b. 8 Dec 1993 Cheptil, Nandi 1.56m 52kg.
At 10000m: AfCh: '16- 3. At HMar: WCh: '18- 2, '20- 6 World road records in Prague Half Marathon 2017: 10k 30:04, 15k 45:37, 20k 1:01:25, HMar 1:04.52, improving at 10k to 29:43 in September and half marathon to 64:51 at Valencia in October 2017.
Progress at HMar, Mar: 2015- 74:06A, 2016- 69:07, 2017- 64:51, 2018- 66:46, 2019- 2:22:28, 2020- 65:58, 2:18:40. pbs: 5000m 15:19.1A '19, 10000m 31:28.38 '16, Road: 10k 29:43 '17, 15k 45:37 '17, 20k 61:25 '17, 25k 1:21:48 '20, 30k 1:38:07 '20.
Won in New York on marathon debut 2019, 2nd Valencia 2020. Married to Nicholas Koech (10k Rd 28:39 '07), son Brandon born 2011. Member of the RunCzech Running Team from 2014.
Pauline Kaveke **KAMULU** b. 30 Dec 1994 Machakos county 1.54m 45kg.
World HMar: '18- 3, World CC: '13- 11J; AfCC: '16- 7.
Progress at 10000m, HMar: 2010- 35:37.83A, 2011- 75:20, 2012- 68:37, 2015- 69:44, 2016- 31:56.70, 72:52; 2017- 31:47.13, 68:04; 2018- 30:41.83, 66:56; 2019- 31:45.04, 68:34. pbs: 3000m 8:46.97 '19, 5000m 14:58.82 '17, Road: 15k 47:34 '18, 20k 63:33 '18, 3000mSt 10:29.73A '11.
Mary Jepkosgei **KEITANY** b. 18 Jan 1982 Kisok, Kabarnet 1.58m 45kg.
At Mar: OG: '12- 4. World HMar: '07- 2, '09- 1. Records: World 25km 2010, 10M, 20km, half marathon 2011, 30km 2017, women's only marathon 2017. HMar: African and Kenyan (2) 2009, marathon: African 2012 & 2017. Commonwealth 25k 1:19:43 & 30k 1:36:05 '17. World W35 HMar 2017 & 2018, 30k & Mar 2017.
Progress at HMar, Mar: 2000- 72:53, 2002- 73:01, 2003- 73:25, 2004- 71:32, 2005- 70:18, 2006- 69:06, 2007- 66:48, 2009- 66:36, 2010- 67:14, 2:29:01; 2011- 65:50, 2:19:19; 2012- 66:49, 2:18:37; 2014- 65:39dh, 2:25:07; 2015- 66:02, 2:23:40; 2016- 68:53, 2:24:26; 2017- 65:13, 2:17:01; 2018- 64:55, 2:22:48; 2019- 67:58, 2:20:58. pbs: 1500m 4:24.33 '99, 10000m 32:18.07 '07; Road: 5k 15:25 '11, 10k 30:45 '11, 15k 46:40 '11, 10M 50:05 '11, 20k 61:34 '18, 25k 1:19:43dh '17, 30k 1:36:05 '17.

17 wins and 3 seconds in 21 half marathons 2006-19 (13 successive wins 2009-16) inc. Great North Run 2014-15 and 2017, RAK 2011-12, 2015. Marathons: won London 2011-12, 2017 (2nd 2015), New York 2014-16, 2018 (2nd 2017 & 2019, 3rd 2010-11). Won World Marathon Majors 2011/12, 2015/16 & 2017/18. Married to Charles Koech (pbs 10k 27:56 & HMar 61:27 '07), son Jared Kipchumba born in June 2008 and daughter Samantha on 5 Apr 2013.
Margaret Chelimo **KIPKEMBOI** b. 9 Feb 1993 1.62m 45kg.
At 5000m: WCh: '17- 5, '19- 2; CG: '18- 2; AfG '15-1; AfCh '16- 2. At 800m: WY: '09- h. World CC: '15- 13; AfCC: '17- 2.
Progress at 5000m, 10000m: 2014- 16:02.19A, 2015- 15:28.6A, 2016- 14:47.24, 31:16.38; 2017- 14:32.82, 2018- 15:01.98, 2019- 14:27.49, 32:04.67A. pbs: 1500m 4:10.8A '17, 2000m 5:40.2+ '20, 3000m 8:24.76 '20, 10kRd 30:42 '20.
Edna Ngeringwony **KIPLAGAT** b. 15 Nov 1979 Eldoret 1.71m 54kg. Corporal in Kenyan Police.
At Mar: OG: '12- 19; WCh: '11-13-15-17-19: 1/1/5/2/4. At 3000m: WJ: '96- 2, '98- 3. World CC: '96-97-06: 5J/4J/13. African record 30km 2008.
Progress at Mar: 2005- 2:50:20, 2010- 2:25:38, 2011- 2:20:46, 2012- 2:19:50, 2013- 2:21:32, 2014- 2:20:21, 2015- 2:27:16, 2016- 2:22:36, 2017- 2:21:52dh, 2018- 2:21:18, 2019- 2:24:13dh. pbs: 3000m 8:53.06 '96, 5000m 15:57.3A '06, 10000m 33:27.0A '07; Road: 5k 15:20 '10, 10k 31:06 '16, 15k 47:57 '10, 10M 54:56 '09, HMar 67:41 '12, 25k 1:21:58 '18, 30k 1:38:23 '18.
Won Los Angeles and New York Marathons 2010, London 2014 (2nd 2011-13), Boston 2017 (2nd 2019); 2nd Chicago & 3rd Tokyo 2016. Won World Marathon Majors 2010/11, 2013/14, 2016/17. Married to Gilbert Koech (10000m 27:55.30 '01, 10k 27:32 '01, Mar 2:13:45 dh '05, 2:14:39 '09); two children.
Florence Jebet **KIPLAGAT** b. 27 Feb 1987 Kapkitony, Keiyo district 1.55m 42kg.
At 5000m: WJ: '06- 2. At 10000m: WCh: '09- 11; CG: '14- 2. World CC: '07- 5, '09- 1; HMar: '10- 1. Won Kenyan 1500m 2007, 10000m 2014, CC 2007 & 2009.
World records 20k and half marathon 2014 & 2015, 15k 2015. Kenyan 10000m record 2009.
Progress at 5000m, 10000m, HMar, Mar: 2006- 15:32.34, 2007- 14:40.74, 31:06.20; 2009- 14:40.14, 30:11.53; 2010- 14:52.64, 32:46.99A, 67:40; 2011- 68:02, 2:19:44; 2012- 30:24.85, 66:38, 2:20:57; 2013- 67:13, 2:21:13; 2014- 31:48.6A, 65:12, 2:20:24; 2015- 65:09, 2:23:33; 2016- 69:19, 2:21:32; 2017- 68:15, 2:26:25; 2018- 2:26:08, 2019- 2:21:50. pbs: 1500m 4:09.0A '07, 3000m 8:40.72 '10, Road: 15k 46:14 '15, 20k 61:54 '15, 30k 1:39:11 '14.
Won half marathon debut in Lille in 2010, followed a month later by World title. Did not

finish in Boston on marathon debut in 2011; won Berlin 2011 and 2013; Chicago 2015-16 (2nd 2014), 2nd London 2014 (3rd 2016). Formerly married to Moses Mosop, daughters Faith and Aisha Chelagat (born April 2008). Niece of William Kiplagat (Mar 2:06:50 '99, 8 WCh '07).
Faith Chepngetich **KIPYEGON** b. 10 Jan 1994 Bornet 1.57m 42kg.
At 1500m: OG: '12- h, '16- 1; WCh: '13-15-17-19: 5/2/1/2; CG: '14- 1; AfCh: '14- 5; WJ: '12- 1; WY: '11- 1. Won DL 2017. World CC: '10-11-13-17: 4J/1J/1J/6; AfCC: '12- 1J, '14- 1.
Records: World 4x1500m 2014, African junior 1500m 2013, African & Commonwealth 1M 2015, Kenyan & Commonwealth 1500m (4) 2013-19, 1000m 2020.
Progress at 800m, 1500m, 5000m: 2010- 4:17.1A, 2011- 2:09.1A, 4:09.48; 2012- 2:03.9A, 4:03.82; 2013- 2:02.8A; 3:56.98, 2014- 3:58.01, 2015- 1:58.02, 3:59.32, 14:31.95; 2016- 3:56.41, 2017- 3:57.04, 2019- 3:54.22, 2020- 1:57.68, 3:59.05. pbs: 2:29.15 '20, 1M 4:16.71 '15, 2000m 5:37.8+ '14, 3000m 8:23.55 '14. Married to **Timothy Kitum** (b. 20 Nov 1994) 800m 3 OG 2013, 2 WJ 2012, 3 WY 2011, 1:43.65 '14. Gave birth to daughter Alyn in June 2017. Sister **Beatrice Mutai** (b. 19 Apr 1987) 11 World CC 2013, 10000m 31:49.81 '18, HMar 69:30 '14.

Purity Cherotich **KIRUI** b. 13 Aug 1991 Kericho 1.62m 47kg.
At 3000mSt: WCh: '17- 10; CG: '14- 1, '18- 3; AfG: '15- 3; AfCh: '14- 6; WJ: '10- 1; Won KEN 2014-15. Progress at 3000mSt: 2008- 10:27.19A, 2009- 10:05.1A, 2010- 9:36.34, 2011- 9:37.85, 2012- 9:35.61, 2013- 9:19.42, 2014- 9:23.43, 2015- 9:17.74, 2016- 9:22.47, 2017- 9:20.07, 2018- 9:21.34. pbs: 800m 2:07.6A '14, 1500m 4:31.83 '08, 5000m 16:13.42 '11. Sister of **Kipyegon Bett** (800m 1:43.76 '16, 1 WJ 2016, 3 WCh 2017, 4-year drugs ban from 24 Feb 2018).

Brigid Jepcheschir **KOSGEI** b. 20 Feb 1994 Kapsait 1.61m 46kg.
World record marathon (& 25k and 30k) and world best half marathon (64:28 to win Great North Run, and 10M 49:21, 20k 61:20) in 2019.
Progress at HMar, Mar: 2015- 2:47:59, 2016- 74:08, 2:24:45, 2017- 66:35, 2:20:22; 2018- 66:49, 2:18:35; 2019- 64:28dh/65:28, 2:14:04; 2020- 2:18:58. Pbs 1Hr 18,930m (dq) '20; Road: 5k 15:39 '19, 10k 30:53 '19, 29:54dh '18; 15k 45:40 '20, 10M 49:21dh '19, 20k 61:20dh '19, 61:29 '20; 25k 1:19:33 '19, 30k: 1:35:18 '19.
Marathon wins: Chicago 2018-19 (2nd 2017), London 2019-20 (2nd 2018), Honolulu 2016-17, Milan 2016. Ran second half of London 2019 in 66:42, fastest ever. Married to Mathew Mitei, daughter Faith Jepchumba born 2014.

Hellen Onsando **OBIRI** b. 13 Dec 1989 Nyangusu, Kisii 1.60m 50kg. Air Force sergeant
At 1500m: OG: '12- 8; WCh: '11- 10 (fell), '13- 3; CG: '14- 6; AfCh: '14- 1; CCp: '14- 4. At 3000m: CCp: '18- 3; WI: '12-14-18: 1/2/4; won WIT 2017. At 5000m: OG: '16- 2; WCh: '17- 1, '19- 1 (5 10000m); CG: '18- 1; AfCh: '18- 1; won DL 2017- 18. World CC: '19- 1. Won KEN 1500m 2011-14.
Records: Two world 4x1500m 2014. African & Commonwealth 3000m 2014, Commonwealth 1M & 5000m 2017, 1M 2018.
Progress at 1500m, 5000m, 10000m: 2011- 4:02.42, 2012- 3:59.68, 16:15.1A, 2013- 3:58.58, 15:49.7A; 2014- 3:57.05, 2016- 3:59.34, 14:25.78; 2017- 4:00.44, 14:18.37; 2018- 3:58.88, 14:21.75; 2019- 14:20.36, 30:35.82; 2020- 4:10.53, 14:22.12. pbs: 800m 2:00.54 '11, 1000m 2:46.00i '12, 1M 4:16.15 '18, 2000m 5:34.83 '17, 3000m 8:20.68 '14, 10k Rd 29:58dh '18. Daughter born in May 2015.

Lilian Kasait **RENGERUK** b. 3 May 1997 1.61m 44kg.
At 5000m: WCh: '19- 5; AfG: '19- 1; AfCh: '18- 5; At 3000m: WJ: '14- 2; WY: '13- 1. World CC: '17- 3, '19- 12 Won KEN 5000m 2017.
Progress at 5000m: 2015- 16:04.61A, 2017- 14:36.80, 2018- 15:01.15, 2019- 14:36.05. pbs: 800m 2:07.6A '17, 1500m 4:22.20 '19, 3000m 8:29.02 '19.

Betsy SAINA b. 30 Jun 1988 Sokosik, Nandi 1.63m 48kg. Bowerman TC, USA. Graduate of Iowa State University, USA
At 10000m: OG: '16- 5; WCh: '15- 8; AfCh: '12- 3. At 3000m: WI: '16- 7. Won NCAA indoor 5000m & CC 2012, 10000m 2013.
Progress at 5000m, 10000m, Mar: 2009- 16:15.74, 36:34.94; 2010- 16:10.69, 33:13.13; 2011- 15:50.74i/16:06.05, 33:13.87; 2012- 15:36.09i, 31:15.97; 2013- 15:12.05, 31:37.22; 2014- 14:39.49, 30:57.30; 2015- 15:00.48, 31:51.35; 2016- 14:44.67, 30:07.78; 2018- 2:22:56, 2019- 2:22:43. pbs: 1M 4:40.98i '13, 2000m 5:45.7 '14, 3000m 8:38.01 '14, 2M 9:16.95 '14, Rd 10k 30:46 '14, 10M 51:55 '14, HMar 67:49 '19, 67:22 short '16. Won Paris marathon 2018.

Eunice Jepkoech **SUM** b. 2 Sep 1988 Burnt Forest, Uasin Gishu 1.72m 53kg. Police.
At 800m: OG: '16- sf; WCh: '11-13-15-19: sf/1/3/5; CG: '14- 1; AfCh: '10- h,'12- 2, '14- 1; CCp: '14- 1; won DL 2013-15. At 1500m: OG: '12- h, Won Kenyan 800m 2012, 2014.
World 4x1500m record 2014, Commonwealth & African 4x800m 2014.
Progress at 800m, 1500m: 2009- 2:07.4A, 2010- 2:00.28, 2011- 1:59.66A, 4:12.41; 2012- 1:59.13, 4:04.26; 2013- 1:57.38, 4:02.05; 2014- 1:57.92, 4:01.54; 2015- 1:56.99, 4:09.7A; 2016- 1:57.47, 4:21.3A; 2017- 1:57.78, 4:13.2A; 2018- 1:59.25, 4:05.38; 2019- 1:58.99A, 2020- 2:02.42. pb 3000m 8:53.12 '12. Daughter Diana Cheruto born 2008.

Norah Jeruto **TANUI** b. 2 Oct 1995 1.71m 57kg. At 3000mSt: AfCh: '16- 1. At 2000mSt: WY: '11- 1. Progress at 3000mSt: 2011- 9:45.1A, 2013- 10:11.4, 2014- 10:01.71A, 2015- 9:55.44, 2016- 9:25.07, 2017- 9:03.70, 2018- 8:59.62, 2019- 9:03.71. pbs: 1500m 4:19,09i '121 4:30.0A '17; 3000m 8:33.61 '18, 5000m 14:51.73 '19, 10kRd 29:51 '20, 2000mSt

6:16.41 '11.
Sister of Daisy Jepkemei.
Agnes Jebet **TIROP** b. 23 Oct 1995 Nandi, Chesumei 1.65m 50kg.
At 5000m: WJ: '12- 3, '14- 3; At 10000m: WCh: '17- 3, '19- 3; AfG: '15- 5. World CC: '13-15-17: 2J/1/5; AfCC: '12- 2J, '14- 1J. Won KEN 10000m 2019.
Progress at 5000m, 10000m: 2011- 16:09.0A, 2012- 15:36.74, 2013- 14:50.36, 2014- 15:00.19, 2015- 32:55.41, 2016- 15:02.67, 2017- 14:33.09, 31:03.50; 2018- 14:24.24, 2019- 14:20.68, 30:25.20; 2020- 15:06.71A. pbs: 1500m 4:12.68 '13, 2000m 5:48.65 '13, 3000m 8:22.92 '20, 10k Rd 30:50 '18, 30:22dh '19; 3000mSt 10:27.4A '12.
Margaret Nyairera **WAMBUI** b. 15 Sep 1995 Endarasha 1.75m 66kg.
At 800m: OG: '16- 3; WCh: '15- h, '17- 4; CG: '18- 2; AfCh: '18- dnf; WJ: '14- 1; WI: '16- 3. At 400m: AfCh: '16- 2/3R. Won KEN 800m 2017.
Progress at 800m: 2014- 2:00.49, 2015- 2:01.32, 2016- 1:56.89, 2017- 1:56.87, 2018- 1:58.07, 2019- 2:00.61. pbs: 200m 24.1A '17, 400m 51.39A/51.97 '16, 600m 1:27.1 '16.
Rosemary Monicah **WANJIRU** b. 9 Dec 1994 1.59m 44kg. Starts Corp., Japan.
At 5000m: AfG: '15- 2; won JPN 2014. At 10000m: WCh: '19- 4. At HMar: WCh: '20- 10.
Progress at 5000m, 10000m: 2011- 15:26.07mx, 2012- 15:40.35, 2013- 15:30.41, 2014- 15:19.00, 2015- 15:15.42, 2016- 15:15.14, 2017- 15:09.68, 31:41.23; 2018- 15:08.61, 32:59.3A; 2019- 30:25.75, 2020- 15:93.49, 30:38.18. pbs: 1500m 4:09.90 '13, 3000m 8:44.24 '18; Road: 10k 29:50 '20, 15k 46:14 '20, 20k 62:10 '20, HMar 65:34 '20.

LATVIA

Governing body: Latvian Athletic Association. Founded 1921.
National Championships first held in 1920 (men), 1922 (women). **2020 Champions: Men:** 100m: Emils Kristofers Jonäss 10.74, 200m: Ilja Petrusenko 21.90, 400m: Arturs Pazters 47.39, 800m: Maksims Sincukovs 1:50.06, 1500m: Janis Razgalis 3:54.68, 5000m: Ugis Jocis 14:53.25/ 30:03.36, HMar: Dmitrijs Serjogins 68:25, 3000mSt: Alberts Blajs 9:09.75, 110mh: Kristaps Sunteiks 15.3, 400mh: Dmitrijs Lasenko 53.98, HJ: Rihards Vaivads 2.05, PV: Mareks Arents 5.10, LJ: Sandis Dzenitis 7.10w, TJ: Rinalds Smilga 14.57, SP: Maris Urtans 15.72, DT: Oskars Vaisjuns 49.29, HT: Igors Sokolovs 60.81, JT: Gatis Cakss 83.80, Dec: Niks Samauskis 6232, 10000mW: Raivo Saulgriezis 42:47.70, 20000mW: Ruslans Smolonskis 1:31:26. **Women**: 100m/200m: Sindija Buksa 11.73/23.73, 400m: Patricija Cirule 56.37, 800m: Liga Velvere 2:02.85, 1500m: Kamilla Vanadzina 4:33.26, 5000m/10000m/HMar: Karina Helmane-Sorocenkova 17:01.60/ 35:45.38/79:31, 3000mSt: Alina Sokunova 11:27.27, 100mh: Marta Marksa 13.97, 400mh: Madara Lungevica 62.67, HJ:

Lasma Zemite 1.80, PV: Ildze Bortascenoka 3.75, LJ/TJ: Ruta Lasmane 6.10/13.82, SP: Linda Ozola 14.18, DT: Inga Mikelsone 45.70, HT: Elva Vestarte 46.20, JT: Lina Muze 60.10, Hep: Kristine Siksaiete 5649, 10000mW/20kW: Modra Ignate 52:15.21/1:46:51.
Gatis CAKSS b. 13 Jun 1995 1.84m 93kg. LSPA.
At JT: WCh: '19- dnq 21; EC: '18- dnq 13; WJ: '14- 1; WY: '11- 8; EU23: '15- 10, '17- 8; EJ: '13- 12. Won LAT 2019-20.
Progress at JT: 2012- 65.18, 2013- 71.47, 2014- 77.26, 2015- 80.06, 2016- 78.45, 2017- 76.94, 2018- 83.89, 2019- 83.72, 2020- 84.56. Pb SP 14.26i '18

Women

Laura IKAUNIECE b. 31 May 1992 Jürmala 1.79m 60kg. Jürmalas SS.
At Hep: OG: '12- 7, '16- 4; WCh: '13- 11, '15- 3, '17- dnf; EC: '12- 2, '14- 6; WJ: '10- 6; WY: '09- 2; EJ: '11- 3; WUG: '13- 1. At Pen: EI: '19- 5; At 100mh: EC: '16- h. Won LAT 100m 2012-13, 200m 2009, 2013; 100mh & HJ 2010.
Six Latvian heptathlon records 2012-17.
Progress at Hep: 2010- 5618, 2011- 6063, 2012- 6414, 2013- 6321, 2014- 6320, 2015- 6516, 2016- 6622, 2017- 6815, 2018- 6574, 2019- 6518. Pbs: 60m 7.58i '16, 100m 11.78 '16, 200m 23.49 '17, 800m 2:09.43 '16, 60mh 8.29i '19, 100mh 13.07 '16, HJ 1.87 '19, LJ 6.64 '17, SP 14.23i '19, 14.03 '18; JT 56.32 '17, Pen 4701i '19.
Won IAAF Challenge 2015. Her mother Vineta Ikauniece set Latvian records at 100m 11.34A '87, 200m 22.49A '87 and 400m 50.71 '88, and her father Aivars Ikaunieks 110mh pb 13.71A '87 and 13.4 '84. Married Rolands Admidins in 2014.
Lina MUZE b. 4 Dec 1992 Smiltene 1.82m 75kg. Smiltene.
At JT: OG: '12- dnq 12; WCh: '13-19: dnq 14/27; EC: '12- 10, 14/16/18: dnq 19/nt/27; WJ: 10- 2; WY: '09- 6; EU23: '13- 1; EJ: '11- 2; WUG: '15- 2. Won LAT 2013, 2018, 2020.
Progress at JT: 2008- 46.03, 2009- 50.86, 2010- 56.64, 2011- 60.64, 2012- 61.04, 2013- 61.97, 2014- 58.02, 2015- 60.48, 2016- 62.09, 2017- 6055, 2018- 63.18, 2019- 64.87, 2020- 63.19.
Madara PALAMEIKA b. 18 Jun 1987 Valdemarpils 1.85m 76kg. Ventspils.
At JT: OG: '12- 8, '16- 10; WCh: '09-13-15-17-19: dnq 26/27/13/21/18, '11- 10; EC: '10-12-14-16-18: 7/8/4/7/9; WJ: '06- dnq 16; EU23: '07- 3, '09- 1; EJ: '05- dnq 17. Won DL 2016, LAT 2009-11, 2014- 15, 2017, 2019. Three Latvian JT records 2009-16.
Progress at JT: 2002- 42.31, 2003- 49.11, 2004- 51.50, 2005- 51.75, 2006- 54.19, 2007- 57.98, 2008- 53.45, 2009- 64.51, 2010- 62.02, 2011- 63.46, 2012- 62.74, 2013- 62.72, 2014- 66.15, 2015- 65.01, 2016- 58.17, 2017- 63.92, 2018- 62.98, 2019- 63.22, 2020- 58.91.

LITHUANIA

Governing body: Athletic Federation of

Lithuania. Founded 1921.
National Championships first held in 1921 (women 1922). 2020 Champions: Men: 100m/200m: Gediminas Truskauskas 10.37/20.83, 400m/800m: Benediktas Mickus 47.88/1:50.99, 1500m/5000m: Simas Bertasius 3:40.34/14:21.65, 10000m: Ignas Brasevicius 29:53.81, HMar: Valdas Dopolskas 69:57, Mar: Andrius Jaksevicius 2:26:00, 3000mSt: Giedrius Valincius 9:32.44, 110mh: Rapolas Saulius 13.99, 400mh: Arturas Janauskas 53.56, HJ: Adrijus Glebauskas 2.25, PV: Osvaldas Gedrimas 4.90, LJ: Tomas Lotuzis 7.38, TJ: Paulius Svarauskas 15.53, SP: Sarunas Banevicius 17.87, DT: Andrius Gudzius 68.16, HT: Tomas Vasiliuskas 62.76, JT: Edis Matusevicius 81.38, Dec: Edgaras Benkunskas 7643, 10kW: Marius Ziukas 40:44, 20kW: Artur Mastianica 1:22:55. Women: 100m: Karolina Deliautaite 11.68, 200m/400m: Agne Serksniene 23.43/52.29, 800m: Gabija Galvydyte 2:11.12, 1500m: Egle Morenaite 4:32.16, 5000m/10000m/HMar: Vaida Zusinaite 16:30.43/34:40.86/75:20, Mar: Diana Lobacevske 2:39:40, 3000mSt: Greta Karinauskaite 10:42.24, 100mh: Gabriele Ceponyte 14.00w, 400mh: Modesta Morauskaite 57.67, HJ: Urta Baikstyte 1.78, PV: Rugile Miklyciute 3.45, LJ: Jogaile Petrokaite 6.42, TJ: Dovilé Kilty 14.18, SP/DT: Ieva Zarankaité 16.80/60.99, HT: Klaudija Bieliasskaite 41.64, JT: Liveta Jasiunaite 60.27, Hep: Beatrice Juskeviciute 5687, 10kW/20kW: Brigita Virbalyte 45:37/1:30:54.

Andrius GUDZIUS b. 14 Feb 1991 Vilkija, Kaunas district 2.00m 130kg. COSMA.
At DT: OG: '16- 12; WCh: '15- dnq 14, '17- 1, '19- 12; EC: '12- 14-16-18: dnq 29/10/dnq 13/1; WJ: '08- 6, '10- 1; WY: '07- 3; EU23: '11- dnq 13, '13- 1; EJ: '09- 5; CCp: '18- 2; WUG: '15- 3. Won DL 2017, LTU 2013-14, 2017-20.
Progress at DT: 2008- 54.72, 2009- 57.17, 2010- 61.85, 2011- 58.50, 2012- 63.39, 2013- 62.40, 2014- 66.11, 2015- 65.51, 2016- 65.18/67.96dh, 2017- 69.21, 2018- 69.59, 2019- 67.73, 2020- 68.68.

Edis MATUSEVICIUS b. 30 Jun 1996 1.84m 79kg. Vilnius. COSMA, Lithuanian Sports University.
At JT: WCh: '17- dnq nt, '19- dnq 22; EC: '16: dnq 21, '18- 10; WJ: '14- 6; WY: '13- dnq 17; EU23: '17- 5; EJ: '13- dnq 21, '15- 3; WUG: '19- 2. Won LTU 2014-20. Three Lithuanian javelin records 2019.
Progress at JT: 2012- 59.69, 2013- 69.39, 2014- 71.52, 2015- 78.82, 2016- 81.28, 2017- 84.78, 2018- 82.67, 2019- 89.17, 2020- 81.38.
Mother Dalia Zaurite-Matuseviciene pbs 400m 51.12 '84, 800m 1:56.7 '88 still LTU record.
Father Edmuntas javelin pb 83.72 '81 old javelin & 76.92 '87)

Women

Airine PALSYTE b. 13 Jul 1992 Kaunas 1.86m 62kg. COSMA. Vilnius University.
At HJ: OG: '12- 11, '16- 13=; WCh: '13- 12, '15- dnq 14=, '17- 7=, '19- dnq 22; WJ: '08- dnq 23, '10- 2; WY: '09- 4; EC: '10-12-14-16-18: dnq 18/9/13/2/4; EJ: '11- 2; EU23: '13- 2; WUG: '11-15- 17: 2/1/3; WI: '16- 4; EI: '15-17-19: 4/1/3; won LTU 2010, 2012-18.
Three LTU high jump records 2011-14 and absolute records 2.00 & 2.01i 17.
Progress at HJ: 2003- 1.45, 2004- 1.40i, 2005- 1.60, 2006- 1.71, 2007- 1.70i/1.55, 2008- 1.80, 2009- 1.86i/1.83, 2010- 1.92, 2011- 1.96, 2012- 1.95, 2013- 1.95, 2014- 1.98, 2015- 1.98i/1.95, 2016- 1.97i/1.96, 2017- 2.01i/1.92, 2018- 1.96, 2019- 1.98i/1.90, 2020- 1.92i. pb 200m 24.78 '12, TJ 12.70i '12.

Brigita VIRBALYTE-DIMSIENE b. 1 Feb 1985 1.65m 50kg. née Virbalyte. Alytus.COSMA. National TV reporter/
At 20kW: OG: '12- 24, '16- 29; WCh: '09-11-13-15- 17: 23/25/18/7/16; EC: '10-14-18- 12/18/4; EU23: 07- 8; WCp: '18- 10; ECp: 17- 8. At 10000mW: WJ: '04- 9; EJ: '03- 4; ECp: '03- 5J. At 5000mW: WY: '01- 5. Won LTU 10kW 2007, 2010, 2012, 2014-18, 2020; 20kW 2009-11, 2013, 2016-18, 2020.
Lithuanian walks records: 10k 2007, 2010, 2012, 2015, 20k 2018, 50k 2010.
Progress at 20kW: 2005- 1:39:16, 2006- 1:38:59, 2007- 1:36:38, 2008- 1:34:36, 2009- 1:32:08, 2010- 1:32:17, 2011- 1:33:24, 2012- 1:31:08, 2013- 1:30:55, 2014- 1:31:00, 2015- 1:30:20, 2016- 1:30:48, 2017- 1:30:45, 2018- 1:27:59, 2019- 1:31:25, 2020- 1:30:54.
pbs: 3000mW 12:05.72 '18, 5000mW 21:17.8 '14, 10kW 42:43 '15, 44:18.53t '20; 50kW 4:25:22 '10.

LUXEMBOURG

Governing body: Fédération Luxembourgeoise d'Athlétisme. Founded 1928.
2020 National Champions: Men: 100m: Pol Bidaine 11.01, 200m/400m: Philippe Hilger 22.22/50.18, 800m: Vivien Henz 1:56.19, 1500m/5000m: Bob Bertemes 4:09.47/15:04.77, 3000mSt: Luc Scheller 9:59.89, 110mh: Pit Steinmetz 16.53, HJ: Quentin Bebon 1.97, PV: Joe Seil 4.50, LJ: Nils Liefgen 6.76, TJ: Louis Müller 13,86, SP: Bob Bertemes 20.33, DT: Valentin Mol 50.97, HT: Konstantin Moill 56.71, JT: Jon Novak 50.84, Dec: Sven Liefgen 4791. Women: 100m/ 200m: Patrizia Ven Der Weken 11.90/24.86, 400m/400mh: Chloé Schmidt 58.17/63.33, 800m: Fanny Arendt 2:13.62, 1500m: Vera Hoffmann 4:24.56, 5000m: Martine Mellina 17:32.06, 3000mSt: Liz Weiler 11:39.96, 100mh/LJ: Marie Damit 15.42/5.36, HJ: Mia Bourscheid 1.55, TJ: Elsa Blond Hanten 10.73, SP: Ann Bertemes 12.54, DT: Nadine Kremer 35.02,, HT: Géraldine Davin 46.06, JT: Noémie Pleimling 57.46.

Bob BERTEMES b. 24 May 1993 Luxembourg 1.87m 117kg. CAB.
At SP: WCh: '15-17-19:- dnq 14/31/26; EC: '16: dnq 16, '18- 6; EU23: '13- dnq 13, '15- 2; WJ: '13- nt; EJ: 11- dnq 23; EI: 15- 5, '19- 5. LUX champion 2011, 2013-15, 2017-19.
22 LUX shot records 2011-19, discus (2) 2019.

Progress at SP: 2010- 14.36, 2011- 16.96, 2012- 17.70, 2013- 18.78, 2014- 19.36, 2015- 20.56i/19.87, 2016- 20.14, 2017- 20.63i/20.18, 2018- 21.00, 2019- 22.22, 2020- 21.26. Pb DT 61.06 '19

MOLDOVA
Governing Body: Federatia de Atletism din Republica Moldova. Founded 1991.
Serghei MARGHIEV b. 6 Nov 1992 Vladikavkaz, North Osetia, Russia 1.94m 99kg.
At HT: OG: '12- dnq 28, '16- 10; WCh: '15- dnq 23, '17- 8, '19- dnq 16; EC: '14-16-18: 9/8/7; WJ: '10- dnq 14; WY: '09- dnq 28; EU23: '13- 5; EJ: '11- 2; WUG: '15- 4, '17- 3. Won Balkan 2013-14, MDA 2012-17. Four MDA HT records 2014-15
Progress at HT: 2011- 67.54, 2012- 75.20, 2013- 74.41, 2014- 78.27, 2015- 78.72, 2016- 78.48, 2017- 77.70, 2018- 76.81, 2019- 78.20, 2020- 75.70
Younger brother of Zalina (qv) and Marina.

Women
Zalina PETRIVSKAYA b. 5 Feb 1988 Vladikavkaz, North Osetia, Russia 1.74m 90kg. née Marghieva. AS-CSPLN.
At HT: OG: '08- dnq 35, '12- dq8, '16- 5; WCh: '09- dq dnq 26, '11- dq8, '15- 8, '17- dnq 19, '19- 4; EC: '10-12-16-18: dq5/dq8/5/6; WJ: '06- 4; WY: '05- 7; EU23: '09- 1; EJ: '07- 5; WUG: '11- dq1, '13- dq3. Won Balkan 2015-18, MDA 2016.
Ten Moldovan hammer records 2005-19 (and 3 disqualified).
Progress at HT: 2005- 61.80, 2006- 65.50, 2007- 65.40, 2008- 70.22, 2009- 71.56, 2015- 73.97, 2016- 74.21, 2017- 73.80, 2018- 72.80, 2019- 74.70; DQ: 2010- 71.50, 2011- 72.93, 2012- 74.47, 2013- 74.28.
Drugs ban announced in 2013 with all results annulled from 2009 Worlds to 2013. Sister **Marina** (now **Nikisenko**) (b. 28 Jun 1986) HT: 72.53 '09, seven MDA records 2007-09, OG: '08- 16: dnq/41/24; WCh: '09/11/15/17- dnq 32/17/25/27; EC: '10-12-16-18: 5/dnq 14/14/24; received a 3-year drugs ban from 24 July 2012.

MOROCCO
Governing Body: Fédération Royale Marocaine d'Athlétisme. Founded 1957.
Soufiane EL BAKKALI b. 7 Jan 1996 Fez 1.88m 70kg.
At 3000mSt: OG: '16- 4; WCh: '17- 2, '19- 3; WJ: '14- 4; AfG: '19- 3; AfCh: '14- 10, '18- 2; CCp: 18- fa; won MedG 2018. World CC: '19- 2 mxR.
Progress at 3000mSt: 2013- 8:52.00, 2014- 8:32.66, 2015- 8:27.79, 2016- 8:14.35, 2017- 8:04.83, 2018- 7:58.15, 2019- 8:03.76, 2020- 8:08.04. pbs: 1500m 3:33.45 '20, 2000m 5:00.55i '19, 3000m 7:41.88i '18, 7:49.68 '16, 5000m 13:10.60i '17, 13:47.76 '14.

Abdelaati IGUIDER b. 25 Mar 1987 Errachidia 1.70m 52kg.
At 1500m(/5000m): OG: '08- 5, '12- 3/6, '16- 5; WCh: '07-09-11-13-15-17-19: h/11/5/sf/3/sf;/sf WJ: '04- 1, '06- 4; AfG: '19- 3; AfCh: '18- 6; WI: '10-12-14-18: 2/1/3/3. At 3000m: WI: '16- 4. World CC: '19- 2 mxR.
Progress at 1500m, 5000m: 2004- 3:35.53, 2005- 3:35.63, 2006- 3:32.68, 2007- 3:32.75, 2008- 3:31.88, 2009- 3:31.47, 2010- 3:34:25, 2011- 3:31.60, 2012- 3:33.99, 13:09.17; 2013- 3:33.29, 2014- 3:29.83, 2015- 3:28.79, 12:59.25; 2016- 3:31.40, 13:08.61; 2017- 3:34.99, 2018- 3:31.59, 2019- 3:31.64, 13:17.74. pbs: 800m 1:46.67 '15, 1000m 2:19.14 '07, 1M 3:49.09 '14, 2000m 4:59.20 '16, 3000m 7:30.09 '16.

Women
Rabab ARRAFI b. 12 Jan 1991 Khourigba 1.77m 64kg. ASOAK.
At (800m)/1500m: OG: '16- h/12; WCh: '13- sf, '15- 4/9, '17- 8, '19- 7/9; AfG: '19 (2); AfCh: 12-14-16-18: 1/3/5&2/2; CCp: 18- 3; WI: '14- dq (3rd), '18- 8; won Is.Sol 2017. MedG 800m & 1500m 2018. At 3000m: WY: '07- 12. Won FrancG 2013, 2017. World CC: '19- 2 mxR.
Moroccan 1500m record 2018 & 2019.
Progress at 800m, 1500m: 2006- 24:21.59, 2011- 2:09.24, 2:04.60, 4:05.80; 2013- 2:00.58, 4:05.22; 2014- 2:03.18i, 4:02.71; 2015- 1:58.55, 4:02.94; 2016- 2:01.49, 4:03.95; 2017- 4:01.75, 2018- 1:57.94, 3:59.15; 2019- 2:00.02, 3:58.84; 2020- 2:02.46i, pbs: 1000m 2:38.11 '19, 1M 4:18.42 '19, 3000m 8:54.92i '19, 9:34.78 '07.

NAMIBIA
Helalia JOHANNES b. 13 Aug 1980 Mahikeng 1.65m 48kg. AGN.
At Mar: OG: '08- 40, 12- 11, '16- 56; WCh: '09-13-17-19: 55/dnf/19/3; CG: '14- 5, '18- 1. At HMar: WCh: '10-16; AfG: '11- 3. Won W.MilG 5000m 2019. NAM records: 5000m 2013, HMar (6) 2007-20, Mar (7) 2008-20. World W40 record 2020.
Progress at Mar: 2008- 2:32:30, 2009- 2:33:26, 2010- 2:34:34, 2011- 2:30:37, 2012- 2:26:09, 2013- 2:29:30, 2014- 2:28:27, 2016-2:32:32, 2017- 2:29:25, 2018- 2:29:28, 2019- 2:22:25, 2020- 2:19:59. Pbs: 5000m 15:44.53A '13, 10000m 34:00.90A '14, road: 10k 30:59 '19, HMar 68:10 '20, 25k 1:21:48 '20, 30k 1:38:31 '20. Won Dublin marathon 2011, 2016; Cape Town 2018, Nagoya 2019.

Beatrice MASILINGI b. 10 Apr 2003 1.72m 66kg.
African youth 200m record 2020 and Namibia records 100m (=), 200m (3) 2020.
Progress at 100m, 200m: 2019- 23.76, 2020- 22.94A/22.71Aw, 50.42A; 2021- 22.69Aw. Pb 100m 11.38A '20.

NETHERLANDS
Governing body: Koninklijke Nederlandse Atletiek Unie (KNAU). Founded 1901.
National Championships first held in 1910 (men), 1921 (women). **2020 Champions: Men**: 100m: 100m: Joris van Gool 10.17, 200m: Taymir Burnet 20.35w, 400m: Jochem Dobber 46.59, 800m: Djoao Lobles 1:50.40, 1500m: Richard Douna 3:45.43, 5000m/10000m: Mike Foppen 13:36.37/27:59.10, 3000mSt: Martin van der Horst 9:24.98,

110mh: Liam van der Schaaf 13.93, 400mh: Nick Smidt 51.12, HJ: Douwe Amels 2.06, PV: Menno Vloon 5.75, LJ:Anton Ediagbonya 7.38w, TJ: Fabian Florant 14.94, SP: Sven Poelmann 19.03, DT: Stephan Dekker 54.48, HT: Denzel Comenentia 70.53, JT: Jurriaan Wouters 76.09, Dec: Rik Taam 8031, 20000mW: Rick Liesting 1:31:31.9, 50kW: Paul Jansen 4:43:35. **Women**: 100m/100mh: Nadine Visser 11.25/13.10, 200m: Lieke Klaver 22.95, 400m: Andrea Bouma 53.87, 800m: Suzanne Voorrips 2:04.58, 1500m: Britt Ummels 4:20.13, 5000m: Diane van Es 15:44.50, 10000m: Jasmijn Lau 32:20.75, 3000mSt: Irene van der Reijken 9:46.09, 400mh: Cathelijn Peeters 60.32, HJ: Britt Weerman 12.86, PV: Femke Pluim 4.30, LJ: Anouk Vetter 6.24, TJ: Danielle Spek 12.66, SP: Jessica Schilder 18.27, DT: Jorinde van Klinken 56.54, HT: Wendy Koolhaas 64.77, JT: Lisanne Schol 59.53, Hep: Anne van de Wiel 5756, 10kW: Anne van Andel 56:42.

Pieter BRAUN b. 21 Jan 1993 Terheojden 1.86m 83kg. Sprint.
At Dec: OG: '16- dnf; WCh: '15- 12, '17- 16, '19- 7; EC: 16- 7, '18- 7; WJ: '12- 16; EU23: '13- 11, '15- 1.
Progress at Dec: 2013- 7540, 2014- 7892, 2015- 8197, 2016- 8058, 2017- 8334, 2018- 8342, 2019- 8306. pbs: 60m 7.20i '20, 100m 10.97 '15, 10.90w '17; 200m 22.15 '16, 400m 48.02 '15, 1000m 2:39.15i '20, 1500m 4:24.29 '18, 60mh 8.08i '16, 110mh 14.13 '15, HJ 2.05 '17, PV 5.05 '16, LJ 7.71 '17, SP 15.40i '21, 15.28 '18; DT 46.89 '19, JT 64.19 '19, Hep 6072i '20.

Menno VLOON b. 11 May 1994 Zaandam 1.77m 77kg. AY Lycurgus.
At PV: WCh: '17: dnq nh; EC: '16- dnq 17=; WJ: '12- dnq 17=; EU23: '15- 8; EI: '21- 5=; Won NED 2014-17, 2020. NED PV record 2017 & indoors 2021.
Progress at PV: 2011- 4.65, 2012- 5.19i/5.15, 2013- 5.32i/5.30, 2014- 5.40, 2015- 5.55, 2016- 5.58, 2017- 5.85, 2018- 5.70i/5.56, 2019- 5.71, 2020- 5.76, 2021- 5.96i. Pbs: 60m 7.01i '16, 100m 11.09 '12, 10.98w '18; 400m 52.31 '12, 1000m 2:58.09i '13, 1500m 5:09.78 '12, 60mh 8.04i '16, 110mh 14.10 '13, HJ 1.89 '13, LJ 7.65i, 7.76w '09, 7.65 '12; SP 14.67 '15, DT 43.38 '14, JT 63.59 '12, Hep 6372i '13.

Women

Femke BOL b. 23 Feb 2000 Amersfoort 1.78m 57kg. Altis.
At 400mh: WCh: '19- sf; EJ: '19- 1. At 400m: EJ: '17- sf; EI: '21 1/1R. Two Dutch 400mh records 2020, European U20 2019, Dutch 400m (5 indoors) 2021.
Progress at 400m, 400mh: 2015- 56.14, 2016- 54.95, 2017- 54.39, 2018- 54.33, 2019- 52.98, 55.32; 2020- 51.13, 53.79; 2021- 50.64i. pbs: 60m 7.73i '20, 200m 23.40 '20, 300mh 38.55 '20.

Nadine BROERSEN b. 29 Apr 1990 Hoorn 1.71m 62kg. AV Sprint Breda.
At Hep: OG: '12- 11, '16- 13; WCh: '13-15-17-19: 10/4/dnf/6; EC: '14- 2, '16- dnf; EU23: '11- 9; EJ: '09- 5; ECp: '14- 1. At Pen: WI: '14- 1; EI: '17- 5. Won NED HJ 2010-11, 2014; LJ 2015; JT 2013, 2018. Four Dutch high jump records 2013-14 and indoors 2014.
Progress at Hep: 2009- 5507, 2010- 5967, 2011- 5932(w)/5854, 2012- 6319, 2013- 6345, 2014- 6539, 2015- 6531, 2016- 6377, 2017- 6326, 2019- 6392. pbs: 200m 24.57 '14, 800m 2:11.11 '14, 60mh 8.32i '13, 100mh 13.39 '14, HJ 1.94 '14, LJ 6.39 '14, 6.40w '16; SP 14.93i '14, 14.82 '15; JT 54.97 '12, Pen 4830i '14. Lost c.200 points in stumbling at last hurdle in first event of 2013 World heptathlon. Won IAAF Combined Events Challenge 2014.

Sifan HASSAN b. '1 Jan' 1993 Adama, Ethiopia 1.70m 49kg. Eindhoven Atletiek.
At 1500m/(5000m): OG: '16- 5 (h 800m); WCh: '15- 3 (sf 800m), '17- 5/3, '19- 1 (1 10000m); EC: '14- 1/2, '16- 2, '18- (1); CCp: '14- 1; WI: '16- 1, '18- 3; EI: '15- 1. At 3000m: WI: '14- 5, '18- 2; CCp: '18- 1; ET: '14- 1. Eur CC: '13- 1 U23, '15- 1. Won DL 1500m 2015, 2019; 5000m 2019.
Records: World 1 mile 2019, 1 Hour 2020, road best 5k 14:44 '19, European 1500m 3000m 2019, 5000m 2018 & 2019, 10000m 2020, 15k, 20k & half marathon 2018, European U23 1500m (3) 2014-15, Dutch 1500m (6) 2014-19, 1M (3) 2015-19, 3000m (4) 2014-19, 5000m (4) 2014-19.
Progress at 800m, 1500m, 5000m, 10000m: 2011- 4:20.13, 2012- 4:08.74, 2013- 2:00.86, 4:03.73. 2014- 1:59.95, 3:57.00, 14:59.23; 2015- 1:58.50, 3:56.05; 2016- 2:00.27, 3:57.13; 2017- 1:56.81, 3:56.14, 14:41.24; 2018- 1:59.35, 3:57.41, 14:22.34; 2019- 3:51.95, 14:22.12, 30:17.62; 2020- 14:37.85, 29:36.67. pbs: 1000m 2:34.68 '15, 1M 4:12.33 '19, 2000m 5:46.1 '14, 5:37e '19; 3000m 8:18.49 '19, 1Hr 18,930m; Road: 15k 46:09 '18, 20k 61:56 '18, HMar 65:15 '18. Came to the Netherlands as a refugee at age 15. Dutch eligibility 29 Nov 2013.

Susan KRUMINS b. 8 Jul 1986 Nijmegen 1.72m 54kg. née Kuijken. Zevenheuvelen. Was at Florida State University, USA.
At 5000m/(10000m): OG: '16- 8/14; WCh: '13- 8, '15- 8/10, '17- 8/5, '19- (7); EC: '14- 3, '16- 4, '18- 6/2. At 1500m: WCh: '09- h; EC: '10- h; EU23: '07- 4. At 3000m: WJ: '04- dnf; EJ: '05- 2; CCp: '14- 3. Eur CC: '05- 3J, '08- 1 U23, '18- 4. Won NED 1500m 2014, 5000m 2016; NCAA 1500m 2009.
Progress at 5000m, 10000m: 2003- 16:41.31, 2006- 16:20.30, 2009- 16:31.68, 2013- 15:04.36, 2014- 15:32.82, 2015- 15:07.38, 31:31.97; 2016- 15:00.69, 31:32.43; 2017- 14:51.25, 31:20.24; 2018- 15:09.65, 31:52.55; 2019- 31:05.40. pbs: 800m 2:02.24 '09, 1000m 2:38.01 '14, 1500m 4:02.25 '17, 1M 4:34.11i '09, 2000m 5:38.37 '13, 3000m 8:34.41 '17 , 3000mSt 10:42.93 '05; Road: 10k 31:11 '19, 15k 47:41 '18, 10M 51:30 '18, HMar 70:32 '17.
In September 2016 married Andrew Krumins, who competed for Australia at the 2001 World Youth Champs, pb 800m 1:47.16 '06.

Dafne SCHIPPERS b. 15 Jun 1992 Utrecht 1.79m 68kg. Hellas.

NETHERLANDS – NEW ZEALAND

At (100m)/200m/4x100mR: OG: '16- 5/2; WCh: '11- sf, '15- 2/1, '17- 3/1, '19- (dns); EC: '12- 5/2R, '14- 1/1, '16- 1/-/1R, '18- 3/2/2R; WJ: '10- 3R; EU23: '13- (1) (3 LJ); CCp: '14- 3/1, '18- 4/2; ET: '14- 1. At 60m: WI: '16- 2, '18- 5; EI: '13-15-19: 4/1/2. At Hep: OG: '12- 10; WCh: '13- 3; WJ: '10- 1; EJ: '09- 4, '11- 1. Won DL 200m 2016, NED 100m 2011-12, 2014-15, 2019; LJ 2012, 2014. European records: 200m 2015, 150m 2020 Dutch records: 100m (5) 2014-15, 200m (5) 2011-15, LJ 2014, Hep 2013 & 2014.
Progress at 100m, 200m, Hep: 2007- 12.09/12.08w, 2008- 12.26/12.01w, 2009- 11.79, 24.21, 5507; 2010- 11.56, 23.70/23.41w, 5967; 2011- 11.19/11.13w, 22.69, 6172; 2012- 11.36, 22.70, 6360; 2013- 11.09, 22.84, 6477; 2014- 11.03, 22.03, 6545; 2015- 10.81, 21.63; 2016- 10.83, 21.88; 2017- 10.95, 22.05; 2018- 10.99, 22.14; 2019- 11.04, 22.45; 2020- 11.26, 22.94. pbs: 60m 7.00i '16, 150m 16.56 '20, 800m 2:08.59 '14, 60mh 8.18i '12, 100mh 13.13 '14, HJ 1.80 '12, LJ 6.78 '14, SP 14.66 '15, JT 42.22 '15.
First Dutch woman to win a medal in World Championships and emulated Fanny Blankers-Koen (1950) by winning EC sprint double 2014. European Athlete of the Year 2014-15.

Anouk VETTER b. 4 Feb 1993 Amsterdam 1.77m 62kg. Sprint.
At Hep: OG: '16- 10; WCh: '15- 12, '17- 3, '19- dnf; EC: '14- 16-18: 7/1/5; WJ: '12- dnf; EJ: '11- dnf. At Pen: EI: '15- 8. Won NED LJ 2017, 2019-20, JT 2019. Dutch heptathlon records 2016 & 2017.
Progress at Hep: 2011- 5549, 2012- 5764, 2013- 5872, 2014- 6316, 2015- 6458, 2016- 6626, 2017- 6636, 2018- 6426, 2019- dnf. pbs: 60m 7.46i '16, 100m 11.61 '16, 11.44w '17, 200m 23.70 '16, 800m 2:17.71 '16, 60mh 8.25i '16, 100mh 13.29 '16, HJ 1.81 '13, LJ 6.41i '12, 6.34 '15, 6.38w '16; SP 16.00 '17, JT 58.41 '17, Pen 4548i '15.
Won Ratingen 2015, Talence 2017. Mother Gerda Blokziel NED JT champion 1987-8. pb 58.22 '86.

Nadine VISSER b. 9 Feb 1995 Hoorn 1.75m 63kg. SAV.
At Hep/(100mh): OG: '16- 19 (h); WCh: '15- 8, '17- 7/7, '19- (6); EC: '14 (h), '16- (sf), '18- (4); WJ: '12- 11, 14- 3 (3); EU23: '15- (3, 11 LJ), '17- (1); EJ: '13- 4; WUG: '17- (1). At 60mh: WI: '18- 3; EI: '17- 19-21: 7/1/1. Won NED 100mh 2020, 100mh 2015, 2020. Dutch 100mh records 2018 & 2019.
Progress at 100mh, Hep: 2011- 13.84, 5171; 2012- 13.50, 5475; 2013- 13.21, 5774; 2014- 12.99, 6110; 2015- 12.81, 6467; 2016- 12.89, 6190; 2017- 12.78/12.57w, 6370; 2018- 12.71, 2019- 12.62, 2020- 12.68. pbs: 60m 7.30i '20, 100m 11.25 '20, 150m 16.94 '20, 200m 23.38 '20, 22.83w '17; 800m 2:13.08 '15, 60mh 7.77i '21 (NED record), HJ 1.80 '14, LJ 6.48 '15, SP 13.89i, 13.64 '17, JT 44.01 '15, Pen 4428i '17.

NEW ZEALAND
Governing body: Athletics New Zealand. Founded as the New Zealand Amateur Athletic Association in 1887, current name from 1989. **National Championships** first held in 1887 (men), 1926 (women). **2020 Champions: Men**: 100m/200m: Edward Osei-Nketia 10.46/20.88, 400m: Luke Mercieca 48.04, 800m: Michael Dawson 1:51.55, 1500m: Nick Willis 3:42.94, 5000m: Hayden Wilde 14:13.86, 10000m: Cameron Graves 29:55.47, 3000mSt Ieuan Van Der Peet 9:20.38, 110mh: James Sandilands 15.23, 400mh: Mike Cochrane 55.15, HJ: Hamish Kerr 2.16, PV: James Steyn 5.32, LJ: Felix McDonald 7.64w, TJ: Andrew Allan 14.66, SP: Tom Walsh 21.70, DT: Alex Parkinson 58.92, HT: Anthony Nobilo 59.94, JT: Alex Wood 68.71, Dec: Max Attwell 7041, 3000mW/10000mW: Quentin Rew 11:58.24/40:42.11. **Women**: 100m/200m: Zoe Hobbs 11.47/23.26w, 400m: Annalies Kalma 55.29, 800m: Katherine Camp 2:05.84, 1500m: Angela Petty 4:18.14, 5000m: Rebekah Greene 16:51.66, 10000m: Lisa Cross 34:56.57, 3000mSt: Amanda Holyer 12:15.14, 100mh: Fiona Morrison 13.62, 400mh: Portia Bing 57.69, HJ: Josephine Reeves 1.83, PV: Imogen Reeves 1.83, LJ: Briana Stephenson 6.08, TJ: Kayla Goodwin 12.87, SP: Valerie Adams 18.73, DT: TeRina Keenan 55.35, HT: Julia Ratcliffe 70.31, JT: Victoria Peeters 57.96, Hep: Christina Ryan 4928, 3000mW/10000mW: Alana Barber 13:16.91/45:34.49.

Jacko GILL b. 20 Dec 1994 Auckland 1.90m 125kg. Takapuna.
At SP: OG: '16- 9; WCh: '15- 8, '17- 9, '19- 7; CG: '14- 11; WJ: '10- 1, '12- 1; WY: '11- 1, YthOG: '10- 2. Oceania champion 2014, 2019.
Five World youth shot records 5kg 23.86 '10, 24.35 and 24.45 '11; 6kg (4) 21.34 to 22.31, 7.26kg (3) in 2011. World junior 6kg record 23.00 '13. Three NZL records 2011.
Progress at SP: 2010- 18.57, 2011- 20.38, 2012- 20.05, 2014- 20.70, 2015- 20.75, 2016- 20.83, 2017- 21.01, 2019- 21.47, 2020- 21.07, 2021- 21.52.
First name actually Jackson. World age 15 and 16 bests for 5kg, 6kg and 7.26kg shot. His father Walter was NZ champion at SP 1987 & 1989, DT 1975, pbs 16.57 '86 & 53.78 (1975); his mother Nerida (née Morris) had discus best of 51.32 and was NZ champion in 1990. His sister Ayla was 6th in WJ hammer 2010.

Tomas WALSH b. 1 Mar 1992 Timaru 1.86m 123kg. South Canterbury.
At SP: OG: '16- 3; WCh: '15- 4, '17- 1, '19- 3; CG: '14- 2, '18- 1; WJ: '10- dnq 16; WY: '09- 6 (dnq 31 DT), CCp: '14- 4, '18- 3; WI: '14-16-18: 3/1/1. Won DL 2016, 2018-19; NZ SP 2010-20, DT 2013, 2018- 19. Shot records: 9 Oceania 2016-19, 13 NZL 2013-19 and 9 OCE indoor 2014-18, Comm 2016 (=) & 2018.
Progress at SP: 2010- 17.57, 2011- 18.83, 2012- 19.33, 2013- 20.61, 2014- 21.26i/21.16, 2015- 21.62, 2016- 22.21, 2017- 22.14, 2018- 22.67, 2019- 22.90, 2020- 21.70, 2021- 21.60. pb DT 53.58 '14.

At World Indoors: set four NZ indoor records in 2014 and three Oceania records in both 2016 and 2018.

Women

Valerie ADAMS b. 6 Oct 1984 Rotorua 1.93m 123kg. Auckland City.
At SP: OG: '04- 7, '08- 1, '12- 1, '16- 2; WCh: '03-05-07-09-11-13: 5/2/1/1/1/1; CG: '02-06-10-14-18: 2/1/1/1/2; WJ: '02- 1; WY: '99- 10, '01- 1; WI: '04-08-10-12-14-16: dnq 10/1/1/1/1/3; WCp: '02- 6, '06- 1, '10- 1. Won WAF 2005, 2007-09, DL 2010-14, 2016; NZL SP 2001-11, 2013-14, 2016, 2018, 2020; DT 2004, HT 2003.
Nine Oceania & Commonwealth shot records 2005-11, 21 NZ 2002-11, 10 OCE indoor 2004-13.
Progress at SP: 1999- 14.83, 2000- 15.72, 2001- 17.08, 2002- 18.40, 2003- 18.93, 2004- 19.29, 2005- 19.87, 2006- 20.20, 2007- 20.54, 2008- 20.56, 2009- 21.07, 2010- 20.86, 2011- 21.24, 2012- 21.11, 2013- 20.98i/20.90, 2014- 20.67i/20.59, 2015- 18.73, 2016- 20.42, 2018- 19.31, 2020- 18.81, 2021- 19.65. pbs: DT 58.12 '04, HT 58.75 '02.
Ten senior global shot titles. IAAF Female Athlete of the Year 2014. Disqualification of Nadezhda Ostapchuk gave her ar 95 win streak 2007-15. Her father came from England and her mother from Tonga. Married New Caledonia thrower Bertrand Vili (SP 17.81 '02, DT 63.66 '09, 4 ECp '07 for France) in November 2004 (divorced in 2010), and Gabriel Price on 2 April 2016. Made a Dame Companion of the New Zealand Order of Merit for services to athletics in the 2017 New Year's Honours. Daughter Kimoana born in October 2017, son Kepaleli born March 2019.

Eliza McCARTNEY b. 11 Dec 1996 Auckland 1.79m 65kg. North Harbour Bays.
At PV: OG: '16- 3; WCh: '17- 9; CG: '18- 2; WJ: '14- 3; WY: '13- 4; WUG: '15- 2; WI: '16- 5, '18- 4. NZ champion 2016. Pole vault records: World junior 2015, Oceania & Commonwealth (6) 2016-18, 11 NZ 2014-18, Oceania indoor 2018.
Progress at PV: 2012- 3.85, 2013- 4.11, 2014- 4.45, 2015- 4.64, 2016- 4.80, 2017- 4.82, 2018- 4.94, 2019- 4.85.

NIGER

Amina SEYNI b. 24 Oct 1996 Niamey 1.67m 54kg.
At 200m: WCh: '19- sf; AfG: '19- 4. Niger records 100m & 200m (2) 2019, 400m (6) 2017-9.
Progress at 200m, 400m: 2017- 24.03, 52.17; 2018- 23.75, 50.69; 2019- 22.58, 49.19.
Does not qualify to compete internationally at 400m due to World Athletics's rule on testosterone limits.

NIGERIA

Governing body: The Athletic Federation of Nigeria. Founded 1944.

Chukwuebuka ENEKWECHI b. 28 Jan 1993 Queens, New York 1.81m 107kg. Was at Purdue University, USA.
At SP: WCh: '17- dnq 25, '19- 8; CG: '18- 2; AfG: '19- 1; AfCh: '18- 1; CCp: '18- 6. Won NGR 2016. Two Nigerian shot records 2019.
Progress at SP: 2013- 19.05, 2014- 19.38, 2015- 19.46, 2016- 20.37, 2017- 21.07, 2018- 21.22, 2019- 21.80, 2020- 21.04i. Pbs: HT 72.77 '15, Wt: 24.39i '15.

Ejowvokoghene **Divine ODUDURU** b. 7 Oct 1996 Ughelli 1.75m 70kg. Texas Tech University.
At (100m)/200m: OG: '16- sf; WCh: '19- sf; WJ: '14- 2; WY: '13- sf/6; AfG: '15- 2, '19- 2/2R; AfC: '14- 6, '16- sf, '18- 2/2R; Af-J: '13- 1/1R, '15-1/1/1R; Af-Y: '13- 1/1/3 MedR. Won NCAA 100m 2019, 200m 2018-19 (& indoor 2019), NGR 2014, 2016. Two Nigerian 200m records 2019.
Progress at 100m, 200m: 2013- 10.61/10.51w, 21.13; 2014- 10.30, 20.66/20.25w; 2015- 10.37, 20.45; 2016- 10.25/10.23w, 20.34; 2017- 10.09w, 20.45w; 2018- 10.10, 20.13; 2019- 9.86, 19.73; 2020- 10.10, 20.22. pbs: 60m 66.52i '19, 150m 15.25 '16, 300m 32.72 '16, 400m 47.35 '20.

Women

Oluwatobiloda '**Tobi' AMUSAN** b. 23 Apr 1997 Ijebu Ode1.56m 57kg. Graduate of University of Texas at El Paso, USA.
At 100mh: OG: '16- sf; WCh: '17- sf, '19- 4; CG: '18- 1/3R; WJ: '16- 5; AfG: '15- 1, '19- 1; Af Ch: '18- 1; CCp: '18- 5/dqR Won Af-J 2015 (1R '13&15), NCAA 2017. At 60mh: WI: '18- 7. At 200m: WY: '13- sf.
Unratified world junior best for 100mh 2016.
Progress at 100mh: 2014- 13.89, 2015- 13.11, 2016- 12.83A/12.79w, 2017- 12.57, 2018- 12.68/12.61w, 2019- 12.48. pbs: 100m 11.50 '16, 200m 22.92A/23.35i/22.60Aw '17, 60mh 7.84i '20, LJ 6.15Ai '17, 6.06 '16.

Ese BRUME b. 20 Jan 1996 Ugheli, Delta State 1.67m 58kg. Was at Eastern Mediterranean University, Famagusta, Cyprus.
At LJ: OG: '16- 5; WCh: '17- dnq 17, '19- 3; CG: '14- 1; WJ: '14- dnq 33; AfG: '15- 4, '19- 1; Af Ch: '14-16-18: 1/1/1; CCp: '14- 5, '18- 5. Won Af-J LJ & 4x100m 2013 & 2015, TJ 2015; NGR LJ 2014, 2016-17.
Progress at LJ: 2012- 6.02, 2013- 6.53, 2014- 6.68, 2015- 6.61, 2016- 6.83, 2017- 6.64/6.68w, 2018- 6.83, 2019- 7.05, 2020- 6.82/6.71. pbs: 100m 11.84 '14, 200m 24.20 '18, 400m 55.53 '16, TJ 13.16A '15.

Blessing OKAGBARE b. 9 Oct 1988 Sapele 1.80m 68kg. Married name Ighoteguonor. Was at University of Texas at El Paso, USA.
At LJ/(100m): OG: '08- 2, '12- dnq 14/8; '16- (sf, sf 200m), WCh: '11- dnq 18/5, '13- 2/6 (3 200m), '15- (8), '17- 8/(sf), '19- h 200m; CG: '14- 1 100m & 200m/2R, '18- 3R; AfG: '07- 2 (4 TJ), '11- 1/2; AfCh: '10- 1/1/1R, '12- 1/2, '14- (1)/1R, '18- 1R; WJ: '06- dnq 17 (dnq 16 TJ); CCp: '10- 6/3/3R, '18- dqR; Won Nigerian 100m 2009-14, 2016;

200m 2013-14, 2016; LJ 2008-09, 2011-13; TJ 2008; NCAA 100m & LJ 2010. African records 100m (2) 2013, 200m 2018, 4x200m 2015, Nigerian & African junior TJ record 2007.
Progress at 100m, 200m, LJ: 2004- 5.85 irreg, 2006- 6.16, 2007- 6.51, 2008- 23.76A, 6.91; 2009- 11.16, 6.73/6.90w; 2010- 11.00/10.98w/10.7Aw, 22.71, 6.88; 2011- 11.08/11.01w, 22.94, 6.78/6.84w; 2012- 10.92, 22.63, 6.97; 2013- 10.79/10.75w, 22.31, 7.00/7.14w; 2014- 10.85, 22.23, 6.86; 2015- 10.80, 22.67, 6.66; 2016- 11.02/10.92w, 22.58, 6.73; 2017- 10.99, 22.87, 6.77; 2018- 10.90/10.72w, 22.04; 2019- 11.04, 22.05. pbs: 60m 7.10i '21, 300m 37.04 '13, 400m 53.34 '15, TJ 14.13 '07.
Majestic winner of Commonwealth Games sprint double in 2014. Married football international Jude Igho Otegheri on 7 Nov 2014.

NORWAY
Governing body: Norges Friidrettsforbund. Founded 1896.
National Championships first held in 1896 (men), 1947 (women, walks 1937). **2020 Champions: Men:** 100m: Even Meinseth 10.69, 200m: Mathias Johansen 21.36, 400m: Fredrik Øvereng 47.21, 800m/1500m: Jakob Ingebrigtsen 1:48.72/3:33.93, 5000m: Narve Nordås 14:02.66, 10000m: Zerei Mezngi 28:04.29, HMar: Marius Vedvik 64:41, 3000mSt: Harald Kårbø 8:53.11, 110mh: Vladimir Vukicevic 14.00, 400mh: Karsten Warholm 48.23, HJ: Sander Skotheim 2.08, PV: Sondre Guttormsen 5.55, LJ/TJ: Henrik Flåtnes 7.62/15.77w, SP: Marcus Thomsen 18.39, DT: Ola Stunes Isene 60.19, HT: Eivind Henriksen 76.40, JT: Kasper Sagen 79.90, Dec: Martin Roe 7990, 5000mW: Tobias Lømo 23:50.79.
Women: 100m: Helene Rønningen 11.76, 200m/400m: Henriette Jæger 23.60/52.90, 800m: Hedda Hynne 2:03.64, 1500m: Amalie Sæten 4:38.30, 5000m: Sigrid Våg 16:15.02, 10000m/HMar: Vienna Dahle 33:28.39/74:16, 3000mSt: Andrea Engesæth 9:57.95, 100mh: Andrea Rooth 13.50, 400mh: Amalie Iuel 55.63, HJ/LJ: Mia Lien 1.80/6.22 PV: Lene Retzius 3.80, TJ: Hedda Kvalvåg 12.73w, SP/DT: Elisabeth Rosvold 13.59/49.76, HT: Beatrice Llano 66.78, JT: Ane Dahlen 54.76, Hep: Telma Eid 5093, 3000mW: Siri Glittenberg 13:37.45.

Håvard HAUKENES b. 22 Apr 1990 Bergen 1.80m 68kg. IL Gular
At 50kW: OG: '16- 7; WCh: '13/17/19- dq, '15- 24; EC: '18- 4. At 20kW: EC: '14- dq. Won NOR 5000mW 2017-18, 20kW 2014, 2016; 50kW 2012. Norwegian record 30k walk 2020.
Progress at 50kW: 2011- 4:04:48, 2012- 3:56:38, 2015- 3:56:50, 2016- 3:46:33, 2017- 3:43:40, 2018- 3:48:35, 2019- 3:42:50; pbs: 3000mW 11:44.17 '15, 11:26.95irr '19; 5000mW 19:19.79 '16, 10000mW 42:39.5 '16, 20kW 1:23:15 '16, 30kW 2:07:42 '20.

Eivind HENRIKSEN b. 14 Sep 1990 Oslo 1.91m 116kg. IK Tjalve

At HT: OG: '12- dnq 11; WCh: '11- dnq 24, '19- 6; EC: '10-12-14-16: dnq – 22/14/17/16; '18- 5; WJ: '08- dnq; WY: '07- 9 (dnq 18 DT); EU23: '11- 12; EJ: '07- dnq 22, '09- 4, NOR champion 2010-20. Six Norwegian hammer records 2011-19.
Progress at HT: 2005- 45.30, 2007- 60.51, 2008- 62.69, 2009- 69.07, 2010- 72.86, 2011- 74.59, 2012- 75.57, 2013- 73.27, 2014- 72.70, 2015- 71.84, 2016- 74.97, 2017- 74.27, 2018- 76.86, 2019- 78.25, 2020- 76.40. Pbs: DT 53.16 '11, JT 56.10 '10, Wt 21.77 '12.

Filip Mangen INGEBRIGTSEN b. 20 Apr 1993 Stavanger 1.87m 75kg. Sandnes IL
At 1500m: OG: '16- h; WCh: '17- 3, '19- sf (dnf 5000m); EC: '14-16-18: h/1/12; WJ: '10- h, '12- 9; EU23: '13- 6. At 800m: WJ: '12- h; EU23: '13- h; EJ: 11- h. Eur CC: '18- 1, '19- 11; Won NOR 800m 2016, 1500m 2013. Norwegian records 1500m 2018, 1M 2019, 1000m 2020.
Progress at 1500m: 2011- 3:51.70, 2012- 3:44.04, 2013- 3:38.76, 2014- 3:40.48, 2015- 3:42.32, 2016- 3:32.43, 2017- 3:32.48. 2018- 3:30.01, 2019- 3:30.82, 2020- 3:30.35. pbs: 800m 1:46.74 '20, 1000m 2:16.46 '20, 1M 3:49.60 '19, 2000m 4:56.91 '20, 3000m 7:49.70 '16, 5000m 13:11.75 '19, 10k Rd 28:47 '18, 2000mSt 5:46.15 '12.
Married Astrid Mangen Cederqvist (60m 7.47i '18, 100m 11.71 '16, 200m 23.56 '18, 400m 55.35i '19) on 15 Sep 2018.

Henrik Børkja INGEBRIGTSEN b. 24 Feb 1991 Stavanger 1.80m 69kg. Sandnes IL
At 1500m/(5000m): OG: '12- 5, '16- sf; WCh: '13- 8, '15- h, '19 (13); EC: '10-12-14-16-18: h/1/2/3&4/& 2; WJ: '10- h; EU23: '11- h, '13- (1); EJ: '09- h; CCp: '14- 4; EI: '15- 6. At 3000m: CCp: 18- 3; EI: '15-17-19: 3/2/3. Won NOR 800m 2013, 1500m 2010, 2012, 2014; 5000m 2015, 2018-19.; CC 2019 Eur CC: '12- 1 U23, '17- 11.
Norwegian records: 1500m (4) 2012-14, 1M (3) 2012-14, 3000m 2019.
Progress at 1500m: 2004- 4:30.63, 2005- 4:22.48, 2006- 4:04.15, 2007- 3:54.08, 2008- 3:50.63, 2009- 3:44.53, 2010- 3:38.61, 2011- 3:39.50, 2012- 3:35.43, 2013- 3:33.95, 2014- 3:31.46, 2015- 3:32.85, 2016- 3:34.57, 2017- 3:38.96, 2018- 3:35.61, 2019- 3:40.23. pbs: 800m 1:48.09 '14, 1M 3:50.72 '14, 2000m 4:53.72 '20, 3000m 7:36.85 '19, 2M 8:22.31 '18, 5000m 13:13.58 '19, 10k Rd 28:41 '18, 2000mSt 5:41.03 '09, 3000mSt 8:52.56 '09.
Younger brothers: **Filip** (qv) and **Jakob** (qv)

Jakob INGEBRIGTSEN b. 19 Sep 2000 Sandnes 1.81m 65kg. Sandnes IL
At 1500m/(5000m): WCh: '19- 4/5; EC: 18- 1/1; WJ: '16- 9, '18- 2/3; EJ: 17- 8/1; EI: '19- 2 (1 3000m), '21- 1 (1 3000m); CCp: 18- 3. At 3000mSt: WCh: '17- h; EJ: '17- 1. World CC: '19- 12J. Won EU20 CC 2016-19, NOR 800m 2020, 1500m 2017- 20, 5000m, 3000mSt 2017.
Records: Two world U20 indoor 1500m 2019. European 2000m 2020, ind 1500m 2021; European U20 1500m (2), 1M, 5000m (3) & 3000m ind 2018 & 2019; U23 1500m & 3000m

2020; NOR 5000m 2019.
Progress at 1500m, 5000m: 2015- 3:48.37, 2016- 3:42.44, 14:38.67; 2017- 3:39.92, 13:35.84; 2018- 3:31.18, 13:17.06; 2019- 3:30.16, 13:02.03; 2020- 3:28.68, 2021- 3:31.60i. pbs: 800m 1:46.44 '20, 1M 3:51.30 '19, 2000m 4:50.01 '20, 3000m 7:27.05 '20, 10kRd 27:54 '19, 3000mSt 8:26.81 '17.
Youngest ever sub-4 min miler at 16 in 2017 and in 2018 the youngest ever male European champion, winning 1500m at 17yr 323d and next day 5000m. Has won a record four European U20 CC titles. European age bests 1500m 11-12 & 14-19, 1M & 5000m 16-19, 3000mSt 16-18.

Ola Stunes ISENE b. 29 Jan 1995 Drammen 1.94m 107kg. IF Sturla.
At DT: WCh: '19- 10; EC: '18- 11; WJ: '14- 5; EU23: '15- nt, '11- 11; NOR champion 2018-20.
Progress at DT: 2013- 50.57, 2014- 55.57, 2015- 59.97, 2016- 61.36, 2017- 61.33, 2018- 63.30, 2019- 67.78, 2020- 64.62. Pb SP 17.34 '16, HT 42.28 '16, JT: 54.12 '12.
His sister Berit has pb DT 48.44 '17.

Sondre Nordstad MOEN b. 12 Jan 1991 Trondheim 1.78m 62kg. SK Vidar.
At Mar: OG: '16- 19; EC: '18- dnf. At 5000m: WCh: '17- h; EC: '10- h; WJ: '08- 14, EJ: '09- 5. At 10000m: WCh: '19- 11; EC: '10- 14, '14- 9; EU23: '11- 1; Eur CC: '07-08-09-10-11: 6J/2J/4J/5J/3 U23. Won NOR 5000m 2011, 10000m 2015, 2019; & HMar 2015, CC 2014.
Records: European marathon 2017, 20,000m, 25,000m & 1 hour 2020 (but illegal shoes); Norwegian half marathon & marathon (2) 2017, 10000m 2019. 20000m & 1 Hr 2020.
Progress at 10000m, Mar: 2007- 30:29.31, 2008- 29:21.92, 2009- 29:17.99, 2010- 29:19.63, 2011- 28:41.66, 2014- 28:40.27, 2015-28:25.23, 2:12:54; 2016- 2:14:17, 2017- 28:15.12, 2:05:48; 2018- 28:37.92, 2019- 27:24.78, 2:06:16; 2020- 28:35.52, 2:09:01. Pbs: 1500m 3:48.65 '14, 3000m 7:52.55 '17, 5000m 13:20.16 '17, 20000m 56:51.60 '20, 25000m 1:12:46.5 '20, 1Hr 21131m '20, 3000mSt 9:10.01 '08, Road: 10M 47:32 '16, 15k 42:26 '17, 20k 56:42 '17, HMar 59:48 '17. Won Fukuoka marathon 2017. European age 17 10000m best 2008.

Karsten WARHOLM b. 28 Feb 1996 Volda 1.87m 78kg. Dimna IL.
At 400mh: OG: '16- sf; WCh: '17- 1, '19- 1; EC: '16- 6, '18- 1 (8 400m); EU23: '17- 1; CCp: '18- 3. At 400m: EC: '14- h; EU23: '17- 2; EJ: '15- 2; EI: '19- 1; At Oct: WY: '13- 1; At Dec: WJ: '14- 10; EJ: '15- 2. Won DL 2019, NOR 400m & 400mh 2015-19, 110mh 2013-14.
Records: European 400mh (4) 2019-20, indoor 400m 2019, four European U23 400mh 2018, NOR: 300m 2018, 400m (2) 2016-17, 400mh (14) 2016-20.
Progress at 400mh: 2014- 52.20, 2015- 51.09, 2016- 48.49, 2017- 48.22, 2018- 47.64, 2019- 46.92, 2020- 46.87. pbs: 60m 6.75i '17, 100m 10.49i '17, 10.52 '16; 200m 20.92i/21.09 '16, 21.00w '15; 300m 32.47i '21, 32.69 '18; 400m 44.87 '17, 1000m 2:45.80i '13, 1500m 4:44.73 '15, 60mh 8.10i '15, 110mh 14.30 '15, HJ 2.05 '14, PV 4.30 '15, LJ 7.66 '15, TJ 14.48i/14.33 '12, SP 9.18 '14, DT 29.40 '14, JT 45.82 '15.
Won many NOR age group titles at wide range of events. EJ silver at 400m & Dec in 2015 even though 400m was in the middle of the decathlon first day. IAAF Rising Star of the Year 2017. Won all his ten races in 2020, now has best ever average of top ten times at 400m hurdles.

Women

Karoline Bjerkeli GRØVDAL b. 14 Jun 1990 Ålesund 1.67m 52kg. IK Tjalve.
At 1500m: WCh: '17- h; ET: '15- 2. At 3000m: EI: '19- 5; At 5000m/(10000m): OG: '12- h, '16- 7/9; WCh: 13- 13, '15- h, '17- dnf; (h 1500m); EC: '10- 9/dnf, '14- 12, '16- (3); EJ: '09- 1; ET: '10- 3. At 3000mSt: WCh: '09- h, '19- 13 (h 5000m); EC: '18- 3; EU23: '11- h; WJ: '06- 5; EJ: '07- 1, '09- 1. At 2000mSt: WY: '07- 3. Eur CC: '06-09-13-15-16-17-18-19: 2J/1J/ 5/3/3/3/3/2. Won NOR 1500m 2013, 2015; 5000m 2008, 2010, 2012, 2014; 3000mSt 2006, 2009-10, 2019. NOR records 1M 2016, 3000mSt 2007 & 2017, 2000m 2018.
Progress at 5000m, 10000m, 3000mSt: 2005- 11:07.5, 2006- 9:55.95, 2007- 15:55.62, 9:33.19; 2008- 16:08.22; 2009- 15:29.82, 9:33.34; 2010- 15:25.40, 9:39.54; 2011- 15:44.92, 9:46.07; 2012- 15:24.86, 2013- 15:16.27mx, 2014- 15:47.63, 2015- 15:15.18, 2016- 14:57.53, 31:14.07; 2017- 15:00.44, 9:13.35; 2018- 9:18.36, 2019- 14:51.66, 9:20.69; 2020- 15:01.13mx. pbs: 800m 2:04.23 '16, 1500m 4:05.57 '18, 1M 4:26.23 '16, 2000m 5:41.04 '18, 3000m 8:37.58 '17, 10k Rd 30:32 '20, HMar 69:41 '12, 2000mSt 6:21.39 '08.

Hedda HYNNE b. 13 Mar 1990 Skien 1.72m 57kg. IK Tjalve.
At 800m: OG: '16- h; WCh: '17/19- sf; EC: '14- h. Won NOR 800m 2014, 2018-20.
NOR records 600m, 800m (2) 2020.
Progress at 800m: 2013- 2:05.11, 2014- 2:0224, 2015- 2:02.74, 2016- 2:00.94, 2017- 1:59.87, 2018- 2:01.46, 2019- 2:00.53, 2020- 1:58.10. pbs: 100m 12.51 '07, 200m 25.58 '13, 300m 39.82 '18, 400m 53.24 '16, 600m 1:26.90 '20, 1500m 4:33.41 '13.

PERU

Governing body: Federación Peruana de Atletismo.

Kimberley GARCÍA b. 19 Oct 1993 Huancayo 1.67m 44kg.
At 20kW: OG: '16- 14; WCh: '13/15/17: 32/dnf/7; WCp: '16- 12, '18- 8; PAm: '15- 5, '19- 2; SAG: '18- 1; SAChs: '14- 1. At 10000mW: WJ: '12- 10. At 5000mW: WY: '09- dnf; YOG: '10- 7.
S.American walks record 10k 2017, 20k 2014. Five Peru 20kW records 2013-18, 10000mW 2018.
Progress at 20kW: 2013- 1:33:57, 2014- 1:29:44, 2015- 1:31:13, 2016- 1:29:38, 2017- 1:29:13, 2018-

PHILIPPINES

1:28:56, 2019- 1:29:14. Pbs: 5000mW 22:57.4 '11, 10000mW 42:56.97 '18.

Ernest John OBIENA b. 17 Nov 1995 Tondo, Manila 1.90m 68kg. University of Santo Tomas.
At PV: WCh: '19- dnq15; AsiG: 18- 7; AsiC: 17- 3, '19- 1; WUG: '19- 1.
17 PHI pole vault records 2014-19 & indoors 2021.
Progress at PV: 2013- 4.90, 2014- 5.21, 2015- 5.45, 2016- 5.55, 2017- 5.61, 2018- 5.51, 2019- 5.81, 2020- 5.80, 2021- 5.86i. Pb 110mh 14.39 '17.

POLAND

Governing body: Polski Zwiazek Lekkiej Atletyki (PZLA). Founded 1919.
National Championships first held in 1920 (men), 1922 (women). **2020 Champions: Men**: 100m: Remigiusz Olszewski 10.51, 200m: Lukasz Krawczuk 21.18 irregular start, 400m: Karol Zalewski 46.35, 800m: Krzysztof Róznicki 1:47.73, 1500m: Michal Rozmys 3:53.09, 5000m: Szymon Kulka 14:03.02, 10000m: Krystian Zalewski 28:59.88, HMar: Adam Nowicki 64:58, Mar: Kamil Jastrzebski 2:12:58, 3000mSt: Mateusz Kaczmarek 8:57.88, 110mh: Damian Czykier 13.92, 400mh: Patryk Dobek 50.07, HJ: Norbert Kobielski 2.26, PV: Pawel Wojciechowski 5.61, LJ: Mateusz Jopek 7.82, TJ: Adrian Swiderski 16.38, SP: Michal Haratyk 20.64, DT: Bartlomiej Stój 63.05, HT: Wojciech Nowicki 80.28, JT: Marcin Krukowski 83.51, Dec: Rafal Horbowicz 7478, 10000mW/20kW: Dawid Tomala 41:39.70/1:24:44, 50kW: Rafal Augustyn 3:47:42. **Women**: 100m: Ewa Swoboda 11.52, 200m: Marlena Gola 23.64, 400m: Justyna Swiety-Ersetic 51.44, 800m: Joanna Józwik 2:04.52, 1500m: Sofia Ennaoui 4:15.89, 5000m/10000m: Katarzyna Jankowska 16:06.02/33:10.52, HMar: Angelika Mach 73:58, Mar: Aleksandra Lisowska 2:30:47, 3000mSt: Matylda Kowal 9:57.16, 100mh: Karolina Koleczek 13.04, 400mh: Joanna Linkiewicz 56.23, HJ: Kamila Licwinko 1.88, PV: Wiktoria Wojewódzka 4.20, LJ: Joanna Kurylo 6.35, TJ: Karolina Mlodawska 13.55, SP: Paulina Guba 18.09, DT: Daria Zabawska 55.28, HT: Katarzyna Furmanek 72.85, JT: Maria Andrejczyk 62.66, Hep: Paulina Ligarska 5648, 5000mW/20kW: Katarzyna Zdzieblo 21:13.69/1:30:41, 50kW: Agnieszka Ellward 4:38:44.

Konrad BUKOWIECKI b. 17 Mar 1997 Olsztyn 1.91m 140kg. KS AZS UWM Olsztyn.
At SP: OG: '16- nt; WCh: '15- dnq, '17- 8, '19- 6; EC: '16- 4, '18- 2; WJ: '14- 1, '16- dq1 & 5 DT; WY: '13- 5; EU23: '17- 1, '19- 1; EJ: '15- 1 (dnq 13 DT); Yth OG: '10- 1; WI: '16- 4, '18- 8; EI: '15- 6, '17- 1; WUG: '17- 2, '19- 1; ET: 17- 3. Won POL 2016, 2019.
Shot records: Four world junior 7.26kg 2015-16, (6kg 23.34dq '16), indoor 6kg (4) 22.38 '15 to 22.96 '16, World youth 5kg 2 out to 22.24 & 5

indoor to 24.24 in 2014; European junior (5) 2015, indoor (3) 2016, U23 indoor 2017 & 2018, out (2) 2019.
Progress at SP: 2014- 17.29i, 2015- 20.78, 2016- 21.14, 2017- 21.97i/21.59, 2018- 22.00i/21.66, 2019- 21.99, 2020- 21.88i/20.88. Pb DT 58.42 '17.
Lost his 2016 World Junior gold with a public warning for a banned stimulant.

Patryk DOBEK b. 13 Feb 1994 Koscierzyna 1.87m 75kg. MKL Szczecin.
At 400mh: OG: '16- h; WCh: '15- 7, '17/19- sf; EC: '14- sf, '18- 5; EU23: '15- 1/2R; ET: '15-17-19: 2/3/1; WUG: '19- 3/3R; Polish champion 2014-20. At 400m: WJ: '12- sf/2R; WY: '11- 3; EJ: '13- 2/2R. At 800m: EI: '21- 1.
Progress at 400mh: 2012- 52.00, 2013- 50.67, 2014- 49.13, 2015- 48.40, 2016- 49.01, 2017- 49.15, 2018- 48.59. 2019- 48.80, 2020- 50.07. pbs: 200m 21.38 '15, 300m 33.34 '13, 400m 46.12 '19, 600m 1:15.78 '14, 800m 1:46.81i '21, 300mh 36.40 '20.

Pawel FAJDEK b. 4 Jun 1989 Swiebodzice 1.86m 118kg. KS Agros Zamosc.
At HT: OG: '12- dnq, '16- dnq 17; WCh: '11-13-15-17-19: 10/1/1/1/1; EC: 14-16-18: 2/1/2; WJ: '08- 4; EU23: '09- 8, '11- 1; WUG: '11-13-15-17: 1/1/1/1; CCp: '14- 3; ET: '11-13-14-15-17: 2/1/2/1/1. Won POL 2012, 2014-16, 2019; Franc G 2013, IAAF HT challenge 2013, 2015-17, 2019.
Two Polish hammer records 2014-15.
Progress at HT: 2008- 64.58, 2009- 72.36, 2010- 76.07, 2011- 78.54, 2012- 81.39, 2013- 82.27, 2014- 83.48, 2015- 83.93, 2016- 82.47, 2017- 83.44, 2018- 81.14, 2019- 80.88, 2020- 79.81. pb Wt 23.22i '14.
Won 16 of 17 competitions in 2015, 13/14 in 2016 and 15/16 in 2017, with respectively the top 12/12/10 performances of the year at hammer. The clear favourite, he failed to qualify with only 72.00 for Olympic final 2016 after 29 successive wins, all over 78m.

Michal HARATYK b. 10 Apr 1992 Cieszyn 1.94m 136kg. KS Sprint Bielsko-Biala.
At SP: OG: '16- dnq 18; WCh: '17- 5, '19- dnq 16; EC: '16- 2, EI: '19- 1, '21- 2; CCp: '18- 4; ET: '19- 1; POL champion 2017, 2020.
Two Polish shot records 2019.
Progress at SP: 2012- 17.72, 2013- 17.24, 2014- 19.95, 2015- 20.10i/19.95, 2016- 21.35i/21.23, 2017- 21.88, 2018- 22.09, 2019- 22.32, 2020- 21.88, 2021- 21.83i. pb DT 53.53 '13.
Elder brother Lukasz SP 18.82 '10.

Marcin KRUKOWSKI b. 14 Jun 1992 Warszawa 1.82m 92kg. KS Warszawianka W-wa.
At JT: OG: '16- dnq 15; WCh: '13-15-17-19: dnq 24/dnq 15/9/7; EC: '16- 6, '18- 4; WJ: '10- dnq 27; WY: '09- 4; EU23: '13- 9; EJ: '11- 2; ET: '19- 3. Won POL 2015-20.
Progress at JT: 2009- 65.95, 2010- 72.10, 2011- 79.19, 2012- 82.58, 2013- 83.04, 2014- 80.66, 2015- 85.20, 2016- 84.74, 2017- 88.09, 2018- 85.32, 2019- 85.72, 2020- 87.07.

Adam KSZCZOT b. 2 Sep 1989 Opoczno 1.78m 64kg. RKS Lódz. Studied organisation and management.
At 800m: OG: '12/16- sf; WCh: '09/13/19- sf, '11-15-17: 6/2/2; EC: '10-14-16-18: 3/1/1/1; WJ: '08- 4; EU23: '09/11- 1; EJ: '07- 3; WI: '10-12-14-18: 3/4/2/1; EI: '09-11-13-17-21: 4/1/1/1/4; CCp: '14- 3; ET: '11-13-14-15-19: 1/1/2/3/1. Won POL 800m 2009-10, 2012, 2014-15; 1500m 2017-18; WIT 2016, 2018. Polish 1000m record 2011 and 2014.
Progress at 800m: 2005- 1:59.57, 2006- 1:51.09, 2007- 1:48.10, 2008- 1:47.16, 2009- 1:45.72, 2010- 1:45.07, 2011- 1:43.30, 2012- 1:43.83, 2013- 1:44.76, 2014- 1:44.02, 2015- 1:43.45, 2016- 1:43.76, 2017- 1:44.84, 2018- 1:44.59, 2019- 1:44.61, 2020- 1:45.64. pbs: 400m 46.51 '11, 600m 1:14.55 '10, 1000m 2:15.72 '14, 1500m 3:38.31 '17.

Marcin LEWANDOWSKI b. 13 Jun 1987 Szczecin 1.80m 64kg. CWZS Zawisza Bydgoszcz. PE student.
At 800m: OG: '08/12- sf, '16- 6; WCh: '09-11-13-15-17: 8/4/4/sf/sf; EC: '10-14-16: 1/5/2; WJ: '06- 4; EU23: '07- 1, '09- 2; WI: '14- dq (3); EI: '09-11-15: 6/2/1; CCp: '10- 2; ECp: '08- 2, '10- 3; won W.MilG 2011. At 1500m: WCh: '17- 6, '19- 3; EC: '18- 2; EJ: '05- 7; WI: '18- 2; EI: '13-17-19-21: 4/1/1/2; CCp: 18- 2; ET: '13-14-15-17-19: 3/3/2/1/1. Won Polish 800m 2011, 2016, 2018 1500m 2008, 2010, 2014, 2016, 2019, 4k CC 2020. Polish records: 1000m 2011 & 2016, 1500m (2) 2019, 2000m 2020.
Progress at 800m, 1500m: 2002- 1:57.86, 2003- 1:53.31, 2004- 1:51.73, 3:52.38; 2005- 1:48.86, 3:48.61; 2006- 1:46.69, 3:43.64; 2007- 1:45.52, 3:42.86; 2008- 1:45.84, 3:44.94; 2009- 1:43.84, 3:44.39; 2010- 1:44.10, 3:40.38; 2011- 1:44.53, 3:40.24; 2012- 1:44.34, 3:37.76i; 2013- 1:43.79, 3:38.98/3:38.34i; 2014- 1:44.03, 3:38.19/3:37.37i; 2015- 1:43.72, 3:52.06/3:38.68i; 2016- 1:43.73, 3:37.69; 2017- 1:44.77, 3:34.04; 2018- 1:44.32, 3:35.06; 2019- 1:43.74, 3:31.46; 2020-1:45.77, 3:33.99. pbs: 400m 47.76 '09, 600m 1:15.17 '14, 1000m 2:14.30 '16, 1M 3:52.34 '19, 2000m 4:57.09 '20, 3000m 7:51.69i '21. Coach is brother Tomasz (1:51.00 '03).

Piotr LISEK b. 16 Aug 1992 Duszniki, Poznan 1.94m 96kg. OSOT Szczecin.
At PV: OG: '16- 4=; WCh: '15-17-19: 3=/2/3; EC: '14-16-18: 6/4=/4; EU23: '13- dnq 17; ET: '15- 3, '19- 1; WI: 16- 3; WI: '18- 3; EI: '15-17-19-21: 3/1/2/3. Won POL 2017, WIT 2018. Two POL pole vault records 2019, three indoors 2015-19.
Progress at PV: 2006- 3.20, 2007- 3.30, 2008- 4.10, 2009- 4.42, 2010- 4.70, 2011- 5.10i/5.00, 2012- 5.20, 2013- 5.60, 2014- 5.82, 2015- 5.90i/5.82, 2016- 5.77i/5.75, 2017- 6.00i/5.89, 2018- 5.94, 2019- 6.02, 2020- 5.90.
6-months drugs ban in 2012. Married to Aleksandra Wisnik (PV 4.15 '14).

Piotr MALACHOWSKI b. 7 Jun 1983 Zuromin 1.94m 135kg. WKS Slask Wroclaw. Army corporal.
At DT: OG: '08- 2, '12- 5, '16- 2; WCh: '07-09-11-13-15-17-19: 12/2/9/2/1/5/dnq 17; EC: '06-10-14-16-18: 6/1/4/1/dnq; WJ: '02- 6; EU23: '03- 9, '05- 2; EJ: '01- 5; CCp: '10- 4; ECp: '06-07-08-09-10-11-14-19: 1/1/3/1/2/3/2/1. Won DL 2010, 2014-16; POL 2005-10, 2012-15, 2018.
Nine Polish discus records 2006-13.
Progress at DT: 1999- 39.48, 2000- 52.04, 2001- 54.19, 2002- 56.84, 2003- 57.83, 2004- 62.04, 2005- 64.74, 2006- 66.21, 2007- 66.61, 2008- 68.65, 2009- 69.15, 2010- 69.83, 2011- 68.49, 2012- 68.94, 2013- 71.84, 2014- 69.28, 2015- 68.29, 2016- 68.15, 2017- 67.68, 2018- 65.78, 2019- 67.23, 2020- 64.87.

Wojciech NOWICKI b. 22 Feb 1989 Bialystok 1.97m 131kg. KS Podlasie Bialystok.
At HT: OG: '16- 3; WCh: '15-17-19: 3/3/4; EC: '16- 3, '18- 1; EU23: '11- 5; CCp: 18- 6; ET: '19- 1. Won POL 2017-18, 2020; IAAF HT challenge 2018, W.MilG 2019.
Progress at HT: 2008- 55.71, 2009- 64.41, 2010- 69.59, 2011- 72.72, 2012- 73.52, 2013- 75.87, 2014- 76.14, 2015- 78.71, 2016- 78.36, 2017- 80.87, 2018- 81.85, 2019- 81.74, 2020- 80.28. pb Wt 22.72i '14.
World number one in 2019 when he was 7-5 against Pawel Fajdek. Their career record is 77-17 in Fajdek's favour 2009-20. Awarded a bronze medal at 2019 Worlds as it was decided that he had been disadvantaged by judging,

Robert URBANEK b. 29 Apr 1987 Leczyca 2.00m 120kg. MKS Aleksandrów Lódzki.
At DT: OG: '12/16- dnq 32/17; WCh: '13-15-17-19: 6/3/7/dnq 23; EC: '12-14-16-18: 6/3/9/dnq 14; EU23: '09- 7; CCp: '14- 6; ET: '15- 1, 17- 2. Won POL 2017.
Progress at DT: 2004- 47.09, 2005- 47.83, 2006- 50.84, 2007- 56.18, 2008- 62.22, 2009- 60.54, 2010- 60.74, 2011- 64.37, 2012- 66.93, 2013- 65.30, 2014- 65.75, 2015- 66.31, 2016- 65.56, 2017- 66.73, 2018- 65.15, 2019- 65.81, 2020- 65.99. pb SP 16.21 '07.

Pawel WOJCIECHOWSKI b. 6 Jun 1989 Bydgoszcz 1.90m 81kg. CWKS Zawisza Bydgoszcz. PE student.
At PV: OG: '12- dnq nh, '16- dnq 16=; WCh: '11-15-17-19: 1/3=/5/dnq 13=; EC: '14-16-18: 2/7=/5; WJ: '08- 2; EU23: '11- 1; EJ: '07- dnq 16; EI: '11-17-19: 4/3/1; CCp: '14- 5. Won W.MilG 2011 & 2019, POL 2015-16, 2018-20.
Polish pole vault record 2011 and 2017.
Progress at PV: 2001- 2.50, 2002- 2.70, 2003- 3.10, 2004- 3.50, 2005- 4.10, 2006- 4.70, 2007- 5.00, 2008- 5.51, 2009- 5.40i/5.22, 2010- 5.60, 2011- 5.91, 2012- 5.62, 2014- 5.80, 2015- 5.84, 2016- 5.84i/5.71, 2017- 5.93, 2018- 5.88i/5.84, 2019- 5.90i/5.87, 2020- 5.70i/5.61.

Women

Maria ANDREJCZYK b. 9 Mar 1996 Sejny 1.74m 77kg. LUKS Hancza Suwalki.
At JT: OG: '16- 4; WCh: '15/19- dnq 28/22; EC: '16- dnq 13; WJ: '14- 5; WY: '13- dnq 26; EJ: '15- 1; WT: '19- 2. Polish champion 2016.
Polish javelin record 2016.

POLAND

Progress at JT: 2010- 28.51, 2011- 41.21, 2012- 44.58, 2014- 56.53, 2015- 62.11, 2016- 67.11, 2018- 54.24, 2019- 63.39, 2020- 65.70.

Sofia ENNAOUI b. 30 Aug 1995 Ben Guerir, Morocco 1.58m 43kg. MKL Szczecin.
At 1500m: OG: '16- 10; WCh: '15/17- sf; EC: '16- 7, '18- 2; WJ: '12- 10, '14- 5; EU23: '15- 2, '17- 2; EJ: '13- 2; CCp: '18- 7; ET: '19- 1; EI: '17- 3, '19- 2. At 800m: WCh: '15- sf; WY: '11- h, At 3000m: WJ: '14- dnf; ET: '15- 1, '17- 1; EI: '15- 6; Eur CC: '13- 2J, '16- 1 U23. Won POL 1500m 2015, 2017, 2019-20. Polish 1000m record 2020.
Progress at 1500m: 2012- 4:13.68, 2013- 4:12.05, 2014- 4:07.34, 2015- 4:04.26. 2016- 4:01.00, 2017- 4:03.35, 2018- 4:02.06, 2019- 4:04.06, 2020- 3:59.70. pbs: 400m 56.07 '15, 800m 2:00.11 '15, 1000m 2:32.30 '20, 1M 4:23.34 '18, 3000m 8:45.29i '17, 8:59.44 '14. Moroccan father, she moved to Poland with her Polish mother at the age of 2.

Joanna FIODOROW b. 4 Mar 1989 Augustów 1.69m 89kg. OS AZS Poznan.
At HT: OG: '12- 7, '16- 9; WCh: '11-15: dnq 21/17, '17- 6, '19- 2; EC: '14-16-18: 3/10/3; WJ: '08- dnq 19; EU23: '09- 4, '11- 2; ET: '14- 2, '19- 2; WUG: '15- 2, '17- 3.
Progress at HT: 2005- 40.96, 2006- 50.18, 2007- 55.93, 2008- 61.22, 2009- 62.80, 2010- 64.66, 2011- 70.06, 2012- 74.18, 2013- 68.92, 2014- 74.39, 2015- 72.67, 2016- 72.98, 2017- 75.09, 2018- 74.39, 2019- 76.35, 2020- 67.81. pbs: SP 12.87 '10, JT 35.56 '09.

Katarzyna FURMANEK b. 19 Feb 1996 1.74m 76kg. KKL Kielce.
At HT: WJ: '14- 7; WY: '13- 6; EU23: '17- 6; EJ: '13- dnq 14, '15- 3; WUG: '19- 3. Won POL 2020.
Progress at HT: 2011- 52.81, 2012- 54.88, 2013- 62.63, 2014- 63.94, 2015- 64.83, 2016- 67.11, 2017- 69.60, 2018- 68.41, 2019- 69.68, 2020- 73.61. pb DT 45.61 '16.

Joanna JÓZWIK b. 30 Jan 1991 Walbrzych 1.68m 53kg. AZS-AWF Warszawa.
At 800m: OG: '16- 5; WCh: '15- 7, '17- sf; EC: '14- 3, '16- 6; WJ: '10- sf; EU23: '11- h, '13- 8; ET: '15- 2; EI: '15- 3, '21- 2. Polish champion 2014-15, 2020.
Progress at 800m: 2007- 2:12.90, 2008- 2:11.55, 2009- 2:07.31, 2010- 2:05.09, 2011- 2:03.15, 2012- 2:05.87, 2013- 2:02.39, 2014- 1:59.63, 2015- 1:58.35, 2016- 1:57.37, 2017- 1:59.29i/2:00.77, 2019- 2:02.80, 2020- 2:01.26, 2021- 2:00.42i. pbs: 200m 24.16 '14, 300m 39.83 '11, 400m 53.08 '14, 600m 1:25.04 '15, 1000m 2:34.93 '16.

Malwina KOPRON b. 16 Nov 1994 Pulawy 1.69m 89kg. AZS UMCS Lublin.
At HT: OG: '16- dnq 15; WCh: '15- dnq 14, '17- 3, '19- dnq 13; EC: '16- 6, '18- 4; WJ: '12- dnq nt; WY: '11- 2; EU23: '15- 3; EJ: '13- 4; WUG: '17- 1, '19- 2; ET: '17- 2. Won POL 2019.
Progress at HT: 2011- 57.03, 2012- 64.88, 2013- 66.11, 2014- 69.30, 2015- 71.27, 2016- 72.74, 2017- 76.85, 2018- 72.72, 2019- 75.23, 2020- 74.18. pb JT 51.66 '12.

Kamila LICWINKO b. 22 Mar 1986 Bielsk Podlaski 1.83m 66kg. née Stepaniuk. KS Podlasie Bialystok.
At HJ: OG: '16- 9; WCh: '09-13-15-17-19: dnq 16/7=/4/3/5; EC: '14- 9=; EU23: '07- 4; EJ: '05- 7; WI: '14- 1=,'16- 3; EI: '09- 8, '15- 3; ET: '13-14-15-17: 2/3=/3/1; WUG: '13- 1. Won POL 2007-09, 2015-17, 2019-20. Polish high jump records 2013 & 2014, three indoor 2015.
Progress at HJ: 1999- 1.46, 2000- 1.61, 2001- 1.66, 2002- 1.75, 2003- 1.75, 2004- 1.84, 2005- 1.86, 2006- 1.85i/1.84, 2007- 1.90, 2008- 1.91, 2009- 1.93, 2010- 1.92i/1.89, 2011- 1.88i, 2012- 1.89, 2013- 1.99, 2014- 2.00i/1.97, 2015- 2.02i/1.99, 2016- 1.99, 2017- 1.99, 2019- 1.98, 2020- 1.94i/1.88.
Married her trainer Michal Licwinko in 2013. Baby born in 2018.

Justyna SWIETY-ERSETIC b. 3 Dec 1992 Racibórz 1.67m 57kg. née Swiety. AZS-AWF Katowice.
At 400m: OG: '16- sf; WCh: '17- h/3R, '19- 7/2R; EC: '12-14-16-18: 4h/sf/6/1&1R; EU23: '13- 3/1R; EJ: '11- 2R; WI: '14-16-18: 4/5&2R/4&2R; EI: '15-17-19-21: 3R/3&1R/6&1R/2; CCp: '18- 6/dq mxR; ET: '19- 1/1R. Won WIT 2020, POL 2013, 2016, 2020 (6 indoor titles).
Progress at 400m: 2009- 55.55, 2010- 55.30, 2011- 55.51, 2012- 52.81, 2013- 52.22, 2014- 52.22, 2015- 52.44, 2016- 51.62, 2017- 51.15, 2018- 50.41, 2019- 50.85, 2020- 51.33, 2021- 51.34i. pbs: 200m 23.81 '14, 300m 36.50 '19, 600m 1:26.68 '14, 800m 2:04.78 '12.
Brilliant relay runner. Married international wrestler Dawid Ersetic on 16 Sep 2017.

Ewa SWOBODA b. 26 Jul 1997 Zory 1.64m 55kg. AZS-AWF Katowice.
At 100m: OG: '16- sf; WCh: '17/19- sf; EC: '18- sf; WJ: '14- 5 (dnf h 200m), '16- 2; WY: '13- 4; EU23: '17- 1, '19- 1/3R; EJ: '15- 1/2R; ET: '15-17-19: 3/2R/3; At 60m: EI: '15-17-19: 8/2/1. Won Polish 100m 2017, 2019-20, WIT 60m 2019.
World junior 60m indoor record 2016.
Progress at 100m, 200m: 2011- 11.97, 2012- 12.02, 2013- 11.54/11.46w, 2014- 11.30, 2015- 11.24/11.21w, 2016- 11.12/11.10w; 2017- 11.24, 2018- 11.13/11.12w, 2019- 11.07, 2020- 11.24. pbs: 60m 7.07i '16, 200m 23.79 '18.

Anita WLODARCZYK b. 8 Aug 1985 Rawicz 1.76m 90kg. AZS-AWF Katowice. PE student.
At HT: OG: '08- 4, '12- 1, '16- 1; WCh: '09-11-13-15-17: 1/5/1/1/1; EC: '10-12-14-16-18: 3/1/1/1/1; EU23: '07- 9; CCp: '14- 1, '18- 2; ET: '09-13-15: 1/2/1. Won POL 2009, 2011-12, 2014-18; Franc G 2013, IAAF HT challenge 2013-18.
Six world hammer records 2009-16, nine Polish records 2009-16.
Progress at HT: 2002- 33.83, 2003- 43.24, 2004- 54.74, 2005- 60.51, 2006- 65.53, 2007- 69.07, 2008- 72.80, 2009- 77.96, 2010- 78.30, 2011- 75.33, 2012- 77.60, 2013- 78.46, 2014- 79.58, 2015- 81.08, 2016- 82.98, 2017- 82.87, 2018- 79.5, 2019- 75.61. pbs: SP

13.25 '06, DT 52.26 '08, Wt 20.09i '14.
In 2015 she had the eight best throws of the year, including when she became first woman to throw hammer over 80m with 81.08 at Cetniewo, and two 80m throws at the World Champs. She had the top 12 performances in 2016 and top 9 in 2017, won all her competitions in 2015- 11, 2016- 12 and 2017- 12 to take her win streak to 42 from a last loss on 16 June 2014 to a loss on 26 May 2018.

PORTUGAL

Governing body: Federação Portuguesa de Atletismo. Founded 1921.
National Championships first held in 1910 (men), 1937 (women). **2020 Champions: Men**: 100m: José Lopes 10.49, 200m: Frederico Curvelo 21.26w, 400m: Ricardo Santos 46.99, 800m: Nuno Pereira 1:49.21, 1500m: Isaac Nader 3:47.19, 3000m/10000m: Samuel Barata 8:06.30/ 28:30.73, 2000mSt (no water jump): Andre Pereira 5:28.50, 110mh: João Oliveira 14.09, 400mh: Edgar Remédios 52.75, HJ: Gerson Baldé 2.23, PV: João Buaró 5.05, LJ: Marcos Chuva 7.58w, TJ: Tiago Pereira 16.94, SP: Tsanko Arnaudov 20.77, DT: Edujose Lima 58.14, HT: Ruben Antunes 68.85, JT: Leandro Ramos 75.78, Pen: Abdel Larrianaga 3820, 3000mW/20kW/ 35kW: João Vieira 11:45.85/1:25:37/2:39:47.
Women: 100m/200m: Lorène Bazolo 11.52/2 3.62w, 400m: Cátia Azevedo 52.70, 800m/1500m: Salomé Afonso 2:07.45/4:23.48, 3000m: Mariana Machado 9:13.60, 10000m: Sara Moreira 33:04.94 (Carla Salomé Richa 32:49.93 dq illegal spikes), 2000mSt (no water jump): Joana Soares 6:09.59, 100mh: Olímpia Barbosa 13.85w, 400mh: Vera Barbosa 57.65, HJ: Anabela Neto 1.74, PV: Marta Onofre 3.90, LJ: Evelise Veiga 6.49, TJ: Patricia Mamona 14.26w, SP: Auriol Dongmo 19.53, DT: Liliana Cá 61.20, HT: Vânia Silva 61.50, JT: Cláudia Ferreira 53.27, Pen: Inès Pires 3316, 3000mW/20kW: Ana Cabecinha 12:43.01/1:30:18.

Nelson ÉVORA b. 20 Apr 1984 Abidjan, Côte d'Ivoire 1.81m 70kg. FC Barcelona.
At (LJ/)TJ: OG: '04- dnq 40, '08- 1, '16- 6; WCh: '05-07-09-11-15-17-19: dnq 14/1/2/5/3/3/dnq 15; EC: '06-14-16-18: 6&4/6/dnq 17/1; WJ: '02- dnq 18/6; EU23: '05- 3; EJ: '03- 1/1; WUG: '09- 1, '11- 1; WI: '06-08-16-18: 6/3/4/3; EI: '07-15-17-19: 5/1/1/2; CCp: '18- 5; ECp: '09- 2/1; Won WAF TJ 2008, POR LJ 2006-07, 2016; TJ 2003-04, 2006-07, 2009-11, 2013-17; WIT 2018.
Six Portuguese triple jump records 2006-07, Cape Verde LJ & TJ records 2001-02.
Progress at TJ: 1999- 14.35, 2000- 14.93i, 2001- 16.15, 2002- 15.87, 2003- 16.43, 2004- 16.85i/16.04, 2005- 16.89, 2006- 17.23, 2007- 17.74, 2008- 17.67, 2009- 17.66/17.82w, 2010- 16.36, 2011- 17.35, 2013- 16.68, 2014- 16.97, 2015- 17.52, 2016- 17.03, 2017- 17.20i/17.19, 2018- 17.40i/17.10, 2019- 17.13, 2020- 16.51i. pbs: HJ 2.07i '05, 1.98 '99; LJ 8.10 '07.

Portugal's first male world champion in 2007. Father from Cape Verde, mother from Côte d'Ivoire, relocating to Portugal when he was five. Switched nationality in 2002. Sister Dorothé (b. 28 May 1991) 400m pb 53.54 '18.

Pedro Pablo PICHARDO Peralta b. 30 Jun 1993 Santiago de Cuba 1.85m 71kg. SL Benfica.
At TJ: WCh: '13- 2, '15- 2, '19- 4; WJ: '12- 1; PAm: '15- 1; WI: '14- 3; EI: '21- 1. Won DL 2018, CAC-J 2012, CUB 2014-15.
Three CAC triple jump records 2015.
Progress at TJ: 2009- 14.55, 2010- 15.35/15.45w, 2011- 16.09, 2012- 16.79, 2013- 17.69, 2014- 17.76, 2015- 18.08, 2017- 17.60, 2018- 17.95, 2019- 17.62, 2020- 17.28/17.40w, 2021- 17.36i. pb LJ 7.81 '15.
Switched from Cuba and attained Portuguese citizenship on 23 Nov 2017 and able to compete for Portugal from 1 Aug 2019. Injured in 2016. Father Jorge was a 2.10 high jumper.

João VIEIRA b. 20 Feb 1976 Portimão 1.74m 58kg. Sporting Clube de Portugal.
At 20kW (50kW): OG: '04- 10, '08- 32, '12- 11/dnf 50k, '16- 31/dnf; WCh: '99-01-03-05-07-09-11-13-15-17-19: dq/dq/17/dnf/25/9/11/3/36/(10)/(2); EC: '98-02-06-10-14-18: 20/12/3/2/dnf/(dnf); WCp: '02-06-12: 11/8/14; ECp: '03-07-13: 4/7/6, '19- (3). At 10000mW: WJ: '94- 11; Won POR 3000mW 2020, 10000mW 2011-13, 2015-19; 20kW 1996, 1999-2007, 2009, 2020, winter 2009, 2011, 2013-14, 2017-19; 35kW 2016-19, 2021; 50kW 2004, 2008, 2012, 2019.
Portuguese records: 5000mW 2000, 10000mW 2011, 2019; 20kW (3) 2002-06, 50kW 2004 & 2012.
World M40 5000m walk record (19:30.20) 2018, Progress at 20kW, 50kW: 1994- 1:33:51, 1995- 1:26:35, 1996- 1:23:49, 1997- 1:20:59, 1998- 1:22:50, 1999- 1:22:26.3t, 2000- 1:22:53, 2001- 1:22:52, 2002- 1:20:44, 2003- 1:20:30, 2004- 1:20:48, 3:52:00; 2005- 1:21:56, 2006- 1:20:09, 2007- 1:20:42, 2008- 1:21:13, 3:52:35; 2009- 1:21:43, 2010- 1:20:49, 2011- 1:22:44, 2012- 1:20:41, 3:45:17; 2013- 1:21:08, 2014- 1:23:20, 2015- 1:21:51, 2016- 1:22:34, 3:49:05; 2017- 1:22:42, 3:45:28; 2018- 1:22:06, 2019- 1:22:06, 3:46:38; 2020- 1:25:37; pbs: 5000m 18:33.16 '00, 10000mW 39:44.91 '11, 39:06R '10; 30kW 2:09:49 '04.
Eleven successive World Champs (second most ever). Partner of Vera Santos. Twin brother Sergio has 20kW pb 1:20:58 '97.

Women

Ana CABECINHA b. 29 Apr 1984 Beja 1.68m 52kg. CO Pechão.
At 20kW: OG: '08- 8, '12- 7, '16- 6; WCh: '11-13-15-17-19: 5/7/4/6/9; EC: '10-14-18: 7/6/8; EU23: '05- 4; WCp '08-10-12-14-16: 11/8/7/8/6; ECp: '13-15-17-19: 4/9/2/5. At 5000mW: WY: '01- 10. At 10000mW: WJ: '02- 12; EJ: '03- 3; won IbAm 2006, 2010; 2nd RWC 2012; POR 3000W 12:43.01; 10000mW 2005, 2008, 2010, 2012, 2014-17, 2019; 20kW 2012-15, 2017, 2019-20.
POR records 10,000m and 20km walk 2008.

PORTUGAL – PUERTO RICO – QATAR

Progress at 20kW: 2004- 1:37:39, 2005- 1:34:13, 2006- 1:31:02, 2007- 1:32:46, 2008- 1:27:46, 2009- 1:33:05, 2010- 1:31:14, 2011- 1:31:08, 2012- 1:28:03, 2013- 1:29:17, 2014- 1:27:49, 2015- 1:28:28, 2016- 1:28:40, 2017- 1:28:57, 2018- 1:29:41, 2019- 1:31:12, 2020- 1:30:18. pbs: 3000mW 12:17.50 '14, 5000mW 21:22.23 '15, 21:21R '12; 10000mW 43:08.17 '08; running 1500m 4:31.73 '07, 3000m 9:44.81i '17, 9:46.08 '13; 5000m 17:57.34 '12.

Susana COSTA b. 22 Sep 1984 Setúbal 1.78m 65kg. Academia Fernanda Ribeiro.
At TJ: OG: '16- 9; WCh: '15: dnq, '17- 11, '19- dnq 20; EC: '12-14-16-18: dnq 13/8/5/11; EI: '17- 7, '19- 5. POR champion 2003, 2005-06, 2018 (LJ 2003); IbAm 2012.
Progress at TJ: 2002- 12.62, 2003- 12.68, 2004- 13.02i/13.00/13.11w, 2005- 13.07i/12.89/13.53w, 2006- 13.12/13.51w, 2007- 13.49i/12.88/13.27w, 2008- 13.77i/13.36, 2009- 12.91, 2010- 12.62/12.75w, 2011- 13.70/13.77w, 2012- 14.19, 14.16, 2014- 14.11, 2015- 14.32, 2016- 14.34, 2017- 14.35, 2018- 14.17, 2019- 14.43i/13.99, 2020- 14.10. pb LJ 5.89 '03, 5.97w '06.

Auriol DONGMO Mekemnang b. 3 Aug 1990 Ngaoundéré, Cameroon 1.73m 95kg. Sporting CP.
At SP (DT): OG: '16- 12; WCh: '15: dnq 20; AfG: '11- 1 (5), 15 1 (5); AfCh: '12- 3, 14- 1 (8), '16- 1 (7); EI: '21- 1. Won WIT 2021, POR 2020, Franc G 2017. Shot records: CMR 2011-19, 2 African indoor 2020, 6 Portuguese 2020 & 2 indoor 2021.
Progress at SP: 2008- 13.34, 2009- 13.74, 2010- 13.70, 2011- 16.03, 2012- 15.41, 2013- 15.88, 2014- 16.84, 2015- 17.64, 2016- 17.92, 2017- 18.37, 2019- 17.90, 2020- 19.53, 2021- 19.65i. pb DT 47.00 '16.
Formerly from Cameroon, eligible for Portugal from 28 March 2020.

Inês HENRIQUES b 1 May 1980 Santarém 1.56m 48kg. CN Rio Maior.
At 50kW: WCh: '17- 1, '19- dnf; EC: '18- 1; ECp: '19- 3. At 20kW: OG: '04-12-16: 25/13/12; WCh: '01-05-07-09-11-13-15: dq/27/7/ 10/8/10/23; EC: '02-06-10-14: 15/12/8/13; EU23: '01- 10; WCp: '06-10-12-16: 13/3/8/8; ECp: '07- 7, '13- 7; Won POR 10000mW 2006, 2009, 2011, 2013, 2018; 20kW 2009, 2011, 2016, 2018; 35kW 2017-18, 50kW 2017. At 5000mW: EJ: '99- 12.
World walks records 50k (2) 2017, 35k 2018.
Progress at 20kW, 50kW: 2000- 1:41:09, 2001- 1:34:49, 2002- 1:34:46.5t, 2003- 1:36:03, 2004- 1:31:23.7t, 2005- 1:33:24, 2006- 1:30:28, 2007- 1:30:24, 2008- 1:31:06, 2009- 1:30:34, 2010- 1:29:36, 2011- 1:30:29, 2012- 1:29:54, 2013- 1:29:30, 2014- 1:29:33, 2015- 1:29:52, 2016- 1:29:00, 2017- 1:30:44, 4:05:56; 2018- 1:29:15, 4:09:21; 2019- 1:38:16, 4:13:57; 2020- 1:35:20. pbs: 3000mW 12:25.36i '13, 12:38.75 '07; 5000mW 21:32.08 '14, 10000mW 43:22.05 '08, 43:09R '10; 35kW 2:45:51 '18.
Inaugural women's world record holder and world champion at 50k walk.

Patrícia MAMONA b. 21 Nov 1988 Lisbon 1.68m 53kg. Sporting CP. Was at Clemson University, USA.
At TJ: OG: '12- dnq 13, '16- 6; WCh: '11-15: dnq 27/16, '17- 9, '19- 8; EC: '10-12-14-16-18: 8/2/dnq 13/1/dnq 16; WJ: '06- 4; WY: '05- 7; EU23: '09- 5; EJ: '07- dnq 15; WI: '14- 4; EI: '13-15-17-19-21: 8/5/2/4/1; WUG: '11- 2. POR champion 2008-17, 2019-20; NCAA 2010-11; WIT 2017.
Nine Portuguese triple jump records 2009-16.
Progress at TJ: 2004- 12.71, 2005- 12.87, 2006- 13.37/13.38w, 2007- 13.24, 2008- 13.51, 2009- 13.83, 2010- 14.12, 2011- 14.42, 2012- 14.52, 2013- 14.02/14.07w, 2014- 14.36/14.49w, 2015- 14.32i/14.19, 2016- 14.65, 2017- 14.42, 2018- 14.19, 2019- 14.44i/14.40, 2020- 14.33i/14.26, 2021- 14.53i. pbs: 200m 24.42 '10, 800m 2:19.70i '09, 60mh 8.41i '09, 100mh 13.53/13.49w '10, HJ 1.69 '04; LJ 6.40i '20, 6.23 '19, Pen 4081i '09, Hep 5293 '11.

PUERTO RICO

Governing body: Federación de Atletismo Amateur de Puerto Rico. Founded 1947.

Wesley VÁZQUEZ b. 27 Mar 1994 Bayamón 1.84m 73kg.
At 800m: OG: '12/16- h; WCh: '13- h, '19- 5; WJ: '12- 4; WY: '11- 7; PAm: '19- 2; PAm-J: '11- 2; C.Cp: '14- 8, '18- 8; WUG: '13- 4. Four PUR 800m records 2012-19, CAC Junior 2012.
Progress at 800m: 2010- 1:51.19, 2011- 1:47.38, 2012- 1:45.29, 2013- 1:45.94, 2014- 1:44.64, 2016- 1:44.75, 2018- 1:46.47, 2019- 1:43.78, 2020- 1:45.18. pbs: 400m 46.67 '20, 600m 1:14.85 '20, 1000m 2:19.94 '14, 1500m 3:46.98 '16, 1M 4:06.50 '15.

Women

Jasmine CAMACHO-QUINN b. 21 Aug 1996 Ladson, South Carolina, USA 1.80m 73kg. Nike. University of Kentucky, USA.
At 100mh: OG: '16- dq sf. NCAA champion 2016, 2018; NACAC U23 2016
CAC 100mh record 2018, 9 PUR records 2016-18, 100m & 300m (2) 2020.
Progress at 100mh: 2013- 14.10, 2014- 13.37, 2016- 12.69/12.45w, 2017- 12.58, 2018- 12.40, 2019- 12.82/12.73w. pbs: 60m 7.59i '16, 100m 11.22 '20, 150m 16.91 '20, 200m 22.45 '20, 300m 36.12 '20, 60mh 7.95i '18, LJ 6.15 '14.
Mother is from Puerto Rico. Her brother Robert Quinn is a defensive end for Miami Dolphins in the NFL.

QATAR

Governing body: Qatar Association of Athletics Federation. Founded 1963.

Mutaz Essa BARSHIM b. 24 Jun 1991 Doha 1.92m 70kg. Team Aspire.
At HJ: OG: '12- 3=, '16- 2; WCh: '11-13-15-17-19: 7/2/4/1/1; WJ: '10- 1; AsiG: '10- 1, '14- 1; AsiC: '11- 1, '15- 3; WI: '12-14-16-18: 9=/1/4/2; CCp: '14- 3; won DL 2014-15, 2017; Asian indoors 2010,

2012, 2014, 2016, 2018; Asi-J 2010, W.Mil G 2011, Arab 2011, 2013, 2015; Gulf 2013.
Five Asian high jump records 2012-14 and indoors (3) 2013-15, 14 Qatar records 2010-13. Progress at HJ: 2008- 2.07, 2009- 2.14, 2010- 2.31, 2011- 2.35, 2012- 2.39, 2013- 2.40, 2014- 2.43, 2015- 2.41, 2016- 2.40, 2017- 2.40, 2018- 2.40, 2019- 2.37. IAAF Male Athlete of the Year 2017. His 2.43 at Brussels in 2014 was the world's best since 1993, second only to Javier Sotomayor. Qatari father (who was a race walker), Sudanese mother. Younger brothers Muamer Aissa Barshim (b. 3 Jan 1994) HJ pb 2.28 '14 and 3rd 2014 Asian Games, and Hamdi Mahamat Alamine 2.27 '18.

Ashraf Amjad EL-SEIFY (Al-Saifi) b. 20 Feb 1995 Egypt 1.83m 100kg.
At HT: OG: '16- 6; WCh: '13- dnq 24, '15- 9, '17- dnq 23, '19- 9; WJ: '12- 1, '14- 1; AsiG: '18- 1; AsiC: '15/19- 2; CCp: '18- 5. Won Asi-J 2014.
Records: world youth 5kg 85.26 '11, world junior 6kg 85.57 '12, Asian junior 2013, three Qatar 2013-16.
Progress at HT: 2013- 76.37, 2014- 71.81, 2015- 78.04, 2016- 78.19, 2017- 76.14, 2018- 77.04, 2019- 76.22, 2020- 73.33, 2021- 74.71.
Former Egyptian, QAT from 30 Mar 2011; able to compete for them from 29 Mar 2012.

Abdelilah HAROUN b. 1 Jan 1997 Sudan 1.78m 73kg.
At 400m: OG: '16- sf; WCh: '17- 3, '19- h; AsiG: '18- 1/1R; AsiC: '15- 1/1R; WJ: '16- 1; WI: '16- 2; CCp: '18-1. Won Asian indoor Champs 2016, 2018, Games 2017; Arab 2015.
Asian 400m records indoors and out 2015, 4x400m 2018; QAT 2015 & 2018. World best 500m indoors 2016.
Progress at 400m: 2014- 45.74, 2015- 44.27, 2016- 44.81, 2017- 44.48, 2018- 44.07, 2019- 47.76. Pbs: 200m 21.16 '18, 500m 59.83i '16, 800m 1:56.06 '17. Qatar citizen from 2 Feb 2015, having lived there from 2013.

Abderrahmane SAMBA b. 5 Sep 1995 Saudi Arabia. 1.87m 80kg.
At 400m: WCh: '17- 7, '19- 3; AsiG: '18- 1/1R; AsiC: '19- 1; CCp: '18- 1.
Three Asian and five Qatar 400mh records 2018, Asian 4x400m record 2018.
Progress at 400mh: 2017- 48.31A/48.44, 2018- 46.98, 2019- 47.27. Pbs: 200m 21.17, '16. 20.94w '15; 400m 44.60A '19, 44.62 '18.
12 successive wins in 400mh finals from August 2017, inc. season's record nine sub-48 times in 2018, to May 2019. Born in Saudi Arabia and then ran in Mauritania (his father's nation) before transferring to Qatar, when he has lived since 6 May 2015, citizen from 1 Oct 2015, cleared to compete from 6 May 2016.

ROMANIA

Governing body: Federatia Romana de Atletism. Founded 1912.
National Championships first held in 1914 (men), 1925 (women). **2020 Champions: Men:** 100m: Petre Rezmives 10.71, 200m/400mh: Vlad Dulcescu 21,35/51.14, 400m: Mihai Pislaru 46.54. 800m: Cristian Voicu 1:51.09, 1500m: Nicolae Coman 4:06.11, 5000m/10000m: Nicolae Soare 14:33.73/30:17.63, 3000mSt: Mihai Cochior 9:13.85, 110mh: Cosmin Dumitrache 14.35, HJ: Mihai Donesan 2.14, PV: Andrei Deliu 4.80, LJ: Gabriel Bitan 7.73, TJ: Florin Visan 16.06, SP: Andrei Toader 18.7641, DT: Alin Firfirica 62.16, HT: Mihaita Micu 68.98, JT: Alexandru Novac 76.88, Dec: Razvan Roman 6898, 20kW: Marcia Mihaila 1:30:42. **Women:** 100m/200m: Marina Baboi 11.63/23.78, 400m: Calelia Gall 53.46, 800m: Cristina Balan 2:07.26, 1500m: Maria Sfarghiu 4:25.49, 5000m/3000mSt: Elena Panaet 16:07.66/ 9:54.60, 10000m: Roxana Rotaru 33:26.03, 100mh: Anamaria Nesteriuc 13.44, 400mh: Sanda Belgyan 58.53, HJ: Daniela Stanciu 1.80, PV: Stefania Dragan 3.40, LJ/TJ: Florentina Iusco 6.31/13.69, SP: Andreea Apachite 14.52, DT: Andrea Lungu 48.84, HT: Bianca Ghelber 71.57, JT: Iona Plavan 50.16, Hep: Florentina Budica 4440, 20kW: Ana Rodean 1:40:02.

Alin Alexandru **FIRFIRICA** b. 3 Nov 1995 Suceava 1.96m 108kg.
At DT: WCh: '19- 4; EC: 18- 7; WJ: '14- dnq 13 (dnq 19 EP); EU23: '15- 1, '17- 2; EJ: '13- dnq 24; WUG: '17- 2, '19- 2. Balkan champion 2019-20, ROU 2015-20, W.MilG 2019.
Progress at DT: 2013- 52.11, 2014- 65.45, 2015- 61.04, 2016- 65.03, 2017- 61.98, 2018- 66.22, 2019- 67.32, 2020- 66.22. pb SP 17.75i '18, 17.31 '17.

Women

Bianca-Florentina **GHELBER** b. 1 Jun 1990 Roman, Neamt district 1.70m 70kg. née Perie. S.C.M. Bacau. Student.
At HT: OG: '08/12- dnq 16/17; WCh: '07/09/17/19: dnq 26/19/24/18, '11-13- 6/9; EC: '10-12-14-18: 4/9/7/dnq 19; WJ: '06/08- 1; WY: '05/07- 1; EU23: '11- 1; EJ: '07/09- 1; WUG: '11- 2, '13- 4; ROU champion 2009-14, 2016-17, 2019-20; Balkan 2013-14, 2020.
Progress at HT: 2003- 47.14, 2004- 57.67, 2005- 65.13, 2006- 67.38, 2007- 67.24, 2008- 69.59, 2009- 69.63, 2010- 73.52, 2011- 72.04, 2012- 70.05, 2013- 71.57, 2014- 71.93, 2016- 66.26, 2017- 69.44, 2018- 70.96, 2019- 70.80, 2020- 72.18. pb SP 13.04i '07.
World age 14 best of 65.13 in 2005. Won seven global or European age-group championships. Daughter Victoria born September 2015. Her younger sister Roxana won the bronze medal in the 2011 World Youth hammer, pb 61.43 '15.

Elena Andreea **PANTUROIU** b. 24 Feb 1995 Ribeira 1.70m 57kg. CS Onesti.
At TJ: OG: '16- dnq 16; WCh: '15/17- dnq 18/14, '19- 11; EC: 16- dnq 16, '18- 4; WJ: '14- 5; WY: '11- dnq 24; EU23: '15- 2, '17- 1; EJ: '13- 2; WI: '16- 5,

134   ROMANIA – RUSSIA

18- 4. Romanian champion 2016, 2018-19.
Progress at TJ: 2011- 12.79, 2012- 12.94i/12.67/13.08w, 2013- 13.26, 2014- 13.93i/13.81/14.20w, 2015- 14.13, 2016- 14.33, 2017- 14.43, 2018- 14.47, 2019- 14.23i/14.12/14.24w, 2020- 13.87i. pbs: 200m 25.94 '12, 800m 2:17.41 '14, 60mh 8.51i '16, 100mh 14.65 '13, HJ 1.80i '17, 1.71 '13; LJ 6.44i/6.14 '15, SP 11.61i '17; JT 31.09 '12, Pen 4309i '17, Hep 5102 '13.

RUSSIA

Governing body: All-Russia Athletic Federation. Founded 1911.
National Championships first held 1908, USSR women from 1922. **2020 Champions: Men**: 100m: Igor Obravtsov 10.36, 200m: Ilfat Sadeyev 21.12, 400m: Maksim Fedyayev 46.15, 800m: Konstantin Kholmogorov 1:46.37, 1500m: Sergey Dubrovskiy 3:44.21, 5000m/10000m: Vladimir Nikitin 13:33.67/28:16.22, HMar: Rinas Akhmadiyev 64:01, Mar: Yuriy Chechun 2:15:05, 3000mSt: Maksim Yakushev 8:23.02, 110mh: Sergey Shubenkov 13.31, 400mh: Timofey Chalyy 49.77, HJ: Ilya Ivanyuk 2.24, PV: Aleksandr Gripich 5.50, LJ: Aleksandr Menkov 8.06w, TJ: Denis Obyortyshev 16.83, SP: Aleksandr Lesnoy 21.04, DT: Aleksey Khudyakov 62.18, HT: Valeriy Pronkin 75.83, JT: Nikolay Orlov 82.33, Dec: Sergey Timshin 7609, 20kW: Vasily Mizinov 1:19:09, 50kW: Dementiy Cheparev 3:43:29. **Women**: 100m/200m: Krisztina Khorosheva 11.66/23.66, 400m: Polina Miller 51.51; 800m/ 1500m: Aleksandra Gulyayeva 2:00.32/4:05.69, 5000m: Svetlana Aplachkina 15:31.34, 10000m/HMar: Yelena Korobkina 32:56.23/70:11, Mar: Sardana Trofimova 2:27:08, 3000mSt: Yekaterina Ivonina 9:16.84, 100mh: Nina Morozova 13.53, 400mh: Vera Rudakova 55.57, HJ: Mariya Lasitskene 1.92, PV: Anzhelika Sidorova 4.70, LJ: Polina Lukyanenkova 6.57, TJ: Yekaterina Koneva 14.73w, SP: Natalya Troneva 16.82, DT: Yekaterina Strokova 63.90; HT: Sofiya Palkina 70.86, JT: Vera Markaryan 56.97, Hep: Aleksandra Butvina 5610, 20kW: Elvira Khasanova 1:27:45, 50kW: Yelena Lashmanova 3:50:42

Mikhail AKIMENKO b. 6 Dec 1995 Prokhladny 1.96m 86kg. Moskva.
At HJ: WCh: '19- 2; WJ: '14- 1; EU23: '15- 6; EJ: '13- 3. RUS champion 2019.
Progress at HJ: 2013- 2.18, 2014- 2.24, 2015- 2.24, 2016- 2.28, 2017- 2.18, 2018- 2.25, 2019- 2.35, 2020- 2.31i/2.19, 2021- 2.31i. pbs: 60mh 7.92i '16, LJ 7.15i '14.

Dementiy CHEPAREV b. 28 Oct 1992. Mordoviya.
At 10000mW: WY: '09- 2; EJ: '11- 8; ECp-J: '11- 3. Won RUS 50kW 2018, 2020.
Progress at 50kW: 2017- 3:43:05, 2018- 3:54:20, 2020- 3:43:29. pbs: 3000mW 11:02.9 '18, 5000mW: 19:13.5i '20, 20:32.82 '16; 10000mW 41:53.76 '09, 41:00R '10; 20kW 1:22:54 '16, 30kW 2:07:00 '18, 35kW: 2:27:26 '20.

Ilya IVANYUK b. 9 Mar 1993 Krasny, Smolensk 1.83m 75kg. Smolensk
At HJ: WCh: '17- 6, '19- 3; EC: '18- 3; WJ: '12- 4; EU23: '13- 6, '15- 1; CCp: '18- 5. Won RUS 2020, W.MilG 2019.
Progress at HJ: 2010- 2.15, 2011- 2.20, 2012- 2.22i/2.12, 2013- 2.27i/2.26, 2014- 2.23, 2015- 2.30, 2016- 2.25i/2.19, 2017- 2.31i/2.30, 2018- 2.31, 2019- 2.35, 2020- 2.33i/2.30.

Aleksandr MENKOV b. 7 Dec 1990 Minusinsk, Krasnoyarsk reg. 1.78m 74kg. Krasnoyarsk VS. Krasnoyarsk State University.
At LJ: OG: '12- 11; WCh: '09-11-13-15-17: dnq 32/6/1/6/4; EC: '14- dnq 13; WI: '12- 3, '14- 5; EU23: '11- 1; EJ: '09- 1; EI: '13- 1; WUG: '13- 2; ET: '11-13-15: 1/1/1. Won DL 2012-13, Russian 2012, 2018, 2020. Two Russian records 2013.
Progress at LJ: 2008- 6.98, 2009- 8.16, 2010- 8.10, 2011- 8.28, 2012- 8.29, 2013- 8.56, 2014- 8.30i/8.02, 2015- 8.27, 2016- 7.91, 2017- 8.32, 2018- 8.41, 2019- 8.30i/8.13, 2020- 7.78/8.06w. pbs: HJ 2.15 '10, TJ 15.20 '09.

Vasiliy MIZINOV b. 29 Dec 1997 Magnitogorsk 1.67m 55kg.
At 20kW: WCh: '19- 2; EC: '18- 3; EU23: '19- 1; ECp: '19- 2; won RUS 2020. At 10000mW: EJ: '15- dq. World junior 5000m walk record 2016.
Progress at 20kW: 2017- 1:21:48, 2018- 1:18:54, 2019- 1:18:32, 2020- 1:19:09, 2021- 1:18:45. pbs: 5000mW: 18:25.5i '19, 18:51.9 '16; 10000mW 38:58.21 '16.

Timur MORGUNOV b. 12 Oct 1996 Kopeysk 1.88m 77kg.
At PV: EC: '18- 2; EJ: '15- 5; CCp: '18- 4. Russian champion 2017, DL 2018.
Progress at PV: 2014- 5.20, 2015- 5.50, 2016- 5.80i/5.55, 2017- 5.80, 2018- 6.00, 2020- 5.86i. pbs: HJ 1.83 '17, LJ 7.25 '17, JT 51.68 '17, Dec 6856 '17.

Valeriy PRONKIN b. 15 Jun 1994 Nizhny Novgorod 1.95m 115kg.
At HT: WCh: '17- 2; WJ: '12- 8; WY: 11- dnq 20 (10 DT); EU23: '15- 2; EJ: '13- 1. Won RUS 2017, 2020.
Progress at HT: 2012- 64.78, 2013- 73.50, 2014- 71.34, 2015- 76.80, 2016- 75.39, 2017- 79.32, 2019- 79.10, 2020- 76.50.

Sergey SHIROBOKOV b. 16 Feb 1999 Malaya Ita, Sharkanskiy Dist, Udmurtia 1.68m 57kg.
At 20kW: WCh: '17- 2; ECp: '17- 12; won RUS 2018-19. At 10000mW: WY: '15- 1; EJ: '17- 1. World U20 10k & 20k walks bests 2018.
Progress at 20kW: 2016- 1:22:31, 2017- 1:18:26, 2018- 1:17:25, 2019- 1:18:42, 2020- 1:19:34 pbs: 5000mW 18:45.7i '18, 10000mW 40:58.0 '16, 38:25R '18.

Ilya SHKURENYOV b. 11 Jan 1991 Linevo, Volgograd reg. 1.91m 82kg. Volgograd Dyn.
At Dec: OG: '12- 16; WCh: '13-15-17-19: 8/4/dnf/4; EC: '12-14-18- 3/3/3/2; WJ: '10- 2; EU23: '11-

5, '13- 2; ECp: '15- 1. Russian champion 2013, 2016-17. At Hep: WI: '12- 4; EI: '13-15-19: 5/1/3. Progress at Dec: 2011- 7894, 2012- 8219, 2013- 8370, 2014- 8498, 2015- 8538, 2016- 8292, 2017- 8601, 2018- 8321, 2019- 8494, 2020- 8086. pbs: 60m 6.98i '15, 100m 10.89 '17, 400m 47.88 '15, 1000m 2:41.65i '13, 1500m 4:24.98 '15, 60mh 7.86i '15, 110mh 13.95 '17, HJ 2.12 '17, PV 5.40 '13, LJ 7.78 '16, 7.81w '20, SP 15.21i/14.71 '19; DT 48.75 '19, JT 63.58 '14, Hep 6353i '15.
Won IAAF Challenge 2015.

Sergey SHUBENKOV b. 4 Oct 1990 Barnaul, Altay Kray 1.90m 75kg. Tyumen State University.
At 110mh: OG: '12- sf; WCh: '11-13-15-17-19: h/3/1/2/2; EC: '12-14-18: 1/1/2; EU23: '11- 1; EJ: '09- 2, WUG: '13- 3; CCp: '14- 1, '18- 1; ET: '13-14-15: 1/1/1. Won DL 2017-18, WMilG 2015 & 2019, Russian 2013, 2016, 2020. At 60mh: EI: '13- 1.
Seven Russian 110mh records 2012-18.
Progress at 110mh: 2010- 13.54, 2011- 13.46, 2012- 13.09, 2013- 13.16/13.10w, 2014- 13.13, 2015- 12.98, 2016- 13.20, 2017- 13.01, 2018- 12.92, 2019- 13.12, 2020- 13.31. pb 60mh 7.49i '13.
Mother Natalya Shubenkova had heptathlon pb 6859 '04; 4th 1988 OG and 3rd 1986 EC.

Women

Klavdiya AFANASYEVA b. 15 Jan 1996.
At 20kmW: WCh: '17- dq; EU23: '17- 1; At 10000mW: EJ: '15- 1; WCp: '14- 6J; ECp: '15- 1J. At 5000mW: WY: '13- 5. won RUS 50kW 2018-19. World 35k & 50k walk bests 2019.
Progress at 20kW, 50kW: 2016- 1:26:47, 2017- 1:28:29, 2018- 4:14:46, 2019- 1:29:40, 3:57:08. pbs: 10000mW 43:36.88 '15, 30kW 2:22:27 '19, 35kW 2:38:24 '19 .

Anna CHICHEROVA b. 22 Jul 1982 Yerevan, Armenia 1.80m 57kg. Moskva VS. Physical culture graduate.
At HJ: OG: '04- 6, '08- dq (3), '12- 1; WCh: '03-05-07-09-11-13-15: 6/4/2=/dq2/1/3=/3; EC: '06- 7=; WJ: '00- 4; WY: '99- 1; EJ: '01- 1; WUG: '05- 1; WI: '03-04-12: 3/2/2=; EI: '05- 1, '07- 5=; ECp: '06- 3. Won RUS 2004, 2007-08, 2011-12, 2015-16.
Progress at HJ: 1998- 1.80, 1999- 1.89, 2000- 1.90, 2001- 1.92, 2002- 2.00i/1.89, 2003- 2.04i/2.00, 2004- 2.04i/1.98, 2005- 2.01i/1.99, 2006- 1.96i/1.95, 2007- 2.03, 2008- 2.04, 2009- 2.02, 2011- 2.07, 2012- 2.06i/2.05, 2013- 2.02, 2014- 2.01, 2015- 2.01, 2016- 1.98, 2018- 1.98, 2019- 2.02i/2.00, 2020- 1.96i/1.90. Moved with family to Russia at the beginning of the 1990s. Married to Gennadiy Chernoval KAZ, pbs 100m 10.18, 200m 20.44 (both 2002), 2 WUG 100m & 200m 2001, 2 AsiG 2002 2002; their daughter Nika born on 7 Sep 2010. Lost her 2008 Olympic bronze medal when a re-test in 2016 showed positive; also lost her 2009 World silver with the 2-year drugs ban.

Reykhan KAGRAMANOVA 1 Jun 1997.
Progress at 20kW: 2017- 1:35:44, 2018- 1:29:50,

2019- 1:30:26, 2020- 1:26:50. pbs: 5000mW 20:21.5i '20, 10000mW: 45:40.65 '18.

Elvira KHASANOVA 10 Jan 2000.
At 5000mW: WY: '17- 3. At 20kW: Russian champion 2020. European and world junior 10000m walk record 2019.
Progress at 20kW: 2019- 1:28:15, 2020- 1:26:43. pbs: 5000mW 20:21.5i '20, 10000mW: 41:45.84 '19.

Darya KLISHINA b. 15 Jan 1991 Tver 1.80m 57kg. Moskva. Model.
At LJ: OG: '16- 9; WCh: '11-13-15-17: 6/6/10/2; EC: '14- 3; WY: '07- 1; EU23: '11- 1; EJ: '09- 1; WI: '10-12-14: 5/4/7; EI: '11-13-17: 1/1/4, WUG: '13- 1; ET: '11-13-15: 1/2/1. RUS champion 2014, 2019.
Progress at LJ: 2005- 5.83, 2006- 6.33/6.47w, 2007- 6.49, 2008- 6.52i/6.20, 2009- 6.80, 2010- 7.03, 2011- 7.05, 2012- 6.93, 2013- 7.01i/6.90/6.98w, 2014- 6.90, 2015- 6.95, 2016- 6.84, 2017- 7.00. 2019- 6.84. The one Russian athlete permitted to compete (as a neutral) at OG '16 and EI '17.

Yekaterina KONEVA b. 25 Sep 1988 Khabarovsk 1.69m 55kg. Khabarovskiy.
At TJ: WCh: '13- 2, '15- 5; EC: '14- 2; WI: '14- 1; WUG: '11-13-15: 1/1/1; CCp: '14- 2; EI: '15- 1; ET: '13-14-15: 2/1/1. RUS champion 2014-15, 2018,. 2020; WMilG LJ & TJ 2015.
Progress at TJ: 2010- 13.93/14.00w, 2011- 14.46, 2012- 14.60i/14.36, 2013- 14.82, 2014- 14.89, 2015- 15.04, 2016- 14.42, 2018- 14.67/14.79w, 2019- 14.81i/14.4, 2020- 14.74w. pbs: 60m 7.39i '07, 100m 11.76 '09, 200m 23.89 '09, LJ 6.82i '15, 6.70/6.80w '11.
Married Sergey Polyanskiy (LJ 8.20 '15, 8 WCh '15) in October 2016, daughter Sofiya born 17 Apr 2017. Two-year drugs ban 2007-09.

Yelena LASHMANOVA b. 9 Apr 1992 Saransk 1.70m 48kg. Biology student at Mordoviya State University.
At 20kmW: OG: '12- 1; WCh: '13- 1; WCp: '12- 1; won RUS 2016-19, 50kW 2020. At 10000mW: WJ: '10- 1; EJ: '11- 1; ECp: '11- 1J. At 5000mW: WY: '09- 1. and 50km 2020, world junior 10,000m 2011. Unratified world record 50k walk & world indoor 10000m walk best 2020.
Progress at 20kW, 50kW: 2012- 1:25:02, 2013- 1:25:49, 2016- 1:24:58, 2017- 1:25:18, 2018- 1:23:39, 2019- 1:24:31, 2020- 3:50:42. pbs: 5000mW 20:04.4i '20, 20:15.6 '16; 10000mW 42:59.48 '11, 30kW 2:17:28 '20, 35k: 2:40:22 '20, .
Best ever debut at 20k walk (2nd 1:26:30 in 2012). Then 14 successive 20k wins 2012-20 plus world best at 50k. Received two-year drugs ban from test on 4 Jan 2014.

Mariya LASITSKENE b. 14 Jan 1993 Prokhladny, Kabardino-Balkar 1.82m 60kg. née Kuchina. Moskva.
At HJ: WCh: '15-17-19: 1/1/1; EC: '14- 2, '18- 1; WJ: '12- 3; WY: '09- 2=; EU23: '15- 12; EJ: '11- 1; WI: '14- 1=. '18- 1; EI: '15- 1, '19- 1; WUG: '13- 2; CCp: '14- 1, '18- 1; ET: '13-14-15: 1/1/1. Won DL

2014, 2017-19; Yth Oly 2010, RUS champion 2014, 2017-20; W.MilG 2015 & 2019, WIT 2018.
World junior indoor high jump record 2011.
Progress at HJ: 2009- 1.87, 2010- 1.91, 2011- 1.97i/1.95, 2012- 1.96i/1.89, 2013- 1.98i/1.96, 2014- 2.01i/2.00, 2015- 2.01, 2016- 2.00, 2017- 2.06, 2018- 2.04, 2019- 2.06, 2020- 2.05i/1.97, 2021- 2.00i.
Married journalist Vladas Lasitskas on 17 Mar 2017. 45 successive wins 23 June 2016 to 30 June 2018 World Indoors, Top seven performances of 2017 and top four in 2018 and 2019.

Darya NIDBAYKINA b. 26 Dec 1994. 1.68m 57kg.
At TJ: EU23: '15- 6; EJ: '13- 5. RUS champion 2019.
Progress at TJ: 2012- 13.02, 2013- 13.53/13.58w, 2014- 13.24, 2015- 13.70, 2016- 13.72i/13.64/13.67w, 2017- 14.21, 2018- 14.20, 2019- 14.64, 2020- 14.17/14.27w. pb LJ 6.04i '18, 5.86 '20.

Margarita NIKIFOROVA b. 19 Aug 1998. Mordoviya – Kemerovskaya.
Progress at 50kW: 2019- 4:05:58, 2020- 3:59:56. pb 20kW: 1:31:57 '18, 30kW 2:22:07 '20, 2:45:16 '20.

Marina NOVIKOVA 1 Mar 1989. née Pandakova. Churvashkaya Reg.
At 20kW: WCp: '14- 10. ECp: '13- 2, '15- 5; WUG: '15- 2.
Progress at 20kW: 2008- 1:38:19, 2011- 1:33:00, 2012- 1:28:29, 2013- 1:27:39, 2014- 1:27:54, 2015- 1:25:03, 2016- 1:27:18, 2020- 1:27:25. pbs: 3000mW: 11:50.30 '16, 5000mW 21:40.41i '13, 10kW 42:09 '20.

Anzhelika SIDOROVA b. 28 Jun 1991 Moskva 1.66m 52kg. Moskva Youth.
At PV: WCh: '15- nh, '17- dnq nh, '19- 1; EC: '14- 1, '18- 4; WJ: '10- 4; EU23: '13- 2; WI: '14- 2=, '18- 2; EI: '13-15-19: 3/1/1; CCp: 18- 1; ET: '13-14-15- 2/1/2. Won RUS 2014-15, 2019-20; WIT 2019.
Progress at PV: 2007- 3.80, 2008- 4.00, 2009- 4.10i/4.00, 2010- 4.30, 2011- 4.40i/4.30, 2012- 4.50, 2013- 4.62i/4.60, 2014- 4.72i/4.70, 2015- 4.80i/4.79, 2016- 4.85, 2017- 4.75, 2018- 4.90i/4.85, 2019- 4.95, 2020- 4.95i/4.80.

Yelena SOKOLOVA b. 23 Jul 1986 Staryi Oskol, Belgorod reg. 1.70m 61kg. née Kremneva. Krasnodarsk krai.
At LJ: OG: '12- 2; WCh: '09- dnq 13, '13- 8, '15/19- dnq 23/24; WJ: '02- dnq; WY: '03- 6 (3 MedR); EU23: '07- 3; EI: '07- 5, '09- 2; WUG: '07- 2, '13- 2. Won DL 2012, RUS 2009, 2012, 2015, 2017-18.
Progress at LJ: 2002- 6.33, 2003- 6.39i?/6.31, 2006- 6.53, 2007- 6.71, 2008- 6.74, 2009- 6.92, 2010- 6.72/6.90w, 2011- 6.76, 2012- 7.07, 2013- 6.91, 2015- 6.70, 2016- 6.59, 2017- 6.85, 2018- 6.70, 2019- 6.81, 2020- 6.46/6.70i. pbs: 60m 7.34i '12, 100m 11.61 '12, TJ 13.15i/12.93 '03.
Son born on 23 Aug 2014.

Yekaterina STROKOVA b. 17 Dec 1989 1.84m 80kg

At DT: WCh: '13/15- dnq 15/17; EC: 14- 9; WJ: '08- dnq 16; EU23: '11-10; ET: '14- 3. Won RUS 2013, 2016 2019-20.
Progress at DT: 2006- 46.86, 2007- 47.83, 2008- 55.82 2009- 56.65, 2010- 58.41, 2011- 59.61, 2012- 63.52, 2013- 63.80, 2014- 65.78, 2015- 64.33, 2016- 65.26, 2017- 52.90, 2018- 58.63, 2019- 63.90, 2020- 63.90. Pb JT 46.34 '05.

SERBIA

Governing body: Athletic Federation of Serbia. Founded in 1921 (as Yugoslav Athletic Federation).
National Championships (Yugoslav) first held in 1920 (men) and 1923 (women). **2020 Champions: Men**: 100m: Aleksa Kijanovic 10.50, 200m/400m: Bosko Kijanovic 21.18/46.58, 800m: Miroslav Dukadinovic 1:51.70, 1500m: Elzan Bibic 3:46.91, 3000m: Nikola Bursac 8:30.19, 5000m/10000m/3000mSt: Milos Milosavljevic 15:31.14/31:44.42/9:12.08, HMar: Ognjen Stojanovic 1:12:10, 110mh/PV/Dec: Aleksandar Grnovic 14.50/4.21/5912, 400mh: Milos Markovic 54.94, HJ: Jasmin Halili 2.11, LJ: Strahinja Jovancevic 7.69, TJ: Milan Mladenovic 14.52, SP/DT: Bogdan Zdravkovic 18.89/49.57, HT: Milos Covic 54.50, JT: Vedran Samac 71.61, 10000mW: Predrag Filipovic 52:56.5, 20kW: Predrag Krstovic 1:46:15 sh. **Women**: 100m: Milana Timanic 11.72, 200m: Tamara Milutinovics 24.31, 400m: Tijana Japundzic 56.34, 800m: Maria Stambolic 2:10.57, 1500m/3000m: Teodora Simovic 4:40.60/10:03.24, 5000m: Aleksandra Kostadinovic 18:24.83, 10000m: Nevena Iovanovic 39:19.39, HMar: Katarina Pohlod 1:25:54, 3000mSt: Sanja Djokovic 12:18.32, 100mh: Anja Lukic 13.34, 400mh: Maja Gajic 61.19, HJ: Zorana Bukvic 1.75, LJ: Milica Gardasevic 6.42, TJ: Marija Stojadinovic 13.25, SP: Zorica Stanic 12.67, DT: Dragana Tomasevic 56.20, HT: Aleksandra Ivanovic 51.45, JT: Marija Vucenovic 58.88, Hep: Marina Zivkovic 5029, 5000mW/ 20kW: Tijana Savicevic 26:29.3/1:59:42 sh.

Asmir KOLASINAC b. 15 Oct 1984 Skopje, Macedonia 1.86m 137kg. Beogradski AC.
At SP: OG: '08- dnq 30, '12- 7, '16- dnq 15; WCh: '09-11-13-15-19: dnq 20/10/10/7/dnq 27; EC: '10- 12-14-16-18: 7/3/5/5/dnq; EU23: '05- dnq; EI: '13- 1, '15- 2; Won Balkan 2011; SRB 2008, 2010- 15, 2018-19.
Progress at SP: 2004- 15.50, 2005- 17.88, 2006- 17.85, 2007- 19.30, 2008- 19.99, 2009- 20.41, 2010- 20.52i/20.38, 2011- 20.50, 2012- 20.85, 2013- 20.80, 2014- 20.79, 2015- 21.58, 2016- 20.96, 2017- 20.87i/19.45, 2018- 20.48, 2019- 20.88, 2020- 21.01i.
Older brother Almir BIH had JT best 68.32 '09.

Women

Ivana SPANOVIC b. 10 May 1990 Zrenjanin 1.76m 65kg. AC Vojvodina, Novi Sad.
At LJ: OG: '08- dnq 28, '12- 8, '16- 3; WCh: '13- 3, '15- 2, '17- 4; EC: '10-12-14-16-18: 8/dnq 14/2/1/

dns; WJ: '06- 7, '08- 1; WY: '05- dnq, '07- 2; EU23: '11- 2; EJ: '07- 5, '09- 2; WUG: '09- 1; CCp: '14- 2; WI: '14-16-18: 3/2/1; EI: '13-15-17-19: 5/1/1/1. Won DL 2016-17, Serbian 2006, 2008, 2011-13, 2019; Balkan 2011, 2013, MedG 2018
11 Serbian long jump records 2009-16 (& 11 indoor 2007-17), indoor records 60m & Pen.
Progress at LJ: 2003- 5.36, 2004- 5.91, 2005- 6.43, 2006- 6.48i/6.38, 2007- 6.53i/6.41, 2008- 6.65, 2009- 6.71, 2010- 6.78, 2011- 6.71/6.74w, 2012- 6.64, 2013- 6.82, 2014- 6.92i/6.88, 2015- 7.02, 2016- 7.10, 2017- 7.24i/6.96, 2018- 6.99/7.04w, 2019- 6.99i/6.85, 2020- 6.80. pbs: 60m 7.31i '15, 100m 11.90 '13, 60mh 8.49i '13, HJ 1.78i '13, 1.65 '05; TJ 13.78 '14, SP 12.40i '13, Pen 4240i '13.
Won first medal for Serbia at World Champs and Olympic Games. Her 7.24 at EI '17 was the world's longest indoor women's LJ for 28 years..

SLOVAKIA

Governing body: Slovak Athletic Federation. Founded 1939.
National Championships first held in 1939.
2020 Champions: Men: 100m/200m: Ján Volko 10.45/21.36, 400m: Simon Bujna 46.68, 800m: Andrej Mitasík 1:53.42, 1500m: Jaroslav Szabo 4:00.66, 5000m/10000m: Tibor Sahajda 14:56.01/30:50.15, HMar/Mar: Marek Hladik 68:32/2:26:08, 3000mSt: Marek Ondrovic 9:41.76, 110mh: Majej Baluch 14.39, 400mh: Martin Kucera 51.06, HJ: Matús Bubeník 2.20, PV: Ján Zmoray 4.90, LJ: Ján Suba 7.06w, TJ: Tomás Veszelka 16.61, SP: Adrián Baran 16.95, DT: Samuel Kovác 55.00, HT: Marcel Lomnicky 76.47, JT: Maximilian Slezak 72.85, 20000mW: Miroslav Uradník 1:25:37.80, 50000mW: Michal Morvay 4:00:54.30.
Women: 100m: Monika Weigertová 11.79, 200m: Viktória Forster 24.53, 400m: Ivreta Putalová 53.19, 800m: Gabriela Gajanová 2:03.16, 1500m: Elena Dusková 4:33.99, 5000m: Liza Hazuchová 16:36.84, 10000m: Silvia Valová 35:41.89, HMar: Silvia Schwaiger 77:51, Mar: Sylvia Sebastian 3:04:28, 3000mSt: Lucia Keszeghová 10:59.51, 100mh: Stanislava Skvarková 13.11, 400mh: Emma Zapletalová 55.19, HJ: Tana Dunajská 1.75, PV: Lujza Paliderová 3.40, LJ: Lucia Vadlejch 6.13w, TJ: Silvia Kaliasová 12.50w, SP: Ivana Kristoficová 13.10, DT: Barbora Jakubcová 47.04, HT: Martina Hrasnová 70.71, JT: Petra Hanuliaková 45.05, 20000mW: Maria Czaková 1:38:16.70.

Marcel LOMNICKY b. 6 Jul 1987 Nitra 1.77m 106kg. TJ Stavbár Nitra. Was at Virginia Tech University, USA.
At HT: OG: '12- dnq 13, '16- 5; WCh: '11-13-15-17-19: dnq 20/7/8/dnq 13/dnq 18; WJ: '04- dnq 17, '06- 3; EC: '10-12-14-16-18: dnq 24/11/7/5/10; EU23: '07- 3, '09- 6; EJ: '05- 8; WUG: '11- 2, '13- 2. SVK champion 2012-17, 2019-20; won NCAA HT 2009, indoor Wt 2012.
Progress at HT: 2005- 64.27, 2006- 69.53, 2007- 72.17, 2008- 72.66, 2009- 71.78, 2010- 74.83, 2011- 75.84, 2012- 77.43, 2013- 78.73, 2014- 79.16, 2015- 77.63, 2016- 77.48, 2017- 77.92, 2018- 77.00, 2019- 77.15, 2020- 76.47. pbs: SP 15.73 '07, DT 43.82 '08, Wt 23.05i '12. Sister Nikola Lomnická (b. 16 Sep 1988) has hammer best 71.58 '14, won NCAA 2010 and was 8th EC 2014; married Andras Haklits CRO at end of 2018.
Matej TÓTH b. 10 Feb 1983 Nitra 1.85m 73kg. Dukla Banská Bystrica.
At 20kW/(50kW): OG: '04- 32, '08- 26, '12- (5), '16- (1); WCh: '05- 21, 07- 14, '09- 8/9, '11- 9/dnf, '13- (4), '15- (1), '19- (dnf); EC: '06-10-14-18: 6/6/(2)/(2); EU23: '03- 6; WCp: '10- (1); ECp: '09-11-13-15: 9/1/3/2. At 10000mW: WJ: '02- 16, WY: '99- 8; EJ: '01- 6. Won SVK 20kW 2005-08, 2010-12, 2015, 2017, 2021; 50kW 2011, 2018, 2020.
Four SVK 50k walk records 2009-15.
Progress at 20kW, 50kW: 1999- 1:34:29, 2000- 1:30:28, 2001- 1:29:33, 2003- 1:13:17, 2004- 1:23:18, 2005- 1:21:38, 2006- 1:21:39, 2007- 1:25:10, 2008- 1:21:24, 2009- 1:20:53, 3:41:32; 2010- 1:22:04, 3:53:30; 2011- 1:20:16, 3:39:46; 2012- 1:20:25, 3:41:24; 2013- 1:20:14, 3:41:07; 2014- 1:19:48, 3:36:21; 2015- 1:20:21, 3:34:38; 2016- 1:29:04, 3:40:58; 2017- 1:24:38, 2018- 3:42:46, 2020- 3:41:15. pbs: 3000mW 10:57.32i '11, 11:05.95 '12; 5000mW 18:34.56i '12, 18:54.39 '11; 10000W 39:45.03 '06, 39:07R '10; 30kW 2:12:44 '13, 35kW 2:34:23 '13.
First ever World and Olympic gold medallist for Slovakia. Won IAAF Race Walking Challenge 2015. Had fourth win at Dudince 50k in 2020.

Women

Martina HRASNOVÁ b. 21 Mar 1983 Bratislava 1.77m 88kg. née Danisová. Dukla Banská Bystrica.
At HT: OG: '08- 6, '12/16- dnq 15/19; WCh: '01-07-13-15: dnq 23/12/18/15, '09- 3, '19- 9; EC: '02 & '06- dnq 26, '12-14-16-18: 2/2/7/dnq 18; WJ: '00- 5, '02- 2; EJ: '99- 4, '01- 2; CCp: '14- 3; WUG: '07- 5, '09- 2. Won SVK SP 2003, 2006; HT 2000-01, 2006, 2008-09, 2011-15, 2018-20.
14 Slovakian hammer records 2001-09.
Progress at HT: 1999- 58.61, 2000- 61.62, 2001- 68.50, 2002- 68.22, 2003- 66.36, 2005- 69.24, 2006- 73.84, 2007- 69.22, 2008- 76.82, 2009- 76.90, 2011- 72.47, 2012- 73.34, 2013- 72.41, 2014- 75.27, 2015- 74.27, 2016- 72.34, 2017- 67.86, 2018- 73.25, 2019- 72.04, 2020- 70.71. pbs: 60m 7.96i '12, SP 15.60i '15, 15.02 '06; DT 43.15 '06, Wt 21.74i '11.
Two-year drugs ban (nandrolone) from July 2003. Daughter Rebeka born on 4 July 2010. Brother of Branislav Danis (HT 69.20 '06). Equalled EC women's record six appearances.

SLOVENIA

Governing body: Atletska Zveza Slovenije. Current organisation founded 1948.
2020 National Champions: Men: 100m: Nick

SLOVENIA – SOUTH AFRICA

Kocevar 10.68, 200m: Jure Grkman 21.15, 400m: Luka Janezic 46.53, 800m: Jan Vukovic 1:49.55, 1500m/3000m: Jan Kokalj 3:51.57/8:21.13, 5000m: Jan Bresan 14:38.13, 10000m: Mitja Krevs 30:37.65, HMar: Primoz Kobe 67:56, 3000mSt: Matevz Cimermancic 9:26.38, 110mh: Filip Jakob Demsar 14.34, 400mh: Peter Hribarsek 53.77, HJ: Sandro Jersin Tomassini 2.12, PV: Robert Renner 5.25, LJ: Dino Subasic 7.35w, TJ: Ziga Vrscaj 15.59, SP: Blaz Zupancic 18.82, DT: Kristjan Ceh 62.37, HT: Nejc Plesko 67.26, JT: Matija Kranjc 73.96. **Women**: 100m/200m: Maja Mihalinec 11.59/23.41, 400m Anita Horvat 53.85, 800m: Jerneja Smonkar 2:09.22, 1500m: Ingrid Zeleznik 4:31.34, 3000m: Marusa Mismas Zrimsek 8:46.44, 5000m/10000m/HMar: Neja Krsinar 17:06.30/34:46.52/76:57, 100mh: Nika Glojnaric 13.51, 400mh: Agata Zupin 57.35, HJ: Lia Apostolovski 1.86, PV: Tina Sutej 4.50, LJ: Maja Bedrac 6.23, TJ: Neja Filipic 13.88, SP/DT: Veronika Domjan 14.69/52.53, HT: Barbara Spiler 66.18, JT: Tina Vaupot 41.29.

Kristjan CEH b. 17 Feb 1999 2.06m 118kg. Ptuj. Student of agronomy at the Faculty of Biotechnology, Maribor.
At DT: WCh: '19: dnq 31; WJ: '18- dnq 15; EU23: 19- 1; WJ: '17 nt. SLO champion 2019-20.
Three SLO discus records 2020,
Progress at DT: 2016- 48.71, 2017- 52.22, 2018- 62.03, 2019- 63.82, 2020- 68.75, 2021- 67.05. Pb SP 17.65i '20, 16.48 '19.

Women

Tina SUTEJ b. 7 Nov 1988 Ljubljana 1.73m 58kg. Kladivar Celje. Studied biology at University of Arkansas, USA.
At PV: OG: '12- dnq 19=, '16- 11; WCh: '11-15-17-19: dnq 12/nh/15=/13=; EC: '10-12-14-16-18: 10/dnq 24/10=/nh/dnq 25=; WJ: '06- 2; WY: '05- 8; EU23: '09- 5; WUG: '11- 2; WI: '14- 10; EI: '17- 8=, '21- 2. SLO champion 2006, 2008-18 (& 5 indoor). 16 SLO pole vault records 2010-20.
Progress at PV: 2004- 3.81, 2005- 4.10, 2006- 4.25, 2007- 4.17i/4.10, 2008- 4.20, 2009- 4.25, 2010- 4.50, 2011- 4.61, 2012- 4.55, 2013- 4.35, 2014- 4.71i/4.50, 2015- 4.55i/4.38, 2016- 4.56, 2017- 4.50, 2018- 4.50, 2019- 4.73, 2020- 4.75, 2021- 4.70i.

SOUTH AFRICA

Governing body: Athletics South Africa. Original body founded 1894.
National Championships first held in 1894 (men), 1929 (women).

Stephen MOKOKA b. 31 Jan 1985 Mahikeng 1.56m 50kg. AGN.
At 10000m: OG: '16- 18; WCh: '11-13-15-17: 13/20/20/20; CG: '18- 6; AfC: '12- 8, '16- 1; WUG: '07-11-13: 3/2/1. At Mar: OG: '12- 49; WCh: '19- 5; At HMar: WCh: '09-12-14-16-20: 8/8/12/10/7; WUG: '13- 2. Won RSA 1500m 2010, 5000m 2013, 2015-16; 10000m 2009-13, 2015-16, 2018; HMar 2008-09, 2011-13, 2019; Mar 2018, CC 2014 (24 titles at all events).
RSA records: 5000m 2015, HMar 2019 & 2020.
Progress at Mar: 2010- 2:08:33, 2011- 2:10:29, 2012- 2:09:43, 2013- 2:09:30, 2014- 2:08:43, 2015- 2:07:40, 2016-2:10:18, 2017- 2:08:35, 2018- 2:08:31, 2019- 2:07:58, 2020- 2:08:05. Pbs: 800m 1:48.87A '14, 1000m 2:23.18A '13, 1500m 3:38.55 '10, 3000m 7:55.92A '11, 5000m 13:11.44 '15, 10000m 27:40.73 '12, 3000mSt 8:56.48 '04; road: 15k 42:18 '20, 10M 46:25 '09, 20k 56:34 '20, HMar 59:36 '19.
Won Shanghai Marathon 2013-14, 2016-17.

Clarence MUNYAI b. 20 Feb 1998 Johannesburg 1.76m 66kg. Tuks, Pretoria.
At 200m: OG: '16- h; WCh: '17- dq h, '19- sf; CG: '18- 4; WJ: 16- 4; AfCh: '16 sf; Af-J: 17- 1. Won RSA 200m 2016. Records: World junior 300m 2017, African junior 200m 2017, South African 200m 2018, African 4x100m 2019.
Progress at 200m: 2014- 21.61A, 2015- 20.77A, 2016- 20.36A/20.40/20.33Aw, 2017- 20.10A/20.31, 2018- 19.69A/20.36, 2019- 20.04, 2020- 20.23A. pbs: 100m 10.10A '18, 300m 31.61 '17.

Ruswahl SAMAAI b. 25 Sep 1991 Paarl 1.78m 73kg. Was at University of Johannesburg.
At LJ: OG: '16- 9; WCh: '15- dnq 20, '17- 3, '19- 5; CG: '14- 3, '18- 3; AfCh: '14-16-18: 3/1/1; CCp: '18- 1; WI: '16- 5, '18- 6; RSA champion 2015.
Progress at LJ: 2009- 6.93A, 2010- 7.41, 2011- 7.75/7.80w, 2012- 7.94A/7.61w, 2013- 7.96A/7.74, 2014- 8.13A/8.08, 2015- 8.38, 2016- 8.38/8.40w, 2017- 8.49A/8.35, 2018- 8.45, 2019- 8.23, 2020- 8.09. pb TJ 16.10A '14.

Akani SIMBINE b. 21 Sep 1993 Kempton Park 1.76m 74kg. Tuks, graduate of the University of Pretoria.
At 100m/(200m): OG: '16- 5; WCh: '13- h, '15- sf/sf, '17- 5/sf, '19- 4; CG: 14- sf/5, '18- 1/2R; AfCh: '14- 8, '16- 3, '18- 1/1R; CCp: '18- 3; WUG: '15- 1. Won RSA 100m 2015, 2017; 200m 2019.
Records: Three South African 100m 2015-16, African 4x100m & 4x200m 2019.
Progress at 100m, 200m: 2010- 10.61A, 2011- 10.57A, 21.27A; 2012- 10.19A, 20.68A; 2013- 10.36, 20.79A/20.78w; 2015- 9.97, 20.23; 2016- 9.89, 20.16; 2017- 9.92A/9.99, 19.95A/20.21; 2018- 9.93, 2019- 9.92, 20.27A, 2020- 9.91A/9.96, 2021- 9.99A. pb 60m 6.60Ai '15, 6.66i '13.

Wayde van NIEKERK b. 15 Jul 1992 Cape Town 1.83m 73kg. University of the Free State, Bloemfontein.
At (200m)/400m: OG: '16- 1; WCh: '13- h, '15- 1, '17- 2/1; CG: '14- sf/2; AfCh: '14- 2, '16- (1); WJ: '10- (4); WUG: '13- 2R; CCp: '14- 4/1R. Won RSA 200m 2011, 2017, 400m 2013-15.
Records: World 400m 2016, 300m 2017, Commonwealth 400m (2) 2015-16, African 300m (3) 2016-17. 400m (3) 2015-16, RSA 200m 2015 & 2017, 400m (5) 2014-16.
Progress at 200m, 400m: 2010- 21.02, 2011- 20.57, 2012- 20.91, 46.43; 2013- 20.84A, 45.09; 2014- 20.19, 44.38; 2015- 19.94, 43.48; 2016- 20.02, 43.03;

2017- 19.84, 43.62; 2019- 47.28A, 2020- 20.31A, 45.58; 2021- 20.10Aw. pbs: 60m 6.62 '20, 100y 9.36 '18, 100m 9.94 '17, 300m 30.81 '17.
The only man to run under 10.0, 20.0 and 44.0, fourth best ever combination 100-200-400 man. Has won three successive global 400m titles.

Women

Mokgadi **Caster SEMENYA** b. 7 Jan 1991 Polokwane, Limpopo Province 1.70m 64kg. NWU Pukke. Student of sports science at North West University, Potchefstroom.
At 800m (/1500m): OG: '12- 1, '16- 1; WCh: '09- 1, '11- 1, '15- sf, '17- 1/3; CG: '18- 1/1; AfG: '15- 1/8; AfCh: '16- 1/1/1R, '18- 1 (1 400m); WJ: '08- h; Afr-J: '09- 1 (1); CCp: '18- 1 (2 400m/2mxR); won DL 2016-18. RSA 400m 2016-17, 800m 2011-12, 2014-18; 1500m 2011, 2016, 2018-19; 5000m 2019. World best 600m 2017. RSA records: 400m (2) 2018, 600m 2012 & 2017, 800m (6) 2009-18, 1000m (3) 2018, 1500m (2) 2018.
Progress at 400m, 800m, 1500m: 2007- 2:09.35, 2008- 2:04.23, 2009- 1:55.45, 4:08.01; 2010- 1:58.16, 2011- 52.54A/53.16, 1:56.35; 2012- 53.62, 1:57.23, 4:12.93; 2013- 1:58.92, 2014- 55.33A, 2:02.66; 2015- 53.12, 1:59.59, 4:21.63; 2016- 50.40, 50.40, 1:55.28, 4:01.99; 2017- 51.53, 1:55.16, 4:02.84; 2018- 49.62, 1:54.25, 3:59.92; 2019- 1:54.98, 4:13.59A. pbs: 200m 23.81A '20, 300m 36.78A '20, 600m 1:21.77 '17, 1000m 2:30.70 '18, 1500m 4:01.99 '16, 2000m 5:38.19 '19, 3000m 9:36.29A '17, 5000m 16:05.97A '19.
Questions over her gender arose at the African Junior and World Champs in 2009, and barred from competing by Athletics South Africa until the IAAF allowed this in July 2010 but saying that medical details remained confidential. With regulations back in place she could not take part at the 2019 Worlds at middle distances.

Sunette **VILJOEN** b. 6 Oct 1983 Johannesburg 1.70m 73kg. NW University, Potchefstroom.
At JT: OG: '04/08- dnq 35/32, '12- 4, '16- 2; WCh: '03/09/19- dnq 16/17/17, '11-13-15: 2/6/3; CG: '06-10-14-18: 1/1/2/3; AfG: '03-07-19: 3/3/3; AfCh: '04-06-08-10-14-16: 1/2/1/1/1/1; WUG: '07- 5, '09- 1, '11- 1; CCp: '10- 1, '14- 2. Won Afro-Asian Games 2003, RSA 2003-04, 2006, 2009-17, 2019. Four African javelin records 2009-12, two Commonwealth 2011-12.
Progress at JT: 1999- 43.89A, 2000- 45.50A, 2001- 50.70A, 2002- 58.33A, 2003- 61.59, 2004- 61.15A, 2005- 57.31, 2006- 60.72, 2007- 58.39, 2008- 62.24A, 2009- 65.43, 2010- 66.38, 2011- 68.38, 2012- 69.35, 2013- 64.51, 2014- 65.32, 2015- 66.62, 2016- 65.14, 2017- 63.49A, 2018- 62.46A, 2019- 61.22A. She played one Test and 17 ODIs for South Africa as an all-rounder at cricket 2000-02. Son Henré born in 2005.

SPAIN

Governing body: Real Federación Española de Atletismo (RFEA). Founded 1920.

SOUTH AFRICA – SPAIN 139

National Championships first held in 1917 (men), 1931 (women). **2020 Champions: Men**: 100m: Pablo Montalvo 10.40, 200m: Daniel Rodríguez 21.08, 400m: Bernat Erta 46.19, 800m: Mariano García 1:47.55, 1500m: Kevin López 3:44.48, 5000m: Abdessamad Oukhelfen 13:47.26, HMar: Tariku Novales 62:34, Mar: Javier Guerra 2:07:27, 3000mSt: Fernando Carro 8:30.31, 110mh: Asier Martínez 13.83, 400mh: Javier Delgado 50.59, HJ: Carlos Rojas 2.26, PV: Isdro Leyva 5.46, LJ: Francisco Javier Cobián 7.79, TJ: Pablo Torrijos 16.88, SP: Carlos Tobalina 18.83, DT: Lois Maikel Martínez 60.02, HT: Javier Cienfuegos 74.92, JT: Odei Jainaga 83.51, Dec: Bruno Comin 7303, 10000mW: Álvaro Martín 41:42.59, 50kW: Ivan Pajuelo 3:57:22. **Women**: 100m: Paula Sevilla 11.52, 200m: Jaël Bestué 23.60, 400m: Andrea Jiménez 53.64, 800m/1500m: Esther Guerrero 2:06.23/4:23.47, 5000m: Marta Pérez 16:08.28, HMar: Elena Loyo 72:22, Mar: Marta Galimany 2:29:02, 3000mSt: Irene Sánchez-Escribano 9:48.57, 100mh: Elbo Parmo 13.68, 400mh: Sara Gallego 57.17, HJ: Cristina Fernando 1.87, PV: Andrea San José 4.32, LJ: Juliet Itoya 6.37, TJ: Patricia Sarrapio 13.67, SP: María Belén Toimil 16.20, DT: Paula Ferrándiz 50.64, HT: Laura Redondo 68.12, JT: Arantza Moreno 55.83, Hep: Claudia Conte 5891, 10000mW: Antia Chamosa 48:35.20, 50kW: Mar Juárez 4:15:46.

Fernando **CARRO** b. 1 Apr 1992 Madrid 1.75m 67kg. New Balance.
At 3000mSt: OG: '16- h; WCh: '15/17- h, 19- 11; EC: '16- 9, '18- 2; EU23: '13- 7, EJ: '11- 4; CCp: '18- 4; ET: 19- 1; Spanish champion 2018-20. At 3000m: WY: '09- h.
Spanish 3000mSt record 2019.
Progress at 3000mSt: 2010- 9:08.41, 2011- 8:54.26, 2012- 8:35.51, 2013- 8:40.74, 2014- 8:36.81, 2015- 8:21.78, 2016- 8:33.69, 2017- 8:29.92, 2018- 8:19.30, 2019- 8:05.69, 2020- 8:13.45. pbs: 1500m 3:35.90 '20, 3000m 7:50.54i '21, 7:51.69 '19; 5000m 13:32.11 '20, 10000m 28:28.68 '18, 10kRd 27:46dh '29, 2000mSt 5:26.78 '20.

Javier **CIENFUEGOS** b. 15 Jul 1990 Montijo, Badajoz 1.93m 134kg. Playas de Castellón.
At HT: OG: '12/16- dnq 14/27; WCh: '09-11-13-15: dnq 24/32/23/29; '19- 7; EC: '10-12-14-18: dnq 18/22/15/15; '16- 12; WJ: '08- 12; WY: '07- dnq 18; EU23: '11- 2; EJ: '07- dnq 20, '09- 3. Spanish champion 2009-10, 2012-16, 2018-20, Ib.Am 2018. Seven Spanish hammer records 2012-19. World U20 6kg record 82.97 '09.
Progress at HT: 2008- 69.25, 2009- 74.77, 2010- 72.19, 2011- 75.31, 2012- 76.21, 2013- 76.71, 2014- 75.03, 2015- 74.76, 2016- 76.37, 2017- 76.63, 2018- 76.10, 2019- 79.38, 2020- 77.52. pbs: DT 48.18 '12, Wt 21.87 '14.

Diego **GARCÍA** b. 19 Jan 1996 Madrid 1.74m 60kg. A.D.Marathon.
At 20kW: WCh: '15-17-19: 29/13/35; EC:'18- 2;

SPAIN

EU23: '17- 1; ECp: '17- 7, '19- 3. At 10kW: WJ: '14- 2; WY: '13- 3; EJ: '15- 1; WCp: '14- 4J; ECp: '15- 1J. Progress at 20kW: 2015- 1:21:45, 2016- 1:21:36, 2017- 1:20:34, 2018- 1:19:18, 2019- 1:18:58, 2021- 1:19:40. pbs: 1MW 5:36.27 '17, 3000mW 11:06.57i '18, 5000mW 19:03.16 '15, 10000mW 39:47.77 '17. Won (1=) IAAF Race Walking Challenge 2018.

Miguel Ángel LÓPEZ b. 3 Jul 1988 Murcia 1.81m 70kg. CA Llano de Brujas-Murcia.
At 20kW: OG: '12- 5, '16- 11 (dnf 50kW); WCh: '11-13-15-17-19: 12/2/1/10/26; EC: '10-14-18: 12/1/6; EU23: '09- 1; WCp: '10- 12, '14- 5; ECp: '11-13-15-17-19: 5/2/1/2/6. At 10kW: WJ: '06- 14; WY: '05- 6; EJ: '05- 9, '07- 8; WCp: '06- 2J; ECp: '07- 2J. Won Spanish 10000mW 2010, 2012-16; 20kW 2010, 2012, 2015, 2019; 50kW 2016. Progress at 20kW: 2008- 1:23:44, 2009- 1:22:23, 2010- 1:23:08, 2011- 1:21:41, 2012- 1:19:49, 2013- 1:21:21, 2014- 1:19:21, 2015- 1:19:14, 2016- 1:20:34, 2017- 1:19:57, 2018- 1:20:54, 2019- 1:21:00, 2021- 1:21:02. pbs: 3000mW 11:39.92 '13, 5000mW 18:46.95 '16, 10000mW 38:06.28 '16, 35kW 2:32:56 '15, 50kW 3:53:52 '16.

Álvaro MARTÍN b. 18 Jun 1994 Llerena, Badajoz 1.81m 62kg. Playas de Castellón.
At 20kW: OG: '12- dnf. '16- 2; WCh: '13-15-17-19: 23/16/8/22; EC: '14- 5, '18- 1; EU23: '15- 2; WCp: '14-16-18: 18/3/8; ECp: '19- 5. At 10kW: WJ: '12- 4; WY: '11- 8; EJ: '13- 3; ECp: '11- 6J. Won Spanish 10000mW 2017-20, 20kW 2016-18. Progress at 20kW: 2012- 1:22:12, 2013- 1:22:25, 2014- 1:20:39, 2015- 1:20:19, 2016- 1:19:36, 2017- 1:19:41, 2018- 1:20:42, 2019- 1:20:50, 2020- 1:35:09+, 2021- 1:20:54. pbs: 5000mW 18:39.65 '15, 10000mW 39:23.51 '16, 35kW 2:37:17 '14, 50kW 3:57:24 '20.

Orlando ORTEGA b. 29 Jul 1991 La Habana 1.85m 75kg. C.A.Adidas.
At 110mh: OG: '16- 2; WCh: '13- h, '17- 7, '19- 5; EC: '18- 3; WJ: '10- h; PAm: '11- 3; ET: 17- 1, '19- 1. Won DL 2016, 2019; Cuban 2011, Spanish 2016-19. At 60mh: EI: '17- 7, '19- 4; WIT 2017. Two Spanish 110mh records 2016.
Progress at 110mh: 2009- 14.11, 2010- 13.99, 2011- 13.29/13.1w, 2012- 13.09, 2013- 13.08, 2014- 13.01, 2015- 12.94, 2016- 13.04, 2017- 13.15/13.09w, 2018- 13.08, 2019- 13.05, 2020- 13.11. pbs: 60m 6.65i '20, 100m 10.62 '11, 150m 15.57 '20, 200m 21.08 '18, 400m 47.84 '09, 50mh 6.66+i '12, 60mh 7.45i '15, 7.48i '17 ESP record.
Left Cuba in 2013; Spanish citizenship on 9 Sep 2015 with eligibility from 29 Jul 2016, just before the Olympic Games. Awarded joint bronze medal at 2019 Worlds as he was impeded when he would surely have won a medal.

Pablo TORRIJOS b. 12 May 1992 Castellón de la Plana 1.87m 78kg. Playas de Castellón.
At TJ: OG: '16- dnq 31; WCh: '15- dnq 20, '17- 10; EC: '16- 8, '18- 5; WY: '09- dnq 14 (dnq 33 LJ); EU23: '13- 8; EJ: '11- 6; CCp: '18- 8; ET: '17- 3; WI: '16- 7; EI: '15- 52, '17- 9. Three Spanish TJ records 2017-20. (& 2 indoors) Progress at TJ: 2009- 15.20, 2010- 15.56, 2011- 16.16i/15.84, 2012- 16.08/16.47w, 2013- 16.28/16.71w, 2014- 16.87, 2015- 17.04/16.61, 2016- 16.89A/16.71, 2017- 16.96, 2018- 16.98/17.23w, 2020- 16.89, 2020- 17.18i/17.09. pb LJ 7.53 '12, 7.56w '14.

Jorge UREÑA b. 8 Oct 1993 Onil, Alicante 1.78m 75kg. Playas de Castellón.
At Dec: WCh: '15- 21, '17- 9; EC: '16- dnf, '18-16; WJ: '12- 20; EU23: '15- 2; ET: '19- 3. Spanish champion 2015-16. At Hep: EI: '15-17-19-21: 7/2/1/2.
Progress at Dec: 2013- 7358, 2014- 7656, 2015- 7983, 2016- 7985, 2017- 8125, 2018- 7934, 2019- 8123. pbs: 60m 6.91i '17, 100m 10.76 '19, 400m 48.36 '19, 1000m 2:40.06i '15, 1500m 4:24.12 '17, 60mh 7.78i '17, 110mh 13.88 '19, HJ 2.11i '20, 2.08 '17; PV 5.02i/5.00 '16, LJ 7.73i '19, 7.54 '16; SP 14.68i '19, 14.36 '17; DT 39.56 '18, JT 64.02 '15, Hep 6249i '17. His father José Antonio Ureña was also a decathlete (7372 '93).

Women

Ana PELETEIRO b. 2 Dec 1995 Ribeira, La Coruña 1.71m 52kg. C.A.Adidas.
At TJ: WCh: '17- 7, '19- 6; EC: '18-3; WJ: '12- 1, '14- 6; WY: '11- 3; EU23: '17- 2; EJ: '13- 3; WI: '18- 3; EI: '17-19-21: 5/1/2; ET: 19- 2. Spanish champion 2015, 2017-18.
Two European youth bests at triple jump 2012. Spanish record 2019.
Progress at TJ: 2011- 13.17, 2012- 14.17, 2013- 13.75i/13.29/13.30w, 2014- 14.07, 2015- 14.03, 2016- 13.91i/13.55, 2017- 14.23, 2018- 14.55, 2019- 14.73i/14.59, 2020- 13.90i, 2021- 14.52i. pbs: 60m 7.56i '14, 100m 11.93 '14, LJ 6.07 '19.

María PÉREZ b. 29 Apr 1996 Orce, Granada 1.56m 48kg. Valencia Esports.
At 20kW: WCh: '17- 10, '19- 8; EC: '18- 1; EU23: '17- 2; WCp: '18- 7; ECp: '17- 6. Won Spanish 10000mW 2019, 20kW 2019, 2021. At 10kW: WJ: '14- 5, WCp: '14- 9J; EJ: '15- 4, ECp: '15- 3J. At 5000mW: WY: '13- 7.
Spanish walks records: 3000m & 20k 2018.
Progress at 20kW: 2015- 1:35:14, 2016- 1:33:44, 2017- 1:29:37, 2018- 1:26:36, 2019- 1:30:55, 2021- 1:28:26. pbs: 3000mW 12:00.87 '18, 5000mW 20:38.16 '18. 10000mW 44:13.83 '16, Rd 43:40 '20.

Julia TAKACS b. 29 Jun 1989 Budapest, Hungary 1.71m 53kg. Playas de Castellón.
At 20kW: OG: '16- 33; WCh: '15- 8; EU23: '09- 5, '11- 1; WCp: '12- 9, '16- 13; ECp: '09- 11, '11- 9; WUG: '11- 1. At 50kW: WCh: '19- 8; EC: '18- 3; WT: '18- 8; ECp: '19- 2. At 10000mW: WJ: '08- 6. Won IbAm 10000mW 2014, Spanish 10000mW 2009, 2011, 2013-15, 2017; 20kW 2013-14, 50kW (2) 2018-19.
Spanish walk records: 3000m & 5000m 2014, 10000m (2) 2013-14, 50k (2) 201-198.
Progress at 20kW, 50kW: 2006- 1:43:49, 2007-

1:38:57, 2008- 1:39:12, 2009- 1:35:04, 2010- 1:30:14, 2011- 1:31:32, 2012- 1:30:37, 2013- 1:28:44, 2014- 1:29:08, 2015- 1:31:23, 2016- 1:29:47, 2017- 1:30:14. 2018- 1:27:58, 4:13:04; 2019- 1:34:24. 4:05:46. pbs: 3000mW 12:11.27 '14, 5000mW 20:30.04 '14, 10000mW 42:23.37 '14, 30kW 2:20:38 '19, 35kW 2:53:59 '19.
She has lived in Spain from the age of 14 and switched from Hungary to Spain 19 June 2008.

SRI LANKA

Governing body: Athletic Association of Sri Lanka. Founded 1922.
National Champions 2020: **Men**: 100m: Himasha Eashan 10.27, 200m/400m: Kalinga Kumarage 20.79/46.25. 800m: G.R.Chathuranga 1:49.82, 1500m: Saman Kumara Fernando 3:47.86, 5000m: Samantha Pushpakumara 14:29.45, 10000m: A K Tharanga 30:42.15, 3000mSt: Udaya Herath 9:00.22, 110mh: Roshan Ranathunga 14.33w, 400mh: Asitha Rathnasena 52.09, HJ: Laksamuda Mendis 2.10, PV: Sachin Janith 4.70, LJ: Sreshan Dhananjaya 7.71, TJ: Sanjaya Jayasinghe 16.32, SP: Samith Fernando 16.12, DT: Z T M Aasik 44.78, HT: Rohana Kumara 50.73, JT: Sampath Ranasinghe 76.10, Dec: Ajith Kumara Karunathilake 7059. **Women**: 100m: Amasha De Silva 11.55, 200m/400m: Nadeesha Ramanayake 24.15/53.47, 800m: Dilshi Kumarasinghe 2:02.80, 1500m: Gayanthika Abeyrathne 4:17.58, 5000m: Nilanthi Ariyadasa 17:13.24, 10000m: H N M Nandasena 35:21.11, 3000mSt: Nilani Rathnayake 10:15.86, 100mh: Ireshani Rajasinghe 13.85, 400mh: Shayama Dulani 62.90, HJ: Muditha Madushani 1.60; PV: Sachini Perera 3.56, LJ: Lakshini Silva 6.33, TJ: Hashini Balasooriya 13.07, SP: Thraika Fernando 14.10, DT: Ishara Perera 38.69, HT: Aruni Lakshika 43.02, JT: Nadeeka Lakmali 53.97, Hep: Lakshini Dissanayaka 3526.

SWEDEN

Governing body: Svenska Friidrottsförbundet. Founded 1895.
National Championships first held in 1896 (men), 1928 (women). **2020 Champions: Men**: 100m: Henrik Larsson 10.37, 200m: Felix Svensson 20.80, 400m: Nick Ekelund-Arenander 46.60, 800m: Andreas Kramer 1:45.53, 1500m: Johan Rogestadt 3:53.99, 5000m: Suldan Hassan 13:57.27, 10000m: Emil Millán de la Oliva 29:49.05, HMar: Samuel Russom ERI 63:47, Mar: Samuel Tsegay ERI 2:14:41, 3000mSt: Simon Sundström 8:48.33, 110mh: Max Hrelja 14.00, 400mh: Oskar Edlund 50.15, HJ: Melwin Holm 2.13, PV: Armand Duplantis 5.63, LJ: Thobias Montler 8.15, TJ: Jesper Hellström 16.09, SP: Wictor Petersson 20.60, DT: Daniel Ståhl 68.74, HT: Ragnar Carlsson 70.83, JT: Kim Amb 83.60, Dec: Fredrik Samuelsson 7854, 20000mW: Perseus Karlström 1:37:12. **Women**: 100m: Nikki Anderberg 11.47, 200m/400m: Moa Hjelmar 23.47/53.39, 800m: Lovisa Lindh 2:04.89, 1500m: Hanna Hermansson 4:16.07, 5000m/10000m: Meraf Bahta 16:27.13/34:07.21, HMar: Charlotta Fougberg 76:51, Mar: Carolina Wikström 2:33:59, 3000mSt: Amélie Svensson 10:17.75, 100mh: Lovissa Karlsson 13.67, 400mh: Hanna Palmqvist 57.33, HJ: Erika Kinsey 1.95, PV: Angelica Bengtsson 4.71, LJ: Khaddi Sagnia 6.72, TJ: Rebecca Abrahamsson 13.56, SP: Fanny Roos 18.59, DT: Vanessa Kamga 56.11, HT: Ida Storm 58.54, JT: Ásdis Hjálmsdóttir Annerud ISL 57.27, Hep: Bianca Salming 6042, 10000mW: Helena Sandmer 1:01:25.

Kim AMB b. 31 Jul 1990 Solna 1.80m 85kg. F Bålsta IK.
At JT: OG: '12/16- dnq 17/17; WCh: '13- 10, '15-11, '19- 8; EC: '12-14-16: 7/dnq/7; WJ: '08- dnq 13; EU23: '11- 4. Swedish champion 2011-13, 2015-16, 2018-20.
Progress at JT: 2007- 55.01, 2008- 69.34, 2009- 66.06, 2010- 77.81, 2011- 80.09, 2012- 81.84, 2013- 84.61, 2014- 84.14, 2015- 82.40, 2016- 84.50, 2017- 82.02, 2018- 77.13, 2019- 86.03, 2020- 86.49. Pb PV 3.45 '06. Father Björn had a best old javelin of 62.60 '79 and sister Emilia JT best of 49.34 '12.

Armand 'Mondo' DUPLANTIS b. 10 Nov 1999 Lafayette, LA, USA 1.83m 79kg. Puma, Upsala IF, Louisiana State University, USA.
At PV: WCh: '17- 9, '19- 2; EC: '18- 1; WJ: '16- 3, '18- 1; WY: '15- 1; EJ: '17- 1; WI: '18- 7=; EI: '21- 1; Won SWE 2020, WIT 2020
Pole vault records: Two world indoor and one outdoor 2020, world junior (4 indoor, 6 out) 2017-18; 8 outdoor, 6 indoor Swedish 2017-20.
Progress at PV: 2007- 2.33, 2008- 2.89, 2009- 3.20, 2010- 3.86, 2011- 3.91, 2012- 3.97i, 2013- 4.45, 2014- 4.60, 2015- 5.30, 2016- 5.51, 2017- 5.90, 2018- 6.05, 2019- 6.00, 2020- 6.18i/6.15, 2021- 6.10i. Pbs: 100m 10.73/10.57w '18, LJ 7.12, 7.15w '17.
Has dual citizenship Sweden/USA; declaration for Sweden confirmed from 9 Jun 2015. Has set world age records from age 7 in 2007. World junior records at 5.95, 6.00 and 6.05 to win EC 2018. IAAF Rising Star of the Year 2018, WA Athlete of the Year 2020. His father Greg (USA) had pb 5.80 '93, his mother Helena Hedlund was a Swedish heptathlete (5314 '83), and his brother Andreas (b. 2 May 1993) had PV pb 5.43i/5.36 '13, WJ: '12- 10, EJ: '11- 9. Maternal grandfather Lars-Åke Hedlund PV pb 3.80 '58.

Perseus KARLSTRÖM b. 2 May 1990 Eskilstuna 1.84m 75kg. né Ibáñez. Eskilstuna FI.
At 20kW: OG: '16- dnf; WCh: '13-15-17-19: 37/dnf/37/3; EC: '14- 15, '18- 20; ECp: '15-17-19: 8/3/1. At 50kW: WT: '18- 8. At 10000mW: WJ: '08- 30; WY: '07- 24; EJ: 09- 9. Won SWE 20k 2012-16, 2018, 2020; 50kW 2013, 2016, 10000mW 2008, 2015-16, 2018-19.
Swedish walks records: 10000m (3) 2017-19, 20k 2016 & 2019
Progress at 20kW, 50kW: 2005- 1:53:39, 2008-

SWEDEN

1:35:31, 2009- 1:31:22, 2010- 1:25:32, 2011- 1:26:20, 2012- 1:23:43, 2013- 1:24:55, 3:52:43; 2014- 1:21:54, 2015- 1:22:44, 2016- 1:19:11, 4:06:33; 2017- 1:20:20, 3:44:35; 2018- 1:20:30, 3:48:54; 2019- 1:18:07, 2020- 1:19:34, 2021- 1:18:45. pbs: 1MW 5:38.18 '17, 3000mW 11:43.3 '20, 5000mW 18:32.56 '19, 10000mW 38:03.95 '19.
His father Enrique Vera was 2nd in World 50kW 1976, pb 3:43:59 '79; mother Siw Gustavsson/Ibáñez/Karlström was 3rd in European 10kW 1986. Brother Anatole Ibáñez (b. 14 Nov 1985) pbs 20kW 1:20:54 '16, 50kW 3:48:42 '14, 12 WCh '19.

Andreas KRAMER b. 13 Apr 1997 Sävedalen 1.90m 73kg. Sävedalens AJK.
At 800m: WCh: '17- sf, '19- h; EC: '18- 2; WJ: '16- sf; EU23: '17- 1, '19- h; EJ: '15- 6; EI: '19- 7; CCp: '18- 4. SWE champion 2017-20.
Swedish 800m record 2020.
Progress at 800m: 2009- 2:22.31, 2010- 2:14.86, 2011- 2:04.58, 2012- 1:57.56, 2013- 1:54.76, 2014- 1:51.59, 2015- 1:49.62, 2016- 1:47.24, 2017- 1:45.13, 2018- 1:45.03, 2019- 1:45.10, 2020- 1:44.47, 2021- 1:45.09i. pbs: 400m 47.75i '19, 1000m 2:18.30 '18, 1500m 3:46.0 '16.
His mother Anne lise (Hollevik) had pbs 800m 2:08.99 '85, 1500m 4:32.7 '86.

Thobias (Nilsson) **MONTLER** b. 15 Feb 1996 Helsingborg 1.87m 72kg. Malmö AI. Was at Keiser University, USA.
At LJ: WCh: '19- 9; EC: '18- 4; WJ: '14- 8; WY: '13- 8; EU23: '17- 3; EJ: '15- 4 (1R); EI: '19- 2, '21- 2. SWE champion 2017-20.
Progress at LJ: 2009- 5.53i/5.60w, 2010- 6.31, 2011- 6.72, 2012- 7.09/7.23w, 2013- 7.37, 2014- 7.67, 2015- 7.73i/7.68, 2016- 7.73i/7.49, 2017- 8.04, 2018- 8.10, 2019- 8.22/8.43w, 2020- 8.22i/8.15, 2021- 8.31i. pbs: 60m 6.82i '21, 100m 10.49 '19, HJ 1.95 '17, TJ: 13.98w? '17.

Simon PETTERSSON b. 3 Jan 1994 Sixarby 1.98m 106kg. Hässelby SK.
At DT: WCh: '17- 11, '19- 9; EC: '18- 4; EU23: '15- 5.
Progress at DT: 2013- 49.71, 2014- 55.39, 2015- 60.25, 2016- 63.10, 2017- 64.88, 2018- 65.84, 2019- 66.39, 2020- 67.72, 2021- 66.32i. pbs: HJ 1.89 '11, PV 4.26i '12, 4.15 '11; LJ 6.82i '12, 6.67 '11; TJ: 14.32/14.39w '11, SP 17.83 '16, HT 58.43 '16, JT 61.06 '16.

Daniel STÅHL b. 27 Aug 1992 Järfälla 2.02m 160kg. Spårvägens FK.
At (SP)/DT: OG: '16- dnq 14; WCh: '15- 5, '17- 2, '19- 1; EC: '14-16-18: dnq 24/5/2; EU23: '13- 4; WJ: '10- (dnq 27); WY: '09- dnq 16/dnq 16; EJ: '11- (dnq 20); CCp: '18- 3; ET: '19- 3. Won DL 2019, SWE SP 2015-16, 2018; DT 2014, 2016-20.
Swedish discus records 2017 & 2019.
Progress at DT: 2008- 40.36, 2009- 44.34, 2010- 50.32, 2011- 55.60, 2012- 62.16, 2013- 61.29, 2014- 66.89, 2015- 64.73, 2016- 68.72, 2017- 71.29, 2018- 69.72, 2019- 71.86, 2020- 71.37. pbs: SP 19.60i '17,

19.38 '16; HT 48.91 '16, JT 50.43 '16.
Father Jan had pbs SP 16.80 & HT 59.14 '80, mother Taina DT 51.90 '82, sister Anneli HT 59.74 '13.

Women

Angelica BENGTSSON b. 8 July 1993 Väckelsång 1.64m 53kg. Hässelby SK.
At PV: OG: '12/16- dnq 19=/14=, WCh: '13-15-17- 19: dnq 16/4=/10/6; EC: '12-14-16-18: 10/5/3/6; WJ: '10- 1, '12- 1; WY: '09- 1; EU23: '13- 3, '15- 1; EJ: '11- 1; YthOG: '10- 1; EI: '15- 3, '17- 3=; ET: '15- 3, '19- 3=. Won SWE 2012, 2014-16, 2020.
Pole vault records: Two world youth 2010; four world junior indoors 2011, two world junior outdoor bests, ten Swedish 2011-19.
Progress at PV: 2004- 2.65, 2005- 3.10, 2006- 3.40, 2007- 3.90, 2008- 4.12, 2009- 4.37, 2010- 4.47, 2011- 4.63i/4.57, 2012- 4.58, 2013- 4.55, 2014- 4.62i/4.50, 2015- 4.70, 2016- 4.66i/4.65, 2017- 4.65, 2018- 4.73, 2019- 4.81i/4.80, 2020- 4.74i/4.73. pbs: LJ 5.66 '16, JT 35.04 '17.
Rising Star Awards: IAAF 2010, European Athletics 2012. Her father Glenn had JT pb 67.08 '82, sisters Victoria (b. 1990) PV 4.00 '09 and Maria (b. 1988) DT 43.95 '07.

Erika KINSEY b. 10 Mar 1988 Nälden 1.85m 68kg. née Wiklund. Trångsvikens IF. Was at University of Central Missouri, USA.
At HJ: OG: '16- dnq 29=; WCh: '15-17-19: dnq 18/21=/19=; EC: '16- dnq 22, '18- 13; WJ: '06- 8; WY: '05- 5; EU23: '09- 8, EJ: '07- 1; WI: '16- 8, '18- 7=; EI: '19- 7; ET: '19- 2. Won SWE 2019-20.
Progress at HJ: 2002- 1.58, 2003- 1.65, 2004- 1.86, 2005- 1.84, 2006- 1.84, 2007- 1.85/1.87i, 2008- 1.91, 2009- 1.88, 2011- 1.84, 2013- 1.75, 2014- 1.88, 2015- 1.97, 2016- 1.93i/1.90, 2017- 1.94, 2018- 1.94, 2019- 1.96, 2020- 1.95. Pbs: LJ 6.51 '19, TJ 13.11 '15, Pen 4041i '20.
Married Daniel Kinsey USA (b. 25 Jul 1986, Dec: 7563 '09) in July 2014. Played ice hockey in Norway. and came back to athletics in 2014.

Michaela MEIJER b. 30 Jul 1993 Göteborg 1.72m 63kg. née Andersen. Örgryte IS.
At PV: OG: '16- dnq 17, WCh: '15-17-19: nh/dnq10/dnq25; EC: '16- 5; WJ: '10- nh; WY: '09- 2; EU23: '15- 2; EJ: '11- dnq 13; EI: '17- 5, '19- 8. SWE champion 2009, 2017.
Swedish pole vault records 2017 & 2020.
Progress at PV: 2005- 2.03, 2006- 2.81i/2.50, 2007- 3.60, 2008- 3.91, 2009- 4.15, 2010- 4.25i/4.20, 2011- 4.26, 2012- 4.14i/3.96, 2014- 4.28, 2015- 4.55, 2016- 4.62i/4.60, 2017- 4.71, 2018- 4.45iu/3.69, 2019- 4.75i/4.70, 2020- 4.83. pbs: 60mh 8.92i '11, 100mh 14.81 '11, HJ 1.61 '09, LJ 5.73i '11, 5.54 '10; SP 11.05 '16, JT 33.40 '15.

Fanny ROOS b. 2 Jan 1995 Ljungby 1.73cm 79kg. Athletics 24Seven SK.
At SP: WCh: '17/19- dnq 20/14; EC: '16- dnq 20, '18- 11; WJ: '12- dnq 13, '14- 6; WY: '11- 10; EU23: '15- 4, '17- 1; EJ: '13- 7; EI: '17-19-21: 4/6/2. Won

SWE 2014-20 (ind 2014-21), DT 2019. Six Swedish shot records 2017-19 and indoors 2021.
Progress at SP: 2011- 13.94, 2012 -14.76, 2013- 15.82, 2014- 16.29, 2015- 17.05, 2016- 17.58, 2017- 18.21, 2018- 18.68, 2019- 19.06, 2020- 18.77, 2021- 19.29i. Pbs: DT: 56.89 '19, HT 57.84 '20, JT 43.60 '16.

Khaddijatou **'Khaddi'** SAGNIA b. 20 Apr 1994 Helsingborg 1.73cm 63kg. Ullevi FK.
At LJ: OG: '16- dnq 27; WCh: '15- 7, '17- dnq 16; EC: '16- 6, '18- 7; WY: '11- 11; EU23: '15- 4; WI: '18- 6; EI: '21- 3. At TJ: WY: '11- 9; YthOG: '10- 1. Won SWE TJ 2011, LJ 2015-18, 2020; 100m 2016. Swedish indoor LJ record 2018.
Progress at LJ: 2007- 5.18i, 2008- 5.56, 2009- 6.03i/5.89/6.00w, 2010- 6.26, 2011- 6.32, 2014- 6.55, 2015- 6.78, 2016- 6.74, 2017- 6.72, 2018- 6.92i/6.71, 2019- 6.81, 2020- 6.92, 2021- 6.82i. Pbs: 60m 7.26i '21, 100m 11.48 '16, 200m 25.14 '14, 60mh 8.14i '18, 100mh 13.93 '15, 13.62w '14; HJ 1.78 '11, TJ 13.65/13.86w '11, JT 41.47 '14, Hep 5287 '11.

SWITZERLAND

Governing body: Schweizerischer Leichtathletikverband (SLV). Formed 1905 as Athletischer Ausschuss des Schweizerischen Fussball-Verbandes.
National Championships first held in 1906 (men), 1934 (women). **2020 Champions: Men:** 100m: Silvan Wicki 10.18, 200m: William Reais 20.24, 400m: Ricky Petrucciani 46.39, 800m: Jonas Schöpfer 1:52.55, 1500m: Tom Elmer 3:54.56, 5000m: Jonas Raess 14:02.09, 10000m Tadesse Abraham 29:17.70, HMar: Andrea Salvisberg 64:44, 3000mSt: Michael Curti 8:53.47, 110mh: Jason Joseph 13.31, 400mh: Dany Barnd 50.07, HJ: Roman Sieber 2.15, PV: Alberto Dominik 5.45, LJ/Dec: Simon Ehammer 7.99/8231, TJ: Simon Sieber 15.31, SP: Stefan Wieland 17.63, DT: Gregori Ott 54.33, HT: Martin Bingisser 57.65, JT: Simon Wieland 76.67, 10000mW: Nathan Bonzon 52:23.0. **Women:** 100m: Ajla Del Ponte 11.27, 200m: Léa Sprunger 23.08, 400m: Silke Lemmens 53.10, 800m: Lora Hoffmann 2:08.73, 1500m/5000m/10000m: Fabienne Schlumpf 4:14.29/16:30.18/32:16.37, HMar: Nicole Egger 73:34, 3000mSt: Shirley Lang 10:36.16, 100mh: Ditaji Kambundji 13.07, 400mh: Yasmin Giger 56.78, HJ: Salome Lang 1.88, PV: Angelica Moser 4.66, LJ/Hep: Annik Kälin 6.49/6167, TJ: Alina Tobler 13.01, SP: Miryam Mazenauer 15.80, DT: Chantal Tanner 48.85, HT: Nicole Zihlmann 65.61, JT: Géraldine Ruckstuhl 47.83, 5000mW/10000mW: Dora Brière 30:11.0/60:41.0.

Simon EHAMMER b. 7 Feb 2000 Urnäsch 1.84m 78kg. TV Teufen.
At Dec: WJ: '18- 3; EJ: '17- 19, '19- 1. Won SUI LJ 2019-20, Dec 2020.
Progress at LJ, Dec: 2017- 7.14, 2018- 7.45, 2019- 7.87, 7735; 2020- 8.15, 8231. pbs: 60m 6.75i '21, 100m 10.50 '20, 200m 21.14 '20, 400m 47.27 '20,

SWEDEN – SWITZERLAND 143

1000m 2:51.20i '20, 1500m 4:42.54 '20, 60mh 7.80i '21, 110mh 13.48 '20, HJ 2.05 '18, PV 5.10 '20, LJ 8.15 '20, SP 15.31i '21, 13.75 '20; DT 36.39 '20, JT 55.00 '20, Hep 6092i '21.

Jason JOSEPH b. 11 Oct 1998 1.88m 85kg. LC Therweil.
At 110mh: WCh: '19- sf; EC: '18- sf; EU23: '19- 1; EJ: '17- 1; SUI champion 2018-20.
Four Swiss records 2018-20.
Progress at 110mh: 2017- 13.93, 2018- 13.39/13.38w, 2019- 13.39/13.38w, 2020- 13.29. pbs: 60m 6.83i '18, 100m 10.56 '17, 10.46w '18; 200m 21.72 '17, 60mh 7.56i '19.

Julien WANDERS b. 18 Mar 1996 Geneva 1.75m 60kg.
At 5000m/(10000m): WCh: '19- h/dnf; EC: '18- 8/7; WJ: '14- 18; EJ: '15- 14; ET: '19- 2. World HMar: '18- 8, '20- 21; Eur CC: '19- 3. Won SUI 1500 2017, 5000m 2016.
Records: European half marathon 2019 (and bests at 15k, 20k), road best 10k 2018 & 2020, U23 HMar 2018, Swiss HMar 2018, 10000m (2) 2019.
Progress at HMar: 2017- 61:43, 2018- 60:09, 2019- 59:13, 2020- 59:55. pbs: 1500m 3:39.30 '19, 3000m 7:43.62 '19, 5000m 13:13.84 '19, 10000m 27:17.29 '19, Road: 10k 27:13 '20, 15k 41:56 '19, 10M: 45:00 '19, 20k 55:46 '19.
Dual citizenship with France.

Women

Ajla DEL PONTE b. 15 Jul 1996 Locarno. Lausanne Universty. 1.68m 59kg. US Ascona.
At 100m: OG: '16- hR; WCh: '19: h/4R; EC: '18- sf; WJ: '14- h; EU23: '17- 5 (h 200m); WUG: '17- 1R, '19- 2/1R. At 60m: EI: '19: 8, '21- 1. Won Swiss 100m 2020.
Progress at 100m: 2014- 11.82, 2015- 11.90/11.89w, 2016- 11.52, 2017- 11.42, 2018- 11.21, 2019- 11.29/11.20w, 2020- 11.08. pbs: 60m 7.03i '21, 150m 16.67 '20, 200m 23.02/22.83w '20, 300m 38.68 '17.

Mujinga KAMBUNDJI b. 17 Jun 1992 Uetendorf 1.68m 59kg. ST Bern.
At 100m/(200m): OG: '16- sf/sf; WCh: '13-15-17-19: (h)/sf&sf/sf&sf/sf&3; EC: '12- h, '14- 4/5, '16- 3/sf, '18- 4/4; WJ: '10- sf/sf; WY: '09- sf/6; EU23: '13- 4/5; EJ: '11- 5/5; ET: '19- (1)/2R; At 60m: WI: '18- 3; EI: '15-17-19: 5/3/5. Won Swiss 100m 2009, 2011-17; 200m 2009, 2012-15, 2017.
Swiss records: 100m (10), 200m (5) 2014-19.
Progress at 100m, 200m: 2007- 12.17, 2008- 12.02, 24.30; 2009- 11.66, 23.87; 2010- 11.70/11.57w, 23.68; 2011- 11.53, 22.70/23.31w; 2012- 11.62, 23.26; 2013- 11.50, 23.24; 2014- 11.20, 22.83; 2015- 11.07, 22.64; 2016- 11.14, 22.78; 2017- 11.07, 22.42; 2018- 10.95, 22.45; 2019- 11.00, 22.26; 2020- 11.21, 23.25. pbs: 60m 7.03i '18, 150m 17.28 '20.
Sister **Ditaji** (b. 20 May 2002) 100mh 7 EY 18, 13/07 '20, 60mh 8.05i '21.

Angelica MOSER b. 9 Oct 1997 Piano, Texas 1.69m 63kg. LC Zürich.

At PV: OG: '16- dnq 23; WCh: '15/17- dnq 25=/13, '19- 13; WJ: '16- 1; EC: '16- 7, '18- dnq 20; EU23: '17- 1, '19- 1; EJ: '15- 1; YOG '14- 1; EI: '19- 4, '21- 1. Swiss champion 2017-20.
Progress at PV: 2012- 3.90, 2013- 4.04, 2014- 4.36, 2015- 4.41, 2016- 4.57, 2017- 4.61, 2018- 4.45, 2019- 4.65i/4.60, 2020- 4.66, 2021- 4.75i. pbs: 60mh 8.68i '19, 100mh 13.88 '19, HJ 1.71 '15, LJ 5.34 '17, SP 12.97, '18, JT 42.06 '17, Hep 5190 '17.
Father Severin 27th in 1988 OG decathlon, pb 7936 '88.

Selina RUTZ-BÜCHEL b. 26 Jul 1991 Mosnang 1.68m 58kg. KTV Bütschwil
At 800m: OG: '16- sf; WCh: '15/17- sf, '19- h; EC: '14-16-18: sf/4/7; WJ: '10- sf; EU23: '11- 5, 13- 3; EJ: '09- 7; WI: '14- 4, '18- 6; EI: '15- 1, '17- 1. Won Swiss 400m 2016, 800m 2011, 2013.
Swiss records 800m 2015, 1000m 2020.
Progress at 800m: 2008- 2:11.68, 2009- 2:06.20, 2010- 2:05.95, 2011- 2:04.25, 2012- 2:04.02, 2013- 2:01.64i/2:01.66, 2014- 2:00.93i/2:01.42, 2015- 1:57.95, 2016- 1:58.77, 2017- 1:59.46, 2018- 2:00.42, 2019- 2:01.32, 2020- 1:58.37. pbs: 400m 52.97 '17, 600m 1:25.45 '15, 1000m 2:35.58 '20, 1500m 4:08.95i '16, 4:10.12 '20.

Léa SPRUNGER b. 5 Mar 1990 Nyon 1.83m 69kg. COVA Nyon.
At 400mh: OG:'16- h; WCh: '15- sf, '17- 5, '19- 4; EC: '16- 3, '18- 1; At Hep: WJ: '08-10; WY: '07- 13; EU23: '11- 16; EJ: '09- 3; At 200m: OG: '12- h; EC: '12/14- sf; at 400m: EI: '17- 5, '19- 1; ET: '19- 2. Won Swiss 200m 2016-17, 2020; 400m 2014, 400mh 2018; WIT 400m 2018. Swiss records: 200m 2016, 400m 2017 & 2018, 400mh 2019.
Progress at 400mh: 2015- 55.60, 2016- 54.92, 2017- 54.29, 2018- 54.33, 2019- 54.06, 2020- 54.98. pbs: 60m 7.31i '20, 100m 11.34 '14, 150m 17.06 '16, 200m 22.38 '16, 300m 35.70 '17, 400m 50.52 '18, 800m 2:23.94 '09, 60mh 8.65i '12, 100mh 14.31 '11, 300mh 39.25 '20, HJ 1.81 '08, LJ 6.14 '08, SP 12.77i '12, 12.63 '11; JT 38.73 '09, Pen 4047i '12, Hep 5651 '11. Older sister Ellen Sprunger (b. 8 Aug 1986) Hep 6124 '12.

SYRIA

Majed El Dein GHAZAL b. 21 Apr 1987 Damascus 1.93m 72kg.
At HJ: OG: '08/12- dnq 24=/28=, 16- 7=; WCh: '09-11-13-15-19: dnq 28=/23=/21/15/25=, '17- 3; AsiG: '10-14-18: dnq 13=/6/3=; AsiC: '11-17-19: 2/3/1; CCp: '18-4. Won WMilG 2015, Is.Sol & Asian Ind G 2017, Med G 2018.
13 Syrian records 2007-16.
Progress at HJ: 2006- 2.09, 2007- 2.17, 2008- 2.21i/2.20, 2009- 2.16, 2010- 2.22, 2011- 2.28, 2012- 2.26, 2013- 2.23, 2014- 2.26, 2015- 2.31, 2016- 2.36, 2017- 2.32, 2018- 2.33, 2019- 2.31.

TAIWAN

Governing body: Chinese Taipei Athletics Association.

National Championships 2020: Men: 100m: Yang Chun-Han 10.13, 200m: Yeh Shou-Po 21.31, 400m: Yu Chen-Yi 47.71, 800m/1500m: Wu Jui-Hsuan 1:53.26/3:58.24, 5000m: Li Ch-Yu 14:59.17, 10000m: Chou Ting-Yin 31:47.88, 3000mSt: Hsu Wei-Po 9:42.67, 110mh: Yang Wei-Ting 14.16, 400mh: Yu Chia-Hsuan 52.14, HJ: Fu Chao-Hsuan 2.14, PV: Hsieh Chia-Han 5.05, LJ: Lin Yu-Tang 7.88, TJ: Lee Kuei-Lung 16.12, SP: Ma Hao-Wei 17.27, DT: Tai Shih-Hao 52.82, HT: Tzeng Hao-Chan 58.58, JT: Cheng Chao-Tsun 85.54, Dec: Huang Han 6738, 10000mW/20kW: Hsu Chia-Wei 43:44.19/1:35:41; **Women**: 100m: Chang Po-Ya 11.87, 200m/400m: Hu Chia-En 24.61/55.45, 800m: Wang Jou-Hsuan 2:18.09, 1500m/3000mSt: Chen Chao-Chun 4:42.41/11:00.35, 5000m: Chang Yu-Chen 17:54.59, 10000m: Tsao Chun-Yu 33:54.81, 100mh: Hsu Lee 13.19, 400mh: Wu Pei-Shan 61.96, HJ: Lee Ching-Ching 1.75, PV: Shen Yi-Ju 4.00, LJ: Huang Shih-Han 6.17w, TJ: Lin Chia-Yu 12.53, SP: Lin Chia-Ying 15.91, DT: Guo Pei-Yu 46.82, HT: Liang Yu-Chieh 55.64, JT: Chiu Yu-Ting 52.66, 10000mW/20kW: Chiang Chia-Jou 49:32.42/1:41:41.

CHENG Chao-Tsun b. 17 Oct 1993 Yangmei 1.82m 88kg.
At JT: WCh: '17- dnq 22, '19- 10; WJ: '10- 8; WY: '09- dnq 12; AsiG: '14- 5, '18-5; AsiC: '11-15-17-19: 11/7/6/1; CCp: '18- 3; WUG: '15- 4, '17- 1. Won Asi-J 2012.
Javelin records: 4 Taiwan 2010-17, Asian 2017.
Progress at JT: 2009- 71.71, 2010- 78.68, 2011- 77.07, 2012- 77.10, 2013- 71.22, 2014- 81.61, 2015- 81.78, 2016- 71.66, 2017- 91.36, 2018- 84.60, 2019- 89.05, 2020- 85.54.

THAILAND

Governing body: Athletic Association of Thailand.
National Championships 2020: Men: 100m/200m: Siripol Punpa 10.34w/20.85, 400m: Aphisit Chumsri 48.13, 800m: Jirayu Pleenaram 1:55.68, 3000mSt: Patikarn Phetchsricha 9:46.14, 110mh: Natthapol Dansongnern 14.68, 400mh: Thanawitch Prasertsub 54.64, HJ: Tawan Kaewdam 2.15, PV: Phatsapong Amsam-Ang 5.30, LJ: Suttisak Singkhon 7.29, TJ: Wisarut Suwachai 15.41, SP: Promrob Janthima 15.98, DT: Thongchai Silamool 49.61, HT: Kittiphong Boonmawan 68.00, JT: Wanchalerm Roscha 62.54, 20000mW: Arthit Sriwichai 1:40:56.35; **Women**: 100m/200m: Suphanich Poolkerd 11.58w/24.01, 400m: Benny Nonthaman 56.34, 3000mSt: Surakan Wanna 12:49.46, 100mh: Natthawai Dawandee 14.74, 400mh: Benny Nonthaman 62.07, HJ: Prangthip Chitkhokhruad 1.64, LJ: Suphawadee Inthathueng 5.72, TJ: Parinya Chueamaroeng 13.18. SP: Areerat Intadit 14.93, DT: Subenrat Insaeng 58.37, HT: Mingkamol Kumphol 52.35, JT: Jariya Wichaidit

THAILAND – TRINIDAD – TURKEY 145

54.83. 20000mW: Kotchaporn Tangriswong 2:00:16.58.

TRINIDAD & TOBAGO

Governing body: National Association of Athletics Administrations of Trinidad & Tobago. Founded 1945, reformed 1971.
National Championships first held in 1946 (men) and 1947 (women). 2020 not held
Machel CEDENIO b. 6 Sep 1995 Pt. Fortin 1.83m 70kg. Simplex.
At 400m/4x400mR: OG: '16- 4; WCh: '15- 7/2R, '17- sf/1R, '19- 7; CG: '18- sf; WJ: '12- 5/3R, '14- 1; WY: '11- 4; PAm: '15- 2/1R, '19- h/3R; WI: '16- res 3R. Won CAC-J 2014, TTO 2016-17, 2019. TTO 400m record 2016.
Progress at 400m: 2010- 48.12, 2011- 46.89, 2012- 46.02, 2013- 45.93, 2014- 45.13, 2015- 44.36, 2016- 44.01, 2017- 44.90, 2018- 45.68, 2019- 44.41, 2020- 45.76. Pbs: 200m 21.15 '13, 300m 31.7+ '16.
Kyle GREAUX b. 26 Apr 1988 Sangre Grande 1.90m 80kg. Abilene Wildcats.
At 200m/4x100mR: OG: '16- h; WCh: '13-15-17-19: h/h/sf/8; CG: '14- sf, '18- 6; PAm: '15- sf, '19- h/2R. Won NACAC 2018, TTO 2015, 2018.
Progress at 200m: 2013- 20.57, 2014- 20.59, 2015- 20.42, 2016- 20.61, 2017- 20.19, 2018- 19.97, 2019- 20.15/20.09St. Pbs: 60m 6.87i '15, 100m 10.16 '17, 150mSt 15.03 '18, 300m 33.34 '16, 400m 47.14 '13.
Father Vernie Greaux was an international athlete at 400-1500m.
Jereem RICHARDS b. 13 Jan 1994 Pt. Fortin 1.83m 66kg. University of Alabama, USA.
At 200m/4x400mR: WCh: '17- 3/1R, '19- sf; WJ: '12- sf/3R, WY: '11- sf; CG: '14- h, '18- 1; PAm: '19- 2; WI: '12- 3R. Won TTO 2017, 2019.
Progress at 200m, 400m: 2011- 21.23, 47.32; 2012- 20.82, 47.17; 2013- 20.72/20.69w, 46.20; 2014- 20.58, 46.15; 2015- 20.72, 45.91; 2016- 46.02, 2017- 19.97, 45.21; 2018- 19.99, 2019- 20.14, 45.92; 2020- 20.71i, 46.55i. Pbs: 60m 6.73 '21, 100m 10.23 '19, 300m 32.10i '18, 500m 1:02.79i '20.
Ran 43.5 400m relay leg at 2017 Worlds.
Keshorn WALCOTT b. 2 Apr 1993 Toco 1.88m 90kg. Rebirth.
At JT: OG: '12- 1, '16- 3; WCh: '13/15- dnq 19/26, '17- 7, 19- 11; CG: '14- 2; WJ: '10- dnq, '12- 1; WY: '09- dnq 13; PAm: '11-15-19: 7/1/2; CAG: '18- 1; CCp: '14- 3. Won CAC-J 2010, 2012; TTO 2012, 2015-16, 2018-19
Javelin records: CAC 2015, nine TTO 2012-15, eight CAC junior 2011-12.
Progress at JT: 2009- 60.02, 2010- 67.01, 2011- 75.77A, 2012- 84.58, 2013- 84.39, 2014- 85.77, 2015- 90.16, 2016- 88.77, 2017- 86.61, 2018- 84.96, 2019- 86.09. pb TJ 14.28 '10.
First Caribbean Olympic champion and youngest ever Olympic champion in throws. Won IAAF Rising Star Award 2012. Elder brother Elton TJ pb 16.43/16.51w '11 & 4 WY '09, aunt Anna Lee Walcott Hep pb 5224 '00.

Women

Tyra GITTENS b. 6 Jun 1998 1.76m 60kg. Texas A&M University, USA.
At Hep: PAm: '19- dnf. Won NCAA indoor HJ & Pen 2021. TTO records: Hep 2018, indoor HJ 2021, LJ (2) 2021, Pen (7) 2018-21.
Progress at HJ, Hep: 2014- 1.78, 2015- 1.84, 2016- 1.85, 5337; 2017- 1.83, 5490w/5324; 2018- 1.86, 6074; 2019- 1.87, 6049; 2020- 1.86i, 2021- 1.93i. Pbs: 200m 23.86 '19, 800m 2:28.22i '21, 60mh 8.27i '21, 100mh 13.21 '18, LJ 6.68i ''21, 6.53 '19; SP: 13.89 '19, JT 41.10 '18, Pen 4746i '21.
Lived in the USA for most of her life. Her father Sterling Gittens was a sprinter.

TURKEY

Governing body: Türkiye Atletizm Federasyonu. Founded 1922.
National Champions 2020: Men: 100m: Kayhan Özer 10.46w, 200m: Oguz Uyar 21.32, 400m: Mohamed El Abbas QAT 46.29, 800m: Musaab Adam M.Ali 1:47.62, 1500m: Mehmet Çelik 3:45.48, 3000m: Ali Kaya 8:08.73, 5000m: Aras Kaya 13:31.50, 10000m: Halil Yasin 30:27.74, Mar: Yavuz Agrali 2:19:23, 3000mSt: Hilal Yego 8:40.26, 110mh: Mikdat Sevler 13.76, 400mh: Berke Akçam 49.78, HJ: Alperin Acet 2.21, PV: Berkay Gürmeric 4.80, LJ: Muammer Demir 7.66w, TJ: Can Özüpek 16.32, SP: Alperan Karahan 17.63, DT: Ömer Sahin 56.48, HT: Özkan Baltaci 76.87, JT: Ümmet Degermenci 71.77, 10000mW/20kW: Salih Korkmaz 39:26.92/1:19:31. Women: 100m/200m: Elif Polat 11.88w/24.65, 400m: Nevin Ince 57.03, 800m: Rahime Tekin 2:11.80, 1500m/3000m: Meryem Akdag 4:23.40/9:11.26, 5000m: Fatma Demir 16:44.98, Mar: Tubay Erdal 2:41:11, 3000mSt: Derya Kunur 10:02.93, 100mh: Özge Soylu 13.55, 400mh: Emel Kirçin-Sanli 58.61, HJ: Buse Savaskan 1.79, PV: Demet Parlak 4.15, LJ: Tugba Aydin 5.97, TJ: Tugba Danismaz 13.81, SP: Aysel Yilmaz 15.07, DT: Eylem Becerek 57.09, HT: Merve Yilmazer 55.28, JT: Münevver Hanci 50.57, 10000mW: Evin Demir 44:43.85.

Esref APAK b. 3 Jan 1982 Kalecik 1.86m 105kg. ENKA.
At HT: OG: '04- 2, '08/12/16- dnq 15/16/24=; WCh: '05-09-11-15-17: dnq 17/27/17/17/16, '07- 11; EC: '06-16-18 dnq 18/dnq/dnq 16; WJ: '00- 1; EU23: '03- 2; EJ: '01- 3; WUG: '05- 2; won Med G 2005, Balkan 2015-16. Turkish 2001-03, 2008-13, Is.Sol 2017. 20 Turkish hammer records 2000-05.
Progress at HT: 1997- 41.26, 1998- 49.22, 1999- 57.93, 2000- 69.97, 2001- 72.82, 2002- 73.24, 2003- 77.57, 2004- 81.27, 2005- 81.45, 2006- 79.80, 2007- 80.31, 2008- 80.36, 2009- 77.11, 2010- 75.22, 2011- 78.04, 2012- 78.28, 2013- 76.94, 2015- 76.82, 2016- 76.45, 2017- 78.00, 2018- 78.59, 2019- 74.45, 2020- 77.56. 2-year drugs ban from 8 Jun 2013. Married to Sema Apak (200m 23.67, 100mh 13.71 '11).

TURKEY – UGANDA

Yasmani COPELLO Escobar. b. 15 Apr 1987 La Habana, Cuba 1.96m 86kg. Fenerbahçe.
At 400mh: OG: '16- 3; WCh: '15- 6, '17- 2, '19- 6; EC: '16- 1, '18- 2; CCp: '18- 4; won Ibero-American 2008, Balkan 2015, Cuban NG 2010. Seven Turkish 400mh records 2015-18.
Progress at 400mh: 2006- 52.30, 2007- 49.99, 2008- 50.08, 2009- 49.56, 2010- 51.23, 2011- 49.76, 2012- 50.28, 2013- 49.89, 2014- 50.62, 2015- 48.46, 2016- 47.92, 2017- 48.24, 2018- 47.81, 2019- 48.25, 2020- 49.04. pbs: 200m 21.44 '09, 300m 32.53 '00, 400m 46.77 '09, 110mh 14.35A '08.
Former Cuban, has lived in Turkey from 2012, acquired citizenship 21 Oct 2013, cleared to compete for them from 30 Apr 2014.

Ramil GULIYEV b. 29 May 1990 Baku, Azerbaijan 1.87m 73kg. Fenerbahçe.
At (100m)/200m: OG: '08- qf, '16- 8; WCh: '09-15-17-19: 7/6/1/5; EC: '14- h/6, '16- 6/2, '18- 1/2R WJ: '06- (h), '08- 5; WY: '07- 2; EJ: '09- 2/1; WUG: '09- 1, '15- 3/3; CCp: '18- 2/2R; ET: '14- 3/2. At 60m: EI: '09- 7. Won EYOF 100m & 200m 2007, Balkan 100m 2014, 2016; 200m 2014-16, TUR 100m 2012, 200m 2016; Is.Sol 100m & 200m 2017, Med G 2018. Records: European Junior 200m 2009; AZE 100m (2) 2009, 200m (4) 2007-09; TUR 100m (2) & 200m (5) 2011-18. European sea-level 200m best 2018.
Progress at 200m: 2006- 21.74, 2007- 20.72, 2008- 20.66, 2009- 20.04, 2010- 20.73, 2011- 20.32, 2012- 20.53, 2013- 20.46, 2014- 20.38, 2015- 19.88, 2016- 20.09, 2017- 20.02/19.98w, 2018- 19.76, 2019- 19.86, 2020- 20.73. pbs: 60m 6.58i '12, 100m 9.97/9.9 '17, 150m 15.38 '20, 300m 32.61 '16.
Switched from Azerbaijan to Turkey on 26 Apr 2011, and cleared to compete for Turkey from 4 Apr 2013. Partner of Yekaterina Zavyalova (née Poistogova) RUS (800m 2 OG 2012 in pb 1:57.53, 4 WCh 2013, 4 EC 2014, 3 EJ 2009).

Women

Yasemin CAN (formerly **Vivian Jemutai** KEN) b. 11 Dec 1996 Kenya 1.66m 49kg. ENKA.
At 5000m/10000m: OG: '16- 6/7; WCh: '17- h/11; EC: '16- 1/1, '18- 3/4; EU23: '17- 1/1; At 3000m: EI: '17- 2. World HMar: '20- 7. World CC: '17- 3 mxR; Eur CC: '16-17-18-19: 1. Won Balkan 5000m & 10000m 2017; TUR 10000m 2016, Is.Sol 2017. European U23 records 10000m (3), 15k Rd 2016
Progress at 5000m, 10000m: 2015- 15:39.90, 32:42.31; 2016- 14:37.61, 30:26.41; 2017- 14:36.82, 31:18.20; 2018- 14:57.63, 32:34.34; 2019- 14:53.92, 30:59.20; 2020- 14:40.70. pbs: 1500m 4:11.54i '17, 4:16.42- 16; 2000m 5:43.0 '18, 3000m 8:33.29 '19, road: 15k 46:24 '20, 20k 62:40 '20, HMar 66:20 '20.
Became a Turkish citizen on 25 May 2015, cleared to compete for them from 13 Mar 2016.

Eda TUGSUZ b. 27 Mar 1997 Antalya 1.71m 68kg.
At JT: WCh: '17- 5, '19- dnq 20; EC: '16- 11, '18- dnq 16; WJ: '14- dnq 21, '16- 3; WY: '13- 5; EU23: '17- 4, '19- 2; EJ: '15- 8; WUG: '17- 4, '19- 3. Won Isl. Sol 2017, Balkan 2016, TUR 2016
6 Turkish javelin records 2016-17, European U23 record 2017.
Progress at JT: 2013- 50.29, 2014- 52.53, 2015- 56.52, 2016- 58.95, 2017- 67.21, 2018- 65.20, 2019- 64.83, 2020- 60.38.

UGANDA
Governing body: Uganda Athletics Federation. Founded 1925.

Joshua Kiprui **CHEPTEGEI** b. 12 Sep 1996 Kapsewui 1.79m 61kg.
At (5000m)/10000m: OG: '16- 8/6; WCh: '15- 9, '17- 2, '19- 1; CG: '18- 1/1; WJ: '14- 4/1; won Afr-J 2015. At HMar: WCh: '20- 4. World CC: '19- 1. Won DL 5000m 2019, UGA 5000m 2014-16.
World records: 5000m & 10000m 2020, road 15k 2018, 10k 2019, 5k 2020. Ugandan 10k Rd 2017.
Progress at 10000m: 2013- 28:53.52A, 2014- 13:32.84, 27:56.26; 2015- 13:28.50A, 27:27.57; 2016- 13:00.60, 27:10.06; 2017- 12:59.83, 26:49.94; 2018- 27:19.62; 2019- 12:57.41, 26:48.36; 2020- 12:35.36, 26:11.00. pbs: 1500m 3:37.82 '16, 3000m 7:33.26 '19, 2M 8:07.54 '19, 3000mSt 8:43.21A '13; Road: 5k 12:51 '20, 10k 26:38 '19, 15k 41:05 '18, 10M 45:15 '18, 20k 56:16 '20, HMar 59:21 '20.
Had big lead at 3/4 distance in World Cross 2017, but faded badly to 30th. Three world records in 2020.

Jacob KIPLIMO b. 14 Nov 2000 Bukwo, Mount Elgon 1.70m 55kg. Emilia Romagna, Italy,
At (5000m)/10000m: OG: '16-(h); WCh: '17- (h); CG: '18- 4; WJ: '16- 3, '18- 6/2. AT HMar: WCh: '20- 1; World CC: '17- 1J, '19- 2. Won World Mountain Running Ch 2015.
Uganda 3000m & half marathon records 2020.
Progress at 5000m, 10000m, HMar: 2015- 29:22.14A, 2016- 13:19.54, 27:26.68; 2017- 13:13.64, 2018- 13:19.66, 27:30.25, 61:53A; 2020- 12:48.63, 57:37. pbs: 1500m 3:50.24 '16, 2000m 4:59.7+ '20, 3000m 7:26.64 '20, 2M 8:25.17 '18, Road: 10k 26:41dh '18, 15k 42:18 '20, 20k 55:55 '20.

Ronald MUSAGALA b. 16 Dec 1992 Iganga, Busoga 1.76m 61kg.
At 1500m (800m): OG: '16- 11; WCh: '13- (sf), '15- h, '17/19- sf; CG: '14- 11 (8), 18- h; AfCh: '18- 3; CCp: "18- 8. Won UGA 800m & 1500m 2013. Five UGA 1500m records 2015-19.
Progress at 1500m: 2012- 3:43.73A, 2013- 3:38.89A, 2014- 3:37.75, 2015- 3:35.01, 2016- 3:36.23, 2017- 3:33.65, 2018- 3:35.33, 2019- 3:30.58. pbs: 800m 1:45.27 '14, 1000m 2:17.11 '14, 1M 4:02.4A'14, 3000m 7:44.78 '18, 5000m 13:24.41 '15.

Women

Sarah CHELANGAT b. 5 Jun 2001 1.58m 42kg.
At 5000m: WCh: '19- h; WJ: '18- 4; AfG: '19- 4, Af-J: '19- 3. At 3000m: WY: '17- 5; Af-J: '18- 2; YOG: '18- 1 (& 1 CC). World CC: '19- 4J.
Uganda records 5000m 2019, 10000m 2020.
Progress at 5000m, 10000m: 2017- 16:32.61A,

2018- 15:29.25, 2019- 15:00.61; 2020- 31:06.46. pbs: 1500m 4:21.62 '17, 3000m 9:11.63 '19.

Peruth CHEMUTAI b. 10 Jul 1999 Bukwo district 1.65m 50kg.
At 3000mSt: OG: '16- h; WCh: '17- h, '19- 5; WJ: '16- 7, '18- 2. World CC: '17- 7J, '19- 5. Comm-Y: '15- 2 1500m & 3000m
Ugandan 3000mSt record 2018.
Progress at 3000mSt:, 2015- 10:19.93A, 2016- 9:31.03, 2017- 9:27.72, 2018- 9:07.94, 2019- 9:11.08. pbs: 1500m 4:17.18 '16, 3000m 9:13.09 '17.

Stella CHESANG b. 1 Dec 1996 Namoryo, Kween district 1.58m 42kg. Uganda Police.
At 5000m: OG: '16- h; WCh: '17- h; WJ: '14- 4; AfG: '19-7; Af-J: '15- 3. At 10000m: WCh: '19- 16; CG: '18- 1; AfCh: '18- 4. At 3000m: WY: '13- 4. Af CC: '18- 5. Won World Mountain Running Ch 2015. Ugandan 5000m record 2019.
Progress at 5000m.10000m: 2012- 16:00.6A, 2013- 43:31.51A, 2014- 15:53.85, 2015- 15:25.01, 2016- 15:10.30, 2017- 15:17.91, 2018- 15:52.51A, 31:39.0A; 2019- 15:00.72, 31:38.70. pbs: 800m 2:08.04A '17, 1500m 4:18.80 '15, 3000m 8:52.39 '15, 10kRd 31:14 '18, 15kRd 47:19 '18.

Halima NAKAAYI b. 16 Oct 1994 Seeta, Mukono 1.60m 66kg.
At 800m: OG: '16- sf, WCh: '17- sf, '19- 1; CG: '18- h; AfG: '19- 3; AfCh: '16-h, 18- 4; WJ: '12- sf; WY: '11- h; Af-J: '13- 4 (&4 400m). At 400m: CG '14- h; won Comm-Y 2011.
Two Uganda 800m records 2018-19, 1000m 2020.
Progress at 800m: 2011- 2:08.12A, 2012- 2:04.84A, 2013- 2:06.6, 2014- 2:07.2A, 2015- 2:05.84A, 2016- 1:58.78, 2017- 2:00.80, 2018- 1:58.39, 2019- 1:58.04, 2020- 2:01.96i. pbs: 400m 53.02A '17, 1000m 2:32.12 '20, 1500m 4:31.34 '16, 1M 4:50.53 '16.

Winnie NANYONDO b. 23 Aug 1993 Mulago 1.64m 48kg.
At 800m/(1500m): OG: '16- h, WCh: '17- h, '19- 4/11; CG: '14- 3, '18- 4/10; AfG: '15- 7; AfCh: '18- 5/5; WJ: '12- 8.
Uganda records 800m 2014, 1500m (2) 2019, 1M (2) 2018-19.
Progress at 800m, 1500m: 2012- 2:02.38, 4:22.62A; 2013- 2:02.96, 4:28.77; 2014- 1:58.63, 4:20.40; 2015- 2:01.97, 4:17.13; 2016- 2:00.57, 2017- 2:00.22, 4:07.93; 2018- 1:59.41, 4:06.05; 2019- 1:58.83, 3:59.56; 2020- 2:00.49, 4:06.13i/4:07.94. pbs: 400m 53.72A '14, 1000m 2:36.13 '18, 1M 4:18.65 '19, 3000m 9:27.25A '19, 5000m 15:57.16 '20.

UKRAINE

Governing body: Ukrainian Athletic Federation. Founded 1991.
National Champions 2020: **Men**: 100m: Oleksandr Sokolov 10.47, 200m: Serhiy Smelyk 21.00, 400m: Oleksandr Pohorilko 46.77, 800m: Yevhen Hutsol 1:49.17, 1500m: Andrii Atamaniuk 3:58.97, 5000m: Vasyl Koval 14:07.92, 10000m/ HMar: Bohdan-Ivan Horodyskyy 29:31.20/ 64:00, 3000mSt: Roman Rostykus 9:07.10, 110mh: Viktor Solyanov 14.11, 400mh: Dmytro Romanchuk 50.60, HJ: Andriy Protsenko 2.30, PV: Artur Bortnikov 5.30, LJ: Yaroslav Isachenkov 7.97, TJ: Ihor Honchar 16.18, SP: Ihor Musiyenko 19.48, DT: Mykyta Nestorenko 55.10, HT: Myhaylo Kokhan 75.39, JT: Oleksandr Nychyporchuk 72.36, Dec: Oleksiy Kasyanov 7716, 20kW: Ivan Losev 1:21:44, 50kW: Ihor Hlavan 3:47:31. **Women**: 100m: Yana Kachur 11.76, 200m: Tetyana Melnyk 23.59, 400m: Anna Ryzhykova 51.70, 800m: Olha Lyakhova 2:03.49, 1500m: Lyudmyla Danylina 4:30.77, 5000m: Yuliya Shmatenko 15:49.59, 10000m: Valeriya Zijenko 32:42.72, HMar: Yevheniya Prokofeyeva 71:14, 3000mSt: Nataliya Strebkova 10:01.77, 100m: Hanna Plotitsyna 13.25, 400mh: Viktoriya Tkachuk 55.60; HJ: Oksana Okuneva 1.92, PV: Maryna Kylypko 4.40, LJ: Maryna Bekh-Romanchuk 6.81, TJ: Iryna Pimenova 13.40, SP: Olha Holodna 16.02, DT: Nataliya Semenova 54.77, HT: Iryna Klymets 71.71, JT: Tetyana Nychyporchuk 54.03, Hep: Alina Shukh 6215, 20kW: Lyudmyla Olyanovska 1:29:18, 50kW: Khrystyna Yudkina 4:32:30.

Bohdan BONDARENKO b. 30 Aug 1989 Kharkiv 1.95m 72kg.
At HJ: OG: '12- 7, '16- 3; WCh: '11-13-15-17-19: dnq 15=/1/2=/9/dnq nh; EC: '12- 11, '14- 1; WJ: '06- 3, '08- 1; EU23: '11- 1; EJ: '07- 9; WUG: '11- 1, CCp: '14- 1; ET: '13- 1. Won DL 2013.
Three UKR high jump records 2013-14.
Progress at HJ: 2005- 2.15, 2006- 2.26, 2007- 2.25i/2.19, 2008- 2.26, 2009- 2.27/2.15, 2010- 2.10, 2011- 2.30, 2012- 2.31, 2013- 2.41, 2014- 2.42, 2015- 2.37, 2016- 2.37, 2017- 2.32, 2019- 2.31.
Missed 2018 season after knee surgery. Married Iryna Pimenova (TJ 13.74 '16) in 2017. His father Viktor had decathlon pb of 7480 '87.

Myhaylo KOKHAN b. 22 Jan 2001 Zaporizhzhia 1.82m 103kg. Dnipropetrovsk.
At HT: WCh: '19- 5; WJ: '18- 2; WY: '17- 1; EJ: '19- 1; EY: '18- 1; YOG: '18- 1. Won Balkan & UKR 2020. European U20 6kg hammer record (84.71) 2019. World Youth 5kg record (87.82) 2018.
Progress at HT: 2017- 71.42, 2018- 70.02, 2019- 77.39, 2020- 77.78.

Andriy PROTSENKO b. 20 May 1988 Kherson 1.94m 80kg. Khersonskaya. Biotechnology graduate.
At HJ: OG: '12- 9, '16- 4=; WCh: '09-11-13-15-17-19: dnq 25/27/23=/17/13=/14=; EC: '10-12: dnq 17/13=, '14-16-18: 2/9=/5=; EU23: '09- 3; EJ: '07- 2; WI: '14- 3, '16- 7; EI: '15- 6, '19- 2=; WUG: '13- 2; ET: '10- 3, '14- 1. Won DL 2019, Balkan 2020, UKR 2012, 2018-20.
Progress at HJ: 2005- 2.10, 2006- 2.18i/2.10, 2007- 2.21, 2008- 2.30, 2009- 2.25 2010- 2.25, 2011- 2.31, 2012- 2.31, 2013- 2.32, 2014- 2.40, 2015- 2.33i/2.32,

UKRAINE

2016- 2.33, 2017- 2.30, 2018- 2.31, 2019- 2.32, 2020- 2.30, 2021- 2.34i.

Maryna ZAKALNYTSKYY b. b. 19 Aug 1994 Verkhnia, Ivano-Frankivska region 1.80m 65kg.
At 50kW: WCh: '17- 26, '19- 9; EC: '18- 1; WCp: '18- 4; ECp: '17- 6.
Progress at 50kW: 2014- 4:07:08, 2015- 3:57:18, 2016- 3:56:30, 2017- 3:53:50, 2018- 3:44:59, 2019- 4:13:28, 2021- 3:46:26. pbs: 20kW 1:21:56 '20.30kW: 2:13:10 '18, 35kW 2:34:48 '16.

Women

Maryna BEKH-ROMANCHUK b. 18 Jul 1995 Starokostiantyniv 1.72m 63kg. née Bekh. Khmelnytska.
At LJ: OG: '16- nj; WCh: '13/17- dnq 24/18, '19- 2; EC: '16- 12, '18-2; WJ: '12- 8, '14- 9; WY: '11- 5; EU23: '15- 6, '17- 3; EJ: '13- 3; WI: '18- 10; EI: '17-19-21: 7/3/1; ET: '17- 3; WUG: '19- 1. Won UKR 2015-20, WIT 2020.
Progress at LJ: 2010- 6.10, 2011- 6.47, 2012- 6.36, 2013- 6.78, 2014- 6.36, 2015- 6.63, 2016- 6.93, 2017- 6.71i/6.59/6.63w, 2018- 6.73/6.86w, 2019- 6.92, 2020- 6.96i/6.87, 2021- 6.96i. Pbs: 60m 7.45i '20, TJ 13.07 '13.
Married (2 Sep 2018) Mykhaylo Romanchuk, who at 1500m swimming won the World short-course title in 2018, and was 2nd at the long-course Worlds in 2017 and 2019. European champion at 400m and 800m freestyle in 2018.

Iryna HERASHCHENKO b. 10 Mar 1995 Kiev 1.81m 61kg.
At HJ: OG: '16- 10; WCh: '15/17/19: dnq 23/13=/23; EC: '14/16- dnq 20/18=; WJ: '12- 7, '14- 5; WY: '11- 2; EU23: '15- 3, '17- 2; WUG: '17- 2, '19- 2; EJ: '13- 3; WI: '18- 7; EI: '19- 5, '21- 2.
Progress at HJ: 2010- 1.83, 2011- 1.87, 2012- 1.90, 2013- 1.92i/1.91, 2014- 1.95i/1.92, 2015- 1.94, 2016- 1.94, 2017- 1.95, 2018- 1.93i/1.88, 2019- 1.99, 2020- 1.94i/1.90, 2021- 1.98i.

Iryna KLYMETS b. 4 Oct 1994 Chetvertnia, Volyn 1.68m 78kg. Lutsk.
At HT: OG: '16- dnq 28; WCh: '17- dnq 21, '19- 5; EC: '18- 11; EU23: '15- 7; EJ: '13- dnq 21; WUG: '19- 1; ET: '19- 3. Won UKR 2018-20.
Progress at HT: 2012- 57.10, 2013- 61.00, 2014- 59.94, 2015- 65.21, 2016- 72.23, 2017- 72.53, 2018- 72.63, 2019- 73.56, 2020- 73.01. Pb Wt 21.35 '18.

Yuliya LEVCHENKO b. 28 Nov 1997 Bakhmut 1.79m 60kg. Kiev.
At HJ: OG: '16- dnq 19; WCh: '15: dnq 24, '17- 2, '19- 4; EC: '18- 9; WJ: '16- 3; WY: '13- 13; EU23: '17- 1, '19- 1; EJ: '15- 6; ET: '19- 1; YOG: '14- 1; WI: '18- 5; EI: '17-19-21: 3/2/4. Won UKR 2018-19.
Progress at HJ: 2013- 1.77, 2014- 1.89, 2015- 1.92, 2016- 1.95, 2017- 2.01, 2018- 1.98i/1.97, 2019- 2.02, 2020- 2.00, 2021- 1.96i.

Yaroslava MAHUCHIKH b. 19 Sep 2001 Dnipro 1.81m 56kg. Dnipropetrovsk.
At HJ: WCh: '19- 2; WY: '17- 1; EJ: '19- 1; EY: '18- 1; YOG: '18- 1; EI: '21- 1; WIT 2020.
High jump indoor records: world U18 2018, World U20 (2) & European U20 (3) 2019, World U20 indoor 2020; UKR 2021.
Progress at HJ: 2015- 1.60, 2016- 1.76, 2017- 1.92A, 2018- 1.98i/1.95, 2019- 2.04, 2020- 2.02i/2.00. 2021- 2.06i.
Youngest ever field event medallist at World Champs. WA Rising Star award for 2019.

Lyudmyla OLYANOVSKA b. 20 Feb 1993 Solobkivtsi, Khmelnitskya 1.72m 57kg. Khmelnitskya.
At 20kW: WCh: '13- 11, '15- 3; EC: '14- 2; WCp: '14- 7; EU23: '13- 1, '15- 2; ECp: '13- 6, '15- 7; Won UKR 2020. At 10000m/10kW: WJ: '12- 4; EJ: '11- 7; WCp: '12- 5J.
Two UKR 20k road walk records 2014-15 (and unofficial 5000m & 10,000m (2)).
Progress at 20kW: 2013- 1:30:26, 2014- 1:27:27, 2015- 1:27:09, 2020- 1:29:13, 2021- 1:29:52. pbs: 3000mW 12:38.43i '13, 5000mW 20:15.71 '14, 10000mW 41:42.5 '14. Four-year ban announced in 2017, backdated to 9 Nov 2015.

Anna RYZHYKOVA b. 24 Nov 1989 Dnipropetrovsk 1.77m 67kg. née Yaroshchuk.
At 400mh/4x400mR: OG: '12- sf/3R; WCh: '11-13-15-19: sf/5/sf/7; EC: '10- 12-14-18: sf/3/h&2R/2; WJ: '08- 6/2R; EU23: '09- 8, '11- 1/2R; WUG: '11- 1, '13- 1; CCp: '18- 3; ET: '13-14-19: 2&1R/1/2. Won Balkan 400m 2020, UKR 400m 2019-20, 400mh 2009-10, 2012, 2018-19. At 200m: EJ: '07- h/2 4x100m.
Progress at 400m 2019,: 2006- 57.52, 2007- 56.46, 2008- 56.09, 2009- 57.23, 2010- 55.60, 2011- 54.77, 2012- 54.35, 2013- 54.77, 2014- 55.00, 2015- 55.16, 2018- 54.47, 2019- 54.45, 2020- 54.93. pbs: 60m 7.74i '06, 200m 23.49 '10, 400m 52.11 '14, LJ 6.05 '13.

Alina SHUKH b. 12 Feb 1999 Izmail, Odessa region 1.75m 60kg. BVUFK Brovary.
At Hep: WCh: '17- 14; EC: '18-15; WY: '15- 3; EU23: '19- 15; EJ: 17- 1; EY: '16- 1; ET: '17- 1; Balkan champion 2019-20, UKR 2020. At Pen: WI: '18- 7. At JT: WJ: '15- 1.
World youth spec heptathlon record 6186 in 2016, world indoor U20 pentathlon record 2017.
Progress at Hep: 2016- 6099, 2017- 6381, 2018- 6177, 2019- 6178, 2020- 6386. pbs: 60m 7.9i/8.26i '18, 200m 25.88 '18, 800m 2:10.93 '18, 60mh 8.78i '19, 8.6 '18; 100mh 14.11 '20, HJ 1.92 '16, LJ 6.29 '17, TJ 12.97 '19, SP 15.08i '19, 14.43 '18; JT 56.54 '17, Pen 4602i '19.

UNITED KINGDOM

Governing body: UK Athletics. Founded 1999 (replacing British Athletics, founded 1991, which succeeded BAAB, founded 1932). The Amateur Athletic Association was founded in 1880 and the Women's Amateur Athletic Association in 1922.

National Championships (first were English Championships 1866-79, then AAA 1880-2006, WAAA from 1922). **2020 UK Champions: Men:** 100m: Harry Aikines-Aryeetey 10.35, 200m: Andrew Morgan-Harrison 20.69w, 400m: Alex Knibbs 46.65, 800m: Daniel Rowden 1:45.94, 1500m: George Mills 3:51.39, 5000m: Marc Scott 13:32.98, HMar: Chris Thompson 61:07, 3000mSt: Phil Norman 8:32.51, 110mh: David King 13.58, 400mh: Alastair Chalmers 49.66, HJ: Joel Clarke-Khan 2.18, PV: Harry Coppell 5.85, LJ: Reynold Banigo 7.81, TJ: Nathan Douglas 15.80, SP: Scott Lincoln 19.65, DT: Nicholas Percy 59.74, HT: Craig Murch 73.24, JT: James Whiteaker 75.99, 5000mW: Callum Wilkinson 19:25.94.
Women: 100m: Imani Lansiquot 11.26w, 200m: Hannah Williams 23.83, 400m: Laviai Nielsen 51.72, 800m: Keely Hodgkinson 2:03.24, 1500m: Laura Weightman 4:09.76, 5000m Jessica Judd 15:37.52, HMar: Lily Partridge 70:50, 3000mSt: Aimee Pratt 9:30.73, 100mh: Cindy Ofili 13.16, 400mh: Jessie Knight 55.80, HJ: Morgan Lake 1.80, PV: Holly Bradshaw 4.35, LJ: Jazmin Sawyers 6.69, TJ: Naomi Ogbeta 13.44, SP: Sophie McKinna 17.88, DT: Kirsty Law 57.95, HT: Jessica Mayho 65.47, JT: Freya Jones 53.12, 5000mW: Gemma Bridge 22:51.15.

Tom BOSWORTH b. 17 Jan 1990 Pembury, Kent 1.84m 64kg. Tonbridge, was at Leeds Metropolitan University.
At 20kW: OG: '16- 6, WCh: '15- 24, '17- dq, '19- 7; EC: '14- 11, '18- 7; CG: '10- 11, '18- 2; WT: '18- 14; ECp: '17- 4, '19- 4; won RWA 2010-11, 2013, 2015-18; UK 5000mW 2011, 2014-18; 10kW 2011, 2013.
World bests: 1Mile W 2017, 3000m indoor & out 2018. UK walk records: 5000m (4) 2011-19, 10k road 2015 & 2020, 20k (3) 2016-18.
Progress at 20kW: 2010- 1:28:24, 2011- 1:27:18, 2012- 1:24:49, 2013- 1:24:44, 2014- 1:22:20, 2015- 1:22:33, 2016- 1:20:13, 2017- 1:20:58, 2018- 1:19:38, 2019- 1:20:53, 2020- 1:23:56. pbs: 1MW: 5:31.08 '17, 3000mW 10:30.28i/10:43.84 '18, 11:29.54 '16; 5000mW 18:20.97i '20, 18:43.28 '17; 10kW 39:10 '20, 41:34.19t '15.

Mohamed FARAH b. 23 March 1983 Mogadishu, Somalia 1.71m 58kg. Newham & Essex Beagles.
At 5000m (/10000m): OG: '08- h, '12- 1/1, '16- 1/1; WCh: '07- 6, '09- 7, '11- 1/2, '13- 1/1, '15- 1/1, '17- 2/1; EC: '06- 2, '10- 1/1, '12- 1, '14- 1/1; CG: '06- 9; WJ: '00- 10; EJ: '01- 1; EU23: '03 & '05- 2; ECp: '08-09-10-13: 1/1/1 &(1)/1. At 3000m: WY: '99- 6; WI: '08- 6, '12- 4; EI: '05-07-09-11: 6/5/1/1; ECp: '05-06: 2/2. World CC: '07- 11, '10- 20; HMar: '16- 3; Eur CC: '99-00-01-04-05-06-08-09: 5J/7J/2J/15/21/1/2/2. Won DL 5000m 2017, UK 5000m 2007, 2011; Mar 2014, 2018-19; HMar 2018-19.
Records: World 1 hour 2020, indoor 2M 2015, European 10000m 2011, HMar best 2019, indoor 5000m 2011 (u) & 2017, 1500m 2013; indoor 2M 2012, 20k and HMar 2015, 15k 2016, Mar 2018; UK 3000m 2016, 2M 2014, 5000m 2010 & 2011, HMar (5) 2011-19, Mar (2) 2018, 20000m & 1Hr 2020.
Progress at 1500m, 5000m, 10000m: 1996- 4:43.9, 1997- 4:06.41, 1998- 3:57.67, 1999- 3:55.78, 2000- 3:49.60, 14:05.72; 2001- 3:46.1, 13:56.31; 2002- 3:47.78, 14:00.5; 2003-3:43.17, 13:38.41; 2004- 3:43.4, c.14:25; 2005- 3:38.62, 13:30.53; 2006- 3:38.02, 13:09.40; 2007- 3:45.2i+, 3:46.50, 13:07.00; 2008- 3:39.66, 13:08.11, 27:44.54; 2009- 3:33.98, 13:09.14; 2010- 12:57.94, 27:28.86; 2011- 12:53.11, 26:46.57; 2012- 3:34.66, 12:56.98, 27:30.42; 2013- 3:28.81, 13:05.88, 27:21.71; 2014- 13:23.42, 28:08.11; 2015- 3:28.93, 13:11.77, 26:50.97; 2016- 3:31.74, 12:59.29, 26:53.71; 2017- 13:00.70, 26:49.51; 2020- 14:06.3+, 28:11.9+. At Mar: 2014- 2:08:21, 2018- 2:05:11, 2019- 2:05:39. pbs: 800m 1:48.69 '03, 1M 3:56.49 '05, 2000m 5:01.8i '09, 5:02.1+ '16; 3000m 7:32.62 '16, 2M 8:03.40i '15, 8:07.85 '14; 15000m 42:17.95 '20, 20000m 56:20.40 '20, 1Hr 21,330m '20, 2000mSt 5:55.72 '00; road 15k 42:03+ '16, 10M 45:32+ '15, 20k 56:27 '15, HMar 59:07dh '19, 59:32 '15, 25k 1:12:36 '18, 30k 1:27:31 '18.
Joined his father in England in 1993. Sixth man to win Olympic 5000m/10,000m double at same Games and uniquely repeated that in 2016. In 2013 became third man to win World 5000m/10000m double and he repeated in 2015; now has record eight global distance running titles. Has 12 wins, including Great North Run 2014-19, and three 2nds in his 15 half marathons. Knighted in the 2017 New Year's Honours. 3rd in London Marathon and 1st in Chicago in 2018.

Miguel FRANCIS b. 28 Mar 1995 Montserrat 1.86m 75kg. Racers TC, Jamaica.
At 200m: WCh: '15/19- sf; WJ: '14- sf; CG: '14- 7R; PAm: '15- 6.
Three Antiguan 200m records 2015-16.
Progress at 100m: 2013- 20.60/20.58w, 2014- 20.71, 2015- 20.05/19.76dt, 2016- 19.88/19.67dt, 2017- 20.44, 2018- 20.38, 2019- 19.97. pbs: 100m 10.23 '19, 150m 14.95 '16, 400m 46.48 '17.
Antigua to UK 24 Sep 2016. Eligible for international competition from 30 Mar 2017.

Tom GALE b. 18 Dec 1998 Wiltshire 1.97m 82kg. Team Bath.
At HJ: CG: '18- dnq 14;WJ: '16- 9; EU23: '19- 2; EJ: '17- 3.
Progress at HJ: 2013- 1.66, 2014- 1.86, 2015- 2.06i/1.96, 2016- 2.18, 2017- 2.30, 2018- 2.23, 2019- 2.27, 2020- 2.33i.

Adam GEMILI b. 6 Oct 1993 London 1.78m 73kg. Blackheath & Bromley.
At 100m/(200m)/4x100mR: OG: '12- sf, '16- (4); WCh: '13- (5), '17- 1R, '19- sf/4/2R; EC: '14- (1)/1R, '16- 1R, '18- (5)/1R; CG: '14- 2/2R, '18 dns F; WJ: '12- 1; EU23: '13- 1/4/1R; EJ: '11- 2/2R; ET: '13/14- 1R. Won UK 200m 2016, 2019.
European 4x100m records 2017 & 2019.
Progress at 100m, 200m: 2009- 11.2, 2010- 10.80/10.72w, 21.87w; 2011- 10.35/10.23w, 20.98;

150   UNITED KINGDOM

2012- 10.05, 20.38; 2013- 10.06, 19.98; 2014- 10.04, 19.98; 2015- 9.97; 2016- 10.11, 19.97; 2017- 10.08/10.03w, 20.35; 2018- 10.11, 20.10; 2019- 10.04/20.03; 2020- 10.28, 20.56. Pb 60m 6.59i '16.
Member of Chelsea youth football academy before playing for Dagenham & Redbridge. Won European Athletics Rising Star award 2014. Mother from Iran, father from Morocco.
Elliot GILES b. 26 May 1994 Birmingham 1.73m 64kg. Birchfield H.
At 800m: OG: '16- h; WCh: '17/19- sf, '19- 5; CG: '18- h,; EC: '16- 3, '18- sf; WI: '18- 4. Won UK 2016-18.
Commonwealth indoor 800m record 2021.
Progress at 800m: 2010- 1:57.93, 2011- 1:53.24, 2015- 1:47.55, 2016- 1:45.54, 2017- 1:44.99, 2018- 1:45.04, 2019- 1:45.03, 2020- 1:44.56, 2021- 1:43.63i. Pbs: 600m 1:18.0+ '19, 1500m 3:36.90i '21, 3:41.27 '17; 1M 3:56.47 '19.
Callum HAWKINS b. 22 Jun 1992 Elderslie, near Paisley 1.66m 52kg. Was at Butler University, USA
At Mar: OG: '16- 9; WCh: '17- 4, '19- 4; CG: '18- dnf. At HMar: EC: '16- 9; At 10000m: CG: '14- 20; At 3000m: EY: '09- 1; Eur CC: '16- 3.
Progress at Mar: 2015- 2:12:17, 2016- 2:10:52, 2017- 2:10:17, 2019- 2:08:14. pbs: 800m 1:55.36 '10, 1500m 3:54.09 '10, 3000m 8:07.98 i'12, 8:10.28 '14; 5000m 13:59.8w '17, 10000m 28:49.57 '14, road: 10k 28:02 '20, 15k 42:37 '17, 10M 47:01 '18, 20k 56:55 '20, HMar 60:00 '17. Older brother Derek: Mar: 2:12:57 '16. 9 CG 2014.
Zharnel HUGHES b. 13 Jul 1995 Sandy Ground, Anguilla 1.90m 79kg. Racers TC, Jamaica.
At (100m)/200m: WCh: '15- 5, '17- sf, '19- 6/sf/2R CG: '18- dq/1R; EC: '16- h, '18- (1)/1R; WJ: '12- sf/h, '14- 5; ET: '17- 1R. Won CAC-J 2014, UK 2015, PAm-J 100m 2013.
Records: European 4x100m 2019. Anguilla: 100m (4), 200m (6) 2012-14.
Progress at 100m, 200m: 2012- 10.42/10.41w, 20.90; 2013- 10.23A/10.39, 20.79/20.77w; 2014- 10.12, 20.32; 2015-10.15, 20.02; 2016- 10.10, 20.62; 2017- 10.12/10.08w, 20.22; 2018- 9.91, 20.23/20.12dq; 2019- 9.95, 20.24/20.00St. pb 400m 46.95 '16.
Switched from Anguilla and cleared to compete for Britain from 19 June 2015. Disqualified after finishing first just ahead but obstructing Jereem Richards at 2018 CG.
Joshua KERR b. 8 Oct 1997 Edinburgh. Edinburgh AC. 1.86m 73kg. New Mexico University, USA,
At 1500m: WCh: '17- h, '19- 6; WJ: '16- 10; EJ: '15- 1. Won NCAA 2017.
Progress at 1500m: 2009- 4:38.25, 2010- 4:30.86, 2011- 4:19.62, 2012- 4:05.26, 2013- 3:58.87, 2014- 3:52.46, 2015- 3:44.12, 2016- 3:41.08, 2017- 3:35.99, 2018- 3:35.01, 2019- 3:32.52, 2020- 3:34.53. pbs: 800m 1:45.35 '19, 1000m 2:17.60 '20, 1M 3:53.48

'19, 3000m 8:10.14 '19, 5000m 13:28.66 '19.
Nick MILLER b. 1 May 1993 Carlisle 1.88m 112kg. Border H, Oklahoma State Univ., USA.
At HT: OG: '16- dnq 22; WCh: '15- 11, '17- 6, 19- 10; EC: '16- dnq 25, '18- 9; CG: '14- 2, '18- 1; WJ: '12- dnq 25; EU23: '13- 9, '15- 1; ET: '15- 2, '17- 3. UK champion 2014-15, 2017-19; NCAA 2016.
Three UK hammer records 2015-18.
Progress at HT: 2010- 49.86, 2011- 57.74, 2012- 67.56, 2013- 71.60, 2014- 74.38, 2015- 77.55, 2016- 76.93, 2017- 77.51, 2018- 80.26, 2019- 78.39. Pbs: DT 45.37 '13, Wt 22.46i '15.
Lawrence OKOYE b. 6 Oct 1991 London 1.98m 137kg. Croydon Harriers.
At DT: OG: '12- 12; EC: '12- 11; EU23: '11- 1; WJ: '10- 6. UK champion 2012.
UKdiscus records 2011 & 012.
Progress at DT: 2011- 67.63, 2012- 68.24, 2019- 60.80, 2020- 65.15.
Having been a brilliant rugby player (wing) and with an offer from Oxford University, gave up athletics for American Football after 2012 Olympics and signed as an offensive tackle for the San Francisco 49ers. He was then briefly with further NFL teams: the Arizona Cardinals in 2015, New York Jets 2015-16, Dallas Cowboys 2016. Returned to athletics in 2019.
Andrew POZZI b. 15 May 1992 Leamington Spa 1.86m 79kg. Stratford-upon-Avon. Bristol University.
At 110mh: OG: '12- h, '16- sf; WCh: '17/19- sf; EC: '16- dns, '18- 6; CG: '18- 6=; EJ: '11- 2. UK champion 2016, 2018. At 60mh: WI: '12-14- 18: 4/4/1; EI: '17-19-21: 1/6/2.
Progress at 110mh: 2009- 14.8, 2011- 13.73/13.66w, 2012- 13.34, 2015- 13.62, 2016- 13.19, 2017- 13.14/13.13w, 2018- 13.28, 2019- 13.28, 2020- 13.14. pbs: 100m 10.44 '18, 60mh 7.43i '17, LJ 6.73 '09.
Daniel ROWDEN b. 9 Sep 1997 Buckhurst Hill.1.77m 61kg. Woodford Green. Student of mechanical engineering at Imperial College, London.
At 800m: EC: '18- sf; WJ: '16- sf; EU23: '17- 2; EJ: '15- sf. Won UK 2020.
Progress at 800m: 2010- 2:19.5, 2011- 2:09.80, 2012- 2:00.62, 2013- 1:53.75, 2014- 1:52.35, 2015- 1:49.32, 2016- 1:48.13, 2017- 1:46.64, 2018- 1:44.97, 2020- 1:44.09. Pb 400m 48.48 '15.
Marc SCOTT b. 21 Dec 1993 Northallerton 1.77m 62kg, Cambridge & Coleridge, Bowerman TC, was at Manchester Metropolitan University & University of Tulsa, USA.
At 5000m: WCh: '17/19- ht; EC: '18- 5; At 10000m: EU23: '15- 6; At 3000m: ET: '17- 2; Eur CC: '15- 4 U23, '18- 9. Won UK 5000m 2018, 2020, NCAA 10000m 2017.
European indoor 5000m record 2020.
Progress at 5000m, 10000m: 2012- 31:54.39, 2013- 14:13.53, 31:00.91; 2014- 14:33,42i, 2015- 13:36.81, 29:30.33; 2016- 13:37.34i, 2017- 13:22.37. 28:07.97;

2018- 13:23.14, 2019- 13:21.97i/13:47.12, 27:56.19; 2020- 13:08.87i/13:32.98, 2021- 13:05.13, 27:10.41. pbs: 1500m 3:35.93 '20, 1M 4:05.36i '17, 3000m 7:36.09 '21, road: 15k 43:49 '19, 10M 46:58 '19, HMar 60:39 '20.

Jake WIGHTMAN b. 11 Jul 1994 Nottingham. 1.82m 67kg. Edinburgh AC. Was at Loughborough University,
At 800m: CG: '18- 4. At 1500m: WCh: "17- sf, '19- 5; EC: '16- 7, '18- 3; CG: '14- h, '18- 3; EJ: '13- 1; ET: '17- 2; WI: '18- 6.
Progress at 800m, 1500m: 2008- 2:18.0, 2009- 4:22.47, 2010- 2:05.40, 4:13.89; 2011- 1:57.35, 3:59.35; 2012- 1:51.6, 3:51.74; 2013- 1:48.01, 3:43.74; 2014- 1:47.93, 3:35.49; 2015- 1:47.36, 3:40.05; 2016- 1:47.13, 3:36.64; 2017- 1:45.42, 3:34.17; 2018- 1:44.61, 3:33.96; 2019- 1:45.08, 3:31.87; 2020- 1:44.18, 3:29.47. pbs: 400m 48.34 '16, 600m 1:17.2 '20, 800m 1:44.18 '20, 1000m 2:16.27 '18, 1M 3:52.02 '19, 3000m 8:13.6 '15, 5000m 15:37.32 '11, 5k Rd 14:18 '17, 10k Rd 30:29 '17.
Father Geoff Wightman (Mar 2:13:17 '91, 6 EC & 8 CG '90, mother Susan Tooby (10000m 32:20.95 '88, 6 CG '86, Mar 2:31:33 & 12 OG '88).

Women

Dina ASHER-SMITH b. 4 Dec 1995 Farnborough 1.65m 55kg. Blackheath & Bromley. Was at King's College, London.
At (100m)/200m/4x100mR: OG: '16- 5/3R; WCh: '13- 3R, '15- 5, '17- 4/2R, '19- 2/1/2R; EC: '14- dnf, '16- 1/2R, '18- 1/1/1R; CG: '18- 3/1R; WJ: '12- 7, '14- (1); EJ: '13- 1/1R; CCp: '18- (2)/2R. At 60m: WI: '16- dns; EI: '15- 2. Won DL 100m 2019, UK 100m 2015, 2018-19.
UK records 100m (5) 2015-19, 200m (3) 2015-19, 4x100m (2) 2016.
Progress at 100m, 200m: 2009- 12.10, 24.83; 2010- 12.00/24.50; 2011- 11.96, 24.16/24.11w; 2012- 11.54, 23.49; 2013- 11.38/11.30w, 23.14; 2014- 11.14/11.93w, 22.61; 2015- 10.99, 22.07; 2016- 11.08, 22.31; 2017- 11.13, 22.22; 2018- 10.85, 21.89; 2019- 10.83, 21.88. pbs: 60m 6.91+ '19, 7.08i '15; 150m 16.70St '17, 17.00 '20; 400m 53.49 '14.

Holly BRADSHAW b. 2 Nov 1991 Preston 1.75m 68kg. née Bleasdale. Blackburn Harriers.
At PV: OG: '12- 6=, '16- 5; WCh: '11-15-17-19: dnq/7/6/4; EC: '18- 3; CG: '18- 4; WI: '12- 3, '14- 9; WJ: '10- 3; EU23: '11- 1; EI: '13-19-21: 1/2/3=.
UK champion 2011-12, 2015-20.
Seven UK pole vault records 2011-17, five indoors 2011-12.
Progress at PV: 2007- 2.30, 2008- 3.10i, 2009- 4.05, 2010- 4.35, 2011- 4.71i/4.70, 2012- 4.87i/4.71, 2013- 4.77i/4.60, 2014- 4.73i, 2015- 4.70, 2016- 4.76i/4.70, 2017- 4.81, 2018- 4.80, 2019- 4.81i/4.80, 2020- 4.73, 2021- 4.85i. pbs: SP 11.81i '17, 11.32 '11, JT 37.60 '11.
World age-19 best 2011, age-20 best 2012.
Married 800m runner Paul Bradshaw (1:47.37 '09) on 25 Oct 2014.

Melissa COURTNEY-BRYANT b. 30 Aug 1993 1.70m 54kg. Poole, was at St. Mary's & Brunel Universities.
At 1500m/(5000m): EC: '16- h, '18- (5); CG: '18- 3/9; EU23: '15- 10; WUG: '17- 5; At 3000m: EI: '19- 3. Eur CC: '17- 1mxR, '18- 8.
Progress at 1500m, 5000m: 2006- 4:52.2, 2007- 4:30.85, 2008- 4:25.40, 2009- 4:28.69, 2010- 4:25.85, 2011- 4:27.87, 2012- 4:28.67, 2013- 4:17.57i/4:17.87, 2014- 4:11.41, 2015- 4:09.74, 16:13.45; 2016- 4:07.55, 2017- 4:05.82, 15:28.95; 2018- 4:03.44, 15:04.75; 2019- 4:05.37, 14:53.82; 2020- 4:01.81, 15:16.50; 2021- 4:04.79i. pbs: 600m 59.93mx '12, 60.0 '12; 800m 2:04.03 '17, 1M 4:23.15 '17, 3000m 8:38.22i '19, 8:39.20 '18; 10kRd 33:57 '14, 33:34sh '15.
Married Ashley Bryant (Dec 8163 '17, 2 CG 2014) in October 2019.

Niamh EMERSON b. 22 Apr 1999 Shirland, Derbyshire 1.79m 68kg. Amber Valley & Erewash.
At Hep: CG: '18- 3; WJ: '18- 1; WY: '15- 13; EJ: '17- 4, EY: '16- 3. At Pen: EI: '19- 2. Comm-Y: '15- 1 HJ, 3 400mh.
Progress at Hep: 2017- 6013, 2018- 6253. pbs: 200m 24.40 '18, 24.18w '20; 800m 2:09.74 '18, 1500m 4:45.11mx '13, 60mh 8.54i '19, 100mh 13.76, 13.71w '18; 400mh 61.07 '15, HJ 1.89 '16, LJ 6.41 '18, SP 13.93i '19, 12.67 '17; JT 43.95 '18, Pen 4731i '19.

Sophie HITCHON b. 11 Jul 1991 Burnley 1.70m 74kg. Blackburn H.
At HT: OG: '12- 8, '16- 3; WCh: '11-13: dnq 25/16, '15- 4, '17- 7; EC: '12-14-16-18: 10/dnq 18/4/8; CG: '14- 3; WJ: '08- 7, '10- 1; WY: '07- dnq 17; EU23: '11- 3, '13- 1; EJ: '09- 3; ET: '13/14- 3; won Comm-Y 2008, UK 2011-12, 2014-18.
13 UK hammer records 2011-16.
Progress at HT: 2006- 40.98, 2007- 54.56, 2008- 60.73, 2009- 63.18, 2010- 66.01, 2011- 69.59, 2012- 71.98, 2013- 72.97, 2014- 71.53, 2015- 73.86, 2016- 74.54, 2017- 73.97, 2018- 73.48, 2019- 67.51. pbs: 100m 12.2/12.40 '09, 200m 25.2 '08, 25.51 '09; SP 10.75 '08.
Married Damien Grulick 15 Sep 2018.

Keely HODGKINSON b. 3 Mar 2002 Wigan 1.68m 54kg. Leigh H, Leeds Beckett University.
At 800m: EJ: '19- 3, EY: '18- 1; EI: '21- 1. Won UK 2020. World indoor U20 800m record 2021.
Progress at 800m: 2013- 2:27.3, 2014- 2:20.01, 2015- 2:29.4, 2016- 2:12.53, 2017- 2:06.85, 2018- 2:04.26, 2019- 2:03.40, 2020- 2:01.16i/2:01.73, 2021- 1:59.03i. Pbs: 400m 54.69mx '20, 56.2 '18; 1500m 4:29.05mx '18, 4:29.1 '17.

Katarina JOHNSON-THOMPSON b. 9 Jan 1993 Liverpool 1.83m 70kg. Liverpool H.
At Hep: OG: '12- 13, '16- 6; WCh: '13-15-17-19: 5/28 & 11 LJ/5 & 5 HJ/1; EC: '18- 2; CG: '18- 1; WY: '09- 1; EU23: '13- 1; EJ: '09- 8, '11- 6. At LJ: WJ: '12- 1 (sf 100mh); WI: '14- 2. At Pen: WI: '18- 1; EI: '15- 1, '19- 1. Won UK LJ 2014.

UNITED KINGDOM

Records: Commonwealth Hep 2019, UK indoor records: HJ (2) 2014-15, LJ & Pen 2015.
Progress at LJ, Hep: 2006- 5.11, 2007- 5.77i/5.65, 2008- 6.11i/5.90/6.07w, 5343; 2009- 6.31, 5481; 2010- 6.25i/5.58, 2011- 6.44, 5787; 2012- 6.51/ 6.81w, 6267; 2013- 6449, 6.56; 2014- 6.92, 6682; 2015- 6.93i/6.79, 5039; 2016- 6.84, 6523; 2017- 6.75, 6691; 2018- 6.71i/6.70, 6759; 2019- 6.85, 6981; 2020- 6.52. pbs: 60m 7.50i '14, 100m 12.35 '08, 12.2 '09, 11.30w '14; 200m 22.79 '16, 300m 38.56i '08, 400m 53.7 '14; 800m 2:07.26 '19, 60mh 8.18i '15, 100mh 13.09 '19, 200mhSt 25.31 '15, 400mh 58.3 '14, HJ 1.98 '16, TJ 12.83, 13.35w '14; SP 13.86 '19, JT 43.93 '19, Pen 5000i '12.
Pbs in the each of the last four events when adding 182 points to her pb for 5th at the 2013 Worlds and 474 points to pentathlon best to win 2015 European Indoors, inc. 6.89 long jump, the best ever in a pentathlon. Four pbs in winning World heptathlon title 2019. Three no-jumps (last by 1 cm) in 2015 WCh Hep LJ. World heptathlon best HJ 1.98 at 2016 OG. Won Götzis heptathlon 2014 & 2019. 29 English age-group titles U15 to U23.

Morgan LAKE b. 12 May 1997 Milton Keynes 1.78m 64kg. Windsor, Slough, Eton & Honslow.
At (Hep)/HJ: OG: '16- 10=; WCh: '15- dnq 14=, '17- 6, '19- dnq 18=; EC: '14- dnq 17=; '16- (dnf), '18- 7; CG: '18- 2; WJ: '14- 1/1; WY: '13- (dnf); EJ: '15- 1; WI: '18- 4. At Pen: WI: '16- 6; EI: '15- 9, '17- 8) HJ. Won UK HJ 2016-20.
World youth indoor pentathlon record 2014.
Progress at HJ, Hep: 2007- 1.28, 2008- 1.50, 2009- 1.57, 2010- 1.70, 2011- 1.76, 2012- 1.80, 2013- 1.90, 2014- 1.94, 6148; 2015- 1.94, 5082; 2016- 1.94, 5951; 2017- 1.96, 2018- 1.97, 2019- 1.97i/1.94, 2020- 1.90i/ 1.82, 2021- 1.96i. pbs: 60m 7.98i '13, 200m 24.59 '14, 800m 2:18.53i '16, 2:21.06 '14; 60mh 8.63i '16, 100mh 14.25 '14, LJ 6.32 '14, TJ 12.35, 12.45w '13; SP 14.85 '14, JT 41.93 '17, Pen 4527i '15.
Record 33 English age-group titles 2010-19 (12 indoors, 21 out). Father Eldon had a TJ pb of 15.43 (1989).

Eilish McCOLGAN b. 25 Nov 1990 Dundee 1.76m 59kg. Dundee Hawkhill, was at Dundee University.
At 800m: OG: '16- 13; WCh: '17- 10, '19- 10; EC: '16- 6, '18- 2; CG: '18- 6 (6 1500m); At 3000m: EI: '17- 3, '19- 7; At 10000m: ET: '19- 2; At 3000mSt: OG: '12- h; WCh: '13- 10, CG: '14- 6; EU23: '11- 6; Won UK 5000m 2019, 3000mSt 2012-14.
Progress at 1500m, 5000m, 10000m: 2002- 5:22.8, 2003- 4:58.14, 2004- 4:36.70, 2005- 4:37.78, 2006- 4:38.00, 2007- 4:35.56, 2008- 4:27.11, 2010- 4:21.38, 2011- 4:14.44, 15:52.69; 2012- 4:11.78mx/4:13.19, 15:44.62; 2013- 4:09.67, 2014- 4:15.23mx, 2016- 4:03.74, 15:05.00; 2017- 4:01.60, 14:48.49, 32:10.59; 2018- 4:04.30, 14:53.05; 2019- 4:00.97, 14:46.17, 31:16.76; 2020- 4:03.74, 14:57.27. pbs: 800m 2:12.22 '08, 1000m 2:40.8+ '19. 1M 4:24.71 '19, 2000m 5:43.1+ '17, 3000m 8:31.00 '17, road: 10M 51:36 '19;

HMar 72:26+ '20, 2000mSt 6:42.24 '11, 3000mSt 9:35.82 '13.
Her mother Liz (10,000m OG: '88- 2, WCh: '91- 1, 30:57.07 '91), father Peter (3000mSt 8:27.93 '91).

Laura MUIR b. 9 May 1993 Milnathort, Kinross 1.62m 54kg. Dundee Hawkhill H. Was at Glasgow University.
At 1500m/(3000m): OG: '16- 7; WCh: '15- 5, '17- 4 (6 5000m), '19- 5; EC: '14- h, '18- 1; CG: '14- 11; WJ: '12- (16); EU23: '13- 3; WI: '18- 2/3; EI: '13- 6, '15- (4), '17- 1/1, 19- 1/1; won DL 2016, 2018. At 800m: WCh: '13- sf. Won UK 800m 2018, 1500m 2015-16. Eur CC: '15- 4 U23.
UK records 1500m (2) 2016, 1000m 2020, Indoor records: Commonwealth 3000m 2017, 1500m 2021; European 1000m & 3000m 2017.
Progress at 1500m, 5000m: 2005- 5:33.16, 2006- 5:12.39, 2007- 4:48.97, 2008- 4:47.92, 2009- 4:58.77, 2010- 4:50.91. 2011- 4:38.90, 2012- 4:14.52mx/ 4:17.81, 2013- 4:07.76, 15:53.68; 2014- 4:00.07, 2015- 3:58.66. 2016- 3:55.22, 2017- 4:00.35, 14:49.12i/ 14:52.07; 2018- 3:58.18, 2019- 3:55.76, 2020- 3:57.40, 2021- 3:59.58i. pbs: 400m 55.36i mx '16, 55.71i '14, 56.78 '12; 800m 1:58.69 '17, 1000m 2:30.82 '20, 1M 4:18.03 '17, 2000m 5:41.5+i '17, 3000m 8:26.41i/8:30.64 '17, 10k Rd 38:23 '11.

Tiffany PORTER b. 13 Nov 1987 Ypsilanti, USA 1.72m 62kg. née Ofili. Doctorate in pharmacy from University of Michigan.
At 100mh: OG: '12- sf, '16- 7; WCh: '11-13-15-17: 4/3/5/h; EC: '14- 1, '16- 3; CG: '14- 2, '18- 6; WJ: '06- 3 (for USA); CCp: '14- 2; ET: '13- 1. At 60mh: WI: '12-14-16: 2/3/3; EI: '11- 2, '21- 3. Won UK 100mh 2011, 2013-16; NCAA 100mh 2007-09 & 60mh indoors 2008-09.
Records: British 100mh (4) 2011-14, 50mh/55mh/ 60mh indoors; world best 4x100mh 2014 & 2015.
Progress at 100mh: 2005- 14.19, 2006- 13.37/ 13.15w, 2007- 12.80, 2008- 12.73, 2009- 12.77/ 12.57w, 2010- 12.85, 2011- 12.56, 2012- 12.65/ 12.47w, 2013- 12.55, 2014- 12.51, 2015- 12.56, 2016- 12.70, 2017- 12.75, 2018- 12.99, 2020- 12.90/ 12.74w. pbs: 60m 7.41i '11, 100m 11.70 '09, 11.63w '08; 200m 23.90 '08, 400m 61.96 '06, LJ 6.48 '09; UK records: 50mh 6.83i '12, 55mh 7.38i '12, 60mh 7.80i '11.
Opted for British nationality in September 2010; her mother being born in London (father in Nigeria). Married US hurdler Jeff Porter (pb 13.08 '12, sf OG '12/16) in May 2011, daughter Chidera Linda born 25 Jul 2019.

Jemma REEKIE b. 6 Mar 1998 1.64m 50kg. Kilbarchan.
At (800m)/1500m. WCh: '19- h; EC: '18- h, EU23: '19- 1/1; EJ: '17- 1 (4 3000m).
Records: Commonwealth 1500m & 1M indoors and UK 800m indoors 2020.
Progress at 800m, 1500m: 2011- 2:25.66, 5:14.72; 2012- 2:17.46, 4:53.32; 2013- 2:12.82, 4:38.99; 2014- 2:09.88, 4:40.58; 2015- 2:10.09, 2016- 2:07.23, 4:24.22; 2017- 2:04.25, 4:12.28; 2018- 2:02.62, 4:06.11; 2019-

2:01.45,4:05.82; 2020- 1:57.91i, 4:00.52i/4:02.20. Pbs: 1000m 2:31.11 '20, 1M 4:17.88i '20, 4:27.00 '189 3000m 9:11.20mx, 9:24.81 '17.

Cindy SEMBER b. 5 Aug 1994 Ypsilanti, USA 1.78m 68kg. née Ofili. Wooford Green & Essex L, University of Michigan.
At 100mh: OG: '16- 4; WCh: '15/19- sf; ET: '19- 4. Won UK 2019-20. AT 60mh: EI: '21- 2, NCAA indoor 2016.
Progress at 100mh: 2012- 13.61, 2013- 13.34/13.30w, 2014- 12.93, 2015- 12.60, 2016- 12.63, 2017- 12.92, 2018- 13.26, 2019- 12.85, 2020- 12.88. pbs: 60m 7.37i '14, 100m 11.39 '15, 200m 23.46/23.43w '16, 60mh 7.88i '21.
Sister of Tiffany Porter. Has dual British/US nationality. Married John Sember March 2020.

Lorraine UGEN b. 22 Aug 1991 London 1.78m 64kg. Blackheath & Bromley. Was at Texas Christian University, USA.
At LJ: OG: '16- 11; WCh: '13- dnq, '15- 5, '17- 5; EC: '16- dnq 18, '18- 9; CG: '14- 5, '18- 4/1R; WJ: '10- dnq 17; EU23: '13- dns F; EJ: '09- dnq 21; WI: '16- 3; EI: 17- 2; won UK 2017-18, NCAA 2013, WIT 2016.
Progress at LJ: 2007- 5.55, 2008- 5.79, 2009- 6.29, 2010- 6.35/6.42w, 2011- 6.54, 2012- 6.74/6.83w, 2013- 6.77, 2014- 6.73Ai/6.59i/6.39/6.40w, 2015- 6.92/6.96w, 2016- 6.93i/6.80/6.82w, 2017- 6.97i/ 6.78, 2018- 7.05, 2019- 6.70, 2020- 6.74i. pbs: 60m 7.50Ai '12, 7.51i '14; 100m 11.32 '18, 11.31w '17; 200m 23.81/23.71w '15, 100mh 15.2/15.42 '08, HJ 1.56 '08, Hep 4307 '08.

Laura WEIGHTMAN b. 1 Jul 1991 Alnwick 1.72m 58kg. Morpeth H. Leeds Met University.
At 1500m: OG: '12- 7, '16- 11; WCh: '13- h, '15- sf, '17- 6; EC: '14- 3, '18- 3; CG: '14- 2; WJ: '10- 6. Won UK 2012, 2014, 2017-18, 2020. At 3000m: ET: '13- 2. At 5000m: WCh: '19- 7; CG: '18- 3. Eur U23 CC: '13- 8.
Progress at 1500m: 2004- 4:50.5, 2005- 4:44.0, 2006- 4:37.20, 2007- 4:26.02, 2008- 4:22.20, 2009- 4:14.9mx/4:19.9, 2010- 4:09.60mx/4:12.82, 2011- 4:07.94mx/4:15.51, 2012- 4:02.99, 2013- 4:05.36, 2014- 4:00.17, 2015- 4:04.70, 2016- 4:04.66, 2017- 4:00.71, 15:08.24; 2018- 4:01.76, 15:25.84; 2019- 4:00.63, 14:44.57; 2020- 4:00.09, 14:35.44. pbs: 400m 58.43 '09, 800m 2:01.87 '17, 1000m 2:37.56 '18, 1M 4:17.60 '19, 2000m 5:38.76+e '19, 5:44.22 '13, 3000m 8:26.07 '19, 10kRd 31:40 '19.

USA

Governing body: USA Track and Field. Founded 1979 as The Athletics Congress, when it replaced the AAU (founded 1888) as the governing body.
National Championships first held in 1876 (men), 1923 (women). **2020 Champions: Men**: Mar: Galen Rupp 2:09:20, 50kW: Andreas Gustafsson 4:12:11; **Women**: Mar: Aliphine Tuliamuk 2:27:23, 50kW: Robyn Stevens 4:37:23

Devon ALLEN b. 12 Dec 1994 Phoenix, Arizona 1.83m 82kg. Nike. Was at University of Oregon.
At 110mh: OG: '16- 5; WCh: '17- sf, '19- 7; CCp: '18- 5; Won US 2014, 2016, 2018; NCAA 2014, 2016.
Progress at 110mh: 2014- 13.16, 2016- 13.03, 2017- 13.10, 2018- 13.23/13.13w, 2019- 13.33, 2020- 13.36. pbs: 60m 6.85Ai '14, 100m 10.26 '18, 200m 20.52 '18, 400m 48.45 '12, 60mh 7.49Ai/7.50i '18, 400mh 51.19 '14.
Football scholarship as a wide receiver, but suffered a knee injury on the opening kickoff of the Rose Bowl at the end of 2014.

Ronnie BAKER b. 15 Oct 1993 Louisville, Kentucky 1.78m 80kg. Nike. Was at Texas Christian University.
At 100m: WUG: '15- 4. At 60m: WI: '18- 3; won NCAA indoor 2015-16, US 2017; WIT 2020.
Progress at 100m: 2011- 10.57, 2012- 10.59/10.55w, 2013- 10.58/10.33w, 2014- 10.21/10.14w, 2015- 10.05/9.94w, 2016- 10.09/9.95w, 2017- 9.98, 2018- 9.87/9.78w, 2019- 10.20, 2020- 10.00. pbs: 60m 6.40Ai/6.44i '18, 200m 20.55 '18, 20.06w '17; 400m 46.18 '13.
World fastest indoor 60m 2016 & 2017.

Kenneth 'Kenny' BEDNAREK b. 14 Oct 1998 Oklahoma 1.85m 84kg.
At 200m: WCh: '19- h.
Progress at 200m, 400m: 2015- 21.48, 47.95; 2016- 21.91/21.54w, 44.42; 2017- 47.03; 2018- 20.43, 46.68; 2019- 19.82A/20.07/19.49Aw, 44.73A/45.62; 2020- 19.80. pb 100m 10.09/10.02w '20.
Won 2019 JUCO titles for Indian Hills Warriors at high altitude in Hobbs, New Mexico 200m 19.82 and 400m 44.73, just the second time sub-20 and sub-45 sec times had been run on the same day; after 19.49w in his heat.

Chris BENARD b. 4 Apr 1990 Tustin, California 1.90m 79kg. Chula Vista Elite. Was at Arizona State University.
At TJ: OG: '16- dnq 16; WCh: '17- 6.
Progress at TJ: 2008- 15.09, 2009- 15.38, 2010- 15.52/16.20w, 2011- 15.80Ai/15.75, 2012- 16.74, 2013- 16.78, 2014- 17.10, 2015- 16.95, 2016- 17.21, 2017- 17.48, 2018- 17.40, 2019- 17.01/17.33w, 2020- 17.02Ai/16.91i. pb LJ 8.10Ai, 7.96 '14.

Rai BENJAMIN b. 27 Jul 1997 Bronx, New York 1.91m 77kg. Nike,was at UCLA, then USC.
At 400mh: WCh: '19- 2/1R; WY: '13- sf; won NCAA 2018, US 2019.
CAC 400m hurdles record 2018, Antiguan records: 400m (2) 2017-18, 400mh (8) 2015-18. Ran on fastest ever indoor 4x400m by USC 2018.
Progress at 400m, 400mh: 2013- 53.13, 2014- 47.17, 52.12; 2015- 46.19, 49.97; 2016- 49.82, 2017- 45.72, 48.33; 2018- 44.74, 47.02; 2019- 44.31, 46.98; 2021- 45.39i. pbs: 60m 6.72i '17, 100m 10.03 '20, 200m 19.99 '18, 300m 32.35i '20.
Parents are from Antigua, but he declined

Antiguan selection for the 2016 Olympic Games and, already a US citizen; was cleared by the IAAF to compete for the USA in October 2018. He is the son of West Indies Test cricketer (fast bowler) Winston Benjamin.

Matthew BOLING b. 20 Jun 2000 Miami, Florida 1.83m 73kg. University of Georgia.
At 100m/200m: WJ: '18- res(2)R 4x400m, PAm-J: '19- 1/1/1R/1R. Won NCAA indoor 200m 2021. World U20 4x100m and 4x400m records 2019.
Progress at 100m, 200m, LJ: 2017- 7.29, 2018- 21.20, 7.30/7.38w; 2019- 10.11A/10.13/9.98w, 20.31A/20.36/20.30w, 8.01; 2020- 20.66i, 2021- 20.19i, 8.07i pbs: 60m 6.64i '21, 400m 45.51i '21, 46.15 '18; HJ 1.98 '17.

Hillary BOR b. 22 Nov 1989 Eldoret, Kenya 1.68m 57kg. Hoka One One. Iowa State Univ.
At 3000mSt: OG: '16- 7; WCh: '17- h, '19- 8. Won US 2019.
Progress at 3000mSt: 2008- 8:36.84, 2009- 8:35.12, 2010- 8:38.05, 2011- 8:40.83, 2012- 8:36.44, 2013- 8:32.41, 2014- 8:38.42, 2015- 8:45.94, 2016- 8:13.68, 2017- 8:11.82, 2018- 8:12.20, 2019- 8:08.41. pbs: 1500m 3:44.30 '08, 1M 4:03.43i '08, 3000m 7:48.73i '20, 2M 8:39.54Ai '17, 5000m 13:05.60i '21, 13:26.81 '18; 10000m 27:38.53 '20, 10M Rd 48:31 '15. US citizen from 31 December 2014 after joining the US Army with his brothers **Emmanuel** (1500m: 4 WUG 3:41.65 in 2007, 3000m 7:44.93i '18, 5000m 13:28.79 '17, 2 US CC 2018) and Julius (1500m 3:41.11 W'10).

Donavan BRAZIER b. 15 Apr 1997 Grand Rapids, Michigan 1.88m 73kg. Nike. Was at Texas A&M University.
At 800m: WCh: '17- sf, '19- 1; won DL 2019, NCAA 2016, US 2017, 2019.
Records: World indoor 600m 2019, North American 800m 2019, indoor 800m (3) 2019-21.
Progress at 800m: 2012- 2:06, 2013- 1:54.36, 2014- 1:48.61, 2015- 1:43.55, 2016- 1:44.14, 2017- 1:43.95, 2018- 1:45.10Ai, 2019- 1:42.34, 2020- 1:43.15, 2021- 1:44.21i. pbs: 400m 46.91i '18, 47.02 '16; 600m 1:13.77i '19, 1000m 2:21.79i '17, 1500m 3:35.85 '20, 1M 3:59.30i '17.

Trayvon BROMELL b 10 Jul 1995 St. Petersburg, Florida 1.75m 71kg. New Balance. Baylor University.
At 100m/4x100mR: OG: '16- 8; WCh: '15- 3=; WJ: '14- 2/1R; PAm-J: 13- 3/1R, won NCAA 2014. At 60m: WI: '16- 1.
Two world junior 100m records 2014.
Progress at 100m, 200m: 2012- 10.40, 21.01; 2013- 10.27/9.99Aw, 20.91/20.86w; 2014- 9.97/9.77w, 20.59/20.23w; 2015- 9.84/9.76w, 20.03/19.86w; 2016- 9.84, 20.30; 2017- 10.22, 2019- 10.54, 2020- 9.90/9.87w. Pbs: 50m 5.72i+ '21, 60m 6.47i '16.
Fastest ever teenager with 9.84 for 100m in 2015.

Chris CARTER b. 11 Mar 1989 Austin 1.86m 80kg. Was at University of Houston.
At TJ: PAm: '11- 6, '19- 6; WI: '14- 6, '18- 5. Won US indoor 2014.
Progress at TJ: 2005- 14.43, 2006- 13.78/14.69w, 2007- 15.88, 2008- 15.41i/15.31/15.69Aw, 2009- 16.34, 2010- 15.98, 2011- 16.86, 2012- 16.61, 2013- 16.69, 2014- 17.15Ai/17.09, 2015- 16.71i/16.70, 2016- 17.18, 2017- 17.10Aidq/16.75i, 2018- 17.20Ai/17.18/17.28w, 2019- 17.18i/16.85/16.87w, 2020- 16.65i. pbs: 400mh 53.90 '07, LJ 7.67 '13, 7.68w '11.

Matthew CENTROWITZ b. 18 Nov 1989 Beltsville, Maryland 1.76m 61kg. Nike Oregon Project. Studied sociology at the Univ. of Oregon.
At 1500m: OG: '12- 4, '16- 1; WCh: '11-13-15-17-19: 3/2/8/h/8; WI: '12- 7, '16- 1. At 5000m WJ: '08- 11. Won US 2011, 2013, 2015-16, 2018; NCAA 2011, PAm-J 2007.
Progress at 1500m: 2007- 3:49.54, 2008- 3:44.98, 2009- 3:36.92, 2010- 3:40.14, 2011- 3:34.46, 2012- 3:31.96, 2013- 3:33.58, 2014- 3:31.09, 2015- 3:30.40, 2016- 3:34.09, 2017- 3:33.41, 2018- 3:31.77, 2019- 3:32.81, 2020- 3:57.93iM. pbs: 800m 1:44.62 '15, 1000m 2:16.67 '16. 1M 3:50.53 '14, 3000m 7:40.74i '16, 2M 8:21.07i '17, 8:40.55 '07; 5000m 13:00.39 '19, 10M Rd 50:39 '18.
Father Matt pbs: 1500m 3:36.60 '76, 3:54.94 '82, 5000m US record 13:12.91 '82, 10000m 28:32.7 '83; h OG 1500m 1976; 1 PAm 5000m 1979. Sister Lauren (b. 25 Sep 1986) 1500m pb 4:10.23 '09.

Paul Kipkemoi **CHELIMO** b. 27 Oct 1990 Iten, Kenya 1.71m 57kg. Nike, formerly US Army. Went to the University of North Carolina.
At 5000m: OG: '16- 2; WCh: '17- 3, '19- 7; WUG: '13- 2 (1500m 6); won US 2017-18. At 3000m: CCp: '18- 1; WI: '16- 7.
Progress at 5000m: 2011- 13:53.02, 2012- 13:21.89, 2013- 13:36.27, 2015- 13:37.02, 2016- 13:03.90, 2017- 13:08.62, 2018- 12:57.55, 2019- 13:04.60, 2021- 13:09.90i. pbs: 1500m 3:39.33 '16, 1M 3:55.96 '18, 3000m 7:31.57 '17, 2M 8:07.59 '19, 10000m 27:43.89 '19; Road: 15k 43:46 '17, 10M 48:19 '15.
Came to the USA in 2010, granted US citizenship on 23 Jul 2014 and cleared to compete for the US from 15 Jun 2015. Reduced his 5000m best from 13:19.54 to 13:03.90 at the 2016 Olympic Games.

Michael CHERRY b. 23 Mar 1995 New York 1.86m 75kg. Was at Louisiana State University.
At 400m/4x400mR: WCh: '17- 2R, '19- 1R/1mxR; WJ: '14- 1R; PAm: '19- 2R; WI: '18- 2/2R; Won US indoor 2018.
World 4x400mxR record 2020
Progress at 400m: 2010- 49.25, 2011- 48.57, 2012- 46.37, 2013- 46.02, 2014- 45.17, 2015- 45.43, 2016- 44.81, 2017- 44.66, 2018- 44.85, 2019- 44.69, 2020- 44.98. pbs: 200m 20.72 '20, 300m 32.37 '20, 600m 1:17.17Ai '16, 1:17.19Ai '19.
Ran fastest 4x400m relay splits at 2019 Worlds: 43.6 in men's final and 44.2 in mixed final.

Will CLAYE b. 13 Jun 1991 Tucson 1.80m 68kg. Puma. Was at University of Oklahoma, then Florida.
At (LJ)/TJ: OG: '12- 3/2, '16- 2; WCh: '11- 9/3,

'13- 3, '15- dnq 19, '17- 2, '19- 2; WI: '12- 4/1, '18- 1; CCp: '14- 2/3; won US 2014, 2016-17; PAm-J and NCAA 2009.
Progress at LJ, TJ: 2007- 14.91/15.19w, 2008- 7.39/7.48w, 15.97; 2009- 7.89/8.00w, 17.19/17.24w; 2010- 7.30w, 16.30; 2011- 8.29, 17.50/17.62w; 2012- 8.25, 17.70i/17.62; 2013- 8.10, 17.52; 2014- 8.19/8.29w, 17.75; 2015- 8.07/8.11w, 17.48/17.50w; 2016- 8.14/8.42w, 17.76; 2017- 7.89, 17.91; 2018- 17.44/17.46w; 2019- 8.21, 18.14. pb 100m 10.64/10.53w '12.
Possibly youngest ever NCAA champion – won 2009 title on his 18th birthday with 17.24w (and US junior record 17.19). First to win Olympic medals at both LJ and TJ since 1936. Married Queen Harrison (qv) on 13 October 2018.

Omar CRADDOCK b. 26 Apr 1991 Killeen, Texas 1.78m 79kg. Was at University of Florida.
At TJ: WCh: '13/19- dnq 13/13, '15- 4; WJ: '10- 3; PAm: '19- 1; WI: '16- 5. Won US 2015, NCAA 2012-13; WIT 2016.
Progress at TJ: 2006- 14.67, 2007- 15.16A, 2008- 15.53, 2009- 14.87i, 2010- 16.56, 2011- 16.57i/16.46, 2012- 16.75i/16.71/16.92w, 2013- 16.92/17.15w, 2014- 16.98/17.26w, 2015- 17.53, 2016- 17.16/17.42w, 2017- 17.08, 2018- 17.40, 2019- 17.68, 2020- 17.14Ai/17.04. pb LJ 7.63i '13, 7.60 '15, 7.70w '12.

Freddie CRITTENDEN b. 3 Aug 1994 St. Louis 1.83m 73kg. Nike. Was at Syracuse University.
At 110mh: PAm: '19- 2.
Progress at 110mh: 2013- 14.36/14.10w, 2014- 13.73, 2015- 13.62, 2016- 13.48/13.43w, 2017- 13.42, 2018- 13.27, 2019- 13.17, 2020- 13.30. pb 60mh 7.53i '19.

Ryan CROUSER b. 18 Dec 1992 Boring, Oregon 2.01m 142kg. Nike. Was at University of Texas.
At SP(/DT): OG: '16- 1; WCh: '17- 6, '19- 2; WY: '09- 1/2; CCp- '18- 2; won US 2016-17, 2019; NCAA 2013-14, indoors 2014.
World indoor shot record 2021.
Progress at SP: 2011- 19.48i, 2012- 20.29i/19.32, 2013- 21.09, 2014- 21.39, 2015- 21.14i/21.11, 2016- 22.52, 2017- 22.65, 2018- 22.53, 2019- 22.90, 2020- 22.91, 2021- 22.82i. pbs: DT 63.90 '14, JT 61.16 '09. 30 throws at 22.20 or better in 2020 (66 in career). Set High School 1.62kg DT record 72.40 '11. His father Mitch SP 20.04i '83, 19.94 '82, DT 67.22 '85; uncle Dean SP 21.07 '82, DT 65.88 '83, won NCAA SP 1982 & DT 1982-3; uncle Brian JT 83.00 '87, old JT 95.10 '85, won NCAA 1982 & 1985, dnq OG 1988 & 1992; Dean's children: Sam SP 17.62 '13, JT 83.30 '15 (dnq 34 OG 16), US junior & HS record '10, won NCAA 2014-15; Haley US junior JT record 55.22 '12, pb 55.65 '18, 4 WY '11.

Marquis DENDY b. 17 Nov 1992 Middleton, Delaware 1.92m 75kg. Nike. Was at University of Florida.
At LJ/(TJ): WCh: '13-15-17: dnq 27/21 (13)/20; WI: '16- 1, '18- 3. At TJ: WJ: '10- 8; won US LJ 2015; NACAC LJ 2012, 2018; NCAA LJ & TJ 2014-15, indoor LJ 2013, 2015-16; TJ 2015.
Progress at LJ, TJ: 2009- 7.20, 15.40; 2010- 7.45, 16.03; 2011- 7.47/7.56w, 15.62; 2012- 8.06i/7.81, 15.55; 2013- 8.28i/8.10/8.29w, 16.25i/16.03; 2014- 8.00, 16.52/17.05w; 2015- 8.39/8.68w, 17.50/17.71w; 2016- 8.42, 16.36; 2017- 8.18/8.39w, 2018- 8.42i/8.29, 2020- 7.78., 2021- 8.21i. pbs: 60m 6.88i '14, 100m 10.31 '15

Jarret EATON b. 24 Jun 1989 Philadelphia 1.83m 82kg. Was at Syracuse University.
At 110mh: PAm: '19- dnf/3R. At 60mh: WI: '16- 4, '18- 2. US indoor 60m champion 2016, 2018; WIT 2019.
Progress at 110mh: 2008- 13.90, 2009- 14.06/13.99w, 2010- 13.83, 2011- 13.63, 2012- 13.44, 2014- 13.71, 2015- 13.41/13.40w, 2016- 13.25, 2017- 13.34, 2018- 13.33, 2019- 13.45. pbs: 55m 6.36i '16, 60m 6.83i '16, 100m 10.96 '17, 60mh 7.43Ai/7.47i '18, 400mh 53.26 '07.

Craig ENGELS b. 1 May 1994 Pfafftown, North Carolina 1.87m 73kg. Nike. Was at North Carolina State, then University of Mississippi.
At 1500m: WCh: '19- 10; WI: '18- 7. Won PAm-J 2013, US 2019.
Progress at 1500m: 2013- 3:45.51, 2015- 3:40.28, 2016- 3:37.66, 2017- 3:35.95, 2018- 3:36.89, 2019- 3:34.04, 2020- 3:35.42. Pbs: 800m 1:44.68 '19, 1000m 2:18.98i '19, 1M 3:51.60 '19, 3000m 7:50.79i '19, 7:53.28 '20; 5000m 14:20.27 '15.

Mason FINLEY b. 7 Oct 1990 Kansas City 2.03m 150kg. Nike. Was at University of Wyoming.
At DT: OG: '16- 11; WCh: '17- 3, '19- dnq 13; WUG: '11- 8 (3 SP). Won US 2016-17, PAm-J SP & DT 2009.
Progress at DT: 2010- 60.18, 2011- 60.65, 2012- 61.40, 2013- 62.48A, 2014- 64.17A, 2015- 64.80A, 2016- 66.72, 2017- 68.03, 2018- 67.06, 2019- 67.13. pbs: SP 20.71i '11, 19.89 '12; WR 19.42i '14.
His father Jared DT 58.34 '79.

Justin GATLIN b. 10 Feb 1982 Brooklyn, NY 1.85m 79kg. XTEP. University of Tennessee.
At 100m/(200m)/4x100mR: OG: '04- 1/3/2R, '12- 3/dq2R, '16- 2/sf; WCh: '05- 1/1, '11- sf, '13- 2/2R, '15- 2/2, '17- 1/2R, '19- 2/1R. At 60m: WI: '03- 1, '12- 1. Won DL 100m 2013-15, US 100m 2005-06, 2012, 2016; 200m 2005, 2015-16; (indoor 60m 2003), NCAA 100m & 200m 2001-02 (& indoor 60m/200m 2002).
N.American 4x100m records 2015 & 2019. World M35 100m records 2017 & 2019.
Progress at 100m, 200m: 2000- 10.36, 2001- 10.08, 20.29/19.86w; 2002: international suspension 10.05/10.00w, 19.86; 2003- 9.97, 20.04; 2004- 9.85, 20.01; 2005- 9.88/9.84w, 20.00; 2006- 9.77dq, 2010- 10.09, 20.63; 2011- 9.95, 20.20; 2012- 9.79, 20.11; 2013- 9.85, 20.21; 2014- 9.77/9.76w, 19.68; 2015- 9.74, 19.57, 2016- 9.80, 19.75; 2017- 9.92, 2018- 10.03, 2019- 9.87, 2020-

10.07/9.99w. pbs: 60m 6.45i '03, 100y 9.10 '14, 400m 48.02 '19, 55mh 7.39i '02, 60mh 7.86i '01, 110mh 13.41dq '02, 13.78/13.74w '01; LJ 7.34i '01, 7.21 '00.
In high school – 110mh 13.66 and 300mh 36.74 on junior hurdles. Ineligible internationally in 2002 after failing a drugs test in 2001 (winning 100m, 200m and 110mh at US Juniors) for a prescribed medication to treat Attention Deficit Disorder. Reinstated by IAAF in July 2002. Won 2005 World 100m by biggest ever winning margin of 0.17 and took US title and tied world record with 9.77 in Doha, but had earlier tested positive for testosterone. Received a four-year ban,. In Brussels on 5 Sep 2014 recorded best-ever one-day sprint double with 9.77 and 19.71.

Cravon GILLESPIE b. 31 Jul 1996 Pasadena, California 1.75m 66kg. University of Oregon.
At 100m: WCh: '19- res 1R; PAm: '19- 6/3R.
Progress at 100m, 200m: 2014- 10.54/10.45w, 2015- 10.45, 21.11; 2016- 10.21/10.04w, 20.20; 2017- 10.37/10.16w, 21.28; 2018- 10.12/10.02w, 20.61; 2019- 9.93, 19.93; 2020- 10.09. pb 60m 6.57i '19.

Quincy HALL b. 31 Jul 1998 1.85m 75kg. Sociology at University of South Carolina.
At 400mh: Won PAm-J 2017, NCAA 2019.
Progress at 400mh: 2014- 52.19, 2015- 51.88, 2016- 53.21, 2017- 49.02, 2018- 49.65, 2019- 48.48. pbs: 200m 21.65 '15, 400m 44.53 '19.

JuVaughn HARRISON b. 30 Apr 1999 Huntsville né Blake 1.96m 75kg. Louisiana State University. Won NCAA HJ & LJ 2019 and indoors 2021.
Progress at HJ, LJ: 2017- 2.14i/2.08, 2018- 2,23, 7.84; 2019- 2.28i/2.27, 8.20; 2020- 2.28i, 8.11i; 2021- 2.30i, 8.45i.
Best ever one-day HJ/LJ combination in 2021 NCAA Indoor double.

Jeffery HENDERSON b. 19 Feb 1989 Sherwood, Arkansas 1.78m 82kg. Was at Florida Memorial University and Stillman College.
At LJ: OG: '16- 1; WCh: '15- 9, '17- dnq 17, '19- 2; PAm: '15- 1; CCp: '18- 3; WI: '16- 4; US champion 2014, 2016, 2018; indoors 2012.
Progress at LJ: 2006- 7.14i, 2007- 7.51i/7.41, 2008- 7.74/7.77w, 2009- 8.15u/7.88/8.19w, 2010- 7.94Ai/7.90i, 2011- 7.78, 2012- 7.91w, 2013- 8.22, 2014- 8.43/8.52w, 2015- 8.52/8.54w, 2016- 8.38/8.59w, 2017- 8.28, 2018- 8.44A/8.20/8.39w, 2019- 8.39. pbs: 55m 6.31i '09, 60m 6.58i '16, 100m 10.18A '13, 10.25 '11, 10.19w '15; 200m 20.65A '13, TJ 14.90i '08.

Darrell HILL b. 17 Aug 1993 Darby, Pennsylvania 1.92m 150kg. Nike. Was at Penn State University.
At SP: OG: '16- dnq 23; WCh: '17- 11, '19- 5; PAm: '15- 4; WI: '18- 6. Won DL 2017, NACAC 2018.
Progress at SP: 2012- 17.62i/17.53, 2013- 19.13, 2014- 20.57, 2015- 20.86, 2016- 21.63, 2017- 22.44, 2018- 22.40, 2019- 22.35. pbs: DT 50.20 '15, Wt 19.12i '15.

Grant HOLLOWAY b. 19 Nov 1997 Chesapeake, Virginia 1.90m 86kg. adidas. University of Florida.
At 110mh: WCh: '19- 1; won NCAA 2017-19 (60m ind 2019, 60mh ind 2017-19). Won WIT 60mh 2021. World 2021 and four North American indoor 60m hurdles records 2019-21.
Progress at 110mh, LJ: 2014- 6.82i, 2015- 7.84, 2016- 7.91i/7.77, 2017- 13.39, 8.05i/8.04; 2018- 13.15, 8.17/8.32w; 2019- 12.98, 2020- 13.19. pbs: 55m 6.22i '16, 60m 6.50i '19, 100m 10.68w '15, 200m 20.66 '19, 300m 32.80i '17, 500m 1:03.35i '16, 60mh 7.29i '21, HJ 2.16 '14.
Wide receiver at American football. Ran 43.88 anchor leg at 2017 NCAAs. Unbeaten in 54 races at 60m hurdles indoors 2014-21.

(Timothy Lamont) **T.J.HOLMES** b. 2 Jul 1995 St. Petersburg, Florida 1.82m 73kg. Sports medicine student at Baylor University.
At 400mh: WCh: '17- 5, '19- 5; WJ: 14- 3.
Progress at 400mh: 2013- 50.61, 2014- 49.90, 2015- 51.48, 2016- 49.31, 2017- 48.44, 2018- 48.30, 2019- 48.20. pbs: 400m 46.45 '18, 600y 1:10.53i '17, 800m 1:56.01 '17, 60mh 7.87i '18, 300mh 35.07 '20.

Bryce HOPPEL b. 5 Sep 1997 Midland, Texas 1.79m 68kg. Mechanical engineering at University of Kansas.
At 800m: WCh: '19- 4; PAm: '19- 4; Won NCAA 2019. N.American indoor 1000m record 2021.
Progress at 800m: 2015- 1:52.97, 2016- 1:49.58, 2017- 1:48.52, 2018- 1:45.67, 2019- 1:44.25, 2020- 1:43.23, 2021- 1:44.37i. pbs: 1000m 2:16.27i '21, 1500m 3:47.98 '19, 1M 4:09.95i '18.

Andrew IRWIN b. 24 Jan 1993 1.90m 84kg. Was at University of Arkansas. Farmer.
At PV: WCh: '17- dnq 15; Won US indoor 2019, NCAA indoor 2012-13.
N.American U20 pole vault record 2012.
Progress at PV: 2010- 5.34i/5.04, 2011- 5.41i/5.35, 2012- 5.72, 2013- 5.70i/5.65, 2014- 5.60i/5.50, 2015- 5.75i/5.65, 2016- 5.45Ai, 2017- 5.75, 2018- 5.87i/5.72, 2019- 5.88i/5.80, 2020- 5.80i.
Sister Stephanie had PV pbs 4.18i '07, 4.16 '08.

Evan JAGER b. 8 Mar 1989 Algonquin, Illinois 1.86m 66kg. Bowerman TC. Was at University of Wisconsin.
At 3000mSt: OG: '12- 6, '16- 2; WCh: '13- 5, '15- 6, '17- 3; CCp: '14- 2; US champion 2012-18. At 1500m: WJ: '08- 8. At 5000m: WCh: '09- h.
Three N.American 3000m steeplechase records 2012-15.
Progress at 5000m, 3000mSt: 2009- 13:22.18, 2012- 8:06.81, 2013- 13:02.40, 8:08.60; 2014- 13:08.63, 8:04.71; 2015- 8:00.45, 2016- 13:16.86, 8:04.01; 2017- 8:01.29, 2018- 8:01.02, 2020- 13:12.13. pbs: 800m 1:50.10i '10, 1:51.04 '08; 1000m 2:20.29i '15, 1500m 3:32.97 '15, 1M 3:53.33 '14, 2000m 4:57.56 '14, 3000m 7:35.16 '12, 2M 8:14.95i '13.
Set US record in only his fifth steeplechase race, improving pb by 10.59 secs. In 2009 3rd in US Champs in only his second race at 5000m.

Sam KENDRICKS b. 7 Sep 1992 Oxford, Mississippi 1.89m 79kg. Nike. Army reservist (2nd Lt.). Was at University of Mississippi.
At PV: OG: '16- 3; WCh: '15-17-19: 9=/1/1; CCp: '18- 1; WUG: '13- 1; WI: '16- 2, '18- 2; Won DL 2017, 2019; US 2014-18, NCAA 2013-4.
N.American pole vault record 2019.
Progress at PV: 2010- 4.68, 2011- 5.18, 2012- 5.50, 2013- 5.81, 2014- 5.75, 2015- 5.86Ai/5.82, 2016- 5.92, 2017- 6.00, 2018- 5.96, 2019- 6.06, 2020- 6.02.

David KENDZIERA b. 9 Sep 1994 1.90m 84kg. Was at University of Illinois.
Progress at 400mh: 2013- 53.32, 2014- 51.10, 2015- 49.56, 2016- 50.97, 2017- 49.00, 2018- 48.42, 2019- 48.69, 2020- 49.35. pbs: 200m 21.61 '15, 21.32w '18; 400m 46.67 '20, 60mh 7.69i '16, 110mh 13.39 '17.

Fred KERLEY b. 7 May 1995 San Antonio, Texas 1.91m 93kg. Nike. Texas A&M University.
At 400m/4x400mR: WCh: '17- 7/2R, '19- 3/1R; WI: '18- 2R, Won NCAA 2017, US 2017, 2019; DL 2018.
Progress at 400m: 2010- 52.30, 2014- 46.38, 2015- 47.15Ai/47.81, 2016- 45.10, 2017- 43.70, 2018- 44.33, 2019- 43.64, 2021- 45.03i. pbs: 100m 10.11 '21, 200m 20.24 '17, 300m 32.10+ '17, 600y 1:11.39i '14, TJ 13.90 '13. Brother **My'Lik** (b. 6 Jun 1996) pb 400m 44.85 '17, WIR 4x400m 2018; sister Virginia 400m 54.38 '17.

Joe KOVACS b. 28 Jun 1989 Bethlehem, Pennsylvania 1.81m 132kg. New York AC. Was at Penn State University.
At SP: OG: '16- 2; WCh: '15-17-19: 1/2/1; CCp: '14- 2; Won DL 2015, US 2014-15.
Progress at SP: 2007- 16.49, 2008- 16.86i, 2009- 18.53, 2010- 19.36i/18.73, 2011- 19.84i/19.15, 2012- 21.08, 2013- 20.82, 2014- 22.03. 2015- 22.56, 2016- 22.13, 2017- 22.57, 2018- 21.02, 2019- 22.91, 2020- 21.34i/21.30., 2021- 22.05i pbs: DT 56.08 '11, HT 61.50 '11, Wt 19.07i '11.
Married to Ashley Muffet SP (17.57i '12, 16.80 '08; DT 57.20 '09).

Erik KYNARD b. 3 Feb 1991 Toledo, Ohio 1.93m 86kg. Nike Jordan. Was at Kansas State University.
At HJ: OG: '12- 2, '16- 6; WCh: '11-13-15-17: dnq 14/5/8=/dnq nh; WJ: '08- dnq 19=; CCp: '14- 5; WI: '14-16-18: 4/3/4; Won DL 2016, US 2013-14, 2016; NCAA 2011-12.
Progress at HJ: 2007- 2.13i/2.05, 2008- 2.23i/2.15, 2009- 2.24i/2.22, 2010- 2.25, 2011- 2.33i/2.31, 2012- 2.34, 2013- 2.37, 2014- 2.37, 2015- 2.37, 2016- 2.35, 2017- 2.31i/2.30, 2018- 2.31i/2.29, 2020- 2.26Ai/2.25i/2.21. pb LJ 7.15i '09.

K.C.LIGHTFOOT b. 11 Nov 1999 Lee's Summit, Missouri 1.88m 75kg. Baylor University.
At PV: WCh: '19- dnq 15. NCAA indoor 2021.
Progress at PV: 2015- 4.49, 2016- 5.11, 2017- 5.40A, 2018- 5.61, 2019- 5.76, 2020- 5.83i/5.82, 2021- 6.00i.
His father had a PV best of 4.95.

Lopez LOMONG b. 1 Jan 1985 1.78m 67kg. Kimotong, South Sudan. Was at Northern Arizona University.
At 1500m: OG: '08- sf; WCh: '09- 8, '13- sf. At 5000m: OG: '12- 10. At 10000m: WCh: '19- 7. At 3000m: WI: '12- 6. Won US 5000m 2019, 10000m 2018-19, NCAA 1500m & indoor 3000m 2007, 5000m 2015, NACAC 5000m 2015, 10000m 2018.
Progress at 1500m, 5000m, 10000m: 2006- 3:45.96; 2007- 3:37.07, 15:07.06A; 2008- 3:36.36, 2009- 3:32.94, 2010- 3:32.20, 2011- 3:33.59, 2012- 3:38.64, 13:11.63; 2013- 3:34.55, 13:07.00i; 2014- 3:38.47, 13:07.95; 2015- 3:41.27, 13:21.32; 2016- 3:50.78, 13:48.48; 2017- 3:38.52, 13:12.27i/13:21.74; 2018- 3:39.40, 28:21.37; 2019- 3:37.62, 13:00.13, 27:04.72; 2020- 12:58.78. pbs: 800m 1:45.58 '08, 1000m 2:20.98 '09, 1M 3:51.21i/ 3:51.45 '13, 3000m 7:37.74i '20, 7:39.81 '14.
Refugee from Sudan. Flagbearer for the USA at 2008 Olympic Games Opening Ceremony.

Wil(bert) **LONDON** III b. 17 Aug 1997 Waco, Texas 1.83m 68kg. Kinesiology student at Baylor University.
At 400m/4x400mR: WCh: '17- sf/2R, '19- 1R/1mxR; WJ: '16- 2/1R; PAm: '19- 4/2R. 2 NACAC U23 2019.
World 4x400mxR record 2020
Progress at 400m: 2013- 50.54, 2014- 47.66, 2015- 45.96, 2016- 45.27, 2017- 44.47, 2018- 44.73, 2019- 44.63. pb 200m 21.10 '16, 20.84w '17.

Matthew **LUDWIG** b. 4 Jul 1996 1.83m 86kg. Was at University of Missouri, then Akron.
At PV: won NCAA 2017.
Progress at PV: 2015- 4.94, 2016- 5.46, 2017- 5.70, 2018- 5.71, 2019- 5.83i/5.67, 2020- 5.90A, 2021- 5.80i. Pb 200m 21.76w '15.

Noah LYLES b. 18 Jul 1997 Gainesville, Florida 1.80m 70kg. adidas.
At 100m: WJ: '16- 1/1R; PAm-J '15- 2 (1 200m); CCp: '18- 1/1R; at 200m: WCh: '19- 1/1R; WY: 13- sf/2Med R; Yth OG: '14- 1, won DL 100m 2019; 200m 2017-19. Won US 100m 2018, 200m 2019, World indoor 300m record 2017. N.American 4x100m record 2019.
Progress at 100m, 200m: 2012- 21.82, 2013- 10.86/10.73w, 21.23; 2014- 10.45, 20.71; 2015- 10.14/10.07w, 20.18; 2016- 10.16/10.08w, 20.09/20.04w; 2017- 9.95w, 19.90; 2018- 9.88/9.86w, 19.65; 2019- 9.86, 19.50; 2020- 10.04/9.93w, 19.76. pbs: 60m 6.57i '18, 150mSt 14.69 '19, 300m 31.87Ai/32.67i '17, 400m 47.04 '16, HJ 2.03i '16.
His younger brother **Josephus** (b. 22 Jul 1998) 1 4x400m WJ '14, 3 200m & 2 400m WY '15; pbs 200m 20.24 '20, 400m 45.09 '18. Their father Kevin had a 400m pb 45.01 '95 and mother Keisha Caine 52.48 '94.

Aaron MALLETT b. 26 Sep 1994 St. Louis, Missouri 1.88m 79kg. University of Iowa.
US indoor 60mh champion 2020.
Progress at 110mh: 2014- 13.86, 2015- 13.59/

USA

13.40w, 2016- 13.48, 2017- 13.37/13.24w, 2018- 13.55, 2019- 13.46, 2020- 13.15. pbs: 60m 6.80 '17, 100m 10.47 '17, 200m 21.29 '17, 60mh 7.54Ai '20, 7.56 '19; 400mh 51.41 '15.

Kahmari MONTGOMERY b. 16 Aug 1997 Plainfield, Illinois 1.84m 72kg. Univ. of Houston.
At 400m: WJ: '16- 5/1R; WUG: '17- 2R; won NCAA 2019.
Progress at 400m: 2014- 46.82, 2015- 46.24, 2016- 45.13, 2017- 46.57i/46.76, 2018- 44.58, 2019- 44.23, 2020- 45.50. pbs: 60m 6.85i '17, 100m 10.50 '15, 200m 20.35/20.32w '19, 300m 33.29 '20.

Clayton MURPHY b. 26 Feb 1995 New Madison, Ohio 1.82m 68kg. Nike. Was at University of Akron.
At 800m: OG: '16- 3; WCh: '15- sf, '19- 8; PAm: '15- 1; CCp: '18- 2. Won US 800m 2016, 2018; NCAA 1500m 2016.
Progress at 800m, 1500m: 2013- 1600m 4:11.72, 2014- 1:50.03, 3:44.53; 2015- 1:45.59, 3:40.69; 2016- 1:42.93, 3:36.23; 2017- 1:43.60, 3:36.34; 2018- 1:43.12, 3:38.93; 2019- 1:44.47, 3:37.40i/3:37.59; 2020- 1:47.59i, 4:00.48Mi. pbs: 600m 1:16.9+ '16, 1000m 2:17.17 '17, 1M 3:51.99 '17, 3000m 8:16.70i '17, 8:19.09 '16; 5000m 14:15.61 '15.

Chris NILSEN b. 13 Jan 1998 Kansas City, Missouri 1.96m 93kg. Was at University of South Dakota.
At PV: WCh: '17- dnq 13; WJ: '16- 7; PAm: '19- 1. Won NCAA 2018-19.
North American U20 pole vault record 2017.
Progress at PV: 2014- 3.73, 2015- 5.18, 2016- 5.60, 2017- 5.75, 2018- 5.86, 2019- 5.95, 2020- 5.93i/5.70, 2021- 5.93i.

Michael NORMAN b. 3 Dec 1997 San Diego 1.85m 78kg. University of Southern California.
At 200m: WJ: '16- 1/1R. At 400m: WCh: '19- sf; won DL 2019, NCAA 2018.
World indoor 400m record (44.52) and ran on fastest ever indoor 4x400m by USC 2018.
Progress at 200m, 400m: 2013- 22.62, 49.54; 2014- 20.82, 46.94; 2015- 20.24, 45.19; 2016- 20.14/20.06w, 45.51; 2017- 20.75i, 44.60; 2018- 19.84, 43.61; 2019- 19.70, 43.45. pb 100m 9.86 '20, 300m 31.9+ '18.
Improved 100m pb in 2020 from 10.27 '16 to 9.86. Mother Nobue born in Japan. His elder sister Michelle had pbs 100m 11.83/11.72 & 200m 24.12/24.06w in 2016. LJ 6.05 '14.

Vernon NORWOOD b. 10 Apr 1992 New Orleans 1.87m 77kg. New Balance. Was at Louisiana State University.
At 400m/4x400mR: WCh: '15- sf/res1R, '19- sf/res1R; WI: '16- 1R, '18- 2R. Won NCAA indoors and out 2015, US indoor 2016.
Progress at 400m: 2011- 47.47, 2012- 45.72A/45.98, 2013- 45.56A/45.67, 2014- 45.02, 2015- 44.44, 2016- 45.00, 2017- 44.47, 2018- 45.47, 2019- 44.40. pbs: 200m 20.77 '15, 20.46w '19; 300m 32.07 '15, 500m 1:00.11i '17, 600y 1:08.80i '13, 600m 1:18.57Ai '15.

Payton OTTERDAHL b. 2 Apr 1996 Rosemount, Minnesota 1.93m 138kg. North Dakota State University.
Won NCAA indoor SP & weight 2019, PAm-J DT 2015.
Progress at SP: 2015- 18.11, 2016- 17.88i/17.61, 2017- 18.62, 2018- 20.96, 2019- 21.81i/21.37, 2020- 21.19, 2021- 21.54i. pbs: DT 62.94 '19, HT 67.08 '19, Wt 24.11i '19.
Brothers Trevor (pbs: SP 18.44i '20, Wt 22.38i '21) and Maxwell (pb SP 19.14i '21).

Nick PONZIO b. 5 Jan 1995 1.83m 132kg. Vel. Graduate of University of Southern California.
Progress at SP: 2014- 18.47, 2015- 19.53, 2016- 19.43i/19.42, 2017- 19.53, 2018- 19.62i/19.32, 2019- 20.73, 2020- 21.72. pb DT 56.47 '15.

Daniel ROBERTS b. 13 Apr 1998 Atlanta 1.86m 77kg. Nike. University of Kentucky.
At 110mh: WCh: '19- h; won US 2019.
Progress at 110mh: 2017- 13.82/13.75w 2018- 13.25, 2019- 13.00. pbs: 60m 6.63i '19, 200m 20.69i '19, 21.42i '19, 21.43 '19; 60mh 7.41i '19.

Jeron ROBINSON b. 30 Apr 1991 Angleton, Texas 1.93m 73kg. Was at Texas A&M-Kingville University.
At HJ: WCh: '17- dnq 26, '19- 11; PAm: '15- 4, '19- 6. Won NACAC 2018, US 2019.
Progress at HJ: 2008- 2.05, 2009- 2.16, 2010- 2.18, 2011- 2.23, 2012- 2.13, 2013- 2.26, 2014- 2.30, 2015- 2.31, 2016- 2.29i/2.26, 2017- 2.30, 2018- 2.31, 2019- 2.30, 2020- 2.25i/2.24

Justin ROBINSON b. 30 Mar 2002 St. Louis, Missouri 1.80m 73kg. Arizona Stata University.
At 400m: WJ: '18- 2R; PAm: '19- 3/2R; won PAm-J 2019.
Records: World U18 400m & U20 4x400m 2019.
Progress at 400m: 2017- 48.03, 2018- 46.20, 2019- 44.84A/45.07, 2020- 44.91. pbs: 60m 6.79i '19, 100m 10.56/10.32w '19, 200m 21.06 '19, 20.67w '20; 300m 32.87i '20., 500m 1:02.39i '20

Michael RODGERS b. 24 Apr 1985 Brenham, Texas 1.78m 73kg. Studied kinesiology at Oklahoma Baptist University.
At 100m/4x100mR: OG: '16- dqR; WCh: '09-13-15-17-19: sf/6&2R/5/2R/sf&1R; PAm: '19- 1/3R; CCp: '14- 2/1R, '18- 1R. At 60m: WI: '08-10-16: 4/2/6. Won US 100m 2009, 2014; indoor 60m 2008; WIT 60m 2016
N.American 4x100m records 2015 & 2019.
Progress at 100m: 2004- 10.55/10.31w, 2005- 10.30/10.25w, 2006- 10.29/10.18w, 2007- 10.10, 10.07w, 2008- 10.06/10.01w, 2009- 9.94/9.9/9.85w, 2010- 10.00/9.99w, 2011- 9.85, 2012- 9.94, 9.90, 2014- 9.91/9.80w, 2015- 9.86, 2016- 9.97, 20.42; 2017- 10.00/9.98w, 2018- 9.89, 2019- 9.97, 2020- 10.12. pbs: 60m 6.48Ai/6.50i '11, 150mSt 15.33 '14, 200m 20.74 '09.
Dropped out of US World Champs team after positive test for stimulant on 19 July 2011 with a 9-month suspension. 45 wind-legal and 18

wind-assisted (+ 1 dq) sub-10sec 100m times 2009-19. Younger sister Alishea Usery won US junior 400m 2009, pb 53.27 '09.
Galen RUPP b. 8 May 1986 Portland 1.80m 62kg. Nike Oregon Project. Studied business at University of Oregon.
At (5000/)10000m: OG: '08- 13, '12- 7/2, '16- 5 (3 Mar); WCh: '07- 11, '09- 8, '11- 9/7, '13- 8/4, '15- 5/5. At 5000m: WJ: '04- 9; PAm-J: '03- 1. At 3000m: WI: '10- 5, '14- 4; WY: '03- 7. Won US 5000m 2012, 10000m 2009-16, Mar 2016, 2020; NCAA 5000m & 10000m (& indoor 3000m & 5000m) 2009, CC 2008.
N.American records: 10000m 2011 & 2014, junior 5000m 2004, 10000m 2005; indoor 5000m (13:11.44) 2011 & 2014, 3000m 2013, 2M 2012, 2014; US 10M 2020.
Progress at 5000m, 10000m, Mar: 2002- 14:34.05, 2003- 14:20.29, 2004- 13:37.91, 29:09.56; 2005- 13:44.72. 28:15.52; 2006- 13:47.04, 30:42.10; 2007- 13:30.49, 27:33.48; 2008- 13:49.8+, 27:36.99; 2009- 13:18.12i/13:42.59+, 27:37.99; 2010- 13:07.35, 27:10.74; 2011- 13:06.86, 26:48.00; 2012- 12:58.90, 27:25.33; 2013- 13:01.37, 27:24.39; 2014- 13:00.99, 26:44.36; 2015- 13:08.38, 27:08.91; 2016- 13:20.69, 27:08.92, 2:10:05; 2017- 13:54.88, 28:18.29, 2:09:20; 2018- 13:34.78i, 2:06:07. pbs: 800m 1:49.87i/1:50.00 '09, 1500m 3:34.15 '14, 1M 3:50.92i/3:52.11 '13, 3000m 7:30.16i '13, 7:43.24 '10, 2M 8:07.41i '14, road: 15k 42:47 '20, 10M 45:54 '20, HMar 59:47 '18.
Won US Olympic Trials on marathon debut 2016, 2nd Boston & 1st Chicago 2017, 1st Prague 2018. Married to Keara Sammons (10000m 33:54.55 '07).

Donald SCOTT b. 23 Feb 1992 Apokpa, Florida 1.83m 84kg. Was at Eastern Michigan University.
At TJ: WCh: '17- dnq 13, '19- 6; PAm-J: '11- 5. Won US 2018-19
Progress at TJ: 2010- 14.86/15.07w, 2011- 15.79, 2012- 15.75, 2013- 15.58i, 2014- 16.02/16.34w, 2015- 16.84i/16.71/16.83w, 2016- 17.02, 2017- 17.25, 2018- 17.37, 2019- 17.43/17.74w, 2020- 17.24Ai/ 16.82i. pb LJ 7.58 '15.
Football scholarship at university.

Trevor STEWART b. 20 May 1997 Henderosn, NC 1.83m 73kg. North Carolina A&T University.
At 400m: Won NACAC U23 2019.
Progress at 400m: 2015- 48.35, 2016- 46.24, 2018- 45.28, 2019- 44.25, 2020- 46.43i. pbs: 100m 10.78 '16, 200m 20.27 '19, 300m 33.35i '19.

Nathan STROTHER b. 6 Sep 1995 Norcross, Georgia 1.83m 70kg. University of Tennessee.
At 400m: WCh: '19- sf/res1R; CCp: '18- 3; WIT 2019.
Progress at 400m: 2014- 47.37, 2015- 45.76, 2016- 45.07, 2017- 45.07, 2018- 44.34, 2019- 44.29, 2020- 47.15i. pbs: 200m 20.76 '18, 300m 33.16i '18.

Christian TAYLOR b. 18 Jun 1990 Fayetteville 1.90m 75kg. Li Ning. Studied at the University of Florida.

At (LJ/)TJ: OG: '12- 1, '16- 1; WCh: '11-13-15-17- 19: 1/4/1/1/1; WI: '12- 2; WJ: '08- 7/8 (res 1 4x400m); WY: '07- 3/1; CCp: '18- 1/1mxR. Won DL 2012-17, 2019; NCAA 2010-11, US 2011-12, NCAA indoor 2009-10.
North American triple jump record 2015.
Progress at LJ, TJ: 2007- 7.29, 15.98; 2008- 7.79i/7.68/7.77w, 16.05; 2009- 8.02i/7.72, 16.98i/ 16.65/16.91w; 2010- 8.19, 17.18i/17.02/17.09w; 2011- 8.00/8.07w/17.96; 2012- 8.12, 17.81; 2013- 8.01/8.07w, 17.66; 2014- 8.09, 17.51; 2015- 8.18, 18.21; 2016- 7.96, 17.86; 2017- 18.11, 2018- 17.81/ 17.86w, 2019- 17.92/17.93w, 2020- 17.57. pbs: 60m 6.79i '11, 100m 10.58 '20, 200m 20.70 '13, 400m 45.07 '18.
18.21 in final round of the 2015 World Champs was the second longest ever legal TJ mark (18.32 from take-off to landing.) Both parents came from Barbados. Fiancée is Austrian Beate Schrott (7 OG 100mh 2012). President of the Athletes Asociation, which he founded in 2019.

Ben TRUE b. 29 Dec 1985 North Yarmouth, Maine 1.83m 70kg. Saucony. Studied art history and architecture at Dartmouth College.
At 5000m: WCh: '15- 6, '19- h. World CC: '13- 6.
Progress at 5000m: 2006- 14:18.61, 2007- 13:14.85, 2010- 13:43.98, 2011- 13:24.11, 2012- 13:20.53, 2013- 13:11.59, 2014- 13:02.74, 2015- 13:05.54, 2016- 13:12.67, 2017- 13:06.74i/13:10.83, 2018- 13:04.11, 2019- 13:09.81. pbs: 800m 1:50.07 '07, 1500m 3:36.05 '16, 1M 3:57.31i '17, 3:57.83 '18; 3000m 7:35.53 '17, 2M 8:11.33i '17, 8:23.76 '18; 10000m 27:14.95 '21; road: 10M 46:48 '11, 15k 43:04 '14. Married to Sarah Groff, 4th 2012 Olympics in triathlon.

Cole WALSH b. 14 Jun 1995 Phoenix 1.90m 80kg. Was at University of Oregon.
At PV: WCh: '19- 10=; WJ: '14- dnq 24.
Progress at PV: 2012- 5.01, 2013- 5.12, 2014- 5.35, 2015- 5.25, 2016- 5.41, 2017- 5.50, 2018- 5.75, 2019- 5.83, 2020- 5.65/5.80idq, 2021- 5.73i.
3-month doping ban from 29 Jan 2020.

Rudy WINKLER b. 6 Dec 1994 Sand Lake, New York 1.86m 102kg. Was at Cornell University.
At HT: OG: '16- dnq 18; WCh: '17- dnq 31, '19- 11; WJ: '12- 11; WY: '11- 9, PAm: '19- 8; PAm-J: '13- 2; NACAC: '16- 2 U23, '18- 4. Won NCAA 2017
Progress at HT: 2013- 64.93, 2014- 63.54, 2015- 70.36, 2016- 76.76, 2017- 75.22, 2018- 73.85, 2019- 77.06, 2020- 80.70/80.72dh. Pbs: DT 51.47 '19, Wt 23.52i '17.
US HS record 77.67 with 12lb hammer 2013.

Jacob WOOTEN b. 22 Apr 1997 Tomball, Texas 1.83m 73kg. Was at Texas A&M University.
Progress at PV: 2011- 3.65i, 2012- 4.26i/3.96; 2013- 4.87i/4.57. 2014- 5.18, 2015- 5.20i/5.18, 2016- 5.46i/5.30, 2017- 5.45, 2018- 5.60i/5.55, 2019- 5.73i/5.71, 2020- 5.90A, 2021- 5.75i.

Isiah YOUNG b. 5 Jan 1990 Junction City, Kansas 1.83m 75kg. University of Mississippi.
At 200m: OG: '12- sf; WCh: '13- sf, '15- h, '17- 8. Progress at 100m, 200m: 2008- 10.96; 2009- 10.44, 21.22; 2010- 10.32, 20.98; 2011- 10.31, 20.81; 2012- 10.09/10.08w, 20.33/20.16w; 2013- 9.99/9.93w, 19.86; 2014- 10.23, 20.58/20.55w; 2015- 10.00/9.82w, 19.93/19.75w; 2016- 10.03, 20.24; 2017- 9.97/9.95w, 20.14/20.12w; 2018- 9.92, 19.93; 2019- 9.99, 20.29/20.15w; 2020- 10.20, 20.76. pb 60m 6.61i '12.

Women

Morolake AKINOSUN b. 17 May 1994 Lagos, Nigeria 1.63m 61kg. Was at University of Texas.
At 100m/4x100mR: OG: '16- res 1R; WCh: '17- 1R, '19- sf/3R; PAm: '15- sf/1R. Won US Indoor 60m 2017.
Progress at 100m, 200m: 2010- 11.94, 24.58/24.07w; 2011- 11.42, 23.49/23.44w; 2012- 11.41, 24.34; 2013- 11.45/11.29w, 23.26/23.18w; 2014- 11.04/10.96w, 22.68/22.17w; 2015- 11.29/10.94w, 22.52; 2016- 10.95, 22.54; 2017- 10.98/10.94w, 2019- 11.17, 22.94; 2020- 23.41. pbs: 50m 6.22+i '21, 60m 7.08Ai/7.17i '17, 150m 16.98 '20.

Nia ALI b. 23 Oct 1988 Norristown 1.70m 64kg. ALTIS. University of Southern California.
At 100mh: OG: '16- 2; WCh: '13- sf, '17- 8, '19- 1; WUG: '11- 1. Won NCAA 2011. At 60mh: WI: '14- 1, '16- 1; won US indoor 2013-14; WIT 2016.
Progress at 100mh: 2005- 14.20, 2006- 13.63/13.55w, 2007- 13.25, 2008- 13.14, 2009- 13.17, 2011- 12.73/12.63w, 2012- 12.78, 2013- 12.48, 2014- 12.75, 2016- 12.55, 2017- 12.52, 2019- 12.34. pbs: 60m 7.43i '14, 200m 23.90 '09, 800m 2:24.55 '07, 60mh 7.80i '14, HJ 1.86 '11, LJ 5.89 '09, SP 13.61 '09, JT 39.24 '09, Hep 5870 '16.
Son Titus born to her and Michael Tinsley in May 2015 and daughter Yuri to her and partner Andre De Grasse in June 2018.

Valarie ALLMAN b. 23 Feb 1995 Newark, Delaware 1.83m 70kg. Stanford University.
At DT: WCh: '17- dnq 28, '19- 7; WJ: '14=- 2; WUG: '17- 2; Won US 2019.
North American discus record 2020.
Progress at DT: 2011- 44.64, 2012- 50.91, 2013- 56.13, 2014- 57.45, 2015- 57.48, 2016- 61.42, 2017- 64.69, 2018- 63.55, 2019- 67.15, 2020- 70.11, 2021- 66.46. pbs: HT 63.65 '18, Wt 21.42i '18.

Brooke ANDERSEN b. 23 Aug 1995 San Diego 1.73m 84kg. Northern Arizona University.
At HT: WCh: '19- dnq 20; WJ: '14- dnq 21; PAm: '19- 2.
Progress at HT: 2013- 48.70, 2014- 59.37, 2015- 63.30, 2016- 65.50, 2017- 68.62, 2018- 74.20, 2019- 76.75. Pb Wt 22.25i '18.

Angie (Anglerne) **ANNELUS** b. 10 Jan 1997 Kansas City 1.68m 57kg. University of Southern California.
At 200m: WCh: '19- 4; won NCAA 2018-19, NACAC-23 2019.
Progress at 200m: 2013- 24.47, 2014- 24.33/24.11w,

2015- 23.30, 2016- 23.22, 2018- 22.64/22.52w, 2019- 22.16. pbs: 60m 7.29i '19, 100m 11.06 '19.

Whitney ASHLEY b. 18 Feb 1989 Riverside, California 1.83m 93kg. Nike. San Diego State University.
At DT: OG: '16- dnq nt; WCh: '13- dnq 23, '15- 9, '17- dnq 13; PAm: '19- 4; NCAA champion 2012.
Progress at DT: 2008- 44.86, 2009- 46.05, 2010- 47.34, 2011- 54.75, 2012- 59.99, 2013- 61.64, 2014- 63.78, 2015- 64.80, 2016- 64.62, 2017- 63.85, 2018- 61.10, 2019- 63.64. pbs: SP 17.62i '16, 17.60 '17; HT 57.14 '11, Wt 19.19i '12.

Jessica BEARD b. 8 Jan 1989 Euclid, Ohio 1.68m 57kg. adidas. Studied psychology at Texas A&M University.
At 400m/4x400mR: WCh: '09- sf/res (1)R, '11- sf/1R, '13- 1R, '15- res 2R, '19- res 1R&1mxR; WJ: '06- 5/1R, '08- 2/1R; PAm-J: '07- 3; won NCAA 2011. World 4x400mxR record 2019,
Progress at 400m: 2004- 55.22, 2005- 52.39, 2006- 51.89, 2007- 51.63, 2008- 51.09A/51.47, 2009- 50.56, 2010- 51.02, 2011- 51.06, 2012- 51.19, 2013- 51.05, 2014- 50.81, 2015- 50.68, 2016- 51.76, 2017- 50.85, 2018- 50.08, 2019- 51.28, 2020- 51.71. pbs: 60m 7.52i '11, 100m 11.48 '16, 150m 17.41 '20, 200m 22.74 '18, 300m 36.65i '15, 36.94 '20.

Gwendolyn **BERRY** b. 29 Jun 1989 St. Louis, Missouri. 1.76m 80kg. Nike/New York AC. Was at University of Southern Illinois.
At HT: OG: '16- dnq 14; WCh: '17- dnq 14, '19- nt; PAm: '19- 1; Won US 2017, indoor weight 2013- 14, 2017. N.American HT record 2017 & 2018. World 20lb weight indoor record record 2017.
Progress at HT: 2008- 53.70, 2009- 59.58, 2010- 62.55, 2011- 70.52, 2012- 71.95, 2013- 73.81, 2014- 72.04, 2015- 72.26, 2016- 73.09/76.12dq, 2017- 76.77, 2018- 77.78, 2019- 76.46, 2020- 70.15. Pbs: SP 16.99 '11, Wt 25.60i '17.
3-month ban from 29 Mar 2016 for use of a stimulant that cost her a North American 'record' of 76.31 and US indoor weight title.

Erica BOUGARD b. 26 Jul 1993 Memphis 1.73m 57kg. Chula Vista Elite. Was at Mississippi State University.
At Hep: WCh: '13-15-17-19: 24/dnf/18/4; WJ: '12- 13; won US 2019. At Pen: WI: '18- 5, won NCAA ind 2013.
Progress at Hep: 2011- 5270, 2012- 5547, 2013- 5990, 2014- 6118, 2015- 6288, 2016- 6170, 2017- 6502, 2018- 6725, 2019- 6668. pbs: 60m 7.64Ai '20, 100m 11.74 '18, 200m 23.28 '17, 400m 54.09 '11, 600m 1:32.78i '18, 800m 2:08.24 '19, 60mh 7.98A '18, 8.03i '15; 100mh 12.78 '19, HJ 1.92 '17, LJ 6.59 '17, TJ 12.76i '18, 12.62 '13; SP 13.02 '18, JT 45.80 '19, Pen 4760Ai '18.

Tori BOWIE b. 27 Aug 1990 Jackson, Mississippi 1.75m 61kg. adidas. Studied psychology at University of Southern Mississippi.
At 100m/(200m): OG: '16- 2/3/1R; WCh: '15- 3, '17- 1/1R, '19- sf (4 LJ). At 60m: WI: '16- 6. Won

US 100m 2015, 200m 2016; NCAA LJ 2011.
Progress at 100m, 200m, LJ: 2008- 12.21w, 6.03w; 2009- 11.82, 23.99, 6.30/6.60w; 2010- 11.76/11.72w, 24.55/23.98w, 6.43/6.50w; 2011- 6.64, 2012- 11.28, 24.06, 6.78; 2013- 11.14/11.04w, 6.91, 2014- 10.80, 22.18, 6.95i/6.82; 2015- 10.81/10.72w, 22.23; 2016- 10.78/10.74w, 21.99; 2017- 10.85/10.80w, 21.77; 2018- 11.01, 22.75; 2019- 11.09, 6.81. pbs: 60m 7.11i '16, 150mSt 16.30 '17 (world best), TJ 13.09i/12.65 '14. First name actually Frentorish.

Mikiah BRISCO b. 14 Jul 1996 Baton Rouge 1.65m 54kg. Was at Louisiana State University.
At 100m: WY: '13- 3; won NCAA 2017; Won US indoor 60m 2020.
Progress at 100m: 2011- 12.02/11.76w, 2012- 11.71, 2013- 11.69/11.59w, 2014- 11.61A/11.53w, 2015- 11.31/11.24w, 2016- 11.24/11.13w, 2017- 10.96, 2018- 11.05/10.99w, 2019- 11.26, 2020- 11.38/11.32w. pbs: 50m 6.26+i '21, 60m 7.04Ai '20, 7.10 '18; 200m 22.59 '18, 60mh 7.89i '17, 100mh 12.85 '17.

Brittany BROWN b. 18 Apr 1995 Upland, California 1.64m 55kg. University of Iowa.
At 200m: WCh: '19- 2. Won US indoor 300m 2019.
Progress at 200m: 2013- 23.78/23.68w, 2014- 22.95, 2015- 22.89, 2017- 22.55/22.30w, 2018- 22.42, 2019- 22.22, 2020- 23.65w. pbs: 60m 7.39i '17, 100m 11.28 '18, 300m 35.91 '19, 400m 53.76i '19, 56.06 '16.

Dezerea BRYANT b. 27 Apr 1993 Milwaukee 1.57m 50kg. Was at Clemson University, then University of Kentucky.
At (100m)/200m: WCh: '19- 5/3R; WJ: '10- 1R, '12- sf/3/1R; Won NCAA 200m 2015, US 200m 2019.
Progress at 100m, 200m: 2007- 25.33, 2009- 11.86/11.76w, 24.02; 2010- 11.59, 23.51; 2012- 11.29, 22.97; 2013- 11.20, 22.87/22.54w; 2014- 11.24/10.96w, 22.68; 2015- 11.00/10.99w, 22.18; 2016- 11.23w, 23.07; 2017- 11.27/11.20w, 22.95; 2018- 10.99, 22.93; 2019- 11.09/11.04w, 22.47; 2020- 11.47/11.35w. pbs: 60m 7.11Ai/7.12i '17; 150m 17.18w '20. 300m 36.70i '15, 400m 54.46 '13.

Quanesha BURKS b. 15 Mar 1995 Ozark, Alabama 1.60m 55kg. University of Alabama
At LJ: WCh: '17- dnq 14; WJ: '14- 5; PAm: '15- 8; WI: '18- 4; Won NCAA 2015, NACAC 2015.
Progress at LJ: 2012- 6.13, 2013- 5.84w, 2014- 6.38, 2015- 6.93A/6.84/6.91w, 2016- 6.80i/6.77, 2017- 6.83/6.90w, 2018- 6.81i/6.59, 2019- 6.70, 2020- 6.76Ai/6.73i. pbs: 60m 7.20i '18, 100m 11.19 '18, 11.18w '17.

Kori CARTER b. 6 Mar 1992 Pasadena, California 1.65m 57kg. Nike. Studied human biology at Stanford University.
At 400mh: WCh: '15- sf, '17- 1, '19- h; WJ: '08- h; CCp: '14- 7; Won US 2014, NCAA 2013. At 100mh: WY: '09- 2.
Progress at 400mh: 2007- 62.21, 2008- 60.22, 2009- 59.89, 2010- 60.47, 2011- 57.10, 2012- 57.60,

2013- 53.21, 2014- 53.84, 2015- 54.41, 2016- 54.47, 2017- 52.95, 2019- 55.09. pbs: 60m 7.78 '20, 100m 11.57 '11, 200m 23.01 '19, 300m 37.53i '21, 60mh 8.00Ai '18, 8.11i '17; 100mh 12.76 '13.

Kristi CASTLIN b. 7 Jul 1988 Douglasville, Georgia 1.70m 75kg. Nike. Political science graduate of Virginia Tech University.
At 100mh: OG: '16- 3; won PAm-J 2007. At 60mh: won US indoors 2012.
World best 4x100mh 2014 & 2015.
Progress at 100mh: 2005- 13.85, 2006- 13.73, 2007- 12.91/12.82w, 2008- 12.81, 2009- 12.89, 2010- 12.83/12.59w, 2011- 12.83/12.68w, 2012- 12.56/ 12.48w, 2013- 12.61, 2014- 12.58, 2015- 12.71, 2016- 12.50, 2017- 12.61, 2018- 12.96, 2019- 12.86/12.78w. pbs: 55m 7.04i '08, 60m 7.47i '08, 100m 11.60 '12, 11.49w '11; 200m 23.46 '12, 50mh 6.81+i '12, 55mh 7.37i '12, 60mh 7.84Ai/7.91i '12, 400mh 60.44 '07. Married to Alonzo Nelson.

Queen CLAYE b. 10 Sep 1988 Loch Sheldrake, New York 1.70m 60kg. née Harrison. Saucony. Studied business marketing at Virginia Tech.
At 100mh: WCh: '13- 5; PAm: '15- 1. At 400mh: OG: '08- sf; WCh: '11- sf; PAm-J: '07- 1 (2 100mh); won NCAA 100mh, 400mh & 60mh indoors 2010. World best 4x100mh 2014 & 2015.
Progress at 100mh, 400mh: 2007- 12.98, 55.81; 2008- 12.70, 54.60; 2009- 13.14/12.98w, 56.03; 2010- 12.61/12.44w, 54.55; 2011- 12.88, 54.78; 2012- 12.62, 55.32; 2013- 12.43, 2014- 12.46, 2015- 12.52/ 12.50w, 2016- 12.57/12.54w, 2017- 12.64, 2018- 12.63, 2019- 12.63. pbs: 400m 52.88 '08, 60mh 7.74Ai/7.75i 17, LJ 5.82i '06.
Married Will Claye (qv) on 13 October 2018.

Christina CLEMONS b. 29 May 1990 Waldorf, Maryland 1.63m 54kg. adidas. née Manning. Was at Ohio State University.
At 100mh: WCh: '17- 5; WUG: '11- 3/2R. At 60mh: WI: '18- 2; WIT 2018 & 2020. Won NCAA 100mh & 60mh ind 2012.
Progress at 100mh: 2008- 13.86, 2009- 13.08, 2010- 13.10, 2011- 12.86/12.72w, 2012- 12.68/ 12.57w, 2014- 13.61, 2015- 13.04, 2016- 12.87/ 12.67w, 2017- 12.54, 2018- 12.56, 2019- 12.58. pbs: 60m 7.23i '12, 100m 11.29 '11, 200m 23.27 '12, 60mh 7.73Ai/7.77i '18, LJ 5.75 '08.
Married Kyle Clemons (400m 44.79 '16, OG: '16- 1R; WCh: '15- 1R; PAm: '15- 3/3R; WI: '14- 3/1R, '16- 1R) in 2018,

Emma COBURN b. 19 Oct 1990 Boulder 1.73m 55kg. New Balance. Marketing graduate of University of Colorado.
At 3000mSt: OG: '12- 8, '16- 3; WCh: '11-15-17-19: 8/5/1/2; CCp: '14- 1; US champion 2011-12, 2014- 19; NCAA 2011, 2013.
Three North American 3000m steeple records 2014 (unratified as no doping test) & 2016-17 (3).
Progress at 3000mSt: 2009- 10:06.21, 2010- 9:51.86, 2011- 9:37.16, 2012- 9:23.54, 2013- 9:28.26, 2014- 9:11.42, 2015- 9:15.59, 2016- 9:07.63, 2017-

USA

9:02.58, 2018- 9:05.06, 2019- 9:02.35. pbs: 800m 2:01.10 '20, 1500m 4:03.82 '20, 1M 4:23.65 '00, 2000m 5:41.11i '15, 3000m 8:39.19i '21, 8:48.60 '17; 2M 9:15.71i '21, 5000m 15:24.76 '21.
Married Joe Bosshard (5000m 13:34.44, 10000m 28:41.56 in 2011) on 14 Oct 2017.

Vashti CUNNINGHAM b. 18 Jan 1998 Las Vegas 1.85m 66kg. Nike, Nevada Gazzelles.
At HJ: OG: '16- 13=; WCh: '17- 10, '19- 3; WI: '16- 1, '18- 2; PAm-J: 15- 1; won US 2017-19, indoors 2016-20. High jump records: World youth (=) 2015, World junior indoor 2016, North American junior 2017.
Progress at HJ: 2012- 1.76, 2013- 1.83, 2014- 1.90, 2015- 1.96, 2016- 1.99i/1.97, 2017- 1.99, 2018- 1.97Ai/1.95, 2019- 2.00, 2020- 1.97Ai. Pb LJ 5.85w '15.
Father Randall Cunningham was a quarterback in the NFL. Her brother Randall (b. 4 Jan 1996) has HJ pbs 2.27i '17, 2.25 '16 and won PAm-J 2015 and NCAA 2016.

Teahna DANIELS b. 25 Mar 1997 Orlando 1.65m 55kg. Was at University of Texas.
At 100m: WCh: '19- 7/3R; WJ: '14- 1R; PAm-J: '15- 3/1R. Won US 2018, NACAC-23 2019, NCAA indoor 60m 2016.
Progress at 100m: 2012- 11.93, 2013- 11.67/11.64w, 2014- 11.31, 2015- 11.24/11.15w, 2016- 11.21, 2017- 11.06, 2018- 11.11, 2019- 10.99, 2020- 11.53. pbs: 60m 7.11i '16, 200m 22.51 '19.

Tara DAVIS b. 20 May 1999 1.68m 59kg. University of Texas.
At LJ: WJ: '18- 3; WY: '15- 1 (9 TJ). Won NCAA indoor 2021.
Progress at LJ: 2014- 6.03, 2015- 6.41, 2016- 6.37A/6.27/6.31w, 2017- 6.73, 2018- 6.71, 2019- 6.58/6.64w, 2020- 6.17i, 2021- 7.14. Pbs: 60m 7.57i '21, 200m 24.52i '21, 400m 57.73 '21, 60mh 7.98i '18, 100mh 12.95 '17, 300mh 43.33 '17, TJ 13.20 '17.

Chase EALEY b. 20 Jul 1994 Springfield, Illinois 1.78m 84kg. Was at Oklahoma State University.
At SP: WCh: '19- 7; PAm-J: '13- 3; Won US indoor and out 2019.
Progress at SP: 2010- 13.78, 2001- 13.61, 2012- 14.40, 2013- 16.01, 2014- 15.86i/15.59, 2015- 17.39, 2016- 18.46, 2017- 17.79, 2018- 17.78, 2019- 19.68, 2020- 19.41. pbs: HT 56.00 '16, JT 44.89 '16, Wt 19.39i '16.

Kendall ELLIS b. 8 Mar 1996 Pembroke Pines, Florida 1.73m 59kg. Was at University of Southern California.
At 400m: WCh: '17- h/res1R, '19- sf/res1R; PAm-J: '15- 3. Won NCAA indoor 400m 2018.
N.American indoor 400m record 50.34 2018.
Progress at 400m: 2011- 54.83i, 2012- 53.22, 2013- 53.80, 2014- 52.95, 2015- 52.32, 2016- 51.82, 2017- 50.00, 2018- 49.99, 2019- 50.38. pb 200m 22.71 '18, 300m 36.8+, 36.97 '19.

Maggie EWEN b. 23 Sep 1994 St. Francis, Minnesota 1.78m 79kg. Nike. Arizona State University.

At SP: WCh: '19- 4; At HT: WCh: '17- dnq 21; won NCAA 2017. At DT: PAm-J: '13- 2. Won US SP 2018, NCAA SP & DT 2018; NACAC SP 2018.
Progress at SP, HT: 2011- 14.71, 2012- 14.78, 2013- 16.67, 2014- 15.90, 2015- 16.33, 60.54; 2016- 16.85i/16.82, 70.50; 2017- 18.12i/17.72, 74.56; 2018- 19.46, 74.53; 2019- 19.47, 75.04; 2020- 18.80i. pbs: DT 62.47 '18, Wt 22.26i '18.
Father Brice HT 66.58 '88.

Allyson FELIX b. 18 Nov 1985 Los Angeles 1.68m 57kg. Nike. Elementary education graduate of University of Southern California.
At 400m/(4x100mR)/4x400mR: OG: '16- 2/1R/1R; At 200m: OG: '04- 2, '08- 2/1R, '12- 1/1R/1R; WCh: '03- qf, '05- 1, '07- 1/1R/1R, '09- 1/1R, '11- 3/1R/1R (2 400m), '13- dnf, '15- 1 400m/2R/2R, '17- 3 400m/1R/1R, '19- res1R/1MxR; WJ: '02- 5; PAm: '03- 3; WI: '10- 1R. At 100m: OG: '12- 5; WY: '01- 1 (1 Medley R). Won DL 200m 2010, 2014-15; 400m 2010, WAF 200m 2005-06, 2009; US 100m 2010, 200m 2004-05, 2007-09, 2012; 400m 2011, 2015-16.
Records: World 4x400mxR 2019, World junior 200m 2004 after unratified mark (no doping test) at age 17 in 2003; W35 indoor 200m 2021.
Progress at 100m, 200m, 400m: 2000- 12.19/11.99w, 23.90; 2001- 11.53, 23.31/23.27w; 2002- 11.40, 22.83/22.69w, 55.01; 2003- 11.29/ 11.12w, 22.11A/22.51, 52.26; 2004- 11.16, 22.18, 51.83A; 2005- 11.05, 22.13, 51.12; 2006- 11.04, 22.11; 2007- 11.01, 21.81, 49.70; 2008- 10.93, 21.93/21.82w, 49.83; 2009- 11.08, 21.88, 49.83; 2010- 11.27, 22.03, 50.15; 2011- 11.26+, 22.32, 49.59; 2012- 10.89, 21.69, 2013- 11.06+, 22.30, 50.19; 2014- 11.01, 22.02, 50.81; 2015- 11.09, 21.98, 49.26; 2016- 22.02, 49.51; 2017- 11.03, 22.33, 49.65; 2018- 11.30, 51.35; 2019- 51.36, 2021- 22.59i. pbs: 50m 6.43i '02, 60m 7.10i '12, 150m 16.36st '13 (world best), 16.81 '20; 300m 36.33i '07.
Women's record 6 Olympic gold medals with 9 medals to equal record and women's record of 18 medals and 13 gold at World Champs including three in 2007 when she had a record 0.53 winning margin at 200m and ran a 48.0 400m relay leg. Ran 47.72 relay leg at the 2015 Worlds. IAAF female Athlete of the Year 2012. Married to Kenneth Ferguson (400mh 48.15 '07, 2/1R WJ 2002); daughter Camryn born 28 Nov 2018. Older brother Wes Felix won World Junior bronze at 200m and gold in WJR at 4x100m in 2002, pbs: 100m 10.23 '05, 200m 20.43 '04.

Phyllis FRANCIS b. 4 May 1992 New York 1.78m 61kg. Nike. Was at University of Oregon.
At 400m/4x400mR: OG: '16- 5/1R; WCh: '15- 7/res2R, '17- 1/1R, '19- 5/1R; PAm-J: '11- 3/1R. Won NCAA indoors 2014.
Progress at 400m: 2010- 55.82i, 2011- 52.93, 2012- 51.22, 2013- 50.86, 2014- 50.46Ai/50.59, 2015- 50.50, 2016- 49.94, 2017- 49.92, 2018- 50.07, 2019- 49.61. pbs: 60m 7.30i '17, 100m 11.35 '18, 11.34w '16; 200m 22.42 '18, 300m 36.15Ai '17, 36.85i '18;

600m 1:27.38i '11, 800m 2:04.83 '08.
Younger sister Claudia pbs 400m 51.55 '16, 800m 2:02.92 '15, 400mh 55.55 '16.

Tori FRANKLIN b. 7 Oct 1992 Westmont, Illinois 1.73m 55kg. Oiselle. Was at Michigan State University.
At TJ: WCh: '17- dnq 13, '19- 9; CCp: '18- 2; WI: '18- 8. Won NACAC U23 2014.
N.American TJ record 2018 & indoors 2020.
Progress at TJ: 2010- 12.53w, 2012- 13.34i/13.02, 2013- 13.36/13.56w, 2014- 13.56i/13.49, 2015- 13.38i/13.30/13.38w, 2016- 13.66i/13.54, 2017- 14.03, 2018- 14.84, 2019- 14.57i/14.36, 2020- 14.64Ai. pbs: 100m 11.88 '16, 200m 24.07 '16, 400m 53.47 '14, LJ 5.87i '16.

Courtney FRERICHS b. 18 Jan 1993 Barrington, Illinois 1.70m 62kg. Bowerman TC. Studied biology at University of Missouri Kansas City then University of New Mexico.
At 3000mSt: OG: '16- 11; WCh: '17- 2, '19- 6; CCp: '18- 2; NCAA champion 2016.
North American 3000mSt record 2018.
Progress at 3000mSt: 2009- 10:06.21, 2010- 9:51.86, 2011- 9:37.16, 2012- 10:34.48, 2013- 9:55.02, 2014- 9:43.07, 2015- 9:31.36, 2016- 9:20.92, 2017- 9:03.77, 2018- 9:00.85, 2019- 9:09.75. pbs: 800m 2:06.33 '20, 1500m 4:07.39 '20, 3000m 8:47.31i/8:47.90 '20, 5000m 14:50.06 '20.
Married to Griffin Humphreys.

English GARDNER b. 22 Apr 1992 Philadelphia 1.62m 50kg. Nike. Was at University of Oregon.
At 100m/4x100mR: OG: '16- 7/1R; WCh: '13- 4/2R, '15- sf/2R, '19- sf; Won US 100m 2016, NCAA 100m 2012-13, indoor 60m 2012.
Progress at 100m, 200m: 2005- 11.99, 24.53; 2007- 11.61, 24.01; 2008- 11.82/11.49w, 24.27/24.19w; 2011- 11.03, 23.02; 2012- 11.10/11.00w, 22.82; 2013- 10.85, 22.62; 2014- 11.01, 22.81; 2015- 10.79/ 10.76w, 22.74; 2016- 10.74, 2017- 11.04, 22.97; 2018- 11.02, 2019- 11.16w. pbs: 60m 7.10i '19, 400m 53.73 '12.

Kate GRACE b. 24 Oct 1988 Sacramento 1.73m 55kg. Nike Bowerman TC. Yale University.
At 800m: OG: '16- 8. US champion 2016. At 1500m: WCh: '17- sf; won NACAC 2018.
Progress at 800m, 1500m: 2007- 2:10.18, 2008- 2:06.12, 4:32.29; 2009- 2:04.72i/2:05.82, 4:30.31; 2010- 2:04.22, 4:24.57; 2011- 2:03.41, 4:20.66; 2012- 2:01.63, 4:10.57; 2013- 1:59.47, 4:07.40; 2014- 2:01.22, 4:07.35; 2016- 1:58.28, 4:05.65; 2017- 1:59.30, 4:03.59; 2018- 2:00.92, 4:04.05; 2019- 1:59.33, 4:02.49. pbs: 400m 55.96 '06, 600m 1:27.8 '16, 1000m 2:35.49i '20, 1M 4:20.70 '18, 3000m 8:46.86i '20, 5k Rd 16:03 '16.

Sara HALL b. 15 Apr 1983 Santa Rosa, California 1.63m 51kg. née Bei. Asics, was at Stanford University.
At HMar: WCh: '16- 15. At 3000m: WI: '12- 8; At 3000mSt: PAm: '11- 1. Won US Mar 2017/
At Mar: 2015- 2:31:14, 2016- 2:30:06, 2017- 2:27:21, 2018- 2:26:20, 2019- 2:22:16, 2020- 2:20:32. Pbs:

800m 2:05.86 '08, 1500m 4:08.55 '08, 1M 4:31.50i '10, 4:35.02 '06; 3000m 5:54.07 '09, 3000m 8:52.35 '10, 5000m 15:20.88 '06, 10000m: 32:35.87 '15, 2000mSt 6:35.64 '11, 3000mSt 9:39.48 '11, road: 10k 32:14 '14, 15k 48:46 '20, 20k 65:29 '20, HMar 68:18 '20, 25k 1:22:43 '20, 30k 1:39:22 '20.
2nd London Marathon 2020.
Married (2005) **Ryan Hall**, US champion CC 2006, HMar & Mar 2007; 10 OG Mar 2008. Pbs: 5000m 13:16.03 '05, 10000m 28:07.93 '07, HMar 59:43 '07, Mar 2:06:17 '08, 2:04:58wdh '11

Kendra 'Keni' HARRISON b. 18 Sep 1992 Clayton, North Carolina 1.63m 52kg. adidas. University of Kentucky.
At 100mh: WC: '15- sf, '17- 4, '19- 2; CCp: '18- 2. Won DL 100mh 2016, NACAC 2018, US 2017-19, NCAA 100mh (& 60mh indoors) 2015. At 60mh: WI: '16- 8, '18- 1.
Records: World and two N.American 100m hurdles 2016, N.American 60mh (=) 2018.
Progress at 100mh, 400mh: 2010- 13.79, 59.19; 2011- 13.49, 59.13; 2012- 13.03/13.02w, 56.72; 2013- 12.88/12.87w, 55.75; 2014- 12.71/12.68w, 54.76; 2015- 12.50/12.46w, 54.09; 2016- 12.20, 2017- 12.28, 2018- 12.36, 2019- 12.43. pbs: 60m 7.23i '20, 100m 11.35 '16, 150m 16.92 '20, 200m 22.81 '18, 300m 36.83i '21, 400m 53.82i '13, 60mh 7.70i '18.

Quanera HAYES b. 7 Mar 1992. Hope Mills, North Carolina 1.72m 59kg. Nike. Was at Livingstone College.
At 400m/4x400mR: WCh: '17- sf/1R; WI: '16- 3/1R, '18- 1R.
North American indoor 300m record 2017.
Progress at 400m: 2010- 56.46, 2012- 54.18A, 2013- 51.54A, 2014- 51.91, 2015- 50.84, 2016- 49.91, 2017- 49.72, 2018- 51.46Ai/53.23, 2019- 53.45. pbs: 60m 7.34i '17, 100m 11.27 '16, 200m 22.55 '17, 300m 35.71i '17. Son born 2018.

Ashley HENDERSON b. 4 Dec 1995 St. Louis, Missouri 1.68m 59kg.adidas. Was at San Diego State University.
Progress at 100m, 200m: 2009- 12.48, 25.12; 2011- 11.97, 24.47; 2012- 11.85/11.84w, 24.35A.23.89w; 2013- 11.93, 24.33; 2014- 11.86, 24.12; 2015- 11.64, 24.09Ai; 2016- 11.21/10.96w, 22.64/22.44w; 2017- 611.01, 22.54A/22.66/22.35w; 2018- 10.96/10.91w, 22.41i/22.49; 2019- 11.22, 23.00; 2020- 11.81, 23.40i. pbs: 60m 7.17A/7.18i '18, 300m 36.95i '21.

Daniella HILL b. 16 May 1991 Mahomet, Illinois 1.78m 95kg. née Bunch. Nike. Was at Purdue University.
At SP: WCh: '17- dnq 18; PAm: '19- 4.
Progress at SP: 2008- 15.10, 2009- 15.20, 2010- 15.22, 2011- 16.07i/15.72, 2012- 16.65i/16.46, 2013- 17.13, 2014- 17.39, 2015- 18.89, 2016- 18.87i/18.18, 2017- 19.64, 2018- 18.18i/18.02, 2019- 18.82. pbs: DT 48.86 '13, HT 58.36 '14, Wt: 22.35i '14.
Married Zachary Hill (SP 19.25i/18.87 '12) on 7 Oct 2017.

Aleia HOBBS b. 24 Feb 1996 New Orleans

1.72m 59kg. Was at Louisiana State University.
At 100m: PAm-J: '15- 2/1R. Won US 2018, NCAA 60m ind & 100m 2018.
Progress at 100m: 2010- 11.95, 2011- 11.75, 2012- 11.77, 2013- 11.68, 2014- 11.49, 2015- 11.13, 2016- 11.34, 2017- 10.85, 2018- 10.90/10.86w, 2019- 11.03/10.83w, 2020- 11.12. pbs: 50m 6.17i '21, 60m 7.07i '18, 200m 22.93 '18.

Shelby HOULIHAN b. 8 Feb 1993 Sioux City, Iowa 1.60m 54kg. Nike Bowerman TC. Was at Arizona State University.
At 1500m: WCh: '19- 4; WI: '18- 4 (5 3000m); CCp: '18- 2;. At 5000m: OG: '16- 11; WCh: '17- 13. Won US 1500m & 5000m 2018-19, CC 2019; NCAA 1500m 2014, NACAC U23 800m 2014.
World record 4x1500m 2020. North American records 1500m 2019, 5000m 2018 & 2020.
Progress at 1500m, 5000m: 2010- 4:31.21, 2011- 4:26.39, 2012- 4:22.95, 2013- 4:13.64, 16:15.85; 2014- 4:10.89, 16:11.63; 2015- 4:09.62, 15:49.72; 2016- 4:03.39, 15:06.14; 2017- 4:06.22, 15:00.37; 2018- 3:57.34, 14:34.45; 2019- 3:54.99, 15:15.50; 2020- 4:02.37, 14:23.92. pbs: 600m 1:32.27 '20, 800m 1:59.92 '19, 1000m 2:37.83 '19, 1M 4:23.68i '20, 4:31.79 '15; 3000m 8:26.66i '20, 8:37.40 '17; 2M 9:31.38i '19.
Her mother Connie Prince Mar pb 2:35:26 '86.

Molly HUDDLE b. 31 Aug 1984 Elmira, New York 1.63m 48kg. Saucony. Was at University of Notre Dame.
At 5000m: OG: '12- 11; WCh: '11-13-17: h/6/12; CCp: '10- 3. At 10000m: OG: '16- 6; WCh: '15- 4, '17- 8, '19- 9. Won US 5000m 2011, 2014, 2016; 10000m 2015-19. World CC: '10- 19, '11- 17.
N. American 5000m (2) records 2010-14, 10000m 2016, 10M, 20k & HMar 2018, 1 Hour 2020.
Progress at 5000m, 10000m: 2003- 15:36.95, 2004- 15:32.55, 2005- 16:12.17i, 2006- 15:40.41, 32:37.87; 2007- 15:17.13, 33:09.27; 2008- 15:25.47, 31:27.12; 2009- 15:53.91, 32:42.11; 2010- 14:44.76, 31:27.12; 2011- 15:10.01, 31:28.66; 2012- 15:01.32, 2013- 14:58.15, 2014- 14:42.64, 30:47.59; 2015- 14:57.23, 31:39.20; 2016- 14:48.14, 30:13:17; 2017- 15:01.64i/15:03.60, 31:24.78; 2018- 15:01.44, 31:52.32; 2019- 15:08.67, 30:58.46; 2020- 15:20.80. pbs: 1500m 4:08.09 '13, 1M 4:26.84 '14, 3000m 8:42.99 '13, 1Hr 17.930m '20; Rd: 15k 48:52 '14, 10M 50:52 '18, 20k 63:48 '18, HMar 67:25 '18, Mar 2:26:33 '19. Married Kurt Benninger CAN (pbs 1500m 3:38.03 '08, 1M 3:56.99 '08, 5000m 13:30.27 '09) in 2009. Has won 27 national titles. 3rd New York 2016 on marathon debut.

Lynna IRBY b. 6 Dec 1998 Merrillville, Indiana 1.68m 55kg. University of Georgia.
At 400m/4x400mR: WJ: '16- 2/1R (1 4x100m); WY: '15- 2 (1 mxR); PAm: '19- 1R. Won NCAA 2018.
Progress at 200m, 400m: 2012- 24.84, 54.62; 2013- 23.77, 54.16; 2014- 24.05, 54.38; 2015- 24.23/23.85w, 51.79; 2016- 23.53, 51.39; 2017- 23.58i, 52.83; 2018- 22.25/22.06w, 49.80; 2019- 22.95, 51.14; 2020- 22.47, 50.50. pbs: 55m 6.94i '17, 60m 7.31i '18, 100m 11.27 '20, 300m 35.99i '21, 36.73 '18.

Kyra JEFFERSON b. 23 Sep 1994 Detroit 1.65m 57kg. Student at University of Florida.
At 200m/4x400mR: PAm: '15- 2/1R. Won NACAC 2015, NCAA 2017.
North American 4x200m indoor record 2018.
Progress at 200m: 2009- 24.27, 2010- 24.24/24.07w, 2011- 23.53, 2012- 24.11i/24.27, 2013- 23.43i, 2014- 22.78, 2015- 22.24, 2016- 22.56, 2017- 22.02, 2018- 22.48, 2019- 22.93, 2020- 22.87/22.69w. pbs: 60m 7.34i '14, 100m 11.17 '16, 150m 17.01 '20, 300m 36.49 '19, 400m 51.50 '15.
Her father Tom Jefferson was at 200m, 3rd at 1984 OG and 4th at 1991 WI; pbs: 200m, 20.26/20.21w '84, 20.1 '88; 100m 10.17 '86, 10.08w '85, 10.1 '88, 9.9w '84; 300m 31.73 '87.

Wadeline JONATHAS b. 19 Feb 1998 Gonaives, Haiti 1.78m. UMass-Boston, then University of South Carolina.
At 400m: WCh: '19- 4/1R; won NCAA 2019.
Progress at 400m: 2016- 55.81, 2017- 52.18, 2018- 53.18, 2019- 49.60, 2020- 51.32i/51.40. pbs: 60m 7.40i '18, 100m 11.84 '17, 11.41w '18; 200m 22.91 '21; HJ 1.62i '17, LJ 6.28i/5.84/6.15w '18. Moved with her family from Haiti to Massachusetts in 2013. Massive improvement with seven 400m pbs in 2019.

Shamier LITTLE b. 20 Mar 1995 Louisville, Kentucky 1.63m 52kg. adidas. Texas A&M University.
At 400mh: WCh: '15- 2, '17- sf; WJ: '12- dnf, '14- 1/1R; PAm: '15- 1/1R; CCp: '18- 2. Won NCAA 2014-16, NACAC 2018, US 2018.
Progress at 400mh: 2011- 57.83, 2012- 57.44, 2013- 58.80, 2014- 55.07, 2015- 53.74, 2016- 53.51, 2017- 52.75, 2018- 53.32, 2019- 53.73. pbs: 60m 7.65i '17, 200m 23.07 '19, 23.01w '17; 300m 36.98i '18; 400m 50.19 '21, 800m 2:16.03i '19, 60mh 8.43i '14, 100mh 13.77 '14, 200mh St 25.88 '19.
Mother Tiffany Mayfield had HJ pb 1.73.

Sydney McLAUGHLIN b. 7 Aug 1999 New Brunswick, New Jersey 1.74m 61kg. New Balance. University of Kentucky.
At 400mh/4x400mR: OG: '16- sf; WCh: '19- 2/1R; WY: '15- 1; won DL 2019, NCAA 2018.
Five World junior 400mh records 2016-18, indoor 300m 2017 & 400m (3) 2018; world youth records 400mh (2) and 400m indoors 2017.
Progress at 400m, 400mh: 2014- 53.78, 55.63; 2015- 52.59, 55.28; 2016- 51.84i/51.87, 54.15; 2017- 51.61i/51.88, 53.82; 2018- 50.07, 52.75; 2019- 50.78, 52.23. pbs: 200m 22.39 '18, 300m 36.12i '17, 500m 1:09.46i '19, 600m 1:28.85 '18, 55mh 7.66i '15, 60mh 8.17i '15, 100mh 13.34 '14, 300mh 38.90 '17, LJ 5.89i '15. 5.81w '14.
IAAF Rising Star of the Year 2018. Her brother **Taylor** (b. 3 Aug 1997) was 2nd at 2016 World Juniors and has a 400mh pb of 48.85 '19; their father Willie had a 400m best of 45.30 '83.

Brianna McNEAL b. 18 Aug 1991 Miami 1.64m 55kg. née Rollins. Nike. Clemson University.
At 100mh: OG: '16- 1; WCh: '13- 1, '15- 4, '19- h; Won US 2013, 2016; NACAC 2012, DL 2018. At 60mh: WI: '16- 2; won US indoor 60mh 2016, NCAA 100mh 2013, indoor 60mh 2011 & 2013. North American 100m hurdles record 2013, world best 4x100mh 2014 & 2015.
Progress at 100mh: 2007- 14.48, 2008- 13.93, 2009- 13.83, 2011- 12.99/12.88w, 2012- 12.70/12.60Aw, 2013- 12.26, 2014- 12.53, 2015- 12.56, 2016- 12.34, 2018- 12.43, 2019- 12.61. pbs: 60m 7.17Ai/7.20i '20, 100m 11.20 '19, 150m 16.41 '20, 200m 22.94 '18, 300m 37.90i '10, 400m 53.93 '13, 60mh 7.76i '16, 400mh 60.58 '09.
Undefeated in 2013: inc. heats 200m- 7, 400m- 1, 60mh- 8, 100mh- 18. Received a one-year ban due to missing three drugs test in 2016.

Tonea MARSHALL b. 17 Oct 1998 Arlington, Texas 1.65m 55kg. Louisiana State University.
At 100mh: won NACAC-23 2019.
Progress at 100mh 2013- 14.61/14.21w, 2014- 14.07/13.73w, 2015- 13.44/13.12w, 2016- 13.04, 2017- 13.14, 2018- 12.88/12.73w, 2019- 12.57A/12.66. pbs: 60m 7.32Ai/7.33i '20, 100m 11.37 '18, 11.37w '19; 200m 23.74i '20, 24.43/24.35w '18; 60mh 7.86i '20, LJ 5.74 '15, 5.94w '16.

Georganne MOLINE b. 6 Mar 1990 Phoenix, Arizona 1.78m 59kg. Nike. Studied psychology and communications at University of Arizona.
At 400mh: OG: '12- 5; WCh: '13- h. At 4x400m: WI: '18- 1R.
Progress at 400mh: 2010- 57.88, 2011- 57.41, 2012- 53.92, 2013- 53.72, 2014- 54.00, 2015- 54.24, 2016- 53.97, 2017- 53.14, 2018- 53.90. pbs: 200m 23.23i '18, 23.37 '13; 400m 51.39i '18, 51.93 '17; 500m 1:08.84i '15, 600m 1:26.70Ai '16, 1:27.15 '15; 800m 2:08.67i '13. 2:09.58 '14; 300mh 39.08 '20.
Seven 400mh pbs in 2012 to 53.92 in OG final.

Sandi MORRIS-Smith b. 8 Jul 1992 Downers Grove, Illinois 1.72m 65kg. Nike. University of Arkansas, formerly North Carolina.
At PV: OG: '16- 2; WCh: '15- 4=, '17- 2, '19- 2; WI: '16- 2, '18- 1; PAm-J: 1- 2; CCp: '18- 3. Won NACAC U23 2014, US 2017-18.
3 N.American outdoor pole vault records 2016.
Progress at PV: 2009- 3.81, 2010- 4.05, 2011- 4.30, 2012- 4.23i/4.15, 2013- 4.43i/4.02, 2014- 4.55, 2015- 4.76, 2016- 5.00, 2017- 4.87i/4.84, 2018- 4.95, 2019- 4.90, 2020- 4.91i/4.81, 2021- 4.88i.
Married Tyrone Smith (LJ 8.34 BER record '17).

Athing MU b. 8 Jun 2002 Trenton, New Jersey 1.78m 56kg. Texas A&M University.
At 800m: PAm: '19- h; PAm-J: '18- 1; YOG: '18- 3&2. World U18 600m best 2019, world indoor U20 400m & 800m 2021.
Progress at 400m, 800m: 2016- 56.02, 2:10.85; 2017- 57.17, 2:07.18; 2018- 54.12, 2:04.51; 2019- 51.98, 2:01.17; 2020- 53.14i, 2:04.08i; 2021- 50.52i, 1:58.40i. pbs: 200m 24.11i '19, 24.22 '18; 300m 37.36i '20, 500m 1:10.22i '20, 600m 1:23.57i '19, 1500m 4:33.04 '17. Family came from Sudan.

Dalilah MUHAMMAD b. 7 Feb 1990 Jamaica, Queens, New York 1.70m 62kg. Nike. Business graduate of University of Southern California.
At 400mh/4x400mR: OG: '16- 1; WCh: '13- 2, '17- 2, '19- 1/1R; WY: '07- 1 (1 MedR); PAm-J: '09- 2; US champion 2013, 2016-17, DL 2017-18.
2 world records 400mh 2019, best 200mh 2018.
Progress at 400mh: 2005- 61.25, 2006- 59.82, 2007- 57.09, 2008- 57.81, 2009- 56.49, 2010- 57.14, 2011- 56.04, 2012- 56.19, 2013- 53.83, 2014- 58.02, 2015- 55.76, 2016- 52.88, 2017- 52.64, 2018- 53.65, 2019- 52.16. pbs: 60m 7.64i '10, 100m 11.42 '13, 150m 17.07 '20, 200m 23.35 '19, 300m 37.42 '20, 400m 50.60 '19, 500m 1:09.66i '17, 600m 1:28.85 '18, 60mh 8.23i '12, 100mh 13.33 '12, 200mh 25.20 '18, HJ 1.75 '10. WA Athlete of the Year 2019.

Katie NAGEOTTE b. 13 Jun 1991 Olmsted Falls, Ohio 1.68m 59kg. New York AC. Was at Ashland University.
At PV: WCh: '19- 7=; PAm: '19- 2; WI: '18- 5; won NACAC 2018.
Progress at PV: 2008- 3.76, 2009- 3.96, 2010- 3.90, 2011- 4.00i, 2012- 3.81, 2013- 4.44, 2014- 4.48, 2015- 4.55, 2016- 4.63i, 4.60, 2017- 4.73, 2018- 4.91Ai/4.80, 2019- 4.86i/4.82, 2020- 4.92. pb 100m 11.91 '20.

Sharika NELVIS b. 10 May 1990 Memphis 1.78m 64kg. adidas. Sociology student at Arkansas State University.
At 100mh: WCh: '15- 8; PAm: '19- 7. At 60mh: WI: '18- 4; WIT 2018. Won NCAA 100mh & indoor 60mh 2014.
World best 4x100mh 2015. North American indoor 60mh record 2018.
Progress at 100mh: 2008- 14.23, 2009- 14.03, 2011- 13.45, 2012- 13.22/12.99w, 2013- 12.84, 2014- 12.71/12.52w, 2015- 12.34, 2016- 12.60, 2017- 12.52, 2018- 12.51, 2019- 12.65, 2020- 13.09. pbs: 60m 7.28i '14, 100m 11.27/11.17w '14, 200m 23.19 '15, 22.70w '14; 400m 54.62 '13, 60mh 7.70Ai/7.80i '18, LJ 6.32i '13, 6.27 '14.

Courtney OKOLO b. 15 Mar 1994 Carrolltown, Texas 1.68m 54kg. Nike. University of Texas.
At 400m/4x400mR: OG: '16- 7; WCh: '19- res1R/1mxR; WI: '16- 1R, '18- 1/1R; PAm: '19- 3/1R; PAm-J: '13- 1/1R. Won NACAC 2015, 4x400m 2018, NCAA 2014, 2016.
World 4x400mxR record 2019, US indoor 500m record 2017.
Progress at 400m: 2009- 56.50, 2010- 54.34, 2011- 53.03, 2012- 52.40, 2013- 51.04, 2014- 50.03, 2015- 50.82A/50.99, 2016- 49.71, 2017- 50.29, 2018- 50.55i/50.65, 2019- 50.81, 2020- 51.52. pbs: 60m 7.52i '14, 100m 11.53 '16, 150m 17.46 '20, 200m 22.93 '15, 22.79i '16; 300m 35.74 '16, 500m 1:07.34i '17, 600y 1:18.24i '15, 600m 1:24.00Ai/1:25.21 '17.

Javianne OLIVER b. 26 Dec 1994 Monroe, Georgia 1.55m 57kg. University of Kentucky.

Won US indoor 60m 2018, WIT 2021, Progress at 100m: 2011- 12.14, 2012- 11.63, 2013- 11.68, 2014- 11.67, 2015- 11.53, 2016- 11.29/11.16w, 2017- 11.16, 2018- 11.10/11.04w, 2019- 11.40/11.34w, 2020- 11.44/11.27w. pbs: 60m 7.02Ai '18, 7.08 '21; 150m 17.11 '20, 200m 23.47 '17, 22.98w '18; 300m 38.35i '18.

Keturah ORJI b. 5 Mar 1996 Hoboken, New Jersey 1.66m 61kg. Atlanta TC. Univ of Georgia.
At TJ (LJ): OG: '16- 4; WCh: '19- 7; WJ: '14- 9; WY: '13- 3 (2); WI: '16- 4, '18- 5; PAm: '19- (2); won US 2016-19, NCAA 2015-18 (& LJ 2018, indoor TJ 2016-18). North American and 3 US triple jump records 2016, N.Am indoors (3) 2017-20.
Progress at TJ: 2012- 12.46/12.51w, 2013- 13.69, 2014- 13.46, 2015- 14.15, 2016- 14.71, 2017- 14.32i/ 14.31, 2018- 14.62, 2019- 14.72, 2020- 14.60Ai. pbs: 60m 7.53i '18, 100m 11.68 '19, LJ 6.81 '18.

Jenna PRANDINI b. 20 Nov 1992 Clovis, California 1.72m 59kg. Puma. Studied psychology at University of Oregon.
At 200m/4x100mR: OG: '16- sf; WCh: '15- sf/2R.
At 100m: CCp: '18- 3/1R; NACAC: '18- 1/1R. Won NCAA 100m 2015, LJ 2014; US 200m 2015, 2018.
Progress at 100m, 200m, LJ: 2008- 12.18/11.74w, 5.86; 2009- 11.81, 24.48/24.02w; 2010- 11.34, 24.61, 6.15/6.29w; 2011- 11.51/11.44w, 23.75/23.51w, 6.20; 2012- 24.07, 2013- 11.31/11.14w, 23.15, 6.15; 2014- 11.11, 22.60, 6.55; 2015- 10.92, 22.20/22.18w, 6.80; 2016- 10.95/10.81w, 22.39; 2017- 11.05, 22.54; 2018- 10.96/10.95w, 22.16; 2019- 11.10, 22.53; 2021- 22.43. pbs: 60m 7.15i '15, 300m 36.68i '21, TJ 12.73/12.98w '10.

DeAnna PRICE b. 8 Jun 1993 Moscow Mills, Missouri 1.74m 105kg. New York AC. Was at Southern Illinois University.
At HT: OG: '16- 8; WCh: '15- dnq 18, '17- 9, '19- 1; WJ: '12- dnq 11; PAm: '15- 4; CCp: '18- 1. NCAA champion 2015-16, NACAC 2018, US indoor 20lb Wt 2018.
Three North American hammer records 2018-19. Progress at HT: 2011- 55.20, 2012- 62.62, 2013- 65.18, 2015- 72.30, 2016- 73.09, 2017- 74.91, 2018- 78.12, 2019- 78.24, 2021- 76.82. Pbs: SP 16.30 '15, DT 53.46 '15, Wt 24.57i '19. Won IAAF HT Challenge 2019.
Married coach J.C. Lambert in October 2018.

Elinor PURRIER b. 20 Feb 1995 Montgomery, Vermont 1.60m 50kg. New Balance. Was at University of New Hampshire.
At 5000m: WCh: '19- 11. At 3000mSt: WJ: '14- 9. N. American indoor records 1M 2020, 2M 2021.
Progress at 1500m (1M): 2012- 4:50.45 (1600m), 2014- 4:36.14i (1M), 2015- 4:18.59, 2016- 4:29,71i (1M), 2017- 4:12.35/4:29.44iM, 2018- 4:07.79/4:26.55iM, 2019- 4:02.34, 15:15.50; 2020- 4:00.20i/4:00.77. pbs: 800m 2:00.70 '20, 1000m c.2:41.2i+ '20, 1M 4:16.85i '20, 4:30.30 '19; 3000m 8:36.41i '12, 8:46.43 '18; 2M 9:10.28i '21, 5000m 14:58.17 '19, 3000mSt 9:43.05 '17.

Colleen QUIGLEY b. 20 Nov 1992 St. Louis, Missouri 1.73m 59kg. Bowerman TC. Was at Florida State University.
At 3000mSt: OG: '16- 8; WCh: '15- 12, '17- h; NCAA champion 2015. At 1500m: WI: '18- 9. World record 4x1500m 2020.
Progress at 3000mSt: 2012- 10:02.53, 2013- 9:38.23, 2014- 9:56.96, 2015- 9:24.92, 2016- 9:20.00, 2017- 9:15.97, 2018- 9:10.27, 2019- 9:11.41. pbs: 800m 2:02.98 '20, 1000m 2:36.53 '18, 1500m 4:03.02 '18, 1M 4:22.86i '19, 3000m 8:28.71i '20, 8:40.23 '21; 5000m 15:10.42 '20.

Brittney REESE b. 9 Sep 1986 Gulfport, Mississippi 1.73m 64kg. Nike. English graduate of University of Mississippi.
At LJ: OG: '08- 4, '12- 1, '16- 2; WCh: '07-09-11-13- 15-17-19: 8/1/1/1/dnq 24/1/dnq 13; WI: '10-12- 16-18: 1/1/1/2; won DL 2010-11, WAF 2009, US 2008-12, 2014, 2016, 2019 (& 3 indoors); NCAA 2008. N.American indoor LJ record 2012.
Progress at LJ: 2004- 6.31, 2006- 5.94, 2007- 6.83, 2008- 6.95, 2009- 7.10, 2010- 6.94/7.05w, 2011- 7.19, 2012- 7.23i/7.15, 2013- 7.25, 2014- 6.92, 2015- 6.97, 2016- 7.31, 2017- 7.13, 2018- 6.89i/6.87/7.19w, 2019- 7.00. pbs: 50m 6.23i '12, 60m 7.24i '11, 100m 11.40 '17, 11.20w '11; HJ 1.88i/1.84 '08, TJ 13.16 '08. Concentrated on basketball at Gulf Coast Community College in 2005-06. Has won eight global titles. She has an adopted son, Alex.

Sha'Carri RICHARDSON b. 25 Mar 2000 Dallas 1.68m 52kg. Louisiana State University. Won NCAA 100m 2019.
World U20 records 100m & 200m 2019.
Progress at 100m, 200m: 2016- 11.34A/11.47, 23.48; 2017- 11.28, 23.28/23.18w; 2018- 11.42w, 24.34w; 2019- 10.75, 22.17; 2020- 10.95/10.79w, 22.00. pb 60m 7.20i '19.

Raevyn ROGERS b. 7 Sep 1996 Houston 1.71m 64kg. Nike, Was at University of Oregon.
At 800m: WCh: '19- 2; WJ: '14- h; WY: '13- 1 (1 MedR); WI: '18- 5/res 1R; PAm–J '15- 1 (1 4x400R), NCAA 2015-17 (indoor 2016-17).
World indoor 4x800m record 2018.
Progress at 800m: 2008- 2:13.12, 2009- 2:06.90, 2010- 2:10.80, 2011- 2:11.09. 2012- 2:05.50, 2013- 2:03.32, 2014- 2:04.40, 2015- 1:59.71, 2016- 2:00.59, 2017- 1:59.10, 2018- 1:57.69, 2019- 1:58.18, 2020- 2:01.01. pbs: 200m 24.34 '10, 400m 52.06 '18, 600m 1:24.88i '99, 1000m 2:37.10 '20.

Shannon ROWBURY b. 19 Sep 1984 San Francisco 1.65m 52kg. Nike Oregon Project. Was at Duke University.
At 1500m: OG: '08- 7, '12- 4, '16- 4; WCh: '09- 3, '11- sf, '15- 7; CCp: '14- 2; Won US 2008-09, NCAA indoor mile 2007. At 3000m: WI: '14- 7, '16- 3; CCp: '10- 2. At 5000m: WCh: '13- 7, '17- 9. WR distance medley 2015, North American records: 2M 2014, 1500m 2015, 5000m 2016.
Progress at 1500m, 5000m: 2004- 4:17.41, 2005- 4:14.81, 2006- 4:12.31, 15:38.42; 2007- 16:59.97i,

2008- 4:00.33, 2009- 4:00.81, 15:12.95; 2010- 4:01.30, 15:00.51; 2011- 4:05.73, 2012- 4:03.15, 2013- 4:01.28, 15:06.10, 2014- 3:59.49, 14:48.68; 2015- 3:56.29, 2016- 3:57.78, 14:38.92; 2017- 4:04.56i/4:04.61, 14:57.55; 2019- 4:15.65, 15:05.99; 2020- 4:02.56, 14:45.11 pbs: 800m 1:59.97 '16, 1000m 2:40.25i '15, 1M 4:20.34 '08, 2000m 5:46.2 '14, 3000m 8:29.93 '14, 2M 9:20.25 '14, 3000mSt 9:59.4 '06.
Former ballet and Irish dancer. Married Pablo Solares (Mexican 1500m record 3:36.67 '09) on 11 April 2015, daughter Sienna b. 30 June 2018.

Raven SAUNDERS b. 15 May 1996 Charleston, SC 1.65m 125kg. Nike. Was at Southern Illinois University, then Mississippi.
At SP: OG: '16- 5; WCh: '17- 10; WJ: 14- 2; CCp: '18- 1. Won PAm-J 2015, NCAA 2015-16.
Progress at SP: 2014- 17.82, 2015- 18.62i/18.35, 2016- 19.35, 2017- 19.76, 2018- 19.74, 2019- 16.95, 2020- 17.84i, 2021- 19.57i. pbs: DT 56.85 '16, HT 56.91 '16, Wt 21.67i '17.
4 indoor and 4 outdoor US junior records 2015.

Sha'Keela SAUNDERS b. 18 Dec 1993 Elizabeth City, North Carolina 1.68m 59kg. adidas. Was at University of Kentucky.
At LJ: WCh: '17- dnq 21, '19- 9; PAm: '15- 3. Won US 2018, NACAC 2018, U23 2014.
Progress at LJ: 2008- 5.92w, 2011- 5.65/5.90w?, 2012- 6.00i, 2014- 6.43, 2015- 6.75, 2016- 6.89, 2017- 6.90i/6.79/6.92w, 2018- 6.77/6.88w, 2019- 6.78, 2020- 6.41/6.50w. pbs: 55m 7.04i '09, 60m 7.49i '18, 100m 11.88 '17, 200m 23.80 '17, 300m 39.08i '09, 39.52 '20; 400m 55.47 '09, 100mh 13.99 '16, TJ 13.32i '17, 13.03/13.34w '16.

Karissa SCHWEIZER b. 4 May 1996 Iowa 1.64m 50kg. Nike Bowerman TC. Was at University of Missouri.
At 5000m WCh: '19- 9. Won NCAA indoor and out 2017-18, indoor 3000m 2018, CC 2016.
World record 4x1500m 2020. North American indoor 3000m record 2020.
Progress at 1500m, 5000m: 2015- 4:26.34, 16:32.91; 2016- 4:17.56, 15:58.09; 2017- 4:15.77, 15:18.69; 2018- 4:06.77, 15:02.44; 2019- 4:08.51, 14:45.18; 2020- 4:00.02, 14:26.34. pbs: 800m 2:02.77 '20, 1000m 2:44.12i '18, 1M 4:24.32i '20, 3000m 8:25.70i '20, 8:40.25 '21; 10000m 30:47.99 '21.

Jennifer SIMPSON b. 23 Aug 1986 Webster City, Iowa 1.65m 50kg. née Barringer. New Balance. Studied political science at University of Colorado.
At 1500m: OG: '12- sf, '16- 3; WCh: '11-13-15-17-19: 1/2/11/2/8; won DL 2014. At 3000mSt: OG: '08- 8; WCh: '07- h, '09- 4; won NCAA 2006, 2008-09. Won US 1500m 2014-17, 5000m 2013, 3000mSt 2009.
North American records: 3000m steeplechase (3) 2008-09, 2 miles indoors 2015, out 2018.
Progress at 1500m, 5000m, 3000mSt: 2006- 16:15.23, 9:53.04, 2007- 4:21.53, 15:48.24, 9:33.95; 2008- 4:11.36, 9:22.26, 2009- 3:59.90, 15:01.70i/ 15:05.25, 9:12.50; 2010- 4:03.63, 15:33.33; 2011- 4:03.54, 15:11.49; 2012- 4:04.07, 2013- 4:00.48, 14:56.26; 2014- 3:57.22, 2015- 3:57.30, 2016- 3:58.19, 2017- 4:00.70, 2018- 3:59.37, 2019- 3:58.42, 15:21.12; 2020- 14:58.67i. pbs: 800m 2:00.45 '13, 1000m 2:38.22 '19, 1M 4:17.30 '18, 2000m 5:45.7 '14, 3000m 8:29.58 '14, 2M 9:16.78 '18.
Married Jason Simpson on 8 Oct 2010. Won the 5th Avenue Mile seven times 2011 and 2013-18.

Emily SISSON b. 12 Oct 1991 Chesterfield, Missouri 1.65m 47kg. New Balance. Was at Providence University. Married to Shane Quinn At 10000m: WCh: '17- 9, '19- 10. At (3000m)/ 5000m: WJ: '10- 10/6; PAM-J: '07- 3. World CC: '10- 18J. Won NCAA 5000m indoors and out 2015.
Progress at 10000m: 2011- 35:07.35, 2013- 33:02.88, 2014- 32:31.06, 2015- 31:38.03, 2016- 32:54.06, 2017- 31:25.64, 2018- 32:06.31, 2019- 30:49.57. pbs: 1M 4:38.49i '13, 4:44.02 '10; 3000m 8:49.61 '18, 5000m 14:55.82 '17, 15kRd 48:09 '21, HMar 67:26 '20, Mar 2:23:08 '19.

Jaide STEPTER-BAYNES b. 25 Sep 1994 Santa Ana, California 1.73m 64kg. Nike. University of Southern California.
At 400m: PAm: '19- dq/1R.
Progress at 400m: 2009- 58.69, 2010- 59.14, 2011- 58.04, 2013- 51.05, 2014- 53.98i, 2015- 52.89i, 2016- 50.91, 2017- 51.12, 2018- 50.63, 2019- 51.18, 2020- 52.53Ai/52.63i. pbs: 200m 22.80 '18, 300m 36.12 '19, 100mh 14.35 '13, 400mh 54.95 '16.
Her mother LaTanya Sheffield was NCAA champion at 400m in 1985, 3rd PAm 1987, 8th OG 1988, pb 54.36 '88.

Jennifer SUHR b. 5 Feb 1982 Fredonia, New York 1.80m 64kg. adidas. née Stuczynski. Graduate of Roberts Wesleyan University, now studying child psychology.
At PV: OG: '08- 2, '12- 1, '16- 7=; WCh: '07-11-13-15-17-19: 10/4/2/4=/dnq nh/7=; PAm: '15- 3; WI: '08-14-16: 2/5=/1; WCp: '06- nh; US champion 2006-10, 2012-16; indoors 2005, 2007-09, 2011-13.
Records: world indoors 2013 & 2016, W35 2018, four N.American 2007-08, six indoors 2009-13.
Progress at PV: 2002- 2.75, 2004- 3.49, 2005- 4.57i/4.26, 2006- 4.68i/4.66, 2007- 4.88, 2008- 4.92, 2009- 4.83i/4.81, 2010- 4.89, 2011- 4.91, 2012- 4.88i/4.81, 2013- 5.02Ai/4.91, 2014- 4.73i/4.71, 2015- 4.82, 2016- 5.03i/4.82, 2017- 4.83, 2018- 4.93, 2019- 4.91, 2020- 4.85Ai. pbs: 55mh 8.07i '05, JT 46.82 '05.
All-time top scorer at basketball at her university

Cassandra TATE b. 11 Sep 1990 Hammond, Louisiana 1.74m 64kg. adidas. Management graduate of Louisiana State University.
At 400m/4x400m: WI: '14- 1R. At 400mh: WCh: '15- 3, '17- 7; won DL 2016, NCAA & NACAC 2012.
Progress at 400mh: 2010- 56.87, 2011- 55.99, 2012- 55.22, 2013- 55.45, 2014- 54.70, 2015- 54.01, 2016-

54.47, 2017- 54.59, 2018- 54.94. 2019- 54.91. pbs: 60m 7.49i '11, 100m 11.79 '08, 11.47w '10; 200m 23.37i '10, 23.68 '09; 400m 52.40Ai '14, 52.51 '15; 60mh 8.61i '09, 100mh 14.21 '08, 14.08w '07; 200mhSt 26.12 '19. Engaged to David Verburg.

Gabrielle THOMAS b. 7 Dec 1996 Florence, Massachussets1.70m 57kg. New Balance. Was at Harvard University.
At 200m. Won NCAA indoor 2018.
Progress at 200m: 2015- 24.22, 2016- 22.47/22.37w 2017- 22.56, 2018- 22.19/22.13w, 2019- 22.69, 2020- 22.63, 2021- 22.17. pbs: 60m 7.21i '21, 100m 11.10 '19, 10.99w '18; 150m 16.89 '20, 300m 35.73i '21, LJ 6.27 '17, 6.61w '18; TJ 12.24i '18, 12.34w '20. Provisionally suspended in 2020 for whereabouts failures but exonerated.

Kendell WILLIAMS b. 14 Jun 1995 Marietta 1.73m 64kg. Was at University of Georgia.
At Hep: OG: '16- 17; WCh: '17- 12, '19- 5; WJ: '12- 8; WY: '11- 11; won US 2017, NCAA 2014, 2016-17, indoor Pen 2014-17. At Pen: WI: '16- 5, 18- 9. At 100mh: WJ: '14- 1; WY: '11- 3.
Progress at Hep: 2011- 5169, 2012- 5578, 2013- 5572A, 2014- 6018, 2015- 6223, 2016- 6402, 2017- 6564, 2019- 6610. pbs: 200m 23.50 '17, 400m 55.61Ai '18, 600m 1:34.92i '18, 800m 2:15.31 '16, 60mh 8.18i '19, 100mh 12.58 '19, 400mh 58.63 '10, HJ 1.88Ai '14, 1.85 '17; LJ 6.69/6.91w '18, SP 13.55i '16, 13.41 '19; JT 46.48 '17, Pen 4703i '16.
Her brother **Devon** (b. 17 Dec 1994) has decathlon pb 8345 '17, WCh: '17-10, '19- dnf WC; won NCAA indoor heptathlon with 6177 '17.

Ajee' WILSON b. 8 May 1994 Neptune, New Jersey 1.69m 55kg. adidas. Studied kinesiology at Temple University, Philadelphia.
At 800m: OG: '16- sf; WCh: '13- 5. '17- 3, '19- 3; WJ: '10- 5, '12- 1; WY: 11- 1; CCp: '14- 2, '18- 2; WI: '16- 2, '18- 2; won DL 2019, US 2014, 2017-19; indoor 2013-14, 2016; NACAC 2018.
Records: WR distance medley 2015, World indoor 4x800m 2018, North American 4x800m 2014, 600m 2017, Indoor 800m 1:58.60 2019, world junior 600m & North American junior 800m 2013.
Progress at 800m: 2008- 2:11.43, 2009- 2:07.08, 2010- 2:04.18, 2011- 2:02.64, 2012- 2:00.91, 2013- 1:58.21, 2014- 1:57.67, 2015- 1:57.87, 2016- 1:59.44, 2017- 1:55.61, 2018- 1:56.45, 2019- 1:57.72, 2020- 1:58.29i, 2021- 1:58.93. pbs: 400m 53.63 '14, 500m 1:09.63i '17, 600m 1:22.39 '17, 1000m 2:34.71i '19, 1500m 4:05.18 '18, 1M 4:33.57 '16, 3000m 10:13.41 '07. Elder sister Jade has 400mh pb 59.90 '12.

Shakima WIMBLEY b. 23 Apr 1995 Fort Lauderdale, Florida 1.87m 61kg. adidas. University of Miami.
At 400m/4x400mR: WCh: '17- 1R, '19- sf; WJ: '14- 1R; PAm: '15- 2/1R; CCp: '18- 5; WI: '18- 2/1R. Won US 2018-19.
Progress at 400m: 2012- 55.11, 2013- 53.67, 2014- 51.68, 2015- 50.84, 2016- 50.90, 2017- 50.36, 2018-

49.52, 2019- 50.20, 2020- 53.82. pbs: 100m 11.99 '13, 200m 22.34 '18, 300m 36.4+ '19, 36.72i '17.

Kara WINGER b. 10 Apr 1986 Seattle 1.83m 84kg. née Patterson. Asics. Studied interior design at Purdue University.
At JT: OG: '08/12/16- dnq 40/30/13; WCh: '09/11/17- dnq 28/20/15, '15- 8, '19- 5; PAm: '15- 2, '19- 1; PAm-J: '05- 2; CCp: '10-14-18: 5/7/3. Won NACAC 2015, US 2008-11, 2014-15, 2017-18. North American javelin record 2010.
Progress at JT: 2003- 44.75, 2004- 48.51, 2005- 52.09, 2006- 56.19, 2008- 61.56, 2009- 63.95, 2010- 66.67, 2011- 62.76, 2012- 60.49, 2013- 57.12, 2014- 62.90, 2015- 66.47, 2016- 61.86, 2017- 64.80, 2018- 64.75, 2019- 64.92, 2020- 64.44. Pb DT 35.17 '11.
Married Russ Winger (SP 21.29i '08, 21.25 '10; DT 66.04 '11, dnq 26 WCh 15) on 28 Sep 2014.

UZBEKISTAN
Governing body: Athletic Federation of Uzbekistan.

Svetlana RADZIVIL b. 17 Jan 1987 Tashkent 1.84m 61kg
At HJ: OG: '08- dnq 16, '12- 7, '16- 13=; WCh: '09- dnq 18=, '11- 7=, '15- 9=, '19- 12; AsiG: '06-10-14-18: 7/1/1/1; AsiC: '09-11-13-15-19: 3/2/2/1/3; WJ: '02- dnq, '04- 13, '06- 1; WY: '03- dnq; CCp: '14- 4, '18- 2; WI: '12- 8. Won Asi-J 2006, Asian indoor 2014, 2016.
Progress at HJ: 2002- 1.84, 2003- 1.78, 2004- 1.88, 2005- 1.85, 2006- 1.91, 2007- 1.91, 2008- 1.93, 2009- 1.91, 2010- 1.95, 2011- 1.95, 2012- 1.97, 2013- 1.94, 2014- 1.96, 2015- 1.94, 2016- 1.94, 2018- 1.96, 2019- 1.96, 2020- 1.93i/1.83.

VENEZUELA
Governing body: Federación Venezolana de Atletismo. Founded 1948.
National Champions 2020: **Men**: 20kW: Yereman Salazar 1:31:07; **Women**: 20kW: Ana Sulbarán 1:48:45.

Women
Yulimar ROJAS b. 21 Oct 1995 Caracas 1.89m 75kg. FC Barcelona, Spain.
At TJ (LJ): OG: '16- 2; WCh: '17- 1, '19- 1; WJ: '14- dnq 17 (11); PAm: '15- 4 (11), 19- 1; SACh: '15- 1, '17- 2; WI: '16- 1, '18- 1; WIT 2020. Won SAm23 LJ & TJ 2014, SAmJ HJ 2011.
Triple jump records: World indoor 2020, South American 2019 and nine indoor 2016-20, Venezuelan records: LJ 2015, TJ (7) 2015-19. U20 HJ 2013.
Progress at TJ: 2014- 13.65, 2015- 14.20, 2016- 15.02, 2017- 14.96, 2018- 14.63i, 2019- 15.41, 2020- 15.43i/14.71. Pbs: 100m 11.94 '13, HJ 1.87 '13, LJ 6.59i '20, 6.57 '15.
Lives in Guadalajara, Spain and coached by Iván Pedroso. First woman to win an Olympic medal for Venezuela. IAAF Rising Star of the Year 2017, WA Athlete of the Year 2020.

WORLD AND CONTINENTAL RECORDS 169

INTRODUCTION TO WORLD LISTS AND INDEX

Records
World, World U20 and U18, Olympic, Area and Continental records are listed for standard events. In running events up to and including 400 metres, only fully automatic times are shown. Marks listed are those which are considered statistically acceptable and thus may differ from official records. These are followed by 'odd events', road bests and bests by over 35/40 masters.

World All-time and Year Lists
Lists are presented in the following format: Mark, Wind reading (where appropriate), Name, Nationality (abbreviated), Date of birth, Position in competition, Meeting name (if significant), Venue, Date of performance.
In standard events the best 30 or so performances are listed followed by the best marks for other athletes. Position, meet and venue details have been omitted beyond 100th in year lists.
In the all-time lists performances which have been world records (or world bests, thus including some unratified marks) are shown with WR against them (or WIR for world indoor records).
Juniors (U20) are shown with-J after date of birth, and Youths (U18) with -Y.

Indexes
These contain the names of all athletes ranked with full details in the world year lists for standard events (and others such as half marathon). The format of the index is as follows:
Family name, First name, Nationality, Birthdate, Height (cm) and Weight (kg), 2020 best mark, Lifetime best (with year) as at the end of 2019.
* indicates an athlete who is profiled in the Biographies section, and ^ one who has been profiled in previous editions.

Altitude aid
Marks set at an altitude of 1000m or higher have been suffixed by the letter "A" in events where altitude may be of significance.
Although there are no separate world records for altitude assisted events, it is understood by experts that in all events up to 400m in length (with the possible exclusion of the 110m hurdles), and in the horizontal jumps, altitude gives a material benefit to performances. For events beyond 800m, however, the thinner air of high altitude has a detrimental effect.
Supplementary lists are included in relevant events for athletes with seasonal bests at altitude who have low altitude marks qualifying for the main list.

Some leading venues over 1000m
Addis Ababa ETH	2365m
Air Force Academy USA	2194
Albuquerque USA	1555
Antananarivo MAD	1350
Assela ETH	2430
Ávila ESP	1128
Bloemfontein RSA	1392
Bogotá COL	2644
Boulder USA	1655
Bozeman USA	1467
Calgary CAN	1045
Cali COL	1046
Ciudad de Guatemala GUA	1402
Ciudad de México MEX	2247
Cochabamba BOL	2558
Colorado Springs USA	1823
Cuenca ECU	2561
Denver USA	1609
El Paso USA	1187
Flagstaff USA	2107
Fort Collins USA	1521
Gabarone BOT	1006
Germiston RSA	1661
Guadalajara MEX	1567
Harare ZIM	1473
Johannesburg RSA	1748
Kampala UGA	1189
Krugersdorp RSA	1740
Levelland USA	1069
Logan USA	1372
Medellín COL	1541
Monachil ESP	2302
Nairobi KEN	1675
Orem USA	1455
Pietersburg RSA	1230
Pocatello USA	1361
Potchefstroom RSA	1351
Pretoria RSA	1400
Provo USA	1380
Pueblo USA	1487
Querétaro MEX	1825
Reno USA	1369
Roodepoort RSA	1623
Rustenburg RSA	1215
Salt Lake City USA	1321
San José CRC	1200
Sasolberg RSA	1488
Secunda RSA	1628
Sestriere ITA	2050
Soría ESP	1056
Windhoek NAM	1725
Xalapa MEX	1356

Some others over 500m
Albertville FRA	550
Almaty KZK	847
Ankara TUR	902
Bangalore, IND	949
Bern SUI	555
Blacksburg USA	634
Boise USA	818
Canberra AUS	581

La Chaux de Fonds SUI	997
Caracas VEN	922
Edmonton CAN	652
Jablonec CZE	598
Las Vegas USA	619
Lausanne SUI	597
León ESP	837
Lubbock USA	981
Madrid ESP	640
Magglingen SUI	751
Malles ITA	980
Moscow, Idaho USA	787
München GER	520
Nampa, Idaho USA	760
Salamanca ESP	806
Santiago de Chile CHI	520
São Paulo BRA	725
Sofia BUL	564
Spokane USA	576
Trípoli GRE	655
Tucson USA	728
Uberlândia BRA	852

350m-500m

Banská Bystrica SVK	362
Fayetteville USA	407
Genève SUI	385
Götzis AUT	448
Johnson City USA	499
Rieti ITA	402
Sindelfingen GER	440
Stuttgart GER	415
Tashkent UZB	477
Zürich SUI	410

Automatic timing
In the main lists for sprints and hurdles, only times recorded by fully automatic timing devices are included.

Hand timing
In the sprints and hurdles supplementary lists are included for races which are hand timed. Athletes with a hand timed best 0.01 seconds or more better than his or her automatically timed best has been included, but hand timed lists have been terminated close to the differential levels considered by the IAAF to be equivalent to automatic times, i.e. 0.24 sec. for 100m, 200m, 100mh, 110mh, and 0.14 sec. for 400m and 400mh. It should be noted that this effectively recognises bad hand timekeeping, for there should be no material difference between hand and auto times, but badly trained timekeepers anticipate the finish, having reacted to the flash at the start.
In events beyond 400m, auto times are integrated with hand timed marks, the latter identifiable by times being shown to tenths. All-time lists also include some auto times in tenths of a second, identified with '.

Indoor marks
Indoor marks are included in the main lists for field events and straightway track events, but not for other track events as track sizes vary in circumference (200m is the international standard) and banking, while outdoor tracks are standardised at 400m. Outdoor marks for athletes with indoor bests are shown in a supplemental list.

Mixed races
For record purposes athletes may not, except in road races, compete in mixed sex races. Statistically there would not appear to be any particular logic in this, and women's marks set in such races are shown in our lists – annotated with mx. In such cases the athlete's best mark in single sex competition is appended.

Field event series
Field event series are given (where known) for marks in the top 30 performances lists.

Tracks and Courses
As well as climatic conditions, the type and composition of tracks and runways will affect standards of performance, as will the variations in road race courses.

Wind assistance
Anemometer readings have been shown for sprints and horizontal jumps in metres per second to one decimal place. If the figure was given to two decimal places, it has been rounded to the next tenth upwards, e.g. a wind reading of +2.01m/s, beyond the IAAF legal limit of 2.0, is rounded to +2.1; or -1.22m/s is rounded up to -1.2.

Drugs bans
The IAAF Council may decertify an athlete's records, titles and results if he or she is found to have used a banned substance before those performances. Performances at or after such a positive finding are shown in footnotes. Such athletes are shown with ¶ after their name in year lists, and in all-time lists if at any stage of their career they have served a drugs suspension of a year or more (thus not including athletes receiving public warnings or 3 month bans for stimulants etc., which for that year only are indicated with a #). This should not be taken as implying that the athlete was using drugs at that time. Nor have those athletes who have subsequently unofficially admitted to using banned substances been indicated; the ¶ is used only for those who have been caught.

Venues
Place names occasionally change. Our policy is to use names in force at the time that the performance was set. Thus Leningrad prior to 1991, Sankt-Peterburg from its re-naming.

Amendments
Keen observers may spot errors in the lists. They are invited to send corrections as well as news and results for 2021.

Peter Matthews
Email p.matthews121@btinternet.com

WORLD & CONTINENTAL RECORDS

As at 23 March 2019. **Key:** W = World, Afr = Africa, Asi = Asia, CAC = Central America & Caribbean, Eur = Europe, NAm = North America, Oce = Oceania, SAm = South America, Com = Commonwealth, W20 = World Junior (U20), W18 = World Youth (U18, not officially ratified by IAAF). h hand timed.
A altitude over 1000m, + timing by photo-electric-cell, # awaiting ratification, § not officially ratified

100 METRES
W,CAC,Com	9.58	Usain BOLT	JAM	Berlin	16 Aug 2009
NAm	9.69	Tyson GAY	USA	Shanghai	20 Sep 2009
Afr	9.85	Olusoji FASUBA	NGR	Doha	12 May 2006
Eur	9.86	Francis OBIKWELU	POR	Athina	22 Aug 2004
	9.86	Jimmy VICAUT	FRA	Saint-Denis 4 Jul 2015 & Montreuil-sous-Bois 7 Jun 2016	
Asi	9.91	Femi Seun OGUNODE	QAT	Wuhan 4 Jun 15 & Gainesville 22 Apr 2016	
	9.91	SU Bingtian	CHN	Madrid 22 Jun 18 & Paris (C) 30 Jun 2018	
Oce	9.93	Patrick JOHNSON	AUS	Mito	5 May 2003
SAm	10.00A	Róbson da SILVA	BRA	Ciudad de México	22 Jul 1988
W20	9.97	Trayvon BROMELL	USA	Eugene	13 Jun 2014
W18	10.15	Anthony SCHWARTZ	USA	Gainesville	31 Mar 2017

200 METRES
W,CAC,Com	19.19	Usain BOLT	JAM	Berlin	20 Aug 2009
NAm	19.32	Michael JOHNSON	USA	Atlanta	1 Aug 1996
Afr	19.68	Frank FREDERICKS	NAM	Atlanta	1 Aug 1996
Eur	19.72A	Pietro MENNEA	ITA	Ciudad de México	12 Sep 1979
SAm	19.81	Alonso EDWARD	PAN	Berlin	20 Aug 2009
Asi	19.88	XIE Zhenye	CHN	London (OS)	21 Jul 2019
Oce	20.06A	Peter NORMAN	AUS	Ciudad de México	16 Oct 1968
W20	19.93	Usain BOLT	JAM	Hamilton, BER	11 Apr 2004
W18	20.13	Usain BOLT	JAM	Bridgetown	20 Jul 2003

400 METRES
W, Afr, Com	43.03	Wayde van NIEKERK	RSA	Rio de Janeiro	14 Aug 2016
NAm	43.18	Michael JOHNSON	USA	Sevilla	26 Aug 1999
CAC	43.48	Sreven GARDINER	BAH	Doha	4 Oct 2019
Asi	43.93	Yousef Ahmed AL-MASRAHI	KSA	Beijing	23 Aug 2015
SAm	44.15	Anthony ZAMBRANO	COL	Doha	4 Oct 2019
Eur	44.33	Thomas SCHÖNLEBE	GDR/GER	Roma	3 Sep 1987
Oce	44.38	Darren CLARK	AUS	Seoul	26 Sep 1988
W20	43.87	Steve LEWIS	USA	Seoul	28 Sep 1988
W18	44.84A	Justin ROBINSON	USA	Albuquerque	8 Jun 2019

800 METRES
W, Afr, Com	1:40.91	David RUDISHA	KEN	London (OS)	9 Aug 2012
Eur	1:41.11	Wilson KIPKETER	DEN	Köln	24 Aug 1997
SAm	1:41.77	Joaquim CRUZ	BRA	Köln	26 Aug 1984
NAm	1:42.34	Donavan BRAZIER	USA	Doha	1 Oct 2019
Asi	1:42.79	Youssef Saad KAMEL	BRN	Monaco	29 Jul 2008
CAC	1:42.85	Norberto TELLEZ	CUB	Atlanta	31 Jul 1996
Oce	1:44.21	Joseph DENG	AUS	Monaco	20 Jul 2018
W20	1:41.73	Nijel AMOS	BOT	London (OS)	9 Aug 2012
W18	1:43.37	Mohamed AMAN	ETH	Rieti	10 Sep 2011

1000 METRES
W, Afr, Com	2:11.96	Noah NGENY	KEN	Rieti	5 Sep 1999
Eur	2:12.18	Sebastian COE	GBR	Oslo	11 Jul 1981
NAm	2:13.9	Rick WOHLHUTER	USA	Oslo	30 Jul 1974
SAm	2:14.09	Joaquim CRUZ	BRA	Nice	20 Aug 1984
Asi	2:14.72	Youssef Saad KAMEL	BRN	Stockholm	22 Jul 2008
Oce	2:16.09	Jeff RISELEY	AUS	Ostrava	17 Jun 2014
CAC	2:17.0	Byron DYCE	JAM	København	15 Aug 1973
W20	2:13.93 §	Abubaker KAKI	SUD	Stockholm	22 Jul 2008
W18	2:17.44	Hamza DRIOUCH	QAT	Sollentuna	9 Aug 2011

1500 METRES
W, Afr	3:26.00	Hicham EL GUERROUJ	MAR	Roma	14 Jul 1998
Com	3:26.34	Bernard LAGAT	KEN	Bruxelles	24 Aug 2001
Eur	3:28.68	Jakob INGEBRIGTSEN	GBR	Monaco	14 Aug 2020
Asi	3:29.14	Rashid RAMZI	BRN	Roma	14 Aug 2006
NAm	3:29.30	Bernard LAGAT	USA	Rieti	28 Aug 2005

Oce	3:29.66	Nick WILLIS	NZL	Monaco	17 Jul 2015
SAm	3:33.25	Hudson Santos de SOUZA	BRA	Rieti	28 Aug 2005
CAC	3:35.03	Maurys CASTILLO	CUB	Huelva	7 Jun 2012
W20	3:28.81	Ronald KWEMOI	KEN	Monaco	18 Jul 2014
W18	3:33.72	Nicholas KEMBOI	KEN	Zürich	18 Aug 2006

1 MILE

W, Afr	3:43.13	Hicham El GUERROUJ	MAR	Roma	7 Jul 1999
Com	3:43.40	Noah NGENY	KEN	Roma	7 Jul 1999
Eur	3:46.32	Steve CRAM	GBR	Oslo	27 Jul 1985
NAm	3:46.91	Alan WEBB	USA	Brasschaat	21 Jul 2007
Asi	3:47.97	Daham Najim BASHIR	QAT	Oslo	29 Jul 2005
Oce	3:48.98	Craig MOTTRAM	AUS	Oslo	29 Jul 2005
SAm	3:51.05	Hudson de SOUZA	BRA	Oslo	29 Jul 2005
CAC	3:56.13	Daniel HERRERA	MEX	Concord, MA	1 Jun 2017
W20	3:49.29	William Biwott TANUI (later ÖZBILEN)	KEN	Oslo	3 Jul 2009
W18	3:54.56	Isaac SONGOK	KEN	Linz	20 Aug 2001

2000 METRES

W, Afr	4:44.79	Hicham EL GUERROUJ	MAR	Berlin	7 Sep 1999
Com	4:48.74	John KIBOWEN	KEN	Hechtel	1 Aug 1998
Eur	4:50.01	Jakob INGEBRIGTSEN	NOR	Oslo	11 Jun 2020
Oce	4:50.76	Craig MOTTRAM	AUS	Melbourne	9 Mar 2006
NAm	4:52.44	Jim SPIVEY	USA	Lausanne	15 Sep 1987
Asi	4:55.57	Mohammed SULEIMAN	QAT	Roma	8 Jun 1995
SAm	5:03.34	Hudson Santos de SOUZA	BRA	Manaus	6 Apr 2002
CAC	5:03.4	Arturo BARRIOS	MEX	Nice	10 Jul 1989
W20	4:56.25	Tesfaye CHERU	ETH	Reims	5 Jul 2011
W18	4:56.86	Isaac SONGOK	KEN	Berlin	31 Aug 2001

3000 METRES

W, Afr, Com	7:20.67	Daniel KOMEN	KEN	Rieti	1 Sep 1996
Eur	7:26.62	Mohammed MOURHIT	BEL	Monaco	18 Aug 2000
Oce	7:28.02	Stewart McSWEYN	AUS	Roma	17 Sep 2020
NAm	7:29.00	Bernard LAGAT	USA	Rieti	29 Aug 2010
Asi	7:30.76	Jamal Bilal SALEM	QAT	Doha	13 May 2005
CAC	7:35.71	Arturo BARRIOS	MEX	Nice	10 Jul 1989
SAm	7:39.70	Hudson Santos de SOUZA	BRA	Lausanne	2 Jul 2002
W20	7:28.19	Yomif KEJELCHA	ETH	Saint-Denis	27 Aug 2016
W18	7:32.37	Abreham CHERKOS Feleke	ETH	Lausanne	11 Jul 2006

5000 METRES

W, Afr, Com	12:35.36	Joshua CHEPTEGEI	UGA	Monaco	14 Aug 2020
NAm	12:47.20	Mohammed AHMED	CAN	Portland	10 Jul 2020
Eur	12:49.71	Mohammed MOURHIT	BEL	Bruxelles	25 Aug 2000
Asi	12:51.96	Albert ROP	BRN	Monaco	19 Jul 2013
Oce	12:55.76	Craig MOTTRAM	AUS	London (CP)	30 Jul 2004
CAC	13:07.79	Arturo BARRIOS	MEX	London (CP)	14 Jul 1989
SAm	13:19.43	Marilson dos SANTOS	BRA	Kassel	8 Jun 2006
W20	12:43.02	Selemon BAREGA	ETH	Bruxelles	31 Aug 2018
W18	12:54.19	Abreham CHERKOS Feleke	ETH	Roma	14 Jul 2006

10,000 METRES

W, Afr, Com	26:11.00	Joshua CHEPTEGEI	UGA	Valencia	7 Oct 2020
Asi	26:38.76	Abdullah Ahmad HASSAN	QAT	Bruxelles	5 Sep 2003
NAm	26:44.36	Galen RUPP	USA	Eugene	30 May 2014
Eur	26:46.57	Mohamed FARAH	GBR	Eugene	3 Jun 2011
CAC	27:08.23	Arturo BARRIOS	MEX	Berlin	18 Aug 1989
Oce	27:23.80	Stewart McSWEYN	AUS	Melbourne	14 Dec 2019
SAm	27:28.12	Marilson dos SANTOS	BRA	Neerpelt	2 Jun 2007
W20	26:41.75	Samuel WANJIRU	KEN	Bruxelles	26 Aug 2005
W18	27:02.81	Ibrahim JEYLAN Gashu	ETH	Bruxelles	25 Aug 2006

HALF MARATHON

W, Afr, Com	57:32	Kibiwott KANDIE	KEN	Valencia	6 Dec 2020
Asi	58:40	Abraham CHEROBEN	BRN	København	17 Sep 2017
Eur	59:13	Julien WANDERS	SUI	Ras Al Khaimah	8 Feb 2019
	59:07 dh	Mo FARAH	GBR	South Shields	8 Sep 2019
SAm	59:33	Marilson dos SANTOS	BRA	Udine	14 Oct 2007
NAm	59:43	Ryan HALL	USA	Houston	14 Jan 2007

WORLD AND CONTINENTAL RECORDS 173

Oce	59:47	Zane ROBERTSON	NZL	Marugame	1 Feb 2015
CAC	60:14	Armando QUINTANILLA	MEX	Tokyo	21 Jan 1996
W20	59:16	Samuel WANJIRU	KEN	Rotterdam	11 Sep 2005
W18	60:38	Faustin BAHA Sulle	TAN	Lille	4 Sep 1999

MARATHON

W, Afr, Com	2:01:39	Eliud KIPCHOGE	KEN	Berlin	16 Sep 2018
Eur	2:04:16	Kaan Kigen ÖZBILEN	TUR	Valencia	1 Dec 2019
Asi	2:04:43	El Hassan EL ABBASSI	BRN	Valencia	2 Dec 2018
NAm	2:05:38	Khalid KHANNOUCHI (ex MAR)	USA	London	14 Apr 2002
SAm	2:06:05	Ronaldo da COSTA	BRA	Berlin	20 Sep 1998
Oce	2:08:16	Steve MONEGHETTI	AUS	Berlin	30 Sep 1990
CAC	2:08:30	Dionicio CERÓN	MEX	London	2 Apr 1995
W20	2:04:32	Tsegaye MEKONNEN	ETH	Dubai	24 Jan 2014
W18	2:11:43	LI He	CHN	Beijing	14 Oct 2001

100 KILOMETRES

W, Asi	6:09:14	Nao KAZAMI	JPN	Yubetsu	24 Jun 2018
NAm	6:09:26	Jim WALMSLEY	USA	Chandler	23 Jan 2021
Eur	6:16:41	Jean-Paul PRAET	BEL	Torhout	24 Jun 1989
SAm	6:18:09	Valmir NUNES	BRA	Winschoten	16 Sep 1995
Com	6:19:20	Stephen WAY	GBR/Eng	Gravesend	3 May 2014
Afr	6:24:06	Bongmusa MTHEMBU	RSA	Los Alcazares	27 Nov 2016
Oce	6:29:26	Tim SLOAN	AUS	Ross-Richmond	23 Apr 1995
CAC	6:54:27	Alfonzo ANSALDO	MEX	Rodenbachm	20 Apr 1985

3000 METRES STEEPLECHASE

W, Asi	7:53.63	Saïf Saaeed SHAHEEN	QAT	Bruxelles	3 Sep 2004
Afr, Com	7:53.64	Brimin KIPRUTO	KEN	Monaco	22 Jul 2011
Eur	8:00.09	Mahiedine MEKHISSI-BENABBAD	FRA	Saint-Denis	6 Jul 2013
NAm	8:00.45	Evan JAGER	USA	Saint-Denis	4 Jul 2015
Oce	8:14.05	Peter RENNER	NZL	Koblenz	29 Aug 1984
SAm	8:14.41	Wander MOURA	BRA	Mar del Plata	22 Mar 1995
CAC	8:25.69	Salvador MIRANDA	MEX	Barakaldo	8 Jul 2000
W20	7:58.66	Stephen CHERONO (now Shaheen)	KEN	Bruxelles	24 Aug 2001
W18	8:12.28	Getnet WALE	ETH	Hengelo	11 Jun 2017

110 METRES HURDLES

W, NAm	12.80	Aries MERRITT	USA	Bruxelles	7 Sep 2012
CAC	12.87	Dayron ROBLES	CUB	Ostrava	12 Jun 2008
Asi	12.88	LIU Xiang	CHN	Lausanne	11 Jul 2006
Com	12.90	Omar McLEOD	JAM	Kingston	24 Jun 2017
Eur	12.91	Colin JACKSON	GBR	Stuttgart	20 Aug 1993
Afr	13.11	Antonio ALKANA	RSA	Praha	5 Jun 2017
SAm	13.18	Gabriel CONSTANTINO	BRA	Székesfehérvár	9 Jul 2019
Oce	13.29	Kyle VANDER-KUYP	AUS	Göteborg	11 Aug 1995
W20	13.12	LIU Xiang (with 3'6" hurdles)	CHN	Lausanne	2 Jul 2002
W20 99cm h	12.99	Wilhem BELOCIAN	FRA	Eugene	24 Jul 2014
	12.99	Damion THOMAS	JAM	Kingston	23 Jun 2018
W18	13.32	Dejour RUSSELL	JAM	Kingston	24 Jun 2017
W18 91cm h	12.87	Zasha ZHOYA	FRA	Angers	6 Jul 2019

400 METRES HURDLES

W, NAm	46.78	Kevin YOUNG	USA	Barcelona	6 Aug 1992
Eur	46.87	Karsten WARHOLM	NOR	Stockhoilm	23 Aug 2020
Asi	46.98	Abderrahman SAMBA	QAT	Paris (C)	30 Jun 2018
CAC, Com	47.02	Rai BENJAMIN	ANT	Eugene	8 Jun 2018
Afr	47.10	Samuel MATETE	ZAM	Zürich	7 Aug 1991
SAm	47.84	Bayano KAMANI	PAN	Helsinki	7 Aug 2005
Oce	48.28	Rohan ROBINSON	AUS	Atlanta	31 Jul 1996
W20	48.02	Danny HARRIS	USA	Los Angeles	17 Jun 1984
W18	48.89	L.J. VAN ZYL	RSA	Kingston	19 Jul 2002
W18 84cm	48.84A	Zazini SOKWAKHANA	RSA	Pretoria	17 Mar 2017

HIGH JUMP

W, CAC	2.45	Javier SOTOMAYOR	CUB	Salamanca	27 Jul 1993
Asi	2.43	Mutaz Essa BARSHIM	QAT	Bruxelles	5 Sep 2014
Eur	2.42	Patrik SJÖBERG	SWE	Stockholm	30 Jun 1987
	2.42 i§	Carlo THRÄNHARDT	FRG	Berlin	26 Feb 1988
	2.42i	Ivan UKHOV	RUS	Praha	25 Feb 2014

2.42   Bohdan BONDARENKO   UKR   New York   14 Jun 2014
NAm   2.40 i§   Holis CONWAY   USA   Sevilla   10 Mar 1991
         2.40   Charles AUSTIN   USA   Zürich   7 Aug 1991
NAm=, Com 2.40   Derek DROUIN   CAN   Des Moines   25 Apr 2014
Afr   2.38   Jacques FREITAG   RSA   Oudtshoorn   5 Mar 2005
Oce   2.36   Tim FORSYTH   AUS   Melbourne   2 Mar 1997
          2.36   Brandon STARC   AUS   Eberstadt   26 Aug 2018
SAm   2.33   Gilmar MAYO   COL   Pereira   17 Oct 1994
W20   2.37   Dragutin TOPIC   YUG   Plovdiv   12 Aug 1990
                    Steve SMITH   GBR   Seoul   20 Sep 1992
W18   2.33   Javier SOTOMAYOR   CUB   La Habana   19 May 1984

POLE VAULT
W, Eur   6.18 i   Armand DUPLANTIS   SWE   Glasgow   15 Feb 2020
          6.15   Armand DUPLANTIS   SWE   Roma   17 Sep 2020
Oce, Com 6.06i   Steve HOOKER   AUS   Boston (R)   7 Feb 2009
          6.05   Dmitriy MARKOV   AUS   Edmonton   9 Aug 2001
NAm   6.06   Sam KENDRICKS   USA   Des Moines   27 Jul 2019
Afr   6.03   Okkert BRITS   RSA   Köln   18 Aug 1995
Asi   5.92i   Igor POTAPOVICH   KAZ   Stockholm   19 Feb 1998
          5.90   Grigoriy YEGOROV   KAZ Stuttgart 19 Aug 1993 & London (CP) 10 Sep 1993
          5.90   Igor POTAPOVICH   KAZ   Nice   10 Jul 1996
SAm   6.03   Thiago BRAZ da SILVA   BRA   Rio de Janeiro   15 Aug 2016
CAC   5.90   Lázaro BORGES   CUB   Daegu   29 Aug 2011
W20   6.05   Armand DUPLANTIS   SWE   Berlin   12 Aug 2018
W18   5.56   Sasha ZHOYA   FRA   Sydney   1 Apr 2019

LONG JUMP
W, NAm   8.95   Mike POWELL   USA   Tokyo   30 Aug 1991
Eur   8.86 A   Robert EMMIYAN   ARM   Tsakhkadzor   22 May 1987
SAm   8.73   Irving SALADINO   PAN   Hengelo   24 May 2008
CAC   8.71   Iván PEDROSO   CUB   Salamanca   18 Jul 1995
Com   8.69   Tajay GAYLE   JAM   Doha   28 Sep 2019
Afr   8.65A   Luvo MANYONGA   RSA   Potchefstroom   22 Apr 2017
Oce   8.54   Mitchell WATT   AUS   Stockholm   29 Jul 2011
Asi   8.48   Mohamed Salim AL-KHUWALIDI   KSA   Sotteville   2 Jul 2006
W20   8.35   Sergey MORGUNOV   RUS   Cheboksary   20 Jun 2012
W18   8.28   Maykel D MASSÓ   CUB   La Habana   28 May 2016

TRIPLE JUMP
W, Eur, Com 18.29   Jonathan EDWARDS   GBR/Eng Göteborg   7 Aug 1995
NAm   18.21   Christian TAYLOR   USA   Beijing   27 Aug 2015
CAC   18.08   Pedro Pablo PICHARDO   CUB   La Habana   28 May 2015
Afr   18.07i   Fabrice ZANGO   BUR   Aubière   16 Jan 2021
          17.66   Fabrice ZANGO   BUR   Doha   29 Sep 2019
SAm   17.90   Jadel GREGÓRIO   BRA   Belém   20 May 2007
Asi   17.59   LI Yanxi   CHN   Jinan   26 Oct 2009
Oce   17.46   Ken LORRAWAY   AUS   London (CP)   7 Aug 1982
W20   17.50   Volker MAI   GDR/GER Erfurt   23 Jun 1985
W18   17.41   Jordan A. DIAZ   CUB   La Habana   8 Jun 2018

SHOT
W, NAm   23.12   Randy BARNES   USA   Los Angeles (Westwood) 20 May 1990
Eur   23.06   Ulf TIMMERMANN   GDR/GER Haniá   22 May 1988
Oce, Com 22.90   Tom WALSH   NZL   Doha   5 Oct 2019
SAm   22.61   Darlan ROMANI   BRA   Stanford   30 Jun 2019
Afr   21.97   Janus ROBBERTS   RSA   Eugene   2 Jun 2001
CAC   21.96   O'Dayne RICHARDS   JAM   Rabat   16 Jul 2017
Asi   21.13   Sultan Abdulmajeed AL-HEBSHI   KSA   Doha   8 May 2009
W20   21.14   Konrad BUKOWIECKI   POL   Oslo   9 Jun 2016
W18   20.38   Jacko GILL   NZL   Auckland (North Shore) 5 Dec 2011
W20 6kg   23.00   Jacko GILL   NZL   Auckland (North Shore) 18 Aug 2013
W18 5kg   24.45   Jacko GILL   NZL   Auckland (North Shore) 19 Dec 2011

DISCUS
W, Eur   74.08   Jürgen SCHULT   GDR/GER Neubrandenburg   6 Jun 1986
NAm   72.34 ¶   Ben PLUCKNETT   USA   Stockholm   7 Jul 1981
          71.32 §   Ben PLUCKNETT   USA   Eugene   4 Jun 1983
CAC   71.06   Luis DELIS   CUB   La Habana   21 May 1983
Com   70.78   Fedric DACRES   JAM   Rabat   16 Jun 2019

WORLD AND CONTINENTAL RECORDS 175

Afr	70.32	Frantz KRUGER	RSA	Salon-de-Provence	26 May 2002
SAm	70.29	Mauricio ORTEGA	COL	Lovelhe	22 Jul 2020
Asi	69.32	Ehsan HADADI	IRI	Tallinn	3 Jun 2008
Oce	68.20	Benn HARRADINE	AUS	Townsville	10 May 2013
W20	65.62 §	Werner REITERER	AUS	Melbourne	15 Dec 1987
W18/20	65.31	Mykyta NESTERENKO	UKR	Tallinn	3 Jun 2008
W20 1.75kg	70.13	Mykyta NESTERENKO	UKR	Halle	24 May 2008
W18 1.5kg	77.50	Mykyta NESTERENKO	UKR	Koncha Zaspa	19 May 2008

¶ Disallowed by the IAAF following retrospective disqualification for drug abuse, but ratified by the AAU/TAC

HAMMER

W, Eur	86.74	Yuriy SEDYKH	UKR/RUS	Stuttgart	30 Aug 1986
Asi	84.86	Koji MUROFUSHI	JPN	Praha	29 Jun 2003
NAm	82.52	Lance DEAL	USA	Milano	7 Sep 1996
Afr	81.27	Mostafa Hicham AL-GAMAL	EGY	Al-Qáhira	21 Mar 2014
Com	80.63	Chris HARMSE	RSA	Durban	15 Apr 2005
Oce	79.29	Stuart RENDELL	AUS	Varazdin	6 Jul 2002
SAm	78.63	Wagner DOMINGOS	BRA	Celje	19 Jun 2016
CAC	78.02	Roberto JANET	CUB	La Habana	28 May 2015
W20	78.33	Olli-Pekka KARJALAINEN	FIN	Seinäjoki	5 Aug 1999
W18	73.66	Vladislav PISKUNOV	UKR	Kyiv	11 Jun 1994
W20 6kg	85.57	Ashraf Amgad EL-SEIFY	QAT	Barcelona	14 Jul 2012
W18 5kg	87.82	Myhaylo KOKHAN	UKR	Györ	7 Jul 2018

JAVELIN

W, Eur	98.48	Jan ZELEZNY	CZE	Jena	25 May 1996
Afr, Com	92.72	Julius YEGO	KEN	Beijing	26 Aug 2015
Asi	91.36	CHENG Chao-Tsun	TPE	Taipei	26 Aug 2017
NAm	91.29	Breaux GREER	USA	Indianapolis	21 Jun 2007
CAC	90.16	Keshorn WALCOTT	TTO	Lausanne	9 Jul 2015
Oce	89.02	Jarrod BANNISTER	AUS	Brisbane	29 Feb 2008
SAm	84.70	Edgar BAUMANN	PAR	San Marcos	17 Oct 1999
W20	86.48	Neeraj CHOPRA	IND	Bydgoszcz	23 Jul 2016
W18 700g	89.34	Braian Ezequiel TOLEDO	ARG	Mar del Plata	6 Mar 2010

DECATHLON

W, Eur	9126	Kevin MAYER	FRA	Talence	16 Sep 2018
NAm	9045	Ashton EATON	USA	Beijing	29 Aug 2015
Com	8847	Daley THOMPSON	GBR/Eng	Los Angeles	9 Aug 1984
Asi	8725	Dmitriy KARPOV	KAZ	Athína	24 Aug 2004
CAC	8654	Leonel SUÁREZ	CUB	La Habana	4 Jul 2009
Afr	8521	Larbi BOURAADA	ALG	Rio de Janeiro	18 Aug 2016
Oce	8492	Ashley MOLONEY	AUS	Brisbane	20 Dec 2020
SAm	8393	Carlos Eduardo CHININ	BRA	São Paulo	8 Jun 2013
W20 Jnr spec	8435	Niklas KAUL	GER	Grosseto	23 Jul 2017
Snr spec	8397	Torsten VOSS	GDR	Erfurt	7 Jul 1982
W18	8104h	Valter KÜLVET	EST	Viimsi	23 Aug 1981
	7829	Valter KÜLVET	EST	Stockholm	13 Sep 1981

4 X 100 METRES RELAY

W, CAC, Com	36.84	JAM (Carter, M Frater, Blake, Bolt)	London (OS)	11 Aug 2012
NAm	37.10	USA (Coleman, Gatlin, Rodgers, N Lyles)	Doha	5 Oct 2019
Eur	37.36	GBR (Gemili, Hughes, Kilty, Mitchell-Blake)	Doha	5 Oct 2019
Asi	37.43	JPN (Tada, Shiraishi, Kiryu, Sani-Brown)	Doha	5 Oct 2019
Afr	37.65	RSA (Dlodlo, Magakwe, Munyai, Simbine)	Doha	4 Oct 2019
SAm	37.72	BRA (R do Nascimento, V dos Santos, D Silva, P de Oliveira)	Doha	5 Oct 2019
Oce	38.17	AUS (Henderson, Jackson, Brimacombe, Marsh)	Göteborg	12 Aug 1995
	38.17	AUS (Alozie, Ntiamoah, McCabe, Ross)	London (OS)	10 Aug 2012
W20	38.62A	USA (A Smith, Ofotan, M Moore, Boling)	San José, CRC	20 Jul 2019
W18	39.97	JAM (Everett, Wilson, Powell, Stephens)	Willemstad	16 Apr 2017

4 X 400 METRES RELAY

W, NAm	2:54.29	USA (Valmon, Watts, Reynolds, Johnson)	Stuttgart	22 Aug 1993
Eur	2:56.60	GBR (Thomas, Baulch, Richardson, Black)	Atlanta	3 Aug 1996
CAC, Com	2:56.72	BAH (Brown, Pinder, Mathieu, Miller)	London (OS)	10 Aug 2012
SAm	2:58.56	BRA (C da Silva, A J dos Santos, de Araújo, Parrela)	Winnipeg	30 Jul 1999
Afr	2:58.68	NGR (Chukwu, Monye, Bada, Udo-Obong)	Sydney	30 Sep 2000
Oce	2:59.70	AUS (Frayne, Clark, Minihan, Mitchell)	Los Angeles	11 Aug 1984
Asi	3:00.56	QAT (Samba, Abbas, El Nour, Haroun)	Jakarta	30 Aug 2018
W20	2:59.30A	USA (F Lewis, Boling, Moorer, J Robinson)	San José, CRC	21 Jul 2019
W18	3:11.66A	TTO (Guevara, Cedenio, Walters, Lewis)	Morelia	1 Jul 2012

WORLD AND CONTINENTAL RECORDS

20 KILOMETRES WALK
W, Asi	1:16:36	Yusuke SUZUKI	JPN	Nomi	15 Mar 2015
Eur	1:17:02	Yohann DINIZ	FRA	Arles	8 Mar 2015
	1:16:43 §	Sergey MOROZOV	RUS	Saransk	8 Jun 2008
SAm	1:17:21	Jefferson PÉREZ	ECU	Saint-Denis	23 Aug 2003
CAC	1:17:46	Julio MARTIÑEZ	GUA	Eisenhüttenstadt	8 May 1999
Oce, Com	1:17:33	Nathan DEAKES	AUS	Cixi	23 Apr 2005
Afr	1:19:02	Hatem GHOULA	TUN	Eisenhüttenstadt	10 May 1997
NAm	1:19:20	Inaki GÓMEZ	CAN	Nomi	20 Mar 2016
W20	1:17:25 §	Sergey SHIROBOKOV	RUS	Cheboksary	9 Jun 2018
W18	1:18:07	LI Gaobo	CHN	Cixi	23 Apr 2005

20,000 METRES TRACK WALK
W, CAC	1:17:25.6	Bernardo SEGURA	MEX	Bergen (Fana)	7 May 1994
Asi	1:18:03.3	BU Lingtang	CHN	Beijing	7 Apr 1994
Eur	1:18:35.2	Stefan JOHANSSON	SWE	Bergen (Fana)	15 May 1992
Oce, Com	1:19:48.1	Nathan DEAKES	AUS	Brisbane	4 Sep 2001
SAm	1:20:23.8	Andrés CHOCHO	ECU	Buenos Aires	5 Jun 2011
NAm	1:21:57.0	Evan DUNFEE	CAN	Moncton	27 Jun 2014
Afr	1:22:51.84	Hatem GHOULA	TUN	Leutkirch	8 Sep 1994
W20	1:20:11.72	LI Gaobo	CHN	Wuhan	2 Nov 2007
W18	1:24:28.3	ZHU Hongjun	CHN	Xian	15 Sep 1999

50 KILOMETRES WALK
W, Eur	3:32:33	Yohann DINIZ	FRA	Zürich	15 Aug 2014
Oce, Com	3:35:47	Nathan DEAKES	AUS	Geelong	2 Dec 2006
Asi	3:36:06	YU Chaohong	CHN	Nanjing	22 Oct 2005
CAC	3:41:09	Erick BARRONDO	GUA	Dudince	23 Mar 2013
NAm	3:41:38	Evan DUNFEE	CAN	Rio de Janeiro	19 Aug 2016
SAm	3:42:57	Andrés CHOCHO	ECU	Ciudad Juárez	6 Mar 2016
Afr	3:53:09	Marc MUNDELL	RSA	Dudince	20 Mar 2021
W20	3:41:10	ZHAO Jianguo	CHN	Wajima	16 Apr 2006
W18	3:45:46	YU Guoping	CHN	Guangzhou	23 Nov 2001

50,000 METRES TRACK WALK
W, Eur	3:35:27.2	Yoahnn DINIZ	FRA	Reims	12 Mar 2011
CAC	3:41:38.4	Raúl GONZÁLEZ	MEX	Bergen (Fana)	25 May 1979
Oce, Com	3:43:50.0	Simon BAKER	AUS	Melbourne	9 Sep 1990
Asi	3:48:13.7	ZHAO Yongshen	CHN	Bergen (Fana)	7 May 1994
NAm	3:52:21.0	Tim BERRETT	CAN	Victoria	29 Oct 2000
SAm	3:57:58.0	Claudio dos SANTOS	BRA	Blumenau	20 Sep 2008
Afr	4:21:44.2	Abdelwahab FERGUÈNE	ALG	Toulouse	25 Mar 1984

World Records at other men's events recognised by World Atletics
1 Hour	21,330 m	Mo FARAH	GBR	Bruxelles	4 Sep 2020
4 x 200m	1:18.63	National team	JAM	Nassau	24 May 2014
		(Nickel Ashmeade, Warren Weir, Jermaine Brown, Yohan Blake)			
4 x 800m	7:02.43	National Team	KEN	Bruxelles	25 Aug 2006
		(Joseph Mutua, William Yiampoy, Ismael Kombich, Wilfred Bungei)			
4 x 1500m	14:22.22	C Cheboi, A Kiplagat, Magut, A Kiprop	KEN	Nassau	25 May 2014
Distance Medley	9:15.50	Merber,Spratling,Johnson,Blankenship	USA	Nassau	3 May 2015

Walking
30km track	2:01:44.1	Maurizio DAMILANO	ITA	Cuneo	3 Oct 1992
U20 10,000m track	38:46.4	Viktor BURAYEV	RUS	Moskva	20 May 2000
U20 10km road	37:44	WANG Zhen	CHN	Beijing	18 Sep 2010

WOMEN

100 METRES
W, NAm	10.49	Florence GRIFFITH JOYNER	USA	Indianapolis	16 Jul 1988
CAC, Com	10.70	Shelly-Ann FRASER	JAM	Kingston	29 Jun 2012
	10.70	Elaine THOMPSON	JAM	Kingston	1 Jul 2016
Eur	10.73	Christine ARRON	FRA	Budapest	19 Aug 1998
Afr	10.78	Murielle AHOURÉ	CIV	Montverde	11 Jun 2016
Asi	10.79	LI Xuemei	CHN	Shanghai	18 Oct 1997
SAm	10.91	Rosângela SANTOS	BRA	London (OS)	6 Aug 2017
Oce	11.11	Melissa BREEN	AUS	Canberra	9 Feb 2014
W20	10.75	Sha'Carri RICHARDSON	USA	Austin	8 Jun 2019
W18	10.94	Briana WILLIAMS	JAM	Kingston	21 Jun 2019

WORLD AND CONTINENTAL RECORDS 177

200 METRES
W, NAm	21.34	Florence GRIFFITH JOYNER	USA	Seoul	29 Sep 1988
Eur	21.63	Dafne SCHIPPERS	NED	Beijing	28 Aug 2015
CAC, Com	21.64	Merlene OTTEY	JAM	Bruxelles	13 Sep 1991
Asi	22.01	LI Xuemei	CHN	Shanghai	22 Oct 1997
Afr	22.04	Blessing OKAGBARE	NGR	Abilene	24 Mar 2018
Oce	22.23	Melinda GAINSFORD-TAYLOR	AUS	Stuttgart	13 Jul 1997
SAm	22.48	Ana Cláudia da SILVA	BRA	São Paulo	6 Aug 2011
W20	22.17	Sha'Carri RICHARDSON	USA	Austin	8 Jun 2019
	22.11A §	Allyson FELIX (no doping control)	USA	Ciudad de México	3 May 2003
W18	22.42	Amy HUNT	GBR	Mannheim	30 Jun 2019

400 METRES
W, Eur	47.60	Marita KOCH	GDR	Canberra	6 Oct 1985
Asi	48.14	Salwa Eid NASER	BRN	Doha	3 Oct 2019
CAC, Com	48.37	Shaunae MILLER-UIBO	BAH	Doha	3 Oct 2019
Oce,	48.63	Cathy FREEMAN	AUS	Atlanta	29 Jul 1996
NAm	48.70	Sanya RICHARDS	USA	Athína	16 Sep 2006
Afr	49.10	Falilat OGUNKOYA	NGR	Atlanta	29 Jul 1996
SAm	49.64	Ximena RESTREPO	COL	Barcelona	5 Aug 1992
W20	49.42	Grit BREUER	GER	Tokyo	27 Aug 1991
W18	50.01	LI Jing	CHN	Shanghai	18 Oct 1997

800 METRES
W, Eur	1:53.28	Jarmila KRATOCHVÍLOVÁ	CZE	München	26 Jul 1983
Afr,W20,Com	1:54.01	Pamela JELIMO	KEN	Zürich	29 Aug 2008
CAC	1:54.44	Ana Fidelia QUIROT	CUB	Barcelona	9 Sep 1989
Asi	1:55.54	LIU Dong	CHN	Beijing	9 Sep 1993
NAm	1:55.61	Ajee' WILSON	USA	Monaco	21 Jul 2017
SAm	1:56.68	Letitia VRIESDE	SUR	Göteborg	13 Aug 1995
Oce	1:58.25	Toni HODGKINSON	NZL	Atlanta	27 Jul 1996
W18	1:57.18	WANG Yuan	CHN	Beijing	8 Sep 1993

1000 METRES
W, Eur	2:28.98	Svetlana MASTERKOVA	RUS	Bruxelles	23 Aug 1996
Afr, Com	2:29.15	Faith KIPYEGON	KEN	Monaco	14 Aug 2020
NAm	2:31.80	Regina JACOBS	USA	Brunswick	3 Jul 1999
SAm	2:32.25	Letitia VRIESDE	SUR	Berlin	10 Sep 1991
CAC	2:33.21	Ana Fidelia QUIROT	CUB	Jerez de la Frontera	13 Sep 1989
Asi	2:33.6 §	Svetlana ULMASOVA	UZB	Podolsk	5 Aug 1979
	2:40.53	ZHAO Jing	CHN	Changbaishan	2 Sep 2014
Oce	2:35.90	Linden HALL	AUS	Melbourne	2 Mar 2021
W20	2:35.4a	Irina NIKITINA	RUS	Podolsk	5 Aug 1979
	2:35.4	Katrin WÜHN	GDR	Potsdam	12 Jul 1984
W18	2:38.58	Jo WHITE	GBR	London (CP)	9 Sep 1977

1500 METRES
W, Afr	3:50.07	Genzebe DIBABA	ETH	Monaco	17 Jul 2015
Asi	3:50.46	QU Yunxia	CHN	Beijing	11 Sep 1993
Eur	3:51.95	Sifan HASSAN	NED	Doha	5 Oct 2019
Com	3:54.22	Faith KIPYEGON	KEN	Doha	5 Oct 2019
NAm	3:54.99	Shelby HOULIHAN	USA	Doha	5 Oct 2019
Oce	4:00.42	Jessica HULL	AUS	Berlin	13 Sep 2020
CAC	4:01.84	Yvonne GRAHAM	JAM	Monaco	25 Jul 1995
SAm	4:05.67	Letitia VRIESDE	SUR	Tokyo	31 Aug 1991
W20	3:51.34	LANG Yinglai	CHN	Shanghai	18 Oct 1997
W18	3:54.52	ZHANG Ling	CHN	Shanghai	18 Oct 1997

1 MILE
W, Eur	4:12.33	Sifan HASSAN	NED	Monaco	12 Jul 2019
Afr	4:14.30	Genzebe DIBABA	ETH	Rovereto	6 Sep 2016
	4:13.31i	Genzebe DIBABA	ETH	Stockholm	17 Feb 2016
Com	4:16.15	Hellen OBIRI	KEN	London (OS)	22 Jul 2018
NAm	4:16.71	Mary SLANEY	USA	Zürich	21 Aug 1985
Asi	4:17.75	Maryam Yusuf JAMAL	BRN	Bruxelles	14 Sep 2007
Oce	4:21.40	Linden HALL	AUS	London (OS)	22 Jul 2018
CAC	4:24.64	Yvonne GRAHAM	JAM	Zürich	17 Aug 1994
SAm	4:30.05	Soraya TELLES	BRA	Bratislava	9 Jun 1988
W20	4:17.57	Zola BUDD	GBR	Zürich	21 Aug 1985
W18	4:30.81	Gelete BURKA	ETH	Heusden	2 Aug 2003

2000 METRES

W, Afr ind	5:23.75i	Genzebe DIBABA	ETH	Sabadell	7 Feb 2017
W, Eur	5:25.36	Sonia O'SULLIVAN	IRL	Edinburgh	8 Jul 1994
Com	5:26.93	Yvonne MURRAY	GBR/Sco	Edinburgh	8 Jul 1994
Afr	5:27.50	Genzebe DIBABA	ETH	Ostrava	17 Jun 2014
Asi	5:29.43+§	WANG Junxia	CHN	Beijing	12 Sep 1993
	5:31.88	Maryam Yusuf JAMAL	BRN	Eugene	7 Jun 2009
NAm	5:32.7	Mary SLANEY	USA	Eugene	3 Aug 1984
Oce	5:37.71	Benita JOHNSON	AUS	Ostrava	12 Jun 2003
W20	5:33.15	Zola BUDD	GBR	London (CP)	13 Jul 1984
W18	5:46.5+	Sally BARSOSIO	KEN	Zürich	16 Aug 1995

3000 METRES

W, Asi	8:06.11	WANG Junxia	CHN	Beijing	13 Sep 1993
Eur	8:18.49	Sifan HASSAN	NED	Stanford	30 Jun 2019
Afr	8:20.27	Letesenbet GIDEY	ETH	Stanford	30 Jun 2019
Com	8:20.68	Hellen OBIRI	KEN	Doha	9 May 2014
NAm	8:25.83	Mary SLANEY	USA	Roma	7 Sep 1985
Oce	8:35.31	Kimberley SMITH	NZL	Monaco	25 Jul 2007
CAC	8:37.07	Yvonne GRAHAM	JAM	Zürich	16 Aug 1995
SAm	9:02.37	Delirde BERNARDI	BRA	Linz	4 Jul 1994
W20	8:28.83	Zola BUDD	GBR	Roma	7 Sep 1985
W18	8:36.45	MA Ningning	CHN	Jinan	6 Jun 1993

5000 METRES

W, Afr	14:06.62	Letesenbet GIDEY	ETH	Valencia	7 Oct 2020
Com	14:18.37	Hellen OBIRI	KEN	Roma	8 Jun 2017
Eur	14:22.12	Sifan HASSAN	NED	London (OS)	21 Jul 2019
NAm	14:23.92	Shelby HOULIHAN	USA	Portland	10 Jul 2020
Asi	14:28.09	JIANG Bo	CHN	Shanghai	23 Oct 1997
Oce	14:43.80	Jessica HULL	AUS	Monaco	14 Aug 2020
CAC	15:04.32	Adriana FERNÁNDEZ	MEX	Gresham	17 May 2003
SAm	15:18.85	Simone Alves da SILVA	BRA	São Paulo	20 May 2011
W20	14:30.88	Tirunesh DIBABA	ETH	Bergen (Fana)	11 Jun 2004
W18	14:45.71	SONG Liqing	CHN	Shanghai	21 Oct 1997

10,000 METRES

W, Afr	29:17.45	Almaz AYANA	ETH	Rio de Janeiro	12 Aug 2016
Asi	29:31.78	WANG Junxia	CHN	Beijing	8 Sep 1993
Com	29:32.53	Vivian CHERUIYOT	KEN	Rio de Janeiro	12 Aug 2016
Eur	29:36.67	Sifan HASSAN	NED	Hengelo	10 Oct 2020
NAm	30:13.17	Molly HUDDLE	USA	Rio de Janeiro	12 Aug 2016
Oce	30:35.54	Kimberley SMITH	NZL	Stanford	4 May 2008
CAC	31:10.12	Adriana FERNANDEZ	MEX	Brunswick	1 Jul 2000
SAm	31:47.76	Carmen de OLIVEIRA	BRA	Stuttgart	21 Aug 1993
W20	30:26.50	Linet MASAI	KEN	Beijing	15 Aug 2008
W18	31:11.26	SONG Liqing	CHN	Shanghai	19 Oct 1997

HALF MARATHON

W, Afr	64:31	Ababel YESHANEH	ETH	Ras Al Khaimah	21 Feb 2020
	64:28 dh	Brigid KOSGEI	KEN	South Shields	8 Sep 2019
W Women only	65:16	Peres JEPCHIRCHIR	KEN	Gdynia	17 Oct 2020
Com	64:51	Joyciline JEPKOSGEI	KEN	Valencia	22 Oct 2017
Eur	65:15	Sifan HASSAN	NED	København	16 Sep 2018
Asi	65:22	Violah JEPCHUMBA	BRN	Praha	1 Apr 2017
Oce	67:11	Kimberley SMITH	NZL	Philadelphia	18 Sep 2011
NAm	67:25	Molly HUDDLE	USA	Houston	14 Jan 2018
CAC	68:34 dh	Olga APPELL	MEX	Tokyo	24 Jan 1993
	69:28	Adriana FERNÁNDEZ	MEX	Kyoto	9 Mar 2003
SAm	70:14	Gladys TEJEDA	PER	Cardiff	26 Mar 2016
W20	66:47	Degitu AZIMERAW	ETH	Ras Al Khaimah	9 Feb 2018
W18	72:31	LIU Zhuang	CHN	Yangzhou	24 Apr 2011

MARATHON

W, Com	2:14:04	Brigid KOSGEI	KEN	Chicago	13 Oct 2019
Wo only	2:17:01	Mary KEITANY	KEN	London	23 Apr 2017
Eur	2:15:25	Paula RADCLIFFE	GBR/Eng	London	13 Apr 2003
Asi	2:19:12	Mizuki NOGUCHI	JPN	Berlin	25 Sep 2005
NAm	2:19:36	Deena KASTOR	USA	London	23 Apr 2006
Oce	2:22:36	Benita JOHNSON	AUS	Chicago	22 Oct 2006

WORLD AND CONTINENTAL RECORDS

CAC	2:22:59	Madai PÉREZ	MEX	Chicago		22 Oct 2006
SAm	2:26:48	Inés MELCHOR	PER	Berlin		28 Sep 2014
W20	2:20:59	Shure DEMISE	ETH	Dubai		23 Jan 2015

100 KILOMETRES

W, Asi	6:33:11	Tomoe ABE	JPN	Yubetsu		25 Jun 2000
NAm	7:00:48	Ann TRASON	USA	Winschoten		16 Sep 1995
Eur	7:04:36	Dominika STELMACH	POL	Pabianice		30 Aug 2020
SAm	7:20:22	Maria VENÂNCIO	BRA	Cubatão		8 Aug 1998
Afr	7:31:47	Helena JOUBERT	RSA	Winschoten		16 Sep 1995
Oce	7:34:35	Kirstin BULL	AUS	Los Alcazares		27 Nov 2016
CAC	8:33:43	Marina VALENCIA	MEX	Monterrey		14 Oct 2007

3000 METRES STEEPLECHASE

W, Afr, Com	8:44.32	Beatrice CHEPKOECH	KEN	Monaco		20 Jul 2018
Asi	8:52.78	Ruth JEBET	BRN	Saint-Denis		27 Aug 2016
Eur	8:58.81	Gulnara GALKINA	RUS	Beijing		17 Aug 2008
NAm	9:00.85	Courtney FRERICHS	USA	Monaco		20 Jul 2018
CAC	9:14.09	Aisha PRAUGHT LEER	JAM	Bruxelles		31 Aug 2018
Oce	9:14.28	Genevieve LaCAZE	AUS	Saint-Denis		27 Aug 2016
SAm	9:25.99	Belén CASETTA	ARG	London (OS)		11 Aug 2017
W20	8:58.78	Celliphine CHESPOL	KEN	Eugene		26 May 2017
W18	9:24.73	Celliphine CHESPOL	KEN	Shanghai		14 May 2016

100 METRES HURDLES

W, NAm	12.20	Kendra HARRISON	USA	London (OS)		22 Jul 2016
Eur	12.21	Yordanka DONKOVA	BUL	Stara Zagora		20 Aug 1988
Oce, Com	12.28	Sally PEARSON	AUS	Daegu		3 Sep 2011
CAC	12.32	Danielle WILLIAMS	JAM	London (OS)		20 Jul 2019
Asi	12.44	Olga SHISHIGINA	KAZ	Luzern		27 Jun 1995
Afr	12.44	Glory ALOZIE NGR Monaco 8 Aug 1998, Bruxelles 28 Aug 1998, Sevilla				28 Aug 1999
SAm	12.67	Yvette LEWIS	PAN	Lahti		17 Jul 2013
W20	12.71	Brittany ANDERSON	JAM	Joensuu		24 Jul 2019
W18	12.84	Tia JONES	USA	Clovis		25 Jun 2016

400 METRES HURDLES

W, NAm	52.16	Dalilah MUHAMMAD	USA	Doha		4 Oct 2019
Eur	52.34	Yuliya PECHONKINA	RUS	Tula		8 Aug 2003
CAC, Com	52.42	Melaine WALKER	JAM	Berlin		20 Aug 2009
Afr	52.90	Nezha BIDOUANE	MAR	Sevilla		25 Aug 1999
Oce	53.17	Debbie FLINTOFF-KING	AUS	Seoul		28 Sep 1988
Asi	53.96	HAN Qing	CHN	Beijing		9 Sep 1993
	53.96	SONG Yinglan	CHN	Guangzhou		22 Nov 2001
SAm	55.60	Gianna WOODRUFF	PAN	Barranquilla		31 Jul 2018
W20	52.75	Sydney McLAUGHLIN	USA	Knoxville		13 May 2018
W18	54.15	Sydney McLAUGHLIN	USA	Eugene		10 Jul 2016

HIGH JUMP

W, Eur	2.09	Stefka KOSTADINOVA	BUL	Roma		30 Aug 1987
Afr, Com	2.06	Hestrie CLOETE	RSA	Saint-Denis		31 Aug 2003
NAm	2.05	Chaunté HOWARD-LOWE	USA	Des Moines		26 Jun 2010
CAC	2.04	Silvia COSTA	CUB	Barcelona		9 Sep 1989
Asi	1.99	Marina AITOVA	KAZ	Athína		13 Jul 2009
Oce	1.99	Eleanor PATTERSON	AUS	Wellington		28 Feb 2020
SAm	1.96	Solange WITTEVEEN	ARG	Oristano		8 Sep 1997
W20	2.04	Yaroslava MAHUCHIKH	UKR	Doha		30 Sep 2019
W18	1.96A	Charmaine GALE	RSA	Bloemfontein		4 Apr 1981
	1.96	Olga TURCHAK	UKR	Donetsk		7 Sep 1984
	1.96	Eleanor PATTERSON	AUS	Townsville		7 Dec 2013
	1.96	Vashti CUNNINGHAM	USA	Edmonton		1 Aug 2015

POLE VAULT

W, Eur	5.06	Yelena ISINBAYEVA	RUS	Zürich		28 Aug 2009
NAm	5.03i	Jennifer SUHR	USA	Brockport		30 Jan 2016
	5.00	Sandi MORRIS	USA	Bruxelles		9 Sep 2016
Com, Oce	4.94	Eliza McCARTNEY	NZL	Jockgrim		17 Jul 2018
CAC	4.91	Yarisley SILVA	CUB	Beckum		2 Aug 2015
SAm	4.87	Fabiana MURER	BRA	São Bernardo do Campo		3 Jul 2016
Asi	4.72	LI Ling	CHN	Shanghai		18 May 2019
Afr	4.42	Elmarie GERRYTS	RSA	Wesel		12 Jun 2000

WORLD AND CONTINENTAL RECORDS

W20	4.71i	Wilma MURTO		FIN	Zweibrucken	31 Jan 2016
	4.64	Eliza McCARTNEY		NZL	Auckland	19 Dec 2015
W18	4.50	Lisa GUNNARSSON	SWE	Pézenas 28 May 2016 & Angers 25 Jun 2016		

LONG JUMP

W, Eur	7.52	Galina CHISTYAKOVA		RUS	Leningrad	11 Jun 1988
NAm	7.49	Jackie JOYNER-KERSEE		USA	New York	22 May 1994
	7.49A §	Jackie JOYNER-KERSEE		USA	Sestriere	31 Jul 1994
SAm	7.26A	Maurren MAGGI		BRA	Bogotá	26 Jun 1999
CAC, Com	7.16A	Elva GOULBOURNE		JAM	Ciudad de México	22 May 2004
Afr	7.12	Chioma AJUNWA		NGR	Atlanta	1 Aug 1996
Oce	7.05	Brooke STRATTON		AUS	Perth	12 Mar 2016
Asi	7.01	YAO Weili		CHN	Jinan	5 Jun 1993
W20	7.14	Heike DAUTE/Drechsler		GDR	Bratislava	4 Jun 1983
W18	6.91	Heike DAUTE/Drechsler		GDR	Jena	9 Aug 1981

TRIPLE JUMP

W, Eur	15.50	Inessa KRAVETS		UKR	Göteborg	10 Aug 1995
Afr, Com	15.39	Françoise MBANGO Etone		CMR	Beijing	17 Aug 2008
SAm	15.31	Caterine IBARGÜEN		COL	Monaco	18 Jul 2014
CAC	15.29	Yamilé ALDAMA		CUB	Roma	11 Jul 2003
Asi	15.25	Olga RYPAKOVA		KAZ	Split	4 Sep 2010
NAm	14.84	Tori FRANKLIN		USA	Baie Mahault	12 May 2018
Oce	14.04	Nicole MLADENIS		AUS	Hobart 9 Mar 2002 & Perth 7 Dec 2003	
W20	14.62	Tereza MARINOVA		BUL	Sydney	25 Aug 1996
W18	14.57	HUANG Qiuyan		CHN	Shanghai	19 Oct 1997

SHOT

W, Eur	22.63	Natalya LISOVSKAYA		RUS	Moskva	7 Jun 1987
Asi	21.76	LI Meisu		CHN	Shijiazhuang	23 Apr 1988
Oce, Com	21.24	Valerie ADAMS		NZL	Daegu	29 Aug 2011
CAC	20.96	Belsy LAZA		CUB	Ciudad de México	2 May 1992
NAm	20.63	Michelle CARTER		USA	Rio de Janeiro	12 Aug 2016
SAm	19.30	Elisângela ADRIANO		BRA	Tunja	14 Jul 2001
Afr	18.43	Vivian CHUKWUEMEKA		NGR	Walnut	19 Apr 2003
W20	20.54	Astrid KUMBERNUSS		GDR	Orimattila	1 Jul 1989
W18	19.08	Ilke WYLUDDA		GDR	Karl-Marx-Stadt	9 Aug 1986

DISCUS

W, Eur	76.80	Gabriele REINSCH		GDR	Neubrandenburg	9 Jul 1988
Asi	71.68	XIAO Yanling		CHN	Beijing	14 Mar 1992
CAC	70.88	Hilda RAMOS		CUB	La Habana	8 May 1992
NAm	70.15	Valerie ALLMAN		USA	Rathdrum	1 Aug 2020
Oce, Com	69.64	Dani STEVENS		AUS	London (OS)	13 Aug 2017
SAm	65.98	Andressa de MORAIS		BRA	Lima	6 Aug 2019
Afr	64.87	Elizna NAUDE		RSA	Stellenbosch	2 Mar 2007
W20	74.40	Ilke WYLUDDA		GDR	Berlin	13 Sep 1988
W18	65.86	Ilke WYLUDDA		GDR	Neubrandenburg	1 Aug 1986

HAMMER

W, Eur	82.98	Anita WLODARCZYK		POL	Warszawa	28 Aug 2016
NAm	78.24	DeAnna PRICE		USA	Des Moines	27 Jul 2019
Asi	77.68	WANG Zheng		CHN	Chengdu	29 Mar 2014
CAC	76.62	Yipsi MORENO		CUB	Zagreb	9 Sep 2008
Com	75.73	Sultana FRIZELL		CAN	Tucson	22 May 2014
SAm	73.74	Jennifer DAHLGREN		ARG	Buenos Aires	10 Apr 2010
Oce	73.47	Lauren BRUCE		NZL	Hastings	20 Sep 2020
Afr	69.70	Amy SÈNE		SEN	Forbach	25 May 2014
W20	73.24	ZHANG Wenxiu		CHN	Changsha	24 Jun 2005
W18	70.60	ZHANG Wenxiu		CHN	Nanning	5 Apr 2003
W18 3kg	76.04	Réka GYURÁTZ		HUN	Zalaegerszeg	23 Jun 2013

JAVELIN

W, Eur	72.28	Barbora SPOTÁKOVÁ		CZE	Stuttgart	13 Sep 2008
CAC	71.70	Osleidys MENÉNDEZ		CUB	Helsinki	14 Aug 2005
Afr, Com	69.35	Sunette VILJOEN		RSA	New York	9 Jun 2012
Oce	68.92	Kathryn MITCHELL		AUS	Gold Coast	11 Apr 2018
Asi	67.98	LU Huihui		CHN	Shenyang	2 Aug 2019
NAm	66.67	Kara PATTERSON		USA	Des Moines	25 Jun 2010
SAm	63.84A	Flor Dennis RUIZ		COL	Cali	25 Jun 2016

WORLD AND CONTINENTAL RECORDS   181

W20	63.96 §	Elina TZÉNGGO	GRE	Ioánnina	1 Aug 2020
	63.86	Yulenmis AGUILAR	CUB	Edmonton	2 Aug 2015
W18	62.93	XUE Juan	CHN	Changsha	27 Oct 2003
W18 500g	68.76	Adriana VILAGOS	SRB	Sremska Mitrovica	7 Mar 2020

HEPTATHLON

W, NAm	7291	Jackie JOYNER-KERSEE	USA	Seoul	24 Sep 1988
Eur	7032	Carolina KLÜFT	SWE	Osaka	26 Aug 2007
Com	6981	Katarina JOHNSON-THOMPSON	GBR/Eng	Doha	4 Oct 2019
Asi	6942	Ghada SHOUAA	SYR	Götzis	26 May 1996
CAC	6742	Yorgelis RODRIGUEZ	CUB	Götzis	27 May 2018
Oce	6695	Jane FLEMMING	AUS	Auckland	28 Jan 1990
Afr	6423	Margaret SIMPSON	GHA	Götzis	29 May 2005
SAm	6285	Evelis AGUILAR	COL	Barranquilla	1 Aug 2018
W20	6542	Carolina KLÜFT	SWE	München	10 Aug 2002
W18	6185	SHEN Shengfei	CHN	Shanghai	18 Oct 1997
U18 spec	6301	Henriette JÆGER	NOR	Moss	13 Sep 2020

DECATHLON

W, Eur	8358	Austra SKUJYTE	LTU	Columbia, MO	15 Apr 2005
Asi	7798 §	Irina NAUMENKO	KAZ	Talence	26 Sep 2004
NAm	7577 §	Tiffany LOTT-HOGAN	USA	Lage	10 Sep 2000
CAC	7245 §	Magalys GARCÍA	CUB	Wien	29 Jun 2002
Afr, Com	6915	Margaret SIMPSON	GHA	Réduit	19 Apr 2007
SAm	6570	Andrea BORDALEJO	ARG	Rosario	28 Nov 2004
Oce	6428	Simone CARRÉ	AUS	Melbourne	11 Mar 2012

4 X 100 METRES RELAY

W, NAm	40.82	USA (Madison, Felix, Knight, Jeter)	London (OS)	10 Aug 2012
CAC, Com	41.07	JAM (Campbell-Brown, Morrison, Thompson, Fraser-Pryce)	Beijing	29 Aug 2015
Eur	41.37	GDR (Gladisch, Rieger, Auerswald, Göhr)	Canberra	6 Oct 1985
Asi	42.23	Sichuan CHN (Xiao Lin, Li Yali, Liu Xiaomei, Li Xuemei)	Shanghai	23 Oct 1997
SAm	42.29	BRA (E dos Santos, Silva, Krasucki, R Santos)	Moskva	18 Aug 2013
Afr	42.39	NGR (Utondu, Idehen, Opara-Thompson, Onyali)	Barcelona	7 Aug 1992
Oce	42.99A	AUS (Massey, Broadrick, Lambert, Gainsford-Taylor)	Pietersburg	18 Mar 2000
W20	43.27	GER (Fehm, Kwadwo, Junk, Montag)	Grosseto	23 Jul 2017
W18	44.05	GDR (Koppetsch, Oelsner, Sinzel, Brehmer)	Athína	24 Aug 1975

4 X 400 METRES RELAY

W, Eur	3:15.17	URS (Ledovskaya, Nazarova, Pinigina, Bryzgina)	Seoul	1 Oct 1988
NAm	3:15.51	USA (D.Howard, Dixon, Brisco, Griffith Joyner)	Seoul	1 Oct 1988
CAC, Com	3:18.71	JAM (Whyte, Prendergast, N Williams-Mills, S Williams)	Daegu	3 Sep 2011
Afr	3:21.04	NGR (Bisi Afolabi, Yusuf, Opara, Ogunkoya)	Atlanta	3 Aug 1996
Oce	3:23.81	AUS (Peris, Lewis, Gainsford-Taylor, Freeman)	Sydney	30 Sep 2000
Asi	3:24.28	Hebei CHN (An X, Bai X, Cao C, Ma Y)	Beijing	13 Sep 1993
SAm	3:26.68	BRA (Coutinho, de Oliveira, Souza, de Lima)	São Paulo	7 Aug 2011
W20	3:24.04A	USA (Holmes, Harris, Hilman, Kayla Davis)	San José, CRC	21 Jul 2019
W18	3:36.98	GBR (Ravenscroft, E McMeekin, Kennedy, Pettett)	Duisburg	26 Aug 1973

10 KILOMETRES WALK   Not currently a World Athletics record event

W, Eur	41:04	Yelena NIKOLAYEVA	RUS	Sochi	20 Apr 1996
Asi	41:16	WANG Yan	CHN	Eisenhüttenstadt	8 May 1999
Oce, Com	41:30	Kerry SAXBY-JUNNA	AUS	Canberra	27 Aug 1988
CAC	42:42	Graciela MENDOZA	MEX	Naumburg	25 May 1997
SAm	43:03	Erica de SENA	BRA	Suzhou	25 Sep 2017
NAm	44:09+	Maria MICHTA-COFFEY	USA	St. Louis	3 Apr 2016
Afr	45:02	Chahinez NASRI	TUN	La Coruña	28 May 2016
W20	41:52 §	Tatyana MINEYEVA	RUS	Penza	5 Sep 2009
W18	43:28	Aleksandra KUDRYASHOVA	RUS	Adler	19 Feb 2006

10,000 METRES TRACK WALK

W, Asi	41:37.9 §	GAO Hongmiao	CHN	Beijing	7 Apr 1994
W, Eur	41:56.23	Nadyezhda RYASHKINA	RUS	Seattle	24 Jul 1990
Oce, Com	41:57.22	Kerry SAXBY-JUNNA	AUS	Seattle	24 Jul 1990
SAm	42:02.99	Sandra Lorena ARENAS	COL	Trujillo	25 Aug 2018
CAC	44:13.88	Alegna GONZÁLEZ	MEX	Tampere	14 Jul 2018
NAm	44:30.1 m	Alison BAKER	CAN	Bergen (Fana)	15 May 1992
	44:06 no kerb	Michelle ROHL	USA	Kenosha	2 Jun 1996
Afr	44:41.8A	Grace Njue WANJIRU	KEN	Thika	5 Mar 2016
W20	42:47.25	Anezka DRAHOTOVÁ	CZE	Eugene	23 Jul 2014
W18	42:56.09	GAO Hongmiao	CHN	Tangshan	27 Sep 1991

… WORLD AND CONTINENTAL RECORDS

20,000 METRES TRACK WALK
W, Eur	1:26:52.3	Olimpiada IVANOVA	RUS	Brisbane	6 Sep 2001
Asi, W20	1:29:32.4 §	SONG Hongjuan	CHN	Changsha	24 Oct 2003
SAm	1:31:02.25	Sandra Lorena ARENAS	COL	Lima	13 Jun 2015
CAC	1:31:53.8A	Mirna ORTIZ	GUA	Ciudad de Guatemala	9 Aug 2014
NAm, Com	1:32:54.0	Rachel SEAMAN	CAN	Moncton	27 Jun 2014
Oce	1:33:40.2	Kerry SAXBY-JUNNA	AUS	Brisbane	6 Sep 2001
Afr	1:36:18.22	Nicolene CRONJE	RSA	Durban	17 Apr 2004
W18	1:34:21.56	WANG Xue	CHN	Wuhan	1 Nov 2007

20 KILOMETRES WALK
W, Eur	1:23:39 §	Yelena LASHMANOVA	RUS	Cheboksary	9 Jun 2018
W, Asi	1:23:49	YANG Jiayu	CHN	Huangshan	20 Mar 2021
Eur	1:25:02	Yelena LASHMANOVA	RUS	London	11 Aug 2012
SAm, W20	1:25:29	Glenda MOREJÓN	ECU	La Coruña	8 Jun 2019
CAC	1:26:17	María Guadeloupe GONZÁLEZ	MEX	Roma	7 May 2016
Oce, Com	1:27:44	Jane SAVILLE	AUS	Naumburg	2 May 2004
NAm	1:29:54	Rachel SEAMAN	CAN	Nomi	15 Mar 2015
Afr	1:30:40A	Grace Njue WANJIRU	KEN	Nairobi	6 Jun 2016
W18	1:30:35	ZHOU Tongmei	CHN	Cixi	23 Apr 2005

50 KILOMETRES WALK
W, Eur	3:50:42	Yelena LASHMANOVA	RUS	Voronovskoye	5 Sep 2020
W, Asi	3:59:15	LIU Hong	CHN	Huangshan	9 Mar 2019
Eur	4:04:50	Eleonora GIORGI	ITA	Alytus	19 May 2019
Oce, Com	4:09:33	Claire TALLENT	AUS	Taicang	5 May 2018
SAm	4:11:12	Johana ORDÓÑEZ	ECU	Lima	11 Aug 2019
CAC	4:13:56A	Mirna ORTIZ	GUA	Ciudad de Guatemala	24 Feb 2019
NAm	4:21:51	Kathleen BURNETT	USA	London	13 Aug 2017
Afr	4:48:00	Natalie le ROUX	RSA	Taicang	5 May 2018

World Records at other track & field events recognised by the IAAF
1 Hour	18,930 m	Sifan HASSAN	NED	Bruxelles	4 Sep 2020
4x200m	1:27.46	L Jenkins, L Colander, N Perry, M Jones	USA	Philadelphia	29 Apr 2000
4x800m	7:50.17	Olizarenko, Gurina, Borisova, Podyalovskaya	USSR	Moskva	5 Aug 1984
4x1500m	16:27.02	Quigley, Cranny, Schweizer, Houlihan	USA	Portland	31 Jul 2020
50,000m track walk	4:34:46.5	Erin TAYLOR-TALCOTT	USA	Banks	9 Mar 2014

MIXED 4 X 400 METRES RELAY
W, NAm	3:09.34	USA (London, Felix, Okolo, Cherry)	Doha	29 Sep 2019
CAC, Com	3:11.78	JAM (Allen, McGregor, James, Francis)	Doha	29 Sep 2019
Asi	3:11.82	BRN (Isah, Jamal, Naser, Abubakar)	Doha	29 Sep 2019
Eur	3:12.27	GBR (Yousif, Clark, Diamond, Rooney)	Doha	29 Sep 2019
SAm	3:16.12	BRA (Henriques, T Silva, Coutinho, L Carvalho)	Doha	28 Sep 2019
Afr	3:16.90	KEN (Momanyi, Thomas, Syombua, A Koech)	Yokohama	11 May 2019
Oce	3:18.55	AUS (Solomon, Goodwin, Rubie, Connolly)	Ostrava	9 Sep 2018

WORLD BESTS AT NON-STANDARD EVENTS
Men
50m	5.47+e	Usain Bolt	JAM	Berlin (in 100m)	16 Aug 2009
60m	6.31+	Usain Bolt	JAM	Berlin (in 100m)	16 Aug 2009
100 yards	9.07	Asafa Powell	JAM	Ostrava	27 May 2010
150m turn	14.44+	Usain Bolt	JAM	Berlin (in 200m)	20 Aug 2009
150m straight	14.35	Usain Bolt	JAM	Manchester	17 May 2009
300m	30.81	Wayde van Niekerk	RSA	Ostrava	28 Jun 2017
500m	59.32	Orestes Rodriguez	CUB	La Habana	15 Feb 2013
600m	1:12.81	Johnny Gray	USA	Santa Monica	24 May 1986
2 miles	7:58.61	Daniel Komen	KEN	Hechtel	19 Jul 1997
2000m Steeple	5:10.68	Mahiedine Mekhissi	FRA	Reims	30 Jun 2010
200mh	22.55	Laurent Ottoz	ITA	Milano	31 May 1995
	22.55	Yoshiro Watanabe	JPN	Izumi	1 Oct 2017
200mh straight	22.10	Andrew Turner	GBR	Manchester	15 May 2011
	22.10	L.J. van Zyl	RSA	Manchester	9 May 2015
220yh straight	21.9	Don Styron	USA	Baton Rouge	2 Apr 1960
300mh	33.78	Karsten Warholm	NOR	Oslo	11 Jun 2020
35lb weight	25.41	Lance Deal	USA	Azusa	20 Feb 1993
Pentathlon (1985 tables)	4282 points	Bill Toomey (7.58, 66.18, 21.3, 44.53, 4:20.3)	USA	London (CP)	16 Aug 1969
Double decathlon	14,571	Joe Detmer	USA	Lynchburg	24/25 Sep 2010

10.93w, 7.30, 200mh 24.25w, 12.27, 5k 18:25.32, 2:02.23, 1.98, 400m 50.43, HT 31.82, 3kSt 11:22.47
15.01, DT 40.73, 200m 22.58, 4.85, 3k 10:25.99, 400mh 53.83, 51.95, 4:26.66, TJ 13.67, 10k 40:27.26

WORLD AND CONTINENTAL RECORDS

U18 Octathlon	6491	Jake Stein	AUS	Villeneuve d'Ascq	7 Jul 201
4x110mh	52.94	USA Richardson, Harris, Merritt, Oliver		Des Moines	25 Apr 2015
1 mile walk	5:31.08	Tom Bosworth	GBR	London (OS)	9 Jul 2017
3000m track walk	10:30.28i	Tom Bosworth	GBR	Glasgow	25 Feb 2018
	10:47.11	Giovanni De Benedictis	ITA	San Giovanni Valdarno	19 May 1990
5000m track walk	18:05.49	Hatem Ghoula	TUN	Tunis	1 May 1997
10,000m track walk	37:25.21	Eiki Takahashi	JPN	Inzai	14 Nov 2020
2 Hours track	29,572m+	Maurizio Damilano	ITA	Cuneo	3 Oct 1992
10 km road walk	37:11	Roman Rasskazov	RUS	Saransk	28 May 2000
U18 10km road	38:57	Li Tianlei	CHN	Beijing	18 Sep 2010
30 km road walk	2:01:13+	Vladimir Kanaykin	RUS	Adler	19 Feb 2006
35 km road walk	2:21:31	Vladimir Kanaykin	RUS	Adler	19 Feb 2006
100 km road walk	8:38:07	Viktor Ginko	BLR	Scanzorosciate	27 Oct 2002

Women

50m	5.93+	Marion Jones	USA	Sevilla (in 100m)	22 Aug 1999
60m	6.81+	Shelly-Ann Fraser-Pryce	JAM	Doha (in 100m)	29 Sep 2019
100 yards	9.91	Veronica Campbell-Brown	JAM	Ostrava	31 May 2011
150m	16.10+	Florence Griffith-Joyner	USA	Seoul (in 200m)	29 Sep 1988
300m	34.41	Shaunae Miller-Uibo	BAH	Ostrava	20 Jun 2019
	34.1+	Marita Koch	GDR	Canberra (in 400m)	6 Oct 1985
500m	1:05.9	Tatána Kocembová	CZE	Ostrava	2 Aug 1984
600m	1:21.77	Caster Semenya	RSA	Berlin	27 Aug 2017
2 miles	8:58.58	Meseret Defar	ETH	Bruxelles	14 Sep 2007
2000m Steeple	5:52.80	Gesa Felicitas Krause	GER	Berlin	1 Sep 2019
200mh	24.8	Yadisleidis Pedroso	ITA	Caserta	6 Apr 2013
	25.20	Dalilah Muhammad	USA	Northridge	10 Mar 2018
300mh	38.16	Zuzana Hejnová	CZE	Cheb	2 Aug 2013
Double heptathlon	10,798	Milla Kelo	FIN	Turku	7/8 Sep 2002
	100mh 14.89, HJ 1.51, 1500m 5:03.74, 400mh 62.18, SP 12.73, 200m 25.16, 100m 12.59				
	LJ 5.73w, 400m 56.10, JT 32.69, 800m 2:23.94, 200mh 28.72, DT 47.86, 3000m 11:48.68				
4x100mh	50.50	USA Rollins, Harper-Nelson, Q Harrison, Castlin		Des Moines	24 Apr 2015
3000m track walk	11:35.34i	Gillian O'Sullivan	IRL	Belfast	15 Feb 2003
	11:48.24	Ileana Salvador	ITA	Padova	29 Aug 1993
5000m track walk	20:01.80	Eleonora Giorgi	ITA	Misterbianco	18 May 2014
25 km road walk	1:56:12+	Eleonora Giorgi	ITA	Catania	31 Jan 2016
30 km road walk	2:19:43	Eleonora Giorgi	ITA	Catania	31 Jul 2016
35 km road walk	2:38:24	Klavdiya Afanasyeva	RUS	Sochi	18 Feb 2019
100 km road walk	10:04:50	Jolanta Dukure	LAT	Scanzorosciate	21 Oct 2007

LONG DISTANCE WORLD BESTS – MEN TRACK

15,000m	0:42:18.7+	Haile Gebrselassie	ETH	Ostrava	27 Jun 2007
10 miles	0:45:23.8+	Haile Gebrselassie	ETH	Ostrava	27 Jun 2007
20,000m	56:20.02+	Bashir Abdi	BEL	Bruxelles	4 Sep 2020
15 miles	1:11:43.1	Bill Rodgers	USA	Saratoga, Cal.	21 Feb 1979
25,000m	1:12:25.4	Moses Mosop	KEN	Eugene	3 Jun 2011
30,000m	1:26:47.4	Moses Mosop	KEN	Eugene	3 Jun 2011
20 miles	1:39:14.4	Jack Foster	NZL	Hamilton, NZ	15 Aug 1971
30 miles	2:40:12.6+	Tyler Andrews	USA	Santa Barbara	13 Apr 2018
50 km	2:42:30.28	C.J.Albertson	USA	Clovis	8 Nov 1920
40 miles	3:48:35	Don Ritchie	GBR	London (Hendon)	16 Oct 1982
50 miles	4:51:49	Don Ritchie	GBR	London (Hendon)	12 Mar 1983
100 km	6:10:20	Don Ritchie	GBR	London (CP)	28 Oct 1978
150 km	10:34:30	Denis Zhalybin	RUS	London (CP)	20 Oct 2002
100 miles	11:28:03	Oleg Kharitonov	RUS	London (CP)	20 Oct 2002
200 km	15:10:27+	Yiannis Kouros	AUS	Adelaide	4-5 Oct 1997
200 miles	27:48:35	Yiannis Kouros	GRE	Montauban	15-16 Mar 1985
500 km	60:23.00+ ??	Yiannis Kouros	GRE	Colac, Aus	26-29 Nov 1984
500 miles	105:42:09+	Yiannis Kouros	GRE	Colac, Aus	26-30 Nov 1984
1000 km	136:17:00	Yiannis Kouros	GRE	Colac, Aus	26-31 Nov 1984
1500 km	10d 17:28:26	Petrus Silkinas	LTU	Nanango, Qld	11-21 Mar 1998
1000 miles	11d 13:54:58+	Petrus Silkinas	LTU	Nanango, Qld	11-22 Mar 1998
2 hours	37.994 km	Jim Alder	GBR	Walton-on-Thames	17 Oct 1964
12 hours	163,785km	Zach Bitter	USA	Phoenix	14 Dec 2013
24 hours	303.506 km	Yiannis Kouros	AUS	Adelaide	4-5 Oct 1997
48 hours	473.797 km	Yiannis Kouros	AUS	Surgères	3-5 May 1996
6 days	1036.8 km	Yiannis Kouros	GRE	Colac, Aus	20-26 Nov 2005

LONG DISTANCE ROAD RECORDS & BESTS – MEN

Where superior to track bests (over 10km) and run on properly measured road courses. (W) WA recognition.

10 km (W)	0:26:24	Rhonex Kipruto	KEN	Valencia	12 Jan 2020

WORLD AND CONTINENTAL RECORDS

15 km	0:41:05	Joseph Cheptegei	UGA	Nijmegen	18 Nov 2018
	0:41:05+	Geoffrey Kamworor	KEN	Copenhagen	15 Sep 2019
10 miles	0:44:24 §	Haile Gebrselassie	ETH	Tilburg	4 Sep 2005
	0:44:45	Paul Koech	KEN	Amsterdam-Zaandam	21 Sep 1997
20 km	0:54:42+	Jacob Kiplimo	KEN	Valencia	6 Dec 2020
25 km	1:11:18	Dennis Kimetto	KEN	Berlin	6 May 2012
30 km	1:26:45+	Eliud Kipchoge	KEN	Berlin	16 Sep 2018
20 miles	1:35:22+	Steve Jones	GBR	Chicago	10 Oct 1985
30 miles	2:37:31+	Thompson Magawana	RSA	Claremont-Kirstenbosch	2 Apr 1988
50 km	2:43:38+	Thompson Magawana	RSA	Claremont-Kirstenbosch	2 Apr 1988
40 miles	3:45:39	Andy Jones	CAN	Houston	23 Feb 1991
50 miles	4:50:08+	Jim Walmsley	USA	Folksam-Sacramento	5 May 2019
200 km	15:08:53+	Denis Zhalybin (at 202.5k)	RUS	Sankt-Peterburg	2-3 Sep 2006
500 km	58:00:50	Yiannis Kouros	GRE	Colac, AUS	20-23 Nov 2005
1000 miles	10d:10:30:35	Yiannis Kouros	GRE	New York	21-30 May 1988

LONG DISTANCE WORLD BESTS – WOMEN TRACK

15 km	0:48:54.91+	Dire Tune	ETH	Ostrava	12 Jun 2008
10 miles	0:54:21.8	Lorraine Moller	NZL	Auckland	9 Jan 1993
20,000m	1:05:26.6	Tegla Loroupe	KEN	Borgholzhausen	3 Sep 2000
25,000m	1:27:05.84	Tegla Loroupe	KEN	Mengerskirchen	21 Sep 2002
30,000m	1:45:50.0	Tegla Loroupe	KEN	Warstein	6 Jun 2003
20 miles	1:59:09 !	Chantal Langlacé	FRA	Amiens	3 Sep 1983
30 miles	3:12:25+	Carolyn Hunter-Rowe	GBR	Barry, Wales	3 Mar 1996
50 km	3:18:52+	Carolyn Hunter-Rowe	GBR	Barry, Wales	3 Mar 1996
40 miles	4:26:43	Carolyn Hunter-Rowe	GBR	Barry, Wales	7 Mar 1993
50 miles	5:48:12.0+	Norimi Sakurai	JPN	San Giovanni Lupatoto	27 Sep 2003
100 km	7:14:05.8	Norimi Sakurai	JPN	San Giovanni Lupatoto	27 Sep 2003
150 km	12:49.23	Mami Kudo	JPN	Soochow	10-11 Dec 2011
100 miles	13:25	Camille Herron	USA	Phoenix	8-9 Dec 2018
200 km	17:07:27+	Camille Herron	USA	Phoenix	8-9 Dec 2018
200 miles	39:09:03	Hilary Walker	GBR	Blackpool	5-7 Nov 1988
500 km	77:53:46	Eleanor Adams	GBR	Colac, Aus.	13-16 Nov 1989
500 miles	130:59:58+	Sandra Barwick	NZL	Campbelltown, AUS	18-23 Nov 1990
1000 km	8d 00:27:06+	Eleanor Robinson	GBR	Nanango, Qld	11-19 Mar 1998
1500 km	12d 06:52:12+	Eleanor Robinson	GBR	Nanango, Qld	11-23 Mar 1998
1000 miles	13d 02:16:49	Eleanor Robinson	GBR	Nanango, Qld	11-24 Mar 1998
2 hrs	32.652 km	Chantal Langlacé	FRA	Amiens	3 Sep 1983
12 hrs	149.208 km	Camille Herron	USA	Phoenix	10 Dec 2017
24 hours	262.192 km	Camille Herron	USA	Phoenix	8-9 Dec 2018
48 hours	385.130 km	Mami Kudo	JPN	Surgères	22-24 May 2010
6 days	883.631 km	Sandra Barwick	NZL	Campbelltown, AUS	18-24 Nov 1990

! Timed on one running watch only

LONG DISTANCE ROAD RECORDS & BESTS - WOMEN

Where superior to track bests (over 10km)

10 km (W)	0:29:43	Joyciline Jepkosgei	KEN	Praha	9 Sep 2017
15 km	0:45:37	Joyciline Jepkosgei	KEN	Praha	1 Apr 2017
10 miles	0:49:29+	Caroline Kipkurui	KEN	Ras Al Khaimah	9 Feb 2018
	0:49:21+ dh	Brigid Kosgei	KEN	South Shields	8 Sep 2019
20 km	1:01:25	Joyciline Jepkosgei	KEN	Praha	1 Apr 2017
	1:01:20+ dh	Brigid Kosgei	KEN	South Shields	8 Sep 2019
25 km	1:19:33	Brigid Kosgei	KEN	Chicago	13 Oct 2019
30 km	1:35:18	Brigid Kosgei	KEN	Chicago	13 Oct 2019
20 miles	1:43:33+	Paula Radcliffe	GBR	London	13 Apr 2003
30 miles	3:01:16+	Frith van der Merwe	RSA	Claremont-Kirstenbosch	25 Mar 1989
50 km	3:07:20	Alyson Dixon	GBR	Brasov	1 Sep 2019
40 miles	4:26:13+	Ann Trason	USA	Houston	23 Feb 1991
50 miles	5:40:18	Ann Trason	USA	Houston	23 Feb 1991
100 miles	12:42:39	Camille Herron	USA	Vienna, Illinois	10-11 Nov 2017
1000 km	7d 01:11:00+	Sandra Barwick	NZL	New York	16-23 Sep 1991
1000 miles	12d 14:38:40	Sandra Barwick	NZL	New York	16-29 Sep 1991
24 hours	270.116k	Camille Herron	USA	Albi	26-27 Oct 2019
48 hrs	401.000k	Patrycja Bereznowska	POL	Athína	26-28 Jan 2018

WORLD INDOOR RECORDS

Men

50 metres	5.56A	Donovan Bailey	CAN	Reno	9 Feb 1996
60 metres	6.34A	Christian Coleman	USA	Albuquerque	18 Feb 2018
100 metres	9.98	Usain Bolt	JAM	Warszawa	23 Aug 2014

WORLD AND CONTINENTAL RECORDS

Event	Mark	Athlete	Nat	Venue	Date
200 metres	19.92	Frank Fredericks	NAM	Liévin	18 Feb 1996
400 metres	44.52	Michael Norman	USA	College Station	10 Mar 2018
800 metres	1:42.67	Wilson Kipketer	DEN	Paris (Bercy)	9 Mar 1997
1000 metres	2:14.20	Ayanleh Souleiman	DJI	Stockholm	17 Feb 2016
1500 metres	3:31.04	Samuel Tefera	ETH	Birmingham	16 Feb 2019
1 mile	3:47.01	Yomif Kejelcha	ETH	Boston (Allston)	3 Mar 2019
2000 metres #	4:49.99	Kenenisa Bekele	ETH	Birmingham	17 Feb 2007
3000 metres	7:24.90	Daniel Komen	KEN	Budapest	6 Feb 1998
2 miles #	8:03.40	Mo Farah	GBR	Birmingham	21 Feb 2015
5000 metres	12:49.60	Kenenisa Bekele	ETH	Birmingham	20 Feb 2004
10000 metres #	27:50.29	Mark Bett	KEN	Gent	10 Feb 2002
50 m hurdles	6.25	Mark McKoy	CAN	Kobe	5 Mar 1986
60 m hurdles	7.29	Grant Holloway	USA	Madrid	24 Feb 2021
110 m hurdles	13.03	Orlando Ortega	CUB	Warszawa	23 Aug 2014
High jump	2.43	Javier Sotomayor	CUB	Budapest	4 Mar 1989
Pole vault	6.18	Armand Duplantis	SWE	Glasgow	15 Feb 2020
Long jump	8.79	Carl Lewis	USA	New York	27 Jan 1984
Triple jump	18.07	Fabrice Zango	BUR	Aubiére	16 Jan 2021
Shot	22.82	Ryan Crouser	USA	Fayetteville	24 Jan 2021
Javelin #	85.78	Matti Närhi	FIN	Kajaani	3 Mar 1996
35 lb weight #	25.86	Lance Deal	USA	Atlanta	4 Mar 1995
3000m walk #	10:30.28	Tom Bosworth	GBR	Glasgow	25 Feb 2018
5000m walk	18:07.08	Mikhail Shchennikov	RUS	Moskva	14 Feb 1995
10000m walk #	38:31.4	Werner Heyer	GDR	Berlin	12 Jan 1980
4 x 200m	1:22.11	United Kingdom		Glasgow	3 Mar 1991
		(Linford Christie, Darren Braithwaite, Ade Mafe, John Regis)			
4 x 400m	3:01.39 §	USA (Texas A&M University)		College Station	10 Mar 2018
		(Ilolo Izu, Robert Grant, Devin Dixon, Mylik Kerley)			
4 x 800m	7:11.30	USA (Hoka New Jersey/New York TC)		Boston (Allston)	25 Feb 2018
		(Joe McCasey, Kyle Merber, Chris Giesting, Jesse Garn)			
Distance Med	9:19.93	USA		New York (Armory)	31 Jan 2015
		(Matthew Centrowitz, Mike Berry, Erik Sowinski, Pat Casey)			
Heptathlon	6645 points	Ashton Eaton	USA	Istanbul	9/10 Mar 2012
		(6.79 60m, 8.16 LJ, 14.56 SP, 2.03 HJ, 7.68 60mh, 5.20 PV, 2:32.77 1000m)			

Women — # events not officially recognised by the IAAF

Event	Mark	Athlete	Nat	Venue	Date
50 metres	5.96+	Irina Privalova	RUS	Madrid	9 Feb 1995
60 metres	6.92	Irina Privalova	RUS	Madrid	11 Feb 1993 & 9 Feb 1995
200 metres	21.87	Merlene Ottey	JAM	Liévin	13 Feb 1993
400 metres	49.59	Jarmila Kratochvílová	CZE	Milano	7 Mar 1982
800 metres	1:55.82	Jolanda Ceplak	SLO	Wien	3 Mar 2002
1000 metres	2:30.94	Maria Lurdes Mutola	MOZ	Stockholm	25 Feb 1999
1500 metres	3:53.09	Gudaf Tsegay	ETH	Liévin	9 Feb 2021
1 mile	4:13.31	Genzebe Dibaba	ETH	Stockholm	17 Feb 2016
2000 metres #	5:23.75	Genzebe Dibaba	ETH	Sabadell	7 Feb 2017
3000 metres	8:16.60	Genzebe Dibaba	ETH	Stockholm	6 Feb 2014
2 miles #	9:00.48	Genzebe Dibaba	ETH	Birmingham	15 Feb 2014
5000 metres	14:18.86	Genzebe Dibaba	ETH	Stockholm	19 Feb 2015
50 m hurdles	6.58	Cornelia Oschkenat	GDR	Berlin	20 Feb 1988
60 m hurdles	7.68	Susanna Kallur	SWE	Karlsruhe	10 Feb 2008
100 m hurdles	12.64	Ludmila Engquist	SWE	Tampere	10 Feb 1997
High jump	2.08	Kajsa Bergqvist	SWE	Arnstadt	4 Feb 2006
Pole vault	5.03	Jenn Suhr	USA	Brockport	30 Jan 2016
Long jump	7.37	Heike Drechsler	GDR	Wien	13 Feb 1988
Triple jump	15.43	Yulimar Rojas	VEN	Madrid	21 Feb 2020
Shot	22.50	Helena Fibingerová	CZE	Jablonec	19 Feb 1977
Javelin #	64.34	Lu Huihui	CHN	Beijing	30 May 2020
20 lb weight #	25.60	Gwen Berry	USA	Albuquerque	4 Mar 2017
3000m walk	11:35.34 un	Gillian O'Sullivan	IRL	Belfast	15 Feb 2003
	11:40.33	Claudia Iovan/Stef	ROU	Bucuresti	30 Jan 1999
5000m walk #	20:04.4	Yelene Lashmanova	RUS	Saransk	27 Dec 2020
10000m walk	43:33.16	Anna Terlyukevich	BLR	Mogilyov	21 Feb 2020
4 x 200m	1:32.41	Russia		Glasgow	29 Jan 2005
		(Yekaterina Kondratyeva, Irina Khabarova, Yuliya Pechonkina, Yuliya Gushchina)			
4 x 400m	3:23.37	Russia		Glasgow	28 Jan 2006
		(Yuliya Gushchina, Olga Kotlyarova, Olga Zaytseva, Olesya Krasnomovets)			
4 x 800m	8:05.89	USA	USA	New York (Armory)	3 Feb 2018
		(Chrishuna Williams, Raevyn Rogers, Charlene Lipsey, Ajee' Wilson)			
Distance Med	10:42.57	New Balance TC	USA	Boston (Roxbury)	7 Feb 2015
		(Sarah Brown, Mahogany Jones, Megan Krumpoch, Brenda Martinez)			
Pentathlon	5013 points	Nataliya Dobrynska	UKR	Istanbul	9 Mar 2012
		(8.38 60mh, 1.84 HJ, 16.51 SP, 6.57 LJ, 2:11.15 800m)			

WORLD INDOOR JUNIOR (U20) RECORDS

First approved by IAAF Council in 2011. **Men**

60 metres	6.51	Mark Lewis-Francis	GBR	Lisboa	11 Mar 2001
200 metres	20.37	Walter Dix	USA	Fayetteville	11 Mar 2005
400 metres	44.80	Kirani James	GRN	Fayetteville	27 Feb 2011
800 metres	1:44.35	Yuriy Borzakovskiy	RUS	Dortmund	30 Jan 2000
1000 metres	2:15.77	Abubaker Kaki	SUD	Stockholm	21 Feb 2008
1500 metres	3:36.02	Jakob Ingebrigtsen	NOR	Düsseldorf	20 Feb 2019
One mile	3:55.02	German Fernandez	USA	College Station	28 Feb 2009
3000 metres	7:32.87	Hagos Gebrhiwet	ETH	Boston (Roxbury)	2 Feb 2013
5000 metres	12:53.29	Isiah Koech	KEN	Düsseldorf	11 Feb 2011
60mh (99cm)	7.34	Sasha Zhoya	FRA	Miramas	22 Feb 2020
High jump	2.35	Volodymyr Yashchenko	URS	Milano	12 Mar 1978
Pole vault	5.88	Armand Duplantis	SWE	Clermont-Ferrand	25 Feb 2018
Long jump	8.22	Viktor Kuznetsov	UKR	Brovary	22 Jan 2005
Triple jump	17.20	Melvin Raffin	FRA	Belgrade	3 Mar 2017
Shot (6kg)	22.48	Konrad Bukowiecki	POL	Torun	8 Jan 2016
Heptathlon	6022	Jente Hauttekeete	BEL	Frankfurt-am-Main	13/14 Feb 2021
(jnr imps)		(7.07, 7.33, 15.64, 2.10 / 8.06, 4.70, 2:46.71)			

Women

60 metres	7.07	Ewa Swoboda	POL	Torun	12 Feb 2016
200 metres	22.40	Bianca Knight	USA	Fayetteville	14 Mar 2008
400 metres	50.36 §	Sydney McLaughlin	USA	College Station	10 Mar 2018
	50.52	Athing Mu	USA	College Station	6 Feb 2021
800 metres	1:58.40 §	Athing Mu	USA	Fayetteville	27 Feb 2021
	1:59.03	Keely Hodgkinson	GBR	Wien	30 Jan 2021
1000 metres	2:35.80	Mary Cain	USA	Boston (Roxbury)	8 Feb 2014
1500 metres	4:01.57	Lemlem Hailu	ETH	Liévin	19 Feb 2020
One mile	4:24.10	Kalkidan Gezahegne	ETH	Birmingham	20 Feb 2010
3000 metres	8:33.56	Tirunesh Dibaba	ETH	Birmingham	20 Feb 2004
5000 metres	14:53.99	Tirunesh Dibaba	ETH	Boston	31 Jan 2004
60m hurdles	7.91 §	Grace Stark	USA	College Station	29 Feb 2019
	7.91A §	Ackera Nugent	JAM	Air Force Academy	26 Feb 2021
High jump	2.02	Yaroslava Mahuchikh	UKR	Karlsruhe	31 Jan 2020
Pole vault	4.71	Wilma Murto	FIN	Zweibrücken	31 Jan 2016
Long jump	6.91 §	Larissa Iapichino	ITA	Ancona	20 Feb 2021
	6.88	Heike Daute	GDR	Berlin	1 Feb 1983
Triple jump	14.37	Ren Ruiping	CHN	Barcelona	11 Mar 1995
Shot	20.51	Heidi Krieger	GDR	Budapest	8 Feb 1984
Pentathlon	4635A §	Kendell Williams	USA	Albuquerque	15 Mar 2014
		(8.21, 1.88, 12.05, 6.32, 2:17.31)			

WORLD VETERANS/MASTERS RECORDS

MEN – aged 35-39

100 metres	9.87	Justin Gatlin (10.2.92)	USA	Stanford	30 Jun 2019
200 metres	20.11	Linford Christie (2.4.60)	GBR	Villeneuve d'Ascq	25 Jun 1995
400 metres	44.54	Chris Brown (15.10.78)	BAH	Eugene	30 May 2015
800 metres	1:43.36	Johnny Gray (19.6.60)	USA	Zürich	16 Aug 1995
1000 metres	2:18.8+	William Tanui (22.2.64)	KEN	Rome	7 Jul 1999
1500 metres	3:32.45	William Tanui (22.2.64)	KEN	Athína	16 Jun 1999
1 mile	3:51.38	Bernard Lagat (12.12.74)	USA	London (CP)	6 Aug 2011
2000 metres	4:58.3+ e	William Tanui 22.2.64	KEN	Monaco	4 Aug 1999
	4:54.74i	Bernard Lagat (12.12.74)	USA	New York	15 Feb 2014
3000 metres	7:29.00	Bernard Lagat (12.12.74)	USA	Rieti	29 Aug 2010
5000 metres	12:53.60	Bernard Lagat (12.12.74)	USA	Monaco	22 Jul 2011
10000 metres	26:51.20	Haile Gebrselassie (18.4.73)	ETH	Hengelo	24 May 2008
20000 metres	56:20.30+	Mo Farah (23.3.83)	GBR	Bruxelles	4 Sep 2020
1 Hour	21,330m	Mo Farah (23.3.83)	GBR	Bruxelles	4 Sep 2020 9
Half Marathon	59:10 dh	Paul Tergat (17.6.69)	KEN	Lisboa	13 Mar 2005
	59:31	Gilbert Masai (20.5.81)	KEN	København	18 Sep 2016
Marathon	2:01:41	Kenenisa Bekele (13.6.82)	ETH	Berlin	29 Sep 2019
3000m steeple	8:04.95	Simon Vroemen (11.5.69)	NED	Bruxelles	26 Aug 2005
110m hurdles	12.96	Allen Johnson (1.3.71)	USA	Athína	17 Sep 2006
400m hurdles	48.10	Felix Sánchez (30.8.77)	DOM	Moskva	13 Aug 2013
High jump	2.31	Dragutin Topic (12.3.71)	SRB	Kragujevac	28 Jul 2009
	2.31	Jamie Nieto (2.11.76)	USA	New York	9 Jun 2012
Pole vault	5.90i	Björn Otto (16.10.77)	GER	Cottbus	30 Jan 2013
	5.90i	Björn Otto		Düsseldorf	8 Feb 2013
	5.90	Björn Otto		Eugene	1 Jun 2013
Long jump	8.50	Larry Myricks (10.3.56)	USA	New York	15 Jun 1991

WORLD AND CONTINENTAL RECORDS

	8.50	Carl Lewis (1.7.61)	USA	Atlanta	29 Jul 1996
Triple jump	17.92	Jonathan Edwards (10.5.66)	GBR	Edmonton	6 Aug 2001
Shot	22.67	Kevin Toth (29.12.67)	USA	Lawrence	19 Apr 2003
Discus	71.56	Virgilijus Alekna (13.2.72)	LTU	Kaunas	25 Jul 2007
Hammer	83.62	Igor Astapkovich (4.1.63)	BLR	Staiki	20 Jun 1998
Javelin	92.80	Jan Zelezny (16.6.66)	CZE	Edmonton	12 Aug 2001
Decathlon	8241	Kip Janvrin (8.7.65)	USA	Eugene	22 Jun 2001
		(10.98, 7.01, 14.21, 1.89, 48.41, 14.72, 45.59, 5.20, 60.41, 4:14.96)			
20 km walk	1:17:02	Yohann Diniz (1.1.78)	FRA	Arles	8 Mar 2015
20000m t walk	1:19:42.1	Yohann Diniz (1.1.78)	FRA	Bogny-sur-Meuse	25 May 2014
50 km walk	3:32:33	Yohann Diniz (1.1.78)	FRA	Zürich	15 Aug 2014
50000m t walk	3:49:29.7	Alain Lemercier (11.1.57)	FRA	Franconville	3 Apr 1994

MEN – aged 40 or over

100 metres	9.93	Kim Collins (5.4.76)	SKN	Bottrop	29 May 2016
200 metres	20.64	Troy Douglas (30.11.62)	NED	Utrecht	9 Aug 2003
400 metres	46.96	Sandro Viana (26.3.77)	BRA	São Bernardo do Campo	1 Jul 2017
800 metres	1:48.05	Anthony Whiteman (13.11.71)	GBR	Manchester (Stretford)	12 Jul 2014
1000 metres	2:24.93i	Vyacheslav Shabunin (27.9.69)	RUS	Moskva	10 Jan 2010
1500 metres	3:40.20i+	Bernard Lagat (12.12.74)	USA	New York (Armory)	14 Feb 2015
	3:41.87	Bernard Lagat		Birmingham	7 Jun 2015
1 mile	3:54.91i+	Bernard Lagat		New York (Armory)	14 Feb 2015
	3:57.91	Bernard Lagat		London (OS)	25 Jul 2015
3000 metres	7:37.92i+	Bernard Lagat (12.12.74)	USA	Metz	25 Feb 2015
	7:42.75	Bernard Lagat		Luzern	14 Jul 2015
5000 metres	13:06.78	Bernard Lagat		Rio de Janeiro	20 Aug 2016
10000 metres	27:49.35	Bernard Lagat		Stanford	1 May 2016
10 km road	27:48	Bernard Lagat (12.12.74)	USA	Manchester	10 May 2015
1 Hour	19.710k	Steve Moneghetti (26.9.62)	AUS	Geelong	17 Dec 2005
Half marathon	60:41 dh	Haile Gebrselassie (18.4.73)	ETH	South Shields	15 Sep 2013
	61:04	Mark Kiptoo (21.6.76)	KEN	Azpeitia	24 Mar 2018
Marathon	2:07:50	Mark Kiptoo (21.6.76)	KEN	Frankfurt	28 Oct 2018
3000m steeple	8:38.40	Angelo Carosi (20.1.64)	ITA	Firenze	11 Jul 2004
110m hurdles	13.97	David Ashford (24.1.63)	USA	Indianapolis	3 Jul 2004
	13.73 ?	David Ashford		Carolina	11 Jul 2003
400m hurdles	49.69	Danny McFarlane (14.2.72)	JAM	Kingston	29 Jun 2012
High jump	2.28	Dragutin Topic (12.3.71)	SRB	Beograd	20 May 2012
Pole vault	5.71i	Jeff Hartwig (25.9.67)	USA	Jonesboro	31 May 2008
	5.70	Jeff Hartwig		Eugene	29 Jun 2008
Long jump	7.68A	Aaron Sampson (20.9.61)	USA	Cedar City, UT	21 Jun 2002
	7.59i	Mattias Sunneborn (27.9.70)	SWE	Sätra	3 Feb 2013
	7.57	Hans Schicker (3.10.47)	FRG	Kitzingen	16 Jul 1989
Triple jump	17.32	Fabrizio Donato (14.8.76	ITA	Pierre-Bénite	9 Jun 2017
Shot	21.41	Brian Oldfield USA (1.6.45)	USA	Innsbruck	22 Aug 1985
Discus	70.28	Virgilijus Alekna (13.2.72)	LTU	Klaipeda	23 Jun 2012
Hammer	82.23	Igor Astapkovich (4.1.63)	BLR	Minsk	10 Jul 2004
Javelin	85.92	Jan Zelezny (16.6.66)	CZE	Göteborg	9 Aug 2006
Pentathlon	3510	Werner Schallau (8.9.38)	FRG	Gelsenkirchen	24 Sep 1978
		6.74, 59.20, 23.0, 43.76, 5:05.7			
Decathlon	7525	Kip Janvrin (8.7.65)	USA	San Sebastián	24 Aug 2005
		11.56, 6.78, 14.01, 1.80, 49.46, 15.40, 42.70, 4.70, 58.43, 4:25.87			
20 km walk	1:20:20	Andriy Kovenko (25.11.73)	UKR	Alushta	28 Feb 2014
20000m t walk	1:24:46.1	Ivan Trotskiy (27.5.76)	BLR	Grodno	23 Jun 2016
50 km walk	3:37:43	Yohann Diniz (1/1.78)	FRA	Alytus	19 May 2019
50000m t walk	3:51:54.5	José Marín (21.1.50)	ESP	Manresa	7 Apr 1990
4x100m	42.18	Great Britain & NI	GBR	London (LV)	19 Aug 2018
		(Jason Carty, Dominic Bradley, Mensah Elliott, Dwain Chambers)			
4x400m	3:20.83	S Allah, K Morning, E Gonera, R Blackwell USA Philadelphia			27 Apr 2001

WOMEN – aged 35-39

100 metres	10.74	Merlene Ottey (10.5.60)	JAM	Milano	7 Sep 1996
200 metres	21.93	Merlene Ottey (10.5.60)	JAM	Bruxelles	25 Aug 1995
400 metres	50.14	Novlene Williams-Mills (26.4.82)	JAM	Kingston	25 Jun 2017
800 metres	1:56.53	Lyubov Gurina (6.8.57)	RUS	Hechtel	30 Jul 1994
1000 metres	2:31.5	Maricica Puica (29.7.50)	ROU	Poiana Brasov	1 Jun 1986
1500 metres	3:57.73	Maricica Puica (29.7.50)	ROU	Bruxelles	30 Aug 1985
1 mile	4:17.33	Maricica Puica (29.7.50)	ROU	Zürich	21 Aug 1985
2000 metres	5:28.69	Maricica Puica (29.7.50)	ROU	London (CP)	11 Jul 1986
3000 metres	8:23.23	Edith Masai (4.4.67)	KEN	Monaco	19 Jul 2002
5000 metres	14:33.84	Edith Masai (4.4.67)	KEN	Oslo	2 Jun 2006
10000 metres	30:30.26	Edith Masai (4.4.67)	KEN	Helsinki	6 Aug 2005
Half Marathon	64:55	Mary Keitany (18.1.82)	KEN	Ras Al Khaimah	9 Feb 2018

WORLD AND CONTINENTAL RECORDS

Event	Mark	Athlete	Nat	Venue	Date
Marathon	2:17:01	Mary Keitany (18.1.82)	KEN	London	23 Apr 2017
3000m steeple	9:33.93	Minori Hayakari (29.11.72)	JPN	Heusden	20 Jul 2008
100m hurdles	12.40	Gail Devers (19.11.66)	USA	Lausanne	2 Jul 2002
400m hurdles	52.94	Marina Styepanova (1.5.50)	RUS	Tashkent	17 Sep 1986
High jump	2.02i	Anna Chicherova (22.7.82	RUS	Moskva	15 Feb 2019
	2.01	Inga Babakova (27.6.67)	UKR	Oslo	27 Jun 2003
	2.01	Ruth Beitia (1.4.79)	ESP	Zürich	17 Aug 2014
Pole vault	4.93	Jenn Suhr (5.2.82)	USA	Austin	14 Apr 2018
Long jump	6.99	Heike Drechsler (16.12.64)	GER	Sydney	29 Sep 2000
Triple jump	14.89	Caterine Ibargüen (12.2.84)	COL	Lausanne	5 Jul 2019
Shot	21.46	Larisa Peleshenko (29.2.64)	RUS	Moskva	26 Aug 2000
	21.47i	Helena Fibingerová (13.7.49)	CZE	Jablonec	9 Feb 1985
Discus	69.60	Faina Melnik (9.6.45)	RUS	Donetsk	9 Sep 1980
Hammer	74.03	Amber Campbell (5.6.81)	USA	Eugene	6 Jul 2016
Javelin	68.92	Kathryn Mitchell (10.7.82)	AUS	Gold Coast	11 Apr 2018
Heptathlon	6533	Jane Frederick (7.4.52)	USA	Talence	27 Sep 1987
		13.60, 1.82, 15.50, 24.73; 6.29, 49.70, 2:14.88			
5000m walk	20:12.41	Elisabetta Perrone (9.7.68)	ITA	Rieti	2 Aug 2003
10km walk	41:41	Kjersti Tysse Plätzer (18.1.72)	NOR	Kraków	30 May 2009
10000m t walk	43:26.5	Elisabetta Perrone (9.7.68)	ITA	Saluzzo	4 Aug 2004
20km walk	1:25:59	Tamara Kovalenko (5.6.64)	RUS	Moskva	19 May 2000
20000m t walk	1:27:49.3	Yelena Nikolayeva (1.2.66)	RUS	Brisbane	6 Sep 2001
50km walk	4:05:56	Inês Henriques (1.5.80)	POR	London	13 Aug 2017
4x100m	47.65	Stafford, Springer, Hutchinson, Baird	TTO	Lyon	16 Aug 2015
4x400m	3:50.80	Mitchell, Mathews, Beadnall, Gabriel	GBR	Gateshead	8 Aug 1999

WOMEN – aged 40 or over

Event	Mark	Athlete	Nat	Venue	Date
100 metres	10.99	Merlene Ottey (10.5.60)	JAM	Thessaloniki	30 Aug 2000
200 metres	22.72	Merlene Ottey (10.5.60)	SLO	Athína	23 Aug 2004
400 metres	53.05A	María Figuerêdo (11.11.63)	BRA	Bogotá	10 Jul 2004
	53.14	María Figuerêdo (11.11.63)	BRA	San Carlos, VEN	19 Jun 2004
800 metres	1:59.25	Yekaterina Podkopayeva (11.6.52)	RUS	Luxembourg	30 Jun 1994
1000 metres	2:36.16	Yekaterina Podkopayeva (11.6.52)	RUS	Nancy	14 Sep 1994
	2:36.08i	Yekaterina Podkopayeva	RUS	Liévin	13 Feb 1993
1500 metres	3:59.78	Yekaterina Podkopayeva (11.6.52)	RUS	Nice	18 Jul 1994
1 mile	4:23.78	Yekaterina Podkopayeva (11.6.52)	RUS	Roma	9 Jun 1993
3000 metres	9:01.1+	Jo Pavey (20.9.73)	GBR	Roma	5 Jun 2014
	8:58.20i	Nuria Fernández (16.8.76)	ESP	Beograd	3 Mar 2017
5000 metres	15:04.87	Jo Pavey (20.9.73)	GBR	Roma	5 Jun 2014
10000 metres	31:25.49	Sinead Diver (17.2.77)	AUS	Doha	29 Sep 2019
1 hour	16.056k	Jackie Fairweather (10.11.67)	AUS	Canberra	24 Jan 2008
Half Marathon	68:48	Lisa Weightman (16.1.79)	AUS	Sunshine Coast	4 Aug 2019
Marathon	2:19:52	Helalia Johannes (13.8.80)	NAM	Valencia	6 Dec 2020
3000m steeple	10:00.75	Minori Hayakari (29.11.72)	JPN	Kumagaya	22 Sep 2013
100 m hurdles	13.20	Patricia Girard (8.4.68)	FRA	Paris	14 Jul 2008
400 m hurdles	58.35	Barbara Gähling (20.1.65)	GER	Erfurt	21 Jul 2007
	58.3 h	Gowry Retchakan (21.6.60)	GBR	Hoo	3 Sep 2000
High jump	1.94i	Venelina Veneva-Mateeva (13.6.74)	BUL	Dobrich 15 Feb & Praha	6 Mar 2015
	1.90	Venelina Veneva-Mateeva	BUL	Plovdiv 12 Jul & Pitesti	27 Jul 2014
Pole vault	4.10	Doris Auer (10.5.71)	AUT	Innsbruck	6 Aug 2011
	4.11 §	Doris Auer	AUT	Wien	5 Jul 2011
Long jump	6.72	Tatyana Ter-Mesrobian (12.5.68)	RUS	Sankt-Peterburg	1 Jun 2009
Triple jump	14.06	Yamilé Aldama (14.8.72)	GBR	Eugene	1 Jun 2013
Shot	19.05	Antonina Ivanova (25.12.32)	RUS	Oryol	28 Aug 1973
	19.16i	Antonina Ivanova	RUS	Moskva	24 Feb 1974
Discus	67.89	Iryna Yatchenko (31.10.65)	BLR	Staiki	29 Jun 2008
Hammer	67.57	Iryna Sekachyova (21.7.76)	UKR	Kyiv	14 Jun 2017
Javelin	61.96	Laverne Eve (16.6.65)	BAH	Monaco	9 Sep 2005
Heptathlon	5449	Tatyana Alisevich (22.1.69)	BLR	Staiki	3 Jun 2010
		14.80, 1.62, 13.92, 26.18, 5.55, 45.44, 2:24.39			
5000m walk	21:46.68	Kelly Ruddick (19.4.73)	AUS	Brisbane	29 Mar 2014
10000m t walk	44:50.19	Susana Feitor (28.1.75)	POR	Leiria	25 Jul 2015
20km walk	1:31:58	Susana Feitor		Rio Maior 18 Apr 2015 & Murcia	17 May 2015
20000m t walk	1:33:28.15t	Teresa Vaill (20.11.62)	USA	Carson	25 Jun 2005
50km walk	4:29:15	Aggelikí Makrí (25.9.78)	GRE	Alytus	19 May 2019
4x100m	48.01	Mogentale, Brims, Bezuidenhout, Strong	AUS	Lahti	8 Aug 2009
4x400m	3:56.02	Seidel, Gazda-Sagolla, Kroner, Heidrich	GER	Potsdam	25 Aug 2002

WORLD AND CONTINENTAL RECORDS SET IN 2020

OUTDOORS – MEN § Not ratified

1500	Eur	3:28.68	Jakob INGEBRIGTSEN	NOR	Monaco	14 Aug 20
2000	Eur	4:50.01	Jakob INGEBRIGTSEN	NOR	Oslo	11 Jun 20
3000	Oce	7:28.02	Stewart McSWEYN	AUS	Roma	17 Sep 20
5000	W, Com	12:35.36	Joshua CHEPTEGEI	UGA	Monaco	14 Aug 20
5k Rd	W, Com	12:51	Joshua CHEPTEGEI	UGA	Monaco	16 Feb 20
10,000	W, Com	26:11.00	Joshua CHEPTEGEI	UGA	Valencia	7 Oct 20
	Oce	27:22.55	Patrick TIERNAN	AUS	Los Angeles	5 Dec 20
10k Rd	W, Com	26:24	Rhonex KIPRUTO	KEN	Valencia	12 Jan 20
	Eur	27:13	Julien WANDERS	SUI	Valencia	12 Jan 20
20,000	Eur	56:51.60+	Sondre Nordstad MOEN	NOR	Kristiansand	7 Aug 20
	W	56:20.02+	Bashir ABDI	BEL	Bruxelles	4 Sep 20
	Com	56:20.30+	Mo FARAH	GBR	Bruxelles	4 Sep 20
20k	W, Com	54:42+	Jacob KIPLIMO	KEN	Valencia	6 Dec 20
HMar	W, Com	57:32	Kibiwott KANDIE	KEN	Valencia	6 Dec 20
25,000	Eur	1:12:46.5t	Sondre Nordstad MOEN	NOR	Oslo	11 Jun 20
50,000	W	2:42:30.28	C.J. ALBERTSON	USA	Clovis	8 Nov 20
1Hr	Eur	21,131 m	Sondre Nordstad MOEN	NOR	Kristiansand	7 Aug 20
	W, Com	21,330 m	Mo FARAH	GBR	Bruxelles	4 Sep 20
300H	W	33.78	Karsten WARHOLM	NOR	Oslo	11 Jun 20
400H	Eur	46.87	Karsten WARHOLM	NOR	Stockholm	23 Aug 20
PV (out)	W	6.15	Armand DUPLANTIS	SWE	Roma	17 Sep 20
DT	SAm	67.03	Mauricio ORTEGA	COL	Lovelhe	29 Feb 20
	SAm	69.60	Juan CAICEDO	ECU	Lovelhe	22 Jul 20
	SAm	70.29	Mauricio ORTEGA	COL	Lovelhe	22 Jul 20
Dec	Oce	8492	Ashley MOLONEY	AUS	Brisbane	20 Dec 20
		(10.36, 7.67w, 13.62, 2.11, 45.82 / 14.17, 43.93, 4.80, 57.77, 4:48.48)				
4x1500R	NAm	14:34.97	Jager, Fisher, McGorty, Lomong	USA	Portland	31 Jul 20
5000W	Asi	18:34.88	Toshikazu YAMANISHI	JPN	Kumagaya	19 Sep 20
	Asi	18:20.14	Koki IKEDA	JPN	Inzai	25 Oct 20
10,000W	W	37:25.21	Eiki TAKAHASHI	JPN	Inzai	14 Nov 20

OUTDOORS – WOMEN

150	W	16.41	Brianna McNEAL	USA	Fort Worth	20 Jul 20
	Eur	16.56	Dafne SCHIPPERS	NED	Ostrava	8 Sep 20
300	Asi	37.08	Seika AOYAMA	JPN	Yamaguchi	18 Oct 20
1000	Afr, Com	2:29.15	Faith KIPYEGON	KEN	Monaco	14 Aug 20
1500	Oce	4:00.42	Jessica HULL	AUS	Berlin	13 Sep 20
5000	NAm	14:23.92	Shelby HOULIHAN	USA	Portland	10 Jul 20
	Oce	14:43.80	Jessica HULL	AUS	Monaco	14 Aug 20
	W	14:06.62	Letesenbet GIDEY	ETH	Valencia	7 Oct 20
10,000	Eur	29:36.67	Sifan HASSAN	NED	Hengelo	10 Oct 20
HMar	W	1:04:31	Ababel YESHANEH	ETH	Ras Al Khaimah	21 Feb 20
	W-wo,Com	1:05:34	Peres JEPCHIRCHIR	KEN	Praha	5 Sep 20
	W-wo,Com	1:05:16	Peres JEPCHIRCHIR	KEN	Gdynia	17 Oct 20
	Eur-wo	1:05:18	Melat Yisak KEJETA	GER	Gdynia	17 Oct 20
30k	Asi	1:38:35	Honami MAEDA	JPN	Ohme	16 Feb 20
Mar	Asi-wo	2:20:29	Mao ICHIYAMA	JPN	Nagoya	8 Mar 20
	W40	2:19:52	Helalia JOHANNES	NAM	Valencia	6 Dec 20
100k	Eur	7:04:36	Dominika STELMACH	POL	Pabianice	30 Aug 20
1Hr	W	18,930 m	Sifan HASSAN	NED	Bruxelles	4 Sep 20
	Afr ,Com	18,341 m	Eva CHERONO	KEN	Bruxelles	4 Sep 20
24Hr	Eur	260,679 k	Malgorzata PAZDA-POZORSKA	POL	Pabianice	30 Aug 20
HJ	Oce	1.99	Eleanor PATTERSON	AUS	Wellington	28 Feb 20
DT	NAm	70.15	Valerie ALLMAN	USA	Rathdrum	1 Aug 20
HT	Oce	71.69 & 72.35	Julia RATCLIFFE	NZL	Hamilton	15 Feb 20
	Oce	73.47	Lauren BRUCE	NZL	Hastings	20 Sep 20
JT/500	W18	68.76	Adriana VILAGOS	SRB	Sremska Mitrovica	7 Mar 20
JT	W20	63.96 §	Elína TZÉNGGO	GRE	Ioánnina	1 Aug 20
HepU18	WU18	6301	Henriette JAEGER	NOR	Moss	13 Sep 20
		(13.21w, 1.69, 14.69, 23.36w / 6.33, 35.71, 2:11.37)				
4x1500R	W	16:27.02	Quigley, Cranny, Schweizer, Houlihan	USA	Portland	31 Jul 20
50kW	W	3:50:42 §	Yelena LASHMANOVA	RUS	Voronovskoye	5 Sep 20

WORLD AND CONTINENTAL RECORDS SET IN JAN-MAR 2021

INDOORS – MEN

500	SAm	1:00.66	Alejandro PERLAZA	COL	Lynchburg	23 Jan 21
800	W35	1:48.75	Tamás KAZI	HUN	Budapest	7 Feb 21
	W35	1:48.74	Tamás KAZI	HUN	Budapest	13 Feb 21
	NAm	1:44.21	Donovan BRAZIER	USA	Staten Island	13 Feb 21
	Com	1:43.63	Elliot GILES	GBR/Eng	Torun	17 Feb 21
1000	NAm	2:16.27	Bryce HOPPEL	USA	Staten Island	13 Feb 21
1500	Eur	3:31.80	Jakob INGEBRIGTSEN	NOR	Liévin	9 Feb 21
	Oce	3:32.35	Oliver HOARE	AUS	Staten Island	13 Feb 21
2M	Oce	8:14.92	Morgan McDONALD	AUS	Staten Island	13 Feb 21
60H	NAm=	7.35	Grant HOLLOWAY	USA	Fayetteville	24 Jan 21
	NAm	7.32	Grant HOLLOWAY	USA	Liévin	9 Feb 21
	NAm=	7.32	Grant HOLLOWAY	USA	Madrid	24 Feb 21
	W	7.29	Grant HOLLOWAY	USA	Madrid	24 Feb 21
PV	W18	5.60	Matvey VOLKOV	BLR	Lódz	12 Feb 21
TJ	W	18.07	Fabrice ZANGO	BUR	Aubière	16 Jan 21
SP	W	22.82	Ryan CROUSER	USA	Fayetteville	24 Jan 21
	Asi	20.80 & 21.10	Abdelrahman MAHMOUD	BRN	Gomel	29 Jan 21
WT	Asi	21.45 twice	Khalil BEDOUI	QAT	Allendale	5 Feb 21
	Asi	21.51	Khalil BEDOUI	QAT	Allendale	12 Feb 21
Hep/U20	W20	6062	Jente HAUTTEKEETE	BEL	Frankfurt-am-Main	14 Feb 21
		7.07, 7.33, 15.64, 2.10 / 8.06, 4.70, 2:46.71				
DMR	W	9:19.42	Oregon University	MIX	Fayetteville	29 Jan 21
		Hocker, Peralta/DOM, Hunter/AUS, Teare				
5000W	W20	18:50.7 §	Sergey KOZHEVNIKOV	RUS	Saransk	27 Dec 20

INDOORS – WOMEN

60	SAm=	7.17	Rosangela SANTOS	BRA	Liévin	9 Feb 21
200	W35	22.59	Allyson FELIX	USA	Fayetteville	21 Feb 21
	Afr	22.75	Favour OFILI	NGR	Fayetteville	27 Feb 21
400	W40	55.44	Aneta LEMIESZ	POL	Torun	23 Jan 21
	W40	55.39	Aneta LEMIESZ	POL	Spala	6 Feb 21
	W20	50.52 §	Athing MU	USA	College Station	6 Feb 21
	CAC	50.21	Shaunae MILLER-UIBO	BAH	Staten Island	13 Feb 21
	W40	54.80	Aneta LEMIESZ	POL	Torun	13 Mar 21
800	W20	1:59.03	Keely HODGKINSON	GBR	Wien	30 Jan 21
	W20	1:58.40 §	Athing MU	USA	Fayetteville	27 Feb 21
1000	W18	2:41.53	Roisin WILLIS	USA	Chicago	20 Feb 21
1500	W	3:53.09	Gudaf TSEGAY	ETH	Liévin	9 Feb 21
	Com	3:59.58	Laura MUIR	GBR	Liévin	9 Feb 21
2M	NAm	9:10.28	Elle PURRIER	USA	Staten Island	13 Feb 21
2000SC	W	5:45.09	Winfred YAVI (no water jumo)	BRN	Liévin	9 Feb 21
60H	W20=	7.91	Ackera NUGENT	JAM	Lubbock	26 Feb 21
LJ	W20	6.91	Larissa IAPICHINO	ITA	Ancona	20 Feb 21
WT	Afr	23.08 & 23.40	Sade OLATOYE	NGR	Geneva, USA	12 Feb 21
	W35	24.93	Erin REESE	USA	Terre Haute	13 Feb 21
Pen	CAC	4746	Tyra GITTENS	TTO	Fayetteville	11 Mar 21
		8.27, 1.93, 13.86, 6.58, 2:28.22				
4x800R	W20	8:37.20	Willis, Goggans, Whittaker, Gorriaran	USA	Virginia Beach	17 Jan 21
3000W	W35	12:21.43	Antigóni DRISBIÓTI	GRE	Pireás	12 Feb 21
5000W	W	20:04.4 §	Yelena LASHMANOVA	RUS	Saransk	27 Dec 20

OUTDOORS – MEN

600	W20	1:14.79	Mohamed Ali GOUANED	ALG	El Djezair	26 Mar 21
100k	NAm	6:09:26	Jim WALMSLEY	USA	Chandler	23 Jan 21
35kW	Afr	2:41:21+	Marc MUNDELL	RSA	Dudince	20 Mar 21
50kW	Afr	3:53:09	Marc MUNDELL	RSA	Dudince	20 Mar 21

OUTDOORS – WOMEN

1000	Oce	2:35.90	Linden HALL	AUS	Melbourne	2 Mar 21
	W18	2:36.72	Claudia HOLLINGSWORTH	AUS	Melbourne	2 Mar 21
5k	W	14:43	Beatrice CHEPKOECH	KEN	Monaco	14 Feb 21
HT	Oce	73.55	Julia RATCLIFFE	NZL	Hastings	26 Mar 21
Hep	SAm	6346	Evelyn AGUILAR	COL	Ibagué	14 Mar 21
		13.88, 1.71, 14.31, 23.75 / 6.51, 43.92, 2:13.71				
20kW	W, Asi	1:23:49	YANG Jiayu	CHN	Huangshan	20 Mar 21
35kW	SAm	2:51:11A	Erica de SENA	BRA	Macas	13 Mar 21

EUROPEAN INDOOR CHAMPIONSHIPS 2021

At Torun, Poland 4-7 March 2021

MEN

60 Metres (6)
1. Lamont Marcell Jacobs ITA 6.47
2. Kevin Kranz GER 6.60
3. Ján Volko SVK 6.61
4. Andrew Robertson GBR 6.63
5. Carlos Nascimento POR 6.65
6. Remigiusz Olszewski POL 6.66
7. Karl Erik Nazarov EST 6.67

400 Metres (6)
1. Óscar Husillos ESP 46.22
2. Tony van Diepen NED 46.25
3. Liemarvin Bonevacia NED 46.30
4. Carl Bengström SWE 46.42
5. Jochem Dobber NED 46.82
6. Luka Janezic SLO 47.22

800 Metres (7)
1. Patryk Dobek POL 1:46.81
2. Mateusz Borkowski POL 1:46.90
3. Jamie Webb GBR 1:46.95
4. Adam Kszczot POL 1:47.23
5. Amel Tuka BIH 1:47.37
6. Pierre-Ambr. Bosse FRA 1:50.13

1500 Metres (5)
1. Jakob Ingebrigtsen NOR 3:37.56
2. Marcin Lewandowski POL 3:38.06
3. Jesús Gómez ESP 3:38.47
4. Ignacio Fontes ESP 3:39.66
5. Piers Copeland GBR 3:39.99
6. Michal Rozmys POL 3:40.11
7. Andrew Coscoran IRL 3:40.38
8. István Szögi HUN 3:40.40

3000 Metres (7)
1. Jakob Ingebrigtsen NOR 7:48.20
2. Isaac Kimeli BEL 7:49.41
3. Adel Mechaal ESP 7:49.47
4. Mohamed Katir ESP 7:49.72
5. Narve G Nordås NOR 7:50.21
6. Hugo Hay FRA 7:51.82
7. Andrew Butchart GBR 7:52.15
8. Jimmy Gressier FRA 7:52.43

60 Metres Hurdles (7)
1. Wilhem Bélocian FRA 7.42
2. Andrew Pozzi GBR 7.43
3. Paolo Dal Molin ITA 7.56
4. Asier Martínez ESP 7.60
5. Aurel Manga FRA 7.63
6. Damien Czykier POL 7.63
7. Koen Smet NED 7.73

High Jump (7)
1. Maksim Nedosekov BLR 2.37
2. Gianmarco Tamberi ITA 2.35
3. Thomas Carmoy BEL 2.26
4. Tobias Potye GER 2.26
5= Andrijus Glebauskas LTU 2.23
5= Dmytro Nikitin UKR 2.23
7. Mateusz Przybylko GER 2.19

Pole Vault (7)
1. Armand Duplantis SWE 6.05*
2. Valentin Lavillenie FRA 5.80
3. Piotr Lisek POL 5.80
4. Oleg Zernikel GER 5.70
5= Menno Vloon NED 5.70
5= Ersu Sasma TUR 5.70
7. Robert Sobera POL 5.50

Long Jump (5)
1. Miltiádis Tentóglou GRE 8.35
2. Thobias Montler SWE 8.31
3. Kristian Pulli FIN 8.24
4. Vladyslav Mazur UKR 8.14
5. Maximilian Entholzner GER 7.87
6. Lazar Anic SRB 7.81
7. Jacob Fincham-Dukes GBR 7.79

Triple Jump (7)
1. Pedro Pablo Pichardo POR 17.30
2. Alexis Copello AZE 17.04
3. Max Hess GER 17.01
4. Tobia Bocchi ITA 16.65
5. Levon Aghasyan ARM 16.55
6. Jesper Hellström SWE 16.45
7. Dimítrios Tsiámis GRE 16.40

Shot (5)
1. Tomás Stanek CZE 21.62
2. Michal Haratyk POL 21.47
3. Filip Mihaljevic CRO 21.31
4. Francisco Belo POR 21.28
5. Wictor Petersson SWE 20.75
6. Armin Sinancevic SRB 20.74
7. Marcus Thomsen NOR 20.28

Heptathlon (6/7)
1. Kevin Mayer FRA 6392
2. Jorge Ureña ESP 6158
3. Pawel Wiesiolek POL 6133
4. Rik Taam NED 6111
5. Risto Lillemets EST 6055
6. Andreas Bechmann GER 5995
7. Dario Dester ITA 5835
8. Darko Pesic MNE 5824

4 x 400 Metres Relay (7)
1. NED 3:06.06 4. BEL 3:06.96
2. CZE 3:06.54 5. ITA 3:07.37
3. GBR 3:06.70

Women – 60 Metres (7)
1. Ajla Del Ponte SUI 7.03
2. Lotta Kemppinen FIN 7.22
3. Jamile Samuel NED 7.22
4. Or. Ombissa-Dzangué FRA 7.23
5. Maja Mihalinec SLO 7.26
6. Carolle Zahi FRA 7.26
7. Jennifer Montag GER 7.29

400 Metres (6)
1. Femke Bol NED 50.63
2. Justyna Swiety-Ersetic POL 51.41
3. Jodie Williams GBR 51.73
4. Phil Healy IRL 51.94
5. Lieke Klaver NED 52.03
6. Andrea Miklos ROU 52.10

800 Metres (7)
1. Keely Hodgkinson GBR-J 2:03.88
2. Joanna Józwik POL 2:04.00
3. Angelika Cichocka POL 2:04.15
4. Ellie Baker GBR 2:04.40
5. Lore Hoffmann SUI 2:04.84
6. Isabelle Boffey GBR 2:07.26

1500 Metres (6)
1. Elise Vanderelst BEL 4:18.44
2. Holly Archer GBR 4:19.91
3. Hanna Klein GER 4:20.07
4. Marta Pérez ESP 4:20.39
5. Esther Guerrero ESP 4:20.45
6. Katie Snowden GBR 4:21.81
7. Darya Borisevich BLR 4:22.98
8. Gesa Felicitas Krause GER 4:24.26

3000 Metres (5)
1. Amy-Eloise Markovc GBR 8:46.43
2. Alice Finot FRA 8:46.54
3. Verity Ockenden GBR 8:46.60
4. Meraf Bahta SWE 8:48.78
5. Amelia Quirk GBR 8:48.82
6. Selamawit Bayoulgn ISR 8:49.13
7. Elena Burkard GER 8:51.09
8. Lucia Rodríguez ESP 8:53.90

60 Metres Hurdles (7)
1. Nadine Visser NED 7.77
2. Cindy Sember GBR 7.89
3. Tiffany Porter GBR 7.92
4. Nooralotta Neziri FIN 7.93
5. Pia Skrzyszowska POL 7.95
6. Luminosa Bogliolo ITA 7.99
7. Zoë Sedney NED 8.00

High Jump (7)
1. Yaroslava Mahuchikh UKR 2.00
2. Iryna Herashchenko UKR 1.98
3. Ella Junnila FIN 1.96
4. Yuliya Levchenko UKR 1.94
5. Daniela Stanciu ROU 1.92
6. Alessia Trost ITA 1.92
7. Marija Vukovic MNE 1.92

Pole Vault (6)
1. Angelica Moser SUI 4.75
2. Tina Sutej SLO 4.70
3= Holly Bradshaw GBR 4.65
3= Irina Zhuk BLR 4.65
5. Eléni-Klaoúdia Pólak GRE 4.65
6. Wilma Murto FIN 4.55
7= Yana Hladiychuk UKR 4.45
7= Fanny Smets BEL 4.45

Long Jump (6)
1. Maryna Bekh-Romanchuk UKR 6.92
2. Malaika Mihambo GER 6.88
3. Khaddi Sagnia SWE 6.75
4. An. Mironchik-Ivanova BLR 6.72
5. Larissa Iapichino ITA-J 6.59
6. Laura Strati ITA 6.57
7. Fatima Diame ESP 6.47

Triple Jump (7)
1. Patricia Mamona POR 14.53
2. Ana Peleteiro ESP 14.52
3. Neele Eckhardt GER 14.52
4. Violetta Skvortsova BLR 14.35
5. Paraskeví Papahrístou GRE 14.31
6. Kristiina Mäkelä FIN 14.23
7. Senni Salminen FIN 14.14

Shot (5)
1. Auriol Dongmo POR 19.34
2. Fanny Roos SWE 19.29
3. Christina Schwanitz GER 19.04
4. Alyona Dubitskaya BLR 18.86
5. Jessica Schilder NED 18.69
6. Sara Gambetta GER 18.34
7. María Toimil ESP 18.01

Pentathlon (5)
1. Nafissatou Thiam 4904
2. Noor Vidts BEL 4791
3. Xénia Krizsán HUN 4644
4. Ivona Dadic AUT 4587
5. Holly Mills GBR 4517
6. Rita Nemes HUN 4486
7. Paulina Ligarska POL 4484
8. Célia Perron FRA 4310

4 x 400 Metres Relay (7)
1. NED 3:27.15* 4. ITA 3:30.32
2. GBR 3:28.20   5. UKR 3:30.38
3. POL 3:29.94   6. GER 3:31.47

WORLD MEN'S ALL-TIME LISTS

Mark	Wind	Name		Nat	Born	Pos	Meet	Venue	Date

100 METRES

Mark	Wind	Name		Nat	Born	Pos	Meet	Venue	Date
9.58 WR	0.9	Usain	Bolt	JAM	21.8.86	1	WCh	Berlin	16 Aug 09
9.63	1.5		Bolt			1	OG	London (OS)	5 Aug 12
9.69 WR	0.0		Bolt			1	OG	Beijing	16 Aug 08
9.69	2.0	Tyson	Gay ¶	USA	9.8.82	1		Shanghai	20 Sep 09
9.69	-0.1	Yohan	Blake	JAM	26.12.89	1	Athl	Lausanne	23 Aug 12
9.71	0.9		Gay			2	WCh	Berlin	16 Aug 09
9.72 WR	1.7		Bolt			1	Reebok	New York (RI)	31 May 08
9.72	0.2	Asafa	Powell	JAM	23.11.82	1rA	Athl	Lausanne	2 Sep 08
9.74 WR	1.7		Powell			1h2	GP	Rieti	9 Sep 07
9.74	0.9	Justin	Gatlin ¶	USA	10.2.82	1	DL	Doha	15 May 15
9.75	1.1		Blake			1	NC	Kingston	29 Jun 12
9.75	1.5		Blake			2	OG	London (OS)	5 Aug 12
9.75	0.9		Gatlin			1	GGala	Roma	4 Jun 15
9.75	1.4		Gatlin			1	Athl	Lausanne	9 Jul 15
9.76	1.8		Bolt			1		Kingston	3 May 08
9.76	1.3		Bolt			1	VD	Bruxelles	16 Sep 11
9.76	-0.1		Bolt			1	GGala	Roma	31 May 12
9.76	1.4		Blake			1	WK	Zürich	30 Aug 12
9.76	0.6	Christian	Coleman	USA	6.3.96	1	WCh	Doha	28 Sep 19
9.77 WR	1.6		Powell			1	Tsik	Athína	14 Jun 05
9.77 WR	1.5		Powell			1	BrGP	Gateshead	11 Jun 06
9.77 WR	1.0		Powell			1rA	WK	Zürich	18 Aug 06
9.77	1.6		Gay			1q1	NC/OT	Eugene	28 Jun 08
9.77	-1.3		Bolt			1	VD	Bruxelles	5 Sep 08
9.77	0.9		Powell			1h1	GP	Rieti	7 Sep 08
9.77	0.4		Gay			1	GGala	Roma	10 Jul 09
9.77	-0.3		Bolt			1	WCh	Moskva	11 Aug 13
9.77	0.6		Gatlin			1	VD	Bruxelles	5 Sep 14
9.77	0.9		Gatlin			1s2	WCh	Beijing	23 Aug 15
9.78	0.0		Powell			1	GP	Rieti	9 Sep 07
9.78	-0.4		Gay			1	LGP	London (CP)	13 Aug 10
9.78	0.9	Nesta	Carter ¶	JAM	10.11.85	1		Rieti	29 Aug 10
9.78	1.0		Powell			1	Athl	Lausanne	30 Jun 11
9.78	-0.3		Gatlin			1	Herc	Monaco	17 Jul 15

(34 performances by 7 athletes)

Mark	Wind	Name		Nat	Born	Pos	Meet	Venue	Date
9.79 WR	0.1	Maurice	Greene	USA	23.7.74	1rA	Tsik	Athína	16 Jun 99
9.80	0.4	Steve	Mullings ¶	JAM	29.11.82	1	Pre	Eugene	4 Jun 11
9.82	1.7	Richard	Thompson	TTO	7.6.85	1	NC	Port of Spain	21 Jun 14

(10)

Mark	Wind	Name		Nat	Born	Pos	Meet	Venue	Date
9.84 WR	0.7	Donovan	Bailey	CAN	16.12.67	1	OG	Atlanta	27 Jul 96
9.84	0.2	Bruny	Surin	CAN	12.7.67	2	WCh	Sevilla	22 Aug 99
9.84	1.3	Trayvon	Bromell	USA	10.7.95	1h4	NC	Eugene	25 Jun 15
9.85 WR	1.2	Leroy	Burrell	USA	21.2.67	1rA	Athl	Lausanne	6 Jul 94
9.85	1.7	Olusoji	Fasuba	NGR	9.7.84	2	SGP	Doha	12 May 06
9.85	1.3	Michael	Rodgers	USA	24.4.85	2	Pre	Eugene	4 Jun 11
9.86 WR	1.2	Carl	Lewis	USA	1.7.61	1	WCh	Tokyo	25 Aug 91
9.86	-0.4	Frank	Fredericks	NAM	2.10.67	1rA	Athl	Lausanne	3 Jul 96
9.86	1.8	Ato	Boldon	TTO	30.12.73	1rA	MSR	Walnut	19 Apr 98
9.86	0.6	Francis	Obikwelu	NGR/POR	22.11.78	2	OG	Athína	22 Aug 04

(20)

Mark	Wind	Name		Nat	Born	Pos	Meet	Venue	Date
9.86	1.4	Keston	Bledman	TTO	8.3.88	1	NC	Port of Spain	23 Jun 12
9.86	1.3	Jimmy	Vicaut	FRA	27.2.92	2	DL	Saint-Denis	4 Jul 15
9.86	0.9	Noah	Lyles	USA	18.7.97	1	DL	Shanghai	18 May 19
9.86	0.8	Divine	Oduduru	NGR	7.10.96	1	NCAA	Austin	7 Jun 19
9.86	1.6	Michael	Norman	USA	3.12.97	1		Fort Worth	20 Jul 20
9.87	0.3	Linford	Christie ¶	GBR	2.4.60	1	WCh	Stuttgart	15 Aug 93
9.87A	-0.2	Obadele	Thompson	BAR	30.3.76	1	WCp	Johannesburg	11 Sep 98
9.87	-0.1	Ronnie	Baker	USA	15.10.93	1	Skol	Chorzów	22 Aug 18
9.88	1.8	Shawn	Crawford ¶	USA	14.1.78	1	Pre	Eugene	19 Jun 04
9.88	0.6	Walter	Dix	USA	31.1.86	2		Nottwil	8 Aug 10

(30)

Mark	Wind	Name		Nat	Born	Pos	Meet	Venue	Date
9.88	0.9	Ryan	Bailey	USA	13.4.89	2		Rieti	29 Aug 10
9.88	1.0	Michael	Frater	JAM	6.10.82	2	Athl	Lausanne	30 Jun 11
9.89	1.6	Travis	Padgett	USA	13.12.86	1q2	NC/OT	Eugene	28 Jun 08
9.89	1.6	Darvis	Patton	USA	4.12.77	1q3	NC/OT	Eugene	28 Jun 08
9.89	1.3	Ngonidzashe	Makusha	ZIM	11.3.87	1	NCAA	Des Moines	10 Jun 11
9.89	1.9	Akani	Simbine	RSA	21.9.93	1	Gyulai	Székesfehérvár	18 Jul 16

100 METRES A-T

Mark	Wind	Name		Nat	Born	Pos	Meet	Venue	Date
9.90	0.4	Nickel	Ashmeade	JAM	7.4.90	1s2	WCh	Moskva	11 Aug 13
9.90	0.6	Andre	De Grasse	CAN	10.11.94	3	WCh	Doha	28 Sep 19
9.91	1.2	Dennis	Mitchell ¶	USA	20.2.66	3	WCh	Tokyo	25 Aug 91
9.91	0.9	Leonard (40)	Scott	USA	19.1.80	2	WAF	Stuttgart	9 Sep 06
9.91	-0.5	Derrick	Atkins	BAH	5.1.84	2	WCh	Osaka	26 Aug 07
9.91	-0.2	Daniel	Bailey	ANT	9.9.86	2	GL	Saint-Denis	17 Jul 09
9.91	0.7	Churandy	Martina	NED	3.7.84	2s1	OG	London (OS)	5 Aug 12
9.91	1.1	James	Dasaolu	GBR	5.9.87	1s2	NC	Birmingham	13 Jul 13
9.91	1.8	Femi Seun	Ogunode ¶	QAT	15.5.91	1	AsiC	Wuhan	4 Jun 15
9.91	1.0	Julian	Forte	JAM	7.1.93	1	ISTAF	Berlin	27 Aug 17
9.91	0.4	Zharnel	Hughes	GBR	13.7.95	1rA		Kingston	9 Jun 18
9.91	0.2		Su Bingtian (48)	CHN	29.8.89	1		Madrid	22 Jun 18
9.92		nine men							

100th man 9.96, 200th 10.03, 300th 10.07, 400th 10.11, 500th 10.13

Doubtful timing: 9.88A 0.2 Sydney Siame ZAM 7.10.97 1 Lusaka 8 Apr 17
Doubtful wind reading: 9.91 -2.3 Davidson Ezinwa NGR22.11.71 1 Azusa 11 Apr 92
Wind-assisted – performances to 9.76, performers listed to 9.88

Mark	Wind	Name		Nat	Born	Pos	Meet	Venue	Date
9.68	4.1	Tyson	Gay ¶	USA	9.8.82	1	NC/OT	Eugene	29 Jun 08
9.69A	5+	Obadele	Thompson	BAR	30.3.76	1		El Paso	13 Apr 96
9.69	4.8	Andre	De Grasse	CAN	10.11.94	1	DL	Stockholm	18 Jun 17
9.72	2.1		Powell			1	Bisl	Oslo	4 Jun 10
9.74	w	Richard	Thompson	TTO	7.6.85	1		Clermont	31 May 14
9.75	3.4		Gay			1h1	NC	Eugene	25 Jun 09
9.75	2.6		Powell			1h2	DL	Doha	14 May 10
9.75	4.3	Darvis	Patton	USA	4.12.77	1rA	TexR	Austin	30 Mar 13
9.75	2.7		De Grasse			1	NCAA	Eugene	12 Jun 15
9.76A	6.1	Churandy	Martina	AHO	3.7.84	1		El Paso	13 May 06
9.76	2.2		Gay			1	GP	New York	2 Jun 07
9.76	2.7		Gatlin			1	Pre	Eugene	31 May 14
9.76	3.7	Trayvon	Bromell	USA	10.7.95	1s1	NC	Eugene	26 Jun 15
9.78	5.2	Carl	Lewis	USA	1.7.61	1	NC/OT	Indianapolis	16 Jul 88
9.78	3.7	Maurice	Greene	USA	23.7.74	1	GP II	Stanford	31 May 04
9.78	2.4	Ronnie	Baker	USA	15.10.93	1	Pre	Eugene	26 May 18
9.79	5.3	Andre	Cason	USA	20.1.69	1h4	NC	Eugene	16 Jun 93
9.80	4.1	Walter	Dix	USA	31.1.86	2	NC/OT	Eugene	29 Jun 08
9.80	2.7	Michael	Rodgers	USA	24.4.85	2	Pre	Eugene	31 May 14
9.82	3.0	Isiah	Young	USA	5.1.90	1		Clermont	16 May 15
9.82	4.9	Remontay	McClain	USA	21.9.92	1h3	NC	Eugene	25 Jun 15
9.83	7.1	Leonard	Scott	USA	19.1.80	1r1	Sea Ray	Knoxville	9 Apr 99
9.83	2.2	Derrick	Atkins	BAH	5.1.84	2	GP	New York	2 Jun 07
9.84	5.4	Francis	Obikwelu	NGR/POR	22.11.78	1		Zaragoza	3 Jun 06
9.84	4.8	Ben Youssef	Meïté	CIV	11.11.86	2	DL	Stockholm	18 Jun 17
9.85	4.8	Dennis	Mitchell ¶	USA	20.2.66	2	NC	Eugene	17 Jun 93
9.85A	3.0	Frank	Fredericks	NAM	2.10.67	1		Nairobi	18 May 02
9.85	4.1	Travis	Padgett	USA	13.12.86	4	NC/OT	Eugene	29 Jun 08
9.85	3.6	Keston	Bledman	TTO	8.3.88	1rA		Clermont	2 Jun 12
9.85	3.2	Charles	Silmon	USA	4.7.91	1s1	NC	Des Moines	21 Jun 13
9.85A	3.0	Kemar	Hyman	CAY	11.10.89	1s2	NACAC	San José, CRC	7 Aug 15
9.86	2.6	Shawn	Crawford ¶	USA	14.1.78	1	GP	Doha	14 May 04
9.86	3.6	Michael	Frater	JAM	6.10.82	2h4	NC	Kingston	23 Jun 11
9.86	3.2	Rakieem "Mookie"	Salaam	USA	5.4.90	2s1	NC	Des Moines	21 Jun 13
9.86	3.7	Diondre	Batson	USA	13.7.92	2s1	NC	Eugene	26 Jun 15
9.86	4.1	Noah	Lyles	USA	18.7.97	1rF		Gainesville	13 Apr 18
9.87	11.2	William	Snoddy	USA	6.12.57	1		Dallas	1 Apr 78
9.87	4.9	Calvin	Smith	USA	8.1.61	1s2	NC/OT	Indianapolis	16 Jul 88
9.87	2.4	Michael	Marsh	USA	4.8.67	1	MSR	Walnut	20 Apr 97
9.87	3.3	Yoshihide	Kiryu	JPN	15.12.95	1r1	TexR	Austin	28 Mar 15
9.87	2.1	Tevin	Hester	USA	10.1.94	1	ACC	Tallahassee	16 May 15
9.88	2.3	James	Sanford	USA	27.12.57	1		Los Angeles (Ww)	3 May 80
9.88	5.2	Albert	Robinson	USA	28.11.64	4	NC/OT	Indianapolis	16 Jul 88
9.88	4.9	Tim	Harden	USA	27.1.74	1	NC	New Orleans	20 Jun 98
9.88	4.5	Coby	Miller	USA	19.10.76	1		Auburn	1 Apr 00
9.88	3.6	Patrick	Johnson	AUS	26.9.72	1		Perth	8 Feb 03
9.88	3.0	Darrel	Brown	TTO	11.10.84	1	NC	Port of Spain	23 Jun 07
9.88	3.7	Ivory	Williams #	USA	2.5.85	1	TexR	Austin	3 Apr 10
9.88	2.4	Reece	Prescod	GBR	29.2.96	3	Pre	Eugene	26 May 18

Drugs disqualification

Mark	Wind	Name		Nat	Born	Pos	Meet	Venue	Date
9.75	1.1		Gay ¶			(1)	NC	Des Moines	21 Jun 13
9.77	1.7		Gatlin ¶	USA	10.2.82	(1)	SGP	Doha	12 May 06

100 – 200 METRES A-T

Mark	Wind	Name		Nat	Born	Pos	Meet	Venue	Date
9.78	2.0	Tim	Montgomery ¶	USA	28.1.75	(1)	GPF	Paris (C)	14 Sep 02
9.79	1.1	Ben	Johnson ¶	CAN	30.12.61	(1)	OG	Seoul	24 Sep 88
9.87	2.0	Dwain	Chambers ¶	GBR	5.4.78	(2)	GPF	Paris (C)	14 Sep 02
9.75w	2.4		Gay			(1s2)	NC	Des Moines	21 Jun 13

200 METRES

Mark	Wind	Name		Nat	Born	Pos	Meet	Venue	Date
19.19 WR	-0.3	Usain	Bolt	JAM	21.8.86	1	WCh	Berlin	20 Aug 09
19.26	0.7	Yohan	Blake	JAM	26.12.89	1	VD	Bruxelles	16 Sep 11
19.30 WR	-0.9		Bolt			1	OG	Beijing	20 Aug 08
19.32 WR	0.4	Michael	Johnson	USA	13.9.67	1	OG	Atlanta	1 Aug 96
19.32	0.4		Bolt			1	OG	London (OS)	9 Aug 12
19.40	0.8		Bolt			1	WCh	Daegu	3 Sep 11
19.44	0.4		Blake			2	OG	London (OS)	9 Aug 12
19.50	-0.1	Noah	Lyles	USA	18.7.97	1	Athl	Lausanne	5 Jul 19
19.53	0.7	Walter	Dix	USA	31.1.86	2	VD	Bruxelles	16 Sep 11
19.54	0.0		Blake			1	VD	Bruxelles	7 Sep 12
19.55	-0.1		Bolt			1	WCh	Beijing	27 Aug 15
19.56	-0.8		Bolt			1		Kingston	1 May 10
19.57	0.0		Bolt			1	VD	Bruxelles	4 Sep 09
19.57	0.4	Justin	Gatlin ¶	USA	10.2.82	1	NC	Eugene	28 Jun 15
19.58	1.3	Tyson	Gay ¶	USA	9.8.82	1	Reebok	New York	30 May 09
19.58	1.4		Bolt			1	Athl	Lausanne	23 Aug 12
19.59	-0.9		Bolt			1	Athl	Lausanne	7 Jul 09
19.62	-0.3		Gay			1	NC	Indianapolis	24 Jun 07
19.63	0.4	Xavier	Carter	USA	8.12.85	1	Athl	Lausanne	11 Jul 06
19.63	-0.9		Bolt			1	Athl	Lausanne	2 Sep 08
19.65	0.0	Wallace	Spearmon	USA	24.12.84	1		Daegu	28 Sep 06
19.65	0.9		Lyles			1	Herc	Monaco	20 Jul 18
19.65	0.2		Lyles			1	DL	Paris (C)	24 Aug 19
19.66 WR	1.7		M Johnson			1	NC	Atlanta	23 Jun 96
19.66	0.0		Bolt			1	WK	Zürich	30 Aug 12
19.66	0.0		Bolt			1	WCh	Moskva	17 Aug 13
19.67	-0.5		Bolt			1	GP	Athína	13 Jul 08
19.67	-0.2		Lyles			1	WK	Zürich	30 Aug 18
19.68	0.4	Frank	Fredericks	NAM	2.10.67	2	OG	Atlanta	1 Aug 96
19.68	-0.1		Gay			1	WAF	Stuttgart	10 Sep 06
19.68	-0.1		Bolt			1	WAF	Thessaloníki	13 Sep 09
19.68	-0.5		Gatlin			1	Herc	Monaco	18 Jul 14
19.68	0.9		Gatlin			1	Pre	Eugene	30 May 15
		(33/10)							
19.69A	-0.5	Clarence	Munyai	RSA	20.2.98	1s1	NC	Pretoria	16 Mar 18
19.70	0.7	Michael	Norman	USA	3.12.97	1	GGala	Roma	6 Jun 19
19.72A WR	1.8	Pietro	Mennea	ITA	28.6.52	1	WUG	Ciudad de México	12 Sep 79
19.73	-0.2	Michael	Marsh	USA	4.8.67	1s1	OG	Barcelona	5 Aug 92
19.73	0.8	Divine	Oduduru	NGR	7.10.96	1	NCAA	Austin	7 Jun 19
19.74	1.4	LaShawn	Merritt ¶	USA	27.6.86	1s3	NC/OT	Eugene	8 Jul 16
19.75	1.5	Carl	Lewis	USA	1.7.61	1	NC	Indianapolis	19 Jun 83
19.75	1.7	Joe	DeLoach	USA	5.6.67	1	OG	Seoul	28 Sep 88
19.75	0.3	Steven	Gardiner	BAH	12.9.95	1		Coral Gables	7 Apr 18
19.76	0.7	Ramil	Guliyev	AZE/TUR	29.5.90	1	EC	Berlin	9 Aug 18
		(20)							
19.77	0.7	Ato	Boldon	TTO	30.12.73	1rA		Stuttgart	13 Jul 97
19.77	0.0	Isaac	Makwala	BOT	29.9.86	1		Madrid	14 Jul 17
19.79	1.2	Shawn	Crawford ¶	USA	14.1.78	1	OG	Athína	26 Aug 04
19.79	0.9	Warren	Weir	JAM	31.10.89	1	NC	Kingston	23 Jun 13
19.80	0.8	Christophe	Lemaitre	FRA	11.6.90	3	WCh	Daegu	3 Sep 11
19.80	2.0	Rasheed	Dwyer	JAM	29.1.89	1s1	PAm	Toronto	23 Jul 15
19.80	-0.3	Andre	De Grasse	CAN	10.11.94	2s2	OG	Rio de Janeiro	17 Aug 16
19.80	1.0	Kenny	Bednarek	USA	14.10.98	1		Montverde	10 Aug 20
19.81	-0.3	Alonso	Edward	PAN	8.12.89	2	WCh	Berlin	20 Aug 09
19.81	0.4	Churandy	Martina	NED	3.7.84	1	Athl	Lausanne	25 Aug 16
		(30)							
19.81	0.1	Akeem	Bloomfield	JAM	10.11.97	1	DL	London (OS)	22 Jul 18
19.83A WR	0.9	Tommie	Smith	USA	6.6.44	1	OG	Ciudad de México	16 Oct 68
19.84	1.7	Francis	Obikwelu	NGR/POR	22.11.78	1s2	WCh	Sevilla	25 Aug 99
19.84	1.2	Wayde	van Niekerk	RSA	15.7.92	1		Kingston	10 Jun 17
19.85	-0.3	John	Capel ¶	USA	27.10.78	1	NC	Sacramento	23 Jul 00
19.85	-0.5	Konstadínos	Kedéris ¶	GRE	11.7.73	1	EC	München	9 Aug 02
19.85	0.0	Nickel	Ashmeade	JAM	4.7.90	2	WK	Zürich	30 Aug 12
19.85	1.9	Ameer	Webb	USA	19.3.91	1	DL	Doha	6 May 16

Mark	Wind	Name		Nat	Born	Pos	Meet	Venue	Date
19.85	-0.5	Christian	Coleman	USA	6.3.96	1q1	NCAA-E	Lexington	27 May 17
19.86A	1.0	Don	Quarrie	JAM	25.2.51	1	PAm	Cali	3 Aug 71
		(40)							
19.86	1.6	Maurice	Greene	USA	23.7.74	2rA	DNG	Stockholm	7 Jul 97
19.86	1.5	Jason	Young	JAM	21.3.91	1	Spitzen	Luzern	17 Jul 12
19.86	1.6	Isiah	Young	USA	5.1.90	1	NC	Des Moines	23 Jun 13
19.87	0.8	Lorenzo	Daniel	USA	23.3.66	1	NCAA	Eugene	3 Jun 88
19.87A	1.8	John	Regis	GBR	13.10.66	1		Sestriere	31 Jul 94
19.87	1.2	Jeff	Williams	USA	31.12.65	1		Fresno	13 Apr 96
19.87	-0.1	Anaso	Jobodwana	RSA	30.7.92	3	WCh	Beijing	27 Aug 15
19.87	-0.1	Alex	Quiñónez	ECU	11.8.89	2	Athl	Lausanne	5 Jul 19
19.88	-0.3	Floyd	Heard	USA	24.3.66	2	NC	Sacramento	23 Jul 00
19.88	0.1	Joshua 'J.J'	Johnson	USA	10.5.76	1	VD	Bruxelles	24 Aug 01
19.88	1.2	Miguel	Francis	ANT/GBR	28.3.95	1		Kingston	11 Jun 16
19.88	0.9		Xie Zhenye	CHN	17.8.93	1	DL	London (OS)	21 Jul 19
		(52)			100th man 20.06, 200th 20.20, 300th 20.28, 400th 20.34, 500th 20.39				

Wind-assisted 4 performances to 19.66, performers listed to 19.86

19.49A	6.1	Kenny	Bednarek	USA	14.10.98	1h4	JUCO	Hobbs, NM	17 May 19
19.58	2.4	Andre	De Grasse	CAN	10.11.94	1	NCAA	Eugene	12 Jun 15
19.61	>4.0	Leroy	Burrell	USA	21.2.67	1	SWC	College Station	19 May 90
19.64A	5.6	Terrance	Laird	USA	12.10.98	1h1	JUCO	Hobbs, NM	17 May 19
19.73	3.3	Shawn	Crawford ¶	USA	14.1.78	1	NC	Eugene	28 Jun 09
19.75	4.1	Isiah	Young	USA	5.1.90	1rA		Clermont	16 May 15
19.83	9.2	Bobby	Cruse	USA	20.3.78	1r2	Sea Ray	Knoxville	9 Apr 99
19.86	4.6	Roy	Martin	USA	25.12.66	1	SWC	Houston	18 May 86
19.86	2.4	Dedric	Dukes	USA	2.4.92	2	NCAA	Eugene	12 Jun 15
19.86	2.4	Trayvon	Bromell	USA	10.7.95	3	NCAA	Eugene	12 Jun 15
19.86	2.9	Danny	Talbot	GBR	1.5.91	1r2		Clermont	15 Apr 17

300 METRES

In 300m races only, not including intermediate times in 400m races

30.81		Wayde	van Niekerk	RSA	15.7.92	1	GS	Ostrava	28 Jun 17
30.85A		Michael	Johnson	USA	13.9.67	1		Pretoria	24 Mar 00
30.97		Usain	Bolt	JAM	21.8.86	1	GS	Ostrava	27 May 10
31.23		LaShawn	Merritt ¶	USA	27.6.86	2		Kingston	11 Jun 16
31.44		Isaac	Makwala	BOT	29.9.86	2	GS	Ostrava	28 Jun 17
31.48		Danny	Everett	USA	1.11.66	1		Jerez de la Frontera	3 Sep 90
31.48		Roberto	Hernández	CUB	6.3.67	2		Jerez de la Frontera	3 Sep 90
31.56		Doug	Walker ¶	GBR	28.7.73	1		Gateshead	19 Jul 98
31.61		Anthuan	Maybank	USA	30.12.69	1		Durham	13 Jul 96
31.61		Clarence	Munyai	RSA	20.2.98	3	GS	Ostrava	28 Jun 17

400 METRES

43.03 WR		Wayde	van Niekerk	RSA	15.7.92	1	OG	Rio de Janeiro	14 Aug 16
43.18 WR		Michael	Johnson	USA	13.9.67	1	WCh	Sevilla	26 Aug 99
43.29 WR		Butch	Reynolds ¶	USA	8.6.64	1	WK	Zürich	17 Aug 88
43.39			Johnson			1	WCh	Göteborg	9 Aug 95
43.44			Johnson			1	NC	Atlanta	19 Jun 96
43.45		Jeremy	Wariner	USA	31.1.84	1	WCh	Osaka	31 Aug 07
43.45		Michael	Norman	USA	3.12.97	1	MSR	Torrance	20 Apr 19
43.48			van Niekerk			1	WCh	Beijing	26 Aug 15
43.48		Steven	Gardiner	BAH	12.9.95	1	WCh	Doha	4 Oct 19
43.49			Johnson			1	OG	Atlanta	29 Jul 96
43.50		Quincy	Watts	USA	19.6.70	1	OG	Barcelona	5 Aug 92
43.50			Wariner			1	DNG	Stockholm	7 Aug 07
43.61			Norman			1	NCAA	Eugene	8 Jun 18
43.62			Wariner			1rA	GGala	Roma	14 Jul 06
43.62			van Niekerk			1	Athl	Lausanne	6 Jul 17
43.64		Fred	Kerley	USA	7.5.95	1	NC	Des Moines	27 Jul 19
43.65			Johnson			1	WCh	Stuttgart	17 Aug 93
43.65		LaShawn	Merritt ¶	USA	27.6.86	2	WCh	Beijing	26 Aug 15
43.66			Johnson			1	NC	Sacramento	16 Jun 95
43.66			Johnson			1rA	Athl	Lausanne	3 Jul 96
43.68			Johnson			1	WK	Zürich	12 Aug 98
43.68			Johnson			1	NC	Sacramento	16 Jul 00
43.70			Kerley			1q1	NCAA-W	Austin	26 May 17
43.71			Watts			1s2	OG	Barcelona	3 Aug 92
43.72		Isaac	Makwala (10)	BOT	29.9.86	1		La Chaux-de-Fonds	5 Jul 15
43.73			van Niekerk			1	Herc	Monaco	21 Jul 17
43.74			Johnson			1	NC	Eugene	19 Jun 93
43.74			Merritt			1	WCh	Moskva	13 Aug 13
43.74		Kirani	James	GRN	1.9.92	1	Athl	Lausanne	3 Jul 14

400 - 600 - 800 METRES A-T

Mark	Wind	Name		Nat	Born	Pos	Meet	Venue	Date
43.75			Johnson			1		Waco	19 Apr 97
43.75			Merritt			1	OG	Beijing	21 Aug 08
	(31/10)								
43.81		Danny	Everett	USA	1.11.66	1	NC/OT	New Orleans	26 Jun 92
43.86A	WR	Lee	Evans	USA	25.2.47	1	OG	Ciudad de México	18 Oct 68
43.87		Steve	Lewis	USA	16.5.69	1	OG	Seoul	28 Sep 88
43.93		Youssef	Al-Masrahi	KSA	31.12.87	1h2	WCh	Beijing	23 Aug 15
43.93		Rusheen	McDonald	JAM	17.8.92	2h2	WCh	Beijing	23 Aug 15
43.94		Akeem	Bloomfield	JAM	10.11.97	2	NCAA	Eugene	8 Jun 18
43.97A		Larry	James	USA	6.11.47	2	OG	Ciudad de México	18 Oct 68
44.01		Machel	Cedenio	TTO	6.9.95	4	OG	Rio de Janeiro	14 Aug 16
44.02		Baboloki	Thebe	BOT	18.3.97	2	Athl	Lausanne	6 Jul 17
	(20)								
44.05		Angelo	Taylor	USA	29.12.78	1	NC	Indianapolis	23 Jun 07
44.07		Abdelilah	Haroun	QAT	.97	1	DL	London (OS)	21 Jul 18
44.09		Alvin	Harrison ¶	USA/DOM	20.1.74	3	NC	Atlanta	19 Jun 96
44.09		Jerome	Young ¶	USA	14.8.76	1	NC	New Orleans	21 Jun 98
44.10		Gary	Kikaya	COD	4.2.78	2	WAF	Stuttgart	9 Sep 06
44.11		Luguelín	Santos	DOM	12.11.92	4	WCh	Beijing	26 Aug 15
44.13		Derek	Mills	USA	9.7.72	1	Pre	Eugene	4 Jun 95
44.13		Nathon	Allen	JAM	28.10.95	3	NCAA	Eugene	8 Jun 18
44.14		Roberto	Hernández	CUB	6.3.67	2		Sevilla	30 May 90
44.15		Anthuan	Maybank	USA	30.12.69	1rB	Athl	Lausanne	3 Jul 96
	(30)								
44.15		Anthony	Zambrano	COL	17.1.98	2	WCh	Doha	4 Oct 19
44.16		Otis	Harris	USA	30.6.82	2	OG	Athína	23 Aug 04
44.17		Innocent	Egbunike	NGR	30.11.61	1rA	WK	Zürich	19 Aug 87
44.18		Samson	Kitur	KEN	25.2.66	2s2	OG	Barcelona	3 Aug 92
44.20A		Charles	Gitonga	KEN	5.10.71	1	NC	Nairobi	29 Jun 96
44.21		Ian	Morris	TTO	30.11.61	3s2	OG	Barcelona	3 Aug 92
44.21A		Emmanuel	Korir	KEN	15.6.95	1	NC	Nairobi	23 Jun 18
44.22		Gil	Roberts	USA	15.3.89	2	NC	Sacramento	24 Jun 17
44.23		Kahmari	Montgomery	USA	16.8.97	1	NCAA	Austin	7 Jun 19
44.24		Tony	McQuay	USA	16.4.90	1s1	NC/OT	Eugene	2 Jul 16
	(40)								
44.25		Karabo	Sibanda	BOT	2.7.98	5	OG	Rio de Janeiro	14 Aug 16
44.25		Trevor	Stewart	USA	20.5.97	2	NCAA	Austin	7 Jun 19
44.26		Alberto	Juantorena	CUB	21.11.50	1	OG	Montreal	29 Jul 76
44.27		Alonzo	Babers	USA	31.10.61	1	OG	Los Angeles	8 Aug 84
44.27		Antonio	Pettigrew ¶	USA	3.11.67	1	NC	Houston	17 Jun 89
44.27		Darold	Williamson	USA	19.2.83	1s1	NCAA	Sacramento	10 Jun 05
44.28		Andrew	Valmon	USA	1.1.65	4	NC	Eugene	19 Jun 93
44.28		Tyree	Washington	USA	28.8.76	1		Los Angeles (ER)	12 May 01
44.29		Derrick	Brew	USA	28.12.77	1	SEC	Athens, GA	16 May 99
44.29		Sanderlei	Parrela	BRA	7.10.74	2	WCh	Sevilla	26 Aug 99
44.29		Nathan	Strother	USA	6.9.95	3	NC	Des Moines	27 Jul 19
	(51)		100th man 44.53, 200th 44.79, 300th 44.98, 400th 45.13, 500th 45.26						
Drugs disqualification									
44.21		Antonio	Pettigrew ¶	USA	3.11.67	(1)		Nassau	26 May 99
Hand timing:	44.1	Wayne	Collett	USA	20.10.49	1	OT	Eugene	9 Jul 72

600 METRES

Mark	Name		Nat	Born	Pos	Meet	Venue	Date
1:12.81	Johnny	Gray	USA	19.6.60	1		Santa Monica	24 May 86
1:13.10	David	Rudisha	KEN	17.12.88	1	DL	Birmingham	5 Jun 16
1:13.2 + ?	John	Kipkurgat	KEN	16.3.44	1		Pointe-à-Pierre	23 Mar 74
1:13.21	Pierre-Ambroise	Bosse	FRA	11.5.92	2	DL	Birmingham	5 Jun 16
1:13.28	Duane	Solomon	USA	28.12.84	1		Burnaby	1 Jul 13

800 METRES

Mark		Name		Nat	Born	Pos	Meet	Venue	Date
1:40.91	WR	David	Rudisha	KEN	17.12.88	1	OG	London (OS)	9 Aug 12
1:41.01	WR		Rudisha			1rA		Rieti	29 Aug 10
1:41.09	WR		Rudisha			1	ISTAF	Berlin	22 Aug 10
1:41.11	WR	Wilson	Kipketer	DEN	12.12.70	1	ASV	Köln	24 Aug 97
1:41.24	WR		Kipketer			1rA	WK	Zürich	13 Aug 97
1:41.33			Rudisha			1		Rieti	10 Sep 11
1:41.51			Rudisha			1	NA	Heusden-Zolder	10 Jul 10
1:41.54			Rudisha			1	DL	Saint-Denis	6 Jul 12
1:41.73	!WR	Sebastian	Coe	GBR	29.9.56	1		Firenze	10 Jun 81
1:41.73	WR		Kipketer			1rA	DNG	Stockholm	7 Jul 97
1:41.73		Nijel	Amos	BOT	15.3.94	2	OG	London (OS)	9 Aug 12

800 – 1000 METRES A-T

Mark	Wind	Name		Nat	Born	Pos	Meet	Venue	Date
1:41.74			Rudisha			1	adidas	New York	9 Jun 12
1:41.77		Joaquim	Cruz	BRA	12.3.63	1	ASV	Köln	26 Aug 84
1:41.83			Kipketer			1	GP II	Rieti	1 Sep 96
1:41.89			Amos			1	Herc	Monaco	12 Jul 19
1:42.01			Rudisha			1	GP	Rieti	6 Sep 09
1:42.04			Rudisha			1	Bisl	Oslo	4 Jun 10
1:42.05		Emmanuel	Korir	KEN	15.6.95	1	DL	London (OS)	22 Jul 18
1:42.12A			Rudisha			1	OT	Nairobi	23 Jun 12
1:42.14			Amos			1	Herc	Monaco	20 Jul 18
1:42.15			Rudisha			1	OG	Rio de Janeiro	15 Aug 16
1:42.17			Kipketer			1	TOTO	Tokyo	16 Sep 96
1:42.20			Kipketer			1	VD	Bruxelles	22 Aug 97
1:42.23		Abubaker	Kaki	SUD	21.6.89	2	Bisl	Oslo	4 Jun 10
1:42.27			Kipketer			1	VD	Bruxelles	3 Sep 99
1:42.28		Sammy	Koskei	KEN	14.5.61	2	ASV	Köln	26 Aug 84
1:42.32			Kipketer			1	GP II	Rieti	8 Sep 02
1:42.33	WR		Coe			1	Bisl	Oslo	5 Jul 79
1:42.34			Cruz			1r1	WK	Zürich	22 Aug 84
1:42.34		Wilfred	Bungei	KEN	24.7.80	2	GP II	Rieti	8 Sep 02
1:42.34		Donavan	Brazier	USA	15.4.97	1	WCh	Doha	1 Oct 19
(31/10)					*! photo-electric cell time*				
1:42.37		Mohammed	Aman	ETH	10.1.94	1	VD	Bruxelles	6 Sep 13
1:42.47		Yuriy	Borzakovskiy	RUS	12.4.81	1	VD	Bruxelles	24 Aug 01
1:42.51		Amel	Tuka	BIH	9.1.91	1	Herc	Monaco	17 Jul 15
1:42.53		Timothy	Kitum	KEN	20.11.94	3	OG	London (OS)	9 Aug 12
1:42.53		Pierre-Ambroise	Bosse	FRA	11.5.92	2	Herc	Monaco	18 Jul 14
1:42.54		Ferguson	Cheruiyot	KEN	30.11.89	2	Herc	Monaco	12 Jul 19
1:42.55		André	Bucher	SUI	19.10.76	1rA	WK	Zürich	17 Aug 01
1:42.58		Vebjørn	Rodal	NOR	16.9.72	1	OG	Atlanta	31 Jul 96
1:42.60		Johnny	Gray	USA	19.6.60	2r1		Koblenz	28 Aug 85
1:42.61		Taoufik	Makhloufi	ALG	29.4.88	2	OG	Rio de Janeiro	15 Aug 16
(20)									
1:42.62		Patrick	Ndururi	KEN	12.1.69	2rA	WK	Zürich	13 Aug 97
1:42.67		Alfred	Kirwa Yego	KEN	28.11.86	2	GP	Rieti	6 Sep 09
1:42.69		Hezekiél	Sepeng ¶	RSA	30.6.74	2	VD	Bruxelles	3 Sep 99
1:42.69		Japheth	Kimutai	KEN	20.12.78	3	VD	Bruxelles	3 Sep 99
1:42.79		Fred	Onyancha	KEN	25.12.69	3	OG	Atlanta	31 Jul 96
1:42.79		Youssef Saad	Kamel	KEN/BRN	29.3.83	2	Herc	Monaco	29 Jul 08
1:42.81		Jean-Patrick	Nduwimana	BDI	9.5.78	2rA	WK	Zürich	17 Aug 01
1:42.82		Duane	Solomon	USA	28.12.84	4	OG	London (OS)	9 Aug 12
1:42.85		Norberto	Téllez	CUB	22.1.72	4	OG	Atlanta	31 Jul 96
1:42.86		Mbulaeni	Mulaudzi	RSA	8.9.80	3	GP	Rieti	6 Sep 09
(30)									
1:42.87		Alfred	Kipketer	KEN	26.12.96	1	DL	Saint-Denis	27 Aug 16
1:42.88		Steve	Cram	GBR	14.10.60	1rA	WK	Zürich	21 Aug 85
1:42.91		William	Yiampoy	KEN	17.5.74	3	GP II	Rieti	8 Sep 02
1:42.93		Clayton	Murphy	USA	26.2.95	3	OG	Rio de Janeiro	15 Aug 16
1:42.95		Boaz	Lalang	KEN	8.2.89	2rA		Rieti	29 Aug 10
1:42.95		Nick	Symmonds	USA	30.12.83	5	OG	London (OS)	9 Aug 12
1:42.97		Peter	Elliott	GBR	9.10.62	1		Sevilla	30 May 90
1:42.97		Ayanleh	Souleiman	DJI	3.12.92	3	Herc	Monaco	17 Jul 15
1:42.98		Patrick	Konchellah	KEN	20.4.68	2	ASV	Köln	24 Aug 97
1:43.03		Kennedy/Kenneth	Kimwetich	KEN	1.1.73	2		Stuttgart	19 Jul 98
(40)									
1:43.05		Jonathan	Kitilit	KEN	24.4.94	3	DL	Saint-Denis	27 Aug 16
1:43.06		Billy	Konchellah	KEN	20.10.62	1	WCh	Roma	1 Sep 87
1:43.07		Yeimer	López	CUB	20.8.82	1		Jerez de la Frontera	24 Jun 08
1:43.08		José Luiz	Barbosa	BRA	27.5.61	1		Rieti	6 Sep 91
1:43.09		Djabir	Saïd-Guerni	ALG	29.3.77	5	VD	Bruxelles	3 Sep 99
1:43.11A		Timothy	Cheruiyot	KEN	20.11.95	1	NC	Nairobi	22 Aug 19
1:43.12		Wycliffe	Kinyamal	KEN	2.7.97	3	DL	London (OS)	22 Jul 18
1:43.13		Abraham Kipchirchir	Rotich	KEN	26.6.93	1	Herc	Monaco	20 Jul 12
1:43.15		Mehdi	Baala	FRA	17.8.78	5	GP II	Rieti	8 Sep 02
1:43.15		Asbel	Kiprop ¶	KEN	30.6.89	2	Herc	Monaco	22 Jul 11
(50)					100th man 1:43.76, 200th 1:4449, 300th 1:44.90, 400th 1:45.2, 500th 1:45.46				

1000 METRES

2:11.96	WR	Noah	Ngeny	KEN	2.11.78	1	GP II	Rieti	5 Sep 99
2:12.18	WR	Sebastian	Coe	GBR	29.9.56	1	OsloG	Oslo	11 Jul 81
2:12.66			Ngeny			1	Nik	Nice	17 Jul 99

1000 – 1500 METRES A-T

Mark	Wind	Name		Nat	Born	Pos	Meet	Venue	Date
2:12.88		Steve	Cram	GBR	14.10.60	1		Gateshead	9 Aug 85
2:13.08		Taoufik	Makhloufi	ALG	29.4.88	1		Tomblaine	1 Jul 15
2:13.40	WR		Coe			1	Bisl	Oslo	1 Jul 80
2:13.49		Ayanleh	Souleiman	DJI	3.12.92	1	Athl	Lausanne	25 Aug 16
2:13.56		Kennedy/Kenneth	Kimwetich	KEN	1.1.73	2	Nik	Nice	17 Jul 99
2:13.62		Abubaker	Kaki	SUD	21.6.89	1	Pre	Eugene	3 Jul 10
2:13.73		Noureddine	Morceli	ALG	28.2.70	1	BNP	Villeneuve d'Ascq	2 Jul 93
2:13.89		Robert	Biwott	KEN	28.1.96	2	Athl	Lausanne	25 Aug 16
2:13.9	WR	Rick	Wohlhuter	USA	23.12.48	1	King	Oslo	30 Jul 74
2:13.95		Jonathan	Kitilit	KEN	24.4.94	3	Athl	Lausanne	25 Aug 16
2:13.96		Mehdi	Baala	FRA	17.8.78	1		Strasbourg	26 Jun 03
		(12)	50th man 2:15.72, 100th 2:16.56, 200th 2:17.45						

1500 METRES

Mark		Name		Nat	Born	Pos	Meet	Venue	Date
3:26.00	WR	Hicham	El Guerrouj	MAR	14.9.74	1	GGala	Roma	14 Jul 98
3:26.12			El Guerrouj			1	VD	Bruxelles	24 Aug 01
3:26.34		Bernard	Lagat	KEN/USA	12.12.74	2	VD	Bruxelles	24 Aug 01
3:26.45			El Guerrouj			1 rA	WK	Zürich	12 Aug 98
3:26.69		Asbel	Kiprop ¶	KEN	30.6.89	1	Herc	Monaco	17 Jul 15
3:26.89			El Guerrouj			1	WK	Zürich	16 Aug 02
3:26.96			El Guerrouj			1	GP II	Rieti	8 Sep 02
3:27.21			El Guerrouj			1	WK	Zürich	11 Aug 00
3:27.34			El Guerrouj			1	Herc	Monaco	19 Jul 02
3:27.37	WR	Noureddine	Morceli	ALG	28.2.70	1	Nik	Nice	12 Jul 95
3:27.40			Lagat			1rA	WK	Zürich	6 Aug 04
3:27.52			Morceli			1	Herc	Monaco	25 Jul 95
3:27.64			El Guerrouj			2rA	WK	Zürich	6 Aug 04
3:27.64		Silas	Kiplagat	KEN	20.8.89	1	Herc	Monaco	18 Jul 14
3:27.65			El Guerrouj			1	WCh	Sevilla	24 Aug 99
3:27.72			Kiprop			1	Herc	Monaco	19 Jul 13
3:27.91			Lagat			2	Herc	Monaco	19 Jul 02
3:28.12		Noah	Ngeny	KEN	2.11.78	2	WK	Zürich	11 Aug 00
3:28.21+			El Guerrouj			1	in 1M	Roma	7 Jul 99
3:28.37			Morceli			1	GPF	Monaco	9 Sep 95
3:28.37			El Guerrouj			1	Herc	Monaco	8 Aug 98
3:28.38			El Guerrouj			1	GP	Saint-Denis	6 Jul 01
3:28.40			El Guerrouj			1	VD	Bruxelles	5 Sep 03
3:28.41		Timothy	Cheruiyot	KEN	20.11.95	1	Herc	Monaco	20 Jul 18
3:28.45			Kiprop			2	Herc	Monaco	18 Jul 14
3:28.45			T Cheruiyot			1	Herc	Monaco	14 Aug 20
3:28.51			Lagat			3	WK	Zürich	11 Aug 00
3:28.57			El Guerrouj			1rA	WK	Zürich	11 Aug 99
3:28.6+			Ngeny			2	in 1M	Roma	7 Jul 99
3:28.68		Jakob	Ingebrigtsen	NOR	19.9.00	2	Herc	Monaco	14 Aug 20
		(30/8)							
3:28.75		Taoufik	Makhloufi	ALG	29.4.88	2	Herc	Monaco	17 Jul 15
3:28.79		Abdelaati	Iguider	MAR	25.3.87	3	Herc	Monaco	17 Jul 15
		(10)							
3:28.80		Elijah	Manangoi	KEN	5.1.93	1	Herc	Monaco	21 Jul 17
3:28.81		Mohamed	Farah	GBR	23.3.83	2	Herc	Monaco	19 Jul 13
3:28.81		Ronald	Kwemoi	KEN	19.9.95	3	Herc	Monaco	18 Jul 14
3:28.95		Fermín	Cacho	ESP	16.2.69	2rA	WK	Zürich	13 Aug 97
3:28.98		Mehdi	Baala	FRA	17.8.78	2	VD	Bruxelles	5 Sep 03
3:29.02		Daniel Kipchirchir	Komen	KEN	27.11.84	1	GGala	Roma	14 Jul 06
3:29.14		Rashid	Ramzi ¶	MAR/BRN	17.7.80	2	GGala	Roma	14 Jul 06
3:29.18		Vénuste	Niyongabo	BDI	9.12.73	2	VD	Bruxelles	22 Aug 97
3:29.29		William	Chirchir	KEN	6.2.79	3	VD	Bruxelles	24 Aug 01
3:29.46	WR	Saïd	Aouita	MAR	2.11.59	1	ISTAF	Berlin	23 Aug 85
		(20)							
3:29.46		Daniel	Komen	KEN	17.5.76	1	Herc	Monaco	16 Aug 97
3:29.47		Augustine	Choge	KEN	21.1.87	1	ISTAF	Berlin	14 Jun 09
3:29.47		Jake	Wightman	GBR	11.7.94	3	Herc	Monaco	14 Aug 20
3:29.50		Caleb	Ndiku	KEN	9.10.92	3	Herc	Monaco	19 Jul 13
3:29.51		Ali	Saïdi-Sief ¶	ALG	15.3.78	1	Athl	Lausanne	4 Jul 01
3:29.53		Amine	Laâlou ¶	MAR	13.5.82	2	Herc	Monaco	22 Jul 10
3:29.58		Ayanleh	Souleiman	DJI	3.12.92	4	Herc	Monaco	18 Jul 14
3:29.66		Nick	Willis	NZL	25.4.83	5	Herc	Monaco	17 Jul 15
3:29.67	WR	Steve	Cram	GBR	14.10.60	1	Nik	Nice	16 Jul 85
3:29.77		Sydney	Maree	USA	9.9.56	1	ASV	Köln	25 Aug 85
		(30)							

1500 METRES - 1 MILE A-T

Mark	Wind	Name		Nat	Born	Pos	Meet	Venue	Date
3:29.77		Sebastian	Coe	GBR	29.9.56	1		Rieti	7 Sep 86
3:29.77		Nixon	Chepseba	KEN	12.12.90	2	Herc	Monaco	20 Jul 12
3:29.91		Laban	Rotich	KEN	20.1.69	2rA	WK	Zürich	12 Aug 98
3:29.91		Aman	Wote	ETH	18.4.84	6	Herc	Monaco	14 Jul 14
3:30.01		Filip	Ingebrigtsen	NOR	20.4.93	3	Herc	Monaco	20 Jul 18
3:30.04		Timothy	Kiptanui	KEN	5.1.80	2	GP	Saint-Denis	23 Jul 04
3:30.07		Rui	Silva	POR	3.8.77	3	Herc	Monaco	19 Jul 02
3:30.10		Robert	Biwott	KEN	28.1.96	7	Herc	Monaco	17 Jul 15
3:30.18		John	Kibowen	KEN	21.4.69	3rA	WK	Zürich	12 Aug 98
3:30.20		Haron	Keitany	KEN	17.12.83	2	ISTAF	Berlin	14 Jun 09
(40)									
3:30.24		Cornelius	Chirchir	KEN	5.6.83	4	Herc	Monaco	19 Jul 02
3:30.33		Ivan	Heshko	UKR	19.8.79	2	VD	Bruxelles	3 Sep 04
3:30.34		Collins	Cheboi	KEN	25.9.87	9	Herc	Monaco	17 Jul 15
3:30.40		Matthew	Centrowitz	USA	18.10.89	10	Herc	Monaco	17 Jul 15
3:30.46		Alex	Kipchirchir	KEN	26.11.84	3	VD	Bruxelles	3 Sep 04
3:30.51		Stewart	McSweyn	AUS	1.6.95	1	DL	Doha	25 Sep 20
3:30.54		Alan	Webb	USA	13.1.83	1	Gaz	Saint-Denis	6 Jul 07
3:30.55		Abdi	Bile	SOM	28.12.62	1		Rieti	3 Sep 89
3:30.57		Reyes	Estévez	ESP	2.8.76	3	WCh	Sevilla	24 Aug 99
3:30.58		William	Tanui	KEN	22.2.64	3	Herc	Monaco	16 Aug 97
3:30.58		Ronald	Musagala	UGA	16.12.92	3	Herc	Monaco	12 Jul 19
(51)		100th man 3:31.75, 200th 3:33.64, 300th 3:34.50, 400th 3:35.28, 500th 3:35.87							

MFN All-time

1 MILE

Mark	Wind	Name		Nat	Born	Pos	Meet	Venue	Date
3:43.13	WR	Hicham	El Guerrouj	MAR	14.9.74	1	GGala	Roma	7 Jul 99
3:43.40		Noah	Ngeny	KEN	2.11.78	2	GGala	Roma	7 Jul 99
3:44.39	WR	Noureddine	Morceli	ALG	28.2.70	1		Rieti	5 Sep 93
3:44.60			El Guerrouj			1	Nik	Nice	16 Jul 98
3:44.90			El Guerrouj			1	Bisl	Oslo	4 Jul 97
3:44.95			El Guerrouj			1	GGala	Roma	29 Jun 01
3:45.19			Morceli			1	WK	Zürich	16 Aug 95
3:45.64			El Guerrouj			1	ISTAF	Berlin	26 Aug 97
3:45.96			El Guerrouj			1	BrGP	London (CP)	5 Aug 00
3:46.24			El Guerrouj			1	Bisl	Oslo	28 Jul 00
3:46.32	WR	Steve	Cram	GBR	14.10.60	1	Bisl	Oslo	27 Jul 85
3:46.38		Daniel	Komen	KEN	17.5.76	2	ISTAF	Berlin	26 Aug 97
3:46.70		Vénuste	Niyongabo	BDI	9.12.73	3	ISTAF	Berlin	26 Aug 97
3:46.76		Saïd	Aouita	MAR	2.11.59	1	WG	Helsinki	2 Jul 87
3:46.78			Morceli			1	ISTAF	Berlin	27 Aug 93
3:46.91		Alan	Webb	USA	13.1.83	1		Brasschaat	21 Jul 07
3:46.92			Aouita			1	WK	Zürich	21 Aug 85
3:47.10			El Guerrouj			1	BrGP	London (CP)	7 Aug 99
3:47.28		Bernard	Lagat	KEN/USA	12.12.74	2	GGala	Roma	29 Jun 01
3:47.30			Morceli			1	VD	Bruxelles	3 Sep 93
3:47.32		Ayanleh	Souleiman (10)	DJI	3.12.92	1	Pre	Eugene	31 May 14
3:47.33	WR	Sebastian	Coe (22/11)	GBR	29.9.56	1	VD	Bruxelles	28 Aug 81
3:47.65		Laban	Rotich	KEN	20.1.69	2	Bisl	Oslo	4 Jul 97
3:47.69		Steve	Scott	USA	5.5.56	1	OsloG	Oslo	7 Jul 82
3:47.79		José Luis	González	ESP	8.12.57	2	Bisl	Oslo	27 Jul 85
3:47.88		John	Kibowen	KEN	21.4.69	3	Bisl	Oslo	4 Jul 97
3:47.88		Silas	Kiplagat	KEN	20.8.89	2	Pre	Eugene	31 May 14
3:47.94		William	Chirchir	KEN	6.2.79	2	Bisl	Oslo	28 Jul 00
3:47.97		Daham Najim	Bashir	KEN/QAT	8.11.78	1	Bisl	Oslo	29 Jul 05
3:48.17		Paul	Korir	KEN	15.7.77	1	GP	London (CP)	8 Aug 03
3:48.23		Ali	Saïdi-Sief ¶ (20)	ALG	15.3.78	1	Bisl	Oslo	13 Jul 01
3:48.28		Daniel Kipchirchir	Komen	KEN	27.11.84	1	Pre	Eugene	10 Jun 07
3:48.38		Andrés Manuel	Díaz	ESP	12.7.69	3	GGala	Roma	29 Jun 01
3:48.40	WR	Steve	Ovett	GBR	9.10.55	1	R-W	Koblenz	26 Aug 81
3:48.50		Asbel	Kiprop ¶	KEN	30.6.89	1	Pre	Eugene	7 Jun 09
3:48.60		Aman	Wote	ETH	18.4.84	3	Pre	Eugene	31 May 14
3:48.78		Haron	Keitany	KEN	17.12.83	2	Pre	Eugene	7 Jun 09
3:48.80		William	Kemei	KEN	22.2.69	1	ISTAF	Berlin	21 Aug 92
3:48.83		Sydney	Maree	USA	9.9.56	1		Rieti	9 Sep 81
3:48.95		Deresse	Mekonnen	ETH	20.10.87	1	Bisl	Oslo	3 Jul 09
3:48.98		Craig	Mottram (30)	AUS	18.6.80	5	Bisl	Oslo	29 Jul 05
3:49.04		Ronald	Kwemoi	KEN	19.9.95	1	Pre	Eugene	27 May 17
3:49.08		John	Walker	NZL	12.1.52	2	OsloG	Oslo	7 Jul 82

1 MILE - 2000 – 3000 METRES A-T

Mark	Wind	Name		Nat	Born	Pos	Meet	Venue	Date
3:49.08		Elijah	Manangoi	KEN	5.1.93	2	Pre	Eugene	27 May 17
3:49.09		Abdelaati	Iguider	MAR	25.3.87	4	Pre	Eugene	31 May 14
3:49.20		Peter	Elliott	GBR	9.10.62	2	Bisl	Oslo	2 Jul 88
3:49.22		Jens-Peter	Herold	GDR	2.6.65	3	Bisl	Oslo	2 Jul 88
3:49.29		William	Biwott/Özbilen	KEN/TUR	5.3.90	2	Bisl	Oslo	3 Jul 09
3:49.31		Joe	Falcon	USA	23.6.66	1	Bisl	Oslo	14 Jul 90
3:49.34		David	Moorcroft	GBR	10.4.53	3	Bisl	Oslo	26 Jun 82
3:49.34		Benjamin (40)	Kipkurui	KEN	28.12.80	3	VD	Bruxelles	25 Aug 00
3:49.38		Andrew	Baddeley	GBR	20.6.82	1	Bisl	Oslo	6 Jun 08
3:49.40		Abdi	Bile	SOM	28.12.62	4	Bisl	Oslo	2 Jul 88
3:49.43		James	Magut	KEN	20.7.90	5	Pre	Eugene	31 May 14
3:49.45		Mike	Boit	KEN	6.1.49	2	VD	Bruxelles	28 Aug 81
3:49.45		Samuel	Tefera	ETH	23.10.99	1	DL	London (OS)	21 Jul 19
3:49.50		Rui	Silva	POR	3.8.77	3	GGala	Roma	12 Jul 02
3:49.56		Fermín	Cacho	ESP	16.2.69	2	Bisl	Oslo	5 Jul 96
3:49.56		Collins	Cheboi	KEN	25.9.87	6	Pre	Eugene	31 May 14
3:49.60		José Antonio	Redolat	ESP	17.2.76	4	GGala	Roma	29 Jun 01
3:49.60		Filip (50)	Ingebrigtsen	NOR	20.4.93	2	DL	London (OS)	21 Jul 19

100th 3:50.90, 200th 3:52.90, 300th 3:54.6, 400th 3:55.66

Indoors

| 3:47.01 | | Yomif | Kejelcha | ETH | 1.8.97 | 1 | | Boston (A) | 3 Mar 19 |
| 3:49.44 | | Edward | Cheserek | KEN | 2.2.94 | 1 | | Boston (A) | 9 Feb 18 |

2000 METRES

4:44.79 WR		Hicham	El Guerrouj	MAR	14.9.74	1	ISTAF	Berlin	7 Sep 99
4:46.88		Ali	Saïdi-Sief ¶	ALG	15.3.78	1		Strasbourg	19 Jun 01
4:47.88 WR		Noureddine	Morceli	ALG	28.2.70	1		Paris (JB)	3 Jul 95
4:48.69		Vénuste	Niyongabo	BDI	9.12.73	1	Nik	Nice	12 Jul 95
4:48.74		John	Kibowen	KEN	21.4.69	1		Hechtel	1 Aug 98
4:50.01		Jakob	Ingebrigtsen	NOR	19.9.00	1		Oslo	11 Jun 20
4:50.08		Noah	Ngeny	KEN	2.11.78	1	DNG	Stockholm	30 Jul 99
4:50.76		Craig	Mottram	AUS	18.6.80	1		Melbourne (OP)	9 Mar 06
4:50.81 WR		Saïd	Aouita	MAR	2.11.59	1	BNP	Paris (JB)	16 Jul 87
4:51.30		Daniel	Komen (10)	KEN	17.5.76	1		Milano	5 Jun 98
4:51.39 WR		Steve	Cram	GBR	14.10.60	1	BGP	Budapest	4 Aug 85

Indoors

| 4:49.99 | | Kenenisa | Bekele | ETH | 13.6.82 | 1 | | Birmingham | 17 Feb 07 |

3000 METRES

7:20.67 WR		Daniel	Komen	KEN	17.5.76	1		Rieti	1 Sep 96
7:23.09		Hicham	El Guerrouj	MAR	14.9.74	1	VD	Bruxelles	3 Sep 99
7:25.02		Ali	Saïdi-Sief ¶	ALG	15.3.78	1	Herc	Monaco	18 Aug 00
7:25.09		Haile	Gebrselassie	ETH	18.4.73	1	VD	Bruxelles	28 Aug 98
7:25.11 WR		Noureddine	Morceli	ALG	28.2.70	1	Herc	Monaco	2 Aug 94
7:25.16			Komen			1	Herc	Monaco	10 Aug 96
7:25.54			Gebrselassie			1	Herc	Monaco	8 Aug 98
7:25.79		Kenenisa	Bekele	ETH	13.6.82	1	DNG	Stockholm	7 Aug 07
7:25.87			Komen			1	VD	Bruxelles	23 Aug 96
7:26.02			Gebrselassie			1	VD	Bruxelles	22 Aug 97
7:26.03			Gebrselassie			1	GP II	Helsinki	10 Jun 99
7:26.5 e			Komen			1	in 2M	Sydney	28 Feb 98
7:26.62		Mohammed	Mourhit ¶	BEL	10.10.70	2	Herc	Monaco	18 Aug 00
7:26.64		Jacob	Kiplimo	UGA	14.11.00	1	G Gala	Roma	17 Sep 20
7:26.69			K Bekele			1	BrGP	Sheffield	15 Jul 07
7:27.05		Jakob	Ingebrigtsen	NOR	19.9.00	2	G Gala	Roma	17 Sep 20
7:27.18		Moses	Kiptanui (10)	KEN	1.10.70	1	Herc	Monaco	25 Jul 95
7:27.26		Yenew	Alamirew	ETH	27.5.90	1	DL	Doha	6 May 11
7:27.3+			Komen			1	in 2M	Hechtel	19 Jul 97
7:27.42			Gebrselassie			1	Bisl	Oslo	9 Jul 98
7:27.50			Morceli			1	VD	Bruxelles	25 Aug 95
7:27.55		Edwin	Soi	KEN	3.3.86	2	DL	Doha	6 May 11
7:27.59		Luke	Kipkosgei	KEN	27.11.75	2	Herc	Monaco	8 Aug 98
7:27.66		Eliud	Kipchoge	KEN	5.11.84	3	DL	Doha	6 May 11
7:27.67			Saïdi-Sief			1	Gaz	Saint-Denis	23 Jun 00
7:27.72			Kipchoge			1	VD	Bruxelles	3 Sep 04
7:27.75		Thomas	Nyariki	KEN	27.9.71	2	Herc	Monaco	10 Aug 96
7:28.00		Yomif	Kejelcha	ETH	1.8.97	1		Göteborg	18 Aug 18
7:28.02		Stewart	McSweyn	AUS	1.6.95	3	G Gala	Roma	17 Sep 20
7:28.04		(30/17)	Kiptanui			1	ASV	Köln	18 Aug 95

3000 METRES - 2 MILES - 5000 METRES A-T

Mark	Wind	Name		Nat	Born	Pos	Meet	Venue	Date
7:28.28		James	Kwalia	KEN/QAT	12.6.84	2	VD	Bruxelles	3 Sep 04
7:28.41		Paul	Bitok	KEN	26.6.70	3	Herc	Monaco	10 Aug 96
7:28.45		Assefa	Mezegebu	ETH	19.6.78	3	Herc	Monaco	8 Aug 98
		(20)							
7:28.67		Benjamin	Limo	KEN	23.8.74	1	Herc	Monaco	4 Aug 99
7:28.70		Paul	Tergat	KEN	17.6.69	4	Herc	Monaco	10 Aug 96
7:28.70		Tariku	Bekele	ETH	21.1.87	1		Rieti	29 Aug 10
7:28.72		Isaac K.	Songok	KEN	25.4.84	1	GP	Rieti	27 Aug 06
7:28.73		Ronald	Kwemoi	KEN	19.9.95	1	DL	Doha	5 May 17
7:28.76		Augustine	Choge	KEN	21.1.87	4	DL	Doha	6 May 11
7:28.93		Salah	Hissou	MAR	16.1.72	2	Herc	Monaco	4 Aug 99
7:28.94		Brahim	Lahlafi	FRA/MAR	15.4.68	3	Herc	Monaco	4 Aug 99
7:29.00		Bernard	Lagat	USA	12.12.74	2		Rieti	29 Aug 10
7:29.09		John	Kibowen	KEN	21.4.69	3	Bisl	Oslo	9 Jul 98
		(30)							
7:29.34		Isaac	Viciosa	ESP	26.12.69	4	Bisl	Oslo	9 Jul 98
7:29.45	WR	Saïd	Aouita	MAR	2.11.59	1	ASV	Köln	20 Aug 89
7:29.92		Sileshi	Sihine	ETH	29.1.83	1	GP	Rieti	28 Aug 05
7:30.09		Ismaïl	Sghyr	MAR/FRA	16.3.72	2	Herc	Monaco	25 Jul 95
7:30.09		Thomas	Longosiwa	KEN	14.1.82	2	SGP	Doha	8 May 09
7:30.09		Abdelaati	Iguider	MAR	25.3.87	2	DL	Saint-Denis	27 Aug 16
7:30.15		Vincent	Chepkok	KEN	5.7.88	5	DL	Doha	6 May 11
7:30.36		Mark	Carroll	IRL	15.1.72	5	Herc	Monaco	4 Aug 99
7:30.36		Hagos	Gebrhiwet	ETH	11.5.94	1	DL	Doha	10 May 13
7:30.43		Isiah	Koech	KEN	19.12.93	1	DNG	Stockholm	17 Aug 12
		(40)							
7:30.50		Dieter	Baumann ¶	GER	9.2.65	6	Herc	Monaco	8 Aug 98
7:30.53		El Hassan	Lahssini	MAR/FRA	1.1.75	6	Herc	Monaco	10 Aug 96
7:30.53		Hailu	Mekonnen	ETH	4.4.80	1	VD	Bruxelles	24 Aug 01
7:30.62		Boniface	Songok	KEN	25.12.80	3	VD	Bruxelles	3 Sep 04
7:30.76		Jamal Bilal	Salem	KEN/QAT	12.9.78	4	SGP	Doha	13 May 05
7:30.78		Mustapha	Essaïd	FRA	20.1.70	7	Herc	Monaco	8 Aug 98
7:30.84		Bob	Kennedy	USA	18.8.70	8	Herc	Monaco	8 Aug 98
7:30.93		Ryan	Hill	USA	31.1.90	4	DL	Saint-Denis	27 Aug 16
7:30.95		Moses	Kipsiro	UGA	2.9.86	1	Herc	Monaco	28 Jul 09
7:30.99		Khalid	Boulami	MAR	7.8.69	1	Nik	Nice	16 Jul 97
7:30.99		Caleb	Ndiku	KEN	9.10.92	2	DNG	Stockholm	17 Aug 12
		(51)		100th man 7:34.32, 200th man 7:38.67, 300th 7:41.04, 400th 7:43.00, 500th 7:44.43					

Indoors

7:24.90 WIR		Komen				1		Budapest	6 Feb 98
7:26.15 WIR		Gebrselassie				1		Karlsruhe	25 Jan 98
7:26.80		Gebrselassie				1		Karlsruhe	24 Jan 99
7:27.80		Alamirew				1	Spark	Stuttgart	5 Feb 11
7:27.93		Komen				1	Spark	Stuttgart	1 Feb 98
7:28.00		Augustine	Choge	KEN	21.1.87	2	Spark	Stuttgart	5 Feb 11
7:30.16		Galen	Rupp	USA	8.5.86	1		Stockholm	21 Feb 13

2 MILES

7:58.61 WR		Daniel	Komen	KEN	17.5.76	1		Hechtel	19 Jul 97
7:58.91			Komen			1		Sydney	28 Feb 98
8:01.08 WR		Haile	Gebrselassie	ETH	18.4.73	1	APM	Hengelo	31 May 97
8:01.72			Gebrselassie			1	BrGP	London (CP)	7 Aug 99
8:01.86			Gebrselassie			1	APM	Hengelo	30 May 99
8:03.50		Craig	Mottram	AUS	18.6.80	1	Pre	Eugene	10 Jun 07
8:03.54 WR			Komen			1		Lappeenranta	14 Jul 96

Indoors

8:03.40		Mohamed	Farah	GBR	23.3.83	1	GP	Birmingham	21 Feb 15
8:04.35		Kenenisa	Bekele	ETH	13.6.82	1	GP	Birmingham	16 Feb 08

5000 METRES

12:35.36 WR		Joshua	Cheptegei	UGA	12.9.96	1	Herc	Monaco	14 Aug 20
12:37.35 WR		Kenenisa	Bekele	ETH	13.6.82	1	FBK	Hengelo	31 May 04
12:39.36 WR		Haile	Gebrselassie	ETH	18.4.73	1	GP II	Helsinki	13 Jun 98
12:39.74 WR		Daniel	Komen	KEN	17.5.76	1	VD	Bruxelles	22 Aug 97
12:40.18			K Bekele			1	Gaz	Saint-Denis	1 Jul 05
12:41.86 WR			Gebrselassie			1	WK	Zürich	13 Aug 97
12:43.02		Selemon	Barega	ETH	20.1.00	1	VD	Bruxelles	31 Aug 18
12:44.39 WR			Gebrselassie			1	WK	Zürich	16 Aug 95
12:44.90			Komen			2	WK	Zürich	13 Aug 97
12:45.09			Komen			1	WK	Zürich	14 Aug 96

A – mark made at an altitude of 1000m or higher, i – indoors, Q – in qualifying competition, WR - world record

5000 - 10000 METRES A-T

Mark	Wind	Name		Nat	Born	Pos	Meet	Venue	Date
12:45.82		Hagos	Gebrhiwet	ETH	11.5.94	2	VD	Bruxelles	31 Aug 18
12:46.53		Eliud	Kipchoge	KEN	5.11.84	1	GGala	Roma	2 Jul 04
12:46.79		Yomif	Kejelcha	ETH	1.8.97	3	VD	Bruxelles	31 Aug 18
12:46.81		Dejen	Gebremeskel	ETH	24.11.89	1	DL	Saint-Denis	6 Jul 12
12:47.04		Sileshi	Sihine (10)	ETH	29.9.83	2	GGala	Roma	2 Jul 04
12:47.20		Mohammed	Ahmed	CAN	5.1.91	1		Portland	10 Jul 20
12:47.53			Gebrhiwet			2	DL	Saint-Denis	6 Jul 12
12:48.09			K Bekele			1	VD	Bruxelles	25 Aug 06
12:48.25			K Bekele			1	WK	Zürich	18 Aug 06
12:48.63		Jacob	Kiplimo	UGA	14.11.00	1	GS	Ostrava	8 Sep 20
12:48.64		Isiah	Koech	KEN	19.12.93	3	DL	Saint-Denis	6 Jul 12
12:48.66		Isaac K.	Songok	KEN	25.4.84	2	WK	Zürich	18 Aug 06
12:48.77		Yenew	Alamirew	ETH	27.5.90	4	DL	Saint-Denis	6 Jul 12
12:48.81		Stephen	Cherono/Shaheen	KEN/QAT	15.10.82	1	GS	Ostrava	12 Jun 03
12:48.98			Komen			1	GGala	Roma	5 Jun 97
12:49.04		Thomas	Longosiwa	KEN	14.1.82	5	DL	Saint-Denis	6 Jul 12
12:49.08			Barega			2	GS	Ostrava	8 Sep 20
12:49.28		Brahim	Lahlafi	MAR	15.4.68	1	VD	Bruxelles	25 Aug 06
12:49.50		John	Kipkoech	KEN	29.12.91	6	DL	Saint-Denis	6 Jul 12
12:49.53			K Bekele			1	Aragón	Zaragoza	28 Jul 07
		(30/19)							
12:49.71		Mohammed	Mourhit ¶ (20)	BEL	10.10.70	2	VD	Bruxelles	25 Aug 00
12:49.87		Paul	Tergat	KEN	17.6.69	3	WK	Zürich	13 Aug 97
12:50.16			Sihine			1	VD	Bruxelles	14 Sep 07
12:50.24		Hicham	El Guerrouj	MAR	14.9.74	2	GS	Ostrava	12 Jun 03
12:50.25		Abderrahim	Goumri ¶	MAR	21.5.76	2	VD	Bruxelles	26 Aug 05
12:50.55		Moses	Masai	KEN	1.6.86	1	ISTAF	Berlin	1 Jun 08
12:50.72		Moses	Kipsiro	UGA	2.9.86	3	VD	Bruxelles	14 Sep 07
12:50.80		Salah	Hissou	MAR	16.1.72	1	GGala	Roma	5 Jun 96
12:50.86		Ali	Saïdi-Sief ¶	ALG	15.3.78	1	GGala	Roma	30 Jun 00
12:51.00		Joseph	Ebuya	KEN	20.6.87	4	VD	Bruxelles	14 Sep 07
12:51.34		Edwin	Soi	KEN	3.3.86	1	Herc	Monaco	19 Jul 13
12:51.45		Vincent	Chepkok	KEN	5.7.88	2	DL	Doha	14 May 10
		(30)							
12:51.78		Nicholas	Kimeli	KEN	29.9.98	2	Herc	Monaco	14 Aug 20
12:51.96		Albert	Rop	KEN/BRN	17.7.92	2	Herc	Monaco	19 Jul 13
12:52.33		Sammy	Kipketer	KEN	29.9.81	2	Bisl	Oslo	27 Jun 03
12:52.45		Tariku	Bekele	ETH	21.1.87	2	ISTAF	Berlin	1 Jun 08
12:52.80		Gebre-egziabher	Gebremariam	ETH	10.9.84	3	GGala	Roma	8 Jul 05
12:52.98		Tilahun	Haile	ETH	13.5.99	1	GGala	Roma	6 Jun 19
12:52.99		Abraham	Chebii	KEN	23.12.79	4	Bisl	Oslo	27 Jun 03
12:53.11		Mohamed	Farah	GBR	23.3.83	1	Herc	Monaco	22 Jul 11
12:53.41		Khalid	Boulami	MAR	7.8.69	4	WK	Zürich	13 Aug 97
12:53.46		Mark	Kiptoo	KEN	21.6.76	1	DNG	Stockholm	6 Aug 10
		(40)							
12:53.58		Imane	Merga	ETH	15.10.88	3	DNG	Stockholm	6 Aug 10
12:53.60		Bernard	Lagat	USA	12.12.74	2	Herc	Monaco	22 Jul 11
12:53.66		Augustine	Choge	KEN	21.1.87	4	GGala	Roma	8 Jul 05
12:53.72		Philip	Mosima	KEN	2.1.77	2	GGala	Roma	5 Jun 96
12:53.84		Assefa	Mezegebu	ETH	19.6.78	1	VD	Bruxelles	28 Aug 98
12:54.07		John	Kibowen	KEN	21.4.69	4	WCh	Saint-Denis	31 Aug 03
12:54.15		Dejene	Berhanu	ETH	12.12.80	3	GGala	Roma	2 Jul 04
12:54.19		Abreham	Cherkos	ETH	23.9.89	5	GGala	Roma	14 Jul 06
12:54.46		Moses	Mosop	KEN	17.7.85	3	Gaz	Saint-Denis	8 Jul 06
12:54.58		James	Kwalia	KEN/QAT	12.6.84	5	Bisl	Oslo	27 Jun 03
		(50)							

100th man 12:59.44, 200th 13:06.76, 300th 13:11.32, 400th 13:13.94, 500th 13:16.87

10,000 METRES

Mark		Name		Nat	Born	Pos	Meet	Venue	Date
26:11.00	WR	Joshua	Cheptegei	UGA	12.9.96	1		Valencia	7 Oct 20
26:17.53	WR	Kenenisa	Bekele	ETH	13.6.82	1	VD	Bruxelles	26 Aug 05
26:20.31	WR		K Bekele			1	GS	Ostrava	8 Jun 04
26:22.75	WR	Haile	Gebrselassie	ETH	18.4.73	1	APM	Hengelo	1 Jun 98
26:25.97			K Bekele			1	Pre	Eugene	8 Jun 08
26:27.85	WR	Paul	Tergat	KEN	17.6.69	1	VD	Bruxelles	22 Aug 97
26:28.72			K Bekele			1	FBK	Hengelo	29 May 05
26:29.22			Gebrselassie			1	VD	Bruxelles	5 Sep 03
26:30.03		Nicholas	Kemboi	KEN/QAT	25.11.83	2	VD	Bruxelles	5 Sep 03
26:30.74		Abebe	Dinkesa	ETH	6.3.84	1	FBK	Hengelo	29 May 05
26:31.32	WR		Gebrselassie			1	Bisl	Oslo	4 Jul 97
26:35.63		Micah	Kogo	KEN	3.6.86	1	VD	Bruxelles	25 Aug 06

10,000, 20,000 METRES – 1 HOUR – HALF MARATHON A-T

Mark	Wind	Name		Nat	Born	Pos	Meet	Venue	Date
26:36.26		Paul	Koech	KEN	25.6.69	2	VD	Bruxelles	22 Aug 97
26:37.25		Zersenay	Tadese	ERI	8.2.82	2	VD	Bruxelles	25 Aug 06
26:38.08 WR		Salah	Hissou (10)	MAR	16.1.72	1	VD	Bruxelles	23 Aug 96
26:38.76		Abdullah Ahmad	Hassan	QAT	4.4.81	3	VD	Bruxelles	5 Sep 03
		(Formerly Albert Chepkurui KEN)							
26:39.69		Sileshi	Sihine	ETH	29.9.83	1	FBK	Hengelo	31 May 04
26:39.77		Boniface	Kiprop	UGA	12.10.85	2	VD	Bruxelles	26 Aug 05
26:41.58			Gebrselassie			2	FBK	Hengelo	31 May 04
26:41.75		Samuel	Wanjiru	KEN	10.11.86	3	VD	Bruxelles	26 Aug 05
26:41.95			Kiprop			3	VD	Bruxelles	25 Aug 06
26:43.16			K Bekele			1	VD	Bruxelles	16 Sep 11
26:43.53 WR			Gebrselassie			1	APM	Hengelo	5 Jun 95
26:43.98		Lucas	Rotich	KEN	16.4.90	2	VD	Bruxelles	16 Sep 11
26:44.36		Galen	Rupp	USA	8.5.86	1	Pre	Eugene	30 May 14
26:46.19			K Bekele			1	VD	Bruxelles	14 Sep 07
26:46.31			K Bekele			1	WCh	Berlin	17 Aug 09
26:46.44			Tergat			1	VD	Bruxelles	28 Aug 98
26:46.57		Mohamed	Farah	GBR	23.3.83	1	Pre	Eugene	3 Jun 11
26:47.89			Koech			2	VD	Bruxelles	28 Aug 98
		(30/17)							
26:48.35		Imane	Merga	ETH	15.10.88	2	Pre	Eugene	3 Jun 11
26:48.95		Hagos	Gebrhiwet	ETH	11.5.94	1	WCT	Hengelo	17 Jul 19
26:48.99		Josphat	Bett	KEN	12.6.90	3	Pre	Eugene	3 Jun 11
		(20)							
26:49.02		Eliud	Kipchoge	KEN	5.11.84	2	FBK	Hengelo	26 May 07
26:49.20		Moses	Masai	KEN	1.6.86	2	VD	Bruxelles	14 Sep 07
26:49.34		Yomif	Kejelcha	ETH	1.8.97	2	WCh	Doha	6 Oct 19
26:49.38		Sammy	Kipketer	KEN	29.9.81	1	VD	Bruxelles	30 Aug 02
26:49.41		Paul	Tanui	KEN	22.12.90	2	Pre	Eugene	30 May 14
26:49.46		Selemon	Barega	ETH	20.1.00	2	WCT	Hengelo	17 Jul 19
26:49.55		Moses	Mosop	KEN	17.7.85	3	FBK	Hengelo	26 May 07
26:49.90		Assefa	Mezegebu	ETH	19.6.78	2	VD	Bruxelles	30 Aug 02
26:50.16		Rhonex	Kipruto	KEN	12.10.99	1	DL	Stockholm	30 May 19
26:50.20		Richard	Limo	KEN	18.11.80	3	VD	Bruxelles	30 Aug 02
		(30)							
26:51.02		Dejen	Gebremeskel	ETH	24.11.89	1		Sollentuna	27 Jun 13
26:51.11		Yigrem	Demelash	ETH	28.1.94	1	OT	Hengelo	29 Jun 16
26:51.16		Emmanuel	Bett	KEN	30.3.83	1	VD	Bruxelles	7 Sep 12
26:51.49		Charles	Kamathi	KEN	18.5.78	1	VD	Bruxelles	3 Sep 99
26:51.68		Vincent	Chepkok	KEN	5.7.88	2	VD	Bruxelles	7 Sep 12
26:52.12		Bedan	Karoki	KEN	21.8.90	4	WCh	London (OS)	4 Aug 17
26:52.23 WR		William	Sigei	KEN	14.10.69	1	Bisl	Oslo	22 Jul 94
26:52.30		Mohammed	Mourhit ¶	BEL	10.10.70	2	VD	Bruxelles	3 Sep 99
26:52.33		Gebre-egziabher	Gebremariam	ETH	10.9.84	4	FBK	Hengelo	26 May 07
26:52.65		Kenneth	Kipkemoi	KEN	2.8.84	3	VD	Bruxelles	7 Sep 12
		(40)							
26:52.65		Geoffrey	Kamworor	KEN	22.11.92	3	Pre	Eugene	29 May 15
26:52.85		Abera	Kuma	ETH	31.8.90	2		Sollentuna	27 Jun 13
26:52.87		John Cheruiyot	Korir	KEN	13.12.81	5	VD	Bruxelles	30 Aug 02
26:52.93		Mark	Bett	KEN	22.12.76	6	VD	Bruxelles	26 Aug 05
26:53.15		Andamlak	Belihu	ETH	20.11.98	4	WCT	Hengelo	17 Jul 19
26:54.25		Mathew	Kisorio ¶	KEN	16.5.89	7	Pre	Eugene	3 Jun 11
26:54.39		Jemal	Yimer	ETH	11.9.96	5	WCT	Hengelo	17 Jul 19
26:54.61		Stephen	Sambu	KEN	3.7.88	4	Pre	Eugene	30 May 14
26:54.64		Mark	Kiptoo	KEN	21.6.76	8	Pre	Eugene	3 Jun 11
26:54.66		William Malel	Sitonik	KEN	1.3.94	2	Pre	Eugene	27 May 16
		(50)	100th man 27:09.92, 200th 27:24.95, 300th 27:33.55, 400th 27:39.92, 500th 27:44.53						

MFN All-time

20,000 METRES – 1 HOUR

56:20.30+	21 330m WR	Mohamed	Farah	GBR	23.3.83	1	VD	Bruxelles	4 Sep 20
56:20.02+ WR	21 322	Bashir	Abdi	BEL	10.2.89	2	VD	Bruxelles	4 Sep 20
56:25.98+ WR	21 285	Haile	Gebrselassie	ETH	18.4.73	1	GS	Ostrava	27 Jun 07
56:55.6+ WR	21 101	Arturo	Barrios	MEX	12.12.63	1		La Flèche	30 Mar 91

HALF MARATHON

Included are times on the slightly downhill course: Newcastle to South Shields 30.5m

57:32	Kibiwott	Kandie	KEN	20.6.96	1	Valencia	6 Dec 20
57:37	Jacob	Kiplimo	UGA	14.11.00	2	Valencia	6 Dec 20
57:49	Rhonex	Kipruto	KEN	12.10.99	3	Valencia	6 Dec 20
57:59	Alexander	Mutiso	KEN	10.9.96	4	Valencia	6 Dec 20
58:01	Geoffrey	Kamworor	KEN	22.11.92	1	København	15 Sep 19

HALF MARATHON – MARATHON A-T

Mark	Wind	Name		Nat	Born	Pos	Meet	Venue	Date
58:11		Philemon	Kiplimo	KEN	10.10.98	5		Valencia	6 Dec 20
58:23	WR	Zersenay	Tadese	ERI	8.2.82	1		Lisboa	21 Mar 10
58:30			Z Tadese			1		Lisboa	20 Mar 11
58:33	WR	Samuel	Wanjiru	KEN	10.11.86	1		Den Haag	17 Mar 07
58:33		Jemal	Yimer	ETH	11.9.96	2		Valencia	28 Oct 18
58:38			Kandie			1		Praha	5 Sep 20
58:40		Abraham	Cheroben (10)	KEN/BRN	11.10.92	1		København	17 Sep 17
58:42		Bedan	Karoki	KEN	21.8.90	1		Ras Al Khaimah	9 Feb 18
58:42		Erick	Kiptanui	KEN	19.4.90	1		Berlin	8 Apr 18
58:42		Stephen	Kiprop	KEN	8.9.99	1		Ras Al Khaimah	8 Feb 19
58:42		Kelvin	Kiptum	KEN	2.12.99	6		Valencia	6 Dec 20
58:44	PP	Solomon	Yego	KEN	10.5.87	1		Ostia	13 Mar 16
58:44		Abadi	Hadis	ETH	6.11.97	3		Valencia	28 Oct 18
58:44			Hadis			2		Ras Al Khaimah	8 Feb 19
58:46		Mathew	Kisorio ¶	KEN	16.5.89	1		Philadelphia	18 Sep 11
58:47		Atsedu	Tsegay	ETH	17.12.91	1		Praha	31 Mar 12
58:48		Sammy	Kitwara ¶	KEN	26.11.86	2		Philadelphia	18 Sep 11
58:48			Cheroben			1		Valencia	19 Oct 14
58:48		Jorum	Okumbo (20)	KEN	10.12.97	2		København	17 Sep 17
58:49			J Kiplimo			1	WCh	Gdynia	17 Oct 20
58:51		Alex	Oloitiptip Korio	KEN	20.12.90	3		København	17 Sep 17
58:52		Patrick	Makau	KEN	2.3.85	1		Ras Al Khaimah	20 Feb 09
58:53	WR		Wanjiru			1		Ras Al Khaimah	9 Feb 07
58:53		Amdework	Walelegn	ETH	11.3.99	1		New Delhi	29 Nov 20
58:54		Stephen	Kibet	KEN	9.11.86	1		Den Haag	11 Mar 12
58:54			Kamworor			1		Ras Al Khaimah	15 Feb 13
58:54			Kandie			2	WCh	Gdynia	17 Oct 20
58:54		Andamlak	Belihu	ETH	20.11.98	2		New Delhi	29 Nov 20
		(33/25)							
58:55	WR	Haile	Gebrselassie	ETH	18.4.73	1		Tempe	15 Jan 06
58:56	dh	Martin	Mathathi	KEN	25.12.85	1	GNR	South Shields	18 Sep 11
58:56		Stanley	Biwott	KEN	21.4.86	2		Ras Al Khaimah	15 Feb 13
58:56		Stephen	Kissa	UGA	1.12.95	3		New Delhi	29 Nov 20
58:58		Geoffrey	Mutai	KEN	7.10.81	3		Ras Al Khaimah	15 Feb 13
		(30)							
58:59		Wilson	Kipsang	KEN	15.3.82	2		Ras Al Khaimah	20 Feb 09
59:01		Kenneth	Kipkemoi	KEN	2.8.84	2		Valencia	19 Oct 14
59:02		Jonathan	Maiyo	KEN	5.5.88	2		Den Haag	11 Mar 12
59:04		Muktar	Edris	ETH	14.1.94	4		New Delhi	29 Nov 20
59:05		Evans	Cheruiyot	KEN	10.5.82	3	WCh	Udine	14 Oct 07
59:05		Ezekiel	Chebii	KEN	3.1.91	1		Lille	1 Sep 12
59:05		Yomif	Kejelcha	ETH	1.8.97	1		Valencia	27 Oct 19
59:06	dh	Paul	Tergat	KEN	17.6.69	1		Lisboa (dh 69m)	26 Mar 00
59:06		Guye	Adola	ETH	20.10.90	1		New Delhi	23 Nov 14
59:06		Alex	Kibet	KEN	20.10.90	3		Ras Al Khaimah	9 Feb 18
		(40)							
59:06		Daniel	Kipchumba Chebii	KEN	12.12.97	1		Verbania	15 Apr 18
59:07		Paul	Kosgei	KEN	22.4.78	1		Berlin	2 Apr 06
59:07	dh	Micah	Kogo	KEN	3.6.86	2	GNR	South Shields	16 Sep 12
59:07		James	Wangari	KEN	23.3.94	1		København	18 Sep 16
59:07		Mang'ata	Ndiwa	KEN	12.12.87	2		Verbania	15 Apr 18
59:07		Benard	Kimeli	KEN	10.9.95	1		Praha	6 Apr 19
59:07	dh	Mohamed	Farah	GBR	23.3.83	1	GNR	South Shields	8 Sep 19
59:07		Bernard Kipkorir	Ngeno	KEN	10.8.96	2		Valencia	27 Oct 19
59:08		Fikadu	Haftu	ETH	21.2.94	3		Ras Al Khaimah	8 Feb 19
59:08		Felix	Kibitok	KEN	9.6.91	2		Praha	6 Apr 19
		(50)							

Short course: 58:51 Paul Tergat KEN 17.6.69 1 Stra Milano 49m sh 30 Mar 96
Excessively downhill: 58:42 Bernard Koech KEN 31.1.88 1 San Diego (dh 86m) 2 Jun 13
Drugs dq: 58:18 (WR) Abraham Kiptum ¶ KEN 15.9.89 (1) Valencia 28 Oct 18

MARATHON

Mark		Name		Nat	Born	Pos	Meet	Venue	Date
2:01:39	WR	Eliud	Kipchoge	KEN	5.11.84	1		Berlin	16 Sep 18
2:01:41		Kenenisa	Bekele	ETH	13.6.82	1		Berlin	29 Sep 19
2:02:37			Kipchoge			1		London	28 Apr 19
2:02:48		Birhanu	Legesse	ETH	11.9.94	2		Berlin	29 Sep 19
2:02:55		Mosinet	Geremew	ETH	12.2.92	2		London	28 Apr 19
2:02:57	WR	Dennis	Kimetto	KEN	22.1.84	1		Berlin	28 Sep 14
2:03:00		Evans	Chebet	KEN	10.11.88	1		Valencia	6 Dec 20
2:03:03			K Bekele			1		Berlin	25 Sep 16

MARATHON A-T

Mark	Wind	Name		Nat	Born	Pos	Meet	Venue	Date
2:03:04		Lawrence	Cherono	KEN	7.8.88	2		Valencia	6 Dec 20
2:03:05			Kipchoge			1		London	24 Apr 16
2:03:13		Emmanuel	Mutai	KEN	12.10.84	2		Berlin	28 Sep 14
2:03:13		Wilson	Kipsang	KEN	15.3.82	2		Berlin	25 Sep 16
2:03:16		Mule	Wasihun (10)	ETH	20.10.93	3		London	28 Apr 19
2:03:16			Legese			3		Valencia	6 Dec 20
2:03:23 WR			W Kipsang			1		Berlin	29 Sep 13
2:03:30		Amos	Kipruto	KEN	16.9.92	4		Valencia	6 Dec 20
2:03.32			Kipchoge			2		Berlin	24 Sep 17
2:03:34		Getaneh	Molla	ETH	10.1.94	1		Dubai	25 Jan 19
2:03:36		Sisay	Lemma	ETH	12.12.90	3		Berlin	29 Sep 19
2:03:38 WR		Patrick	Makau	KEN	2.3.85	1		Berlin	25 Sep 11
2:03:40		Herpana	Negassa	ETH	11.9.93	2		Dubai	25 Jan 19
2:03:42			W Kipsang			1		Frankfurt	30 Oct 11
2:03:45			Kimetto			1		Chicago	13 Oct 13
2:03:46		Guye	Adola	ETH	20.10.90	2		Berlin	24 Sep 17
2:03:51		Stanley	Biwott	KEN	21.4.86	2		London	24 Apr 16
2:03:51		Kinde	Atanaw	ETH	15.4.93	1		Valencia	1 Dec 19
2:03:52			Mutai			2		Chicago	13 Oct 13
2:03:58			W Kipsang			1		Tokyo	26 Feb 17
2:03:59 WR		Haile	Gebrselassie	ETH	18.4.73	1		Berlin	28 Sep 08
2:04:00			Kipchoge			1		Berlin	27 Sep 15
2:04:00			Geremew			1		Dubai	26 Jan 18
2:04:02		Leul	Gebrselassie	ETH	20.9.93	2		Dubai	26 Jan 18
	(32/20)								
2:04:06		Tamirat	Tola	ETH	11.8.91	3		Dubai	26 Jan 18
2:04:06		Asefa	Mengistu	ETH	18.1.85	4		Dubai	26 Jan 18
2:04:11		Marius	Kipserem	KEN	17.5.88	1		Rotterdam	7 Apr 19
2:04:12		Reuben Kiprop	Kipyego	KEN	21.8.96	5		Valencia	6 Dec 20
2:04:15		Geoffrey	Mutai	KEN	7.10.81	1		Berlin	30 Sep 12
2:04:16		Kaan Kigen	Özbilen	TUR	15.1.86	2		Valencia	1 Dec 19
2:04:23		Ayele	Abshero	ETH	28.12.90	1		Dubai	27 Jan 12
2:04:24		Tesfaye	Abera	ETH	31.3.92	1		Dubai	22 Jan 16
2:04:27		Duncan	Kibet	KEN	25.4.78	1		Rotterdam	5 Apr 09
2:04:27		James Kipsang	Kwambai	KEN	28.2.83	2		Rotterdam	5 Apr 09
	(30)								
2:04:28		Sammy	Kitwara ¶	KEN	26.11.86	2		Chicago	12 Oct 14
2:04:32		Tsegaye	Mekonnen	ETH	15.6.95	1		Dubai	24 Jan 14
2:04:32		Dickson	Chumba	KEN	27.10.86	3		Chicago	12 Oct 14
2:04:33		Hayle	Lemi Berhanu	ETH	13.9.94	2		Dubai	22 Jan 16
2:04:38		Tsegaye	Kebede	ETH	15.1.87	1		Chicago	7 Oct 12
2:04:40		Solomon	Deksisa	ETH	11.3.94	3		Amsterdam	21 Oct 18
2:04:43		El Hassan	El Abbassi	BRN	13.4.84	2		Valencia	2 Dec 18
2:04:44		Abdiwak	Tura	ETH	.95	7		Dubai	26 Jan 18
2:04:45		Lelisa	Desisa	ETH	14.1.90	1		Dubai	25 Jan 13
2:04:46		Titus	Ekiru	KEN	2.1.92	1		Milano	7 Apr 19
	(40)								
2:04:46		Mekuant	Ayenew	ETH	.91	1		Sevilla	23 Feb 20
2:04:48		Yemane	Tsegay Adhane	ETH	8.4.85	1		Rotterdam	15 Apr 12
2:04:48		Berhanu	Shiferaw	ETH	31.5.93	2		Dubai	25 Jan 13
2:04:49		Tadesse	Tola	ETH	31.10.87	3		Dubai	25 Jan 13
2:04:49		Shura	Kitata	ETH	9.6.96	2		London	22 Apr 18
2:04:49		Bashir	Abdi	BEL	10.2.89	2		Tokyo	1 Mar 20
2:04:50		Dino	Sefir	ETH	28.5.88	2		Dubai	27 Jan 12
2:04:50		Getu	Feleke	ETH	28.11.86	2		Rotterdam	15 Apr 12
2:04:51		Abebe	Degefa	ETH	20.5.84	4		Valencia	1 Dec 19
2:04:52		Feyisa	Lilesa (50)	ETH	1.2.90	2		Chicago	7 Oct 12
2:04:52		Endeshaw	Negesse	ETH	13.3.88	4		Dubai	25 Jan 13
2:04:53		Bernard	Koech	KEN	31.1.88	5		Dubai	25 Jan 13
2:04:53		Mathew	Kisorio ¶	KEN	16.5.89	3		Valencia	2 Dec 18
2:04:53		Gelmisa	Chalu	ETH		6		Valencia	6 Dec 20
	(54)								

100th man 2:05:49, 200th 2:06:43, 300th 2:07:18, 400th 2:07:49, 500th 2:08:15

Downhill point-to-point course – Boston marathon is downhill overall (139m) and sometimes strongly wind-aided.

2:03:02		Geoffrey	Mutai	KEN	7.10.81	1		Boston	18 Apr 11
2:03:06		Moses	Mosop	KEN	17.7.85	2		Boston	18 Apr 11

Uncertain distance

2:04:04		Marius	Kipserem	KEN	17.5.88	1		Abu Dhabi	7 Dec 18
2:04:16 drugs dq	Abraham	Kiptum ¶	KEN	5.9.89	(2)		Abu Dhabi	7 Dec 18

Illegally paced: 1:59:41 Eliud Kipchoge KEN 5.11.84 1 Wien 20 Oct 19
2:00:25 Eliud Kipchoge KEN 5.11.84 1 Monza 6 May 17

206   2000m – 3000m STEEPLECHASE A-T

Mark	Wind	Name		Nat	Born	Pos	Meet	Venue	Date

2000 METRES STEEPLECHASE
5:10.68		Mahiedine	Mekhissi-Benabbad	FRA	15.3.85	1		Reims	30 Jun 10
5:13.47		Bouabdellah	Tahri	FRA	20.12.78	1		Tomblaine	25 Jun 10
5:14.43		Julius	Kariuki	KEN	12.6.61	1		Rovereto	21 Aug 90
5:14.53		Saïf Saaeed	Shaheen	QAT	15.10.82	1	SGP	Doha	13 May 05

3000 METRES STEEPLECHASE
7:53.63 WR		Saïf Saaeed	Shaheen	KEN/QAT	15.10.82	1	VD	Bruxelles	3 Sep 04
7:53.64		Brimin	Kipruto	KEN	31.7.85	1	Herc	Monaco	22 Jul 11
7:54.31		Paul Kipsiele	Koech	KEN	10.11.81	1	GGala	Roma	31 May 12
7:55.28 WR		Brahim	Boulami ¶	MAR	20.4.72	1	VD	Bruxelles	24 Aug 01
7:55.51			Shaheen			1	VD	Bruxelles	26 Aug 05
7:55.72 WR		Bernard	Barmasai	KEN	6.5.74	1	ASV	Köln	24 Aug 97
7:55.76		Ezekiel	Kemboi	KEN	25.5.82	2	Herc	Monaco	22 Jul 11
7:56.16		Moses	Kiptanui	KEN	1.10.70	2	ASV	Köln	24 Aug 97
7:56.32			Shaheen			1	Tsik	Athína	3 Jul 06
7:56.34			Shaheen			1	GGala	Roma	8 Jul 05
7:56.37			P K Koech			2	GGala	Roma	8 Jul 05
7:56.54			Shaheen			1	WK	Zürich	18 Aug 06
7:56.58			P K Koech			1	DL	Doha	11 May 12
7:56.81		Richard	Mateelong	KEN	14.10.83	2	DL	Doha	11 May 12
7:56.94			Shaheen			1	WAF	Monaco	19 Sep 04
7:57.28			Shaheen			1	Tsik	Athína	14 Jun 05
7:57.29		Reuben	Kosgei	KEN	2.8.79	2	VD	Bruxelles	24 Aug 01
7:57.32			P K Koech			3	Herc	Monaco	22 Jul 11
7:57.38			Shaheen			1	WAF	Monaco	14 Sep 03
7:57.42			P K Koech			2	WAF	Monaco	14 Sep 03
7:58.09			Boulami			1	Herc	Monaco	19 Jul 02
7:58.10			S Cherono			2	Herc	Monaco	19 Jul 02
7:58.15		Soufiane	El Bakkali (10)	MAR	7.1.96	1	Herc	Monaco	20 Jul 18
7:58.41		Jairus	Birech	KEN	14.12.92	1	VD	Bruxelles	5 Sep 14
7:58.50			Boulami			1	WK	Zürich	17 Aug 01
7:58.66			S Cherono			3	VD	Bruxelles	24 Aug 01
7:58.80			P K Koech			1	VD	Bruxelles	14 Sep 07
7:58.83			Birech			1	DL	Saint-Denis	4 Jul 15
7:58.85			Kemboi			1	SGP	Doha	8 May 09
7:58.98			Barmasai			1	Herc	Monaco	4 Aug 99
		(30/11)							
7:59.08 WR		Wilson	Boit Kipketer	KEN	6.10.73	1	WK	Zürich	13 Aug 97
8:00.09		Mahiedine	Mekhissi-Benabbad	FRA	15.3.85	2	DL	Saint-Denis	6 Jul 13
8:00.12		Conseslus	Kipruto	KEN	8.12.94	1	DL	Birmingham	5 Jun 16
8:00.45		Evan	Jager	USA	8.3.89	2	DL	Saint-Denis	4 Jul 15
8:01.18		Bouabdellah	Tahri	FRA	20.12.78	3	WCh	Berlin	18 Aug 09
8:01.36		Lamecha	Girma	ETH	26.11.00	2	WC	Doha	4 Oct 19
8:01.67		Abel	Mutai	KEN	2.10.88	2	GGala	Roma	31 May 12
8:01.69		Kipkirui	Misoi	KEN	23.12.78	4	VD	Bruxelles	24 Aug 01
8:03.41		Patrick	Sang	KEN	11.4.64	3	ASV	Köln	24 Aug 97
		(20)							
8:03.57		Ali	Ezzine	MAR	3.9.78	1	Gaz	Saint-Denis	23 Jun 00
8:03.57		Hillary	Yego	KEN	2.4.92	3	DL	Shanghai	18 May 13
8:03.74		Raymond	Yator	KEN	7.4.81	3	Herc	Monaco	18 Aug 00
8:03.81		Benjamin	Kiplagat	UGA	4.3.89	2	Athl	Lausanne	8 Jul 10
8:03.89		John	Kosgei	KEN	13.7.73	3	Herc	Monaco	16 Aug 97
8:04.95		Simon	Vroemen ¶	NED	11.5.69	2	VD	Bruxelles	26 Aug 05
8:05.01		Eliud	Barngetuny	KEN	20.5.73	1	Herc	Monaco	25 Jul 95
8:05.12		Benjamin	Kigen	KEN	5.7.93	2	Herc	Monaco	12 Jul 19
8:05.21		Getnet	Wale	ETH	20.7.99	4	WCh	Doha	4 Oct 19
8:05.23		Djilali	Bedrani	FRA	1.10.93	5	WCh	Doha	4 Oct 19
		(30)							
8:05.35 WR		Peter	Koech	KEN	18.2.58	1	DNG	Stockholm	3 Jul 89
8:05.37		Philip	Barkutwo	KEN	6.10.66	2		Rieti	6 Sep 92
8:05.4 WR		Henry	Rono	KEN	12.2.52	1		Seattle	13 May 78
8:05.43		Christopher	Kosgei	KEN	14.8.74	2	WK	Zürich	11 Aug 99
8:05.51		Julius	Kariuki	KEN	12.6.61	1	OG	Seoul	30 Sep 88
8:05.68		Wesley	Kiprotich	KEN	1.8.79	4	VD	Bruxelles	3 Sep 04
8:05.69		Fernando	Carro	ESP	1.4.92	4	Herc	Monaco	12 Jul 19
8:05.72		Abraham	Kibiwot	KEN	6.4.96	5	Herc	Monaco	12 Jul 19
8:05.75		Mustafa	Mohamed	SWE	1.3.79	1	NA	Heusden-Zolder	28 Jul 07
8:05.88		Bernard	Mbugua Nganga	KEN	17.1.85	2	ISTAF	Berlin	11 Sep 11
		(40)							

3000m STEEPLECHASE – 110m HURDLES A-T

Mark	Wind	Name		Nat	Born	Pos	Meet	Venue	Date
8:05.99		Joseph	Keter	KEN	13.6.69	1	Herc	Monaco	10 Aug 96
8:06.13		Tareq Mubarak	Taher	BRN	24.3.84	3	Tsik	Athína	13 Jul 09
8:06.16		Roba	Gari	ETH	12.4.82	3	DL	Doha	11 May 12
8:06.48		Chala	Beyo	ETH	18.1.96	2	DL	Rabat	16 Jun 19
8:06.77		Gideon	Chirchir	KEN	24.2.66	2	WK	Zürich	16 Aug 95
8:06.88		Richard	Kosgei	KEN	29.12.70	2	GPF	Monaco	9 Sep 95
8:06.96		Gilbert	Kirui	KEN	22.1.94	2	DL	London (OS)	27 Jul 13
8:07.02		Brahim	Taleb	MAR	16.2.85	2	NA	Heusden-Zolder	28 Jul 07
8:07.13		Paul	Kosgei	KEN	22.4.78	2	GP II	Saint-Denis	3 Jul 99
8:07.18		Obaid Moussa (50)	Amer ¶	KEN/QAT	18.4.85	4	OG	Athína	24 Aug 04

100th man 8:11.18, 200th 8:16.57, 300th 8:20.34, 400th 8:22.8, 500th 8:24.97
7:53.63 Shaheen formerly Stephen Cherono KEN
Drugs disqualification: 7:53.17 Brahim Boulami ¶ MAR 20.4.72 1 WK Zürich 16 Aug 02

110 METRES HURDLES

Mark	Wind	Name		Nat	Born	Pos	Meet	Venue	Date
12.80 WR	0.3	Aries	Merritt	USA	24.7.85	1	VD	Bruxelles	7 Sep 12
12.87 WR	0.9	Dayron	Robles	CUB	19.11.86	1	GS	Ostrava	12 Jun 08
12.88 WR	1.1		Liu Xiang	CHN	13.7.83	1rA	Athl	Lausanne	11 Jul 06
12.88	0.5		Robles			1	Gaz	Saint-Denis	18 Jul 08
12.89	0.5	David	Oliver	USA	24.4.82	1	DL	Saint-Denis	16 Jul 10
12.90	1.1	Dominique	Arnold	USA	14.9.73	2rA	Athl	Lausanne	11 Jul 06
12.90	1.6		Oliver			1	Pre	Eugene	3 Jul 10
12.90	0.7	Omar	McLeod	JAM	25.4.94	1	NC	Kingston	24 Jun 17
12.91 WR	0.5	Colin	Jackson	GBR	18.2.67	1	WCh	Stuttgart	20 Aug 93
12.91 WR	0.3		Liu Xiang			1	OG	Athína	27 Aug 04
12.91	0.2		Robles			1	DNG	Stockholm	22 Jul 08
12.92 WR	-0.1	Roger	Kingdom	USA	26.8.62	1	WK	Zürich	16 Aug 89
12.92	0.9	Allen	Johnson	USA	1.3.71	1	NC	Atlanta	23 Jun 96
12.92	0.2		Johnson			1	VD	Bruxelles	23 Aug 96
12.92	1.5		Liu Xiang			1	GP	New York	2 Jun 07
12.92	0.0		Robles			1	WAF	Stuttgart	23 Sep 07
12.92	-0.3		Merritt			1	OG	London (OS)	8 Aug 12
12.92	0.6	Sergey	Shubenkov (10)	RUS	4.10.90	1	Gyulai	Székesfehérvár	2 Jul 18
12.93 WR	-0.2	Renaldo	Nehemiah	USA	24.3.59	1	WK	Zürich	19 Aug 81
12.93	0.0		Johnson			1	WCh	Athína	7 Aug 97
12.93	-0.6		Liu Xiang			1	WAF	Stuttgart	9 Sep 06
12.93	0.1		Robles			1	OG	Beijing	21 Aug 08
12.93	1.7		Oliver			1	NC	Des Moines	27 Jun 10
12.93	-0.3		Oliver			1	WK	Zürich	19 Aug 10
12.93	1.2		Merritt			1	NC/OT	Eugene	30 Jun 12
12.93	0.6		Merritt			1	LGP	London (CP)	13 Jul 12
12.93	0.0		Merritt			1	Herc	Monaco	20 Jul 12
12.94	1.6	Jack	Pierce	USA	23.9.62	1s2	NC	Atlanta	22 Jun 96
12.94	1.8		Oliver			1	Pre	Eugene	4 Jun 11
12.94	0.1		Merritt			1s2	OG	London (OS)	8 Aug 12
12.94	0.8	Hansle	Parchment	JAM	17.6.90	1	DL	Saint-Denis	5 Jul 14
12.94	0.5	Orlando (32/14)	Ortega	CUB/ESP	29.7.91	1	DL	Saint-Denis	4 Jul 15
12.95	1.5	Terrence	Trammell	USA	23.11.78	2	GP	New York	2 Jun 07
12.95	0.2	Pascal	Martinot-Lagarde	FRA	22.9.91	1	Herc	Monaco	18 Jul 14
12.97	1.0	Ladji	Doucouré	FRA	28.3.83	1	NC	Angers	15 Jul 05
12.98	0.6	Mark	Crear	USA	2.10.68	1		Zagreb	5 Jul 99
12.98	1.5	Jason	Richardson	USA	4.4.86	1s3	NC/OT	Eugene	30 Jun 12
12.98	0.8	Grant (20)	Holloway	USA	19.11.97	1	NCAA	Austin	7 Jun 19
12.99	1.2	Ronnie	Ash	USA	2.7.88	1s1	NC	Sacramento	29 Jun 14
13.00	0.5	Anthony	Jarrett	GBR	13.8.68	2	WCh	Stuttgart	20 Aug 93
13.00	0.6	Anier	García	CUB	9.3.76	1	OG	Sydney	25 Sep 00
13.00	0.8	Daniel	Roberts	USA	13.4.98	2	NCAA	Austin	7 Jun 19
13.01	0.3	Larry	Wade ¶	USA	22.11.74	1rA	Athl	Lausanne	2 Jul 99
13.02	1.5	Ryan	Wilson	USA	19.12.80	3	GP	New York	2 Jun 07
13.02	1.7	David	Payne	USA	24.7.82	3	WCh	Osaka	31 Aug 07
13.03	-0.2	Greg	Foster	USA	4.8.58	2	WK	Zürich	19 Aug 81
13.03	1.0	Reggie	Torian	USA	22.4.75	1	NC	New Orleans	21 Jun 98
13.03	1.0	Devon (30)	Allen	USA	12.12.94	1	NC/OT	Eugene	9 Jul 16
13.05	1.4	Tony	Dees ¶	USA	6.8.63	1		Vigo	23 Jul 91
13.05	-0.8	Florian	Schwarthoff	GER	7.5.68	1	NC	Bremen	2 Jul 95
13.05	-0.1	Ronald	Levy	JAM	30.10.92	1	DL	Paris (C)	1 Jul 17
13.08	1.2	Mark	McKoy	CAN	10.12.61	1	BNP	Villeneuve-d'Ascq	2 Jul 93

110m - 400m HURDLES A-T

Mark	Wind	Name		Nat	Born	Pos	Meet	Venue	Date
13.08	0.0	Stanislav	Olijar	LAT	22.3.79	2	Athl	Lausanne	1 Jul 03
13.08	1.2	Jeff	Porter	USA	27.11.85	3	NC/OT	Eugene	30 Jun 12
13.09	2.0	Antwon	Hicks	USA	12.3.83	2s2	NC/OT	Eugene	6 Jul 08
13.09	0.6	Garfield	Darien	FRA	22.12.87	1	GS	Ostrava	28 Jun 17
13.11	0.5	Aleec	Harris	USA	31.10.90	4	DL	Saint-Denis	4 Jul 15
13.11	1.8	Antonio (40)	Alkana	RSA	12.4.90	1	Odlozil	Praha	5 Jun 17
13.12	1.5	Falk	Balzer ¶	GER	14.12.73	2	EC	Budapest	22 Aug 98
13.12	1.0	Duane	Ross ¶	USA	5.12.72	3	WCh	Sevilla	25 Aug 99
13.12	1.9	Anwar	Moore	USA	5.3.79	1	ModR	Modesto	5 May 07
13.12	0.0	Dimitri	Bascou	FRA	20.7.87	2	Herc	Monaco	15 Jul 16
13.13	1.6	Igor	KovácÖ	SVK	12.5.69	1	DNG	Stockholm	7 Jul 97
13.13	2.0	Dexter	Faulk	USA	14.4.84	2	GS	Ostrava	17 Jun 09
13.14	0.1	Ryan	Brathwaite	BAR	6.6.88	1	WCh	Berlin	20 Aug 09
13.14	0.0	Andrew	Riley	JAM	6.9.88	4	DL	Saint-Denis	6 Jul 13
13.14	-0.1	Andrew	Pozzi	GBR	15.5.92	2	DL	Paris (C)	1 Jul 17
13.15	0.3	Robin	Korving	NED	29.7.74	5rA	Athl	Lausanne	2 Jul 99
13.15	0.1	Dwight	Thomas	JAM	23.9.80	2	Bisl	Oslo	9 Jun 11
13.15	0.3	Balázs	Baji	HUN	9.6.89	4	Gyulai	Székesfehérvár	4 Jul 17
13.15	0.3	Aaron (53)	Mallett	USA	26.9.94	1	DL	Doha	25 Sep 20

100th man 13.26, 200th 13.38, 300th 13.45, 400th 13.51, 500th 13.56

Rolling start but accepted by race officials
| 13.10A | 2.0 | Falk | Balzer ¶ | GER | 14.12.73 | 1 | WCp | Johannesburg | 13 Sep 98 |

Doubtful timing: Scheessel 4 Jun 95 +1.3 1. Mike Fenner GER 24.4.71 13.06, 2. Eric Kaiser ¶ GER 7.3.71 13.08

Wind-assisted marks *Performances to 12.94, performers to 13.14*

12.87	2.6	Roger	Kingdom	USA	26.8.62	1	WCp	Barcelona	10 Sep 89
12.87	2.4		Liu Xiang	CHN	13.7.83	1	Pre	Eugene	2 Jun 12
12.89	3.2	David	Oliver	USA	24.4.82	1s1	NC/OT	Eugene	6 Jul 08
12.91	3.5	Renaldo	Nehemiah	USA	24.3.59	1	NCAA	Champaign	1 Jun 79
12.94A	2.8		Jackson			1rA		Sestriere	31 Jul 94
12.98	3.1	Ronnie	Ash	USA	2.7.88	1	NACAC	Miramar	9 Jul 10
13.00	2.6	Anwar	Moore	USA	5.3.79	1	DrakeR	Des Moines	28 Apr 07
13.05	3.6	Ryan	Brathwaite	BAR	6.6.88	1		Austin	2 May 09
13.05	2.1	Dimitri	Bascou	FRA	20.7.87	1	NC	Angers	26 Jun 16
13.06	2.1	Mark	McKoy	CAN	10.12.61	1	Gugl	Linz	13 Aug 92
13.12	2.4	Dexter	Faulk	USA	14.4.84	4	Pre	Eugene	2 Jun 12
13.13	5.8	Andrew	Pozzi	GBR	15.5.92	1		Clermont	15 Apr 17
13.14	2.9	Igor	Kazanov	LAT	24.9.63	1r1	Znam	Leningrad	8 Jun 86
13.14	4.7	Lawrence	Clarke	GBR	12.3.90	1h1		Madrid	7 Jul 12
13.14	3.8	Wayne	Davis	TTO	22.8.91	1	NCAA	Eugene	8 Jun 13
13.14	3.0	Wilhem	Belocian	FRA	22.6.95	1	NC	Saint Etienne	28 Jul 19

Hand timing
12.7		Sergey	Shubenkov	RUS	4.10.90	1		Barnaul	2 Jul 16
12.8	1.0	Renaldo	Nehemiah	USA	24.3.59	1		Kingston	11 May 79
12.9	0.0	Yordan	O'Farrill	CUB	9.2.93	1	Barr	La Habana	23 May 14

Wind-assisted
12.8	2.4	Colin	Jackson	GBR	18.2.67	1		Sydney	10 Jan 90
12.9	4.1	Mark	Crear	USA	2.10.68	1rA	S&W	Modesto	8 May 93
12.9	3.1	William	Sharman	GBR	12.9.84	1r2		Madrid	2 Jul 10

400 METRES HURDLES

46.78 WR		Kevin	Young	USA	16.9.66	1	OG	Barcelona	6 Aug 92
46.87		Karsten	Warholm	NOR	28.2.96	1	DL	Stockholm	23 Aug 20
46.92			Warholm			1	WK	Zürich	29 Aug 19
46.98		Abderrahman	Samba	QAT	5.9.95	1	DL	Paris (C)	30 Jun 18
46.98		Rai	Benjamin	ANT/USA	27.7.97	2	WK	Zürich	29 Aug 19
47.02 WR		Edwin	Moses	USA	31.8.55	1		Koblenz	31 Aug 83
47.02			Benjamin		27.7.97	1	NCAA	Eugene	8 Jun 18
47.03		Bryan	Bronson ¶	USA	9.9.72	1	NC	New Orleans	21 Jun 98
47.07			Warholm			1	G Gala	Roma	17 Sep 20
47.08			Warholm			1	ISTAF	Berlin	13 Sep 20
47.10		Samuel	Matete	ZAM	27.7.68	1rA	WK	Zürich	7 Aug 91
47.10			Warholm			1	Herc	Monaco	14 Aug 20
47.12			Warholm			1	DL	London (OS)	20 Jul 19
47.13 WR			Moses			1		Milano	3 Jul 80
47.14			Moses			1	Athl	Lausanne	14 Jul 81
47.16			Benjamin			1	Pre	Stanford	30 Jun 19
47.17			Moses			1	ISTAF	Berlin	8 Aug 80
47.18			Young			1	WCh	Stuttgart	19 Aug 93
47.19		Andre	Phillips	USA	5.9.59	1	OG	Seoul	25 Sep 88

400 METRES HURDLES - HIGH JUMP A-T

Mark	Wind	Name		Nat	Born	Pos	Meet	Venue	Date
47.23		Amadou	Dia Bâ	SEN	22.9.58	2	OG	Seoul	25 Sep 88
47.23			Benjamin	USA		1	NC	Des Moines	27 Jul 19
47.24		Kerron	Clement (10)	USA	31.10.85	1	NC	Carson	26 Jun 05
47.25		Félix	Sánchez	DOM	30.8.77	1	WCh	Saint-Denis	29 Aug 03
47.25		Angelo	Taylor	USA	29.12.78	1	OG	Beijing	18 Aug 08
47.26			Warholm			1	DL	Paris (C)	24 Aug 19
47.27			Moses			1	ISTAF	Berlin	21 Aug 81
47.27			Samba			1	DL	Shanghai	18 May 19
47.30		Bershawn	Jackson	USA	8.5.83	1	WCh	Helsinki	9 Aug 05
47.32			Moses			1		Koblenz	29 Aug 84
47.32			Jackson			1	NC	Des Moines	26 Jun 10
		(30/13)							
47.37		Stéphane	Diagana	FRA	23.7.69	1	Athl	Lausanne	5 Jul 95
47.38		Danny	Harris ¶	USA	7.9.65	1	Athl	Lausanne	10 Jul 91
47.43		Ja0es	Carter	USA	7.5.78	2	WCh	Helsinki	9 Aug 05
47.48		Harald	Schmid	FRG	29.9.57	1	EC	Athína	8 Sep 82
47.53		Hadi Souaʼan	Al-Somaily	KSA	21.8.76	2	OG	Sydney	27 Sep 00
47.54		Derrick	Adkins	USA	2.7.70	1	Athl	Lausanne	5 Jul 95
47.54		Fabrizio	Mori	ITA	28.6.69	2	WCh	Edmonton	10 Aug 01
		(20)							
47.54		Kyron	McMaster	IVB	3.1.97	3	DL	Paris (C)	30 Jun 18
47.60		Winthrop	Graham	JAM	17.11.65	1	WK	Zürich	4 Aug 93
47.63		Johnny	Dutch	USA	20.1.89	2	NC	Des Moines	26 Jun 10
47.66A		L.J. 'Louis'	van Zyl	RSA	20.7.85	1		Pretoria	25 Feb 11
47.67		Bennie	Brazell	USA	2.6.82	2	NCAA	Sacramento	11 Jun 05
47.69		Jehue	Gordon	TTO	15.12.91	1	WCh	Moskva	15 Aug 13
47.70		Michael	Tinsley	USA	21.4.84	2	WCh	Moskva	15 Aug 13
47.72		Javier	Culson	PUR	25.7.84			Ponce	8 May 10
47.75		David	Patrick	USA	12.6.60	4	NC/OT	Indianapolis	17 Jul 88
47.78		Boniface Mucheru Tumuti		KEN	2.5.92	2	OG	Rio de Janeiro	18 Aug 16
		(30)							
47.79		Nicholas	Bett	KEN	14.6.92	1	WCh	Beijing	25 Aug 15
47.81		Llewellyn	Herbert	RSA	21.7.77	3	OG	Sydney	27 Sep 00
47.81		Yasmani	Copello	CUB/TUR	15.4.87	2	EC	Berlin	9 Aug 18
47.82 WR		John	Akii-Bua	UGA	3.12.49	1	OG	München	2 Sep 72
47.82		Kriss	Akabusi	GBR	28.11.58	3	OG	Barcelona	6 Aug 92
47.82		Periklis	Iakovákis	GRE	24.3.79	2	GP	Osaka	6 May 06
47.84		Bayano	Kamani	PAN	17.4.80	2s1	WCh	Helsinki	7 Aug 05
47.84		David	Greene	GBR	11.4.86	2	DL	Saint-Denis	6 Jul 12
47.89		Dai	Tamesue	JPN	3.5.78	3	WCh	Edmonton	10 Aug 01
47.91		Calvin	Davis	USA	2.4.72	1s2	OG	Atlanta	31 Jul 96
		(40)							
47.92		Aleksandr	Vasilyev	BLR	26.7.61	2	ECp	Moskva	17 Aug 85
47.93		Kenji	Narisako	JPN	25.7.84	3	GP	Osaka	6 May 06
47.93		Jeshua	Anderson	USA	22.6.89	1	NC	Eugene	26 Jun 11
47.93		Omar	Cisneros	CUB	19.11.89	1s3	WCh	Moskva	13 Aug 13
47.94		Eric	Thomas	USA	1.12.73	1	GGala	Roma	30 Jun 00
47.97		Maurice	Mitchell	USA	14.5.71	2rA	WK	Zürich	14 Aug 96
47.97		Joey	Woody	USA	22.5.73	3	NC	New Orleans	21 Jun 98
47.97		Thomas	Barr	IRL	24.7.92	4	OG	Rio de Janeiro	18 Aug 16
47.98		Sven	Nylander	SWE	1.1.62	4	OG	Atlanta	1 Aug 96
48.00		Danny	McFarlane	JAM	14.2.72	1s2	OG	Athína	24 Aug 04
		(50)		100th man 48.39, 200th man 48.85, 300th man 49.11, 400th 49.33, 500th 49.48					
Best at low altitude:		47.66	van Zyl	1	GS	Ostrava	31 May 13
Drugs disqualification		47.15	Bronson ¶ (1)	GWG	Uniondale, NY	19 Jul 98

HIGH JUMP

Mark		Name		Nat	Born	Pos	Meet	Venue	Date
2.45 WR		Javier	Sotomayor ¶	CUB	13.10.67	1		Salamanca	27 Jul 93
2.44 WR			Sotomayor			1	CAC	San Juan	29 Jul 89
2.43 WR			Sotomayor			1		Salamanca	8 Sep 88
2.43i WR			Sotomayor			1	WI	Budapest	4 Mar 89
2.43		Mutaz Essa	Barshim	QAT	24.6.91	1	VD	Bruxelles	5 Sep 14
2.42 WR		Patrik	Sjöberg	SWE	5.1.65	1	DNG	Stockholm	30 Jun 87
2.42i WR		Carlo	Thränhardt	FRG	5.7.57	1		Berlin	26 Feb 88
2.42			Sotomayor			1		Sevilla	5 Jun 94
2.42i		Ivan	Ukhov	RUS	29.3.86	1		Praha	25 Feb 14
2.42		Bohdan	Bondarenko	UKR	30.8.89	1	adidas	New York	14 Jun 14
2.42			Barshim			2	adidas	New York	14 Jun 14
2.41 WR		Igor	Paklin	KGZ	15.6.63	1	WUG	Kobe	4 Sep 85
2.41i WR			Sjöberg			1		Pireás	1 Feb 87
2.41i			Sotomayor			1	WI	Toronto	14 Mar 93

MEN All-time

HIGH JUMP A-T

Mark	Wind	Name		Nat	Born	Pos	Meet	Venue	Date
2.41			Sotomayor			1	NC	La Habana	25 Jun 94
2.41			Sotomayor			1	TSB	London (CP)	15 Jul 94
2.41			Bondarenko			1	Athl	Lausanne	4 Jul 13
2.41			Bondarenko			1	WCh	Moskva	15 Aug 13
2.41i			Ukhov			1		Chelyabinsk	16 Jan 14
2.41			Ukhov			1	DL	Doha	9 May 14
2.41			Barshim			1	GGala	Roma	5 Jun 14
2.41			Barshim			1		Eberstadt	22 Aug 14
2.41i			Barshim			1		Athlone	18 Feb 15
2.41	(24/7)		Barshim			1	Pre	Eugene	30 May 15
2.40 WR		Rudolf	Povarnitsyn	UKR	13.6.62	1		Donetsk	11 Aug 85
2.40		Sorin	Matei	ROU	6.7.63	1	PTS	Bratislava	20 Jun 90
2.40i		Hollis	Conway (10)	USA	8.1.67	1	WI	Sevilla	10 Mar 91
2.40		Charles	Austin	USA	19.12.67	1	WK	Zürich	7 Aug 91
2.40		Vyacheslav	Voronin	RUS	5.4.74	1	BrGP	London (CP)	5 Aug 00
2.40i		Stefan	Holm	SWE	25.5.76	1	EI	Madrid	6 Mar 05
2.40i		Aleksey	Dmitrik	RUS	12.4.84	1		Arnstadt	8 Feb 14
2.40		Derek	Drouin	CAN	6.3.90	1	DrakeR	Des Moines	25 Apr 14
2.40		Andriy	Protsenko	UKR	20.5.88	2	Athl	Lausanne	3 Jul 14
2.40		Danil	Lysenko	RUS	19.5.97	1	Herc	Monaco	20 Jul 18

To 2.40 Most performances: Sotomayor 21, Barshim 13, Bondarenko 7, Ukhov 5, Sjöberg 4, Thränhardt 2 for 63/7

Mark	Wind	Name		Nat	Born	Pos	Meet	Venue	Date
2.39 WR			Zhu Jianhua	CHN	29.5.63	1		Eberstadt	10 Jun 84
2.39i WIR		Dietmar	Mögenburg	FRG	15.8.61	1		Köln	24 Feb 85
2.39i		Ralf	Sonn	GER	17.1.67	1		Berlin	1 Mar 91
	(20)								
2.39		Gianmarco	Tamberi	ITA	1.6.92	1	Herc	Monaco	15 Jul 16
2.38i		Gennadiy	Avdeyenko	UKR	4.11.63	2	WI	Indianapolis	7 Mar 87
2.38		Sergey	Malchenko	RUS	2.11.63	1		Banská Bystrica	4 Sep 88
2.38		Dragutin	Topic ¶	YUG	12.3.71	1		Beograd	1 Aug 93
2.38i		Steve	Smith	GBR	29.3.73	2		Wuppertal	4 Feb 94
2.38i		Wolf-Hendrik	Beyer	GER	14.2.72	1		Weinheim	18 Mar 94
2.38		Troy	Kemp	BAH	18.6.66	1	Nik	Nice	12 Jul 95
2.38		Artur	Partyka	POL	25.7.69	1		Eberstadt	18 Aug 96
2.38i		Matt	Hemingway	USA	24.10.72	1	NC	Atlanta	4 Mar 00
2.38i		Yaroslav	Rybakov	RUS	22.11.80	1		Stockholm	15 Feb 05
	(30)								
2.38		Jacques	Freitag	RSA	11.6.82	1		Oudtshoorn	5 Mar 05
2.38		Andriy	Sokolovskyy	UKR	16.7.78	1	GGala	Roma	8 Jul 05
2.38i		Linus	Thörnblad	SWE	6.3.85	2	NC	Göteborg	25 Feb 07
2.38		Andrey	Silnov	RUS	9.9.84	1	LGP	London (CP)	25 Jul 08
2.38		Zhang Guowei		CHN	4.6.91	2	Pre	Eugene	30 May 15
2.37		Valeriy	Sereda	RUS	30.6.59	1		Rieti	2 Sep 84
2.37		Tom	McCants	USA	27.11.62	1	Owens	Columbus	8 May 88
2.37		Jerome	Carter	USA	25.3.63	2	Owens	Columbus	8 May 88
2.37		Sergey	Dymchenko	UKR	23.8.67	1		Kyiv	16 Sep 90
2.37i		Dalton	Grant	GBR	8.4.66	1	EI	Paris	13 Mar 94
	(40)								
2.37i		Jaroslav	Bába	CZE	2.9.84	2		Arnstadt	5 Feb 05
2.37		Jesse	Williams	USA	27.12.83	1	NC	Eugene	26 Jun 11
2.37		Robbie	Grabarz	GBR	3.10.87	3	Athl	Lausanne	23 Aug 12
2.37		Erik	Kynard	USA	3.2.91	2	Athl	Lausanne	4 Jul 13
2.37		Donald	Thomas	BAH	1.7.84	1	Gyulai	Székesfehérvár	18 Jul 16
2.36 WR		Gerd	Wessig	GDR	16.7.59	1	OG	Moskva	1 Aug 80
2.36		Sergey	Zasimovich	KAZ	6.9.62	1		Tashkent	5 May 84
2.36		Eddy	Annys	BEL	15.12.58	1		Gent	26 May 85
2.36Ai		Jim	Howard	USA	11.9.59	1		Albuquerque	25 Jan 86

and 20 more men at 2.36 (45 to 2.37) 100th man 2.34, 200th 2.31, 300th 2.30, 400th 2.28, 500th 2.28

Best outdoor marks for athletes with indoor bests

2.41	Ukhov	1	DL	Doha	9 May 14	2.36	Mögenburg	3	Eberstadt	10 Jun 84
2.39	Conway	1	USOF	Norman	30 Jul 89	2.36	Howard	1	Rehlingen	8 Jun 87
2.38	Avdeyenko	2=	WCh	Roma	6 Sep 87	2.36	Zvara	1	Praha	23 Aug 87
2.37	Thränhardt	2		Rieti	2 Sep 84	2.36	Grant	4	WCh	Tokyo	1 Sep 91
2.37	Smith	1	WJ	Seoul	20 Sep 92	2.36	Hoen	1		Oslo	1 Jul 97
2.37	Holm	1		Athína	13 Jul 08	2.36	Bába	2=	GGala	Roma	8 Jul 05
						2.36	Dmitrik	1	NC	Chelyabinsk	23 Jul 11

Ancillary jumps – en route to final marks

2.40	Sotomayor	8 Sep 88	2.40	Sotomayor	29 Jul 89	2.40	Sotomayor	5 Jun 94
2.40	Bondarenko	14 Jun 14	2.40	Barshim	14 Jun 14	2.40	Barshim	5 Sep 14

A – mark made at an altitude of 1000m or higher, i – indoors, Q – in qualifying competition, WR - world record

POLE VAULT

Mark	Wind	Name		Nat	Born	Pos	Meet	Venue	Date
6.18i	WR	Armand	Duplantis	SWE	10.11.99	1		Glasgow	15 Feb 20
6.17i	WR		Duplantis			1		Toruń	8 Feb 20
6.16i	WR	Renaud	Lavillenie	FRA	18.9.86	1		Donetsk	15 Feb 14
6.15i	WR	Sergey	Bubka	UKR	4.12.63	1		Donetsk	21 Feb 93
6.15	WOR		Duplantis			1	G Gala	Roma	17 Sep 20
6.14i	WIR		Bubka			1		Liévin	13 Feb 93
6.14A	WR		Bubka			1		Sestriere	31 Jul 94
6.13i	WIR		Bubka			1		Berlin	21 Feb 92
6.13	WR		Bubka			1	TOTO	Tokyo	19 Sep 92
6.12i	WIR		Bubka			1	Mast	Grenoble	23 Mar 91
6.12	WR		Bubka			1		Padova	30 Aug 92
6.11i	WIR		Bubka			1		Donetsk	19 Mar 91
6.11	WR		Bubka			1		Dijon	13 Jun 92
6.10i	WR		Bubka			1		San Sebastián	15 Mar 91
6.10	WR		Bubka			1	MAI	Malmö	5 Aug 91
6.09	WR		Bubka			1		Formia	8 Jul 91
6.08i	WIR		Bubka			1	NC	Volgograd	9 Feb 91
6.08	WR		Bubka			1	Znam	Moskva	9 Jun 91
6.08i			Lavillenie			1		Bydgoszcz	31 Jan 14
6.07	WR		Bubka			1	Super	Shizuoka	6 May 91
6.07i			Duplantis			1		Liévin	19 Feb 20
6.07			Duplantis			1	Athl	Lausanne	2 Sep 20
6.06	WR		Bubka			1	Nik	Nice	10 Jul 88
6.06i		Steve	Hooker	AUS	16.7.82	1		Boston (R)	7 Feb 09
6.06		Sam	Kendricks	USA	7.9.92	1	NC	Des Moines	27 Jul 19
6.05	WR		Bubka			1	PTS	Bratislava	9 Jun 88
6.05i			Bubka			1		Donetsk	17 Mar 90
6.05i			Bubka			1		Berlin	5 Mar 93
6.05			Bubka			1	GPF	London (CP)	10 Sep 93
6.05i			Bubka			1	Mast	Grenoble	6 Feb 94
6.05			Bubka			1	ISTAF	Berlin	30 Aug 94
6.05			Bubka			1	GPF	Fukuoka	13 Sep 97
6.05		Maksim	Tarasov	RUS	2.12.70	1	GP II	Athína	16 Jun 99
6.05		Dmitriy	Markov	BLR/AUS	14.3.75	1	WCh	Edmonton	9 Aug 01
6.05			Lavillenie			1	Pre	Eugene	30 May 15
6.05			Duplantis			1	EC	Berlin	12 Aug 18
		(36/7)							
6.04		Brad	Walker	USA	21.6.81	1	Pre	Eugene	8 Jun 08
6.03		Okkert	Brits	RSA	22.8.73	1	ASV	Köln	18 Aug 95
6.03		Jeff	Hartwig	USA	25.9.67	1		Jonesboro	14 Jun 00
		(10)							
6.03		Thiago	Braz da Silva	BRA	16.12.93	1	OG	Rio de Janeiro	15 Aug 16
6.02i	WIR	Rodion	Gataullin	RUS	23.11.65	1	NC	Gomel	4 Feb 89
6.02		Piotr	Lisek	POL	16.8.92	1	Herc	Monaco	12 Jul 19
6.01		Igor	Trandenkov	RUS	17.8.66	1	NC	Sankt Peterburg	4 Jul 96
		Hit bar hard, but kept it on with his hand illegally. Next best 5.95						Dijon	26 May 96
6.01		Tim	Mack	USA	15.9.72	1	WAF	Monaco	18 Sep 04
6.01		Yevgeniy	Lukyanenko	RUS	23.1.85	1	EAF	Bydgoszcz	1 Jul 08
6.01	sq	Björn	Otto	GER	16.10.77	1		Aachen	5 Sep 12
6.00		Tim	Lobinger	GER	3.9.72	1	ASV	Köln	24 Aug 97
6.00i		Jean	Galfione	FRA	9.6.71	1	WI	Maebashi	6 Mar 99
6.00i		Danny	Ecker	GER	21.7.77	1		Dortmund	11 Feb 01
		(20)							
6.00		Toby	Stevenson	USA	19.11.76	1eA	CalR	Modesto	8 May 04
6.00		Paul	Burgess	AUS	14.8.79	1		Perth	25 Feb 05
6.00Ai		Shawnacy	Barber	CAN	27.5.94	1		Reno	15 Jan 16
6.00		Timur	Morgunov	RUS	12.10.96	2	EC	Berlin	12 Aug 18
5.98		Lawrence	Johnson	USA	7.5.74	1		Knoxville	25 May 96
5.97		Scott	Huffman	USA	30.11.64	1	NC	Knoxville	18 Jun 94
5.96		Joe	Dial	USA	26.10.62	1		Norman	18 Jun 87
5.95		Andrei	Tivontchik	GER	13.7.70	1	ASV	Köln	16 Aug 96
5.95		Michael	Stolle	GER	17.12.74	1	Herc	Monaco	18 Aug 00
5.95		Romain	Mesnil	FRA	13.6.77	1		Castres	6 Aug 03
		(30)							
5.95		Chris	Nilsen	USA	13.1.98	1	NCAA	Austin	5 Jun 19
5.94i		Philippe	Collet	FRA	13.12.63	1	Mast	Grenoble	10 Mar 90
5.94		Raphael	Holzdeppe	GER	28.9.89	1	NC	Nürnberg	26 Jul 15
5.93i	WIR	Billy	Olson	USA	19.7.58	1		East Rutherford	8 Feb 86

POLE VAULT A-T 211

MFN All-time

212   POLE VAULT – LONG JUMP A-T

Mark	Wind	Name		Nat	Born	Pos	Meet	Venue	Date
5.93i		Tye	Harvey	USA	25.9.74	2	NC	Atlanta	3 Mar 01
5.93		Alex	Averbukh	ISR	1.10.74	1	GP	Madrid (C)	19 Jul 03
5.93		Pawel	Wojciechowski	POL	6.6.89	2	Athl	Lausanne	6 Jul 17
5.92		István	Bagyula	HUN	2.1.69	1	Gugl	Linz	5 Jul 91
5.92		Igor	Potapovich	KAZ	6.9.67	2		Dijon	13 Jun 92
5.92		Dean	Starkey	USA	27.3.67	1	Banes	São Paulo	21 May 94
		(40)							
5.91 WR		Thierry	Vigneron	FRA	9.3.60	2	GGala	Roma	31 Aug 84
5.91i		Viktor	Ryzhenkov	UZB	25.8.66	2		San Sebastián	15 Mar 91
5.91A		Riaan	Botha	RSA	8.11.70	1		Pretoria	2 Apr 97
5.91		Malte	Mohr	GER	24.7.86	1		Ingolstadt	22 Jun 12
5.91		Konstadinos	Filippídis ¶	GRE	26.11.86	1	DL	Saint-Denis	4 Jul 15
5.90		Pierre	Quinon	FRA	20.2.62	2	Nik	Nice	16 Jul 85
5.90i		Ferenc	Salbert	HUN/FRA	5.8.60	1	Mast	Grenoble	14 Mar 87
5.90		Miroslaw	Chmara	POL	9.5.64	1	BNP	Villeneuve d'Ascq	27 Jun 88
5.90i		Grigoriy	Yegorov	KAZ	12.1.67	1		Yokohama	11 Mar 90
5.90		Denis	Petushinskiy ¶	RUS	28.6.67	1	Znam	Moskva	13 Jun 93
		(50)							
5.90i		Pyotr	Bochkaryov	RUS	3.11.67	1	El	Paris (B)	12 Mar 94
5.90		Jacob	Davis	USA	29.4.78	1	TexR	Austin	4 Apr 98
5.90		Viktor	Chistyakov	RUS/AUS	9.2.75	1		Salamanca	15 Jul 99
5.90		Pavel	Gerasimov	RUS	29.5.79	1		Rüdlingen	12 Aug 00
5.90		Nick	Hysong	USA	9.12.71	1	OG	Sydney	29 Sep 00
5.90		Giuseppe	Gibilisco	ITA	5.1.79	1	WCh	Saint-Denis	28 Aug 03
5.90i		Igor	Pavlov	RUS	18.7.79	1	El	Madrid	5 Mar 05
5.90		Lázaro	Borges	CUB	19.6.86	2	WCh	Daegu	29 Aug 11
5.90i		Dmitriy	Starodubtsev	RUS	3.1.86	1		Chelyabinsk	18 Dec 11

(61) with 5.90A Jacob Wooten & Matt Ludwig 22 Feb 20   100th 5.82, 200th 5.75, 300th 5.70, 400th 5.65, 500th 5.60
Best outdoor marks for athletes with lifetime bests indoors

6.00		Gataullin	1	Tokyo	16 Sep 89	5.93	Ecker	1		Ingolstadt	26 Jul 98
6.00		Hooker	1	Perth	27 Jan 08	5.93	Barber	2	DL	London (OS)	25 Jul 15
5.98		Galfione	1	Amiens	23 Jul 99	5.90	Yegorov	2	WCh	Stuttgart	19 Aug 93

Exhibition or Market Square competitions   Ancillary jump: 6.05i Bubka   13 Feb 93
6.00		Jean		Galfione	FRA	9.6.71	1		Besançon	23 May 97
5.95		Viktor		Chistiakov	RUS/AUS	9.2.75	1		Chiari	8 Sep 99
5.90		Pyotr		Bochkaryov	RUS	3.11.67	1		Karlskrona	28 Jun 96

LONG JUMP

Mark	Wind	Name		Nat	Born	Pos	Meet	Venue	Date
8.95 WR	0.3	Mike	Powell	USA	10.11.63	1	WCh	Tokyo	30 Aug 91
8.90A WR	2.0	Bob	Beamon	USA	29.8.46	1	OG	Ciudad de México	18 Oct 68
8.87	-0.2	Carl	Lewis	USA	1.7.61	*	WCh	Tokyo	30 Aug 91
8.86A	1.9	Robert	Emmiyan	ARM	16.2.65	1		Tsakhkadzor	22 May 87
8.79	1.9		Lewis			1	TAC	Indianapolis	19 Jun 83
8.79i WR	-		Lewis			1		New York	27 Jan 84
8.76	1.0		Lewis			1	USOF	Indianapolis	24 Jul 82
8.76	0.8		Lewis			1	NC/OT	Indianapolis	18 Jul 88
8.75	1.7		Lewis			1	PAm	Indianapolis	16 Aug 87
8.74	1.4	Larry	Myricks ¶	USA	10.3.56	2	NC/OT	Indianapolis	18 Jul 88
8.74A	2.0	Erick	Walder ¶	USA	5.11.71	1		El Paso	2 Apr 94
8.74	1.2	Dwight	Phillips	USA	1.10.77	1	Pre	Eugene	7 Jun 09
8.73	1.2	Irving	Saladino	PAN	23.1.83	1	FBK	Hengelo	24 May 08
8.72	-0.2		Lewis			1	OG	Seoul	26 Sep 88
8.71	-0.4		Lewis			1	Pepsi	Los Angeles (Ww)	13 May 84
8.71	0.1		Lewis			1	OT	Los Angeles	19 Jun 84
8.71	1.9	Iván	Pedroso	CUB	17.12.72	1		Salamanca	18 Jul 95
8.71i		Sebastian	Bayer (10)	GER	11.6.86	1	El	Torino	8 Mar 09
8.70	0.8		Myricks			1	NC	Houston	17 Jun 89
8.70	0.7		Powell			1		Salamanca	27 Jul 93
8.70	1.6		Pedroso			1	WCh	Göteborg	12 Aug 95
8.69	0.5	Tajay	Gayle	JAM	2.8.96	1	WC	Doha	28 Sep 19
8.68	1.0		Lewis			Q	OG	Barcelona	5 Aug 92
8.68	1.6		Pedroso			1		Lisboa	17 Jun 95
8.68	1.7	Juan Miguel	Echevarría	CUB	11.8.98	1		Bad Langensalza	30 Jun 18
8.67	0.4		Lewis			1	WCh	Roma	5 Sep 87
8.67	-0.7		Lewis			1	OG	Barcelona	6 Aug 92
8.66	0.8		Lewis			*	MSR	Walnut	26 Apr 87
8.66	1.0		Myricks			1		Tokyo	23 Sep 87
8.66	0.9		Powell			1	BNP	Villeneuve d'Ascq	29 Jun 90
8.66A	1.4		Lewis			*		Sestriere	31 Jul 94
8.66	0.3		Pedroso			1		Linz	22 Aug 95

LONG JUMP A-T

Mark	Wind	Name		Nat	Born	Pos	Meet	Venue	Date
8.66	1.6	Loúis	Tsátoumas	GRE	12.2.82	1		Kalamáta	2 Jun 07
8.66	1.0		Echevarría			1	GS	Ostrava	13 Jun 18
		(34/13)							
8.65A	1.3	Luvo	Manyonga ¶	RSA	18.11.91	1	NC	Potchefstroom	22 Apr 17
8.63	0.5	Kareem	Streete-Thompson	CAY/USA	30.3.73	1	GP II	Linz	4 Jul 94
8.62	0.7	James	Beckford	JAM	9.1.75	1		Orlando	5 Apr 97
8.59i		Miguel	Pate	USA	13.6.79	1	NC	New York	1 Mar 02
8.58	1.8	Jarrion	Lawson	USA	6.5.94	2	NC/OT	Eugene	3 Jul 16
8.56i	-	Yago	Lamela	ESP	24.7.77	2	WI	Maebashi	7 Mar 99
8.56	0.2	Aleksandr	Menkov	RUS	7.12.90	1	WCh	Moskva	16 Aug 13
		(20)							
8.54	0.9	Lutz	Dombrowski	GDR	25.6.59	1	OG	Moskva	28 Jul 80
8.54	1.7	Mitchell	Watt	AUS	25.3.88	1	DNG	Stockholm	29 Jul 11
8.53	1.2	Jaime	Jefferson	CUB	17.1.62	1	Barr	La Habana	12 May 90
8.52	0.7	Savanté	Stringfellow	USA	6.11.78	1	NC	Stanford	21 Jun 02
8.52	1.8	Jeff	Henderson	USA	19.2.89	*	PAm	Toronto	22 Jul 15
8.51	1.7	Roland	McGhee	USA	15.10.71	2		São Paulo	14 May 95
8.51	1.7	Greg	Rutherford	GBR	17.11.86	1		Chula Vista	24 Apr 14
8.50	0.2	Llewellyn	Starks	USA	10.2.67	2		Rhede	7 Jul 91
8.50	1.3	Godfrey Khotso	Mokoena	RSA	6.3.85	2	GP	Madrid	4 Jul 09
8.49	2.0	Melvin	Lister	USA	29.8.77	1	SEC	Baton Rouge	13 May 00
		(30)							
8.49	0.6	Jai	Taurima	AUS	26.6.72	2	OG	Sydney	28 Sep 00
8.49	0.7	Christian	Reif	GER	24.10.84	1		Weinheim	31 May 14
8.49A	-0.8	Ruswahl	Samaai	RSA	25.9.91	2	NC	Potchefstroom	22 Apr 17
8.48	0.8	Joe	Greene	USA	17.2.67	3		São Paulo	14 May 95
8.48	0.6	Mohamed Salim	Al-Khuwalidi	KSA	19.6.81	1		Sotteville-lès-Rouen	2 Jul 06
8.47	1.9	Kevin	Dilworth	USA	14.2.74	1		Abilene	9 May 96
8.47	0.9	John	Moffitt	USA	12.12.80	2	OG	Athína	26 Aug 04
8.47	-0.2	Andrew	Howe	ITA	12.5.85	2	WCh	Osaka	30 Aug 07
8.47	0.0		Li Jinzhe	CHN	1.9.89	1		Bad Langensalza	28 Jun 14
8.47A	0.7		Wang Jianan	CHN	27.8.96	1		Guiyang	16 Jun 18
		(40)							
8.46	1.2	Leonid	Voloshin	RUS	30.3.66	1	NC	Tallinn	5 Jul 88
8.46	1.6	Mike	Conley	USA	5.10.62	2		Springfield	4 May 96
8.46	1.8	Cheikh Tidiane	Touré	SEN/FRA	25.1.70	1		Bad Langensalza	15 Jun 97
8.46	0.3	Ibrahin	Camejo	CUB	28.6.82	1		Bilbao	21 Jun 08
8.46	1.3	Luis	Rivera	MEX	21.6.87	1	WUG	Kazan	12 Jul 13
8.45	2.0	Nenad	Stekic	YUG	7.3.51	1	PO	Montreal	25 Jul 75
8.45	0.8	Marquise	Goodwin	USA	19.11.90	1		Baie Mahault	14 May 16
8.44	1.7	Eric	Metcalf	USA	23.1.68	1	NC	Tampa	17 Jun 88
8.44A	1.8	Michel	Tornéus	SWE	26.5.86	1		Monachil	10 Jul 16
8.43	0.8	Jason	Grimes	USA	10.9.59	*	NC	Indianapolis	16 Jun 85
8.43	1.8	Giovanni	Evangelisti	ITA	11.9.61	1		San Giovanni Valdarno	16 May 87
8.43i	-	Stanislav	Tarasenko	RUS	23.7.66	1		Moskva	26 Jan 94
8.43	0.1	Luis Felipe	Méliz	CUB/ESP	11.8.79	2	OD	Jena	3 Jun 00
8.43	-0.2	Ignisious	Gaisah	GHA/NED	20.6.83	2	GGala	Roma	14 Jul 06
8.43	0.7		Shi Yuhao	CHN	26.9.98	2	DL	Shanghai	12 May 18
		(55)							

100th man 8.34, 200th 8.25, 300th 8.19, 400th 8.15, 500th 8.11

Best at low altitude: 8.62 1 Manyonga 1 FBK Hengelo 11 Jun 17 8.61 1.3 Emmiyan 1 GWG Moskva 6 Jul 86 8.58 1.8 Walder 1 Springfield 4 May 86 8.45 -1.2 Samaai 1 AfrC Asaba 2 Aug 18

Wind-assisted marks performances to 8.72, performers to 8.47

8.99A	4.4	Mike	Powell	USA	10.11.63	1		Sestriere	21 Jul 92
8.96A	1.2+	Iván	Pedroso	CUB	17.12.72	1		Sestriere	29 Jul 95
8.95A	3.9		Powell			1		Sestriere	31 Jul 94
8.92	3.3	Juan Miguel	Echevarría	CUB	11.8.98	1	NC	La Habana	10 Mar 19
8.91	2.9	Carl	Lewis	USA	1.7.61	2	WCh	Tokyo	30 Aug 91
8.90	3.7		Powell			1	S&W	Modesto	16 May 92
8.83	2.1		Echevarría			1	DL	Stockholm	10 Jun 18
8.79	3.0		Pedroso			1	Barr	La Habana	21 May 92
8.78	3.1	Fabrice	Lapierre	AUS	17.10.83	1	NC	Perth	18 Apr 10
8.77	3.9		Lewis			1	Pepsi	Los Angeles (Ww)	18 May 85
8.77	3.4		Lewis			1	MSR	Walnut	26 Apr 87
8.73	4.6		Lewis			Q	NC	Sacramento	19 Jun 81
8.73	3.2		Lewis			Q	NC	Indianapolis	17 Jun 83
8.73A	2.6		Powell			1		Sestriere	31 Jul 91
8.73	4.8		Pedroso			1		Madrid	20 Jul 95
8.72	2.2		Lewis			1	NYG	New York	24 May 92
8.72A	3.9		Lewis			2		Sestriere	31 Jul 94
8.68	4.9	James	Beckford	JAM	9.1.75	1	JUCO	Odessa, Tx	19 May 95
8.68	3.7	Marquis	Dendy	USA	17.11.92	1	NC	Eugene	25 Jun 15

214   LONG JUMP - TRIPLE JUMP A-T

Mark	Wind	Name		Nat	Born	Pos	Meet	Venue	Date
8.66A	4.0	Joe	Greene	USA	17.2.67	2		Sestriere	21 Jul 92
8.64	3.5	Kareem	Streete-Thompson	CAY/USA	30.3.73	2	NC	Knoxville	18 Jun 94
8.63	3.9	Mike	Conley	USA	5.10.62	2	NC	Eugene	20 Jun 86
8.59	2.9	Jeff	Henderson	USA	19.2.89	1	NC/OT	Eugene	3 Jul 16
8.57	5.2	Jason	Grimes	USA	10.9.59	1	vFRG,AFR	Durham	27 Jun 82
8.53	4.9	Kevin	Dilworth	USA	14.2.74	1		Fort-de-France	27 Apr 02
8.51	3.7	Ignisious	Gaisah	GHA	20.6.83	1	AfCh	Bambous	9 Aug 06
8.49	2.6	Ralph	Boston	USA	9.5.39	1	OT	Los Angeles	12 Sep 64
8.49	4.5	Stanislav	Tarasenko	RUS	23.7.66	2		Madrid	20 Jun 95
8.48	2.8	Kirill	Sosunov	RUS	1.11.75	1		Oristano	18 Sep 95
8.48	3.4	Peter	Burge	AUS	3.7.74	1		Gold Coast (RB)	10 Sep 00
8.48	2.1	Brian	Johnson	USA	25.3.80	1	Conseil	Fort-de-France	8 May 08
8.48	2.8	Lamont Marcell	Jacobs	ITA	26.9.94	1	NC-23	Bressanone	10 Jun 16

Exhibition: 8.46 Yuriy Naumkin RUS 4.11.68 1   Iglesias 6 Sep 96
Best outdoors
8.56 1.3 Lamela 1 Torino 24 Jun 99   8.49 1.6 Bayer 1 NC Ulm 4 Jul 09
8.46A 0.0 Pate 1 Cd. de México 3 May 03 and 8.45 1.5 2 NC Stanford 21 Jun 02, 8.48w 5.6 1 Fort Worth 21 Apr 01
Ancillary marks – other marks during series (to 8.67/8.70w)
8.84	1.7	Lewis	30 Aug 91	8.89Aw	2.4	Pedroso	29 Jul 95	8.75w	2.1	Lewis	16 Aug 87
8.71	0.6	Lewis	19 Jun 83	8.84Aw	3.8	Powell	21 Jul 92	8.75Aw	3.4	Powell	21 Jul 92
8.68	0.3	Lewis	18 Jul 88	8.83w	2.3	Lewis	30 Aug 91	8.73w	2.4	Lewis	18 May 85
8.68	0.0	Lewis	30 Aug 91	8.80Aw	4.0	Powell	21 Jul 92	8.73w		Powell	16 May 92
8.67	-0.2	Lewis	5 Sep 87	8.78Aw		Powell	21 Jul 92	8.71Aw		Powell	31 Jul 91

TRIPLE JUMP

Mark	Wind	Name		Nat	Born	Pos	Meet	Venue	Date
18.29 WR	1.3	Jonathan	Edwards	GBR	10.5.66	1	WCh	Göteborg	7 Aug 95
18.21	0.2	Christian	Taylor	USA	18.6.90	1	WCh	Beijing	27 Aug 15
18.14	0.4	Will	Claye	USA	13.6.91	1		Long Beach	29 Jun 19
18.11	0.8		Taylor			1	Pre	Eugene	27 May 17
18.09	-0.4	Kenny	Harrison	USA	13.2.65	1	OG	Atlanta	27 Jul 96
18.08	0.0	Pedro Pablo	Pichardo	CUB	30.6.93	1	Barr	La Habana	28 May 15
18.06	0.8		Pichardo			1	DL	Doha	15 May 15
18.06	1.1		Taylor			1	Athl	Lausanne	9 Jul 15
18.06	0.4		Claye			1	DL	Paris (C)	24 Aug 19
18.04	0.3	Teddy	Tamgho	FRA	15.6.89	1	WCh	Moskva	18 Aug 13
18.04	0.8		Taylor			2	DL	Doha	15 May 15
18.01	0.4		Edwards			1	Bisl	Oslo	9 Jul 95
18.00	1.3		Edwards			1	McD	London (CP)	27 Aug 95
17.99	0.5		Edwards			1	EC	Budapest	23 Aug 98
17.99	1.8		Pichardo			2	Athl	Lausanne	9 Jul 15
17.98 WR	1.8		Edwards			1		Salamanca	18 Jul 95
17.98	1.2		Tamgho			1	DL	New York	12 Jun 10
17.97 WR	1.5	Willie	Banks	USA	11.3.56	1	TAC	Indianapolis	16 Jun 85
17.96	0.1		Taylor			1	WCh	Daegu	4 Sep 11
17.96	-0.4		Pichardo			1	GGala	Roma	4 Jun 15
17.95	0.6		Pichardo			1	DL	Doha	4 May 18
17.94	0.0		Pichardo			1		La Habana	8 May 15
17.93	1.6		Harrison			1	DNG	Stockholm	2 Jul 90
17.92	1.6	Khristo	Markov	BUL	27.1.65	1	WCh	Roma	31 Aug 87
17.92	1.9	James	Beckford	JAM	9.1.75	1	JUCO	Odessa, TX	20 May 95
17.92i	WIR -		Tamgho			1	EI	Paris (Bercy)	6 Mar 11
17.92	0.7		Edwards			1	WCh	Edmonton	6 Aug 01
17.92	0.9		Taylor			1	WCh	Doha	29 Sep 19
17.91i	WIR -		Tamgho			1	NC	Aubière	20 Feb 11
17.91	1.4		Tamgho			1	Athl	Lausanne	30 Jun 11
17.91	0.9		Claye			1	NC	Sacramento	23 Jun 17
		(31/9)							
17.90	1.0	Vladimir	Inozemtsev (10)	UKR	25.5.64	1	PTS	Bratislava	20 Jun 90
17.90	0.4	Jadel	Gregório	BRA	16.9.80	1	GP	Belém	20 May 07
17.89A WR	0.0	João Carlos	de Oliveira	BRA	28.5.54	1	PAm	Ciudad de México	15 Oct 75
17.87	1.7	Mike	Conley	USA	5.10.62	1	NC	San José	27 Jun 87
17.86	1.3	Charles	Simpkins	USA	19.10.63	1	WUG	Kobe	2 Sep 85
17.85	0.9	Yoelbi	Quesada	CUB	4.8.73	1	WCh	Athína	8 Aug 97
17.83i	WIR -	Aliecer	Urrutia	CUB	22.9.74	1		Sindelfingen	1 Mar 97
17.83i	WIR -	Christian	Olsson	SWE	25.1.80	1	WI	Budapest	7 Mar 04
17.81	1.0	Marian	Oprea	ROU	6.6.82	1	Athl	Lausanne	5 Jul 05
17.81	0.1	Phillips	Idowu	GBR	30.12.78	1	EC	Barcelona	29 Jul 10
17.78	1.0	Nikolay	Musiyenko	UKR	16.12.59	1	Znam	Leningrad	7 Jun 86
		(20)							
17.78	0.6	Lázaro	Betancourt ¶	CUB	18.3.63	1	Barr	La Habana	15 Jun 86

TRIPLE JUMP - SHOT A-T   215

Mark	Wind	Name		Nat	Born	Pos	Meet	Venue	Date
17.78	0.8	Melvin	Lister	USA	29.8.77	1	NC/OT	Sacramento	17 Jul 04
17.77	1.0	Aleksandr	Kovalenko	RUS	8.5.63	1	NC	Bryansk	18 Jul 87
17.77i WIR	-	Leonid	Voloshin	RUS	30.3.66	1		Grenoble	6 Feb 94
17.77i		Fabrice	Zango	BUR	25.6.93	1		Paris	2 Feb 20
17.75	0.3	Oleg	Protsenko	RUS	11.8.63	1	Znam	Moskva	10 Jun 90
17.74	1.4	Nelson	Évora	POR	20.4.84	1	WCh	Osaka	27 Aug 07
17.73i		Walter	Davis	USA	2.7.79	1	WI	Moskva	12 Mar 06
17.73i	-	Fabrizio	Donato	ITA	14.8.76	2	EI	Paris (Bercy)	6 Mar 11
17.72i		Brian	Wellman	BER	8.9.67	1	WI	Barcelona	12 Mar 95
		(30)	El-Sheryf now Seref Osmanoglou TUR						
17.72	1.3	Sheryf	El-Sheryf	UKR	2.1.89	1	EU23	Ostrava	17 Jul 11
17.70i		Daniele	Greco	ITA	1.3.89	1	EI	Göteborg	2 Mar 13
17.69	1.5	Igor	Lapshin	BLR	8.8.63	1		Stayki	31 Jul 88
17.69i		Yoandri	Betanzos	CUB	15.2.82	2	WI	Doha	14 Mar 10
17.68	0.4	Danil	Burkenya	RUS	20.7.78	1	NC	Tula	31 Jul 04
17.68A	1.6	Alexis	Copello	CUB	12.8.85	1		Ávila	17 Jul 11
17.68	0.0	Omar	Craddock	USA	26.4.91	1		Long Beach	20 Apr 19
17.66	1.7	Ralf	Jaros	GER	13.12.65	1	ECp	Frankfurt-am-Main	30 Jun 91
17.65	1.0	Aleksandr	Yakovlev	UKR	8.9.57	1	Znam	Moskva	6 Jun 87
17.65	0.8	Denis	Kapustin	RUS	5.10.70	2	Bisl	Oslo	9 Jul 98
		(40)							
17.64	1.4	Nathan	Douglas	GBR	4.12.82	1	NC	Manchester (SC)	10 Jul 05
17.63	0.9	Kenta	Bell	USA	16.3.77	1c2	MSR	Walnut	21 Apr 02
17.62i	-	Yoel	García	CUB	25.11.73	2		Sindelfingen	1 Mar 97
17.62	-0.2	Arne David	Girat	CUB	26.8.84	3	ALBA	La Habana	25 Apr 09
17.60	0.6	Vladimir	Plekhanov	RUS	11.4.58	2	NC	Leningrad	4 Aug 85
17.59i	-	Pierre	Camara	FRA	10.9.65	1	WI	Toronto	13 Mar 93
17.59	0.3	Vasiliy	Sokov	RUS	7.4.68	1	NC	Moskva	19 Jun 93
17.59	0.8	Charles	Friedek	GER	26.8.71	1		Hamburg	23 Jul 97
17.59	0.9	Leevan	Sands	BAH	16.8.81	3	OG	Beijing	21 Aug 08
17.59	0.0		Li Yanxi	CHN	26.6.84	1	NG	Jinan	26 Oct 09
		(50)	100th man 17.41, 200th 17.20, 300th 17.04, 400th 16.92, 500th 16.82						

Wind-assisted marks – performances to 17.91, performers to 17.60

Mark	Wind	Name		Nat	Born	Pos	Meet	Venue	Date
18.43	2.4	Jonathan	Edwards	GBR	10.5.66	1	ECp	Villeneuve d'Ascq	25 Jun 95
18.20	5.2	Willie	Banks	USA	11.3.56	1	NC/OT	Indianapolis	16 Jul 88
18.17	2.1	Mike	Conley	USA	5.10.62	1	OG	Barcelona	3 Aug 92
18.08	2.5		Edwards			1	BrGP	Sheffield	23 Jul 95
18.05	2.4		Claye			2	Pre	Eugene	27 May 17
18.03	2.9		Edwards			1	GhG	Gateshead	2 Jul 95
18.01	3.7		Harrison			1	NC	Atlanta	15 Jun 96
17.97	7.5	Yoelbi	Quesada	CUB	4.8.73	1		Madrid	20 Jun 95
17.93	5.2	Charles	Simpkins	USA	19.10.63	2	NC/OT	Indianapolis	16 Jul 88
17.93	3.4		Taylor			1	Gyulai	Székesfehérvár	9 Jul 19
17.92	3.4	Christian	Olsson	SWE	25.1.80	1	GP	Gateshead	13 Jul 03
17.91	3.2		Simpkins			1	NC	Eugene	21 Jun 86
17.82	2.5	Nelson	Évora	POR	20.4.84	1	NC	Seixal	26 Jul 09
17.81	4.6	Keith	Connor	GBR	16.9.57	1	CG	Brisbane	9 Oct 82
17.76A	2.2	Kenta	Bell	USA	16.3.77	1		El Paso	10 Apr 04
17.75		Gennadiy	Valyukevich	BLR	1.6.58	1		Uzhgorod	27 Apr 86
17.75	7.1	Brian	Wellman	BER	8.9.67	2		Madrid	20 Jun 95
17.74	2.7	Donald	Scott	USA	23.2.92	1	NC	Des Moines	26 Jul 19
17.73	4.1	Vasiliy	Sokov	RUS	7.4.68	1		Riga	3 Jun 89
17.71	2.4	Marquis	Dendy	USA	17.11.92	1	NCAA	Eugene	12 Jun 15
17.69	3.9	Alexis	Copello	CUB	12.8.85	1	ALBA	La Habana	25 Apr 09
17.63	4.3	Robert	Cannon	USA	9.7.58	3	NC/OT	Indianapolis	16 Jul 88

Best outdoor marks for athletes with indoor bests

					17.65	1.4	Betanzos 2	ALBA La Habana	25 Apr 09
17.79	1.4	Olsson	1	OG	Athína	22 Aug 04	17.67w	5.4 1	Bilbao	1 Jul 06
17.75	1.0	Voloshin	2	WCh	Tokyo	26 Aug 91	17.62A	0.1 Wellman	1	El Paso	15 Apr 95
17.71	-0.7	Davis	1	NC	Indianapolis	25 Jun 06	17.60	1.9 Donato	1	Milano	7 Jun 00
17.70	1.7	Urrutia	1	GP II	Sevilla	6 Jun 96	17.63w	2.8 1 EC	Helsinki	30 Jun 12
17.66	0.5	Zango	3	WCh	Doha	29 Sep 19	17.67w	3.4 Greco	1 NC	Bressanone	8 Jul 19

Low altitude best: 17.65 0.1 Copello 1 Barr La Habana 30 May 09

Ancillary marks – other marks during series (to 17.92)

18.16	WR	1.3	Edwards	7 Aug 95	17.93	0.2	Pichardo	28 May 15	18.39w	3.7	Edwards	25 Jun 95
18.02		0.8	Taylor	9 Jul 15	17.92i		Tamgho	6 Mar 11	18.06w	4.9	Banks	16 Jul 88
17.99		0.1	Harrison	27 Jul 96								

SHOT

23.12	WR		Randy		Barnes ¶	USA	16.6.66	1		Los Angeles (Ww)	20 May 90
23.10					Barnes			1	Jenner	San José	26 May 90
23.06	WR		Ulf		Timmermann	GDR	1.11.62	1	Veniz	Haniá	22 May 88
22.91	WR		Alessandro		Andrei	ITA	3.1.59	1		Viareggio	12 Aug 87

216 SHOT A-T

Mark	Wind	Name		Nat	Born	Pos	Meet	Venue	Date
22.91		Joe	Kovacs	USA	28.6.89	1	WC	Doha	5 Oct 19
22.91		Ryan	Crouser	USA	18.12.92	1		Marietta	18 Jul 20
22.90			Crouser			2	WC	Doha	5 Oct 19
22.90		Tom	Walsh	NZL	1.3.92	3	WCh	Doha	5 Oct 19
22.86		Brian	Oldfield	USA	1.6.45	1	ITA	El Paso	10 May 75
22.75		Werner	Günthör	SUI	1.6.61	1		Bern	23 Aug 88
22.74			Crouser			1		Long Beach	20 Apr 19
22.74			Crouser			1	Hanz	Zagreb	14 Sep 20
22.72			Crouser			1		Des Moines	29 Aug 20
22.70			Crouser			1	Skol	Chorzów	6 Sep 20
22.67		Kevin	Toth ¶	USA	29.12.67	1	KansR	Lawrence	19 Apr 03
22.67			Walsh			1		Auckland	25 Mar 18
22.67			Crouser			1		Tucson	18 May 19
22.66i WIR			Barnes			1	Sunkist	Los Angeles	20 Jan 89
22.65			Crouser			1	NC	Sacramento	25 Jun 17
22.64 WR		Udo	Beyer (10)	GDR	9.8.55	1		Berlin	20 Aug 86
22.62 WR			Timmermann			1		Berlin	22 Sep 85
22.62			Crouser			1	NC	Des Moines	26 Jul 19
22.61			Timmermann			1		Potsdam	8 Sep 88
22.61		Darlan	Romani	BRA	9.4.91	1	Pre	Stanford	30 Jun 19
22.60			Timmermann			1	vURS	Tallinn	21 Jun 86
22.60			Walsh			1	WK	Zürich	30 Aug 18
22.60i			Crouser			1	NC	Albuquerque	15 Feb 20
22.59			Crouser			1		Beograd	17 Sep 20
22.58i			Crouser			1		Manhattan, KS	5 Dec 20
22.57			Kovacs			1		Tucson	18 May 17
		(30/11)							
22.54		Christian	Cantwell	USA	30.9.80	1	GP II	Gresham	5 Jun 04
22.52		John	Brenner	USA	4.1.61	1	MSR	Walnut	26 Apr 87
22.51		Adam	Nelson	USA	7.7.75	1		Gresham	18 May 02
22.44		Darrell	Hill	USA	17.8.93	1	VD-DLF	Bruxelles	31 Aug 17
22.43		Reese	Hoffa	USA	8.10.77	1	LGP	London (CP)	3 Aug 07
22.32		Michal	Haratyk	POL	10.4.92	1		Warszawa	28 Jul 19
22.28		Ryan	Whiting	USA	24.11.86	1	DL	Doha	10 May 13
22.25		Konrad	Bukowiecki	POL	17.3.97	1	Skol	Chorzów	14 Sep 19
22.24		Sergey	Smirnov	RUS	17.9.60	2	vGDR	Tallinn	21 Jun 86
		(20)							
22.22		Bob	Bertemes	LUX	24.5.93	1		Cessange	4 Aug 19
22.21		Dylan	Armstrong	CAN	15.1.81	1	NC	Calgary	25 Jun 11
22.20		John	Godina	USA	31.5.72	1		Carson	22 May 05
22.20		David	Storl	GER	27.7.90	1	Athl	Lausanne	9 Jul 15
22.17i		Tomás	Stanek	CZE	13.6.91	1		Düsseldorf	6 Feb 18
22.10		Sergey	Gavryushin	RUS	27.6.59	1		Tbilisi	31 Aug 86
22.10		Cory	Martin	USA	22.5.85	1		Tucson	22 May 10
22.09		Sergey	Kasnauskas	BLR	20.4.61	1		Stayki	23 Aug 84
22.09i		Mika	Halvari	FIN	13.2.70	1		Tampere	7 Feb 00
22.02i WIR		George	Woods	USA	11.2.43	1	LAT	Inglewood	8 Feb 74
		(30)							
22.02		Dave	Laut	USA	21.12.56	1		Koblenz	25 Aug 82
22.00 WR		Aleksandr	Baryshnikov	RUS	11.11.48	1	vFRA	Colombes	10 Jul 76
21.99		Leonardo	Fabbri	ITA	15.4.97	1	NC	Padova	30 Aug 20
21.98		Gregg	Tafralis ¶	USA	9.4.58	1		Los Gatos	13 Jun 92
21.97		Janus	Robberts	RSA	10.3.79	1	NCAA	Eugene	2 Jun 01
21.96		Mikhail	Kostin	RUS	10.5.59	1		Vitebsk	20 Jul 86
21.96		O'Dayne	Richards	JAM	14.12.88	2	DL	Rabat	16 Jul 17
21.95		Tomasz	Majewski	POL	30.8.81	1	DNG	Stockholm	30 Jul 09
21.93		Remigius	Machura ¶	CZE	3.7.60	1		Praha	23 Aug 87
21.92		Carl	Myerscough ¶	GBR	21.10.79	1	NCAA	Sacramento	13 Jun 03
		(40)							
21.87		C.J.	Hunter ¶	USA	14.12.68	2	NC	Sacramento	15 Jul 00
21.85 WR		Terry	Albritton	USA	14.1.55	1		Honolulu	21 Feb 76
21.84		Filip	Mihaljevic	CRO	31.7.94	1		Slovenska Bistrica	25 May 19
21.83i		Aleksandr	Bagach ¶	UKR	21.11.66	1		Brovary	21 Feb 99
21.82 WR		Al	Feuerbach	USA	14.1.48	1		San José	5 May 73
21.82		Andy	Bloom	USA	11.8.73	1	GPF	Doha	5 Oct 00
21.81		Yuriy	Bilonog ¶	UKR	9.3.74	1	NC	Kiev	3 Jul 03
21.81i		Payton	Otterdahl	USA	2.4.96	1		Brookings, SD	23 Feb 19
21.80		Chukwuebuka	Enekwechi	NGR	28.1.93	1		Schifflange	18 Aug 19
21.78 WR		Randy	Matson	USA	5.3.45	1		College Station	22 Apr 67
		(50)							

100th man 21.35, 200th 20.89, 300th 20.56, 400th 20.28, 500th 20.06

SHOT - DISCUS A-T

Mark	Wind	Name		Nat	Born	Pos	Meet	Venue	Date
Not recognised by GDR authorities:		22.11	Rolf Oesterreich	GDR	24.8.49	1		Zschopau	12 Sep 76
Best outdoor mark for athlete with indoor best:		22.01	Stanek			1		Schönebeck	2 Jun 17
Drugs disqualification									
22.84			Barnes			(1)		Malmö	7 Aug 90
22.10		Andrey	Mikhnevich ¶	BLR	12.7.76	(1)		Minsk	11 Aug 11
21.82		Mike	Stulce ¶	USA	21.7.69	(1)		Brenham	9 May 90

Ancillary marks – other marks during series (to 22.64)

22.84 WR	Andrei	12 Aug 87	22.73	Crouser	18 Jul 20	22.70	Günthör	23 Aug 88
22.76	Barnes	20 May 90	22.72 WR	Andrei	12 Aug 87	22.70	Crouser	29 Aug 20
22.74	Andrei	12 Aug 87	22.71	Crouser	5 Oct 19	22.68	Crouser	29 Aug 20
22.73	Crouser	20 Apr 19						

DISCUS

Mark	Wind	Name		Nat	Born	Pos	Meet	Venue	Date
74.08	WR	Jürgen	Schult	GDR	11.5.60	1		Neubrandenburg	6 Jun 86
73.88		Virgilijus	Alekna	LTU	13.2.72	1	NC	Kaunas	3 Aug 00
73.38		Gerd	Kanter	EST	6.5.79	1		Helsingborg	4 Sep 06
72.02			Kanter			1eA		Salinas	3 May 07
71.88			Kanter			1eA		Salinas	8 May 08
71.86	WR	Yuriy	Dumchev	RUS	5.8.58	1		Moskva	29 May 83
71.86		Daniel	Ståhl	SWE	27.8.92	1		Bottnaryd	29 Jun 19
71.84		Piotr	Malachowski	POL	7.6.83	1	FBK	Hengelo	8 Jun 13
71.70		Róbert	Fazekas ¶	HUN	18.8.75	1		Szombathely	14 Jul 02
71.64			Kanter			1		Kohila	25 Jun 09
71.56			Alekna			1		Kaunas	25 Jul 07
71.50		Lars	Riedel	GER	28.6.67	1		Wiesbaden	3 May 97
71.45			Kanter			1		Chula Vista	29 Apr 10
71.37			Ståhl			1		Sollentuna	10 Aug 20
71.32		Ben	Plucknett ¶	USA	13.4.54	1	Pre	Eugene	4 Jun 83
71.29			Ståhl			1		Sollentuna	29 Jun 17
71.26		John	Powell (10)	USA	25.6.47	1	NC	San José	9 Jun 84
71.26		Rickard	Bruch	SWE	2.7.46	1		Malmö	15 Nov 84
71.26		Imrich	Bugár	CZE	14.4.55	1	Jenner	San José	25 May 85
71.25			Fazekas			1	WCp	Madrid (C)	21 Sep 02
71.25			Alekna			1	Danek	Turnov	20 May 08
71.18		Art	Burns	USA	19.7.54	1		San José	19 Jul 83
71.16	WR	Wolfgang	Schmidt	GDR	16.1.54	1		Berlin	9 Aug 78
71.14			Plucknett			1		Berkeley	12 Jun 83
71.14		Anthony	Washington	USA	16.1.66	1eA		Salinas	22 May 96
71.12			Alekna			1	WK	Zürich	11 Aug 00
71.08			Alekna			1		Réthimno	21 Jul 06
71.06		Luis Mariano	Delís ¶	CUB	12.12.57	1	Barr	La Habana	21 May 83
71.06			Riedel			1	WK	Zürich	14 Aug 96
71.00			Bruch			1		Malmö	14 Oct 84
		(30/16)							
70.98		Mac	Wilkins	USA	15.11.50	1	WG	Helsinki	9 Jul 80
70.82		Aleksander	Tammert	EST	2.2.73	1		Denton	15 Apr 06
70.78		Fedrick	Dacres	JAM	28.2.94	1	DL	Rabat	16 Jun 19
70.66		Robert	Harting	GER	18.10.84	1	Danek	Turnov	22 May 12
		(20)							
70.54		Dmitriy	Shevchenko ¶	RUS	13.5.68	1		Krasnodar	7 May 02
70.38	WR U	Jay	Silvester	USA	27.8.37	1		Lancaster	16 May 71
70.32		Frantz	Kruger	RSA/FIN	22.5.75	1		Salon-de-Provence	26 May 02
70.29		Mauricio	Ortega	COL	4.8.94	1		Lovelhe	22 Jul 20
70.06		Romas	Ubartas ¶	LTU	26.5.60	1		Smalininkay	8 May 88
70.00		Juan	Martínez ¶	CUB	17.5.58	2	Barr	La Habana	21 May 83
69.95		Zoltán	Kövágó ¶	HUN	10.4.79	1		Salon-de-Provence	25 May 06
69.91		John	Godina	USA	31.5.72	1		Salinas	19 May 98
69.90		Jason	Young ¶	USA	27.5.81	1		Lubbock	26 Mar 10
69.70		Géjza	Valent	CZE	3.10.53	2		Nitra	26 Aug 84
		(30)							
69.62		Knut	Hjeltnes ¶	NOR	8.12.51	2	Jen	San José	25 May 85
69.62		Timo	Tompuri	FIN	9.6.69	1		Helsingborg	8 Jul 01
69.60		Juan José	Caicedo	ECU	20.7.92	2		Lovelhe	22 Jul 20
69.59		Andrius	Gudzius	LTU	14.2.91	2	DL	Stockholm	10 Jun 18
69.50		Mario	Pestano	ESP	8.4.78	1	NC	Santa Cruz de Tenerife	27 Jul 08
69.46		Al	Oerter	USA	19.9.36	1	TFA	Wichita	31 May 80
69.44		Georgiy	Kolnootchenko	BLR	7.5.59	1	vUSA	Indianapolis	3 Jul 82
69.40		Art	Swarts ¶	USA	14.2.45	1		Scotch Plains	8 Dec 79
69.36		Mike	Buncic	USA	25.7.62	1		Fresno	6 Apr 91
69.32		Ehsan	Hadadi	IRI	21.1.85	1		Tallinn	3 Jun 08
69.35		Gudni Valur	Gudnason	ISL	11.10.95	1		Reykjavik	16 Sep 20
		(40)							

MEN All-time

218   DISCUS – HAMMER A-T

Mark	Wind	Name		Nat	Born	Pos	Meet	Venue	Date
69.28		Vladimir	Dubrovshchik	BLR	7.1.72	1	NC	Staiki	3 Jun 00
69.26		Ken	Stadel	USA	19.2.52	2	AAU	Walnut	16 Jun 79
68.98		Lukas	Weisshaidinger	AUT	20.2.92	1		Rehlingen	20 May 18
68.94		Adam	Setliff	USA	15.12.69	1		Atascadero	25 Jul 01
68.91		Ian	Waltz	USA	15.4.77	1		Salinas	24 May 06
68.90		Jean-Claude	Retel	FRA	11.2.68	1		Salon-de-Provence	17 Jul 02
68.88		Vladimir	Zinchenko	UKR	25.7.59	1		Dnepropetrovsk	16 Jul 88
68.76		Jarred	Rome	USA	21.12.76	2cA		Chula Vista	6 Aug 11
68.75		Kristian	Ceh	SLO	17.2.99	1		Maribor	23 Jun 20
(50)		100th man 67.39, 200th 65.61, 300th 64.54, 400th 63.53, 500th 62.63							
Subsequent to or at drugs disqualification				! recognised as US record					
72.34!		Ben	Plucknett ¶	USA	13.4.54	(1)	DNG	Stockholm	7 Jul 81
71.20			Plucknett			(1)	CalR	Modesto	16 May 81
70.84		Kamy	Keshmiri ¶	USA	23.1.69	(1)		Salinas	27 May 92
Sloping ground									
72.08		John	Powell	USA	25.6.47	1		Klagshamn	11 Sep 87
69.80		Stefan	Fernholm	SWE	2.7.59	1		Klagshamn	13 Aug 87
69.44		Adam	Setliff	USA	15.12.69	1		La Jolla	21 Jul 01
Ancillary marks – other marks during series (to 71.00)									
72.35 Alekna 3 Aug 00 72.30 Kanter 4 Sep 06 71.08 Plucknett 4 Jun 83									

HAMMER

Mark		Name		Nat	Born	Pos	Meet	Venue	Date
86.74 WR		Yuriy	Sedykh	RUS	11.6.55	1	EC	Stuttgart	30 Aug 86
86.66 WR			Sedykh			1	vGDR	Tallinn	22 Jun 86
86.34 WR			Sedykh			1		Cork	3 Jul 84
86.04		Sergey	Litvinov	RUS	23.1.58	1	OD	Dresden	3 Jul 86
85.74			Litvinov			2	EC	Stuttgart	30 Aug 86
85.68			Sedykh			1	BGP	Budapest	11 Aug 86
85.60			Sedykh			1	PTG	London (CP)	13 Jul 84
85.60			Sedykh			1	Drz	Moskva	17 Aug 84
85.20			Litvinov			2		Cork	3 Jul 84
85.14			Litvinov			1	PTG	London	11 Jul 86
85.14			Sedykh			1	Kuts	Moskva	4 Sep 88
85.02			Sedykh			1	BGP	Budapest	20 Aug 84
84.92			Sedykh			2	OD	Dresden	3 Jul 86
84.90		Vadim	Devyatovskiy ¶	BLR	20.3.77	1		Staiki	21 Jul 05
84.88			Litvinov			1	GP-GG	Roma	10 Sep 86
84.86		Koji	Murofushi	JPN	8.10.74	1	Odlozil	Praha	29 Jun 03
84.80			Litvinov			1	OG	Seoul	26 Sep 88
84.72			Sedykh			1	GWG	Moskva	9 Jul 86
84.64			Litvinov			2	GWG	Moskva	9 Jul 86
84.62		Igor	Astapkovich	BLR	4.1.63	1	Expo	Sevilla	6 Jun 92
84.60			Sedykh			1	8-N	Tokyo	14 Sep 84
84.58			Sedykh			1	Znam	Leningrad	8 Jun 86
84.51		Ivan	Tikhon ¶	BLR	24.7.76	1	NC	Grodno	9 Jul 08
84.48		Igor	Nikulin	RUS	14.8.60	1	Athl	Lausanne	12 Jul 90
84.46			Sedykh			1		Vladivostok	14 Sep 88
84.46			Tikhon			1		Minsk	7 May 04
84.40		Jüri	Tamm	EST	5.2.57	1		Banská Bystrica	9 Sep 84
84.36			Litvinov			2	vGDR	Tallinn	22 Jun 86
84.32			Tikhon			1		Staiki	8 Aug 03
84.26			Sedykh			1	Nik	Nice	15 Jul 86
	(30/8)								
84.19		Adrián	Annus ¶	HUN	28.6.73	1		Szombathely	10 Aug 03
83.93		Pawel	Fajdek	POL	4.6.89	1	Kuso	Szczecin	9 Aug 15
	(10)								
83.68		Tibor	Gécsek ¶	HUN	22.9.64	1		Zalaegerszeg	19 Sep 98
83.46		Andrey	Abduvaliyev	TJK/UZB	30.6.66	1		Adler	26 May 90
83.43		Aleksey	Zagornyi	RUS	31.5.78	1		Adler	10 Feb 02
83.40 @		Ralf	Haber	GDR	18.8.62	1		Athína	16 May 88
		82.54				1		Potsdam	9 Sep 88
83.38		Szymon	Ziółkowski	POL	1.7.76	1	WCh	Edmonton	5 Aug 01
83.30		Olli-Pekka	Karjalainen	FIN	7.3.80	1		Lahti	14 Jul 04
83.04		Heinz	Weis	GER	14.7.63	1	NC	Frankfurt	29 Jun 97
83.00		Balázs	Kiss	HUN	21.3.72	1	GP II	Saint-Denis	4 Jun 98
82.78		Karsten	Kobs	GER	16.9.71	1		Dortmund	26 Jun 99
82.69		Krisztián	Pars	HUN	18.2.82	1	EC	Zürich	16 Aug 14
	(20)				@ competitive meeting but unsanctioned by GDR federation				
82.64		Günther	Rodehau	GDR	6.7.59	1		Dresden	3 Aug 85
82.62		Sergey	Kirmasov ¶	RUS	25.3.70	1		Bryansk	30 May 98

HAMMER – JAVELIN A-T

Mark	Wind	Name		Nat	Born	Pos	Meet	Venue	Date
82.62		Andrey	Skvaruk	UKR	9.3.67	1		Koncha-Zaspa	27 Apr 02
82.58		Primoz	Kozmus	SLO	30.9.79	1		Celje	2 Sep 09
82.54		Vasiliy	Sidorenko	RUS	1.5.61	1		Krasnodar	13 May 92
82.52		Lance	Deal	USA	21.8.61	1	GPF	Milano	7 Sep 96
82.40		Plamen	Minev	BUL	28.4.65	1	NM	Plovdiv	1 Jun 91
82.38		Gilles	Dupray	FRA	2.1.70	1		Chelles	21 Jun 00
82.28		Ilya	Konovalov ¶	RUS	4.3.71	1	NC	Tula	10 Aug 03
82.24		Benjaminas	Viluckis	LIT	20.3.61	1		Klaipeda	24 Aug 86
		(30)							
82.24		Vyacheslav	Korovin	RUS	8.9.62	1		Chelyabinsk	20 Jun 87
82.23		Vladislav	Piskunov ¶	UKR	7.6.78	2		Koncha-Zaspa	27 Apr 02
82.22		Holger	Klose	GER	5.12.72	1		Dortmund	2 May 98
82.16		Vitaliy	Alisevich	BLR	15.6.67	1		Parnu	13 Jul 88
82.08		Ivan	Tanev	BUL	1.5.57	1	NC	Sofia	3 Sep 88
82.00		Sergey	Alay ¶	BLR	11.6.65	1		Stayki	12 May 92
81.88		Jud	Logan ¶	USA	19.7.59	1		State College	22 Apr 88
81.85		Wojciech	Nowicki	POL	22.2.89	1	Gyulai	Székesfehérvár	2 Jul 18
81.81		Libor	Charfreitag	SVK	11.9.77	3	Odlozil	Praha	29 Jun 03
81.79		Christophe	Épalle	FRA	23.1.69	1		Clermont-Ferrand	30 Jun 00
		(40)							
81.78		Christoph	Sahner	FRG	23.9.63	1		Wemmetsweiler	11 Sep 88
81.70		Aleksandr	Seleznyov	RUS	25.1.63	2		Sochi	22 May 93
81.66		Aleksandr	Krykun	UKR	1.3.68	1		Kiev	29 May 04
81.64		Enrico	Sgrulletti	ITA	24.4.65	1		Ostia	9 Mar 97
81.56		Sergey	Gavrilov	RUS	22.5.70	1	Army	Rostov	16 Jun 96
81.56		Zsolt	Németh	HUN	9.11.71	1		Veszprém	14 Aug 99
81.52		Juha	Tiainen	FIN	5.12.55	1		Tampere	11 Jun 84
81.49		Valeriy	Svyatokho	BLR	20.7.81	1	NCp	Brest	27 May 06
81.45		Esref	Apak ¶	TUR	3.1.82	1	Cezmi	Istanbul	4 Jun 05
81.44		Yuriy	Tarasyuk	BLR	11.4.57	1		Minsk	10 Aug 84
		(50)		100th man 80.14, 200th 77.80, 300th 76.14, 400th 74.84, 500th 73.80					

Drugs disqualification: 86.73　Ivan Tikhon ¶　BLR　24.7.76　(1)　NC　Brest　3 Jul 05

Ancillary marks – other marks during series (to 84.85)

86.68	Sedykh	30 Aug 86	85.82	Sedykh	22 Jun 86	85.42	Sedykh	11 Aug 86	85.20	Sedykh	3 Jul 84
86.62	Sedykh	30 Aug 86	85.52	Sedykh	13 Jul 84	85.28	Sedykh	30 Aug 86	85.04	Sedykh	13 Jul 84
86.00	Sedykh	3 Jul 84	85.46	Sedykh	30 Aug 86	85.26	Sedykh	11 Aug 86	84.98	Sedykh	4 Sep 86
86.00	Sedykh	22 Jun 86	85.42	Litvinov	3 Jul 86	85.24	Sedykh	11 Aug 86	84.92	Litvinov	3 Jul 86

JAVELIN

Mark	Wind	Name		Nat	Born	Pos	Meet	Venue	Date
98.48 WR		Jan	Zelezny	CZE	16.6.66	1		Jena	25 May 96
97.76		Johannes	Vetter	GER	26.3.93	1	Skol	Chorzów	6 Sep 20
95.66 WR			Zelezny			1	McD	Sheffield	29 Aug 93
95.54A WR			Zelezny			1		Pietersburg	6 Apr 93
94.64			Zelezny			1	GS	Ostrava	31 May 96
94.44			Vetter			1		Luzern	11 Jul 17
94.02			Zelezny			1		Stellenbosch	26 Mar 97
93.90		Thomas	Röhler	GER	30.9.91	1	DL	Doha	5 May 17
93.88			Vetter			1		Thum	18 Aug 17
93.09		Aki	Parviainen	FIN	26.10.74	1		Kuortane	26 Jun 99
92.80			Zelezny			1	WCh	Edmonton	12 Aug 01
92.72		Julius	Yego	KEN	4.1.89	1	WCh	Beijing	26 Aug 15
92.70			Vetter			1	ECp-w	Leiria	11 Mar 18
92.61		Sergey	Makarov	RUS	19.3.73	1		Sheffield	30 Jun 02
92.60		Raymond	Hecht	GER	11.11.68	1	Bisl	Oslo	21 Jul 95
92.42			Zelezny			1	GS	Ostrava	28 May 97
92.41			Parviainen			1	ECp-1A	Vaasa	24 Jun 01
92.28			Zelezny			1	GPF	Monaco	9 Sep 95
92.28			Hecht			1	WK	Zürich	14 Aug 96
92.12			Zelezny			1	McD	London (CP)	27 Aug 95
92.12			Zelezny			1	TOTO	Tokyo	15 Sep 95
92.06		Andreas	Hofmann	GER	16.12.91	1		Offenburg	2 Jun 18
91.82			Zelezny			1	McD	Sheffield	4 Sep 94
91.78			Röhler			1	DL	Doha	4 May 18
91.69		Kostadínos	Gatsioúdis	GRE	17.12.73	1		Kuortane	24 Jun 00
91.68			Zelezny			1	GP	Gateshead	1 Jul 94
91.59		Andreas	Thorkildsen (10)	NOR	1.4.82	1	Bisl	Oslo	2 Jun 06
91.56			Vetter			2	DL	Doha	4 May 18
91.53		Tero	Pitkämäki	FIN	19.12.82	1		Kuortane	26 Jun 05
91.53			Röhler			1	GS	Ostrava	28 Jun 17
		(30/11)							

JAVELIN - DECATHLON A-T

Mark	Wind	Name		Nat	Born	Pos	Meet	Venue	Date
91.46 WR		Steve	Backley	GBR	12.2.69	1		Auckland (NS)	25 Jan 92
91.36			Cheng Chao-Tsun	TPE	17.10.93	1	WUG	Taipei	26 Aug 17
91.29		Breaux	Greer	USA	19.10.76	1	NC	Indianapolis	21 Jun 07
90.73		Vadims	Vasilevskis	LAT	5.1.82	1		Tallinn	22 Jul 07
90.61		Magnus	Kirt	EST	10.4.90	1		Kuortane	22 Jun 19
90.60		Seppo	Räty	FIN	27.4.62	1		Nurmijärvi	20 Jul 92
90.44		Boris	Henry	GER	14.12.73	1		Linz	9 Jul 97
90.16		Keshorn	Walcott	TTO	2.4.93	1	Athl	Lausanne	9 Jul 15
89.73		Jakub	Vadlejch	CZE	10.10.90	2	WCh	London (OS)	12 Aug 17
(20)									
89.21		Ihab	Abdelrahman ¶	EGY	1.5.89	1	DL	Shanghai	18 May 14
89.17		Edis	Matusevicius	LTU	30.6.96	1	NC	Palanga	27 Jul 19
89.16A		Tom	Petranoff	USA	8.4.58	1		Potchefstroom	1 Mar 91
89.15			Zhao Qinggang	CHN	24.7.85	1	AsiG	Incheon	2 Oct 14
89.10 WR		Patrik	Bodén	SWE	30.6.67	1		Austin	24 Mar 90
89.06		Bernhard	Seifert	GER	15.2.93	2		Offenburg	26 May 19
89.02		Jarrod	Bannister ¶	AUS	3.10.84	1	NC	Brisbane	29 Feb 08
88.98		Antti	Ruuskanen	FIN	21.2.84	1	NC	Pori	2 Aug 15
88.90		Aleksandr	Ivanov	RUS	25.5.82	1	Znam	Tula	7 Jun 03
88.84		Dmitriy	Tarabin	RUS	29.10.91	1	NC	Moskva	24 Jul 13
(30)									
88.75		Marius	Corbett	RSA	26.9.75	1	CG	Kuala Lumpur	21 Sep 98
88.70		Peter	Blank	GER	10.4.62	1	NC	Stuttgart	30 Jun 01
88.36		Matthias	de Zordo	GER	21.2.88	1	VD	Bruxelles	16 Sep 11
88.34		Vitezslav	Vesely	CZE	27.2.83	Q	OG	London (OS)	8 Aug 12
88.32		Petr	Frydrych	CZE	13.1.88	3	WCh	London (OS)	12 Aug 17
88.29		Julian	Weber	GER	29.8.94	2	ISTAF	Berlin	3 Sep 16
88.24		Matti	Närhi	FIN	17.8.75	1		Soini	27 Jul 97
88.22		Juha	Laukkanen	FIN	6.1.69	1		Kuortane	20 Jun 92
88.20		Gavin	Lovegrove	NZL	21.10.67	1	Bisl	Oslo	5 Jul 96
88.09		Marcin	Krukowski	POL	14.6.92	1	NC	Bialystok	21 Jul 17
(40)									
88.06		Neeraj	Chopra	IND	24.12.97	1	AsiG	Jakarta	27 Aug 18
88.02		Oliver	Helander	FIN	1.1.97	1		Pietersaari	7 Jul 18
88.01		Ioánnis	Kiriazis	GRE	19.1.96	1	TexR	Austin	31 Mar 17
88.00		Vladimir	Ovchinnikov	RUS	2.8.70	1		Tolyatti	14 May 95
87.83		Andrus	Värnik	EST	27.9.77	1		Valga	19 Aug 03
87.82		Harri	Hakkarainen	FIN	16.10.69	1		Kuortane	24 Jun 95
87.60		Kazuhiro	Mizoguchi	JPN	18.3.62	1	Jenner	San José	27 May 89
87.40		Vladimir	Sasimovich ¶	BLR	14.9.68	2		Kuortane	24 Jun 95
87.34		Andrey	Moruyev	RUS	6.5.70	1	ECp	Birmingham	25 Jun 94
87.31		Anderson	Peters	GRN	21.10.97	1	PAm	Lima	10 Aug 19
(50)		100th man 85.11, 200th 83.00, 300th 81.02, 400th 79.86, 500th 78.92							

Ancillary marks – other marks during series (to 91.68) new javelin introduced in 1986
| 95.34 | Zelezny | 29 Aug 93 | 92.88 | Zelezny | 25 May 96 | 92.26 | Zelezny | 26 Mar 97 |
| 93.06 | Vetter | 11 Jul 17 | 92.30 | Zelezny | 26 Mar 97 | 91.88 | Zelezny | 27 Aug 95 |

Javelins with roughened tails, now banned by the IAAF
96.96 WR		Seppo	Räty	FIN	27.4.62	1		Punkalaidun	2 Jun 91
94.74 Irreg			Zelezny			1	Bisl	Oslo	4 Jul 92
91.98 WR			Räty			1	Super	Shizuoka	6 May 91
90.82		Kimmo	Kinnunen	FIN	31.3.68	1	WCh	Tokyo	26 Aug 91

DECATHLON

9126 WR	Kevin	Mayer		FRA	10.2.92	1		Talence		16 Sep 18
	10.55/0.3	7.80/1.2	16.00	2.05	48.42		13.75/-1.1	50.54	5.45	71.80	4:36.11
9045 WR	Ashton	Eaton		USA	21.1.88	1	WCh	Beijing		29 Aug 15
	10.23/-0.4	7.88/0.0	14.52	2.01	45.00		13.69/-0.2	43.34	5.20	63.63	4:17.52
9039 WR		Eaton				1	NC/OT	Eugene		23 Jun 12
	10.21/0.4	8.23/0.8	14.20	2.05	46.70		13.70/-0.8	42.81	5.30	58.87	4:14.48
9026 WR	Roman	Sebrle		CZE	26.11.74	1		Götzis		27 May 01
	10.64/0.0	8.11/1.9	15.33	2.12	47.79		13.92/-0.2	47.92	4.80	70.16	4:21.98
8994 WR	Tomás	Dvorák		CZE	11.5.72	1	ECp	Praha		4 Jul 99
	10.54/-0.1	7.90/1.1	16.78	2.04	48.08		13.73/0.0	48.33	4.90	72.32	4:37.20
8902		Dvorák				1	WCh	Edmonton		7 Aug 01
	10.62/1.5	8.07/0.9	16.57	2.00	47.74		13.80/-0.4	45.51	5.00	68.53	4:35.13
8900		Dvorák				1		Götzis		4 Jun 00
	10.54/1.3	8.03/0.0	16.68	2.09	48.36		13.89/-1.0	47.89	4.85	67.21	4:42.33
8893		Sebrle				1	OG	Athína		24 Aug 04
	10.85/1.5	7.84/0.3	16.36	2.12	48.36		14.05/1.5	48.72	5.00	70.52	4:40.01
8893		Eaton				1	OG	Rio de Janeiro		18 Aug 16
	10.46/-0.1	7.94/1.7	14.73	2.01	46.07		13.80/0.7	45.49	5.20	59.77	4:23.33

DECATHLON AT 221

Mark	Wind	Name		Nat	Born	Pos	Meet	Venue			Date
8891 WR		Dan	O'Brien	USA	18.7.66	1		Talence			5 Sep 92
	10.43w/2.1	8.08/1.8	16.69	2.07	48.51		13.98/-0.5	48.56	5.00	62.58	4:42.10
8869			Eaton			1	OG	London (OS)			9 Aug 12
	10.35/0.4	8.03/0.8	14.66	2.05	46.90		13.56/0.1	42.53	5.20	61.96	4:33.59
8847 WR		Daley	Thompson	GBR	30.7.58	1	OG	Los Angeles			9 Aug 84
	10.44/-1.0	8.01/0.4	15.72	2.03	46.97		14.33/-1.1	46.56	5.00	65.24	4:35.00
8844w			O'Brien			1	TAC	New York			13 Jun 91
	10.23	7.96	16.06	2.08	47.70		13.95W/4.2	48.08	5.10	57.40	4:45.54
8842			Sebrle			1		Götzis			30 May 04
	10.92/0.5	7.86w/3.3	16.22	2.09	48.59		14.15/0.3	47.44	5.00	71.10	4:34.09
8837			Dvořák			1	WCh	Athína			6 Aug 97
	10.60/0.8	7.64/-0.7	16.32	2.00	47.56		13.61/0.8	45.16	5.00	70.34	4:35.40
8834			Mayer			2	OG	Rio de Janeiro			18 Aug 16
	10.81/-0.4	7.60/0.1	15.76	2.04	48.28		14.02/0.7	46.78	5.40	65.04	4:25.49
8832 WR		Jürgen	Hingsen	FRG	25.1.58	1	OT	Mannheim			9 Jun 84
	10.70w/2.9	7.76/-1.6	16.42	2.07	48.05		14.07/0.2	49.36	4.90	59.86	4:19.75
8832		Bryan	Clay	USA	3.1.80	1	NC/OT	Eugene			30 Jun 08
	10.39/-0.4	7.39/-1.6	15.17	2.08	48.41		13.75/1.9	52.74	5.00	70.55	4:50.97
8825 WR			Hingsen			1		Bernhausen			5 Jun 83
	10.92/0.0	7.74	15.94	2.15	47.89		14.10	46.80	4.70	67.26	4:19.74
8824			O'Brien			1	OG	Atlanta			1 Aug 96
	10.50/0.7	7.57/1.4	15.66	2.07	46.82		13.87/0.3	48.78	5.00	66.90	4:45.89
8820			Clay			2	OG	Athína			24 Aug 04
	10.44w/2.2	7.96/0.2	15.23	2.06	49.19		14.13/1.5	50.11	4.90	69.71	4:41.65
8817			O'Brien			1	WCh	Stuttgart			20 Aug 93
	10.57/0.9	7.99/0.4	15.41	2.03	47.46		14.08/0.0	47.92	5.20	62.56	4:40.08
8815		Erki	Nool	EST	25.6.70	2	WCh	Edmonton			7 Aug 01
	10.60/1.5	7.63/2.0	14.90	2.03	46.23		14.40/0.0	43.40	5.40	67.01	4:29.58
8812			O'Brien			1	WCh	Tokyo			30 Aug 91
	10.41/-1.6	7.90/0.8	16.24	1.91	46.53		13.94/-1.2	47.20	5.20	60.66	4:37.50
8811			Thompson			1	EC	Stuttgart			28 Aug 86
	10.26/2.0	7.72/1.0	15.73	2.00	47.02		14.04/-0.3	43.38	5.10	62.78	4:26.16
8809			Eaton			1	WCh	Moskva			11 Aug 13
	10.35/-0.5	7.73/0.3	14.39	1.93	46.02		13.72/0.4	45.00	5.20	64.83	4:29.80
8807			Sebrle			1		Götzis			1 Jun 03
	10.78/-0.2	7.86/1.2	15.41	2.12	47.83		13.96/0.0	43.42	4.90	69.22	4:28.63
8800			Sebrle			1		Götzis			2 Jun 02
	10.95/0.5	7.79/1.8	15.50	2.12	48.35		13.89/1.6	48.02	5.00	68.97	4:38.16
8800			Sebrle			1	EC	München			8 Aug 02
	10.83/1.3	7.92/0.8	15.41	2.12	48.48		14.04/0.0	46.88	5.10	68.51	4:42.94
8795		Damian	Warner (10)	CAN	4.11.89	1	Hypo	Götzis			27 May 18
	10.31/0.6	7.81/0.5	14.83	2.03	47.72		13.56/0.0	47.32	4.80	61.94	4:26.59
8792		Uwe	Freimuth	GDR	10.9.61	1	OD	Potsdam			21 Jul 84
	11.06/0.4	7.79/1.2	16.30	2.03	48.43		14.66/1.9	46.58	5.15	72.42	4:25.19
(31/11)											
8790		Trey	Hardee	USA	7.2.84	1	WCh	Berlin			20 Aug 09
	10.45/0.2	7.83/1.9	15.33	1.99	48.13		13.86/0.3	48.08	5.20	68.00	4:48.91
8784		Tom	Pappas	USA	6.9.76	1	NC	Stanford			22 Jun 03
	10.78/0.2	7.96/1.4	16.28	2.17	48.22		14.13/1.7	45.84	5.20	60.77	4:48.12
8762		Siegfried	Wentz	FRG	7.3.60	2		Bernhausen			5 Jun 83
	10.89	7.49/	15.35	2.09	47.38		14.00	46.90	4.80	70.68	4:24.90
8735		Eduard	Hämäläinen	FIN/BLR	21.1.69	1		Götzis			29 May 94
	10.50w/2.1	7.26/1.0	16.05	2.11	47.63		13.82/-3.0	49.70	4.90	60.32	4:35.09
8727		Dave	Johnson	USA	7.4.63	1		Azusa			24 Apr 92
	10.96/0.4	7.52w/4.5	14.61	2.04	48.19		14.17/0.3	49.88	5.28	66.96	4:29.38
8725		Dmitriy	Karpov	KAZ	23.7.81	3	OG	Athína			24 Aug 04
	10.50w/2.2	7.81/-0.9	15.93	2.09	46.81		13.97/1.5	51.65	4.60	55.54	4:38.11
8709		Aleksandr	Apaychev	UKR	6.5.61	1	vGDR	Neubrandenburg			3 Jun 84
	10.96/	7.57/	16.00	1.97	48.72		13.93/	48.00	4.90	72.24	4:26.51
8706		Frank	Busemann	GER	26.2.75	2	OG	Atlanta			1 Aug 96
	10.60/0.7	8.07/0.8	13.60	2.04	48.34		13.47/0.3	45.04	4.80	66.86	4:31.41
8698		Grigoriy	Degtyaryov	RUS	16.8.58	1	NC	Kyiv			22 Jun 84
	10.87/0.7	7.42/0.1	16.03	2.10	49.75		14.53/0.3	51.20	4.90	67.08	4:23.09
(20)											
8694		Chris	Huffins	USA	15.4.70	1	NC	New Orleans			20 Jun 98
	10.31w/3.5	7.76w/2.5	15.43	2.18	49.02		14.02/1.0	53.22	4.60	61.59	4:59.43
8691		Niklas	Kaul	GER	11.2.98	1	WCh	Doha			4 Oct 19
	11.27/0.3	7.19/0.6	15.10	2.02	48.48		14.64/0.7	49.20	5.00	79.05	4:15.70
8680		Torsten	Voss	GDR	24.3.63	1	WCh	Roma			4 Sep 87
	10.69/-0.3	7.88/1.2	14.98	2.10	47.96		14.13/0.1	43.96	5.10	58.02	4:25.93

MEN All-time

222   DECATHLON – 4x100m RELAY A-T

Mark	Wind	Name	Nat	Born	Pos	Meet	Venue	Date
8670		Michael Schrader	GER	1.7.87	2	WCh	Moskva	11 Aug 13
	10.73/-0.5	7.85/0.2 14.56		1.99	47.66		14.29/0.4	46.44 5.00 65.67	4:25.38
8667 WR		Guido Kratschmer	FRG	10.1.53	1		Bernhausen	14 Jun 80
	10.58w/2.4	7.80/ 15.47		2.00	48.04		13.92/	45.52 4.60 66.50	4:24.15
8663		Rico Freimuth	GER	14.3.88	1		Ratingen	25 Jun 17
	10.44w/3.3	7.60/1.5 14.87		2.01	48.76		13.87/0.7	51.56 4.90 62.33	4:37.04
8654		Leonel Suárez	CUB	1.9.87	1	CAC	La Habana	4 Jul 09
	11.07/0.7	7.42/0.8 14.39		2.09	47.65		14.15/-0.6	46.07 4.70 77.47	4:27.29
8644		Steve Fritz	USA	1.11.67	4	OG	Atlanta	1 Aug 96
	10.90/0.8	7.77/0.9 15.31		2.04	50.13		13.97/0.3	49.84 5.10 65.70	4:38.26
8644		Maurice Smith	JAM	28.9.80	2	WCh	Osaka	1 Sep 07
	10.62/0.7	7.50/0.0 17.32		1.97	47.48		13.91/-0.2	52.36 4.80 53.61	4:33.52
8634 WR		Bruce Jenner	USA	28.10.49	1	OG	Montreal	30 Jul 76
	10.94/0.0	7.22/0.0 15.35		2.03	47.51		14.84/0.0	50.04 4.80 68.52	4:12.61
	(30)							
8627		Robert Zmelík	CZE	18.4.69	1		Götzis	31 May 92
	10.62w/2.1	8.02/0.2 13.93		2.05	48.73		13.84/1.2	44.44 4.90 61.26	4:24.83
8626		Michael Smith	CAN	16.9.67	1		Götzis	26 May 96
	11.23/-0.6	7.72/0.6 16.94		1.97	48.69		14.77/-2.4	52.90 4.90 71.22	4:41.95
8617		Andrey Kravchenko	BLR	4.1.86	1		Götzis	27 May 07
	10.86/0.2	7.90/0.9 13.89		2.15	47.46		14.05/-0.1	39.63 5.00 64.35	4:29.10
8605		Arthur Abele	GER	30.7.86	1		Ratingen	26 Jun 16
	10.95/-0.6	748/0.4 15.79		1.98	49.43		14.07/-0.9	46.20 4.90 71.89	4:24.12
8604		Maicel Uibo	EST	27.12.92	2	WCh	Doha	4 Oct 19
	11.10/0.3	7.46/0.2 15.12		2.17	50.44		14.43/0.2	46.64 5.40 63.83	4:31.51
8603		Dean Macey	GBR	12.12.77	3	WCh	Edmonton	7 Aug 01
	10.72/-0.2	7.59/0.4 15.41		2.15	46.21		14.34/0.0	46.96 4.70 54.61	4:29.05
8601		Ilya Shkurenyov	RUS	11.1.91	1	NC	Smolensk	10 Jun 17
	10.89/0.7	7.58/0.9 14.15		2.12	49.00		13.95/1.4	44.91 5.30 60.29	4:28.35
8583w		Jón Arnar Magnússon	ISL	28.7.69	1	ECp-2	Reykjavík	5 Jul 98
	10.68/2.0	7.63/2.0 15.57		2.07	47.78		14.33W/5.2	44.53 5.00 64.16	4:41.60
	8573				3		Götzis	31 May 98
	10.74/0.5	7.60/-0.2 16.03		2.03	47.66		14.24/0.7	47.82 5.10 59.77	4:46.43
8580		Kai Kazmirek	GER	28.1.91	4	OG	Rio de Janeiro	18 Aug 16
	10.78/-0.1	7.69/-1.0 14.20		2.10	46.75		14.62/0.7	43.25 5.00 64.60	4:31.25
8574		Christian Plaziat	FRA	28.10.63	1	EC	Split	29 Aug 90
	10.72/-0.6	7.77/1.1 14.19		2.10	47.10		13.98/0.7	44.36 5.00 54.72	4:27.83
	(40)							
8574		Aleksandr Yurkov	UKR	21.7.75	4		Götzis	4 Jun 00
	10.69/0.9	7.93/1.8 15.26		2.03	49.74		14.56/-0.9	47.85 5.15 58.92	4:32.49
8571		Lev Lobodin	RUS	1.4.69	3	EC	Budapest	20 Aug 98
	10.66w/2.2	7.42/0.2 15.67		2.03	48.65		13.97/0.9	46.55 5.20 56.55	4:30.27
8566		Sebastian Chmara	POL	21.11.71	1		Alhama de Murcia	17 May 98
	10.97w/2.9	7.56/1.2 16.03		2.10	48.27		14.32/1.8	44.39 5.20 57.25	4:29.66
8558		Pascal Behrenbruch	GER	19.1.85	1	EC	Helsinki	28 Jun 12
	10.93/0.8	7.15/-0.8 16.89		1.97	48.54		14.16/0.2	48.24 5.00 67.45	4:34.02
8554		Attila Zsivoczky	HUN	29.4.77	5		Götzis	4 Jun 00
	10.64w/2.1	7.24/-1.0 15.72		2.18	48.13		14.87/-0.9	45.64 4.65 63.57	4:23.13
8548		Paul Meier	GER	27.7.71	3	WCh	Stuttgart	20 Aug 93
	10.57/0.9	7.57/1.1 15.45		2.15	47.73		14.63/0.0	45.72 4.60 61.22	4:32.05
8547		Igor Sobolevskiy	UKR	4.5.62	2	NC	Kyiv	22 Jun 84
	10.64/0.7	7.71/0.2 15.93		2.01	48.24		14.82/0.3	50.54 4.40 67.40	4:32.84
8539(w)		Lindon	GRN	28.2.93	1	SEC	Columbia, SC	12 May 17
	10.64w/3.6	7.35w/2.1 15.18		2.05	48.74		14.45/1.8	55.22 4.70 68.97	4:55.91
8539		Eelco Sintnicolaas	NED	7.4.87	2	Hypo	Götzis	28 May 17
	10.57/0.5	7.61/0.6 14.62		1.91	48.37		14.16/-1.2	43.52 5.40 62.13	4:30.32
8534		Siegfried Stark	GDR	12.6.55	1	OT	Halle	4 May 80
	11.10w	7.64 15.81		2.03	49.53		14.86w	47.20 5.00 68.70	4:27.7
8534w/8478		Antonio Peñalver	ESP	1.12.68	1		Alhama de Murcia	24 May 92
(7.19w/4.0)		10.76w/3.9	7.42W/6.2 16.50		2.12	49.50		14.32/0.8	47.38 5.00 59.32	4:39.94
	(51)							

100th man 8364, 200th 8204, 300th 8105, 400th 8012, 500th 7935

4 x 100 METRES RELAY

36.84 WR	JAM	N Carter 10.1, Frater 8.9, Blake 9.0, Bolt 8.8		1	OG	London (OS)	11 Aug 12
37.04 WR	JAM	N Carter, Frater, Blake, Bolt		1	WCh	Daegu	4 Sep 11
37.10	USA	Coleman, Gatlin, Rodgers, N.Lyles 8.77		1	WCh	Doha	5 Oct 19
37.27	JAM	Powell, Blake, Ashmeade, Bolt		1	OG	Rio de Janeiro	19 Aug 16
37.31	JAM	Mullings, Frater, Bolt, Powell		1	WCh	Berlin	22 Aug 09
37.36	JAM	Carter, Bailey-Cole, Ashmeade, Bolt		1	WCh	Moskva	18 Aug 13
37.36	JAM	Carter, Powell, Ashmeade, Bolt		1	WCh	Beijing	29 Aug 15
37.36	GBR	Gemili, Hughes, Kilty, Mitchell-Blake 8.91		2	WCh	Doha	5 Oct 19

4 x 100m - 4 x 200m RELAY A-T   223

Mark	Wind	Name	Nat	Born	Pos	Meet	Venue	Date
37.38		USA Demps, Patton, Kimmons, Gatlin			1h2	OG	London (OS)	10 Aug 12
37.38		USA Rodgers, Gatlin, Gay, R.Bailey			1	W.Rly	Nassau	2 May 15
37.39		JAM Carter, Frater, Blake, Bailey-Cole			1h1	OG	London (OS)	10 Aug 12
37.40 WR		USA Marsh, Burrell, Mitchell, C Lewis			1	OG	Barcelona	8 Aug 92
37.40 WR		USA Drummond, Cason, D Mitchell, L Burrell			1s1	WCh	Stuttgart	21 Aug 93
37.41		JAM Carter, Powell, Dwyer, Ashmeade			1h2	WCh	Beijing	29 Aug 15
37.43		JPN Tada, Shiraishi, Kiryu, Sani Brown 8.96			3	WCh	Doha	5 Oct 19
37.45		USA Kimmons, Spearmon, Gay, Rodgers			1	WK	Zürich	19 Aug 10
37.47		GBR Ujah, Gemili, Talbot, Mitchell-Blake			1	WCh	London (OS)	12 Aug 17
37.48		USA Drummond, Cason, D Mitchell, L Burrell			1	WCh	Stuttgart	22 Aug 93
37.50 WR		USA Cason, Burrell, Mitchell, C Lewis			1	WCh	Tokyo	1 Sep 91
37.52		USA Rodgers, Gatlin, Bacon, Coleman			2	WCh	London (OS)	12 Aug 17
37.56		GBR Gemili, Hughes, Kilty, Mitchell-Blake			1h1	WCh	Doha	4 Oct 19
37.58		USA 'Red' Silmon, Rodgers, Salaam, Gatlin			1	Herc	Monaco	19 Jul 13
37.58		JAM Livermore, Bailey-Cole, Ashmeade, Bolt			1	CG	Glasgow	2 Aug 14
37.59		USA Drummond, Montgomery, B Lewis, Greene			1	WCh	Sevilla	29 Aug 99
37.59		USA Conwright, Spearmon, Gay, Smoots			1	WCp	Athína	16 Sep 06
37.60		JPN Yamagata, Iizuka, Kiryu, Cambridge			2	OG	Rio de Janeiro	19 Aug 16
37.60		GBR Ujah, Hughes, Kilty, Mitchell-Blake			1	DL	London (OS)	21 Jul 19
37.61		USA Drummond, Williams, B Lewis, Greene			1	OG	Sydney	30 Sep 00
37.61		USA Kimmons, Gatlin, Gay, Bailey			1	Herc	Monaco	20 Jul 11
37.61		GBR Ujah, Hughes, Gemili, Mitchell-Blake			1	DL	London (OS)	22 Jul 18
		(30 performances by teams from 4 nations) Further bests by nations:						
37.62		TTO Brown, Burns, Callander, Thompson			2	WCh	Berlin	22 Aug 09
37.64		CAN Haynes, A.Brown, Rodney, De Grasse			3	OG	Rio de Janeiro	19 Aug 16
37.65		RSA Dlodlo, Magakwe, Munyai, Simbine			1h2	WCh	Doha	4 Oct 19
37.72		BRA do Nascimento, V dos Santos, D Silva, de Oliveira			4	WCh	Doha	5 Oct 19
37.79 WR		FRA Morinière, Sangouma 8.90, Trouabal, Marie-Rose			1	EC	Split	1 Sep 90
37.79		CHN Su Bingtian, Xu Zhouzheng, Wu Zhiqiang, Xie Zhenye			3h2	WCh	Doha	4 Oct 19
		(10)						
37.91		NED Van Gool, Burnet, Paulina, Martina			5h2	WCh	Doha	4 Oct 19
37.94		NGR O Ezinwa, Adeniken, Obikwelu, D Ezinwa			1s2	WCh	Athína	9 Aug 97
37.98		TUR Barnes, Harvey, Hekimoglu, Guliyev			2	EC	Berlin	12 Aug 18
38.00		CUB Simón, Lamela, Isasi, Aguilera			3	OG	Barcelona	8 Aug 92
38.01		ANT Walsh, D.Bailey, Jarvis, Francis			4h2	WCh	Beijing	29 Aug 15
38.02		URS Yevgenyev, Bryzgin, Muravyov, Krylov			2	WCh	Roma	6 Sep 87
38.02		GER Reus, Unger, Kosenkow, Jakubczyk			1		Weinheim	27 Jul 13
38.11		ITA Cattaneo, Jacobs, Manenti, Tortu			4h1	WCh	Doha	4 Oct 19
38.12		GHA Duah, Nkansah, Zakari, Tuffour			1s1	WCh	Athína	9 Aug 97
38.17		AUS Henderson, Jackson, Brimacombe, Marsh			1s2	WCh	Göteborg	12 Aug 95
		(20)						
38.31		POL Masztak, Kuc, Kubaczyk, Krynski			6h2	OG	London (OS)	10 Aug 12
38.41		SKN Lestrod, Rogers, Adams, Lawrence			6h1	OG	London (OS)	10 Aug 12
38.41		BAR S.Brathwaite, Burke, B.Ellis, Hoyte			1	CAG	Barranquilla	2 Aug 18
38.45		AHO Goeloe, Raffaela, Duzant, Martina			6	WCh	Helsinki	13 Aug 05
38.46		URS/RUS Zharov, Krylov, Fatun, Goremykin			4	EC	Split	1 Sep 90
38.46		ESP Viles, Ruiz, Hortelano, Rodríguez			4h1	WCh	Moskva	18 Aug 13
38.47		HKG Tang Yik Chun, Lai Chun Ho, Ng Ka Fung, Tsui Chi Ho			1		Taipei	26 May 12
38.52		BAH Griffith, Fraser, Hart, T.Smith			3h1	CG	Glasgow	1 Aug 14
38.52		DOM De Oloe, Andujar, Del Carmen, Martinez			1	IbAm	Rio de Janeiro	16 May 16
38.53		UKR Rurak, Osovich, Kramarenko, Dologodin (30)			1	ECp	Madrid	1 Jun 96
Multi-nation team								
37.46		Racers TC Bailey/ANT, Blake JAM, Forsythe JAM, Bolt JAM			1	LGP	London (CP)	25 Jul 09
Hand timed								
38.3 A		UKR Kravtsov, Smelyk, Suprun, Ibrahimov			2		Erzurum	10 Jun 17
One man disqualified for drugs								
37.04		USA Kimmons 10.1, Gatlin 8.9, Gay ¶ 9.0, Bailey 9.0			(2)	OG	London (OS)	11 Aug 12
37.10 (WR)		JAM N Carter ¶, Frater, Bolt, Powell			(1)	OG	Beijing	22 Aug 08
37.91		NGR Asonze ¶, Obikwelu, Effiong, Aliu			(3)	WCh	Sevilla	29 Aug 99

4 x 200 METRES RELAY

1:18.63 WR	JAM Ashmeade 20.5, Weir 19.2, J Brown 19.6, Y Blake 19.4		1	WRly	Nassau	24 May 14
1:18.68 WR	USA - Santa Monica Track Club					
	Marsh 20.0, Burrell 19.6, Heard 19.7, C Lewis 19.4		1	MSR	Walnut	17 Apr 94
1:19.10	World All-Stars		2	MSR	Walnut	17 Apr 94
	Drummond USA 20.4, Mitchell USA 19.3, Bridgewater USA 20.3, Regis GBR 19.1					
1:19.11 WR	Santa Monica TC/USA M.Marsh, L Burrell, Heard, C Lewis		1	Penn	Philadelphia	25 Apr 92
1:19.16	USA Red Team Crawford, Clay, Patton, Gatlin		1	PennR	Philadelphia	26 Apr 03
1:19.20	CAN Smellie, Rodney, De Grasse, A.Brown		1	FlaR	Gainesville	2 Apr 16
1:19.38 WR	Santa Monica TC/USA Everett, Burrell, Heard, C Lewis		1	R-W	Koblenz	23 Aug 89

MFN All-time

224 4x200m – 4x400m RELAY A-T

Mark	Wind	Name	Nat	Born	Pos	Meet	Venue	Date
1:19.39		USA Blue Drummond, Crawford, B Williams, Greene			1	PennR	Philadelphia	28 Apr 01
1:19.42		CAN Smellie, Rodney, De Grasse, Brown			1	W.Rly	Nassau	23 Apr 17
1:19.45		Santa Monica TC/USA DeLoach, Burrell, C.Lewis, Heard			1	Penn	Philadelphia	27 Apr 91
Best non-US nations								
1:20.42		RSA Magakwe, van Wyk, Dambile, Simbine			2	WRly	Yokohama	12 May 19
1:20.51		SKN A Adams, L Roland, BJ Lawrence, A Clarke			2	WRly	Nassau	24 May 14
1:20.66		FRA Lemaitre, Fonsat, Bassaw, Romain			3	WRly	Nassau	25 May 14
1:21.10		ITA Tilli, Simionato, Bongiorno, Mennea			1		Cagliari	29 Sep 83
1:21.22		POL Tulin, Balcerzak, Pilarczyk, Urbas			2		Gdansk	14 Jul 01
1:21.29		GBR Adam, Mafe, Christie, Regis			1	4N	Birmingham	23 Jun 89

4 x 400 METRES RELAY

Mark		Nat	Names	Pos	Meet	Venue	Date
2:54.29	WR	USA	Valmon 44.5, Watts 43.6, Reynolds 43.23, Johnson 42.94	1	WCh	Stuttgart	22 Aug 93
2:55.39		USA	Merritt 44.4, Taylor 43.7, Neville 44.16, Wariner 43.18	1	OG	Beijing	23 Aug 08
2:55.56		USA	Merritt 44.4, Taylor 43.7, Williamson 44.32, Wariner 43.10	1	WCh	Osaka	2 Sep 07
2:55.74	WR	USA	Valmon 44.6, Watts 43.00, M Johnson 44.73, S Lewis 43.41	1	OG	Barcelona	8 Aug 92
2:55.91		USA	O Harris 44.5, Brew 43.6, Wariner 43.98, Williamson 43.83	1		Athína	28 Aug 04
2:55.99		USA	L Smith 44.62, A Harrison 43.84, Mills 43.66, Maybank 43.87	1	OG	Atlanta	3 Aug 96
2:56.16A	WR	USA	Matthews 45.0, Freeman 43.2, James 43.9, Evans 44.1	1	OG	Ciud. México	20 Oct 68
2:56.16	WR	USA	Everett 43.79, S Lewis 43.69, Robinzine 44.74, Reynolds 43.94	1	OG	Seoul	1 Oct 88
2:56.60		GBR	I Thomas 44.92, Baulch 44.19, Richardson 43.62, Black 43.87	2	OG	Atlanta	3 Aug 96
2:56.65		GBR	Thomas 44.8, Black 44.2, Baulch 44.08, Richardson 43.57	2	WCh	Athína	10 Aug 97
2:56.69		USA	Kerley 44.5, Cherry 43.6, London 44.43, Benjamin 44.19	1	WCh	Doha	6 Oct 19
2:56.72		BAH	Brown 44.9, Pinder 43.5, Mathieu 44.25, Miller 44.01	1	OG	London (OS)	10 Aug 12
2:56.75		JAM	McDonald 44.5, Haughton 44.4, McFarlane 44.37, Clarke 43.51	3	WCh	Athína	10 Aug 97
2:56.91		USA	Rock 44.7, Brew 44.3, Williamson 44.40, Wariner 43.49	1	WCh	Helsinki	14 Aug 05
2:57.05		USA	Nellum 45.2, Mance 43.5, McQuay 43.41, Taylor 44.85	2	OG	London (OS)	10 Aug 12
2:57.25		USA	Verburg 44.9, McQuay 44.1, C Taylor 44.6, L Merritt 43.8	1	WRly	Nassau	25 May 14
2:57.29		USA	Everett 45.1, Haley 44.0, McKay 44.20, Reynolds 44.00	1	WCh	Roma	6 Sep 87
2:57.30		USA	Hall 45.3, McQuay 43.2, Roberts 44.79, Merritt 43.97	1	OG	Rio de Janeiro	20 Aug 16
2:57.32		USA	Ramsey 44.9, Mills 44.6, Reynolds 43.74, Johnson 44.11	1	WCh	Göteborg	13 Aug 95
2:57.32		BAH	McKinney 44.9, Moncur 44.6, A Williams 44.34, Brown 43.42	2	WCh	Helsinki	14 Aug 05
2:57.53		GBR	Black 44.7, Redmond 44.0, Regis 44.22, Akabusi 44.59	1	WCh	Tokyo	1 Sep 91
2:57.57		USA	Valmon 44.9, Watts 43.4, D.Everett 44.31, Pettigrew 44.93	2	WCh	Tokyo	1 Sep 91
2:57.59		BAH	L Williams 45.0, Pinder 43.8, C Brown 44.2, Mathieu 44.6	2	WRly	Nassau	25 May 14
2:57.82		USA	Verburg 44.9, McQuay 44.3, Nellum 44.38, Merritt 44.18	1	WCh	Beijing	30 Aug 15
2:57.86		USA	Taylor 45.4, Wariner 43.6, Clement 44.72, Merritt 44.16	1	WCh	Berlin	23 Aug 09
2:57.87		USA	L Smith 44.59, Rouser 44.33, Mills 44.32, Maybank 44.63	1s2	OG	Atlanta	2 Aug 96
2:57.90		JAM	Bloomfield 44.9, Allen 44.2, Thomas 44.3, Gaye 44.5	2	WCh	Doha	6 Oct 19
2:57.91		USA	Nix 45.59, Armstead 43.97, Babers 43.75, McKay 44.60	1	OG	Los Angeles	11 Aug 84
2:57.97		JAM	McDonald, Haughton McFarlane, D Clarke	1	PAm	Winnipeg	30 Jul 99
2:58.00		POL	Rysiukiewicz 45.6, Czubak 44.2, Haczek 44.0, Mackowiak 44.2	2	GWG	Uniondale, NY	22 Jul 98
		(30/5	plus 6 times for teams that contained an athlete who was subsequently banned for drugs abuse				
2:58.12		TTO	Solomon 46.1, Richards 43.4, Cedenio 44.41, L. Gordon 44.08	1	WCh	London (OS)	13 Aug 17
2:58.52		BEL	Watrin 46.0, D.Borlée 44.1, D.Borlée 44.71, K.Borlée 43.67	4	OG	Rio de Janeiro	20 Aug 16
2:58.56		BRA	Cl. da Silva 44.6, A dos Santos 45.1, de Araújo 45.0, Parrela 43.9	2	PAm	Winnipeg	30 Jul 99
2:58.68		NGR	Chukwu 45.18, Monye 44.49, Bada 44.70, Udo-Obong 44.31	1	OG	Sydney	30 Sep 00
2:58.96		FRA	Djhone 45.4, Keita 44.7, Diagana 44.69, Raquil 44.15	2	WCh	Saint-Denis	31 Aug 03
		(10)					
2:59.06		BOT	Makwala 44.9, Sibanda 43.9, Nkobolo 44.94, Maotoanong 45.28	5	OG	Rio de Janeiro	20 Aug 16
2:59.13		CUB	Martínez 45.6, Herrera 44.38, Tellez 44.81, Hernández 44.34	1h2	OG	Barcelona	7 Aug 92
2:59.21		RSA	Pistorius 45.54, Mogawane 43.97, de Beer 44.24, Victor 45.20	3h1	WCh	Daegu	1 Sep 11
2:59.45		RUS	Denmukhametov 46.0, Trenikin 44.5, Kudryavtsev 44.63, Ivashko 44.29	4h1	WCh	Beijing	29 Aug 15
2:59.50		COL	Perlaza 45.4, Palomeque 44.7, Solís 45.0, Zambrano 44.4	4	WCh	Doha	6 Oct 19
2:59.63		KEN	D Kitur 45.9, S Kitur 45.13, Kipkemboi 44.76, Kemboi 44.33	3h2	OG	Barcelona	7 Aug 92
2:59.70		AUS	Frayne 45.38, Clark 43.86, Minihan 45.07, Mitchell 45.39	4	OG	Los Angeles	11 Aug 84
2:59.86		GDR	Möller 45.8, Schersing 44.63, Carlowitz 45.3, Schönlebe 44.1	1	vURS	Erfurt	23 Jun 85
2:59.95		YUG	Jovkovic, Djurovic, Macev, Brankovic 44.3	2h3	WCh	Tokyo	31 Aug 91
2:59.96		FRG	Dobeleit 45.7, Henrich 44.3, Itt 45.12, Schmid 44.93	4	WCh	Roma	6 Sep 87
		(20)					
3:00.15		DOM	Cuesta 45.4, Soriano 43.8, J.Santos 46.58, L.Santos 44.36	6h2	WCh	Beijing	29 Aug 15
3:00.56		QAT	Samba 44.6, M.Abbas 45.2, El Nour 46.43, Haroun 44.41	1	AsiG	Jakarta	30 Aug 18
3:00.64		SEN	Diarra 46.53, Dia 44.94, Ndiaye 44.70, Faye 44.47	4	OG	Atlanta	3 Aug 96
3:00.65		ESP	Husillos 45.4, Búa 45.3, Echeverry 45.26, García 44.75	5	WCh	London (OS)	13 Aug 17
3:00.76		JPN	Karube 45.88, Ito 44.86, Osakada 45.08, Omori 44.94	5	OG	Atlanta	3 Aug 96
3:00.79		ZIM	Chiwira 46.2, Mukomana 44.6, Ngidhi 45.79, Harnden 44.20	2h3	WCh	Athína	9 Aug 97
3:00.82A		VEN	A Ramírez 45.7, Aguilar 45.3, Acevedo 44.7, Longart 45.2	3	PAm	Guadalajara	28 Oct 11
3:00.91		IND	Kunhu, Anas, Dharun, Rajiv	1		Bengaluru	10 Jun 16
3:01.12		FIN	Lönnqvist 46.7, Salin 45.1, Karttunen 44.8, Kukkoaho 44.5	6	OG	München	10 Sep 72
3:01.26		IRL	Gregan 46.1, Murphy 45.2, Barr 45.05, English 44.96	(30) 8h2	WCh	Beijing	29 Aug 15

4 x 400m – 4 x 800m – 4x1500m – 3000m - 5000m WALKS A-T

Mark	Wind	Name	Nat	Born	Pos	Meet	Venue	Date

Including subsequently banned athlete
2:54.20(WR) USA Young 44.3, Pettigrew ¶ 43.2, Washington 43.5, Johnson 43.2 (1) GWG Uniondale, NY 22 Jul 98
2:56.35   USA A Harrison 44.36, Pettigrew 44.17, C Harrison 43.53, Johnson 44.29 (1) OG Sydney   30 Sep 00
2:56.45   USA J Davis 45.2, Pettigrew 43.92, Taylor 43.92, M Johnson 43.49   (1) WCh Sevilla   29 Aug 99
2:56.47   USA Young 44.6, Pettigrew 43.1, Jones 44.80, Washington 44.80   (1) WCh Athína   10 Aug 97
2:56.60   USA Red Taylor 45.0, Pettigrew 44.2, Washington 43.7, Johnson 43.7 (1) PennR Philadelphia 29 Apr 00
2:57.54   USA Byrd 45.9, Pettigrew 43.9, Brew 44.03, Taylor 43.71   1 WCh Edmonton 12 Aug 01
2:58.06   RUS Dyldin 45.5, Frolov 44.6, Kokorin 44.34, Alekseyev ¶ 43.56 3 OG Beijing   23 Aug 08

4 x 800 METRES RELAY

7:02.43 WR KEN Mutua 1:46.73, Yiampoy 1:44.38, Kombich 1:45.92, Bungei 1:45.40 1 VD Bruxelles 25 Aug 06
7:02.82   USA   2 VD Bruxelles 25 Aug 06
      J Harris 1:47.05, Robinson 1:44.03, Burley 1:46.05, Krummenacker 1:45.69
7:03.89 WR GBR Elliott 1:49.14, Cook 1:46.20, Cram 1:44.54, Coe 1:44.01   1 London (CP) 30 Aug 82
7:04.70   RSA van Oudtshoorn 1:46.9, Sepeng 1:45.2, Kotze 1:48.3, J Botha 1:44.3 1 Stuttgart   6 Jun 99
7:06.66   QAT Sultan 1:45.81, Al-Badri 1:46.71, Suleiman 1:45.89, Ali Kamal 1:48.25 4 VD Bruxelles 25 Aug 06
7:07.40   URS Masunov, Kostetskiy, Matvetev, Kalinkin   1   Moskva   5 Aug 84
7:08.5 WR FRG Kinder 1:46.9, Adams 1:47.7, Bogatzki 1:47.9, Kemper 1:46.2   1 Wiesbaden 13 Aug 66
7:08.89   POL Konieczny 1:48.9, Krawczyk 1:49.1, Lewandowski 1:45.9, Kszczot 1:44.8 2 WRly Nassau 24 May 14

4 x 1500 METRES RELAY

14:22.22 WR KEN C Cheboi 3:38.5, S Kiplagat 3:32.4, Magut 3:39.0, A Kiprop 3:32.3 1 WRly Nassau 25 May 14
14:36.23 WR KEN W Biwott 3:38.5, Gathimba 3:39.5, G Rono 3:41.4, Choge 3:36.9   1 VD Bruxelles   4 Sep 09
14:38.8 WR FRG Wessinghage 3:38.8, Hudak 3:39.1, Lederer 3:44.6, Fleschen 3:36.3 1 Köln   16 Aug 77
14:39.97 Nike Bowerman 'B' (USA) Jager c.3:39, Fisher 3:37, McGorty 3:38, Lomong 3:39 1 Portland 31 Jul 20
14:40.4 WR NZL Polhill 3:42.9, Walker 3:40.4, Dixon 3:41.2, Quax 3:35.9   1 Oslo   22 Aug 73
14:40.80 USA Casey 3:38.2, Torrence 3:36.6, Leer 3:39.3, Manzano 3:46.7   2 WRly Nassau 25 May 14
14:41.22 ETH Gebremedhin 3:39.9, Fida 3:37.5, Z Alemayehu 3:46.5, Wote 3:37.3 3 WRly Nassau 25 May 14
14:45.63 URS Kalutskiy, Yakovlev, Legeda, Lotarev   1 Leningrad 4 Aug 85
14:46.04 AUS Gregson 3:39.1, McEntee 3:44.9, Birmingham 3:38.3, Williamsz 3:43.7 4 WRly Nassau 25 May 14
14:46.16 Larios, ESP Jiménez 3:40.9, Pancorbo 3:41.2, A García 3:43.9, Viciosa 3:40.2 1 Madrid   5 Sep 97
14:48.2   FRA Bégouin 3:44.5, Lequement 3:44.3, Philippe 3:42.2, Dien 3:37.2 2 Bourges 23 Jun 79
Mixed Team: 14:44.31 Ali BRN, Birgen KEN, N Kemboi KEN, Campbell IRL   2 VD Bruxelles 4 Sep 09

4 x 1 MILE RELAY

15:49.08 IRL Coghlan 4:00.2, O'Sullivan 3:55.3, O'Mara 3:56.6, Flynn 3:56.98 1 Dublin   17 Aug 85
15:59.57 NZL Rogers 3:57.2, Bowden 4:02.5, Gilchrist 4:02.8, Walker 3:57.07   1 Auckland   2 Mar 83

4 x 110m/120y HURDLES

52.94   USA Blue Richardson, Harris, Merritt, Oliver   1 DrakeR Des Moines 25 Apr 15
53.08   All Stars Riley JAM, R Brathwaite BAR, Parchment JAM, Swift BAR 2 DrakeR Des Moines 25 Apr 15
53.31y USA Red Oliver, Herring, Brown, Merritt   1 PennR Philadelphia 25 Apr 08
53.36   USA Bramlett, Moore, Payne, Merritt   1 DNG Stockholm   7 Aug 07

3000 METRES TRACK WALK

10:43.84	Tom	Bosworth	GBR	17.1.90	1	Anniv	London (OS)	21 Jul 18
10:47.08	Lebogang	Shange	RSA	1.8.90	2	Anniv	London (OS)	21 Jul 18
10:47.11	Giovanni	De Benedictis	ITA	8.1.68	1		S.Giovanni Valdarno	19 May 90
10:52.44+	Yohann	Diniz	FRA	1.1.78	1	in 5k	Villeneuve d'Ascq	27 Jun 08
10:54.70	Dane	Bird-Smith	AUS	15.7.92	1		Brisbane	11 Feb 17

Indoors
10:30.28	Tom	Bosworth	GBR	17.1.90	1	GP	Glasgow	25 Feb 18
10:31.42	Andreas	Erm	GER	12.3.76	1		Halle	4 Feb 01
10:49.33	Christopher	Linke	GER	24.10.88	1		Erfurt	9 Feb 18
10:50.0	Denis	Nizhegorodov	RUS	26.7.80	1		Saransk	4 Dec 06
10:52.15	Nils	Brembach	GER	23.2.93	2		Erfurt	9 Feb 18
10:52.77	Callum	Wilkinson	GBR	14.3.97	2	GP	Glasgow	25 Feb 18
10:53+	Mikhail	Shchennikov	RUS	24.12.67	1	in 5k	Moskva	14 Feb 95
10:53.3	Igor	Yerokhin	RUS	4.9.85	2		Saransk	4 Dec 06
10:54.61	Carlo	Mattioli	ITA	23.10.54	1		Milano	6 Feb 80

5000 METRES TRACK WALK

18:05.49	Hatem	Ghoula	TUN	7.6.73	1		Tunis	1 May 97
18:17.22	Robert	Korzeniowski	POL	30.7.68	1		Reims	3 Jul 92
18:18.01	Yohann	Diniz	FRA	1.1.78	1		Villeneuve d'Ascq	27 Jun 08
18:20.14	Koki	Ikeda	JPN	3.5.98	1		Inzai	25 Oct 20
18:26.70	Yuta	Koga	JPN	15.7.99	2		Inzai	25 Oct 20
18:27.34	Francisco Javier	Fernández ¶	ESP	6.3.77	1		Villeneuve d'Ascq	8 Jun 07

Indoors
18:07.08	Mikhail	Shchennikov	RUS	24.12.67	1		Moskva	14 Feb 95
18:08.86	Ivano	Brugnetti	ITA	1.9.76	1	NC	Ancona	17 Feb 07
18:11.41	Ronald	Weigel	GDR	8.8.59	1mx		Wien	13 Feb 88

5000m, 10,000m - 20 KILOMETRES WALK A-T

Mark	Wind	Name		Nat	Born	Pos	Meet	Venue	Date
18:11.8		Valeriy	Borchin ¶	RUS	11.9.86	1		Saransk	30 Dec 10
18:15.25		Grigoriy	Kornev	RUS	14.3.61	1		Moskva	7 Feb 92
18:15.54		Andrey	Ruzavin	RUS	28.3.86	1		Samara	30 Jan 14
18:16.54 ?		Frants	Kostyukevich	BLR	4.4.63	2	NC	Gomel	4 Feb 89
18:16.76		Yohann	Diniz	FRA	1.1.78	1		Reims	7 Dec 14
18:19.97		Giovanni	De Benedictis	ITA	8.1.68	1	EI	Genova	28 Feb 92
18:20.97		Tom	Bosworth	GBR	17.1.90	1	NC	Glasgow	23 Feb 20
18:21.76		Ruslan	Dmytrenko	UKR	22.3.86	2		Samara	30 Jan 14
18:22.25		Andreas	Erm	GER	12.3.76	1	NC	Dortmund	25 Feb 01
18:23.18		Rishat	Shafikov	RUS	23.1.70	1		Samara	1 Mar 97
18:24.13		Francisco Javier	Fernández ¶	ESP	6.3.77	1		Belfast	17 Feb 07
18:27.15		Alessandro	Gandellini	ITA	30.4.73	1	NC	Genova	12 Feb 00
18:27.80		Jozef	Pribilinec	SVK	6.7.60	2	WI	Indianapolis	7 Mar 87
18:27.95		Stefan	Johansson	SWE	11.4.67	3	EI	Genova	28 Feb 92
Drugs dq: 18:17.13		Vladimir	Kanaykin ¶	RUS	21.3.85	(2)	Winter	Moskva	5 Feb 12
18:26.82		Sergey	Bakulin ¶	RUS	13.11.86	(3)	Winter	Moskva	5 Feb 12

10,000 METRES TRACK WALK

Mark	Wind	Name		Nat	Born	Pos	Meet	Venue	Date
37:25.21		Eiki	Takahashi	JPN	19.11.92	1		Inzai	14 Nov 20
37:25.90		Koki	Ikeda	JPN	3.5.98	2		Inzai	14 Nov 20
37:35.00		Yuta	Koga	JPN	15.7.99	3		Inzai	14 Nov 20
37:53.09		Francisco Javier	Fernández ¶	ESP	6.3.77	1	NC	Santa Cruz de Tenerife	27 Jul 08
37:58.08		Daisuke	Matsunaga	JPN	24.3.95	1		Kitami	7 Jul 18
37:58.6		Ivano	Brugnetti	ITA	1.9.76	1		Sesto San Gioavnni	23 Jul 05
38:02.60		Jozef	Pribilinec	SVK	6.7.60	1		Banská Bystrica	30 Aug 85
38:03.95		Perseus	Karlström	AUS	24.7.55	1		Sydney	25 Sep 86
38:06.28		Miguel Ángel	López	ESP	3.7.88	1	NC	Gijón	24 Jul 16
38:06.6		David	Smith (10)	AUS	24.7.55	1		Sydney	25 Sep 86
38:08.13		Yohann	Diniz	FRA	1.1.78	1	NC	Reims	12 Jul 14
38:10.23		Yusuke	Suzuki	JPN	2.1.88	1		Abashiri	16 Jul 15
38:12.13		Ronald	Weigel	GDR	8.8.59	1		Potsdam	10 May 86
38:18.0+		Valdas	Kazlauskas	LTU	23.2.58	1		Moskva	18 Sep 83
38:20.0		Moacir	Zimmermann	BRA	30.12.83	1		Blumenau	7 Jun 08
38:23.73			Wang Zhen	CHN	24.8.91	1		Genova	8 Feb 15
38:24 0+		Bernardo	Segura	MEX	11.2.70	1	SGP	Fana	7 May 94
38:23.95		Masatora	Kawano	JPN	23.10.98	4		Inzai	14 Nov 20
38:24.23		Dane	Bird-Smith	AUS	15.7.92	1	NC	Sydney	31 Mar 17
38:24.31		Hatem	Ghoula (20)	TUN	7.6.73	1		Tunis	30 May 98

20 KILOMETRES WALK

Mark	Wind	Name		Nat	Born	Pos	Meet	Venue	Date
1:16:36 WR		Yusuke	Suzuki	JPN	2.1.88	1	AsiC	Nomi	15 Mar 15
1:16:43		Sergey	Morozov ¶	RUS	21.3.88	1	NC	Saransk	8 Jun 08
1:17:02		Yohann	Diniz	FRA	1.1.78	1	NC	Arles	8 Mar 15
1:17:15		Toshikazu	Yamanishi	JPN	15.2.96	1	AsiC	Nomi	17 Mar 19
1:17:16 WR		Vladimir	Kanaykin ¶	RUS	21.3.85	1	RWC	Saransk	29 Sep 07
1:17:21 WR		Jefferson	Pérez	ECU	1.7.74	1	WCh	Saint-Denis	23 Aug 03
1:17:22 WR		Francisco Javier	Fernández ¶	ESP	6.3.77	1		Turku	28 Apr 02
1:17:23		Vladimir	Stankin	RUS	2.1.74	1	NC-w	Adler	8 Feb 04
1:17:24			Diniz			1		Lugano	15 Mar 15
1:17:24		Masatora	Kawano	JPN	23.10.98	2		Nomi	17 Mar 19
1:17:25		Sergey	Shirobokov (10)	RUS	16.2.99	1	NC	Cheboksary	9 Jun 18
1:17:25		Koki	Ikeda	JPN	3.5.98	3		Nomi	17 Mar 19
1:17:25.6t		Bernardo	Segura	MEX	11.2.70	1	SGP	Bergen (Fana)	7 May 94
1:17:26		Eiki	Takahashi	JPN	19.11.92	1	NC	Kobe	18 Feb 18
1:17:33		Nathan	Deakes	AUS	17.8.77	1		Cixi	23 Apr 05
1:17:36			Kanaykin			1	NC	Cheboksary	17 Jun 07
1:17:36			Wang Zhen	CHN	24.8.91	1		Taicang	30 Mar 12
1:17:36			Yamanishi			1	NC	Kobe	16 Feb 20
1:17:38		Valeriy	Borchin ¶	RUS	11.9.86	1	NC-w	Adler	28 Feb 09
1:17:40			Chen Ding	CHN	5.8.92	2		Taicang	30 Mar 12
1:17:41			Zhu Hongjun	CHN	18.8.83	2		Cixi	23 Apr 05
1:17:41			Yamanishi			2	NC	Kobe	18 Feb 18
1:17:41			Yamanishi			1		La Coruña	8 Jun 19
1:17:43			Diniz			1		Lugano	18 Mar 12
1:17:45		Massimo	Stano	ITA	27.2.92	2		La Coruña	8 Jun 19
1:17:46		Julio	Martínez (20)	GUA	27.9.73	1		Eisenhüttenstadt	8 May 99
1:17:46		Roman	Rasskazov	RUS	28.4.79	1	NC	Moskva	19 May 00
1:17:46		Daisuke	Matsunaga	JPN	24.3.95	3	NC	Kobe	18 Feb 18
1:17:47			Suzuki			4		Nomi	17 Mar 19
1:17:52			Fernández			1		La Coruña	4 Jun 05
		(30/22)							

20 - 30 KILOMETRES WALK A-T

Mark	Wind	Name		Nat	Born	Pos	Meet	Venue	Date
1:17:52		Isamu	Fujisawa	JPN	12.10.87	5		Nomi	17 Mar 19
1:17:53			Cui Zhide	CHN	11.1.83	3		Cixi	23 Apr 05
1:17:54			Wang Kaihua	CHN	16.2.94	1		Huangshan	4 Mar 17
1:17:56		Alejandro	López	MEX	9.2.75	2		Eisenhüttenstadt	8 May 99
1:18:03.3tWR			Bo Lingtang	CHN	12.8.70	1	NC	Beijing	7 Apr 94
1:18:05		Dmitriy	Yesipchuk	RUS	17.11.74	1	NC-w	Adler	4 Mar 01
1:18:06		Viktor	Burayev ¶	RUS	23.8.82	2	NC-w	Adler	4 Mar 01
1:18:06		Vladimir	Parvatkin	RUS	10.10.84	1	NC-w	Adler	12 Mar 05
		(30)							
1:18:07		Perseus	Karlström	SWE	2.5.90	4		La Coruña	8 Jun 19
1:18:07			Li Gaobo	CHN	4.5.89	4		Cixi	23 Apr 05
1:18:12		Artur	Meleshkevich	BLR	11.4.75	1		Brest	10 Mar 01
1:18:13 WR		Pavol	Blazek	SVK	9.7.58	1		Hildesheim	16 Sep 90
1:18:13			Wang Hao	CHN	16.8.89	1	NG	Jinan	22 Oct 09
1:18:14		Mikhail	Khmelnitskiy	BLR	24.7.69	1	NC	Soligorsk	13 May 00
1:18:14		Noé	Hernández	MEX	15.3.78	4	WCh	Saint-Denis	23 Aug 03
1:18:16		Vladimir	Andreyev	RUS	7.9.66	2	NC	Moskva	19 May 00
1:18:17		Ilya	Markov	RUS	19.6.72	2	NC-w	Adler	12 Mar 05
1:18:18		Yevgeniy	Misyulya	BLR	13.3.64	1		Eisenhüttenstadt	11 May 96
		(40)							
1:18:18		Sergey	Bakulin ¶	RUS	13.11.86	2	NC-w	Adler	23 Feb 08
1:18:20 WR		Andrey	Perlov	RUS	12.12.61	1	NC	Moskva	26 May 90
1:18:20		Denis	Nizhegorodov	RUS	26.7.80	3	NC-w	Adler	4 Mar 01
1:18:22		Robert	Korzeniowski	POL	30.7.68	1		Hildesheim	9 Jul 00
1:18:23		Andrey	Makarov	BLR	2.1.71	2	NC	Soligorsk	13 May 00
1:18:24		Alex	Schwazer ¶	ITA	26.12.84	1		Lugano	14 Mar 10
1:18:25		Erick	Barrondo	GUA	14.6.91	3		Lugano	18 Mar 12
1:18:27		Daniel	García	MEX	28.10.71	2	WCp	Podebrady	19 Apr 97
1:18:27			Xing Shucai	CHN	4.8.84	5		Cixi	23 Apr 05
1:18:30			Yu Chaohong	CHN	12.12.76	6		Cixi	23 Apr 05
		(50)		100th man 1:19:14, 200th 1:20:07, 300th 1:20:46, 400th 1:21:26, 500th 1:21:52					
Drugs disqualification									
1:16:53		Vladimir	Kanaykin ¶	RUS	21.3.85	(2)	NC	Saransk	8 Jun 08
1:17:30		Alex	Schwazer ¶	ITA	26.12.84	(1)		Lugano	18 Mar 12
1:17:47		Andrey	Ruzavin ¶	RUS	28.3.86	(1)	NC-w	Sochi	18 Feb 12
1:17:52			Morozov ¶			(2)	NC-w	Sochi	18 Feb 12
1:18:25		Andrey	Krivov ¶	RUS	14.11.85	(3)	NC-w	Sochi	18 Feb 12
1:18:28		Pyotr	Trofimov ¶	RUS	28.11.83	1	NC-w	Sochi	23 Feb 08
1:18:29		Stanislav	Yemelyanov ¶	RUS	23.10.90	(4)	NC-w	Sochi	18 Feb 12

30 KILOMETRES WALK

Mark		Name		Nat	Born	Pos	Meet	Venue	Date
2:01:13+		Vladimir	Kanaykin ¶	RUS	21.3.85	1	in 35k	Adler	19 Feb 06
2:01:44.1t		Maurizio	Damilano	ITA	6.4.57	1		Cuneo	3 Oct 92
2:01:47+			Kanaykin			1	in 35k	Adler	13 Mar 05
2:02:27+			Kanaykin			1	in 35k	Adler	8 Feb 04
2:02:41		Andrey	Perlov	RUS	12.12.61	1	NC-w	Sochi	19 Feb 89
2:02:45		Yevgeniy	Misyulya	BLR	13.3.64	1		Mogilyov	28 Apr 91
2:03:06		Daniel	Bautista	MEX	4.8.52	1		Cherkassy	27 Apr 80
2:03:50+		Vladimir	Parvatkin	RUS	10.10.84	2	in 35k	Adler	19 Feb 06
2:03:56.5t		Thierry	Toutain	FRA	14.2.62	1		Héricourt	24 Mar 91
2:04:00		Aleksandr	Potashov	BLR	12.3.62	1		Adler	14 Feb 93
2:04:24		Valeriy	Spitsyn	RUS	5.12.65	1	NC-w	Sochi	22 Feb 92
2:04:30		Vitaliy	Matsko (10)	RUS	8.6.60	2	NC-w	Sochi	19 Feb 89
2:04:48		Sergey	Bakulin ¶	RUS	13.11.86	1	NC-w	Sochi	19 Feb 18
2:04:49+		Semyon	Lovkin	RUS	14.7.77	1=	in 35k	Adler	1 Mar 03
2:04:49+		Stepan	Yudin	RUS	3.4.80	1=	in 35k	Adler	1 Mar 03
2:04:50+		Sergey	Kirdyapkin ¶	RUS	16.1.80	2	in 35k	Adler	13 Mar 05
2:04:55.5t		Guillaume	Leblanc	CAN	14.4.62	1		Sept-Iles	16 Jun 90
2:05:01		Sergey	Katureyev	RUS	29.9.67	2	NC-w	Sochi	22 Feb 92
2:05:05		Pyotr	Pochenchuk	UKR	26.7.54	2		Cherkassy	27 Apr 80
2:05:06		Nathan	Deakes	AUS	17.8.77	1	NC	Hobart	27 Aug 06
2:05:08+		Denis	Nizhegorodov	RUS	26.7.80	3	in 35k	Adler	19 Feb 06
2:05:09		Mikhail	Shchennikov (20)	RUS	24.12.67	1	NC-w	Sochi	11 Feb 96

35 KILOMETRES WALK

Mark		Name		Nat	Born	Pos	Meet	Venue	Date
2:21:31		Vladimir	Kanaykin ¶	RUS	21.3.85	1	NC-w	Adler	19 Feb 06
2:23:17			Kanaykin			1	NC-w	Adler	8 Feb 04
2:23:17			Kanaykin			1	NC-w	Adler	13 Mar 05
2:24:25		Semyon	Lovkin	RUS	14.7.77	1	NC-w	Adler	1 Mar 03
2:24:25		Sergey	Bakulin ¶	RUS	13.11.86	1	NC-w	Adler	1 Mar 09
2:24:50		Denis	Nizhegorodov	RUS	26.7.80	2	NC-w	Adler	19 Feb 06

35 - 50 KILOMETRES WALK A-T

Mark	Wind	Name		Nat	Born	Pos	Meet	Venue	Date
2:24:53			Bakulin			1	NC-w	Sochi	19 Feb 18
2:24:56			Nizhegorodov			2	NC-w	Adler	1 Mar 09
2:25:19		Andrey	Ruzavin ¶	RUS	28.3.86	3	NC-w	Adler	1 Mar 09
2:25:38		Stepan	Yudin	RUS	3.4.80	2	NC-w	Adler	1 Mar 03
2:25:58		German	Skurygin ¶	RUS	15.9.63	1	NC-w	Adler	20 Feb 98
2:25:59		Mikhail	Ryzhov ¶	RUS	17.12.91	1	NC-w	Sochi	18 Feb 12
2:26:16		Alex	Schwazer ¶	ITA	26.12.84	1		Montalto Di Castro	24 Jan 10
2:26:25		Aleksey	Voyevodin ¶ (10)	RUS	9.8.70	2	NC-w	Adler	8 Feb 04
2:26:29		Yuriy	Andronov	RUS	6.11.71	4	NC-w	Adler	1 Mar 09
2:26:33		Ivan	Noskov	RUS	16.7.88	2	NC-w	Sochi	18 Feb 12
2:26:36		Igor	Yerokhin ¶	RUS	4.9.85	1	NC-w	Sochi	26 Feb 11
2:26:46		Oleg	Ishutkin	RUS	22.7.75	1	NC-w	Adler	9 Feb 97
2:27:02		Yevgeniy	Shmalyuk	RUS	14.1.76	1	NC-w	Adler	20 Feb 00
2:27:07		Dmitriy	Dolnikov	RUS	19.11.72	2	NC-w	Adler	20 Feb 98
2:27:07		Sergey	Sharipov	RUS	14.4.92	1	NC-w	Sochi	18 Feb 17
2:27:21		Pavel	Nikolayev	RUS	18.12.77	3	NC-w	Adler	20 Feb 98
DQ: 2:25:42		Sergey	Kirdyapkin ¶	RUS	18.6.80	(1)	NC-w	Sochi	18 Feb 12
2:25:54		Mikhail	Ryzhov	RUS	17.12.91	(1)	NC-w	Sochi	27 Feb 15

50 KILOMETRES WALK

Mark		Name		Nat	Born	Pos	Meet	Venue	Date
3:32:33 WR		Yohann	Diniz	FRA	1.1.78	1	EC	Zürich	15 Aug 14
3:33:12			Diniz			1	WCh	London	13 Aug 17
3:34:14 WR		Denis	Nizhegorodov	RUS	26.7.80	1	WCp	Cheboksary	11 May 08
3:34:38		Matej	Tóth	SVK	10.2.83	1		Dudince	21 Mar 15
3:35:27.2t WR			Diniz			1		Reims	12 Mar 11
3:35:29			Nizhegorodov			1	NC	Cheboksary	13 Jun 04
3:35:47		Nathan	Deakes	AUS	17.8.77	1	NC	Geelong	2 Dec 06
3:36:03 WR		Robert	Korzeniowski	POL	30.7.68	1	WCh	Saint-Denis	27 Aug 03
3:36:04		Alex	Schwazer ¶	ITA	26.12.84	1	NC	Rosignano Solvay	11 Feb 07
3:36:06			Yu Chaohong	CHN	12.12.76	1	NG	Nanjing	22 Oct 05
3:36:13			Zhao Chengliang	CHN	1.6.84	2	NG	Nanjing	22 Oct 05
3:36:20			Han Yucheng	CHN	16.12.78	1	NC	Nanning	27 Feb 05
3:36:21			Tóth			2	EC	Zürich	15 Aug 14
3:36:39 WR			Korzeniowski			1	EC	München	8 Aug 02
3:36:42		German	Skurygin ¶ (10)	RUS	15.9.63	2	WCh	Saint-Denis	27 Aug 03
3:36:45		Masatora	Kawano	JPN	23.10.98	1		Takahata	27 Oct 19
3:36:53		Jared	Tallent	AUS	17.10.84	1	OG	London	11 Aug 12
3:37:04			Schwazer			2	WCp	Cheboksary	11 May 08
3:37:09			Schwazer			1	OG	Beijing	22 Aug 08
3:37:16			Si Tianfeng	CHN	17.6.84	2	OG	London	11 Aug 12
3:37:26 WR		Valeriy	Spitsyn	RUS	5.12.65	1	NC	Moskva	21 May 00
3:37:39		Satoshi	Maruo	JPN	28.11.91	2		Takahata	27 Oct 19
3:37:41 WR		Andrey	Perlov	RUS	12.12.61	1	NC	Leningrad	5 Aug 89
3:37:41		Ivan	Noskov ¶	RUS	16.7.88	3	EC	Zürich	15 Aug 14
3:37:43			Diniz			1	ECp	Alytus	19 May 19
3:37:46		Andreas	Erm	GER	12.3.76	3	WCh	Saint-Denis	27 Aug 03
3:37:48			Diniz			1	NC	St.Sebastien-sur-Loire	13 Mar 16
3:37:54		Robert	Heffernan	IRL	20.2.78	3	OG	London	11 Aug 12
3:37:56			Heffernan			1	WCh	Moskva	14 Aug 13
3:37:58			Xing Shucai	CHN	4.8.84	2	NC	Nanning	27 Feb 05
	(30/20)								
3:38:01		Aleksey	Voyevodin ¶	RUS	9.8.70	4	WCh	Saint-Denis	27 Aug 03
3:38:02			Wang Qin	CHN	8.5.94	1		Huangshan	9 Mar 19
3:38:08		Sergey	Kirdyapkin ¶	RUS	16.1.80	1	WCh	Helsinki	12 Aug 05
3:38:08		Igor	Yerokhin ¶	RUS	4.9.85	1	NC	Saransk	8 Jun 08
3:38:17 WR		Ronald	Weigel	GDR	8.8.59	1	IM	Potsdam	25 May 86
3:38:29		Vyacheslav	Ivanenko	RUS	3.3.61	1	OG	Seoul	30 Sep 88
3:38:43		Valentí	Massana	ESP	5.7.70	1	NC	Orense	20 Mar 94
3:39:01			Li Jianbo	CHN	14.11.86	4	OG	London	11 Aug 12
3:39:07		Yusuke	Suzuki	JPN	2.1.88	1	NC	Wajima	14 Apr 19
3:39:17			Dong Jimin	CHN	10.10.83	4	NC	Nanning	27 Feb 05
	(30)								
3:39:21		Vladimir	Potemin	RUS	15.1.80	2	NC	Moskva	21 May 00
3:39:22		Sergey	Korepanov	KAZ	9.5.64	1	WCp	Mézidon-Canon	2 May 99
3:39:34		Valentin	Kononen	FIN	7.3.69	1		Dudince	25 Mar 00
3:39:45		Hartwig	Gauder	GDR	10.11.54	3	OG	Seoul	30 Sep 88
3:39:47		Tomohiro	Noda	JPN	24.1.96	1	NC	Takahata	28 Oct 18
3:39:54		Jesús Angel	García	ESP	17.10.69	1	WCp	Podebrady	20 Apr 97
3:40:02		Aleksandr	Potashov	BLR	12.3.62	1	NC	Moskva	27 May 90
3:40:07		Andrey	Plotnikov	RUS	12.8.67	2	NC	Moskva	27 May 90

50 - 100 KM WALK – WOMEN 100m A-T

Mark	Wind	Name		Nat	Born	Pos	Meet	Venue	Date
3:40:08		Tomasz	Lipiec ¶	POL	10.5.71	2	WCp	Mézidon-Canon	2 May 99
3:40:12		Oleg	Ishutkin	RUS	22.7.75	2	WCp	Podebrady	20 Apr 97
		(40)							
3:40:12		Yuki	Yamazaki	JPN	16.1.84	1		Wajima	12 Apr 09
3:40:13		Nikolay	Matyukhin	RUS	13.12.68	3	WCp	Mézidon-Canon	2 May 99
3:40:19		Takayuki	Tanii	JPN	14.2.83	2	AsiG	Incheon	1 Oct 14
3:40:20		Hirooki	Arai	JPN	18.5.88	1	NC	Wajima	19 Apr 15
3:40:23			Gadasu Alatan	CHN	27.1.84	3	NG	Nanjing	22 Oct 05
3:40:39		Igor	Hlavan	UKR	25.9.90	3	WCh	Moskva	14 Aug 13
3:40:40		Vladimir	Kanaykin ¶	RUS	21.3.85	1	NC	Saransk	12 Jun 05
3:40:46 WR		José	Marin	ESP	21.1.50	1	NC	Valencia	13 Mar 83
3:40:46		Yuriy	Andronov ¶	RUS	6.11.71	1		Moskva	11 Jun 12
3:40:57.9t		Thierry	Toutain	FRA	14.2.62	1		Héricourt	29 Sep 96
		(50)							

100th man 3:43:36, 200th 3:48:04, 300th 3:51:19, 400th 3:53:24, 500th 3:55:28

Drugs disqualification

3:35:59		Sergey	Kirdyapkin ¶	RUS	16.1.80	(1)	OG	London	11 Aug 12
3:36:55		Vladimir	Kanaykin ¶	RUS	21.3.85	(2)	WCp	Cheboksary	11 May 08
3:37:54		Igor	Yerokhin ¶	RUS	4.9.85	(5)	OG	London	11 Aug 12
3:38:46		Sergey	Bakulin ¶	RUS	13.11.86	(1)	NC	Saransk	12 Jun 11
3:38:58		Mikhail	Ryzhov ¶	RUS	17.12.91	(2)	WCh	Moskva	14 Aug 13

100 KILOMETRES WALK

8:38.07	Viktor	Ginko	BLR	7.12.65	1		Scanzorosciate	27 Oct 02
8:43:30		Ginko			1		Scanzorosciate	29 Oct 00
8:44:28		Ginko			1		Scanzorosciate	19 Oct 03
8:48:28	Modris	Liepins	LAT	30.8.66	1		Scanzorosciate	28 Oct 01
8:54:35	Aleksey	Rodionov	RUS	5.3.57	1		Scanzorosciate	15 Nov 98

WOMEN'S ALL-TIME WORLD LISTS

100 METRES

10.49 WR	0.0	Florence	Griffith Joyner	USA	21.12.59	1q1	NC/OT	Indianapolis	16 Jul 88
		@ Probably strongly wind-assisted, but recognised as a US and world record							
10.61(WR)	1.2		Griffith Joyner			1	NC/OT	Indianapolis	17 Jul 88
10.62	1.0		Griffith Joyner			1q3	OG	Seoul	24 Sep 88
10.64	1.2	Carmelita	Jeter	USA	24.11.79	1		Shanghai	20 Sep 09
10.65A	1.1	Marion	Jones ¶	USA	12.10.75	1	WCp	Johannesburg	12 Sep 98
10.67	-0.1		Jeter			1	WAF	Thessaloníki	13 Sep 09
10.70 (WR)	1.6		Griffith Joyner			1s1	NC/OT	Indianapolis	17 Jul 88
10.70	-0.1		Jones			1	WCh	Sevilla	22 Aug 99
10.70	2.0		Jeter			1	Pre	Eugene	4 Jun 11
10.70	0.6	Shelly-Ann	Fraser-Pryce	JAM	27.12.86	1	NC	Kingston	29 Jun 12
10.70	0.3	Elaine	Thompson	JAM	28.6.92	1	NC	Kingston	1 Jul 16
10.71	0.1		Jones			1		Chengdu	12 May 98
10.71	2.0		Jones			1s2	NC	New Orleans	19 Jun 98
10.71	-0.3		Fraser-Pryce			1	WCh	Moskva	12 Aug 13
10.71	0.5		Thompson			1	OG	Rio de Janeiro	13 Aug 16
10.71	0.8		Thompson			1	NC	Kingston	23 Jun 17
10.71	0.1		Fraser-Pryce			1	WCh	Doha	29 Sep 19
10.72	2.0		Jones			1	NC	New Orleans	20 Jun 98
10.72	0.0		Jones			1	Herc	Monaco	8 Aug 98
10.72	0.0		Jones			1	Athl	Lausanne	25 Aug 98
10.72	-0.3		Fraser-Pryce			1	VD	Bruxelles	6 Sep 13
10.72	0.6		Thompson			1	VD	Bruxelles	9 Sep 16
10.73	2.0	Christine	Arron	FRA	13.9.73	1	EC	Budapest	19 Aug 98
10.73	0.1		Fraser-Pryce			1	WCh	Berlin	17 Aug 09
10.73	0.6		Thompson			1	NC	Kingston	21 Jun 19
10.73	0.6		Fraser-Pryce			2	NC	Kingston	21 Jun 19
10.74	1.3	Merlene	Ottey	JAM/SLO	10.5.60	1	GPF	Milano	7 Sep 96
10.74	0.2		Fraser-Pryce			1	DL	Saint-Denis	4 Jul 15
10.74	1.0	English	Gardner	USA	22.4.92	1	NC	Eugene	3 Jul 16
10.74	0.2		Fraser-Pryce			1	Athl	Lausanne	5 Jun 19
10.75	0.6		Jones			1	GGala	Roma	14 Jul 98
		(29/8) and 5 performances at 10.75							
10.75	0.4	Kerron	Stewart	JAM	16.4.84	1	GGala	Roma	10 Jul 09
10.75	1.6	Sha'Carri	Richardson (10)	USA	25.3.00	1	NCAA	Austin	8 Jun 19
10.76 WR	1.7	Evelyn	Ashford	USA	15.4.57	1	WK	Zürich	22 Aug 84
10.76	1.1	Veronica	Campbell-Brown	JAM	15.5.82	1	GS	Ostrava	31 May 11
10.77	0.9	Irina	Privalova	RUS	22.11.68	1rA	Athl	Lausanne	6 Jul 94
10.77	0.7	Ivet	Lalova-Collio	BUL	18.5.84	1	ECp-1A	Plovdiv	19 Jun 04

100 METRES A-T

Mark	Wind	Name		Nat	Born	Pos	Meet	Venue	Date
10.78A	1.0	Dawn	Sowell	USA	27.3.66	1	NCAA	Provo	3 Jun 89
10.78	1.8	Torri	Edwards ¶	USA	31.1.77	1s2	OT	Eugene	28 Jun 08
10.78	1.6	Murielle	Ahouré	CIV	23.8.87	1		Montverde	11 Jun 16
10.78	1.0	Tianna	Bartoletta'	USA	30.8.85	2	NC	Eugene	3 Jul 16
10.78	1.0	Tori	Bowie	USA	27.8.90	3	NC	Eugene	3 Jul 16
10.79	0.0		Li Xuemei	CHN	5.1.77	1	NG	Shanghai	18 Oct 97
		(20)							
10.79	-0.1	Inger	Miller	USA	12.6.72	2	WCh	Sevilla	22 Aug 99
10.79	1.1	Blessing	Okagbare	NGR	9.10.88	1	DL	London (OS)	27 Jul 13
10.81	WR 1.7	Marlies	Göhr'	GDR	21.3.58	1	OD	Berlin	8 Jun 83
10.81	-0.3	Dafne	Schippers	NED	15.6.92	2	WCh	Beijing	24 Aug 15
10.82	-1.0	Gail	Devers	USA	19.11.66	1	OG	Barcelona	1 Aug 92
10.82	0.4	Gwen	Torrence	USA	12.6.65	2	GPF	Paris	3 Sep 94
10.82	-0.3	Zhanna	Pintusevich-Block ¶	UKR	6.7.72	1	WCh	Edmonton	6 Aug 01
10.82	-0.7	Sherone	Simpson	JAM	12.8.84	1	NC	Kingston	24 Jun 06
10.82	0.9	Michelle-Lee	Ahye ¶	TTO	10.4.92	1	NC	Port of Spain	24 Jun 17
10.83	1.7	Marita	Koch	GDR	18.2.57	2	OD	Berlin	8 Jun 83
		(30)							
10.83	-1.0	Juliet	Cuthbert	JAM	9.4.64	2	OG	Barcelona	1 Aug 92
10.83	0.1	Ekateríni	Thánou ¶	GRE	1.2.75	2s1	WCh	Sevilla	22 Aug 99
10.83	0.1	Dina	Asher-Smith	GBR	4.12.95	2	WCh	Doha	29 Sep 19
10.84	1.3	Chioma	Ajunwa ¶	NGR	25.12.70	1		Lagos	11 Apr 92
10.84	1.9	Chandra	Sturrup	BAH	12.9.71	1	Athl	Lausanne	5 Jul 05
10.84	1.8	Kelly-Ann	Baptiste ¶	TTO	14.10.86	1		Clermont	5 Jun 10
10.85	2.0	Anelia	Nuneva	BUL	30.6.62	1h1	NC	Sofia	2 Sep 88
10.85	1.0	Muna	Lee	USA	30.10.81	1	OT	Eugene	28 Jun 08
10.85	2.0	Barbara	Pierre	HAI/USA	28.4.87	1s1	NC	Des Moines	21 Jun 13
10.85	2.0	Aleia	Hobbs	USA	24.2.96	1		Baton Rouge	29 Apr 17
		(40)							
10.85	1.5	Marie Josée	Ta Lou	CIV	18.11.88	1	DL	Doha	4 May 18
10.86	0.6	Silke	Gladisch'	GDR	20.6.64	1	NC	Potsdam	20 Aug 87
10.86	1.2	Chryste	Gaines ¶	USA	14.9.70	1	WAF	Monaco	14 Sep 03
10.86	2.0	Marshevet	Hooker/Myers	USA	25.9.84	2	Pre	Eugene	4 Jun 11
10.87	1.8	Octavious	Freeman	USA	20.4.92	2	NC	Des Moines	21 Jun 13
10.88	0.4	Lauryn	Williams	USA	11.9.83	2	WK	Zürich	19 Aug 05
10.89	1.8	Katrin	Krabbe ¶	GDR	22.11.69	1		Berlin	20 Jul 88
10.89	0.0		Liu Xiaomei	CHN	11.1.72	2	NG	Shanghai	18 Oct 97
10.89	1.5	Allyson	Felix	USA	18.11.85	5	OG	London (OS)	4 Aug 12
10.90	1.4	Glory	Alozie	NGR/ESP	30.12.77	1		La Laguna	5 Jun 99
10.90	1.8	Shalonda	Solomon	USA	19.12.85	2		Clermont	5 Jun 10
		(51)		100th women 10.98, 200th 11.08, 300th 11.14, 400th 11.19, 500th 11.23					

Doubtful wind reading

10.83	0.0	Sheila	Echols	USA	2.10.64	1q2	NC/OT	Indianapolis	16 Jul 88
10.86	0.0	Diane	Williams	USA	14.12.60	2q1	NC/OT	Indianapolis	16 Jul 88

Probably semi-automatic timing: 10.87 1.9 Lyudmila Kondratyeva RUS 11.4.58 1 Leningrad 3 Jun 80

Wind-assisted performances to 10.72 and performers to 10.86

10.54	3.0		Griffith Joyner			1		OG	Seoul	25 Sep 88
10.60	3.2		Griffith Joyner			1h1	NC/OT	Indianapolis	16 Jul 88
10.68	2.2		Jones			1	DNG	Stockholm	1 Aug 00
10.70	2.6		Griffith Joyner			1s2	OG	Seoul	25 Sep 88
10.71	2.2		Fraser-Pryce			1	Pre	Eugene	1 Jun 13
10.71	2.4		Thompson			1		Kingston	7 May 16
10.72	3.0		Jeter			1s1	NC	Eugene	26 Jun 09
10.72	3.2	Tori	Bowie	USA	27.8.90	1s2	NC	Eugene	26 Jun 15
10.72	4.5	Tawanna	Meadows	USA	4.8.86	1		Lubbock	6 May 17
10.72	2.7	Blessing	Okagbare	NGR	9.10.88	1	TexasR	Austin	31 Mar 18
10.76	3.4	Marshevet	Hooker/Myers	USA	25.9.84	1q1	NC/OT	Eugene	27 Jun 08
10.77	2.3	Gail	Devers	USA	19.11.66	1	Jen	San José	28 May 94
10.77	2.3	Ekateríni	Thánou ¶	GRE	1.2.75	1		Rethymno	28 May 99
10.78	5.0	Gwen	Torrence	USA	12.6.65	1q3	NC/OT	Indianapolis	16 Jul 88
10.78	3.3	Muna	Lee	USA	30.10.81	2	NC	Eugene	26 Jun 09
10.79	3.3	Marlies	Göhr'	GDR	21.3.58	1	NC	Cottbus	16 Jul 80
10.80	2.9	Pam	Marshall	USA	16.8.60	1	NC	Eugene	20 Jun 86
10.80	2.8	Heike	Drechsler'	GDR	16.12.64	1	Bisl	Oslo	5 Jul 86
10.81	3.6	Jenna	Prandini	USA	20.11.92	1h4	NC	Eugene	2 Jul 16
10.82	2.2	Silke	Gladisch/Möller	GDR	20.6.64	1s1	WCh	Roma	30 Aug 87
10.83	3.9	Sheila	Echols	USA	2.10.64	1h2	NC/OT	Indianapolis	16 Jul 88
10.84	2.9	Candyce	McGrone	USA	24.3.89	2		Lubbock	6 May 17
10.84	2.9	Alice	Brown	USA	20.9.60	2	NC	Eugene	20 Jun 86
10.86	3.4	Lauryn	Williams	USA	11.9.83	2q1	NC/OT	Eugene	27 Jun 08
10.86	3.2	Jasmine	Todd	USA	23.12.93	3s2	NC	Eugene	26 Jun 15

100 – 200 METRES A-T   231

Mark	Wind	Name	Nat	Born	Pos	Meet	Venue	Date
Hand timing: 10.6	0.1	Zhanna Pintusevich ¶	UKR	6.7.72	1		Kiev	12 Jun 97
Drugs disqualification								
10.75	-0.4	Jones ¶			(1)	OG	Sydney	23 Sep 00
10.83	1.6	Kelly-Ann Baptiste ¶	TTO	14.10.86	(1)	NC	Port of Spain	22 Jun 13
10.85	0.9	Kelli White ¶	USA	1.4.77	(1)	WCh	Saint-Denis	24 Aug 03
10.79w	2.3	Kelli White ¶	USA	1.4.77	(1)		Carson	1 Jun 03

200 METRES

Mark	Wind	Name	Nat	Born	Pos	Meet	Venue	Date
21.34WR	1.3	Florence	Griffith Joyner	USA	21.12.59	1	OG	Seoul	29 Sep 88
21.56W	1.7		Griffith Joyner			1s1	OG	Seoul	29 Sep 88
21.62A	-0.6	Marion	Jones ¶	USA	12.10.75	1	WCp	Johannesburg	11 Sep 98
21.63	0.2	Dafne	Schippers	NED	15.6.92	1	WCh	Beijing	28 Aug 15
21.64	0.8	Merlene	Ottey	JAM	10.5.60	1	VD	Bruxelles	13 Sep 91
21.66	-1.0		Ottey			1	WK	Zürich	15 Aug 90
21.66	0.2	Elaine	Thompson	JAM	28.6.92	2	WCh	Beijing	28 Aug 15
21.69	1.0	Allyson	Felix	USA	18.11.85	1	NC/OT	Eugene	30 Jun 12
21.71WR	0.7	Marita	Koch	GDR	18.2.57	1	v CAN	Karl-Marx-Stadt	10 Jun 79
21.71WR	0.3		Koch			1	OD	Potsdam	21 Jul 84
21.71WR	1.2	Heike	Drechsler'	GDR	16.12.64	1	NC	Jena	29 Jun 86
21.71WR	-0.8		Drechsler			1	EC	Stuttgart	29 Aug 86
21.72	1.3	Grace	Jackson	JAM	14.6.61	2	OG	Seoul	29 Sep 88
21.72	-0.1	Gwen	Torrence (10)	USA	12.6.65	1s2	OG	Barcelona	5 Aug 92
21.74	0.4	Marlies	Göhr'	GDR	21.3.58	1	NC	Erfurt	3 Jun 84
21.74	1.2	Silke	Gladisch'	GDR	20.6.64	1	WCh	Roma	3 Sep 87
21.74	0.6	Veronica	Campbell-Brown	JAM	15.5.82	1	OG	Beijing	21 Aug 08
21.74	-0.4	Shaunae	Miller-Uibo	BAH	15.4.94	1	WK	Zürich	29 Aug 19
21.75	-0.1	Juliet	Cuthbert	JAM	9.4.64	2s2	OG	Barcelona	5 Aug 92
21.76	0.3		Koch			1	NC	Dresden	3 Jul 82
21.76	0.7		Griffith Joyner			1q1	OG	Seoul	28 Sep 88
21.76	-0.8		Jones			1	WK	Zürich	13 Aug 97
21.77	-0.1		Griffith Joyner			1q2	NC/OT	Indianapolis	22 Jul 88
21.77	1.0		Ottey			1	Herc	Monaco	7 Aug 93
21.77	-0.3		Torrence			1	ASV	Köln	18 Aug 95
21.77	0.6	Inger	Miller	USA	12.6.72	1	WCh	Sevilla	27 Aug 99
21.77	1.5	Tori	Bowie	USA	27.8.90	1	Pre	Eugene	27 May 17
21.78	-1.3		Koch			1	NC	Leipzig	11 Aug 85
21.78	-0.1		Thompson			1	OG	Rio de Janeiro	17 Aug 16
21.79	1.7		Gladisch			1	NC	Potsdam	22 Aug 87
		(30/17)						
21.81	-0.1	Valerie	Brisco-Hooks	USA	6.7.60	1	OG	Los Angeles	9 Aug 84
21.83	-0.2	Evelyn	Ashford	USA	15.4.57	1	WCp	Montreal	24 Aug 79
21.85	0.3	Bärbel	Wöckel'	GDR	21.3.55	2	OD	Potsdam	21 Jul 84
		(20)						
21.87	0.0	Irina	Privalova	RUS	22.11.68	2	Herc	Monaco	25 Jul 95
21.88	0.9	Dina	Asher-Smith	GBR	4.12.95	1	WCh	Doha	2 Oct 19
21.93	1.3	Pam	Marshall	USA	16.8.60	1	NC/OT	Indianapolis	23 Jul 88
21.95	0.3	Katrin	Krabbe ¶	GDR	22.11.69	1	EC	Split	30 Aug 90
21.97	1.9	Jarmila	Kratochvílová	CZE	26.1.51	1	PTS	Bratislava	6 Jun 81
21.99	0.9	Chandra	Cheeseborough	USA	10.1.59	2	NC	Indianapolis	19 Jun 83
21.99	1.1	Marie-José	Pérec	FRA	9.5.68	1	BNP	Villeneuve d'Ascq	2 Jul 93
21.99	1.1	Kerron	Stewart	JAM	16.4.84	2	NC	Kingston	29 Jun 08
22.00	1.1	Sherone	Simpson	JAM	12.8.84	1	NC	Kingston	25 Jun 06
22.00	1.3	Sha'Carri	Richardson	USA	25.3.00	1		Montverde	10 Aug 20
		(30)						
22.01	-0.5	Anelia	Nuneva'	BUL	30.6.62	1	NC	Sofia	16 Aug 87
22.01	0.0	Li	Xuemei	CHN	5.1.77	1	NG	Shanghai	22 Oct 97
22.01	0.6	Muna	Lee	USA	30.10.81	4	OG	Beijing	21 Aug 08
22.01	0.2	Candyce	McGrone	USA	24.3.89	4	WCh	Beijing	28 Aug 15
22.02	1.1	Kyra	Jefferson	USA	23.9.94	1	NCAA	Eugene	10 Jun 17
22.04A	0.7	Dawn	Sowell	USA	27.3.66	1	NCAA	Provo	2 Jun 89
22.04	0.5	Blessing	Okagbare	NGR	9.10.88	1		Abilene	24 Mar 18
22.05	1.1	Shericka	Jackson	JAM	16.7.94	1	DL	Paris (c)	30 Jun 18
22.06A	0.7	Evette	de Klerk'	RSA	21.8.65	1		Pietersburg	8 Apr 89
22.07	-0.1	Mary	Onyali	NGR	3.2.68	1	WK	Zürich	14 Aug 96
		(40)						
22.08	0.8	Marie Josée	Ta Lou	CIV	18.11.88	2	WCh	London (OS)	11 Aug 17
22.09	-0.3	Sanya	Richards-Ross	USA	26.2.85	1	DL	New York	9 Jun 12
22.09	-0.2	Shelly-Ann	Fraser-Pryce	JAM	27.12.86	2	DL	London (OS)	8 Aug 12
22.09	1.5	Deajah	Stevens	USA	19.5.95	1	Pac 12	Eugene	14 May 17
22.10	-0.1	Kathy	Cook'	GBR	3.5.60	4	OG	Los Angeles	9 Aug 84

WOMEN All-time

200 - 300 - 400 METRES A-T

Mark	Wind	Name		Nat	Born	Pos	Meet	Venue	Date
22.11	1.0	Carmelita	Jeter	USA	24.11.79	2	NC/OT	Eugene	30 Jun 12
22.11	0.1	Myriam	Soumaré	FRA	29.10.86	2	VD	Bruxelles	5 Sep 14
22.13	1.2	Ewa	Kasprzyk	POL	7.9.57	2	GWG	Moskva	8 Jul 86
22.14	-0.6	Carlette	Guidry	USA	4.9.68	1	NC	Atlanta	23 Jun 96
22.15	1.0	Shalonda	Solomon	USA	19.12.85	1	NC	Eugene	26 Jun 11
22.16	0.9	Jenna	Prandini	USA	20.11.92	1	DL	London (OS)	22 Jul 18
22.16	1.3	Angie	Annelus	USA	10.1.97	1	NCAA	Austin	8 Jun 19
		(52)	100th woman 22.31, 200th 22.51, 300th 22.66, 400th 22.76, 500th 22.85						
Wind-assisted			*Performers listed to 22.11*						
21.80	3.2	Kimberlyn	Duncan	USA	2.8.91	1	NC	Des Moines	23 Jun 13
21.82	3.1	Irina	Privalova	RUS	22.11.68	1	Athl	Lausanne	6 Jul 94
21.91	2.8	Muna	Lee	USA	30.10.81	1		Fort-de-France	10 May 08
21.97	5.3	Shania	Collins	USA	14.11.96	1h5	NCAA-E	Tampa	25 May 18
22.01	2.9	Michelle-Lee	Ahye	TTO	10.4.92	1		San Marcos	25 Apr 15
22.06	3.8	Jeneba	Tarmoh	USA	27.9.89	1	NC	Sacramento	29 Jun 14
22.06	2.4	Lynna	Irby	USA	6.12.98	1h6	NCAA-E	Tampa	25 May 18
Hand timing									
21.9	-0.1	Svetlana	Goncharenko	RUS	28.5.71	1		Rostov-na-Donu	31 May 98
21.6w	2.5	Pam	Marshall	USA	16.8.60	1	NC	San José	26 Jun 87
Drugs disqualification									
22.05	-0.3	Kelli	White ¶	USA	1.4.77	(1)	WCh	Saint-Denis	28 Aug 03

300 METRES

34.41		Shaunae	Miller-Uibo	BAH	15.4.94	1	GS	Ostrava	20 Jun 19
35.00+		Marie-José	Pérec	FRA	9.5.68	1	in 400	Tokyo	27 Aug 91
35.06+		Jarmila	Kratochvílová	CZE	26.1.51	1	in 400	Helsinki	10 Aug 83
35.09+		Salwa Eid	Naser	BRN	23.5.98	1	in 400	Doha	3 Oct 19

400 METRES

47.60 WR		Marita	Koch	GDR	18.2.57	1	WCp	Canberra	6 Oct 85
47.99 WR		Jarmila	Kratochvílová	CZE	26.1.51	1	WCh	Helsinki	10 Aug 83
48.14		Salwa Eid	Naser	BRN	23.5.98	1	WCh	Doha	3 Oct 19
48.16 WR			Koch			1	EC	Athína	8 Sep 82
48.16			Koch			1	Drz	Praha	16 Aug 84
48.22			Koch			1	EC	Stuttgart	28 Aug 86
48.25		Marie-José	Pérec	FRA	9.5.68	1	OG	Atlanta	29 Jul 96
48.26			Koch			1	GO	Dresden	27 Jul 84
48.27		Olga	Vladykina'	UKR	30.6.63	2	WCp	Canberra	6 Oct 85
48.37		Shaunae	Miller-Uibo	BAH	15.4.94	2	WCh	Doha	3 Oct 19
48.45			Kratochvílová			1	NC	Praha	23 Jul 83
48.59		Tatána	Kocembová'	CZE	2.5.62	2	WCh	Helsinki	10 Aug 83
48.60 WR			Koch			1	ECp	Torino	4 Aug 79
48.60			Vladykina			1	ECp	Moskva	17 Aug 85
48.61			Kratochvílová			1	WCp	Roma	6 Sep 81
48.63		Cathy	Freeman	AUS	16.2.73	2	OG	Atlanta	29 Jul 96
48.65			Bryzgina'			1	OG	Seoul	26 Sep 88
48.70		Sanya	Richards	USA	26.2.85	1	WCp	Athína	16 Sep 06
48.73			Kocembová			2	Drz	Praha	16 Aug 84
48.77			Koch			1	v USA	Karl-Marx-Stadt	9 Jul 82
48.82			Kratochvílová			1	Ros	Praha	23 Jun 83
48.83		Valerie	Brisco	USA	6.7.60	1	OG	Los Angeles	6 Aug 84
48.83			Pérec			1	OG	Barcelona	5 Aug 92
48.83			Richards			1	VD	Bruxelles	4 Sep 09
48.85			Kratochvílová			2	EC	Athína	8 Sep 82
48.86			Kratochvílová			1	WK	Zürich	18 Aug 82
48.86			Koch			1	NC	Erfurt	2 Jun 84
48.87			Koch			1	VD	Bruxelles	27 Aug 82
48.88			Koch			1	OG	Moskva	28 Jul 80
48.89 WR			Koch			1		Potsdam	29 Jul 79
48.89			Koch			1		Berlin	15 Jul 84
48.89		Ana Gabriela	Guevara	MEX	4.3.77	1	WCh	Saint-Denis	27 Aug 03
		(32/11)							
49.05		Chandra	Cheeseborough	USA	10.1.59	2	OG	Los Angeles	6 Aug 84
49.07		Tonique	Williams-Darling	BAH	17.1.76	1	ISTAF	Berlin	12 Sep 04
49.10		Falilat	Ogunkoya	NGR	12.5.68	3	OG	Atlanta	29 Jul 96
49.11		Olga	Nazarova ¶	RUS	1.6.65	1s1	OG	Seoul	25 Sep 88
49.16		Antonina	Krivoshapka ¶	RUS	21.7.87	1	NC	Cheboksary	5 Jul 12
49.19		Mariya	Pinigina'	UKR	9.2.58	3	WCh	Helsinki	10 Aug 83
49.19		Amina	Seyni	NIG	24.10.96	2	Athl	Lausanne	5 Jul 19
49.24		Sabine	Busch	GDR	21.11.62	2	NC	Erfurt	2 Jun 84

400 – 600 – 800 METRES A-T

Mark	Wind	Name		Nat	Born	Pos	Meet	Venue	Date
49.26		Allyson (20)	Felix	USA	18.11.85	1	WCh	Beijing	27 Aug 15
49.28	WR	Irena	Szewinska'	POL	24.5.46	1	OG	Montreal	29 Jul 76
49.28		Pauline	Davis-Thompson	BAH	9.7.66	4	OG	Atlanta	29 Jul 96
49.29		Charity	Opara ¶	NGR	20.5.72	1	GGala	Roma	14 Jul 98
49.30		Petra	Müller'	GDR	18.7.65	1		Jena	3 Jun 88
49.30		Lorraine	Fenton'	JAM	8.9.73	2	Herc	Monaco	19 Jul 02
49.32		Shericka	Williams	JAM	17.9.85	2	WCh	Berlin	18 Aug 09
49.33		Amantle	Montsho ¶	BOT	4.7.83	1	Herc	Monaco	19 Jul 13
49.40		Jearl	Miles-Clark	USA	4.9.66	1	NC	Indianapolis	14 Jun 97
49.41		Christine	Ohuruogu	GBR	17.5.84	1	WCh	Moskva	12 Aug 13
49.42		Grit (30)	Breuer ¶	GER	16.2.72	2	WCh	Tokyo	27 Aug 91
49.43		Kathy	Cook'	GBR	3.5.60	3	OG	Los Angeles	6 Aug 84
49.43A		Fatima	Yusuf	NGR	2.5.71	1	AfG	Harare	15 Sep 95
49.47		Aelita	Yurchenko	UKR	1.1.65	2	Kuts	Moskva	4 Sep 88
49.47		Shericka	Jackson	JAM	16.7.94	3	WCh	Doha	3 Oct 19
49.48		Francena	McCorory	USA	20.10.88	1	NC	Sacramento	28 Jun 14
49.49		Olga	Zaytseva	RUS	10.11.84	1	NCp	Tula	16 Jul 06
49.52		Shakima	Wimbley	USA	23.4.95	1	NC	Des Moines	23 Jun 18
49.53		Vanya	Stambolova ¶	BUL	28.11.83	1	GP	Rieti	27 Aug 06
49.56		Bärbel	Wöckel'	GDR	21.3.55	1		Erfurt	30 May 82
49.56		Monique (40)	Hennagan	USA	26.5.76	1	NC/OT	Sacramento	17 Jul 04
49.57		Grace	Jackson	JAM	14.6.61	1	Nik	Nice	10 Jul 88
49.58		Dagmar	Rübsam'	GDR	3.6.62	3	NC	Erfurt	2 Jun 84
49.59		Marion	Jones ¶	USA	12.10.75	1r6	MSR	Walnut	16 Apr 00
49.59		Katharine	Merry	GBR	21.9.74	1	GP	Athína	11 Jun 01
49.60		Wadeline	Jonathas	USA	19.2.98	4	WCh	Doha	3 Oct 19
49.61		Ana Fidelia	Quirot	CUB	23.3.63	1	PAm	La Habana	5 Aug 91
49.61		Phyllis	Francis	USA	4.5.92	5	WCh	Doha	3 Oct 19
49.62		Caster	Semenya	RSA	7.1.91	2	C.Cup	Ostrava	8 Sep 18
49.63		Novlene	Williams-Mills	JAM	26.4.82	1		Shanghai	23 Sep 06
		(49) 4 at 49.64		100th woman 50.08, 200th 50.70, 300th 51.05, 400th 51.25, 500th 51.45					
Hand timing									
48.9		Olga	Nazarova ¶	RUS	1.6.65	1	NP	Vladivostok	13 Sep 88
49.2A		Ana Fidelia	Quirot	CUB	23.3.63	1	AmCp	Bogotá	13 Aug 89
Drugs disqualification									
49.28		Yuliya	Gushchina	RUS	4.3.83	(2)	NC	Cheboksary	5 Jul 12
49.35		Anastasiya	Kapachinskaya ¶	RUS	21.11.79	(1)	NC	Cheboksary	22 Jul 11

600 METRES

Mark	Name		Nat	Born	Pos	Meet	Venue	Date
1:21.77	Caster	Semenya	RSA	7.1.91	1	ISTAF	Berlin	27 Aug 17
1:22.39	Ajee'	Wilson	USA	8.5.94	2	ISTAF	Berlin	27 Aug 17
1:22.63	Ana Fidelia	Quirot	CUB	23.3.63	1		Guadalajara, ESP	25 Jul 97
1:22.87	Maria Lurdes	Mutola	MOZ	27.10.72	1		Liège (NX)	27 Aug 02

800 METRES

Mark		Name		Nat	Born	Pos	Meet	Venue	Date
1:53.28	WR	Jarmila	Kratochvílová	CZE	26.1.51	1		München	26 Jul 83
1:53.43	WR	Nadezhda	Olizarenko'	UKR	28.11.53	1	OG	Moskva	27 Jul 80
1:54.01		Pamela	Jelimo	KEN	5.12.89	1	WK	Zürich	29 Aug 08
1:54.25		Caster	Semenya	RSA	7.1.91	1	DL	Paris (C)	30 Jun 18
1:54.44		Ana Fidelia	Quirot	CUB	23.3.63	1	WCp	Barcelona	9 Sep 89
1:54.60			Semenya			1	Herc	Monaco	20 Jul 18
1:54.68			Kratochvílová			1	WCh	Helsinki	9 Aug 83
1:54.77			Semenya			1	C.Cup	Ostrava	9 Sep 18
1:54.81		Olga	Mineyeva	RUS	1.9.52	2	OG	Moskva	27 Jul 80
1:54.82			Quirot			1	ASV	Köln	24 Aug 97
1:54.85	WR		Olizarenko			1	Prav	Moskva	12 Jun 80
1:54.87			Jelimo			1	OG	Beijing	18 Aug 08
1:54.94	WR	Tatyana	Kazankina ¶	RUS	17.12.51	1	OG	Montreal	26 Jul 76
1:54.97			Jelimo			1	Gaz	Saint-Denis	18 Jul 08
1:54.98			Semenya			1	DL	Doha	3 May 19
1:54.99			Jelimo			1	ISTAF	Berlin	1 Jun 08
1:55.04			Kratochvílová			1	OsloG	Oslo	23 Aug 83
1:55.05		Doina	Melinte	ROU	27.12.56	1	NC	Bucuresti	1 Aug 82
1:55.1	'		Mineyeva			1	Znam	Moskva	6 Jul 80
1:55.16			Jelimo			1	VD	Bruxelles	5 Sep 08
1:55.16			Semenya			1	WCh	London (OS)	13 Aug 17
1:55.19		Maria Lurdes	Mutola	MOZ	27.10.72	1	WK	Zürich	17 Aug 94

WOMEN All-time

800 – 1000 METRES A-T

Mark	Wind	Name		Nat	Born	Pos	Meet	Venue	Date
1:55.19		Jolanda	Ceplak ¶ (10)	SLO	12.9.76	1rA	NA	Heusden	20 Jul 02
1:55.26		Sigrun	Wodars/Grau	GDR	7.11.65	1	WCh	Roma	31 Aug 87
1:55.27			Semenya			1	Herc	Monaco	21 Jul 17
1:55.27			Semenya			1	WK	Zürich	30 Aug 18
1:55.28			Semenya			1	OG	Rio de Janeiro	20 Aug 16
1:55.29			Mutola			2	ASV	Köln	24 Aug 97
1:55.32		Christine	Wachtel	GDR	6.1.65	2	WCh	Roma	31 Aug 87
1:55.33			Semenya			1	Herc	Monaco	15 Jul 16
		(30/12)							
1:55.42		Nikolina	Shtereva	BUL	25.1.55	2	OG	Montreal	26 Jul 76
1:55.46		Tatyana	Providokhina	RUS	26.3.53	3	OG	Moskva	27 Jul 80
1:55.47		Francine	Niyonsaba	BDI	5.5.93	2	Herc	Monaco	21 Jul 17
1:55.54		Ellen	van Langen	NED	9.2.66	1	OG	Barcelona	3 Aug 92
1:55.54			Liu Dong	CHN	24.12.73	1	NG	Beijing	9 Sep 93
1:55.56		Lyubov	Gurina	RUS	6.8.57	3	WCh	Roma	31 Aug 87
1:55.60		Elfi	Zinn	GDR	24.8.53	3	OG	Montreal	26 Jul 76
1:55.61		Ajee'	Wilson	USA	8.5.94	3	Herc	Monaco	21 Jul 17
		(20)							
1:55.68		Ella	Kovacs	ROU	11.12.64	1	RomIC	Bucuresti	2 Jun 85
1:55.69		Irina	Podyalovskaya	RUS	19.10.59	1	Izv	Kyiv	22 Jun 84
1:55.74		Anita	Weiss'	GDR	16.7.55	4	OG	Montreal	26 Jul 76
1:55.87		Svetlana	Masterkova	RUS	17.1.68	1	Kuts	Moskva	18 Jun 99
1:55.96		Lyudmila	Veselkova	RUS	25.10.50	2	EC	Athína	8 Sep 82
1:55.96		Yekaterina	Podkopayeva'	RUS	11.6.52	1		Leningrad	27 Jul 83
1:55.99		Liliya	Nurutdinova ¶	RUS	15.12.63	2	OG	Barcelona	3 Aug 92
1:56.00		Tatyana	Andrianova	RUS	10.12.79	1	NC	Kazan	18 Jul 08
1:56.0 WR		Valentina	Gerasimova	KAZ	15.5.48	1	NC	Kyiv	12 Jun 76
1:56.0		Inna	Yevseyeva	UKR	14.8.64	1		Kyiv	25 Jun 88
		(30)							
1:56.04		Janeth	Jepkosgei	KEN	13.12.83	1	WCh	Osaka	28 Aug 07
1:56.09		Zulia	Calatayud	CUB	9.11.79	1	Herc	Monaco	19 Jul 02
1:56.1		Ravilya	Agletdinova'	BLR	10.2.60	2	Kuts	Podolsk	21 Aug 82
1:56.15		Natoya	Goule	JAM	30.3.91	3	Herc	Monaco	20 Jul 18
1:56.2 '		Totka	Petrova ¶	BUL	17.12.56	1		Paris (C)	6 Jul 79
1:56.2		Tatyana	Mishkel	UKR	10.6.52	3	Kuts	Podolsk	21 Aug 82
1:56.21		Martina	Kämpfert'	GDR	11.11.59	4	OG	Moskva	27 Jul 80
1:56.21		Zamira	Zaytseva	UZB	16.2.53	2		Leningrad	27 Jul 83
1:56.21		Kelly	Holmes	GBR	19.4.70	2	GPF	Monaco	9 Sep 95
1:56.24			Qu Yunxia	CHN	8.12.72	2	NG	Beijing	9 Sep 93
		(40)							
1:56.40		Jearl	Miles-Clark	USA	4.9.66	3	WK	Zürich	11 Aug 99
1:56.42		Paula	Ivan	ROU	20.7.63	1	Balk	Ankara	16 Jul 88
1:56.43		Hasna	Benhassi	MAR	1.6.78	2	OG	Athína	23 Aug 04
1:56.44		Svetlana	Styrkina	RUS	1.1.49	5	OG	Montreal	26 Jul 76
1:56.51		Slobodanka	Colovic	YUG	10.1.65	1		Beograd	17 Jun 87
1:56.53		Patricia	Djaté	FRA	3.1.71	3	GPF	Monaco	9 Sep 95
1:56.56		Ludmila	Formanová	CZE	2.1.74	4	WK	Zürich	11 Aug 99
1:56.57		Zoya	Rigel	RUS	15.10.52	3	EC	Praha	31 Aug 78
1:56.59		Natalya	Khrushchelyova	RUS	30.5.73	2	NC	Tula	31 Jul 04
1:56.60		Natalya	Tsyganova	RUS	7.2.71	1	NC	Tula	25 Jul 00
1:56.6		Tamara	Sorokina'	RUS	15.8.50	5	Kuts	Podolsk	21 Aug 82
		(51)		100th woman 1:57.38, 200th 1:58.37, 300th 1:59.15, 400th 1:59.6, 500th 2:00.02					
Indoors:	1:55.85	Stephanie	Graf	AUT	26.4.73	2	EI	Wien	3 Mar 02
Drugs disqualification									
1:54.85		Yelena	Soboleva ¶	RUS	3.10.82	(1)	NC	Kazan	18 Jul 08
1:55.87		Mariya	Savinova ¶	RUS	13.8.85	(1)	WCh	Daegu	4 Sep 11

1000 METRES

Mark		Name		Nat	Born	Pos	Meet	Venue	Date
2:28.98 WR		Svetlana	Masterkova	RUS	17.1.68	1	VD	Bruxelles	23 Aug 96
2:29.15		Faith	Kipyegon	KEN	10.1.94	1	Herc	Monaco	14 Aug 20
2:29.34 WR		Maria Lurdes	Mutola	MOZ	27.10.72	1	VD	Bruxelles	25 Aug 95
2:30.6 WR		Tatyana	Providokhina	RUS	26.3.53	1		Podolsk	20 Aug 78
2:30.67 WR		Christine	Wachtel	GDR	6.1.65	1	ISTAF	Berlin	17 Aug 90
2:30.70		Caster	Semenya	RSA	7.1.91	1	ISTAF	Berlin	2 Sep 18
2:30.82		Laura	Muir	GBR	9.5.93	2	Herc	Monaco	14 Aug 20
2:30.85		Martina	Kämpfert'	GDR	11.11.59	1		Berlin	9 Jul 80
2:31.06		Ciara	Mageean	IRL	12.3.92	3	Herc	Monaco	14 Aug 20
2:31.11		Jemma	Reekie (10)	GBR	6.3.98	4	Herc	Monaco	14 Aug 20
2:31.50		Natalya	Artyomova ¶	RUS	5.1.63	1	ISTAF	Berlin	10 Sep 91
2:31.5 A		Maricica	Puica	ROU	29.7.50	1		Poiana Brasov	1 Jun 86
2:31.51		Sandra	Gasser ¶	SUI	27.7.62	1		Jerez de la Frontera	13 Sep 89

1500 METRES A-T

1500 METRES

Mark	Wind	Name		Nat	Born	Pos	Meet	Venue	Date
3:50.07 WR		Genzebe	Dibaba	ETH	8.2.91	1	Herc	Monaco	17 Jul 15
3:50.46 WR			Qu Yunxia	CHN	8.12.72	1	NG	Beijing	11 Sep 93
3:50.98			Jiang Bo	CHN	13.3.77	1	NG	Shanghai	18 Oct 97
3:51.34			Lang Yinglai	CHN	22.8.79	2	NG	Shanghai	18 Oct 97
3:51.92			Wang Junxia	CHN	9.1.73	2	NG	Beijing	11 Sep 93
3:51.95		Sifan	Hassan	ETH/NED	1.1.93	1	WCh	Doha	5 Oct 19
3:52.47 WR		Tatyana	Kazankina ¶	RUS	17.12.51	1	WK	Zürich	13 Aug 80
3:53.91			Yin Lili ¶	CHN	11.11.79	3	NG	Shanghai	18 Oct 97
3:53.96		Paula	Ivan'	ROU	20.7.63	1	OG	Seoul	1 Oct 88
3:53.97			Lan Lixin (10)	CHN	14.2.79	4	NG	Shanghai	18 Oct 97
3:54.11			Dibaba			1		Barcelona	8 Jul 15
3:54.22		Faith	Kipyegon	KEN	10.1.94	2	WCh	Doha	5 Oct 19
3:54.23		Olga	Dvirna	RUS	11.2.53	1	NC	Kyiv	27 Jul 82
3:54.38		Gudaf	Tsegay	ETH	23.1.97	3	WCh	Doha	5 Oct 19
3:54.52			Zhang Ling	CHN	13.4.80	5	NG	Shanghai	18 Oct 97
3:54.99		Shelby	Houlihan	USA	8.2.93	4	WCh	Doha	5 Oct 19
3:55.0 ' WR			Kazankina ¶			1	Znam	Moskva	6 Jul 80
3:55.01			Lan Lixin			1h2	NG	Shanghai	17 Oct 97
3:55.07			Dong Yanmei	CHN	16.2.77	6	NG	Shanghai	18 Oct 97
3:55.22		Laura	Muir	GBR	9.5.93	1	DL	Saint-Denis	27 Aug 16
3:55.30		Hassiba	Boulmerka	ALG	10.7.68	1	OG	Barcelona	8 Aug 92
3:55.30+			Hassan			1	in 1M	Monaco	12 Jul 19
3:55.33		Süreyya	Ayhan ¶	TUR	6.9.78	1	VD	Bruxelles	5 Sep 03
3:55.38			Qu Yunxia			2h2	NG	Shanghai	17 Oct 97
3:55.47			Zhang Ling			3h2	NG	Shanghai	17 Oct 97
3:55.47			G Dibaba			1	DL	Rabat	16 Jun 19
3:55.60			Ayhan			1	WK	Zürich	15 Aug 03
3:55.68		Yuliya	Chizhenko ¶	RUS	30.8.79	1	Gaz	Saint-Denis	8 Jul 06
3:55.76			Muir			5	WCh	Doha	5 Oct 19
3:55.82			Dong Yanmei			4h2	NG	Shanghai	17 Oct 97
	(30/20)								
3:56.12		Gabriela	DeBues-Stafford	CAN	13.9.95	6	WCh	Doha	5 Oct 19
3:56.14		Zamira	Zaytseva	UZB	16.2.53	2	NC	Kyiv	27 Jul 82
3:56.18		Maryam	Jamal	BRN	16.9.84	1	GP	Rieti	27 Aug 06
3:56.29		Shannon	Rowbury	USA	19.9.84	3	Herc	Monaco	17 Jul 15
3:56.31			Liu Dong	CHN	24.12.73	5h2	NG	Shanghai	17 Oct 97
3:56.43		Yelena	Soboleva ¶	RUS	3.10.82	2	Gaz	Saint-Denis	8 Jul 06
3:56.50		Tatyana	Pozdnyakova	RUS	4.3.56	3	NC	Kyiv	27 Jul 82
3:56.54		Abeba	Aregawi	ETH/SWE	5.7.90	1	GGala	Roma	31 May 12
3:56.63		Nadezhda	Ralldugina	UKR	15.11.57	1	Drz	Praha	18 Aug 84
3:56.65		Yekaterina	Podkopayeva'	RUS	11.6.52	1		Rieti	2 Sep 84
	(30)								
3:56.7 '		Lyubov	Smolka	UKR	29.11.52	2	Znam	Moskva	6 Jul 80
3:56.7		Doina	Melinte	ROU	27.12.56	1		Bucuresti	12 Jul 86
3:56.77+		Svetlana	Masterkova	RUS	17.1.68	1	WK	Zürich	14 Aug 96
3:56.8 '		Nadezhda	Olizarenko'	UKR	28.11.53	3	Znam	Moskva	6 Jul 80
3:56.91		Lyudmila	Rogachova	RUS	30.10.66	2	OG	Barcelona	8 Aug 92
3:56.91		Tatyana	Tomashova ¶	RUS	1.7.75	1	EC	Göteborg	13 Aug 06
3:56.97		Gabriela	Szabo	ROU	14.11.75	1	Herc	Monaco	8 Aug 97
3:57.03			Liu Jing	CHN	3.2.71	6h2	NG	Shanghai	17 Oct 97
3:57.05		Svetlana	Guskova	MDA	19.8.59	4	NC	Kyiv	27 Jul 82
3:57.05		Hellen	Obiri	KEN	13.12.89	1	Pre	Eugene	31 May 14
	(40)								
3:57.12		Mary	Decker/Slaney	USA	4.8.58	1	vNord	Stockholm	26 Jul 83
3:57.22		Maricica	Puica	ROU	29.7.50	1		Bucuresti	1 Jul 84
3:57.22		Jennifer	Simpson'	USA	23.8.86	2	DL	Saint-Denis	5 Jul 14
3:57.40		Suzy	Favor Hamilton	USA	8.8.68	1	Bisl	Oslo	28 Jul 00
3:57.4 '		Totka	Petrova	BUL	17.12.56	1	Balk	Athína	11 Aug 79
3:57.41		Jackline	Maranga	KEN	16.12.77	3	Herc	Monaco	8 Aug 97
3:57.46			Zhang Linli	CHN	6.3.73	3	NG	Beijing	11 Sep 93
3:57.71		Christiane	Wartenberg'	GDR	27.10.56	2	OG	Moskva	1 Aug 80
3:57.71		Carla	Sacramento	POR	10.12.71	4	Herc	Monaco	8 Aug 97
3:57.72		Galina	Zakharova	RUS	7.9.56	1	NP	Baku	14 Sep 84
	(50)		100th woman 3:59.70, 200th 4:01.80, 300th 4:03.66, 400th 4:04.97, 500th 4:05.97						

Indoors: 3:55.17 WIR   G Dibaba   1   Karlsruhe   1 Feb 14

Drugs disqualification

3:56.15		Mariem	Alaoui Selsouli ¶	MAR	8.4.84	(1)	DL	Saint-Denis	6 Jul 12
3:56.62		Asli	Çakir Alptekin ¶	TUR	20.8.85	(2)	DL	Saint-Denis	6 Jul 12
3:57.65		Anna	Alminova ¶	RUS	17.1.85	(1)	DL	Saint-Denis	16 Jul 10

WOMEN All-time

236   1 MILE – 2000 - 3000 METRES A-T

Mark	Wind	Name		Nat	Born	Pos	Meet	Venue	Date
1 MILE									
4:12.33	WR	Sifan	Hassan	NED	1.1.93	1	Herc	Monaco	12 Jul 19
4:12.56	WR	Svetlana	Masterkova	RUS	17.1.68	1	WK	Zürich	14 Aug 96
4:14.30		Genzebe	Dibaba	ETH	8.2.91	1		Rovereto	6 Sep 16
4:14.71			Hassan			1	DL	London (OS)	22 Jul 18
4:15.61	WR	Paula	Ivan'	ROU	20.7.63	1	Nik	Nice	10 Jul 89
4:15.8		Natalya	Artyomova ¶	RUS	5.1.63	1		Leningrad	5 Aug 84
4:16.14		Gudaf	Tsegay	ETH	23.1.97	2	DL	London (OS)	22 Jul 18
4:16.15		Hellen	Obiri	KEN	13.12.89	3	DL	London (OS)	22 Jul 18
4:16.71	WR	Mary	Slaney (Decker)	USA	4.8.58	1	WK	Zürich	21 Aug 85
4:16.71		Faith	Kipyegon	KEN	10.1.94	1	VD	Bruxelles	11 Sep 15
Indoors									
4:13.31	WIR	Genzebe	Dibaba	ETH	8.2.91	1	Globen	Stockholm	17 Feb 16
Drugs dq: 4:15.63		Yelena	Soboleva ¶	RUS	3.10.82	(1)		Moskva	29 Jun 07
2000 METRES									
5:25.36	WR	Sonia	O'Sullivan	IRL	28.11.69	1	TSB	Edinburgh	8 Jul 94
5:26.93		Yvonne	Murray	GBR	4.10.64	2	TSB	Edinburgh	8 Jul 94
5:27.50		Genzebe	Dibaba	ETH	8.2.91	1	GS	Ostrava	17 Jun 14
5:28.69	WR	Maricica	Puica	ROU	29.7.50	1	PTG	London (CP)	11 Jul 86
5:28.72		Tatyana	Kazankina ¶	RUS	17.12.51	1		Moskva	4 Aug 84
5:29.43+			Wang Junxia	CHN	9.1.73	1h2	NG	Beijing	12 Sep 93
5:29.64		Tatyana	Pozdnyakova	UKR	4.3.56	2		Moskva	4 Aug 84
Indoors:									
5:23.75		Genzebe	Dibaba	ETH	8.2.91	1		Sabadell	7 Feb 17
3000 METRES									
8:06.11	WR		Wang Junxia	CHN	9.1.73	1	NG	Beijing	13 Sep 93
8:12.18			Qu Yunxia	CHN	8.12.72	2	NG	Beijing	13 Sep 93
8:12.19	WR		Wang Junxia			1h2	NG	Beijing	12 Sep 93
8:12.27			Qu Yunxia			2h2	NG	Beijing	12 Sep 93
8:16.50			Zhang Linli	CHN	6.3.73	3	NG	Beijing	13 Sep 93
8:18.49		Sifan	Hassan	NED	1.1.93	1	Pre	Stanford	30 Jun 19
8:19.78			Ma Liyan	CHN	6.9.68	3h2	NG	Beijing	12 Sep 93
8:20.07		Konstanze	Klosterhalfen	GER	18.2.97	2	Pre	Stanford	30 Jun 19
8:20.27		Letesenbet	Gidey	ETH	20.3.98	3	Pre	Stanford	30 Jun 19
8:20.68		Hellen	Obiri	KEN	13.12.89	1	DL	Doha	9 May 14
8:21.14		Mercy	Cherono	KEN	7.5.91	2	DL	Doha	9 May 14
8:21.26			Ma Liyan			4	NG	Beijing	13 Sep 93
8:21.29		Genzebe	Dibaba (10)	ETH	8.2.91	4	Pre	Stanford	30 Jun 19
8:21.42		Gabriela	Szabo	ROU	14.11.75	1	Herc	Monaco	19 Jul 02
8:21.64		Sonia	O'Sullivan	IRL	28.11.69	1	TSB	London (CP)	15 Jul 94
8:21.84			Zhang Lirong	CHN	3.3.73	5	NG	Beijing	13 Sep 93
8:22.06	WR		Zhang Linli			1h1	NG	Beijing	12 Sep 93
8:22.20		Paula	Radcliffe	GBR	17.12.73	2	Herc	Monaco	19 Jul 02
8:22.22		Almaz	Ayana	ETH	21.11.91	1		Rabat	14 Jun 15
8:22.34			Ayana			1	WK	Zürich	3 Sep 15
8:22.44			Zhang Lirong			2h1	NG	Beijing	12 Sep 93
8:22.54			Obiri			1	DL	Doha	25 Sep 20
8:22.62	WR	Tatyana	Kazankina ¶	RUS	17.12.51	1		Leningrad	26 Aug 84
8:22.92		Agnes	Tirop	KEN	23.10.95	2	DL	Doha	25 Sep 20
8:22.92		Beatrice	Chepkoech	KEN	6.7.91	3	DL	Doha	25 Sep 20
8:23.11			Ayana			1	DL	Doha	6 May 16
8:23.14			Obiri			1	Herc	Monaco	21 Jul 17
8:23.23		Edith	Masai	KEN	4.4.67	3	Herc	Monaco	19 Jul 02
8:23.26		Olga	Yegorova ¶ (20)	RUS	28.3.72	1	WK	Zürich	17 Aug 01
8:23.55		Faith	Kipyegon	KEN	10.1.94	3	DL	Doha	9 May 14
		(30/21)							
8:24.41		Viola	Kibiwot	KEN	22.12.83	4	DL	Doha	9 May 14
8:24.51+		Meseret	Defar	ETH	19.11.83	1	in 2M	Bruxelles	14 Sep 07
8:24.76		Margaret	Kipkemboi	KEN	9.2.93	4	DL	Doha	25 Sep 20
8:25.13		Hyvin	Jepkemoi	KEN	13.1.92	5	DL	Doha	25 Sep 20
8:25.23		Gudaf	Tsegay	ETH	23.1.97	6	DL	Doha	25 Sep 20
8:25.40		Yelena	Zadorozhnaya	RUS	3.12.77	2	GGala	Roma	29 Jun 01
8:25.56		Tatyana	Tomashova ¶	RUS	1.7.75	3	GGala	Roma	29 Jun 01
8:25.62		Berhane	Adere	ETH	21.7.73	3	WK	Zürich	17 Aug 01
8:25.83		Mary	Slaney	USA	4.8.58	1	GGala	Roma	7 Sep 85
		(30)							
8:25.92		Gelete	Burka	ETH	15.2.86	2	DNG	Stockholm	25 Jul 06
8:26.07		Laura	Weightman	GBR	1.7.91	5	Pre	Stanford	30 Jun 19

3000 - 5000 METRES A-T

Mark Wind	Name		Nat	Born	Pos	Meet	Venue	Date
8:26.48	Zahra	Ouaziz	MAR	20.12.69	2	WK	Zürich	11 Aug 99
8:26.53	Tatyana	Samolenko' ¶	UKR	12.8.61	1	OG	Seoul	25 Sep 88
8:26.78 WR	Svetlana	Ulmasova	UZB	4.2.53	1	NC	Kyiv	25 Jul 82
8:27.12 WR	Lyudmila	Bragina	RUS	24.7.43	1	v USA	College Park	7 Aug 76
8:27.15	Paula	Ivan'	ROU	20.7.63	2	OG	Seoul	25 Sep 88
8:27.62	Getenesh	Wami	ETH	11.12.74	4	WK	Zürich	17 Aug 01
8:27.83	Maricica	Puica	ROU	29.7.50	2	GGala	Roma	7 Sep 85
8:28.33	Janet	Kisa	KEN	5.3.92	3	Herc	Monaco	15 Jul 16
(40)								
8:28.41	Sentayehu	Ejigu	ETH	21.6.85	1	Herc	Monaco	22 Jul 10
8:28.51	Irene	Jelagat	KEN	10.12.88	7	DL	Doha	9 May 14
8:28.66	Vivian	Cheruiyot	KEN	11.9.83	2	WAF	Stuttgart	23 Sep 07
8:28.80	Marta	Domínguez	ESP	3.11.75	3	WK	Zürich	11 Aug 00
8:28.83	Zola	Budd'	GBR	26.5.66	3	GGala	Roma	7 Sep 85
8:28.87	Maryam	Jamal	BRN	16.9.84	1	Bisl	Oslo	29 Jul 05
8:29.02	Yvonne	Murray	GBR	4.10.64	3	OG	Seoul	25 Sep 88
8:29.02	Lilian	Rengeruk	KEN	3.5.97	3	DL	Doha	3 May 19
8:29.05	Caroline	Kipkirui	KEN	26.5.94	1	DL	Doha	4 May 18
8:29.06	Priscah	Cherono	KEN	27.6.80	3	WAF	Stuttgart	23 Sep 07
(50)	100th woman 8:34.10, 200th 8:41.23, 300th 8:45.77, 400th 8:48.46							
Indoors:								
8:16.60 WIR	Genzebe	Dibaba	ETH	8.2.91	1		Stockholm	6 Feb 14
8:23.72 WIR	Meseret	Defar	ETH	19.11.83	1	Spark	Stuttgart	3 Feb 07
8:23.74	Meselech	Melkamu	ETH	27.4.85	2	Spark	Stuttgart	3 Feb 07
8:25.27	Sentayehu	Ejigu	ETH	21.6.85	2	Spark	Stuttgart	6 Feb 10
8:25.70	Karissa	Schweizer	USA	4.5.96	1		Boston (A)	27 Feb 20
8:26.41	Laura	Muir	GBR	9.5.93	1		Karlsruhe	4 Feb 17
8:27.86 WIR	Liliya	Shobukhova ¶	RUS	13.11.77	1	NC	Moskva	17 Feb 06
8:28.49	Anna	Alminova ¶	RUS	17.1.85	2	Spark	Stuttgart	7 Feb 09
8:28.66	Shelby	Houlihan	USA	8.2.93	2		Boston (A)	27 Feb 20
8:28.71	Colleen	Quigley	USA	20.11.92	3		Boston (A)	27 Feb 20
8:29.00	Olesya	Syreva ¶	RUS	25.11.83	2	NC	Moskva	17 Feb 06

5000 METRES

Mark Wind	Name		Nat	Born	Pos	Meet	Venue	Date
14:06.62 WR	Letesenbet	Gidey	ETH	20.3.98	1		Valencia	7 Oct 20
14:11.15 WR	Tirunesh	Dibaba	ETH	1.10.85	1	Bisl	Oslo	6 Jun 08
14:12.59	Almaz	Ayana	ETH	21.11.91	1	GGala	Roma	2 Jun 16
14:12.88	Meseret	Defar	ETH	19.11.83	1	DNG	Stockholm	22 Jul 08
14:14.32		Ayana			1	DL	Shanghai	17 May 15
14:15.41	Genzebe	Dibaba	ETH	8.2.91	1	DL	Saint-Denis	4 Jul 15
14:16.31		Ayana			1		Rabat	22 May 16
14:16.63 WR		Defar			1	Bisl	Oslo	15 Jun 07
14:18.37	Hellen	Obiri	KEN	13.12.89	1	GGala	Roma	8 Jun 17
14:18.89		Ayana			1	VD	Bruxelles	9 Sep 16
14:19.76		G Dibaba			1	Pre	Eugene	30 May 15
14:20.36		Obiri			1	DL	London (OS)	21 Jul 19
14:20.68	Agnes	Tirop	KEN	23.10.95	2	DL	London (OS)	21 Jul 19
14:20.87	Vivian	Cheruiyot	KEN	11.9.83	1	DNG	Stockholm	29 Jul 11
14:21.29		G Dibaba			1	Bisl	Oslo	11 Jun 15
14:21.75		Obiri			1	DL	Rabat	13 Jul 18
14:21.97		Ayana			2	DL	Saint-Denis	4 Jul 15
14:22.12	Sifan	Hassan	NED	1.1.93	3	DL	London (OS)	21 Jul 19
14:22.34		Hassan			2	DL	Rabat	13 Jul 18
14:22.47		Obiri			1	DL	Shanghai	13 May 17
14:22.51		Cheruiyot			2	Bisl	Oslo	15 Jun 07
14:23.14		Gidey			3	DL	Rabat	13 Jul 18
14:23.33	Senbere	Teferi (10)	ETH	3.5.95	4	DL	Rabat	13 Jul 18
14:23.46		T Dibaba			1	GP	Rieti	7 Sep 08
14:23.68		T Dibaba			1	DL	Saint-Denis	6 Jul 13
14:23.75	Liliya	Shobukhova ¶	RUS	13.11.77	1	NC	Kazan	19 Jul 08
14:23.92	Shelby	Houlihan	USA	8.2.93	1		Portland	10 Jul 20
14:24.24		Tirop			5	DL	Rabat	13 Jul 18
14:24.53 WR		Defar			1		New York (RI)	3 Jun 06
14:24.68 WR	Elvan	Abeylegesse ¶	TUR	11.9.82	1	Bisl	Bergen (Fana)	11 Jun 04
(30/13)								
14:26.34	Karissa	Schweizer	USA	4.5.96	2		Portland	10 Jul 20
14:26.76	Konstanze	Klosterhalfen	GER	18.2.97	1	NC	Berlin	3 Aug 19
14:27.49	Margaret	Kipkemboi	KEN	9.2.93	2	WCh	Doha	5 Oct 19
14:27.55	Caroline	Kipkirui	KEN	26.5.94	2	VD-DLF	Bruxelles	1 Sep 17
14:28.09 WR		Jiang Bo	CHN	13.3.77	1	NG	Shanghai	23 Oct 97

WOMEN All-time

5000 - 10,000 METRES A-T

Mark	Wind	Name		Nat	Born	Pos	Meet	Venue	Date
14:28.39		Sentayehu	Ejigu	ETH	21.6.85	2	DL	Saint-Denis	16 Jul 10
14:29.11		Paula	Radcliffe	GBR	17.12.73	1	ECpS	Bydgoszcz	20 Jun 04
14:29.32		Olga	Yegorova ¶	RUS	28.3.72	1	ISTAF	Berlin	31 Aug 01
		(20)							
14:29.32		Berhane	Adere	ETH	21.7.73	1	Bisl	Oslo	27 Jun 03
14:29.50		Viola	Kibiwot	KEN	22.12.83	2		Rabat	22 May 16
14:29.60		Tsehay	Gemechu	ETH	12.12.98	4	WCh	Doha	5 Oct 19
14:29.82			Dong Yanmei	CHN	16.2.77	2	NG	Shanghai	23 Oct 97
14:30.42		Sally	Kipyego	KEN	19.12.85	2	WK	Zürich	8 Sep 11
14:30.88		Getenesh	Wami	ETH	11.12.74	1	NA	Heusden-Zolder	5 Aug 00
14:31.14		Linet	Masai	KEN	5.12.89	2	DL	Shanghai	23 May 10
14:31.20		Gelete	Burka	ETH	15.2.86	2	GS	Ostrava	27 Jun 07
14:31.48		Gabriela	Szabo	ROU	14.11.75	1	ISTAF	Berlin	1 Sep 98
14:31.91		Meselech	Melkamu	ETH	27.4.85	3	DL	Shanghai	23 May 10
		(30)							
14:31.91		Sylvia	Kibet	KEN	28.3.84	4	DL	Shanghai	23 May 10
14:31.95		Faith	Kipyegon	KEN	10.1.94	2	Pre	Eugene	30 May 15
14:32.08		Zahra	Ouaziz	MAR	20.12.69	2	ISTAF	Berlin	1 Sep 98
14:32.33			Liu Shixiang ¶	CHN	13.1.71	3h1	NG	Shanghai	21 Oct 97
14:32.74		Ejagayehu	Dibaba	ETH	25.6.82	3	Bisl	Bergen (Fana)	11 Jun 04
14:33.04		Werknesh	Kidane	ETH	21.11.81	2	Bisl	Oslo	27 Jun 03
14:33.13		Gulnara	Galkina'	RUS	9.7.78	2	NC	Kazan	19 Jul 08
14:33.30		Etenesh	Diro	ETH	10.5.91	4	VD	Bruxelles	9 Sep 16
14:33.49		Lucy Wangui	Kabuu	KEN	24.3.84	2	Bisl	Oslo	6 Jun 08
14:33.84		Edith	Masai	KEN	4.4.67	3	Bisl	Oslo	2 Jun 06
		(40)							
14:33.95		Mercy	Cherono	KEN	7.5.91	2	GGala	Roma	2 Jun 16
14:35.30		Priscah	Jepleting/Cherono	KEN	27.6.80	4	Bisl	Oslo	2 Jun 06
14:35.44		Laura	Weightman	GBR	1.7.91	3	Herc	Monaco	14 Aug 20
14:36.05		Lilian	Rengeruk	KEN	3.5.97	5	WCh	Doha	5 Oct 19
14:36.45 WR		Fernanda	Ribeiro	POR	23.6.69	1		Hechtel	22 Jul 95
14:36.52		Mariem Alaoui	Selsouli ¶	MAR	8.4.84	1	G Gala	Roma	13 Jul 07
14:36.82		Yasemin	Can	TUR	11.12.96	4	GGala	Roma	8 Jun 17
14:37.07		Jéssica	Augusto	POR	8.11.81	5	DL	Saint-Denis	16 Jul 10
14:37.33 WR		Ingrid	Kristiansen'	NOR	21.3.56	1		Stockholm	5 Aug 86
14:38.09		Mariya	Konovalova ¶	RUS	14.8.74	3	NC	Kazan	19 Jul 08
		(50)							

100th woman 14:45.71, 200th 14:59.68, 300th 15:06.75, 400th 15:11.46, 500th 15:16.44

Indoors:
14:18.06 WIR			G Dibaba			1	XL-G	Stockholm	19 Feb 15
14:24.37 WIR			Defar			1		Stockholm	18 Feb 09
14:24.79			Defar			1	GE Galan	Stockholm	10 Feb 10

Drugs disqualification
14:36.79		Alemitu	Bekele ¶	TUR	17.9.77	4	VD	Bruxelles	27 Aug 10

10,000 METRES

Mark	Wind	Name		Nat	Born	Pos	Meet	Venue	Date
29:17.45 WR		Almaz	Ayana	ETH	21.11.91	1	OG	Rio de Janeiro	12 Aug 16
29:31.78 WR			Wang Junxia	CHN	9.1.73	1	NG	Beijing	8 Sep 93
29:32.53		Vivian	Cheruiyot	KEN	11.9.83	2	OG	Rio de Janeiro	12 Aug 16
29:36.67		Sifan	Hassan	NED	1.1.93	1		Hengelo	10 Oct 20
29:42.56		Tirunesh	Dibaba	ETH	1.10.85	3	OG	Rio de Janeiro	12 Aug 16
29:53.51		Alice Aprot	Nawowuna	KEN	2.1.94	4	OG	Rio de Janeiro	12 Aug 16
29:53.80		Meselech	Melkamu	ETH	27.4.85	1		Utrecht	14 Jun 09
29:54.66			T Dibaba			1	OG	Beijing	15 Aug 08
29:59.20		Meseret	Defar	ETH	19.11.83	1	NC	Birmingham	11 Jul 09
30:01.09		Paula	Radcliffe	GBR	17.12.73	1	EC	München	6 Aug 02
30:04.18		Berhane	Adere (10)	ETH	21.7.73	1	WCh	Saint-Denis	23 Aug 03
30:07.00			Ayana			1	OT	Hengelo	29 Jun 16
30:07.15		Werknesh	Kidane	ETH	21.11.81	2	WCh	Saint-Denis	23 Aug 03
30:07.20			Sun Yingjie ¶	CHN	3.10.77	3	WCh	Saint-Denis	23 Aug 03
30:07.78		Betsy	Saina	KEN	30.6.88	5	OG	Rio de Janeiro	12 Aug 16
30:08.06			Defar			1		Sollentuna	27 Jun 13
30:11.53		Florence	Kiplagat	KEN	27.2.87	2		Utrecht	14 Jun 09
30:11.87		Wude	Ayalew	ETH	4.7.87	3		Utrecht	14 Jun 09
30:12.53		Lornah	Kiplagat (KEN)	NED	1.5.74	4	WCh	Saint-Denis	23 Aug 03
30:13.17		Molly	Huddle	USA	31.8.84	6	OG	Rio de Janeiro	12 Aug 16
30:13.37			Zhong Huandi	CHN	28.6.67	2	NG	Beijing	8 Sep 93
30:13.74 WR		Ingrid	Kristiansen'	NOR	21.3.56	1	Bisl	Oslo	5 Jul 86
30:15.67			T Dibaba			1		Sollentuna	28 Jun 05
30:16.32			Ayana			1	WCh	London (OS)	5 Aug 17
30:17.15			Radcliffe			1	GP	Gateshead	27 Jun 04

10,000 METRES - HALF MARATHON A-T   239

Mark	Wind	Name		Nat	Born	Pos	Meet	Venue	Date
30:17.49		Derartu	Tulu	ETH	21.3.72	1	OG	Sydney	30 Sep 00
30:17.62			Hassan	NED	1.1.93	1	WCh	Doha	28 Sep 19
30:18.39		Ejegayehu	Dibaba	ETH	25.6.82	2		Sollentuna	28 Jun 05
30:19.39			Kidane			1	GP II	Stanford	29 May 05
30:20.44		Hitomi	Niiya	JPN	26.2.88	1	NC	Osaka	4 Dec 20
		(30/22)							
30:21.23		Letesenbet	Gidey	ETH	20.3.98	2	WCh	Doha	28 Sep 19
30:21.67		Elvan	Abeylegesse ¶	TUR	11.9.82	1	ECp	Antalya	15 Apr 06
30:22.22		Shalane	Flanagan	USA	8.7.81	2	OG	Beijing	15 Aug 08
30:22.48		Getenesh	Wami	ETH	11.12.74	2	OG	Sydney	30 Sep 00
30:22.88		Fernanda	Ribeiro	POR	23.6.69	3	OG	Sydney	30 Sep 00
30:23.07		Alla	Zhilyayeva	RUS	5.2.69	5	WCh	Saint-Denis	23 Aug 03
30:24.36			Xing Huina	CHN	25.2.84	1	OG	Athína	27 Aug 04
30:25.20		Agnes	Tirop	KEN	23.10.95	3	WCh	Doha	28 Sep 19
		(30)							
30:26.20		Galina	Bogomolova	RUS	15.10.77	6	WCh	Saint-Denis	23 Aug 03
30:26.37		Sally	Kipyego	KEN	19.12.85	2	OG	London (OS)	3 Aug 12
30:26.41		Yasemin	Can	TUR	11.12.96	7	OG	Rio de Janeiro	12 Aug 16
30:26.50		Linet	Masai	KEN	5.12.89	3	OG	Beijing	15 Aug 08
30:26.66		Gelete	Burka	ETH	23.1.86	8	OG	Rio de Janeiro	12 Aug 16
30:26.70		Belaynesh	Oljira	ETH	26.6.90	3	Pre	Eugene	1 Jun 12
30:29.21mx		Philes	Ongori	KEN	19.7.86	1mx		Yokohama	23 Nov 08
30:29.23		Gladys	Cherono	KEN	12.5.83	2	GS	Ostrava	27 Jun 13
30:29.36		Liliya	Shobukhova ¶	RUS	13.11.77	1	NC	Cheboksary	23 Jul 09
30:30.26		Edith	Masai	KEN	4.4.67	5	WCh	Helsinki	6 Aug 05
		(40)							
30:31.03		Mariya	Konovalova ¶	RUS	14.8.74	2	NC	Cheboksary	23 Jul 09
30:31.42		Inga	Abitova ¶	RUS	6.3.82	1	EC	Göteborg	7 Aug 06
30:32.03		Tegla	Loroupe	KEN	9.5.73	3	WCh	Sevilla	26 Aug 99
30:32.36		Susanne	Wigene	NOR	12.2.78	2	EC	Göteborg	7 Aug 06
30:32.72		Lidiya	Grigoryeva ¶	RUS	21.1.74	3	EC	Göteborg	7 Aug 06
30:35.54		Kimberley	Smith	NZL	19.11.81	2		Stanford	4 May 08
30:35.75		Rosemary	Wanjiru	KEN	9.12.94	4	WCh	Doha	28 Sep 19
30:35.82		Hellen	Obiri	KEN	13.12.89	5	WCh	Doha	28 Sep 19
30:35.91		Birhane	Ababel	ETH	10.6.90	4	GS	Ostrava	27 Jun 13
30:36.75		Netsanet	Gudeta	ETH	12.2.91	4	OT	Hengelo	29 Jun 16
		(50)							

100th woman 31:03.62, 200th 31:21.36, 300th 31:36.90, 400th 31:48.21, 500th 31:56.47

Drugs dq: 29:56.34 Elvan Abeylegesse ¶ TUR 11.9.82 (2) OG Beijing 15 Aug 08

WOMEN All-time

HALF MARATHON

Slightly downhill courses included: Newcastle-South Shields 30.5m, Tokyo 33m (to 1998), Lisboa (Spring to 2008) 69m

64:28	dh	Brigid	Kosgei	KEN	20.2.94	1	GNR	South Shields	8 Sep 19
64:31	WR	Ababel	Yeshaneh	ETH	22.7.91	1	RAK	Ras Al Khaimah	21 Feb 20
64:46		Yalemzerf	Yehualaw	ETH	3.8.99	1		New Delhi	29 Nov 20
64:49			Kosgei			2	RAK	Ras Al Khaimah	21 Feb 20
64:51	WR	Joyciline	Jepkosgei	KEN	8.12.93	1		Valencia	22 Oct 17
64:52	WR		Jepkosgei			1		Praha	1 Apr 17
64:52		Fancy	Chemutai	KEN	20.3.95	1	RAK	Ras Al Khaimah	9 Feb 18
64:55		Mary	Keitany	KEN	18.1.82	2	RAK	Ras Al Khaimah	9 Feb 18
65:04		Joan	Chelimo	KEN	10.11.90	1		Praha	7 Apr 18 65:06
WR		Peres	Jepchirchir	KEN	27.9.93	1	RAK	Ras Al-Khaymah	10 Feb 20
65:06		Ruth	Chepngetich (10)	KEN	8.8.94	2		New Delhi	29 Nov 20
65:07		Caroline	Kipkirui	KEN	26.5.94	3	RAK	Ras Al Khaimah	9 Feb 18
65:09	WR	Florence	Kiplagat	KEN	27.2.87	1		Barcelona	15 Feb 15
65:12	WR		F Kiplagat			1		Barcelona	16 Feb 14
65:13			Keitany			2	RAK	Ras Al-Khaymah	10 Feb 17
65:15		Sifan	Hassan	NED	1.1.93	1		København	16 Sep 18
65:16			Jepchirchir			1	WCh	Gdynia	17 Oct 20
65:18		Melat	Kejeta	ETH/GER	27.9.92	2	WCh	Gdynia	17 Oct 20
65:18		Genzebe	Dibaba	ETH	8.2.91	1		Valencia	6 Dec 20
65:19			Yehualaw			3	WCh	Gdynia	17 Oct 20
65:21			Yeshaneh			3		New Delhi	29 Nov 20
65:22		Violah	Jepchumba ¶	BRN	23.10.90	2		Praha	1 Apr 17
65:28			Kosgei			1		Manama	15 Mar 19
65:29			Chepngetich			1		Istanbul	7 Apr 19
65:32		Senbere	Teferi	ETH	3.5.95	1		Valencia	27 Oct 19
65:34		Rosemary	Wanjiru	KEN	9.12.94	3	RAK	Ras Al Khaimah	21 Feb 20
65:34			Jepchirchir			1		Praha	5 Sep 20
65:36			Chemutai			2		Valencia	22 Oct 17
65:37			J Chelimo			4	RAK	Ras Al Khaimah	9 Feb 18

HALF MARATHON - MARATHON A-T

Mark	Wind	Name		Nat	Born	Pos	Meet	Venue	Date
65:39	dh		Keitany			1	GNR	South Shields	7 Sep 14
65:39		Zeineba	Yimer	ETH	17.6.98	4	WCh	Gdynia	17 Oct 20
65:39		Sheila	Chepkirui	KEN	27.12.90	2		Valencia	6 Dec 20
		(30/20)							
65:40	dh	Paula	Radcliffe	GBR	17.12.73	1	GNR	South Shields	21 Sep 03
65:44	dh	Susan	Chepkemei	KEN	25.6.75	1		Lisboa (60m dh)	1 Apr 01
65:45	dh	Priscah	Jeptoo	KEN	26.6.84	1	GNR	South Shields	15 Sep 13
65:45		Netsanet	Gudeta	ETH	12.2.91	2	RAK	Ras Al Khaimah	8 Feb 19
65:52		Edith	Chelimo	KEN	16.7.86	1		Cardiff	1 Oct 17
65:57		Birhane	Dibaba	ETH	11.9.93	1		København	15 Sep 19
66:00		Tsehay	Gemechu	ETH	12.12.98	1		New Delhi	20 Oct 19
66:01		Roza	Dereje	ETH	6.5.97	1		Barcelona	10 Feb 19
66:01		Evaline	Chirchir	KEN	10.5.98	4	RAK	Ras Al Khaimah	21 Feb 20
66:04		Cynthia	Limo	KEN	18.12.89	1		Ra's Al-Khaymah	12 Feb 16
		(30)							
66:07		Gladys	Cherono	KEN	12.5.83	2		Ra's Al-Khaymah	12 Feb 16
66:07		Degitu	Azimeraw	ETH	24.1.99	4	RAK	Ras Al Khaimah	8 Feb 19
66:09		Lucy Wangui	Kabuu	KEN	24.3.84	1		Ra's Al-Khaymah	15 Feb 13
66:09	dh	Meseret	Defar	ETH	19.11.83	2	GNR	South Shields	15 Sep 13
66:09		Chemtai	Salpeter	ISR	12.12.88	2		Praha	6 Apr 19
66:11		Eunice	Chumba	BRN	23.5.93	1		København	17 Sep 17
66:11		Gelete	Burka	ETH	23.1.86	1		Valencia	28 Oct 18
66:13		Alia Mohamed	Saeed	UAE	18.5.91	2		Valencia	28 Oct 18
66:14		Worknesh	Degefa	ETH	28.10.90	2		Praha	2 Apr 16
66:14		Valary	Aiyabei	KEN	8.6.91	5	RAK	Ras Al Khaimah	8 Feb 19
		(40)							
66:19		Joyce	Chepkirui	KEN	20.8.88	1		Praha	5 Apr 14
66:20		Yasemin	Can	TUR	1.8.92	7	WCh	Gdynia	17 Oct 20
66:25	WR	Lornah	Kiplagat	NED	1.5.74	1	WCh	Udine	14 Oct 07
66:26		Genet	Yalew	ETH	31.12.92	3		Ra's Al-Khaymah	12 Feb 16
66:27		Rita	Jeptoo ¶	KEN	15.2.81	3		Ra's Al-Khaymah	15 Feb 13
66:28		Mamitu	Daska	ETH	16.10.83	2		Ra's Al-Khaymah	13 Feb 15
66:29		Mercy Wacera	Ngugi	KEN	17.12.88	1		Houston	17 Jan 16
66:31		Pauline	Korikwiang	KEN	1.3.88	4		Valencia	28 Oct 18
66:33		Dorcas	Tuitoek	KEN	31.1.98	2		Istanbul	7 Apr 19
66:34		Vivian	Cheruiyot	KEN	11.9.83	1		Lisboa	17 Mar 19
		(50)							
			100th woman 67:23, 200th 68:25, 300th 69:02, 400th 69:27, 500th 69:46						

MARATHON

Mark		Name		Nat	Born	Pos	Meet	Venue	Date
2:14:04	WR	Brigid	Kosgei	KEN	20.2.94	1		Chicago	13 Oct 19
2:15:25	WR	Paula	Radcliffe	GBR	17.12.73	1		London	13 Apr 03
2:17:01		Mary	Keitany	KEN	18.1.82	1		London	23 Apr 17
2:17:08		Ruth	Chepngetich	KEN	8.8.94	1		Dubai	25 Jan 19
2:17:18	WR		Radcliffe			1		Chicago	13 Oct 02
2:17:16		Peres	Jepchirchir	KEN	27.9.93	1		Valencia	6 Dec 20
2:17:41		Worknesh	Degefa	ETH	28.10.90	2		Dubai	25 Jan 19
2:17:42			Radcliffe			1		London	17 Apr 05
2:17:45		Lonah Chemtai	Salpeter	ISR	12.12.88	1		Tokyo	1 Mar 20
2:17:56		Tirunesh	Dibaba	ETH	1.10.85	2		London	23 Apr 17
2:18:11		Gladys	Cherono	KEN	12.5.83	1		Berlin	16 Sep 18
2:18:20			Kosgei			1		London	28 Apr 19
2:18:30		Roza	Dereje (10)	ETH	6.5.97	1		Valencia	1 Dec 19
2:18:31			Dibaba			1		Chicago	8 Oct 17
2:18:31		Vivian	Cheruiyot	KEN	11.9.83	1		London	22 Apr 18
2:18:33		Azmera	Abreha	ETH	31.1.98	2		Valencia	1 Dec 19
2:18:34		Ruti	Aga	ETH	16.1.94	2		Berlin	16 Sep 18
2:18:35			Kosgei			1		Chicago	7 Oct 18
2:18:35			Chepngetich			1		Istanbul	11 Nov 18
2:18:35		Birhane	Dibaba	ETH	11.9.93	2		Tokyo	1 Mar 20
2:18:37			Keitany			1		London	22 Apr 12
2:18:40		Joyciline	Jepkosgei	KEN	8.12.93	2		Valencia	6 Dec 20
2:18:46			B Dibaba			3		Valencia	1 Dec 19
2:18:47	WR	Catherine	Ndereba	KEN	21.7.72	1		Chicago	7 Oct 01
2:18:52			V Cheruiyot			4		Valencia	1 Dec 19
2:18:55			T Dibaba			3		Berlin	16 Sep 18
2:18:56			Radcliffe			1		London	14 Apr 02
2:18:58		Tiki	Gelana	ETH	22.10.87	1		Rotterdam	15 Apr 12
2:18:58			B Kosgei			1		London	4 Oct 20
2:19:10		Valary	Aiyabei	KEN	8.6.91	1		Frankfurt	27 Oct 19
		(30/18)							

MARATHON – STEEPLECHASE A-T   241

Mark	Wind	Name		Nat	Born	Pos	Meet	Venue	Date
2:19:12		Mizuki	Noguchi	JPN	3.7.78	1		Berlin	25 Sep 05
2:19:19		Irina	Mikitenko (20)	GER	23.8.72	1		Berlin	28 Sep 08
2:19:26		Degitu	Azimeraw	ETH	24.1.99	1		Amsterdam	20 Oct 19
2:19:28		Zeineba	Yimer	ETH	17.6.98	5		Valencia	1 Dec 19
2:19:30		Feyse	Tadese	ETH	19.11.88	2		Dubai	26 Jan 18
2:19:31		Aselefech	Mergia	ETH	23.1.85	1		Dubai	27 Jan 12
2:19:34		Lucy Wangui	Kabuu	KEN	24.3.84	2		Dubai	27 Jan 12
2:19:36		Deena	Kastor	USA	14.2.73	1		London	23 Apr 06
2:19:36		Yebrgual	Melese	ETH	18.4.90	3		Dubai	26 Jan 18
2:19:38		Worknesh	Degefa	ETH	28.10.90	1		Dubai	24 Jan 20
2:19:39			Sun Yingjie ¶	CHN	3.10.77	1		Beijing	19 Oct 03
2:19:41		Yoko	Shibui	JPN	14.3.79	1		Berlin	26 Sep 04
		(30)							
2:19:41		Tirfi	Tsegaye	ETH	25.11.84	1		Dubai	22 Jan 16
2:19:44		Florence	Kiplagat	KEN	27.2.87	1		Berlin	25 Sep 11
2:19:46 WR		Naoko	Takahashi	JPN	6.5.72	1		Berlin	30 Sep 01
2:19:47		Sarah	Chepchirchir	KEN	27.7.84	1		Tokyo	26 Feb 17
2:19:50		Edna	Kiplagat	KEN	15.11.79	2		London	22 Apr 12
2:19:51			Zhou Chunxiu	CHN	15.11.78	1	Dong-A	Seoul	12 Mar 06
2:19:52		Mare	Dibaba	ETH	20.10.89	3		Dubai	27 Jan 12
2:19:52		Tigist	Girma	ETH	12.7.93	2		Amsterdam	20 Oct 19
2:19:52		Helalia	Johannes	NAM	13.8.80	3		Valencia	6 Dec 20
2:19:54		Zeineba	Yimer	ETH	17.6.98	4		Valencia	6 Dec 20
		(40)							
2:19:57		Rita	Jeptoo ¶	KEN	15.2.81	1		Chicago	13 Oct 13
2:20:11		Guteni	Shone	ETH	17.11.91	2		Dubai	24 Jan 20
2:20:13		Haftamnesh	Tesfay	ETH	28.4.94	5		Dubai	26 Jan 18
2:20:14		Priscah	Jeptoo	KEN	26.6.84	3		London	22 Apr 12
2:20:14		Ashete	Bekere	ETH	17.4.88	1		Berlin	29 Sep 19
2:20:24		Workenesh	Edesa	ETH	11.9.92	6		Valencia	1 Dec 19
2:20:29		Mao	Ichiyama	JPN	29.5.97	1		Nagoya	8 Mar 20
2:20:30		Bezunesh	Bekele	ETH	29.1.83	4		Dubai	27 Jan 12
2:20:30		Aberu	Kebede	ETH	12.9.89	1		Berlin	30 Sep 12
2:20:30		Sutume	Asefa	ETH	11.12.94	3		Tokyo	1 Mar 20
		(50)	100th woman 2:21:53, 200th 2:23:50, 300th 2:25:15, 400th 2:26:15, 500th 2:26:58						

WOMEN All-time

Downhill point-to-point course – Boston marathon is downhill overall (139m) and sometimes strongly wind-aided.
| 2:19:59 D | | Buzunesh | Deba | ETH | 8.9.87 | 2 | | Boston | 21 Apr 14 |

Drugs disqualification
2:18:20		Liliya	Shobukhova ¶	RUS	13.11.77	1		Chicago	9 Oct 11
2:20:23			Wei Yanan ¶	CHN	6.12.81	1		Beijing	20 Oct 02
2:18:57 D		Rita	Jeptoo ¶	KEN	15.2.81	1		Boston	21 Apr 14

2000 METRES STEEPLECHASE

Mark	Name		Nat	Born	Pos	Meet	Venue	Date
5:52.80	Gesa Felicitas	Krause	GER	3.8.92	1	ISTAF	Berlin	1 Sep 19
5:56.28	Marusa	Mismas	SLO	24.10.94	1		Ljubljana	16 Jul 20
5:56.83	Winfred	Yavi	BRN	31.12.99	2	ISTAF	Berlin	1 Sep 19
6:00.07	Luiza	Gega	ALB	5.11.88	3	ISTAF	Berlin	1 Sep 19
6:02.16	Virginia	Nyambura	KEN	20.7.93	1	ISTAF	Berlin	6 Sep 15
6:02.47	Beatrice	Chepkoech	KEN	6.7.91	2	ISTAF	Berlin	6 Sep 15
6:03.38	Wioletta	Janowska	POL	9.6.77	1		Gdansk	15 Jul 06

3000 METRES STEEPLECHASE

Mark		Name		Nat	Born	Pos	Meet	Venue	Date
8:44.32 WR		Beatrice	Chepkoech	KEN	6.7.91	1	Herc	Monaco	20 Jul 18
8:52.78 WR		Ruth	Jebet ¶	KEN/BRN	17.11.96	1	DL	Saint-Denis	27 Aug 16
8:55.10			Chepkoech			1	VD	Bruxelles	31 Aug 18
8:55.29			Jebet			1	WK-DLF	Zürich	24 Aug 17
8:55.58			Chepkoech			1	Pre	Stanford	30 Jun 19
8:57.84			Chepkoech			1	WCh	Doha	30 Sep 19
8:58.78		Celliphine	Chespol	KEN	23.3.99	1	Pre	Eugene	26 May 17
8:58.81 WR		Gulnara	Samitova/Galkina	RUS	9.7.78	1	OG	Beijing	17 Aug 08
8:59.36			Chepkoech			1	DL	Paris (C)	30 Jun 18
8:59.62		Norah	Tanui	KEN	2.10.95	2	VD	Bruxelles	31 Aug 18
8:59.75			Jebet			1	OG	Rio de Janeiro	15 Aug 16
8:59.84			Chepkoech			2	WK-DLF	Zürich	24 Aug 17
8:59.88			Chepkoech			1	AfrC	Asaba	5 Aug 18
8:59.97			Jebet			2	DL	Shanghai	14 May 16
9:00.11		Hyvin	Jepkemoi	KEN	13.1.92	2	Pre	Eugene	28 May 16
9:00.12			Jepkemoi			1	DL	Doha	5 May 17
9:00.70			Chepkoech			2	Pre	Eugene	26 May 17
9:00.85		Courtney	Frerichs	USA	18.1.93	2	Herc	Monaco	20 Jul 18
9:01.57			Chepkoech			2	DL	Doha	5 May 17

3000m STEEPLECHASE – 100m HURDLES A-T

Mark	Wind	Name		Nat	Born	Pos	Meet	Venue	Date
9:01.59 WR		Samitova/Galkina				1		Iráklio	4 Jul 04
9:01.60		Jepkemoi				3	VD	Bruxelles	31 Aug 18
9:01.69		Chepkoech				1	DL	Paris (C)	1 Jul 17
9:01.71		Chepkoech				1	WK	Zürich	29 Aug 19
9:01.82		Chespol				2	DL	Paris (C)	30 Jun 18
9:01.96		Jepkemoi				2	DL	Saint-Denis	27 Aug 16
9:01.99		Jebet				3	DL	Doha	5 May 17
9:02.35		Emma	Coburn	USA	19.10.90	2	WCh	Doha	30 Sep 19
9:02.58			Coburn			1	WCh	London (OS)	11 Aug 17
9:03.30		Gesa Felicitas	Krause	GER	3.8.92	3	WCh	Doha	30 Sep 19
9:03.52			Jebet			3	Pre	Eugene	26 May 17
(30/9)									
9:05.36		Habiba	Ghribi (10)	TUN	9.4.84	1	VD	Bruxelles	11 Sep 15
9:05.68		Winfred	Yavi	BRN	31.12.99	4	WCh	Doha	30 Sep 19
9:06.57		Yekaterina	Volkova ¶	RUS	16.2.78	1	WCh	Osaka	27 Aug 07
9:06.66		Daisy	Jepkemei	KEN	13.2.96	4	WK	Zürich	29 Aug 19
9:07.06		Sofia	Assefa	ETH	14.11.87	1	FBK	Hengelo	11 Jun 17
9:07.14		Milcah	Chemos Cheywa	KEN	24.2.86	1	Bisl	Oslo	7 Jun 12
9:07.41		Eunice	Jepkorir	KEN	17.2.82	2	OG	Beijing	17 Aug 08
9:07.94		Peruth	Chemutai	UGA	10.7.99	6	Herc	Monaco	20 Jul 18
9:08.23		Roseline	Chepngetich	KEN	17.6.97	7	Herc	Monaco	20 Jul 18
9:08.39		Yuliya	Zaripova' ¶	RUS	26.4.86	2	WCh	Berlin	17 Aug 09
9:09.19		Tatyana	Petrova	RUS	8.4.83	2	WCh	Osaka	27 Aug 07
(20)									
9:09.39		Marta	Dominguez ¶	ESP	3.11.75	1		Barcelona	25 Jul 09
9:09.61		Hiwot	Ayalew	ETH	6.3.90	3	Bisl	Oslo	7 Jun 12
9:10.27		Colleen	Quigley	USA	20.11.92	1	ISTAF	Berlin	2 Sep 18
9:12.50		Jennifer	Simpson'	USA	23.8.86	5	WCh	Berlin	17 Aug 09
9:12.55		Lydia	Chepkurui	KEN	23.8.84	2	WCh	Moskva	13 Aug 13
9:13.16		Ruth	Bisibori	KEN	2.1.88	7	WCh	Berlin	17 Aug 09
9:13.22		Gladys	Kipkemboi	KEN	15.10.86	2	GGala	Roma	10 Jun 10
9:13.25		Etenesh	Diro	ETH	10.5.91	6	DL	Paris (C)	1 Jul 17
9:13.35		Karoline Bjerkeli	Grøvdal	NOR	14.6.90	1	NC	Sandnes	26 Aug 17
9:13.46		Anna Emilie	Møller	DEN	28.7.97	7	WCh	Doha	30 Sep 19
(30)									
9:13.53		Gülcan	Mingir ¶	TUR	21.5.89	1	Pavlov	Sofia	9 Jun 12
9:13.85		Virginia	Nyambura	KEN	20.7.93	3	Herc	Monaco	17 Jul 15
9:14.09		Aisha	Praught Leer	JAM	14.12.89	8	VD	Bruxelles	31 Aug 18
9:14.28		Genevieve	LaCaze/Gregson	AUS	4.8.89	6	DL	Saint-Denis	27 Aug 16
9:15.04		Dorcus	Inzikuru	UGA	2.2.82	1	SGP	Athína	14 Jun 05
9:16.51 WR		Alesya	Turova	BLR	6.12.79	1		Gdansk	27 Jul 02
9:16.68		Yekaterina	Ivonina	RUS	14.6.94	1	NC	Kazan	20 Jul 18
9:16.85		Cristina	Casandra	ROU	21.10.77	4	OG	Beijing	17 Aug 08
9:16.94		Mercy	Njoroge	KEN	10.6.86	2	DL	Doha	6 May 11
9:17.15		Wioletta	Frankiewicz/Janowska	POL	9.6.77	1	SGP	Athína	3 Jul 06
(40)									
9:17.74		Purity	Kirui	KEN	13.8.91	5	VD	Bruxelles	11 Sep 15
9:17.85		Zemzem	Ahmed	ETH	27.12.84	7	OG	Beijing	17 Aug 08
9:18.03		Lydia	Rotich	KEN	8.8.88	3	Bisl	Oslo	4 Jun 10
9:18.35		Donna	MacFarlane	AUS	18.6.77	3	Bisl	Oslo	6 Jun 08
9:18.54		Antje	Möldner-Schmidt	GER	13.6.84	9	WCh	Berlin	17 Aug 09
9:18.54		Jéssica	Augusto	POR	8.11.81	1		Huelva	9 Jun 10
9:18.85		Leah	O'Connor	USA	30.8.92	6	Pre	Eugene	28 May 16
9:19.48		Stephanie	Garcia	USA	3.5.88	8	DL	Saint-Denis	27 Aug 16
9:19.76		Lalita	Babar	IND	2.6.89	4h2	OG	Rio de Janeiro	13 Aug 16
9:19.93		Luiza	Gega	ALB	5.11.88	9	WCh	Doha	30 Sep 19
(50)		100th woman 9:27.53, 200th 9:38.31, 300th 9:45.24, 400th 9:51.16, 500th 9:55.71							
Drugs disqualification									
9:05.02		Yuliya	Zaripova	RUS	26.4.86	(1)	DNG	Stockholm	17 Aug 12
9:07.32		Marta	Dominguez ¶	ESP	3.11.75	(1)	WCh	Berlin	17 Aug 09

100 METRES HURDLES

12.20 WR 0.3	Kendra	Harrison	USA	18.9.92	1	DL	London (OS)	22 Jul 16
12.21 WR 0.7	Yordanka	Donkova	BUL	28.9.61	1		Stara Zagora	20 Aug 88
12.24 0.9		Donkova			1h		Stara Zagora	28 Aug 88
12.24 0.5		K Harrison			1	Pre	Eugene	28 May 16
12.25 WR 1.4	Ginka	Zagorcheva	BUL	12.4.58	1	v TCH,GRE	Drama	8 Aug 87
12.26 WR 1.5		Donkova			1	Balk	Ljubljana	7 Sep 86
12.26 1.7	Lyudmila	Narozhilenko ¶	RUS	21.4.64	1rB		Sevilla	6 Jun 92
	(later Ludmila Engquist SWE)							

100 METRES HURDLES A-T

Mark	Wind	Name		Nat	Born	Pos	Meet	Venue	Date
12.26	1.2	Brianna	Rollins/McNeal	USA	18.8.91	1	NC	Des Moines	22 Jun 13
12.27	-1.2		Donkova			1		Stara Zagora	28 Aug 88
12.28	1.8		Narozhilenko			1	NC	Kyiv	11 Jul 91
12.28	0.9		Narozhilenko			1rA		Sevilla	6 Jun 92
12.28	1.1	Sally	Pearson'	AUS	19.9.86	1	WCh	Daegu	3 Sep 11
12.28	0.1		K Harrison			1	Gyulai	Székesfehérvár	4 Jul 17
12.29 WR	-0.4		Donkova			1	ASV	Köln	17 Aug 86
12.32	1.6		Narozhilenko			1		Saint-Denis	4 Jun 92
12.32	0.8	Danielle	Williams	JAM	14.9.92	1	DL	London (OS)	20 Jul 19
12.33	1.4		Donkova			1		Fürth	14 Jun 87
12.33	-0.3	Gail	Devers	USA	19.11.66	1	NC	Sacramento	23 Jul 00
12.34	-0.5		Zagorcheva			1	WCh	Roma	4 Sep 87
12.34	1.9	Sharika	Nelvis	USA	10.5.90	1h3	NC	Eugene	26 Jun 15
12.34	1.2		Rollins			1	NC	Eugene	8 Jul 16
12.34	0.3	Nia	Ali (10)	USA	23.10.88	1	WCh	Doha	6 Oct 19
12.35 WR	0.1		Donkova			1h2	ASV	Köln	17 Aug 86
12.35	-0.2		Pearson			1	OG	London (OS)	7 Aug 12
12.35	0.9	Jasmin	Stowers	USA	23.9.91	1	DL	Doha	15 May 15
12.36 WR	1.9	Grazyna	Rabsztyn	POL	20.9.52	1	Kuso	Warszawa	13 Jun 80
12.36 WR	-0.6		Donkova			1	NC	Sofia	13 Aug 86
12.36	1.1		Donkova			1		Schwechat	15 Jun 88
12.36	0.3		Pearson			1s2	WCh	Daegu	3 Sep 11
12.36	1.4		K Harrison			1	Towns	Athens GA	8 Apr 16
12.36	0.6		K Harrison			1	DL	London (OS)	22 Jul 18
		(31/12)							
12.37	1.5	Joanna	Hayes	USA	23.12.76	1	OG	Athína	24 Aug 04
12.37	-0.2	Dawn	Harper Nelson	USA	13.5.84	2	OG	London (OS)	7 Aug 12
12.39	1.5	Vera	Komisova'	RUS	11.6.53	1	GGala	Roma	5 Aug 80
12.39	1.8	Natalya	Grigoryeva ¶	UKR	3.12.62	2	NC	Kyiv	11 Jul 91
12.40	1.2	Jasmine	Camacho-Quinn	PUR	21.8.96	1	SEC	Knoxville	13 May 18
12.40	0.6	Janeek	Brown	JAM	14.5.98	1	NCAA	Austin	8 Jun 19
12.41	0.5	Alina	Talay	BLR	14.5.89	1		St. Pölten	31 May 18
12.42	1.8	Bettine	Jahn	GDR	3.8.58	1	OD	Berlin	8 Jun 83
		(20)							
12.42	2.0	Anjanette	Kirkland	USA	24.2.74	1	WCh	Edmonton	11 Aug 01
12.43	-0.9	Lucyna	Kalek (Langer)	POL	9.1.56	1		Hannover	19 Aug 84
12.43	-0.3	Michelle	Perry	USA	1.5.79	1s1	NC	Carson	26 Jun 05
12.43	0.2	Lolo	Jones	USA	5.8.82	1s1	OG	Beijing	18 Aug 08
12.43	1.2	Queen	Harrison	USA	10.9.88	2	NC	Des Moines	22 Jun 13
12.44	-0.5	Gloria	Uibel (-Siebert)	GDR	13.1.64	2	WCh	Roma	4 Sep 87
12.44	-0.8	Olga	Shishigina ¶	KAZ	23.12.68	1	Spitzen	Luzern	27 Jun 95
12.44	0.4	Glory	Alozie	NGR/ESP	30.12.77	1	Herc	Monaco	8 Aug 98
12.44	0.2	Damu	Cherry ¶	USA	29.11.77	2rA	Athl	Lausanne	11 Jul 06
12.45	1.3	Cornelia	Oschkenat'	GDR	29.10.61	1		Neubrandenburg	11 Jun 87
		(30)							
12.45	1.4	Brigitte	Foster-Hylton	JAM	7.11.74	1	Pre	Eugene	24 May 03
12.45	1.5	Olena	Krasovska	UKR	17.8.76	2	OG	Athína	24 Aug 04
12.45	1.4	Virginia	Powell/Crawford	USA	7.9.83	1	GP	New York	2 Jun 07
12.46	0.7	Perdita	Felicien	CAN	29.8.80	1	Pre	Eugene	19 Jun 04
12.47	1.1	Marina	Azyabina	RUS	15.6.63	1s2	NC	Moskva	19 Jun 93
12.47	1.1	Danielle	Carruthers	USA	22.12.79	2	WCh	Daegu	3 Sep 11
12.48	-0.2	Kellie	Wells	USA	16.7.82	3	OG	London (OS)	7 Aug 12
12.48	0.2	Tobi	Amusan	NGR	23.4.97	1h5	WCh	Doha	5 Oct 19
12.49	0.9	Susanna	Kallur	SWE	16.2.81	1	ISTAF	Berlin	16 Sep 07
12.49	1.0	Priscilla	Lopes-Schliep	CAN	26.8.82	2	VD	Bruxelles	4 Sep 09
		(40)							
12.50	0.0	Vera	Akimova'	RUS	5.6.59	1		Sochi	19 May 84
12.50	-0.1	Delloreen	Ennis-London	JAM	5.3.75	3	WCh	Osaka	29 Aug 07
12.50	0.8	Josephine	Onyia ¶	NGR/ESP	17.5.86	1	ISTAF	Berlin	1 Jun 08
12.50	1.2	Kristi	Castlin	USA	7.7.88	2	NC	Eugene	8 Jul 16
12.51	1.4	Miesha	McKelvy	USA	26.7.76	2	Pre	Eugene	24 May 03
12.51	0.7	Tiffany	Porter'	USA/GBR	13.11.87	2	C.Cup	Marrakech	14 Sep 14
12.52	-0.4	Michelle	Freeman	JAM	5.5.69	1s1	WCh	Athína	10 Aug 97
12.52	0.6	Chanel	Brissett	USA	10.8.99	2	NCAA	Austin	8 Jun 19
12.53	0.2	Tatyana	Reshetnikova	RUS	14.10.66	1rA	GP II	Linz	4 Jul 94
12.53	-0.4	Svetla	Dimitrova ¶	BUL	27.1.70	1	Herc	Stara Zagora	16 Jul 94
12.53	1.0	Melissa	Morrison	USA	9.7.71	1	DNG	Stockholm	5 Aug 98
		(51)							

100th woman 12.65, 200th 12.78, 300th 12.88, 400th 12.97, 500th 13.03

Wind assisted performances to 12.35, performers to 12.50

| 12.28 | 2.7 | Cornelia | Oschkenat' | GDR | 29.10.61 | 1 | | Berlin | 25 Aug 87 |

100 - 400 METRES HURDLES A-T

Mark	Wind	Name		Nat	Born	Pos	Meet	Venue	Date
12.29	3.5		Donkova			1	Athl	Lausanne	24 Jun 88
12.29	2.7	Gail	Devers	USA	19.11.66	1	Pre	Eugene	26 May 02
12.29	3.8	Lolo	Jones	USA	5.8.82	1	NC/OT	Eugene	6 Jul 08
12.30	2.8		Rollins			1s1	NC	Des Moines	22 Jun 13
12.33	2.3		Rollins			1h3	NC	Des Moines	21 Jun 13
12.35	2.4	Bettine	Jahn	GDR	3.8.58	1	WCh	Helsinki	13 Aug 83
12.35	3.7	Kellie	Wells	USA	16.7.82	1		Gainesville	16 Apr 11
12.37	2.7	Gloria	Uibel/Siebert'	GDR	13.1.64	2		Berlin	25 Aug 87
12.37	3.4	Danielle	Carruthers	USA	22.12.79	1s1	NC	Eugene	26 Jun 11
12.40	2.1	Michelle	Freeman	JAM	5.5.69	1	GPF	Fukuoka	13 Sep 97
12.41	2.2	Olga	Shishigina ¶	KAZ	23.12.68	1rA	Athl	Lausanne	5 Jul 95
12.42	2.4	Kerstin	Knabe	GDR	7.7.59	2	WCh	Helsinki	13 Aug 83
12.43	2.7	Yvette	Lewis	USA/PAN	16.3.85	1	MSR	Walnut	20 Apr 13
12.44	2.6	Melissa	Morrison	USA	9.7.71	1		Carson	22 May 04
12.45	2.1	Perdita	Felicien	CAN	29.8.80	1	NC	Victoria	10 Jul 04
12.47	3.0	Tiffany	Porter	USA/GBR	13.11.87	1		Gainesville	21 Apr 12
12.48	3.8	Kristi	Castlin	USA	7.7.88	1		Clermont	2 Jun 12
12.50	2.7	Svetla	Dimitrova ¶	BUL	27.1.70	1		Saint-Denis	10 Jun 94
Probably hand timed			Officially 12.36, but subsequent investigations showed this unlikely to have been auto-timed						
12.4	0.7	Svetla	Dimitrova ¶	BUL	27.1.70	1		Stara Zagora	9 Jul 97
Hand timed									
12.3 WR	1.5	Anneliese	Ehrhardt	GDR	18.6.50	1	NC	Dresden	22 Jul 73
12.3		Marina	Azyabina	RUS	15.6.63	1		Yekaterinburg	30 May 93
12.0w		Yordanka	Donkova	BUL	28.9.61	1		Sofia	3 Aug 86
12.1w	2.1	Ginka	Zagorcheva	BUL	12.4.58	2		Sofia	3 Aug 86

400 METRES HURDLES

Mark		Name		Nat	Born	Pos	Meet	Venue	Date
52.16 WR		Dalilah	Muhammad	USA	7.2.90	1	WCh	Doha	4 Oct 19
52.20 WR			Muhammad			1	NC	Des Moines	28 Jul 19
52.23		Sydney	McLaughlin	USA	7.8.99	2	WCh	Doha	4 Oct 19
52.34 WR		Yuliya	Nosova-Pechonkina'	RUS	21.4.78	1	NC	Tula	8 Aug 03
52.42		Melaine	Walker	JAM	1.1.83	1	WCh	Berlin	20 Aug 09
52.47		Lashinda	Demus	USA	10.3.83	1	WCh	Daegu	1 Sep 11
52.61 WR		Kim	Batten	USA	29.3.69	1	WCh	Göteborg	11 Aug 95
52.62		Tonja	Buford-Bailey	USA	13.12.70	2	WCh	Göteborg	11 Aug 95
52.63			Demus			1	Herc	Monaco	28 Jul 09
52.64			Walker			1	OG	Beijing	20 Aug 08
52.64			Muhammad			1	NC	Sacramento	25 Jun 1
52.70		Natalya	Antyukh	RUS	26.6.81	1	OG	London (OS)	8 Aug 12
52.73			Walker			2	WCh	Daegu	1 Sep 11
52.74 WR		Sally	Gunnell	GBR	29.7.66	1	WCh	Stuttgart	19 Aug 93
52.74			Batten			1	Herc	Monaco	8 Aug 98
52.75		Shamier	Little (10)	USA	20.3.95	2	NC	Sacramento	25 Jun 17
52.75			McLaughlin			1	SEC	Knoxville	13 May 18
52.77		Faní	Halkiá ¶	GRE	2.2.79	1s2	OG	Athína	22 Aug 04
52.77			Demus			2	OG	London (OS)	8 Aug 12
52.79		Sandra	Farmer-Patrick	USA	18.8.62	2	WCh	Stuttgart	19 Aug 93
52.79		Kaliese	Spencer	JAM	6.5.87	1	LGP	London (CP)	5 Aug 11
52.82		Deon	Hemmings	JAM	9.10.68	1	OG	Atlanta	31 Jul 96
52.82			Halkiá			1		Athína	25 Aug 04
52.82			Demus			1	GGala	Roma	10 Jun 10
52.83		Zuzana	Hejnová	CZE	19.12.86	1	WCh	Moskva	15 Aug 13
52.84			Batten			1	WK	Zürich	12 Aug 98
52.85			McLaughlin			1	WK	Zürich	29 Aug 19
52.88			Muhammad			1	NC	Eugene	10 Jul 16
52.88			McLaughlin			2	NC	Des Moines	27 Jul 19
52.89		Daimí	Pernía	CUB	27.12.76	1	WCh	Sevilla	25 Aug 99
		(30/16)							
52.90		Nezha	Bidouane	MAR	18.9.69	2	WCh	Sevilla	25 Aug 99
52.94 WR		Marina	Styepanova'	RUS	1.5.50	1s	Spart	Tashkent	17 Sep 86
52.95		Sheena	Johnson/Tosta	USA	1.10.82	1	NC/OT	Sacramento	11 Jul 04
52.95		Kori	Carter	USA	3.6.92	3	NC	Sacramento	25 Jun 17
		(20)							
53.02		Irina	Privalova	RUS	22.11.68	1	OG	Sydney	27 Sep 00
53.11		Tatyana	Ledovskaya	BLR	21.5.66	1	WCh	Tokyo	29 Aug 91
53.11		Ashley	Spencer	USA	8.6.93	4	NC	Sacramento	25 Jun 17
53.14		Georganne	Moline	USA	6.3.90	5	NC	Sacramento	25 Jun 17
53.17		Debbie	Flintoff-King	AUS	20.4.60	1	OG	Seoul	28 Sep 88
53.20		Josanne	Lucas	TTO	14.5.84	3	WCh	Berlin	20 Aug 09

400 METRES HURDLES - HIGH JUMP A-T

Mark	Wind	Name		Nat	Born	Pos	Meet	Venue	Date
53.21		Marie-José	Pérec	FRA	9.5.68	2	WK	Zürich	16 Aug 95
53.22		Jana	Pittman/Rawlinson	AUS	9.11.82	1	WCh	Saint-Denis	28 Aug 03
53.24		Sabine	Busch	GDR	21.11.62	1	NC	Potsdam	21 Aug 87
53.25		Ionela	Târlea-Manolache	ROU	9.2.76	2	GGala	Roma	7 Jul 99
		(30)							
53.28		Tiffany	Ross-Williams	USA	5.2.83	1	NC	Indianapolis	24 Jun 07
53.32		Sandra	Glover	USA	30.12.68	3	WCh	Helsinki	13 Aug 05
53.36		Andrea	Blackett	BAR	24.1.76	4	WCh	Sevilla	25 Aug 99
53.36		Brenda	Taylor	USA	9.2.79	2	NC/OT	Sacramento	11 Jul 04
53.37		Tetyana	Tereshchuk	UKR	11.10.69	3s2	OG	Athína	22 Aug 04
53.46		Janieve	Russell	JAM	14.11.93	2	Athl	Lausanne	5 Jul 18
53.47		Janeene	Vickers	USA	3.10.68	3	WCh	Tokyo	29 Aug 91
53.48		Margarita	Ponomaryova'	RUS	19.6.63	3	WCh	Stuttgart	19 Aug 93
53.55		Sara Slott	Petersen	DEN	9.4.87	2	OG	Rio de Janeiro	18 Aug 16
53.58		Cornelia	Ullrich'	GDR	26.4.63	2	NC	Potsdam	21 Aug 87
		(40)							
53.63		Ellen	Fiedler'	GDR	26.11.58	3	OG	Seoul	28 Sep 88
53.65Amx		Myrtle	Bothma'	RSA	18.2.64	mx		Pretoria	12 Mar 90
53.74A						1		Johannesburg	18 Apr 86
53.67		Perri	Shakes-Drayton	GBR	21.12.88	2	DL	London (OS)	26 Jul 13
53.68		Vania	Stambolova ¶	BUL	28.11.83	1		Rabat	5 Jun 11
53.72		Yekaterina	Bikert	RUS	13.5.80	2	NC	Tula	30 Jul 04
53.74		Ristananna	Tracey	JAM	9.5.92	3	WCh	London (OS)	10 Aug 17
53.74		Rushell	Clayton	JAM	18.10.92	3	WCh	Doha	4 Oct 19
53.77		Irina	Davydova	RUS	27.5.88	1	EC	Helsinki	29 Jun 12
53.79		Femke	Bol	NED	23.2.00	1		Papendal	18 Jul 20
53.84		Natasha	Danvers	GBR	19.9.77	3	OG	Beijing	20 Aug 08
		(50)	100th woman 54.39, 200th 55.22, 300th 55.68, 400th 56.01, 500th 56.30						
Drugs disqualification: 53.38			Jiang Limei ¶	CHN	.3.70	(1)		Shanghai	22 Oct 97

HIGH JUMP

2.09 WR	Stefka	Kostadinova	BUL	25.3.65	1	WCh	Roma	30 Aug 87
2.08 WR		Kostadinova			1	NM	Sofia	31 May 86
2.08i WIR	Kajsa	Bergqvist	SWE	12.10.76	1		Arnstadt	4 Feb 06
2.08	Blanka	Vlasic	CRO	8.11.83	1	Hanz	Zagreb	31 Aug 09
2.07 WR	Lyudmila	Andonova ¶	BUL	6.5.60	1	OD	Berlin	20 Jul 84
2.07 WR		Kostadinova			1		Sofia	25 May 86
2.07		Kostadinova			1		Cagliari	16 Sep 87
2.07		Kostadinova			1	NC	Sofia	3 Sep 88
2.07i WIR	Heike	Henkel'	GER	5.5.64	1	NC	Karlsruhe	8 Feb 92
2.07		Vlasic			1	DNG	Stockholm	7 Aug 07
2.07	Anna	Chicherova ¶	RUS	22.7.82	1	NC	Cheboksary	22 Jul 11
2.06		Kostadinova			1	ECp	Moskva	18 Aug 85
2.06		Kostadinova			1		Fürth	15 Jun 86
2.06		Kostadinova			1		Cagliari	14 Sep 86
2.06		Kostadinova			1		Wörrstadt	6 Jun 87
2.06		Kostadinova			1		Rieti	8 Sep 87
2.06i WIR		Kostadinova			1		Pireás	20 Feb 88
2.06		Bergqvist			1		Eberstadt	26 Jul 03
2.06	Hestrie	Cloete	RSA	26.8.78	1	WCh	Saint-Denis	31 Aug 03
2.06	Yelena	Slesarenko	RUS	28.2.82	1	OG	Athína	28 Aug 04
2.06		Vlasic			1		Thessaloníki	30 Jul 07
2.06		Vlasic			1	ECp-1B	Istanbul	22 Jun 08
2.06		Vlasic			1	GP	Madrid	5 Jul 08
2.06	Ariane	Friedrich	GER	10.1.84	1	ISTAF	Berlin	14 Jun 09
2.06i		Vlasic			1		Arnstadt	6 Feb 10
2.06i		Chicherova			1		Arnstadt	4 Feb 12
2.06	Mariya	Lasitskene' (10)	RUS	14.1.93	1	Athl	Lausanne	6 Jul 17
2.06		Lasitskene			1	GS	Ostrava	20 Jun 19
	(48/10)	33 performances at 2.05						
2.05 WR	Tamara	Bykova	RUS	21.12.58	1	Izv	Kyiv	22 Jun 84
2.05	Inga	Babakova	UKR	27.6.67	1		Tokyo	15 Sep 95
2.05i	Tia	Hellebaut	BEL	16.2.78	1	EI	Birmingham	3 Mar 07
2.05	Chaunté	Lowe'	USA	12.1.84	1	NC	Des Moines	26 Jun 10
2.04	Silvia	Costa	CUB	4.5.64	1	WCp	Barcelona	9 Sep 89
2.04i	Alina	Astafei	GER	7.6.69	1		Berlin	3 Mar 95
2.04	Venelina	Veneva ¶	BUL	13.6.74	1		Kalamáta	2 Jun 01
2.04i	Antonietta	Di Martino	ITA	1.6.78	1		Banská Bystrica	9 Feb 11
2.04	Irina	Gordeyeva	RUS	9.10.86	1		Eberstadt	19 Aug 12
2.04	Brigetta	Barrett	USA	24.12.90	1	NC	Des Moines	22 Jun 13

246 HIGH JUMP – POLE VAULT A-T

Mark	Wind	Name		Nat	Born	Pos	Meet	Venue	Date
		(20)							
2.04		Yaroslava	Mahuchikh	UKR	19.9.01	2	WCh	Doha	30 Sep 19
2.03 WR		Ulrike	Meyfarth	FRG	4.5.56	1	ECp	London (CP)	21 Aug 83
2.03		Louise	Ritter	USA	18.2.58	1		Austin	8 Jul 88
2.03		Tatyana	Motkova	RUS	23.11.68	2		Bratislava	30 May 95
2.03		Níki	Bakoyiánni	GRE	9.6.68	2	OG	Atlanta	3 Aug 96
2.03i		Monica	Iagar/Dinescu	ROU	2.4.73	1		Bucuresti	23 Jan 99
2.03i		Marina	Kuptsova	RUS	22.12.81	1	EI	Wien	2 Mar 02
2.03		Svetlana	Shkolina	RUS	9.3.86	3	OG	London (OS)	11 Aug 12
2.02i		Susanne	Beyer'	GDR	24.6.61	2	WI	Indianapolis	8 Mar 87
2.02		Yelena	Yelesina	RUS	4.4.70	1	GWG	Seattle	23 Jul 90
		(30)							
2.02		Viktoriya	Styopina	UKR	21.2.76	3	OG	Athína	28 Aug 04
2.02		Ruth	Beitia	ESP	1.4.79	1	NC	San Sebastián	4 Aug 07
2.02i		Kamila	Licwinko'	POL	22.3.86	1	NC	Torun	21 Feb 15
2.02		Elena	Vallortigara	ITA	21.9.91	2	DL	London (OS)	22 Jul 18
2.02		Nafissatou	Thiam	BEL	19.8.94	1H	Déca	Talence	22 Jun 19
2.02		Yuliya	Levchenko	UKR	28.11.97	1	E v USA	Minsk	10 Sep 19
2.01 WR		Sara	Simeoni	ITA	19.4.53	1	v Pol	Brescia	4 Aug 78
2.01		Olga	Turchak	UKR	5.3.67	2	GWG	Moskva	7 Jul 86
2.01A		Desiré	du Plessis	RSA	20.5.65	1		Johannesburg	16 Sep 86
2.01i		Gabriele	Günz	GDR	8.9.61	2		Stuttgart	31 Jan 88
		(40)							
2.01		Heike	Balck	GDR	19.8.70	1	vUSSR-j	Karl-Marx-Stadt	18 Jun 89
2.01i		Ioamnet	Quintero	CUB	8.9.72	1		Berlin	5 Mar 93
2.01		Hanne	Haugland	NOR	14.12.67	1	WK	Zürich	13 Aug 97
2.01i		Tisha	Waller	USA	1.12.70	1	NC	Atlanta	28 Feb 98
2.01		Yelena	Gulyayeva ¶	RUS	14.8.67	2		Kalamáta	23 May 98
2.01		Vita	Palamar	UKR	12.10.77	2=	WK	Zürich	15 Aug 03
2.01		Amy	Acuff	USA	14.7.75	4	WK	Zürich	15 Aug 03
2.01		Iryna	Myhalchenko	UKR	20.1.72	1		Eberstadt	18 Jul 04
2.01		Emma	Green Tregaro	SWE	8.12.84	2	EC	Barcelona	1 Aug 10
2.01i		Airine	Palsyte	LTU	13.7.92	1	EI	Beograd	4 Mar 17
		(50)	100th woman 1.98, 200th 1.95, 300th 1.93, 400th 1.92, 500th 1.91							

Best outdoor marks
2.05	Henkel	1	WCh Tokyo	31 Aug 91	2.02	Iagar/Dinescu	1		Budapest	6 Jun 98
2.05	Hellebaut	1	OG Beijing	23 Aug 08	2.02	Kuptsova	1	FBK	Hengelo	1 Jun 03
2.03	Di Martino	1	ECp-1B Milano	24 Jun 07	2.01	Astafei	2		Wörrstadt	27 May 95

Ancillary jumps: 2.06 Kostadinova 30 Aug 87, 2.05i Henkel 8 Feb 92, 2.05i Bergqvist 4 Feb 06, 2.05 Vlasic 31 Aug 09

POLE VAULT

Mark		Name		Nat	Born	Pos	Meet	Venue	Date
5.06 WR	Yelena		Isinbayeva	RUS	3.6.82	1	WK	Zürich	28 Aug 09
5.05 WR			Isinbayeva			1	OG	Beijing	18 Aug 08
5.04 WR			Isinbayeva			1	Herc	Monaco	29 Jul 08
5.03 WR			Isinbayeva			1	GGala	Roma	11 Jul 08
5.03i WIR	Jennifer		Suhr	USA	5.2.82	1		Brockport	30 Jan 16
5.02Ai WIR			Suhr			1	NC	Albuquerque	2 Mar 13
5.01 WR			Isinbayeva			1	WCh	Helsinki	12 Aug 05
5.01i WIR			Isinbayeva			1	XL Galan	Stockholm	23 Feb 12
5.01i			Suhr			1		Fredonia	1 Oct 16
5.00 WR			Isinbayeva			1	LGP	London (CP)	22 Jul 05
5.00i WIR			Isinbayeva			1		Donetsk	15 Feb 09
5.00	Sandi		Morris	USA	8.7.92	1	VD	Bruxelles	9 Sep 16
4.95 WR			Isinbayeva			1	GP	Madrid	16 Jul 05
4.95i WIR			Isinbayeva			1		Donetsk	16 Feb 08
4.95i			Morris			1	NC	Portland	12 Mar 16
4.95i			Morris			1	WI	Birmingham	3 Mar 18
4.95			Morris			1		Greenville	27 Jul 18
4.95	Anzhelika		Sidorova	RUS	28.6.91	1	WCh	Doha	29 Sep 19
4.95i			Sidorova			1		Moskva	29 Feb 20
4.94	Eliza		McCartney	NZL	11.12.96	1		Jockgrim	17 Jul 18
4.93 WR			Isinbayeva			1	Athl	Lausanne	5 Jul 05
4.93			Isinbayeva			1	VD	Bruxelles	26 Aug 05
4.93i WIR			Isinbayeva			1		Donetsk	10 Feb 07
4.93			Isinbayeva			1	LGP	London (CP)	25 Jul 08
4.93			Morris			1		Houston	23 Jul 16
4.93			Suhr			1		Austin	14 Apr 18
4.92 WR			Isinbayeva			1	VD	Bruxelles	3 Sep 04
4.92			Stuczynski/Suhr			1	NC/OT	Eugene	6 Jul 08
4.92			McCartney			1		Mannheim	23 Jun 18

POLE VAULT A-T

Mark	Wind	Name		Nat	Born	Pos	Meet	Venue	Date
4.92i			Sidorova			1	NC	Moskva	25 Feb 20
4.92		Katie	Nageotte	USA	13.6.91	1		Marietta	1 Aug 20
		(31/6)							
4.91		Yarisley	Silva	CUB	1.6.87	1		Beckum	2 Aug 15
4.91		Ekateríni	Stefanídi	GRE	4.2.90	1	WCh	London (OS)	6 Aug 17
4.90i		Demi	Payne	USA	30.9.91	2	Mill	New York (A)	20 Feb 16
4.88 WR		Svetlana	Feofanova	RUS	16.7.80	1		Iráklio	4 Jul 04
		(10)							
4.87i		Holly	Bleasdale/Bradshaw	GBR	2.11.91	1		Villeurbanne	20 Jan 12
4.87		Fabiana	Murer	BRA	16.3.81	1	NC	São Bernardo do Campo	3 Jul 16
4.85i		Anna	Rogowska	POL	21.5.81	1	EI	Paris (Bercy)	6 Mar 11
4.83		Stacy	Dragila	USA	25.3.71	1	GS	Ostrava	8 Jun 04
4.83		Nikoléta	Kiriakopoúlou	GRE	21.3.86	1	DL	Saint-Denis	4 Jul 15
4.83		Michaela	Meijer	SWE	30.7.93	1		Norrköping	1 Aug 20
4.82		Monika	Pyrek	POL	11.8.80	2	WAF	Stuttgart	22 Sep 07
4.82		Silke	Spiegelburg	GER	17.3.86	1	Herc	Monaco	20 Jul 12
4.82		Alysha	Newman	CAN	29.6.94	1	DL	Paris (C)	24 Aug 19
4.81		Alana	Boyd	AUS	10.5.84	1		Sippy Downs	2 Jul 16
		(20)							
4.81i		Angelica	Bengtsson	SWE	8.7.93	2		Clermont-Ferrand	24 Feb 19
4.80		Martina	Strutz	GER	4.11.81	2	WCh	Daegu	30 Aug 11
4.80i		Nicole	Büchler	SUI	17.12.83	4	WI	Portland	17 Mar 16
4.78		Tatyana	Polnova	RUS	20.4.79	2	WAF	Monaco	19 Sep 04
4.78i		Robeilys	Peinado	VEN	26.11.97	2		Liévin	19 Feb 20
4.77		Annika	Becker	GER	12.11.81	1	NC	Wattenscheid	7 Jul 02
4.76		Jirina	Ptácníková'	CZE	20.5.86	1		Plzen	4 Sep 13
4.75		Katerina	Badurová	CZE	18.12.82	2	WCh	Osaka	28 Aug 07
4.75i		Yuliya	Golubchikova	RUS	27.3.83	1		Athína (P)	13 Feb 08
4.75Ai		Kylie	Hutson	USA	27.11.87	2	NC	Albuquerque	2 Mar 13
		(30)							
4.75i		Lisa	Ryzih	GER	27.9.88	2	EI	Beograd	4 Mar 17
4.75		Ninon	Guillon-Romarin	FRA	15.4.95	8	Herc	Monaco	20 Jul 18
4.73		Chelsea	Johnson	USA	20.12.83	1		Los Gatos	26 Jun 08
4.73		Anastasiya	Savchenko	RUS	15.11.89	1	NCp	Yerino	15 Jun 13
4.73		Olivia	Gruver	USA	29.7.97	1		Stanford	29 Mar 19
4.73		Tina	Sutej	SLO	7.11.88	1		Velenje	15 Sep 19
4.72i		Kym	Howe	AUS	12.6.80	2		Donetsk	10 Feb 07
4.72i		Jillian	Schwartz	USA/ISR	19.9.79	1		Jonesboro	15 Jun 08
4.72		Carolin	Hingst	GER	18.9.80	1		Biberach	9 Jul 10
4.72		Li Ling		CHN	6.7.89	2=	DL	Shanghai	18 May 19
		(40)							
4.72		Irina	Zhuk	BLR	26.1.93	1	NC	Minsk	20 Aug 20
4.72		Nina	Kennedy	AUS	5.4.97	1		Perth	16 Dec 20
4.71Ai		Mary	Saxer Sibears	USA	21.6.87	1	NC	Albuquerque	23 Feb 14
4.71i		Marion	Fiack	FRA	13.10.92	1		Aubière	10 Jan 15
4.71i		Wilma	Murto	FIN	11.6.98	1		Zweibrücken	31 Jan 16
4.70		Yvonne	Buschbaum	GER	14.7.80	1	NC	Ulm	29 Jun 03
4.70		Vanessa	Boslak	FRA	11.6.82	2	ECp-S	Málaga	28 Jun 06
4.70		Angelina	Zhuk/Krasnova	RUS	7.2.91	1	EU23	Tampere	13 Jul 13
4.70		Kristen	Brown	USA	26.5.92	1		Chula Vista	26 Jun 16
4.70		Lexi	Weeks/Jacobus	USA	20.11.96	3	NC	Eugene	10 Jul 16
		(50)							
4.70		Xu Huiqin		CHN	4.9.93	3		Jockgrim	17 Jul 19
4.70		Emily	Grove	USA	22.5.93	2		Omaha	1 Aug 19
4.70i		Morgann	LeLeux	USA	14.11.92	1		Baton Rouge	21 Feb 20
4.70		Eléni-Klaoúdia	Pólak	GRE	9.9.96	1		Athína (AK)	18 Jul 20
		(54)	100th woman 4.60, 200th 4.45, 300th 4.40, 400th 4.31, 500th 4.26						

Outdoor bests

4.83	Rogowska	2	VD	Bruxelles	26 Aug 05	4.73	Ryzih	3		Rottach-Egern	15 Jul 17
4.81	Bradshaw	1		Rottach-Egern	15 Jul 17	4.71	Payne	1		Hammond	8 May 15
4.80	Bengtsson	6	WCh	Doha	29 Sep 19	4.70	Hutson	1		Terre Haute	15 Jun 13
4.78	Büchler	2	DL	Doha	6 May 16	4.70	Saxer	1		Chula Vista	6 Jun 13
4.75	Golubchikova	4	OG	Beijing	18 Aug 08	4.70	Peinado	1		SAmG Cochabamba	7 Jun 18

Ancillary jumps: Isinbayeva: 4.97 15 Feb 09, 4.96 WR 22 Jul 05, 4.95 18 Aug 08, 4.93 29 Jul 08, 4.92i 23 Feb 12
Exhibition: 4.72 Anastasiya Shvedova RUS 3.5.79 1 Aosta 5 Jul 08

LONG JUMP

7.52 WR	1.4	Galina	Chistyakova	RUS	26.7.62	1	Znam	Leningrad	11 Jun 88
7.49	1.3	Jackie	Joyner-Kersee	USA	3.3.62	1	NYG	New York	22 May 94
7.49A	1.7		Joyner-Kersee			1		Sestriere	31 Jul 94
7.48	1.2	Heike	Drechsler	GER	16.12.64	1	v ITA	Neubrandenburg	9 Jul 88

LONG JUMP A-T

Mark	Wind	Name		Nat	Born	Pos	Meet	Venue	Date
7.48	0.4		Drechsler			1	Athl	Lausanne	8 Jul 92
7.45 WR	0.9		Drechsler'			1	v USSR	Tallinn	21 Jun 86
7.45 WR	1.1		Drechsler			1	OD	Dresden	3 Jul 86
7.45 WR	0.6		Joyner-Kersee			1	PAm	Indianapolis	13 Aug 87
7.45	1.6		Chistyakova			1	BGP	Budapest	12 Aug 88
7.44 WR	2.0		Drechsler			1		Berlin	22 Sep 85
7.43 WR	1.4	Anisoara	Cusmir/Stanciu	ROU	28.6.62	1	RomIC	Bucuresti	4 Jun 83
7.42	2.0	Tatyana	Kotova ¶	RUS	11.12.76	1	ECp-S	Annecy	23 Jun 02
7.40	1.8		Daute' (Drechsler)			1		Dresden	26 Jul 84
7.40	0.7		Drechsler			1	NC	Potsdam	21 Aug 87
7.40	0.9		Joyner-Kersee			1	OG	Seoul	29 Sep 88
7.39	0.3		Drechsler			1	WK	Zürich	21 Aug 85
7.39	0.5	Yelena	Byelevskaya'	BLR	11.10.63	1	NC	Bryansk	18 Jul 87
7.39			Joyner-Kersee			1		San Diego	25 Jun 88
7.37i WR	-		Drechsler			1	v2N	Wien	13 Feb 88
7.37A	1.8		Drechsler			1		Sestriere	31 Jul 91
7.37		Inessa	Kravets ¶	UKR	5.10.66	1		Kyiv	13 Jun 92
7.36	0.4		Joyner			1	WCh	Roma	4 Sep 87
7.36	1.8		Byelevskaya			2	Znam	Leningrad	11 Jun 88
7.36	1.8		Drechsler			1		Jena	28 May 92
7.35	1.9		Chistyakova			1	GPB	Bratislava	20 Jun 90
7.34	1.6		Daute'			1		Dresden	19 May 84
7.34	1.4		Chistyakova			2	v GDR	Tallinn	21 Jun 86
7.34			Byelevskaya			1		Sukhumi	17 May 87
7.34	0.7		Drechsler			1	v USSR	Karl-Marx-Stadt	20 Jun 87
7.33	0.4		Drechsler			1	v USSR	Erfurt	22 Jun 85
7.33	2.0		Drechsler			1		Dresden	2 Aug 85
7.33	-0.3		Drechsler			1	Herc	Monaco	11 Aug 92
7.33	0.4	Tatyana	Lebedeva ¶	RUS	21.7.76	1	NC	Tula	31 Jul 04
		(33/8)							
7.31	1.5	Yelena	Kokonova'	UKR	4.8.63	1	NP	Alma-Ata	12 Sep 85
7.31	1.9	Marion	Jones ¶	USA	12.10.75	1	Pre	Eugene	31 May 98
		(10)							
7.31	1.7	Brittney	Reese	USA	9.9.86	1	NC	Eugene	2 Jul 16
7.30	-0.8	Malaika	Mihambo	GER	3.2.94	1	WCh	Doha	6 Oct 19
7.27	-0.4	Irina	Simagina/Meleshina	RUS	25.5.82	2	NC	Tula	31 Jul 04
7.26A	1.8	Maurren	Maggi ¶	BRA	25.6.76	1	SACh	Bogotá	26 Jun 99
7.24	1.0	Larisa	Berezhnaya	UKR	28.2.61	1		Granada	25 May 91
7.24i		Ivana	Spanovic	SRB	10.5.90	1	EI	Beograd	5 Mar 17
7.21	1.6	Helga	Radtke	GDR	16.5.62	2		Dresden	26 Jul 84
7.21	1.9	Lyudmila	Kolchanova	RUS	1.10.79	1		Sochi	27 May 07
7.20 WR	-0.5	Valy	Ionescu	ROU	31.8.60	1	NC	Bucuresti	1 Aug 82
7.20	2.0	Irena	Ozhenko'	LTU	13.11.62	1		Budapest	12 Sep 86
		(20)							
7.20	0.8	Yelena	Sinchukova'	RUS	23.1.61	1	BGP	Budapest	20 Jun 91
7.20	0.7	Irina	Mushayilova	RUS	6.1.67	1	NC	Sankt-Peterburg	14 Jul 94
7.17	1.8	Irina	Valyukevich	BLR	19.11.59	2	NC	Bryansk	18 Jul 87
7.17	0.6	Tianna	Bartoletta'	USA	30.8.85	1	OG	Rio de Janeiro	17 Aug 16
7.16		Iolanda	Chen	RUS	26.7.61	1		Moskva	30 Jun 88
7.16A	-0.1	Elva	Goulbourne	JAM	21.1.80	1		Ciudad de México	22 May 04
7.16	1.6	Sosthene	Moguenara	GER	17.10.89	1		Weinheim	28 May 16
7.14	1.8	Nijole	Medvedeva ¶	LTU	20.10.60	1		Riga	4 Jun 88
7.14	1.2	Mirela	Dulgheru	ROU	5.10.66	1	Balk G	Sofia	5 Jul 92
7.13	2.0	Olga	Kucherenko ¶	RUS	5.11.85	1		Sochi	27 May 10
		(30)							
7.12	1.6	Sabine	Paetz/John'	GDR	16.10.57	2		Dresden	19 May 84
7.12	0.9	Chioma	Ajunwa ¶	NGR	25.12.70	1	OG	Atlanta	2 Aug 96
7.12	1.3	Naide	Gomes	CPV/POR	10.11.79	1	Herc	Monaco	29 Jul 08
7.11	0.8	Fiona	May	GBR/ITA	12.12.69	2	EC	Budapest	22 Aug 98
7.11	1.3	Anna	Nazarova ¶	RUS	3.2.86	1	Mosc Ch	Moskva	20 Jun 12
7.10	1.6	Chelsea	Hayes	USA	9.2.88	2	NC/OT	Eugene	1 Jul 12
7.09 WR	0.0	Vilhelmina	Bardauskiené	LTU	15.6.53	Q	EC	Praha	29 Aug 78
7.09	1.5	Ljudmila	Ninova	AUT	25.6.60	1	GP II	Sevilla	5 Jun 94
7.08	0.5	Marieta	Ilcu ¶	ROU	16.10.62	1	RumIC	Pitesti	25 Jun 89
7.08	1.9	Anastasiya	Mironchik-Ivanova	BLR	13.4.89	1		Minsk	12 Jun 12
		(40)							
7.07	0.0	Svetlana	Zorina	RUS	2.2.60	1		Krasnodar	15 Aug 87
7.07	0.5	Yelena	Sokolova	RUS	23.7.86	2	OG	London (OS)	8 Aug 12
7.07	0.4	Shara	Proctor	AIA/GBR	16.9.88	2	WCh	Beijing	28 Aug 15
7.06	0.4	Tatyana	Kolpakova	KGZ	18.10.59	1	OG	Moskva	31 Jul 80

LONG JUMP – TRIPLE JUMP A-T

Mark	Wind	Name	Name	Nat	Born	Pos	Meet	Venue	Date
7.06	-0.1	Niurka	Montalvo	CUB/ESP	4.6.68	1	WCh	Sevilla	23 Aug 99
7.06		Tatyana	Ter-Mesrobyan	RUS	12.5.68	1		Sankt Peterburg	22 May 02
7.05	0.6	Lyudmila	Galkina	RUS	20.1.72	1	WCh	Athína	9 Aug 97
7.05	-0.4	Eunice	Barber	FRA	17.11.74	1	WAF	Monaco	14 Sep 03
7.05	1.1	Darya	Klishina	RUS	15.1.91	1	EU23	Ostrava	17 Jul 11
7.05	2.0	Brooke	Stratton	AUS	12.7.93	1		Perth	12 Mar 16
7.05	1.2	Lorraine	Ugen	GBR	22.8.91	1	NC	Birmingham	1 Jul 18
7.05	0.9	Ese	Brume	NGR	20.1.96	1	NC	Bursa	4 Aug 19
(52)			100th woman 6.94, 200th 6.83, 300th 6.77, 400th 6.72, 500th 6.67						

Wind assisted Performances to 7.35, performers to 7.07

Mark	Wind	Name	Name	Nat	Born	Pos	Meet	Venue	Date
7.63A	2.1	Heike	Drechsler	GER	16.12.64	1		Sestriere	21 Jul 92
7.45	2.6		Joyner-Kersee			1	NC/OT	Indianapolis	23 Jul 88
7.39	2.6		Drechsler			1		Padova	15 Sep 91
7.39	2.9		Drechsler			1	Expo	Sevilla	6 Jun 92
7.39A	3.3		Drechsler			2		Sestriere	31 Jul 94
7.36	2.2		Chistyakova			1	Znam	Volgograd	11 Jun 89
7.35	3.4		Drechsler			1	NC	Jena	29 Jun 86
7.23A	4.3	Fiona	May	ITA	12.12.69	1		Sestriere	29 Jul 95
7.22	4.3	Anastasiya	Mironchik-Ivanova	BLR	13.4.89	1	NC	Grodno	6 Jul 12
7.19A	3.7	Susen	Tiedtke ¶	GER	23.1.69	1		Sestriere	28 Jul 93
7.17	3.6	Eva	Murková	SVK	29.5.62	1		Nitra	26 Aug 84
7.15	2.8	Janay	DeLoach-Soukup	USA	12.10.85	Q	NC/OT	Eugene	29 Jun 12
7.14A	4.5	Marieke	Veltman	USA	18.9.71	2		Sestriere	29 Jul 95
7.14	2.2	Blessing	Okagbare	NGR	9.10.88	2	DL	Doha	10 May 13
7.12A	5.8	Níki	Xánthou	GRE	11.10.73	3		Sestriere	29 Jul 95
7.12A	4.3	Nicole	Boegman	AUS	5.3.67	4		Sestriere	29 Jul 95
7.09	2.9	Renata	Nielsen	DEN	18.5.66	2		Sevilla	5 Jun 94
7.08	2.2	Lyudmila	Galkina	RUS	20.1.72	1		Thessaloniki	23 Jun 99
7.07A	5.6	Valentina	Uccheddu	ITA	26.10.66	5		Sestriere	29 Jul 95
7.07A	2.7	Sharon	Couch	USA	13.9.67	1		El Paso	12 Apr 97
7.07A	w	Erica	Johansson	SWE	5.2.74	1		Vygieskraal	15 Jan 00

Best outdoors: 7.10 0.3 Spanovic 1 Beograd 11 Sep 16
Best at low altitude:
7.06 0.8 Maggi ¶ 1 Milano 3 Jun 03 | 7.12w 3.4 May 1 NC Bologna 25 May 96
         7.17w 2.6 1 São Paulo 13 Apr 02 |
Ancillary marks – other marks during series (to 7.34/7.36w)
7.45 WR 1.0 Chistyakova 11 Jun 88 | 7.47Aw 3.1 Drechsler 21 Jul 92 | 7.38w 2.2 Chistyakova 11 Jun 88
7.37   Drechsler   9 Jul 88 | 7.39Aw 3.1 Drechsler 21 Jul 92 | 7.36w   Joyner-Kersee 31 Jul 94

TRIPLE JUMP

Mark	Wind	Name	Name	Nat	Born	Pos	Meet	Venue	Date
15.50 WR	0.9	Inessa	Kravets ¶	UKR	5.10.66	1	WCh	Göteborg	10 Aug 95
15.43i WIR		Yulimar	Rojas	VEN	21.10.95	1		Madrid	21 Feb 20
15.41	1.5		Rojas			1		Andújar	6 Sep 19
15.39	0.5	Françoise	Mbango	CMR	14.4.76	1	OG	Beijing	17 Aug 08
15.37	-0.6		Rojas			1	WCh	Doha	5 Oct 19 15.36i
WIR		Tatyana	Lebedeva ¶	RUS	21.7.76	1	WI	Budapest	6 Mar 04
15.34	-0.5		Lebedeva			1		Iráklio	4 Jul 04
15.33	-0.1		Kravets			1	OG	Atlanta	31 Jul 96
15.33	1.2		Lebedeva			1	Athl	Lausanne	6 Jul 04
15.32	0.5		Lebedeva			1	Super	Yokohama	9 Sep 00
15.32	0.9	Hrisopiyí	Devetzí ¶	GRE	2.1.76	Q	OG	Athína	21 Aug 04
15.31	0.0	Caterine	Ibargüen	COL	12.2.84	1	Herc	Monaco	18 Jul 14
15.30	0.6		Mbango			1	OG	Athína	23 Aug 04
15.29	0.3	Yamilé	Aldama	CUB/SUD/GBR	14.8.72	1	GGala	Roma	11 Jul 03
15.28	0.3		Aldama			1	GP	Linz	2 Aug 04
15.28	0.9	Yargelis	Savigne	CUB	13.11.84	1	WCh	Osaka	31 Aug 07
15.27	1.3		Aldama			1	GP	London (CP)	8 Aug 03
15.25	-0.8		Lebedeva			1	WCh	Edmonton	10 Aug 01
15.25	-0.1		Devetzí			2	OG	Athína	23 Aug 04
15.25	1.7	Olga	Rypakova	KAZ	30.11.84	1	C.Cup	Split	4 Sep 10
15.23	0.8		Lebedeva			1		Réthimno	23 Jun 04
15.23	0.6		Lebedeva			1	Tsik	Athína	3 Jul 06
15.21	1.2		Aldama			2		Réthimno	23 Jun 04
15.20	0.0	Sarka	Kaspárková (10)	CZE	20.5.71	1	WCh	Athína	4 Aug 97
15.20	-0.3	Tereza	Marinova	BUL	5.9.77	1	OG	Sydney	24 Sep 00
15.20	1.3		Savigne			1	Vard	Réthimno	14 Jul 08
15.19	0.5		Lebedeva			1	Athl	Lausanne	11 Jul 06
15.18	0.3	Iva	Prandzheva ¶	BUL	15.2.72	2	WCh	Göteborg	10 Aug 95
15.18	-0.2		Lebedeva			1	WCh	Saint-Denis	26 Aug 03
15.17	0.4		Ibargüen			1	OG	Rio de Janeiro	14 Aug 16

(30/12(

TRIPLE JUMP – SHOT A-T

Mark	Wind	Name		Nat	Born	Pos	Meet	Venue	Date
15.16	0.1	Rodica	Mateescu ¶	ROU	13.3.71	2	WCh	Athína	4 Aug 97
15.16i	WIR -	Ashia	Hansen	GBR	5.12.71	1	EI	Valencia	28 Feb 98
15.16	0.7	Trecia	Smith	JAM	5.11.75	2	GP	Linz	2 Aug 04
15.14	1.9	Nadezhda	Alekhina	RUS	22.9.78	1	NC	Cheboksary	26 Jul 09
15.09 WR	0.5	Anna	Biryukova	RUS	27.9.67	1	WCh	Stuttgart	21 Aug 93
15.09	-0.5	Inna	Lasovskaya	RUS	17.12.69	1	ECCp-A	Valencia	31 May 97
15.08i		Marija	Sestak	SLO	17.4.79	1		Athína (P)	13 Feb 08
15.07	-0.6	Paraskeví	Tsiamíta	GRE	10.3.72	Q	WCh	Sevilla	22 Aug 99
		(20)							
15.04	1.7	Yekaterina	Koneva ¶	RUS	25.9.88	2	Pre	Eugene	30 May 15
15.03i	WIR	Iolanda	Chen	RUS	26.7.61	1	WI	Barcelona	11 Mar 95
15.03	1.9	Magdelin	Martinez	ITA	10.2.76	1		Roma	26 Jun 04
15.02	0.9	Anna	Pyatykh ¶	RUS	4.4.81	3	EC	Göteborg	8 Sep 06
15.00	1.2	Kène	Ndoye	SEN	20.11.78	2		Iráklio	4 Jul 04
14.99	0.2	Olha	Saladukha	UKR	4.6.83	1	EC	Helsinki	29 Jun 12
14.98	1.8	Sofia	Bozhanova ¶	BUL	4.10.67	1		Stara Zagora	16 Jul 94
14.98	0.2	Baya	Rahouli	ALG	27.7.79	1	MedG	Almeria	1 Jul 05
14.96	0.7	Yelena	Hovorova	UKR	18.9.73	4	OG	Sydney	24 Sep 00
14.94i	–	Cristina	Nicolau	ROU	9.8.77	1	NC	Bucuresti	5 Feb 00
		(30)							
14.94i		Oksana	Udmurtova	RUS	1.2.82	1		Tartu	20 Feb 08
14.93	0.0	Shanieka	Ricketts'	JAM	2.2.92	1	WK	Zürich	29 Aug 19
14.90	1.0		Xie Limei	CHN	27.6.86	1		Urumqi	20 Sep 07
14.85	1.2	Viktoriya	Gurova' ¶	RUS	22.5.82	3	NC	Kazan	19 Jul 08
14.84	0.0	Tori	Franklin	USA	7.10.92	1		Baie-Mahault	12 May 18
14.83i	-	Yelena	Lebedenko	RUS	16.1.71	1		Samara	1 Feb 01
14.83	0.5	Yelena	Oleynikova	RUS	9.12.76	1	Odlozil	Praha	17 Jun 02
14.79	1.7	Irina	Mushayilova	RUS	6.1.67	1	DNG	Stockholm	5 Jul 93
14.78i		Adelina	Gavrila	ROU	26.11.78	1		Bucuresti	3 Feb 08
14.78	-0.1	Hanna	Minenko	UKR/ISR	25.9.89	2	WCh	Beijing	24 Aug 15
		(40)							
14.77	0.9	Liadagmis	Povea	CUB	6.2.96	3	Athl	Lausanne	5 Jul 19
14.76	0.9	Galina	Chistyakova	RUS	26.7.62	1	Spitzen	Luzern	27 Jun 95
14.76	1.1	Gundega	Sproģe ¶	LAT	12.12.72	3		Sheffield	29 Jun 97
14.76	0.4	Kseniya	Detsuk	BLR	23.4.86	*	NCp	Brest	26 May 12
14.73	-1.3	Paraskeví	Papahrístou	GRE	17.4.89	1		Athína (F)	8 Jun 16
14.73i		Ana	Peleteiro	ESP	2.12.95	1	EI	Glasgow	3 Mar 19
14.72	1.8		Huang Qiuyan	CHN	25.1.80	1	NG	Guangzhou	22 Nov 01
14.72	1.7	Keturah	Orji	USA	5.3.96	3	DL	Paris (C)	24 Aug 19
14.71	1.4	Athanasía	Pérra	GRE	2.2.83	1	NC	Athína	16 Jun 12
14.70i		Oksana	Rogova	RUS	7.10.78	1		Volgograd	6 Feb 02
		(50)		100th woman 14.46, 200th 14.18, 300th 14.03, 400th 1390, 500th 13.77					

Wind assisted   Performances to 15.18, performers to 14.75

Mark	Wind	Name		Nat	Born	Pos	Meet	Venue	Date
15.24A	4.2	Magdelin	Martinez	ITA	10.2.76	1		Sestriere	1 Aug 04
15.18	2.1		Ibargüen			1	Pre	Eugene	30 May 15
15.17	2.4	Anna	Pyatykh ¶	RUS	4.4.81	2	SGP	Athína	3 Jul 06
15.10	2.7	Keila	Costa	BRA	6.2.83	1		Uberlandia	6 May 07
15.06	2.6	Olga	Saladukha	UKR	4.6.83	1	DNG	Stockholm	29 Jul 11
15.05	3.1	Liadagmis	Povea	CUB	6.2.96	1	NC	La Habana	8 Mar 19
14.99	6.8	Yelena	Hovorova	UKR	18.9.73	1	WUG	Palma de Mallorca	11 Jul 99
14.85	2.5	Gabriela	Petrova	BUL	29.6.92	1	ET-2	Stara Zagora	20 Jun 15
14.84	4.1	Galina	Chistyakova	RUS	26.7.62	1		Innsbruck	28 Jun 95
14.83	8.3		Ren Ruiping	CHN	1.2.76	1		Taiyun	21 May 95
14.83	2.2	Heli	Koivula-Kruger	FIN	27.6.75	2	EC	München	10 Aug 02
14.81	2.4	Kseniya	Detsuk	BLR	23.4.86	1	NCp	Brest	26 May 12
14.78	2.7	Kimberly	Williams	JAM	3.11.88	3	Pre	Eugene	1 Jun 13
14.77	2.3	Paraskeví	Papahrístou	GRE	17.4.89	1		Ankara	5 Jun 12
14.75	4.2	Jelena	Blazevica	LAT	11.5.70	1	v2N	Kaunas	23 Aug 97

Best outdoor mark for athlete with all-time best indoors

15.15	1.7	Hansen	1	GPF	Fukuoka	13 Sep 97	14.85	1.4	Udmurtova 1	Padova	31 Aug 08
15.03	1.1	Sestak	6	OG	Beijing	17 Aug 08	14.75	1.1	Gavrila 3	GP II Rieti	7 Sep 03
14.97WR	0.9	Chen	1	NC	Moskva	18 Jun 93	14.70	1.3	Nicolau 1	EU23 Göteborg	1 Aug 99

Ancillary marks – other marks during series (to 15.19)

15.30	0.5	Mbango	23 Aug 04	15.28	-0.3	Ledebeva		4 Jul 04	15.21 -0.2 Mbango	23 Aug 04
15.29i		Rojas	21 Feb 20	15.25i	WIR	Ledebeva		6 Mar 04	15.19 1.0 Lebedeva	3 Jul 06
									15.19 1.3 Mbango	17 Aug 0

Drugs disqualification

15.32	0.5		Lebedeva		(2)	OG	Beijing	17 Aug 08
15.23	1.6		Devetzi ¶		(3)	OG	Beijing	17 Aug 08
15.22	1.5		Devetzí ¶		(1)		Thessaloníki	9 Jul 08

A – mark made at an altitude of 1000m or higher,   i – indoors,   Q – in qualifying competition,   WR - world record

SHOT A-T

Mark	Wind	Name		Nat	Born	Pos	Meet	Venue	Date
22.63 WR		Natalya	Lisovskaya	RUS	16.7.62	1	Znam	Moskva	7 Jun 87
22.55			Lisovskaya			1	NC	Tallinn	5 Jul 88
22.53 WR			Lisovskaya			1		Sochi	27 May 84
22.53			Lisovskaya			1		Kyiv	14 Aug 88
22.50i WIR		Helena	Fibingerová	CZE	13.7.49	1		Jablonec	19 Feb 77
22.45 WR		Ilona	Slupianek' ¶	GDR	24.9.56	1		Potsdam	11 May 80
22.41			Slupianek			1	OG	Moskva	24 Jul 80
22.40			Slupianek			1		Berlin	3 Jun 83
22.38			Slupianek			1		Karl-Marx-Stadt	25 May 80
22.36 WR			Slupianek			1		Celje	2 May 80
22.34			Slupianek			1		Berlin	7 May 80
22.34			Slupianek			1	NC	Cottbus	18 Jul 80
22.32 WR			Fibingerová			1		Nitra	20 Aug 77
22.24			Lisovskaya			1	OG	Seoul	1 Oct 88
22.22			Slupianek			1		Potsdam	13 Jul 80
22.19		Claudia	Losch	FRG	10.1.60	1		Hainfeld	23 Aug 87
22.14i			Lisovskaya			1	NC	Penza	7 Feb 87
22.13			Slupianek			1		Split	29 Apr 80
22.06			Slupianek			1		Berlin	15 Aug 78
22.06			Lisovskaya			1		Moskva	6 Aug 88
22.05			Slupianek			1	OD	Berlin	28 May 80
22.05			Slupianek			1		Potsdam	31 May 80
22.04			Slupianek			1		Potsdam	4 Jul 79
22.04			Slupianek			1		Potsdam	29 Jul 79
21.99 WR			Fibingerová			1		Opava	26 Sep 76
21.98			Slupianek			1		Berlin	17 Jul 79
21.96			Fibingerová			1	GS	Ostrava	8 Jun 77
21.96			Lisovskaya			1	Drz	Praha	16 Aug 84
21.96			Lisovskaya			1		Vilnius	28 Aug 88
21.95		(30/4)	Lisovskaya			1	IAC	Edinburgh	29 Jul 88
21.89 WR		Ivanka	Khristova	BUL	19.11.41	1		Belmeken	4 Jul 76
21.86		Marianne	Adam	GDR	19.9.51	1	v URS	Leipzig	23 Jun 79
21.76		Li Meisu		CHN	17.4.59	1		Shijiazhuang	23 Apr 88
21.73		Natalya	Akhrimenko	RUS	12.5.55	1		Leselidze	21 May 88
21.69		Viktoriya	Pavlysh ¶	UKR	15.1.69	1	EC	Budapest	20 Aug 98
21.66		Sui Xinmei ¶		CHN	29.1.65	1		Beijing	9 Jun 90
		(10)							
21.61		Verzhinia	Veselinova	BUL	18.11.57	1		Sofia	21 Aug 82
21.60i		Valentina	Fedyushina	UKR	18.2.65	1		Simferopol	28 Dec 91
21.58		Margitta	Droese/Pufe	GDR	10.9.52	1		Erfurt	28 May 78
21.57 @		Ines	Müller'	GDR	2.1.59	1		Athína	16 May 88
21.45						1		Schwerin	4 Jun 86
21.53		Nunu	Abashidze ¶	UKR	27.3.55	2	Izv	Kyiv	20 Jun 84
21.52		Huang Zhihong		CHN	7.5.65	1	NC	Beijing	27 Jun 90
21.46		Larisa	Peleshenko ¶	RUS	29.2.64	1	Kuts	Moskva	26 Aug 00
21.45 WR		Nadezhda	Chizhova	RUS	29.9.45	1		Varna	29 Sep 73
21.43		Eva	Wilms	FRG	28.7.52	2	HB	München	17 Jun 77
21.42		Svetlana	Krachevskaya'	RUS	23.11.44	2	OG	Moskva	24 Jul 80
		(20)	@ competitive meeting, but unsanctioned by GDR federation						
21.31 @		Heike	Hartwig'	GDR	30.12.62	2		Athína	16 May 88
21.27						1		Haniá	22 May 88
21.27		Liane	Schmuhl	GDR	29.6.61	1		Cottbus	26 Jun 82
21.24		Valerie	Adams	NZL	6.10.84	1	WCh	Daegu	29 Aug 11
21.22		Astrid	Kumbernuss	GDR/GER	5.2.70	1	WCh	Göteborg	5 Aug 95
21.21		Kathrin	Neimke	GDR	18.7.66	2	WCh	Roma	5 Sep 87
21.19		Helma	Knorscheidt	GDR	31.12.56	1		Berlin	24 May 84
21.15i		Irina	Korzhanenko ¶	RUS	16.5.74	1	NC	Moskva	18 Feb 99
21.10		Heidi	Krieger	GDR	20.7.65	1	EC	Stuttgart	26 Aug 86
21.09		Nadezhda	Ostapchuk ¶	BLR	12.10.80	1		Minsk	21 Jul 05
21.06		Svetlana	Krivelyova ¶	RUS	13.6.69	1	OG	Barcelona	7 Aug 92
		(30)							
21.05		Zdenka	Silhavá' ¶	CZE	15.6.54	2	NC	Praha	23 Jul 83
21.01		Ivanka	Petrova-Stoycheva	BUL	3.2.51	1	NC	Sofia	28 Jul 79
21.00		Mihaela	Loghin	ROU	1.6.52	1		Formia	30 Jun 84
21.00		Cordula	Schulze	GDR	11.9.59	4	OD	Potsdam	21 Jul 84
20.96		Belsy	Laza	CUB	5.6.67	1		Ciudad de México	2 May 92
20.95		Elena	Stoyanova ¶	BUL	23.1.52	2	Balk	Sofia	14 Jun 80
20.91		Svetla	Mitkova	BUL	17.6.64	1		Sofia	24 May 87
20.80		Sona	Vasícková	CZE	14.3.62	1		Praha	2 Jun 88

252 SHOT – DISCUS A-T

Mark	Wind	Name		Nat	Born	Pos	Meet	Venue	Date
20.77		Christina	Schwanitz	GER	24.12.85	1		Beijing	20 May 15
20.72		Grit	Haupt/Hammer	GDR	4.6.66	3		Neubrandenburg	11 Jun 87
	(40)								
20.70		Natalya	Mikhnevich' ¶	BLR	25.5.82	2	NC	Grodno	8 Jul 08
20.63		Michelle	Carter	USA	12.10.85	1	OG	Rio de Janeiro	12 Aug 16
20.61		María Elena	Sarría	CUB	14.9.54	1		La Habana	22 Jul 82
20.61		Yanina	Korolchik' ¶	BLR	26.12.76	1	WCh	Edmonton	5 Aug 01
20.60		Marina	Antonyuk	RUS	12.5.62	1		Chelyabinsk	10 Aug 86
20.54			Zhang Liuhong	CHN	16.1.69	1	NC	Beijing	5 Jun 94
20.53		Iris	Plotzitzka	FRG	7.1.66	1	ASV	Köln	21 Aug 88
20.50i		Christa	Wiese	GDR	25.12.67	2	NC	Senftenberg	12 Feb 89
20.47		Nina	Isayeva	RUS	6.7.50	1		Bryansk	28 Aug 82
20.47		Cong Yuzhen		CHN	22.1.63	2	IntC	Tianjin	3 Sep 88
	(50)		100th woman 19.73, 200th 18.99, 300th 18.35, 400th 17.96, 500th 17.63						

Best outdoor marks

21.08	Fedyushina	1	Leselidze	15 May 88	20.82	Korzhanenko ¶	1	Rostov na Donu	30 May 98
						21.06 drugs dq	(1) OG	Athína	18 Aug 04

Ancillary marks – other marks during series (to 22.09)

22.33	Slupianek	2 May 80	22.12	Slupianek	13 Jul 80
22.20	Slupianek	13 Jul 80	22.11	Slupianek	7 May 80
22.60 Lisovskaya (WR) 7 Jun 87	22.19	Lisovskaya	5 Jul 88	22.10	Slupianek	25 May 80
22.40 Lisovskaya 14 Aug 88	22.14	Slupianek	25 May 80	22.09	Slupianek	7 May 80
22.34 Slupianek 11 May 80	22.14	Slupianek	13 Jul 80			

Drugs disqualification

21.70i	Nadezhda	Ostapchuk ¶	BLR	12.10.80	(1)	NC	Mogilyov	12 Feb 10

DISCUS

Mark		Name		Nat	Born	Pos	Meet	Venue	Date
76.80 WR		Gabriele	Reinsch	GDR	23.9.63	1	v ITA	Neubrandenburg	9 Jul 88
74.56 WR		Zdenka	Silhavá' ¶	CZE	15.6.54	1		Nitra	26 Aug 84
74.56		Ilke	Wyludda	GDR	28.3.69	1	NC	Neubrandenburg	23 Jul 89
74.44			Reinsch			1		Berlin	13 Sep 88
74.40			Wyludda			2		Berlin	13 Sep 88
74.08		Diana	Gansky'	GDR	14.12.63	1	v USSR	Karl-Marx-Stadt	20 Jun 87
73.90			Gansky			1	ECp	Praha	27 Jun 87
73.84		Daniela	Costian ¶	ROU	30.4.65	1		Bucuresti	30 Apr 88
73.78			Costian			1		Bucuresti	24 Apr 88
73.42			Reinsch			1		Karl-Marx-Stadt	12 Jun 88
73.36 WR		Irina	Meszynski	GDR	24.3.62	1	Drz	Praha	17 Aug 84
73.32			Gansky			1		Neubrandenburg	11 Jun 87
73.28		Galina	Savinkova'	RUS	15.7.53	1	NC	Donetsk	8 Sep 84
73.26 WR			Savinkova			1		Leselidze	21 May 83
73.26			Sachse/Gansky			1		Neubrandenburg	6 Jun 86
73.24			Gansky			1		Leipzig	29 May 87
73.22		Tsvetanka	Khristova ¶	BUL	14.3.62	1		Kazanlak	19 Apr 87
73.10		Gisela	Beyer	GDR	16.7.60	1	OD	Berlin	20 Jul 84
73.04			Gansky			1		Potsdam	6 Jun 87
73.04			Wyludda			1	ECp	Gateshead	5 Aug 89
72.96			Savinkova			1	v GDR	Erfurt	23 Jun 85
72.94			Gansky			2	v ITA	Neubrandenburg	9 Jul 88
72.92		Martina	Opitz/Hellmann	GDR	12.12.60	1	NC	Potsdam	20 Aug 87
72.90			Costian			1		Bucuresti	14 May 88
72.78			Hellmann			2		Neubrandenburg	11 Jun 87
72.78			Reinsch			1	OD	Berlin	29 Jun 88
72.72			Wyludda			1		Neubrandenburg	23 Jun 89
72.70			Wyludda			1	NC-j	Karl-Marx-Stadt	15 Jul 88
72.54			Gansky			1	NC	Rostock	25 Jun 88
72.52			Hellmann			1		Frohburg	15 Jun 86
72.52			Khristova			1	BGP	Budapest	11 Aug 86
	(31/10)								
72.14		Galina	Murashova	LTU	22.12.55	2	Drz	Praha	17 Aug 84
71.80 WR		Maria	Vergova/Petkova	BUL	3.11.50	1	NC	Sofia	13 Jul 80
71.68			Xiao Yanling ¶	CHN	27.3.68	1		Beijing	14 Mar 92
71.58		Ellina	Zvereva' ¶	BLR	16.11.60	1	Znam	Leningrad	12 Jun 88
71.50 WR		Evelin	Schlaak/Jahl	GDR	28.3.56	1		Potsdam	10 May 80
71.41		Sandra	Perkovic	CRO	21.6.90	1		Bellinzona	18 Jul 17
71.30		Larisa	Korotkevich	RUS	3.1.67	1	RusCp	Sochi	29 May 92
71.22		Ria	Stalman	NED	11.12.51	1		Walnut	15 Jul 84
		Disallowed as Dutch record in 2016 after Stalman admitted drugs use							
70.88		Hilda Elia	Ramos ¶	CUB	1.9.64	1		La Habana	8 May 92
70.80		Larisa	Mikhalchenko	UKR	16.5.63	1		Kharkov	18 Jun 88
	(20)								

DISCUS – HAMMER A-T

Mark	Wind	Name		Nat	Born	Pos	Meet	Venue	Date
70.68		Maritza	Martén	CUB	16.8.63	1	Ib Am	Sevilla	18 Jul 92
70.65		Denia	Caballero	CUB	13.1.90	1		Bilbao	20 Jun 15
70.50 WR		Faina	Melnik	RUS	9.6.45	1	Znam	Sochi	24 Apr 76
70.34 @		Silvia	Madetzky	GDR	24.6.62	3		Athína	16 May 88
69.34						1		Halle	26 Jun 87
70.15		Valarie	Allman	USA	23.2.95	1		Rathdrum	1 Aug 20
70.02		Natalya	Sadova ¶	RUS	15.7.72	1		Thessaloniki	23 Jun 99
69.86		Valentina	Kharchenko	RUS	.49	1		Feodosiya	16 May 81
69.72		Svetla	Mitkova	BUL	17.6.64	2	NC	Sofia	15 Aug 87
69.68		Mette	Bergmann	NOR	9.11.62	1		Florø	27 May 95
69.64		Dani	Stevens	AUS	26.5.88	2	WCh	London (OS)	13 Aug 17
(30)									
69.51		Franka	Dietzsch	GER	22.1.68	1		Wiesbaden	8 May 99
69.50		Florenta	Craciunescu'	ROU	7.5.55	1	Balk	Stara Zagora	2 Aug 85
69.39		Yaimé	Pérez	CUB	29.5.91	1		Sotteville-lès-Rouen	16 Jul 19
69.17		Gia	Lewis-Smallwood	USA	1.4.79	1	Déca	Angers	30 Aug 14
69.14		Irina	Yatchenko ¶	BLR	31.10.65	1		Staiki	31 Jul 04
69.08		Carmen	Romero	CUB	6.10.50	1	NC	La Habana	17 Apr 76
69.08		Mariana	Ionescu/Lengyel	ROU	14.4.53	1		Constanta	19 Apr 86
68.92		Sabine	Engel	GDR	21.4.54	1	v URS,POL	Karl-Marx-Stadt	25 Jun 77
68.89		Nadine	Müller	GER	21.11.85	1	ECp-w	Bar	18 Mar 12
68.80A		Nicoleta	Grasu	ROU	11.9.71	1		Poiana Brasov	7 Aug 99
(40)									
68.64		Margitta	Pufe'	GDR	10.9.52	1	ISTAF	Berlin	17 Aug 79
68.62			Yu Hourun	CHN	9.7.64	1		Beijing	6 May 88
68.62			Hou Xuemei	CHN	27.2.62	1	IntC	Tianjin	4 Sep 88
68.60		Nadezhda	Kugayevskikh	RUS	19.4.60	1		Oryol	30 Aug 83
68.58		Lyubov	Zverkova	RUS	14.6.55	1	Izv	Kyiv	22 Jun 84
68.52		Beatrice	Faumuiná	NZL	23.10.74	1	Bisl	Oslo	4 Jul 97
68.49		Julia	Fischer/Harting	GER	1.4.90	1	Werfer	Halle	21 May 16
68.38		Olga	Burova'	RUS	17.9.63	2	RusCp	Sochi	29 May 92
68.18		Tatyana	Lesovaya	KAZ	24.4.56	1		Alma-Ata	23 Sep 82
68.18		Irina	Khval	RUS	17.5.62	1		Moskva	8 Jul 88
68.18		Barbara	Hechevarría	CUB	6.8.66	2		La Habana	17 Feb 89
(51)									

Unofficial meeting: Berlin 6 Sep 88: 1. Martina Hellmann 78.14, 2. Ilke Wyludda 75.36
Downhill: 69.44 Suzy Powell USA 3.9.76 1 La Jolla 27 Apr 02
Drugs disqualification: 70.69 Darya Pishchalnikova ¶ RUS 19.7.85 (1) NC Cheboksary 5 Jul 12
Ancillary marks – other marks during series (to 72.92)

73.32	Reinsch	13 Sep 88	73.28	Gansky	27 Jun 87	73.10	Reinsch	9 Jul 88
73.28	Gansky	11 Jun 87	73.16	Wyludda	13 Sep 88	73.06	Gansky	27 Jun 87
72.92	Hellmann	20 Aug 87						

100th woman 66.00, 200th 63.94, 300th 62.16, 400th 60.58, 500th 59.45

HAMMER

Mark		Name		Nat	Born	Pos	Meet	Venue	Date
82.98 WR		Anita	Włodarczyk	POL	8.8.85	1	Skol	Warszawa	28 Aug 16
82.87			Włodarczyk			1	Skol	Cetniewo	29 Jul 17
82.29 WR			Włodarczyk			1	OG	Rio de Janeiro	14 Aug 16
81.08 WR			Włodarczyk			1	Skol	Cetniewo	1 Aug 15
80.85			Włodarczyk			1	WCh	Beijing	27 Aug 15
80.79			Włodarczyk			1	NC	Białystok	23 Jul 17
80.26			Włodarczyk			1		Cetniewo	12 Jul 16
79.80			Włodarczyk			1	Skol	Warszawa	15 Aug 17
79.73			Włodarczyk			1	DL	Doha	6 May 17
79.72			Włodarczyk			1	GS	Ostrava	27 Jun 17
79.61			Włodarczyk			1	Kuso	Szczecin	18 Jun 16
79.59			Włodarczyk			1	NC	Lublin	22 Jul 18
79.58 WR			Włodarczyk			1	ISTAF	Berlin	31 Aug 14
79.48			Włodarczyk			1	Werfer	Halle	21 May 16
79.45			Włodarczyk			1		Forbach	29 May 16
79.42 WR		Betty	Heidler	GER	14.10.83	1		Halle	21 May 11
78.94			Włodarczyk			1	EC	Berlin	12 Aug 18
78.76			Włodarczyk			1	EC	Zürich	15 Aug 14
78.74			Włodarczyk			1	AWC	London (OS)	14 Jul 18
78.69			Włodarczyk			1	NC	Bydgoszcz	26 Jun 16
78.54			Włodarczyk			1	GS	Ostrava	19 May 16
78.51		Tatyana	Lysenko ¶	RUS	9.10.83	1	NC	Cheboksary	5 Jul 12
78.46			Włodarczyk			2	WCh	Moskva	16 Aug 13
78.30 WR			Włodarczyk			1	EAF	Bydgoszcz	6 Jun 10
78.28			Włodarczyk			1	ET	Cheboksary	21 Jun 15
78.24			Włodarczyk			1	NC	Kraków	21 Jul 15
78.24		DeAnna	Price	USA	8.6.93	1	NC	Des Moines	27 Jul 19

254   HAMMER – JAVELIN A-T

Mark	Wind	Name		Nat	Born	Pos	Meet	Venue	Date
78.22			Wlodarczyk			1		Dubnica nad Vahom	21 Aug 13
78.18			Lysenko			1	OG	London (OS)	10 Aug 12
	(30/4)								
77.78		Gwen	Berry	USA	29.6.89	1	Kuso	Chorzów	8 Jun 18
77.68			Wang Zheng	CHN	14.12.87	1		Chengdu	29 Mar 14
77.33			Zhang Wenxiu ¶	CHN	22.3.86	1	AsiG	Incheon	28 Sep 14
77.32		Oksana	Menkova ¶	BLR	28.3.82	1		Staiki	29 Jun 08
77.26 WR		Gulfiya	Khanafeyeva ¶	RUS	4.6.82	1	NC	Tula	12 Jun 06
77.13		Oksana	Kondratyeva	RUS	22.11.85	1	Znam	Zhukovskiy	30 Jun 13
	(10)								
76.90		Martina	Hrasnová' ¶	SVK	21.3.83	1		Trnava	16 May 09
76.85		Malwina	Kopron	POL	16.11.94	1	WUG	Taipei	26 Aug 17
76.83		Kamila	Skolimowska	POL	4.11.82	1	SGP	Doha	11 May 07
76.75		Brooke	Andersen	USA	23.8.95	1		Rathdrum	1 Jun 19
76.72		Mariya	Bespalova ¶	RUS	21.5.86	2		Zhukovskiy	23 Jun 12
76.66		Olga	Tsander	BLR	18.5.76	1		Staiki	21 Jul 05
76.63		Yekaterina	Khoroshikh ¶	RUS	21.1.83	2	Znam	Moskva	24 Jun 06
76.62		Yipsi	Moreno	CUB	19.11.80	1	GP	Zagreb	9 Sep 08
76.56		Alena	Matoshko	BLR	23.6.82	2		Minsk	12 Jun 12
76.35		Joanna	Fiodorow	POL	4.3.89	2	WCh	Doha	28 Sep 19
	(20)								
76.33		Darya	Pchelnik ¶	BLR	20.12.81	2		Staiki	29 Jun 08
76.26		Hanna	Malyshik	BLR	4.2.94	1		Brest	27 Apr 18
76.21		Yelena	Konevtsova	RUS	11.3.81	3		Sochi	26 May 07
76.17		Anna	Bulgakova ¶	RUS	17.1.88	1	NC	Moskva	24 Jul 13
76.07 WR		Mihaela	Melinte ¶	ROU	27.3.75	1		Rüdlingen	29 Aug 99
76.05		Kathrin	Klaas	GER	6.2.84	5	OG	London (OS)	10 Aug 12
75.73		Amanda	Bingson	USA	20.2.90	1	NC	Des Moines	22 Jun 13
75.73		Sultana	Frizell	CAN	24.10.84	1		Tucson	22 May 14
75.68		Olga	Kuzenkova ¶	RUS	4.10.70	1	NCp	Tula	4 Jun 00
75.43		Janeah	Stewart	USA	21.7.96	2		Bloomington	22 Jun 19
	(30)								
75.29		Hanna	Skydan	UKR/AZE	14.5.92	1	Isl.Sol	Baku	16 May 17
75.23		Alexandra	Tavernier	FRA	13.12.93	1		Kladno	16 Sep 20
75.09		Yelena	Rigert'	RUS	2.12.83	1	Kuts	Moskva	15 Jul 13
75.08		Ivana	Brkljacic	CRO	25.1.83	2	Kuso	Waszawa	17 Jun 07
75.04		Maggie	Ewen	USA	23.9.94	4	NC	Des Moines	27 Jul 19
75.02			Luo Na	CHN	8.10.93	1	WWerf	Halle	26 May 18
74.77		Jeneva	McCall/Stevens	USA	28.10.89	2		Dubnica nad Vahom	21 Aug 1
74.70		Zalina	Petrivskaya' ¶	MDA	5.2.88	1	NC	Chisinau	22 Jun 19
74.66		Manuèla	Montebrun	FRA	13.11.79	1	GP II	Zagreb	11 Jul 05
74.65		Mariya	Smolyachkova	BLR	10.2.85	2		Staiki	19 Jul 08
	(40)								
74.54		Sophie	Hitchon	GBR	11.7.91	3	OG	Rio de Janeiro	15 Aug 1
74.52		Iryna	Sekachyova	UKR	21.7.76	1	NC	Kyiv	2 Jul 08
74.20		Jessica	Cosby Toruga	USA	31.5.82	3		Tucson	22 May 14
74.17		Tugçe	Sahutoglu ¶	TUR	1.5.88	1		Izmir	19 May 12
74.10		Iryna	Novozhylova	UKR	7.1.86	1		Kyiv	19 May 12
74.03		Amber	Campbell	USA	5.6.81	1	NC	Eugene	6 Jul 16
73.90		Arasay	Thondike	CUB	28.5.86	1		La Habana	18 Jun 09
73.87		Erin	Gilreath	USA	11.10.80	1	NC	Carson	25 Jun 05
73.74		Jennifer	Dahlgren	ARG	21.4.84	1		Buenos Aires	10 Apr 10
73.64		Rosa	Rodríguez	VEN	2.7.86	1		Barquisimeto	16 May 13
	(50)		100th woman 71.33, 200th 68.12, 300th 66.52, 400th 64.75, 500th 63.89						

Downhill: 75.20 Manuéla Montebrun FRA 13.11.79 1 Vineuil 18 May 03

Ancillary marks – other marks during series to 78.80 – all by Wlodarczyk

81.77	28 Aug 16	80.73	29 Jul 17	80.31	28 Aug 16	79.67	12 Jul 16	79.39	12 Jul 16
81.74	14 Aug 16	80.69	29 Jul 17	80.27	27 Aug 15	79.62	12 Jul 16	79.31	27 Aug 15
81.63	29 Jul 17	80.42	29 Jul 17	79.68	28 Aug 16	79.60	14 Aug 16	79.27	27 Jun 17
81.27	28 Aug 16	80.40	14 Aug 16	79.68	27 Jun 17	79.58	12 Jul 16	79.23	15 Aug 17

Drugs disqualification

78.69		Oksana	Menkova ¶	BLR	28.3.82	(1)		Minsk	18 Jul 12
78.61			Lysenko			(1)		Sochi	26 May 07
78.19			Menkova			(1)		Brest	28 Apr 12
78.19			Menkova			(1)		Minsk	12 Jun 12
78.80		Tatyana	Lysenko ¶	RUS	9.10.83	(1)	WCh	Moskva	16 Aug 13
77.36		Gulfiya	Khanafeyeva ¶	RUS	4.6.82	(2)		Sochi	26 May 07

JAVELIN

| 72.28 WR | | Barbora | Spotáková | CZE | 30.6.81 | 1 | WAF | Stuttgart | 13 Sep 08 |
| 71.70 WR | | Osleidys | Menéndez | CUB | 14.11.79 | 1 | WCh | Helsinki | 14 Aug 05 |

JAVELIN A-T

Mark	Wind	Name		Nat	Born	Pos	Meet	Venue	Date
71.58			Spotáková			2	WCh	Daegu	2 Sep 11
71.54	WR		Menéndez			1		Réthimno	1 Jul 01
71.53			Menéndez			1	OG	Athína	27 Aug 04
71.42			Spotáková			1	OG	Beijing	21 Aug 08
70.53		Mariya	Abakumova ¶	RUS	15.1.86	1	ISTAF	Berlin	1 Sep 13
70.20		Christina	Obergföll	GER	22.8.81	1	ECp-S	München	23 Jun 07
70.03			Obergföll			2	WCh	Helsinki	14 Aug 05
69.82			Menéndez			1	WUG	Beijing	29 Aug 01
69.81			Obergföll			1		Berlin (Elstal)	31 Aug 08
69.75			Abakumova			1		Berlin (Elstal)	25 Aug 13
69.57			Obergföll			1	WK	Zürich	8 Sep 11
69.55			Spotáková			1	OG	London (OS)	9 Aug 12
69.53			Menéndez			1	WCh	Edmonton	7 Aug 01
69.48	WR	Trine	Hattestad	NOR	18.4.66	1	Bisl	Oslo	28 Jul 00
69.45			Spotáková			1	Herc	Monaco	22 Jul 11
69.35		Sunette	Viljoen	RSA	6.1.83	1	DL	New York	9 Jun 12
69.34			Abakumova			1	ECp-w	Castellón	16 Mar 13
69.15			Spotáková			1		Zaragoza	31 May 08
69.09			Abakumova			Q	WCh	Moskva	16 Aug 13
69.05			Obergföll			1	WCh	Moskva	18 Aug 13
68.94			Abakumova			1	WK	Zürich	29 Aug 13
68.92		Kathryn	Mitchell	AUS	10.7.82	1	CG	Gold Coast	11 Apr 18
68.91			Hattestad			1	OG	Sydney	30 Sep 00
68.86			Obergföll			1	NC	Kassel	24 Jul 11
68.81			Spotáková			1	Odlozil	Praha	16 Jun 08
68.76			Obergföll			Q	WCh	Daegu	1 Sep 11
68.73			Spotáková			2	DL	New York	9 Jun 12
68.66			Spotáková			1	GGala	Roma	10 Jun 10
		(30/7)							
68.43		Sara	Kolak	CRO	22.6.95	1	Athl	Lausanne	6 Jul 17
68.34		Steffi	Nerius	GER	1.7.72	2		Berlin (Elstal)	31 Aug 08
67.98			Lu Huihui ¶	CHN	26.6.89	1	WCT	Shenyang	2 Aug 19
		(10)							
67.90		Christin	Hussong	GER	17.3.94	1	EC	Berlin	10 Aug 18
67.70		Kelsey	Barber	AUS	21.9.91	1	Spitzen	Luzern	9 Jul 19
67.69		Katharina	Molitor	GER	8.11.83	1	WCh	Beijing	30 Aug 15
67.67		Sonia	Bisset	CUB	1.4.71	1		Salamanca	6 Jul 05
67.51		Miréla	Manjani/Tzelíli	GRE	21.12.76	2	OG	Sydney	30 Sep 00
67.47		Tatyana	Kholodovich	BLR	21.6.91	1	Bisl	Oslo	7 Jun 18
67.40		Nikola	Ogrodníková	CZE	18.8.90	1		Offenburg	26 May 19
67.32		Linda	Stahl	GER	2.10.85	1	adidas	New York	14 Jun 14
67.30		Vera	Rebrik	RUS	25.2.89	1	NC-w	Adler	19 Feb 16
67.29		Hanna	Hatsko-Fedusova	UKR	3.10.90	1	NC	Kirovohrad	26 Jul 14
		(20)							
67.29			Liu Shiying	CHN	24.9.93	1	NC	Shaoxing	15 Sep 20
67.21		Eda	Tugsuz	TUR	27.3.97	1	Isl.Sol	Baku	18 May 17
67.20		Tatyana	Shikolenko	RUS	10.5.68	1	Herc	Monaco	18 Aug 00
67.16		Martina	Ratej	SLO	2.11.81	2	DL	Doha	14 May 10
67.11		Maria	Andrejczyk	POL	9.3.96	Q	OG	Rio de Janeiro	16 Aug 16
66.91		Tanja	Damaske	GER	16.11.71	1	NC	Erfurt	4 Jul 99
66.83		Kimberley	Mickle	AUS	28.12.84	1		Melbourne	22 Mar 14
66.80		Louise	McPaul/Currey	AUS	24.1.69	1		Gold Coast (RB)	5 Aug 00
66.67		Kara	Patterson/Winger	USA	10.4.86	1	NC	Des Moines	25 Jun 10
66.53		Marcelina	Witek	POL	2.6.95	1		Białogard	5 May 18
		(30)							
66.25			Li Lingwei	CHN	26.1.89	2	WCh	London (OS)	9 Aug 17
66.18		Madara	Palameika	LAT	18.6.87	1	VD	Bruxelles	9 Sep 16
66.17		Goldie	Sayers	GBR	16.7.82	1	LGP	London (CP)	14 Jul 12
66.00		Haruka	Kitaguchi	JPN	16.3.98	1		Kitakyushu	27 Oct 19
65.91		Nikola	Brejchová'	CZE	25.6.74	1	GP	Linz	2 Aug 04
65.47			Zhang Li	CHN	17.1.89	1	AsiG	Incheon	1 Oct 14
65.30		Claudia	Coslovich	ITA	26.4.72	1		Ljubljana	10 Jun 00
65.29		Xiomara	Rivero	CUB	22.11.68	1		Santiago de Cuba	17 Mar 01
65.17		Karen	Forkel	GER	24.9.70	2	NC	Erfurt	4 Jul 99
65.08		Ana Mirela	Termure ¶	ROU	13.1.75	1	NC	Bucuresti	10 Jun 01
		(40)							
64.90		Paula	Huhtaniemi'	FIN	17.2.73	1	NC	Helsinki	10 Aug 03
64.89		Yekaterina	Ivakina	RUS	4.12.64	4	Bisl	Oslo	28 Jul 00
64.87		Kelly	Morgan	GBR	17.6.80	1	NC	Birmingham	14 Jul 02
64.87		Lina	Muze	LAT	4.12.92	2	DL	Shanghai	18 May 19

JAVELIN - HEPTATHLON A-T

Mark	Wind	Name	Nat	Born	Pos	Meet	Venue	Date
64.83		Christina Scherwin	DEN	11.7.76	3	WAF	Stuttgart	9 Sep 06
64.83		Liz Gleadle	CAN	5.12.88	1		Kawasaki	10 May 15
64.75		Brittany Borman	USA	1.7.89	2		Kawasaki	10 May 15
64.62		Joanna Stone	AUS	4.10.72	2		Gold Coast (RB)	5 Aug 00
64.62		Nikolett Szabó	HUN	3.3.80	1		Pátra	22 Jul 01
64.61		Oksana Makarova	RUS	21.7.71	2	ECp	Paris (C)	19 Jun 99
		(50)						
		100th woman 62.75, 200th 59.69, 300th 57.79, 400th 56.73						

Drugs dq:

| 71.99 | | Mariya Abakumova ¶ | RUS | 15.1.86 | 1 | WCh | Daegu | 2 Sep 11 |

Also Abakumova: 70.78 2 OG Beijing 21 Aug 08, 68.92 Q WCh Berlin 16 Aug 09, 68.89 1 DL Doha 14 May 10
Ancillary marks – other marks during series (to 68.90)

71.25	Abakumova	2 Sep 11	69.32	Abakumova	21 Aug 08	68.95	Obergföll	8 Sep 11
69.42	Menéndez	7 Aug 01	69.22	Spotáková	21 Aug 08	Spec. changed from 1 May 1999.		
69.35	Abakumova	25 Aug 13	69.08	Abakumova	21 Aug 08			

HEPTATHLON

7291 WR		Jackie	Joyner-Kersee	USA	3.3.62	1	OG	Seoul	24 Sep 88
		12.69/0.5	1.86	15.80	22.56/1.6	7.27/0.7	45.66	2:08.51	
7215 WR			Joyner-Kersee			1	NC/OT	Indianapolis	16 Jul 88
		12.71/-0.9	1.93	15.65	22.30/ 0.0	7.00/-1.3	50.08	2:20.70	
7158 WR			Joyner-Kersee			1	USOF	Houston	2 Aug 86
		13.18/-0.5	1.88	15.20	22.85/1.2	7.03w/2.9	50.12	2:09.69	
7148 WR			Joyner-Kersee			1	GWG	Moskva	7 Jul 86
		12.85/0.2	1.88	14.76	23.00/0.3	7.01/-0.5	49.86	2:10.02	
7128			Joyner-Kersee			1	WCh	Roma	1 Sep 87
		12.91/0.2	1.90	16.00	22.95/1.2	7.14/0.9	45.68	2:16.29	
7044			Joyner-Kersee			1	OG	Barcelona	2 Aug 92
		12.85/-0.9	1.91	14.13	23.12/0.7	7.10/1.3	44.98	2:11.78	
7032		Carolina	Klüft	SWE	2.2.83	1	WCh	Osaka	26 Aug 07
		13.15/0.1	1.95	14.81	23.38/0.3	6.85/1.0	47.98	2:12.56	
7013		Nafissatou	Thiam	BEL	19.8.94	1	Hypo	Götzis	28 May 17
		13.34/-0.7	1.98	14.51	24.40/-1.6	6.56/0.8	59.32	2:15.24	
7007		Larisa	Nikitina ¶	RUS	29.4.65	1	NC	Bryansk	11 Jun 89
		13.40/1.4	1.89	16.45	23.97/1.1	6.73w/4.0	53.94	2:15.31	
7001			Klüft			1	WCh	Saint-Denis	24 Aug 03
		13.18/-0.4	1.94	14.19	22.98/1.1	6.68/1.0	49.90	2:12.12	
6985		Sabine	Braun	GER	19.6.65	1		Götzis	31 May 92
		13.11/-0.4	1.93	14.84	23.65/2.0	6.63w/2.9	51.62	2:12.67	
6981		Katarina	Johnson-Thompson	GBR	9.1.93	1	WCh	Doha	4 Oct 19
		13.09/0.6	1.95	13.86	23.08/1.0	6.77/0.2	43.93	2:07.26	
6979			Joyner-Kersee			1	NC	San José	24 Jun 87
		12.90/2.0	1.85	15.17	23.02/0.4	7.25/2.3	40.24	2:13.07	
6955		Jessica	Ennis-Hill	GBR	28.1.86	1	OG	London (OS)	4 Aug 12
		12.54/1.3	1.86	14.28	22.83/-0.3	6.48/-0.6	47.49	2:08.65	
6952			Klüft			1	OG	Athína	21 Aug 04
		13.21/0.2	1.91	14.77	23.27/-0.1	6.78/0.4	48.89	2:14.15	
6946 WR		Sabine	Paetz'	GDR	16.10.57	1		Potsdam	6 May 84
		12.64/0.3	1.80	15.37	23.37/0.7	6.86/-0.2	44.62	2:08.93	
6942		Ghada	Shouaa	SYR	10.9.72	1		Götzis	26 May 96
		13.78/0.3	1.87	15.64	23.78/0.6	6.77/0.6	54.74	2:13.61	
6935 WR		Ramona	Neubert (10)	GDR	26.7.58	1	v USSR	Moskva	19 Jun 83
		13.42/1.7	1.82	15.25	23.49/0.5	6.79/0.7	49.94	2:07.51	
6910			Joyner			1	MSR	Walnut	25 Apr 86
		12.9/0.0	1.86	14.75	23.24w/2.8	6.85/2.1	48.30	2:14.11	
6906			Ennis			1		Götzis	27 May 12
		12.81/0.0	1.85	14.51	22.88/1.9	6.51/0.8	47.11	2:09.00	
6897			John'			2	wOG	Seoul	24 Sep 88
		12.85/0.5	1.80	16.23	23.65/1.6	6.71/ 0.0	42.56	2:06.14	
6889		Eunice	Barber	FRA	17.11.74	1		Arles	5 Jun 05
		12.62w/2.9	1.91	12.61	24.12/1.2	6.78w/3.4	53.07	2:14.66	
6887			Klüft			1	WCh	Helsinki	7 Aug 05
		13.19/-0.4	1.82	15.02	23.70/-2.5	6.87/0.2	47.20	2:08.89	
6878			Joyner-Kersee			1	NC	New York	13 Jun 91
		12.77	1.89	15.62	23.42	6.97/0.4	43.28	2:22.12	
6875			Nikitina			1	ECp-A	Helmond	16 Jul 89
		13.55/-2.1	1.84	15.99	24.29/-2.1	6.75/-2.5	56.78	2:18.67	
6861			Barber			1	WCh	Sevilla	22 Aug 99
		12.89/-0.5	1.93	12.37	23.57/0.5	6.86/-0.3	49.88	2:15.65	
6859		Natalya	Shubenkova	RUS	25.9.57	1	NC	Kyiv	21 Jun 84
		12.93/1.0	1.83	13.66	23.57/-0.3	6.73/0.4	46.26	2:04.60	

HEPTATHLON A-T

Mark	Name		Nat	Born	Pos	Meet	Venue		Date
6858	Anke	Vater/Behmer	GDR	5.6.61	3	OG	Seoul		24 Sep 88
	13.20/0.5	1.83	14.20	23.10/1.6		6.68/0.1	44.54	2:04.20	
6847		Nikitina			1	WUG	Duisburg		29 Aug 89
	13.47	1.81	16.12	24.12		6.66	59.28	2:22.07	
(30/13)									
6845 WR		Neubert			1	v URS	Halle		20 Jun 82
	13.58/1.8	1.83	15.10	23.14/1.4		6.84w/2.3	42.54	2:06.16	
6845	Irina	Belova ¶	RUS	27.3.68	2	OG	Barcelona		2 Aug 92
	13.25/-0.1	1.88	13.77	23.34/0.2		6.82/0.0	41.90	2:05.08	
6836	Carolin	Schäfer	GER	5.12.91	2	Hypo	Götzis		28 May 17
	13.09/1.0	1.86	14.76	23.36/0.7		6.57/0.9	49.80	2:14.73	
6832	Lyudmila	Blonska ¶	UKR	9.11.77	2	WCh	Osaka		26 Aug 07
	13.25/0.1	1.92	14.44	24.09/0.3		6.88/1.0	47.77	2:16.68	
6831	Denise	Lewis	GBR	27.8.72	1		Talence		30 Jul 00
	13.13/1.0	1.84	15.07	24.01w/3.6		6.69/-0.4	49.42	2:12.20	
6815	Laura	Ikauniece-Admidina	LAT	31.5.92	3	Hypo	Götzis		28 May 17
	13.10/1.0	1.77	13.53	23.49/-2.9		6.64/0.8	56.17	2:11.76	
6808	Brianne	Theisen-Eaton	CAN	18.12.88	1	Hypo	Götzis		31 May 15
	13.05/-0.2	1.89	13.73	23.34/1.4		6.72/0.9	42.96	2:09.37	
6803	Jane	Frederick	USA	7.4.52	1		Talence		16 Sep 84
	13.27/1.2	1.87	15.49	24.15/1.6		6.43/0.2	51.74	2:13.55	
(20)									
6778	Nataliya	Dobrynska	UKR	29.5.82	2	EC	Barcelona		31 Jul 10
	13.59/-1.6	1.86	15.88	24.23/-0.2		6.56/0.3	49.25	2:12.06	
6768w	Tatyana	Chernova ¶	RUS	29.1.88	1		Arles		3 Jun 07
	13.04w/6.1	1.82	13.57	23.59w/5.2		6.61/1.2	53.43	2:15.05	
6765	Yelena	Prokhorova	RUS	16.4.78	1	NC	Tula		23 Jul 00
	13.54/-2.8	1.82	14.30	23.37/-0.2		6.72/1.0	43.40	2:04.27	
6750		Ma Miaolan	CHN	18.1.70	1	NG	Beijing		12 Sep 93
	13.28/1.5	1.89	14.98	23.86/		6.64/	45.82	2:15.33	
6742	Yorgelis	Rodríguez	CUB	25.1.95	2	Hypo	Götzis		27 May 18
	13.48/0.3	1.86	14.95	23.96/-0.6		6.58w/2.3	48.65	2:12.73	
6741	Heike	Drechsler	GER	16.12.64	1		Talence		11 Sep 94
	13.34/-0.3	1.84	13.58	22.84/-1.1		6.95/1.0	40.64	2:11.53	
6735(w)	Hyleas	Fountain	USA	14.1.81	1	NC	Des Moines		26 Jun 10
	12.93w/2.6	1.90	13.73	23.28w/3.3		6.79w/2.7	42.26	2:17.80	
6725	Erica	Bougard	USA	26.7.93	3	Hypo	Götzis		27 May 18
	12.80/1.5	1.86	13.02	23.31/0.4		6.62/1.1	41.97	2:08.42	
6703	Tatyana	Blokhina	RUS	12.3.70	1		Talence		11 Sep 93
	13.69/-0.6	1.91	14.94	23.95/-0.4		5.99/-0.3	52.16	2:09.65	
6702	Chantal	Beaugeant ¶	FRA	16.2.61	2		Götzis		19 Jun 88
	13.10/1.6	1.78	13.74	23.96w/3.5		6.45/0.2	50.96	2:07.09	
(30)									
6695	Jane	Flemming	AUS	14.4.65	1	CG	Auckland		28 Jan 90
	13.21/1.4	1.82	13.76	23.62w/2.4		6.57/1.6	49.28	2:12.53	
6683	Jennifer	Oeser	GER	29.11.83	3	EC	Barcelona		31 Jul 10
	13.37/-1.0	1.83	13.82	24.07/-0.3		6.68/-0.3	49.17	2:12.28	
6681	Kristina	Savitskaya	RUS	10.6.91	1	NC	Cheboksary		3 Jun 12
	13.52/0.0	1.88	15.27	24.61/0.0		6.65/0.0	46.83	2:14.73	
6660	Ines	Schulz	GDR	10.7.65	3		Götzis		19 Jun 88
	13.56/0.4	1.84	13.95	23.93w/2.8		6.70/0.7	42.82	2:06.31	
6658	Svetla	Dimitrova ¶	BUL	27.1.70	2		Götzis		31 May 92
	13.41/-0.7	1.75	14.72	23.06w/2.4		6.64/1.9	43.84	2:09.60	
6649	Lilli	Schwarzkopf	GER	28.8.83	2	OG	London (OS)		4 Aug 12
	13.26/0.9	1.83	14.77	24.77/0.9		6.30/-0.7	51.73	2:10.50	
6646	Natalya	Grachova	UKR	21.2.52	1	NC	Moskva		2 Aug 82
	13.80	1.80	16.18	23.86		6.65w/3.5	39.42	2:06.59	
6636	Anouk	Vetter	NED	4.2.93	3	WCh	London (OS)		6 Aug 17
	13.31/0.0	1.77	15.09	24.36/-0.4		6.32/-0.4	58.41	2:19.43	
6635	Sibylle	Thiele	GDR	6.3.65	2	GWG	Moskva		7 Jul 86
	13.14/0.6	1.76	16.00	24.18		6.62/1.0	45.74	2:15.30	
6635	Svetlana	Buraga	BLR	4.9.65	3	WCh	Stuttgart		17 Aug 93
	12.95/0.1	1.84	14.55	23.69/0.0		6.58/-0.2	41.04	2:13.65	
(40)									
6633	Natalya	Roshchupkina	RUS	13.1.78	2	NC	Tula		23 Jul 00
	14.05/-2.8	1.88	14.28	23.47/-0.2		6.45/0.4	44.34	2:07.93	
6623	Judy	Simpson'	GBR	14.11.60	3	EC	Stuttgart		30 Aug 86
	13.05/0.8	1.92	14.73	25.09/0.0		6.56w/2.5	40.92	2:11.70	
6619	Liliana	Nastase	ROU	1.8.62	4	OG	Barcelona		2 Aug 92
	12.86/-0.9	1.82	14.34	23.70/0.2		6.49/-0.3	41.30	2:11.22	
6619	Xénia	Krizsán	HUN	13.1.93	2		Talence		23 Jun 19
	13.36/0.3	1.78	14.29	24.38/0.4		6.23/1.0	53.27	2:08.16	

WOMEN All-time

258   HEPTATHLON – DECATHLON - 4x100m

Mark	Wind	Name			Nat	Born	Pos	Meet	Venue		Date
6616 (w)		Malgorzata	Nowak'		POL	9.2.59	1	WUG	Kobe		31 Aug 85
	13.27w/4.0	1.95		15.35		24.20/0.0		6.37w/3.9	43.36	2:20.39	
6610		Kendell	Williams		USA	14.6.95	2	NC	Des Moines		28 Jul 19
	12.84/1.6	1.85		13.41		23.91/-0.8		6.83w/2.3	44.31	2:20.92	
6604		Remigija	Nazaroviene'		LTU	2.6.67	2	URSch	Bryansk		11 Jun 89
	13.26/1.4	1.86		14.27		24.12/0.7		6.58/0.9	40.94	2:09.98	
6604		Irina	Tyukhay		RUS	14.1.67	3		Götzis		28 May 95
	13.20/-0.7	1.84	14.97			24.33/1.7		6.71/0.5	43.84	2:17.64	
6599A		Jessica	Zelinka		CAN	3.9.81	1	NC	Calgary		28 Jun 12
	12.76/-0.6	1.77		14.74		23.42w/2.1		5.98w/2.9	46.60	2:08.95	
6599		Austra	Skujytė		LTU	12.8.79	3	OG	London (OS)		4 Aug 12
	14.00/0.7	1.92		17.31		25.43/0.9		6.25/-0.6	51.13	2:20.59	
(50)			100th woman 6425, 200th 6235, 300th 6132, 400th 6046, 500th 5973								

Drugs disqualification

6880		Tatyana	Chernova ¶		RUS	29.1.88	(1)	WCh	Daegu		30 Aug 11
	13.32/0.9	1.83		14.17		23.50/-1.5		6.61/-0.7	52.95	2:08.04	
6618		Lyudmyla	Yosypenko ¶		UKR	24.9.84	(4)	OG	London (OS)		4 Aug 12
	13.25/0.9	1.83		13.90		23.68/0.6		6.31/-0.6	49.63	2:13.28	

DECATHLON

8358 WR		Austra		Skujyte			LTU	12.8.79	1		Columbia, MO	15 Apr 05
	12.49/1.6	46.19	3.10		48.78	57.19		14.22w/2.4	6.12/1.6	16.42	1.78	5:15.86
8150 WR		Marie		Collonvillé			FRA	23.11.73	1		Talence	26 Sep 04
	12.48/0.4	34.69	3.50		47.19	56.15		13.96/0.4	6.18/1.0	11.90	1.80	5:06.09
7921		Jordan		Gray			USA	28.12.95	1	NC	San Mateo	23 Jun 19
	12.16/0.5	6.18/-0.4	12.86		1.65	57.41		14.10/1.1	39.09		3.71 39.83	5:26.14

4 x 100 METRES RELAY

40.82 WR	USA	Madison (-Bartoletta), Felix, Knight, Jeter	1	OG	London (OS)	10 Aug 12
41.01	USA	Bartoletta, Felix, Gardner, Bowie	1	OG	Rio de Janeiro	19 Aug 16
41.07	JAM	Campbell-Brown, Morrison, Thompson, Fraser-Pryce	1	WCh	Beijing	29 Aug 15
41.29	JAM	Russell, Stewart, Calvert, Fraser-Pryce	1	WCh	Moskva	18 Aug 13
41.36	JAM	C.Williams, Thompson, Campbell-Brown, Fraser-Pryce	2	OG	Rio de Janeiro	19 Aug 16
41.37 WR	GDR	Gladisch, Rieger, Auerswald, Göhr	1	WCp	Canberra	6 Oct 85
41.41	JAM	Fraser-Pryce, Simpson, Campbell-Brown, Stewart	2	OG	London (OS)	10 Aug 12
41.44	JAM	Whyte, Fraser-Pryce, J Smith, Jackson	1	WCh	Doha	5 Oct 19
41.47	USA	Gaines, Jones, Miller, Devers	1	WCh	Athina	9 Aug 97
41.49	RUS	Bogoslovskaya, Malchugina, Voronova, Privalova	1	WCh	Stuttgart	22 Aug 93
41.49	USA	Finn, Torrence, Vereen, Devers	2	WCh	Stuttgart	22 Aug 93
41.52	USA	Gaines, Jones, Miller, Devers	1h1	WCh	Athina	8 Aug 97
41.53 WR	GDR	Gladisch, Koch, Auerswald, Göhr	1		Berlin	31 Jul 83
41.55	USA	Brown, Williams, Griffith, Marshall	1	ISTAF	Berlin	21 Aug 87
41.56	USA	B Knight, Felix, Myers, Jeter	1	WCh	Daegu	4 Sep 11
41.58	USA	Brown, Williams, Griffith, Marshall	1	WCh	Roma	6 Sep 87
41.58	USA	L.Williams, Felix, Lee, Jeter	1		Cottbus	8 Aug 09
41.60 WR	GDR	Müller, Wöckel, Auerswald, Göhr	1	OG	Moskva	1 Aug 80
41.60	JAM	Simpson, Morrison, Thompson, Fraser-Pryce	1	WK	Zürich	3 Sep 15
41.61A	USA	Brown, Williams, Cheeseborough, Ashford	1	USOF	USAF Academy	3 Jul 83
41.62	GER	Pinto, Mayer, Lückenkemper, Haase	1		Mannheim	29 Jul 16
41.63	USA	Brown, Williams, Cheeseborough, Ashford	1	v GDR	Los Angeles	25 Jun 83
41.64	USA	Madison, Tarmoh, Knight, L Williams	1h1	OG	London (OS)	9 Aug 12
41.65	USA	Brown, Bolden, Cheeseborough, Ashford	1	OG	Los Angeles	11 Aug 84
41.65	GDR	Gladisch, Koch, Auerswald, Göhr	1	ECp	Moskva	17 Aug 85
41.65	JAM	C.Williams, Thompson, Facey, Campbell-Brown	1	WK	Zürich	1 Sep 16
	(26 performances by 4 nations) from here just best by nation					
41.77	GBR	Philip, Henry, Asher-Smith, Neita	3	OG	Rio de Janeiro	19 Aug 16
41.78	FRA	Girard, Hurtis, Félix, Arron	1	WCh	Saint-Denis	30 Aug 03
41.92	BAH	Fynes, Sturrup, Davis-Thompson, Ferguson	1	WCh	Sevilla	29 Aug 99
42.03	TTO	Baptiste, Ahye, Thomas, Hackett	3	WCh	Beijing	29 Aug 15
42.04	UKR	Povh, Stuy, Ryemyen, Bryzgina	3	OG	London (OS)	10 Aug 12
42.04	NED	Samuel, Schippers, van Schagen, Sedney (10)	1	EC	Amsterdam	10 Jul 16
42.08mx	BUL	Pavlova, Nuneva, Georgieva, Ivanova	mx		Sofia	8 Aug 84
		42.29 Pencheva, Nuneva, Georgieva, Donkova	1		Sofia	26 Jun 88
42.18	SUI	Del Ponte, Atcho, Kambundji, Kora	4	WCh	Doha	5 Oct 19
42.23	CHN	(Sichuan) Xiao Lin, Li Yali, Liu Xiaomei, Li Xuemei	1	NG	Shanghai	23 Oct 97
42.29	BRA	E dos Santos, Silva, Krasucki, R Santos	2h3	WCh	Moskva	18 Aug 13
42.39	NGR	Utondu, Idehen, Opara-Thompson, Onyali	2h2	OG	Barcelona	7 Aug 92
42.54	BEL	Borlée, Mariën, Ouédraogo, Gevaert	2	OG	Beijing	22 Aug 08
42.56	BLR	Nesterenko, Sologub, Nevmerzhitskaya, Dragun	3	WCh	Helsinki	13 Aug 05
42.59	FRG	Possekel, Helten, Richter, Kroniger	2	OG	Montreal	31 Jul 76
42.60	CAN	Emmanuel, Hyacinthe, Fofanah, Bingham	3h1	WCh	Beijing	29 Aug 15

4 x 100m - 4x 200m RELAY A-T   259

Mark	Wind	Name	Nat	Born	Pos	Meet	Venue	Date
42.67	GHA	Owusu-Agyapong, Acheampong, Gyaman, Amponsah			1		Cape Coast	8 Jul 16
	(20)							
42.68	POL	Popowicz, Korczynska, Jeschke, Wedler			3	EC	Barcelona	1 Aug 10
42.73	BRN	Jassim, Odiong, Al-Khaldi, Naser			1	AsiG	Jakarta	30 Aug 18
42.89	CUB	Ferrer, López, Duporty, Allen			6	WCh	Stuttgart	22 Aug 93
42.90	ITA	Herrera Abreu, Hooper, Bongiorni, Siragusa			5h2	WCh	Doha	4 Oct 19
42.92	KAZ	Kashafutdinova, Zyabkina, Rakhmanova, Safronova			1		Almaty	4 Jul 16
42.98	CZE/TCH	Sokolová, Soborová, Kocembová, Kratochvilová			1	WK	Zürich	18 Aug 82
42.99A	AUS	Massey, Broadrick, Lambert, Gainsford-Taylor			1		Pietersburg	18 Mar 00
43.03A	COL	M.Murillo, Palacios, Obregón, D Murillo			2	SAm-r	Bogotá	10 Jul 04
43.07	GRE	Tsóni, Kóffa, Vasarmídou, Thánou			2	MedG	Bari	18 Jun 97
43.25A	RSA	Hartman, Moropane, Holtshausen, Seyerling			2		Pietersburg	18 Mar 00
	(30)							

Best at low altitude

43.03	COL	M.Murillo, Palacios, Obregón, N.González			3h2	WCh	Helsinki	12 Aug 05
43.18	AUS	Wilson, Wells, Robertson, Boyle			5	OG	Montreal	31 Jul 76

4 x 200 METRES RELAY

1:27.46 WR	USA Blue	Jenkins, Colander-Richardson, Perry, M Jones	1		PennR	Philadelphia	29 Apr 00
1:28.15 WR	GDR	Göhr, R.Müller, Wöckel, Koch	1			Jena	9 Aug 80
1:28.77	Tumbleweed, TC	Henry GBR, Onuora GBR, Bartoletta USA, Schippers NED	1		FlaR	Gainesville	1 Apr 17
1:28.77	PURE Athletics	Baptiste TTO, Wimbley USA, Bowie USA, Henry-Robinson JAM	1		FlaR	Gainesville	31 Mar 18
1:28.78	Un of Oregon USA	Dunmore, Cunliffe, Stevens, Washington	2		FlaR	Gainesville	1 Apr 17
1:29.04	JAM	Levy, Jackson, Forbes, Thompson	1		W.Rly	Nassau	22 Apr 17
1:29.25	PURE Athletics	Baptiste TTO, Wimbley, Henry, Miller-Uibo BAH	1		FlaR	Gainesville	30 Mar 19
1:29.42	Texas A & M (USA)	Tarmoh, Mayo, Beard, Lucas	1		Penn R	Philadelphia	24 Apr 10
1:29.45	USA Solomon, Meadows, Knight, K Duncan		1		WRly	Nassau	25 May 14
1:29.61	GBR	Henry A Onuora, B Williams, A Philip	2		WRly	Nassau	25 May 14
Drugs dq:	1:29.40	USA Red Colander, Gaines, Miller, M Jones ¶	(1)		Penn	Philadelphia	24 Apr 04

4 x 400 METRES RELAY

3:15.17 WR	URS		1		OG	Seoul	1 Oct 88
		Ledovskaya 50.12, O.Nazarova 47.82, Pinigina 49.43, Bryzgina 47.80					
3:15.51	USA		2		OG	Seoul	1 Oct 88
		D.Howard 49.82, Dixon 49.17, Brisco 48.44, Griffith Joyner 48.08					
3:15.92 WR	GDR	G.Walther 49.8, Busch 48.9, Rübsam 49.4, Koch 47.8	1		NC	Erfurt	3 Jun 84
3:16.71	USA	Torrence 49.80, Malone 49.4, Kaiser-Brown 49.48, Miles 48.78	1		WCh	Stuttgart	22 Aug 93
3:16.87	GDR	Emmelmann 50.9, Busch 48.8, Müller 48.9, Koch 48.21	1		EC	Stuttgart	31 Aug 86
3:16.87	USA	Trotter 50.3, Felix 48.1, McCorory 49.39, Richards-Ross 49.10	1		OG	London (OS)	11 Aug 12
3:17.83	USA	Dunn 50.5, Felix 48.8, Demus 50.14, Richards 48.44	1		WCh	Berlin	23 Aug 09
3:18.09	USA	Richards-Ross 49.3, Felix 49.4, Beard 49.84, McCorory 49.52	1		WCh	Daegu	3 Sep 11
3:18.29	USA		1		OG	Los Angeles	11 Aug 84
		Leatherwood 50.50, S.Howard 48.83, Brisco-Hooks 49.23, Cheeseborough 49.73					
3:18.29	GDR	Neubauer 50.58, Emmelmann 49.89, Busch 48.81, Müller 48.99	3		OG	Seoul	1 Oct 88
3:18.38	RUS		2		WCh	Stuttgart	22 Aug 93
		Ruzina 50.8, Alekseyeva 49.3, Ponomaryova 49.78, Privalova 48.47					
3:18.43	URS	Ledovskaya 51.7, Dzhigalova 49.2, Nazarova 48.87, Bryzgina 48.67	1	WCh	Tokyo	1 Sep 91
3:18.54	USA	Wineberg 51.0, Felix 48.6, Henderson 50.06, Richards 48.93	1		OG	Beijing	23 Aug 08
3:18.55	USA	Trotter 51.2, Felix 48.0, Wineberg 50.24, Richards 49.07	1		WCh	Osaka	2 Sep 07
3:18.58	URS	I.Nazarova, Olizarenko, Pinigina, Vladykina	1		ECp	Moskva	18 Aug 85
3:18.63	GDR	Neubauer 51.4, Emmelmann 49.1, Müller 48.64, Busch 49.48	1		WCh	Roma	6 Sep 87
3:18.71	JAM	Whyte 50.0, Prendergast 49.6, Williams-Mills 49.84, Williams 49.22	2	WCh	Daegu	3 Sep 11
3:18.92	USA	P Francis 50.5, McLaughlin 48.8, Muhammad 49.43, Jonathas 50.20	1	WCh	Doha	6 Oct 19
3:19.01	USA	Trotter 49.8, Henderson 49.7, Richards 49.81, Hennagan 49.73 (1)	OG			Athína	28 Aug 04
		Note team was disqualified as Crystal Cox (subject of retrospective drugs ban) ran for them in the heat					
3:19.02	USA	Hayes 50.4, Felix 48.7, Wimbley 49.58, Francis 50.28	1		WCh	London (OS)	13 Aug 17
3:19.04 WR	GDR	Siemon' 51.0, Busch 50.0, Rübsam 50.2, Koch 47.9	1		EC	Athína	11 Sep 82
3:19.06	USA	Okolo 51.13, Hastings 49.7, Francis 49.82, Felix 49.66	1		OG	Rio de Janeiro	20 Aug 16
3:19.12	URS	Baskakova, I.Nazarova, Pinigina, Vladykina	1		Drz	Praha	18 Aug 84
3:19.13	JAM	Day 50.5, Jackson 49.4, McPherson 50.19, Williams-Mills 49.14	1	WCh	Beijing	30 Aug 15
3:19.23 WR	USA	Maletzki 50.05, Rohde 49.00, Streidt 49.51, Brehmer 49.77	1		OG	Montreal	31 Jul 76
3:19.39	USA	Francis 51.40, Hastings 49.93, Richards-Ross 48.79, McCorory 49.27	1	W.Rly	Nassau	3 May 15
		(26/5 with USSR and Russia counted separately)					
3:20.04	GBR	Ohuruogu 50.6, Okoro 50.9, McConnell 49.79, Sanders 48.76	3		WCh	Osaka	2 Sep 07
3:20.32	CZE/TCH		2		WCh	Helsinki	14 Aug 83
		Kocembová 48.93, Matejkovicová 52.13, Moravcíková 51.51, Kratochvílová 47.75					
3:21.04	NGR	Afolabi 51.9, Yusuf 49.72, Opara 51.29, Ogunkoya 48.90	2		OG	Atlanta	3 Aug 96
3:21.21	CAN	Crooks 50.30, Richardson 50.22, Killingbeck ¶ 50.62, Payne 50.07	2	OG	Los Angeles	11 Aug 84
3:21.88	BLR	Yushchenko 51.40, Khlyustova 50.7, I Usovich 49.97, S Usovich 49.78	5	WCh	Osaka	2 Sep 07
	(10)						

260 RELAYS – WALKS

Mark	Wind	Name	Nat	Born	Pos	Meet	Venue	Date
3:21.89		POL Baumgart-Witan 51.0, Wyciszkiewicz 50.0, Holub-Kowalik 50.7, Swiety-Ersetic 50.1			2	WCh	Doha	6 Oct 19
3:21.94		UKR Dzhigalova, Olizarenko, Pinigina, Vladykina			1	URS Ch	Kyiv	17 Jul 86
3:22.34		FRA Landre 51.3, Dorsile 51.1, Elien 50.54, Pérec 49.36			1	EC	Helsinki	14 Aug 94
3:22.49		FRG Thimm 50.81, Arendt 49.95, Thomas 51.50, Abt 50.23			4	OG	Seoul	1 Oct 88
3:23.21		CUB Díaz 51.1, Calatayud 51.2, Clement 50.47, Terrero 50.46			6	OG	Beijing	23 Aug 08
3:23.81		AUS Peris-K 51.71, Lewis 51.69, Gainsford-T 51.06, Freeman 49.35			4	OG	Sydney	30 Sep 00
3:24.28		CHN (Hebei) An X, Bai X, Cao C, Ma Y			1	NG	Beijing	13 Sep 93
3:25.16		ITA Chigbolu 52.1, Spacca 51.3, Folorunso 51.44, Grenot 50.18			4h2	OG	Rio de Janeiro	19 Aug 16
3:25.68		ROU Ruicu 52.69, Rîpanu 51.09, Barbu 52.64, Tîrlea 49.26			2	ECp	Paris (C)	20 Jun 99
3:25.7a (20)		FIN Eklund 53.6, Pursiainen 50.6, Wilmi 51.6, Salin 49.9			2	EC	Roma	8 Sep 74
3:25.81		BUL Ilieva, Stamenova, Penkova, Damyanova			1	v Hun,Pol	Sofia	24 Jul 83
3:26.33		GRE Kaidantzi 53.2, Goudenoúdi 51.6, Boudá 51.76, Halkiá 49.75			3	ECpS	Bydgoszcz	20 Jun 04
3:26.36		BAH L Clarke 52.4, Strachan 51.9, Cox 50.91, Amertil 51.07			6h2	OG	Rio de Janeiro	19 Aug 16
3:26.58		BEL Claes 52.5, Vervaet 51.2, Couckuyt 52.2, Laus 50.7			4h2	WCh	Doha	5 Oct 19
3:26.68		BRA (Bovespa) Coutinho, de Oliveira, Sousa, de Lima			1	NC	São Paulo	7 Aug 11
3:26.86		BOT Moroko 53.3, Botlogetswe 50.9, Matlhaku 53.00, Montsho 49.59			3 CG	Gold Coast	14 Apr 18
3:26.89		IND R Kaur 53.1, Beenamol 51.4, Soman 52.51, M Kaur 49.85			3h2	OG	Athína	27 Aug 04
3:26.98		NED			6h1	OG	Rio de Janeiro	19 Aug 16
		Ghafoor 52.4, Lisanne de Witte 51.0, van Leuveren 50.99, Laura de Witte 52.49						
3:27.08		CMR Nguimgo 51.7, Kaboud 52.1, Atangana 51.98, Béwouda 51.35			7	WCh	Saint-Denis	31 Aug 03
3:27.14		MEX Rodríguez 53.3, Medina 51.2, Vela 52.94, Guevara 49.70			4h2	WCh	Osaka	1 Sep 07
Drugs disqualification								
3:18.82		RUS Gushchina 50.6, Litvinova 49.2, Firova 49.20, Kapachinskaya 49.82			(2)	OG	Beijing	23 Aug 08
3:19.36		RUS			(3)	WCh	Daegu	3 Sep 11
		Krivoshapka 50.3, Antyukh 50.0, Litvinova 49.96, Kapachinskaya ¶ 49.22						
3:21.85		BLR Kozak 52.0, Khlyustova 50.3, I Usovich 49.85, S Usovich 49.69			(4)	OG	Beijing	23 Aug 08

4 x 800 METRES RELAY

7:50.17 WR	USSR Olizarenko, Gurina, Borisova, Podyalovskaya		1		Moskva	5 Aug 84
7:51.62	USSR II Ruchayeva, Agletdinova, Zvagintseva, Zhukova		2		Moskva	5 Aug 84
7:52.24	USSR Podkopayeva, Zvyagintseva, Olizarenko, Agletdinova		1		Leningrad	4 Aug 85
7:52.3 WR	USSR		1		Podolsk	16 Aug 76
	Providokhina 1:58.4, Gerasimova 1:59.2, Styrkina 1:57.3, Kazankina ¶ 1:57.4					
7:54.10 WR	GDR Zinn, Hoffmeister, Weiss, Klapezynski		1	NC	Karl-Marx-Stadt	6 Aug 76
8:00.62	USA Price 2:01.30, Vessey 2:00.92, Ludlow 1:59.50, Montaño 1:58.90		1	WRly	Nassau	3 May 15

4 x 1500 METRES RELAY

16:27.02 WR	Nike Bowerman (USA) Quigley c.4:08, Cranny 4:09, Schweizer 4:06, Houlihan 4:04	1	WRly	Portland	31 Jul 20
16:33.58 WR	KEN M Cherono 4:07.5, Kipyegon 4:08.5, Jelagat 4:10.5, Obiri 4:07.1	1	WRly	Nassau	24 May 14
16:55.33	USA Kampf 4:09.2, Mackey, Grace, Martinez 4:10.2	2	WRly	Nassau	24 May 14
17:08.65	AUS Buckman 4:08.1, Delaney 4:15.5, McGowan, Duncan 4:16.0	3	WRly	Nassau	25 May 14

3000 METRES WALK (TRACK)

11:48.24 WR	Ileana	Salvador	ITA	16.1.62	1		Padova	29 Aug 93
11:50.30	Marina	Pandakova	RUS	1.3.89	1		Moskva	28 Jul 16
11:51.26 WR	Kerry	Saxby-Junna	AUS	2.6.61	1		Melbourne	7 Feb 91
11:52.01	Beate	Anders/Gummelt	GER	4.2.68	1		Lapinlahti	27 Jun 93

5000 METRES WALK (TRACK)

20:01.80 WR	Eleonora	Giorgi	ITA	14.9.89	1		Misterbianco	18 May 14
20:02.60 WR	Gillian	O'Sullivan	IRL	21.8.76	1	NC	Dublin (S)	13 Jul 02
20:03.0 WR	Kerry	Saxby-Junna	AUS	2.6.61	1		Sydney	11 Feb 96
20:07.52 WR	Beate	Anders/Gummelt	GDR	4.2.68	1	vURS	Rostock	23 Jun 90
20:11.45	Sabine	Zimmer/Krantz	GER	6.2.81	1	NC	Wattenscheid	2 Jul 05
20:12.41	Elisabetta	Perrone	ITA	9.7.68	1	NC	Rieti	2 Aug 03
20:15.71	Lyudmyla	Olyanovska ¶	UKR	20.2.93	1		Kyiv	4 Jun 14
20:18.87	Melanie	Seeger	GER	8.1.77	1	NC	Braunschweig	10 Jul 04
20:21.69	Annarita	Sidoti	ITA	25.7.69	1	NC	Cesenatico	1 Jul 95
Indoors								
20:04.4	Yelena	Lashmanova	RUS	9.4.92	1		Saransk	27 Dec 20
20:21.5	Reykhan	Kagramanova	RUS	1.6.97	2		Saransk	27 Dec 20
20:21.9	Elvira	Khasanova	RUS	10.1.00	3		Saransk	27 Dec 20

10 KILOMETRES WALK

41:04 WR	Yelena	Nikolayeva	RUS	1.2.66	1	NC	Sochi	20 Apr 96
41:16		Wang Yan	CHN	3.5.71	1		Eisenhüttenstadt	8 May 99
41:16	Kjersti	Plätzer (Tysse)	NOR	18.1.72	1	NC	Os	11 May 02
41:17	Irina	Stankina	RUS	25.3.77	1	NC-w	Adler	9 Feb 97
41:24	Olimpiada	Ivanova ¶	RUS	26.8.70	2	NC-w	Adler	9 Feb 97

10 – 20 KILOMETRES WALK A-T   261

Mark	Wind	Name		Nat	Born	Pos	Meet	Venue	Date
41:25			Yang Jiayu	CHN	18.2.96	1		Wenzhong	15 Dec 20
41:28		Antonella	Palmisano	ITA	6.8.91	1	NC	Modena	18 Oct 20
41:29 WR		Larisa	Ramazanova	RUS	23.9.71	1	NC	Izhevsk	4 Jun 95
41:30 WR		Kerry	Saxby-Junna	AUS	2.6.61	1	NC	Canberra	27 Aug 88
41:30			O Ivanova			2	NC	Izhevsk	4 Jun 95
41:31		Yelena	Gruzinova (10)	RUS	24.12.67	2	NC	Sochi	20 Apr 96
41:37.9t			Gao Hongmiao	CHN	17.3.74	1	NC	Beijing	7 Apr 94
41:38		Rossella	Giordano	ITA	1.12.72	1		Naumburg	25 May 97
41:41			Nikolayeva			2		Naumburg	25 May 97
41:41			Tysse Plätzer			1		Kraków	30 May 09
41:42		Olga	Kaniskina ¶	RUS	19.1.85	2		Kraków	30 May 09
41:42.5t		Lyudmyla	Olyanovska ¶	UKR	20.2.93	1		Mukachevo	1 Nov 14
41:45			Liu Hongyu	CHN	11.1.75	2		Eisenhüttenstadt	8 May 99
41:45.84t		Elvira	Khasanova	RUS	10.1.00	1		Cheboksary	3 Aug 19
41:46		Annarita	Sidoti	ITA	25.7.69	1		Livorno	12 Jun 94
41:46			O Ivanova			1	NC/w	Adler	11 Feb 96
		(21/17)							
41:48			Li Chunxiu	CHN	13.8.69	1	NG	Beijing	8 Sep 93
41:48	+	Yelena	Lashmanova	RUS	9.4.92	1	in 20k	Cheboksary	9 Jun 18
41:50		Yelena	Arshintseva	RUS	5.4.71	1	NC-w	Adler	11 Feb 95
		(20)							
41:51		Beate	Anders/Gummelt	GER	4.2.68	2		Eisenhüttenstadt	11 May 96
41:52		Tatyana	Mineyeva ¶	RUS	10.8.90	1	NCp-j	Penza	5 Sep 09
41:52		Tatyana	Korotkova	RUS	24.4.80	1		Buy	19 Sep 10
41:53		Tatyana	Sibileva	RUS	17.5.80	1	RWC-F	Beijing	18 Sep 10
41:56		Yelena	Sayko	RUS	24.12.67	2	NC/w	Adler	11 Feb 96
41:56.23t		Nadezhda	Ryashkina	RUS	22.1.67	1	GWG	Seattle	24 Jul 90
41:59		Marina	Pandakova	RUS	1.3.89	1		Podolsk	8 May 16
42:01		Tamara	Kovalenko	RUS	5.6.64	3	NC-w	Adler	11 Feb 95
42:01		Olga	Panfyorova	RUS	21.8.77	1	NC-23	Izhevsk	16 May 98
42:02.99t		Sandra	Arenas	COL	17.9.93	1	IbAm	Trujillo	26 Aug 18
		(30)							
42:03		Lina	Bikulova	RUS	1.10.88	1		Bui	13 Sep 14
42:04+		Vera	Sokolova ¶	RUS	8.6.87	1=	in 20k	Sochi	26 Feb 11
42:04+		Tatyana	Shemyakina	RUS	3.9.87	1=	in 20k	Sochi	26 Feb 11
42:05+		Margarita	Turova	BLR	28.12.80	1+	in 20k	Adler	12 Mar 05
42:06		Valentina	Tsybulskaya	BLR	19.2.68	4		Eisenhüttenstadt	8 May 99
42:06		Nadezhda	Sergeyeva	RUS	12.3.94	1		Mis	3 May 19
42:07		Ileana	Salvador	ITA	16.1.62	1		Sesto San Giovanni	1 May 92
42:09		Elisabetta	Perrone	ITA	9.7.68	4		Eisenhüttenstadt	11 May 96
42:11		Nina	Alyushenko	RUS	29.5.68	3	NC	Izhevsk	4 Jun 95
42:12+		Elmira	Alembekova ¶	RUS	30.6.90	1	in 20k	Sochi	27 Feb 15
42:12+		Svetlana	Vasilyeva	RUS	24.7.92	3	in 20k	Sochi	27 Feb 15
		(41)		50th woman 42:16, 100th 42:57, 200th 43:48, 300th 44:21, 400th 44:46					
Drugs dq: 42:04+ Anisya			Kirdyapkina ¶	RUS	23.10.89	(1=)	in 20k	Sochi	26 Feb 11
Best track times									
41:57.22		Kerry	Saxby-Junna	AUS	2.6.61	2	GWG	Seattle	24 Jul 90
41:57.29		Antonella	Palmisano	ITA	6.8.91	1		Orvieto	23 Apr 17
42:00.4A			Yang Jiayu	CHN	18.2.96	1		Huehot	8 May 20
42:11.5		Beate	Anders/Gummelt	GER	4.2.68	1	SGP	Fana	15 May 92

20 KILOMETRES WALK

1:23:39	Yelena	Lashmanova	RUS	9.4.92	1	NC	Cheboksary	9 Jun 18
1:24:31		Lashmanova			1	RUS-w	Sochi	17 Feb 19
1:24:38 WR		Liu Hong	CHN	12.5.87	1		La Coruña	6 Jun 15
1:24:47	Elmira	Alembekova ¶	RUS	30.6.90	1	NC-w	Sochi	27 Feb 15
1:24:50	Olimpiada	Ivanova ¶	RUS	26.8.70	1	NC-w	Adler	4 Mar 01
1:24:56	Olga	Kaniskina ¶	RUS	19.1.85	1	NC-w	Adler	28 Feb 09
1:24:58		Lashmanova			1	NC	Cheboksary	25 Jun 16
1:25:02 WR		Lashmanova			1	OG	London	11 Aug 12
1:25:03	Marina	Pandakova	RUS	1.3.89	2	NC-w	Sochi	27 Feb 15
1:25:04	Svetlana	Vasilyeva	RUS	24.7.92	3	NC-w	Sochi	27 Feb 15
1:25:08 WR	Vera	Sokolova	RUS	8.6.87	1	NC-w	Sochi	26 Feb 11
1:25:11		Kaniskina			1	NC-w	Adler	23 Feb 08
1:25:11	Anisya	Kirdyapkina ¶	RUS	23.10.89	1	NC-w	Sochi	20 Feb 10
1:25:12		Lu Xiuzhi (10)	CHN	26.10.93	1	WCT	Beijing	20 Mar 15
1:25:16		Qieyang Shenjie	CHN	11.11.90	2	OG	London	11 Aug 12
1:25:18	Tatyana	Gudkova	RUS	23.1.78	1	NC	Moskva	19 May 00
1:25:18		Lashmanova			1	NC-w	Sochi	18 Feb 17
1:25:20	Olga	Polyakova	RUS	23.9.80	2	NC	Moskva	19 May 00

WOMEN All-time

50 KILOMETRES WALK A-T

Mark	Wind	Name		Nat	Born	Pos	Meet	Venue	Date
1:25:22		Yekaterina	Medvedyeva	RUS	29.3.94	2	NC-w	Sochi	18 Feb 17
1:25:26			Sokolova			2	NC-w	Adler	28 Feb 09
1:25:26			Kirdyapkina			3	NC-w	Adler	28 Feb 09
1:25:27			Alembekova			1	NC-w	Sochi	18 Feb 12
1:25:29		Irina	Stankina	RUS	25.3.77	3	NC	Moskva	19 May 00
1:25:29		Glenda	Morejón	ECU	30.5.00	1		La Coruña	8 Jun 19
1:25:30			Kirdyapkina			2	NC-w	Adler	23 Feb 08
1:25:32		Yelena	Shumkina ¶	RUS	24.1.88	4	NC-w	Adler	28 Feb 09
1:25:34			Yang Jiayu	CHN	18.2.96	2		La Coruña	8 Jun 19
1:25:35			Sokolova			2	NC-w	Sochi	20 Feb 10
1:25:37			Qieyang Shenjie			1	NGP	Huangshan	10 Mar 19
1:25:38			Sokolova			4	NC-w	Sochi	27 Feb 15
	(30/18)								
1:25:46		Tatyana	Shemyakina	RUS	3.9.87	3	NC-w	Adler	23 Feb 08
1:25:52		Larisa	Yemelyanova	RUS	6.1.80	5	NC-w	Adler	28 Feb 09
	(20)								
1:25:52		Tatyana	Sibileva	RUS	17.5.80	3	NC-w	Sochi	20 Feb 10
1:25:59		Tamara	Kovalenko	RUS	5.6.64	4	NC	Moskva	19 May 00
1:26:11		Margarita	Turova	BLR	28.12.80	1	NC	Nesvizh	15 Apr 06
1:26:14		Irina	Petrova	RUS	26.5.85	2	NC-w	Adler	19 Feb 06
1:26:16		Lyudmila	Arkhipova	RUS	25.11.78	5	NC-w	Adler	23 Feb 08
1:26:17		Eleonora	Giorgi	ITA	14.9.89	2	ECp	Murcia	17 May 15
1:26:17		María Guadalupe	González ¶	MEX	9.1.89	1	WCp	Roma	7 May 16
1:26:22 WR			Wang Yan	CHN	3.5.71	1	NG	Guangzhou	19 Nov 01
1:26:22 WR		Yelena	Nikolayeva	RUS	1.2.66	1	ECp	Cheboksary	18 May 03
1:26:23			Wang Liping	CHN	8.7.76	2	NG	Guangzhou	19 Nov 01
	(30)								
1:26:27		Sofiya	Brodatskaya	RUS	4.10.95	3	NC-w	Sochi	18 Feb 17
1:26:28		Iraida	Pudovkina	RUS	2.11.80	1	NC-w	Adler	12 Mar 05
1:26:29			Wang Na	CHN	29.5.95	2	NGP	Huangshan	4 Mar 17
1:26:34		Tatyana	Kalmykova	RUS	10.1.90	1	NC	Saransk	8 Jun 08
1:26:35			Liu Hongyu	CHN	11.1.75	3	NG	Guangzhou	19 Nov 01
1:26:36		Antonella	Palmisano	ITA	6.8.91	3	WCh	London	13 Aug 17
1:26:36		María	Pérez	ESP	29.4.96	1	EC	Berlin	11 Aug 18
1:26:46			Song Hongjuan	CHN	4.7.84	1	NC	Guangzhou	20 Mar 04
1:26:43		Elvira	Khasanova	RUS	10.1.00	1	NC-w	Sochi	17 Feb 20
1:26:47		Irina	Yumanova ¶	RUS	6.11.90	3	NC-w	Sochi	18 Feb 12
	(40)								
1:26:47		Klavdiya	Afanasyeva	RUS	15.1.96	3	NC	Cheboksary	25 Jun 16
1:26:50		Natalya	Fedoskina	RUS	25.6.80	2	ECp	Dudince	19 May 01
1:26:50		Reykhan	Kagramanova	RUS	1.6.97	2	NC-w	Sochi	17 Feb 20
1:26:53		Anezka	Drahotová	CZE	22.7.95	4	ECp	Murcia	17 May 15
1:26:57		Lyudmila	Yefimkina	RUS	22.8.81	3	NC-w	Adler	19 Feb 06
1:26:59		Erica	de Sena	BRA	3.5.85	4	WCh	London	13 Aug 17
1:27:07		Kjersti	Tysse Plätzer	NOR	18.1.72	2	OG	Beijing	21 Aug 08
1:27:09		Elisabetta	Perrone	ITA	9.7.68	3	ECp	Dudince	19 May 01
1:27:09		Lyudmyla	Olyanovska ¶	UKR	20.2.93	7	ECp	Murcia	17 May 15
1:27:12		Elisa	Rigaudo	ITA	17.6.80	3	OG	Beijing	21 Aug 08
	(50)		100th best woman 1:28:15, 200th 1:29:58, 300th 1:31:20, 400th 1:32:24, 500th 1:33:46						
Drugs dq:		1:25:09 Anisya	Kirdyapkina ¶	RUS	23.10.89	(2)	NC-w	Sochi	26 Feb 11
1:25:09			Kaniskina			(2)	OG	London	11 Aug 12
1:26:46		Mariya	Ponomaryova ¶	RUS	18.6.95	(3)	NC	Cheboksary	25 Jun 16
1:27:08		Anna	Lukyanova ¶	RUS	23.4.91	(5)	NC-w	Sochi	18 Feb 12

30/35 KILOMETRES WALK

	2:38:24	Klavdiya	Afanasyeva	RUS	15.1.96	1	NC-w	Sochi	17 Feb 19
2:17:28	2:40:22+	Yelena	Lashmanova	RUS	9.4.92	1	in 50k	Voronovskoye	5 Sep 20
2:19:43		Eleonora	Giorgi	ITA	14.9.89	1		Catania	31 Jan 16
2:21:29+	2:43:43		Giorgi			1	NC	Grosseto	26 Jan 20
	2:43:56	Vera	Sokolova	RUS	8.6.87	1	NC-w	Sochi	17 Feb 20
	2:44:00	Margarita	Nikiforova	RUS	19.8.98	2	NC-w	Sochi	17 Feb 19
2:22:07	2:45:16+		Nikiforova			2	in 50k	Voronovskoye	5 Sep 20
2:22:20+	2:45:21		Giorgi			1		Gioiosa Marea	27 Jan 19
2:22:27+			Afanasyeva			1	in 50k	Cheboksary	15 Jun 19
2:22:47	2:45:51	Inês	Henriques	POR	1.5.80	1		Porto de Mos	7 Jan 18
2:24:33	2:48:13	Olga	Shargina	RUS	24.7.96	1	NC-w	Sochi	19 Mar 18
	2:49:04	Anastasiya	Kalashnikova	RUS	29.6.97	3	NC-w	Sochi	17 Feb 20
	2:49:18	Kristina	Lyubushkina	RUS	19.9.95	4	NC-w	Sochi	17 Feb 20
	2:49:23		Liang Rui	CHN	18.6.94	1		Huangshan	4 Mar 18
	2:50:01	Aleksandra	Bushkova	RUS	13.1.97	3	NC-w	Sochi	17 Feb 19
	2:50:05	Nadezhda	Mokeyeva	RUS	10.1.96	4	NC-w	Sochi	17 Feb 19

50 – 100 KILOMETRES WALK A-T

Mark	Wind	Name		Nat	Born	Pos	Meet	Venue	Date

50 KILOMETRES WALK

Mark	Wind	Name	Surname	Nat	Born	Pos	Meet	Venue	Date
3:50:42		Yelena	Lashmanova	RUS	9.4.92	1	NC	Voronovskoye	5 Sep 20
3:57:08		Klavdiya	Afanasyeva	RUS	15.1.96	1	NC	Cheboksary	15 Jun 19
3:59:15 WR			Liu Hong	CHN	12.5.87	1	NGP	Huangshan	9 Mar 19
3:59:56		Margarita	Nikiforova	RUS	19.8.98	2	NC	Voronovskoye	5 Sep 20
4:03:51			Li Maocuo	CHN	20.10.92	2	NGP	Huangshan	9 Mar 19
4:04:36 WR			Liang Rui	CHN	18.6.94	1	WTC	Taicang	5 May 18
4:04:50		Eleonora	Giorgi	ITA	14.9.89	1	ECp	Alytus	19 May 19
4:05:46		Julia	Takacs	ESP	29.6.89	2	ECp	Alytus	19 May 19
4:05:56 WR		Inês	Henriques	POR	1.5.80	1	WCh	London	13 Aug 17
4:05:58			Nikiforova			2	NC	Cheboksary	15 Jun 19
4:07:30			Ma Faying (10)	CHN	30.8.93	3	NGP	Huangshan	9 Mar 19
4:08:26 WR			Henriques			1		Porto de Mós	15 Jan 17
4:08:58			Yin Hang	CHN	7.2.97	2	WCh	London	13 Aug 17
4:09:09			Yin Hang			2	WTC	Taicang	5 May 18
4:09:21			Henriques			1	EC	Berlin	7 Aug 18
4:09:33		Claire	Tallent/Woods	AUS	6.7.81	3	WTC	Taicang	5 May 18
4:10:59 WR		Monica	Svensson	SWE	26.12.78	1		Scanzorosciate	21 Oct 07
4:11:01		Raquel	González	ESP	16.11.89	1	NC	El Vendrell	10 Feb 19
4:11:12		Johana	Ordóñez	ECU	12.12.87	1	PAm	Lima	11 Aug 19
4:12:16 WR		Yelena	Ginko	BLR	30.7.76	1		Scanzorosciate	17 Oct 04
4:12:26			Liang Rui			1	NC	Weinan	8 Sep 18
4:12:44		Alina	Tsviliy	UKR	18.9.94	2	EC	Berlin	7 Aug 18
4:12:44			Woods			1		Santee	26 Jan 19
4:12:56		Paola	Pérez	ECU	21.12.89	4	WTC	Taicang	5 May 18
4:13:04			Takacs			1	NC	Burjassot	25 Feb 18
4:13:04			Li Maocuo			1	NGP	Chifeng	3 Jul 18
4:13:28			Ma Faying			5	WTC	Taicang	5 May 18
4:13:56A		Mirna	Ortiz	GUA	28.2.87	1		Ciudad de Guatemala	24 Feb 19
4:13:57			Henriques			3	ECp	Alytus	19 May 19
4:14:25		Mária (30/20)	Czaková	SVK	2.10.88	1		Dudince	24 Mar 18
4:14:31			Jiang Pengqin	CHN	5.9.95	4	NGP	Huangshan	9 Mar 19
4:14:49			Bai Tiantian	CHN	14.8.98	5	NGP	Huangshan	9 Mar 19
4:15:33			Wang Yingliu	CHN	1.3.92	6	NGP	Huangshan	9 Mar 19
4:15:42		Mayra Carolina	Herrera	GUA	20.12.88	1		Owego	9 Sep 17
4:15:46		Mar	Juárez	ESP	27.9.93	1	NC	Torrevieja	16 Feb 19
4:15:50		Valentyna	Myronchuk	UKR	10.8.94	4	ECp	Alytus	19 May 19
4:16:27		Jolanta	Dukure	LAT	20.9.79	1		Paralepa	9 Sep 06
4:16:39		Anastasiya	Yatsevich	BLR	18.1.85	5	ECp	Alytus	19 May 19
4:17:07		Olena	Sobchuk	UKR	23.11.95	6	ECp	Alytus	19 May 19
4:17:29		Nadezhda (30)	Dorozhuk	BLR	23.1.90	7	ECp	Alytus	19 May 19
4:18:26		Anastasiya	Kalashnikova	RUS	29.6.97	3	NC	Voronovskoye	5 Sep 20
4:18:56		Ainhoa	Pinedo	ESP	17.2.83	2	NC	Burjassot	25 Feb 18
4:19:04		Magaly	Bonilla	ECU	8.2.92	11	WTC	Taicang	5 May 18
4:19:56		Masumi	Fuchise	JPN	2.9.86	1		Wajima	14 Apr 19
4:19:57		Khrystyna	Yudkina	UKR	4.12.84	8	ECp	Alytus	19 May 19
4:20:17		Ivana	Renic	CRO	21.8.96	2		Dudince	23 Mar 19
4:20:36		Erika	Morales	MEX	10.12.86	1		Hauppage	24 Oct 18
4:20:49			Yang Shuqing	CHN	30.8.96	3	WCh	London	13 Aug 17
4:21:51		Kathleen	Burnett	USA	10.7.88	4	WCh	London	13 Aug 17
4:22:23		Nadezhda (40)	Mokeyeva	RUS	10.1.96	3	NC	Cheboksary	15 Jun 19
4:22:24		Kristina	Lyubushkina	RUS	19.9.95	4	NC	Voronovskoye	5 Sep 20
4:22:36		Aleksandra	Bushkova	RUS	13.1.97	2	NC	Cheboksary	9 Jun 18
4:22:46		Viviane	Lyra	BRA	29.7.93	4	PAm	Lima	11 Aug 19
4:22:47			Chi Meijiao	CHN	28.6.96	8	NGP	Huangshan	9 Mar 19
4:22:57		Evelin	Inga	PER	16.4.98	1	PAmCp	Lázaro Cardenas	21 Apr 19
4:23:15		Vasylyna	Vitovshchyk	UKR	30.4.90	5	EC	Berlin	7 Aug 18
4:25:22		Brigita	Virbalyte-Dimsiene	LTU	1.2.85	1		Villa di Serio	17 Oct 10
4:26:10		Mariavittoria	Becchetti	ITA	12.12.94	11	ECp	Alytus	19 May 19
4:26:42			Chen Yumin	CHN	8.2.97	9	NGP	Huangshan	9 Mar 19
4:27:13		Olga (50)	Shargina	RUS	24.7.96	3	NC	Cheboksary	9 Jun 18

100 KILOMETRES WALK

Mark	Wind	Name	Surname	Nat	Born	Pos	Meet	Venue	Date
10:04:50		Jolanta	Dukure	LAT	20.9.79	1		Scanzorosciate	21 Oct 07
10:13:56		Kora	Boufflért	FRA	23.4.66	1		Roubaix	9 Oct 94
10:20:02		Lyudmila	Lyubomirova	RUS	13.11.62	1		Perpignan	15 Oct 95

264 JUNIOR MEN ALL-TIME

Mark	Wind	Name		Nat	Born	Pos	Meet	Venue	Date

JUNIOR MEN'S ALL-TIME LISTS

100 METRES
9.97	1.8	Trayvon	Bromell	USA	10.7.95	1	NCAA	Eugene	13 Jun 14
10.00	1.6	Trentavis	Friday	USA	5.6.95	1h1	NC-j	Eugene	5 Jul 14
10.01	0.0	Darrel	Brown	TTO	11.10.84	1q3	WCh	Saint-Denis	24 Aug 03
10.01	1.6	Jeffery	Demps	USA	8.1.90	2q1	NC/OT	Eugene	28 Jun 08
10.01	0.9	Yoshihide	Kiryu	JPN	15.12.95	1h3	Oda	Hiroshima	29 Apr 13
10.03	0.7	Marcus	Rowland	USA	11.3.90	1	PAm-J	Port of Spain	31 Jul 09
10.03	1.7	Lala Muhammad	Zohri	INA	1.7.00	3		Osaka	19 May 19
10.04	1.7	DeAngelo	Cherry	USA	1.8.90	1h4	NCAA	Fayetteville	10 Jun 09
10.04	0.2	Christophe	Lemaitre	FRA	11.6.90	1	EJ	Novi Sad	24 Jul 09
10.04	1.9	Abdullah Abkar	Mohammed	KSA	.97	1	MSR	Norwalk	15 Apr 16

Wind assisted to 10.02
9.77	4.2	Trayvon	Bromell	USA	10.7.95	1	Big 12	Lubbock	18 May 14
9.83	7.1	Leonard	Scott	USA	19.1.80	1		Knoxville	9 Apr 99
9.96	4.5	Walter	Dix	USA	31.1.86	1rA	TexR	Austin	9 Apr 05
9.96	5.0	André	De Grasse	CAN	10.11.94	1	JUCO	Hutchinson, KS	18 May 13
9.97	??	Mark	Lewis-Francis	GBR	4.9.82	1q3	WCh	Edmonton	4 Aug 01
9.98	5.0	Tyreek	Hill	USA	1.3.94	2	JUCO	Hutchinson, KS	18 May 13
9.98	4.2	Matthew	Boling	USA	20.6.00	1		Webster, TX	27 Apr 19
10.02	2.8	DeAngelo	Cherry	USA	1.8.90	1h2	NC-j	Eugene	26 Jun 09
10.02	2.4	Marcus	Rowland	USA	11.3.90	1	NC-j	Eugene	26 Jun 09

200 METRES
19.93	1.4	Usain	Bolt	JAM	21.8.86	1		Hamilton, BER	11 Apr 04
20.04	0.1	Ramil	Guliyev	AZE	29.5.90	1	WUG	Beograd	10 Jul 09
20.07	1.5	Lorenzo	Daniel	USA	23.3.66	1	SEC	Starkville	18 May 85
20.09	1.6	Noah	Lyles	USA	18.7.97	4	NC/OT	Eugene	9 Jul 16
20.10A	1.7	Clarence	Munyai	RSA	20.2.98	2		Pretoria	4 Mar 17
20.13	1.7	Roy	Martin	USA	25.12.66	1		Austin	11 May 85
20.14	1.8	Tyreek	Hill	USA	1.3.94	1		Orlando	26 May 12
20.14	1.6	Michael	Norman	USA	3.12.97	5	NC/OT	Eugene	9 Jul 16
20.16A	-0.2	Riaan	Dempers	RSA	4.3.77	1	NC-j	Germiston	7 Apr 95
20.18	1.0	Walter	Dix	USA	31.1.86	1s2	NCAA	Sacramento	9 Jun 05
20.20A	0.5	Tlotliso Gift	Leotlela	RSA	12.5.98	3	NC	Potchefstroom	22 Apr 17
20.21A	1.4	Baboloki	Thebe	BOT	18.3.97	1	NC-j	Gaborone	22 May 16

Wind assisted to 20.14
19.86	4.0	Justin	Gatlin	USA	10.2.82	1h2	NCAA	Eugene	30 May 01
20.01	2.5	Derald	Harris	USA	5.4.58	1		San José	9 Apr 77
20.02	2.7	Khance	Meyers	USA	11.1.99	1	JUCO	El Dorado	19 May 18
20.03	2.9	Trentavis	Friday	USA	5.6.95	1	NC-j	Eugene	6 Jul 14
20.04	3.3	Noah	Lyles	USA	18.7.97	1h1	NC/OT	Eugene	7 Jul 16
20.06	2.8	Michael	Norman	USA	3.12.97	1h4	NC/OT	Eugene	7 Jul 16
20.07	3.4	Maxwell	Willis	USA	2.9.98	1h1	Big 12	Lawrence	13 May 17
20.08	9.2	Leonard	Scott	USA	19.1.80	2r2		Knoxville	9 Apr 99
20.10	4.6	Stanley	Kerr	USA	19.6.67	2r2	SWC	Houston	18 May 86

400 METRES
43.87		Steve	Lewis	USA	16.5.69	1	OG	Seoul	28 Sep 88
44.22A		Baboloki	Thebe	BOT	18.3.97	1	NC-j	Gaborone	21 May 16
44.25		Karabo	Sibanda	BOT	2.7.98	5	OG	Rio de Janeiro	14 Aug 16
44.27		Abdelilah	Haroun	QAT	1.1.97	2		La Chaux-de-Fonds	5 Jul 15
44.36		Kirani	James	GRN	1.9.92	1	WK	Zürich	8 Sep 11
44.66		Hamdam Odha	Al-Bishi	KSA	5.5.81	1	WJ	Santiago de Chile	20 Oct 00
44.66		LaShawn	Merritt	USA	27.6.86	1		Kingston	7 May 05
44.69		Darrell	Robinson	USA	23.12.63	2		Indianapolis	24 Jul 82
44.71A		Luguelín	Santos	DOM	12.11.93	2	PAm	Guadalajara	26 Oct 11
44.73A		James	Rolle	USA	2.2.64	1	USOF	USAF Academy	2 Jul 83
44.75		Darren	Clark	AUS	6.9.65	4	OG	Los Angeles	8 Aug 84
44.75		Deon	Minor	USA	22.1.73	1s1	NCAA	Austin	5 Jun 92

800 METRES
1:41.73		Nijel	Amos	BOT	15.3.94	2	OG	London (OS)	9 Aug 12
1:42.37		Mohammed	Aman	ETH	10.1.94	1	VD	Bruxelles	6 Sep 13
1:42.53		Timothy	Kitum	KEN	20.11.94	3	OG	London (OS)	9 Aug 12
1:42.69		Abubaker	Kaki	SUD	21.6.89	1	Bisl	Oslo	6 Jun 08
1:43.13		Abraham Kipchirchir	Rotich	KEN	26.6.93	1	Herc	Monaco	20 Jul 12
1:43.40		Leonard	Kosencha	KEN	21.8.94	2	Herc	Monaco	20 Jul 12
1:43.55		Donavan	Brazier	USA	15.4.97	1	NCAA	Eugene	10 Jun 16
1:43.56		Robert	Biwott	KEN	28.1.96	2		Barcelona	8 Jul 15

Mark	Wind	Name		Nat	Born	Pos	Meet	Venue	Date
1:43.64		Japheth	Kimutai	KEN	20.12.78	3rB	WK	Zürich	13 Aug 97
1:43.76		Kipyegon	Bett	KEN	2.1.98	2	ISTAF	Berlin	3 Sep 16
1:43.81		Edwin	Melly	KEN	24.3.94	2		Rieti	9 Sep 12

1000 METRES

2:13.93		Abubaker	Kaki	SUD	21.6.89	1	DNG	Stockholm	22 Jul 08
2:15.00		Benjamin	Kipkurui	KEN	28.12.80	5	Nik	Nice	17 Jul 99
2:16.84		Ali	Hakimi	TUN	24.4.76	1		Lindau	28 Jul 95

1500 METRES

3:28.81		Ronald	Kwemoi	KEN	19.9.95	3	Herc	Monaco	18 Jul 14
3:30.10		Robert	Biwott	KEN	28.1.96	7	Herc	Monaco	17 JUl 15
3:30.16		Jakob	Ingebrigtsen	NOR	19.9.00	2	Athl	Lausanne	5 Jul 19
3:30.24		Cornelius	Chirchir	KEN	5.6.83	4	Herc	Monaco	19 Jul 02
3:31.13		Mulugueta	Wondimu	ETH	28.2.85	2rA	NA	Heusden	31 Jul 04
3:31.42		Alex	Kipchirchir	KEN	26.11.84	5	VD	Bruxelles	5 Sep 03
3:31.49		George	Manangoi	KEN	29.11.00	6	Herc	Monaco	12 Jul 19
3:31.54		Isaac	Songok	KEN	25.4.84	1	NA	Heusden	2 Aug 03
3:31.63		Samuel	Tefera	ETH	23.10.99	2	DL	Shanghai	12 May 18
3:31.64		Asbel	Kiprop	KEN	30.6.89	1	GGala	Roma	11 Jul 08
3:31.70		William	Biwott	KEN	5.3.90	3	GGala	Roma	10 Jul 09

1 MILE

3:49.29		William	Biwott	KEN	5.3.90	2	Bisl	Oslo	3 Jul 09
3:49.77		Caleb	Ndiku	KEN	9.10.92	5	Pre	Eugene	4 Jun 11
3:50.25		Alex	Kipchirchir	KEN	26.11.84	2	GP II	Rieti	7 Sep 03
3:50.39		James	Kwalia	KEN	12.6.84	1	FBK	Hengelo	1 Jun 03
3:50.41		Noah	Ngeny	KEN	2.11.78	2	Nik	Nice	16 Jul 97
3:50.69		Cornelius	Chirchir	KEN	5.6.83	5	GGala	Roma	12 Jul 02
3:50.83		Nicholas	Kemboi	KEN	18.12.89	6	Bisl	Oslo	6 Jun 08

2000 METRES

4:56.25		Tesfaye	Cheru	ETH	2.3.93	1		Reims	5 Jul 11
4:56.86		Isaac	Songok	KEN	25.4.84	6	ISTAF	Berlin	31 Aug 01
4:58.18		Soresa	Fida	ETH	27.5.93	4		Reims	5 Jul 11
4:58.76		Jairus	Kipchoge	KEN	15.12.92	7		Reims	5 Jul 11

3000 METRES

7:28.19		Yomif	Kejelcha	ETH	1.8.97	1	DL	Saint-Denis	27 Aug 16
7:28.78		Augustine	Choge	KEN	21.1.87	2	SGP	Doha	13 May 05
7:29.11		Tariku	Bekele	ETH	21.1.87	2	GP	Rieti	27 Aug 06
7:30.36		Hagos	Gebrhiwet	ETH	11.5.94	1	DL	Doha	10 May 13
7:30.43		Isiah	Koech	KEN	19.12.93	1	DNG	Stockholm	17 Aug 12
7:30.67		Kenenisa	Bekele	ETH	13.6.82	2	VD	Bruxelles	24 Aug 01
7:30.91		Eliud	Kipchoge	KEN	5.11.84	2	VD	Bruxelles	5 Sep 03
7:32.17		Selemon	Barega	ETH	20.1.00	1	Bisl	Oslo	13 Jun 19
7:32.37		Abreham	Cherkos	ETH	23.9.89	2	Athl	Lausanne	11 Jul 06
7:32.72		John	Kipkoech	KEN	29.12.91	4		Rieti	29 Aug 10
7:33.00		Hailu	Mekonnen	ETH	4.4.80	2		Stuttgart	6 Jun 99
7:33.01		Levy	Matebo	KEN	3.11.89	2	GP	Rieti	7 Sep 08

5000 METRES

12:43.02		Selemon	Barega	ETH	20.1.00	1	VD	Bruxelles	31 Aug 18
12:47.53		Hagos	Gebrhiwet	ETH	11.5.94	2	DL	Saint-Denis	6 Jul 12
12:48.64		Isiah	Koech	KEN	19.12.93	3	DL	Saint-Denis	6 Jul 12
12:52.61		Eliud	Kipchoge	KEN	5.11.84	2	Bisl	Oslo	27 Jun 03
12:53.66		Augustine	Choge	KEN	21.1.87	4	GGala	Roma	8 Jul 05
12:53.72		Philip	Mosima	KEN	2.1.77	2	GGala	Roma	5 Jun 96
12:53.81		Tariku	Bekele	ETH	21.1.87	4	GGala	Roma	14 Jul 06
12:53.98		Yomif	Kejelcha	ETH	1.8.97	1	VD	Bruxelles	11 Sep 15
12:54.07		Sammy	Kipketer	KEN	29.9.81	2	GGala	Roma	30 Jun 00
12:54.19		Abreham	Cherkos	ETH	23.9.89	5	GGala	Roma	14 Jul 06
12:54.58		James	Kwalia	KEN	12.6.84	2	Bisl	Oslo	27 Jun 03
12:56.15		Daniel	Komen	KEN	17.5.76	2	GG	Roma	8 Jun 95

10,000 METRES

26:41.75		Samuel	Wanjiru	KEN	10.11.86	3	VD	Bruxelles	26 Aug 05
26:49.46		Selemon	Barega	ETH	20.1.00	2	WCT	Hengelo	17 Jul 19
26:55.73		Geoffrey	Kirui	KEN	16.2.93	6	VD	Bruxelles	16 Sep 11
26:57.56		Yigrem	Demelash	ETH	28.1.94	4	VD	Bruxelles	7 Sep 12
27:02.81		Ibrahim	Jeylan	ETH	12.6.89	4	VD	Bruxelles	25 Aug 06

JUNIOR MEN ALL-TIME

Mark	Wind	Name		Nat	Born	Pos	Meet	Venue	Date
27:04.00		Boniface	Kiprop	UGA	12.10.85	5	VD	Bruxelles	3 Sep 04
27:04.45		Bernard	Kipyego	KEN	16.7.86	4	FBK	Hengelo	29 May 05
27:06.35		Geoffrey	Kipsang	KEN	28.11.92	10	Pre	Eugene	3 Jun 11
27:06.47		Habtanu	Fikadu	ETH	13.3.88	8	FBK	Hengelo	26 May 07
27:07.29		Moses	Masai	KEN	1.6.86	7	VD	Bruxelles	3 Sep 04
27:08.94		Andamlak	Belihu	ETH	20.11.98	10	WCh	London(OS)	4 Aug 17
27:09.92		Aron	Kifle	ERI	20.2.98	11	WCh	London (OS)	4 Aug 17
27:11.18		Richard	Chelimo	KEN	21.4.72	1	APM	Hengelo	25 Jun 91

HALF MARATHON

Mark		Name		Nat	Born	Pos	Meet	Venue	Date
59:16		Samuel	Wanjiru	KEN	10.11.86	1		Rotterdam	11 Sep 05
59:21		Stephen	Kiprop	KEN	8.9.99	5		Valencia	28 Oct 18
59:22		Amdework	Walelegn	ETH	11.3.99	2		New Delhi	21 Oct 18
59:31		Geoffrey	Kipsang	KEN	28.11.92	2		New Delhi	27 Nov 11
59:36		Tilahun	Regassa	ETH	18.1.90	1		Lille	6 Sep 08
59:37		Bravin	Kiptoo	KEN	26.2.01	7		Valencia	6 Dec 20
59:38		Faustin	Baha	TAN	30.5.82	4		Lisboa	26 Mar 00
59:51		Andamlak	Belihu	ETH	20.11.98	2		New Delhi	19 Nov 17
59:57		Eric	Ndiema	KEN	28.12.92	4		Den Haag	14 Mar 10
60:09		Ghirmay	Ghebrselassie	ERI	14.11.95	1		Paderborn	30 Mar 13

MARATHON

Mark		Name		Nat	Born	Pos	Meet	Venue	Date
2:04:32		Tsegaye	Mekonnen	ETH	15.6.95	1		Dubai	24 Jan 14
2:06:07		Eric	Ndiema	KEN	28.12.92	3		Amsterdam	16 Oct 11
2:06:15		Bazu	Worku	ETH	15.9.90	2		Paris	5 Apr 09
2:08:17		Edwin	Kibet	KEN	7.7.96	5		Eindhoven	11 Oct 15
2:08:51		Berhanu	Shiferaw	ETH	31.5.93	1		Taiyuan	2 Sep 12
2:08:53		Shura	Kitata	ETH	9.6.96	3		Shanghai	8 Nov 15
2:09:08		Ghirmay	Gebrselassie	ERI	14.11.95	6		Chicago	12 Oct 14
2:09:12		Feyisa	Lilesa	ETH	1.2.90	1		Dublin	26 Oct 09
2:10:00		Samuel	Rutto	KEN	?.95	1		Torino	16 Nov 14
2:10:01		Ernest	Ngeno	KEN	20.5.95	2		Torino	16 Nov 14

3000 METRES STEEPLECHASE

Mark		Name		Nat	Born	Pos	Meet	Venue	Date
7:58.66		Stephen	Cherono	KEN	15.10.82	3	VD	Bruxelles	24 Aug 01
8:01.16		Conseslus	Kipruto	KEN	8.12.94	1	DL	Shanghai	18 May 13
8:01.36		Lemecha	Girma	ETH	26.11.00	2	WC	Doha	4 Oct 19
8:03.74		Raymond	Yator	KEN	7.4.81	3	Herc	Monaco	18 Aug 00
8:05.21		Getnet	Wale	ETH	16.7.00	4	WCh	Doha	4 Oct 19
8:05.52		Brimin	Kipruto	KEN	31.7.85	1	FBK	Hengelo	31 May 04
8:06.96		Gilbert	Kirui	KEN	22.1.94	2	DL	London (OS)	27 Jul 13
8:07.18		Moussa	Omar Obaid	QAT	18.4.85	4	OG	Athína	24 Aug 04
8:07.69		Paul	Kosgei	KEN	22.4.78	5	DNG	Stockholm	7 Jul 97
8:07.71		Hillary	Yego	KEN	2.4.92	3	DL	Shanghai	15 May 11
8:08.37		Amos	Kirui	KEN	9.2.98	4	GGala	Roma	8 Jun 17

110 METRES HURDLES (106cm)

Mark	Wind	Name		Nat	Born	Pos	Meet	Venue	Date
13.12	1.6		Liu Xiang	CHN	13.7.83	1rB	Athl	Lausanne	2 Jul 02
13.23	0.0	Renaldo	Nehemiah	USA	24.3.59	1r2	WK	Zürich	16 Aug 78
13.32	0.7	Dejour	Russell	JAM	1.4.00	4	NC	Kingston	24 Jun 17
13.36	-0.6	Shunsuke	Izumiya	JPN	26.1.00	2	NC	Fukuoka	30 Jun 19
13.40	-1.0		Shi Dongpeng	CHN	6.1.84	1	NC	Shanghai	14 Sep 03
13.44	-0.8	Colin	Jackson	GBR	18.2.67	1	WJ	Athína	19 Jul 86
13.44	-0.8	Damion	Thomas	JAM	29.6.99	2s3	NCAA-W	Eugene	6 Jun 18
13.46	1.8	Jon	Ridgeon	GBR	14.2.67	1	EJ	Cottbus	23 Aug 85
13.46	-1.6	Dayron	Robles	CUB	19.11.86	1	PAm-J	Windsor	29 Jul 05
13.47	1.9	Holger	Pohland	GDR	5.4.63	2	vUSA	Karl-Marx-Stadt	10 Jul 82
13.47	1.2	Aries	Merritt	USA	24.7.85	4	NCAA	Austin	12 Jun 04
13.47	0.2		Xie Wenjun	CHN	11.7.90	2	GP	Shanghai	20 Sep 08

Wind assisted

13.26	2.9	Shunsuke	Izumiya	JPN	26.1.00	1		Osaka	19 May 19
13.39	2.3	Damion	Thomas	JAM	29.6.99	2h2	SEC	Knoxville	12 May 18
13.41	2.6	Dayron	Robles	CUB	19.11.86	2	CAC	Nassau	10 Jul 05
13.42	4.5	Colin	Jackson	GBR	18.2.67	2	CG	Edinburgh	27 Jul 86
13.42	2.6	Antwon	Hicks	USA	12.3.83	1	WJ	Kingston	21 Jul 02

99 cm Hurdles

12.99	0.5	Wilhem	Belocian	FRA	22.6.95	1	WJ	Eugene	24 Jul 14
12.99	0.3	Damion	Thomas	JAM	29.6.99	1		Kingston	23 Jun 18
13.00	0.3	Orlando	Bennett	JAM	12.10.99	2		Kingston	23 Jun 18
13.06	0.5	Tyler	Mason	JAM	15.1.95	2	WJ	Eugene	24 Jul 14
13.08	2.0	Wayne	Davis	USA	2.7.90	1	PAm-J	Port of Spain	31 Jul 09

JUNIOR MEN ALL-TIME 267

Mark	Wind	Name		Nat	Born	Pos	Meet	Venue	Date
13.10	-0.8	Dejour	Russell	JAM	1.4.00	1		Kingston	24 Mar 18
13.14	1.6	Eddie	Lovett	USA	25.6.92	1	PAm-J	Miramar	23 Jul 11
13.17	-0.7	David	Omoregie	GBR	1.11.95	1	NC-j	Bedford	22 Jun 14
13.18	1.0	Yordan	O'Farrill	CUB	9.2.93	1	WJ	Barcelona	12 Jul 12
Wind assisted to 13.14									
13.03	2.9	Eddie	Lovett	USA	25.6.92	1h1	PAm-J	Miramar	23 Jul 11
13.09	-0.8	Wayne	Pinnock	JAM	25.10.00	1	N.Sch	Kingston	30 Mar 19
13.11	?	Rasheed	Broadbelt	JAM	13.8.00	1		Kingston	7 Apr 19
13.11	2.7	Eric	Edwards	USA	3.1.00	1	PAm-J	San José, CRC	19 Jul 19
Hand timed: 12.9y Renaldo			Neherniah	USA	24.3.59	1		Jamaica, NY	30 May 77

400 METRES HURDLES

48.02		Danny	Harris	USA	7.9.65	2s1	OT	Los Angeles	17 Jun 84
48.26		Jehue	Gordon	TTO	15.12.91	4	WCh	Berlin	18 Aug 09
48.28		Alison	dos Santos	BRA	3.6.00	7	WCh	Doha	30 Sep 19
48.51		Kerron	Clement	USA	31.10.85	1	WJ	Grosseto	16 Jul 04
48.52		Johnny	Dutch	USA	20.1.89	5	NC/OT	Eugene	29 Jun 08
48.62		Brandon	Johnson	USA	6.3.85	2	WJ	Grosseto	16 Jul 04
48.68		Bayano	Kamani	USA	17.4.80	1	NCAA	Boise	4 Jun 99
48.68		Jeshua	Anderson	USA	22.6.89	1	WJ	Bydgoszcz	11 Jul 08
48.72		Angelo	Taylor	USA	29.12.78	2	NCAA	Bloomington	6 Jun 97
48.73		Zazini	Sokwakhana	RSA	23.1.00	2	WUG	Napoli	11 Jul 19
48.74		Vladimir	Budko	BLR	4.2.65	2	DRZ	Moskva	18 Aug 84

HIGH JUMP

2.37		Dragutin	Topic	YUG	12.3.71	1	WJ	Plovdiv	12 Aug 90
2.37		Steve	Smith	GBR	29.3.73	1	WJ	Seoul	20 Sep 92
2.36		Javier	Sotomayor	CUB	13.10.67	1		Santiago de Cuba	23 Feb 86
2.35i		Vladimir	Yashchenko	UKR	12.1.59	1	EI	Milano	12 Mar 78
2.34						1	Prv	Tbilisi	16 Jun 78
2.35		Dietmar	Mögenburg	FRG	15.8.61	1		Rehlingen	26 May 80
2.34		Tim	Forsyth	AUS	17.8.73	1	Bisl	Oslo	4 Jul 92
2.33			Zhu Jianhua	CHN	29.5.63	1	AsiG	New Delhi	1 Dec 82
2.33		Patrik	Sjöberg	SWE	5.1.65	1	OsloG	Oslo	9 Jul 83
2.33		Maksim	Nedosekov	BLR	21.1.98	1	EJ	Grosseto	22 Jul 17
2.32i		Jaroslav	Bába	CZE	2.9.84	3		Arnstadt	8 Feb 03
2.32			Huang Haiqiang	CHN	8.2.88	1	WJ	Beijing	17 Aug 06

POLE VAULT

6.05		Armand	Duplantis	SWE	10.11.99	1	EC	Berlin	12 Aug 18
5.80		Maksim	Tarasov	RUS	2.12.70	1	vGDR-j	Bryansk	14 Jul 89
5.80		Raphael	Holzdeppe	GER	28.9.89	2		Biberach	28 Jun 08
5.80i		Emmanouíl	Karalís	GRE	20.10.99	5=	WI	Birmingham	4 Mar 18
5.75		Konstadínos	Filippídis	GRE	26.11.86	2	WUG	Izmir	18 Aug 05
5.75		Chris	Nilsen	USA	13.1.98	3	NC	Sacramento	24 Jun 17
5.72		Andrew	Irwin	USA	23.1.93	1	SEC	Baton Rouge	13 May 12
5.71		Lawrence	Johnson	USA	7.5.74	1		Knoxville	12 Jun 93
5.71		Germán	Chiaraviglio	ARG	16.4.87	1	WJ	Beijing	19 Aug 06
5.71		Shawnacy	Barber	CAN	27.5.94	2	TexR	Austin	29 Mar 13

LONG JUMP

8.35	1.1	Sergey	Morgunov	RUS	9.2.93	1	NC-j	Cheboksary	19 Jun 12
8.34	0.0	Randy	Williams	USA	23.8.53	Q	OG	München	8 Sep 72
8.33	2.0	Maykel	Massó	CUB	8.5.99	1		Madrid	14 Jul 17
8.31	0.8		Shi Yuhao	CHN	26.9.98	1		Beijing	25 Jun 17
8.30	1.8	Miltiádis	Tentóglou	GRE	18.3.98	1	NC	Pátra	18 Jun 17
8.28	0.8	Luis Alberto	Bueno	CUB	22.5.69	1		La Habana	16 Jul 88
8.28	0.8	Juan Miguel	Echevarría	CUB	11.8.98	2		Madrid	14 Jul 17
8.28	1.6	Lester	Lescay	CUB	15.10.01	1		Camagüey	23 Feb 20
8.27	1.7	Eusebio	Cáceres	ESP	10.9.91	Q	EC	Barcelona	30 Jul 10
8.25	0.9		Wang Jianan	CHN	27.8.96	3	DL	Shanghai	17 May 15
8.24	0.2	Eric	Metcalf	USA	23.1.68	1	NCAA	Indianapolis	6 Jun 86
8.24	1.8	Vladimir	Ochkan	UKR	13.1.68	1	vGDR-j	Leningrad	21 Jun 87
Wind assisted									
8.40	3.2	Kareem	Streete-Thompson	CAY	30.3.73	1		Houston	5 May 91
8.35	2.2	Carl	Lewis	USA	1.7.61	1	NCAA	Austin	6 Jun 80
8.34	2.3	Juan Miguel	Echevarría	CUB	11.8.98	1		Padova	16 Jul 17
8.29	2.3	James	Beckford	JAM	9.1.75	1		Tempe	2 Apr 94

TRIPLE JUMP

| 17.50 | 0.4 | Volker | Mai | GDR | 3.5.66 | 1 | vURS | Erfurt | 23 Jun 85 |

268 JUNIOR MEN ALL-TIME

Mark	Wind	Name		Nat	Born	Pos	Meet	Venue	Date
17.42	1.3	Khristo	Markov	BUL	27.1.65	1	Nar	Sofiya	19 May 84
17.41	1.0	Jordan	Díaz	CUB	23.2.01	1		La Habana	8 Jun 18
17.40A	0.4	Pedro	Pérez	CUB	23.2.52	1	PAm	Cali	5 Aug 71
17.40	0.8	Ernesto	Revé	CUB	26.2.92	1		La Habana	10 Jun 11
17.31	-0.2	David	Girat Jr.	CUB	26.8.84	Q	WCh	Saint-Denis	23 Aug 03
17.29	1.3	James	Beckford	JAM	9.1.75	1		Tempe	2 Apr 94
17.27		Aliecer	Urrutia	CUB	22.9.74	1		Artemisa	23 Apr 93
17.27	1.6	Cristian	Nápoles	CUB	27.11.98	2	NC	La Habana	17 Mar 17
17.24	0.7	Lázaro	Martínez	CUB	3.11.97	2		La Habana	1 Feb 14
17.23	0.2	Yoelbi	Quesada	CUB	4.8.73	1	NC	La Habana	13 May 92
Wind assisted									
17.33	2.1	Teddy	Tamgho	FRA	15.6.89	1	WJ	Bydgoszcz	11 Jul 08
17.24	2.5	Will	Claye	USA	13.6.91	1	NCAA	Fayetteville	13 Jun 09

SHOT

Mark		Name		Nat	Born	Pos	Meet	Venue	Date
21.14		Konrad	Bukowiecki #	POL	17.3.97	2	Bisl	Oslo	9 Jun 16
21.05i		Terry	Albritton	USA	14.1.55	1	AAU	New York	22 Feb 74
20.38						2	MSR	Walnut	27 Apr 74
20.83i		Jordan	Geist	USA	21.7.98	1		Greensburg	22 Dec 16
20.62						1		Tucson	9 Dec 17
20.65		Mike	Carter	USA	29.10.60	1	vSU-j	Boston	4 Jul 79
20.43		David	Storl	GER	27.7.90	2		Gerlingen	6 Jul 09
20.41		Adrian	Piperi	USA	20.1.99	1q	NCAA-W	Sacramento	26 May 18
20.39		Janus	Robberts	RSA	10.3.79	1	NC	Germiston	7 Mar 98
20.38		Jacko	Gill	NZL	10.12.94	1		Auckland (NS)	5 Dec 11
20.20		Randy	Matson	USA	5.3.45	2	OG	Tokyo	17 Oct 64
20.20		Udo	Beyer	GDR	9.8.55	2	NC	Leipzig	6 Jul 74
Drugs disqualification									
20.54		Andrei	Toader ¶	ROU	26.5.97	(1)	ROU IC	Pitesti	4 Jun 16
6 kg Shot									
23.00		Jacko	Gill	NZL	10.12.94	1		Auckland	18 Aug 13
22.94		Konrad	Bukowiecki	POL	17.3.97	1	NC-j	Suwalki	3 Jul 16
		23.34 drugs dq				(1)	WJ	Bydgoszcz	19 Jul 16
22.73		David	Storl	GER	27.7.90	1		Osterode	14 Jul 09
22.30		Andrei	Toader	ROU	26.5.97	2	WJ	Bydgoszcz	19 Jul 16
22.15i		Oleg	Tomashevich	BLR	31.5.00	1		Vitebsk	20 Jan 19
22.07		Kyle	Blignaut	RSA	9.11.99	1	WJ	Tampere	10 Jul 18
22.06		Adrian	Piperi	USA	20.1.99	2	WJ	Tampere	10 Jul 18
22.02		Jordan	Geist	USA	21.7.98	1	PAm-J	Trujillo	23 Jul 17
21.96		Edis	Elkasevic	CRO	18.2.83	1	NC-j	Zagreb	29 Jun 02

DISCUS

Mark		Name		Nat	Born	Pos	Meet	Venue	Date
65.62		Werner	Reiterer	AUS	27.1.68	1		Melbourne	15 Dec 87
65.31		Mykyta	Nesterenko	UKR	15.4.91	3		Tallinn	3 Jun 08
63.64		Werner	Hartmann	FRG	20.4.59	1	vFRA	Strasbourg	25 Jun 78
63.26		Sergey	Pachin	UKR	24.5.68	2		Moskva	25 Jul 87
63.25		Connor	Bell	NZL	21.6.01	1		Hastings	25 Jan 20
63.22		Brian	Milne	USA	7.1.73	1		State College	28 Mar 92
62.58		Matthew	Denny	AUS	2.6.96	2	WUG	Gwangju	11 Jul 15
62.52		John	Nichols	USA	23.8.69	1		Baton Rouge	23 Apr 88
62.43		Martin	Markovic	CRO	13.1.96	1	NC-w	Split	8 Mar 15
62.36		Tulake	Nuermaimaiti	CHN	8.3.82	2	NG	Guangzhou	21 Nov 01
1.75kg Discus									
70.13		Mykyta	Nesterenko	UKR	15.4.91	1		Halle	24 May 08
68.48		Martin	Markovic	CRO	13.1.96	1	NC-j	Varazdin	28 Jun 15
68.02		Bartlomiej	Stój	POL	15.5.96	1	EJ	Eskilstuna	19 Jul 15
67.40		Connor	Bell	NZL	21.6.01	1	NC	Christchurch	7 Mar 20
67.32		Margus	Hunt	EST	14.7.87	1	WJ	Beijing	16 Aug 06
66.88		Traves	Smikle	JAM	7.5.92	1		Kingston	31 Mar 11
66.81		Matthew	Denny	AUS	2.6.96	1		Brisbane	23 Nov 14
66.47		Moaaz Mohamed	Ibrahim	QAT	8.2.99	1		Cape Town	3 Feb 18
66.45		Gordon	Wolf	GER	17.1.90	1		Halle	23 May 09
66.41		Roje	Stona	JAM	26.2.99	1	Carifta	Willemstad	15 Apr 17

HAMMER

Mark		Name		Nat	Born	Pos	Meet	Venue	Date
78.33		Olli-Pekka	Karjalainen	FIN	7.3.80	1	NC	Seinäjoki	5 Aug 99
78.14		Roland	Steuk	GDR	5.3.59	1	NC	Leipzig	30 Jun 78
78.00		Sergey	Dorozhon	UKR	17.2.64	1		Moskva	7 Aug 83
77.78		Myhaylo	Kokhan	UKR	22.1.01	3	Gyulai	Székesfehérvár	19 Aug 20
76.67		Hristos	Frantzeskákis	GRE	26.4.00	1	Balk C	Pravets	2 Sep 19
76.54		Valeriy	Gubkin	BLR	3.9.67	2		Minsk	27 Jun 86

JUNIOR MEN ALL-TIME 269

Mark	Wind	Name		Nat	Born	Pos	Meet	Venue	Date
76.42		Ruslan	Dikiy	TJK	18.1.72	1		Togliatti	7 Sep 91
76.37		Ashraf Amjad	El-Seify	QAT	20.2.95	1		Doha	10 Apr 13
75.52		Sergey	Kirmasov	RUS	25.3.70	1		Kharkov	4 Jun 89
75.42		Szymon	Ziolkowski	POL	1.7.76	1	EJ	Nyíregyhazá	30 Jul 95

6kg Hammer

Mark		Name		Nat	Born	Pos	Meet	Venue	Date
85.57		Ashraf Amjad	El-Seify	QAT	20.2.95	1	WJ	Barcelona	14 Jul 12
82.97		Javier	Cienfuegos	ESP	15.7.90	1		Madrid	17 Jun 09
82.84		Quentin	Bigot	FRA	1.12.92	1		Bondoufle	16 Oct 11
82.64		Bence	Halász	HUN	4.8.97	1	NC-j	Szombathely	25 Jun 16
82.62		Yevgeniy	Aydamirov	RUS	11.5.87	1	NC-j	Tula	22 Jul 06
81.75		Hlib	Piskunov	UKR	25.11.98	1	EJ	Grosseto	21 Jul 17
81.73		Aleksandr	Shimanovich	BLR	9.2.98	1		Brest	28 Apr 17
81.34		Krisztián	Pars	HUN	18.2.82	1		Szombathely	2 Sep 01
81.32		Hristos	Frantzeskákis	GRE	26.4.00	1		Tripolí	5 May 18
81.16		Özkan	Baltaci	TUR	13.2.94	1		Ankara	31 Jul 13

JAVELIN

Mark		Name		Nat	Born	Pos	Meet	Venue	Date
86.48		Neeraj	Chopra	IND	24.12.97	1	WJ	Bydgoszcz	23 Jul 16
84.73		Myhaylo	Kokhan	UKR	22.1.01	1	EJ	Borås	19 Jul 19
84.69		Zigismunds	Sirmais	LAT	6.5.92	2		Bauska	22 Jun 11
84.58		Keshorn	Walcott	TTO	2.4.93	1	OG	London (OS)	11 Aug 12
84.22		Hristos	Frantzeskákis	GRE	26.4.00	2	EJ	Borås	19 Jul 19
83.87		Andreas	Thorkildsen	NOR	1.4.82	1		Fana	7 Jun 01
83.55		Aleksandr	Ivanov	RUS	25.5.82	2	NC	Tula	14 Jul 01
83.07		Robert	Oosthuizen	RSA	23.1.87	1	WJ	Beijing	19 Aug 06
82.52		Harri	Haatainen	FIN	5.1.78	4		Leppävirta	25 May 96
82.52		Till	Wöschler	GER	9.6.91	1	WJ	Moncton	23 Jul 10

DECATHLON

8397	Torsten	Voss		GDR	24.3.63	1	NC	Erfurt	7 Jul 82
	10.76	7.66	14.41	2.09	48.37	14.37	41.76	4.80	62.90	4:34.04
8257	Yordani	García		CUB	21.11.88	8	WCh	Osaka	1 Sep 07
	10.73/0.7	7.15/0.2	14.94	2.09	49.25	14.08/-0.2	42.91	4.70	68.74	4:55.42
8130	Ayden	Owens		PUR	28.5.00	1		Azusa	18 Apr 19
	10.43/1.1	7.53	13.41	1.90	47.66	13.91w/2.2	43.14	4.60	51.21	4:28.90
8114	Michael	Kohnle		FRG	3.5.70	1	EJ	Varazdin	26 Aug 89
	10.95	7.09/0.1	15.27	2.02	49.91	14.40	45.82	4.90	60.82	4:49.43
8104	Valter	Külvet		EST	19.2.64	1		Viimsi	23 Aug 81
	10.7	7.26	13.86	2.09	48.5	14.8	47.92	4.50	60.34	4:37.8
8103	Ashley	Moloney		AUS	13.3.00	1	Oce Ch	Townsville	26 Jun 19
	10.59/1.0	7.52/1.0	13.48	1.92	46.75	14.29/1.2	42.36	5.00	54.38	4:53.73
8082	Daley	Thompson		GBR	30.7.58	1	ECp/s	Sittard	31 Jul 77
	10.70/0.8	7.54/0.7	13.84	2.01	47.31	15.26/2.0	41.70	4.70	54.48	4:30.4
8041		Qi Haifeng		CHN	7.8.83	1	AsiG	Busan	10 Oct 02
	11.09/0.2	7.22/0.0	13.05	2.06	49.09	14.54/0.0	43.16	4.80	61.04	4:35.17
8036	Christian	Schenk		GDR	9.2.65	5		Potsdam	21 Jul 84
	11.54	7.18	14.26	2.16	49.23	15.06	44.74	4.20	65.98	4:24.11

IAAF Junior specification with 99cm 110mh, 6kg shot, 1.75kg Discus

8435	Niklas	Kaul		GER	11.2.98	1	EJ	Grosseto	23 Jul 17
	11.48/-1.3	7.20/1.6	15.37	2.05	48.42	14.55/-0.2	48.49	4.70	68.05	4:15.51
8238	Markus	Rooth		NOR	22.12.01	1		Oslo	28 Jun 20
	11.03/0.0	7.53/0.6	15.81	1.97	49.56	14.18/1.5	46.07	4.75	59.80	4:39.79
8190	Ashley	Moloney		AUS	13.3.00	1	WJ	Tampere	11 Jul 18
	10.51/-0.3	7.06/1.1	12.83	2.10	46.86	14.13/-0.3	47.39	4.60	53.67	4:42.65
8141	Johannes	Erm		EST	26.3.98	2	EJ	Grosseto	23 Jul 17
	11.06/0.7	7.42/-0.3	13.44	1.92	48.17	14.66/0.9	43.61	4.50	54.19	4:28.96
8135	Jiri	Sykora		CZE	20.1.95	1	WJ	Eugene	23 Jul 14
	10.92/0.5	7.35/2.0	15.50	1.94	49.00	14.23/-0.1	48.55	4.40	60.56	4:42.10
8131	Arkadiy	Vasilyev		RUS	19.1.87	1		Sochi	27 May 06
	11.28/-0.8	7.70/2.0	14.59	2.00	49.17	14.67/0.6	46.30	4.70	56.96	4:32.10

10,000 METRES WALK

Mark		Name		Nat	Born	Pos	Meet	Venue	Date
38:46.4		Viktor	Burayev	RUS	23.8.82	1	NC-j	Moskva	20 May 00
38:54.75		Ralf	Kowalsky	GDR	22.3.62	1		Cottbus	24 Jun 81
38:58.21		Vasiliy	Mizinov	RUS	29.12.97	1	NC-j	Cheboksary	25 Jun 16
39:08.23		Daisuke	Matsunaga	JPN	24.3.95	1		Tama	14 Dec 13
39:18.63		Hiroto	Jusho	JPN	11.1.00	3		Nagasaki	8 Dec 19
39:28.63		Toshizaku	Yamanishi	JPN	15.2.96	2		Osaka	13 Sep 15
39:28.45		Andrey	Ruzavin	RUS	28.3.86	1	EJ	Kaunas	23 Jul 05
39:30.15		Yuga	Yamashita	JPN	6.2.96	1		Tama	12 Dec 15
39:35.01		Stanislav	Yemelyanov	RUS	23.10.90	1	WJ	Bydgoszcz	11 Jul 08

JUNIOR MEN ALL-TIME

Mark	Wind	Name		Nat	Born	Pos	Meet	Venue	Date

20 KILOMETRES WALK
1:17:25		Sergey	Shirobokov	RUS	16.2.99	1	NC	Chgeboksary	9 Jun 18
1:18:06		Viktor	Burayev	RUS	23.8.82	2	NC-w	Adler	4 Mar 01
1:18:07			Li Gaobo	CHN	23.7.89	4		Cixi	23 Apr 05
1:18:44			Chu Yafei	CHN	5.9.88	5		Yangzhou	22 Apr 06
1:18:52			Chen Ding	CHN	5.8.92	3		Taicang	22 Apr 11
1:18:57			Bai Xuejin	CHN	6.6.87	7		Yangzhou	22 Apr 06
1:19:02		Éder	Sánchez	MEX	21.5.86	11		Cixi	23 Apr 05
1:19:14			Xu Xingde	CHN	12.6.84	3	NC	Yangzhou	12 Apr 03
1:19:34			Li Jianbo	CHN	14.11.86	16		Cixi	23 Apr 05

4 x 100 METRES RELAY
38.62A	USA	A Smith, Ofotan, M Moore, Boling		1	PAm-J	San José, CRC	20 Jul 19
38.66	USA	Kimmons, Omole, I Williams, L Merritt		1	WJ	Grosseto	18 Jun 04
38.96	JAM	Nairne, C Taylor, Matherson, Stephens		2	WJ	Tampere	124 Jul 18
39.01	JPN	Oseto, Hashimoto, Cambridge, Kanamori		1h1	WJ	Barcelona	13 Jul 12
39.05	GBR	Edgar, Grant, Benjamin, Lewis-Francis		1	WJ	Santiago de Chile	22 Oct 00
39.13	GER	Gurski, Vartel, Giese, Eitel		3	WJ	Bydgoszcz	23 Jul 16
39.17	TTO	Simpson, Burns, Holder, Brown		3	WJ	Kingston	21 Jul 02
39.29	BRA	de Araújo, Monteiro, R dos Santos Jnr, Rocha		2h1	WJ	Barcelona	13 Jul 12
39.31	POL	Bijowski, Slowikowski, Zalewski, Jabłonski		3h1	WJ	Barcelona	13 Jul 12

4 x 400 METRES RELAY
2:59.30A	USA-J	F Lewis 45.9, Boling 44.5, Moorer 45.2, J Robinson 43.7	1	PAm	San José, CRC	21 Jul 19
3:00.33	USA	Herron 45.1, Shinnick 45.1, Hooper 44.73, J Lyles 45.36	1	PAm-J	Trujillo	23 Jul 17
3:00.99A	JAM	Whitehorne, Farr, McPherson, Cox	2	PAm	San José, CRC	21 Jul 19
3:02.81	BOT	Poo, Thebe, Sibanda, Talane	2	WJ	Bydgoszcz	24 Jul 16
3:02.84A	BRA	L da Silva, B da Silva, Vilar, Hernandes da Silva	3	PAm	San José, CRC	21 Jul 19
3:03.86A	BAR	Nicholas, Hoyte-Small, Griffith, Gale	4	PAm	San José, CRC	21 Jul 19
3:03.77	JAM	Chambers, Carpenter, James, C Taylor	2	PAm-J	Trujillo	23 Jul 17
3:03.80	GBR	Grindley, Patrick, Winrow, Richardson	2	WJ	Plovdiv	12 Aug 90
3:04.05	ITA	Gjetja 47.1, Romano 45.6, Sibilio 46.06, Scotti 45.31	1	WJ	Tampere	15 Jul 18
3:04.11	JPN	Walsh, Yui, Kitagawa, Kato	2	WJ	Eugene	27 Jul 14

JUNIOR WOMEN'S ALL-TIME LISTS

100 METRES
10.75	1.6	Sha'Carri	Richardson	USA	25.3.00	1	NCAA	Austin	8 Jun 19
10.88	2.0	Marlies	Oelsner	GDR	21.3.58	1	NC	Dresden	1 Jul 77
10.89	1.8	Katrin	Krabbe	GDR	22.11.69	1rB		Berlin	20 Jul 88
10.94	0.6	Briana	Williams	JAM	21.3.02	3	NC	Kingston	21 Jun 19
10.98	2.0	Candace	Hill	USA	11.2.99	1		Shoreline	20 Jun 15
10.99	0.9	Angela	Tenorio	ECU	27.1.96	2	PAm	Toronto	22 Jul 15
10.99	1.7	Twanisha	Terry	USA	24.1.99	1	MSR	Torrance	21 Apr 18
11.02	1.5	Tamara	Clark	USA	9.1.99	3	SEC	Knoxville	13 May 18
11.03	1.7	Silke	Gladisch	GDR	20.6.64	3	OD	Berlin	8 Jun 83
11.03	0.6	English	Gardner	USA	22.4.92	1	Pac10	Tucson	14 May 11
11.04	1.4	Angela	Williams	USA	30.1.80	1	NCAA	Boise	5 Jun 99
11.04	1.6	Kiara	Grant	JAM	8.10.00	6	NCAA	Austin	8 Jun 19

Wind assisted to 11.03
10.96	3.7	Angela	Williams	USA	30.1.80	1		Las Vegas	3 Apr 99
10.96	2.6	Twanisha	Terry	USA	24.1.99	1	Pac-12	Stanford	13 May 18
10.97	3.3	Gesine	Walther	GDR	6.10.62	4	NC	Cottbus	16 Jul 80
11.01	5.4	Kaylin	Whitney	USA	9.3.98	3	Athl	Lausanne	9 Jul 15
11.02	2.1	Nikole	Mitchell	JAM	5.6.74	1	Mutual	Kingston	1 May 93
11.03	2.2	Dina	Asher-Smith	GBR	4.12.95	1		Mannheim	5 Jul 14

200 METRES
22.11A	-0.5	Allyson	Felix	USA	18.11.85	1		Ciudad de México	3 May 03
22.18	0.8					2	OG	Athína	25 Aug 04
22.17	1.3	Sha'Carri	Richardson	USA	25.3.00	2	NCAA	Austin	8 Jun 19
22.19	1.5	Natalya	Bochina	RUS	4.1.62	2	OG	Moskva	30 Jul 80
22.37	1.5	Sabine	Rieger	GDR	6.11.63	2	vURS	Cottbus	26 Jun 82
22.39	1.5	Sydney	McLaughlin	USA	7.8.99	1	FlaR	Gainesville	29 Mar 18
22.42	0.4	Gesine	Walther	GDR	6.10.62	1		Potsdam	29 Aug 81
22.42	1.7	Amy	Hunt	GBR	15.5.02	1J		Mannheim	30 Jun 19
22.43	0.8	Bianca	Knight	USA	2.1.89	1	Reebok	New York (RI)	31 May 08
22.43A	-0.7	Candace	Hill	USA	11.2.99	1	WY	Calí	19 Jul 15
22.45	0.5	Grit	Breuer	GER	16.2.72	2	ASV	Köln	8 Sep 91
22.45	0.9	Shaunae	Miller	BAH	15.4.94	2	NC	Freeport	22 Jun 13
22.47	0.4	Kaylin	Whitney	USA	9.3.98	4	NC	Eugene	28 Jun 15

JUNIOR WOMEN ALL-TIME

Mark	Wind	Name		Nat	Born	Pos	Meet	Venue	Date
Indoors									
22.40		Bianca	Knight	USA	2.1.89	1r2	NCAA	Fayetteville	15 Mar 08
Wind assisted									
22.25	5.6	Bianca	Knight	USA	2.1.89	5	NC/OT	Eugene	6 Jul 08
22.34	2.3	Katrin	Krabbe	GDR	22.11.69	1	WJ	Sudbury	30 Jul 88
22.38	2.1	Candace	Hill	USA	11.2.99	1		Montverde	11 Jun 16
22.41	3.1	Shaunae	Miller	BAH	15.4.94	1		Athens, GA	13 Apr 13
22.41	2.6	Gina	Lückenkemper	GER	21.11.96	1	EJ	Eskilstuna	18 Jul 15
22.44	2.5	Lauren Rain	Williams	USA	25.7.99	1		Norwalk	21 May 16

400 METRES

49.42		Grit	Breuer	GER	16.2.72	2	WCh	Tokyo	27 Aug 91
49.77		Christina	Brehmer	GDR	28.2.58	1		Dresden	9 May 76
49.88		Salwa Eid	Naser	BRN	23.5.98	2	VD	Bruxelles	1 Sep 17
49.89		Sanya	Richards	USA	26.2.85	2	NC/OT	Sacramento	17 Jul 04
50.01			Li Jing	CHN	14.2.80	1	NG	Shanghai	18 Oct 97
50.07		Sydney	McLaughlin	USA	7.8.99	1	FlaR	Gainesville	30 Mar 18
50.19		Marita	Koch	GDR	18.2.57	3	OD	Berlin	10 Jul 76
50.42A		Beatrice	Masilingi	NAM	10.4.03	1		Pretoria	12 Dec 20
50.46		Kendall	Baisden	USA	5.3.95	2	Big 12	Lubbock	18 May 14
50.50		Ashley	Spencer	USA	8.6.93	1	WJ	Barcelona	13 Jul 12
50.59		Fatima	Yusuf	NGR	2.5.71	1	HGP	Budapest	5 Aug 90

800 METRES

1:54.01		Pamela	Jelimo	KEN	5.12.89	1	WK	Zürich	29 Aug 08
1:55.45		Caster	Semenya	RSA	7.1.91	1	WCh	Berlin	19 Aug 09
1:56.59		Francine	Niyonsaba	BDI	5.5.93	1	VD	Bruxelles	7 Sep 12
1:57.18			Wang Yuan	CHN	8.4.76	2h2	NG	Beijing	8 Sep 93
1:57.45		Hildegard	Ullrich	GDR	20.12.59	5	EC	Praha	31 Aug 78
1:57.62			Lang Yinglai	CHN	22.8.79	1	NG	Shanghai	22 Oct 97
1:57.63		Maria	Mutola	MOZ	27.10.72	4	WCh	Tokyo	26 Aug 91
1:57.74		Sahily	Diago	CUB	26.8.95	1	Barr	La Habana	25 Jul 14
1:57.77			Lu Yi	CHN	10.4.74	4	NG	Beijing	9 Sep 93
1:57.86		Katrin	Wühn	GDR	19.11.65	1		Celje	5 May 84
1:58.16			Lin Na	CHN	18.1.80	3	NG	Shanghai	22 Oct 97

1500 METRES

3:51.34			Lang Yinglai	CHN	22.8.79	2	NG	Shanghai	18 Oct 97
3:53.91			Yin Lili	CHN	11.11.79	3	NG	Shanghai	18 Oct 97
3:53.97			Lan Lixin	CHN	14.2.79	4	NG	Shanghai	18 Oct 97
3:54.52			Zhang Ling	CHN	13.4.80	5	NG	Shanghai	18 Oct 97
3:56.98		Faith	Kipyegon	KEN	10.1.94	2	DL	Doha	10 May 13
3:59.53		Dawit	Seyaum	ETH	27.7.96	1		Marrakech	8 Jun 14
3:59.60		Gelete	Burka	ETH	15.2.86	5	GP	Rieti	28 Aug 05
3:59.81			Wang Yuan	CHN	8.4.76	7	NG	Beijing	11 Sep 93
3:59.96		Zola	Budd	GBR	26.5.66	3	VD	Bruxelles	30 Aug 85
4:00.05			Lu Yi	CHN	10.4.74	8	NG	Beijing	11 Sep 93
4:00.18		Gudaf	Tsegay	ETH	23.1.97	3	Pre	Eugene	28 May 16

3000 METRES

8:28.83		Zola	Budd	GBR	26.5.66	3	GG	Roma	7 Sep 85
8:33.63		Meskerem	Mamo	ETH	13.4.99	7	DL	Doha	4 May 18
8:34.03		Lemlem	Hailu	ETH	21.5.01	9	DL	Doha	3 May 19
8:35.76		Beyenu	Degefu	ETH	12.7.99	8	DL	Doha	4 May 18
8:35.89		Sally	Barsosio	KEN	21.3.78	2	Herc	Monaco	16 Aug 97
8:36.45			Ma Ningning	CHN	1.6.76	4	NC	Jinan	6 Jun 93
8:36.87		Alemitu	Haroye	ETH	9.5.95	14	VD	Bruxelles	5 Sep 14
8:37.68		Alemaz	Teshale	ETH	5.7.99	6	Hanz	Zagreb	4 Sep 18
8:38.61		Kalkedan	Gezahegn	ETH	8.5.91	5	WAF	Thessaloníki	13 Sep 09
8:38.97		Linet	Masai	KEN	5.12.89	5	GP	Rieti	9 Sep 07
8:39.13		Agnes	Tirop	KEN	23.10.95	3		Rieti	8 Sep 13
Indoors									
8:39.55		Fantu	Worku	ETH	29.3.99	3		Ostrava	25 Jan 18

5000 METRES

14:30.88		Tirunesh	Dibaba	ETH	1.10.85	2	Bisl	Bergen (Fana)	11 Jun 04
14:33.32		Letesenbet	Gidey	ETH	20.3.98	3	GGala	Roma	8 Jun 17
14:35.18		Sentayehu	Ejigu	ETH	21.6.85	4	Bisl	Bergen (Fana)	11 Jun 04
14:39.96			Yin Lili	CHN	11.11.79	4	NG	Shanghai	23 Oct 97
14:43.29		Emebet	Anteneh	ETH	13.1.92	5	Bisl	Oslo	9 Jun 11
14:45.33			Lan Lixin	CHN	14.2.79	2h2	NG	Shanghai	21 Oct 97
14:45.71			Song Liqing	CHN	20.1.80	3h2	NG	Shanghai	21 Oct 97

JUNIOR WOMEN ALL-TIME

Mark	Wind	Name		Nat	Born	Pos	Meet	Venue	Date
14:45.90			Jiang Bo	CHN	13.3.77	1		Nanjing	24 Oct 95
14:45.98		Pauline	Korikwiang	KEN	1.3.88	7	Bisl	Oslo	2 Jun 06
14:46.12		Beatrice	Chebet	KEN	5.3.00	7	DL	London (OS)	21 Jul 19
14:46.71		Sally	Barsosio	KEN	21.3.78	3	VD	Bruxelles	22 Aug 97
14:47.13		Mercy	Cherono	KEN	7.5.91	7	DL	Shanghai	23 May 10

10,000 METRES

Mark	Wind	Name		Nat	Born	Pos	Meet	Venue	Date
30:26.50		Linet	Masai	KEN	5.12.89	4	OG	Beijing	15 Aug 08
30:31.55			Xing Huina	CHN	25.2.84	7	WCh	Saint-Denis	23 Aug 03
30:39.41			Lan Lixin	CHN	14.2.79	2	NG	Shanghai	19 Oct 97
30:39.98			Yin Lili	CHN	11.11.79	3	NG	Shanghai	19 Oct 97
30:53.53		Girmawit	Gebrzihair	ETH	21.11.01	8		Hengelo	17 Jul 19
30:57.54		Tsige	Gebreselama	ETH	30.9.00	9		Hengelo	17 Jul 19
30:59.92		Merima	Hashim	ETH	.81	3	NA	Heusden-Zolder	5 Aug 00
31:06.20		Lucy	Wangui	KEN	24.3.84	1rA		Okayama	27 Sep 03
31:06.46		Sarah	Chelangat	UGA	5.6.01	3		Hengelo	10 Oct 20
31:11.26			Song Liqing	CHN	20.1.80	7	NG	Shanghai	19 Oct 97
31:15.38		Sally	Barsosio	KEN	21.3.78	3	WCh	Stuttgart	21 Aug 93

HALF MARATHON

Mark	Wind	Name		Nat	Born	Pos	Meet	Venue	Date
66:47		Degitu	Azimeraw	ETH	24.1.99	6	RAK	Ras Al Khaimah	9 Feb 18
67:51		Meseret	Belete	ETH	16.9.99	8		København	16 Sep 18
67:57		Gelana	Abebe	ETH	18.1.90	4		Ras Al Khaimah	20 Feb 09
68:21		Valentine	Kipketer	KEN	5.1.93	1		Lille	3 Sep 11
68:36		Merima	Mohamed	ETH	10.6.92	2		New Delhi	21 Nov 10
68:38		Medhin	Beyene	ETH	5.4.02	1		Boulogne-Billancourt	17 Nov 19
68:41		Evelyne	Kimwei	KEN	25.8.87	1		Kobe	19 Nov 06
68:53		Shure	Demise	ETH	21.1.96	4		Ostia	2 Mar 14
69:05		Delillah	Asiago	KEN	24.2.72	1	GWR	Exeter	5 May 91
69:10		Muliye	Dekebo	ETH	13.3.98	5		Ostia	12 Mar 17

MARATHON

Mark	Wind	Name		Nat	Born	Pos	Meet	Venue	Date
2:20:59		Shure	Demise	ETH	21.1.96	4		Dubai	23 Jan 15
2:21:32		Bedatu	Hirpa	ETH	28.4.99	3		Frankfurt	28 Oct 18
2:22:38			Zhang Yingying	CHN	4.1.90	1	NC	Xiamen	5 Jan 08
2:23:06		Merima	Mohamed	ETH	10.6.92	3		Toronto	26 Sep 10
2:23:37			Liu Min	CHN	29.11.83	1		Beijing	14 Oct 01
2:23:57			Zhu Xiaolin	CHN	20.4.84	4		Beijing	20 Oct 02
2:25:23		Azmera	Abreha	ETH	.98	3		Amsterdam	15 Oct 17
2:25:48			Jin Li	CHN	29.5.83	6		Beijing	14 Oct 01
2:26:34			Wei Yanan	CHN	6.12.81	1		Beijing	15 Oct 00
2:27:05			Chen Rong	CHN	18.5.88	1		Beijing	21 Oct 07

3000 METRES STEEPLECHASE

Mark	Wind	Name		Nat	Born	Pos	Meet	Venue	Date
8:58.78		Celliphine	Chespol	KEN	23.3.99	1	Pre	Eugene	26 May 17]
9:07.94		Peruth	Chemutai	UGA	10.7.99	6	Herc	Monaco	20 Jul 18
9:10.74		Winfred	Yavi	BRN	31.12.99	9	Herc	Monaco	20 Jul 18
9:20.37		Birtukan	Adamu	ETH	29.4.92	4	GGala	Roma	26 May 11
9:20.55		Ruth	Chebet	KEN/BRN	17.11.96	4	WK	Zürich	28 Aug 14
9:20.65		Tigist	Mekonen	BRN	7.7.97	8	Herc	Monaco	17 Jul 15
9:22.51		Almaz	Ayana	ETH	21.11.91	3	VD	Bruxelles	27 Aug 14
9:23.4A		Mercy	Wanjiru	KEN	2.3.99	1		Nairobi	6 Jun 18
9:23.59		Mercy	Chepkurui	KEN	16.9.00	5	DL	Shanghai	18 May 19
9:23.92		Fancy	Cherono	KEN	2.8.01	3	AfrC	Asaba	5 Aug 18
9:24.51		Ruth	Bisibori	KEN	2.1.88	1		Daegu	3 Oct 07

100 METRES HURDLES

Mark	Wind	Name		Nat	Born	Pos	Meet	Venue	Date
12.71	1.3	Brittany	Anderson	JAM	31.1.01	1		Joensuu	24 Jul 19
12.74	1.7	Dior	Hall	USA	2.1.96	3	NCAA	Eugene	13 Jun 15
12.75	1.7	Chanel	Brissett	USA	10.8.99	1	Pac-12	Stanford	13 May 18
12.83A	0.4	Tobi	Amusan	NGR	23.4.97	1		El Paso	30 Apr 16
12.84	1.5	Aliuska	López	CUB	29.8.69	2	WUG	Zagreb	16 Jul 87
12.84	1.2	Tia	Jones	USA	8.9.00	1h1	NC-j	Clovis	25 Jun 16
12.85	2.0	Elvira	German	BLR	19.6.97	1	WJ	Bydgoszcz	24 Jul 16
12.86	1.4	Cortney	Jones	USA	18.6.99	2s2	NCAA	Eugene	7 Jun 18
12.87	2.0	Kendell	Williams	USA	14.6.95	1	NC-j	Eugene	6 Jul 14
12.87	2.0	Rushelle	Burton	JAM	4.12.97	2	WJ	Bydgoszcz	24 Jul 16
12.88	1.5	Yelena	Ovcharova	UKR	17.6.76	2	ECp	Villeneuve d'Ascq	25 Jun 95
Wind assisted									
12.79	3.8	Tobi	Amusan	NGR	23.4.97	2	NCAA	Eugene	11 Jun 16
12.81	3.4	Anay	Tejeda	CUB	3.4.83	1	WJ	Kingston	21 Jul 02

Mark	Wind	Name		Nat	Born	Pos	Meet	Venue	Date
12.82	2.1	Kristi	Castlin	USA	7.7.88	1		College Park	21 Apr 07
12.83	3.7	Tara	Davis	USA	20.5.99	1		Clovis	3 Jun 17

400 METRES HURDLES

Mark		Name		Nat	Born	Pos	Meet	Venue	Date
52.75		Sydney	McLaughlin	USA	7.8.99	1	SEC	Knoxville	13 May 18
54.40			Wang Xing	CHN	30.11.86	2	NG	Nanjing	21 Oct 05
54.58		Ristananna	Tracey	JAM	5.9.92	2	NC	Kingston	24 Jun 11
54.70		Lashinda	Demus	USA	10.3.83	1	WJ	Kingston	19 Jul 02
54.93		Li Rui		CHN	22.11.79	1	NG	Shanghai	22 Oct 97
55.05A		Zeney	van der Walt	RSA	22.5.00	2	NC	Pretoria	17 Mar 18
55.07		Shamier	Little	USA	20.3.95	1	NCAA	Eugene	13 Jun 14
55.11		Kaliese	Spencer	JAM	6.4.87	1	WJ	Beijing	17 Aug 06
55.15		Huang Xiaoxiao		CHN	3.3.83	2	NG	Guangzhou	22 Nov 01
55.20		Lesley	Maxie	USA	4.1.67	2	TAC	San Jose	9 Jun 84
55.20A		Jana	Pittman	AUS	9.11.82	1		Pietersburg	18 Mar 00
55.20		Anna	Cockrell	USA	28.8.97	1	WJ	Bydgoszcz	22 Jul 16

Drugs disqualification:
54.54		Peng Yinghua ¶	CHN	21.2.79	(2)	NG	Shanghai	22 Oct 97

HIGH JUMP

Mark		Name		Nat	Born	Pos	Meet	Venue	Date
2.04		Yaroslava	Mahuchikh	UKR	19.9.011	2	WCh	Doha	30 Sep 19
2.01		Olga	Turchak	UKR	5.3.67	2	GWG	Moskva	7 Jul 86
2.01		Heike	Balck	GDR	19.8.70	1	vURS-j	Karl-Marx-Stadt	18 Jun 89
2.00		Stefka	Kostadinova	BUL	25.3.65	1		Sofia	25 Aug 84
2.00		Alina	Astafei	ROU	7.6.69	1	WJ	Sudbury	29 Jul 88
1.99i		Vashti	Cunningham	USA	18.1.98	1	NC	Portland	12 Mar 16
1.99						1	NC	Sacramento	23 Jun 17
1.98		Silvia	Costa	CUB	4.5.64	2	WUG	Edmonton	11 Jul 83
1.98		Yelena	Yelesina	RUS	5.4.70	1	Druzh	Nyíregyháza	13 Aug 88
1.97		Svetlana	Isaeva	BUL	18.3.67	2		Sofia	25 May 86
1.97i		Mariya	Kuchina	RUS	14.1.93	1		Trinec	26 Jan 11
1.96		six women							

POLE VAULT

Mark		Name		Nat	Born	Pos	Meet	Venue	Date
4.71i		Wilma	Murto	FIN	11.6.98	1		Zweibrücken	31 Jan 16
4.52						2	PNG	Turku	29 Jun 16
4.64		Eliza	McCartney	NZL	11.12.96	1		Auckland	19 Dec 15
4.63i		Angelica	Bengtsson	SWE	8.7.93	2		Stockholm	22 Feb 11
4.58						1		Sollentuna	5 Jul 12
4.61		Alyona	Lutkovskaya	RUS	15.3.96	1		Irkutsk	21 May 15
4.60i		Hanna	Shelekh	UKR	14.7.93	3		Donetsk	11 Feb 12
4.60i		Roberta	Bruni	ITA	8.3.94	1	NC	Ancona	17 Feb 13
4.60		Robeilys	Peinado	VEN	26.11.97	1		Barquisimeto	20 May 15
4.60		Lisa	Gunnarsson	SWE	20.8.99	2	TexasR	Austin	31 Mar 18
4.59		Nina	Kennedy	AUS	5.4.97	1		Perth	14 Feb 15
4.57		Angelica	Moser	SUI	9.10.97	1		Frauenkappelen	1 Aug 16
4.55i		Aksana	Gataullina	RUS	17.7.00	1		Sankt Peterburg	23 Feb 18
4.55						2	NC	Kazan	20 Jul 18

LONG JUMP

Mark	Wind	Name		Nat	Born	Pos	Meet	Venue	Date
7.14	1.1	Heike	Daute	GDR	16.12.64	1	PTS	Bratislava	4 Jun 83
7.03	1.3	Darya	Klishina	RUS	15.1.91	1	Znam	Zhukovskiy	26 Jun 10
7.00	-0.2	Birgit	Grosshennig	GDR	21.2.65	2		Berlin	9 Jun 84
6.94	-0.5	Magdalena	Khristova	BUL	25.2.77	2		Kalamáta	22 Jun 96
6.91	0.0	Anisoara	Cusmir	ROU	28.6.62	1		Bucuresti	23 May 81
6.90	1.4	Beverly	Kinch	GBR	14.1.64	*	WCh	Helsinki	14 Aug 83
6.88	0.6	Natalya	Shevchenko	RUS	28.12.66	2		Sochi	26 May 84
6.84		Larisa	Baluta	UKR	13.8.65	2		Krasnodar	6 Aug 83
6.83	1.7	Kate	Hall	USA	12.1.97	1		Greensboro NC	21 Jun 15
6.82	1.8	Fiona	May	GBR	12.12.69	*	WJ	Sudbury	30 Jul 88
6.81	1.6	Carol	Lewis	USA	8.8.63	1	TAC	Knoxville	20 Jun 82
6.81	1.4	Yelena	Davydova	KZK	16.11.67	1	NC-j	Krasnodar	17 Jul 85

Wind assisted to 6.82
7.27	2.2	Heike	Daute	GDR	16.12.64	1	WCh	Helsinki	14 Aug 83
6.93	4.6	Beverly	Kinch	GBR	14.1.64	5	WCh	Helsinki	14 Aug 83
6.88	2.1	Fiona	May	GBR	12.12.69	1	WJ	Sudbury	30 Jul 88
6.84	2.8	Anu	Kaljurand	EST	16.4.69	2		Riga	4 Jun 88

TRIPLE JUMP

Mark	Wind	Name		Nat	Born	Pos	Meet	Venue	Date
14.62	1.0	Tereza	Marinova	BUL	5.9.77	1	WC	Sydney	25 Aug 96
14.57	0.2		Huang Qiuyan	CHN	25.1.80	1	NG	Shanghai	19 Oct 97

274 JUNIOR WOMEN ALL-TIME

Mark	Wind	Name		Nat	Born	Pos	Meet	Venue	Date
14.52	0.6	Anastasiya	Ilyina	RUS	16.1.82	q	WJ	Santiago de Chile	20 Oct 00
14.46	1.0		Peng Fengmei	CHN	2.7.79	1		Chengdu	18 Apr 98
14.43	0.6	Kaire	Leibak	EST	21.5.88	1	WJ	Beijing	17 Aug 06
14.38	-0.7		Xie Limei	CHN	27.6.86	1	AsiC	Inchon	1 Sep 05
14.37i	-		Ren Ruiping	CHN	1.2.76	3	WI	Barcelona	11 Mar 95
	14.36		0.0			1	NC	Beijing	1 Jun 94
14.36	0.0	Dailenys	Alcántara	CUB	10.8.91	3	Barr/NC	La Habana	29 May 09
14.35		Yana	Borodina	RUS	21.4.92	1J	Mosc Ch	Moskva	15 Jun 11
14.32	-0.1	Yelena	Lysak ¶	RUS	19.10.75	1		Voronezh	18 Jun 94
14.29	1.2	Mabel	Gay	CUB	5.5.83	1		La Habana	5 Apr 02
14.28	0.9	Valeriya	Kanatova	UZB	29.8.92	3	NCp	Tashkent	12 Jun 11
Wind assisted									
14.83	8.3		Ren Ruiping	CHN	1.2.76	1	NC	Taiyuan	21 May 95
14.55	3.7	Dailenis	Alcántara	CUB	10.8.91	1	Barr/NC	La Habana	21 Mar 10
14.43	2.7	Yelena	Lysak ¶	RUS	19.10.75	1	WJ	Lisboa	21 Jul 94

SHOT

20.54		Astrid	Kumbernuss	GDR	5.2.70	1	vFIN-j	Orimattila	1 Jul 89
20.51i		Heidi	Krieger	GDR	20.7.65	2		Budapest	8 Feb 84
	20.24					5		Split	30 Apr 84
20.23		Ilke	Wyludda	GDR	28.3.69	1	NC-j	Karl-Marx-Stadt	16 Jul 88
20.12		Ilona	Schoknecht	GDR	24.9.56	2	NC	Erfurt	23 Aug 75
20.02			Cheng Xiaoyan	CHN	30.11.75	3	NC	Beijing	5 Jun 94
19.90		Stephanie	Storp	FRG	28.11.68	1		Hamburg	16 Aug 87
19.63			Wang Yawen	CHN	23.8.73	1		Shijiazhuang	25 Apr 92
19.57		Grit	Haupt	GDR	4.6.66	1		Gera	7 Jul 84
19.48		Ines	Wittich	GDR	14.11.69	5		Leipzig	29 Jul 87
19.46			Gong Lijiao	CHN	24.1.89	Q	OG	Beijing	16 Aug 08
19.42		Simone	Michel	GDR	18.12.60	3	vSU	Leipzig	23 Jun 79
19.23			Zhang Zhiying	CHN	19.7.73	1	NC-j	Hangzhou	8 May 92

DISCUS

74.40		Ilke	Wyludda	GDR	28.3.69	2		Berlin	13 Sep 88
	75.36	unofficial meeting				2		Berlin	6 Sep 88
67.38		Irina	Meszynski	GDR	24.3.62	1		Berlin	14 Aug 81
67.00		Jana	Günther	GDR	7.1.68	6	NC	Potsdam	20 Aug 87
66.80		Svetla	Mitkova	BUL	17.6.64	1		Sofia	2 Aug 83
66.60		Astrid	Kumbernuss	GDR	5.2.70	1		Berlin	20 Jul 88
66.34		Franka	Dietzsch	GDR	22.1.68	2		Saint-Denis	11 Jun 87
66.30		Jana	Lauren	GDR	28.6.70	1	vURS-j	Karl-Marx-Stadt	18 Jun 89
66.08			Cao Qi	CHN	15.1.74	1	NG	Beijing	12 Sep 93
65.96		Grit	Haupt	GDR	4.6.66	3		Leipzig	13 Jul 84
65.22		Daniela	Costian	ROU	30.4.65	3		Nitra	26 Aug 84
65.20			Liu Fengying	CHN	26.1.79	Q	NC	Chengdu	1 Jun 97
64.52		Martina	Opitz	GDR	12.12.60	3	NC	Karl-Marx-Stadt	12 Aug 79

HAMMER

73.24			Zhang Wenxiu	CHN	22.3.86	1	NC	Changsha	24 Jun 05
71.71		Kamila	Skolimowska	POL	4.11.82	1	GPF	Melbourne	9 Sep 01
71.34		Silja	Kosonen	FIN	16.12.02	2		Somero	26 Jul 20
70.62		Alexandra	Tavernier	FRA	13.12.93	1	WJ	Barcelona	14 Jul 12
70.39		Mariya	Smolyachkova	BLR	10.2.85	1		Staiki	26 Jun 04
70.39		Réka	Gyurátz	HUN	31.5.96	1		Budapest	23 May 15
69.73		Natalya	Zolotukhina	UKR	4.1.85	1		Kyiv	24 Jul 04
69.63		Bianca	Perie	ROU	1.6.90	1	NC-j	Bucuresti	14 Aug 09
69.32		Sofiya	Palkina	RUS	9.6.98	2		Zhukovskiy	16 Jun 17
69.25		Audrey	Ciofani	FRA	13.3.96	1		Gagny	10 May 15
68.98		Ayamey	Medina	CUB	21.2.98	2	Barr	La Habana	27 May 16
68.74		Arasay	Thondike	CUB	28.5.86	2	Barr	La Habana	2 May 05

JAVELIN

63.96		Elína	Tzéngго	GRE	2.9.02	1	NC	Ioánnina	1 Aug 20
63.86		Yulenmis	Aguilar	CUB	3.8.96	1	PAm-J	Edmonton	2 Aug 15
63.01		Vira	Rebryk	UKR	25.2.89	1	WJ	Bydgoszcz	10 Jul 08
62.93			Xue Juan	CHN	10.2.86	1	NG	Changsha	27 Oct 03
62.11		Maria	Andrejczyk	POL	9.3.96	1	Skol	Cetniewo	1 Aug 15
62.09			Zhang Li	CHN	17.1.89	1		Beijing	25 May 08
61.99			Wang Yaning	CHN	4.1.80	1	NC	Huizhou	14 Oct 99
61.96		Sofi	Flink	SWE	8.7.95	Q	WCh	Moskva	16 Aug 13
61.79		Nikolett	Szabó	HUN	3.3.80	1		Schwechat	23 May 99
61.61			Chang Chunfeng	CHN	4.5.88	1	NC-j	Chengdu	4 Jun 07
61.49			Liang Lili	CHN	16.11.83	1	NC	Benxi	1 Jun 02

JUNIOR WOMEN ALL-TIME   275

Mark	Wind	Name		Nat	Born	Pos	Meet	Venue		Date

HEPTATHLON

Mark	Wind	Name		Nat	Born	Pos	Meet	Venue		Date
6768w		Tatyana	Chernova	RUS	29.1.88	1		Arles		3 Jun 07
	13.04w/6.1	1.82	13.57	23.59w/5.2	6.61/1.2		53.43	2:15.05		
6542		Carolina	Klüft	SWE	2.2.83	1	EC	München		10 Aug 02
	13.33/-0.3	1.89	13.16	23.71/-0.3	6.36/1.1		47.61	2:17.99		
6465		Sibylle	Thiele	GDR	6.3.65	1	EJ	Schwechat		28 Aug 83
	13.49	1.90	14.63	24.07	6.65		36.22	2:18.36		
6436		Sabine	Braun	FRG	19.6.65	1	vBUL	Mannheim		9 Jun 84
	13.68	1.78	13.09	23.88	6.03		52.14	2:09.41		
6428		Svetla	Dimitrova ¶	BUL	27.1.70	1	NC	Sofia		18 Jun 89
	13.49/-0.7	1.77	13.98	23.59/-0.2	6.49/0.7		40.10	2:11.10		
6403		Emilia	Dimitrova	BUL	13.11.67	6	GWG	Moskva		7 Jul 86
	13.73	1.76	13.46	23.17	6.29		43.30	2:09.85		
6381		Alina	Shukh	UKR	12.2.99	1	EJ	Grosseto		21 Jul 17
	14.46/-1.7	1.87	13.87	25.97/0.3	6.33w/3.2		54.51	2:13.52		
6357		Géraldine	Ruckstuhl	SUI	24.2.98	2	EJ	Grosseto		21 Jul 17
	13.98/-1.5	1.81	13.54	24.74/0.1	5.97/1.1		54.32	2:12.56		
6298		Nafissatou	Thiam	BEL	19.8.94	1	EJ	Rieti		19 Jul 13
	13.87/1.2	1.89	14.26	25.15/-0.6	6.37/0.1		46.94	2:24.89		
6276		Larisa	Nikitina	RUS	29.4.65	8	URS Ch	Kyiv		21 Jun 84
	13.87/1.6	1.86	14.04	25.26/-0.7	6.31/0.1		48.62	2:22.76		
6267		Katarina	Johnson-Thompson	GBR	9.1.93	15	OG	London (OS)		4 Aug 12
	13.48/0.9	1.89	11.32	23.73/-0.5	6.19/-0.4		38.37	2:10.76		
Drugs disqualification: 6534 Svetla Dimitrova BUL 27.1.70 (3) ECp Helmond										16 Jul 89
	13.30/1.0	1.84	14.35	23.33/-2.2	6.47/-1.4		39.20	2:13.56		

10 KILOMETRES WALK

Mark		Name		Nat	Born	Pos	Meet	Venue	Date
41:45.84t		Elvira	Khasanova	RUS	10.1.00	1		Cheboksary	3 Aug 19
41:52		Tatyana	Mineyeva	RUS	10.8.90	1	NCp-j	Penza	5 Sep 09
41:55		Irina	Stankina	RUS	25.3.77	1	NC-wj	Adler	11 Feb 95
41:57			Gao Hongmiao	CHN	17.3.74	2	NG	Beijing	8 Sep 93
42:15+		Anisya	Kirdyapkina	RUS	23.10.89	1=	in 20k	Adler	23 Feb 08
42:29		Tatyana	Kalmykova	RUS	10.1.90	1	NC-wj	Adler	23 Feb 08
42:31		Irina	Yumanova	RUS	17.6.90	2	NC-wj	Adler	23 Feb 08
42:43.0	t	Svetlana	Vasilyeva	RUS	24.7.92	1	NC-wj	Sochi	27 Feb 11
42:44			Long Yuwen	CHN	1.8.75	3	NC	Shenzen	18 Feb 93

20 KILOMETRES WALK

Mark	Name		Nat	Born	Pos	Meet	Venue	Date
1:25:29	Glenda	Morejón	ECU	30.5.00	1		La Coruña	8 Jun 19
1:25:30	Anisya	Kirdyapkina	RUS	23.10.89	2	NC-w	Adler	23 Feb 08
1:26:36	Tatyana	Kalmykova	RUS	10.1.90	1	NC	Saransk	8 Jun 08
1:27:01		Lu Xiuzhi	CHN	26.10.93	2		Taicang	30 Mar 12
1:27:16		Song Hongjuan	CHN	4.7.84	1	NC	Yangzhou	14 Apr 03
1:27:24		Wu Quanming	CHN	16.11.01	3	NGP	Huangshan	10 Mar 19
1:27:34		Jiang Jing	CHN	23.10.85	2	WCp	Naumburg	2 May 04
1:27:35	Natalya	Fedoskina	RUS	25.6.80	2	WCp	Mézidon-Cannon	2 May 99
1:27:37		Bai Yanmin	CHN	29.6.87	1	NG	Nanjing	20 Oct 05
1:28:08	Anezka	Drahotová	CZE	22.7.95	3	EC	Zürich	14 Aug 14

4 X 100 METRES RELAY

Mark		Team	Runners		Pos	Meet	Venue	Date
43.27	GER	Fehm, Kwadwo, Junk, Montag			1h3	EJ	Grosseto	23 Jul 17
43.29	USA (Blue)	Knight, Tarmoh, Olear, Mayo			1		Eugene	8 Aug 06
43.40	JAM	Simpson, Stewart, McLaughlin, Facey			1	WJ	Kingston	20 Jul 02
43.44A	NGR	Utondu, Iheagwam, Onyali, Ogunkoya			1	AfrG	Nairobi	9 Aug 87
43.68	FRA	Vouaux, Jacques-Sebastien, Kamga, Banco			3	WJ	Grosseto	18 Jul 04
43.81	GBR	Miller, Asher-Smith, S Wilson, Henry			1	EJ	Rieti	21 Jul 13
43.87	URS	Lapshina, Doronina, Bulatova, Kovalyova			1	vGDR-j	Leningrad	20 Jun 87
43.90	IRL	Scott, Moses, Neville. Jumbo-Gula			2	WJ	Tampere	14 Jul 18
43.98	BRA	Silva, Leoncio, Krasucki, Santos			2	PAm-J	São Paulo	7 Jul 07

4 X 400 METRES RELAY

Mark		Team	Runners	Pos	Meet	Venue	Date
3:24.04A	USA	Holmes, Harris, Holman, K Davis		1	PAm-J	San José, CRC	21 Jul 19
		3:27.60 Anderson, Kidd, Smith, Hastings		1	WJ	Grosseto	18 Jul 04
3:28.39	GDR	Derr, Fabert, Wöhlk, Breuer		1	WJ	Sudbury	31 Jul 88
3:29.66	JAM	Stewart, Morgan, Walker, Hall		1	PennR	Philadelphia	28 Apr 01
3:30.03	RUS	Talko, Shapayeva, Soldatova, Kostetskaya		2	WJ	Grosseto	18 Jul 04
3:30.38	AUS	Scamps, R Poetschka, Hanigan, Andrews		1	WJ	Plovdiv	12 Aug 90
3:30.46	GBR	Wall, Spencer, James, Miller		2	WJ	Kingston	21 Jul 02
3:30.68A	CAN	Gale, Rynda, Marsh, Léger		2	PAm-J	San José, CRC	21 Jul 19
3:30.72	BUL	Kireva, Angelova, Rashova, Dimitrova		3	v2N	Sofia	24 Jul 83
3:30.84	NGR	Abugan, Odumosu, Eze, Adesanya		2	WJ	Beijing	20 Aug 06

MEN'S WORLD LISTS 2020

60 METRES INDOORS

Mark	Name		Nat	Born	Pos	Meet	Venue	Date	
6.37A	Christian	Coleman	USA	6.3.96	1	NC	Albuquerque	15	Feb
6.44	Ronnie	Baker	USA	15.10.93	1		Liévin	19	Feb
6.44		Baker			1		Madrid	21	Feb
6.48A		Coleman			1h1	NC	Albuquerque	15	Feb
6.48	Demek	Kemp	USA	26.4.96	2		Madrid	21	Feb
6.49A	Marvin	Bracy	USA	15.12.93	2	NC	Albuquerque	14	Feb
6.49		Baker			1h1		Liévin	19	Feb
6.50		Kemp			1		Boston (R)	25	Jan
6.50		Baker			1	GP	G;asgow	15	Feb
6.50		Kemp			2		Liévin	19	Feb
6.50		Baker			1h1		Madrid	21	Feb
6.51A		Coleman			1s1	NC	Albuquerque	15	Feb
(12/4)									
6.53	Raymond	Ekevwo	NGR	23.3.99	1		Fayetteville	1	Feb
6.53	Chijindu	Ujah	GBR	5.3.94	1		Düsseldorf	4	Feb
6.53A	Brandon	Carnes	USA	6.3.95	1h3	NC	Albuquerque	14	Feb
6.56					2		Düsseldorf	4	Feb
6.55	Ján	Volko	SVK	2.11.96	3		Madrid	21	Feb
6.55	Emmanuel	Wells	USA	20.10.97	1		Seattle	29	Feb
6.56	Warren	Fraser	BAH	8.7.91	1		Clemson	14	Feb
(10)									
6.56A	Kevaughn	Rattray	JAM	16.4.96	1		Albuquerque	14	Feb
6.62					3	Millrose	New York (A)	8	Feb
6.56A	Maurice	Eaddy	USA	4.6.95	2s1	NC	Albuquerque	15	Feb
6.56	Shuhei	Tada	JPN	24.6.96	1h2		Madrid	21	Feb
6.57	Raheem	Chambers	JAM	6.10.97	2		Nashville	18	Jan
6.57	Jaylen	Mitchell	USA		1		Lubbock	31	Jan
6.57	Luca	Lai	ITA	24.6.92	1h1		Magglingen	1	Feb
6.58	Keitavious	Walter	USA	16.4.96	1h1		Iowa City	18	Jan
6.58A	Langston	Jackson	USA	24.11.00	1h2		Albuquerque	8	Feb
6.61					1s2		Lexington	25	Jan
6.58	Brendon	Stewart	USA	29.7.00	2		Clemson	14	Feb
6.58	Waseem	Williams	JAM	8.1.97	1	Big 10	Geneva, OH	29	Feb
6.58	Cravont	Charleston	USA	2.1.98	1	ACC	Notre Dame	29	Feb
(20)									
6.59	Joris	van Gool	NED	4.4.98	2		Torun	8	Feb
6.59	Mike	Rodgers	USA	24.4.85	4		Liévin	19	Feb
6.59	Kenroy	Higgins	USA		1rB		Seattle	29	Feb
6.59	Kevin	Kranz	GER	20.6.98	1		Frankfurt	12	Dec
6.60	Kenzo	Cotton	USA	13.5.96	1		Fayetteville	17	Jan
6.60	Julian	Reus	GER	29.4.88	1		Chemnitz	7	Feb
6.60	Richard	Kilty	GBR	2.9.89	3		Torun	8	Feb
6.60	Emre Zafer	Barnes	TUR	7.11.88	1	ISTAF	Berlin	14	Feb
6.60	Bolade	Ajomale	CAN	31.8.95	1		Staten Island	14	Feb
6.60	Deniz	Almas	GER	17.7.97	1	NC	Leipzig	22	Feb
(30)									
6.60	Filippo	Tortu	ITA	15.6.98	1	NC	Ancona	23	Feb
6.61	Andre	Ewers	JAM	7.6.95	1h1		Columbia SC	7	Feb
6.61	Remigiusz	Olszewski	POL	20.9.92	4		Torun	8	Feb
6.61	Taylor	Banks	USA	10.10.00	3		Clemson	14	Feb
6.61	TJ	Brock	USA	3.2.98	1		Lubbock	15	Feb
6.61	Jhevaughn	Matherson	JAM	27.2.99	1h2	ACC	Notre Dame	28	Feb
6.61	Travis	Collins	USA	26.2.96	1		Birmingham	29	Feb
6.62	Cameron	Burrell	USA	11.9.94	1		Houston	17	Jan
6.62	Jacolby	Shelton	USA		1		Lubbock	24	Jan
6.62	Andrew	Robertson	GBR	17.12.90	1		Wien	1	Feb
(40)									

6.62	Markus	Fuchs	AUT	14.11.95	8 Feb
6.62	Kristoffer	Hari	DEN	23.12.97	14 Feb
6.62A	Jonte	Baker	USA	23.5.97	15 Feb
6.62	Silvan	Wicki	SUI	13.2.95	15 Feb
6.62	Derrius	Rodgers	USA	15.10.97	21 Feb
6.62	Davonte	Burnett	USA	27.2.00	22 Feb
6.63	Theo	Etienne	GBR	3.9.96	19 Jan
6.63	Chris	Royster	USA	26.1.92	1 Feb
6.63A	Remontay	McClain	USA	21.9.92	1 Feb
6.63	Oliver	Bromby	GBR	30.3.98	5 Feb
6.63	Eugene	Amo-Dadzie	GBR	22.6.92	8 Feb

6.63	Lamont Marcell	Jacobs	ITA	26.9.94	19 Feb
6.63	Nesta	Carter	JAM	11.10.85	19 Feb
6.64	Gaston	Bouchereau	USA	.98	18 Jan
6.64	Philipp	Corucle	GER	18.7.97	18 Jan
6.64	Zdenek	Stromsík	CZE	25.11.94	21 Jan
6.64	Giovanni	Cellario	ITA	22.11.94	25 Jan
6.64	Christopher	Grant	JAM	9.9.98	1 Feb
6.64	Hassan	Taftian	IRI	4.5.93	4 Feb
6.64	Mario	Burke	BAR	18.3.97	5 Feb
6.64	Amaury	Golitin	FRA	28.1.97	5 Feb
6.64	Ojie	Edoburun	GBR	2.6.96	12 Feb

60 – 100 METRES

Mark	Wind	Name		Nat	Born	Pos	Meet	Venue		Date
6.64		Charlie	Dobson	GBR	20.10.99	14 Feb	6.64	Julian	Wagner	GER	18.3.98	22 Feb
6.64		Lance	Lang	USA-J	1.2.01	14 Feb	6.64	Courtney	Lindsey	USA	18.11.98	22 Feb
6.64		Michael	Pohl	GER	18.11.89	22 Feb		(67)			

OUTDOORS

Mark	Wind	Name		Nat	Born	Pos	Meet	Venue		Date
6.56A	w?	Phatutshedzo	Maswanganye	RSA-J	1.2.01	1		Pretoria		7 Feb
6.62	0.6	Justin	Gatlin	USA	10.2.82	23 Jul	6.63w	2.4 Cordero	Gray	USA	9.5.89	30 Jul
6.62A	1.0	Wayde	van Niekerk	RSA	15.7.92	10 Nov					

100 METRES

Mark	Wind	Name		Nat	Born	Pos	Meet	Venue		Date
9.86	1.6	Michael	Norman	USA	3.12.97	1		Fort Worth	20 Jul
9.90	1.4	Trayvon	Bromell	USA	10.7.95	1h3		Clermont	24 Jul
9.91A	1.7	Akani	Simbine	RSA	21.9.93	1h3		Pretoria	14 Mar
9.96	0.3		Simbine			1	G Gala	Roma	17 Sep
9.97	1.9	Andre	De Grasse	CAN	10.11.94	1h2		Clermont	24 Jul
9.99	1.6		Bromell			1h2		Montverde	10 Aug
10.00	1.1	Ronnie	Baker	USA	15.10.93	1		Fort Worth	23 Jul
10.01A	1.3		Simbine			1		Pretoria	14 Mar
10.02	-0.2		Simbine			1		Bellinzona	15 Sep
10.03A	-1.8		Simbine			1s1		Pretoria	14 Mar
10.03	0.3	Julian	Forte	JAM	7.1.93	1		Kingston	18 Jul
10.03	1.6	Rai	Benjamin	USA	27.7.97	2		Fort Worth	20 Jul
10.03	1.0	Aska	Cambridge	JPN	31.5.93	1		Fukui	29 Aug
		[13/8]							
10.04	1.4	Noah	Lyles	USA	18.7.97	2h3		Clermont	24 Jul
10.04A	1.4	Yoshihide	Kiryu	JPN	15.12.95	1		Fujiyoshida	1 Aug
		[10]							
10.04	0.2	Andre	Ewers	JAM	7.6.95	1r1		Jacksonville	8 Aug
10.04	1.8	Kyree	King	USA	9.7.94	1h1		Montverde	10 Aug
10.04	0.3	Arthur Gue	Cissé	CIV	29.12.96	2	G Gala	Roma	17 Sep
10.06A	0.8	Phatutshedzo	Maswanganye	RSA-J	1.2.01	1s1-J		Pretoria	14 Mar
10.07	1.1	Justin	Gatlin	USA	10.2.82	2		Fort Worth	23 Jul
10.07	-0.2	Filippo	Tortu	ITA	15.6.98	2		Bellinzona	15 Sep
10.08A	-0.9	Henricho	Bruintjies	RSA	16.7.93	1s3		Pretoria	14 Mar
10.08	1.4	Deniz	Almas	GER	17.7.97	1		Weinheim	1 Aug
10.09	1.7	Cravon	Gillespie	USA	31.7.96	1		Prairie View	6 Aug
10.09	1.8	Kenny	Bednarek	USA	14.10.98	2h1		Montverde	10 Aug
		[20]							
10.09	0.9	Jeff	Demps	USA	8.1.90	1		Des Moines	29 Aug
10.10A		Wayde	van Niekerk	RSA	15.7.92	1		Bloemfontein	21 Feb
10.10	1.8	Divine	Oduduru	NGR	7.10.96	1rB		Clermont	24 Jul
10.10	1.6	Lamont Marcell	Jacobs	ITA	26.9.94	1		Trieste	1 Aug
10.11	2.0	Silvan	Wicki	SUI	13.2.95	1		Bulle	11 Jul
10.11	1.9	Senoj-Jay	Givans	JAM	30.12.93	2h2		Clermont	24 Jul
10.11	0.1	Felipe Barci	dos Santos	BRA	8.10.98	1s2	NC	São Paulo	11 Dec
10.12	1.5	Jack	Hale	AUS	22.5.98	1h2		Perth	1 Feb
10.12	0.9	Devin	Quinn	USA	8.6.96	2		Des Moines	29 Aug
10.12	0.3	Michael	Rodgers	USA	24.4.85	5	G Gala	Roma	17 Sep
		[30]							
10.12	1.4	Paulo André	de Oliveira	BRA	20.8.98	1s1	NC	São Paulo	11 Dec
10.13	2.0	Shota	Iizuka	JPN	25.6.91	1		Shizuoka	2 Aug
10.13	-0.5		Yang Chun-Han	TPE	1.1.97	1	NC	Taipei	4 Dec
10.14	1.8	Kendal	Williams	USA	23.9.95	2rB		Clermont	24 Jul
10.14	1.6	Joshua	Hartmann	GER	9.6.99	1		Zeven	25 Jul
10.14	1.8	Soshi	Mizukubo	JPN	1.3.99	1		Niigata	12 Sep
10.15	0.6	Aaron	Brown	CAN	27.5.92	1rB		Montverde	10 Aug
10.15	0.0	Yohan	Blake	JAM	26.12.89	1		Kingston	22 Aug
10.16	1.5	Rohan	Browning	AUS	31.12.97	1h1		Perth	1 Feb
10.16	1.8	Nickel	Ashmeade	JAM	7.4.90	3rB		Clermont	24 Jul
		[40]							
10.16	0.4	K.M.Yupon	Abeykoon	SRI	31.12.94	1		Dessau	8 Sep
10.16	0.7	Mouhamadou	Fall	FRA	25.2.92	1	NC	Albi	12 Sep
10.17A	1.7	Simon	Magakwe	RSA	25.5.85	2h3		Pretoria	14 Mar
10.17	1.3	Chijindu	Ujah	GBR	5.3.94	2	PNG	Turku	11 Aug
10.17	1.1	Joris	van Gool	NED	4.4.98	1	NC	Utrecht	29 Aug
10.18	0.5		He Yuhong	CHN-J	2.2.01	1		Chengdu	24 Jul
10.18	1.5	Jaylen	Bacon	USA	5.8.96	1rC		Clermont	24 Jul
10.18	1.6	Nesta	Carter	JAM	11.10.85	1rB		Kingston	25 Jul
10.18	2.0	Maurice	Eaddy	USA	4.6.95	3rB		Montverde	10 Aug
10.18	1.5	Shuhei	Tada	JPN	24.6.96	1h2		Fukui	29 Aug
		[50]							

MEN 2020

100 - 150 METRES

Mark	Wind	Name	Nat	Born	Pos	Meet	Venue	Date
10.19	1.6	Rodrigo do Nascimento	BRA	26.9.94			29 Feb	
10.19	1.6	Przemysław Słowikowski	POL	20.11.93			26 Jul	
10.19	1.0	Yuki Koike	JPN	13.5.95			29 Aug	
10.19	0.7	Amaury Golitin	FRA	28.1.97			12 Sep	
10.20	0.0	Isiah Young	USA	5.1.90			4 Jul	
10.20	0.1	Tyquendo Tracey	JAM	10.6.93			8 Aug	
10.20	1.8	Bruno Dede	JPN	7.10.99			12 Sep	
10.21	0.9	Oshane Bailey	JAM	9.8.89			29 Feb	
10.21	0.8	Jan Veleba	CZE	6.12.86			8 Jun	
10.21	0.1	Romario Williams	JAM	17.11.95			8 Aug	
10.21	0.2	Sean Safo-Antwi	GHA	31.10.90			15 Aug	
10.21	0.9	Akihiro Higashida	JPN	13.12.95			29 Aug	
10.22A	1.4	Clarence Munyai	RSA	26.9.98			7 Mar	
10.22	2.0	Luca Lai	ITA	24.6.92			11 Jul	
10.22	1.8	Ryota Suzuki	JPN	25.6.99			12 Sep	
10.23	0.0	Kenroy Anderson	JAM	27.6.87			29 Feb	
10.23	0.2	Egwero Ogho-Oghene	NGR	26.11.88			14 Mar	
10.23	0.4	Elijah Hall	USA	22.8.94			17 Aug	
10.23	1.2	Ramil Guliyev	TUR	29.5.90			28 Aug	
10.24	1.5	Jake Doran	AUS	17.11.00			1 Feb	
10.24	0.0	Roberto Skyers	CUB	12.11.91			6 Mar	
10.24	1.5	Julian Reus	GER	29.4.88			3 Jul	
10.24	1.0	Remigiusz Olszewski	POL	20.9.92			8 Aug	
10.24	1.9	Chris Ius	AUS	10.2.00			28 Nov	
10.24	1.4	Derick Silva	BRA	23.4.98			11 Dec	
10.24	0.5	Franco Florio	ARG	30.5.00			18 Dec	
10.25A	0.7	Duke Kuali	RSA	26.5.98			14 Mar	
10.25	0.8	Ján Volko	SVK	2.11.96			8 Jun	
10.25	1.0	Dominik Kopec	POL	5.3.95			26 Jul	
10.25	0.7	Ippei Takeda	JPN	13.3.97			23 Aug	
		(79)				100th 10.29		

Wind assisted

9.87	2.5	Trayvon	Bromell	USA	10.7.95	1	Montverde	10 Aug
9.93	4.0	Noah	Lyles	USA	18.7.97	1h1	Montverde	4 Jul
9.93	2.3		Lyles			1	Clermont	24 Jul
9.96	2.1	Julian	Forte	JAM	7.1.93	1	Kingston	25 Jul
9.97	2.3		De Grasse			2	Clermont	24 Jul
9.99	4.0	Justin	Gatlin	USA	10.2.82	2h1	Montverde	4 Jul
10.02	4.2	Reynier	Mena	CUB	21.11.96	1	La Habana	20 Mar
10.02	2.5	Kenny	Bednarek	USA	14.10.98	3	Montverde	10 Aug
10.03	5.6	Andrew	Robertson	GBR	17.12.90	1	Nuneaton	23 Aug
10.03	2.8	Felipe Bardi	dos Santos	BRA	8.10.98	1h4	Bragança Paulista	31 Oct
10.05	3.6	Przemysław	Słowikowski	POL	20.11.93	1	Jelenia Góra	26 Jul
10.06	2.2	Rohan	Browning	AUS	31.12.97	1	Perth	1 Feb
10.07	4.2	Roberto	Skyers	CUB	12.11.91	2	La Habana	20 Mar
10.07	2.1	Yohan	Blake	JAM	26.12.89	2	Kingston	25 Jul
10.10	2.2	Jack	Hale	AUS	22.5.98	2	Perth	1 Feb
10.11	2.8	Derick	Silva	BRA	23.4.98	2h4	Bragança Paulista	31 Oct
10.12	2.5	Charles	Dobson	GBR	20.10.99	1	Dagenham	23 Aug
10.12	5.6	Harry	Aikines-Aryeetey	GBR	29.8.88	2	Nuneaton	23 Aug
10.13	2.9		Xie Zhenye	CHN	17.8.93	1	Shanghai	23 Aug
10.13	4.0	Rodrigo	do Nascimento	BRA	26.9.94	1	Campinas	2 Dec
10.15	3.6	Karol	Kwiatowski	POL	20.8.96	26 Jul		
10.16	2.5	Ján	Volko	SVK	2.11.96	12 Jul		
10.16	4.0	Erik	Cardoso	BRA	3.3.00	2 Dec		
10.17	2.9	Jake	Penny	AUS	2.5.96	1 Mar		
10.17	4.2	Jenns Reynold Fernández		CUB-J	4.1.01	20 Mar		
10.18	4.0	Alonso	Edward	PAN	8.12.89	4 Jul		
10.18	2.8	Aldemir Gomes da Silva		BRA	8.6.92	31 Oct		
10.19	2.2	Edward	Osei-Nketia	NZL-J	8.5.01	23 Feb		
10.19	2.1	Romario	Williams	JAM	17.11.95	25 Jul		
10.20	2.5	Elijah	Hall	USA	22.8.94	30 Jul		
10.21	2.5	Seye	Ogunlewe	NGR	30.8.91	23 Aug		
10.21	4.1	Franco	Florio	ARG	30.5.00	21 Nov		
10.23A		Ferdinand	Omurwa	KEN	2.1.96	5 Mar		

Low altitude best: 10.06 1.0 Kiryu 2 Fukui 29 Aug
Hand timing - Wind assisted: 9.9w 2.5 Roberto Skyers CUB 12.11.91 1 La Habana 28 Feb

JUNIORS

2 juniors in main list. Further juniors:

10.27	0.7	Hiroki	Yanagita	JPN-Y	25.7.03	4h3	Tokyo	23 Aug
10.28A	1.2	Elviano	Johnson	RSA	11.11.02	1h3	Pretoria	14 Mar
10.29A	-0.5	Sinesipho	Dambile	RSA	2.3.02	2	Pretoria	14 Mar
10.29A	0.8	Eckardt	Potgieter	RSA	13.6.02	2s1	Pretoria	14 Mar
10.29	1.5	Ryiem	Robertson [Forde]	JAM	23.5.01	2rC	Clermont	24 Jul
10.29	-0.4	Erriyon	Knighton	USA-Y	29.1.04	1	Satellite Beach, FL	8 Aug

Wind assisted

10.17	4.2	Jenns Reynold	Fernández	CUB	4.1.01	3	La Habana	20 Mar
10.19	2.2	Edward	Osei-Nketia	NZL	8.5.01	1	Auckland (Waitakere)	23 Feb
10.22A	2.6	Eckardt	Potgieter	RSA	13.6.02	1h2	Pretoria	14 Mar
10.25w	4.2	Shainer	Reginfo	CUB	8.4.02	5	La Habana	20 Mar
10.28w	2.5	Joel	Pascall-Menzie	GBR	3.11.02	3	Dagenham	23 Aug

150 METRES

15.05	1.9	Silvan	Wicki	SUI	13.2.95	1	Langenthal	13 Jun
15.07		Steven	Gardiner	BAH	12.9.95	1rA	Marietta	15 Aug
15.08A		Akani	Simbine	RSA	21.9.93	1	Johannesburg	14 Feb
15.08	1.8	Jaron	Flournoy	USA	24.11.95	1rA	Fort Worth	20 Jul
15.13A		Clarence	Munyai	RSA	20.2.98	2	Johannesburg	14 Feb
15.15	0.5	Arthur Gue	Cissé	CIV	29.12.96	1	GS	Ostrava	8 Sep

200 METRES

19.76	0.7	Noah	Lyles	USA	18.7.97	1	Herc	Monaco	14 Aug
19.80	1.0	Kenny	Bednarek	USA	14.10.98	1	Montverde	10 Aug
19.94	0.8		Lyles			1	Clermont	25 Jul

200 METRES

Mark	Wind	Name		Nat	Born	Pos	Meet	Venue	Date	
19.96	1.0	Steven	Gardiner	BAH	12.9.95	1rB		Clermont	25	Jul
20.06	1.0		Bednarek			1		Montverde	4	Jul
20.13	1.3		Lyles			1	Gyulai	Székesfehérvár	19	Aug
20.19	0.8		Bednarek			2		Clermont	25	Jul
20.19	-0.6		Gardiner			1		Marietta	1	Aug
		[8/3]								
20.22	0.8	Divine	Oduduru	NGR	7.10.96	3		Clermont	25	Jul
20.23A	0.7	Clarence	Munyai	RSA	20.2.98	1s3		Pretoria	13	Mar
20.23	0.9	Arthur Gue	Cissé	CIV	29.12.96	1	DL	Doha	25	Sep
20.24	1.0	Josephus	Lyles	USA	22.7.98	2rB		Clermont	25	Jul
20.24	0.8	Andre	De Grasse	CAN	10.11.94	4rA		Clermont	25	Jul
20.24	1.2	Aaron	Brown	CAN	27.5.92	1rB		Montverde	10	Aug
20.24	0.2	William	Reals	SUI	4.5.99	1	NC	Basel	11	Sep
		[10]								
20.31A		Wayde	van Niekerk	RSA	15.7.92	1		Bloemfontein	21	Feb
20.33	0.3	Erriyon	Knighton	USA-Y	29.1.04	1		Satellite Beach, FL	7	Aug
20.35	1.3	Eseosa	Desalu	ITA	19.2.94	2	Gyulai	Székesfehérvár	19	Aug
20.37	1.6	Reynier	Mena	CUB	21.11.96	1		La Habana	21	Mar
20.39	0.9	Julian	Forte	JAM	7.1.93	2	DL	Doha	25	Sep
20.40	1.2	Lucas	Carvalho	BRA	16.7.93	1	NC	São Paulo	12	Dec
20.41	1.2	Aldemir Gomes	da Silva	BRA	8.6.92	2	NC	São Paulo	13	Dec
20.44A	1.2	Sinesipho	Dambile	RSA-J	2.3.02	1	Keino	Nairobi	3	Oct
20.45	1.9	Silvan	Wicki	SUI	13.2.95	1		Bern	27	Jun
20.45	0.8	Nathon	Allen	JAM	28.10.95	5rA		Clermont	25	Jul
		[20]								
20.45	1.2	Alonso	Edward	PAN	8.12.89	2rB		Montverde	10	Aug
20.46	1.8	Romario	Williams	JAM	17.11.95	1		Kingston	9	Aug
20.47	1.6	Nickel	Ashmeade	JAM	7.4.90	1rC		Clermont	25	Jul
20.47	1.2	Shota	Iizuka	JPN	25.6.91	1		Kumagaya	20	Sep
20.49A	0.0	Sydney	Siame	ZAM	7.10.97	1		Ndola	22	Feb
20.50A	-0.5	Phatutshedzo Maswanganye		RSA-J	1.2.01	1h3		Pretoria	13	Mar
20.50	0.7	Antonio	Infantino	ITA	22.3.91	15	Aug	20.64A	0.1	Luxolo Adams RSA 1.8.96 13 Mar
20.51	1.4	Yoshihide	Kiryu	JPN	15.12.95	10	Aug	20.64	1.6	Aldrich Bailey USA 6.2.94 23 Jul
20.52	1.9	Yancarlos	Martínez	DOM	8.7.92	9	Feb	20.64	1.7	Jan Veleba CZE 6.12.86 31 Jul
20.52	1.4	Antonio	Watson	JAM-J	11.9.01	6	Mar	20.64	0.7	Deniz Almas GER 17.7.97 14 Aug
20.52	1.5	Paulo André de Oliveira		BRA	20.8.98	12	Dec	20.65	0.0	Christophe Lemaitre (50) FRA 11.6.90 9 Jul
20.53A	0.7	Eckardt	Potgieter	RSA-J	13.6.02	1	Mar	20.65	-1.4	Robert Gregory USA-J .01 7 Aug
20.54	1.0	Kyree	King	USA	9.7.94	10	Aug	20.65	1.4	Soshi Mizukubo JPN 1.3.99 10 Aug
20.56	1.5	Keigo	Yasuda	JPN	21.2.00	29	Aug	20.65	1.5	Koki Kasatani JPN 31.12.98 29 Aug
20.56	1.6	Arnoldo Lazael Romero		CUB	5.4.00	21	Mar	20.66	0.1	John Gikas AUS 7.10.99 27 Jan
20.56	1.3	Adam	Gemili	GBR	6.10.93	19	Aug	20.66A	0.4	Abdulaziz Mohamed QAT-J 20.10.01 10 Mar
20.56	1.2	Felipe Bardi dos Santos		BRA	8.10.98	13	Dec	20.66	-0.8	Rasheed Dwyer JAM 29.1.89 18 Jul
20.58	0.5	Lucas	Vilar	BRA-J	10.3.01	18	Dec	20.67	-0.5	Robin Erewa GER 24.6.91 1 Aug
20.59	1.9	Lidio	Feliz	DOM	24.6.97	9	Feb	20.67	0.8	Kojo Musah DEN 15.4.96 2 Aug
20.60	1.9	Matthew	Hudson-Smith	GBR	26.10.94	25	Jul	20.67	0.7	Amaury Golitin FRA 28.1.97 13 Sep
20.61	1.6	Jaron	Flournoy	USA	24.11.96	23	Jul	20.68A	1.0	Daniel Stokes USA 20.8.97 14 Mar
20.61	1.5	Keigo	Yasuda	JPN	21.2.00	29	Aug	20.68	0.9	Kazuma Higuchi JPN 14.9.99 29 Aug
20.61A	1.2	Tazana	Kamanga-Dyrbak	DEN-J	12.1.02	3	Oct	20.68	0.7	Sasha Zhoya FRA-J 25.6.02 13 Sep
20.62	-0.8	Yohan	Blake	JAM	26.12.89	18	Jul	20.69A	-0.2	Ngoni Makusha ZIM 22.6.94 13 Mar
20.63	1.0	Deon	Lendore	TTO	28.10.92	6	Aug	20.69	0.3	Davide Re ITA 16.3.93 4 Jul
20.63	-0.2	Jiří	Polák	CZE	22.4.98	9	Aug	20.69	1.3	Elijah Hall USA 22.8.94 19 Aug
								(65)		100th 20.80

Indoors

20.43		Terrance	Laird	USA	12.10.98	1		Fayetteville	15 Feb
20.49		Micaiah	Harris	USA	19.12.98	1		Fayetteville	1 Feb
20.58Ai		Langston	Jackson	USA	24.11.00	8 Feb	20.66	Matthew Boling USA 20.6.00	15 Feb
20.61		Karayme	Bartley	JAM	96	21 Feb	20.66	Andrew Morgan-Harrison GBR 9.3.98	16 Feb
							20.68	Caleb Boger USA-J 19.2.01	7 Mar

Wind assisted

20.35	5.2	Taymir	Burnet	NED	1.10.92	1	NC	Utrecht	30 Aug
20.55	3.5	Da'Marcus Fleming		USA-J	21.12.01	7 Mar	20.64A	4.7 Nicholas Ferns RSA 14.1.97	12 Dec
							20.66	2.6 Javon Francis JAM 14.12.94	30 Jul

Hand timing: 20.0 Duke Kuali RSA 26.5.98 1 Johannesburg 8 Feb

JUNIORS
2 juniors in main list. 5 performances by 4 men to 20.55 (& 1 wind-assisted). Additional mark and further juniors:

Dambile		20.47A -0.5 1h3			Pretoria			13 Mar	
20.50A	-0.5	Phatutshedzo	Maswanganye	RSA	1.2.01	2h3		Pretoria	13 Mar
20.52	1.4	Antonio	Watson	JAM	11.9.01	1		Kingston	6 Mar
20.53A	0.7	Eckardt	Potgieter	RSA	13.6.02	2		Pretoria	1 Mar
20.58	0.5	Lucas	Vilar	BRA	10.3.01	1	NC-23	Bragança Paulista	18 Dec
20.61A	1.2	Tazana	Kamanga-Dyrbak	DEN	12.1.02	3	Keino	Nairobi	3 Oct
20.65	-1.4	Robert	Gregory	USA	.01	1		Satellite Beach, FL	7 Aug
20.66A	0.4	Abdulaziz	Mohamed	QAT	20.10.01	1		Potchefstroom	10 Mar
20.68	0.7	Sasha	Zhoya	FRA	25.6.02	2	NC	Albi	13 Sep
20.70	1.4	Deandre	Watkin	JAM	9.10.02	2		Kingston	6 Mar
20.71A	-1.8	Letsile	Tebogo	BOT-Y	7.6.03	1		Gaborone	14 Mar

200 - 300 - 400 METRES

Mark	Wind	Name		Nat	Born	Pos	Meet	Venue	Date
20.75	-0.2	Da'Marcus	Fleming	USA	21.12.01	1		Tampa	10 Mar
20.68i		Caleb	Boger	USA-J	19.2.01	1	JUCO	Lynchburg	7 Mar
20.72i		Kennedy	Lightner	USA	1.1.01	1r2		Fayetteville	15 Feb
Wind assisted: 20.55w 3.5		Da'Marcus Fleming USA-J 21.12.01				1		Tampa	7 Mar
20.67w	2.4	Justin	Robinson	USA	30.3.02	1rB		Des Moines	29 Aug
20.72w	2.4	Kaishin	Shimada	JPN	25.11.02	1		Shizuoka	27 Sep

300 METRES

Mark		Name		Nat	Born	Pos	Meet	Venue	Date
31.83		Steven	Gardiner	BAH	12.9.95	1		Alachua, FL	5 Jul
31.95			Gardiner			1		Alachua	27 Jun
32.10A		Sinesipho	Dambile	RSA-J	2.3.02	1		Pretoria	7 Feb
32.13A		Thapelo	Phora	RSA	21.11.91	2		Pretoria	7 Feb
32.37		Michael	Cherry	USA	23.3.95	1		Fort Worth	23 Jul
32.46	Sinan	Ören	TUR	10.2.98	18 Jul	32.57	Luka	Janezic	SLO	14.11.95	13 Jun
32.53	Yasmani	Copello	TUR	15.4.87	18 Jul	32.59	William	Reais	SUI	4.5.99	13 Jun
32.55	Asa	Guevara	TTO	20.12.95	27 Jun	32.63A	Pavel	Maslák	CZE	21.2.91	4 Feb
32.55	Zakithi	Nene	RSA	2.4.98	5 Dec	32.68A	Gideon	Narib	NAM	27.5.90	17 Oct

Indoors

| 32.28 | | Jacory | Patterson | USA | 2.2.00 | 1 | | Blacksburg | 18 Jan |
| 32.35 | | Rai | Benjamin | USA | 27.7.97 | 1 | Millrose | New York (A) | 8 Feb |

400 METRES

Mark		Name		Nat	Born	Pos	Meet	Venue	Date
44.91		Justin	Robinson	USA-J	30.3.02	1		Marietta	15 Aug
44.98		Michael	Cherry	USA	23.3.95	2		Marietta	15 Aug
45.05		Karsten	Warholm	NOR	28.2.96	1	DL	Stockholm	23 Aug
45.07		Akeem	Bloomfield	JAM	10.11.97	1		Clermont	24 Jul
45.21		Edoardo	Scotti	ITA	9.5.00	1	G Gala	Roma	17 Sep
45.25		Youssef Mohamed	Dagher	KUW	15.7.93	2	G Gala	Roma	17 Sep
45.31		Davide	Re	ITA	16.3.93	1		Savona	16 Jul
45.37		Steven	Solomon	AUS	16.5.93	1		Canberra	13 Feb
45.40		Josephus	Lyles	USA	22.7.98	2		Clermont	24 Jul
45.46		Ludvy	Vaillant	FRA	15.3.95	1	NC	Albi	13 Sep
[10]									
45.47		Karol	Zalewski	POL	7.8.93	1	Kuso	Chorzów	25 Aug
45.50		Kahmari	Montgomery	USA	16.8.97	1	Gyulai	Székesfehérvár	19 Aug
45.53		Lucas	Carvalho	BRA	16.7.93	1	NC	São Paulo	11 Dec
45.55		Matthew	Hudson-Smith	GBR	26.10.94	1		Montverde	4 Jul
45.56		Jhon	Perlaza	COL	26.8.94	2		Montverde	4 Jul
45.58		Wayde	van Niekerk	RSA	15.7.92	1		Bellinzona	15 Sep
45.59		Jakub	Krzewina	POL	10.10.89	1	Maniak	Szczecin	16 Aug
45.64A		Boitumelo	Masilo	BOT	5.8.95	1rA		Gaborone	14 Mar
45.64		Joachim	Dobber	NED	8.7.97	4	G Gala	Roma	17 Sep
45.65		Deon	Lendore	TTO	28.10.92	1		Prairie View	30 Jul
[20]									
45.65		Vladimir	Aceti	ITA	16.10.98	1		La Chaux-de-Fonds	15 Aug
45.65		Rabah	Yousif	GBR	11.12.86	5	G Gala	Roma	17 Sep
45.76A	Baboloki	Thebe	BOT	18.3.97	14 Mar	45.84	Tony	van Diepen	NED	17.4.96	6 Sep
45.76	Machel	Cedenio	TTO	6.9.95	29 Aug	45.88	Kennedy	Luchembe	ZAM-J	8.7.01	6 Sep
45.77A	Emmanuel	Bamidele	NGR	6.7.99	7 Mar	45.96	Mohammad Nasser Abbas	QAT	28.10.96	25 Sep
45.78	Luka	Janezic	SLO	14.11.95	17 Sep	45.98A	Ditiro	Nzamani	BOT	29.1.00	15 Feb
45.78	Mizuki	Obuchi	JPN	19.2.97	3 Nov	45.98	LaShawn	Merritt	USA	27.6.86	24 Jul
45.80	Marvin	Schlegel	GER	2.1.98	9 Aug	45.99	Isayah	Boers	NED	19.6.99	15 Sep
45.81	Anderson	Henriques	BRA	3.3.92	11 Dec	46.00	Matej	Krsek	CZE	13.5.00	22 Aug
45.82	Alex	Beck	AUS	7.2.92	13 Feb	46.01	Manuel	Sanders	GER	3.4.98	9 Aug
45.82A	Samuel	García	ESP	4.12.91	14 Mar	46.03	Kaito	Kawabata	JPN	17.8.98	24 Oct
45.82	Ashley	Moloney	AUS	13.3.00	19 Dec	46.05	Rafal	Omelko	POL	16.1.89	20 Jun
45.83	Rikuya	Ito	JPN	10.11.98	25 Aug	46.09	Daniel	Atinaya	NGR	98	6 Nov
45.83	Daichi	Inoue	JPN	27.4.99	11 Sep	46.10A	Leungo	Scotch	BOT	28.2.96	28 Feb
45.84	Charles	Dobson	GBR	20.10.99	16 Aug	46.10	Rusheen	McDonald	JAM	17.8.92	25 Jul

Indoors [# = Track with circumference exceeding 200m] (47)

45.44		Randolph	Ross	USA-J	1.1.01	1		Lubbock	31 Jan
45.51		Bryce	Deadmon	USA	26.3.97	1rA	SEC	College Station	29 Feb
45.56#		Wayne	Lawrence	USA/JAM	21.11.98	1rA	Big 10	Geneva, OH	29 Feb
45.62		Jamal	Walton	CAY	25.11.98	2	SEC	College Station	29 Feb
45.66#		Jacory	Patterson	USA	2.2.00	1	ACC	Notre Dame	29 Feb
45.78	Jonathan	Jones	BAR	6.2.99	14 Feb	45.97#	Tyler	Johnson	USA	11.2.98	29 Feb
45.84	Kyron	McMaster	IVB	3.1.97	15 Feb	45.99	Quincy	Hall	USA	31.7.98	22 Feb
45.86A	Rashard	Clark	USA	4.11.94	15 Feb	46.00A	Kyle	Clemons	USA	27.8.90	15 Feb
45.96	Elija	Godwin	USA	1.7.99	29 Feb	46.01	Tyler	Terry	USA	3.12.97	29 Feb
45.97	Derrick	Mokaleng	RSA	18.6.97	15 Feb	46.05	Jeremy	Farr	JAM	20.11.00	15 Feb

JUNIORS also 1 in main list

| 45.88 | | Kennedy | Luchembe | ZAM | 8.7.01 | 1 | | Madrid | 6 Sep |

400 - 600 - 800 METRES

Mark	Name		Nat	Born	Pos	Meet	Venue	Date
46.19	Bernat	Erta	ESP	15.2.01	1	NC	Getafe	13 Sep
46.29A	Ivan Danny	Geldenhuys	RSA	9.8.01	1		Pretoria	14 Mar
46.29	Oliver	Murcko	SVK	3.5.01	3	PTS	Samorín	11 Sep

500 METRES

Mark	Name		Nat	Born	Pos	Meet	Venue	Date
1:00.30	Davide	Re	ITA	16.3.93	1		Rieti	23 Jul
1:00.82	Pablo Sánchez-Valladares ESP 12.11.97				22 Sep			
Indoors								
1:00.73	Tai					Burgess	USA 15.4.99	25 Jan

600 METRES

Mark	Name		Nat	Born	Pos	Meet	Venue	Date
1:14.85	Wesley	Vázquez	PUR	27.3.94	1		Caguas	1 Aug
1:15.07	Donavan	Brazier	USA	15.4.97	1	Gyulai	Székesfehérvár	19 Aug
1:15.86	Nijel	Amos	BOT 15.3.94	17 Jul		1:16.40A Kabelo	Mohlosi	RSA 20.1.93 14 Feb
Indoors								
1:14.39	Donavan	Brazier	USA	15.4.97	1		Boston (R)	25 Jan
1:15.16	Devin	Dixon	USA	22.9.97	1		Lubbock	1 Feb

800 METRES

Mark	Name		Nat	Born	Pos	Meet	Venue	Date
1:43.15	Donavan	Brazier	USA	15.4.97	1	Herc	Monaco	14 Aug
1:43.23	Bryce	Hoppel	USA	5.9.97	2	Herc	Monaco	14 Aug
1:43.76		Brazier			1	DL	Stockholm	23 Aug
1:43.84		Brazier			1		Newberg	31 Jul
1:44.09	Daniel	Rowden	GBR	9.9.97	1	Hanz	Zagreb	15 Sep
1:44.14	Marco	Arop	CAN	20.9.98	3	Herc	Monaco	14 Aug
1:44.16	Ferguson Rotich	Cheruiyot	KEN	30.11.89	1	DL	Doha	25 Sep
1:44.18	Jake	Wightman	GBR	11.7.94	1	GS	Ostrava	8 Sep
[8/6]								
1:44.47	Andreas	Kramer	SWE	13.4.97	2	GS	Ostrava	8 Sep
1:44.51	Amel	Tuka	BIH	9.1.91	3	GS	Ostrava	8 Sep
1:44.56	Benjamin	Robert	FRA	4.11.98	4	Herc	Monaco	14 Aug
1:44.56	Elliot	Giles	GBR	26.5.94	2	DL	Doha	25 Sep
[10]								
1:44.75	Max	Burgin	GBR-J	20.5.02	1		Manchester (Str)	11 Aug
1:44.81	Edose	Ibadin	NGR	27.2.93	1		Alexandria, VA	1 Aug
1:44.82	Tony	van Diepen	NED	17.4.96	4	GS	Ostrava	8 Sep
1:44.83	Kyle	Langford	GBR	2.2.96	5	Herc	Monaco	14 Aug
1:44.93	Marc	Reuther	GER	23.6.96	6	Herc	Monaco	14 Aug
1:44.96	Peter	Bol	AUS	22.2.94	7	Herc	Monaco	14 Aug
1:45.18	Wesley	Vázquez	PUR	27.3.94	5	GS	Ostrava	8 Sep
1:45.21A	Joseph	Deng	AUS	7.7.98	2	Keino	Nairobi	3 Oct
1:45.26	Collins	Kipruto	KEN	12.4.94	2	Quercia	Rovereto	8 Sep
1:45.52A	Wycliffe	Kinyamal	KEN	2.7.97	3	Keino	Nairobi	3 Oct
[20]								
1:45.57	Guy	Learmonth	GBR	20.4.92	3	Skol	Chorzów	6 Sep
1:45.60	Álvaro	de Arriba	ESP	2.6.94	7	Hanz	Zagreb	15 Sep
1:45.64	Adam	Kszczot	POL	2.9.89	4	Skol	Chorzów	6 Sep
1:45.68A	Cornelius	Tuwei	KEN	24.5.93	4	Keino	Nairobi	3 Oct
1:45.71	Saúl	Ordóñez	ESP	10.4.94	1	NA	Heusden-Zolder	6 Sep
1:45.77	Marcin	Lewandowski	POL	13.6.87	5	Skol	Chorzów	6 Sep
1:45.96	Djoão	Lobles	NED-J	14.1.01	4	NA	Heusden-Zolder	6 Sep
1:46.13	Michael	Saruni	KEN	18.6.95	1		Nashville	15 Aug
1:46.16	Eliott	Crestan	BEL	22.2.99	4	NA	Heusden-Zolder	6 Sep
1:46.18	Balázs	Vindics	HUN	28.3.94	1		Veszprém	2 Jul
[30]								
1:46.23A	Tshepo	Tshite	RSA	15.1.97	1		Pretoria	13 Mar
1:46.24	Piers	Copeland	GBR	26.11.98	3		Göteborg	29 Aug
1:46.24	Filip	Sasínek	CZE	8.1.96	4		Göteborg	29 Aug
1:46.26	Lukás	Hodbod	CZE	2.3.96	5	Szew	Bydgoszcz	19 Aug
1:46.28	Mateusz	Borkowski	POL	2.4.97	7	Skol	Chorzów	6 Sep
1:46.29	Vincent	Crisp	USA	17.8.97	2		Alexandria, VA	1 Aug
1:46.3A	Edwin	Melly	KEN	23.4.94	1		Nairobi	5 Mar
1:46.31	Michal	Rozmys	POL	13.3.95	8	Skol	Chorzów	6 Sep
1:46.33	Thiago	André	BRA	4.8.95	1	NC	São Paulo	11 Dec
1:46.37	Baptiste	Mischler	FRA	23.11.97	1		Décines-Charpieu	29 Aug
[40]								
1:46.37	Konstantin	Kholmogorov	RUS	7.2.96	1	NC	Chelyabinsk	9 Sep
1:46.38A	Nicholas	Kipkoech ¶	KEN	22.10.92	6	Keino	Nairobi	3 Oct
1:46.41	Catalin	Tecueanu	ROU	9.9.99	3	Quercia	Rovereto	8 Sep
1:46.42	Quamel	Prince	GUY	20.4.94	2		Nashville	15 Aug
1:46.44	Jakob	Ingebrigtsen	NOR	19.9.00	1	Boysen	Oslo	30 Jun
[45]								

800 METRES

Mark	Name		Nat	Born		Pos	Meet	Venue		Date
1:46.52	Mason	Cohen	AUS	19.9.96	29 Feb	1:47.05	Jan	Fris	CZE	19.12.95	29 Aug
1:46.56	Robert	Downs	USA	17.8.94	15 Aug	1:47.10A	Peter	Kiptum	KEN	22.12.98	5 Mar
1:46.59A	Kabelo	Mohlosi	RSA	20.1.93	10 Mar	1:47.10	Eduardo	Romero	ESP	27.1.99	1 Aug
1:46.59	Jesús	Gómez	ESP	24.4.91	17 Aug	1:47.10	George	Mills	GBR	12.5.99	11 Aug
1:46.64	Dylan	Stenson	AUS	30.9.88	29 Feb	1:47.10	Pablo Sánchez-Valladares		ESP	12.11.97	24 Aug
1:46.64	Simone	Barontini	ITA	5.1.99	8 Sep	1:47.10	Craig	Engels	USA	1.5.94	29 Aug
1:46.67	Alex	Amankwah	GHA	2.3.92	22 Aug	1:47.1A	Noah	Kibet	KEN-Y	12.4.04	21 Nov
1:46.67	Jakub	Davidík	CZE-J	20.1.02	8 Sep	1:47.12	Guilherme	Kurtz	BRA	27.8.94	11 Dec
1:46.68	Renaud	Rosière	FRA	27.9.93	29 Aug	1:47.20	Sergey	Dubrovskiy	RUS	20.1.95	9 Sep
1:46.69	Josh	Kerr	GBR	8.10.97	21 Aug	1:47.24	Mariano	Garcia	ESP	25.9.97	10 Aug
1:46.74	Filip	Ingebrigtsen	NOR	20.4.93	30 Jun	1:47.27	Krzysztof	Róznicki	POL-Y	29.8.03	3 Jul
1:46.74	Javier	Mirón	ESP	13.12.99	24 Aug	1:47.28	Christoph	Kessler	GER	28.4.95	1 Aug
1:46.78	Joshua	Lay	GBR	11.4.00	21 Aug	1:47.28	Daichi	Setoguchi	JPN	4.8.98	13 Sep
1:46.78	Timothy	Cheruiyot	KEN	20.11.95	25 Sep	1:47.29	Leandro Alves Prates		BRA	4.8.98	11 Dec
1:46.81	Erik	Sowinski	USA	21.12.89	25 Sep	1:47.3A	Jackson	Kivuva	KEN	11.8.88	5 Mar
1:46.82	Alex	Botterill	GBR	18.1.00	21 Aug	1:47.30	Mikuto	Kaneko	JPN-J	6.11.01	23 Aug
1:46.86	Erik	Martinsson	SWE	25.9.96	10 Aug	1:47.30	Sho	Kawamoto	JPN	1.3.93	5 Sep
1:46.87	Eduardo	Moreira	BRA-J	9.1.01	11 Dec	1:47.32	Dennis	Biederbick	GER	9.8.97	1 Aug
1:46.93	Yusuf	Bizimana	GBR	6.9.00	15 Sep	1:47.39	Alexis	Miellet	FRA	5.5.95	29 Aug
1:46.94	Filip	Snejdr	CZE	16.4.95	19 Aug	1:47.41	Matheus	Pessoa	BRA	9.4.96	11 Dec
1:46.94	Andrés	Arroyo	PUR	7.6.95	6 Sep	1:47.42	Jackson	Lunn	AUS-J	16.10.01	22 Feb
1:46.96	Felix	Francois	SWE	8.11.90	16 Aug	1:47.42	Matthew	Scott	AUS	2.5.97	22 Feb
1:47.01	Gabriel	Aquaro	ITA	2.4.97	8 Sep	1:47.46	Djilali	Bedrani	FRA	1.10.93	29 Aug
1:47.02	Jun-ya	Matsumoto	JPN	28.9.00	13 Sep	1:47.49	Konstantin	Plokhotnikov	RUS	24.3.97	28 Aug
Indoors						[92]					
1:46.01	Isaiah	Harris		USA	18.10.96	3	Millrose	New York (A)			8 Feb
1:46.31	Mariano	Garcia		ESP	25.9.97	3		Madrid			21 Feb
1:46.38	Mostafa	Smaïli		MAR	9.1.97	1		Karlsruhe			31 Jan
1:46.60	Adrian	Ben		ESP	4.8.98	21 Feb	1:47.12	Isaiah	Jewett	USA	2.2.97	1 Feb
1:46.84	Andrew	Osagie		GBR	19.2.88	23 Feb	1:47.21	Robert	Farken	GER	20.9.97	2 Feb
1:47.01	Erik	Nzikwinkunda		BDI	18.3.97	7 Feb	1:47.26	Josh	Hoey	USA	1.11.99	1 Feb
1:47.01	Brannon	Kidder		USA	18.11.93	8 Feb	1:47.37	Johnny	Gregorek	USA	7.12.91	24 Sep
1:47.11	Colby	Alexander		USA	13.6.91	24 Feb	1:47.48	Tamás	Kazi	HUN	16.5.85	23 Feb

JUNIORS
2 in main list. 4 performances by 3 men to 1:46.80. Additional marks and further juniors:

Burgin	1:46.02	6	DL	Stockholm		23 Aug			
1:46.67	Jakub	Davidík		CZE	20.1.02	11	GS	Ostrava	8 Sep
1:46.87	Eduardo	Moreira		BRA	9.1.01	2	NC	São Paulo	11 Dec
1:47.1A	Noah	Kibet		KEN-Y	12.4.04	1h1		Nairobi	21 Nov
1:47.27	Krzysztof	Róznicki		POL-Y	29.8.03	1s1		Sopot	3 Jul
1:47.30	Mikuto	Kaneko		JPN	6.11.01	1		Tokyo	23 Aug
1:47.42	Jackson	Lunn		AUS	16.10.01	3		Sydney	22 Feb
1:47.85A	Edmund	Du Plessis		RSA	5.4.02	1		Pretoria	13 Mar

1000 METRES

2:16.46	Filip	Ingebrigtsen	NOR	20.4.93	1		Oslo		11 Jun
2:17.05	Filip	Sasínek	CZE	8.1.96	16 Aug	2:18.55	Jake	Heyward	GBR	26.4.99	17 Jul
2:17.29	Ignacio	Fontes	ESP	22.6.98	16 Aug	**Indoors**					
2:17.30	Michal	Rozmys	POL	13.3.95	16 Aug	2:17.41	Bryce	Hoppel	USA	5.9.97	25 Jan
2:17.60	Josh	Kerr	GBR	8.10.97	17 Jul	2:17.51	Jake	Wightman	GBR	11.7.94	25 Jan
2:18.15	Sam	Prakel	USA	29.10.94	17 Jul	2:18.01	Abraham	Alvarado	USA	4.8.95	11 Jan
2:18.44	Ismael	Debjani	BEL	25.9.90	9 Aug	2:18.36	Rob	Napolitano	USA	3.11.94	14 Feb
2:18.49	Vincent	Ciattei	USA	21.1.95	17 Jul	2:18.81	Saúl	Ordóñez	ESP	10.4.94	25 Jan

1500 METRES

3:28.45	Timothy	Cheruiyot	KEN	20.11.95	1	Herc	Monaco	14 Aug
3:28.68	Jakob	Ingebrigtsen	NOR	19.9.00	2	Herc	Monaco	14 Aug
3:29.47	Jake	Wightman	GBR	11.7.94	3	Herc	Monaco	14 Aug
3:30.25		Cheruiyot			1	DL	Stockholm	23 Aug
3:30.35	Filip	Ingebrigtsen	NOR	20.4.93	4	Herc	Monaco	14 Aug
3:30.51	Stewart	McSweyn	AUS	1.6.95	1	DL	Doha	25 Sep
3:30.69		J.Ingebrigtsen			1	VD	Bruxelles	4 Sep
3:30.74		J.Ingebrigtsen			2	DL	Stockholm	23 Aug
3:31.48		McSweyn			3	DL	Stockholm	23 Aug
3:32.17		McSweyn			1	Hanz	Zagreb	15 Sep
3:32.69	Yomif	Kejelcha	ETH	1.8.97	5	Herc	Monaco	14 Aug
3:32.97	Selemon	Barega	ETH	20.1.00	2	DL	Doha	25 Sep
3:33.07	Jesús	Gómez	ESP	24.4.91	6	Herc	Monaco	14 Aug
3:33.45	Soufiane	El Bakkali	MAR	7.1.96	3	DL	Doha	25 Sep
3:33.46		Gómez			4	DL	Stockholm	23 Aug
3:33.72	Ignacio	Fontes (10)	ESP	22.6.98	1		Castellón	24 Aug
3:33.77	Lamecha	Girma	ETH	26.11.00	4	DL	Doha	25 Sep
3:33.92		J.Ingebrigtsen			1	GS	Ostrava	8 Sep

1500 METRES

Mark	Name		Nat	Born	Pos	Meet	Venue	Date	
3:33.93		J.Ingebrigtsen			1	NC	Bergen	19	Sep
3:33.99	Marcin	Lewandowski	POL	13.6.87	7	Herc	Monaco	14	Aug
	[20/12]								
3:34.07	James	West	GBR	30.1.96	5	DL	Doha	25	Sep
3:34.14	Kumari	Taki	KEN	6.5.99	2	GS	Ostrava	8	Sep
3:34.53	Josh	Kerr	GBR	8.10.97	1		Newberg	31	Jul
3:34.63	Charlie	Da'Vall Grice	GBR	7.11.93	8	Herc	Monaco	14	Aug
3:34.63	Oliver	Hoare	AUS	29.1.97	1		Nashville	15	Aug
3:34.83	Matthew	Ramsden	AUS	23.7.97	3	Hanz	Zagreb	15	Sep
3:34.89	Mohammed	Ahmed	CAN	5.1.91	1		Portland	21	Jul
3:34.98	Saul	Ordóñez	ESP	10.4.94	2		Castellón	24	Sep
	[20]								
3:35.00	Pierrik	Jocteur-Monrozier	FRA	23.3.98	9	Herc	Monaco	14	Aug
3:35.02	Filip	Sasínek	CZE	8.1.96	4	GS	Ostrava	8	Sep
3:35.07	Elzan	Bibic	SRB	8.1.99	4	Hanz	Zagreb	15	Sep
3:35.22	Ryan	Gregson	AUS	26.4.90	5	Hanz	Zagreb	15	Sep
3:35.26	Yemaneberhan	Crippa	ITA	15.10.96	1		Rovereto	5	Aug
3:35.32	Piers	Copeland	GBR	26.11.98	8	DL	Doha	25	Sep
3:35.34	Kalle	Berglund	SWE	11.3.96	10	Herc	Monaco	14	Aug
3:35.42	Craig	Engels	USA	1.5.94	11	Herc	Monaco	14	Aug
3:35.43A	Abel	Kipsang	KEN	12.3.93	3	Keino	Nairobi	3	Oct
3:35.59	William	Paulson	CAN	17.11.94	2		Newberg	31	Jul
	[30]								
3:35.60	Adam Ali	Musaab	QAT	17.4.95	9	DL	Doha	25	Sep
3:35.85	Donavan	Brazier	USA	15.4.97	1		Portland	3	Jul
3:35.87	Azeddine	Habz	FRA	19.7.93	2		Marseille	3	Sep
3:35.90	Fernando	Carro	ESP	1.4.92	3		Castellón	24	Aug
3:35.93	Marc	Scott	GBR	21.12.93	2		Portland	21	Jul
3:35.98	Kevin	López	ESP	12.6.90	3		Marseille	3	Sep
3:36.01	Mike	Foppen	NED	29.11.96	9	GS	Ostrava	8	Sep
3:36.04	Jimmy	Gressier	FRA	4.5.97	10	GS	Ostrava	8	Sep
3:36.11	Johnny	Gregorek	USA	7.12.91	1		Bethel, CT	13	Sep
3:36.14	Quentin	Tison	FRA	16.4.96	1		Pontoise	19	Sep
	[40]								
3:36.23	Grant	Fisher	USA	22.4.97	3		Portland	21	Jul
3:36.31	Evan	Jager	USA	8.3.89	4		Portland	21	Jul
3:36.35	Vincent	Ciattei	USA	21.1.95	4		Newberg	31	Jul
3:36.39	Baptiste	Mischler	FRA	23.11.97	5		Marseille	3	Sep
3:36.54	Sam	Prakel	USA	29.10.94	2		Nashville	15	Aug
3:36.59	Mohamed	Katir	ESP	17.2.98	4		Castellón	24	Jul
3:36.67	Bethwel	Birgen	KEN	6.8.88	10	DL	Doha	25	Sep
3:36.7+	João	Bussotti Neves	ITA	10.5.93	4		San Donato Milanese	5	Sep
3:36.72	George	Mills	GBR	12.5.99	6	Hanz	Zagreb	15	Sep
3:36.83	Tripp	Hurt	USA	30.10.92	3		Nashville	15	Aug
	[50]								
3:36.92	Joshua	Lay	GBR	11.4.00	5		Bellinzona	15	Sep
3:36.95	Nassim	Hassaous	ESP	23.3.94	5		Castellón	24	Aug
3:36.97	Boaz	Kiprugut	KEN	18.5.98	2	NA	Heusden-Zolder	6	Sep
3:37.12	Sean	McGorty	USA	8.3.95	5		Portland	21	Jul
3:37.12	Colby	Alexander	USA	13.6.91	2		Bethel, CT	13	Sep
3:37.13	Salim	Keddar	ALG	23.11.93	3		Pontoise	19	Sep
3:37.15	Hamza	Driouch	QAT	16.11.94	11	DL	Doha	25	Sep
3:37.16	Willy	Fink	USA	7.3.94	4		Nashville	15	Aug
3:37.20	Matt	Hughes	CAN	3.8.89	8	Hanz	Zagreb	15	Sep
3:37.36	Woody	Kincaid	USA	21.9.92	6		Portland	21	Jul
	[60]								
3:37.42	Morgan	McDonald	AUS	23.4.96	5		Nashville	15	Aug
3:37.43	Mahadi	Abdi Ali	NED	8.11.95	4	NA	Heusden-Zolder	6	Sep
3:37.46	Jonas	Raess	SUI	8.3.94	6		Bellinzona	15	Sep
3:37.55	Joe	Klecker	USA	16.11.96	6		Nashville	15	Aug
3:37.56	Johan	Rogestedt	SWE	27.1.93	9	Hanz	Zagreb	15	Sep
3:37.59A	Vincent	Keter	KEN-J	11.3.02	4	Keino	Nairobi	3	Oct
3:37.60	Isaac	Kimeli	BEL	9.3.94	5	NA	Heusden-Zolder	6	Sep
3:37.64	Graham	Crawford	USA	29.12.92	7		Nashville	15	Aug
3:37.70	Yani	Khelaf	FRA	7.2.98	8		Marseille	3	Sep
3:37.84	Tom	Elmer	SUI	1.4.97	7		Bellinzona	15	Sep
	[70]								
3:37.89	Ismael	Debjani	BEL	25.9.90	1		Nivelles	7	Aug
3:37.93	David	Bustos	ESP	25.8.90	6	NA	Heusden-Zolder	6	Sep
3:38.01	Simas	Bertasius	LTU	31.10.93	4		Poznan	11	Sep
3:38.03	Djilali	Bedrani	FRA	1.10.93	2		Tournefeuille	8	Aug

1500 METRES – 1 MILE

Mark	Name		Nat	Born	Pos	Meet	Venue		Date
3:38.04	Marc	Tortell	GER	26.12.97	6		Castellón		24 Aug
3:38.04	Samuel	Tanner	NZL	24.8.00	1		Wanganui		1 Dec
3:38.15	Tim	Van De Velde	BEL	1.2.00	7	NA	Heusden-Zolder		6 Sep
3:38.16	Ryan	Hill	USA	31.1.90	7		Portland		21 Jul
3:38.26	Paul	Robinson	IRL	24.5.91	10	Hanz	Zagreb		15 Sep
3:38.27	Vincent [80]	Kibet	KEN	6.5.91	13	DL	Doha		25 Sep
3:38.29	Marius	Probst	GER	20.8.95	6 Sep				
3:38.30	Neil	Gourley	GBR	7.2.95	23 Aug				
3:38.33	Ronald	Kwemoi	KEN	19.9.95	4 Jul				
3:38.48	Rob	Napolitano	USA	3.11.94	13 Jan				
3:38.53	Yassin	Bouih	ITA	24.11.96	15 Sep				
3:38.69	Mikael	Johnsen	DEN	4.2.92	6 Sep				
3:38.69	Adam	Kszczot	POL	2.9.89	11 Sep				
3:38.70	Henry	Wynne	USA	18.4.95	31 Jul				
3:38.73	Hugo	Hay	FRA	28.3.97	6 Sep				
3:38.83	Mohamed	Mohumed	GER	24.3.99	19 Jul				
3:38.84	Abderrahman	El Khayami	ESP	11.8.95	24 Aug				
3:38.87	Mehdi	Belhadj	FRA	10.6.95	3 Sep				
3:38.88	Topi	Raitanen	FIN	7.2.96	1 Aug				
3:38.90	Mohad Abdikadar Sheikh Ali		ITA	12.6.93	15 Sep				
3:38.92	Sergio	Paniagua	ESP	26.10.95	24 Aug				
3:38.94	Michal	Rozmys	POL	13.3.95	8 Sep				
3:39.04	Jake	Heyward	GBR	26.4.99	31 Jul				
3:39.05	Jan	Fris	CZE	19.12.95	9 Aug				
3:39.15	Narve Gilje	Nordås	NOR	30.9.98	3 Sep				
3:39.19	David [100]	Nikolli	ALB	20.6.94	5 Aug				
3:39.23	Justus	Soget	KEN	22.10.99	4 Jul				
3:39.24	Thiago	André	BRA	4.8.95	13 Dec				
3:39.38	Enrique	Herreros	ESP	15.9.99	24 Aug				
3:39.40	István	Szögi	HUN	12.9.95	25 Jul				
3:39.61	Ahmed	Abdelwahed	ITA	26.5.96	8 Sep				
3:39.66	Josh	Thompson	USA	9.5.93	30 Jun				
3:39.66	Lopez	Lomong	USA	1.1.85	30 Jun				
3:39.66	Maximilan	Thorwirth	GER	9.1.95	25 Jul				
3:39.67	Kristian Uldbjerg	Hansen	DEN	15.8.96	29 Aug				
3:39.68	Benjamin	Rubio	FRA	15.4.91	29 Aug				
3:39.69	Mats	Hauge	NOR	16.7.97	3 Sep				
3:39.70	Karl	Bebendorf	GER	7.5.96	25 Jul				
3:39.70	Stijn	Baeten	BEL	3.6.94	15 Aug				
3:39.90	Jonathan	Davies	GBR	28.10.94	15 Sep				
3:39.97	Isaac	Nader	POR	17.8.99	24 Aug				
3:40.03	Dillon	Maggard	USA	16.10.95	15 Aug				
3:40.08	Emil	Danielsson	SWE	5.9.97	23 Aug				
3:40.1+	Pietro	Riva	ITA	1.5.97	5 Sep				
3:40.12	Suldan	Hassan	SWE	1.4.98	8 Jul				
3:40.24	Eric	Avila	USA	3.10.89	21 Aug				
3:40.28	Cameron	Griffith	AUS	31.8.96	15 Aug				

Indoors

Mark	Name		Nat	Born	Pos	Venue		Date
3:34.77	Josh	Thompson	USA	9.5.93	1	Boston (A)		27 Feb
3:35.54	Samuel	Tefera	ETH	23.10.99	1	Liévin		19 Feb
3:36.13	Justyn	Knight	CAN	19.7.96	1	Boston (A)		28 Feb
3:36.22	Bethwel	Birgen	KEN	6.8.88	1	Glasgow		15 Feb
3:36.40	Chris	O'Hare	GBR	23.11.90	2	Boston (A)		28 Feb
3:36.51	Brannon	Kidder	USA	18.11.93	1	Boston (A)		27 Feb
3:36.82	Abraham	Alvarado	USA	4.8.95	3	Boston (A)		27 Feb
3:37.81	Izaic	Yorks	USA	17.4.94	3	Boston (A)		28 Feb
3:37.98	Andrew	Coscoran	IRL	18.6.96	3	Boston (A)		1 Feb
3:38.03	Rob	Napolitano	USA	3.11.94	4	Boston (A)		28 Feb
3:38.30	Eric	Avila	USA	3.10.89	28 Feb			
3:38.55	Kebede	Endale	ETH	22.6.00	14 Feb			
3:39.13	Thiago	André	BRA	4.8.95	8 Feb			
3:39.51	Nanami	Arai	JPN	26.12.94	27 Feb			

JUNIORS

Mark	Name		Nat	Born	Pos	Meet	Venue		Date
3:37.59A	Vincent	Keter	KEN	11.3.02	4	Keino	Nairobi		3 Oct
3:37.95i	1	Metz				9 Feb			
3:40.73	Jakub	Davidík	CZE	20.1.02	5		Kladno		16 Sep
3:40.9A	Melese	Nberet	ETH	20.1.01	2		Addis Ababa		6 Dec
3:41.90	Mos Aboynnachat	Bollerød	NOR	2.11.01	8		Kuortane		1 Aug
3:42.16	Henry	McLucjie	GBR	3.5.02	3		London (BP)		15 Sep
3:42.47	Sven	Wagner	GER	20.12.01	5		Pfungstadt		1 Aug
3:42.60	Pol	Oriach	ESP	20.9.02	2		Gavà		29 Jul

Indoors

| 3:41.44 | Thomas | Keen | GBR | 16.6.01 | 3 | Wien | 1 Feb |
| 3:42.21 | Kazuto | Iizawa | JPN | 2.2.01 | 5rB | Boston (A) | 28 Feb |

1 MILE

Mark	Name		Nat	Born	Pos	Venue		Date
3:50.61	Stewart	McSweyn	AUS	1.6.95	1	Penguin		29 Dec
3:51.23	Matthew	Ramsden	AUS	23.7.97	1	San Donato Milanese		5 Sep
3:52.08	Yemaneberhan	Crippa	ITA	15.10.96	2	San Donato Milanese		5 Sep
3:52.38	Ryan	Gregson	AUS	26.4.90	3	San Donato Milanese		5 Sep
3:53.35	Oliver	Hoare	AUS	29.1.97	1	Columbia, SC		29 Aug
3:56.18	Tripp	Hurt	USA	30.10.92	25 Jul			
3:56.62	Narve Gilje	Nordås	NOR	30.9.98	12 Aug			
3:56.87	Osama	Zoghlami	ITA	19.6.94	5 Sep			
3:57.11	Nick	Harris	USA	31.5.94	25 Jul			
3:57.25	Mats	Hauge (10)	NOR	16.7.97	12 Aug			
3:57.30	Jye	Edwards	AUS	6.3.98	19 Dec			
3:57.38	Jacob	Boutera	NOR	29.4.96	12 Aug			
3:57.54	João	Bussotti Neves	ITA	10.5.93	5 Sep			
3:57.86	Colby	Alexander	USA	13.6.91	2 Oct			
3:57.87	Kieran	Tuntivate	THA	16.2.97	15 Aug			
3:57.90 [16]	Pietro	Riva	ITA	1.5.97	5 Sep			

Indoors

3:55.41	Charles	Hunter	AUS	20.7.96		Boston (A)	28 Feb
3:55.50	Cooper	Teare	USA	18.8.99	2	Boston (A)	28 Feb
3:55.61	Chris	O'Hare	GBR	23.11.90	1	Millrose	New York (A)	8 Feb
3:55.62#	Yared	Nuguse	USA	1.6.99	1	ACC	Notre Dame	29 Feb
3:55.86	Samuel	Tefera	ETH	23.10.99	1	Athlone	12 Feb

1M - 2000 - 3000 METRES

Mark	Name		Nat	Born	Pos	Meet	Venue		Date
3:56.50#	Evan	Jager	USA	8.3.89	1		Feb		1 Feb
3:56.56	Rob	Napolitano	USA	3.11.94	8	Feb	3:57.19#	Sean	McGorty USA 8.3.95 1 Feb
3:56.72	Nick	Willis	NZL	25.4.83	8	Feb	3:57.36	Kieran	Tuntivate THA 16.2.97 15 Feb
3:56.77	José Carlos	Villareal	MEX	10.5.97	8	Feb	3:57.43#	James	West GBR 30.1.96 15 Feb
3:56.85	Craig	Engels	USA	1.5.94	25	Jan	3:57.66#	Ryan	Adams USA 25.7.96 18 Jan
3:56.85	Andrew	Coscoran	IRL	18.6.96	25	Jan	3:57.66	Sam	Ellis USA 20.10.98 15 Feb
3:56.90	George	Beamish	NZL	24.10.96	8	Feb	3:57.67#	Ben	Blankenship USA 15.12.88 18 Jan
3:56.99	Filip	Ingebrigtsen	NOR	20.4.93	8	Feb	3:57.81	Sam	Prakel USA 29.10.94 8 Feb
3:57.03#	Waleed	Suliman	USA	22.9.98	18	Jan	3:57.88	Mick	Stanovsek AUS 16.1.97 28 Feb
3:57.03	Eric	Jenkins	USA	24.11.91	8	Feb	3:57.93#	George	Kusche RSA 6.8.98 1 Feb
							3:57.93	Matthew	Centrowitz USA 18.10.89 28 Feb

JUNIORS

3:59.54	Leo	Daschbach	USA	4.10.01	1		El Dorado Hills	23 May
3:58.20i	Cole	Hooker	USA	6.6.01	5		Boston (A)	28 Feb

2000 METRES

Mark	Name		Nat	Born	Pos	Meet	Venue	Date
4:50.01	Jakob	Ingebrigtsen	NOR	19.9.00	1		Oslo	11 Jun
4:53.72	Henrik	Ingebrigtsen	NOR	24.2.91	2		Oslo	11 Jun
4:55.44	Matthew	Ramsden	AUS	23.7.97	1	Szew	Bydgoszcz	19 Aug
4:56.91	Filip	Ingebrigtsen	NOR	20.4.93	3		Oslo	11 Jun
4:57.09	Marcin	Lewandowski	POL	13.6.87	2	Szew	Bydgoszcz	19 Aug
4:57.60	Filip	Sasínek	CZE	8.1.96	3	Szew	Bydgoszcz	19 Aug
4:57.61	Piers	Copeland	GBR	26.11.98	4	Szew	Bydgoszcz	19 Aug
4:57.87	Lamecha	Girma	ETH	26.11.00	5	Szew	Bydgoszcz	19 Aug
4:57.98	Michal	Rozmys	POL	13.3.95	6	Szew	Bydgoszcz	19 Aug
4:58.26	Getnet	Wale	ETH	16.7.00	7	Szew	Bydgoszcz	19 Aug
4:58.92	Mike	Foppen	NED	29.11.96	1		Bern	24 Jul
4:59.47+	Stewart	McSweyn	AUS	1.6.95	1	in 3000	Roma	17 Sep
4:59.7+	Jacob	Kiplimo	UGA	14.11.00	2	in 3000	Roma	17 Sep
4:59.71	Kalle	Berglund	SWE	11.3.96	1		Sollentuna	10 Aug
5:00.23	Andreas	Almgren	SWE	12.6.95	2		Sollentuna	10 Aug
5:00.47	Jonas	Raess	SUI	8.3.94	2		Bern	24 Jul
5:00.53	Robin	Hendrix	BEL	14.1.95	3		Bern	24 Jul
5:00.72	Mohamed	Ahmed	CAN	5.1.91	8 Aug	5:01.75	Hugo	Hay FRA 28.3.97 24 Jul
5:00.73	Neil	Gourley	GBR	7.2.95	10 Aug	5:02.0+e	Yemaneberhan	Crippa ITA 15.10.96 17 Sep
5:01.32	Tom	Elmer	SUI	1.4.97	24 Jul	5:02.31	Matt	Hughes CAN 3.8.89 10 Aug

3000 METRES

Mark	Name		Nat	Born	Pos	Meet	Venue	Date
7:26.64	Jacob	Kiplimo	UGA	14.11.00	1	G Gala	Roma	17 Sep
7:27.05	Jakob	Ingebrigtsen	NOR	19.9.00	2	G Gala	Roma	17 Sep
7:28.02	Stewart	McSweyn	AUS	1.6.95	3	G Gala	Roma	17 Sep
7:35.2+	Joshua	Cheptegei	UGA	12.9.96	1	Herc	Monaco	14 Aug
7:38.27	Yemaneberhan	Crippa	ITA	15.10.96	4	G Gala	Roma	17 Sep
7:39.75	Mike	Foppen	NED	29.11.96	5	G Gala	Roma	17 Sep
7:40.62	Ouassim	Oumaiz	ESP	30.3.99	1		Barcelona (S)	22 Sep
7:41.54+	Selemon	Barega	ETH	20.1.00	1	in 5000	Ostrava	8 Sep
7:42.5+	Lamecha	Girma	ETH	26.11.00	2	in 5000	Ostrava	8 Sep
7:43.18	Elzan	Bibic	SRB	8.1.99	2		Barcelona (S)	22 Sep
(10)								
7:43.48	Marc	Scott	GBR	21.12.93	1		Bromley	21 Aug
7:43.79	James	West	GBR	30.1.96	2		Bromley	21 Aug
7:44.13	Mohamed	Katir	ESP	17.2.98	3		Barcelona (S)	22 Sep
7:45.24	Abdessamad	Oukhefen	ESP	18.12.98	4		Barcelona (S)	22 Sep
7:45.46	Sean	Tobin	IRL	20.7.94	5		Barcelona (S)	22 Sep
7:45.75	Jonathan	Davies	GBR	28.10.94	3		Bromley	21 Aug
7:45.81	Alexander	Yee	GBR	18.2.98	4		Bromley	21 Aug
7:45.90	Nassim	Hassaous	ESP	23.3.94	6		Barcelona	22 Jul
7:46.10+	Grant	Fisher	USA	22.4.97	1		Portland	10 Jul
7:46.31+	Evan	Jager	USA	8.3.89	2		Portland	10 Jul
(20)								
7:46.48+	Sean	McGorty	USA	8.3.95	3		Portland	10 Jul
7:46.64+	Mohammed	Ahmed	CAN	5.1.91	4		Portland	10 Jul
7:46.86+	Lopez	Lomong	USA	1.1.85	5		Portland	10 Jul
7:47.04+	Woody	Kincaid	USA	21.9.92	6		Portland	10 Jul
7:47.48	Isaac	Kimeli	BEL	9.3.94	6	G Gala	Roma	17 Sep
7:48.08	Matthew	Ramsden	AUS	23.7.97	17 Sep	7:50.03	Pietro	Riva ITA 1.5.97 17 Sep
7:48.63	Osama	Zoglami	ITA	19.6.94	17 Sep	7:50.13	Ben	Blankenship USA 15.12.88 21 Aug
7:49.03	Dan	Kiplangat	KEN	4.6.96	4 Jul	7:50.57	Narve Gilje	Nordås NOR 30.9.98 29 Jul
7:49.90	Hyuga	Endo	JPN	5.8.98	4 Jul	7:50.72	Eric	Jenkins USA 24.11.91 7 Sep
						7:51.61	Zach	Facioni AUS 3.4.99 21 Nov

Indoors

7:32.80	Getnet	Wale	ETH	16.7.00	1		Liévin	19 Feb
7:33.19	Selemon	Barega	ETH	20.1.00	2		Liévin	19 Feb

MEN 2020

3000 METRES

Mark	Name		Nat	Born	Pos	Meet	Venue	Date	
7:34.58	Birhanu	Yemataw	BRN	27.2.96	3		Liévin	19	Feb
7:34.94	Lamecha	Girma	ETH	26.11.00	4		Liévin	19	Feb
7:35.78	Berihu	Aregawi	ETH-J	28.2.01	5		Liévin	19	Feb
7:36.21	Bethwel	Birgen	KEN	6.8.88	3		Düsseldorf	4	Feb
7:37.74	Lopez	Lomong	USA	1.1.85	1		Boston (A)	27	Feb
7:38.03	Ryan	Hill	USA	31.1.90	2		Boston (A)	27	Feb
7:38.25	Evan	Jager	USA	8.3.89	3		Boston (A)	27	Feb
7:38.85	Tilahun	Haile	ETH	13.5.99	6		Liévin	19	Feb
7:39.94	Vladimir	Nikitin	RUS	5.8.92	1		Moskva	9	Feb
7:39.99	Grant	Fisher	USA	22.4.97	4		Boston (A)	27	Feb
7:40.25	Davis	Kiplangat	KEN	10.7.98	5		Düsseldorf	4	Feb
7:41.31	Justus	Soget	KEN	22.10.99	3		Karlsruhe	31	Jan
7:41.40	Djilali	Bedrani	FRA	1.10.93	7		Liévin	19	Feb
7:41.94	Travis	Mahoney	USA	25.7.90	5		Boston (A)	27	Feb
7:43.73	Luis	Grijalva	GUA	10.4.99	1		Boston (A)	15	Feb
7:44.21	Willy	Fink	USA	7.3.94	1		Boston (A)	1	Feb
7:44.31	Daniel	Estrada	MEX	30.5.93	2		Boston (A)	15	Feb
7:44.67	George	Beamish	NZL	24.10.96	3		Boston (A)	15	Feb
7:45.08	Adel	Mechaal	ESP	5.12.90	8		Madrid	21	Feb
7:45.50	Kieran	Lumb	CAN	2.8.98	4		Boston (A)	15	Feb
7:45.67	Jonas	Raess	SUI	8.3.94	6		Düsseldorf	4	Feb
7:45.70	Tyler	Day	USA	18.12.96	5		Boston (A)	15	Feb
7:45.87	Abraham	Seme	ETH-J	7.11.01	8		Liévin	19	Feb
7:46.30	Graham	Crawford	USA	29.12.92	7		Boston (A)	15	Feb
7:46.32	Soufiyan	Bouqantar	MAR	30.8.93	9		Liévin	19	Feb
7:46.36	Justyn	Knight	CAN	19.7.96	1	Millrose	New York (A)	8	Feb
7:46.45#	Cooper	Teare	USA	18.8.99	4		Seattle	14	Feb
7:46.71#	Yared	Nuguse	USA	1.6.99	1		Notre Dame	8	Feb
7:46.74	Edward	Cheserek	KEN	2.2.94	2	GP	Boston (R)	25	Jan
7:47.37	Ben	Flanagan	CAN	11.1.95	8		Boston (A)	15	Feb
7:47.57	Joe	Klecker	USA	16.11.96	2	Millrose	New York (A)	8	Feb
7:47.85	Matt	Baxter	NZL	6.8.94	9		Boston (A)	15	Feb
7:47.93	Isaac	Updike	USA	21.3.92	10		Boston (A)	15	Feb
7:47.99#	Hyuga	Endo	JPN	5.8.98	7		Seattle	14	Feb

Mark	First	Last	Nat	Born	Pos	Date		Mark	First	Last	Nat	Born	Pos	Date	
7:48.17	Jordan	Gusman	MLT	30.1.94	8	Feb		7:50.22	Kyle	Mau	USA	27.8.96	14	Feb	
7:48.34	Andreas	Almgren	SWE	12.6.95	22	Feb		7:50.37	Paul	Chelimo	USA	27.10.90	8	Feb	
7:48.44	Mason	Ferlic	USA	5.8.93	14	Feb		7:50.61	Maximilan	Thorwirth	GER	9.1.95	4	Feb	
7:48.54	Jimmy	Gressier	FRA	4.5.97	19	Feb		7:50.64	Marcel	Fehr	GER	20.6.92	4	Feb	
7:48.57	John	Gay	CAN	7.11.96	14	Feb		7:50.80#	Cameron	Griffith	AUS	31.8.96	14	Feb	
7:48.73	Hillary	Bor	USA	22.11.89	8	Feb		7:50.90	Jordan	Mann	USA	12.1.93	8	Feb	
7:49.01#	Alexander	Ostberg	USA	15.2.97	14	Feb		7:50.93	George	Kusche	RSA	6.8.98	8	Feb	
7:49.15	Kieran	Tuntivate	THA	16.2.97	1	Feb		7:51.00#	Jack	Rowe	GBR	30.1.96	14	Feb	
7:49.19	Edwin	Kurgat	KEN	.96	8	Feb		7:51.13	Benjamin	Kigen	KEN	5.7.93	21	Feb	
7:49.45	Ryan	Adams	USA	25.7.96	25	Jan		7:51.17	Andreas	Vojta	AUT	9.6.89	21	Feb	
7:49.55	Andrew	Bayer	USA	3.2.90	14	Feb		7:51.29	Robin	Hendrix	BEL	14.1.95	16	Feb	
7:49.65	Eric	Avila	USA	3.10.89	8	Feb		7:51.30	Rabie	Doukkana	FRA	6.12.87	19	Feb	
7:49.65	Luc	Bruchet	CAN	23.2.91	14	Feb		7:51.57	Ari	Klau	USA	.97	15	Feb	
7:49.67	Chala	Beyo	ETH	18.1.96	19	Feb		7:51.59	Wesley	Kiptoo	KEN		8	Feb	
7:49.82	Carlos	Mayo	ESP	18.9.95	24	Jan		7:51.78	Paul	Tanui	KEN	22.12.90	8	Feb	
7:50.00	Jacob	Thomson	USA	29.11.94	25	Jan		7:51.79	Dillon	Maggard	USA	16.10.95	8	Feb	

JUNIORS

Mark	Name		Nat	Born	Pos	Venue	Date	
8:00.2A	Gideon	Rono	KEN-Y	22.2.03	1	Nairobi	22	Mar
8:00.5A	Enmmanuel	Kiplagat	KEN		2	Nairobi	22	Mar

Indoors 2 in main list, 4 performances by 2 men to 7:54.0

Aregawi	7:36.85	1		Metz		9 Feb		
Seme	7:50.59	9		Madrid		21 Feb		
7:54.43	Anas	Essayi	MAR	18.3.01	2	Mondeville	1	Feb
7:56.97	Nico	Young	USA	27.7.02	11	Millrose	New York (A)	8 Feb

5000 METRES

Mark	Name		Nat	Born	Pos	Meet	Venue	Date	
12:35.36	Joshua	Cheptegei	UGA	12.9.96	1	Herc	Monaco	14	Aug
12:47.20	Mohammed	Ahmed	CAN	5.1.91	1		Portland	10	Jul
12:48.63	Jacob	Kiplimo	UGA	14.11.00	1	GS	Ostrava	8	Sep
12:49.08	Selemon	Barega	ETH	20.1.00	2	GS	Ostrava	8	Sep
12:51.78	Nicholas	Kimeli	KEN	29.9.98	2	Herc	Monaco	14	Aug
12:58.78	Lopez	Lomong	USA	1.1.85	2		Portland	10	Jul
13:02.26	Yemaneberhan	Crippa	ITA	15.10.96	3	GS	Ostrava	8	Sep
13:07.73 +		Kimeli			1		Valencia	7	Oct
13:08.32A		Kimeli			1	Keino	Nairobi	3	Oct
13:08.91A	Berihu	Aregawi	ETH-J	28.2.01	2	Keino	Nairobi	3	Oct
13:09.83	Stewart	McSweyn	AUS	1.6.95	1		Göteborg	29	Aug
[11/9]									

5000 METRES

Mark	Name		Nat	Born	Pos	Meet	Venue	Date	
13:10.64	Jonathan	Ndiku (10)	KEN	18.9.91	1		Kumagaya	20	Sep
13:11.10	Benard	Koech	KEN	25.11.99	2		Kumagaya	20	Sep
13:11.22	Sean	McGorty	USA	8.3.95	1		Portland	30	Jun
13:11.32	Jacob	Krop	KEN-J	4.6.01	3	Herc	Monaco	14	Aug
13:11.68	Grant	Fisher	USA	22.4.97	2		Portland	30	Jun
13:12.12	Evan	Jager	USA	8.3.89	3		Portland	30	Jun
13:12.84	Yomif	Kejelcha	ETH	1.8.97	1	FBK	Hengelo	10	Oct
13:13.06	Mike	Foppen	NED	29.11.96	4	Herc	Monaco	14	Aug
13:13.14	Ouassim	Oumaiz	ESP	30.3.99	5	Herc	Monaco	14	Aug
13:15.28	Ryan	Hill	USA	31.1.90	4		Portland	30	Jun
13:15.77	Jimmy [20]	Gressier	FRA	4.5.97	7	Herc	Monaco	14	Aug
13:15.83	Justus	Soget	KEN	22.10.99	1		Konosu	24	Oct
13:16.61	Benard	Kimeli	KEN	10.9.95	1		Fukagawa	8	Jul
13:16.63	Matthew	Ramsden	AUS	23.7.97	2		Göteborg	29	Aug
13:16.75	Luis	Grijalva	GUA	10.4.99	1		San Juan Capistrano	4	Dec
13:17.13	Cooper	Teare	USA	18.8.99	2		San Juan Capistrano	4	Dec
13:17.40	Titus	Wambua	KEN	14.8.97	1		Chitose	18	Jul
13:17.55	Drew	Hunter	USA	5.9.97	3		San Juan Capistrano.	4	Dec
13:17.95	Abdessamad	Oukhelfen	ESP	18.12.98	5	GS	Ostrava	8	Sep
13:18.01	Suldan	Hassan	SWE	1.4.98	3		Göteborg	29	Aug
13:18.49	Yuta [30]	Bando	JPN	21.11.96	1	NC	Osaka	4	Dec
13:18.57	Sam	Atkin	GBR	14.3.93	4		San Juan Capistrano	4	Dec
13:18.68	Eric	Avila	USA	3.10.89	5		San Juan Capistrano	4	Dec
13:18.76	Richard	Yator	KEN	6.4.98	3		Fukagawa	8	Jul
13:18.99	Hyuga	Endo	JPN	5.8.98	2		Chitose	18	Jul
13:19.10	Ronald	Kwemoi	KEN	19.9.95	2		Konosu	24	Oct
13:19.65	Henrik	Ingebrigtsen	NOR	24.2.91	1	Boysen	Oslo	29	Jun
13:20.08	Jonas	Raess	SUI	8.3.94	4		Göteborg	29	Aug
13:20.39	Vincent	Yegon	KEN	5.12.00	2		Abashiri	15	Jul
13:21.22	Wesley	Ledama	KEN	2.7.99	3		Chitose	18	Jul
13:21.39	Amos [40]	Kurgat	KEN	7.3.92	3	JPN Ch	Osaka	4	Dec
13:21.59	Victor	Korir	KEN-J	21.3.02	4		Chitose	18	Jul
13:21.78	Edward	Cheserek	KEN	2.2.94	1		Van Nuys	22	Aug
13:22.40	Anthony	Maina	KEN-Y	27.3.03	4		Fukagawa	8	Jul
13:22.42	Dominic	Lagat	KEN	15.5.98	3		Kumagaya	20	Sep
13:22.44	Charles	Philibert-Thiboutot	CAN	31.12.90	6		San Juan Capistrano	4	Dec
13:22.58	Jackson Kavesa	Muema	KEN-J	3.9.01	5		Fukagawa	8	Jul
13:23.52	Evans	Keitany	KEN	27.11.99	6		Fukagawa	8	Jul
13:23.71	Mohamed	Mohumed	GER	24.3.99	1	NA	Heusden-Zolder	6	Sep
13:23.97	Per	Svela	NOR	19.3.92	8	Herc	Monaco	14	Aug
13:23.99	Samuel [50]	Masai	KEN-J	20.3.01	1		Machida	3	Oct
13:24.03	Andreas	Vojta	AUT	9.6.89	6	GS	Ostrava	8	Sep
13:24.13	Saïd	El Otmani	ITA	14.10.91	7	GS	Ostrava	8	Sep
13:24.29	Hiroki	Matsueda	JPN	20.5.93	5		Chitose	18	Jul
13:24.54	Matthew	Kimeli	KEN	4.1.98	3	FBK	Hengelo	10	Oct
13:25.06	Ryan	Gregson	AUS	26.4.90	5		Göteborg	29	Aug
13:25.28	Alex	Cherono	KEN	30.12.00	1		Toyota	26	Sep
13:25.29	Benuel	Mogeni	KEN-J	11.3.01	5		Kumagaya	20	Sep
13:25.52	Robin	Hendrix	BEL	14.1.95	2	NA	Heusden-Zolder	6	Sep
13:25.65	Charles	Wanjiku	KEN	16.5.00	2		Yokohama	6	Dec
13:25.76	Andrew [60]	Lorot	KEN	2.12.97	3		Konosu	24	Oct
13:25.87	Yamato	Yoshii	JPN-J	14.2.02	6	NC	Osaka	4	Dec
13:26.56	Elzan	Bibic	SRB	8.1.99	8	GS	Ostrava	8	Sep
13:26.70	Muthoni	Muiru	KEN	27.3.98	3		Yokohama	6	Dec
13:26.85	Thierry	Ndikumwenayo	BDI	26.3.97	1		Castellón	24	Aug
13:26.92	Simon	Saidimu	KEN	12.10.00	4		Konosu	24	Oct
13:26.96	Charles	Karanja	KEN	8.11.00	4		Yokohama	6	Dec
13:27.34	Taku	Fujimoto	JPN	11.9.99	2		Toyota	26	Sep
13:27.37	Cleophas	Kandie	KEN	14.8.00	3		Shibetsu	4	Jul
13:27.47	Hugo	Hay	FRA	28.3.97	6		Göteborg	29	Aug
13:27.84A	Samuel [70]	Kibet	UGA-J	23.9.01	4	Keino	Nairobi	3	Oct

13:28.30	Shu	Hasegawa	JPN	25.11.97	15 Jul	13:28.98	Joe	Klecker	USA	16.11.96	22 Aug
13:28.33	Oliver	Hoare	AUS	29.1.97	22 Aug	13:29.34	Kiprono	Sitonik	KEN-J	10.11.01	15 Nov
13:28.59	Evans	Yego	KEN	5.9.95	3 Oct	13:29.59	Emil Millán	de la Oliva	SWE-J	24.7.01	29 Aug
13:28.70	Shoya	Kawase	JPN	9.7.98	4 Dec	13:30.15	Alexander	Mutiso	KEN	10.9.96	8 Jul

5000 - 10,000 METRES

Mark	Name		Nat	Born	Pos	Meet	Venue	Date
13:30.41	Yuhei	Urano	JPN	1.11.97				20 Sep
13:30.52	Samson	Ndirangu	KEN	14.5.94				15 Nov
13:30.65	Matt	Hughes	CAN	3.8.89				29 Aug
13:30.79	David	Ngure	KEN	10.8.98				18 Jul
13:31.24	Jonathan	Davies	GBR	28.10.94				29 Aug
13:31.50	Aras	Kaya	TUR	4.4.94				4 Sep
13:31.84	Eric	Speakman	NZL	29.8.90				18 Dec
13:32.11	Fernando	Carro	ESP	1.4.92				4 Jul
13:32.41	Sam	Parsons	GER	18.6.94				4 Dec
13:32.5A	Robert Kiprop	Koech	KEN	25.2.97				5 Mar
13:32.92	Matthew	Centrowitz	USA	18.10.89				4 Dec
13:32.95	Cole	Hocker	USA-J	6.6.01				4 Dec
13:32.98	Marc	Scott	GBR	21.12.93				5 Dec
13:32.99	Luc	Bruchet	CAN	23.2.91				5 Dec
13:33.1A	Emmanuel	Kiprop	KEN	21.8.99				5 Mar
13:33.15	José Ignacio	Gimenez	ESP	7.1.95				6 Sep
13:33.39	Narve Gilje	Nordås	NOR	30.9.98				29 Jun
13:33.40	Emmanuel	Kipchirchir	KEN-Y	27.11.03				12 Sep
13:33.43	Brian	Barraza	USA	16.5.95				4 Dec
13:33.5A	Gideon	Rono	KEN-Y	22.2.03				20 Nov
13:33.53	Tetsuya	Yoroizaka (100)	JPN	20.3.90				27 Sep
13:33.67	Vladimir	Nikitin	RUS	5.8.92				8 Sep
13:33.69	Sergio	Jiménez	ESP	7.1.95				4 Jul
13:33.79	James	Rungaru	KEN	14.1.93				24 Oct
13:33.8A	Rhonex	Kipruto	KEN	12.10.99				5 Mar
13:33.83	Suguru	Osako	JPN	23.5.91				27 Sep
13:33.92	Philemon Kiplagat	Ruto	KEN-J	20.9.01				17 Oct
13:33.97	Tatsuhiko	Ito	JPN	23.3.98				18 Jul
13:34.05	Tom	Anderson	GBR	12.1.90				4 Dec
13:34.10	Haruki	Minatoya	JPN	25.4.96				20 Sep
13:34.50	Ismael	Debjani	BEL	25.9.90				6 Sep
13:34.54	Jinnosuke	Matsumura	JPN	22.3.95				4 Dec
13:34.57	Keisuke	Morita	JPN	19.10.95				4 Dec
13:34.67	Kazuki	Tamura	JPN	16.7.95				17 Oct
13:34.71	Yuki	Sato	JPN	26.11.86				17 Oct
13:34.74	Kosuke	Ishida	JPN-J	21.8.02				27 Sep
13:34.82	Maximilan	Thorwirth	GER	9.1.95				11 Jul
13:34.88	Julien	Wanders	SUI	18.3.96				29 Aug
13:34.91	Kasey	Knevelbaard	USA	2.9.96				4 Dec
13:34.97	Julian	Oakley	NZL	23.6.93				18 Dec
13:34.98	Dan	Kiplangat	KEN	4.6.96				12 Sep
13:35.24	Aritaka	Kajiwara	JPN	16.6.88				4 Dec
13:35.26	Stan	Niesten	NED	19.11.96				6 Sep
13:35.38	James	Bunuka	KEN	1.11.97				15 Nov
13:35.44	Jun	Nobuto	JPN	24.12.91				18 Jul
13:35.56	Samuel	Fitwi Sibhatu	GER	1.1.97				15 Aug
13:35.61	Fabien	Palcau	FRA	22.6.97				12 Sep
13:35.63	Ryota	Matono	JPN	17.8.92				4 Dec
13:35.65	Kosei	Yamaguchi	JPN	19.8.91				26 Sep
13:35.68	Bedan	Karoki	KEN	21.8.90				26 Sep
13:35.71	Kisaisa	Ledama	KEN	28.6.98				3 Oct
13:35.88	Takuya	Hanyu	JPN	8.11.97				4 Dec
13:35.9A	Collins	Koros	KEN	27.12.90				5 Mar
13:36.19	Shuichi	Kondo	JPN	27.7.95				30 Sep
13:36.39	Tamaki	Fujimoto	JPN-J	14.1.01				15 Nov
13:36.55	Koki	Takada	JPN	13.6.93				18 Jul
13:36.57	Taishi	Ito	JPN-Y	2.2.03				15 Nov
13:36.68	Simon	Debognies	BEL	16.7.96				29 Aug
13:36.86	Yuya	Yoshida	JPN	23.4.97				30 Sep
13:36.92	Yuichiro	Ueno	JPN	29.7.85				15 Nov
13:36.94	Seiya	Shigeno	JPN	23.12.96				15 Nov
13:37.28	Ren	Tazawa	JPN	11.11.00				8 Jul
13:37.34	Keita	Yoshida	JPN	31.8.98				3 Oct
13:37.37	Daiji	Kawai	JPN	22.9.91				18 Jul
13:37.38	Keijiro	Mogi	JPN	21.10.95				8 Jul
13:37.57	Farah	Abdulkarim	CAN	9.11.96				15 Aug
13:37.59	Zeray	Kbrom Mezenghi	NOR	12.1.86				29 Jun
13:37.83	Hideyuki	Taaka	JPN	9.10.90				15 Jul
13:37.85	Jack	Rowe	GBR	30.1.96				5 Sep
(149)								

Indoors

Mark	Name		Nat	Born	Pos	Meet	Venue	Date
13:08.25	Shadrack	Kipchirchir	USA	22.2.89	1		Boston (A)	28 Feb
13:08.87	Marc	Scott	GBR	21.12.93	2		Boston (A)	28 Feb
13:09.05	Edward	Cheserek	KEN	2.2.94	3		Boston (A)	28 Feb
13:10.07	Eric	Jenkins	USA	24.11.91	4		Boston (A)	28 Feb
13:12.53	Emmanuel	Bor	USA	14.4.88	5		Boston (A)	28 Feb
13:13.38	Matt	Hughes	CAN	3.8.89	6		Boston (A)	28 Feb
13:15.72	Paul	Tanui	KEN	22.12.90	1		Boston (A)	25 Jan
13:16.95	Tyler	Day	USA	18.12.96	2		Boston (A)	25 Jan
13:17.15	Willy	Fink	USA	7.3.94	7		Boston (A)	28 Feb
13:21.17	Hillary	Bor	USA	22.11.89	8		Boston (A)	28 Feb
13:24.07	Vladimir	Nikitin	RUS	5.8.92	1	NC	Moskva	27 Feb
13:24.67	Andrew	Bayer	USA	3.2.90	9		Boston (A)	28 Feb
13:27.61	Matt	Baxter	NZL	6.8.94	25 Jan			
13:27.68	Jordan	Mann	USA	12.1.93	28 Feb			
13:28.35	Jacob	Thomson	USA	29.11.94	28 Feb			
13:28.55	Alex	Masai	KEN	97	28 Feb			
13:29.61	Ryohei	Sakaguchi	JPN	5.4.97	28 Feb			
13:31.07	Ben	Flanagan	CAN	11.1.95	28 Feb			
13:31.25	Brian	Barraza	USA	16.5.95	28 Feb			
13:31.44	Mason	Ferlic	USA	5.8.93	28 Feb			
13:31.50#	Morgan	Beadlescomb	USA	1.6.98	14 Feb			
13:33.35	Jordan	Gusman	MLT	30.1.94	28 Feb			
13:33.44	Kiseki	Shiozawa	JPN	17.12.98	28 Feb			
13:36.36#	Peter	Seufer	USA	18.2.97	14 Feb			
13:36.62#	Jackson	Mestler	USA	27.12.97	14 Feb			
13:36.81	Anatoliy	Rybakov	RUS	27.2.85	27 Feb			
13:37.73	Donn	Cabral	USA	12.12.89	28 Feb			

JUNIORS

9 juniors in main list. 8 performances by 6 men to 13:25.0. Additional marks and further juniors:

Krop	13:11.88A	3	Keino Nairobi			14 Aug		
Masai	13:23.55	1	Yokohama			6 Dec		
13:29.34	Kiprono		Sitonik (10)	KEN	10.11.01	2	Yokohama	15 Nov
13:29.59	Emil Millán		de la Oliva	SWE	24.7.01	7	Göteborg	29 Aug
13:33.40	Emmanuel		Kipchirchir	KEN-Y	27.11.03	1	Okayama	12 Sep
13:33.5A	Gideon		Rono	KEN-Y	22.2.03	1	Nairobi	20 Nov
13:33.92	Philemon		Ruto	KEN	20.9.01	1	Hadano	17 Oct
13:34.74	Kosuke		Ishida	JPN	21.8.02	3	Hadano	27 Sep
13:36.39	Tamaki		Fujimoto	JPN	14.1.01	1	Yokohama	15 Nov
13:36.57	Taishi		Ito	JPN-Y	2.2.03	8	Yokohama	15 Nov
13:39.16	Duncan		Kisaisa	KEN-Y	4.1.03	6	Yokohama	6 Dec

10,000 METRES

Mark	Name		Nat	Born	Pos	Venue	Date
26:11.00	Joshua	Cheptegei	UGA	12.9.96	1	Valencia	7 Oct
26:58.97	Nicholas	Kimeli	KEN	29.9.98	1	Leiden	19 Sep
27:01.42	Richard	Yator	KEN	6.4.98	1	Kumagaya	19 Sep
27:01.74		Yator			1	Yokohama	14 Nov

10,000 METRES

Mark	Name		Nat	Born	Pos	Meet	Venue	Date	
27:01.95	Jonathan	Ndiku	KEN	18.9.91	2		Yokohama	14	Nov
27:02.39	Benard	Koech	KEN	25.11.99	2		Kumagaya	19	Sep
27:02.80	Bedan	Karoki	KEN	21.8.90	3		Kumagaya	19	Sep
27:07.29		Ndiku			1		Hadano	27	Sep
27:08.91		Karoki			1rA		Tajimi	9	Oct
27:12.98		Kimeli			2		Valencia	7	Oct
27:14.84		Koech			1		Fukagawa	8	Jul
27:15.97		Karoki			2		Fukagawa	8	Jul
27:18.75	Akira	Aizawa	JPN	18.7.97	1	NC	Osaka	4	Dec
27:19.42		Koech			2	JPN Ch	Osaka	4	Dec
27:20.34	Cleophas	Kandie	KEN	14.8.00	4		Kumagaya	19	Sep
27:22.06	Eric	Jenkins	USA	24.11.91	1		San Juan Capistrano	5	Dec
27:22.55	Patrick	Tiernan (10)	AUS	11.9.94	2		San Juan Capistrano	5	Dec
27:23.47		Ndiku			1		Abashiri	15	Jul
27:23.58	Edward	Cheserek	KEN	2.2.94	3		San Juan Capistrano	5	Dec
27:25.73	Tatsuhiko	Ito	JPN	23.3.98	3	NC	Osaka	4	Dec
27:26.58	Sam	Atkin	GBR	14.3.93	4		San Juan Capistrano	5	Dec
27:28.92	Kazuki	Tamura	JPN	16.7.95	4	NC	Osaka	4	Dec
27:28.97	Shadrack	Kipchirchir	USA	22.2.89	3		Valencia	7	Oct
27:30.09	Charles	Wanjiku	KEN	16.5.00	1		Sagamihara	23	Nov
27:30.81	Alexander	Mutiso	KEN	10.9.96	5		Kumagaya	19	Sep
27:31.13		Koech			1		Isahaya	11	Oct
27:34.48	Stephen	Kissa	UGA	1.12.95	4		Valencia	7	Oct
27:34.86	Daiji	Kawai	JPN	22.9.91	5	NC	Osaka	4	Dec
27:35.57	Justus	Soget (20)	KEN	22.10.99	1		Hachioji	21	Nov
27:35.57	Joe [30/21]	Klecker	USA	16.11.96	5		San Juan Capistrano	5	Dec
27:36.08	Evans	Keitany	KEN	27.11.99	2		Hachioji	21	Nov
27:36.29	Tetsuya	Yoroizaka	JPN	20.3.90	6	NC	Osaka	4	Dec
27:36.37	Samuel	Masai	KEN-J	20.3.01	3		Hachioji	21	Nov
27:36.93	Suguru	Osako	JPN	23.5.91	7	NC	Osaka	4	Dec
27:37.29	Wesley	Kiptoo	KEN		6		San Juan Capistrano	5	Dec
27:38.48	Vincent	Yegon	KEN	5.12.00	1		Konosu	21	Nov
27:38.53	Hillary	Bor	USA	22.11.89	7		San Juan Capistrano	5	Dec
27:39.20	Robert	Brandt	USA	2.11.96	8		San Juan Capistrano	5	Dec
27:39.50	Titus [30]	Wambua	KEN	14.8.97	4		Hachioji	21	Nov
27:39.80	Vincent	Raimoi	KEN	16.7.96	1		Chitose	18	Jul
27:41.10	Solomon	Boit	KEN	1.10.99	2		Leiden	19	Sep
27:41.30	Joseph	Ndirangu	KEN	9.9.94	2		Chitose	18	Jul
27:41.84	Yuki	Sato	JPN	26.11.86	8	NC	Osaka	4	Dec
27:42.99	Kiprono	Sitonik	KEN-J	10.11.01	5		Hachioji	21	Nov
27:44.65	Frank	Lara	USA	25.9.95	9		San Juan Capistrano	5	Dec
27:45.08	Andrew	Lorot	KEN	2.12.97	6		Hachioji	21	Nov
27:45.87	Philemon Kiplagat	Ruto	KEN-J	20.9.01	7		Hachioji	21	Nov
27:46.01	Simon	Saidimu	KEN	12.10.00	8		Hachioji	21	Nov
27:46.09	Ren [40]	Tazawa	JPN	11.11.00	10	NC	Osaka	4	Dec
27:47.49	Kisaisa	Ledama	KEN	28.6.98	10		Hachioji	21	Nov
27:47.55	Yuma	Hattori	JPN	13.11.93	7		Kumagaya	19	Sep
27:48.27	Stanley	Waithaka	KEN	9.4.00	1		Yokohama	5	Dec
27:48.64	Nicholas	Kosimbei	KEN	10.1.96	3rA		Sagamihara	9	Oct
27:49.16	Kengo	Suzuki	JPN	11.6.95	8		Kumagaya	19	Sep
27:49.38	Silas	Kingori	KEN	5.1.98	1rB		Hachioji	21	Nov
27:49.53	Girma	Mecheso	USA	16.1.88	2		Van Nuys	29	Aug
27:50.09	Kenta	Murayama	JPN	23.2.93	11	NC	Osaka	4	Dec
27:50.43	Philip	Muluwa	KEN-J	3.3.02	2rB		Hachioji	21	Nov
27:50.93	Dominic [50]	Langat	KEN	15.5.98	11		Hachioji	21	Nov
27:51.27	Robert	Mwei	KEN	11.4.98	9		Kumagaya	19	Sep
27:52.27	Tatsuya	Maruyama	JPN	29.7.94	12	NC	Osaka	4	Dec
27:52.35	Takashi	Ichida	JPN	16.6.92	1rB	NC	Osaka	4	Dec
27:52.89	Victor	Korir	KEN-J	14.8.02	12		Hachioji	21	Nov
27:53.17	Connor	McMillan	USA	15.11.95	10		San Juan Capistrano	5	Dec
27:53.95	Evans	Yego	KEN	5.9.95	13		Hachioji	21	Nov
27:54.06	Yuhi	Nakaya	JPN	11.6.99	2rB	NC	Osaka	4	Dec
27:55.07	Shinobu	Kubota	JPN	12.12.91	14		Hachioji	21	Nov
27:55.40	Alex	Cherono	KEN	30.12.00	5rA		Tajimi	9	Oct

MEN 2020

10,000 METRES

Mark	Name		Nat	Born	Pos	Meet	Venue	Date	
27:55.59	Naoki	Ota	JPN	13.10.99	3rB	NC	Osaka	4	Dec
[60]									
27:56.78	Yusuke	Nishiyama	JPN	7.11.94	6rA		Tajimi	9	Oct
27:56.81	Patrick	Mathenge	KEN	2.11.96	15		Hachioji	21	Nov
27:57.36	Keijiro	Mogi	JPN	21.10.95	13	NC	Osaka	4	Dec
27:58.40	Tatsuya	Oike	JPN	18.5.90	14	NC	Osaka	4	Dec
27:58.52	Yohei	Ikeda	JPN	22.6.98	15	NC	Osaka	4	Dec
27:58.63	Yuta	Aoki	JPN	27.4.97	16	NC	Osaka	4	Dec
27:59.10	Mike	Foppen	NED	29.11.96	3		Leiden	19	Sep
27:59.40	Hiroto	Inoue	JPN	6.1.93	17	NC	Osaka	4	Dec
27:59.95	Dan	Kiplangat	KEN	4.6.96	5		Fukagawa	8	Jul
28:00.29	Simon	Kariuki	KEN	13.2.92	3rB		Hachioji	21	Nov
[70]									
28:01.29	Shuho	Dairokuno	JPN	23.12.92	4rB	NC	Osaka	4	Dec
28:02.29	Enoch	Omwamba	KEN	4.4.93	5		Abashiri	15	Jul
28:03.13	Joel	Mwaura	KEN	20.1.99	10		Kumagaya	19	Sep
28:03.30	Vincent	Kipkemoi	KEN	3.1.99	11		Kumagaya	19	Sep
28:03.33	Yusuke	Ogura	JPN	16.4.93	18	NC	Osaka	4	Dec
28:03.56	Charles Kamau	Karanja	KEN	5.8.97	4rB		Hachioji	21	Nov
28:03.81	Taisei	Nakamura	JPN	5.10.97	17		Hachioji	21	Nov
28:03.94	Kazuya	Nishiyama	JPN	5.11.98	2		Nobeoka	17	Oct
28:04.05	Florian	Carvalho	FRA	9.3.89	1	NC	Pace	29	Aug
28:04.29	Zerei	Kbrom Mezngi	NOR	12.1.86	1	NC	Bergen (Fana)	20	Sep
[80]									
28:04.32	Zachery	Panning	USA	29.3.95	12		San Juan Capistrano	5	Dec
28:04.56	Minato	Oishi	JPN	19.5.88	19	NC	Osaka	4	Dec
28:05.37	Yuhei	Urano	JPN	1.11.97	20	NC	Osaka	4	Dec
28:05.66	James	Bunuka	KEN	1.11.97	1		Niigata	11	Sep
28:06.21	Muthoni	Muiru	KEN	27.3.98	18		Hachioji	21	Nov
28:06.56	Shoma	Funatsu	JPN	25.9.97	2		Yokohama	5	Dec
28:06.88	Benjamin	Flanagan	CAN	11.1.95	3		Lake Balboa, CA	29	Aug
28:06.90A	Paul	Tanui	KEN	22.12.90	1		Nairobi	3	Oct
28:06.91	Shin-ichiro	Nakamura	JPN	14.4.93	3		Yokohama	5	Dec
28:07.01	Fabien	Palcau	FRA	22.6.97	2	NC	Pace	29	Aug
[90]									
28:07.34	Sho	Nagato	JPN	13.1.97	4		Yokohama	5	Dec
28:07.62	Reid	Buchanan	USA	3.2.93	13		San Juan Capistrano	5	Dec
28:07.69	Jackson Kavesa	Muema	KEN-J	3.9.01	19		Hachioji	21	Nov
28:07.70	Conner	Mantz	USA	8.12.96	4		Lake Balboa, CA	29	Aug
28:07.89	Masahiro	Fukumoto	JPN	8.4.97	5		Yokohama	5	Dec
28:08.10	Boniface	Mulwa	KEN	16.4.00	6		Abashiri	15	Jul
28:08.20	Ben	Blankenship	USA	15.12.88	5		Lake Balboa, CA	29	Aug
28:08.25	Shunya	Kikuchi	JPN	26.7.98	5rB		Hachioji	21	Nov
28:08.27	Mehdi	Frere	FRA	27.7.96	3	NC	Pace	29	Aug
28:08.27	Yuki	Suzuki	JPN	1.11.95	1rC		Yokohama	14	Nov
[100]									

28:08.29	Akito	Terui	JPN	11.5.94	5 Dec	28:12.07	Masaya	Taguchi	JPN	20.5.92	5 Dec
28:08.61	Yamato	Yoshii	JPN-J	14.2.02	14 Nov	28:12.13	Ryuto	Igawa	JPN	5.9.00	21 Nov
28:08.83	Kiseki	Shiozawa	JPN	17.12.98	4 Dec	28:12.37	Jun	Nobuto	JPN	24.12.91	15 Jul
28:08.94	Seiya	Amano	JPN	16.3.98	4 Dec	28:12.53	Reed	Fischer	USA	9.7.95	5 Dec
28:09.05	Watari	Tochigi	JPN	8.5.95	21 Nov	28:12.63	Naoki	Aiba	JPN	24.1.91	4 Dec
28:09.14	Kyohei	Hosoya	JPN	31.8.95	21 Nov	28:12.63	Noritoshi	Hara	JPN	6.12.95	5 Dec
28:09.19	Atsuya	Imai	JPN	30.3.97	14 Nov	28:13.01	Noah	Kiplimo	KEN	22.11.00	21 Nov
28:09.23	Tadashi	Isshiki	JPN	5.6.94	21 Nov	28:13.12	Takato	Suzuki	JPN	23.7.97	18 Jul
28:09.27	Ryoma	Takeuchi	JPN	29.5.92	5 Dec	28:13.50	Kiyoshi	Koga	JPN	30.4.96	21 Nov
28:09.50	Jun	Nobuto	JPN	24.12.91	4 Dec	28:13.73	Naoki	Chiba	JPN	8.10.98	5 Dec
28:09.64	Wesley	Ledama	KEN	2.7.99	21 Nov	28:13.84	Kota	Murayama	JPN	23.2.93	15 Jul
28:10.41	Shoya	Kawase	JPN	9.7.98	21 Nov	28:13.93	Yuto	Kawamura	JPN	21.11.97	5 Dec
28:10.51	Ryota	Natori	JPN	21.7.98	27 Sep	28:14.52	Hidekatu	Hijikata	JPN	27.6.97	5 Dec
28:10.79	Hiroto	Fujimagari	JPN	26.5.97	14 Nov	28:14.65	Takato	Imai	JPN	2.11.96	14 Nov
28:10.84	Yudai	Okamoto	JPN	29.12.91	21 Nov	28:14.85	Atsushi	Yamato	JPN	13.3.97	9 Oct
28:10.86	Mitsunori	Asaoka	JPN	11.1.93	21 Nov	28:14.86	Arsène	Guillorel	FRA	14.8.83	29 Aug
28:11.05	Alex	Masai	KEN	.97	5 Dec	28:14.86	Tetta	Shiratani	JPN-J	24.8.01	5 Dec
28:11.20	Yohei	Suzuki	JPN	23.5.94	18 Jul	28:15.10	David	Ngure	KEN	10.8.98	21 Nov
28:11.64	Tomoya	Ogikubo	JPN	11.12.97	27 Sep	28:15.13	Masaya	Komachi	JPN	30.1.96	5 Dec
28:11.73+	Robert	Keter	KEN	.89	4 Sep	28:15.40	Tomohiro	Chimori	JPN	27.12.00	5 Dec
28:11.76	Yuma	Kaiki	JPN	14.12.98	14 Nov	28:15.41	Sydney	Gidabuday	USA	21.8.96	5 Dec
28:11.76	Yenablo	Biyazen	ETH	29.1.00	5 Dec	28:15.57	Hiroki	Suzuki	JPN	27.7.94	4 Dec
28:11.79+	Peter	Kiprotich	KEN	20.12.98	4 Sep	28:15.65	John	Reniewicki	USA	3.10.95	5 Dec
28:11.9+	Mohamed	Farah	GBR	23.3.83	4 Sep	28:15.66	Takahiro	Nakamura	JPN	24.8.83	21 Nov
28:11.94	Benuel	Mogeni	KEN-J	11.3.01	4 Dec	28:16.05	Yuki	Matsumura	JPN	14.1.93	5 Dec
28:12.0+	Bashir	Abdi	BEL	10.2.89	4 Sep	28:16.06	Simon	Bedard	FRA	3.1.97	5 Dec
28:12.05	Kosei	Yamaguchi	JPN	19.8.91	9 Oct	28:16.10	Kazuto	Kawabata	JPN	20.12.95	21 Nov
28:12.06	Abdihamid	Nur	USA	14.10.00	5 Dec	28:16.40	Victor	Kiplangat	UGA	19.11.99	7 Oct

10,000 METRES - 1 HOUR - 10k ROAD

Mark	Name	Nat	Born	Pos Meet	Venue	Date
28:16.44	Vladimir Nikitin	RUS	5.8.92	21 Aug		
28:16.59	Kento Kikutani	JPN	8.5.94	9 Oct		
28:16.62	Masato Kikuchi	JPN	18.9.90	21 Nov		
28:16.67	Mizuki Higashi	JPN	30.8.94	4 Dec		
28:16.93	Shohei Kurata	JPN	5.8.92	15 Jul		
28:16.95	Takehiro Shishikura	JPN	19.6.98	21 Nov		
28:17.33	Luc Bruchet	CAN	23.2.91	21 Nov		
28:17.55	Kieran Lumb	CAN	2.8.98	21 Nov		
28:17.56	Yuji Onoda	JPN	3.9.96	21 Nov		
28:17.58	Kyosuke Teshima	JPN	14.6.99	21 Nov		
28:17.84	Taiga Nakanishi	JPN	27.5.00	21 Nov		
28:18.10	John Gay	CAN	7.11.96	21 Nov		
28:18.14	Haruki Minatoya	JPN	25.4.96	15 Jul		
28:18.50	Chihiro Miyawaki	JPN	28.8.91	9 Oct		
28:18.57	Brogan Austin	USA	5.10.91	5 Dec		
28:18.71	Naoki Okamoto	JPN	26.5.84	26 Sep		
28:18.73	Tadesse Getahon	ISR	20.12.97	6 Dec		
28:18.89	Anatoliy Rybakov	RUS	27.2.85	21 Aug		
28:19.05	Shun Yuzawa	JPN	21.9.96	18 Jul		
28:19.07	Yuya Yoshida	JPN	23.4.97	11 Oct		
28:19.25	Takuya Fujikawa	JPN	17.12.92	21 Nov		
28:19.26	Yuichi Fukuda	JPN	10.4.98	21 Nov		
28:19.27	Masatoshi Sakata	JPN	17.8.94	9 Oct		
28:19.38	Bernard Kimani	KEN	10.9.93	21 Nov		
28:19.44	Ken Nakayama	JPN	24.2.97	15 Jul		
28:19.48	Shuichi Kondo	JPN	27.7.95	21 Nov		
28:19.61	Toshinori Watanabe	JPN	27.6.93	21 Nov		
28:19.77	Yoshiki Kushida	JPN	21.4.00	21 Nov		
28:20.09	Luka Musembi	KEN	12.12.00	18 Oct		
28:20.10	Takuya Hanyu	JPN	8.11.97	9 Oct		
28:20.13	Takuto Miura	JPN	4.12.99	21 Nov		
28:20.22	Taisei Nakamura	JPN	5.10.97	15 Jul		
28:20.40	Kensuke Yamaguchi	JPN	3.5.99	21 Nov		
28:20.42	Hibiki Aogaki	JPN-J	20.3.02	5 Dec		
28:20.54	Tomoki Ota	JPN	17.10.97	9 Oct		
28:20.55	Narve Gilje Nordås	NOR	30.9.98	20 Sep		
28:20.63	Gaku Hoshi	JPN	17.9.98	23 Nov		
28:21.33	Daniel Kitonyi	KEN	12.1.94	18 Oct		
28:21.38	Benjamin Choquert	FRA	17.4.86	29 Aug		
28:21.50	Masaki Sakuda	JPN	6.5.96	21 Nov		
28:21.79	Shota Higuchi	JPN	5.12.00	5 Dec		
28:21.93	Hiroki Nagayama	JPN	20.7.96	17 Oct		
28:22.27	Masaki Kodama	JPN-J	3.1.02	21 Nov		
28:22.28A	Enos Kales	KEN	10.7.97	3 Oct		
28:22.28	Nagiya Mori	JPN	3.7.99	14 Nov		
28:22.42	Jesus Ramos	ESP	29.4.96	18 Dec		
28:23.21	Emil Millán de la Oliva	SWE-J	24.7.01	19 Sep		
[200]	230 under 28:30.0					

JUNIORS
6 juniors in main list. 8 performances by 7 men to 28:10.0. Additional marks and further juniors:
Ruto	27:46.67	2		Tajimi		4 Oct	
28:08.61	Yamato	Yoshii	JPN	14.2.02	3	Yokohama	14 Nov
28:11.94	Benuel	Mogeni	KEN	11.3.01	6rB	Osaka	4 Dec
28:14.86	Tetta	Shiratori	JPN	24.8.01	14	Yokohama	5 Dec
28:20.42	Hibiki	Aogaki (10)	JPN	20.3.02	18	Yokohama	5 Dec
28:22.27	Masaki	Kodama	JPN	3.1.02	6	Tokorozawa	21 Nov
28:23.21	Emil Millán	de la Oliva	SWE	24.7.01	4	Leiden	19 Sep
28:23.87	Mebuki	Suzuki	JPN	3.6.01	2	Sagamihara	23 Nov
28:30.48	Kyosuke	Hanao	JPN	20.12.01	5	Sagimihara	23 Nov
28:30.64	Yushin	Akatsu	JPN	19.6.01	6	Sagimihara	23 Nov
28:32.41	Patrick	Kinyanyu	KEN-Y	14.9.03	2	Konosu	21 Nov
28:32.52A	Peter Muiruri	Kamau	KEN	28.12.01	4 Kenio	Nairobi	3 Oct
28:35.28	Kotaro	Kondo	JPN	30.1.01	8	Sagimihara	23 Nov
28:37.50	Kosuke	Ishida	JPN	21.8.02	1	isesaki	31 Oct
28:39.63	Ken	Tansho (20)	JPN	7.2.01	8	Hadano	18 Oct

20,000M 1 HOUR

56:20.30	21,330m	Mohamed	Farah		GBR	23.3.83	1	VD Bruxelles	4 Sep
56:20.02	21,322	Bashir	Abdi		BEL	10.2.89	2	VD Bruxelles	4 Sep
57:50.25	20,772	Mourad	Amdouni		FRA	21.1.88	1	Bastia	19 Sep
57:55.0	20,703+	Sondre Nordstad	Moen (illegal shoes)	NOR	12.1.91	1	Oslo	11 Jun
58:53.6	20,384	Girnaw	Amare		ISR	26.10.87	1	Tel Aviv	26 Jan

10 KILOMETRES ROAD

26:24	Rhonex	Kipruto	KEN	12.10.99	1	Valencia	12 Jan
27:12	Benard	Kimeli	KEN	10.9.95	2	Valencia	12 Jan
27:13	Julien	Wanders	SUI	18.3.96	3	Valencia	12 Jan
27:18	Daniel	Simiyu	KEN	18.9.95	1	Berlin	26 Sep
27:25+	Kibiwott	Kandie	KEN	20.6.96	in HMar	Valencia	6 Dec
27:25+	Jacob	Kiplimo	UGA	14.11.00	in HMar	Valencia	6 Dec
27:25+		R Kipruto			in HMar	Valencia	6 Dec
27:25+	Alexander	Mutiso	KEN	10.9.96	in HMar	Valencia	6 Dec
27:25+	Philemon	Kiplimo	KEN	10.10.98	in HMar	Valencia	6 Dec
27:25+	Kelvin	Kiptum	KEN	2.12.99	in HMar	Valencia	6 Dec
27:25+	Bravin	Kiptoo	KEN-J	26.2.01	in HMar	Valencia	6 Dec
27:30	Jacob	Krop	KEN-J	4.6.01	4	Valencia	12 Jan
27:32	Shadrack	Koech	KEN	5.9.97	5	Valencia	12 Jan

Where faster than track bests

27:42	Mourad	Amdouni	FRA	21.1.88	1	Barcelona	31 Dec
27:50	Djilali	Bedrani	FRA	1.10.93	7	Valencia	12 Jan
27:50+	Amdework	Walelegn	ETH	11.3.99	in HMar	New Delhi	29 Nov
27:50+	Andamlak	Belihu	ETH	20.11.98	in HMar	New Delhi	29 Nov
27:50+	Victor	Kiplangat	UGA	19.11.99	in HMar	New Delhi	29 Nov
27:50+	Leonard	Barsoton	KEN	21.10.94	in HMar	Ras Al Khaimah	21 Feb
27:51+	Muktar	Edris	ETH	14.1.94	in HMar	New Delhi	29 Nov
27:51+	Tesfahun	Akalnew	ETH	29.4.99	in HMar	New Delhi	29 Nov
27:51+	Shadrack	Korir Kiminin	KEN	10.2.96	in HMar	New Delhi	29 Nov

10 - 15 - 20 KM ROAD - HALF MARATHON

Mark	Name		Nat	Born	Pos	Meet	Venue	Date	
27:51+	Abrar	Osman	ERI	24.6.89		in HMar	New Delhi	29	Nov
28:00	Chala	Regasa	ETH	30.4.97	8		Valencia	12	Jan
28:00	Amine	Souida	MAR		1		Casablanca	9	Feb
28:01	Sikiyas	Misganaw	ETH	29.4.00	9		Valencia	12	Jan
28:02	Callum	Hawkins	GBR	22.6.92	10		Valencia	12	Jan
28:04+	Viktor	Kiplangat	UGA	19.11.99		in HMar	Barcelona	16	Feb
28:04+	Boniface	Kibiwot	KEN			in HMar	Barcelona	16	Feb
28:05	Lawi	Kosgei	KEN	14.1.99	11		Valencia	12	Jan
28:05+	Victor	Chumo	KEN	1.1.87		in HMar	Barcelona	16	Feb
28:05+	Moses	Koech	KEN	5.8.97		in HMar	Barcelona	16	Feb
28:05+	Josphat Kiptoo	Boit	KEN	25.11.95		in HMar	New Delhi	29	Nov
28:06	Solomon	Kipchoge	KEN		1		Chonburi	28	Jan
28:06	Carlos	Mayo	ESP	18.9.95	2		Barcelona	31	Dec
28:07+	Benard	Ngeno	KEN	10.8.96		in HMar	Houston	19	Jan
28:07+	Abel	Kipchumba	KEN	3.2.94		in HMar	Houston	19	Jan
28:07+	Gabriel	Geay	TAN	10.9.96		in HMar	Houston	19	Jan
28:07+	Tola	Shura Kitata	ETH	9.6.96		in HMar	Houston	19	Jan
28:07+	Bethwel	Yegon	KEN	.94		in HMar	Houston	19	Jan
28:07+	Geoffrey	Koech	KEN	28.8.93		in HMar	Houston	19	Jan
28:07+	Mande	Bushendich	UGA	7.4.97		in HMar	Barcelona	16	Feb
28:07+	Joseph Karanja	N'Ganga	KEN	.89		in HMar	Ras Al Khaimah	21	Feb
28:08	Richard	Douma	NED	17.4.93	12		Valencia	12	Jan
28:08	Daniele	Meucci	ITA	7.10.85	13		Valencia	12	Jan
28:08+	Jemal	Yimer	ETH	11.9.96		in HMar	Houston	19	Jan
28:08+	Brett	Robinson	AUS	8.5.91		in HMar	Houston	19	Jan
28:08+	Noah	Kipkemboi	KEN	.93		in HMar	Barcelona	16	Feb
28:08+	Mule	Wasihun	ETH	20.10.93		in HMar	Ras Al Khaimah	21	Feb
28:08+	Alfred	Barkach	KEN	2.3.97		in HMar	Ras Al Khaimah	21	Feb
28:08+	Vincent	Raimoi	KEN	16.7.96		in HMar	Ras Al Khaimah	21	Feb
28:08+	Maxwell	Rotich	KEN	5.8.98		in HMar	Ras Al Khaimah	21	Feb
28:08+	Edwin Kiprop	Kiptoo	KEN	14.8.93		in HMar	Ras Al Khaimah	21	Feb
28:08+	Solomon	Berihu	ETH	2.10.99		in HMar	Ras Al Khaimah	21	Feb
28:08+	Avinash	Sable	IND	13.9.94		in HMar	New Delhi	29	Nov
28:08	Eyob Ghebrehiwet Faniel		ITA	26.11.92	2		Madrid	31	Dec

28:09	Juan Antoio	Pérez	ESP	6.11.88	12 Jan	28:13	Paul	Chelimo	USA	27.10.90 31 Dec
28:09+	Abdallah	Mande	UGA	10.5.95	21 Feb	28:15	Carlos	Mayo	ESP	18.9.95 9 Feb
28:09	Jonas	Leandersson	SWE	26.1.91	8 Nov	28:15+	Razini	Lemeteki	KEN	21.12.98 17 Oct
28:10	Ben	Connor	GBR	17.10.92	12 Jan	28:17	Haymanot	Alew	ETH	11.11.97 26 Jan
28:10	Yassine	Zaki	MAR		9 Feb	28:17	Isaac	Kimeli	BEL	9.3.94 11 Oct
28:10	Simon	Boch	GER	18.4.94	8 Nov	28:18	Raphael	Montoya	FRA	24.11.95 31 Dec
28:11	Javier	Guerra	ESP	10.11.83	12 Jan	28:20	Zerei	Kbrom Mezngi	NOR	12.1.86 17 Oct
28:11	Samuel	Fitwi Sibhatu	GER	1.1.97	12 Jan	28:22	Hamid	El Janati	MAR	9 Feb
28:12	Mohamed	El Talhaoui	MAR	.91	9 Feb	28:22	Vladimir	Nikitin	RUS	5.8.92 20 Sep
28:12	David	Nilsson	SWE	16.4.87	8 Nov	28:22	Robin	Hendrix	BEL	14.1.95 11 Oct
28:13	Sondre Nordstad Moen		NOR	12.1.91	25 Jul	28:22	Abdelaati	Iguider	MAR	25.3.87 12 Dec
28:13	Jimmy	Gressier	FRA	4.5.97	31 Dec					

Downhill 86m: Nov 22, Alcobendas: 1. Fernando Carro 27:46, 2. Jorge Blanco 27:51, 3. Jesús Ramos 27:56; 4. Nicolás Cuestas URU 28:14

15/20 KILOMETRES ROAD

See also in Half Marathon lists

15k	20k								
42:00	56:41	Shadrack	Korir Kimining	KEN	10.2.96		in HMar	New Delhi	29 Nov
42:04	57:02	Stephen	Kissa	UGA	1.12.95		in HMar	Barcelona	16 Feb
42:10	56:54		Barsoton				in HMar	Ras Al Khaimah	21 Feb
42:15	56:43	Andamlak	Belihu	ETH	20.11.98		in HMar	Houston	19 Jan
42:15		Julien	Wanders	SUI	18.3.96		in HMar	Ras Al Khaimah	21 Feb
	56:58	Abrar	Osman	ERI	24.6.89		in HMar	New Delhi	29 Nov
	57:00	Moses	Koech	KEN	5.8.97		in HMar	Den Haag	8 Mar
42:16	57:49	Solomon	Berihu	ETH	2.10.99		in HMar	Ras Al Khaimah	21 Feb
42:27	57:50	Edwin Kiprop	Kiptoo	KEN	14.8.93		in HMar	Ras Al Khaimah	21 Feb

HALF MARATHON

	20k	15k								
57:32	54:43	41:10	Kibiwott	Kandie	KEN	20.6.96	1		Valencia	6 Dec
57:37	54:42	41:11	Jacob	Kiplimo	UGA	14.11.00	2		Valencia	6 Dec
57:49	54:50	41:10	Rhonex	Kipruto	KEN	12.10.99	3		Valencia	6 Dec
57:59	54:57	41:10	Alexander	Mutiso	KEN	10.9.96	4		Valencia	6 Dec
58:11	55:07	41:11	Philemon	Kiplimo	KEN	10.10.98	5		Valencia	6 Dec
58:38				Kandie			1		Praha	5 Sep
58:42	55:43	41:31	Kelvin	Kiptum	KEN	2.12.99	6		Valencia	6 Dec
58:49	55:55	42:18		J Kiplimo			1	WCh	Gdynia	17 Oct

HALF MARATHON 293

Mark			Name	Nat	Born	Pos	Meet	Venue	Date
58:53	56:00	42:00	Amdework	Walelegn	ETH	11.3.99	1		New Delhi	29 Nov
58:54	55:58	42:17		Kandie			2	WCh	Gdynia	17 Oct
58:54	56:00	42:00	Andamlak	Belihu	ETH	20.11.98	2		New Delhi	29 Nov
58:56	56:00	42:00	Stephen	Kissa	UGA	1.12.95	3		New Delhi	29 Nov
58:58	56:07	42:09		Kandie			1		Ras Al Khaimah	21 Feb
59:04	56:02	42:00	Muktar	Edris	ETH	14.1.94	4		New Delhi	29 Nov
59:08	56:09	42:17		Walelegn			3	WCh	Gdynia	17 Oct
59:09				Mutiso			1		Santa Pola	19 Jan
59:10	56:00	42:00	Leonard	Barsoton	KEN	21.10.94	5		New Delhi	29 Nov
59:16	56:15	42:04		Mutiso			2		Ras Al Khaimah	21 Feb
59:21	56:16	42:19	Joshua	Cheptegei	UGA	12.9.96	4	WCh	Gdynia	17 Oct
59:22	56:11	42:00	Tesfahun	Akalnew	ETH	29.4.99	6		New Delhi	29 Nov
59:25	56:30	42:14	Jemal	Yimer	ETH	11.9.96	1		Houston	19 Jan
59:26	56:30	42:14	Benard	Ngeno	KEN	10.8.96	2		Houston	19 Jan
59:26	56:18	42:00	Victor	Kiplangat	UGA	19.11.99	7		New Delhi	29 Nov
59:27	56:30	42:14	Shadrack	Korir Kimining	KEN	10.2.96	3		Houston	19 Jan
59:28	56:30	42:14		P Kiplimo			4		Houston	19 Jan
59:32	56:29	42:18		Belihu			5	WCh	Gdynia	17 Oct
59:34	56:29	42:18		Barsoton			6	WCh	Gdynia	17 Oct
59:35	56:32	42:15	Abel	Kipchumba	KEN	3.2.94	5		Houston	19 Jan
59:36	56:30	?	Geoffrey	Koech	KEN	28.8.93	6		Houston	19 Jan
59:36	56:34	42:18	Stephen	Mokoka	RSA	31.1.85	7	WCh	Gdynia	17 Oct
			[30/20]							
59:37	56:34	41:58	Bravin	Kiptoo	KEN-J	26.2.01	7		Valencia	6 Dec
59:40	56:39	42:19	Mourad	Amdouni	FRA	21.1.88	8	WCh	Gdynia	17 Oct
59:42	56:37	42:15	Gabriel	Geay	TAN	10.9.96	7		Houston	19 Jan
59:42	56:39	42:18	Benard	Kimeli	KEN	10.9.95	9	WCh	Gdynia	17 Oct
59:45	56:41	42:19	Leul	Gebrselassie	ETH	20.9.93	10	WCh	Gdynia	17 Oct
59:47	56:46	42:15	Tola	Shura Kitata	ETH	9.6.96	8		Houston	19 Jan
59:47	56:43	42:13	Mule	Wasihun	ETH	20.10.93	3		Ras Al Khaimah	21 Feb
59:49	56:46	42:33	Alfred	Barkach	KEN	2.3.97	4		Ras Al Khaimah	21 Feb
59:51	56:49	42:17	Vincent	Raimoi	KEN	16.7.96	5		Ras Al Khaimah	21 Feb
59:55	56:52	42:43	Julien	Wanders	SUI	18.3.96	8		Valencia	6 Dec
			[30]							
59:56			Geoffrey	Kusuro	UGA	12.2.89	2		Santa Pola	19 Jan
59:57	56:48	42:39	Brett	Robinson	AUS	8.5.91	1		Marugame	2 Feb
59:58	57:02	42:24	Victor	Chumo	KEN	1.1.87	1		Barcelona	16 Feb
59:58	57:00	42:40	Dawit	Wolde	ETH	19.5.91	1		Den Haag	8 Mar
60:00	56:55	42:39	Yusuke	Ogura	JPN	16.4.93	2		Marugame	2 Feb
60:00	57:02	42:25	Moses	Koech	KEN	5.8.97	3		Barcelona	16 Feb
60:00	56:59	42:39	Bernard	Kimani	KEN	10.9.93	3		Den Haag	8 Mar
60:01	56:55	42:39	Callum	Hawkins	GBR	22.6.92	3		Marugame	2 Feb
60:01	57:03	42:28	Hailemariyam	Kiros	ETH	5.2.97	11	WCh	Gdynia	17 Oct
60:03	56:59	42:39	Leonard	Langat	KEN	7.8.90	4		Den Haag	8 Mar
			[40]							
60:04			Henry	Ronoh	KEN	12.12.96	1		Napoli	23 Feb
60:04	57:02	42:37	Hamza	Sahli	MAR	10.5.93	12	WCh	Gdynia	17 Oct
60:06	56:52	42:40	Taku	Fujimoto	JPN	11.9.89	4		Marugame	2 Feb
60:06	57:02	42:25	Abrar	Osman	ERI	24.6.89	4		Barcelona	16 Feb
60:06			Benson	Kipruto	KEN	17.3.91	3		Praha	5 Sep
60:06	57:10	43:06	Carlos	Mayo	ESP	18.9.95	9		Valencia	6 Dec
60:12	56:57	42:15	Jake	Robertson	NZL	14.11.89	10		Houston	19 Jan
60:13	56:55	42:15	Joseph Karanja	N'Ganga	KEN	.89	8		Ras Al Khaimah	21 Feb
60:13	57:01	42:42	Razini	Lemeteki	KEN	21.12.98	1		Tachikawa	17 Oct
60:14	57:04	42:25	Mande	Bushendich	UGA	7.4.97	6		Barcelona	16 Feb
			[50]							
60:17	57:14	42:37	Mohamed	El Aaraby	MAR	12.11.89	13	WCh	Gdynia	17 Oct
60:18	57:00	42:39	James	Rungaru	KEN	14.1.93	6		Den Haag	8 Mar
60:20	57:01	42:15	Maxwell	Rotich	KEN	5.8.98	9		Ras Al Khaimah	21 Feb
60:20			Amos	Kurgat	KEN	7.3.92	4		Praha	5 Sep
60:22	57:08	42:38	Kenenisa	Bekele	ETH	13.6.82	1		London	1 Mar
60:22	57:17	42:47	Galen	Rupp (10M 45:54+)	USA	8.5.86	1		Dorena	30 Oct
60:23	57:04	42:42	Noah	Kiplimo	KEN	22.11.00	3		Tachikawa	17 Oct
60:24	57:21	42:40	Precious	Mashele	RSA	13.10.90	14	WCh	Gdynia	17 Oct
60:26	57:18	42:29	Mouhcine	Outalha	MAR	15.12.98	15	WCh	Gdynia	17 Oct
60:27			Mohamed	Farah	GBR	23.3.83	1		Larne	12 Sep
			[60]							
60:30	57:27	42:37	Othmane	El Goumri	MAR	28.5.92	17	WCh	Gdynia	17 Oct
60:30	57:32		Avinash	Sable	IND	13.9.94	10		New Delhi	29 Nov
60:31	57:27	42:45	Jake	Smith	GBR	19.5.98	18	WCh	Gdynia	17 Oct

MEN 2020

294 HALF MARATHON

Mark			Name		Nat	Born	Pos	Meet	Venue		Date	
60:34	57:09	42:43	James	Bunuka	KEN	1.11.97	4		Tachikawa		17	Oct
60:35	57:24	42:22	Abdallah	Mande	UGA	10.5.95	10		Ras Al Khaimah		21	Feb
60:39			Marc	Scott	GBR	21.12.93	2		Larne		12	Sep
60:40			Joel	Mwangi	KEN	3.6.85	1		Verona		16	Feb
60:40			Felix	Kipkoech	KEN	1.2.98	5		Praha		5	Sep
60:40	57:40	43:03	Bohdan-Ivan	Horodyskyy	UKR	18.5.94	20	WCh	Gdynia		17	Oct
60:42			Evans Kipkorir	Cheruiyot	KEN	24.9.91	3		Napoli		23	Feb
			[70]									
60:43	57:29	42:42	Masato	Kikuchi	JPN	18.9.90	5		Marugame		2	Feb
60:44			Joel	Mwaura	KEN	20.1.99	1		Kumamoto		19	Jan
60:44			Eyob	Ghebrehiwet Faniel	ITA	26.11.92	1		Sevilla		26	Jan
60:46			Hailemariam	Atsebha	ETH	14.3.86	2		Sevilla		26	Jan
60:47			Vestus	Chemjor	KEN	.87	3		Santa Pola		19	Jan
60:47			Timothy	Kosgei	KEN	1.1.97	6		Praha		5	Sep
60:49	57:30	42:41	Yuta	Shitara	JPN	18.12.91	6		Marugame		2	Feb
60:49			Kiyoshi	Koga	JPN	30.4.96	2		Yamaguchi		9	Feb
60:50			Hiroki	Suzuki	JPN	27.7.94	3		Yamaguchi		9	Feb
60:50	57:30	42:18	Guye	Adola	ETH	20.10.90	22	WCh	Gdynia		17	Oct
		[80]										
60:51	57:47	42:51	Collen	Mulaudzi	RSA	8.4.91	23	WCh	Gdynia		17	Oct
60:51	57:41	42:37	Aras	Kaya	TUR	4.4.94	24	WCh	Gdynia		17	Oct
60:52	57:56		Tadesse	Getahon	ISR	20.12.97	25	WCh	Gdynia		17	Oct
60:53			Patrick	Mwaka	KEN	2.11.92	4		Yamaguchi		9	Feb
60:54	Shin		Kimura	JPN	8.2.94	9 Feb	61:08	Naoki	Koyama	JPN	12.5.96	9 Feb
60:55	Yusuke		Nishiyama	JPN	7.11.94	9 Feb	61:08	Stephen	Scullion	IRL	9.11.88	12 Sep
60:55	Ben		Connor	GBR	17.10.92	12 Sep	61:09	Shohei	Otsuka	JPN	13.8.94	2 Feb
60:56	Hosea		Chirchir	KEN	.84	19 Jan	61:09	Vladimir	Nikitin	RUS	5.8.92	4 Oct
60:56	Jun		Nobuto	JPN	24.12.91	9 Feb	61:10	Solomon	Berihu	ETH	2.10.99	21 Feb
60:56	Solomon		Koech	KEN	.97	16 Feb	61:10	Teshome	Dirirsa	ETH	25.4.94	23 Feb
60:57	Ezra		Tanui	KEN	.97	2 Feb	61:11	José Luis	Santana	MEX	29.9.89	17 Oct
60:57	Takahiro		Nakamura	JPN	24.8.83	9 Feb	61:14	Tsubasa	Ichiyama	JPN	8.4.96	9 Feb
60:58	Masashi		Nonaka	JPN	10.11.95	9 Feb	61:16	Suguru	Osako	JPN	23.5.91	30 Oct
60:58	Florian		Carvalho	FRA	9.3.89	17 Oct	61:18	Shoya	Kawase	JPN	9.7.98	2 Feb
60:58	Maru		Teferi	ISR	17.2.92	17 Oct	61:18	Tuyoshi	Bando	JPN	12.12.96	9 Feb
60:59	Daisuke		Horiai	JPN	18.12.96	9 Feb	61:20	Juan	Pacheco	MEX	11.12.90	17 Oct
61:01	Ryota		Sato	JPN	15.11.95	9 Feb	61:21	Ayad	Lamdassem	ESP	11.10.81	17 Oct
61:02	Yusuke		Baba	JPN	15.6.96	9 Feb	61:21	Javier	Guerra	ESP	10.11.83	6 Dec
61:03	Patrick		Mathenge	KEN	2.11.96	2 Feb	61:23	Tatsuya	Oike	JPN	18.5.90	9 Feb
61:03	Noritoshi		Hara	JPN	16.12.95	9 Feb	61:23	Enyew	Mekonnen	ETH	7.4.94	21 Feb
	[100]						61:26	Kenta	Murayama	JPN	23.2.93	9 Feb
61:03	Josphat Kiptoo		Boit (57:47)	KEN	25.11.95	29 Nov	61:26	Ismael	Kalale	KEN	25.5.95	16 Feb
61:05	Daisuke		Hosomori	JPN	5.5.94	9 Feb	61:27	Takumi	Kiyotani	JPN	24.1.89	9 Feb
61:05	Edwin Kiprop		Kiptoo	KEN	14.8.93	21 Feb	61:28	Sondre Nordstad	Moen	NOR	12.1.91	16 Feb
61:06	Yuki		Sato	JPN	26.11.86	2 Feb		[133]				
61:07	Chris		Thompson	GBR	17.4.81	1 Mar						

JUNIORS

59:37		Bravin	Kiptoo	KEN	26.2.01	7	Valencia	6	Dec
61:41		Ryuji	Miura	JPN	11.2.02	5	Tachikawa	17	Oct
61:47		Yamato	Yoshii	JPN	14.2.02	10	Tachikawa	17	Oct
61:51		Yosaku	Nomura	JPN	8.3.01	12	Tachikawa	17	Oct
62:09		Jazuki	Ishii	JPN	30.12.01	21	Tachikawa	17	Oct
62:13		Tamaki	Fujimoto	JPN	14.1.01	22	Tachikawa	17	Oct

25/30 KILOMETRES ROAD
See also in Marathon lists

25k	30k								
	1:27:42	Philemon	Kacheran	KEN	4.7.92	in Mar	Valencia	6	Dec
1:13:03	1:27:43	Lelisa	Desisa	ETH	14.1.90	in Mar	Valencia	6	Dec
1:13:15	1:29:22	Noah	Kipkemboi	KEN	.93	in Mar	Valencia	6	Dec
1:13:25	1:28:28	Hiroto	Inoue	JPN	6.1.93	in Mar	Tokyo	1	Mar
1:13:42		Fentahun	Hunegnaw	ETH		in Mar	Valencia	6	Dec
1:13:54	1:29:12	Chihiro	Miyawaki	JPN	28.8.91	in Mar	Tokyo	1	Mar

MARATHON

	25k	30k								
2:03:00	1:13:03	1:27:42	Evans	Chebet	KEN	10.11.88	1	Valencia	6	Dec
2:03:04	1:13:03	1:27:43	Lawrence	Cherono	KEN	7.8.88	2	Valencia	6	Dec
2:03:16	1:13:02	1:27:42	Birhanu	Legese	ETH	11.9.94	3	Valencia	6	Dec
2:03:30	1:13:02	1:27:42	Amos	Kipruto	KEN	16.9.92	4	Valencia	6	Dec
2:04:12	1:13:03	1:27:42	Reuben Kiprop	Kipyego	KEN	21.8.96	5	Valencia	6	Dec
2:04:15	1:13:15	1:27:42		Legese				Tokyo	1	Mar
2:04:46	1:14:24	1:28:40	Mekuant	Ayenew	ETH	.91	1	Sevilla	23	Feb
2:04:49	1:13:25	1:28:28	Bashir	Abdi	BEL	10.2.89	2	Tokyo	1	Mar

MARATHON

Mark			Name		Nat	Born	Pos	Meet	Venue	Date	
2:04:51	1:13:15	1:27:42	Sisay	Lemma	ETH	12.12.90	3		Tokyo	1	Mar
2:04:53	1:13:02	1:27:42	Gelmisa	Chalu	ETH		6		Valencia	6	Dec
2:05:05	1:14:23	1:28:40	Barnabas	Kiptum	KEN	8.12.86	2		Sevilla	23	Feb
2:05:05	1:13:02	1:27:43	Abel	Kirui	KEN	4.6.82	7		Valencia	6	Dec
2:05:15	1:13:03	1:27:42	Abebe	Negewo Degefa	ETH	20.5.84	8		Valencia	6	Dec
2:05:29	1:13:32	1:28:40	Suguru	Osako	JPN	23.5.91	4		Tokyo	1	Mar
2:05:29	1:13:02	1:27:43	Leul	Gebrselassie	ETH	20.9.93	9		Valencia	6	Dec
2:05:37	1:13:02	1:27:43	Philemon	Rono	KEN	8.2.91	10		Valencia	6	Dec
2:05:41	1:14:23	1:29:02	Tola	Shura Kitata	ETH	9.6.96	1		London	4	Oct
2:05:42	1:14:22	1:29:00	Vincent	Kipchumba Torotich	KEN	3.8.90	2		London	4	Oct
2:05:45	1:14:23	1:29:01		Lemma			3		London	4	Oct
2:05:53	1:13:03	1:27:43	Oqbe	Kibrom	ERI	1.1.98	11		Valencia	6	Dec
2:06:04	1:14:22	1:29:01	Mosinet	Geremew	ETH	12.2.92	4		London	4	Oct
2:06:08	1:14:22	1:29:01	Mule	Wasihun (20)	ETH	20.10.93	5		London	4	Oct
2:06:15	1:14:18	1:29:43	Olika	Adugna	ETH	12.9.99	1		Dubai	24	Jan
2:06:15	1:13:25	1:28:28	Bedan	Karoki	KEN	21.8.90	5		Tokyo	1	Mar
2:06:17	1:14:19	1:29:40	Erick	Kiptanui	KEN	19.4.90	2		Dubai	24	Jan
2:06:18	1:14:19	1:29:40	Ayana	Tsedat	ETH	18.2.96	3		Dubai	24	Jan
2:06:18	1:14:20	1:29:41	Tesfaye	Ambesa	ETH	.97	4		Dubai	24	Jan
2:06:21	1:14:19	1:29:41	Yitayal	Atnafu	ETH	20.1.93	5		Dubai	24	Jan
2:06:22	1:14:20	1:29:40	Yihunilign	Adane	ETH	29.2.96	6		Dubai	24	Jan
2:06:22	1:13:22	1:28:28	El Hassan	El Abbassi	BRN	13.4.84	6		Tokyo	1	Mar
2:06:23	1:14:18	1:29:41	Aychew	Bantie	ETH	12.9.95	7		Dubai	24	Jan
2:06:23	1:13:15	1:27:42	Asefa	Mengistu	ETH	18.1.85	7		Tokyo	1	Mar
			(32/30)								
2:06:24	1:14:25	1:28:56	Regasa	Mindaye	ETH	20.4.80	3		Sevilla	23	Feb
2:06:26	1:14:20	1:29:40	Seifu	Tura	ETH	19.6.97	8		Dubai	24	Jan
2:06:27	1:14:24	1:28:56	Workneh	Tiruneh	ETH	30.9.84	4		Sevilla	23	Feb
2:06:31	1:14:19	1:29:41	Bekele	Zewedu	ETH		10		Dubai	24	Jan
2:06:32	1:14:41		Hicham	Laqouahi	MAR	13.6.89	1		Marrakech	26	Jan
2:06:34	1:14:19	1:29:40	Beshah	Yerssie	ETH	1.10.98	11		Dubai	24	Jan
2:06:35	1:14:50	1:30:08	Ayad	Lamdassem	ESP	11.10.81	12		Valencia	6	Dec
2:06:41	1:14:23	1:29:00	Tamirat	Tola	ETH	11.8.91	6		London	4	Oct
2:06:42	1:14:22	1:29:02	Benson	Kipruto	KEN	17.3.91	7		London	4	Oct
2:06:43	1:14:24	1:28:56	Michael	Kunyuga	KEN	27.7.87	5		Sevilla	23	Feb
			(40)								
2:06:45	1:13:53	1:29:05	Ryu	Takaku	JPN	18.2.93	8		Tokyo	1	Mar
2:06:47	1:14:23	1:28:56	Bazu	Worku	ETH	15.9.90	6		Sevilla	23	Feb
2:06:47	1:14:49	1:30:07	Felix	Kandie	KEN	10.4.87	13		Valencia	6	Dec
2:06:49	1:14:22	1:29:02	Eliud	Kipchoge	KEN	5.11.84	8		London	4	Oct
2:06:54	1:13:53	1:29:05	Daisuke	Uekado	JPN	11.12.93	9		Tokyo	1	Mar
2:07:03	1:14:51	1:30:08	Hamid	Ben Daoud	ESP	19.2.96	14		Valencia	6	Dec
2:07:05	1:13:52	1:29:05	Toshiki	Sadakata	JPN	4.3.92	10		Tokyo	1	Mar
2:07:05	1:14:32	1:29:31	Yuya	Yoshida	JPN	23.4.97	1		Fukuoka	6	Dec
2:07:09	1:14:19	1:29:41	Zelalem	Bacha	BRN	10.1.88	12		Dubai	24	Jan
2:07:09	1:14:22	1:29:46	Abdi	Nageeye	NED	2.3.89	15		Valencia	6	Dec
			(50)								
2:07:18	1:14:50	1:30:08	Amanal	Petros	GER	17.5.95	16		Valencia	6	Dec
2:07:19			Eyob Ghebrehiwet	Faniel	ITA	26.11.92	7		Sevilla	23	Feb
2:07:20		1:30:14	Maru	Teferi	ISR	17.2.92	8		Sevilla	23	Feb
2:07:20	1:13:53	1:29:05	Shin	Kimura	JPN	8.2.94	11		Tokyo	1	Mar
2:07:23	1:14:24	1:29:01	Alemayehu	Mekonnen Lema	ETH	12.10.92	9		Sevilla	23	Feb
2:07:23	1:13:52	1:29:05	Yusuke	Ogura	JPN	16.4.93	12		Tokyo	1	Mar
2:07:26		1:29:41	Balew	Yihunle	ETH	21.9.98	13		Dubai	24	Jan
2:07:26	1:14:49	1:30:08	Lucas	Rotich	KEN	16.4.90	17		Valencia	6	Dec
2:07:27		1:30:21	Javier	Guerra	ESP	10.11.83	10		Sevilla	23	Feb
			(60)								
2:07:27	1:13:52	1:29:06	Yuta	Shimoda	JPN	31.3.96	13		Tokyo	1	Mar
2:07:28		1:30:20	Girmaw	Amare	ISR	26.10.87	11		Sevilla	23	Feb
2:07:31	1:13:53	1:28:43	Masato	Kikuchi	JPN	18.9.90	14		Tokyo	1	Mar
2:07:32			Feleke	Zegeye	ETH	.88	2		Marrakech	26	Jan
2:07:38		1:30:18	Shohei	Otsuka	JPN	13.8.94	2		Fukuoka	6	Dec
2:07:39	1:13:51	1:28:43	Tadashi	Isshiki	JPN	5.6.94	15		Tokyo	1	Mar
2:07:40			Dadi	Gemeda	ETH	.82	2		Marrakech	26	Jan
2:07:43			Lemi	Dumecha	ETH		1		Castellón	16	Feb
2:07:45		1:30:20	Haimro	Alame	ISR	8.6.90	13		Sevilla	23	Feb
2:07:45	1:13:52	1:29:05	Yuta	Shitara	JPN	18.12.91	16		Tokyo	1	Mar
			(70)								
2:07:51	1:14:20	1:29:41	Abdi	Fufa	ETH	27.9.95	14		Dubai	24	Jan
2:07:55	1:14:24	1:29:18	Belachew	Alemayehu	ETH	26.10.85	14		Sevilla	23	Feb

296 MARATHON - 100 KILOMETRES - 24 HOURS

Mark			Name		Nat	Born	Pos	Meet	Venue	Date
2:07:56	1:13:20	1:28:13	Simon	Kariuki	KEN	1.4.96	17		Tokyo	1 Mar
2:07:58			Abdi	Kebede	ETH	11.9.97	4		Marrakech	26 Jan
2:08:01			Hamza	Sahli	MAR	10.5.93	1		Oita	2 Feb
2:08:02			Fikre	Worknerh	ETH	11.5.88	5		Marrakech	26 Jan
2:08:03			Gizaw	Bekele	ETH	13.12.87	6		Marrakech	26 Jan
2:08:03			Natsuki	Terada	JPN	30.8.91	3		Fukuoka	6 Dec
2:08:05			Stephen	Mokoka	RSA	31.1.85	2		Otsu	8 Mar
2:08:06			Abdela	Godana	ETH	11.9.92	2		Oita	2 Feb
2:08:09			Derara	Hurisa	ETH	12.7.97	1		Mumbai	19 Jan
2:08:12	1:13:17	1:28:38	Getaneh	Tamire	ETH	10.1.94	19		Tokyo	1 Mar
2:08:16			Birhan	Nebebew	ETH	14.8.94	1		Xiamen	5 Jan
2:08:17			Michael	Githae	KEN	26.8.94	4		Fukuoka	6 Dec
2:08:20			Ayele	Abshero	ETH	28.12.90	2		Mumbai	19 Jan
2:08:21			Naoya	Sakuda	JPN	17.12.94	5		Fukuoka	6 Dec
2:08:22		1:30:08	Daniel	Mateo	ESP	31.8.89	18		Valencia	6 Dec
2:08:26			Birhanu	Teshome	ETH	.97	3		Mumbai	19 Jan
2:08:36			Kelkile	Gezahegn	ETH	1.10.96	1		Houston	19 Jan
2:08:37	1:14:18	1:29:40	Naoki	Okamoto	JPN	26.5.84	20		Tokyo	1 Mar
2:08:41			Jackson	Kiprop	UGA	20.10.86	4		Mumbai	19 Jan
2:08:41			Hiribo	Shano	ETH	.99	2		Castellón	16 Feb
2:08:44	1:14:35	1:30:06	Shohei	Kurata	JPN	5.8.92	21		Tokyo	1 Mar
2:08:45	1:14:01	1:29:23	Takuya	Fujikawa	JPN	17.12.92	22		Tokyo	1 Mar
2:08:45		1:30:06	Yuji	Iwata	JPN	9.7.87	23		Tokyo	1 Mar
2:08:46			Reuben	Kerio	KEN	2.6.94	2		Xiamen	5 Jan
2:08:47			Alemu	Gemechu	ETH	.95	6		Marrakech	26 Jan
2:08:48			Gezahagn	Mengistu	ETH	.93	3		Castellón	16 Feb
2:08:48			Felix	Kiprotich	KEN	7.12.88	3		Otsu	8 Mar
2:08:50		(100)		Peng Jianhua	CHN	18.12.96	1 NC		Nanjing	29 Nov
2:08:50			Kaan Kigen	Özbilen	TUR	15.1.86	19		Valencia	6 Dec
2:08:52	Birhanu	Gebru	ETH	27.1.87	5 Jan	2:09:23	Alphonce	Felix	TAN	14.2.92	8 Mar
2:08:52	Minato	Oishi (1:29:21)	JPN	19.5.88	1 Mar	2:09:25	Marius	Kipserem (1:29:01)	KEN	17.5.88	4 Oct
2:08:53	Tsukasa	Koyama	JPN	21.1.92	2 Feb	2:09:26	Okubay	Tsegay	ERI	.86	6 Dec
2:08:54	Tadu	Abate	ETH	11.9.97	24 Jan	2:09:28	Shoya	Okuno	JPN	10.4.93	8 Mar
2:08:55	Mehdi	Frere	FRA	27.7.96	6 Dec	2:09:31	Yoshiki	Takenouchi	JPN	25.5.92	6 Dec
2:08:56	Abdi Ali	Gelelchu	BRN	1.8.97	19 Jan	2:09:34	Hiroto	Inoue	JPN	6.1.93	1 Mar
2:08:56		Yang Shaohui	CHN	9.7.92	29 Nov	2:09:36	Tatsuya	Maruyama	JPN	29.7.94	20 Dec
2:08:59	Marin	Hehir	USA	19.9.99	20 Dec	2:09:38	Colin	Bennie	USA	3.6.95	20 Dec
2:09:01	Paul	Maina	KEN	31.12.92	19 Jan	2:09:41	Kenji	Yamamoto	JPN	17.11.89	1 Mar
2:09:01	Shengo	Kebede	ETH	.89	16 Feb	2:09:42	Scott	Fauble	USA	5.11.91	20 Dec
2:09:01	Sondre Nordstad	Moen	NOR	12.1.91	4 Oct	2:09:45	Juan	Pacheco	MEX	11.12.90	6 Dec
2:09:03	Tseveenravdan	Byambajav	MGL	7.7.90	2 Feb	2:09:45	Ian	Butler	USA		20 Dec
2:09:03		Duo Bujie	CHN	16.2.94	29 Nov	2:09:46	Scott	Smith	USA	13.7.96	20 Dec
2:09:04	Chihiro	Miyawaki	JPN	28.8.91	1 Mar	2:09:49	Stephen	Scullion	IRL	9.11.88	4 Oct
2:09:06	Takuya	Fukatsu	JPN	10.11.87	2 Feb	2:09:49	Jorge	Castelblanco	PAN	23.9.87	6 Dec
2:09:07	Kento	Kikutani	JPN	8.5.94	2 Feb	2:09:50	Hidekazu	Hijikata	JPN	27.6.97	1 Mar
2:09:09	Noah	Droddy	USA	22.9.90	20 Dec	2:09:50	Kenya	Sonota	JPN	30.5.93	8 Mar
2:09:10	Dereje	Adugna	ETH	9.1.95	26 Jan	2:09:51	Bekele	Muluneh	ETH		26 Jan
2:09:11	Belay	Asefa	ETH	17.6.92	24 Jan	2:09:51	Yimer	Getahun	ISR	28.6.92	23 Feb
2:09:13	Desmond	Mokgobu	RSA	23.11.88	6 Dec	2:09:51	Melkam	Jamber	ISR	23.6.91	23 Feb
2:09:15	Abera	Kuma	ETH	31.8.90	19 Jan	2:09:53	Youssef	Sbaai	MAR	2.5.80	23 Feb
2:09:15	Hassan	Chahdi	FRA	7.5.89	6 Dec	2:09:55	Koji	Kobayashi	JPN	16.1.89	2 Feb
2:09:17	Stanley	Bett	KEN	13.12.86	23 Feb	2:09:55	Iván	Fernández	ESP	10.6.88	23 Feb
2:09:17	Nicolas	Navarro	FRA	12.3.91	6 Dec	2:09:55		Chen Tianyu	CHN	11.5.97	29 Nov
2:09:18	Shoma	Yamamoto	JPN	10.4.95	8 Mar	2:09:55	Mick	Iacofano	USA	26.9.94	20 Dec
2:09:18	Paul	Lonyangata	KEN	12.12.92	20 Dec	2:09:56	Yago	Rojo	ESP	23.3.95	6 Dec
2:09:19	Haruki	Minatoya	JPN	25.4.96	2 Feb	2:09:56	Camilo Raúl	Santiago	ESP	22.12.82	6 Dec
2:09:19	Yohanes	Gebregergish	ERI	1.1.89	6 Dec	2:09:57	Paul	Kuira	KEN	25.1.91	6 Dec
2:09:20	Galen	Rupp	USA	8.5.86	29 Feb	2:09:59	Eulalio	Muñoz (153)	ARG	16.7.95	6 Dec

Downhill 122m Santa Monica 8 Mar: 1. Bayelign Teshager ETH 9.2.00 2:08:27, 2. John Langat KEN 31.12.96 2:08:44
3. Wilson Chebet KEN 12.7.85 2:09:17, 4. Michael Chege KEN 15.11.91 2:09:30
Drugs disqualification: 2:07:16   Jacob   Kendagor ¶   KEN   24.8.84   2   Marrakech   26 Jan

100 KILOMETRES

6:43:13	Aleksandr	Sorokin	LTU	30.9.81	1	POL Ch	Pabianice	30 Aug
6:50:17	Grant	Schmidlechner	AUS	21.9.78	9	Jan		
6:54:17	Dariusz	Novynski	POL	7.4.80	30	Aug		

24 HOURS

277.484km	Zoltán	Csécsei	HUN	25.7.84	1	NC	Balatonalmádi	25 Oct
266.887	Ivan	Penalba	ESP	6.10.91	1		Deventer	20 Sep
260.027	Leszek	Malyszek	POL	6.6.81	1	NC	Pabianice	30 Aug
256.143 t	Jacob	Moss	USA	8.7.93	1		Hampton, GA	15 Nov
255.772	Rafal	Kot	POL	21.12.79	2	NC	Pabianice	30 Aug

24 HOURS - 2000m - 3000m STEEPLECHASE

Mark	Name		Nat	Born	Pos	Meet	Venue		Date
253.355	Simen	Holvik	NOR	6.3.77	19 Sep	248.505	Valentin	Costa	FRA 27.8.66 11 Oct
252.989	Hironori	Nomoto	JPN	24.8.87	9 Feb	248.203	Krzysztof	Braczyk	POL 27.7.71 30 Aug
252.036	Andrzej	Mazur	POL	5.1.74	30 Aug	**Indoor**			
250.108 t	Nicholas	Coury	USA	1.10.87	12 Dec	253.958	Jari	Soikkeli	FIN 11.2.70 23 Feb
248.981 t	Ryan	Montgomery	USA	26.4.94	12 Dec	249.761	Edward	McCroarty	IRL 13.2.77 23 Feb

2000 METRES STEEPLECHASE

5:23.84	Konstantin	Plokhotnikov	RUS	24.3.97	1		Chelyabinsk		27 Aug
5:26.78	Fernando	Carro	ESP	1.4.92	22 Sep	5:30.86	Martin	Grau	GER 26.3.92 12 Jul
5:26.81	Karl	Bebendorf	GER	7.5.96	12 Jul	**No water jump**			
5:27.43	Daniel	Arce	ESP	22.4.92	29 Aug	5:28.50	André	Pereira	POR 10.8.95 8 Aug
						5:28.92	Fernando	Serrão	POR 8.4.93 8 Aug

3000 METRES STEEPLECHASE

Mark	Name		Nat	Born	Pos	Meet	Venue	Date
8:08.04	Soufiane	El Bakkali	MAR	7.1.96	1	Herc	Monaco	14 Aug
8:08.78	Leonard	Bett	KEN	3.11.00	2	Herc	Monaco	14 Aug
8:13.43	Djilali	Bedrani	FRA	1.10.93	3	Herc	Monaco	14 Aug
8:13.45	Fernando	Carro	ESP	1.4.92	4	Herc	Monaco	14 Aug
8:16.25	Matt	Hughes	CAN	3.8.89	5	Herc	Monaco	14 Aug
8:16.57	Topi	Raitanen	FIN	7.2.96	6	Herc	Monaco	14 Aug
8:17.60A	Abraham	Kibiwot	KEN	6.4.96	1		Keino Nairobi	3 Oct
8:19.37	Ryuji	Miura	JPN-J	11.2.02	1		Chitose	18 Jul
8:19.40	Daniel	Arce	ESP	22.4.92	7	Herc	Monaco	14 Aug
8:19.60	Philemon Kiplagat	Ruto	KEN-J	20.9.01	2		Chitose	18 Jul
[10]								
8:20.56	Konstantin	Plokhotnikov	RUS	24.3.97	1		Zhukovskiy	30 Jul
8:21.05	Louis	Gilavert	FRA	1.1.98	1		Décines-Charpieu	29 Aug
8:22.06	Mehdi	Belhadj	FRA	10.6.95	2		Décines-Charpieu	29 Aug
8:22.57	Lemecha	Girma	ETH	26.11.00	8	Herc	Monaco	14 Aug
8:23.02	Maksim	Yakushev	RUS	15.3.92	1	NC	Chelyabinsk	9 Sep
8:23.60	Phil	Norman	GBR	20.10.89	2	PNG	Turku	11 Aug
8:24.19	Kosei	Yamaguchi	JPN	19.8.91	1	NC	Osaka	4 Dec
8:24.38	Jonathan	Ndiku	KEN	18.9.91	1		Kumagaya	19 Sep
8:24.72	Jimmy	Gressier	FRA	4.5.97	3		Décines-Charpieu	29 Aug
8:24.87	Ole	Hesselbjerg	DEN	23.4.90	9	Herc	Monaco	14 Aug
[20]								
8:25.35	Simon	Sundström	SWE	4.2.98	4		Décines-Charpieu	29 Aug
8:25.77	Abdellah	Riahi	FRA	13.10.94	5		Décines-Charpieu	29 Aug
8:25.85	Ryuma	Aoki	JPN	16.6.97	4		Chitose	18 Jul
8:26.22	Ala	Zoghlami	ITA	19.6.94	1	NC	Modena	17 Oct
8:27.27	Gatien	Airiau	FRA	9.6.93	6		Décines-Charpieu	29 Aug
8:27.45	Osama	Zoghlami	ITA	19.6.94	2	NC	Modena	17 Oct
8:27.58	Geoffrey	Kipkemboi	KEN	.96	1		São Paulo	6 Dec
8:27.60	Yuriy	Kloptsov	RUS	22.12.89	3	NC	Chelyabinsk	9 Sep
8:28.01	Yasunari	Kusu	JPN	21.8.93	3	NC	Osaka	4 Dec
8:28.33	Leonardo	Feletto	ITA	26.6.95	1		San Biagio di Callalta	13 Sep
[30]								
8:30.54	Sebastián	Martos	ESP	20.6.89	1		Castellón	24 Aug
8:31.42	Salim Mohamed	Salim	EGY	1.10.93	1		El Mahdi	9 Dec
8:31.88	Seiya	Shigeno	JPN	23.12.96	4	NC	Osaka	4 Dec
8:32.10	Ibrahim	Ezzaydouni	ESP	28.4.91	3	NC	Madrid	12 Sep
8:32.12	Alexis	Phelut	FRA	31.3.98	3	PNG	Turku	11 Aug
8:32.71	Altobeli	da Silva	BRA	3.12.90	2	GP	São Paulo	6 Dec
8:32.98	Ibrahim	Chakir	ESP	4.9.94	2		Castellón	24 Aug
8:33.22	Andreu	Blanes	ESP	14.10.91	2			24 Aug
8:33.61	Mark	Pearce	GBR	19.1.96	5 Sep	8:36.29	Hillary/Hilal Yego (50)	TUR 2.4.92 20 Aug
8:33.64	Tim	Stegemann	GER	4.8.92	25 Jul	8:36.58	Nahuel Carabaña	AND 10.11.99 24 Aug
8:33.99	James	Nipperess	AUS	21.5.90	23 Feb	8:36.72	Zak Seddon	GBR 28.6.94 11 Aug
8:34.11	Taisei	Ogino	JPN	7.11.97	19 Sep	8:37.36	Jun Shinoto	JPN 2.4.85 19 Sep
8:34.55	Kazuya	Shiojiri	JPN	8.11.96	4 Dec	8:37.49	Alvaro Gutierrez	ESP 20.5.98 24 Aug
8:34.96	Jakob	Abrahamsen	DEN	29.7.94	19 Sep	8:37.85	Wilberforce Kones	KEN 19.9.93 6 Dec
8:35.05	Ahmed	Abdelwahed	ITA	26.5.96	10 Oct	8:38.25	Konstantin Wedel	GER 22.11.93 25 Jul
8:35.17	Yohannes	Chiappinelli	ITA	18.8.97	11 Aug	8:38.35	Hironori Tsuetaki	JPN 8.5.93 27 Mar
8:35.6A	Amos	Serem	KEN-J	28.8.02	5 Mar	8:38.48	Yusuke Uchikoshi	JPN 11.8.94 23 Feb
8:35.85	Getnet	Wale	ETH	16.7.00	14 Aug	8:38.75	Tim van der Welde	BEL 1.2.00 11 Aug
8:36.26	Martin	Grau	GER	26.3.92	11 Aug	8:39.70	Daniel Jarvis	GBR 21.10.95 5 Sep
						[60]		

JUNIORS
2 juniors in main list. 5 performances by 2 men to 8:30.0. Additional marks and further juniors:

Miura	8:28.51	1	NC	Nigata		11 Sep			
Ruto	8:24.38	2		Kumagaya		19 Sep	8:24.74	2	JPN Ch Osaka 4 Dec
8:35.6A	Amos	Serem		KEN	28.8.02	2		Nairobi	5 Mar
8:43.0A	Abraham	Seme		ETH	7.11.01	1		Addis Ababa	27 Dec
8:49.92	Hikaru	Kitamura		JPN	18.1.02	2		Niigata	11 Sep

60 METRES HURDLES

Mark	Name		Nat	Born	Pos	Meet	Venue	Date	
7.38	Grant	Holloway	USA	19.11.97	1		Clemson	14	Feb
7.47	Pascal	Martinot-Lagarde	FRA	22.9.91	1		Liévin	19	Feb
7.48		Holloway			1s3		Clemson	14	Feb
7.48	Andy	Pozzi	GBR	15.5.92	1		Madrid	21	Feb
7.51	Trey	Cunningham	USA	26.8.98	2		Clemson	14	Feb
7.52		Cunningham			1		Lubbock	31	Jan
7.52		Pozzi			1		Paris	2	Feb
7.52		Holloway			1h6		Clemson	14	Feb
7.52	Yaqoub	Al-Yoha	KUW	31.1.93	2		Madrid	21	Feb
7.53		Pozzi			1		Torun	8	Feb
7.53		Al-Yoha			2		Madrid	21	Feb
	(11/5)								
7.54	Jarret	Eaton	USA	24.6.89	2		Torun	8	Feb
7.54	Damian	Czykier	POL	10.8.92	3		Torun	8	Feb
7.54A	Aaron	Mallett	USA	26.9.94	1	NC	Albuquerque	15	Feb
7.59					1		Iowa City	18	Jan
7.54	Orlando	Ortega	ESP	29.7.91	1s1	NC	Ourense	29	Feb
7.55	Artem	Makarenko	RUS	23.4.97	1		Moskva	9	Feb
	(10)								
7.56	Valdó	Szücs	HUN	29.6.95	1	NC	Budapest	23	Feb
7.59	Konstadínos	Douvalídis	GRE	10.3.87	1		Metz	9	Feb
7.59	Gregor	Traber	GER	2.12.92	1	NC	Leipzig	22	Feb
7.60	Jaylan	McConico	USA	17.8.98	1		Fayetteville	14	Feb
7.61	Caleb	Parker	USA	26.6.98	1h1		Lubbock	31	Jan
7.61	Taio	Kanai	JPN	28.9.95	1h1	NC	Osaka	1	Feb
7.61	Milan	Trajkovic	CYP	17.3.92	5		Torun	8	Feb
7.61	Eric	Edwards Jr.	USA	3.1.00	2		Fayetteville	14	Feb
7.62	Gabriel	Constantino	BRA	9.2.95	3		Madrid	21	Feb
7.62	Damian	Warner	CAN	4.11.89	1h1		Baton Rouge	21	Feb
	(20)								
7.64	Daniel	Roberts	USA	13.4.98	1	Millrose	New York (A)	8	Feb
7.64	Robert	Dunning	USA	23.6.97	1		Lubbock	15	Feb
7.65A	Brendan	Ames	USA	6.10.88	1s2	NC	Albuquerque	15	Feb
7.65A	Chad	Zallow	USA	25.4.97	4	NC	Albuquerque	15	Feb
7.65	Aurel	Manga	FRA	24.7.92	1	NC	Liévin	29	Feb
7.66	Konstantin	Shabanov	RUS	17.11.89	2		Yekaterinburg	7	Jan
7.66	Greggmar	Swift	BAR	16.2.91	1		Seattle	18	Jan
7.66	Cory	Poole	USA	29.7.99	4		Clemson	14	Feb
7.66	Jason	Joseph	SUI	11.10.98	1	NC	St. Gallen	16	Feb
7.66	Petr	Svoboda	CZE	10.10.84	1	NC	Ostrava	22	Feb
	(30)								
7.67	David	Efremov	KAZ	15.1.99	1	NC	Ust-Kamenogorsk	18	Jan
7.67	Shyheim	Wright	USA	19.12.98	1		University Park	31	Jan
7.67	Jeanice	Laviolette	FRA	25.1.00	1	NC-23	Saint-Brieuc	9	Feb
7.67	John	Burt	USA	10.2.97	1s1		Clemson	14	Feb
7.67A	Aleec	Harris	USA	31.10.90	5	NC	Albuquerque	15	Feb
7.67		Xie Wenjun	CHN	11.7.90	1h1		Lubbock	21	Feb
7.68	Shiunsuke	Izumiya	JPN	26.1.00	2h1	NC	Osaka	1	Feb
7.68A	Michael	Dickson	USA	25.1.97	2h1	NC	Albuquerque	14	Feb
7.71					7		Liévin	19	Feb
7.68	Damion	Thomas	JAM	29.6.99	3		Fayetteville	14	Feb
7.68	Michael	Obasuyi	BEL	12.8.99	3h1		Madrid	21	Feb
	(40)								
7.68	Artur	Noga	POL	2.5.88	2	NC	Torun	1	Mar
7.69	Shuwei	Ishikawa	JPN	29.5.95	1	NC	Osaka	1	Feb
7.69	Shusei	Nomoto	JPN	25.10.95	3h1	NC	Osaka	1	Feb
7.69	Elmo	Lakka	FIN	10.4.93	4		Paris	2	Feb
7.70	Braxton	Canady	USA	13.1.98	1h4	ACC	Notre Dame	28	Feb
7.70	Rasheem	Brown	CAY	22.3.00	1	NAIA	Brookings	7	Mar
7.71	Devon	Brooks	USA		1		Columbia SC	7	Feb
7.71	Just	Kwaou-Mathey	FRA	4.12.99	2	NC-23	Saint-Brieuc	9	Feb
7.71	Enrique	Llopis	ESP	15.10.00	1	NC-23	Salamanca	15	Feb
7.71	João	Oliveira (50)	POR	15.5.92	1h2	NC	Pombal	1	Mar
7.71	Kurt	Powdar	USA-J	9.6.01	1h1	JUCO	Lynchburg	6	Mar
7.72	Paris	Williams	USA	19.8.98	17 Jan	7.73	Higashi Tomasu Ishida	JPN	14.4.97	1 Feb
7.72	Mattia	Montini	ITA	7.5.99	26 Jan	7.73	Stephon Torrence	USA	8.2.98	7 Feb
7.72	Lafranz	Campbell	JAM	19.10.97	14 Feb	7.73	Hassane Fofana	ITA	28.4.92	8 Feb
7.72A	Sam	Brixey	USA	2.5.98	14 Feb	7.73	Oladayo Akindele	USA	18.9.96	28 Feb
7.72	Lorenzo	Perini	ITA	22.7.94	22 Feb	7.73A	Tanner Conner	USA		29 Feb
7.73	Devon	Allen	USA	12.12.94	18 Jan	7.74	Maliek Kendall	USA	1.9.97	1 Feb

110 METRES HURDLES

Mark		Name		Nat	Born	Pos Meet	Venue	Date
7.74A		Zhu Shenglong	CHN	25.1.00	1 Feb	7.74 Brithton	Senior JAM	7.10.00 29 Feb
7.74	Liam	van der Schaaf	NED	8.10.98	9 Feb	7.74 Jamal	Britt USA	11 Dec

110 METRES HURDLES

Mark	Wind	Name		Nat	Born	Pos	Meet	Venue	Date
13.11	0.8	Orlando	Ortega	ESP	29.7.91	1	Herc	Monaco	14 Aug
13.14	0.8	Andrew	Pozzi	GBR	15.5.92	1	Herc	Monaco	14 Aug
13.15	-0.3		Ortega			1		Marseille	3 Sep
13.15	0.1		Pozzi			1	G Gala	Roma	17 Sep
13.15	0.3	Aaron	Mallett	USA	26.9.94	1	DL	Doha	25 Sep
13.17	1.1		Pozzi			1	PNG	Turku	11 Aug
13.18	0.8	Wilhem	Bélocian	FRA	22.6.95	3	Herc	Monaco	14 Aug
13.19	0.8	Grant	Holloway	USA	19.11.97	4	Herc	Monaco	14 Aug
13.20	0.0		Belocian			1	NC	Albi	13 Sep
13.21	0.3		Ortega			1	Gyulai	Székesfehérvár	19 Aug
	[10/5]								
13.24	0.4		Xie Wenjun	CHN	11.7.90	1	NC	Shaoxing	16 Sep
13.27	1.4	Taio	Kanai	JPN	28.9.95	1		Fukui	29 Aug
13.29	0.4	Jason	Joseph	SUI	11.10.98	1h2	NC	Basel	12 Sep
13.30	0.3	Freddie	Crittenden	USA	3.8.94	3	Gyulai	Székesfehérvár	19 Aug
13.31	0.0	Sergey	Shubenkov	RUS	4.10.90	1	NC	Chelyabinsk	8 Sep
	[10]								
13.34	1.4	Shun-ya	Takayama	JPN	3.9.94	2		Fukui	29 Aug
13.36	0.8	Devon	Allen	USA	12.12.94	2r1		Clermont	25 Jul
13.39	1.4	Shuhei	Ishikawa	JPN	29.5.95	3		Fukui	29 Aug
13.40	0.6	Antonio	Alkana	RSA	12.4.90	3		Bellinzona	15 Sep
13.45	1.4	Shusei	Nomoto	JPN	25.10.95	4		Fukui	29 Aug
13.45	0.8	Shunsuke	Izumiya	JPN	26.1.00	2s1	NC	Niigata	2 Oct
13.47	-0.4	Rasheed	Broadbell	JAM	13.8.00	1		Kingston	18 Jul
13.47	0.0		Zeng Jianhang	CHN	17.9.98	1		Shanghai	23 Aug
13.48	1.0	Simon	Ehammer	SUI	7.2.00	2	NC	Basel	12 Sep
13.49	1.0	Konstadínos	Douvalídis	GRE	10.3.87	1	NC	Patra	8 Aug
	[20]								
13.50	0.6	Enrique	Llopis	ESP	15.10.00	1		Madrid	6 Sep
13.51	0.9	David	King	GBR	13.6.94	2rB	Gyulai	Székesfehérvár	19 Aug
13.52	0.0	Jeanice	Laviolette	FRA	25.1.00	2	NC	Albi	13 Sep
13.53	0.2	Vitaliy	Parakhonko	BLR	18.8.93	1		Minsk	25 Jun
13.53	0.9	Vladimir	Vukicevic	NOR	6.5.91	3rB	Gyulai	Székesfehérvár	19 Aug
13.53	1.7	Lorenzo	Perini	ITA	22.7.94	1	NC	Padova	29 Aug
13.54	0.6	Michael	Dickson	USA	25.1.97	1		Des Moines	29 Aug
13.54	1.8	Kevin	Mayer	FRA	10.2.92	1		Saint-Paul, Réunion	19 Dec
13.55	1.2	Roger Valentín	Iribarne	CUB	2.1.96	1h1		Camagüey	6 Feb
13.55	0.6	Cameron	Fillery	GBR	2.11.98	1	Szew	Bydgoszcz	19 Aug
	[30]								
13.57	1.2	Yordan	O'Farrill	CUB	9.2.93	2h1		Camagüey	6 Feb
13.57	1.5	Ryuta	Fujii	JPN	29.7.96	1h2		Fukui	29 Aug
13.57	0.0	Michael	Obasuyi	BEL	12.8.99	3	Hanz	Zagreb	15 Sep
13.57	1.1	Jonathas	Brito	BRA	30.11.92	1	NC	São Paulo	11 Dec
13.58	-0.1	Valdó	Szücs	HUN	29.6.95	1h1	NC	Budapest	8 Aug
13.59	0.4	Genta	Masuno	JPN	24.5.93	2s2	NC	Niigata	2 Oct
13.60	1.8	Matthias	Bühler	GER	2.9.86	1h1		Regensburg	26 Jul
13.60	1.4	Yusuke	Takahashi	JPN	5.7.96	6		Fukui	29 Aug
13.60	0.4		Ning Xiaohan	CHN	24.1.00	3	NC	Shaoxing	16 Sep
13.60	0.1	Yacoub Mohamed Al-Yoha		KUW	31.1.93	5	G Gala	Roma	17 Sep
	[40]								
13.60	0.3	Gabriel	Constantino	BRA	9.2.95	4	DL	Doha	25 Sep
13.60	0.8	Hiromasa	Yokochi	JPN	1.10.00	5s1	NC	Niigata	2 Oct
13.60	0.9		Yang Wei-Ting	TPE	22.9.94	1h		Taipei	4 Oct
13.61	0.8	Paolo	Dal Molin	ITA	31.7.87	5	Herc	Monaco	14 Aug
13.61	0.0	Justin	Kawaou-Mathey	FRA	4.12.99	3	NC	Albi	13 Sep
13.61	0.4	Higashi Tomasu	Ishida	JPN	14.4.97	3s2	NC	Niigata	2 Oct
13.61	0.4	Rashid	Muratake	JPN-J	6.2.02	4s2	NC	Niigata	2 Oct
13.63	-0.3	Pascal	Martinot Lagarde	FRA	22.9.91	3		Marseille	3 Sep
13.64	1.4	Anthony Tyrell	Kuriki	JPN	17.9.96	8		Fukui	29 Aug
13.64	1.1	Rafael	Pereira	BRA	8.4.97	2	NC	São Paulo	11 Dec
	[50]								
13.66	0.6	Damian	Czykier	POL	10.8.92	2	Szew	Bydgoszcz	19 Aug
13.66	0.4		Zhang Honglin	CHN	12.1.94	4	NC	Shaoxing	16 Sep
13.66	1.1	Eduardo	de Deus	BRA	8.10.95	3	NC	São Paulo	11 Dec
13.67	0.8	Nick	Hough	AUS	20.10.93	8 Mar	13.69 0.0 Konstantin Shabanov	RUS	17.11.89 8 Sep
13.67	0.6	Erik	Balnuweit	GER	21.9.88	1 Aug	13.69 0.0	Chen Kuei-Ju TPE	22.9.93 1 Nov
13.68	-0.9	Petr	Svoboda	CZE	10.10.84	22 Aug	13.70 1.2 Elmo	Lakka FIN	10.4.93 15 Aug
13.69	1.6	Mikdat	Sevler	TUR	21.9.98	28 Aug	13.70 1.2 Asier	Martínez ESP	22.4.00 27 Sep

300   110 - 300 - 400 METRES HURDLES

Mark		Name		Nat	Born	Pos	Meet	Venue		Date
13.71	0.0	Balázs	Baji	HUN	9.6.89	1	Aug	13.82 0.2 Aleec Harris USA 31.10.90		15 Aug
13.73	-0.6	Fanor Andrés	Escobar	COL	17.12.97	6	Dec	13.83 0.8 Kim Byung-jun KOR 15.8.91		28 Jul
13.74	1.6	Hassane	Fofana	ITA	28.4.92	16	Jul	13.83 1.5 Keiso Pedriks EST 30.4.94		22 Aug
13.74	1.3	Chad	Zallow	USA	25.4.97	29	Aug	13.84 2.0 Hideki Omuro JPN 25.7.90		29 Aug
13.75	0.9	Bálint	Szeles	HUN	9.11.98	19	Aug	13.85 0.4 Mizuki Kondo JPN-Y 28.3.03		3 Nov
13.79	1.2	Ryo	Tokuoka	JPN	27.9.99	21	Oct	13.86 0.2 Georg Fleischhauer GER 21.10.88		8 Aug
13.80	0.4	Raphael	Mohamed	FRA	2.2.98	25	Jul	13.86 1.5 Takumu Furuya JPN 12.3.97		29 Aug
13.80	0.6	Dawid	Zebrowski	POL	8.1.97	19	Aug	13.86 0.5 Ryohei Terada JPN 15.7.98		13 Sep
13.81	0.8	Nicholas	Andrews	AUS	2.2.97	8	Mar	13.86 -0.3 Rikuto Higuchi JPN 19.8.99		13 Sep
13.81	-0.6	Koen	Smet	NED	9.8.92	18	Jul	13.86 -0.5 Sun Zhenjiang CHN 25.1.99		16 Sep
13.81	0.5	Max	Hrelja	SWE	30.1.98	5	Sep	13.86 1.2 Koichiro Shimizu JPN 15.2.00		21 Oct
13.81	-0.6	Paulo Henrique	da Silva	BRA	29.6.95	6	Dec	[84] 100th 13.93		

Wind assisted

13.20	2.5		Xie Wenjun	CHN	11.7.90	1		Shanghai	19 Jul
13.32	2.5		Zeng Jianhang	CHN	17.9.98	2		Shanghai	19 Jul
13.46	4.1	Nick	Hough	AUS	20.10.93	1		Auckland (Waitakere)	23 Feb
13.46	2.6	Konstadínos	Douvalídis	GRE	10.3.87	1		Vári	15 Jul
13.48	2.6	Vladimir	Vukicevic	NOR	6.5.91	1		Espoo	5 Aug
13.54	2.4	Yusuke	Takahashi	JPN	5.7.96	2h1		Fukui	29 Aug
13.55	2.9	Mikdat	Sevler	TUR	21.1.98	1		Bursa	19 Aug
13.56A	3.8	Ruan	de Vries	RSA	1.2.86	1		Pretoria	14 Mar
13.71	4.1	Jacob	McCorry	AUS	20.11.97	23 Feb	13.78 2.4 Raphael Mohamed FRA 2.2.98		25 Jul
13.72		Matteo	Ngo	FRA	23.3.98	14 Aug	13.79 2.4 Mizuki Kondo JPN-Y 28.3.03		29 Aug
13.75	3.4	Ryan	Fontenot	USA	4.5.86	30 Jul	13.83 2.5 Yang Quanlei CHN 26.10.99		19 Jul
13.76	4.1	Josh	Hawkins	NZL	9.2.94	23 Feb			

Hand timing: La Habana 28 Feb +1.6 1. Roger Valentín Iribarne CUB 2.1.96 13.5
13.5   1.6   Roger Valentín   Iribarne   CUB   2.1.96 1   La Habana   28 Feb

JUNIORS

13.61	0.4	Rashid	Muratake	JPN	6.2.02	4s2	NC	Niigata	2 Oct
		13.63	0.1 2h3 NC	Niigata	2 Oct	13.65 -0.4 2		Tokyo	23 Aug
		13.69	0.1 1s	Niigata	13 Sep	13.69 -0.3 1		Niigata	13 Sep
13.85	0.4	Mizuki	Kondo	JPN-Y	28.3.03	2		Niigata	3 Nov
13.93	0.9	Paul	Chabauty	FRA	20.1.01	1rB	NC	Albi	13 Sep
13.95	-1.6	Koki	Fujihara	JPN-J	31.5.02	1		Uji	6 Nov
13.97	-0.3	Akira	Tawada	JPN	3.3.01	6		Niigata	13 Sep

Wind assisted
13.79w 2.4   Mizuki   Kondo   JPN-Y   28.3.03 5h1   Fukui   29 Aug

110 Metres Hurdles – 99 cm hurdles

13.27	-1.2	Sasha	Zhoya	FRA	25.6.02	1		Madrid	4 Oct
		13.28	-0.3 1	Marseille	3 Sep	3 performances by 2 men to 13.40			
13.28	0.6	Rashiddo	Muratake	JPN	6.2.02	1		Hiroshima	23 Oct
13.51	1.6	Jaheim	Stern	JAM	.02	1		Kingston	6 Mar
13.51	0.6	Kazuki	Kurokawa	JPN	17.6.01	2		Hiroshim	23 Oct

Wind assisted
13.53   2.1   Paul   Chabauty   FRA   20.1.01 1   Pontoise   30 Aug

300 METRES HURDLES

33.78		Karsten	Warholm	NOR	28.2.96	1	Bisl	Oslo	11 Jun
34.93		Sinan	Ören	TUR	10.2.98	1		Anjara	18 Jul
35.07		Timothy TJ	Holmes	USA	2.7.95	1		Marietta	29 Jul
35.35		Alastair	Chalmers	GBR	31.3.00	1		St.Peter Port	12 Jul
35.37		Dany	Brand	SUI	23.2.96	1		Meilen	20 Jun
35.72		Mario	Lambrughi	ITA	5.2.92	1		Milano	26 Sep

400 METRES HURDLES

46.87		Karsten	Warholm	NOR	28.2.96	1	DL	Stockholm	23 Aug
47.07			Warholm			1	G Gala	Roma	17 Sep
47.08			Warholm			1	ISTAF	Berlin	13 Sep
47.10			Warholm			1	Herc	Monaco	14 Aug
47.62			Warholm			1	GS	Ostrava	8 Sep
48.23			Warholm			1	NC	Bergen	20 Sep
48.69		Ludvy	Vaillant	FRA	15.3.95	2	G Gala	Roma	17 Sep
48.72		Rasmus	Mägi	EST	4.5.92	3	G Gala	Roma	17 Sep
		[8/3]							
49.04		Yasmani	Copello	TUR	15.4.87	2	Herc	Monaco	14 Aug
49.11		Wilfried	Happio	FRA	22.9.98	1		La Chaux-de-Fonds	15 Aug
49.12		Tatsuhiro	Yamamoto	JPN	23.4.97	1		Niigata	13 Sep
49.19		Kazuki	Kurokawa	JPN-J	17.6.01	2		Niigata	13 Sep
49.31		Takatoshi	Abe	JPN	12.11.91	1		Tokyo	23 Aug
49.33A		Mehdi	Pirjahan	IRI	23.9.99	1		Tehran	2 Oct

400 METRES HURDLES

Mark	Name		Nat	Born	Pos	Meet	Venue	Date	
49.35	David	Kendziera	USA	9.9.94	4	G Gala	Roma	17	Sep
	[10]								
49.40	Kyohei	Yoshida	JPN	12.10.97	3		Niigata	13	Sep
49.41	Nick	Smidt	NED	12.5.97	2		La Chaux-de-Fonds	15	Aug
49.49	Constantin	Preis	GER	16.5.98	1		Luzern	3	Jul
49.60	Ramsey	Angela	NED	6.11.99	1		Bern	24	Jul
49.63A	Masaki	Toyoda	JPN	17.1.98	1		Fujiyoshida	6	Sep
49.66	Alastair	Chalmers	GBR	31.3.00	1	NC	Manchester	5	Sep
49.68	Efekemo	Okoro	GBR	21.2.92	1		Nuneaton	2	Aug
49.69	Carl	Bengtström	SWE	13.1.00	1	vFIN	Tampere	6	Sep
49.71	Maté	Koroknai	HUN	13.1.93	1		Székesfehérvár	5	Sep
49.77	Timofey	Chalyy	RUS	7.4.94	1	NC	Chelyabinsk	9	Sep
	[20]								
49.78	Emil	Agyekum	GER	22.5.99	2	NC	Braunschweig	9	Aug
49.78	Berke	Akcam	TUR-J	10.4.02	1		Istanbul	4	Sep
49.79	Masaya	Oda	JPN	11.5.95	1		Osaka	24	Oct
49.83	Mario	Lambrughi	ITA	5.2.92	1		Alba	29	Jul
49.89	Hiromu	Yamauchi	JPN	24.8.99	4		Niigata	13	Sep
49.92A	Bassem Awad Al-Hemeida		QAT	28.9.00	10 Mar	50.25	Kotaro	Miyao	JPN	12.7.91	5	Sep
49.93	Vít	Müller	CZE	31.8.96	9 Aug	50.25	Takayuki	Kishimoto	JPN	6.5.90	3	Nov
49.95	Maksims	Sincukovs	LAT	26.6.98	5 Aug	50.26	Keisuke	Nozawa	JPN	7.6.91	24	Oct
49.98	Mitsuru	Sugai	JPN	7.1.94	5 Sep	50.27	Yuki	Matsushita	JPN	9.9.91	15	Aug
50.00	Thomas	Barr	IRL	24.7.92	15 Sep	50.31	Sales	Inglin	SUI	27.8.99	15	Sep
50.00	Shinnosuke	Hase	JPN	11.6.96	26 Sep	50.35	Kakeru	Inoue	JPN	19.3.96	3	Nov
50.02	Chris	Douglas	AUS	10.2.97	22 Feb	50.44	Seamus	Derbyshire	GBR	27.1.00	23	Aug
50.05	Yusuke	Hataura	JPN	5.10.98	13 Sep	50.46	Alessandro	Sibilio	ITA	27.4.99	20	Sep
50.06A	Le Roux	Hamman	RSA	6.1.92	13 Mar	50.47		Peng Ming-Yang	TPE	10.6.98	4	Nov
50.07	Patryk	Dobek	POL	13.2.94	29 Aug	50.48	Lucirio	Garrido	VEN	4.10.88	15	Aug
50.07	Dany	Brand	SUI	23.2.96	12 Sep	50.48	Mahau	Suguimati	BRA	13.11.84	13	Dec
50.11	Chris	McAlister	GBR	3.12.95	2 Aug	50.49	Atsushi	Yamada	JPN	3.7.91	24	Oct
50.12	Hiroya	Kawagoe	JPN	21.9.97	1 Oct	50.50	Oskari	Mörö	FIN	31.1.93	6	Sep
50.14	Vladimir	Lysenko	RUS	10.6.98	30 Aug	50.51	Timothy	Emo-Oghene	NGR	20.11.98	1	Mar
50.15	Oskar	Edlund	SWE-J	16.11.02	16 Aug	50.53	Tuomas	Lehtinen	FIN	4.8.98	16	Aug
50.19		Feng Zhiqiang	CHN	14.4.98	30 May	50.53	Kazunari	Takada	JPN	27.11.97	23	Aug
50.20	Alain-Hervé	Mfomkpa	SUI	4.6.96	27 Jun	50.53	Martin	Kucera	SVK	10.5.90	11	Sep
50.20	Gabriel	Mikolajewski	POL	16.3.99	29 Aug	50.53	Yusuke	Ishida	JPN	25.5.95	26	Sep
50.22A	Masayuki	Obayashi	JPN	6.2.96	6 Sep	50.54	Ren	Miyoshi	JPN	27.11.98	10	Aug
50.23	Sinan	Ören	TUR	10.2.98	7 Aug	50.55	Márcio	Teles	BRA	27.1.94	13	Dec
50.23	Artur	Langowski Terezan	BRA	8.5.91	13 Dec	50.56A	Takeshi	Iwamoto	JPN	13.7.96	6	Sep
50.24	Joshua	Abuaku	GER	7.7.96	3 Jul	50.58	Oaulo Andrés	Ibáñez	ESA	28.10.98	28	Dec
50.25A	Cornel	Fredericks	RSA	3.3.90	21 Feb	50.59	Javier	Delgado (71)	ESP	9.6.96	13	Sep

JUNIORS
2 juniors in main list. 2 performances by 2 men to 50.00. Further juniors:

50.15	Oskar	Edlund	SWE-J	16.11.02	1	NC	Uppsala	16	Aug
50.67	Kouhei	Kanno	JPN	20.6.02	1		Kami	23	Jul
50.73	Ryosuke	Takahashi	JPN-Y	20.6.03	1		Nagoya	24	Jul
50.87A	Marthinus	Du Preez	RSA		1		Pretoria	7	Mar
50.88	Devontie	Archer	JAM	26.5.92	1		Kingston	6	Mar

HIGH JUMP

2.33i	Darryl	Sullivan	USA	28.12.97	1		Blacksburg, VA	18	Jan
				2.05/1 2.10/1 2.15/2 2.18/2 2.27/3 2.33/2					
2.33i	Tom	Gale	GBR	18.12.98	1		Hustopece	8	Feb
				2.15/1 2.20/1 2.24/2 2.27/1 2.30/2 2.33/3 2.35/xxx					
	2.31i 3		Banská Bystrica	11 Feb	2.10/1 2.15/1 2.20/1 2.25/1 2.28/3 2.31/3 2.33/xxx				
2.33i	Luis Enrique	Zayas	CUB	7.6.97	1		Banská Bystrica	11	Feb
				2.20/1 2.25/1 2.31/1 2.33/1 2.35/xxx					
2.33i	Jamal	Wilson	BAH	1.9.88	2		Banská Bystrica	11	Feb
				2.10/1 2.15/1 2.20/1 2.25/1 2.28/2 2.31/2 2.33/2 2.35/xxx					
2.33i	Ilya	Ivanyuk	RUS	9.3.93	1	NC	Moskva	26	Feb
				2.10/1 2.15/1 2.20/1 2.24/1 2.28/1 2.33/4 jump-off					
2.33	Maksim	Nedosekov	BLR	21.1.98	1		Minsk	14	Aug
				2.02/1 2.07/1 2.15/1 2.20/x 2.22/2 2.26/2 2.31/xx 2.33/1 2.36/xx 2.37/x					
2.31i	Mikhail	Akimenko	RUS	6.12.95	1		Chelyabinsk	16	Jan
				2.15/2 2.19/1 2.23/1 2.26/1 2.31/2 2.36/xxx					
	2.31i 1		Moskva	3 Mar	2.10/1 2.15/1 2.20/1 2.24/1 2.28/1 2.31/1 2.34/xxx				
2.31i	Naoto	Tobe	JPN	31.3.92	1	EST Ch	Tallinn	23	Feb
				2.16/1 2.22/1 2.28/3 2.31/3 2.34/xxx					
2.31i	Gianmarco	Tamberi	ITA	1.6.92	1		Siena	29	Feb
				2.13/1 2.21/1 2.28/2 2.31/3 2.34/xxx					
2.31	Tomohiro	Shinno	JPN	17.8.96	1		Kumagaya	20	Sep
	(12/10)			2.10/1- 2.16/1 2.19/1 2.22/2 2.25/3 2.28/2 2.31/3 2.33/xxx					

HIGH JUMP

Mark	Name		Nat	Born	Pos	Meet	Venue	Date
2.30i	Nikita	Anishchenkov	RUS	25.7.92	1		Moskva	27 Jan
2.30i	Earnie	Sears	USA	4.12.98	1		Lubbock	1 Feb
2.30i	Sylwester	Bednarek	POL	28.4.89	2		Hustopece	8 Feb
2.30	Brandon	Starc	AUS	24.11.93	1		Sydney	22 Feb
2.30		Woo Sang-hyuk	KOR	23.4.96	1		Canberra	29 Feb
2.30	Loïc	Gasch	SUI	13.8.94	1		Aarau	31 Jul
2.30	Andriy	Protsenko	UKR	20.5.88	1	NC	Lutsk	30 Aug
2.29i	Norbert	Kobielski	POL	28.1.97	1	NC	Toruń	29 Feb
2.28i	Edgar	Rivera	MEX	13.2.91	1		Wuppertal	24 Jan
2.28i	Paulo	Conceição	POR	29.12.93	1		Luxembourg	1 Feb
	[20]							
2.28i	Juvaughn	Harrison [Blake]	USA	30.4.99	1		Fayetteville	15 Feb
2.28i		Zhang Guowei	CHN	4.6.91	2		Siena	29 Feb
2.28	Mateusz	Przybylko	GER	9.3.92	1	NC	Braunschweig	9 Aug
2.28	Keitaro	Fujita	JPN	2.10.97	1		Osaka	24 Oct
2.28	Ryoichi	Akamatsu	JPN	2.5.95	1		Yokosuka	3 Nov
2.27i	Konstadínos	Baniótis	GRE	6.11.86	1		Lucenec	6 Feb
2.27i	Matthew	Sawe	KEN	2.7.88	6		Hustopece	8 Feb
2.27i	Andriy	Kovalyov	UKR	11.6.92	1	NC	Sumy	22 Feb
2.27	Thomas	Carmoy	BEL	16.2.00	1		Bruxelles	9 Aug
2.27	Takashi	Eto	JPN	5.2.91	1		Tokyo	23 Aug
	[30]							
2.27	Thiago Julio	Moura	BRA	27.11.95	1		Campinas	26 Sep
2.27	Hamish	Kerr	NZL	17.8.96	1		Auckland (NS)	18 Dec
2.26i	Fernando	Ferreira	BRA	13.12.94	2		Nehvizdy	22 Jan
2.26i	Trey	Culver	USA	18.7.96	2		Lubbock	1 Feb
2.26iA	Erik	Kynard	USA	3.2.91	1	NC	Albuquerque	14 Feb
2.26iA	Shelby	McEwen	USA	6.4.96	2	NC	Albuquerque	14 Feb
2.26i	Brenton	Foster	AUS	26.2.98	1		Blacksburg, VA	22 Feb
2.26	Douwe	Amels	NED	16.9.91	1		Rhede	25 Jul
2.26	Dmytro	Yakovenko	UKR	17.9.92	2	NC	Lutsk	30 Aug
2.26	Carlos	Rojas	ESP	10.4.95	1	NC	Alocobendas	12 Sep
	[40]							
2.25i	Darius	Carbin	USA	4.3.98	1		Clemson	11 Jan
2.25i	Clayton	Brown	JAM	8.12.96	1		Fayetteville	1 Feb
2.25i	Adrijus	Glebauskas	LTU	20.11.94	1		Kaunas	1 Feb
2.25i	Eric	Richards	USA	1.8.98	1		Houston	1 Feb
2.25i	Marek	Bahník	CZE	10.5.99	1	NC	Ostrava	2 Feb
2.25i	Tihomir	Ivanov	BUL	11.7.94	1	NC	Sofia	2 Feb
2.25i	Oleh	Doroshchuk	UKR-J	4.7.01	1		Sumy	4 Feb
2.25i	Tejaswin	Shankar	IND	21.12.98	1		Ames	15 Feb
2.25i	Jeron	Robinson	USA	30.4.91	1		Houston	29 Feb
2.25	Victor	Korst	POR	21.10.96	1		Lisboa	27 Jun
	[50]							
2.25	Alperen	Acet	TUR	2.4.98	1		Denizli	6 Aug
2.25	Raul	Spank	GER	13.7.88	1		Berlin	22 Aug
2.25	Tobias	Potye	GER	16.3.95	2		Sinn	29 Aug
2.25	Naoto	Hasegawa	JPN	15.11.96	3		Yamaguchi	18 Oct
2.24i	William	Grimsey	GBR	14.12.96	1		Loughborough	11 Jan
2.24	Joel	Baden	AUS	1.2.96	1		Geelong	18 Jan
2.24i	Luis Joel	Castro	PUR	28.1.91	2		Udine	29 Jan
2.24i	Vadym	Kravchuk	UKR	28.10.96	1		Weinheim	7 Feb
2.24i	Matús	Bubeník	SVK	14.11.89	8		Hustopece	8 Feb
2.24i	Nikita	Kurbanov	RUS	13.4.99	1	NC-23	Sankt Peterburg	14 Feb
	[60]							
2.24i	Dmytro	Nikitin	UKR	31.7.99	1		Istanbul	15 Feb
2.24i	Andrey	Churylo	BLR	19.5.93	1	NC	Mogilev	21 Feb
2.24i	David	Smith	GBR	14.7.91	2	NC	Glasgow	23 Feb
2.24i	Matvey	Rudnik	RUS	8.6.99	4	NC	Moskva	26 Feb
2.24		Chen Long	CHN-J	13.11.02	1		Chengdu	15 May
2.24	Aleksandr	Asanov	RUS	30.3.95	2	NC	Chelyabinsk	10 Sep
2.24		Li Jialun	CHN	16.4.95	1	NC	Shaoxing	16 Sep
2.24i	Daniyil	Tsyplakov	RUS	29.7.92	1		Krasnodar	20 Dec
2.23i	Kyle	Landon	USA	16.10.94	25 Jan			
2.23i	Perry	Christie	USA	18.2.99	8 Feb			
2.23i	Greg	Lauray	USA	15.10.98	8 Feb			
2.23iA	Keenon	Laine	USA	12.6.97	14 Feb			
2.23i	Justice	Summerset	USA	20.1.98	14 Feb			
2.23i	Zack	Anderson	USA	3.6.98	21 Feb			
2.23i	Jyles	Etienne	BAH	17.3.99	29 Feb			
2.23i	Michael	Burke	USA	23.1.97	29 Feb			
2.23	Gerson	Baldé	POR	28.1.00	8 Aug			

2.22i	Roberto	Vilches	MEX	21.5.99	17 Jan
2.22	Oscar	Miers	AUS-J	21.11.01	25 Jan
2.22i	Vernon	Turner	USA	21.8.98	31 Jan
2.22iA	Eure	Yáñez	VEN	20.5.93	2 Feb
2.22i	Kelechi	Aguocha	GBR-J	10.2.01	8 Feb
2.22iA	Jason	Smith	USA	19.12.98	13 Feb
2.22iA	Benjamin	Milligan	USA	29.5.97	13 Feb
2.22i	Michael	Mason	CAN	30.9.86	15 Feb
2.22i	Daniel	Armstrong	USA	24.2.98	22 Feb

POLE VAULT

Mark	Name		Nat	Born		Pos	Meet		Venue		Date
2.22i	Alexis	Sastre	ESP	3.12.93	29 Feb	2.20i	Silvano	Chesani	ITA	17.7.88	11 Feb
2.22	Sandro	Jersin Tomassini	SLO-Y	30.1.04	19 Jul	2.20	Nauraj Singh	Randhawa	MAS	27.1.92	22 Feb
2.21i	Tequan	Claitt	USA	18.7.97	25 Jan	2.20i	Marco	Fassinotti	ITA	29.4.89	23 Feb
2.21i	Donald	Thomas	BAH	1.7.84	29 Jan	2.20i	Bryson	Deberry	USA	13.6.99	25 Feb
2.21i	Bradley	Adkins	USA	30.12.93	1 Feb	2.20i	Semyen	Pozdnyakov	RUS	28.11.92	26 Feb
2.21	Daniel	Kosonen	FIN	17.9.00	11 Jun	2.20	Lushane	Wilson	JAM	11.9.98	29 Feb
2.21	Stefano	Sottile	ITA	26.1.98	25 Jun	2.20i	Rahman	Minor	USA	28.11.98	29 Feb
2.21	Arttu	Mattila	FIN-J	3.3.01	27 Jul	2.20	Keegan	Fourie	RSA	7.9.91	4 Mar
2.21	Yuto	Seko	JPN	16.3.98	2 Aug	2.20	Jonas	Wagner	GER	29.5.97	18 Jul
2.21	Fabian	Delryd	SWE	15.10.96	10 Aug	2.20	Adónios	Mérlos	GRE	4.4.99	22 Jul
2.21	Dániel	Jankovics	HUN	1.3.95	26 Aug	2.20	Viktor	Lonskyy	UKR	27.10.95	16 Aug
2.20i	Erick	Portillo	MEX	5.10.00	24 Jan	2.20	Falk	Wendrich	GER	12.6.95	16 Aug
2.20i	Allen	Gordon	USA	28.8.98	24 Jan	2.20	Aleksey	Fadeyev	RUS	9.5.00	10 Sep
2.20i	Caleb	Parker (100)	USA	26.6.98	25 Jan	2.20		Sun Zhao	CHN	8.2.90	16 Sep
2.20i	Nathan	Ismar	FRA	30.3.99	30 Jan	2.20		Wang Yu	CHN	18.8.91	16 Sep
2.20	Sebastien	Micheau	FRA	3.5.98	30 Jan	2.20	Ryo	Sato	JPN	21.7.94	3 Oct
2.20	Jordan	Wesner	USA	10.6.97	2 Feb	2.20	Kazuhiro	Ota	JPN	11.6.95	3 Oct
2.20i	Chris	Baker	GBR	2.20.91	8 Feb	2.20	Hiromi	Takahari	JPN	13.11.87	3 Oct
2.20i	Nicolas	De Luca	ITA	7.4.93	8 Feb	2.20		Vu Duc Anh	VIE	6.2.98	13 Nov

[124]

Best outdoor marks

2.30	Wilson	1	Nassau	11 Jan		2.25	Glebauskas	1 NC	Palanga		7 Aug
2.30	Tamberi	1	Ancona	28 Jun		2.25	Anishchenkov	1	Chelyabinsk		27 Aug
2.30	Ivanyuk	1	Bryansk	29 Aug		2.25	Rivera	1	Sinn		29 Aug
2.28	Kobielski	1	Plock	16 Aug		2.24	Tobe	3	Tokyo		23 Feb
2.26	Ferreira	1	São Bernardo do Campo	1 Mar							
2.23	Doroshchuk	13 Aug	2.21	Kynard	1 Aug	2.20	T Ivanov	9 Aug	2.20	Nikitin	30 Aug
2.22	Churylo	25 Jun	2.21	Bubeník	15 Aug	2.20	Baker	16 Aug	2.20	Sawe	3 Oct
2.22	Bahnik	4 Jul	2.20	Zayas	22 Mar	2.20	Robinson	29 Aug			

JUNIORS

2 juniors in main list. Additional juniors:

2.22	Oscar	Miers	AUS	21.11.01	1		Brisbane (Nathan)	25 Jan
2.22i	Kelechi	Aguocha	GBR	10.2.01	1e2		Hustopece	8 Feb
2.22	Sandro	Jersin Tomassini	SLO-Y	30.1.04	1	NC-j	Novo Mesto	19 Jul
2.21	Arttu	Mattila	FIN	3.3.01	1		Äänekoski	27 Jul
2.18i	Romaine	Beckford	JAM	9.7.02	1		Lubbock	21 Feb
2.18	Yonatan	Kapitolnik	ISR	25.11.02	1		Tel Aviv	19 Jul
2.18	Elton	Petronilho	BRA	27.12.01	1	NC-23	Bragança Paulista	18 Dec

POLE VAULT

6.18i		Armand		Duplantis		SWE	10.11.99	1		Glasgow	15 Feb
				5.50/1 5.75/2 5.84/1 6.00/1 6.18/i							
	6.17i	1		Torun	8 Feb	5.52/1 5.72/1 5.92/1 6.01/1 6.17/2					
	6.15	1	G Gala	Roma	17 Sep	5.45/1 5.70/1 5.80/1 5.85/2 6.00/1 6.15/2					
	6.07i	1		Liévin	19 Feb	5.60/1 5.80/1 5.90/1 6.07/1 6.19/xxx					
	6.07	1	Athl	Lausanne	2 Sep	5.62/1 5.82/1 5.87/1 5.92/1 5.97/1 6.02/1 6.07/1 6.15/x					
	6.01i	1		Clermont-Ferrand	23 Feb	5.65/1 5.87/1 6.01/1 6.19/xxx					
	6.01	1	DL	Stockholm	23 Aug	5.53/1 5.73/1 5.83/1 6.01/1 6.15/xxx					
	6.00i	1		Düsseldorf	4 Feb	5.40/1 5.55/1 5.70/2 5.80/1 5.90/1 5.95/1 6.00/2 6.17/xxx					
	6.00	1	Herc	Monaco	14 Aug	5.60/1 5.70/3 5.80/1 6.00/3 6.15/xxx					
	6.00	1	VD	Bruxelles	4 Sep	5.50/1 5.70/1 5.80/1 6.00/1 6.15/xxx					
	5.94	1		Göteborg	4 Jul	5.35/1 5.50/1 5.60/1 5.70/2 5.85/1 5.94/3 6.19/xxx					
	5.91	1	ISTAF	Berlin	13 Sep	5.57/1 5.82/x 5.91/2 6.15/xxx					
6.02		Sam		Kendricks		USA	7.9.92	2	Athl	Lausanne	2 Sep
				5.32/1 5.52/1 5.62/2 5.72/1 5.77/1 5.82/1 5.87/1 5.92/1 5.97/1 6.02/1 6.07/1							
	6.01i	1		Rouen	8 Feb	5.39/1 5.54/1 5.64/1 5.74/1 5.80/1 5.86/1 6.01/3					
	5.90i	2		Liévin	19 Feb	5.40/1 5.60/1 5.70/1 5.80/2 5.90/3 5.95/x					
	5.87i	3		Clermont-Ferrand	23 Feb	5.65/1 5.80/1 5.87/1 6.01/xxx					
5.94i		Renaud		Lavillenie		FRA	18.9.86	2		Clermont-Ferrand	23 Feb
				5.65/1 5.80/1 5.87/1 5.94/1 6.01/xxx							
5.93i		Chris		Nilsen		USA	13.1.98	1		Lincoln	21 Feb
				5.38/1 5.53/1 5.63/2 5.73/1 5.84/2 5.93/2							
5.90A		Jacob		Wooten		USA	22.4.97	1		Ciudad de México	22 Feb
				5.52/1 5.62/2 5.72/2 5.82/1 5.90/2 6.00/xxx							
5.90A		Matthew		Ludwig		USA	5.7.96	2		Ciudad de México	22 Feb
				5.52/3 5.62/2 5.72/2 5.82/3 6.00/xxx							
5.90		Piotr		Lisek		POL	16.8.92	1	Maniak	Szczecin	16 Aug
	(21/7)			5.35/1 5.70/1 5.80/2 5.90/2							
5.86i		Timur		Morgunov		RUS	12.10.96	1		Moskva	9 Feb
5.85		Harry		Coppell		GBR	11.7.96	1	NC	Manchester	4 Sep
5.83i		K.C.		Lightfoot		USA	11.11.99	1		Ames	15 Feb
	[10]										
5.82iA		Kyle		Pater		USA	24.12.94	1		Air Force Academy	18 Jan

POLE VAULT

Mark	Name		Nat	Born	Pos	Meet	Venue	Date	
5.82A	Audie	Wyatt	USA	30.4.96	3		Ciudad de México	22	Feb
5.82	Claudio Michel	Stecchi	ITA	23.11.91	1		Chiari	8	Sep
5.82	Thiago	Braz da Silva	BRA	16.12.93	3	ISTAF	Berlin	13	Sep
5.81	Bo Kanda	Lita Baehre	GER	29.4.99	2		Leverkusen	16	Aug
5.80i	Andrew	Irwin	USA	24.1.93	1		Norman	4	Jan
5.80	Kurtis	Marschall	AUS	25.4.97	1		Perth	1	Feb
5.80iA	Branson	Ellis	USA	19.7.00	2	NC	Albuquerque	14	Feb
5.80i	Zachery	Bradford	USA	29.11.99	1		Fayetteville	15	Feb
5.80i	Ben [20]	Broeders	BEL	21.6.95	3		Liévin	19	Feb
5.80		Jin Min-sub	KOR	2.9.92	1		Sydney	1	Mar
5.80	Ernest John	Obiena	PHI	17.11.95	3	G Gala	Roma	17	Sep
5.76	Raphael	Holzdeppe	GER	28.9.89	3		Leverkusen	16	Aug
5.76	Menno	Vloon	NED	11.5.94	1		Leiden	19	Sep
5.75i	Rutger	Koppelaar	NED	1.5.93	1	NC	Apeldoorn	22	Feb
5.75i	Reese	Watson	USA	8.10.93	1		Navasota	7	Mar
5.74i	Valentin	Lavillenie	FRA	16.7.91	3=		Rouen	8	Feb
5.74i	Mathieu	Collet	FRA	15.3.95	5		Rouen	8	Feb
5.73	Austin	Miller	USA	1.6.94	1		Mooresville, NC	22	Jul
5.72i	Alioune Sène [30]		FRA	3.2.96	1		Orléans	11	Jan
5.70i	Konstadinos	Filippídis	GRE	26.11.86	3		Cottbus	29	Jan
5.70i	Torben	Blech	GER	12.2.95	3		Düsseldorf	4	Feb
5.70i	Pål Haugen	Lillefosse	NOR-J	4.6.01	2		Ulsteinvik	28	Feb
5.70i	Pawel	Wojciechowski	POL	6.6.89	1	NC	Torun	1	Mar
5.70	Tray	Oates	USA	14.3.95	1		Marietta	8	Aug
5.65iA	Nate	Richartz	USA	2.11.94	8	NC	Albuquerque	14	Feb
5.65iA	Carson	Waters	USA	5.6.96	9	NC	Albuquerque	14	Feb
5.65i	Adam	Coulon	USA	5.10.97	2		Fayetteville	14	Feb
5.65	Angus	Armstrong	AUS	17.3.97	1		Perth	7	Mar
5.65i	Drew Volz [40]		USA	20.11.92	3		Navasota	7	Mar
5.65	Sondre	Guttormsen	NOR	1.6.99	1		Ski	2	Jun
5.65	Cole	Walsh #	USA	14.6.95	1		Marietta	15	Aug
5.64i		Yao Jie	CHN	21.9.90	2		Szczecin	25	Feb
5.64i	Robert	Sobera	POL	19.1.91	3		Szczecin	25	Feb
5.62i	Brandon	Bray	USA	24.4.97	1		Lubbock	21	Feb
5.62A	Jorge	Luna	MEX	8.6.96	4		Ciudad de México	22	Feb
5.62A	Garrett	Starkey	USA	7.10.93	5		Ciudad de México	22	Feb
5.62	Thibaut	Collet	FRA	17.6.99	6	Athl	Lausanne	2	Sep
5.61i	Mateusz	Jerzy	POL	29.3.95	1		Łódź	1	Jan
5.61i	Dmitry [50]	Zhelyabin	RUS	20.5.90	2		Chelyabinsk	16	Jan
5.61i	Zach	McWhorter	USA	7.1.99	1		New York (A)	25	Jan
5.61i	Hussain Asim	Al-Hizam	KSA	4.1.98	2		Lincoln	8	Feb
5.61iA	Dylan	Bell	USA	21.7.93	2		Colorado Springs	21	Feb
5.60i	Charlie	Myers	GBR	12.6.97	1		Gateshead	16	Jan
5.60i	Adam	Hague	GBR	29.8.97	1		Sheffield	22	Jan
5.60i	Jan	Kudlicka	CZE	29.4.88	3		Chemnitz	7	Feb
5.60i	Igor	Bychkov	ESP	7.3.87	2		Madrid	21	Feb
5.60i	Devin	King	USA	12.3.96	1		Baton Rouge	21	Feb
5.60i	Ersu	Sasma	TUR	30.9.99	1		Istanbul	23	Feb
5.60i	Georgiy [60]	Gorokhov	RUS	20.4.93	2		Moskva	29	Feb
5.60	Oleg	Zernikel	GER	16.4.95	1		Hechingen	4	Jul
5.60	Seito	Yamamoto	JPN	11.3.92	1		Tokyo	23	Aug
5.60	Koki	Kuruma	JPN	25.3.96	1	NC	Niigata	2	Oct
5.60	Germán	Chiaraviglio	ARG	16.4.87	1		Concordia	7	Nov
5.58	Ethan	Cormont	FRA	29.9.00	3	NC	Albi	12	Sep
5.57i	Romain	Gavillon	FRA	4.11.98	1eB		Clermont-Ferrand	22	Feb
5.55i	Ilya	Mudrov	RUS	17.11.91	1		Yaroslavl	11	Jan
5.55i	Jules	Cypres	FRA	9.8.97	5		Rennes	15	Feb
5.55i	Clayton	Fritsch	USA	29.12.98	2		College Station	22	Feb
5.55i	Aleksandr [70]	Gripich	RUS	21.9.86	4	NC	Moskva	26	Feb
5.55	Kyle	Rademeyer	RSA-J	29.1.02	1		Paarl	21	Nov
5.54i	Arnaud	Art	BEL	28.1.93	1e2		Rouen	8	Feb
5.54i	Mikko	Paavola	FIN	16.1.98	1		Mustasaari	20	Dec
5.53i	Axel	Chapelle	FRA	24.4.95	4		Bordeaux	18	Jan
5.53	Melker	Svärd Jacobsson	SWE	8.1.94	2	NC	Uppsala	16	Aug
5.52A	José Rodolfo	Pacho	ECU	30.1.96	7		Ciudad de México	22	Feb

POLE VAULT - LONG JUMP

Mark	Name		Nat	Born	Pos	Meet	Venue	Date	
5.52	Tommi	Holttinen	FIN	3.5.97	1		Espoo	27	Jun
5.52	Masaki	Ejima	JPN	6.3.99	1		Setagaya	15	Aug
5.52	Dan	Bárta	CZE	24.2.98	1	NC-23	Jablonec	19	Sep
5.51i	Ethan	Bray	USA	18.5.97	2		Vermillion	8	Feb
	[80]								
5.51 u	Keaton	Daniel	USA-J	8.4.01	4		Menifee	26	Jun
5.51	Baptiste	Thiery	FRA-J	29.6.01	1		Frauenkappelen	1	Aug
5.51	Kazuki	Furusawa	JPN-J	5.7.02	1		Maebashi	8	Aug
5.51	Urho	Kujanpää	FIN	18.5.97	1		Vaasa	30	Aug
5.51	Isidro	Leyva	ESP	25.4.99	1	NC-23	Sevilla	26	Sep
5.50i	Diogo	Ferreira	POR	30.7.90	26 Jan				
5.50i	Shawnacy	Barber	CAN	27.5.94	29 Jan				
5.50i	Karsten	Dilla	GER	17.7.89	31 Jan				
5.50i	Ivan	Horvat	CRO	17.8.93	1 Feb				
5.50i	Max	Mandusic	ITA	12.6.98	2 Feb				
5.50iA	Larry	Still	USA	7.11.96	7 Feb				
5.50i	Antonio	Ruiz	MEX	4.11.96	15 Feb				
5.50i	Adrián	Vallés	ESP	16.3.95	21 Feb				
5.50i	Didac	Salas	ESP	19.5.93	21 Feb				
5.50i	Matvey	Volkov	RUS/BLR-Y	13.3.04	29 Feb				
5.50i	Mikhail	Shmykov	RUS-J	15.2.01	29 Feb				
5.50	Valco	van Wyk	RSA	26.7.00	4 Mar				
5.50		Huang Bokai	CHN	26.9.96	5 Jun				
5.50		Zhang Wei	CHN	22.3.94	5 Jun				
5.50	Lev	Skorish (100)	ISR	12.4.96	28 Jul				
5.50	Emmanouïl	Karalis	GRE	20.10.99	9 Aug				
5.50	Matthias	Orban	FRA	21.1.00	12 Sep				
5.50	Kosei	Takekawa	JPN	16.12.97	2 Oct				
5.50	Shingo	Sawa	JPN	28.9.96	2 Oct				
5.47i	Keon	Howe	USA	8.12.96	28 Feb				
5.46i	Chase	Smith	USA	1.4.97	15 Feb				
5.46i	Matthew	Peare	USA	19.6.98	28 Feb				
5.46	Mareks	Arents	LAT	6.8.86	5 Aug				
5.45i	Luke	Winder	USA	2.8.95	4 Jan				
5.45iA	Chris	Pillow	USA	8.7.93	10 Jan				
5.45iA	Scott	Marshall	USA	30.6.95	24 Jan				
5.45iA	Cole	Riddle	USA	9.4.99	1 Feb				
5.45iA	Deakin	Volz	USA	12.1.97	1 Feb				
5.45i	Jake	Albright	USA	22.12.93	14 Feb				

5.45i	Michael	Carr	USA	18.9.96	14 Feb
5.45i	Ilya	Prosvirin	RUS	28.2.95	17 Feb
5.45	Declan	Carruthers	AUS	7.9.97	29 Feb
5.45	Robin	Emig	FRA-J	6.6.01	12 Aug
5.45	Dominik	Alberto	SUI	28.4.92	11 Sep
5.45	Simen	Guttormsen	NOR-J	19.1.01	19 Sep
5.43	Stephen	Clough	AUS	4.11.96	1 Feb
5.42i	Nikandros	Stylianou	CYP	22.8.89	1 Feb
5.41Ai	Trey	Devereaux	USA	7.5.97	8 Feb
5.41i	Eerik	Haamer	EST-J	6.1.01	6 Mar
5.41	Matej	Scerba	CZE	9.12.98	8 Aug
5.41	Thomas	Van Der Plaetsen	BEL	24.12.90	29 Aug
5.41	Nikolai	van Huyssteen	RSA-J	8.8.02	4 Nov
5.40i	Gordon	Porsch	GER	11.3.95	25 Jan
5.40	Nick	Southgate	NZL	9.4.94	25 Jan
5.40i	Viktor	Pintusov	RUS	7.2.00	28 Jan
5.40i	Tyce	Hruza	USA	7.10.00	31 Jan
5.40i	Theódoros-Panayiótis Hrisanthópoulos		GRE	21.6.93	15 Feb
5.40i	Haze	Farmer	USA-J	22.6.01	14 Feb
5.40i	Philip	Kass	GER	23.11.98	23 Feb
5.40	Takuma	Ishikawa	JPN	7.11.97	23 Aug
5.40	Istar	Dapena	ESP	3.8.96	6 Sep
5.40	Lamin	Krubally	GAM	13.2.95	19 Sep
5.39i	Noah	Zastrow	USA	.99	29 Feb
5.38i	Stanley	Joseph	FRA	24.10.91	18 Jan
5.38i	Rubem	Miranda	POR	10.6.93	19 Jan
5.38i	Mike	Vani	USA	20.6.91	22 Feb
5.38i	Samuel	Young	USA		29 Feb
5.38	Scott	Houston (143)	USA	11.6.90	24 Jun

Best outdoor marks

5.82	Lightfoot	1ex	Russellville	24 Jul
5.82	R.Lavillenie	3 DL	Doha	25 Sep
5.80	Broeders	2 G Gala	Roma	17 Sep
5.70	Nilsen	2	Dessau	8 Sep
5.70	V.Lavillenie	2 NC	Albi	12 Sep
5.62	Blech	3	Vught	1 Aug
5.62	Wojciechowski	8 Athl	Lausanne	2 Sep
5.61A	Pater	? 1	Boulder	6 Apr
5.50	Vallés	14 Aug	5.50 Yao Jie	29 Oct
5.50	Gripich	9 Sep	5.46 Paavola	5 Aug

5.61	Lillefosse	2	Oslo	11 Jun
5.61u	Richartz	1	Menifee	26 Jun
5.60	Sobera	5 Szew	Bydgoszcz	19 Aug
5.60	Filippídis	4	Dessau	8 Sep
5.55	Cypres	3 Maniak	Szczecin	16 Aug
5.55	Gorokhov	1	Bryansk	29 Aug
5.52	Sasma	1	Bursa	29 Aug
5.51	Kudlicka	1 NC	Plzen	8 Aug
5.45	Mandusic	17 Aug	5.40 Hrisanthópoulos	9 Aug
5.41	Hague	16 Aug	5.40 Pintusov	9 Sep
5.40	Kass	12 Jun	5.40 Prosvirin	9 Sep

Drugs disqualification: 5.80i Cole Walsh # USA 14.6.95 (3) Rouen 8 Feb

JUNIORS

5 juniors in main list. 10 performances (inc. 5 indoors) by 2 men to 5.54. Additional marks and further juniors:

Lillefosse 2+	5.65i	1 NC	Baerum	2 Feb	5.60i	1	Athlone	12 Feb
	5.61i	3	Berlin	14 Feb	5.60	2	Göteborg	4 Jul
	5.60i	1	Stockholm	25 Jan	5.54i	1	Bergen	4 Jun
Rademeyer	5.54	1	Paarl	14 Nov				
5.50i	Matvey	Volkov	RUS/BLR-Y	13.3.04	3		Moskva	29 Feb
5.50i	Mikhail	Shmykov	RUS	15.2.01	4		Moskva	29 Feb
5.45	Robin	Emig	FRA	6.6.01	1		Cannes La Bacca	12 Aug
5.45	Simen	Guttormsen	NOR	19.1.01	3	NC	Bergen (Fana)	19 Sep
5.41i	Eerik	Haamer (10)	EST	6.1.01	1		Tartu	6 Mar
5.41	Nikolai	van Huyssteen	RSA	8.8.02	1		Paarl	4 Nov
5.40i	Haze	Farmer	USA	22.6.01	1		Fayetteville	15 Feb
5.31i	Gabe	Gilfillan	USA	5.10.01	1		Houston	8 Feb
5.30		Song Haoyang	CHN	17.6.02	1		Xi'an	28 Sep
5.30i	Tomoya	Karasawa	JPN	17.5.02	1		Yoshioka	22 Nov
5.30i	Takumi	Kobayashi	JPN	2.9.01	1		Yoshioka	6 Dec

LONG JUMP

| 8.41i | Juan Miguel | Echevarría | CUB | 11.8.98 | 1 | | Madrid | 21 Feb |
| | | | | 8.33 | 8.31 | p | x | p | 8.41 |

306 LONG JUMP

Mark	Wind	Name		Nat	Born	Pos	Meet	Venue		Date	
	8.25	-0.9 1 NC	La Habana		22 Mar	x		8.25	x	p	x	7.97
8.36	0.3		Wang Jianan	CHN	27.8.96	1	NC	Shaoxing		15 Sep
					8.21		8.36	x		x	p	8.29/0.2
8.33	0.5		Huang Changzhou	CHN	20.8.94	2	NC	Shaoxing		15 Sep
					8.33		8.29/0.6	8.24	8.23	8.23	8.12
	8.28	0.5 1	Nanjing		4 Sep	8.28	p		p	8.28
8.29	-0.6	Yuki	Hashioka	JPN	23.1.99	1		Niigata		11 Sep
					7.92		8.06	x		8.29
8.28	1.6	Lester	Lescay	CUB-J	15.10.01	1		Camagüey		23 Feb
					x		8.08	x	8.04	8.28	7.98w
8.27	1.8	Kristian	Pulli	FIN	2.9.94	1		Espoo		11 Jun
					8.27		7.98	8.02		8.13	p	p
8.26	1.9	Maykel	Massó	CUB	8.5.99	2		Camagüey		23 Feb
					7.76		7.97	8.26		7.80	p	7.90
8.26i		Miltiádis	Tentóglou	GRE	18.3.98	1	NC	Pireás		29 Feb
					7.96		7.94	x		8.11	8.16	8.26
		[10/8]								
8.23	1.6	Tajay	Gayle	JAM	2.8.96	*		Kingston		11 Jul
8.23	0.1		Zhang Yaoguang	CHN	21.6.93	2		Nanjing		4 Sep
		[10]								
8.22i		Thobias	Montler	SWE	15.2.96	1	NC	Växjö		23 Feb
8.20	1.4	Darcy	Roper	AUS	31.3.98	1		Canberra		25 Jan
8.20A	0.3	Cheswill	Johnson	RSA	30.9.97	1		Johannesburg		1 Feb
8.20		Shown-D	Thompson	JAM	20.1.97	1		Spanish Town		8 Feb
8.19i		Carey	McLeod	JAM	14.4.98	1	SEC	College Station		29 Feb
8.16	1.1	Alexsandro	Melo	BRA	29.9.95	1	NC	São Paulo		12 Dec
8.15	1.3	Simon	Ehammer	SUI	7.2.00	1		Schaffhausen		27 Jun
8.13	-0.8	Augustin	Bey	FRA	6.6.95	1		Bruxelles		9 Aug
8.12	1.4	Filippo	Randazzo	ITA	27.4.96	1		Savona		16 Jul
8.11i		Juvaughn	Harrison [Blake]	USA	30.4.99	1		Fayetteville		14 Feb
		[20]								
8.10	0.6	Vladislav	Bulakhov	BLR	23.1.99	1	NC	Minsk		2 Aug
8.10	0.2	Radek	Juska	CZE	8.3.93	1	NC	Plzen		9 Aug
8.09i		Rayvon	Grey	USA	2.12.97	1		Fayetteville		1 Feb
8.09	1.5	Ruswahl	Samaai	RSA	25.9.91	1	DL	Stockholm		23 Aug
8.08i		Bachana	Khorava	GEO	15.3.93	1		Tbilisi		2 Feb
8.06	1.5	Aléxandros-Víktor	Peristéris	GRE	16.3.96	1		Kalamáta		29 Jul
8.06	0.3	Julian	Howard	GER	3.4.89	1		Weinheim		1 Aug
8.05i		Justin	Hall	USA	12.2.98	1		Lubbock		14 Feb
8.05	0.0	Strahinja	Jovancevic	SRB	28.2.93	1		Berane		11 Sep
8.04	1.3	Marko	Ceko	CRO	3.8.00	1	NC	Zagreb		8 Aug
		[30]								
8.02i		Steffin	McCarter	USA	19.1.97	1		Houston		17 Jan
8.02i		LaQuarn	Nairn	BAH	31.7.96	2	SEC	College Station		29 Feb
8.01i		Anatoliy	Ryapolov	RUS	31.1.97	1	NC	Moskva		26 Feb
8.00i		Isaac	Grimes	USA	7.2.98	1		Lubbock		1 Feb
8.00i		Gabriele	Chilá	ITA	17.9.97	1	NC	Ancona		22 Feb
8.00i		O'Brien	Wasome	JAM	24.1.97	1	Big 12	Ames		29 Feb
7.99	0.9	Henry	Smith	AUS	9.4.96	3		Canberra		25 Jan
7.99i		Eusebio	Cáceres	ESP	10.9.91	1		Karlsruhe		29 Jan
7.99i		Jarod	Biya	SUI	22.5.00	2	Fra Ch	Liévin		29 Feb
7.99	1.1	Artyom	Primak	RUS	14.1.93	2		Chelyabinsk		9 Sep
		[40]								
7.99	-0.1	Hibiki	Tsuha	JPN	21.1.98	1	NC	Niigata		2 Oct
7.98iA		KeAndre	Bates	USA	24.5.96	1	NC	Albuquerque		14 Feb
7.98	-0.3	Lin Yu-Tang		TPE	11.5.00	1		Kaohsiung		3 Nov
7.97i		Ja'Mari	Ward	USA	21.3.98	3	SEC	College Station		29 Feb
7.97	1.4	Maximilian	Entholzner	GER	18.8.94	1		Castellón		24 Aug
7.97	1.9	Yaroslav	Isachenkov	UKR	2.3.95	1	NC	Lutsk		29 Aug
7.96i		Corion	Knight	USA	18.8.96	1		Clemson		25 Jan
7.96		Mehakpreet	Singh	IND	26.3.95	1		Panchkula		25 Mar
7.96	0.5	Daiki	Oda	JPN	15.1.96	1		Setagaya		4 Apr
7.96	0.5	Antonino	Trio	ITA	4.6.93	1		Palermo		25 Jul
		[50]								
7.95	1.7	Mateusz	Jopek	POL	14.2.96	1		Olomouc		27 Jun
7.95	1.9	Andrzej	Kuch	POL	27.10.91	1		Czestochowa		25 Jul
7.94i		Izmir	Smajlaj	ALB	29.3.93	16 Feb	7.93i		Jean Marie Okutu	ESP	4.8.88	29 Feb
7.94i		Gao Xinglong	CHN	12.3.94	21 Feb	7.93	0.8	Jules	Pommery	FRA-J	22.01.01	28 Aug
7.94	2.0	Maykel Yorges	Vidal	CUB	6.1.00	7 Mar	7.93	1.1	Samory Fraga	Bandeira	BRA	29.11.96	11 Dec
7.94	-1.0	Reynold	Banigo	GBR	13.8.98	30 Aug	7.92i		Vladyslav	Mazur	UKR	21.11.96	10 Jan
7.93iA		Malik	Moffett	USA	11.4.94	14 Feb	7.92	1.1	Shunsuke	Izumiya	JPN	26.1.00	24 Jul
7.93iA		Treyshon	Malone	USA	7.12.96	29 Feb	7.91i		Damar	Forbes	JAM	18.9.90	1 Feb

LONG JUMP - TRIPLE JUMP

Mark	Wind	Name		Nat	Born	Pos	Meet	Venue	Date
7.91i		László	Szabó	HUN	22.11.91	2			Feb
7.91iA		Charles	Brown	USA	28.5.97	14			Feb
7.91	1.7	Kazuma	Adachi	JPN	16.10.97	24			Jul
7.91	1.0	Hans-Christian Hausenberg		EST	18.9.98	9			Aug
7.90i		Shotaro	Shiroyama	JPN	6.3.95	2			Feb
7.89i		Sergiy	Nykyforov	UKR	6.2.94	21			Feb
7.89	1.4	Lin Chia-Hsing		TPE	13.7.99	11			Mar
7.89		Zhang Jingqiang		CHN	8.5.96	30			May
7.89	1.2	István	Virovecz	HUN	1.12.89	1			Aug
7.89	0.6	Filip	Pravdica	CRO	28.7.95	8			Aug
7.89	1.8	Daniel	Segers	BEL-J	1.2.01	16			Aug
7.89	1.1	Natsuki	Mainaga	JPN-Y	12.7.03	18			Sep
7.88Ai		Jason	Smith	USA	19.12.98	14			Feb
7.88i		Ivo	Tavares	POR	31.1.96	22			Feb
7.88	1.8	Jeremy	Andrews	AUS	3.11.92	23			Feb
7.88	-0.4	Emanuel	Archibald	GUY	9.9.94	29			Feb
7.88A		Sikhumbuzo Nkosi		RSA	.98	7			Mar
7.88	0.2	Artyom	Huryin	BLR	17.2.98	26			Jun
7.88	0.0	Tenju	Togawa	JPN	8.1.97	11			Sep
7.88	1.3	Yuto	Toriumi	JPN-J	4.10.01	25			Oct
7.88i		Artyom	Chermoshanskiy	RUS-J	7.2.01	15			Dec
7.87	1.8	Kakeru	Komori	JPN	3.10.91	18			Jul
7.87	1.3	Yuto	Adachi	JPN	16.12.00	10			Oct
7.86	1.7	Henry	Frayne	AUS	14.4.90	1			Feb
7.86i		Fabian	Edoki	NGR	30.3.98	29			Feb
7.86	1.9	Hiromichi	Yoshida	JPN	8.8.99	29			Aug
7.85i		Tom	Campagne	FRA	14.11.00	9			Feb
7.85	2.0	James	Lelliott	GBR	11.2.93	9			Aug
7.84iA		Kyle	Darrow	USA	12.4.95	8			Feb
7.84	1.5	Andrea	Pianti	ITA	2.6.97	25			Jul
7.83i		Allen	Gordon	USA	.99	25			Jan
7.83A		Peter	Makgato	RSA	5.5.96	21			Feb
7.83	1.5	Mikita	Lapatenko	BLR	6.6.95	17			Jul
7.83	1.9	Jack	Roach	GBR	8.1.95	9			Aug
7.83	1.2	Tomasz	Jaszczuk	POL	9.3.92	13			Aug
7.83	1.3	Al Assane	Fofana (100)	FRA	6.3.98	13			Sep
7.82i		Héctor	Santos	ESP	6.1.98	12			Jan
7.82i		Denzel	Harper	USA	5.4.98	1			Feb
7.82i		Fyodor	Kiselkov	RUS	3.6.95	26			Feb
7.82	1.4	Gianluca	Puglisi	GER	10.4.96	1			Aug
7.81	0.7	Chris	Mitrevski	AUS	12.7.96	11			Mar
7.81iA		Abraham	Seaneke	GHA	31.5.96	1			Feb
7.81i		Dan	Bramble	GBR	14.10.90	23			Feb
7.81	0.0	Christopher Ullmann		SUI	21.8.93	1			Aug
7.81	1.4	Yann	Randrianasolo	FRA	3.2.94	20			Aug
7.81	1.9	Hiroyuki	Fukasawa	JPN	10.12.92	8			Sep
7.81	1.8	Gai	Kitagawa	JPN-Y	21.7.03	26			Sep
7.80	1.7	Ulises	Costa	BRA	11.2.96	15			Feb
7.80i		Holland	Martin	BAH	7.6.98	15			Feb
7.80i		Francisco Javier Cobian		ESP	21.7.89	29			Feb
7.80	0.0	Joseph	Edafiadhe	NGR	22.12.96	29			Feb
7.80i		Mateusz	Rózanski	POL	11.8.98	1			Mar
7.80	1.6	Tremaine	Browne	GUY	1.3.00	14			Mar
		[117]							

Wind assisted

8.52	4.5	Tajay	Gayle	JAM	2.8.96	1		Kingston	11 Jul
8.52w						x	p	8.18w	x 8.23
8.07	3.5	Lin Yu-Tang		TPE	11.5.00	1		Taipei	11 Mar
8.06	2.5	Aleksandr	Menkov	RUS	7.12.90	1	NC	Chelyabinsk	9 Sep
8.05	2.7	Hiromichi	Yoshida	JPN	8.8.99	1		Fukui	29 Aug
8.04	2.5	Daiki	Oda	JPN	15.1.96	2		Fukui	29 Aug
8.00	3.8	Joshua	Cowley	AUS-J	13.3.01	2		Canberra	25 Jan
7.99		Johnathan	Baker	USA		1		Katy	29 Feb
7.96	2.1	Artyom	Huryin	BLR	17.2.98	1		Minsk	26 Jun
7.96	4.9	Kakeru	Komori	JPN	3.10.91	1		Okinawa	23 Nov
7.94	2.7	Chris	Mitrevski	AUS	12.7.96	25	Jan	7.91	2.7 Yann Randrianasolo FRA 3.2.94 13 Sep
7.94	3.3	Tom	Campagne	FRA	14.11.00	3	Jul	7.88	2.4 Riku Ito JPN-J 16.1.01 25 Oct
7.93	2.9	Jeremy	Andrews	AUS	3.11.92	1	Feb	7.87	2.5 Ulises Costa BRA 11.2.96 15 Jan
7.93	2.3	Emanuel	Archibald	GUY	9.9.94	14	Mar	7.86	3.2 Gabriel Bitan ROU 23.7.98 8 Aug
7.93	2.5	Boris	Linkov	BUL	24.7.00	9	Aug	7.84	3.4 Christopher Ullmann SUI 21.8.93 11 Jul
								7.81	3.4 Andreas Carlsson SWE 5.4.95 4 Jul
								7.80	0.1 Campagne 3 NC Albi 13 Sep

Best outdoor marks

| 8.15 | 0.0 | Montler | 1 | NC | Uppsala | 16 Aug |

JUNIORS

4 performances by 2 men to 7.90.

8.28	1.6	Lester	Lescay	CUB	15.10.01	1		Camagüey	23 Feb
		8.21	0.2 1		La Habana	7 Mar	8.08 -0.1 1	La Habana	14 Feb
7.93	0.8	Jules	Pommery	FRA	22.01.01	1		Pierre-Bénite	28 Aug
7.89	1.8	Daniel	Segers	BEL	1.2.01	1	NC	Bruxelles	16 Aug
7.89	1.1	Natsuki	Mainaga	JPN-Y	12.7.03	1		Osaka	18 Sep
7.88	1.3	Yuto	Toriumi	JPN	4.10.01	2		Hiroshima	25 Oct
7.88i		Artyom	Chermoshanskiy	RUS	7.2.01	1		Moskva	15 Dec
7.81	1.8	Gai	Kitagawa	JPN-Y	21.7.03	1		Shizuoka	26 Sep
7.75	0.3	Riku	Ito	JPN	16.1.01	3	NC	Niigata	11 Sep
7.74	-0.5	Joshua	Cowley	AUS	13.3.01	*		Canberra	25 Jan
7.73i		Scott	Joseph (10)	CAN	.01	1		Edmonton	6 Mar
7.73A	1.9	Weiré	Olivier	NZL	4.11.02	1		Potchefstroom	17 Nov

Wind assisted

8.00	3.8	Joshua	Cowley	AUS	13.3.01	2		Canberra	25 Jan
7.88	2.4	Riku	Ito	JPN	16.1.01	1		Hiroshima	25 Oct
7.75	2.6	Oliver	Koletzko	GER-Y	.03	1		Wiesbaden	4 Jul
7.73	3.8	Gabriel Luiz	Boza	BRA-Y	7.3.03	1		Bragança Paulista	20 Nov

TRIPLE JUMP

17.77i		Fabrice	Zango	BUR	25.6.93	1		Paris	2 Feb
		17.51i	1		Liévin	19 Feb	17.42	15.47	17.77	x	16.67	17.47
		17.43	1.1 1	Gyulai	Székesfehérvár	19 Aug	17.03	17.25	17.34	17.51	x	x
		17.42	-0.5 2	GS	Ostrava	8 Sep	17.21	17.40/1.0	x	17.43	x	17.12
		17.31i	1		Madrid	21 Feb	17.30/-0.3	17.42	16.76	p	p	17.28
17.57	-0.8	Christian	Taylor	USA	18.6.90	1	ISTAF	Berlin		13 Sep
								x	17.09	17.22	x	17.31
								16.88	16.61	17.02	x	17.57

MFN 2020

TRIPLE JUMP

Mark	Wind	Name		Nat	Born	Pos	Meet	Venue		Date	
17.46	-0.4	1 GS	Ostrava	8 Sep	16.82		16.89w	17.12 p	x	17.46	
17.34	1.0	2 Gyulai	Székesfehérvár	19 Aug	17.02		x	x	17.34	17.25	17.34
17.30	1.5	Andy	Díaz	CUB	25.12.95	x		16.74	17.30	La Habana	21 Mar
		(19/3)								17.06 x	x
17.28	1.0	Pedro Pablo	Pichardo	POR	30.6.93	3	Gyulai	Székesfehérvár			19 Aug
17.24iA		Donald	Scott	USA	23.2.92	1	NC	Albuquerque			15 Feb
17.18i		Pablo	Torrijos	ESP	12.5.92	1	NC	Ourense			1 Mar
17.18	2.0	Cristian	Nápoles	CUB	27.11.98	2	NC	La Habana			21 Mar
17.17	0.8	Max	Hess	GER	13.7.96	2	ISTAF	Berlin			13 Sep
17.16i		Lasha	Gulelauri	GEO	26.5.93	1		Tbilisi			2 Feb
17.15i		Nazim	Babayev	AZE	8.10.97	2		Liévin			19 Feb
		(10)									
17.14iA		Omar	Craddock	USA	26.4.91	2	NC	Albuquerque			15 Feb
17.13			Fang Yaoqing	CHN	20.4.96	1		Beijing			31 Jul
17.10iA		Alexsandro	Melo	BRA	26.9.95	1	SAmC	Cochabamba			2 Feb
17.08	2.0	Lázaro	Martínez	CUB	3.11.97	3	NC	La Habana			21 Mar
17.07i		Jordan	Díaz	CUB-J	23.2.01	3		Liévin			19 Feb
17.07i		Melvin	Raffin	FRA	9.8.98	2		Madrid			21 Feb
17.05	1.0	Henry Daniel	Rosique	CUB	4.1.97	2		Camagüey			22 Feb
17.03	0.5	Jean Marc	Pontvianne	FRA	6.8.94	1		Montpellier			30 Jul
17.02iA		Chris	Benard	USA	4.4.90	3	NC	Albuquerque			15 Feb
17.02i		Jordan	Scott	JAM	29.6.97	1		Clemson			15 Feb
		[20]									
17.00iA		KeAndre	Bates	USA	24.5.96	4	NC	Albuquerque			15 Feb
16.99i			Wu Ruiting	CHN	29.11.95	3		Madrid			21 Feb
16.94	0.4	Tiago	Pereira	POR	19.9.93	1		Lisboa (U)			8 Aug
16.92	0.6	Alexis	Copello	AZE	12.8.85	4	Gyulai	Székesfehérvár			19 Aug
16.91i		Dmitriy	Chizhikov	RUS	6.12.93	1		Moskva			28 Jan
16.91i	1.0		Zhu Yaming	CHN	4.5.94	4		Liévin			19 Feb
16.84i		Clive	Pullen	JAM	18.10.94	2		Clemson			15 Feb
16.83	1.4		Su Wen	CHN	10.2.99	1		Shanghai			23 Aug
16.83	1.0	Denis	Obyortyshev	RUS	16.2.97	1	NC	Chelyabinsk			11 Sep
16.83	1.9	Aleksey	Fyodorov	RUS	25.5.91	1		Sochi			20 Sep
		[30]									
16.79	1.1	Andrea	Dallavalle	ITA	31.10.99	1	NC	Padova			30 Aug
16.78	0.9	Andy Eugenio	Hechavarría	CUB	14.9.00	4	NC	La Habana			21 Mar
16.75	0.0	Hikaru	Ikehata	JPN	31.8.94	1		Tokyo			26 Jul
16.72	1.5	Enzo	Hodebar	FRA	17.5.99	3	NC	Albi			12 Sep
16.70i		Maksim	Nesterenko	BLR	1.9.92	1		Gomel			8 Feb
16.69	0.2	Tomás	Veszelka	SVK	9.7.95	1	PTS	Samorin			11 Sep
16.68i		Carey	McLeod	JAM	14.4.98	3		Clemson			15 Feb
16.68	1.1	Benjamin	Compaoré	FRA	5.8.87	4	NC	Albi			12 Sep
16.67		Levon	Aghasyan	ARM	19.1.95	1		Vanadzor			30 Aug
16.66	0.7	Julian	Konle	AUS	4.6.97	1		Melbourne			6 Feb
		[40]									
16.65i		Chris	Carter	USA	11.3.89	1		Houston			1 Feb
16.65	-0.7	Jesper	Hellström	SWE	27.7.95	3	ISTAF	Berlin			13 Sep
16.65	1.1	Almir	dos Santos	BRA	4.9.93	1		Porto Alegre			13 Nov
16.64i		Jah-Nhal	Perinchief	BER	31.12.97	2		Lubbock			1 Feb
16.64	1.2	Aleksandr	Yurchenko	RUS	30.7.92	3	NC	Chelyabinsk			11 Sep
16.62iA		Mateus Daniel	de Sá	BRA	21.11.95	2	SAmC	Cochabamba			2 Feb
16.62iA		John	Warren	USA	2.3.96	5	NC	Albuquerque			15 Feb
16.62i		Edoardo	Accetta	ITA	28.3.94	1	NC	Ancona			23 Feb
16.62	2.0	Tobia	Bocchi	ITA	7.4.97	2		Trieste			1 Aug
16.60	0.0	Marcos	Ruiz	ESP	10.3.95	2	NC	Alcobendas			12 Sep
		[50]									
16.59	0.8		Li Pangshuai	CHN	9.4.92	1		Shanghai			10 May
16.59	-0.8	Simo	Lipsanen	FIN	13.9.95	1	vSWE	Tampere			5 Sep
16.56i		O'Brien	Wasome	JAM	24.1.97	4		Clemson			15 Feb
16.54			Liu Mingxuan	CHN	16.5.97	2		Beijing			31 Jul
16.53	1.2	Jay Shah	Pradeep	IND	11.10.97	1		Moodbridi			6 Jan
16.52iA		Maximiliano	Díaz	ARG	15.11.88	3	SAmC	Cochabamba			2 Feb
16.52i		Yoann	Rapinier	FRA	29.9.89	4		Paris			2 Feb
16.52	1.9	Vitaliy	Pavlov	RUS	12.1.97	3		Bryansk			30 Aug
16.51i		Nelson	Évora	POR	20.4.84	1	NC	Pombal			29 Feb
16.50i		Clayton	Brown	JAM	8.12.96	1	SEC	College Station			29 Feb
		[60]									
16.49iA		Brandon	Roulhac	USA	13.12.83	6	NC	Albuquerque			15 Feb
16.48i		Chengetayi	Mapaya	ZIM	19.12.98	1		Lubbock			15 Feb
16.48	1.3	Kirill	Kovalenko	RUS	20.1.94	*		Bryansk			30 Aug

TRIPLE JUMP - SHOT

Mark	Wind	Name		Nat	Born	Pos	Meet	Venue	Date
16.47i		Troy	Doris	GUY	12.4.89		15 Feb		
16.47i		Samuele	Cerro	ITA	21.3.95		23 Feb		
16.45	0.8	Alberto	Álvarez	MEX	8.3.91		17 Feb		
16.41	-0.2	Nikólaos	Andrikópoulos	GRE	17.4.97		22 Jul		
16.41	0.1	Can	Özüpek	TUR	2.2.96		20 Aug		
16.41	1.7	Anton	Buldov	RUS	14.6.00		30 Aug		
16.40i		Elvijs	Misans	LAT	8.4.89		29 Feb		
16.40	0.6	Simone	Biasutti	ITA	1.10.99		1 Aug		
16.39i		Pávlos	Bóftsis	GRE	17.9.92		1 Feb		
16.39i		Jonathan	Seremes	FRA	3.9.00		1 Mar		
16.39	0.7		Liu Shijie	CHN	16.10.98		10 May		
16.39A	0.8	Hamid Reza	Kia	IRI-J	4.2.01		25 Aug		
16.38	0.5	Mohammed	Hammadi	MAR	8.8.97		16 Feb		
16.38i		Quentin	Mouyabi	FRA	8.10.98		1 Mar		
16.38	0.4	Yuki	Yamashita	JPN	9.11.95		26 Jul		
16.38	-1.9	Adrian	Swiderski	POL	26.9.86		1 Sep		
16.37i		Razvan	Grecu	ROU	23.12.99		1 Feb		
16.37	1.7	Philipp	Kronsteiner	AUT	25.4.97		15 Aug		
16.36	0.7	Jaak Joonas	Uudmäe	EST	6.4.94		8 Aug		
16.35i		Karol	Hoffmann	POL	1.6.89		7 Feb		
16.35i		Ramon	Adalía	ESP	23.11.98		16 Feb		
16.35	-0.1	Riku	Ito	JPN-J	16.1.01		13 Sep		
16.34i		Alphonso	Jordan	USA	1.11.87		15 Feb		
16.34	0.7	Jiří	Vondráček	CZE	9.9.88		8 Aug		
16.32	0.7	Sanjaya	Jayasinghe	SRI	20.4.82		29 Dec		
16.31i		Dimitrios	Tsiámis	GRE	12.1.82		28 Feb		
16.30iA		Alvaro	Cortez	CHI	27.10.95		2 Feb		
16.29i		Armani	Wallace	USA	11.2.97		25 Jan		
16.28	1.7	Ayo	Ore	AUS	23.4.97		25 Jan		
16.28i		Adil	Gandou	MAR	18.8.93		1 Mar		
16.27i		Odaine	Lewis	JAM	13.12.96		24 Jan		
16.27i		Chris	Welch	USA	8.12.99		22 Feb		
16.27	0.4	Sergey	Laptev	RUS	7.2.91		11 Sep		
16.26i		Andreas	Pantazis	GRE	4.6.00		9 Feb		
16.25i		Owayne	Owens	JAM	8.3.00		29 Feb		
16.24i		Harold	Corréa	FRA	26.6.88		4 Jan		
16.24	1.2	Zdenek	Kubát	CZE	9.4.98		8 Aug		
		[100]							

Wind assisted

17.40	2.3	Pedro Pablo	Pichardo	POR	30.6.93	1		Lisboa (U)	9 Jul
					17.20w	17.40w	17.11	15.57 p	17.17
17.33	2.5		Zango			1	NC	Albi	12 Sep
					16.86	16.61	17.33w	x p	p
16.75	2.5	Kirill	Kovalenko	RUS	20.1.94	2		Bryansk	30 Aug
16.60A	3.9	Maximiliano	Díaz	ARG	15.11.88	1		Salta	24 Oct
16.59	4.8	Thomas	Gogois	FRA	24.6.00	1		Vénissieux	6 May

Best outdoor marks

17.09	1.6	Torrijos		1	Castellón	29 Jul	16.90	0.2 Wu Ruiting	1 NC	Shaoxing	17 Sep
17.04	0.3	Craddock		1	Walnut	9 Jul	16.86	1.0 Zhu Yaming	1	Dalian	14 Jul
16.44	-0.4	de Sá			13 Dec		16.48	-1.2 Melo	1 NC	São Paulo	13 Dec
16.39	1.5	Carter			6 Aug	16.33A	-0.7 M Díaz	24 Oct	16.27	1.1 Nesterenko	1 Aug
16.33	0.3	Adalia			12 Sep	16.31	0.0 Hoffmann	13 Sep	16.44w	M Díaz	20 Dec

Best at low altitude

16.82i		J Scott	2		New York (A)	25 Jan	16.42i		Bates		25 Jan
							16.31	0.5	M Diaz		20 Dec

JUNIORS

17.07i		Jordan	Díaz	CUB	23.2.01	3		Liévin	19 Feb
16.35	-0.1	Riku	Ito	JPN	16.1.01	1		Niigata	13 Sep
16.18	0.3	Yusniel	Jorrín	CUB	2.2.01	5		La Habana	8 Feb
16.16	1.8	Vladyslav	Shepeliev	UKR	12.9.01	2	NC	Lutsk	30 Aug

SHOT

22.91		Ryan	Crouser	USA	18.12.92	1		Marietta	18 Jul
					22.15	21.65	22.24	21.83	22.73	22.91
	22.74	1	Hanz	Zagreb	14 Sep	21.03	22.10	22.74	x	22.59	22.31
	22.72	1		Des Moines	29 Aug	22.27	22.72	22.70	22.63	22.68	22.44
	22.70	1	Skol	Chorzów	6 Sep	22.53	22.59	22.70	22.52	x	22.42
	22.60i	1	NC	Albuquerque	15 Feb	21.84	22.05	x	22.60	22.18	x
	22.59	1		Beograd	17 Sep	22.59	22.32	x	22.57	22.55	22.37
	22.58i	1		Manhattan, KS	5 Dec	21.71	21.91	21.78	21.96	22.58	21.97
	22.56	1		Des Moines	25 Aug	22.56	22.50	x	22.08	22.20	x
	22.43	1	GS	Ostrava	8 Sep	21.79	22.08	22.31	22.43	x	22.21
	22.19i	1	Mill	New York (A)	8 Feb	21.24	21.09	21.59	21.69	22.19	x
	21.87	1		Marietta	11 Jul	x	21.83	x	21.53	21.87	x
21.99		Leonardo	Fabbri	ITA	15.4.97	1	NC	Padova	30 Aug
					x	21.25	20.88	x	21.99	x
21.88i		Konrad	Bukowiecki	POL	17.3.97	1		Ostrava	5 Feb
					20.94	x		20.24	20.49	x	21.88
21.88		Michal	Haratyk	POL	10.4.92	1	Kuso	Chorzów	25 Aug
					21.37	21.33	x	20.64	21.88	21.10
21.86i		Tomás	Stanek	CZE	13.6.91	1		Toruń	8 Feb
					20.91	20.97	21.86	21.23	21.47	x
21.84i		Filip	Mihaljevic	CRO	31.7.94	1		Beograd	27 Feb
					20.98	20.91	20.93	21.38	21.84	x
21.72		Nick	Ponzio	USA	5.1.95	1		Kutztown	24 Jul
					20.73	21.32	21.48	X	21.27	21.72
21.70		Tom	Walsh	NZL	1.3.92	1	NC	Christchurch	6 Mar
	(18/8)				21.10	21.06	21.00	21.70	50.67	20.96
21.52		Darlan	Romani	BRA	9.4.91	1		Bragança Paulista	14 Mar
21.34i		Joe	Kovacs	USA	28.6.89	2	Millrose	New York (A)	8 Feb
	[10]									
21.29		Mohamed	Hamza	EGY	30.8.96	1		El Maadi	31 Dec

310 SHOT

Mark	Name		Nat	Born	Pos	Meet	Venue	Date	
21.21i	Giorgi	Mujaridze	GEO	22.3.98	1	NC	Tbilisi	8	Feb
21.21	Bob	Bertemes	LUX	24.5.93	1		Hassloch	27	Jun
21.20	David	Storl	GER	27.7.90	3		Zagreb	14	Sep
21.19	Payton	Otterdahl	USA	2.4.96	3		Des Moines	29	Aug
21.15i	Wictor	Petersson	SWE	1.5.98	1	NC-23	Göteborg	1	Mar
21.13i	Armin	Sinancevic	SRB	14.8.96	1		Beograd	1	Feb
21.11	Mostafa Amr	Hassan	EGY	16.12.95	1		Cairo	27	Feb
21.07	Jacko	Gill	NZL	20.12.94	2	NC	Christchurch	6	Mar
21.06i	Mesud	Pezer	BIH	27.8.94	2		Beograd	27	Feb
	[20]								
21.05	Nikólaos	Skarvélis	GRE	2.2.93	2		Scottsdale	28	Jun
21.04i	Chukwuebuka	Enekwechi	NGR	28.1.93	4		Torun	8	Feb
21.04	Aleksandr	Lesnoy	RUS	28.7.88	1	NC	Chelyabinsk	9	Sep
21.03	Marcus	Thomsen	NOR	7.1.98	1		Oslo	11	Jun
21.02i	Andrew	Liskowitz	USA	22.5.97	1	Big 10	Geneva, OH	29	Feb
21.01i	Asmir	Kolasinac	SRB	15.10.84	1		Beograd	18	Jan
20.98i	Adrian	Piperi	USA	20.1.99	1	Big 12	Ames	29	Feb
20.94i	Francisco	Belo	POR	27.3.91	3		Ostrava	5	Feb
20.91i	Jordan	Geist	USA	21.7.98	2		Flagstaff	21	Feb
20.90i	Tim	Nedow	CAN	16.10.90	1		Notre Dame	8	Feb
	[30]								
20.79i	Andrei	Toader	ROU	26.5.97	1	NC	Bucuresti	29	Feb
20.77	Tsanko	Arnaudov	POR	14.3.92	1	NC	Lisboa (U)	8	Aug
20.75	Kyle	Blignaut	RSA	9.11.99	1		Pretoria	9	Dec
20.74i	Shahin	Mehrdelan	IRI	21.6.95	1		Tehran	9	Jan
20.70	Zane	Weir	RSA/ITA	7.9.95	1		Borgo Valsugana	20	Sep
20.70	Jason	van Rooyen	RSA	4.2.97	1		Pretoria	12	Dec
20.65	Scott	Lincoln	GBR	7.5.93	1	LI	Loughborough	16	Aug
20.63i	McKay	Johnson	USA	15.4.98	1		Albuquerque	1	Feb
20.62i	Maksim	Afonin	RUS	6.1.92	1	NC	Moskva	26	Feb
20.60	Jakub	Szyszkowski	POL	21.8.91	1		Lublin	25	Jul
	[40]								
20.56	Josh	Freeman	USA	22.8.94	1		Carbondale	25	Jan
20.52	Aleksey	Nichipor	BLR	10.4.93	1	NCp	Brest	17	Jul
20.50i	Jonathan	Tharaldsen	USA	18.2.97	1		Lexington	25	Jan
20.48i	Roger	Steen	USA	17.5.92	4	NC	Albuquerque	15	Feb
20.47i	Pavel	Derkach	RUS	2.11.93	2	NC	Moskva	26	Feb
20.45i	Josh	Awotunde	USA	12.6.95	4	Millrose	New York (A)	8	Feb
20.43i	Turner	Washington	USA	10.2.99	1		Flagstaff	10	Jan
20.35i	Daniel	McArthur	USA	17.3.98	1		Blacksburg	18	Jan
20.33	Uziel	Muñoz	MEX	8.9.95	1		Monterrey	16	May
20.33i	Kristoffer	Thomsen	DEN	21.2.96	1		Fort Wayne	29	Feb
	[50]								
20.27	Maksim	Sidorov	RUS	13.5.86	3	NC	Chelyabinsk	9	Sep
20.22	Orazio	Cremona	RSA	1.7.89	1		Johannesburg	14	Mar
20.21i	Willie	Morrison	USA/PHI	23.11.96	2		Notre Dame	8	Feb
20.20i	Josh	Sobota	USA	23.6.00	2		Lexington	25	Jan
20.16	Ashinia	Miller	JAM	6.6.93	1		Ogre	15	Aug
20.15i	Kemal	Mesic	BIH	4.8.85	5		Beograd	27	Feb
20.14i	Jonathan	Jones	USA	23.4.91	2		Albuquerque	25	Jan
20.13i	Carlos	Tobalina	ESP	2.8.85	6		Madrid	21	Feb
20.13i	Tobias	Dahm	GER	23.5.87	2	NC	Leipzig	22	Feb
20.09	Christian	Zimmermann	GER	9.7.94	1		Germering	25	Jul
	[60]								
20.08i	Jonah	Wilson	USA	2.2.99	1		Seattle	1	Feb
20.07i	Rajindra	Campbell	JAM	29.2.96	1		Pittsburg	1	Mar
20.06i	Alex	Renner	USA	28.12.93	1		Fargo	8	Feb
20.04i	David	Pless	USA	19.11.90	5	Millrose	New York (A)	8	Feb
20.03i	Dennis	Lewke	GER	23.7.93	3	NC	Leipzig	22	Feb
20.01	Simon	Bayer	GER	23.11.95	1		Waiblingen	19	Jul
20.01	William	Braido	BRA	18.3.92	1		Campinas	26	Sep
20.00i	Ihor	Musiyenko	UKR	22.8.93	1	NC	Sumy	20	Feb
20.00	Kiriákos	Zótos	GRE	17.1.96	1		Argos Orestikó	15	Jul
19.98	Roman	Kokoshko	UKR	16.8.96	1		Vinnitsa	24	Jul
	[70]								
19.97i	Demyan	Seskin	RUS	4.8.97	5	NC	Moskva	26	Feb
19.94	Konstantin	Lyadusov	RUS	2.3.88	4	NC	Chelyabinsk	9	Sep
19.93	T'Mond	Johnson	USA	29.7.97	1		Kutztown	26	Jun
19.91	Nick	Vena	USA	16.4.93	2		Kutztown	26	Jun
19.90	Jan Josef	Jeuschede	GER	23.4.93	1		Eppstein	15	Sep
19.89i	Joseph	Maxwell	CAN	3.4.98	2		Clemson	15	Feb

SHOT

Mark	Name		Nat	Born	Pos Meet	Venue		Date
19.85i	Ayomidotun	Ogundeji	NGR	24.2.96	3	Iowa City		18 Jan
19.85	Ryan	Ballantyne	NZL	8.1.99	1	Wellington		28 Feb
19.84	Damien	Birkinhead	AUS	8.4.93	1	Geelong		26 Jan
19.81	Jander	Heil	EST	20.4.97	1	Tallinn		18 Aug
19.80	Oleg	Tomashevich	BLR	31.5.00	1	Minsk		25 Jun
[80]								
19.74	Frédéric	Dagée	FRA	11.12.92	12 Sep	19.26i	Jordan	West	USA	27.6.99	1 Feb
19.72	Matt	Katnik	USA	10.10.96	7 Mar	19.25i	Patrick	Cronie	NED	5.11.89	16 Feb
19.72	Tomas	Djurovic	MNE	14.2.94	27 Jun	19.25	Bogdan	Zdravkovic	SRB	27.3.99	22 Aug
19.71i	Burger	Lambrechts	RSA	6.8.98	1 Feb	19.24i	Corey	Murphy	USA	3.11.96	1 Feb
19.68		Liu Yang	CHN	29.10.86	27 May	19.24		Feng Jie	CHN	18.1.86	18 Sep
19.67i	Connor	Bandel	USA	21.10.97	29 Feb	19.21i	Darius	King	USA	.98	8 Feb
19.67	Nazareno	Sasia	ARG-J	5.1.01	19 Dec	19.21i	Jabari	Bennett	USA	28.12.99	29 Feb
19.65	Sebastian	Lukszo	POL	29.7.94	11 Jul	19.20i	Anastásios	Latifíllári	GRE	8.8.96	28 Feb
19.64i	Viktor	Samolyuk	UKR	5.9.86	20 Feb	19.18	Lucas	Warning	USA	3.2.95	7 Aug
19.61i	Borja	Vivas	ESP	26.5.84	29 Feb	19.16i	Kyle	Mitchell	JAM	16.7.98	29 Feb
19.60i	Josh	Johnson	USA	18.10.99	29 Feb	19.14i	Maxwell	Otterdahl	USA-J	31.5.01	29 Feb
19.57i	Eldred	Henry	IVB	18.9.94	24 Jan	19.13	Lorenzo	Del Gatto	ITA	8.7.94	23 Feb
19.57i	Alex	Talley	USA	.98	29 Feb	19.09i	Benik	Abramyan	GEO	31.7.85	8 Feb
19.54i	Isaac	Odugbesan	NGR	22.4.98	29 Feb	19.06i	John	Meyer	USA	1.12.99	29 Feb
19.53	Ignacio	Carballo	ARG	12.8.94	19 Dec	19.05i	Kevin	Nedrick	JAM	11.1.98	8 Feb
19.51		Tian Zhizhong	CHN	15.12.92	18 Sep	19.04	Leif	Arrhenius	SWE	15.7.86	19 Sep
19.51	William	Dourado	BRA	6.1.94	14 Mar	19.03	Sven	Poelman	NED	5.6.97	29 Aug
19.50i	Jalil	Brewer	USA	21.5.98	25 Jan	19.02i	Tyson	Jones	USA	21.10.99	18 Jan
19.50i	Dmitriy	Karpuk	BLR	5.11.99	8 Feb	19.02i	Martin	Novák	CZE	5.10.92	23 Feb
19.49i	Zachary	Short (100)	HON	29.10.97	7 Feb	19.02i	Terrell	Adams	USA	19.3.98	23 Feb
19.49i	Eric	Favors	IRL	16.11.96	15 Feb	18.99	Jan	Parol	POL	11.11.95	15 Aug
19.49	Andrzej	Gudro	POL	8.4.94	8 Aug	18.94		Li Jun	CHN	2.1.93	23 Aug
19.48i	Hamza	Alic	BIH	20.1.79	27 Feb	18.94i	Veljko	Nedeljkovic	SRB	26.5.98	26 Dec
19.44i	Andrei	Gag	ROU	27.4.91	29 Feb	18.93i	Grant	Voeks	USA	10.9.97	8 Feb
19.43	Wellington	Morais	BRA	6.9.96	13 Dec	18.92	Alexander	Kolesnikoff	AUS	30.9.00	2 Aug
19.42i	Dennis	Lukas	GER	15.2.94	25 Jan	18.91		Chen Xiaodong	CHN	29.9.97	18 Sep
19.42	Mohamed Reza Tayebi		IRI	30.3.98	17 Sep	18.90i	Santiago	Basso	USA	16.12.98	1 Feb
19.41i	Garrett	Appier	USA	15.10.92	8 Feb	18.89i	Ralph	Casper	USA	.98	1 Mar
19.40i	Nathan	Esparza	USA	24.4.98	1 Feb	18.87	Vincenzo	D'Agostino	ITA	20.3.96	29 Jul
19.40i	Nikolas	Curtiss	USA	25.8.97	8 Feb	18.86	Jesper	Arbinge	SWE	27.3.97	6 Aug
19.39i	Sebastiano	Bianchetti	ITA	20.1.96	23 Feb	18.85i	Nikita	Zhidkov	RUS	29.2.88	9 Jan
19.38	Odisséas	Mouzenídis	GRE	30.6.99	8 Jul	18.85i	Ivan	Ivanov	KAZ	3.1.92	18 Jan
19.37i	Cooper	Campbell	USA	3.2.99	5 Dec	18.82i	Christopher	Licata	USA		23 Feb
19.36i	Kord	Ferguson	USA	16.9.95	15 Feb	18.82	Biaz	Zupancic	SLO	6.4.95	25 Jul
19.33i	Jaylen	Simmons	USA	5.11.98	1 Mar	18.80i	Ladislav	Prásil	CZE	17.5.90	2 Feb
19.32	Viktor	Gardenkrans	SWE	30.7.95	16 Aug	18.80i	Mattijs	Mols	NED	22.4.00	22 Feb
19.31i	Charles	Lenford	USA	17.3.98	25 Jan	18.80	Rafal	Kownatke	POL	24.3.85	8 Aug
19.29	Valentin	Moll	GER	24.8.99	5 Jul	[155]					

Best outdoor marks

21.69	Mihaljevic	1		Split	7 Mar	20.88	Bukowiecki	4	Skol	Chorzów	6 Sep
21.30	Kovacs	2		Zagreb	14 Sep	20.54	Afonin	2		Adler	19 Sep
21.24	Stanek	1		Domazlice	26 Jul	20.37	Pezer	1		Zenica	7 Oct
20.94	Petersson	2		Oslo	11 Jun	19.92	Derkach	5	NC	Chelyabinsk	9 Sep
20.91	Geist	2		San Tan Valley	23 Aug	19.88	Mesic	2		Zenica	7 Oct
19.71	Toader		22 Aug	19.48	Musiyenko	29 Aug	19.15	Lukas		9 Aug	18.96	Novák	27 Jun
19.66	Tobalina		25 Jan	19.29	Thomsen	20 Jun	19.14	Favors		18 Jul	18.91	Latifíllári	8 Jul
19.63	Belo		24 Jun	19.22	Karpuk	25 Jun	19.03	Bennett		24 Jul	18.83	Seskin	19 Sep

Online competitions

20.10	Oleg	Tomashevich	BLR	31.5.00	1	Vitebsk	30 Apr
19.58	Dmitriy	Karpuk	BLR	5.11.99	1	Brest	30 Apr

JUNIORS

19.67	Nazareno	Sasia	ARG	5.1.01	1	NC	Rosario	19 Dec
19.14i	Maxwell	Otterdahl	USA	31.5.01	3		Fort Wayne	29 Feb
18.71	Carmelo Alessandro	Musci	ITA	30.5.01	3		Savona	16 Jul
18.56	Lewis	Byng	GBR	29.9.01	2		Loughborough	16 Aug
18.48	Aliaksei	Aleksandrovich	BLR	2.1.01	3		Minsk	25 Jun
18.41	Riccardo	Ferrara	ITA	22.1.01	1		Reggio Calabria	17 Oct
18.39	Eric	Maihöfer	GER	16.6.01	1		Halle	15 Aug
18.23	Muhamet	Ramadani	KOS	11.8.02	1		Mitrovice	28 Jun

6 KG SHOT

20.98	Carmelo Alessandro	Musci	ITA	30.5.01	1	Molfetta	27 Sep
	20.57	1	Castilione della Pescaiai	25 Jul	3 performances by 2 men to 20.20		
20.54i	Aleksey	Aleksandrovich	BLR	2.1.01	1	Minsk	26 Feb
	20.29			2.1.01	1	Brest	8 Jul
20.47	Piotr	Gozdziewicz	POL	23.3.01	1	Karpacz	20 Sep
20.45	Nazareno	Sasia	ARG	5.1.01	1	Paraná	21 Nov
20.42	Eric	Maihöfer	GER	16.6.01	1	Heilbronn	25 Jul
20.32	Juan C.	Vázquez	CUB	13.2.02	1	La Habana	7 Mar

312 SHOT - DISCUS

Mark	Name		Nat	Born	Pos	Meet	Venue	Date
20.26	Lewis	Byng	GBR	29.9.01	1		Harrow	26 Sep
19.87	Wojciech	Marok	POL	12.9.01	1		Ciechanów	28 Aug
19.69i	Jakub	Héza	CZE	23.5.00	1		Olomouc	23 Dec
19.69	Riccardo	Ferrara	ITA	22.1.01	2		Castiglione della Pescaia	25 Jul
19.53	Miguel	Gómez	ESP	2.1.01	1		Cartagena	31 Oct
19.39A	Mohamed	Daouda Tolo	KSA		1		Taïf	11 Sep
19.38i	Alperen	Karahan	TUR	27.10.00	1		Istanbul	29 Dec
19.34i	Semen	Borodayev	RUS	4.5.02	1	NC-j	Volgograd	6 Feb

DISCUS

Mark			Name		Nat/Info	Born	Pos		Venue		Date
71.37			Daniel	Ståhl	SWE	27.8.92	1		Sollentuna		10 Aug
						68.38 x	71.37 x	x	x		
	70.25	1		Helsingborg	21 Jun	66.35 65.25	70.25	68.34	68.41	63.62	
	69.23	1	PNG	Turku	11 Aug	x x	69.23	x	x	x	
	69.20	1	vFIN	Tampere	5 Sep	66.95 x	69.20	x	69.01	65.94	
	69.17	1	DL	Stockholm	23 Aug	x 69.17	67.36	67.44	x	68.57	
	68.87	1	Hanz	Zagreb	15 Sep	66.97 68.87	67.55	68.87	67.16	x	
	68.74	1	NC	Uppsala	15 Aug	65.26 x	x	x	6874	x	
	68.72	1		Växjö	12 Jul	67.56 x	64.81	64.74	68.72	66.38	
	68.54	1		Hässelby	17 Sep	68.30 68.54	67.03	x			
	68.48	1		Kuortane	1 Aug	x 65.91	67.51	68.48	x	66.70	
	68.10	1		Karlstad	8 Jul	68.10 63.50	65.95	66.07	x	64.45	
	68.10	1		Göteborg	6 Aug	x x	68.07	x	x	68.10	
70.29			Mauricio	Ortega	COL	4.8.94	1		Lovelhe		22 Jul
						x 59.49	61.65	70.29	x	x	
69.67			Fedrick	Dacres	JAM	28.2.94	1		Kingston		8 Feb
69.60			Juan José	Caicedo	ECU	20.7.92	2		Lovelhe		22 Jul
						53.85 69.60	p	48.17	p		
69.35			Gudni Valur	Gudnason	ISL	11.10.95	1		Reykjavik		16 Sep
						61.05 63.09	65.71	62.29	69.35	x	
68.75			Kristian	Ceh	SLO	17.2.99	1		Maribor		23 Jun
						x 67.71	x	68.75	x	68.63	
68.68			Andrius	Gudzius	LTU	14.2.91	1		Klaipeda		8 Jul
						x 68.06	68.68	66.00	x		
	68.41	1		Ogre	15 Aug	67.15 x	67.62	x	65.74	68.41	
	68.22	2	Hanz	Zagreb	15 Sep	66.65 64.92	x	66.65	68.22	67.81	
	68.16	1	NC	Palanga	7 Aug	x 66.60	68.16	67.32	64.17	67.55	
68.63			Lukas	Weisshaidinger	AUT	20.2.92	1e1		Schwechat		25 May
						x 63.25	68.63	66.31	65.82	x	
	68.56	1		Schwechat	31 May	x 63.70	67.37	68.56	x	p	
	68.19	1e2		Schwechat	25 May	x 67.21	68.19	66.13	x	67.49	
	(24/8)										
67.72			Simon	Pettersson	SWE	3.1.94	2	DL	Stockholm		23 Aug
66.54			Chad	Wright	JAM	25.3.91	2		Kingston		8 Feb
	[10]										
66.46A			Niklas	Arrhenius	USA	10.9.82	1		Provo		26 Sep
66.22			Alin Alexandru	Firfirica	ROU	3.11.95	1		Bucuresti		1 Mar
65.99			Robert	Urbanek	POL	29.4.87	1		Aleksandrów Lódski		27 Jun
65.47			Matthew	Denny	AUS	2.6.96	1		Wellington		28 Feb
65.15			Lawrence	Okoye	GBR	6.10.91	1		Magdeburg		22 Jul
64.87			Piotr	Malachowski	POL	7.6.83	1		Spala		8 Aug
64.86			Danijel	Furtula	MNE	31.7.92	1		Split		7 Mar
64.66			Traves	Smikle	JAM	7.5.92	2		Kingston		6 Mar
64.66			Lois Maikel	Martínez	ESP	3.6.81	1		Castellón		28 Aug
64.62			Ola Stunes	Isene	NOR	29.1.95	1		Spikkestad		6 Jun
	[20]										
64.40			Marek	Bárta	CZE	8.12.92	1		Praha		10 Jun
64.35			Alex	Rose	SAM	7.11.91	1		Kutztown		1 Aug
64.24			David	Wrobel	GER	13.2.91	1		Schönebeck		24 Jul
64.24			Claudio	Romero	CHI	10.7.00	1c2		Santiago de Chile		30 Dec
64.16			Martin	Kupper	EST	31.5.89	1		Randvere		16 Sep
63.99			Jorge	Fernández	CUB	2.10.87	1		La Habana		14 Feb
63.94			Bartlomiej	Stój	POL	15.5.96	4	Skol	Chorzów		6 Sep
63.66			Clemens	Prüfer	GER	13.8.97	3		Schönebeck		24 Jul
63.51			Philip	Milanov	BEL	6.7.91	1		Marseille		3 Sep
63.37			Kord	Ferguson	USA	19.6.95	1		Marietta		28 Nov
	[30]										
63.35			Sven Martin	Skagestad	NOR	13.1.95	3		Helsingborg		21 Jun
63.25			Connor	Bell	NZL-J	21.6.01	1		Hastings		25 Jan
63.04			Lolassonn	Djouhan	FRA	18.5.91	2		Marseille		3 Sep

DISCUS

Mark	Name		Nat	Born	Pos	Meet	Venue	Date
63.03	János	Huszák	HUN	5.2.92	1	NC-w	Szombathely	7 Mar
63.02	Nick	Percy	GBR	5.12.94	1		Bournemouth	20 Sep
63.00	Martin	Markovic	CRO	13.1.96	2	NC	Split	7 Mar
62.88A	Leif	Arrhenius	SWE	15.7.86	2		Orem	18 May
62.86	Aleksey	Khudyakov	RUS	31.3.95	1		Adler	11 Feb
62.65	Henning	Prüfer	GER	7.3.96	3		Neubrandenburg	27 May
62.59	Yuji	Tsutsumi	JPN	22.12.89	1		Tama	27 Mar
	[40]							
62.46	Sam	Mattis	USA	19.3.94	2		Kutztown	1 Aug
62.07i	Martin	Wierig	GER	10.6.87	1		Berlin	14 Feb
61.87	Giovanni	Faloci	ITA	13.10.85	1	NC-w	Padova	29 Aug
61.68	Daniel	Jasinski	GER	5.8.89	2	NC	Braunschweig	8 Aug
61.46	Oskar	Stachnik	POL	1.3.98	2		Lódz	12 Jul
61.29	Josh	Syrotchen	USA	19.4.94	3		Kutztown	1 Aug
61.28i	Christoph	Harting	GER	10.4.90	2		Berlin	14 Feb
61.24	Reggie	Jagers	USA	13.8.94	3		Spanish Town	18 Jan
61.20	Róbert	Szikszai	HUN	30.9.94	2	NC-w	Szombathely	7 Mar
61.16	Axel	Härstedt	SWE	28.2.87	1		Malmö	11 Jul
	[50]							
61.16	Henrik	Janssen	GER	19.5.98	4		Schönebeck	24 Jul
61.05	Jordan	Young	CAN	21.6.93	2		Hamilton, NZL	15 Feb
60.97A	Werner	Visser	RSA	27.2.98	1		Pretoria	9 Dec
60.90	Aleksandr	Dobrenhkiy	RUS	11.3.94	1		Adler	20 Sep
60.87	Gleb	Sidorchenko	RUS	15.5.86	2		Adler	20 Sep
60.86	Alexander	Parkinson	NZL	8.9.94	4		Wellington	28 Feb
60.79	Douglas	dos Reis	BRA	9.12.95	1		São Bernardo do Campo	29 Feb
60.79	Torben	Brandt	GER	19.5.95	4		Magdeburg	22 Jul
60.77	Yevgeniy	Bogutskiy	BLR	7.9.99	1		Minsk	22 Dec
60.67	Christian	Zimmermann	GER	9.7.94	1		Erding	19 Jul
60.66	Domantas	Poska	LTU	10.1.96	2		Klaipeda	8 Jul
	[60]							
60.61	Aleksey	Sysoyev	RUS	8.3.85	3		Adler	20 Sep
60.54	Aleksas	Abromavicius	LTU	6.12.84	3		Klaipeda	8 Jul
60.40	Jakob	Gardenkrans	SWE	15.8.97	5		Sollentuna	10 Aug
60.35	JeVaughn	Shaw	JAM	2.1.94	1		Marietta	1 Aug
60.28	Tomás	Vonavka	CZE	4.6.90	2		Zlín	15 Aug
60.18	Jordan	Roach	USA	25.3.93	5		Wellington	28 Feb
60.02	Yasiel	Sotero	ESP-J	28.12.01	2		Castellón	29 Feb
60.01	Victor	Hogan	RSA	25.7.89	1		Paarl	4 Mar
59.99	Emil	Mikkelsen	DEN	17.4.90	1		Odense	7 Jun
59.88	Pridu	Niit	EST	27.1.90	1		Tallinn	20 Sep
	[70]							

59.86	Apostolos	Parellis	CYP	24.7.85	7 Aug	58.66	Muhd Irfan	Shamsuddin	MAS	16.8.95	23 Sep
59.86	Marin	Premeru	CRO	29.8.90	15 Sep	58.62	Tom	Reux	FRA	24.2.99	15 Feb
59.85	Zaorawar "Robbie"	Otal	USA	12.7.99	28 Nov	58.62	Gerd	Kanter	EST	6.5.79	9 Aug
59.79		Sun Shichen	CHN	23.7.97	7 Aug	58.60	Voislav	Grubisa	BIH	12.7.97	19 Jul
59.76	Mario Alberto	Díaz	CUB	8.12.99	14 Feb	58.48	George	Armstrong	GBR	8.12.97	5 Sep
59.59	Korbinian	Hässler	GER	8.2.00	18 Jul	58.47	Mitchell	Cooper	AUS	2.6.95	28 Feb
59.58	Gustav	Liberg	SWE	3.5.95	21 Mar	58.46	Glendford	Watson	JAM	11.7.95	6 Mar
59.56	Alessio	Manucci	ITA	7.7.98	26 Sep	58.38	Frantz	Kruger	FIN	22.5.75	14 Aug
59.54A	Dewald	van Heerden	RSA	4.4.91	7 Mar	58.30	Emanuel	Sousa	POR	4.4.99	7 Mar
59.30	Tadej	Hribar	SLO	1.2.87	13 Jun	58.22	Anyel E.	Álvarez	CUB	25.2.00	14 Feb
59.09	Iáson	Thanópoulos	GRE	6.8.94	9 Aug	58.22	José Lorenzo	Hernández	ESP	11.2.97	7 Mar
59.05	Lucas	Nervi	CHI-J	31.8.01	29 Dec	58.19	Tuergong	Abuduaini	CHN	16.6.97	18 Sep
59.00	Marshall	Hall	NZL	7.10.88	18 Jan	58.14	Edujose	Lima	POR	2.3.96	8 Aug
58.95	Nazzareno	Di Marco	ITA	30.4.85	25 Jul	58.14	Shehab	Abdalaziz	EGY	8.8.98	31 Dec
58.85	Alessio	Manucci	ITA	7.7.98	18 Jul	58.07	Oskari	Perälampi	FIN	24.7.85	25 Jul
58.67	Aleksandr	Kirya	RUS	23.3.92	20 Sep	58.00	Hossein	Rasouli	IRI	22.12.99	2 Oct
							[102]				

JUNIORS

63.25	Connor		Bell	NZL	21.6.01	2		Hastings	25 Jan
62.43		2		Wellington	28 Feb	59.79	1	Tauranga	18 Jan
61.12		2		Sydney	22 Feb	59.66	2	Melbourne	6 Feb
60.00		3		Hamilton	15 Feb	58.75	4	Christchurch	8 Mar
60.02	Yasiel		Sotero	ESP	28.12.01	2		Castellón	29 Feb
59.05	Lucas		Nervi	CHI	31.8.01	2		Santiago de Cuba	29 Dec
58.67		1		Montevideo	8 Dec	10 performances by 3 men to 58.50			
57.68	Mykolas		Alekna	LTU	18.9.02	2		Vilnius	22 Aug
56.90	Enrico		Saccomano	ITA	12.2.01	3	NC	Padova	29 Aug
56.56	Uladzislau		Puchko	BLR	18.3.02	2	NC	Minsk	2 Aug
55.28	Carmelo Alessandro		Musci	ITA	30.5.01	5	NC	Padova	29 Aug

+ intermediate time in longer race, A made at an altitude of 1000m or higher, D made in a decathlon, h made in a heat, qf quarter-final, sf semi-final, i indoors, Q qualifying round, r race number, -J juniors, -Y youths (b. 2003 or later)

DISCUS - HAMMER

Mark	Name	Nat	Born	Pos	Meet	Venue	Date
1.75kg DISCUS							
67.40	Connor Bell	NZL	21.6.01	1	NC	Christchurch	7 Mar
65.63	1 Hastings		20 Sep	64.78	1	Hastings	13 Sep
66.35	Lucas Nervi	CHI	31.8.01	1		Santiago de Chile	19 Dec
65.39	1 Santiago de Chile		7 Nov	64.74	1	Santiago de Chile	14 Nov
65.89	Yasiel Brayan Sotero	ESP	28.12.01	1	NC-w	Castellón	23 Feb
65.12	1 Las Palmas		11 Jan	64.68	1	Fuerteventura	4 Jan
64.97	Carmelo Alessandro Musci	ITA	30.5.01	1		Molfetta	26 Sep
	10 performances by 4 men to 64.00						
62.71	Matteo Maulana	GER	16.12.02	1		Großolbersdorf	11 Jul
62.19	Mykolas Alekna	LTU	18.9.02	1	NC-j	Vilnius	25 Jul
62.11	Fabian Weinberg	NOR	26.5.01	1		Kristiansand	28 May
62.04	Vladislav Puchko	BLR	18.3.02	1		Minsk	14 Aug
61.75	Enrico Saccomano	ITA	12.2.01	1		Livorno	26 Sep
61.43	Ralford Mullings	JAM	22.11.02	1		Kingston	6 Mar
60.07	Lukas Winkler	GER	.02	1		Halle	1 Feb

HAMMER

Mark	Name	Nat	Born	Pos	Meet	Venue	Date
80.70	Rudy Winkler	USA	6.12.94	1		Wallkill, NY	26 Jul
	77.97 79.45 75.78 77.09 80.70 80.34						
80.28	Wojciech Nowicki	POL	22.2.89	1	NC	Wloclawek	28 Aug
	78.36 79.46 80.28 x 79.40 80.25						
80.09	1 Kuso Chorzów	25 Aug	76.81 78.65 80.09 77.90 78.12 x				
78.88	2 Skol Chorzów	6 Sep	75.78 x 76.96 78.88 76.51 x				
78.52	1 Chorzów	20 Jun	x 75.96 78.38 77.86 x 78.52				
78.50	1 Spala	8 Aug	77.08 78.33 78.50 78.47 78.39 78.18				
78.07	1 Gyulai Székesfehérvár	19 Aug	75.64 76.63 76.60 77.54 78.07 x				
79.88	Bence Halász	HUN	4.8.97	1	NC	Budapest	9 Aug
	77.68 x x 79.88 79.74 77.77						
78.86	1 Szombathely	6 Jun	only best throw measured				
78.79	1 Szombathely	4 Jul	only best throw measured				
78.69	1 Budapest	13 Sep	77.55 x x x 78.69 x				
78.56	1 Budapest	1 Aug	x 75.35 x x 75.03 78.56				
78.55	1 Szombathely	25 Jul	77.86 78.55 x x x x				
78.43	1 Pardubice	22 Jul	x x 72.40 78.43 77.23 x				
78.18	2 Kuso Chorzów	25 Aug	x x 78.18 x x x				
79.81	Pawel Fajdek	POL	4.6.89	1	Skol	Chorzów	6 Sep
	x 79.81 x x x x						
78.62	1 Lodz	16 Sep	x 77.31 x 78.62 76.94 x				
78.61	2 NC Wloclawek	28 Aug	76.86 78.61 x x x x				
78.05	3 Kuso Chorzów	25 Aug	76.37 78.05 x x 77.22 76.95				
78.06	1 Poznan	11 Sep	x 73.76 x 75.19 78.06 x				
79.05	Aaron Kangas	FIN	3.7.97	1		Espoo	5 Aug
	(22/5)		74.63 74.82 77.06 x 77.29 79.05				
77.78	Myhaylo Kokhan	UKR-J	22.1.01	3	Gyulai	Székesfehérvár	19 Aug
77.56	Esref Apak	TUR	3.1.82	1		Mersin	22 Feb
77.52	Javier Cienfuegos	ESP	15.7.90	1		Montijo	8 Feb
77.33	Özkan Baltaci	TUR	13.2.94	1		Bursa	28 Aug
77.31	Aleksey Sokirskiy	RUS	16.3.85	1		Adler	25 Feb
	[10]						
77.10	Hilmar Örn Jónsson	ISL	6.5.96	1		Hafnarfjörður	27 Aug
76.78	Hrístos Frantzeskákis	GRE	26.4.00	3	Skol	Chorzów	6 Sep
76.50	Valeriy Pronkin	RUS	15.6.94	1		Bryansk	29 Aug
76.61	Gabriel Enrique Kehr	CHI	3.9.96	1		Temuco	28 Dec
76.47	Marcel Lomnicky	SVK	6.7.87	1	NC	Trnava	29 Aug
76.42	Quentin Bigot	FRA	1.12.92	1	NC	Albi	12 Sep
76.41	Pavel Boreysha	BLR	16.2.91	1		Minsk	14 Aug
76.40	Eivind Henriksen	NOR	14.9.90	1	NC	Bergen	18 Sep
76.22	Daniel Haugh	USA	3.5.95	1		Marietta	18 Jul
76.12	Denis Lukyanov	RUS	14.7.89	1		Adler	20 Sep
	[20]						
76.11	Diego del Real	MEX	6.3.94	1		Ciudad de México	18 Jan
75.85	Miháil Anastasákis	GRE	3.12.94	2	NC	Pátra	8 Aug
75.70	Serghei Marghiev	MDA	6.11.92	1	NC	Chisinau	25 Aug
75.67	Andrey Romanov	RUS	19.9.94	1	NC	Chelyabinsk	11 Sep
75.45	Yuriy Vasilchenko	BLR	4.1.94	2		Minsk	14 Aug
75.07	Aleksandr Shimanovich	BLR	9.2.98	1		Minsk	20 Feb
75.00	Nikolay Bashan	BLR	18.11.92	2	NC	Minsk	31 Jul
74.98	Taylor Campbell	GBR	30.6.96	1		Loughborough	7 Mar
74.96	Zakhar Makhrosenko	BLR	10.10.91	2		Minsk	20 Feb

HAMMER 315

Mark	Name		Nat	Born	Pos	Meet	Venue	Date	
74.96	Humberto [30]	Mansilla	CHI	22.5.96	1		Temuco	14	Mar
74.92	Henri	Liipola	FIN	24.4.94	2		Somero	25	Jul
74.89	Krisztián	Pars	HUN	18.2.82	2		Budapest	13	Sep
74.51	Aleksi	Jaakkola	FIN	17.11.97	1		Pori	20	Jul
74.50	Mostafa	Al-Gamal	EGY	1.10.88	1		El Maadi	31	Dec
74.42	Denzel	Comenentia	NED	25.11.95	1		Hilversum	20	Aug
74.28	Thomas	Mardal	NOR	16.4.97	1		Byrkjelo	30	Jul
74.13	Simone	Falloni	ITA	26.9.91	1		Lucca	23	Feb
74.11	Ragnar	Carlsson	SWE	16.11.00	1		Falun	16	Dec
73.85	Dániel	Rába	HUN	24.4.98	2		Szombathely	6	Jun
73.61	Yann [40]	Chaussinand	FRA	11.5.98	2	NC	Albi	12	Sep
73.40	Alaa El-Din	El-Ashry	EGY	6.1.91	2		El Maadi	31	Dec
73.33	Ashraf Amjad	El-Seify	QAT	20.2.95	2	TUR Ch	Istanbul	4	Sep
73.24	Craig	Murch	GBR	27.6.93	1	NC	Manchester	5	Sep
73.23	Tristan	Schwandke	GER	23.5.92	1		St Gallen	23	May
73.23	Hassan Mohamed	Mahmoud	EGY	10.2.84	1		El Maadi	1	Dec
73.22	Alberto	González	ESP	1.6.98	1	NC-23	Sevilla	26	Sep
73.05	Tuomas	Seppänen	FIN	16.5.86	4		Pori	29	Aug
72.94	Hlib	Piskunov	UKR	25.11.98	2	NC	Lutsk	29	Aug
72.91		Wang Qi	CHN-J	10.2.01	1		Nanjing	30	May
72.84	Sergey [50]	Kolomoyets	BLR	11.8.89	2		Minsk	17	Jan
72.68	Serhiy	Perevoznikov	UKR	7.4.95	1		Mukachevo	14	Feb
72.65	Giorgio	Olivieri	ITA	5.11.00	1		Imola	16	Jul
72.59	Osian	Jones	GBR	23.6.93	3		Loughborough	7	Mar
72.54	Mergen	Mammedov	TKM	24.12.90	1	NC	Ashgabat	4	Jun
72.37	Marco	Lingua	ITA	4.6.78	1		Marianao Comense	1	Feb
72.28	Hugo	Tavernier	FRA	1.12.99	3		Kladno	16	Sep
72.02	Patrik	Hájek	CZE	11.11.98	1		Kolín	30	May
71.94	Pedro José	Martin	ESP	12.8.92	2		Motril	7	Mar
71.89		Wang Shizhu	CHN	20.2.89	1	NC	Shaoxing	16	Sep
71.79	Enguerrand [60]	Decroix Tetu	FRA	1.1.97	2		Leverkusen	26	Jul
71.78	Arkadiusz	Rogowski	POL	30.3.93	1		Warszawa	16	Aug
71.65	Marcin	Wrotynski	POL	11.3.96	1		Torun	28	Jul
71.60	Jake	Norris	GBR	30.6.99	1		London (He)	11	Jul
71.58	Yasmani	Fernández	CUB	7.4.95	1		La Habana	13	Feb
71.51	Bence	Pásztor	HUN	5.2.95	4	NC	Szombathely	7	Mar
71.44	Balázs	Varga	HUN	30.1.98	4	NC	Budapest	9	Aug
71.32	Joaquín	Gómez	ARG	14.10.96	1		Buenos Aires	21	Nov
71.30	Myhaylo	Havrylyuk	UKR	19.1.99	2		Mukachevo	14	Feb
71.26	Igor	Yevseyev	RUS	27.3.96	5		Bryansk	29	Aug
71.21	Oscar [70]	Vestlund	SWE	27.4.93	5	vFIN	Tampere	5	Sep
71.18	Roope	Auvinen	FIN	17.2.98	2		Somero	20	Sep
71.07	Yuriy	Shayunov	BLR	22.10.87	5		Minsk	20	Feb
71.06	Giacomo	Proserpio	ITA	22.4.97	1		Mariano Comense	22	Feb
71.05	Sukhrob	Khodjayev	UZB	21.5.93	1	NC	Tashkent	26	Dec
71.03	Ryota	Kashimura	JPN	13.8.91	1	NC	Niigata	2	Oct

70.94	Allan	Wolski	BRA	18.1.90	14	Mar
70.82	António Vital	Silva	POR	23.1.88	22	Feb
70.62	Iván	Menglebéi	GRE	25.1.95	8	Aug
70.54	Oleg	Dubitskiy	BLR	14.10.90	16	Jul
70.46	Naoki	Uematsu	JPN	13.11.94	24	Oct
70.45	Merlin	Hummel	GER-J	4.1.02	27	Jun
70.43	Roberto	Janet	CUB	29.8.86	14	Mar
70.39	Wágner	Domingos	BRA	23.6.83	7	Mar
70.32	Donát	Varga	HUN	8.4.00	9	Aug
70.31	Alan	Cumming	RSA	21.3.96	14	Mar
70.27	Nejc	Plesko	SLO	9.10.92	7	Jun
70.23	Takahiro	Kobata	JPN	9.3.97	2	Oct
70.20	Roberto	Sawyers	CRC	17.10.86	5	Dec
70.11	Carel	Haasbroek	RSA	27.2.98	14	Mar
70.08	Marco	Kammer	FIN	26.2.98	26	Aug
70.05	Gleb	Volik	RUS	17.12.96	25	Feb
70.04	Yudai	Kimura	JPN	19.10.96	18	Oct
70.00	Amanmurad	Hommadov	TKM	28.1.89	4	Jun
69.99	Aléxios	Prodanás	GRE	22.2.97	8	Aug
69.91	Benedek	Doma	HUN-J	17.10.01	24	Sep
69.87		Lee Yun-chul	KOR	28.3.82	25	Jun
69.85	Ruben	Antunes	POR	5.5.99	22	Feb

69.83	Israel	Oloyede	USA	.98	12	Dec
69.77	Jean-Baptiste	Bruxelle	FRA-J	9.7.02	12	Sep
69.76	Pavel	Krivitskiy (100)	BLR	17.4.84	20	Feb
69.61	Shota	Fukuda	JPN	28.11.00	13	Sep
69.40	Alexandros	Poursanides	CYP	23.1.93	7	Feb
69.30	Décio	Andrade	POR	25.1.97	6	Mar
69.27	Chris	Bennett	GBR	17.12.89	7	Mar
69.18	Adam	Kelly	EST	6.7.97	15	Aug
68.98	Ilya	Yevgenyev	RUS	31.7.98	25	Feb
68.98	Mihaita	Micu	ROU	27.9.99	4	Sep
68.94	Yeóryios	Korakídis	GRE	16.11.98	8	Aug
68.93	Markus	Kokkonen	FIN	17.5.95	20	Sep
68.89	Gábor	Czeller	HUN	3.7.99	13	Dec
68.81	Yushiro	Hosaka	JPN	16.10.91	22	Aug
68.73	Kunihiro	Sumi	JPN	27.2.94	19	Jul
68.70	Tommi	Remes	FIN	20.1.94	6	Jun
68.69	Ralf	de Oliveira	BRA	8.7.93	10	Oct
68.66	Denis	Shabasov	BLR	27.3.00	20	Feb
68.57	José Manuel	Padilla	MEX	26.6.96	15	Feb
68.50	Ned	Weatherly	AUS	12.1.98	6	Feb
68.47		Jiang He	CHN	20.7.98	30	May
68.35	Luis	da Silva	BRA	10.7.96	1	Nov

MFN 2020

HAMMER - JAVELIN

Mark	Name		Nat	Born		Pos	Meet	Venue		Date
68.34	Miroslav	Pavlícek	CZE	31.3.87	18 Jul	68.19	Tomas	Vasiliauskas	LTU	28.11.97 15 Aug
68.29	Dawid	Piłat	POL-J	6.2.02	28 Aug	68.12	Dan	Morari	MDA	29.6.98 1 Feb
68.28	Valentin	Andreev	BUL-J	19.1.02	15 Aug	68.07	Ákos	Hudi	HUN	10.8.91 7 Mar
68.27	Danylo	Fedorov	UKR-J	22.8.01	15 Aug	68.00	Chris	Shorthouse	GBR	23.6.88 25 Jul
68.20	Reza	Moghaddam	IRI	17.11.88	25 Aug	68.00	Kittipong	Boonwaman	THA	16.5.96 10 Dec
							[159]			
Downhill: 80.72dh	Rudy	Winkler	USA	6.12.94	1			Middletown, NY		13 Sep

77.74 - 80.18 - x - 80.72 - x - 80.37

JUNIORS

2 juniors in main list. 9 performances by 2 men over 72.00.

Kokhan	77.62	1		Mukachevo	14 Feb	75.39	1	NC	Lutsk	29 Aug
	76.42	1		Pärnu	22 Aug	75.16	4	Kuso	Chorzów	25 Aug
	75.73	4	Skol	Chorzów	6 Sep	74.69	1		Ankara	18 Jul
	75.43	1		Balk Ch Cluj-Napoca	19 Sep					
70.45	Merlin		Hummel	GER	4.1.02	1			Berlin	27 Jun
69.91	Benedek		Doma	HUN	17.10.01	2			Szombathely	24 Sep
69.77	Jean-Baptiste		Bruxelle	FRA	9.7.02	4	NC		Albi	12 Sep
68.29	Dawid		Piłat	POL	6.2.02	5	NC		Włocławek	28 Aug
68.28	Valentin		Andreev	BUL	19.1.02	1			Balchik	15 Aug
68.27	Danylo		Fedorov	UKR	22.8.01	1			Lutsk	15 Aug
66.98	Oréstis		Dousákis	GRE	2.5.02	6	NC		Pátra	8 Aug

6kg HAMMER

83.32	Myhaylo	Kokhan	UKR	22.1.01	1	Balk-J	Istanbul	12 Sep
	80.50	1	NC-j Lusk	12 Aug	79.80	1		Antalya	9 Jan
79.75	Merlin	Hummel	GER	4.1.02	1	NC-j	Heilbronn	4 Sep
77.53	Dawid	Piłat	POL	6.2.02	1		Stalowa Wola	22 Aug
77.36	Benedek	Doma	HUN	17.10.01	1		Szombathely	25 Jul
76.73	Jean-Baptiste	Bruxelle	FRA	9.7.02	1		Antony	25 Jul
76.38	Jan	Doležálek	CZE	23.5.02	1	NC-j	Ostrava	5 Sep
76.24	Valentin	Andreev	BUL	19.1.02	2	Balk-J	Istanbul	12 Sep
76.14	Ronald A.	Mencia	CUB	26.8.02	1	NC	La Habana	20 Mar
75.74	Tomasz	Ratajczyk	POL	20.9.02	1		Bydgoszcz	26 Jul
74.78	Danylo	Fedorov	UKR	22.8.01	3	Balk-J	Istanbul	12 Sep
73.80	Oréstis	Dousákis	GRE	2.5.02	1		Trípoli	8 Jul
72.93	Artur	Moskalenko	BLR	7.4.01	1q		Brest	9 Jul
72.72	Sören	Hilbig	GER	14.6.02	1		Königslutter	18 Jul
72.32	Oskari	Lahtinen	FIN	2.2.01	1		Pori	20 Jul

JAVELIN

97.76	Johannes	Vetter	GER	26.3.93	1	Skol	Chorzów		6 Sep
				83.77	86.41	97.76	94.84	89.95	87.28
	91.49	1	PNG	Turku	11 Aug	91.49	87.59	88.57	86.42 p p
	90.86	1	Kuso	Chorzów	25 Aug	86.81	90.86	86.40	90.00 p 89.00
	87.36	1	NC	Braunschweig	9 Aug	84.84	84.38	87.36	x x 85.88
	87.26	1	ISTAF	Berlin	13 Sep	83.85	87.26	83.57	83.49 83.93 83.97
	86.94	1		Kuortane	1 Aug	80.69	x	81.69	84.19 86.94
	86.17	1		Dessau	8 Sep	79.56	84.16	x	81.97 81.29 86.17
87.86A	Neeraj	Chopra	IND	24.12.97	1		Potchefstroom		28 Jan
				81.63	82.00	82.57	87.86	p p	
87.07	Marcin	Krukowski	POL	14.6.92	1	Sidlo	Sopot		13 Aug
				80.43	x	87.07	76.56		
86.49	Kim	Amb	SWE	31.7.90	1		Zweibrücken		25 Jul
				86.49	p	x	p		
86.05	Aleksey	Kotkovets	BLR	7.6.98	1	NC	Minsk		1 Aug
	(11/5)			83.09	x	86.05	x	x	x
85.54		Cheng Chao-Tsun	TPE	17.10.93	1	NC	Bangkok		5 Dec
85.50	Rocco	van Rooyen	RSA	23.12.92	1		Paarl		4 Nov
85.47A	Shivpal	Singh	IND	6.7.95	1		Potchefstroom		10 Mar
85.24	Andreas	Hofmann	GER	16.12.91	2	PNG	Turku		11 Aug
84.56	Gatis	Cakss	LAT	13.6.95	1		Ogre		14 Aug
	[10]								
84.41	Adrian	Mardare	MDA	20.6.95	2		Dessau		8 Sep
84.31	Jakub	Vadlejch	CZE	10.10.90	1		Kladno		1 Jun
84.10	Odel	Jainaga	ESP	14.10.97	1		Madrid		6 Sep
84.05	Genki	Dean	JPN	30.12.91	1		Tokyo		23 Aug
83.40	Mark	Slavov	BUL	17.3.94	2	Balk Ch	Cluj-Napoca		20 Sep
83.03	Vitezslav	Vesely	CZE	27.2.83	1		Ostrava		22 Aug
82.70	Nikolay	Orlov	RUS	7.1.99	1		Moskva		26 Aug
82.22	Norbert	Rivasz-Tóth	HUN	6.5.96	4	PNG	Turku		11 Aug
82.20	Lassi	Etelätalo	FIN	30.4.88	1	NC	Turku		16 Aug

JAVELIN

Mark	Name		Nat	Born	Pos	Meet	Venue	Date	
81.85	Janis	Svens Griva	LAT	23.4.93	2		Ogre	14	Aug
	[20]								
81.73	Kennosuke	Sogawa	JPN	12.7.94	1		Nara	18	Jul
81.73	Ryohei	Arai	JPN	23.6.91	1		Osaka	24	Oct
81.65	Liam	O'Brien	AUS	13.4.96	1		Brisbane	14	Nov
81.51	Cameron	McEntyre	AUS	10.2.99	1		Sydney (Bankstown)	24	Oct
81.38	Edis	Matusevicius	LTU	30.6.96	1	NC	Palanga	8	Aug
81.36	Toni	Kuusela	FIN	21.1.94	1		Vantaa	27	Jun
81.22	Petr	Frydrych	CZE	13.1.88	2	Odlozil	Praha	8	Jun
81.15	Pavel	Meleshko	BLR	24.11.92	1		Brest	29	Sep
81.13		Ma Qun	CHN	8.2.94	1	NC	Shaoxing	15	Sep
80.75	Vladislav	Panasenkov	RUS	22.5.96	1		Bryansk	16	Aug
	[30]								
80.64	Ihad	Abdelrahman	EGY	1,5,89	1		El Maadi	11	Dec
80.55	Takuto	Kominami	JPN	26.7.95	1		Kitakami	10	Aug
80.50	Anderson	Peters	GRN	21.10.97	1		St George's	1	Aug
80.37	Dejan	Mileusnic	BIH	16.11.91	1	NC	Zenica	8	Aug
80.23	Dmitriy	Tarabin	RUS	29.10.91	2	NCp	Bryansk	30	Aug
80.21	Hamish	Peacock	AUS	15.10.90	1		Hobart	16	Feb
80.15	Mateusz	Kwasniewski	POL	16.7.95	1		Lódz	4	Jul
80.11	Tino	Mäkelä	FIN	31.7.99	1	NC-23	Kemi	23	Jul
80.00	Emin	Öncel	TUR	1.5.97	1		Mersin	23	Feb
79.94	Mauro	Fraresso	ITA	13.1.93	1		Castiglione della Pescaia	25	Jul
	[40]								
79.90	Kasper	Sagen	NOR	19.4.99	1	NC	Bergen	20	Sep
79.80	Nicolás	Quijera	ESP	24.6.96	2	NC	Madrid	12	Sep
79.78	Roberto	Bertolini	ITA	9.10.85	2		Castiglione della Pescaia	25	Jul
79.70	Manu	Quijera	ESP	13.1.98	1		Motril	7	Mar
79.70	Nikolay	Klimuk	BLR	20.12.96	2		Minsk	26	Jun
79.45	Cyprian	Mrzygłód	POL	2.2.98	2		Spala	8	Aug
79.39	Riley	Dolezal	USA	16.11.85	1		Rathdrum, ID	1	Aug
79.22	Antti	Ruuskanen	FIN	21.2.84	2	NC	Turku	16	Aug
79.15A	Phil-Mar	van Rensburg	RSA	23.6.89	1		Secunda	7	Mar
79.12	Jami	Kinnunen	FIN	31.3.95	1		Kuortane	13	Jun
	[50]								
79.11	Aleksandr	Kozlowski	BLR	6.2.95	1		Minsk	20	Feb
79.04	Alexandru	Novac	ROU	24.3.97	2	Balk Ch	Cluj-Napoca	20	Sep
78.99	Jaroslav	Jílek	CZE	22.10.89	2	Odlozil	Praha	8	Jun
78.98	Piotr	Lebioda	POL	28.5.92	3		Suwalki	23	Sep
78.90	Dawid	Wegner	POL	23.4.00	3	Sidlo	Sopot	13	Aug
78.75	Timothy	Herman	BEL	19.10.90	1		Karlstad	8	Jul
78.73		Huang Shih-Feng	TPE	2.3.92	1		Taipei	11	Mar
78.54	Hubert	Chmielak	POL	19.6.89	1		Kołobrzeg	19	Sep
78.42	Topias	Laine	FIN-J	12.7.00	1		Jyväskylä	1	Sep
78.17	Valeriy	Izotov	BLR	12.4.97	2		Brest	16	Jul
	[60]								
78.12	Kohei	Hasegawa	JPN	1.1.90	2		Kitakami	10	Aug
78.11	Arthur Wiborg	Petersen	DEN	18.8.99	2		Bålsta	18	Jul
78.07	Tatsuya	Sakamoto	JPN	4.5.96	3	NC	Niigata	1	Oct
77.96	Unmet	Degirmenci	TUR	23.7.98	2		Bursa	29	Aug
77.81	James	Whiteaker	GBR	8.10.98	1		Nuneaton	2	Aug
77.61A	Rohit	Yadav	IND-J	6.6.01	2		Potchefstroom	28	Jan
77.60	Norbert	Bonvecchio	ITA	14.8.85	1		Vittorio Veneto	27	Sep
77.56	Teemu	Narvi	FIN	2.7.00	2	NC-23	Kemi	23	Aug
77.29A	Johannes	Grobler	RSA	6.8.97	8	Dec			
77.29	Baha Sharif	Mohamed	EGY	29.9.95	11	Dec			
77.04	Toni	Keränen	FIN	16.6.98	23	Aug			
77.00	Rolands	Strobinders	LAT	14.4.92	15	Jul			
76.88	Simon	Wieland	SUI	16.12.00	20	Jun			
76.86	Ivan	Filippov	RUS	28.8.96	17	Feb			
76.84	Teemu	Wirkkala	FIN	14.1.84	16	Aug			
76.81	Kenji	Ogura	JPN	8.6.95	23	Aug			
76.73	Cedric	Sorgelos	BEL	14.4.00	29	Aug			
76.72	Leandro	Ramos	POR	21.9.00	29	Jul			
76.71A	Alex	Kiprotich	KEN	10.10.94	3	Oct			
76.67	Lasse	Saarinen	FIN	10.3.97	1	Jun			
76.56	Jarmo	Marttila	FIN	24.10.92	1	Jun			
76.53	Boris	Bezdolniy	RUS	1.4.97	30	Aug			
76.52	Artur	Felfner	UKR-Y	17.10.03	13	Sep			
76.37	Kazunori	Yagi	JPN	31.1.94	19	Sep			
76.36	Ryosuke	Kamei	JPN	29.4.97	31	Oct			
76.33	Dagbjartur Dadi	Jónsson	ISL	13.11.97	25	Jul			
76.24	Tom	Egbers	NED	11..11.99	16	Aug			
76.18	Gen	Naganuma	JPN	31.3.98	1	Oct			
76.16	Nash	Lowis	AUS	6.11.99	15	Feb			
76.16	Newton	Katoky	IND	.90	4	Mar			
76.16		Zhu Kai	CHN	24.8.98	7	Aug			
76.13	Anro	van Eeden	RSA	19.5.99	28	Feb			
76.10	Luiz Maurício	da Silva	BRA	17.1.00	13	Dec			
76.10	R.M.Sumedha	Ranasinghe	SRI	26.9.91	7	Dec			
76.09	Jurriaan	Wouters	NED	18.4.93	30	Aug			
76.07	Vedran	Samac	SRB	22.1.90	20	Sep			
		Zhao Qinggang	CHN	24.7.85	15	Sep			
75.78									
75.71	Lukas	Moutarde	FRA	1.4.98	12	Sep			
75.60	Osmany	Laffita	CUB	14.8.94	14	Feb			
75.59	Yashvir	Singh (100)	IND-J	22.10.01	11	Jan			
75.55	Teo	Takala	FIN	6.6.94	27	Jul			
75.55	Teuraiterai	Tupala	PYF	6.2.00	27	Feb			
75.54	Yugo	Masuda	JPN	18.4.98	1	Oct			
75.54	Pavel	Sasimovich	BLR	5.9.99	1	Mar			
75.46	Roberto	Orlando	ITA	5.8.95	8	Sep			
75.39	Giovanni	Diaz	PAR	23.3.94	29	Nov			

MEN 2020

318 JAVELIN - HEPTATHLON

Mark	Name		Nat	Born	Pos	Meet	Venue		Date	
75.27	Aleksi	Yli-Mannila	FIN-J	6.1.01	19 Sep	74.60	Denis	Canepa	ITA	3.5.93	3 Oct
75.21		Nam Tae-jong	KOR	11.9.97	27 Jun	74.41	Norberto	Fontana	ITA	12.8.98	20 Sep
75.21	Capers	Williamson	USA	13.10.92	16 Aug	74.37	Pavel	Kuvryshin	RUS	9.7.98	11 Feb
75.13		Hu Haoran	CHN	28.9.98	15 Sep	74.32		Kim Woo-jung	KOR	6.1.97	11 Jul
75.02A	Arshdeep	Singh	IND	5.4.99	10 Mar	74.29	Yusaku	Iwao	JPN-J	12.4.02	23 Aug
74.98	Jakob	Nauck	GER	13.11.99	15 Aug	74.18	Denis	Both	ROU	21.8.97	22 Aug
74.92	Bruno	Schürch	SUI	30.1.96	12 Sep	74.17		Liu Qizhen	CHN	17.9.95	15 Sep
74.88	Yeóryios	Hristakákos	GRE	26.6.98	8 Jul	74.07	Máté	Járvás	HUN-J	31.1.01	9 Aug
74.80	Niklas	Sagawe	GER	16.4.00	24 Jun	74.07	Eryk	Kolodziejczak	POL-J	4.2.02	23 Sep
74.69	William	White	AUS	27.11.95	1 Feb	[125]					

Unofficial due to irregularities: 87.62u Rocco van Rooyen   RSA   23.12.92 1   Paarl   28 Nov
Unsanctioned on-line competition: 85.54u Adrian Mardare   MDA   20.6.95   Chisinau   2 Aug

JUNIORS
2 juniors in main list. 7 performances by 3 men over 76.50. Additional marks and further juniors:

Laine	78.16	1	Jyväskylä	1 Sep	76.72	Q	NC	Turku	15 Aug
	77.47	1	NC-j Kemi	23 Aug	76.52	5	NC	Turku	16 Aug
76.52	Artur	Felfner	UKR-Y	17.10.03	1	Balk-J	Istanbul		13 Sep
75.59	Yashvir	Singh	IND	22.10.01	1		Guwahati		11 Jan
75.27	Aleksi	Yli-Mannila	FIN	6.1.01	1		Lahti		19 Sep
74.29	Yusaku	Iwao	JPN	12.4.02	6		Tokyo		23 Aug
74.07	Máté	Járvás	HUN	31.1.01	2	NC	Budapest		9 Aug
74.07	Eryk	Kolodziejczak	POL	4.2.02	1-j		Suwalki		23 Sep
73.60		Wang Cong	CHN	31.1.01	1		Jinan		15 Apr
73.57	Howard	McDonald (10)	AUS	23.8.01	1		Mackay		4 Oct
73.37	Devoux	Deysel	RSA	30.3.01	1		San Antonio		6 Mar
73.28	Pablo	Costas	ESP	10.5.01	4		Motril		7 Mar
73.12A	Al Fathi	Ganji	IRI	21.4.01	1		Tehran		25 Aug
73.06	Jhonatam	Maullu	ITA	3.4.01	1		Cagliari		3 Sep
72.85	Filip	Dominkovic	SLO	18.2.02	1		Celje		6 Feb

INDOOR HEPTATHLON

6320	Artem	Makarenko	RUS	23.4.97	1	NC	Kirov		17 Feb
	6.75	7.64	14.33	2.06	7.72	4.80	2:40.57		
6209	Garrett	Scantling	USA	19.5.93	1	NC	Annapolis		8 Feb
	6.93	7.45	16.25	1.99	7.91	5.20	2:52.26		
6143	Jorge	Ureña	ESP	8.10.93	1	NC	Ourense		1 Mar
	6.95	7.54	14.44	2.11	7.91	4.65	2:44.15		
6114	Johannes	Erm	EST	26.3.98	1		Fayetteville		1 Feb
	6.99	7.59	14.56	1.96	8.03	4.80	2:36.02		
6110#		Scantling			1		Lexington		25 Jan
	6.95	7.12	16.21	2.02	7.91	5.10	2:52.82		
6097	Andreas	Bechmann	GER	28.9.99	1	NC	Leverkusen		2 Feb
	6.96	7.50	14.26	2.09	8.43	5.00	2:42.37		
6072	Pieter	Braun	NED	21.1.93	1	NC	Apeldoorn		9 Feb
	7.20	7.54	15.03	2.01	8.18	4.93	2:39.15		
6050	Pawel	Wiesiolek	POL	13.8.91	1	NC	Torun		1 Mar
	6.96	7.28	14.63	2.05	8.20	5.10	2:48.47		
6019	Karel	Tilga	EST	5.2.98	2		Fayetteville		1 Feb
	7.18	7.42	15.45	2.05	8.40	4.70	2:36.34		
5996	Risto	Lillemets	EST	20.11.97	2		Tallinn		9 Feb
	7.11	7.25	15.00	2.05	8.21	5.10	2:49.83		
5994	Kyle	Garland (10)	USA	28.5.00	3		Fayetteville		1 Feb
	6.95	7.37	13.70	2.14	8.03	4.40	2:42.82		
5963	Manuel	Eitel	GER	28.1.97	1		Aubière		12 Jan
	6.81	7.41	14.64	1.98	8.22	4.82	2:50.27		
5958	Oleksiy	Kasyanov	UKR	26.8.85	3		Tallinn		9 Feb
	6.97	7.41	15.05	1.96	8.04	4.60	2:43.99		
5939	Simone	Cairoli	ITA	13.1.90	1	NC	Ancona		23 Feb
	7.05	7.52	13.53	2.04	8.23	4.70	2:42.10		
5924	Maicel	Uibo	EST	27.12.92	4		Tallinn		9 Feb
	7.31	7.09	14.82	2.11	8.50	5.20	2:47.03		
5915	Simon	Ehammer	SUI	7.2.00	1	NC	Magglingen		2 Feb
	6.94	7.75	12.98	1.95	7.86	4.70	2:51.14		
5910	Taavi	Tsernjavski	EST	4.3.95	5		Tallinn		9 Feb
	7.09	7.26	14.49	1.96	8.17	4.80	2:40.35		
5907	Rafael	Raap	NED	18.3.99	2		Apeldoorn		9 Feb
	6.99	7.30	13.50	2.04	8.30	4.93	2:46.74		
5889	Ondrej	Kopecky	CZE	16.5.98	1	NC	Praha (OJ)		9 Feb
	7.12	7.12	12.87	2.01	8.08	5.20	2:46.67		
5885	T.J.	Lawson	USA	25.1.97	4		Fayetteville		1 Feb
	7.03	7.45	14.71	2.02	8.74	4.80	2:42.63		

HEPTATHLON - DECATHLON 319

Mark	Name		Nat	Born	Pos	Meet	Venue		Date
5883	Tim	Nowak	GER	13.8.95	2		Aubière		12 Jan
	7.33	7.13 14.96	2.04	8.34		4.82	2:38.68		
5848#	Leo	Neugebauer GER	19.6.00	29 Feb	5759	Mihail	Dudas	SRB	1.11.89 23 Feb
5843#	Maximilian	Vollmer GER	12.3.98	29 Feb	5757	Stepan	Kekin	RUS	13.11.00 17 Feb
5833#	Zachary	Lorbeck USA		29 Feb	5726	Karl Robert	Saluri	EST	6.8.93 9 Feb
5808	Fredrik	Samuelsson SWE	16.2.95	2 Feb	5714	Jack	Flood	USA	15.9.95 8 Feb
5799	Ludovic	Besson FRA	27.1.98	1 Mar	5712	Gary	Haasbroek	AUS	15.3.99 1 Feb
5797	Scott	Filip USA	28.1.95	8 Feb	5707	Jérémy	Lelièvre	FRA	8.2.91 12 Jan
5794	Sergey	Timshin RUS	25.11.92	17 Feb	5706	Markus	Ballengee	USA	8.1.98 29 Feb
5787	Jeremy	Taiwo USA	15.1.90	25 Jan	5705	Ruben	Gado	FRA	13.12.93 9 Feb
5782	Adam Sebastian	Helcelet CZE	27.10.91	9 Feb	5703	Romain	Martin	FRA	12.7.88 1 Feb
5775	Joseph	Delgado USA	8.1.95	18 Jan					

DECATHLON

Mark	Name		Nat	Born	Pos	Meet	Venue		Date
8552	Kevin	Mayer	FRA	10.2.92	1		Saint-Paul, Réunion		19 Dec
	10.68/-0.5	7.40/0.6 16.20	1.97	48.87		13.54/1.8	50.32 4.65	67.66	4:47.74
8492	Ashley	Moloney	AUS	13.3.00	1		Brisbane (Nathan)		20 Dec
	10.36/-0.3	7.67w/2.3 13.62	2.11	45.82		14.17/1.6	43.93 4.80	57.77	4:48.48
8367	Cedric	Dubler	AUS	13.1.95	2		Brisbane (Nathan)		20 Dec
	10.79/-0.3	7.62/0.0 13.24	2.11	47.84		14.34/1.6	41.70 5.00	62.48	4:41.05
8364	Felipe Vinícius	dos Santos	BRA	30.7.94	1	NC	São Paulo		12 Dec
	10.40/+0.8	7.64/-1.4 14.04	2.07	48.01		14.01/-1.4	42.46 4.90	59.82	4:55.83
8260	Axel	Hubert	FRA	16.2.96	1	NC	Aubagne		20 Sep
	11.03/0.0	7.42w/3.4 15.82	1.98	50.75		14.31/-0.4	41.88 4.90	69.69	4:39.62
8231	Simon	Ehammer	SUI	7.2.00	1	NC	Langenthal		9 Aug
	10.50/1.2	7.81/-0.6 13.75	2.01	47.27		13.73/0.6	36.19 4.90	52.88	4:42.54
8202	Vitaliy	Zhuk	BLR	10.9.96	1	NC	Minsk		1 Aug
	11.03/0.5	7.03/-2.1 15.39	2.01	49.11		14.85/-2.0	49.08 4.60	62.98	4:28.83
8133	Risto	Lillemets	EST	20.11.97	1	NC	Tallinn		9 Aug
	10.94/1.6	7.22/0.8 14.96	1.99	50.30		14.69w/2.1	46.39 4.85	63.84	4:42.18
8100	Maksim	Andraloits	BLR	17.6.97	2	NC	Minsk		1 Aug
	10.95/0.5	7.08/-0.1 15.37	2.07	49.12		14.45/-2.0	45.14 4.90	57.38	4:54.08
8086	Taavi	Tsernjavski	EST	4.3.95	1		Rakvere		8 Jul
	10.98/1.6	7.22/1.5 15.13	1.96	49.35		14.69/-1.5	46.16 4.80	59.86	4:39.76
	(10)								
8086	Ilya	Shkurenyov	RUS	11.1.91	1		Adler		24 Sep
	11.16/2.0	7.35/1.1 14.10	1.99	49.64		14.58/0.6	47.39 5.00	59.75	4:46.08
8031	Rik	Taam	NED	17.1.97	1	NC	Emmeloord		6 Sep
	10.80w/2.4	7.07/0.6 14.52	1.97	48.92		14.62/0.3	42.23 4.70	57.53	4:26.53
8027(w)	Thomas	Van Der Plaetsen	BEL	24.12.90	1	NC	Deinze		26 Sep
	11.22w/3.8	7.48/1.0 13.07	2.05	51.32		14.60w/3.6	47.66 5.20	56.53	4:48.25
7990	Leonel	Suárez	CUB	1.9.87	1	NC	La Habana		21 Mar
	11.70/-0.4	7.10w/2.5 14.59	2.05	51.35		15.03/-0.1	45.38 4.50	72.77	4:27.68
7990	Martin	Roe	NOR	1.4.92	1	NC	Fagernes		9 Aug
	11.03/-1.1	7.50/1.5 14.93	1.94	50.96		14.98w/2.4	45.14 4.80	61.88	4:43.33
7978	Makenson	Gletty	FRA	2.4.99	5		Saint-Paul, Réunion		19 Dec
	10.81/-0.5	6.80/1.4 15.37	2.00	50.79		14.11/1.8	45.01 4.55	61.64	4:45.01
7879A	Fredriech	Pretorius	RSA	4.8.95	1		Pretoria		14 Mar
	11.01/0.1	7.44w/2.5 13.60	1.96	50.62		14.65/1.1	43.81 4.90	58.25	4:50.19
7854	Fredrik	Samuelsson	SWE	16.2.95	1		Ljungby		2 Aug
	11.15/-0.4	7.42/1.9 14.09	2.01	50.54		15.25/-1.8	43.60 4.85	60.82	4:52.70
7829	Edward	Mikhan	BLR	7.6.89	3	NC	Minsk		1 Aug
	10.78/0.5	7.06/0.0 14.54	1.92	49.20		15.15/-2.0	47.59 4.40	56.27	4:39.62
7829	Rafael	Raap	NED	18.3.97	2	NC	Emmeloord		6 Sep
	10.95w/2.4	7.21/1.7 13.05	1.97	49.89		14.69/0.3	43.00 4.80	56.63	4:40.36
	[20]								
7761	Benjamin	Hougardy	BEL	8.12.95	6		Saint-Paul, Réunion		19 Dec
	11.00/1.2	7.23/0.3 13.55	1.97	49.27		14.89w/2.2	37.08 4.85	53.53	4:32.14
7753	José Fernando	Santana	BRA	27.3.99	2	NC	São Paulo		12 Dec
	10.93/0.8	7.10/-0.1 13.48	1.95	49.13		14.05/1.4	43.23 4.60	60.68	5:11.89
7742		Hu Yufei	CHN	9.11.93	1		Nanjing		30 Apr
	11.24/0.9	7.09w/2.1 15.17	1.92	49.90		14.52/-0.8	41.48 4.80	53.93	4:44.87
7739	Akihiko	Nakamura	JPN	23.10.90	1	NC	Nagano		27 Sep
	11.02/0.2	7.08/-1.7 12.42	1.97	49.39		14.21/0.7	35.99 4.90	52.33	4:27.06
7738	Ruben	Gado	FRA	13.12.93	2	NC	Aubagne		20 Sep
	10.90/0.0	7.09/1.7 13.32	1.89	49.12		15.01/1.1	42.04 5.00	50.85	4:34.08
7718	Briander	Rivero	CUB	23.4.91	2	NC	La Habana		21 Mar
	11.24/-0.4	7.30w/2.1 14.50	2.02	50.71		14.48/-0.1	42.47 4.30	53.84	4:39.21
7716	Oleksiy	Kasyanov	UKR	26.8.85	1	NC	Lutsk		29 Aug
	11.12/-1.5	7.35/0.7 14.98	1.97	50.94		14.73/-1.6	47.87 4.60	45.30	4:47.95
7694	Toralv	Opsal	NOR	9.3.98	1		Oslo		28 Jun
	11.20/0.0	7.41/1.9 13.97	1.97	49.88		15.20/0.3	40.13 4.85	43.73	4:23.44

DECATHLON

Mark	Name	Nat	Born	Pos	Meet	Venue	Date
7684	Keisuke Ushiro	JPN	24.7.86	2	NC	Nagano	27 Sep
	11.41/0.2 6.90/-0.6 15.11	2.00	52.11		15.14/1.1	44.51 4.90 61.33	4:57.26
7670	Jannis Wolff	GER	98	1	NC	Vaterstetten	23 Aug
	10.77/1.7 6.85/0.2 13.15	1.94	49.49		15.04/0.2	41.05 4.60 57.71	4:38.04
	[30]						
7668	Finley Gaio	SUI	15.4.99	2	NC	Langenthal	9 Aug
	10.94/1.2 7.32/-1.2 13.30	1.92	48.76		14.05/0.6	37.50 4.70 50.63	4:50.70
7665	Alec Diamond	AUS	9.8.97	3		Brisbane (Nathan)	20 Dec
	11.04/-0.3 7.57/0.0 14.51	1.99	49.96		14.60/1.6	44.43 4.60 46.01	5:07.51
7655	Dario Dester	ITA	22.7.00	1		Firenze	2 Aug
	10.92w/2.3 7.09/0.7 13.75	1.93	48.68		14.70/0.0	37.23 4.70 53.58	4:43.50
7653	Hideru Kawakami	JPN	18.3.00	1		Niigata	12 Sep
	10.66/-0.4 7.27/-1.0 11.55	1.93	48.72		14.17/1.9	37.12 4.50 57.15	4:48.29
7651	Dan Golubovic	AUS	29.11.93	4		Brisbane (Nathan)	20 Dec
	11.09/-0.3 7.09/-0.3 14.92	1.99	50.20		14.57/1.6	50.42 4.60 41.60	5:00.88
7643	Edgaras Benkunskas	LTU	28.5.99	1	NC	Palanga	8 Aug
	11.15/1.8 6.92/1.3 13.40	2.07	50.27		14.68/0.0	39.50 4.50 61.22	4:53.15
7641	Malik Diakité	GER	13.3.00	2	NC	Vaterstetten	23 Aug
	10.90/1.7 6.86/0.5 13.01	1.94	48.79		14.93/0.2	40.98 4.40 54.24	4:27.13
7637	Artem Lukyanenko	RUS	30.1.90	2		Adler	24 Sep
	11.37/2.0 7.04/1.3 14.50	1.93	51.45		14.64/0.6	41.73 4.90 53.52	4:41.43
7625	Stepan Kekin	RUS	13.11.00	1	NC-23	Chelyabinsk	10 Sep
	11.03/-0.2 7.33/1.4 13.76	1.85	51.18		14.40/-0.2	42.98 5.30 54.32	5:24.55
7622	Ludovic Besson	FRA	27.1.98	7		Saint-Paul, Réunion	19 Dec
	11.02/-0.5 6.80/0.2 15.57	1.91	50.32		14.35/1.8	42.98 4.55 52.96	4:55.10
	[40]						
7619	Shun Taue	JPN	30.5.97	3	NC	Nagano	27 Sep
	11.01/0.2 7.07/-0.5 12.98	1.91	49.12		14.15/0.7	36.66 4.30 56.50	4:29.57
7614	Léon Mak	NED	5.9.00	3	NC	Emmeloord	6 Sep
	10.95w/2.4 6.66w/3.1 13.60	1.94	49.64		14.87/0.3	46.53 4.80 48.64	4:45.91
7609	Sergey Timshin	RUS	25.11.92	1		Chelyabinsk	10 Sep
	11.42/-0.2 7.44/0.7 13.78	2.03	50.45		15.10/-0.2	41.89 4.60 51.53	4:46.66
7603	Kazuma Katayama	JPN	14.6.95	4	NC	Nagano	27 Sep
	10.83/0.8 6.84/-1.1 13.34	1.94	50.06		15.23/1.4	42.56 4.70 57.03	4:48.47
7601	Jan Ruhrmann	GER	14.7.97	3	NC	Vaterstetten	23 Aug
	11.27/1.5 6.73/0.0 14.43	1.91	50.90		15.64/-0.5	45.04 4.40 61.21	4:26.30
7575w	Ondrej Kopecky	CZE	16.5.98	1		Plzen	20 Jun
	11.02W/4.8 7.25/1.1 12.13	1.95	50.28		14.62w/2.6	42.85 4.60 51.35	4:41.70
7574	Marcus Nilsson	SWE	3.5.91	2	NC	Ljungby	2 Aug
	11.60/0.3 7.01w/2.3 14.49	1.95	52.15		15.71/-1.8	46.94 4.75 57.62	4:39.63
7570	Tristan Marcy	FRA	5.1.00	1	NC-23	Aubagne	20 Sep
	10.79/1.4 7.09w/3.4 11.88	2.01	49.67		14.46/0.1	37.99 4.60 45.50	4:31.81
7545	Jordan de Souza	BRA	30.7.98	3	NC	São Paulo	12 Dec
	10.74/0.8 7.03/-1.4 12.45	1.92	47.77		14.32/1.4	38.86 4.30 46.85	4:41.47
7516	Niels Pittomvils	BEL	18.7.92	1	NC	Bruxelles	16 Aug
	11.61/-1.3 6.96/0.1 13.96	1.99	50.91		15.01/0.0	41.91 4.80 52.31	4:42.33
	[50]						
7512	Yevgeniy Sarantsev	RUS	5.2.88	10 Sep			
7511	Lucas Catanhede	BRA	3.11.94	12 Dec			
7496	Keisuke Okuda	JPN	23.10.96	27 Sep			
7478	Rafal Horbowicz	POL	1.4.98	4 Oct			
7477	Tsuyoshi Shimizu	JPN	21.12.93	27 Sep			
7473	Yevgeniy Likhanov	RUS	10.1.95	10 Sep			
7454	Martijn Hoogewerf	NED	12.5.98	6 Sep			
7443	Lorenzo Naidon	ITA	15.6.99	2 Aug			
7432	Hiroyoshi Ushiro	JPN	25.10.94	24 Jul			
7430	Chris Helwick	USA	18.3.85	4 Oct			
7428	Guo Qi	CHN	28.12.90	3 Jun			
7423	Gaël Quérin	FRA	26.6.87	19 Dec			
7418	Yevgeniy Chernov	RUS	9.11.91	10 Sep			
7415	Leonel Uusimäki	FIN	30.6.98	19 Jul			
7411	Matthias Steinmann	SUI	5.6.92	9 Aug			
	(65)						

JUNIORS

7152	Ville Toivonen	FIN	8.4.02	3	NC	Turku	15 Aug
	11.38/0.2 6.84/1.5 12.34	1.92	54.40		15.18/1.3	41.15 4.12 64.77	4:46.42
7098	Chen Xinghua	CHN	5.5.02	6	NC	Shaojing	16 May
	10.91/1.6 7.15/0.5 11.62	1.89	48.92		14.69/0.2	34.47 4.10 42.29	4:44.15

IAAF junior specification – with 99cm 110mh, 6kg SP, 1.75kg DT

8238	Markus Rooth	NOR	22.12.01	1		Oslo	28 Jun
	11.03/0.0 7.53/0.6 15.81	1.97	49.56		14.18/1.5	46.07 4.75 59.80	4:39.79
8116	Sven Roosen	NED	27.7.01	1	NC-j	Emmeloord	6 Sep
	10.71/2.5 7.26w/2.7 15.17	1.82	48.22		13.81/0.2	45.89 4.40 57.44	4:28.15
7849	Baptiste Thiery	FRA	29.6.01	1	NC-j	Aubagne	20 Sep
	10.94/1.7 7.1w9/2.1 12.24	1.95	49.78		14.89/0.5	40.34 5.50 49.50	4:32.27
7839	Sander Skotheim	NOR	31.5.02	2		Oslo	28 Jun
	11.43/0.0 7.09/1.4 14.16	2.03	50.51		14.61/1.5	45.85 4.65 56.42	4:35.60
7833 (w)	Jente Hautterkeete	BEL	14.3.02	1	NC-j	Deinze	27 Sep
	10.88w/2.7 7.16/2.0 15.19	1.96	50.13		14.10w/3.3	44.02 4.40 49.03	4:36.63

DECATHLON - RELAYS - 3000m - 5000m WALK

Mark	Name	Nat	Born	Pos	Meet	Venue	Date
7666 (w)	Frantisek Doubek	CZE	4.4.02	1		Plzen	21 Jun
	11.04w/3.4 7.18/1.2 14.52	1.89	50.64		14.67w/3.3 41.83 4.40 60.19		4:45.94
7607	Marcel Meyer	GER	1.1.01	1	NC-j	Vaterstetten	22 Aug
	11.08/0.8 6.64/0.6 14.70	1.95	48.64		14.32/1.3 40.77 4.60 47.80		4:41.89
7553	Sven Jansons	NED	19.7.01	2	NC-j	Emmeloord	6 Sep
	10.65/2.5 6.13/2.0 14.40	2.00	49.63		14.27/0.2 42.11 4.40 46.16		4:36.97
7498	Nils Laserich	GER	.01	2	NC-j	Vaterstetten	22 Aug
	11.13/0.8 7.15/-0.6 15.07	1.83	49.32		14.94/0.4 40.48 4.10 54.86		4:39.09
7349	Fabian Amherd	SUI	19.1.01	1	NC-j	Langenthal	9 Aug
	11.63/1.5 6.48/-0.2 14.67	1.95	50.65		14.89/-0.1 41.28 4.30 52.33		4:30.67
7291	Jack Turner	GBR	11.7.01	2	NOR-j	Fagernes	9 Aug
	11.32/-0.2 7.07/0.0 13.17	1.94	50.54		14.43w/2.2 43.13 4.20 48.15		4:58.00
7281	Teo Bastien	FRA	3.10.02	2	NC-j	Aubagne	20 Sep
	11.15/0.9 7.17w/2.1 12.69	2.01	53.49		14.54/-0.1 41.44 4.50 50.12		5:05.59
7272	Raydel Tasé	CUB	1.1.02	1	NC-j	La Habana	21 Mar
	11.12/-0.4 6.89/3.1 13.24	1.93	50.18		14.27/-0.1 38.93 3.80 49.73		4:38.09
7252	Andreu Boix	ESP	30.5.02	1	NC-j	Madrid	4Octug
	11.52/-1.2 7.16/1.6 12.26	1.98	50.53		15.13/-1.0 39.39 4.50 48.80		4:46.89

4 X 100 METRES

38.56	Sprintec Lions JAM/BRN Fisher BRN, ?, ?, D.Gaye JAM			1		Kingston	8 Feb
38.59	Racers Track Club JAM/GBR			1		Kingston	29 Feb
	A.Smith, Hughes GBR, Seville, Francis GBR						
38.75	Sprintec JAM Powell, ?, ?, ?			2		Kingston	8 Feb
38.90	CUB H.Pérez, Skyers, Mena, Romero			1	NC	La Habana	22 Mar
38.90	CZE Zálesky, Veleba, Polák, Jirka			1		Zlin	15 Aug
38.96	Hosei University, Japan JPN Kuwata, R.Higuchi, Eto, K.Higuchi			1h1		Yokohama	16 Oct
39.00	CHN Huang Y, Chen G, Zhang R, Mo Y			1	NC	Shaoxing	16 Sep
39.17	TPE Wei Tai-Sheng, Yang Chun-Hao, Peng Ming-Yang, Wang Wei-Hsu			1		Taipei	12 Mar
39.35A RSA 22 Feb	39.47 AUS 13 Feb	39.70 RUS 11 Sep	39.81 USA 7 Mar
39.40 TUR 28 Aug	39.49 BRA 12 Dec	39.72 SUI 20 Sep	39.87 UKR 19 Sep

4 X 400 METRES

3:03.16	USA	1		Claremont	15 Feb
3:04.32	Nihon University, JPN Uike, Shoji, Inoue, Yamamoto	1		Niigata	13 Sep
3:05.17	Sprintec JAM/CAN Rodney/CAN, C.Hinds, R.Williams, Gaye	1		Kingston	29 Feb
3:06.32 RUS 11 Sep	3:06.35 TUR 20 Apr	3:07.2A KEN 6 Mar	3:08.15 BRA 13 Dec
				3:08.32 CHN 18 Sep
Indoors					
3:02.77i	Texas A&M USA/CAY Walton CAY, Orange, Deadmon, Dixon	1		Lubbock	1 Feb
3:04.12i	North Carolian A&T USA	2		Lubbock	1 Feb

4 X 1500 METRES RELAY

14:39.97	Nike Bowerman 'B' (USA)	1		Portland	31 Jul
	Jager c.3:39, Fisher 3:37, McGorty 3:38, Lomong 3:39				
14:44.69	Nike Bowerman 'A' (mixed nations)	2		Portland	31 Jul
	M Scott GBR, Ahmed CAN, R Hill, Kincaid				

3000 METRES TRACK WALK

11:07.21	Miroslav	Úradník	SVK	24.3.96	1	PTS	Samorin	11 Sep
11:21.38	Leo	Köpp	GER	23.5.98	1		Strausberg	12 Sep
11:22.47	Majej	Tóth	SVK	10.2.83	2	PTS	Samorin	11 Sep
11:33.03	Declan	Tingay	AUS	6.2.99	6 Nov	11:33.61 João Vieira POR 20.2.76 11 Jul
						11:37.72 Michal Morvay SVK 19.8.96 11 Sep
Indoors							
11:04.57+	Tom	Bosworth	GBR	17.1.90	1	in 5kW	Glasgow	23 Feb
11:29.5+	Francesco	Fortunato	ITA	13.12.94	1	in 5kW	Ancona	22 Feb
11:30.29	Sahin	Senoduncu	TUR	24.4.94	11 Jan	11:31.97 Dawid Tomala POL 27.8.89 25 Jan
11:30.65+	Salih	Korkmaz	TUR	14.4.97	11 Jan	11:33.13 Federico Tontodonati ITA 30.10.89 4 Jan

5000 METRES TRACK WALK

18:20.14	Koki	Ikeda	JPN	3.5.98	1		Inzai	25 Oct
18:26.70	Yuta	Koga	JPN	15.7.99	2		Inzai	25 Oct
18:28.26	Masatora	Kawano	JPN	23.10.98	3		Inzai	25 Oct
18:34.88	Toshikazu	Yamanishi	JPN	15.2.96	1		Kumagaya	19 Sep
18:51.25	Eiki	Takahashi	JPN	19.11.92	2		Kumagaya	19 Sep
18:53.19	Aleksandr	Lyakhovich	BLR	4.7.89	1	NC	Minsk	1 Aug
18:57.40	Kevin	Campion	FRA	23.5.88	1		Eu	17 Jul
19:06.68	Perseus	Karlström	SWE	2.5.90	1		Melborne	7 Mar
19:09.89	Tomohiro	Noda	JPN	24.1.96	3		Kumagaya	19 Sep
19:11.45	Saoshi	Maruo	JPN	28.11.91	4		Kumagaya	19 Sep
19:19.22	Subaru	Ishida	JPN	4.6.99	1		Kashihara	25 Nov

5000m – 10,000m WALK

Mark	Name		Nat	Born	Pos	Meet	Venue	Date	
19:20.14	Miguel Ángel	López	ESP	3.7.88	25	Feb	19:33.69 Kazuki Takahashi JPN	17.6.96	19 Sep
19:23.88	Ihor	Hlavan	UKR	25.9.90	15	Aug	19:34.6 Federico Tontodonati ITA	30.10.89	26 Aug
19:25.92	Oleh	Syvystun	UKR	15.9.97	15	Aug	19:35.01 Viktor Shumik UKR	21.5.98	15 Aug
19:25.94	Callum	Wilkinson	GBR	14.3.97	5	Sep	19:35.58 Isamu Fujisawa JPN	12.10.87	19 Sep
19:26.00	Hiroto	Jusho	JPN	11.1.00	25	Oct	19:35.75 Iván López ESP	29.3.97	25 Feb
19:26.08	Mikita	Kolyada	BLR	15.7.00	1	Aug	19:35.97 Anatoliy Gomelov BLR	29.5.96	1 Aug
19:28.59	Majej	Tóth	SVK	10.2.83	15	Sep	19:38.37 Aleksi Ojala FIN	9.12.92	5 Aug
19:29.40	Nazar	Kovalenko	UKR	9.2.87	15	Aug	19:39.36 Miroslav Úradník SVK	24.3.96	25 Jul
19:30.72	Yuki	Murao	JPN	9.8.98	25	Oct	19:39.66 Ivan Banzeruk UKR	9.2.90	15 Aug
19:30.79	Salih	Korkmaz	TUR	14.4.97	29	Aug	19:39.74 Álvaro Martín ESP	18.6.94	19 Sep
19:32.11	David	Kuster	FRA	25.3.99	12	Jul	19:39.75 Kai Kobayashi JPN	28.2.93	19 Sep

Indoors

Mark	Name			Born	Pos	Meet	Venue	Date	
18:20.97	Tom	Bosworth	GBR	17.1.90	1	NC	Glasgow	23	Feb
18:41.89	Gabriel	Bordier	FRA	8.10.97	1		Nantes	18	Jan
18:50.22	Francesco	Fortunato	ITA	13.12.94	1	NC	Ancona	22	Feb
18:50.7	Sergey	Kozhevnikov	RUS-J	9.5.01	1		Saransk	27	Dec
18:51.8	Sergey	Shiroborokov	RUS	16.2.99	2		Saransk	27	Dec
18:58.9	Aleksey	Kudashkin	RUS	1.2.97	3		Saransk	27	Dec
19:02.08		Lyakhovich			1	NC	Mogilyov	22	Feb
19:02.14	Vasiliy	Mizinov	RUS	29.12.97	1		Chelyabinsk	6	Jan
19:13.29	Mikita	Kolyada	BLR	15.7.00	2	NC	Mogilyov	22	Feb
19:13.5	Dementiy	Cheparev	RUS	28.10.92	4		Saransk	27	Dec
19:13.59	Salih	Korkmaz	TUR	14.4.97	1		Istanbul	11	Jan
19:19.55	Marius	Ziukas	LTU	29.6.85	1	NC	Klaipeda	22	Feb
19:22.54	Ihor	Hlavan	UKR	25.9.90	31	Jan	19:31.2 Kiril Shutov RUS	24.9.97	6 Jan
19:26.42	Anatoliy	Gomelov	BLR	29.5.96	22	Feb	19:33.5 Maksim Pyanzin RUS-Y	.03	27 Dec
19:27.6	Sergey	Rakov	RUS	13.6.99	27	Dec	19:35.9 Aleksandr Garin RUS	28.12.99	27 Dec
19:28.6	Maksim	Krasnov ¶	RUS	10.2.96	6	Jan	19:38.2 Sergey Sharipov RUS	14.4.92	27 Dec
19:30.13	Artur	Mastianica	LTU	30.7.92	22	Feb	19:38.98 João Vieira POR	20.2.76	29 Feb
							19:39.34 Serhiy Svitlychnyy UKR	13.7.94	19 Jan

10,000 METRES TRACK WALK

Mark	Name		Nat	Born	Pos	Meet	Venue	Date	
37:25.21	Eiki	Takahashi	JPN	19.11.92	1		Inzai	14	Nov
37:25.90	Koki	Ikeda	JPN	3.5.98	2		Inzai	14	Nov
37:35.00	Yuta	Koga	JPN	15.7.99	3		Inzai	14	Nov
38:23.95	Masatora	Kawano	JPN	23.10.98	4		Inzai	14	Nov
38:41.45		Ikeda			1		Niigata	12	Sep
38:50.9	Perseus	Karlström	SWE	2.5.90	1		Melbourne (Un)	12	Jan
39:04.0A		Wang Kaihua	CHN	16.2.94	1		Huehot	8	May
39:26.92	Salih	Korkmaz	TUR	14.4.97	1	NC	Istanbul	5	Sep
39:30.8	Rhydian	Cowley	AUS	4.1.91	1		Melbourne (Parkville)	27	Jan
39:37.45	Aleksandr	Lyakhovich	BLR	4.7.89	1		Minsk	2	Aug
39:39.04	Veli-Matti	Partanen	FIN	28.10.91	2	vSWE	Tampere	5	Sep
39:48.14	Federico	Tontodonati	ITA	30.10.89	1		Bergamo	10	Sep
39:50.5	Evan	Dunfee	CAN	28.9.90	3		Melbourne (Parkville)	27	Jan
39:52.05	Callum	Wilkinson	GBR	14.3.97	1	IRL Ch	Dublin (S)	29	Aug
39:52.86	Ryutaro	Yamamoto	JPN	17.9.98	1		Sagamihara	22	Nov
39:54.30	Aleksi	Ojala	FIN	9.12.92	3	vSWE	Tampere	5	Sep
39:58.08	Hiroto	Jusho	JPN	11.1.00	1		Sagamihara	22	Nov
40:10.	David	Kuster	FRA	25.3.99	19	Jul	40:18.51 Mikita Kolyada BLR	15.7.00	2 Aug
40:10.25		Wang Rui	CHN	6.1.96	8	May	40:19.81 Ryo Hamanishi JPN	24.4.00	14 Nov
40:10.3	Marius	Ziukas	LTU	29.6.85	27	Jan	40:20.41 Subaru Ishida JPN	4.6.99	13 Dec
40:10.6	Isamu	Fujisawa	JPN	12.10.87	12	Jan	40:32.18 Anatoliy Gomelov BLR	29.5.96	2 Aug
40:14.13		Zhang Jun	CHN	20.7.98	8	May	40:37.64 Artur Mastianica LTU	30.7.92	5 Sep

10 KILOMETRES ROAD WALK

Where superior to track times. See also intermediate times in second column of 20k list.

Mark	Name		Nat	Born	Pos	Meet	Venue	Date	
38:00	Vasiliy	Mizinov	RUS	29.12.97	1		Voronovo	23	Aug
38:03+		Zhang Jun	CHN	20.7.98	1		Wuzhong	13	Dec
38:18		Chen Ding	CHN	5.8.92	1		Wuzhong	15	Dec
38:18		Zhang Jun			2		Wuzhong	15	Dec
38:16+		Wang Kaihua	CHN	16.2.94	2	in 15k	Wuzhong	13	Dec
38:23		Wang Kaihua			3		Wuzhong	15	Dec
38:38		Wang Kaihua				in 15k	Suqian	20	Dec
38:30+		Cai Zelin	CHN	11.4.91		in 15k	Suqian	20	Dec
38:51		Li Kewen	CHN	7.3.99	4		Wuzhong	15	Dec
38:51		Xu Hao	CHN	6.2.99	1B		Wuzhong	15	Dec
39:04	Sergey	Kozhevnikov	RUS-J	9.5.01	1	NC-wj	Sochi	17	Feb
39:06	Francesco	Fortunato	ITA	13.12.94	1		Modena	18	Oct
39:10	Tom	Bosworth	GBR	17.1.90	1	NC	Coventry	1	Mar
39:13+		Zhang Yao	CHN	11.1.00		in 15k	Suqian	20	Dec
39:16+		Zong Hong	CHN	7.11.95		in 15k	Wuzhong	13	Dec
39:16+		Sun Shuai	CHN	15.9.99		in 15k	Wuzhong	13	Dec
39:17	Gabriel	Bordier	FRA	8.10.97	1	NC	Albi	13	Sep

10 - 20 KILOMETRES WALK

Mark	Name			Nat	Born	Pos	Meet	Venue		Date	
39:29+			Wen Yongjie	CHN	28.9.99		in 15k	Wuzhong		13	Dec
39:33			Gao Wenkui	CHN	28.7.95	3rB		Wuzhong		15	Dec
39:34		Dmitriy	Gramachkov	RUS-Y	9.3.03	2		Voronovo		2	Aug
39:36+		Fumitaka	Oikawa	JPN	5.4.95		in 20k	Kobe		16	Feb
39:41			Wang Qin	CHN	8.5.94	6		Wuzhong		15	Dec
39:42			Li Xingfu	CHN-J	18.7.02	7		Wuzhong		15	Dec
39:43+			Zhang Jiaxu	CHN	4.1.00		in 15k	Wuzhong		13	Dec
39:48+			Zhu Xiaoqiang	CHN	21.4.00		in 15k	Wuzhong		13	Dec
39:49			Zeng Qingcun	CHN	3.4.95	8		Wuzhong		15	Dec
39:52		Callum	Wilkinson	GBR	14.3.97	2		Göteborg		5	Aug
39:58+			Lin Jixiang	CHN	16.3.94		in 15k	Wuzhong		13	Dec
40:02	Aleksey		Ishmametev	RUS	21.7.00	23 Aug	40:19	Luis Alberto	Amezcua	ESP	1.5.92 25 Jan
40:08+			Cui Lihong	CHN	13.5.99	13 Dec	40:20	David	Kenny	IRL	10.1.99 5 Aug
40:11			Zhu Guowen	CHN	20.8.97	15 Dec	40:20		Chen Tiancai	CHN-J	15.1.01 19 Sep
40:13	Artemiy		Celine	RUS-J	4.1.01	17 Feb	40:23+		Choi Byung-kwang	KOR	7.4.91 15 Feb
40:14+			Zheng Qingcun	CHN	3.4.95	13 Dec	40:25+		Wei Xubao	CHN	1.2.93 13 Dec
40:15	Håvard		Haukenes	NOR	22.4.90	5 Aug	40:25+		Zhou Yangjun	CHN	17.10.96 13 Dec
40:15			Xu Chunyang	CHN-J	7.3.01	19 Sep	40:26	Andrea	Agrusti	ITA	30.8.95 18 Oct
40:17+			Cao Wenlong	CHN	4.3.98	13 Dec	40:28		Amit	IND-Y	25.12.03 16 Feb
40:18	Diego		García	ESP	19.1.96	6 Dec	40:31	Kiril	Grudkin	RUS-J	12.10.02 17 Feb
							40:31	Federico	Tontodonati	ITA	30.10.89 18 Oct

JUNIORS

See main list for top 3 juniors. Further juniors:

40:13		Artemiy	Celine	RUS	4.1.01	2	NC-wj	Sochi	17	Feb
40:15			Xu Chunyang	CHN	7.3.01	1	NC-j	Taian	19	Sep
40:20			Chen Tiancai	CHN	15.1.01	2	NC-j	Taian	19	Sep
40:28			Amit	IND-Y	25.12.03	1	NC-j	Ranchi	16	Feb
40:31		Kiril	Grudkin	RUS	12.10.02	3	NC-wj	Sochi	17	Feb
40:40		Anton	Kurbatov	RUS	10.2.01	4	NC-wj	Sochi	17	Feb
40:51			Lei Chao	CHN	13.3.01	4	NC-j	Taian	19	Sep
40:54			Zhang Tianji	CHN	29.12.02	5	NC-j	Taian	19	Sep
40:55			Kang Minglong	CHN	16.11.02	6	NC-j	Taian	19	Sep
40:59		Danila	Martynov	RUS-Y	1.5.04	1	NC-wy	Sochi	17	Feb
41:00			Li Shaowei	CHN	20.8.02	8	NC-j	Taian	19	Sep

20 KILOMETRES WALK

20k	10k			Nat	Born	Pos	Meet	Venue	Date	
1:17:36	38:49	Toshikazu	Yamanishi	JPN	15.2.96	1	NC	Kobe	16	Feb
1:18:22	39:21	Koki	Ikeda	JPN	3.5.98	1		Nomi	15	Mar
1:18:29	39:22	Eiki	Takahashi	JPN	19.11.92	2		Nomi	15	Mar
1:18:36	39:22	Yusuke	Suzuki	JPN	2.1.88	3		Nomi	15	Mar
1:18:42	39:22	Yutaro	Koga	JPN	15.7.99	4		Nomi	15	Mar
1:19:07	38:50		Ikeda			2	NC	Kobe	16	Feb
1:19:09	38:00	Vasiliy	Mizinov	RUS	29.12.97	1	NC	Voronovskoe	5	Sep
1:19:31		Salih	Korkmaz	TUR	14.4.97	1		Antalya	16	Feb
1:19:34	39:08	Perseus	Karlström	SWE	2.5.90	3	JPN Ch	Kobe	16	Feb
1:19:34	39:50	Sergey	Shiroborokov	RUS	16.2.99	1		Sochi	17	Feb
1:19:43	40:01		Karlström			1		Podebrady	10	Oct
1:19:46	39:39		Wang Kaihua	CHN	16.2.94	1		Jinzhou	29	Jul
1:19:53	38:50		Takahashi			4	NC	Kobe	16	Feb
1:19:58	40:02	Matteo	Giupponi	ITA	8.10.88	2		Podebrady	10	Oct
1:20:01			Suzuki			1		Tokyo	1	Jan
1:20:15	39:28	Isamu	Fujisawa	JPN	12.10.87	5	NC	Kobe	16	Feb
1:20:19	40:04	Gabriel	Bordier	FRA	8.10.97	3		Podebrady	10	Oct
1:20:24	39:21		Fujisawa			5		Nomi	15	Mar
1:20:26	38:58	Tomohiro	Noda	JPN	24.1.96	6	NC	Kobe	16	Feb
1:20:32	39:30	Hirooki	Arai	JPN	18.5.88	7	NC	Kobe	16	Feb
1:20:41	39:30	Satoshi	Maruo	JPN	28.11.91	8	NC	Kobe	16	Feb
1:20:46		Eduard	Zabuzhenko	UKR	18.4.98	1	Balk Ch	Ivano-Frankivsk	14	Mar
1:20:47	39:30		Koga			9	NC	Kobe	16	Feb
1:20:49		Motofumi	Suwa	JPN	22.10.99	2		Tokyo	1	Jan
1:20:49	39:51	Yutaro	Murayama	JPN	29.9.98	6		Nomi	15	Mar
1:20:49	40:02		Wang Kaihua			2		Taian	19	Sep
		[26/19]								
1:21:02	40:20	Aleksey	Kudashkin	RUS	1.2.97	2		Sochi	17	Feb
		[20]								
1:21:10		Ivan	Losev	UKR	26.1.86	2		Alytus	18	Sep
1:21:12		Nazar	Kovalenko	UKR	9.2.87	3		Alytus	18	Sep
1:21:21		Callum	Wilkinson	GBR	14.3.97	4		Alytus	18	Sep
1:21:34		Sandeep Kumar	Sangwan	IND	1.5.86	1	NC	Ranchi	15	Feb
1:21:35		Viktor	Shumik	UKR	21.5.98	2	Balk Ch	Ivano-Frankivsk	14	Mar
1:21:35	40:01	Kevin	Campion	FRA	23.5.88	4		Podebrady	10	Oct
1:21:36		Serhiy	Svitlychnyy	UKR	13.7.94	2		Antalya	16	Feb

20 - 30 KILOMETRES WALK

Mark		Name		Nat	Born	Pos	Meet	Venue	Date	
1:21:38	40:21	Roma	Yevstifeyev	RUS	19.9.92	3		Sochi	17	Feb
1:21:47		Sahin	Senoduncu	TUR	24.4.94	3		Antalya	16	Feb
1:21:53		Brian	Pintado	ECU	29.7.95	1		Macas	15	Feb
	[30]									
1:21:56		Maryan	Zakalnytskyy	UKR	19.8.94	5		Antalya	16	Feb
1:21:59		Rahul	Rohila	IND	5.7.96	2	NC	Ranchi	15	Feb
1:22:02		Sergey	Kozhevnikov	RUS-J	9.5.01	2	NC	Voronovskoe	5	Sep
1:22:03			Cai Zelin	CHN	11.4.91	2	NC	Taian	19	Sep
1:22:04	39:51	Fumitaka	Oikawa	JPN	5.4.95	7		Nomi	15	Mar
1:22:06		Aleksandr	Lyakhovich	BLR	4.7.89	5		Alytus	18	Sep
1:22:11	40:17	Federico	Tontodonati	ITA	30.10.89	5		Podebrady	10	Oct
1:22:12			Chen Ding	CHN	5.8.92	3	NC	Taian	19	Sep
1:22:12			Joo Hyun-myung	KOR	31.5.97	1		Yecheon	20	Oct
1:22:12		Erick	Barrondo	GUA	16.9.96	1		San Jerónimo	12	Dec
	[40]									
1:22:16		Wayne	Snyman	RSA	8.3.85	1		Dublin	7	Mar
1:22:16		José	Ortiz	GUA	8.3.00	2		San Jerónimo	12	Dec
1:22:16		José Oswaldo	Calel	GUA	8.8.98	3		San Jerónimo	12	Dec
1:22:20		Leo	Köpp	GER	23.5.98	1		Biberach	18	Oct
1:22:23			Choi Byung-kwang	KOR	7.4.91	1	NC	Jeongseon	27	Jun
1:22:27		Vikash	Singh	IND	6.7.96	2	NC	Ranchi	15	Feb
1:22:28		Kai	Kobayashi	JPN	28.2.93	11	NC	Kobe	16	Feb
1:22:29		Ihor	Hlavan	UKR	25.9.90	6		Antalya	16	Feb
1:22:30		Miroslav	Uradnik	SVK	24.3.96	6		Podebrady	10	Oct
1:22:31		Stefano	Chiesa	ITA	25.5.96	7		Podebrady	10	Oct
	[50]									
1:22:32		Evan	Dunfee	CAN	28.9.90	2		Adelaide	9	Feb
1:22:34		Subaru	Ishida	JPN	4.6.99	8		Nomi	15	Mar
1:22:37		Hiroto	Jusho	JPN	11.1.00	5		Tokyo	1	Jan
1:22:38		Yevgeniy	Dobrynkin	RUS	19.7.97	3	NC	Voronovskoe	5	Sep
1:22:41	40:18	Carl	Dohmann	GER	18.5.90	8		Podebrady	10	Oct
1:22:42		Francesco	Fortunato	ITA	13.12.94	9		Podebrady	10	Oct
1:22:52		David	Hurtado	ECU	21.4.99	2		Macas	15	Feb
1:22:52			Zhang Jun	CHN	20.7.98	2		Jinzhou	29	Jul
1:22:53		Aleksandr	Garin	RUS	28.12.99	1	NC-23	Voronovskoe	5	Sep
1:22:54			Yin Jiaxing	CHN	16.3.94	1		Shilin	16	Jan
	[60]									
1:22:55		Artur	Mastianica	LTU	30.7.92	6		Alytus	18	Sep
1:22:56			Li Xiaobin	CHN	10.10.99	4	NC	Taian	19	Sep
1:22:56A		Samuel	Gathimba	KEN	26.10.87	1		Nairobi	3	Oct
1:23:01		Dane	Bird-Smith	AUS	15.7.92	9	Feb			
1:23:05.5	t	Caio	Bonfim	BRA	19.3.91	12	Dec			
1:23:06		Marius	Ziukas	LTU	29.6.85	9	Feb			
1:23:06		Nikolay	Maksimov	RUS	21.12.99	5	Sep			
1:23:07		David	Kenny	IRL	10.1.99	7	Mar			
1:23:08		Tatsuhiko	Nagayama	JPN	24.12.99	15	Mar			
1:23:08		Taki	Naruoka	JPN	17.4.98	15	Mar			
1:23:13		Brandon	Segura	MEX	30.4.96	12	Dec			
1:23:15		Takumi	Suzuki	JPN	14.1.99	15	Mar			
1:23:15			Ceng Qingcun	CHN	3.4.95	29	Jul			
1:23:16		Teodorico	Caporaso	ITA	14.9.87	10	Oct			
1:23:17		Devender	Singh	IND	5.12.83	15	Feb			
1:23:17			Kim Min-kyu	KOR	28.2.99	20	Oct			
1:23:22		Máté	Helebrandt	HUN	12.1.89	27	Sep			
1:23:23		Ivan	Baburkin	RUS	2.1.00	5	Sep			
1:23:25			Guo Kuizhijia	CHN	20.11.99	16	Jan			
1:23:26			Li Kewen	CHN	7.3.99	29	Jul			
1:23:33			Wen Yongjie	CHN	28.9.99	29	Jul			
1:23:37		Aleksey	Ishmametev	RUS	21.7.00	5	Sep			

1:23:39			Yin Jun	CHN	16.3.00	29	Jul
1:23:42		Kazuhiro	Tateiwa	JPN	5.11.99	15	Mar
1:23:43			Niu Wenchao	CHN	20.4.98	19	Sep
1:23:46		Salavat	Ilkayev	RUS	14.9.00	17	Feb
1:23:46		Abdulselam	Imük	TUR	10.10.99	14	Mar
1:23:47		Ivan	Banzeruk	UKR	9.2.90	16	Feb
1:23:49.7	t	Aleksi	Ojala	FIN	9.12.92	13	Aug
1:23:52		Manuel	Soto	COL	28.1.94	10	Oct
1:23:56		Maksim	Krasnov	RUS	10.2.96	17	Feb
1:23:56		Tom	Bosworth	GBR	17.1.90	20	Dec
1:23:57.5	t	Matheus	Correa	BRA	22.8.99	12	Dec
1:23:59		Daisuke	Matsunaga	JPN	24.3.95	1	Jan
1:24:02		José Alejandro	Barrondo	GUA	16.2.99	12	Dec
1:24:04		Krishnan	Ganapathi	IND	29.6.89	15	Dec
1:24:05		Kazuki	Takahashi	JPN	17.6.96	16	Feb
1:24:05			Zhu Xiaoqiang	CHN	21.4.00	29	Jul
1:24:06		Georgiy	Sheyko	KAZ	24.8.89	14	Mar
1:24:09			Song Huazhang	CHN	13.2.99	16	Jan
	[100]						
1:24:09			Xu Hao	CHN	6.2.99	19	Sep

Drugs disqualification
| 1:22:46 | 39:31 | Maksim | Krasnov ¶ | RUS | 10.2.96 | (4) | NC | Voronovskoe | 5 | Sep |

JUNIORS

1:22:02		Sergey	Kozhevnikov	RUS	9.5.01	2	NC	Voronovskoe	5	Sep
1:25:21			Li Junran	CHN	12.3.02	9		Jinzhou	29	Jul
1:26:33		Óscar	Pop	GUA	29.10.01	9		San Jerónimo	12	Dec
1:26:56			Zhao Xiangfei	CHN	27.9.02	15		Jinzhou	29	Jul

30 KILOMETRES WALK

2:07:42		Håvard	Haukenes	NOR	22.4.90	1	IRL Ch	Cork	19	Dec
2:10:40		David	Kenny	IRL	10.1.99	2	NC	Cork	19	Dec
2:11:02		Brendan	Boyce	IRL	15.10.86	3	NC	Cork	19	Dec
2:13:34+		Matej	Tóth	SVK	10.2.83	1	in 50k	Dudince	24	Oct

30 - 35 - 50 KILOMETRES WALK 325

Mark	Name		Nat	Born	Pos	Meet	Venue	Date

35 KILOMETRES WALK

Mark	Name		Nat	Born	Pos	Meet	Venue	Date
2:27:26	Dementiy	Cheparev	RUS	28.10.92	1	NC-w	Sochi	17 Feb
2:27:41	Kirill	Frolov	RUS	29.9.93	2	NC-w	Sochi	17 Feb
2:28:14	Sergey	Sharipov	RUS	14.4.92	3	NC-w	Sochi	17 Feb
2:29:42	Ivan	Noskov	RUS	16.7.88	4	NC-w	Sochi	17 Feb
2:30:12	Sergey	Rakov	RUS	13.6.99	5	NC-w	Sochi	17 Feb
2:34:28		Sun Song	CHN	15.12.96	1		Jinzhou	29 Jul
2:34:55	Federico	Tontodonati	ITA	30.10.89	1		Grosseto	26 Jan
2:35:28+	Matej	Tóth	SVK	10.2.83	1	in 50k	Dudince	24 Oct
2:36:00		Meng Zhongkai	CHN	15.12.97	2		Jinzhou	29 Jul
2:36:56A	Bernardo Uriel	Barrondo	GUA	5.6.93	1		Ciudad de Guatemala	2 Feb
2:36:59		Zhaxi Yangben	CHN	15.4.96	3		Jinzhou	29 Jul

50 KILOMETRES WALK

Mark	Name		Nat	Born	Pos	Meet	Venue	Date
3:41:15	Matej	Tóth	SVK	10.2.83	1		Dudince	24 Oct
3:43:29	Dementiy	Cheparev	RUS	28.10.92	1	NC	Voronovskoe	5 Sep
3:43:46	Sergey	Sharipov	RUS	14.4.92	2	NC	Voronovskoe	5 Sep
3:47:31	Ihor	Hlavan	UKR	25.9.90	1	NC	Ivano-Frankivsk	18 Oct
3:47:42	Rafal	Augustyn	POL	14.5.84	2		Dudince	24 Oct
3:48:37	Sergey	Rakov	RUS	13.6.99	3	NC	Voronovskoe	5 Sep
3:48:57	Andrés	Chocho	ECU	4.11.83	3		Dudince	24 Oct
3:49:45	Karl	Junghannß	GER	6.4.96	4		Dudince	24 Oct
3:49:47	Serhiy	Budza	UKR	6.12.84	2	NC	Ivano-Frankivsk	18 Oct
3:51:17	Ivan	Noskov	RUS	16.7.88	4	NC	Voronovskoe	5 Sep
	[10]							
3:52:19		Zhaxi Yangben	CHN	15.4.96	1	NC	Taian	20 Sep
3:52:58	Valeriy	Litanyuk	UKR	2.4.94	3	NC	Ivano-Frankivsk	18 Oct
3:53:29	Anton	Radko	UKR	2.6.95	4	NC	Ivano-Frankivsk	18 Oct
3:55:27	Arnis	Rumbenieks	LAT	4.4.88	5	UKR Ch	Ivano-Frankivsk	18 Oct
3:55:48		Wang Rui	CHN	6.1.96	2	NC	Taian	20 Sep
3:56:02	Ruslans	Smolonskis	LAT	15.12.96	1	ESP Ch	Torrevieja	16 Feb
3:56:17	Alex	Wright	IRL	19.12.90	5		Dudince	24 Oct
3:56:28.4 t	Vit	Hlavac	CZE	26.2.97	1	NC	Trnava	5 Dec
3:56:31	Rafal	Fedaczynski	POL	3.12.80	6		Dudince	24 Oct
3:56:40	Nikolay	Tikhonov	RUS	20.4.97	5	NC	Voronovskoe	5 Sep
	[20]							
3:56:48	Bernardo Uriel	Barrondo	GUA	5.6.93	1		San Jerónimo	12 Dec
3:57:18	Aleksey	Terentyev	RUS	19.7.91	6	NC	Voronovskoe	5 Sep
3:57:21.3 t	Lukás	Gdula	CZE	6.12.91	2	NC	Trnava	5 Dec
3:57:22	Iván	Pajuelo	ESP	27.8.93	2	NC	Torrevieja	16 Feb
3:57:24	Álvaro	Martín	ESP	18.6.94	3	NC	Torrevieja	16 Feb
3:57:34	Nathaniel	Seiler	GER	6.4.96	7		Dudince	24 Oct
3:59:01		Gong Fanglong	CHN	12.7.98	3	NC	Taian	20 Sep
3:59:41	Andriy	Marchuk	UKR	12.12.98	6		Ivano-Frankivsk	18 Oct
4:01:24	David	Kuster	FRA	25.3.99	1		Tilburg	4 Oct
4:02:55	Aleksandr	Aysabakiyev	RUS	10.12.89	7	NC	Voronovskoe	5 Sep
	[30]							

4:03:08		Sun Song	CHN	15.12.96	20 Sep	4:08:33	Jakub	Jelonek	POL	7.7.85	24 Oct
4:03:52	Mathieu	Bilodeau	CAN	27.11.83	25 Jan	4:09:38	Kirill	Shutov	RUS	24.4.97	5 Sep
4:04:27		Peng Shiyi	CHN	16.9.98	20 Sep	4:09:44	Gurpreet	Singh	IND	9.7.84	16 Feb
4:08:10	Sanabam Daman Singh		IND	15.10.89	16 Feb		[37]				

World Athletics have determined that the long distance walk for Championships should be at 35k rather than 50k, so here are the World and Continental records for 35k:

MEN 35 KILOMETRES WALK

W, Eur	2:21:31	Vladimir KANAYKIN	RUS	Adler	19 Feb 2006
Oce, Com	2:29:11+	Nathan DEAKES	AUS	Geelong	2 Dec 2006
Asi	2:30:13	Daisuke MATSUNAGA	JPN	Wajima	14 Apr 2010
CAC	2:30:43	Raúl GONZALEZ	MEX	Eschborn	30 Sep 1979
NAm	2:34:39+	Evan DUNFEE	CAN	Rio de Janeiro	19 Aug 2016
SAm	2:34:40	Claudio VILLANUEVA	ECU	Súcua	15 Apr 2017
Afr	2:41:21+	Marc MUNDELL	RSA	Dudince	20 Mar 2021
W20	2:29:26 dt?	Sergey RAKOV	RUS	Kostroma	9 Sep 2018

WOMEN 35 KILOMETRES WALK

W, Eur	2:38:24	Klavdiya AFANASYEVA	RUS	Sochi	17 Feb 2019
Asi	2:49:23	LIANG Rui	CHN	Huangshan	4 Mar 2018
Oce, Com	2:53:34+	Claire TALLENT	AUS	Taicang	5 May 2018
SAm	2:51:11A	Erica de SENA	BRA	Macas	13 Mar 2021
NAm	3:00:43+	Kathleen BURNETT	USA	London	13 Aug 2017
CAC	3:02:38+	Mayra HERRERA	GUA	Taicang	5 May 2018
Afr	3:20:25+	Natalie le ROUX	RSA	Taicang	5 May 2018

326 60 METRES

Mark	Name		Nat	Born	Pos	Meet	Venue	Date	

WOMEN'S WORLD LISTS 2020

60 METRES INDOORS

Mark	First	Last	Nat	Born	Pos	Meet	Venue	Date	
7.04A	Mikiah	Brisco	USA	14.7.96	1	NC	Albuquerque	15	Feb
7.04A	Javianne	Oliver	USA	26.12.94	1h1	NC	Albuquerque	15	Feb
7.08A		Brisco			1		Albuquerque	25	Jan
7.08A		Oliver			2	NC	Albuquerque	15	Feb
7.09	Kristina	Makarenko	RUS	28.2.97	1	NC	Moskva	25	Feb
7.10A	Julien	Alfred	LCA-J	10.6.01	2		Albuquerque	25	Jan
7.10A		Brisco			1h2	NC	Albuquerque	15	Feb
7.11	Gina	Bass	GAM	3.5.95	1		Liévin	19	Feb
7.12	Murielle	Ahouré	CIV	23.8.87	2		Liévin	19	Feb
(9/6)									
7.14A	Destiny	Smith-Barnett	USA	26.7.96	1h1		Flagstaff	1	Feb
7.15	Cambrea	Sturgis	USA	27.3.99	1		Lexington	11	Jan
7.15A	Twanisha (Tee Tee)	Terry	USA	24.1.99	3		Albuquerque	25	Jan
7.16	Morolake	Akinosun	USA	17.5.94	2	Millrose	New York (A)	8	Feb
(10)									
7.16	Shelly-Ann	Fraser-Pryce	JAM	27.12.86	1	Müller	Glasgow	15	Feb
7.17	Jayla	Kirkland	USA	13.2.99	1		Clemson	11	Jan
7.17	Chelsea	Francis	USA	14.10.96	1		Houston	31	Jan
7.17A	Brianna	McNeal	USA	18.8.91	3	NC	Albuquerque	15	Feb
7.17	Ka'tia	Seymour	USA	3.10.97	1	ACC	Notre Dame	29	Feb
7.18	Brandee	Presley	USA	11.6.00	1		Birmingham	10	Jan
7.18	Briana	Williams	JAM-J	21.3.02	3	Millrose	New York (A)	8	Feb
7.18	Celera	Barnes	USA	2.12.98	1=		Clemson	14	Feb
7.19	Tamari	Davis	USA-Y	15.2.03	1		Columbia SC	18	Jan
7.19	Semira	Killebrew	USA-J	30.3.01	3		Clemson	14	Feb
(20)									
7.19	Aleia	Hobbs	USA	24.2.96	1h3		Baton Rouge	21	Feb
7.20	Shania	Collins	USA	19.11.96	1		Karlsruhe	31	Jan
7.20	Kiara	Grant	JAM	8.10.00	1		University Park	31	Jan
7.20		Liang Xiaojing	CHN	7.4.97	1h1		Fayetteville	14	Feb
7.20	Maia	McCoy	USA	9.12.96	4		Clemson	14	Feb
7.20A	Quanesha	Burks	USA	15.3.95	5	NC	Albuquerque	15	Feb
7.20	Ajla	Del Ponte	SUI	15.7.96	1	NC	St. Gallen	15	Feb
7.20	Lanae-Tava	Thomas	USA-J	28.1.01	1h1		Seattle	28	Feb
7.21	Brianna	Duncan	USA	6.10.98	2		Fayetteville	1	Feb
7.21A	Tamara	Clark	USA	9.1.99	1h2		Albuquerque	8	Feb
(30)									
7.21	Viktoriya	Ratnikova	UKR	15.5.99	1	NC	Sumy	20	Feb
7.21	Lisa Marie	Kwayie	GER	27.10.96	1	NC	Leipzig	22	Feb
7.22	Malaika	Mihambo	GER	3.2.94	2	NC	Leipzig	22	Feb
7.22	Maja	Mihalinec	SLO	17.12.89	1		Beograd	27	Feb
7.22	Aaliyah	Birmingham	USA	2.9.97	2	Big 12	Ames	29	Feb
7.23	Kendra	Harrison	USA	18.9.92	1h2		Houston	17	Jan
7.23	Kortnei	Johnson	USA	11.8.97	1		Lubbock	18	Jan
7.23	Kiara	Parker	USA	28.10.96	1h4		Iowa City	18	Jan
7.23	Kristsina	Timanovskaya	BLR	19.11.96	2		Mondeville	1	Feb
7.23	Klára	Seidlová	CZE	10.3.94	1		Ostrava	5	Feb
(40)									
7.23	Asha	Philip	GBR	25.10.90	1		Athlone	12	Feb
7.23	Thelma	Davies	USA	8.5.00	2		Fayetteville	14	Feb
7.23	Rebekah	Smith	USA	1.5.98	2		Baton Rouge	21	Feb
7.24	Symone	Mason	USA	31.8.99	2		Lubbock	18	Jan
7.24	Crystal	Emmanuel	CAN	27.11.91	1		Columbia SC	7	Feb
7.24	Halle	Hazzard	GRN	4.2.99	1s2		Clemson	14	Feb
7.24	Abby	Steiner	USA	24.11.99	2s2		Clemson	14	Feb
7.24	Lisa	Mayer	GER	2.5.96	3	NC	Leipzig	22	Feb
7.24	N'ketia	Seedo	NED-Y	7.6.03	1	NC	Apeldoorn	22	Feb
7.25	Myasia	Jacobs	USA	8.1.94	3		Houston	31	Jan
(50)									
7.25	Cynthia	Leduc	FRA	16.2.97	1		Paris	2	Feb
7.25	Alfreda	Steele	USA	19.12.97	3s2		Clemson	14	Feb
7.25A	Marybeth	Price	USA	6.4.95	7	NC	Albuquerque	15	Feb
7.25	Lisa	Wickham	TTO	13.8.94	1		Birmingham	15	Feb
7.25	Farzaneh	Fasihi	IRI	3.1.93	1		Istanbul	16	Feb
7.25	Jacious	Sears	USA-J	14.8.01	2h1	ACC	Notre Dame	28	Feb
7.26	Yasmin	Kwadwo	GER	9.11.90	22 Feb	7.27		Sydney	Conley	USA	11.12.93	17 Jan
7.27	Gabriele	Cunningham	USA	22.2.98	11 Jan	7.27		Kayla	White	USA	24.9.96	25 Jan

60 – 100 METRES

Mark	Wind	Name		Nat	Born	Pos	Meet	Venue	Date
7.27		Joella	Lloyd	ANT-J	4.12.02	14 Feb	7.27A	Cassondra Hall	USA 23.9.97 28 Feb
7.27		Caitland	Smith	USA	24.3.96	15 Feb			

Best at low altitude

7.13		Oliver	1 Mill	New York (A)	8 Feb		7.18	Terry	1=	Clemson	14 Feb
7.15		Alfred	1	Fayetteville	1 Feb		7.20	McNeal	1	Houston	31 Jan
7.16		Brisco	1	Baton Rouge	10 Jan		7.23	Clark	2	Birmingham	10 Jan
							7.26	Burks	1h3	Baton Rouge	10 Jan

Outdoors

Mark	Wind	Name		Nat	Born	Pos	Venue	Date
7.15	-1.1	Briana	Williams	JAM-J	21.3.02	1	Kingston	25 Jan
7.24	-1.1	Natasha	Morrison	JAM	17.11.92	2	Kingston	25 Jan
7.27	-0.3	Tamari	Davis	USA-Y	15.2.03	1	Marietta	29 Jul

100 METRES

Mark	Wind	Name		Nat	Born	Pos	Meet	Venue	Date
10.85	0.2	Elaine	Thompson-Herah	JAM	28.6.92	1	GGala	Roma	17 Sep
10.86	0.9	Shelly-Ann	Fraser-Pryce	JAM	27.12.86	1r1		Kingston	8 Aug
10.87	1.4		Fraser-Pryce			1A2		Kingston	8 Aug
10.87	0.0		Thompson-Herah			1	DL	Doha	25 Sep
10.88	0.3		Thompson-Herah			1B2		Kingston	8 Aug
10.92	0.8		Thompson-Herah			1r2		Kingston	8 Aug
10.95	1.1	Sha'Carri	Richardson	USA	25.3.00	1h1		Montverde	10 Aug
10.98	1.4	Shaunae	Miller-Uibo	BAH	15.4.94	1r1		Clermont	24 Jul
		(8/4)							
11.08	0.7	Ajla	Del Ponte	SUI	15.7.96	1		Bulle	11 Jul
11.11	0.3	Rebekka	Haase	GER	2.1.93	1		Regensburg	26 Jul
11.12	0.2	Aleia	Hobbs	USA	24.2.96	2	GGala	Roma	17 Sep
11.14	0.5	Hannah	Cunliffe	USA	9.1.96	2		Montverde	4 Jul
11.14	0.2	Marie Josée	Ta Lou	CIV	18.11.88	3	GGala	Roma	17 Sep
11.15	1.9	Natalliah	Whyte	JAM	9.8.97	2h2		Clermont	24 Jul
		(10)							
11.15	1.4	Tamari	Davis	USA-Y	15.2.03	2		Clermont	24 Jul
11.16	0.1	Imani	Lansiquot	GBR	17.12.97	1		Leverkusen	16 Aug
11.16A	1.0	Gabriela Anahí	Suárez	ECU-J	2.2.01	1		Quito	12 Dec
11.18	1.5	Kayla	White	USA	24.9.96	1		Des Moines	29 Aug
11.19	1.3	Lisa Marie	Kwayie	GER	27.10.96	2		Regensburg	26 Jul
11.20	1	Shashalee	Forbes	JAM	10.5.96	2A2		Kingston	8 Aug
11.20A	0.6	Rhodah	Njobvu	ZAM	29.1.94	1		Lusaka	6 Dec
11.21	1.8	Mujinga	Kambundji	SUI	17.6.92	1		Langenthal	5 Aug
11.21	2.0	Tatjana	Pinto	GER	2.7.92	1h5		La Chaux-de-Fonds	15 Aug
11.22	0.9	Jasmine	Camacho-Quinn	PUR	21.8.96	1h3		Clermont	24 Jul
		(20)							
11.23	1.4	Jennifer	Montag	GER	11.2.98	2		Wetzlar	18 Jul
11.23	1.1	Basant	Hemida (Awad)	EGY	28.9.96	1		Kladno	18 Sep
11.24	1.3	Ewa	Swoboda	POL	26.7.97	2	Szew	Bydgoszcz	19 Aug
11.25	0.3	Natasha	Morrison	JAM	17.11.92	2B2		Kingston	8 Aug
11.25	1.1	Kortnei	Johnson	USA	11.8.97	2h1		Montverde	10 Aug
11.25	1.2	Nadine	Visser	NED	9.2.95	1	NC	Utrecht	29 Aug
11.26	0.1	Dafne	Schippers	NED	15.6.92	1	ISTAF	Berlin	13 Sep
11.27	1.4	Lynna	Irby	USA	6.12.98	4		Clermont	24 Jul
11.27	1.5	Kristina	Knott	PHI	25.9.95	2		Des Moines	29 Aug
11.27	0.0	Kristal	Awuah	GBR	7.8.99	4	DL	Doha	25 Sep
		(30)							
11.28	1.3	Marije	van Hunenstijn	NED	2.3.95	23 Aug	11.35	-0.2	Mei	Kodama	JPN	8.6.99	12 Sep
11.28	0.6	Carolle	Zahi	FRA	12.6.94	12 Sep	11.36	-0.8	Murielle	Ahouré	CIV	23.8.87	1 Aug
11.29	1.1	Tia	Clayton	JAM-Y	17.8.04	19 Feb	11.38	1.6	Zoe	Hobbs	NZL	11.9.97	25 Jan
11.29	1.3	Amelie-Sophie	Lederer	GER	22.4.94	26 Jul	11.38	1.1	Brandy	Hall	JAM-J	4.9.02	19 Feb
11.29	-0.1	Lisa	Nippgen	GER	2.4.97	1 Aug	11.38	0.0	Grace	Nwokocha	NGR-J	7.4.01	1 Mar
11.30	0.0	Anna	Bongiorni	ITA	15.9.93	16 Jul	11.38	0.4	Mikiah	Brisco	USA	14.7.96	15 Aug
11.30	0.3	Vitória	Rosa	BRA	12.1.96	6 Dec	11.38	0.0	Wided	Atatou	FRA	15.7.99	12 Sep
11.31	0.2	Ge Manqi		CHN	13.10.97	23 May	11.38	1.1	Irene	Siragusa	ITA	23.6.93	16 Sep
11.31	0.9	Ivet	Lalova-Collio	BUL	18.5.84	23 Jul	11.38A	1.5	Beatrice	Masilingi	NAM-Y	10.4.03	17 Dec
11.31	0.4	Gina	Lückenkemper	GER	21.11.96	14 Aug	11.39	1.1	Corinna	Schwab	GER	5.4.99	10 Jul
11.31	1.3	Daryll	Neita	GBR	29.8.96	19 Aug	11.39	0.7	Rani	Rosius	BEL	25.4.00	16 Aug
11.32	1.5	Yunisleidy	de la C.García	CUB	11.8.99	20 Mar	11.39	1.1	Amy	Hunt	GBR-J	15.5.02	29 Aug
11.32	0.2	Lilly	Kaden	GER-J	6.9.01	5 Sep	11.39	0.8	Arialis Josega Gandulla		CUB	22.6.95	8 Sep
11.33	1.2	Naomi	Sedney	NED	17.12.94	29 Aug	11.40	-1.7	Aries	Sánchez	VEN	1.3.96	10 Jan
11.33	0.8	Ana Carolina	Azevedo	BRA	19.5.98	17 Dec	11.40	0.7	Laura	Moreira	CUB	10.1.00	6 Mar
11.34	0.9	Laura	Müller	GER	4.5.96	11 Jul	11.41	-0.2	Inna	Eftimova	BUL	16.8.98	25 Jul
11.35	1.5	Kevona	Davis	JAM-J	20.12.01	16 Mar	11.41	0.2	Talea	Prepens	GER-J	28.12.01	5 Sep
11.35	1.4	Lisa	Mayer	GER	2.5.96	18 Jul	11.41	0.3	Ángela	Tenorio	ECU	27.1.96	6 Dec
11.35	0.9	Gloria	Hooper	ITA	3.3.92	23 Jul	11.42	1.3	Sophia	Junk	GER	1.3.99	26 Jul
							11.42	0.2	Anthonique	Strachan	BAH	22.8.93	17 Sep

Wind assisted

10.73	3.0	Elaine	Thompson-Herah	JAM	28.6.92	1		Kingston	25 Jul

100 - 150 - 200 METRES

Mark	Wind	Name		Nat	Born	Pos	Meet	Venue		Date	
10.79	2.7	Sha'Carri	Richardson	USA	25.3.00	1		Fort Worth		23	Jul
10.83	2.1		Richardson			1		Montverde		4	Jul
10.94	2.8		Richardson			1h2		Montverde		10	Aug
11.05	3.0	Shashalee	Forbes	JAM	10.5.96	2		Kingston		25	Jul
11.15	2.1	Kortnei	Johnson	USA	11.8.97	2		Montverde		10	Aug
11.22	2.7	Brianna	McNeal	USA	18.8.91	2		Fort Worth		23	Jul
11.25	2.3	Tynia	Gaither	BAH	16.3.93	1		Prairie View		6	Aug
11.26	2.6	Wuided	Atatou	FRA	15.7.99	1h2	NC	Albi		12	Sep
11.27	2.8	Javianne	Oliver	USA	26.12.94	2h2		Montverde		4	Jul
11.29	6.2	Dalia	Kaddari	ITA-J	23.3.01	25	Jul	11.36	2..2 Irene Siragusa ITA	23.6.93	29 Aug
11.32	2.7	Mikiah	Brisco	USA	14.7.96	23	Jul	11.37	7.6 Grace Nwokocha NGR-J	7.4.01	5 Feb
11.35	2.8	Dezerea	Bryant	USA	27.4.93	4	Jul	11.37	2.9 Rafailía Spanoudáki-Hatzirīga GRE	7.6.94	15 Jul
11.35	2.2	Zaynab	Dosso	ITA	12.9.99	29	Aug	11.39	2.8 Lorène Bazolo POR	4.5.83	15 Aug
11.35	2.1	Amy	Hunt	GBR-J	15.5.02	4	Sep	11.39 mxw Sophia Fighera AUS	10.4.98	6 Dec
11.36	3.3	Karolina	Koleczek	POL	15.1.93	25	Jul	11.40	2.3 Olivia Fotopoulou CYP	20.12.96	25 Aug
								11.42	2.6 Jessie Saint-Marc FRA	16.7.91	12 Sep

Best at low altitude: 11.39 0.3 Suárez 6 Dec
Drugs disqualification: 11.42A 1.2 TebogoMamathu ¶ RSA 27.5.95 14 Mar

JUNIORS
2 juniors in main list. Additional juniors:

11.29	1.1	Tia	Clayton	JAM-Y	17.8.04	1		Spanish Town	19	Feb
11.32	0.2	Lilly	Kaden	GER	6.9.01	1	NC-j	Heilbronn	5	Sep
11.35	1.5	Kevona	Davis	JAM	20.12.01	1h3		Kingston	16	Mar
11.38	1.1	Brandy	Hall	JAM	4.9.02	2		Spanish Town	19	Feb
11.38	0.0	Grace	Nwokocha	NGR	7.4.01	1		Ado-Ekite	1	Mar
11.38A	1.5	Beatrice	Masilingi	NAM-Y	10.4.03	1		Windhoek	17	Dec
11.39	1.8	Amy	Hunt	GBR	15.5.02	1		Göteborg	29	Aug
11.41	0.2	Talea	Prepens (10)	GER	28.12.01	2	NC-J	Heilbronn	5Sepg	

Wind assisted
T Davis 11.18 2.1 1h1 Clermont 24 Jul
| 11.29 | 6.2 | Dalia | Kaddari | ITA | 23.3.01 | 1 | | Cagliari | 25 | Jul |
| 11.35 | 2.1 | Amy | Hunt | GBR | 15.5.02 | 3 | NC | Manchester | 4 | Sep |

150 METRES

16.41	1.1	Brianna	McNeal	USA	18.8.91	1		Fort Worth		20	Jul
16.56	0.6	Dafne	Schippers	NED	15.6.92	1	GS	Ostrava		8	Sep
16.67	0.3	Ajla	Del Ponte	SUI	15.7.96	1		Meilen		20	Jun
16.78	0.6		Del Ponte			2	GS	Ostrava		8	Sep
16.81	-2.6	Allyson	Felix	USA	18.11.85	1		Walnut		9	Jul
16.89	0.0	Gabrielle	Thomas	USA	7.12.96	1		Marietta		29	Jul
16.89	0.0	Lieke	Klaver	NED	20.8.98	3	GS	Ostrava		8	Sep
16.91	0.0	Jasmine	Camacho-Quinn	PUR	21.8.96	2		Marietta		29	Jul
16.92	1.1	Kendra	Harrison	USA	18.9.92	2		Fort Worth		20	Jul
16.94	0.6	Nadine	Visser	NED	9.2.95	4	GS	Ostrava		8	Sep
16.98	0.0	Morolake	Akinosun	USA	17.5.94	3		Marietta		29	Jul
16.99	0.6	Marie Josée	Ta Lou	CIV	18.11.88	5	GS	Ostrava		8	Sep
17.00	-0.2	Tamari	Davis	USA-Y	15.2.03	29	Jul	17.07	1.1 Dalailah Muhammad USA	7.2.90	20 Jul
17.00mx	1.1	Dina	Asher-Smith	GBR	4.12.95	18	Sep	17.09	0.6 Nikola Bendová CZE	4.11.99	8 Sep
			17.12	0.4			11	Sep	17.11 1.0 Javianne Oliver USA	26.12.94	20 Jul
17.01	-0.2	Kyra	Jefferson	USA	23.9.94	1		17.15 -2.5 Shaunae Miller-Uibo BAH	15.4.94	9 Jul

200 METRES

21.98	2.0	Shaunae	Miller-Uibo	BAH	15.4.94	1		Clermont		25	Jul
22.00	1.3	Sha'Carri	Richardson	USA	25.3.00	1		Montverde		10	Aug
22.19	0.7	Elaine	Thompson-Herah	JAM	28.6.92	1rA		Kingston		9	Aug
			(3/3)								
22.45	2.0	Jasmine	Camacho-Quinn	PUR	21.8.96	2		Clermont		25	Jul
22.47	2.0	Lynna	Irby	USA	6.12.98	3		Clermont		25	Jul
22.57	0.9	Shelly-Ann	Fraser-Pryce	JAM	27.12.86	1rB		Kingston		9	Aug
22.63	-0.1	Gabrielle	Thomas	USA	7.12.96	2		Marietta		29	Jul
22.66	1.3	Lieke	Klaver	NED	20.8.98	1r		La Chaux-de-Fonds		15	Aug
22.67	0.7	Anthonique	Strachan	BAH	22.8.93	2rA		Kingston		9	Aug
22.69	1.8		Ge Manqi	CHN	13.10.97	1		Fuzhou		24	May
			(10)								
22.70	0.7	Shericka	Jackson	JAM	16.7.94	3rA		Kingston		9	Aug
22.80	1.5	Quanera	Hayes	USA	7.3.92	1r2		Clermont		25	Jul
22.86	1.0	Kevona	Davis	JAM-J	20.12.01	1		Santa Cruz		25	Jan
22.87	0.6	Kyra	Jefferson	USA	23.9.94	1		Marietta		22	Aug
22.88	1.3	Shakima	Wimbley	USA	23.4.95	2		Montverde		10	Aug
22.91	0.8	Marije	van Hunenstijn	NED	2.3.95	1		Papendal		18	Jul
22.91	0.7	Basant	Hemida	EGY	28.9.96	1		Kladno		16	Sep

200 - 300 METRES

Mark	Wind	Name		Nat	Born	Pos	Meet	Venue		Date
22.94	0.7	Dafne	Schippers	NED	15.6.92	2	Gyulai	Székesfehérvár		19 Aug
22.94A	1.8	Beatrice	Masilingi	NAM-Y	10.4.03	1		Pretoria		9 Dec
22.98	0.7	Carolle	Zahi (20)	FRA	12.6.94	1	NC	Albi		13 Sep
23.01	1.3	Kortnei	Johnson	USA	11.8.97	10 Aug	23.15	-0.5 Rebekka	Haase GER	2.1.93 9 Aug
23.01	0.0	Ana Carolina	Azevedo	BRA	19.5.98	13 Dec	23.16	0.7 Nikola	Bendová CZE	4.11.99 16 Sep
23.02	0.8	Ajla	Del Ponte	SUI	15.7.96	18 Jul	23.17	1.5 Jessica	Beard USA	8.1.89 25 Jul
23.04	0.2	Shashalee	Forbes	JAM	10.5.96	9 Aug	23.17	-0.1 Remi	Tsuruta JPN	18.4.97 3 Oct
23.04A	0.7	Kristal	Awuah	GBR	7.8.99	3 Oct	23.18	0.1 Yana	Kachur UKR	13.1.97 16 Aug
23.06	0.0	Vitória	Rosa	BRA	12.1.96	13 Dec	23.18	-0.2 Maja	Mihalinec SLO	17.12.89 2 Sep
23.07	-0.4	Favour	Ofili	NGR-J	31.12.02	15 Feb	23.20	1.6 Rafailía	Spanoudáki-Hatzirígа	GRE
23.07	-0.7	Jessica-Bianca	Wessolly	GER	11.12.96	9 Aug				7.6.94 9 Aug
23.07A	0.9	Rhodah	Njobwu	ZAM	29.1.74	6 Dec	23.23	-1.0 Corinna	Schwab GER	5.4.99 25 Jul
23.08	1.5	Léa	Sprunger	SUI	5.3.90	12 Sep	23.23	0.3 Dalia	Kaddari ITA-J	23.3.01 25 Sep
23.09		Gulsunbi	Sharifova	TJK	2.12.97	11 Apr	23.24	1.0 Kristina	Timanovskaya BLR	19.11.96 26 Jun
23.12	0.7	Wided	Atatou	FRA	15.7.99	19 Sep	23.25	0.7 Mujinga	Kambundji SUI	17.6.92 19 Aug
23.13	1.9	Ivet	Lalova-Collio	BUL	18.5.84	16 Jul	23.26	-1.6 Jacinta	Beecher AUS	31.1.98 8 Mar
23.14	-0.7	Laura	Müller	GER	11.12.95	9 Aug	23.26	0.6 Yunisleidy de la C. García	CUB	11.8.99 21 Mar
23.14	-0.7	Lisa Marie	Kwayie	GER	27.10.96	9 Aug	23.27	0.8 Gloria	Hooper ITA	3.3.92 23 Jul

Wind assisted

22.52	3.7		Irby			1		Des Moines		29 Aug
22.69	3.7	Kyra	Jefferson	USA	23.9.94	2		Des Moines		29 Aug
22.71A	2.7	Beatrice	Masilingi	NAM-Y	10.4.03	1		Pretoria		12 Dec
22.83	2.1	Ajla	Del Ponte	SUI	15.7.96	1		Bulle		11 Jul
23.05	2.7	Hannah	Williams	GBR	23.4.98	23 Aug	23.21	3.8 Kristina	Knott PHI	25.9.95 25 Jul
23.08	3.7	Tynia	Gaither	BAH	16.3.93	29 Aug	23.25	2.3 Line	Kloster NOR	27.2.90 15 Aug
23.09	3.6	Rebekka	Haase	GER	2.1.93	10 Jul	23.26	4.5 Zoe	Hobbs NZL	11.9.97 8 Mar
							23.27	4.5 Rosie	Elliott NZL	6.11.97 8 Mar

Indoors

22.57		Abby	Steiner	USA	24.11.99	1	SEC	College Station	29 Feb
22.66		Anavia	Battle	USA	28.3.99	1		Clemson	15 Feb
22.69		Tamara	Clark	USA	9.1.99	2	SEC	College Station	29 Feb
22.76		Symone	Mason	USA	31.8.99	1rB	SEC	College Station	29 Feb
22.80		Thelma	Davies	USA	8.5.00	1		Fayetteville	15 Feb
22.93		Kynnedy	Flannel	USA	12.7.00	1rB		Clemson	15 Feb
22.99		Julien	Alfred	LCA-J	10.6.01	3		Clemson	15 Feb
23.02		Cambrea	Sturgis	USA	27.3.99	1		Twanisha Terry USA	24.1.99 21 Feb
23.02		Lanae-Tava	Thomas	USA-J	28.1.01	21 Feb	23.22	Caisja Chandler USA	18.6.00 29 Feb
23.10		Phil	Healy	IRL	19.11.94	12 Feb	23.23	Savyon Toombs USA	2.6.98 1 Feb
23.11		Kendra	Harrison	USA	18.9.92	15 Feb	23.23	Amarachi Pipi GBR	26.11.95 23 Feb
23.12		Danielle	Williams	JAM	14.9.92	18 Jan	23.25	Kiara Grant JAM	8.10.00 11 Jan
23.13		Ka'tia	Seymour	USA	3.10.97	1 Feb	23.26	Janeek Brown JAM	14.5.98 21 Feb
23.16		Tristan	Evelyn	BAR	25.1.98	29 Feb	23.28	Celera Barnes USA	2.12.98 15 Feb
23.18		Jayda	Eckford	USA	7.8.00	29 Feb	23.28	Ashley Spencer USA	8.6.93 22 Feb

Oversized track

22.82#		Ka'tia	Seymour	USA	3.10.97	1	ACC	Notre Dame	29 Feb
23.24#		Devine	Parker	BAH	2.9.00	29 Feb	**Best outdoors at low altitude:** 23.20 -1.2 Awuah	19 Sep

JUNIORS

2 juniors in main list. 1 performance (+2w) by 2 women to 22.86. Additional marks and further juniors:

23.07	-0.4	Favour	Ofili	NGR	31.12.02	1		Akure	15 Feb
23.23	0.3	Dalia	Kaddari	ITA	23.3.01	3		Bellinzona	25 Sep
23.34	1.5	Shenese	Walker	JAM-Y	23.1.03	1		Kingston	6 Mar
23.37	1.5	Brandy	Hall	JAM	4.9.02	2		Kingston	6 Mar
23.39	-0.7	Talea	Prepens	GER	28.12.01	5	NC	Braunscheig	9 Aug
23.38i		Dajour	Miles	USA	25,.7.01	1h2	SEC	College Station	28 Feb

Wind assisted:

Masilingi	22.81A 2.8	1	Windhoek		14 Nov
23.36	2.1	Henriette	Jæger	NOR-Y 30.6.03 1H	Moss	12 Sep

300 METRES

36.12		Jasmine	Camacho-Quinn	PUR	21.8.96	1		Alachua		5 Jul
36.48			Camacho-Quinn			1		Alachua		27 Jun
36.51		Natasha	Hastings	USA	23.7.86	1		Prairie View		23 Jul
36.54		Cynthia	Bolingo Mbongo	BEL	12.1.93	1		Heusden		6 Sep
36.78A		Caster	Semenya	RSA	7.1.91	14 Feb	37.22A	Taylon	Bieldt RSA	7.1.91 14 Feb
36.84		Jessica	Beard	USA	8.1.89	5 Jul	37.22	Lada	Vondrová CZE	6.9.99 1 Jun
37.05		Justyna	Swiety-Ersetic	POL	3.12.92	20 Jun	37.36	Kaylin	Whitney USA	9.3.98 23 Jul
37.08		Seiko	Aoyama	JPN	1.5.96	18 Oct	37.40	Nikola	Bendová CZE	4.11.99 27 Aug

Indoors

36.52		Gabrielle	Thomas	USA	7.12.96	1		Boston (R)		25 Jan
36.56		Tamara	Clark	USA	9.1.99	1		Birmingham AL		10 Jan
37.07		Shamier	Little	USA	20.3.95	15 Feb	37.36	Taylor	Manson USA	29.9.99 11 Jan
37.09		Anna	Kielbasinska	POL	26.6.90	15 Feb	37.36	Athing	Mu USA-J	8.6.02 19 Jan
37.15		Caitlan	Tate	USA	16.9.98	17 Jan	37.36	Kendall	Ellis USA	8.3.96 25 Jan
37.17		Doneisha	Anderson	BAH	21.9.00	11 Jan	37.38	Kayla	Davis USA-Y	21.12.03 19 Jan
37.21		Danielle	Williams	JAM	14.9.92	25 Jan				

WOMEN 2020

400 METRES

Mark	Wind	Name		Nat	Born	Pos	Meet	Venue	Date	
50.42A		Beatrice	Masilingi	NAM-Y	10.4.03	1		Pretoria	12	Dec
50.44A			Masilingi			1		Pretoria	9	Dec
50.50		Lynna	Irby	USA	6.12.98	1	Herc	Monaco	14	Aug
50.52		Shaunae	Miller-Uibo	BAH	15.4.94	1		Montverde	4	Jul
	(4/3)									
50.98		Lieke	Klaver	NED	20.8.98	1	GGala	Roma	17	Sep
50.99A			Masilingi			1	Keino	Nairobi	3	Oct
51.13		Femke	Bol	NED	23.2.00	1		Bern	24	Jul
51.22A		Amantle	Montsho	BOT	4.7.83	1		Gaborone	14	Mar
51.23		Wadeline	Jonathas	USA	19.2.98	1	Kuso	Chorzów	25	Aug
51.33		Justyna	Swiety-Ersetic	POL	3.12.92	1	Skol	Chorzów	6	Sep
51.35		Lada	Vondrová	CZE	6.9.99	1		Praha (J)	4	Jul
51.51		Polina	Miller	RUS	9.6.00	1	NC	Chelyabinsk	9	Sep
	(10)									
51.52		Courtney	Okolo	USA	15.3.94	1		Marietta	1	Aug
51.57A		Christine	Mboma	NAM-Y	22.5.03	2	NYG	Rietfontein	18	Dec
51.65		Barbora	Malíková	CZE-J	30.12.01	1	NC	Plzen	9	Aug
51.67		Janieve	Russell	JAM	14.11.93	1		Kingston	25	Jul
51.70		Anna	Ryzhykova	UKR	24.11.89	1	NC	Lutsk	30	Aug
51.70		Laviai	Nielsen	GBR	13.3.96	1	PTS	Samorín	11	Sep
51.71		Jessica	Beard	USA	8.1.89	2		Marietta	1	Aug
51.71		Kseniya	Aksyonova	RUS	14.1.88	2	NC	Chelyabinsk	9	Sep
51.73		Corinna	Schwab	GER	5.4.99	1	NC	Braunschweig	9	Aug
51.76		Shericka	Jackson	JAM	16.7.94	2		Kingston	8	Aug
	(20)									
51.80		Agné	Serksniené	LTU	18.2.88	2	GGala	Roma	17	Sep
51.84		Patience Okon	George	NGR	25.11.91	1		Benin City	14	Mar
51.84		Alina	Luchsova	BLR-J	30.8.01	1		Brest	8	Jul
51.84		Kateryna	Klymyuk	UKR	2.6.95	2	NC	Lutsk	30	Aug
51.85		Viktoriya	Tkachuk	UKR	8.11.94	1		Lutsk	15	Aug
51.88		Marileidy	Paulino	DOM	25.10.96	1		Santo Domingo	9	Feb
51.88		Karolina	Pahlitzsch	GER	5.4.94	2	NC	Braunschweig	9	Aug
51.99		Kaylin	Whitney	USA	9.3.98	2		Montverde	4	Jul
51.99A		Mary	Moraa	KEN	15.1.00	2	Keino	Nairobi	3	Oct
52.01		Camelia	Gal ¶	ROU	18.10.92	1	NC	Cluj-Napolca	23	Aug
	(30)									
52.04		Iga	Baumgart-Witan	POL	11.4.89	3	Skol	Chorzów	6	Sep
52.06		Bendere	Oboya	AUS	17.4.00	1		Melbourne	6	Feb
52.15		Tabata	Carvalho	BRA	23.4.96	1		Bragança Paulista	14	Mar
52.15		Ruth Sophia	Spelmeyer	GER	19.9.90	3	NC	Braunschweig	9	Aug
52.15		Malgorzata	Holub-Kowalik	POL	30.10.92	3	Kuso	Chorzów	25	Aug
52.20		Stephenie Ann	McPherson	JAM	25.11.88	1		Kingston	8	Aug
52.21		Alica	Schmidt	GER	8.11.98	9 Aug		52.54	Emma	Zapletalová	SVK	24.3.00	22 Aug
52.21		Yasmin	Liverpool	GBR	15.1.99	23 Aug		52.55	Efejiro	Idamamadudu	NGR	15.12.98	3 Mar
52.26		Patrycja	Wyciszkiewicz	POL	8.1.94	29 Aug		52.55	Camille	Laus	BEL	23.5.93	9 Aug
52.36		Aauri Lorena	Bokesa	ESP	14.12.88	24 Jul		52.57	Jessica	Turner	GBR	8.8.95	5 Sep
52.36		Natalia	Kaczmarek	POL	17.1.98	13 Aug		52.61	Rebecca	Bennett	AUS	1.3.99	22 Feb
52.37 mx		Laura	Müller	GER	11.12.95	15 Aug		52.62	Alina	Lohvynenko	UKR	18.7.90	30 Aug
52.72						30 Aug		52.62	Yennifer	Padilla	COL	1.1.90	6 Dec
52.38		Seiko	Aoyama	JPN	1.5.96	23 Jul		52.62	Anneliese	Rubie-Renshaw	AUS	22.4.92	21 Nov
52.41		Junelle	Bromfield	JAM	8.2.98	9 Aug		52.66	Amandine	Brossier	FRA	15.8.95	13 Sep
52.42		Jessie	Knight	GBR	15.6.94	23 Aug		52.67	Rushell	Clayton	JAM	18.10.92	25 Jul
52.43A		Line	Kloster	NOR	27.2.90	14 Mar		52.67		Yang Huizhen	CHN	13.8.92	15 Sep
52.44		Tiffani	Silva	BRA	6.5.99	17 Sep		52.68	Shamier	Little	USA	20.3.95	22 Aug
52.45		Anita	Horvat	SLO	7.9.96	14 Aug		52.68	Amy	Hillyard	GBR	28.10.95	23 Aug
52.46		Christine	Botlogetswe	BOT	1.10.95	15 Feb		52.70	Ella	Connolly	AUS	13.7.00	11 Jan
52.46			Quach Thi Lan	VIE	18.10.95	11 Nov		52.70	Ellie	Beer	AUS-Y	3.1.03	22 Feb
52.48		Sokhna	Lacoste	FRA	25.8.00	13 Sep		52.70	Cátia	Azevedo	POR	9.3.94	8 Aug
52.49		Nadine	Gonska	GER	23.1.90	9 Aug		52.70	Alice	Mangione	ITA	19.1.97	29 Aug
52.49			Nguyen Thi Huyen	VIE	19.5.93	11 Nov		52.70		Lu Guojuan	CHN-J	6.9.02	15 Sep
52.50		Raevyn	Rogers	USA	7.9.96	19 Aug		52.73	Kornelia	Lesiewicz	POL-Y	14.8.03	19 Sep
52.51		Ivona	Pulalová	SVK	24.3.88	4 Jul		52.75	Chrisann	Gordon	JAM	18.9.94	1 Aug
52.51		Léa	Sprunger	SUI	5.3.90	30 Aug		52.77	Brenda	Cataria-Byll	GER-J	6.9.01	8 Aug
52.52		Henriette	Jæger	NOR-Y	30.6.03	22 Aug		52.77	Ayomide	Folorunso	ITA	17.10.96	8 Sep
52.53		Alena	Mamina	RUS	30.5.90	9 Sep		52.77A	Leni	Shida	UGA	22.5.94	3 Oct
52.54		Favour	Ofili	NGR-J	31.12.02	3 Mar		52.78	Oneka	McAnnuff	JAM-Y	3.9.03	6 Mar

Indoors

51.57		Jessie	Knight	GBR	15.6.94	1	DL	Glasgow	15	Feb
51.60#		Bailey	Lear	USA-J	17.3.01	1		Seattle	29	Feb
51.81#		Kennedy	Simon	USA	12.2.00	1	Big 12	Ames	29	Feb
51.90		Lisanne	de Witte	NED	10.9.92	2		Torun	8	Feb
51.93		Léa	Sprunger	SUI	5.3.90	3		Torun	8	Feb

400 - 500 - 600 - 800 METRES

Mark	Name		Nat	Born	Pos	Meet	Venue		Date
51.98A	Na'Asha	Robinson	USA	23.1.97	2	NC	Albuquerque		15 Feb
52.02	Antonina	Krivoshapka	RUS	21.7.87	1	NC	Moskva		26 Feb
52.05#	Maggie	Barrie	SLE	29.5.96	1		Lexington		25 Jan
52.06	Doneisha	Anderson	BAH	21.9.00	1		Clemson		15 Feb
52.06#	Kaelin	Roberts	USA	6.1.99	2		Seattle		29 Feb
52.07A	Shae	Anderson	USA	7.4.99	1		Albuquerque		14 Feb
52.07A	Quanera	Hayes	USA	7.3.92	3	NC	Albuquerque		15 Feb
52.08	Alexis	Holmes	USA	28.1.00	1	SEC	College Station		29 Feb
52.14	Kyra	Constantine	CAN	1.8.98	1rB		Clemson		14 Feb
52.15	Stephanie	Davis	USA	7.2.99	1rB	SEC	College Station		29 Feb
52.22	Amber Anning		GBR	18.11.00	14 Feb	52.54	Shamier Little	USA 20.3.95	21 Feb
52.25	Amalie Hammild Iuel		NOR	17.4.91	1 Feb	52.56	Ayomide Folorunso	ITA 17.10.96	31 Jan
52.25	Syaira Richardson		USA	29.10.98	29 Feb	52.58	Megan Moss	BAH-J 22.3.02	14 Feb
52.31	Taylor Manson		USA	29.9.99	29 Feb	52.64#	Ashlan Best	CAN 11.2.99	29 Feb
52.37	Andrea Miklos		ROU	17.4.99	16 Feb	52.65	Phil Healy	IRL 19.11.94	1 Feb
52.40#	Stacey-Ann Williams		JAM	8.3.99	29 Feb	52.71#	Brittny Ellis	USA 1.9.97	29 Feb
52.42#	Caitlan Tate		USA	16.9.98	29 Feb	52.74A	A'Keyla Mitchell	USA 25.11.95	14 Feb
52.44	Yekaterina Renzhina		RUS	18.10.94	26 Feb	52.74A	T'Sheila Mungo	USA 21.9.93	15 Feb
52.44	Natassha McDonald		CAN	27.1.97	29 Feb	52.77	Tiana Wilson	USA 19.7.00	21 Feb
52.53A	Jaide Stepter		USA	25.9.94	15 Feb	52.78	Aliyah Abrams	GUY 3.4.97	22 Feb

Best at low altitude: 52.63 Stepter 18 Jan
Hand timed: 51.9mx Jessie Knight GBR 15.6.94 1 Nuneaton 12 Jul

JUNIORS
4 juniors in main list. 6 performances by 3 women to 51.75. Additional marks and further juniors:

Masilingi	50.99A	1	Keino Nairobi		3 Oct	51.07A	1	NYG Windhoek	17 Dec
52.52	Henriette		Jæger	NOR-Y	20.6.03	1		Trondheim	22 Aug
52.54	Favour		Ofili	NGR	31.12.02	1		Ekiti	3 Mar
52.70	Ellie		Beer	AUS-Y	3.1.03	3		Sydney	22 Feb
52.70			Lu Guojuan	CHN	6.9.02	2	NC	Shaoxing	15 Sep
52.73	Kornelia		Lesiewicz	POL-Y	14.8.03	1	NC-J	Radom	19 Sep
52.77	Brenda		Cataria-Byll (10)	GER	6.9.01	6	NC	Braunschweig	9 Aug
52.78	Oneka		McAnnuff	JAM-Y	3.9.03	1		Kingston	6 Mar
52.58 i	Megan		Moss	BAH-J	22.3.02	3		Clemson	14 Feb

500 METRES INDOORS

| 1:09.54 | Lada | Vondrová | CZE | 6.9.99 | 1 | | Praha (Strahov) | | 13 Jan |

600 METRES

1:26.38	Lore	Hoffmann	SUI	25.7.96	1		Lausanne		30 Aug
1:26.79mx	Barbora	Malíková	CZE-J	30.12.01	1		Opva		23 Jun
1:26.90	Hedda	Hynne	NOR	13.3.90	1		Trondheim		28 Feb
1:27.20	Nia Akins		USA	7.7.98	17 Jul	1:27.90	Joanna Józwik	POL 30.1.91	20 Jun
1:27.24	Olivia Baker		USA	12.6.96	30 Jul		Indoors		
1:27.43	Sadi Henderson		USA	12.4.96	17 Jul	1:27.64	Kayla Johnson	USA 1.5.99	1 Feb
1:27.49	Chanelle Price		USA	22.8.90	17 Jul				

800 METRES

1:57.68	Faith	Kipyegon	KEN	10.1.94	1	DL	Doha	25 Sep
1:58.10	Hedda	Hynne	NOR	13.3.90	1		Bellinzona	15 Sep
1:58.37	Selina	Büchel	SUI	26.7.91	2		Bellinzona	15 Sep
1:58.50	Lore	Hoffmann	SUI	25.7.96	3		Bellinzona	15 Sep
1:58.63	Jemma	Reekie	GBR	6.3.98	1	Kuso	Chorzów	25 Aug
1:58.84	Laura	Muir	GBR	9.5.93	1	GS	Ostrava	8 Sep
1:58.87		Reekie			4		Bellinzona	15 Sep
1:58.92	Rose Mary	Almanza	CUB	13.7.92	1h1	NC	La Habana	20 Mar
1:59.05		Almanza			1	NC	La Habana	20 Mar
1:59.22	Esther	Guerrero	ESP	7.2.90	2	DL	Doha	25 Sep
	(10/8)							
1:59.69	Ciara	Mageean	IRL	12.3.92	1		Bern	24 Jul
1:59.87	Adelle	Tracey (10)	GBR	27.5.93	3	DL	Doha	25 Sep
2:00.07	Aleksandra	Gulyayeva	RUS	30.4.94	1	NCp	Bryansk	30 Aug
2:00.10A	Felistus	Mpande	ZAM	29.5.96	1		Ndola	22 Feb
2:00.11	Noélie	Yarigo	BEN	26.12.85	1	Szew	Bydgoszcz	19 Aug
2:00.11	Habitam	Alemu	ETH	9.7.97	4	DL	Doha	25 Sep
2:00.12mx	Chanelle	Price	USA	22.8.90	1r1		Newberg	21 Aug
2:00.12	Sofia	Ennaoui	POL	30.8.95	2	Kuso	Chorzów	25 Aug
2:00.16	Cory	McGee	USA	29.5.92	1		Van Nuys	22 Aug
2:00.28	Alexandra	Bell	GBR	4.11.92	1	Maniak	Szczecin	16 Aug
2:00.29	Heather	MacLean	USA	31.8.95	1		Wellesley	11 Aug
2:00.31	Ce'Aira	Brown	USA	4.11.93	1		Nashville	15 Aug
	(20)							
2:00.39	Kaela	Edwards	USA	8.12.93	2		Nashville	15 Aug

800 METRES

Mark	Name		Nat	Born	Pos	Meet	Venue	Date	
2:00.43	Natoya	Goule	JAM	30.3.91	1		Marietta	25	Jul
2:00.47	Christina	Hering	GER	9.10.94	3	Kuso	Chorzów	25	Aug
2:00.49	Winnie	Nanyondo	UGA	23.8.93	5	DL	Doha	25	Sep
2:00.61	Anna	Sabat	POL	9.11.93	5	Szew	Bydgoszcz	19	Aug
2:00.70mx	Elle	Purrier	USA	20.2.95	1		West Hartford	27	Jul
2:00.82	Katharina	Trost	GER	28.6.95	6	Szew	Bydgoszcz	19	Aug
2:00.88	Georgia	Griffith	AUS	5.12.96	2		Canberra	13	Feb
2:00.89	Angelika	Sarna	POL	1.10.97	7	Szew	Bydgoszcz	19	Aug
2:01.00	Inessa	Gusarova	RUS	29.10.95	2	NCp	Bryansk	30	Aug
(30)									
2:01.01	Nadia	Power	IRL	11.1.98	3	Quercia	Rovereto	8	Sep
2:01.01	Lindsey	Butterworth	CAN	27.9.92	4	Quercia	Rovereto	8	Sep
2:01.02	Raevyn	Rogers	USA	7.9.96	2	DL	Stockholm	23	Aug
2:01.06	Angelika	Cichocka	POL	15.3.88	6	DL	Doha	25	Sep
2:01.08	Renelle	Lamote	FRA	26.12.93	6		Trieste	1	Aug
2:01.08	Shelby	Houlihan	USA	8.2.93	1		Portland	7	Aug
2:01.09	Rebecca	Mehra	USA	25.10.94	2		Van Nuys	22	Aug
2:01.10	Emma	Coburn	USA	19.10.90	3		Van Nuys	22	Aug
2:01.11	Sahily	Diago	CUB	26.8.95	2h	NC	La Habana	20	Mar
2:01.20mx	Joanna	Józwik	POL	30.1.91	1		Warszawa	5	Jul
(40)									
2:01.26	Gabriela	Gajanová	SVK	12.10.99	1	PTS	Šamorín	11	Sep
2:01.30	Svetlana	Uloga	RUS	23.11.86	1		Sochi	20	Sep
2:01.34	Elena	Bellò	ITA	18.1.97	3	Maniak	Szczecin	16	Aug
2:01.37	Claudia	Bobocea	ROU	11.6.92	4	GS	Ostrava	8	Sep
2:01.44	Olha	Lyakhova	UKR	18.3.92	7	Kuso	Chorzów	25	Aug
2:01.53	Bregje	Sloot	NED	28.1.00	6		Bellinzona	15	Sep
2:01.54	Catriona	Bissett	AUS	1.3.94	2		Melbourne	12	Mar
2:01.58	Morgan	Mitchell	AUS	3.10.94	4		Van Nuys	22	Aug
2:01.60	Sara	Kuivisto	FIN	18.8.91	2	PTS	Šamorín	11	Sep
2:01.73	Linden	Hall	AUS	29.6.91	3		Melbourne	12	Mar
(50)									
2:01.73	Keely	Hodgkinson	GBR-J	3.3.02	5	Quercia	Rovereto	8	Sep
2:01.77	Cynthia	Anais	FRA	18.1.88	3		Marseille	3	Sep
2:01.83	Eleonora	Vandi	ITA	15.3.96	3		Heusden-Zolder	6	Sep
2:01.88	Isabelle	Boffey	GBR	13.4.00	1		Kladno	16	Sep
2:01.89	Hannah	Segrave	GBR	14.4.95	1		Columbia SC	29	Aug
2:01.91	Khahisa	Mhlanga	GBR	26.12.99	1rB		Bromley	21	Aug
2:01.91mx	Katie	Snowden	GBR	9.3.94	1		Coulsdon	12	Sep
2:01.92	Maité	Bouchard	CAN	24.8.95	2		Sherbrooke	12	Aug
2:02.07	Nia	Akins	USA	7.7.98	2		Newberg	31	Jul
2:02.07	Tanja	Spill	GER	16.12.95	2	NC	Braunschweig	9	Aug
(60)									
2:02.07	Lucia	Stafford	CAN	17.8.98	3		Sherbrooke	12	Aug
2:02.16A	Prudence	Sekgodiso	RSA-J	5.1.02	1		Pretoria	13	Mar

Mark	Name		Nat	Born	Pos	Mark	Name		Nat	Born	Pos
2:02.22	Shelayna	Oskan-Clarke	GBR	20.1.90	25 Sep	2:02.98	Colleen	Quigley	USA	20.11.92	7 Aug
2:02.32	Brenda	Martinez	USA	8.9.87	22 Aug	2:02.99	Georgie	Hartigan	IRL	1.3.96	21 Aug
2:02.4A	Werkwuha	Getachew	ETH		26 Dec	2:03.01	Anastasiya	Yeremyants	RUS-J	22.3.01	27 Aug
2:02.41	Samantha	Watson	USA	10.11.99	22 Aug	2:03.02	Marta	Pen	POR	31.7.93	15 Sep
2:02.42	Eunice	Sum	KEN	2.9.88	25 Sep	2:03.14	Barbora	Malíková	CZE-J	30.12.01	6 Sep
2:02.52	María de L	Calderín	CUB	14.5.00	20 Mar	2:03.17	Louise	Shanahan	IRL	26.1.97	21 Aug
2:02.58mx	Majtie	Kolberg	GER	5.12.99	19 Jul	2:03.20	Sadi	Henderson	USA	12.4.96	21 Aug
2:02.61	Britt	Ummels	NED	24.8.93	19 Sep	2:03.20	Maeliss	Trapeau	FRA	28.9.99	3 Sep
2:02.65	Elise	Vanderelst	BEL	27.1.98	1 Aug	2:03.20	W.K.L.A.	Nimali	SRI	19.9.89	27 Dec
2:02.66	Hanna	Hermansson	SWE	18.5.89	15 Sep	2:03.24	Lovisa	Lindh	SWE	9.7.91	10 Aug
2:02.69	Liga	Velvere	LAT	10.2.90	14 Aug	2:03.27A	Mary	Moraa	KEN	15.1.00	5 Mar
2:02.77mx	Síofra	Cléirigh Büttner	IRL	21.7.95	27 Jul	2:03.30	Renée	Eykens	BEL	8.6.96	8 Sep
2:02.77	Karissa	Schweizer	USA	4.5.96	7 Aug	2:03.41	Olga	Onufriyenko	RUS	8.3.99	8 Sep
2:02.77	Suzanne	Voorrips	NED	11.10.93	6 Sep	2:03.43	Sabrina	Southerland	USA	18.12.95	31 Jul
2:02.78	Buanka	Kéri	HUN	19.4.94	16 Sep	2:03.45	Julia	Rizk	USA	14.6.96	22 Aug
2:02.80	Dilshi S.	Kumarasinghe	SRI	11.5.99	27 Dec	2:03.46	Hanna	Klein	GER	6.4.93	1 Aug
2:02.90	Daily	Cooper	CUB-J	11.3.02	20 Mar	2:03.47	Mirte	Fannes	BEL	9.2.99	6 Sep
2:02.90	Sophia	Gorriaran	USA-Y	20.6.05	22 Aug	2:03.48	Ellie	Baker	GBR	3.6.98	21 Aug
2:02.97	Katherine	Camp	NZL	6.2.92	13 Feb	2:03.49	Anastasiya	Yermolayeva	RUS	18.4.92	8 Sep
2:02.97	Lena	Kandissounon	FRA	26.11.98	9 Aug	(94)					

Indoors

Mark	Name		Nat	Born	Pos	Meet	Venue	Date	
1:57.91	Jemma	Reekie	GBR	6.3.98	1		Glasgow	1	Feb
1:58.29	Ajee'	Wilson	USA	8.5.94	1	Millrose	New York (A)	8	Feb
1:58.44	Laura	Muir	GBR	9.5.93	2		Glasgow	1	Feb
1:59.35	Natoya	Goule	JAM	30.3.91	2	Millrose	New York (A)	8	Feb
2:00.71	Nia	Akins	USA	7.7.98	1		Boston (A)	14	Feb
2:00.76	Cynthia	Anais	FRA	18.1.88	2		Boston (A)	14	Feb
2:00.93	Maité	Bouchard	CAN	24.8.95	1		Boston (A)	28	Feb

800 - 1000 -1500 METRES

Mark	Name		Nat	Born	Pos	Meet	Venue		Date	
2:00.96	Gabriela	DeBues-Stafford	CAN	13.9.95	4		Glasgow		1	Feb
2:00.98	Melissa	Bishop-Nriagu	CAN	5.8.88	2		Boston (A)		28	Feb
2:01.16	Keely	Hodgkinson	GBR-J	3.3.02	1		Wien		1	Feb
2:01.93	Delia	Sclabas	SUI	8.11.00	2		Metz		9	Feb
2:01.96	Halimah	Nakaayi	UGA	16.10.94	2		Liévin		19	Feb
2:02.06	Brenna	Detra	USA	13.8.95	5		Boston (A)		28	Feb
2:02.11	Shannon	Osika	USA	15.6.93	1		Ann Arbor		1	Feb
2:02.41	Sanne	Wolters-Verstegen NED 10.11.85	1 Feb	2:02.95	Emily	Richards	USA	21.7.95	14	Feb
2:02.52	Liga	Velvere LAT 10.2.90	12 Feb	2:03.01	Juliette	Whittaker	USA-Y	1.12.03	28	Feb
2:02.55#	Aaliyah	Miller USA 28.8.98	15 Feb	2:03.02	Amber	Tanner	USA	24.1.98	14	Feb
2:02.75	Carley	Thomas AUS 26.12.00	28 Feb	2:03.05	Roisin	Willis	USA-Y	6.8.04	28	Feb
2:02.82A	Hanna	Green USA 16.10.94	14 Feb	2:03.11	Diana	Mezuliáníková	CZE	10.4.92	1	Feb
2:02.86	Olivia	Baker USA 12.6.96	8 Feb	2:03.31	Ellie	Baker	GBR	3.6.98	12	Feb
2:02.95	Allie	Wilson USA 31.3.96	18 Jan	2:03.32	Mari	Smith	GBR	14.11.96	12	Feb
				2:03.40	Michaela	Meyer	USA	4.7.98	28	Feb

Best in women only race

| 2:01.26 | Józwik | 5 | Kuso | Chorzów | 25 Aug | 2:02.40 | Snowden | 21 Aug | 2:02.77 Kolberg | 9 Aug |
| 2:01.47 | Price | 1 | | Portland | 3 Jul | 2:03.16i | Cléirigh Büttner 28 Feb | | | |

Drugs disqualification: 2:02.07A Nelly Jepkosgei ¶ BRN 14.7.91 (1) Keino Nairobi 3 Oct

JUNIORS
2 juniors in main list. 3 performances by 2 women to 2:02.2. Additional mark and further juniors:

2:02.90	Daily	Cooper	CUB	11.3.02	4h	NC	La Habana	20 Mar
2:02.90	Sophia	Gorriaran	USA-Y	20.6.05	3		Memphis	22 Aug
2:03.01	Anastasiya	Yeremyants	RUS	22.3.01	1		Bryansk	27 Aug
2:03.02	Marta	Pen	POR	31.7.93	3	Hanz	Zagreb	15 Sep
2:03.14	Barbora	Malíková	CZE	30.12.01	1	NC-j	Ostrava	6 Sep
2:03.27A	Mary	Moraa	KEN	15.1.00	1		Nairobi	5 Mar
2:04.70	Bailey	Goggans	USA-Y	30.3.03	1		Marble Falls	1 Aug
2:04.77	Svitlana	Zhulzhyk	UKR	19.7.02	1		Lutsk	18 Aug
2:04.77	Olga	Rodioshkina	RUS	10.2.01	4h3	NC	Chelyabinsk	9 Sep

Indoors

2:03.01	Juliette	Whittaker	USA-Y	1.12.03	1		Staten Island	28 Feb
2:03.05	Roisin	Willis	USA-Y	6.8.04	1rB		Boston (A)	28 Feb
2:03.80	Hirut	Meshesha	ETH	20.1.01	2		Val-de-Reuil	14 Feb
2:04.08	Athing	Mu	USA	8.6.02	3		Winston-Salem	8 Feb

1000 METRES

2:29.15	Faith	Kipyegon	KEN	10.1.94	1	Herc	Monaco	14 Aug
2:29.92		Kipyegon			1	VD	Bruxelles	4 Sep
2:30.82	Laura	Muir	GBR	9.5.93	2	Herc	Monaco	14 Aug
2:31.06	Ciara	Mageean	IRL	12.3.92	3	Herc	Monaco	14 Aug
2:31.11	Jemma	Reekie	GBR	6.3.98	4	Herc	Monaco	14 Aug
2:32.12	Halimah	Nakaayi	UGA	16.10.94	5	Herc	Monaco	14 Aug
2:32.30	Sofia	Ennaoui	POL	30.8.95	6	Herc	Monaco	14 Aug
2:32.82		Kipyegon			1		Hengelo	10 Oct
2:35.58	Selina	Büchel	SUI	26.7.91	7	Herc	Monaco	14 Aug
2:35.64	Esther	Guerrero	ESP	7.2.90	2	VD	Bruxelles	4 Sep
2:36.54+	Winnie	Nanyondo	UGA	23.8.93	8	Herc	Monaco	14 Aug
2:37.05	Konstanze	Klosterhalfen	GER	18.2.97	1		Blue River	17 Jul
2:37.10	Raevyn	Rogers	USA	7.9.96	9	Herc	Monaco	14 Aug
2:37.26	Lindsey	Butterworth	CAN	27.9.92	3	VD	Bruxelles	4 Sep
2:37.86	Elise	Vanderelst	BEL	27.1.88	4	VD	Bruxelles	4 Sep
2:38.02	Rebecca	Mehra USA 25.10.94	17 Jul	2:38.73	Lucia	Stafford	CAN	17.8.98	2 Aug
2:38.03	Aleksandra	Gulyayeva RUS 30.4.94	22 Aug	2:39.14	Sara	Kuivisto	FIN	18.8.91	2 Sep
2:38.48	Eleonora	Vandi ITA 15.3.96	4 Sep	2:39.15	Renée	Eykens	BEL	8.6.96	4 Sep

Indoors

2:33.47		Muir			1		Glasgow	15 Feb
2:35.49	Kate	Grace	USA	24.10.88	1		Boston (A)	28 Feb
2:37.17	Aleksandra	Gulyayeva	RUS	30.4.94	1		Orenburg	25 Jan
2:37.95	Adelle	Tracey	GBR	27.5.93	2	DL	Glasgow	15 Feb
2:37.96	Katharina	Trost	GER	28.6.95	3	DL	Glasgow	15 Feb
2:38.77	Laurence	Côté CAN 9.2.91	28 Feb	2:40.18	Angelika	Cichocka	POL	15.3.88	15 Feb
2:39.19	Madeleine	Kelly CAN 28.12.95	14 Feb	2:40.22	Hanna	Hermansson	SWE	18.5.89	15 Feb
2:39.96	Melissa	Bishop-Nriagu CAN 5.8.88	14 Feb	2:40.42	Jenna	Westaway	CAN	19.6.94	25 Jan

1500 METRES

3:57.40	Laura	Muir	GBR	9.5.93	1	ISTAF	Berlin	13 Sep
3:57.86		Muir			1	DL	Stockholm	23 Aug
3:58.24		Muir			1	Skol	Chorzów	6 Sep
3:59.05	Faith	Kipyegon	KEN	10.1.94	1	GS	Ostrava	8 Sep
3:59.70	Sofia	Ennaoui	POL	30.8.95	2	Skol	Chorzów	6 Sep
4:00.02	Karissa	Schweizer	USA	4.5.96	1		Portland	21 Jul

1500 METRES

Mark	Name		Nat	Born	Pos	Meet	Venue	Date	
4:00.09	Laura	Weightman	GBR	1.7.91	2	ISTAF	Berlin	13	Sep
4:00.42	Jessica	Hull	AUS	22.10.96	3	ISTAF	Berlin	13	Sep
4:00.77	Elle	Purrier	USA	20.2.95	1		Wellesley Hills	11	Aug
	(9/7))								
4:01.31	Claudia	Bobocea	ROU	11.6.92	3	Skol	Chorzów	6	Sep
4:01.81	Melissa	Courtney-Bryant	GBR	30.8.93	3	DL	Stockholm	23	Aug
4:02.20	Jemma	Reekie	GBR	6.3.98	1		Marseille	3	Sep
	(10)								
4:02.37	Shelby	Houlihan	USA	8.2.93	1		Portland	30	Jun
4:02.56	Shannon	Rowbury	USA	19.9.84	5	ISTAF	Berlin	13	Sep
4:02.58	Winny	Chebet	KEN	20.12.90	4	DL	Stockholm	23	Aug
4:03.05	Marusa	Mismas	SLO	24.10.94	3		Marseille	3	Sep
4:03.13	Esther	Guerrero	ESP	7.2.90	7	DL	Stockholm	23	Aug
4:03.64	Cory	McGee	USA	29.5.92	1		Nashville	15	Aug
4:03.74	Eilish	McColgan	GBR	25.11.90	8	DL	Stockholm	23	Aug
4:03.82	Emma	Coburn	USA	19.10.90	2		Nashville	15	Aug
4:03.98	Colleen	Quigley	USA	20.11.92	2		Portland	21	Jul
4:04.75	Lemlem	Hailu	ETH-J	21.5.01	4	Skol	Chorzów	6	Sep
	(20)								
4:04.90	Hanna	Klein	GER	6.4.93	4	GS	Ostrava	8	Sep
4:05.03+	Danielle	Jones	USA	21.8.96	3M	in 1M	Marion	25	Jul
4:05.16	Linden	Hall	AUS	29.6.91	1		Sydney	22	Feb
4:05.27	Nozomi	Tanaka	JPN	4.9.99	1		Tokyo	23	Aug
4:05.35	Jenny	Blundell	AUS	9.5.94	2		Sydney	22	Feb
4:05.69	Aleksandra	Gulyayeva	RUS	30.4.94	1	NC	Chelyabinsk	8	Sep
4:05.76	Elise	Vanderelst	BEL	27.1.98	2		Heusden-Zolder	6	Sep
4:06.35	Georgia	Griffith	AUS	5.12.96	3		Sydney	22	Feb
4:06.79A	Mercy	Cherono	KEN	7.5.91	3	Keino	Nairobi	3	Oct
4:06.85	Elena	Burkard	GER	10.2.92	6	GS	Ostrava	8	Sep
	(30)								
4:06.91	Marta	Pen	POR	31.7.93	3		Heusden-Zolder	6	Sep
4:07.07	Hanna	Hermansson	SWE	18.5.89	7	GS	Ostrava	8	Sep
4:07.24A	Edina	Jebitok	KEN-J	10.11.01	4	Keino	Nairobi	3	Oct
4:07.30	Simona	Vrzalová	CZE	7.4.88	8	GS	Ostrava	8	Sep
4:07.39	Courtney	Frerichs	USA	18.1.93	1		Portland	21	Jul
4:07.47	Klaudia	Kazimierska	POL-J	3.9.01	6	Skol	Chorzów	6	Sep
4:07.47	Adelle	Tracey	GBR	27.5.93	1		London (BP)	15	Sep
4:07.94	Elise	Cranny	USA	8.5.96	3		Portland	21	Jul
4:07.94	Winnie	Nanyondo	UGA	23.8.93	9	GS	Ostrava	8	Sep
4:08.17	Inessa	Gusarova	RUS	29.10.95	1h1	NC	Chelyabinsk	10	Sep
	(40)								
4:08.23	Habitam	Alemu	ETH	9.7.97	8	Skol	Chorzów	6	Sep
4:08.30	Helen	Schlachtenhaufen	USA	14.3.95	2		Wellesley Hills	11	Aug
4:08.30	Christina	Hering	GER	9.10.94	10	ISTAF	Berlin	13	Sep
4:08.45	Rebecca	Mehra	USA	25.10.94	1		Van Nuys	29	Aug
4:08.48	Karisa	Nelson	USA	12.6.96	2		Newberg	31	Jul
4:08.66	Emily	Lipari	USA	19.11.92	3		Nashville	15	Aug
4:08.68A	Josephine	Kiplangat	KEN	10.10.98	5	Keino	Nairobi	3	Oct
4:08.81	Yolanda	Ngarambe	SWE	14.9.91	4		Nashville	15	Aug
4:08.92	Eleanor	Fulton	USA	17.5.93	4		Newberg	31	Jul
4:09.40	Genevieve	Gregson	AUS	4.8.89	2		London (BP)	15	Sep
	(50)								
4:09.43	Katharina	Trost	GER	28.6.95	1		Leipzig	17	Jul
4:09.44	Amy-Eloise	Neale	GBR	5.8.95	5		Nashville	15	Aug
4:09.62	Kaela	Edwards	USA	8.12.93	2		Van Nuys	29	Aug
4:09.63	Katie	Snowden	GBR	9.3.94	3		Göteborg	29	Aug
4:09.78	Amalie	Sæten	NOR	1.12.97	3	PNG	Turku	11	Aug
4:09.82	Megan	Mansy	USA	27.3.94	6		Nashville	15	Aug
4:09.82	Maureen	Koster	NED	3.7.92	12	ISTAF	Berlin	13	Sep
4:10.00	Helen	Lobun	KEN	18.3.99	2		Shibetsu	4	Jul
4:10.00	Yekaterina	Ivonina	RUS	14.6.94	1		Sochi	19	Sep
4:10.03	Jessica	Judd	GBR	7.1.95	2		Bromley	21	Aug
	(60)								
4:10.12	Selina	Büchel	SUI	26.7.91	27 Jun	4:10.77	Marielle	Hall	USA	28.1.92	21 Jul
4:10.27	Linn	Söderholm	SWE	5.5.96	23 Aug	4:10.79	Dana	Giordano	USA	30.12.93	18 Jul
4:10.27	Renata	Plis	POL	5.2.85	6 Sep	4:10.87	Mariana	Machado	POR	12.11.00	6 Sep
4:10.31	Lauren	Johnson	USA	4.5.87	15 Aug	4:10.99	Ciara	Mageean	IRL	12.3.92	23 Aug
4:10.32	Aude	Korotchansky	FRA	12.9.91	3 Sep	4:11.12	Alice	Finot	FRA	9.2.91	3 Sep
4:10.43	Meraf	Bahta	SWE	21.8.96	29 Aug	4:11.19	Caterina	Granz	GER	14.3.94	19 Aug
4:10.50	Britt	Ummels	NED	24.8.93	8 Sep	4:11.25	Rosie	Clarke	GBR	17.11.91	11 Aug
4:10.53	Hellen	Obiri	KEN	13.12.89	23 Aug	4:11.25	Leah	Falland	USA	30.8.92	15 Aug
4:10.67	Cynthia	Baire	KEN-J	2.12.02	4 Jul	4:11.25	Danielle	Aragon	USA	1.7.94	22 Aug

1500 METRES

Mark	Name		Nat	Born		Pos	Meet	Venue		Date
4:11.27	Gaia	Sabbatini	ITA	10.6.99	6 Sep					
4:11.30	Olga	Vovk	RUS	13.2.93	19 Sep					
4:11.37	Svetlana	Aplachkina	RUS	28.11.92	8 Sep					
4:11.40	Berenice	Fulcheron	FRA	17.2.00	3 Sep					
4:11.44	Vera	Hoffmann	LUX	2.11.96	6 Sep					
4:11.54	Revee	Walcott-Nolan	GBR	6.3.95	15 Sep					
4:11.75	Ran	Urabe	JPN	16.6.95	23 Aug					
4:11.83	Dominique	Scott	RSA	24.6.92	29 Aug					
4:12.12	Alicia	Monson	USA	13.5.98	15 Aug					
4:12.19	Amelia	Quirk	GBR	18.12.99	15 Sep					
4:12.23	Dina	Aleksandrova	RUS	9.8.92	19 Sep					
4:12.38	Amy	Griffiths	GBR	22.3.96	19 Aug					
4:12.57	Erin	Wallace	GBR	18.5.00	19 Aug					
4:12.62	Marisa	Howard	USA	9.8.92	31 Jul					
4:12.63	Solange Andreia	Pereira	ESP	12.12.89						24 Aug
4:12.68	Anastasiya	Aleksandrova	RUS	16.2.94						8 Sep
4:12.75	Lucia	Rodríguez	ESP	26.7.98						24 Aug
4:12.78	Sarah	Billings	AUS	7.3.98						22 Feb
4:12.83	Lauren	Reid	AUS	21.7.85						22 Feb
4:12.91	Madeline	Murray	GBR	19.10.93						22 Feb
4:12.93	Diane	van Es	NED	22.3.99						6 Sep
4:13.09	Abbey	Caldwell	AUS-J	3.7.01						22 Dec
4:13.1A	Quailyne	Kiprop	KEN	1.5.99						5 Mar
4:13.13	Elena	Bellò	ITA	18.1.97						3 Sep
4:13.14	Kaede	Hagitani	JPN	10.10.00						23 Aug
4:13.26	Sinclaire	Johnson	USA	13.4.98						22 Feb
4:13.27mx	Vera	Coutellier	GER	11.9.95						22 Aug
4:13.28	Marta	García	ESP	1.1.98						6 Sep
4:13.49	Rose	Davies	AUS	21.12.99						22 Feb

Illegal pacing: 4:06.56 mx Caterina Granz GER 14.3.94 1 Berlin 28 Aug

Indoors
3:59.87+	Konstanze	Klosterhalfen	GER	18.2.97	1	Millrose	New York (A)	8 Feb
4:00.09	Gudaf	Tsegay	ETH	23.1.97	1		Torun	8 Feb
4:00.20+	Elle	Purrier	USA	20.2.95	2	Millrose	New York (A)	8 Feb
4:00.52+	Jemma	Reekie	GBR	6.3.98	3	Millrose	New York (A)	8 Feb
4:00.60		Tsegay			1		Liévin	19 Feb
4:00.80+	Gabriela	DeBues-Stafford	CAN	13.9.95	4	Millrose	New York (A)	8 Feb
4:01.57	Lemlem	Hailu	ETH-J	21.5.01	2		Liévin	19 Feb
4:02.09	Beatrice	Chepkoech	KEN	6.7.91	1		Düsseldorf	4 Feb
4:02.46	Rababe	Arrafi	MAR	12.1.91	3		Torun	8 Feb
4:02.96	Axumawit	Embaye	ETH	18.10.94	2		Düsseldorf	4 Feb
4:04.24	Dawit	Seyaum	ETH	27.7.96	2	DL	Glasgow	15 Feb
4:05.29	Heather	MacLean	USA	31.8.95	1		Boston (A)	28 Feb
4:05.84	Yelena	Korobkina	RUS	25.11.90	1		Moskva	9 Feb
4:05.91	Fireweyni	Hailu	ETH-J	12.2.01	4		Madrid	21 Feb
4:06.13	Winnie	Nanyondo	UGA	23.8.93	3		Düsseldorf	4 Feb
4:06.39	Fantu	Worku	ETH	29.3.99	4		Düsseldorf	4 Feb
4:06.42	Ciara	Mageean	IRL	12.3.92	3		Boston (R)	25 Jan
4:06.49	Emily	Lipari	USA	19.11.92	2		Boston (A)	28 Feb
4:06.77	Darya	Borisevich	BLR	6.4.90	5		Torun	8 Feb
4:07.09+	Nikki	Hiltz	USA	23.10.94	5	Millrose	New York (A)	8 Feb
4:07.37	Marta	Pérez	ESP	19.4.93	6		Madrid	21 Feb
4:07.40	Tigist	Ketema	ETH	15.9.98	2		Ostrava	5 Feb
4:07.51	Anna	Shchagina	RUS	7.12.91	2		Moskva	9 Feb
4:08.24	Dina	Aleksandrova	RUS	9.8.92	3		Moskva	9 Feb
4:08.36	Hanna	Green	USA	16.10.94	1rB		Boston (A)	28 Feb
4:08.41	Kristiina	Mäki	CZE	22.9.91	9	DL	Glasgow	15 Feb
4:08.69	Katie	Mackey	USA	12.11.87	2rB		Boston (A)	28 Feb
4:08.81	Jessica	Harris	USA	14.3.96	3rB		Boston (A)	28 Feb
4:09.32A	Shannon	Osika	USA	15.6.93	4	NC	Albuquerque	15 Feb
4:09.98	Amanda	Eccleston	USA	18.6.90	4rB		Boston (A)	28 Feb
4:10.01	Mariah	Kelly	CAN	19.8.91	7		Boston (R)	25 Jan
4:10.22	Lucia	Stafford	CAN	17.8.98	1 Feb				
4:11.96	Siofra	Cléirigh Büttner	IRL	21.7.95	1 Feb				
4:10.29	Anastasiya	Aleksandrova	RUS	16.2.94	9 Feb				
4:12.14	Lianne	Farber	USA	12.6.92	28 Feb				
4:10.31	Dana	Giordano	USA	30.12.93	28 Feb				
4:12.34	Whittni	Orton	USA		25 Jan				
4:11.03	Martyna	Galant	POL	26.1.95	8 Feb				
4:12.56	Yekaterina	Ishova	RUS	17.1.89	9 Feb				
4:11.20	Heather	Kampf	USA	19.1.87	1 Feb				
4:12.71	Katie	Rainsberger	USA	18.8.98	28 Feb				
4:11.48	Viktória	Gyürkés	HUN	15.10.92	5 Feb				
4:12.80	Raquel	Lambdin	USA	23.7.93	28 Feb				
4:11.73	Rachel	Schneider	USA	1.11.91	1 Feb				
4:13.06	Luiza	Gega	ALB	5.11.88	16 Feb				
4:11.88	Diana	Mezuliáníková	CZE	10.4.92	5 Feb				
4:13.13	Angel	Piccirillo	USA	8.1.94	28 Feb				

Best in women only race: 4:11.19 Granz GER 19 Aug

JUNIORS
3 juniors in main list + 1 indoors. 12 performances (inc. 6 indoors) by 5 women to 4:11.0. Additional marks and further juniors:

L Hailu 2+	4:05.50	5	GS	Ostrava	8 Sep	4:06.42	1	Keino	Nairobi	3 Oct
	4:01.79i	2		Torun	8 Feb	4:05.24i	2		Madrid	21 Feb
	4:05.08i	1		Otrava	5 Feb	4:08.32i	3		Karlsruhe	31 Jan
4:10.67	Cynthia	Baire		KEN	2.12.02	1		Kagoshima	4 Jul
4:13.09	Abbey	Caldwell		AUS	3.7.01	1		Melbourne (BH)	22 Dec
4:14.32	Yuri	Tazaki		JPN	13.2.01	2		Kumagaya	18 Sep
4:15.62	Nanaka	Yonezawa		JPN-Y	28.2.04	2	NC	Niigata	2 Oct
4:15.8A	Purity	Chepkurui		KEN-Y	14.10.04	1h2		Nairobi	20 Nov
4:16.94i	Zerfe	Wondemagegn		ETH	26.10.02	1		Mondeville	1 Feb

1 MILE

4:21.81	Cory	McGee	USA	29.5.92	1	Marion	25 Jul
4:23.33	Danielle	Jones	USA	21.8.96	2	Marion	25 Jul

1 MILE - 2000 - 3000 METRES

Mark	Name		Nat	Born	Pos	Meet	Venue		Date	
4:23.65	Emma	Coburn	USA	19.10.90	3		Marion		25	Jul
4:29.35	Katharina	Trost	GER	28.6.95	1		Leverkusen		16	Aug
4:31.73	Marta	Pen	POR	31.7.93	22 Sep	4:32.50	Nadia	Power	IRL	11.1.98 22 Sep
4:31.91	Caterina	Granz	GER	14.3.94	16 Aug	4:33.02	Simona	Vrzalová	CZE	7.4.88 2 Sep
4:32.26	Marta	Pérez	ESP	19.4.93	22 Sep	4:33.57	Keely	Small	AUS-J	9.6.01 19 Dec

Indoors

Mark	Name		Nat	Born	Pos	Meet	Venue		Date	
4:16.85	Elle	Purrier	USA	20.2.95	1	Millrose	New York (A)		8	Feb
4:17.26	Konstanze	Klosterhalfen	GER	18.2.97	2	Millrose	New York (A)		8	Feb
4:17.88	Jemma	Reekie	GBR	6.3.98	3	Millrose	New York (A)		8	Feb
4:19.73	Gabriela	DeBues-Stafford	CAN	13.9.95	4	Millrose	New York (A)		8	Feb
4:23.68#	Shelby	Houlihan	USA	8.2.93	1		Seattle		1	Feb
4:24.32#	Karissa	Schweizer	USA	4.5.96	2		Seattle		1	Feb
4:24.45	Nikki	Hiltz	USA	23.10.94	5	Millrose	New York (A)		8	Feb
4:25.98	Heather	MacLean	USA	31.8.95	6	Millrose	New York (A)		8	Feb
4:28.06#	Hanna	Green	USA	16.10.94	3		Seattle		1	Feb
4:28.79	Shannon	Osika	USA	15.6.93	8	Millrose	New York (A)		8	Feb
4:29.76	Whittni	Orton	USA		2		New York (A)		25	Jan
4:31.34	Yolanda	Ngarambe	SWE	14.9.91	8 Feb	4:33.36	Sarah	MacPherson	CAN	8.5.91 25 Jan
4:31.42	Lucia	Stafford	CAN	17.8.98	25 Jan	4:33.37#	Julia	Heymach	USA	20.11.98 15 Feb
4:31.89	Laura	Galván	MEX	5.10.91	25 Jan	4:33.38	Jenna	Westaway	CAN	19.6.94 14 Feb
4:32.36	Julie-Anne	Staehli	CAN	21.12.93	14 Feb	4:33.55	Mariah	Kelly	CAN	19.8.91 14 Feb
4:32.61	Rebecca	Mehra	USA	25.10.94	8 Feb	4:33.59	Jessica	Harris	USA	14.3.96 8 Feb
4:32.85#	Julie	Labach	CAN	14.11.96	15 Feb	4:33.71	Ella	Donaghu	USA	13.4.98 1 Feb
4:32.95	Danae	Rivers	USA	3.2.98	8 Feb	4:33.97	Leah	O'Connor	USA	30.8.92 14 Feb

JUNIORS

Mark	Name		Nat	Born	Pos	Meet	Venue	Date	
4:33.57	Keely	Small	AUS	9.6.01	1		Sydney	19	Dec
4:34.82	Klaudia	Kazimierska	POL	3.9.01	1		Bialogard	26	Sep

2000 METRES

Mark	Name		Nat	Born	Pos	Meet	Venue	Date	
5:39.70+	Hellen	Obiri	KEN	13.12.89	1	in 3000	Doha	25	Sep
5:39.8+	Beatrice	Chepkoech	KEN	6.7.91	2	in 3000	Doha	25	Sep
5:39.9+	Agnes	Tirop	KEN	23.10.95	3	in 3000	Doha	25	Sep
5:40.1+	Lemlem	Hailu	ETH-J	21.5.01	4	in 3000	Doha	25	Sep
5:40.2+	Margaret	Kipkemboi	KEN	9.2.93	5	in 3000	Doha	25	Sep
5:40.3+	Hyvin	Jepkemoi	KEN	13.1.92	6	in 3000	Doha	25	Sep
5:40.4+	Gudaf	Tsegay	ETH	23.1.97	7	in 3000	Doha	25	Sep
5:40.5+	Laura	Weightman	GBR	1.7.91	8	in 3000	Doha	25	Sep
5:40.6+	Jessica	Hull	AUS	22.10.96	9	in 3000	Doha	25	Sep
5:41.0+	Tsehay	Gemechu	ETH	12.12.98	10	in 3000	Doha	25	Sep
5:41.30	Esther	Guerrero	ESP	7.2.90	1		Olot	21	Jul
5:42.73+	Beatrice	Chepkoech	KEN	6.7.91	7 Oct	5:43+?+	Letesenbet Gidey	ETH	20.3.98 7 Oct

Indoors

Mark	Name		Nat	Born	Pos	Meet	Venue	Date	
5:40.33+	Shelby	Houlihan	USA	8.2.93	1m		Boston (A)	27	Feb
5:40.6+	Karissa	Schweizer	USA	4.5.96	2m		Boston (A)	27	Feb
5:40.9+	Colleen	Quigley	USA	20.11.92	3m		Boston (A)	27	Feb
5:41.87+	Kate	Grace	USA	24.10.88	4m		Boston (A)	27	Feb
5:44.43	Yelena	Korobkina	RUS	25.11.90	7 Jan	5:44.7+	Fantu	Worku	ETH	29.3.99 31 Jan

3000 METRES

Mark	Name		Nat	Born	Pos	Meet	Venue	Date	
8:22.54	Hellen	Obiri	KEN	13.12.89	1	DL	Doha	25	Sep
8.22.92	Agnes	Tirop	KEN	23.10.95	2	DL	Doha	25	Sep
8:22.92	Beatrice	Chepkoech	KEN	6.7.91	3	DL	Doha	25	Sep
8:24.76	Margaret	Kipkemboi	KEN	9.2.93	4	DL	Doha	25	Sep
8:25.13	Hyvin	Jepkemoi	KEN	13.1.92	5	DL	Doha	25	Sep
8:25.23	Gudaf	Tsegay	ETH	23.1.97	6	DL	Doha	25	Sep
8:26.31	Laura	Weightman	GBR	1.7.91	7	DL	Doha	25	Sep
8:31.85+		Chepkoech			1	in 5000	Valencia	7	Oct
8:31.9+	Letesenbet	Gidey	ETH	20.3.98	2	in 5000	Valencia	7	Oct
8:33.42	Tsehay	Gemechu	ETH	12.12.98	8	DL	Doha	25	Sep
8:35.78	Lemlem	Hailu (10)	ETH-J	21.5.01	9	DL	Doha	25	Sep
8:36.03	Jessica (12/11)	Hull	AUS	22.10.96	10	DL	Doha	25	Sep
8:39.88	Quailyne	Kiprop	KEN	1.5.99	11	DL	Doha	25	Sep
8:40.26	Shannon	Rowbury	USA	19.9.84	1		Blue River	17	Jul
8:40.88	Eilish	McColgan	GBR	25.11.90	12	DL	Doha	25	Sep
8:41.35	Nozomi	Tanaka	JPN	4.9.99	1		Fukagawa	8	Jul
8:43.08	Maureen	Koster	NED	3.7.92	1		Vight	1	Aug
8:43.33	Helen	Lobun	KEN	18.3.99	2		Fukagawa	8	Jul
8:44.92	Elena	Burkard	GER	10.2.92	1		Winnenden	18	Jul
8:46.44	Marusa	Mismas	SLO	24.10.94	1		Celje	26	Jul
8:47.89+	Elise (20)	Cranny	USA	8.5.96	1	in 5000	Portland	10	Jul

3000 METRES

Mark	Name		Nat	Born	Pos	Meet	Venue	Date	
8:47.90+	Courtney	Frerichs	USA	18.1.93	2	in 5000	Portland	10	Jul
8:48.12	Kaede	Hagitani	JPN	10.10.00	3		Fukagawa	8	Jul
8:48.14+	Shelby	Houlihan	USA	8.2.93	3	in 5000	Portland	10	Jul
8:48.37+	Karissa	Schweizer	USA	4.5.96	4	in 5000	Portland	10	Jul
8:48.48	Gwen	Jorgensen	USA	25.4.86	5	in 5000	Portland	10	Jul
8:48.72	Marielle	Hall	USA	28.1.92	6	in 5000	Portland	10	Jul
8:48.93	Colleen	Quigley	USA	20.11.92	7	in 5000	Portland	10	Jul
8:49+ ?	Sifan	Hassan	NED	1.1.93	1	in 10k	Hengelo	10	Oct
8:50.40	Beatrice	Chebet	KEN	5.3.00	13	DL	Doha	25	Sep
8:51.20	Linden	Hall	AUS	29.6.91	1		Melbourne (BH)	22	Dec
(30)									
8:51.36mx	Alina	Reh	GER	23.5.97	1mx		Erfurt	3	Jul
8:52.17	Margaret	Ekidor	KEN-J	26.6.02	1		Yokohama	6	Dec
8:52.22	Yelena	Korobkina	RUS	25.11.90	1		Moskva	27	Aug
8:52.22	Agnes	Mwikali	KEN-J	15.12.02	1		Takamatsu	10	Oct
8:52.80	Ririka	Hironaka	JPN	24.11.00	1		Kumagaya	18	Sep
8:53.04	Cynthia	Baire	KEN-J	2.12.02	1		Hioki	17	Oct
8:53.46mx	Diane	van Es	NED	22.3.99	1		Utrecht	10	Jul
8:53.60	Viktória	Gyürkés	HUN	15.10.92	1		Veszprém	18	Aug
8:54.09	Amelia	Quirk	GBR	18.12.99	1		Bromley	21	Aug
8:54.54	Lauren	Ryan	AUS	15.3.98	2		Melbourne (BH)	22	Dec
(40)									
8:54.57	Judith	Jepngetich	KEN-J	24.12.02	1		Unnan	10	Oct
8:54.83+	Sheila	Chelangat	KEN	11.4.98	2	in 5000	Ostrava	8	Sep
8:54.9u mx	Chloe	Tighe	AUS	28.9.90	2		Sydney (Bankstown)	26	Jul
8:56.11	Melissa	Courtney-Bryant	GBR	30.8.93	25 Sep	8:59.82mx	Molly	Huddle	USA	31.8.84	22 Aug
8:56.72	Verity	Ockenden	GBR	31.8.91	21 Aug	9:00.79	Svetlana	Aplachkina	RUS	28.11.92	27 Aug
8:57.12	Rebecca	Mwangi	KEN-J	15.6.01	25 Sep	9:01.36mx	Imogen	Stewart	AUS-Y	27.7.05	27 Nov
8:57.16	Esther	Wambui	KEN-Y	8.5.03	12 Sep	9:02.19	Klara	Lukan	SLO	8.9.00	23 Jun
8:57.20	Joan	Chepkemoi	KEN	24.11.93	18 Jul	9:02.43mx	Linn	Nilsson	SWE	15.10.90	1 Aug
8:57.60	Jessica	Judd	GBR	7.1.95	25 Aug	9:02.8A	Judy	Chepkoech	KEN-Y	1.1.04	20 Nov
8:57.64	Yasemin	Can	TUR	11.12.96	19 Aug	9:02.86	Azusa	Mihara	JPN-Y	16.2.03	18 Jul
8:57.86	Winnie	Jerotich	KEN	27.11.99	18 Jul	9:03.12mx	Emily	Brichacek	AUS	7.7.90	29 Feb
8:58.53	Caitlin	Adams	AUS	7.7.97	11 Mar	9:03.42mx	Sofie	Van Accom	BEL	7.6.89	20 Jul
8:58.83 mx	Irene	van der Reijken	NED	13.8.93	10 Jul	9:03.59	Yekaterina	Ishova	RUS	17.1.89	22 Aug
8:58.9u mx	Rose	Davies	AUS	21.12.99	26 Jul	9:03.60	Nanaka	Yonezawa	JPN-Y	28.2.04	26 Sep
	9:00.17				21 Nov	9:04.02	Aude	Korotchansky	FRA	12.9.91	19 Sep
8:58.99 mx	Martha	Mokaya	KEN	1.3.00	24 Oct	9:04.22	Luiza	Gega	ALB	5.11.88	4 Aug
8:59.30	Georgia	Hansen	AUS	20.12.98	11 Mar	9:04.78	Mel	Lawrence	USA	29.8.89	31 Jul
8:59.57mx	Hanna	Hermansson	SWE	18.5.89	1 Aug	9:04.89	Darya	Borisevich	BLR	6.4.90	17 Jul

Illegally paced

| 9:00.27mx | Camille | Buscomb | NZL | 11.7.90 | 1 | | Hamilton | 29 | Jul |

Indoors

8:25.70	Karissa	Schweizer	USA	4.5.96	1		Boston (A)	27	Feb
8:26.66	Shelby	Houlihan	USA	8.2.93	2		Boston (A)	27	Feb
8:28.71	Colleen	Quigley	USA	20.11.92	3		Boston (A)	27	Feb
8:37.58	Fantu	Worku	ETH	29.3.99	1		Karlsruhe	31	Jan
8:39.64	Winfred	Yavi	BRN	31.12.99	1		Val-de-Reuil	14	Feb
8:44.10	Beyenu	Degefa	ETH	12.7.99	3		Eaubonne	17	Feb
8:44.46	Luiza	Gega	ALB	5.11.88	3		Karlsruhe	31	Jan
8:45.76	Tsigie	Gebreselama	ETH	30.9.00	3		Val-de-Reuil	14	Feb
8:45.84	Wondemagegn	Zerfe	ETH-J	26.10.02	4		Val-de-Reuil	14	Feb
8:46.86#	Kate	Grace	USA	24.10.88	2		Seattle	1	Feb
8:47.31#	Courtney	Frerichs	USA	18.1.93	3		Seattle	1	Feb
8:47.74	Roseline	Chepngetich	KEN	17.6.97	5		Val-de-Reuil	14	Feb
8:47.82	Aberash	Minsewo	ETH-J	22.2.01	5		Eaubonne	17	Feb
8:47.97	Julie-Anne	Staehli	CAN	21.12.93	1rE		Boston (R)	24	Jan
8:48.27	Ciara	Mageean	IRL	12.3.92	1		Athlone	12	Feb
8:48.73#	Emily	Infeld	USA	21.3.90	1		Seattle	14	Feb
8:48.74	Gloria	Kite	KEN	29.12.98	4		Karlsruhe	31	Jan
8:48.85	Selamawit	Bayoulgn	ISR	24.3.94	6		Eaubonne	17	Feb
8:48.92	Nicole	Hutchinson	CAN	17.6.97	1		New York (A)	25	Jan
8:48.94	Allie	Ostrander	USA	24.12.96	1	Millrose	New York (A)	8	Feb
8:49.49	Rosie	Clarke	GBR	17.11.91	2		Athlone	12	Feb
8:49.63#	Whittni	Orton	USA		2		Seattle	14	Feb
8:49.74	Laura	Galván	MEX	5.10.91	3	Millrose	New York (A)	8	Feb
8:49.78	Melissa	Courtney-Bryant	GBR	30.8.93	1		Dortmund	9	Feb
8:50.04+	Konstanze	Klosterhalfen	GER	18.2.97	1	in 5000	Boston (A)	27	Feb
8:50.99	Yelena	Korobkina	RUS	25.11.90	1	NC	Moskva	25	Feb
8:51.06	Claudia	Bobocea	ROU	11.6.92	5		Karlsruhe	31	Jan
8:51.39#	Vanessa	Fraser	USA	27.7.95	4		Seattle	1	Feb
8:51.49	Jenny	Simpson	USA	23.8.86	1		Winston-Salem	8	Feb

WOMEN 2020

3000 - 5000 METRES

Mark	Name		Nat	Born	Pos	Meet	Venue	Date	
8:51.78	Dana	Giordano	USA	30.12.93	1		Boston (A)	14	Feb
8:51.91	Taylor	Werner	USA	1.5.98	4	Millrose	New York (A)	8	Feb
8:52.53	Anna	Shchagina	RUS	7.12.91	2	NC	Moskva	25	Feb
8:52.94	Heidi	See	AUS	9.8.89	2		New York (A)	25	Jan
8:53.06	Erika	Kemp	USA	26.1.95	5	Millrose	New York (A)	8	Feb
8:53.69	Alicia	Monson	USA	13.5.98	6	Millrose	New York (A)	8	Feb
8:54.19#	Jessica	Tonn	USA	15.2.92	5		Seattle	1	Feb
8:54.40	Megan	Mansy	USA	27.3.94	2		Boston (A)	14	Feb
8:54.43	Emily	Lipari	USA	19.11.92	3		New York (A)	25	Jan
8:54.66	Weini	Kelati	ERI	1.12.96	7	Millrose	New York (A)	8	Feb
8:54.72#	Ella	Donaghu	USA	13.4.98	3		Seattle	14	Feb

Mark	Name		Nat	Born	Pos Date	Mark	Name		Nat	Born	Pos Date
8:55.26#	Mel	Lawrence	USA	29.8.89	1 Feb	8:59.83	Svetlana	Aplachkina	RUS	28.11.92	25 Feb
8:55.56	Yekaterina	Ivonina	RUS	14.6.94	25 Feb	8:59.93	Victoria	Gerlach	USA	2.6.94	14 Feb
8:55.67#	Katie	Izzo	USA	22.12.96	14 Feb	8:59.97+	Katrina	Coogan	USA	15.11.93	25 Jan
8:56.24#	Katie	Rainsberger	USA	18.8.98	14 Feb	9:00.05	Natalya	Aristarkhova	RUS	31.10.89	25 Feb
8:56.35	Mercy	Chepkurui	KEN	16.9.00	17 Feb	9:00.15#	Katie	Mackey	USA	12.11.87	18 Jan
8:56.54+	Elle	Purrier	USA	20.2.95	25 Jan	9:00.42	Shannon	Osika	USA	15.6.93	25 Jan
8:56.54	Amy-Eloise	Neale	GBR	5.8.95	25 Jan	9:00.50#		Xu Shuangshuang	CHN	6.4.96	1 Feb
8:56.60+	Emma	Coburn	USA	19.10.90	25 Jan	9:00.76	Amanda	Eccleston	USA	18.6.90	25 Jan
8:56.63#	Carina	Viljoen	RSA	15.4.97	14 Feb	9:00.89	Allie	Schadler	USA	7.7.99	28 Feb
8:56.76 mx	Samrawit	Mengsteab	SWE	15.4.90	1 Feb	9:00.95#	Eleanor	Fulton	USA	17.5.93	1 Feb
8:56.82	Grace	Forbes	USA	13.10.00	28 Feb	9:01.08#	Mariah	Kelly	CAN	19.8.91	18 Jan
8:56.89+	Dominique	Scott	RSA	24.6.92	25 Jan	9:01.36	Paige	Stoner	USA	31.1.96	25 Jan
8:57.63	Amy	Cashin	AUS	28.7.94	28 Feb	9:01.51	Alexandra	Lucki	CAN	30.7.96	14 Feb
8:57.84	Regan	Yee	CAN	4.7.95	8 Feb	9:01.67#	Carmela	Cardama	ESP	4.12.96	14 Feb
8:58.14+	Jessica	O'Connell	CAN	10.2.89	25 Jan	9:02.11	Olga	Vovk	RUS	13.2.93	25 Feb
8:58.23	Josette	Norris	USA	15.12.95	14 Feb	9:02.89	Anastasiya	Aleksandrova	RUS	16.2.94	25 Jan
8:59.19#	Allie	Buchalski	USA	12.1.95	18 Jan	9:04.50	Abbie	McNulty	USA	25.2.96	25 Jan
8:59.21+	Stephanie	Garcia	USA	3.5.88	25 Jan	9:04.75	Bri	Ilarda	AUS	19.2.96	28 Feb
8:59.28	Erin	Teschuk	CAN	25.10.94	14 Feb	9:04.78	Maja	Alm	DEN	10.7.88	23 Feb
8:59.38i#	Jessica	Lawson	USA	25.1.99	14 Feb						

JUNIORS

5 juniors in main list + 2 indoors. 7 performances (2 indoors) by 7 women to 8:55.0 and further juniors:

8:57.12	Rebecca	Mwangi	KEN-	15.6.01	2	Miyoshia	25	Sep
8:57.16	Esther	Wambui	KEN-Y	8.5.03	1	Miyoshi	12	Sep
9:01.36mx	Imogen	Stewart	AUS-Y	27.7.05	1	Canberra	27	Nov
9:02.8A	Judy	Chepkoech	KEN-Y	1.1.04	1	Nairobi	20	Nov
9:02.86	Azusa	Mihara (10)	JPN-Y	16.2.03	6	Chitose	18	Jul
9:03.60	Nanaka	Yonezawa	JPN-Y	28.2.04	1	Ichinoseki	26	Sep
9:05.17	Kokone	Sugimori	JPN-Y	19.11.04	2	Ichinoseki	26	Sep

2 MILES – INDOORS

9:29.17	Elle	Purrier	USA	20.2.95	1	Boston (R)	25	Jan
9:31.98	Dominique	Scott	RSA	24.6.92	2	Boston (R)	25	Jan
9:32.81	Emma	Coburn	USA	19.10.90	3	Boston (R)	25	Jan

Boston (R) 25 Jan: 4, 9:36.52 Katrina Coogan USA; 5. 9:36.79 Jessica O'Connell CAN; 6. 9:39.11 Stephanie Garcia USA

5000 METRES

14:06.62	Letesenbet	Gidey	ETH	20.3.98	1		Valencia	7 Oct
14:22.12	Hellen	Obiri	KEN	13.12.89	1	Herc	Monaco	14 Aug
14:23.92	Shelby	Houlihan	USA	8.2.93	1		Portland	10 Jul
14:26.34	Karissa	Schweizer	USA	4.5.96	2		Portland	10 Jul
14:26.57		Gidey			2	Herc	Monaco	14 Aug
14:35.44	Laura	Weightman	GBR	1.7.91	3	Herc	Monaco	14 Aug
14:37.85	Sifan	Hassan	NED	1.1.93	1	GS	Ostrava	8 Sep
14:38e+		Hassan			1	in 10k	Hengelo	10 Oct
14:40.51	Sheila	Chelangat	KEN	11.4.98	2	GS	Ostrava	8 Sep
14:40.70	Yasemin	Can	TUR	11.12.96	3	GS	Ostrava	8 Sep
14:43.80	Jessica	Hull	AUS	22.10.96	4	Herc	Monaco	14 Aug
14:45.11	Shannon	Rowbury (10)	USA	19.9.84	5	Herc	Monaco	14 Aug
14:46.22	Gudaf	Tsegay	ETH	23.1.97	4	GS	Ostrava	8 Sep
14:48.02	Elise	Cranny	USA	8.5.96	1		Portland	30 Jun
14:50.06	Courtney (15/13)	Frerichs	USA	18.1.93	2		Portland	30 Jun
14:54.03	Tsehay	Gemechu	ETH	12.12.98	5	GS	Ostrava	8 Sep
14:55.01	Beatrice	Chepkoech	KEN	6.7.91	6	Herc	Monaco	14 Aug
14:55.32	Rebecca	Mwangi	KEN-J	15.6.01	1		Kumagaya	20 Sep
14:55.83	Hitomi	Niiya	JPN	26.2.88	2		Kumagaya	20 Sep
14:57.37	Eilish	McColgan	GBR	25.11.90	7	Herc	Monaco	14 Aug
14:59.37	Ririka	Hironaka	JPN	24.11.00	3		Kumagaya	20 Sep
15:02.62	Nozomi (20)	Tanaka	JPN	4.9.99	1		Abashiri	15 Jul

5000 METRES

Mark	Name		Nat	Born	Pos	Meet	Venue	Date	
15:03.09	Helen	Lobun	KEN	18.3.99	2		Abashiri	15	Jul
15:03.49	Rosemary	Wanjiru	KEN	9.12.94	1		Fukagawa	8	Jul
15:04.32	Joan	Chepkemoi	KEN	24.11.93	3		Abashiri	15	Jul
15:05.78	Kaede	Hagitani	JPN	10.10.00	4		Abashiri	15	Jul
15:06.66	Mao	Ichiyama	JPN	29.5.97	1		Chitose	18	Jul
15:06.71A	Agnes	Tirop	KEN	23.10.95	2	Keino	Nairobi	3	Oct
15:07.13	Cynthia	Baire	KEN-J	2.12.02	2		Chitose	18	Jul
15:07.52mx	Judith	Jepngetich	KEN-J	24.12.02	1		Hiroshima	29	Nov
15:09.32	Agnes	Mwikali	KEN-J	15.12.02	1		Kasaoka	3	Nov
15:09.63	Tabitha	Kamau	KEN	3.7.00	3	JPN Ch	Osaka	4	Dec
	(30)								
15:10.01	Lauren	Paquette	USA	27.6.86	1		Van Nuys	22	Aug
15:10.10	Margaret	Ekidor	KEN-J	26.6.02	1		Niigata	29	Oct
15:10.31mx	Fabienne	Schlumpf	SUI	17.11.90	1	NC	Bulle	21	Aug
15:10.42	Colleen	Quigley	USA	20.11.92	3		Portland	30	Jun
15:11.11A	Margaret	Kipkemboi	KEN	9.2.93	3	Keino	Nairobi	3	Oct
15:11.50	Kellyn	Taylor	USA	22.7.86	2		Van Nuys	22	Aug
15:13.38A	Tsigie	Gebreselama	ETH	30.9.00	4	Keino	Nairobi	3	Oct
15:13.44	Zeyituna	Husan	ETH	12.1.99	3		Chitose	18	Jul
15:14.71	Alicia	Monson	USA	13.5.98	3		Van Nuys	22	Aug
15:14.84	Winnie	Jerotich	KEN	27.11.99	5		Abashiri	15	Jul
	(40)								
15:16.50	Melissa	Courtney-Bryant	GBR	30.8.93	6	GS	Ostrava	8	Sep
15:16.52	Sayaka	Sato	JPN	27.5.94	5		Kumagaya	20	Sep
15:17.72	Emily	Lipari	USA	19.11.92	3		San Juan Capistrano	4	Dec
15:18.03	Sharon	Lokedi	KEN	10.3.95	4		Van Nuys	22	Aug
15:18.06	Dana	Giordano	USA	30.12.93	4		San Juan Capistrano	4	Dec
15:18.25	Gwen	Jorgensen	USA	25.4.86	4		Portland	30	Jun
15:18.56	Esther	Wambui	KEN-Y	8.5.03	2		Kasaoka	3	Nov
15:18.82	Stella	Rutto	KEN	12.12.96	1		Cluj-Napoca	5	Sep
15:19.21	Stephanie	Bruce	USA	14.1.84	5		Van Nuys	22	Aug
15:19.67	Mikuni	Yada	JPN	29.10.99	4		Chitose	18	Jul
	(50)								
15:19.79A	Joyce	Chepkemoi Tele	KEN	3.5.95	5	Keino	Nairobi	3	Oct
15:20.02	Pauline	Kamulu	KEN	30.12.94	1		Inzai	26	Sep
15:20.60	Genevieve	Gregson	AUS	4.8.89	3		Melbourne	6	Feb
15:20.80	Molly	Huddle	USA	31.8.84	1		Newton	7	Sep
15:20.93	Maureen	Koster	NED	3.7.92	7	GS	Ostrava	8	Sep
15:21.0mx	Anna Emilie	Møller	DEN	28.7.97	1		Aarhus	1	Aug
15:21.44	Laura	Petersen	DEN	28.12.00	8	GS	Ostrava	8	Sep
15:22.14	Jenny	Blundell	AUS	9.5.94	4		Melbourne	6	Feb
15:23.88	Kasumi	Nishihara	JPN	1.3.89	5	NC	Osaka	4	Dec
15:24.24	Momoka	Kawaguchi	JPN	28.6.98	6	NC	Osaka	4	Dec
	(60)								
15:24.61	Yuri	Tazaki	JPN-J	13.2.01	7	NC	Osaka	4	Dec

15:25.14	Yuna	Wada	JPN	7.8.99	4 Dec
15:25.22	Linden	Hall	AUS	29.6.91	6 Feb
15:25.94	Shiori	Yano	JPN	11.2.95	18 Jul
15:26.34	Yuka	Ando	JPN	16.3.94	20 Sep
15:26.42mx	Diane	van Es	NED	22.3.99	7 Aug
15:26.48	Isobel	Batt-Doyle	AUS	14.9.95	2 Dec
15:27.46mx	Alina	Reh	GER	23.5.97	26 Jul
15:27.46	Elly	Henes	USA	13.10.98	7 Sep
15:27.54	Meraf	Bahta	SWE	24.6.89	8 Sep
15:27.57mx	Elena	Burkard	GER	10.2.92	16 Jun
15:27.89	Elaina	Tabb	USA	17.12.91	7 Sep
15:28.24mx	Camille	Buscomb	NZL	11.7.90	18 Dec
15:28.51	Dominique	Scott	RSA	24.6.92	22 Aug
15:29.03	Rino	Goshima	JPN	29.10.97	4 Dec
15:29.14	Laura	Galván	MEX	5.10.91	4 Dec
15:29.18	Sara	Miyake	JPN	26.7.99	18 Jul
15:29.43	Chemtai	Salpeter	ISR	12.12.88	21 Jun
15:29.65	Emily	Brichacek	AUS	7.7.90	6 Feb
15:29.91	Misuzu	Nakahara	JPN	29.11.94	4 Dec
15:30.04	Maho	Shimizu	JPN	7.5.95	15 Jul
15:30.15	Rose	Davies	AUS	21.12.99	6 Feb
15:30.86	Marielle	Hall	USA	28.1.92	30 Jun
15:31.34	Svetlana	Aplachkina	RUS	28.11.92	8 Sep
15:31.45	Danielle	Jones	USA	21.8.96	22 Aug
15:31.49	Rina	Nabeshima	JPN	16.12.93	20 Sep
15:31.51	Honami	Maeda	JPN	17.7.96	18 Jul
15:31.61	Miyaka	Sugata	JPN-J	9.3.01	20 Sep
15:31.87	Svetlana	Karamasheva	RUS	24.5.88	8 Sep
15:31.97	Hannah	Everson	USA	21.4.94	15 Aug

15:32.17	Caitlin	Adams	AUS	7.7.97	6 Feb
15:32.46	Harumi	Okamoto	JPN	7.2.98	4 Nov
15:32.77	Rika	Kaseda	JPN	2.3.99	14 Nov
15:32.93	Yekaterina	Ishova	RUS	17.1.89	8 Sep
15:32.96	Sakiho	Tsutsui	JPN	19.1.96	22 Sep
15:32.98	Eleanor	Fulton	USA	17.5.93	4 Dec
15:33.04	Aude	Korotchansky	FRA	12.9.91	19 Jul
15:33.04	Martha	Mokaya	KEN	1.3.00	5 Dec
15:33.47	Allie	Schadler	USA	7.7.99	4 Dec
15:33.54	Yuki	Nakamura (100)	JPN-J	22.8.00	4 Dec
15:33.78	Anastasiya	Aleksandrova	RUS	16.2.94	8 Sep
15:34.02	Haruka	Yamaguchi	JPN	7.7.87	15 Jul
15:34.22	Rina	Miyata	JPN	5.6.00	4 Jul
15:34.28	Sarah	Lancaster	USA	1.12.87	4 Dec
15:34.47	Jenna	Hutchins	USA-Y	25.3.04	11 Dec
15:34.75	Natosha	Rogers	USA	7.5.91	15 Aug
15:35.17	Annie	Rodenfels	USA	24.7.96	11 Dec
15:36.05	Kim	Conley	USA	14.3.86	4 Dec
15:36.47	Misaki	Tanabe	JPN	31.8.95	4 Dec
15:36.58	Amy-Eloise	Neale	GBR	5.8.95	7 Sep
15:36.61A	Beatrice	Chebet	KEN	5.3.00	3 Oct
15:36.68	Heidi	See	AUS	9.8.89	4 Dec
15:37.13mx	Francesca	Tommasi	ITA	8.8.98	16 Jun
15:37.37	Mary	Sipuko	KEN	10.5.99	22 Sep
15:37.43	Rei	Ohara	JPN	10.8.92	14 Nov
15:37.44	Seira	Fuwa	JPN-Y	25.3.03	6 Dec
15:37.52	Jessica	Judd	GBR	7.1.95	4 Dec
15:37.60	Grace	Barnett	USA	29.6.95	4 Dec
15:38.08	Akane	Ogasawara	JPN-J	25.2.01	5 Dec

340 5000 - 10,000 METRES

Mark	Name		Nat	Born	Pos	Meet	Venue	Date
15:38.27	Rosiin	Flanagan	IRL	2.5.97	4 Dec	15:39.34	Irene Sánchez-Escribano ESP	25.9.92 4 Aug
15:38.27	Mana	Taniguchi	JPN	29.5.99	5 Dec	15:39.57	Miku Moribayashi JPN	5.9.99 5 Dec
15:37.39mx	Linn	Nilsson	SWE	15.10.90	25 Jul	15:39.63	Shiho Kaneshige JPN	7.6.89 4 Dec
15:38.33	Marusa	Mismas	SLO	24.10.94	13 Jun	15:39.66	Liv Westphal FRA	22.12.93 14 Aug
15:38.53	Maggie	Montoya	USA	2.5.95	11 Jul	15:39.76	Renata Plis POL	5.2.85 11 Sep
15:38.95	Juri	Ichikawa	JPN	25.3.98	14 Nov	15:39.80	Stephanie Garcia USA	3.5.88 4 Dec
15:39.32	Kayoko	Fukushi	JPN	25.3.82	27 Sep	15:39.85	Misaki Eguchi JPN	30.3.95 5 Dec
15:39.33	Tomomi Musembi Takamatsu JPN			23.2.00	5 Dec	15:40.00	Naomi Musson (135) KEN	6.12.98 5 Dec

Illegal shoes – disqualified: 15:01.13 Karoline Bjerkeli Grøvdal NOR 14.6.90 1 Oslo (Bisl) 26 Sep

Indoors

14:30.79	Konstanze	Klosterhalfen	GER	18.2.97	1		Boston (A)	27 Feb
14:48.51	Vanessa	Fraser	USA	27.7.95	2		Boston (A)	27 Feb
14:51.91	Emily	Infeld	USA	21.3.90	3		Boston (A)	27 Feb
14:58.67	Jenny	Simpson	USA	23.8.86	1		Boston (A)	14 Feb
15:07.44	Emily	Lipari	USA	19.11.92	1		Boston (A)	1 Feb
15:10.98	Gwen	Jorgensen	USA	25.4.86	5		Boston (A)	27 Feb
15:12.33	Jessica	Tonn	USA	15.2.92	6		Boston (A)	27 Feb
15:13.04	Sharon	Lokedi	KEN	10.3.95	2		Boston (A)	1 Feb
15:14.76	Erika	Kemp	USA	26.1.95	7		Boston (A)	27 Feb
15:17.11	Danielle	Jones	USA	21.8.96	2		Boston (A)	14 Feb
15:19.71	Allie	Ostrander	USA	24.12.96	8		Boston (A)	27 Feb
15:20.73	Marielle	Hall	USA	28.1.92	9		Boston (A)	27 Feb
15:20.84	Dominique	Scott	RSA	24.6.92	3		Boston (A)	1 Feb
15:25.11	Nicole	Hutchinson	CAN	17.6.97	1 Feb	15:32.72	Amy-Eloise Neale GBR	5.8.95 27 Feb
15:25.59	Heidi	See	AUS	9.8.89	27 Feb	15:33.17	Regan Yee CAN	4.7.95 15 Feb
15:26.22	Makena	Morley	USA	21.11.96	14 Feb	15:37.35	Mercy Chelangat KEN	11.7.97 15 Feb

JUNIORS

7 juniors in main list. 10 performances by 6 women to 15:20.0. Additional marks and further juniors:

Baire	15:11.29 1	Isahaya		11 Oct	15:21.54 1	Minamasatsuma	29 Aug
	15:14.30 1	Kagshima		5 Jul			
Mwikali	15:15.14 1	Miyoshi		26 Sep			
15:31.60	Chika	Sugata	JPN	3.9.01	9	Kumagaya	20 Sep
15:33.54	Yuki	Nakamura	JPN	22.8.00	12 NC	Osaka	4 Nov
15:37.44	Seira	Fuwa	JPN-Y	25.3.03	1	Yokohama	6 Dec
15:38.08	Akane	Ogasawara	JPN	25.2.01	2	Yamaguchi	5 Dec

10,000 METRES

29:36.67	Sifan	Hassan	NED	1.1.93	1		Hengelo	10 Oct
30:20.44	Hitomi	Niiya	JPN	26.2.88	1	NC	Osaka	4 Dec
30:38.18	Rosemary	Wanjiru	KEN	9.12.94	1		Abashiri	15 Jul
30:57.73	Tsehay	Gemechu	ETH	12.12.98	2		Hengelo	10 Oct
31:06.46	Sarah	Chelangat	UGA-J	5.6.01	3		Hengelo	10 Oct
31:07.60mx	Kellyn	Taylor	USA	22.7.86	1		Santa Barbara	1 Sep
31:08.09	Evaline	Chirchir	KEN	10.5.98	4		Hengelo	10 Oct
31:09.79	Rachel	Schneider	USA	18.7.91	1		San Juan Capistrano	5 Dec
31:10.08	Weini	Kelati	ERI	1.12.96	2		San Juan Capistrano	5 Dec
31:10.84	Alicia	Monson (10)	USA	13.5.98	3		San Juan Capistrano	5 Dec
	(10./10)							
31:11.07	Sharon	Lokedi	KEN	10.3.95	4		San Juan Capistrano	5 Dec
31:11.56	Mao	Ichiyama	JPN	29.5.97	2	NC	Osaka	4 Oct
31:12.28	Natosha	Rogers	USA	7.5.91	5		San Juan Capistrano	5 Dec
31:15.65		Taylor			6		San Juan Capistrano	5 Dec
31:22.86	Danielle	Shanahan	USA	13.8.94	7		San Juan Capistrano	5 Dec
31:23.30		Ichiyama			2		Abashiri	15 Jul
31:24.47	Stephanie	Bruce	USA	14.1.84	8		San Juan Capistrano	5 Dec
31:25.17	Gloria	Kite	KEN	29.12.98	5		Hengelo	10 Oct
31:30.19	Sayaka	Sato	JPN	27.5.94	3	NC	Osaka	4 Dec
31:31.52	Rina	Nabeshima	JPN	16.12.93	4	NC	Osaka	4 Dec
31:34.39	Mikuni	Yada	JPN	29.10.99	5	NC	Osaka	4 Dec
31:34.94	Honami	Maeda	JPN	17.7.96	1		Fukagawa	8 Jul
	(20)							
31:35.63	Erika	Kemp	USA	26.1.95	9		San Juan Capistrano	5 Dec
31:36.04	Ayumi	Hagiwara	JPN	1.6.92	6	NC	Osaka	4 Dec
31:36.19	Sakiho	Tsutsui	JPN	19.1.96	7	NC	Osaka	4 Dec
31:37.71	Yuka	Ando	JPN	16.3.94	8	NC	Osaka	4 Dec
31:39.86	Rika	Kaseda	JPN	2.3.99	9	NC	Osaka	4 Dec
31:40.67	Therese	Johaug	NOR	25.6.88	1		Oslo	11 Jun
31:45.27	Elaina	Tabb	USA	17.12.91	10		San Juan Capistrano	5 Dec
31:45.83	Tabitha	Kamau	KEN	3.7.00	1		Yamaguchi	5 Dec
31:46.84	Shiori	Yano	JPN	11.2.95	10	NC	Osaka	4 Dec
31:48.72	Olivia	Pratt	USA	21.1.94	11		San Juan Capistrano	5 Dec
	(30)							

10,000 METRES 341

Mark	Name		Nat	Born	Pos	Meet	Venue	Date
31:52.45+	Sheila	Chelangat	KEN	11.4.98		in 1 hour	Bruxelles	4 Sep
31:53.72mx	Lauren	Paquette	USA	27.6.86	3		Santa Barbara	1 Sep
31:54.63	Laura	Galván	MEX	5.10.91	12		San Juan Capistrano	5 Dec
32:06.46	Mizuki	Matsuda	JPN	31.5.95	2		Kumagaya	18 Sep
32:06.87	Maggie	Montoya	USA	2.5.95	14		San Juan Capistrano	5 Dec
32:07.79	Zeyituna	Husan	ETH	12.1.99	2		Isahaya	11 Oct
32:08.67	Narumi	Kobayashi	JPN	17.4.00	4		Abashiri	15 Jul
32:09.37	Maria	Mettler	USA	14.3.99	1B		San Juan Capistrano	5 Dec
32:09.57	Vanessa	Fraser	USA	27.7.95	15		San Juan Capistrano	5 Dec
32:09.82	Carrie (40)	Verdon	USA	8.3.94	2B		San Juan Capistrano	5 Dec
32:09.91	Misaki	Nishida	JPN	7.8.91	11	NC	Osaka	4 Dec
32:10.29	Ikumi	Fukura	JPN	11.8.97	12	NC	Osaka	4 Dec
32:10.31	Jaci	Smith	USA	5.1.97	1		NewYork	23 Oct
32:10.56	Hikari	Onishi	JPN	26.4.00	13	NC	Osaka	4 Dec
32:10.69	Shuri	Ogasawara	JPN	3.10.00	14	NC	Osaka	4 Dec
32:11.66	Yuka	Suzuki	JPN	14.9.99	15	NC	Osaka	4 Dec
32:11.92	Samantha	Palmer	USA	17.6.91	3B		San Juan Capistrano	5 Dec
32:11.93	Jessica	Watychowicz	USA	27.1.91	4B		San Juan Capistrano	5 Dec
32:12.06	Elly	Henes	USA	13.10.98	16		San Juan Capistrano	5 Dec
32:12.22	Gwen (50)	Jorgensen	USA	25.4.86	17		San Juan Capistrano	5 Dec
32:12.28	Fiona	O'Keeffe	USA	24.5.98	5B		San Juan Capistrano	5 Dec
32:12.49	Helen	Tola	ETH	21.11.94	1		Uster	26 Jun
32:13.04mx	Isobel	Batt-Doyle	AUS	14.9.95	1		Adelaide	24 Oct
32:13.23	Misaki	Kato	JPN	15.6.91	1		Miyoshi	26 Sep
32:13.54	Amy	Davis	USA	15.2.97	18		San Juan Capistrano	5 Dec
32:14.23	Maya	Weigel	USA	1.7.95	6B		San Juan Capistrano	5 Dec
32:15.10	Natsumi	Matsushita	JPN	22.1.95	2r2		Yamaguchi	5 Dec
32:15.69	Aysede	Bayisa	ETH	16.4.87	3		Lake Balboa	29 Aug
32:15.88	Momoka	Kawaguchi	JPN	28.6.98	6		Abashiri	15 Jul
32:16.37mx	Fabienne (60)	Schlumpf	SUI	17.11.90	1	NC	Uster	26 Jun
32:16.97	Miki	Hirai	JPN	12.2.96	3r2		Yamaguchi	5 Dec
32:17.65	Kayoko	Fukushi	JPN	25.3.82	3		Osaka	25 Sep
32:19.37	Cailie	Logue	USA	4.1.99	19		San Juan Capistrano	5 Dec
32:19.65mx	Laura	Petersen	DEN	28.12.00	1mx		Odense	1 Aug
32:20.75	Jasmijn	Lau	NED	11.3.99	1		Leiden	19 Sep
32:22.56	Emily	Durgin	USA	15.5.94	20		San Juan Capistrano	5 Dec
32:25.41	Bo	Ummels	NED	24.8.93	2		Leiden	19 Sep
32:28.89	Katie	Izzo	USA	22.12.96	21		San Juan Capistrano	5 Dec
32:28.90mx	Haruka	Yamaguchi	JPN	7.7.87	1		Tokyo	24 Jul
32:30.13	Paige (70)	Stoner	USA	31.1.96	6		Lake Balboa	29 Aug
32:31.37	Nao	Yamamoto	JPN	20.10.96	15 Jul	32:42.38	Yuri Karasawa JPN 25.11.95	5 Dec
32:31.69	Luiza	Gega	ALB	5.11.88	11 Aug	32:42.72	Valeriya Zinenko UKR 6.11.95	15 Aug
32:32.03	Alia	Gray	USA	12.11.88	5 Dec	32:44.99	Kaori Morita JPN 19.9.95	4 Oct
32:32.07	Hisami	Ishii	JPN	10.8.95	5 Dec	32:45.81mx	Domenika Mayer GER 9.10.90	11 Jul
32:33.06	Sarah	Pagano	USA	23.7.91	5 Dec	32:46.94mx	Carolina Wikström SWE 4.9.93	23 Jun
32:33.44	Keira	D'Amato	USA	21.10.84	18 Jul	32:47.00	Jessa Hanson (100) USA 7.2.97	5 Dec
32:34.09	Anne-Marie	Blaney	USA	9.9.93	5 Dec	32:47.17	Akane Yabushita JPN 6.6.91	5 Dec
32:35.26	Winnie	Jerotich	KEN	27.11.99	5 Dec	32:47.57	Kaena Takeyama JPN 30.10.95	5 Dec
32:35.52	Hannah	Everson	USA	21.4.94	5 Dec	32:49.08	Maxena Morley USA 21.11.96	29 Aug
32:35.92mx	Jessica	Stenson	AUS	15.8.87	24 Oct	32:49.93	Carla Salomé Rocha POR 25.4.90	18 Dec
32:37.35	Semira	Mezeghrane-Saad	FRA	29.12.79	29 Aug	32:52.12	Brenda Flores MEX 4.9.91	5 Dec
32:37.47	Susan	Jeptoo	FRA	7.3.87	29 Aug	32:52.19	Kaede Okajima JPN 5.10.99	5 Dec
32:37.90	Wakana	Itsuki	JPN	7.4.94	5 Dec	32:52.83	Yuki Nakamura JPN 22.8.00	15 Jul
32:38.20	Jeralyn	Poe	USA	22.7.98	5 Dec	32:52.89	Allie Kieffer USA 16.9.87	23 Oct
32:38.56mx	Emma	Wilson	USA	3.11.00	12 Dec	32:53.14	Madoka Nakano JPN 14.8.91	5 Dec
32:38.78	Yukina	Ueda	JPN	7.2.98	5 Dec	32:53.47	Ryo Koido JPN 19.9.97	5 Dec
32:39.95	Rei	Ohara	JPN	10.8.90	5 Dec	32:53.77	Yevheniya Prokofyeva UKR 5.6.95	15 Aug
32:40.00	Alexis	Zeis	USA	.96	5 Dec	32:54.38	Yuka Hori JPN 13.6.96	15 Jul
32:40.57	Ursula	Sánchez	MEX	15..9.87	5 Dec	32:55.25	Valeria Straneo ITA 5.4.76	27 Sep
32:41.56	Moeno	Shimizu	JPN	20.3.97	5 Dec	32:56.23	Yelena Korobkina RUS 25.11.90	21 Aug
32:42.08	Yuna	Daito	JPN	27.10.97	5 Dec	32:57.57	Mao Uesugi JPN 16.8.95	5 Dec
32:42.37mx	Tara	Palm	AUS	28.7.85	24 Oct	32:59.83	Genevieve Gregson (116) AUS 4.8.89	1 Aug

Best in women only race: 32:01.25 Lauren Paquette USA 27.6.86 13 San Juan Capistrano 5 Dec

JUNIORS

| 31:06.46 | Sarah | Chelangat | UGA | 5.6.01 | 3 | | Hengelo | 10 Oct |
| 33:16.49 | Rinka | Hida | JPN | 11.1.01 | 1 | | Kashihara | 28 Nov |

1 HOUR

| 18.930m | Sifan | Hassan | NED | 1.1.93 | 1 | | Bruxelles | 4 Sep |

WOMEN 2020

1 HOUR - 10 KILOMETRES ROAD

Mark	Name		Nat	Born	Pos	Meet	Venue		Date	
18.904 dq	Brigid	Kosgei	KEN	20.2.94	dq		Bruxelles		4	Sep
18,571	Lonah Chemtai	Salpeter	ISR	12.12.88	2		Bruxelles		4	Sep
18,341	Eva	Cherono	KEN	15.8.96	3		Bruxelles		4	Sep
17,974	Helen	Tola	ETH	21.11.94	4 Sep	17,955	Sarah	Lahti	SWE 18.2.95	4 Sep
						17,930	Molly	Huddle	USA 31.8.84	1 Nov

10 KILOMETRES ROAD

Mark	Name		Nat	Born	Pos	Meet	Venue	Date	
29:46	Sheila	Chepkirui	KEN	27.12.90	1		Valencia	12	Jan
29:50	Rosemary	Wanjiru	KEN	9.12.94	2		Valencia	12	Jan
29:51	Norah	Tanui	KEN	2.10.95	3		Valencia	12	Jan
30:18+	Ababel	Yeshaneh	ETH	22.7.91		in HMar	Ras Al Khaimah	21	Feb
30:18+	Brigid	Kosgei	KEN	20.2.94		in HMar	Ras Al Khaimah	21	Feb
30:30+	Yalemzerf	Yehualaw	ETH	3.8.99		in HMar	Ras Al Khaimah	21	Feb
30:32+	Peres	Jepchirchir	KEN	27.9.93	1	in HMar	Praha	5	Sep
30:32	Karoline Bjerkeli	Grøvdal	NOR	14.6.90	1		Hole	17	Oct
30:33+		Wanjiru				in HMar	Ras Al Khaimah	21	Feb
30:34+	Evaline	Chirchir	KEN	10.5.98		in HMar	Ras Al Khaimah	21	Feb
30:34+	Joan	Chelimo	KEN	10.11.90		in HMar	Ras Al Khaimah	21	Feb
30:43	Margaret	Kipkemboi	KEN	9.2.93	1		Bolzano	31	Dec
30:44	Dorcas	Tuitoek	KEN	31.1.96	2		Bolzano	31	Dec
30:47+	Fancy	Chemutai	KEN	20.3.95		in HMar	Ras Al Khaimah	21	Feb
30:47+	Yasemin	Can	TUR	11.12.96		in HMar	Gdynia	17	Oct
30:47+	Joyciline	Jepkosgei	KEN	8.12.93		in HMar	Gdynia	17	Oct
30:47+		Yeshaneh				in HMar	Gdynia	17	Oct
30:47+	Zeineba	Yimer	ETH	17.6.98		in HMar	Gdynia	17	Oct
30:47+		Jepchirchir				in HMar	Gdynia	17	Oct
30:47+		Yehualaw				in HMar	Gdynia	17	Oct
30:47+	Melat	Kejeta	GER	27.9.92		in HMar	Gdynia	17	Oct
30:47		Tanui			3		Bolzano	31	Dec
30:49+		Yehualaw				in HMar	New Delhi	29	Nov
30:50	Bosena	Mulate	ETH	.00	4		Valencia	12	Jan
30:50+	Ruth	Chepngetich	KEN	8.8.94		in HMar	New Delhi	29	Nov
30:50+		Yeshaneh				in HMar	New Delhi	29	Nov
30:50+	Irene	Cheptai	KEN	4.2.92		in HMar	New Delhi	29	Nov
(26/20)									
30:52+	Netsanet	Gudeta	ETH	12.2.91		in HMar	Gdynia	17	Oct
30:53	Hellen	Obiri	KEN	13.12.89	1		Barcelona	31	Dec
30:57+	Dorcas	Kimeli	KEN	5.7.97		in HMar	Gdynia	17	Oct
30:57+	Brillian	Kipkoech	KEN	9.3.95		in HMar	Gdynia	17	Oct
30:59	Helen	Tola	ETH	21.11.94	1		Berlin	26	Sep
31:00+	Vivian	Kiplagat	KEN	9.11.91		in HMar	Ras Al Khaimah	21	Feb
31:00+	Genzebe	Dibaba	ETH	8.2.91		in HMar	Valencia	6	Oct
31:00+	Senbere	Teferi	ETH	3.5.95		in HMar	Valencia	6	Oct
31:01+	Degitu	Azimeraw	ETH	24.1.99		in HMar	Ras Al Khaimah	21	Feb
31:06+	Tsehay	Gemechu	ETH	12.12.98		in HMar	New Delhi	29	Nov
31:09	Lonah Chemtai	Salpeter	ISR	12.12.88	5		Valencia	12	Jan
31:09+	Magdalena	Shauri	TAN	25.2.96		in HMar	Ras Al Khaimah	21	Feb
Where better than 10,000m track times									
31:23	Selemawit	Bayoulgn	ISR	24.3.94	1		Tiberias	3	Jan
31:26	Alice	Reh	GER	23.5.97	1		Berlin	7	Jun
31:32+	Asnakech	Awoke	ETH	.94		in HMar	Barcelona	16	Feb
31:32+	Roza	Dereje	ETH	9.5.97		in HMar	Barcelona	16	Feb
31:33+	Helaria	Johannes	NAM	13.8.80	1	in HMar	Marugame	2	Feb
31:33+	Ashete	Bekere	ETH	17.4.88		in HMar	Barcelona	16	Feb
31:33+	Eva	Cherono	KEN	15.8.96		in HMar	New Delhi	29	Nov
31:35+	Meseret	Gola	ETH	30.12.97		in HMar	Gdynia	17	Oct
31:39	Agnes	Mwikali	KEN-J	15.12.02	1		Okayama	20	Dec
31:49	Yelena	Korobkina	RUS	25.11.90	1		Moskva	20	Sep
31:55	Rediet	Danile	ETH		6		Valencia	12	Jan
31:58+	Brenda	Jepleting	KEN			in HMar	Valencia	6	Oct
31:59+	Sinead	Diver	AUS	17.2.77	2	in HMar	Marugame	2	Feb
32:00	Rachael	Chebet	UGA	5.11.96	7		Valencia	12	Jan
32:00+	Charlotte	Purdue	GBR	10.6.91	3m		Marugame	2	Feb
32:00+	Tadu	Teshome	ETH-J	9.6.01		in HMar	Ras Al Khaimah	21	Feb
32:00	Genevieve	Gregson	AUS	4.8.89	1		Launceston	13	Dec
32:01	Yasemin	Can	TUR	1.8.92	1		Chunburi	26	Jan
32:02	Meraf	Bahta	SWE	21.8.96	1	NC	Anderstorp	11	Oct
32:02+	Emily	Sisson	USA	12.10.91		in HMar	Valencia	6	Oct
32:02	Rose	Davies	AUS	21.12.99	2		Launceston	13	Dec
32:03	Desta	Burka	ETH-J	17.4.01	2		Okayama	20	Dec

10 KM ROAD - HALF MARATHON

Mark	Name		Nat	Born	Pos	Meet	Venue	Date	
32:04	Naomi	Mussoni	KEN	6.12.98	3		Okayama	20	Dec
32:07	Pauline	Kamulu	KEN	30.12.94	2		Chonburi	26	Jan
32:08	Karolina	Nadolska	POL	6.9.81	8		Valencia	12	Jan
32:09	Liv	Westphal	FRA	22.12.93	1		Nice	5	Jan
32:10	Isobel	Batt-Doyle	AUS	14.9.95	3		Launceston	13	Dec
32:11	Zahra	El Boudadi	MAR		1		Casablanca	9	Feb
32:13A	Caroline	Gotonga	KEN	.96	2		Nairobi	8	Mar
32:14+	Fabienne	Schlumpf	SUI	17.11.90		in HMar	Gdynia	17	Oct
32:14	Tara	Palm	AUS	28.7.85	4		Launceston	13	Dec
32:15+	Juliet	Chekwel	UGA	25.5.90		in HMar	Gdynia	17	Oct
32:16	Mekdes	Woldu	ERI	20.10.92	2		Nice	5	Jan
32:17	Hajiba	Hasnaoui	MAR	18.4.88	2		Casablanca	9	Feb
32:17	Jessica	Judd	GBR	7.1.95	1		Partington	1	Mar
32:17	Sarah	Lahti	SWE	18.2.95	2		Albi	11	Dec
32:18	Gudaf	Tsegay	ETH	23.1.97	1		Jaén	18	Jan
32:19	Misaki	Hayashida	JPN	7.12.99	2		Yamaguchi	9	Feb
32:20	Miriam	Dattke	GER	24.6.98	3		Berlin	7	Jun
32:22	Miku	Moribayashi	JPN	5.9.99	4		Okayama	20	Dec
32:24	Gerda	Steyn	RSA	3.3.90	1		Dubai	24	Jan
32:24	Fatiha	Asmid	MAR	.92	1		Casablanca	9	Feb
32:26	Eilish	McColgan	GBR	25.11.90	2		Partington	1	Mar
32:29+	Goytatom	Gebreselassie	ETH	15.1.95		in HMar	Houston	19	Jan
32:29+	Ruti	Aga	ETH	16.1.94		in HMar	Houston	19	Jan
32:29+	Caroline	Rotich	KEN	13.5.84		in HMar	Houston	19	Jan
32:29+	Gelete	Burka	ETH	23.1.86		in HMar	Houston	19	Jan
32:29+	Monicah	Ngige Wanjuhi	KEN	7.11.93		in HMar	Houston	19	Jan
32:29+	Bontu	Edao	BRN	12.12.97		in HMar	Houston	19	Jan
32:32+	Sara	Hall	USA	15.4.83	19 Jan				
32:33+	Glenrose	Xaba	RSA	31.12.94	17 Oct				
32:34	Musuzu	Nakahara	JPN	29.11.94	20 Dec				
32:38	Carolina	Wikström	SWE	4.9.93	11 Oct				
32:39+		Choi Kyung-sun	KOR	16.3.92	2 Feb				
32:39	Aleksandra	Aleksandrova	RUS	16.2.94	20 Sep				
32:39	Nana	Sato	JPN	24.9.89	20 Dec				
32:40+	Molly	Seidel	USA	12.7.94	19 Jan				
32:40+	Katy	Jermann	USA	20.4.92	19 Jan				
32:40+	Charlott	Arter	GBR	18.6.91	16 Feb				
32:40+	Nazret	Weldu	ERI	1.1.90	29 Nov				
32:40+	Bekelech	Gudeta	ETH	11.10.97	29 No				
32:40+	Aliphine	Tuliamuk	USA	5.4.89	19 Jan				
32:40	Yumi	Yoshikawa	JPN	31.10.90	20 Dec				
32:41+	Mimi	Belete	BRN	9.6.88	29 Nov				
32:41	Mao	Uesugi	JPN	16.8.95	20 Dec				
32:42	Jennifer	Nesbitt	GBR	24.1.95	11 Jan				
32:42	Etenesh	Diro	ETH	10.5.91	26 Jan				
32:42	Ryo	Koido	JPN	19.9.97	20 Dec				
32:43	Shannon	Rowbury	USA	19.9.84	2 Feb				
32:43	Wafa	El Ghazour	MAR	17.2.88	9 Feb				
32:43	Ann Marie	McGlynn	IRL	22.2.80	18 Jul				
32:43	Chiara	Scherrer	SUI	24.1.96	27 Sep				
32:45	Toshika	Tamura	JPN	6.6.90	26 Jan				

15K, 20K See below in 15k and Half Marathon lists

HALF MARATHON

	20k	15k								
64:31	61:11	45:41	Ababel	Yeshaneh	ETH	22.7.91	1	RAK	Ras Al Khaimah	21 Feb
64:46	61:32	46:15	Yalemzerf	Yehualaw	ETH	3.8.99	1		New Delhi	29 Nov
64:49	61:29	45:40	Brigid	Kosgei	KEN	20.2.94	2	RAK	Ras Al Khaimah	21 Feb
65:06	61:44	46:15	Ruth	Chepngetich	KEN	8.8.94	2		New Delhi	29 Nov
65:16	62:04	46:24	Peres	Jepchirchir	KEN	27.9.93	1	WCh	Gdynia	17 Oct
65:18	62:04	46:25	Melat	Kejeta	GER	27.9.92	2	WCh	Gdynia	17 Oct
65:18	62:00	46:34	Genzebe	Dibaba	ETH	8.2.91	1		Valencia	6 Oct
65:19	62:04	46:25		Yehualaw			3	WCh	Gdynia	17 Oct
65:21	61:52	46:15		Yehualaw			3		New Delhi	29 Nov
65:34	62:10	46:14	Rosemary	Wanjiru	KEN	9.12.94	3	RAK	Ras Al Khaimah	21 Feb
65:34				Jepchirchir			1		Praha	5 Sep
65:39	62:17	46:24	Zeineba	Yimer	ETH	17.6.98	4	WCh	Gdynia	17 Oct
65:39	62:15	46:34	Sheila	Chepkirui (10)	KEN	27.12.90	2		Valencia	6 Oct
65:41	62:17	46:24		Yeshaneh			5	WCh	Gdynia	17 Oct
65:51	62:29	46:38	Senbere	Teferi	ETH	3.5.95	3		Valencia	6 Oct
65:58	62:27	46:24	Joyciline	Jepkosgei	KEN	8.12.93	6	WCh	Gdynia	17 Oct
66:01	62:34	46:13	Evaline	Chirchir	KEN	10.5.98	4	RAK	Ras Al Khaimah	21 Feb
66:16	62:42	46:13	Joan	Chelimo	KEN	10.11.90	5	RAK	Ras Al Khaimah	21 Feb
66:20	62:40	46:24	Yasemin	Can	TUR	1.8.92	7	WCh	Gdynia	17 Oct
66:35	63:14	46:24		Yehualew			6	RAK	Ras Al Khaimah	21 Feb
66:37	63:15	47:24	Ashete	Bekere	ETH	17.4.88	1		Barcelona	16 Feb
66:37	63:16	47:00	Magdalena	Shauri	TAN	25.2.96	7	RAK	Ras Al Khaimah	21 Feb
66:38	63:13	47:03	Hitomi	Niiya	JPN	26.2.88	1		Houston	19 Jan
66:38	63:16	47:00	Vivian	Kiplagat	KEN	9.11.91	8	RAK	Ras Al Khaimah	21 Feb
66:43	63:18		Irene	Cheptai (20)	KEN	4.2.92	4		New Delhi	29 Nov
66:46	63:18	47:08	Netsanet	Gudeta	ETH	12.2.91	8	WCh	Gdynia	17 Oct
66:47			Violah	Lagat	KEN	13.3.89	1		Napoli	23 Feb
				(27/22)						

HALF MARATHON

Mark			Name		Nat	Born	Pos	Meet	Venue	Date	
66:56	63:29	47:09	Brillian	Kipkoech	KEN	9.3.95	9	WCh	Gdynia	17	Oct
67:02	63:26	47:01	Degitu	Azimeraw	ETH	24.1.99	9	RAK	Ras Al Khaimah	21	Feb
67:04	63:28	47:23	Asnakech	Awoke	ETH	.94	2		Barcelona	16	Feb
67:07			Brenda	Jepleting	KEN				Praha	5	Sep
67:10	63:34	47:24	Dorcas	Kimeli	KEN	5.7.97	3		Barcelona	16	Feb
67:16			Edith	Chelimo	KEN	16.7.86	4		Praha	5	Sep
67:16	63:55		Tsehay	Gemechu	ETH	12.12.98	5		New Delhi	29	Nov
67:18	63:54		Eva	Cherono	KEN	15.8.96	6		New Delhi	29	Nov
			(30)								
67:18	63:52	47:32	Dorcas	Tuitoek	KEN	31.1.96	4		Valencia	6	Oct
67:26	64:02	48:04	Emily	Sisson	USA	12.10.91	5		Valencia	6	Oct
67:57			Birho	Gidey	ETH	.00	2		Napoli	23	Feb
68:02	64:22	47:08	Fancy	Chemutai	KEN	20.3.95	10	RAK	Ras Al Khaimah	21	Feb
68:10	64:36	48:05	Helalia	Johannes	NAM	13.8.80	1		Marugame	2	Feb
68:13	64:50	48:40	Caroline	Kipkirui	KEN	26.5.94	3		Houston	19	Jan
68:18			Sara	Hall	USA	15.4.83	1		Dorena	7	Aug
68:19	64:53	48:40	Goytatom	Gebreselassie	ETH	15.1.95	4		Houston	19	Jan
68:23	64:46	48:20	Charlotte	Purdue	GBR	10.6.91	2		Marugame	2	Feb
68:25	64:56	48:41	Ruti	Aga	ETH	16.1.94	6		Houston	19	Jan
			(40)								
68:31	65:01	47:54	Lonah Chemtai	Salpeter	ISR	12.12.88	12	WCh	Gdynia	17	Oct
68:35	65:03	48:48		Choi Kyung-sun	KOR	16.3.92	3		Marugame	2	Feb
68:38	64:59	47:24	Roza	Dereje	ETH	9.5.97	4		Barcelona	16	Feb
68:38	65:14	48:36	Fabienne	Schlumpf	SUI	17.11.90	13	WCh	Gdynia	17	Oct
68:44	65:19	48:52	Juliet	Chekwel	UGA	25.5.90	14	WCh	Gdynia	17	Oct
68:50	65:15	48:27	Sinead	Diver	AUS	17.2.77	4		Marugame	2	Feb
68:53	65:22	48:41	Caroline	Rotich	KEN	13.5.84	7		Houston	19	Jan
68:55	65:21	48:41	Stephanie	Twell	GBR	17.8.89	8		Houston	19	Jan
68:56	65:12	48:13	Mao	Ichiyama	JPN	29.5.97	5		Marugame	2	Feb
68:57			Keira	D'Amato	USA	21.10.84	1		Shelby Township	28	Oct
			(50)								
69:01			Irene	Kimais	KEN	10.10.98	1		Adana	5	Jan
69:02	65:25	48:25	Meseret	Gola	ETH	30.12.97	15	WCh	Gdynia	17	Oct
69:04+	65:33	49:13	Birhane	Dibaba	ETH	11.9.93	in Mar		Valencia	6	Oct
69:05	65:29	48:43	Gelete	Burka	ETH	23.1.86	10		Houston	19	Jan
69:05+	65:33	49:13	Tigist	Girma	ETH	12.7.93	in Mar		Valencia	6	Dec
69:06+	65:19	48:32	Valary	Aiyabei	KEN	8.6.91	in Mar		London	4	Oct
69:09			Vivian	Chepkurui	KEN	.98	6		Praha	5	Sep
69:12	65:43	49:35	Kaena	Takeyama	JPN	30.10.95	1		Yamaguchi	9	Feb
69:14	65:43	49:35	Sakiho	Tsutsui	JPN	19.1.96	2		Yamaguchi	9	Feb
69:16	65:45	49:35	Ayano	Ikemitsu	JPN	18.4.91	3		Yamaguchi	9	Feb
			(60)								
69:16+			Selly	Chepyego	KEN	3.10.85	in Mar		Tokyo	1	Mar
69:16+			Azmera	Gebru	ETH	21.10.95	in Mar		Tokyo	1	Mar
69:17+			Sutume	Asefa	ETH	11.12.94	in Mar		Tokyo	1	Mar
69:24	65:54	49:44	Zeyituna	Husan	ETH	12.1.99	1		Okayama	20	Dec
69:26	65:57	49:15	Glenrose	Xaba	RSA	31.12.94	16	WCh	Gdynia	17	Oct
69:28	65:57	49:45	Joan	Kipkemoi Rotich	KEN	27.11.93	2		Okayama	20	Dec
69:29	65:34	48:41	Monicah	Ngige Wanjuhi	KEN	7.11.93	11		Houston	19	Jan
69:32			Nancy	Kiprop	KEN	.79	2		Santa Pola	19	Jan
69:34	66:03	49:20	Molly	Huddle	USA	31.8.84	12		Houston	19	Jan
69:35	66:05		Molly	Seidel	USA	12.7.94	13		Houston	19	Jan
			(70)								
69:35	66:04	49:20	Katy	Jermann	USA	20.4.92	14		Houston	19	Jan
69:37	66:05	49:26	Lindsay	Flanagan	USA	24.1.91	15		Houston	19	Jan
69:38			Andrea	Seccafien	CAN	27.8.90	6		Marugame	2	Feb
69:40	66:12	49:32	Becky	Wade	USA	9.2.89	16		Houston	19	Jan
69:41	66:07	49:20	Natasha	Wodak	CAN	17.12.81	17		Houston	19	Jan
69:42			Miriam	Dattke	GER	24.6.98	1		Dresden	8	Nov
69:44			Joyline	Chemutai	KEN	31.12.94	1		Den Haag	8	Mar
69:44			Emma	Bates	USA	8.7.92	2		Shelby Township	28	Oct
69:47	66:09	48:53	Bontu	Edao	BRN	12.12.97	18		Houston	19	Jan
69:47	66:25		Nazret	Weldu	ETH	1.1.90	7		New Delhi	29	Nov
			(80)								
69:49			Atalel	Anmut	ETH	.99	2		Adana	5	Jan
69:49	66:07	49:29	Aliphine	Tuliamuk	USA	5.4.89	19		Houston	19	Jan
69:50	66:25		Mimi	Belete	BRN	9.6.88	8		New Delhi	29	Nov
69:52			Sarah	Lahti	SWE	18.2.95	2		Dresden	8	Nov
69:53+			Shitaye	Eshete	BRN	21.5.90	in Mar		Tokyo	1	Mar
69:54	66:25		Bekelech	Gudeta	ETH	11.10.97	9		New Delhi	29	Nov
69:54+	66:17	49:44	Mizuki	Matsuda	JPN	31.5.95	in Mar		Osaka	26	Jan

HALF MARATHON - MARATHON

Mark			Name		Nat	Born	Pos	Meet	Venue		Date
69:54+	66:18	49:44	Fatuma	Sado	ETH	11.10.91		in Mar	Osaka		26 Jan
69:54+	66:18	49:44	Haftamnesh	Tesfay	ETH	28.4.94		in Mar	Osaka		26 Jan
69:54+	66:18	49:44	Stella (90)	Barsosio	KEN	12.3.93		in Mar	Osaka		26 Jan
69:55	66:11	49:35	Juri	Ichikawa	JPN	25.3.98	4		Yamaguchi		9 Feb
69:57	66:28		Tadu	Teshome	ETH-J	9.6.01	12	RAK	Ras Al Khaimah		21 Feb
69:57+			Alemu	Megertu	ETH	12.10.97		in Mar	London		4 Oct
69:58	66:22		Ikumi	Fukura	JPN	11.8.97	5		Yamaguchi		9 Feb
70:01	66:22	49:17	Charlotte	Arter	GBR	18.6.91	5		Barcelona		16 Feb
70:01+	66:06	49:01	Vivian	Cheruiyot	KEN	11.9.83		in Mar	London		4 Oct
70:04	66:16		Nao	Yamamoto)	JPN	20.10.96	9 Feb				
70:05+			Hawi	Feysa	ETH	1.2.99	24 Jan				
70:05+			Dera	Dida	ETH	26.10.96	24 Jan				
70:05+			Tigist	Abayechew	ETH	22.2.94	24 Jan				
70:05+			Bedatu	Hirpa	ETH	28.4.99	24 Jan				
70:05+			Guteni	Shone	ETH	17.11.91	24 Jan				
70:06			Maggie	Montoya	USA	2.5.95	19 Jan				
70:08	66:35		Alina	Reh	GER	23.5.97	16 Feb				
70:10+			Askale	Merachi	ETH	4.1.87	19 Jan				
70:11			Yelena	Korobkina	RUS	25.11.90	6 Sep				
70:12			Laura	Thweatt	USA	17.12.88	19 Jan				
70:13			Rachael	Cliff	CAN	1.4.88	19 Jan				
70:13	66:33		Maki	Izumida	JPN	22.1.96	9 Feb				
70:13	66:37		Rachel	Chebet	UGA	5.11.96	9 Feb				
70:17	66:37		Mao	Uesugi	JPN	16.8.95	9 Feb				
70:18	66:53		Doreen	Chemutai	UGA	23.10.96	17 Oct				
70:19	66:53		Charlotta	Fougberg	SWE	19.6.85	17 Oct				
70:19	66:55		Ursula	Sánchez	MEX	15.9.87	17 Oct				
70:20	66:54		Andrea	Ramírez	MEX	5.12.92	17 Oct				
70:21	66:54		Ayara	Harada	JPN	14.4.98	20 Dec				
70:22	66:55		Daniela	Torres	MEX	23.7.94	17 Oct				
70:24	66:47		Sarah	Inglis	GBR	28.8.91	19 Jan				
70:25	66:49		Shuri	Ogasawara	JPN	3.10.00	20 Dec				
70:26+	66:50		Yuka	Ando	JPN	16.3.94	8 Mar				
70:26+	66:50		Purity	Rionoripo	KEN	10.6.93	8 Mar				
70:26+			Hirut	Tibebu	ETH	13.12.94	8 Mar				
70:26+			Helen	Tola	ETH	21.11.94	8 Mar				
70:26+			Eunice	Chumba	BRN	28.11.94	8 Mar				
70:26	66:52		Mirai	Waku	JPN	1.7.95	20 Dec				
70:27			Daisy	Kimeli	KEN	28.11.94	5 Jan				
70:27+	66:50		Sayaka	Sato	JPN	27.5.94	8 Mar				
70:27+	66:50		Ai	Hosoda	JPN	27.11.95	8 Mar				
70:27+			Debele	Beyene	ETH	12.9.95	8 Mar				
70:28			Hannah	Everson	USA	21.4.94	19 Jan				
70:28	66:37		Rei	Ohara	JPN	10.8.90	26 Jan				
70:29	66:49		Yumi	Yoshikawa	JPN	31.10.90	26 Jan				
70:29	66:54		Yukari	Abe	JPN	21.8.99	20 Dec				
70:30	66:56		Florencia	Borelli	ARG	30.10.92	17 Oct				
70:32			Yevheniya	Prokopyeva	UKR	5.6.95	17 Oct				
70:33			Sofiya	Yaremchuk	UKR	3.6.94	12 Jan				
70:34			Zhang Deshun		CHN	21.2.96	13 Dec				
70:35			Ellie	Pashley	AUS	10.12.88	2 Feb				
70:36			Brenda	Flores	MEX	4.9.91	17 Oct				
70:39			Wakana	Itsuki	JPN	7.4.94	9 Feb				
79:39			Honami	Maeda	JPN	17.7.96	20 Dec				
70:40			Arisa	Nakao	JPN	.00	20 Dec				
70:41			Hitomi	Mizuguchi	JPN	12.8.96	20 Dec				
70:42			Jaci	Smith	USA	5.1.97	19 Jan				
70:45			Nell	Rojas	USA	27.11.87	19 Jan				
70:45			Kanako	Takemoto	JPN	12.6.96	20 Dec				
70:49			Yukina	Ueda	JPN	7.2.98	26 Jan				
70:49			Laura	Hottenrott	GER	14.5.92	17 Oct				
70:49			Natsumi	Matsushita	JPN	22.1.95	9 Feb				
70:50			Lily	Partridge	GBR	9.3.91	1 Mar				
70:50			Fortunate	Chidzivo	ZIM	16.3.87	17 Oct				
70:52A			Lucy	Cheruiyot	KEN	4.1.97	16 Feb				
70:52			Izabela	Paszkiewicz	POL	9.1.88	17 Oct				
70:55			Gerda	Steyn	RSA	3.3.90	21 Feb				
70:56			Agrie	Belachew	ETH	20.1.99	5 Jan				
70:56A			Belaynesh	Oljira	ETH	26.6.90	16 Feb)				

Short course: Tempe 19 Jan 286.5m short (c. 1 minute): 1. Kellyn Taylor USA 69:13, 2. Stephanie Bruce 69:13

In addition to those shown in Marathon list: **30k** 1:38:35 Honami Maeda (20k 65:46) 1 Ome 16 Feb

MARATHON WOMEN 2020

	25k	30k	Name		Nat	Born	Pos	Venue	Date
2:17:16	1:21:47	1:38:07	Peres	Jepchirchir	KEN	27.9.93	1	Valencia	6 Dec
2:17:45	1:22:00	1:38:25	Lonah Chemtai	Salpeter	ISR	12.12.88	1	Tokyo	1 Mar
2:18:35	1:22:01	1:38:25	Birhane	Dibaba	ETH	11.9.93	2	Tokyo	1 Mar
2:18:40	1:21:48	1:38:07	Joyciline	Jepkosgei	KEN	8.12.93	2	Valencia	6 Dec
2:18:58	1:21:17	1:38:18	Brigid	Kosgei	KEN	20.2.94	1	London	4 Oct
2:19:38	1:21:49	1:38:31	Worknesh	Degefa	ETH	28.10.90	1	Dubai	24 Jan
2:19:52	1:21:48	1:38:07	Helalia	Johannes	NAM	13.8.80	3	Valencia	6 Dec
2:19:54	1:21:48	1:38:07	Zeineba	Yimer	ETH	17.6.98	4	Valencia	6 Dec
2:19:56	1:21:48	1:38:08	Tigist	Girma	ETH	12.7.93	5	Valencia	6 Dec
2:19:56	1:21:48	1:38:15	Degitu	Azimeraw (10)	ETH	24.1.99	6	Valencia	6 Dec
2:20:05	1:21:48	1:38:08	Ruti	Aga	ETH	16.1.94	7	Valencia	6 Dec
2:20:11	1:23:01	1:39:35	Guteni	Shone	ETH	17.11.91	2	Dubai	24 Jan
2:20:29	1:23:30	1:40:31	Mao	Ichiyama	JPN	29.5.97	1	Nagoya	8 Mar
2:20:30	1:22:00	1:38:25	Sutume	Asefa	ETH	11.12.94	3	Tokyo	1 Mar
2:20:32	1:22:43	1:39:22	Sara	Hall	USA	15.4.83	1	Chandler	20 Dec
2:20:57	1:21:50	1:38:53	Joan	Chelimo	KEN	10.11.90	8	Valencia	6 Dec
2:21:42	1:22:00	1:38:26	Selly	Chepyego	KEN	3.10.85	4	Tokyo	1 Mar
2:21:47	1:22:52	1:39:51	Mizuki	Matsuda	JPN	31.5.95	1	Osaka	26 Jan
2:21:55	1:23:02	1:39:35	Bedatu	Hirpa	ETH	28.4.99	3	Dubai	24 Jan
2:21:56	1:22:00	1:38:37		Girma			5	Tokyo	1 Mar
2:22:01	1:23:34	1:40:30		Hall			2	London	4 Oct
2:22:05	1:21:17	1:38:19	Ruth	Chepngetich	KEN	8.8.94	3	London	4 Oct
			(22/20)						
2:22:06			Diana	Kipyogei	KEN	5.5.94	1	Istanbul	8 Nov
2:22:40	1:22:52	1:39:51	Mimi	Belete	BRN	9.6.88	2	Osaka	26 Jan
2:22:41	1:23:30	1:40:36	Yuka	Ando	JPN	16.3.94	2	Nagoya	8 Mar
2:22:45	1:23:02	1:39:35	Tigist	Abayechew	ETH	22.2.94	4	Dubai	24 Jan
2:22:51	1:22:23	1:39:28	Ashete	Bekere	ETH	17.4.88	4	London	4 Oct

MARATHON

Mark			Name		Nat	Born	Pos	Meet	Venue	Date	
2:22:52	1:23:17	1:40:24	Dera	Dida	ETH	26.10.96	5		Dubai	24	Jan
2:22:56	1:23:30	1:40:36	Purity	Rionoripo	KEN	10.6.93	3		Nagoya	8	Mar
2:22:56	1:24:55	1:41:54	Keira	D'Amato	USA	21.10.84	2		Chandler	20	Dec
2:22:58	1:22:00	1:38:58	Azmera	Gebru	ETH	21.10.95	6		Tokyo	1	Mar
2:23:03	1:23:00	1:39:55	Sintayehu	Lewetegn	ETH	9.5.96	3		Osaka	26	Jan
			(30)								
2:23:13	1:25:17	1:42:05	Juliet	Chekwel	UGA	25.5.90	1		Sevilla	23	Feb
2:23:17	1:23:30		Hirut	Tibebu	ETH	13.12.94	4		Nagoya	8	Mar
2:23:27	1:23:30	1:40:33	Sayaka	Sato	JPN	27.5.94	5		Nagoya	8	Mar
2:23:29	1:23:37	1:40:46	Askale	Merachi	ETH	4.1.87	1		Houston	19	Jan
2:23:31	1:23:01	1:40:16	Meskerem	Assefa	ETH	3.10.91	4		Osaka	26	Jan
2:23:36	1:23:03	1:40:30	Hawi	Feysa	ETH	1.2.99	6		Dubai	24	Jan
2:23:39	1:25:18	1:42:05	Gada	Bontu	ETH		2		Sevilla	23	Feb
2:23:49	1:25:18	1:42:05	Sifan	Melaku	ETH	18.4.97	3		Sevilla	23	Feb
2:23:52	1:23:29		Helen	Tola	ETH	21.11.94	6		Nagoya	8	Mar
2:24:14	1:25:18	1:42:08	Josephine	Jepkoech	KEN	21.4.89	4		Sevilla	23	Feb
			(40)								
2:24:23	1:23:29	1:40:30	Alemu	Megertu	ETH	12.10.97	5		London	4	Oct
2:24:27	1:24:17	1:41:18	Fancy	Chemutai	KEN	20.3.94	10		Valencia	6	Dec
2:24:30	1:25:17	1:42:04	Purity	Changwony	KEN	.90	5		Sevilla	23	Feb
2:24:30			Hiwot	Gebrekidan	ETH	11.5.95	2		Istanbul	8	Nov
2:24:47			Biruktayit	Eshetu	ETH	29.9.90	2		Houston	19	Jan
2:24:50			Malindi	Elmore	CAN	13.3.80	3		Houston	19	Jan
2:24:51			Amane	Beriso	ETH	13.10.91	1		Mumbai	19	Jan
2:24:54			Meseret	Belete	ETH	16.9.99	4		Houston	19	Jan
2:25:08	1:23:30		Debele	Beyene	ETH	12.9.95	7		Nagoya	8	Mar
2:25:13		1:42:56	Molly	Seidel	USA	12.7.94	6		London	4	Oct
			(50)								
2:25:22	1:22:06	1:39:45	Senbere	Teferi	ETH	3.5.95	7		Tokyo	1	Mar
2:25:22	1:23:00	1:39:22	Kellyn	Taylor	USA	22.7.86	3		Chandler	20	Dec
2:25:40	1:25:40	1:42:38	Emma	Bates	USA	8.7.92	4		Chandler	20	Dec
2:26:02			Lisa	Weightman	AUS	16.1.79	5		Osaka	26	Jan
2:26:12			Medina	Armino	ETH	22.10.97	1		Xiamen	5	Jan
2:26:19		1:43:53	Natasha	Wodak	CAN	17.12.81	5		Chandler	20	Dec
2:26:24	1:23:17	1:43:55	Bornes	Kitur	KEN	23.11.86	6		Osaka	26	Jan
2:26:28			Mesera	Hussen	ETH	22.6.95	2		Xiamen	5	Jan
2:26:34	1:23:40	1:41:35	Ai	Hosoda	JPN	27.11.95	8		Nagoya	8	Mar
2:26:34		1:43:58	Andrea	Ramírez	MEX	5.12.92	6		Chandler	20	Dec
			(60)								
2:26:35		1:44:40	Haruka	Yamaguchi	JPN	7.7.87	7		Osaka	26	Jan
2:26:39			Li Zhixuan		CHN	23.3.94	1		Shanghai	29	Nov
2:26:42			Afera	Godfay	ETH	25.9.91	3		Xiamen	5	Jan
2:26:42	1:26:38	1:44:11	Carolina	Wikström	SWE	4.9.93	11		Valencia	6	Dec
2:26:51			Gerda	Steyn	RSA	3.3.90	7		London	4	Oct
2:26:54			Hiwot	Ayalew	ETH	6.3.90	4		Xiamen	5	Jan
2:26:55	1:26:39	1:44:11	Deborah	Schöneborn	GER	13.3.94	12		Valencia	6	Dec
2:26:59	1:25:14	1:43:02	Buzunesh	Deba	ETH	8.9.87	7		Dubai	24	Jan
2:26:59			Li Dan		CHN	1.5.95	1	NC	Nanjing	29	Nov
2:27:03			Yebrgual	Melese	ETH	18.4.90	5		Xiamen	5	Jan
			(70)								
2:27:07	1:26:56	1:44:10	Gladys	Tejeda	PER	30.9.85	6		Sevilla	23	Feb
2:27:07			Sinead	Diver	AUS	17.2.77	8		London	4	Oct
2:27:08			Jing Mingming		CHN	10.12.96	3	NC	Nanjing	29	Nov
2:27:08			Sardana	Trofimova	RUS	28.3.88	1	NC	Sochi	6	Dec
2:27:08	1:26:38	1:44:11	Marta	Galimany	ESP	5.10.85	13		Valencia	6	Dec
2:27:14			Rodah	Tanui	KEN	25.4.91	2		Mumbai	19	Jan
2:27:17	1:23:01	1:40:42	Fatuma	Sado	ETH	11.10.91	8		Osaka	26	Jan
2:27:20			Berhane	Gebrekidan	ETH	13.3.99	6		Xiamen	5	Jan
2:27:22			Tsehay	Gebre	ETH	11.9.92	7		Xiamen	5	Jan
2:27:23			Aliphine	Tuliamuk/Bolton	USA	5.4.89	1	OT	Atlanta	29	Feb
			(80)								
2:27:29			Darya	Mykhaylova	UKR	29.4.89	9		London	4	Oct
2:27:34	1:24:02	1:43:24	Shitaye	Eshete	BRN	21.5.90	8		Tokyo	1	Mar
2:27:39			Webalem	Ayele	ETH	.89	1		Castellón	16	Feb
2:27:41			Zinash	Debebe	ETH	12.10.96	8		Xiamen	5	Jan
2:27:42	1:25:15	1:43:23	Shure	Demise	ETH	21.1.96	9		Tokyo	1	Mar
2:27:50	1:23:00	1:41:01	Haftamnesh	Tesfay	ETH	28.4.94	9		Osaka	26	Jan
2:27:50	1:25:24	1:43:36	Bekelu	Beji	ETH	21.8.99	7		Sevilla	23	Feb
2:27:51			Hanae	Tanaka	JPN	12.2.90	10		Osaka	26	Jan
2:27:54			Ayaka	Inoue	JPN	19.6.91	11		Osaka	26	Jan
2:27:56			Hawi	Alemu	ETH	24.1.98	1		Marrakech	26	Jan
			(90)								

MARATHON - 100 KM - 24 HOURS - STEEPLECHASE

Mark			Name		Nat	Born	Pos	Meet	Venue		Date
2:27:57			Naomi	Rotich	KEN	5.4.94	2		Castellón		16 Feb
2:28:03			Munkhzaya	Bayartsogt	MGL	10.10.93	12		Osaka		26 Jan
2:28:03			Giovanna	Epis	ITA	11.10.88	1	NC	Reggio Emilia		13 Dec
2:28:05	1:25:46	1:43:36	Melkau	Gizaw	ETH	17.9.90	8		Sevilla		23 Feb
2:28:07			Souad	Kanbouchia	MAR	12.8.82	2		Marrakech		26 Jan
2:28:12	1:24:17	1:42:26	Rei	Ohara	JPN	10.8.90	13		Osaka		26 Jan
2:28:18			Valary	Aiyabei	KEN	8.6.91	4 Oct	2:28:48	Susan	Jeptoo	FRA	7.3.87	26 Jan
2:28:20			Asayech	Ayalew	ETH	.94	26 Jan	2:28:51	Shiho	Kaneshige	JPN	7.6.89	26 Jan
2:28:23			Chaltu	Negassa	ETH	20.9.92	26 Jan	2:28:51	Misaki	Nishida	JPN	7.8.91	26 Jan
2:28:24			Andrea	Bonilla (100)	ECU	5.12.86	6 Dec	2:28:52	Zerfie	Limeneh	ETH	10.2.97	5 Jan
2:28:25			Anja	Scherl	GER	12.4.86	23 Feb	2:28:52	Sally	Kipyego	USA	19.12.85	29 Feb
2:28:25			Elena	Loya	ESP	11.1.83	6 Dec	2:28:52	Matea	Parlov Kostro	CRO	2.6.92	6 Dec
2:28:28			Andtrea	Deelstra	NED	6.3.95	6 Dec	2:28:55	Christina	Foigberg	SWE	19.6.85	13 Dec
2:28:35			Luisa	Dmitriyeva	RUS	5.5.91	6 Sep	2:28:56	Haven	Hailu	ETH	10.9.98.98	19 Jan
2:28:39			Reia	Iwade	JPN	8.12.94	8 Mar	2:28:58	Marcela Cristina	Gómez	ARG	19.2.84	23 Feb
2:28:42			Rabea	Schöneborn	GER	13.3.94	6 Dec	2:28:59	Hanna	Lindholm	SWE	28.11.79	23 Feb
2:28:43				Zhang Deshun	CHN	21.2.96	6 Dec	2:29:00	Rkia	El Moukim	MAR	22.2.88	26 Jan
2:28:43			Paige	Stoner	USA	31.1.96	20 Dec	**Drugs disqualification**					
2:28:48			Katharina	Steinruck	GER	22.8.89	26 Jan	2:27:57	Viktoriya	Khapilina ¶	UKR	23.4.92	11 Oct
2:28:48			Mizuki	Tanimoto	JPN	18.12.94	26 Jan						

100 KILOMETRES

Mark			Name	Nat	Born	Pos	Meet	Venue	Date
7:04:36			Dominika	Stelmach	POL	28.2.82	1	NC	Pabianice	30 Aug
7:38:58			Gitana	Akmanaviciute	LTU	.86	1		Vilnius	9 Jul
7:46:57			Noora	Honkala	FIN	1.07.92	2		Vilnius	19 Jul
7:54:21			Veronika	Jurisic	CRO	6.04.77	2		Slavonski Brod	7 Mar
7:55:33			Bouchra	Eriksen	DEN	22.09.76	1		Viborg	22 Aug
8:02:33			Hana	Vicarová	CZE	24.10.88	5 Dec	8:07:13	Elizabeth	Howard	USA	.72	29 Feb
8:06:09			Antonija	Orlic	CRO	4.11.77	7 Mar						

24 HOURS

Mark		Name		Nat	Born	Pos	Meet	Venue	Date
260.679		Malgorzata	Pazda-Pozorska	POL	16.02.82	1	NC	Pabianice	30 Aug
251.452		Therese	Falk	NOR	5.08.75	1		Stjørdal	19 Sep
241.218		Patrycja	Bereznowska	POL	17.10.75	2	NC	Pabianice	30 Aug
236.561	t	Joasia	Zakrzewski	GBR	19.01.76	1		Bruce	26 Jul
233.611		Aneta	Rajda	POL	6.05.76	3	NC	Pabianice	30 Aug
233.342		Svetlana	Zétényi	HUN	10.07.76	1		Balatonmádi	25 Oct
232.546		Corinne	Gruffaz	FRA	13.07.73	1		Ville-de-Vierzon	11 Oct
232.015		Irene	Kinnegim	NED	8.01.75	1		Deventre	20 Sep
231.376		Aoife	Mundow	IRL	13.10.82	1		Athína	12 Jan
229.897		Milena	Grabska-Grzegorczyk	POL	18.06.78	1		Brugg	18 Oct
229.556	t	Marisa	Lizak	USA	6.07.79	1		Phoenix	12 Dec
228.962		Diana	Dzaviza	LAT	17.04.87	1		Bernau	3 Oct

2000 METRES STEEPLECHASE

Mark	Name		Nat	Born	Pos	Meet	Venue	Date
5:56.28	Marusa	Mismas	SLO	24.10.94	1		Ljubljana	16 Jul
6:11.79	Elizabeth	Bird	GBR	4.10.94	1		Pontoise	15 Aug
6:12.80	Anna	Tropina	RUS	3.11.98	1		Chelyabinsk	27 Aug
6:13.03	Irene	Sánchez-Escribano	ESP	25.9.92	2		Pontoise	15 Aug
6:16.46	Michelle	Finn	IRL	16.12.89	1		Barcelona (S)	22 Sep
6:16.74	Flavie	Renouard	FRA	10.9.00	3		Pontoise	15 Aug
6:18.48	Aimee	Pratt	GBR	3.10.97	4		Pontoise	15 Aug
6:19.21	Lili	Tóth	HUN	17.9.98	1		Budapest	26 Jul
6:19.23	Gréta	Varga	HUN-Y	19.12.03	2		Budapest	26 Jul
6:19.56	Clara	Viñarás	ESP	8.9.932	2		Barcelona (S)	22 Sep
6:21.83	Claire	Palou	FRA-J	26.12.01	15 Aug	6:27.49	Gesa-Felicitas Krause	GER	3.8.92	12 Jul
6:22.73	Lidia	Campo	ESP	26.3.91	22 Sep	6:28.36	Carolina Robles	ESP	4.12.91	22 Sep
No water jump									
6:09.59	Joana	Soares	POR	8.9.93	1	NC	Ribeira Brava	8 Aug
6:19.92	Alice	Finot	FRA	9.2.91	8 Aug	6:26.86	Emilia Pisoeiro	POR	9.1.86	8 Aug

JUNIORS also Varga in main list

| 6:21.83 | Claire | Palou | FRA | 26.12.01 | 5 | | Pontoise | 15 Aug |
| 6:33.70 | Olivia | Gürth | GER | 31.5.02 | 1 | | Heilbronn | 4 Sep |

3000 METRES STEEPLECHASE

Mark	Name		Nat	Born	Pos	Meet	Venue	Date
9:06.14	Hyvin	Jepkemoi	KEN	13.1.92	1	ISTAF	Berlin	13 Sep
9:10.07	Beatrice	Chepkoech	KEN	6.7.91	2	ISTAF	Berlin	13 Sep
9:16.84	Yekaterina	Ivonina	RUS	14.6.94	1	NC	Chelyabinsk	9 Sep
9:20.68	Marusa	Mismas	SLO	24.10.94	3	ISTAF	Berlin	13 Sep
9:23.86	Olga	Vovk	RUS	13.2.93	2	NC	Chelyabinsk	9 Sep
9:27.35	Natalya	Aristarkhova	RUS	31.10.89	3	NC	Chelyabinsk	9 Sep
9:28.12	Anna	Tropina	RUS	3.11.98	4	NC	Chelyabinsk	9 Sep

WOMEN 2020

348 3000m STEEPLECHASE - 60 METRES HURDLES

Mark	Name		Nat	Born	Pos	Meet	Venue	Date	
9:29.05A		Chepkoech			1	Keino	Nairobi	3	Oct
	(8/7)								
9:30.73	Aimee	Pratt	GBR	3.10.97	1	NC	Manchester (SC)	5	Sep
9:32.90	Stella	Rutto	KEN	12.12.96	1	ROU Ch	Cluj-Napoca	4	Sep
9:32.95	Rosie	Clarke	GBR	17.11.91	5	ISTAF	Berlin	13	Sep
	(10)								
9:34.80	Irene	van der Reijken	NED	13.8.93	6	ISTAF	Berlin	13	Sep
9:35.67	Elena	Burkard	GER	10.2.92	7	ISTAF	Berlin	13	Sep
9:38.04	Michelle	Finn	IRL	16.12.89	1		Sydney	22	Feb
9:41.38	Nataliya	Strebkova	UKR	6.3.95	1	Bal Ch	Cluj-Napoca	19	Sep
9:44.00	Paige	Campbell	AUS	27.6.96	2		Sydney	22	Feb
9:44.01	Genevieve	Gregson	AUS	4.8.89	8	ISTAF	Berlin	13	Sep
9:45.37	Alice	Finot	FRA	9.2.91	2		Decines-Charpieu	29	Aug
9:45.70	Mercy	Chepkurui	KEN	16.9.00	9	ISTAF	Berlin	13	Sep
9:46.14	Roseline	Chepngetich	KEN	17.6.97	3	Keino	Nairobi	3	Oct
9:48.57	Irene	Sánchez-Escribano	ESP	25.9.92	1	NC	Madrid (V)	13	Sep
	(20)								
9:48.62	Martina	Merlo	ITA	19.2.93	2		Espoo	5	Aug
9:48.76	Yukari	Ishizawa	JPN	16.4.88	1	NC	Osaka	4	Oct
9:49.45	Reimi	Yoshimura	JPN	22.4.00	2	NC	Osaka	4	Oct
9:50.05	Yuno	Yamanaka	JPN	25.12.00	1		Kumagaya	19	Sep
9:50.17	Linn	Söderholm	SWE	5.5.96	1		Göteborg	29	Aug
9:50.73	Isabel	Mattuzzi	ITA	23.4.95	1	Maniak	Szczecin	16	Aug
9:51.02A	Fancy	Cherono	KEN-J	2.8.01	4	Keino	Nairobi	3	Oct
9:51.27	Chiara	Scherrer	SUI	24.1.96	1		Regensdorf	8	Aug
9:52.19	Yui	Yabuta	JPN	4.3.96	3	NC	Osaka	4	Oct
9:52.99A	Winfred	Yavi	BRN	31.12.99	5	Keino	Nairobi	3	Oct
	(30)								
9:53.68	Lili	Tóth	HUN	17.9.98	13 Sep	9:59.13	Anna	Petrova	RUS 15.7.94 9 Sep
9:53.75A	Peruth	Chemutai	UGA	10.7.99	3 Oct	9:59.35	Jasmijn	Bakker	NED 11.10.99 30 Aug
9:54.60	Elena	Panaet	ROU	5.6.93	4 Sep	9:59.72	Tatiane Raquel da Silva		BRA 10.6.90 11 Dec
9:55.01	Yuzu	Nishide	JPN	25.1.00	4 Oct	10:01.08	Soyoka	Segawa	JPN 28.7.94 19 Sep
9:55.21	Elizabeth	Bird	GBR	4.10.94	13 Sep	10:01.22		Zhang Xinyan	CHN 9.2.94 18 Sep
9:55.46	Lea	Meyer	GER	16.9.97	13 Sep	10:01.59	Semra	Karaslan	TUR 18.1.98 20 Aug
9:56.53		Xu Shuangshuang	CHN	6.4.96	18 Sep	10:02.76	Patrycja	Kapala	POL 26.3.97 13 Sep
9:56.64	Claire	Palou	FRA-J	26.12.01	29 Aug	10:02.8A	Mercy	Wanjiru	KEN 2.3.99 5 Mar
9:56.64	Flavie	Renouard	FRA	10.9.00	29 Aug	10:02.85	Agnes Thurid Gers		GER 4.8.97 8 Aug
9:56.83	Matylda	Kowal	POL	11.1.89	13 Sep	10:02.93	Derya	Kunur	TUR 1.9.99 4 Sep
9:57.83	Özlem	Kaya	TUR	20.4.90	20 Aug	10:03.09	Victoria	Gerlach	USA 2.6.94 29 Aug
9:57.95	Andrea	Engesæth	NOR-J	6.7.01	19 Sep	10:03.24	Silvia	Oggioni	ITA 18.8.95 17 Oct
9:58.12	Yumi	Yoshikawa	JPN	31.10.90	4 Oct	10:03.27	Violetta	Malyshenok	RUS 27.2.96 29 Aug
9:58.30	Clara	Viñarás	ESP	8.9.93	13 Sep	10:03.29	Joana	Soares	POR 8.9.93 11 Jul
9:58.31	Yuki	Akiyama	JPN	26.8.94	23 Aug	10:04.2A	Dorothy	Kimutai	KEN-J 15.12.02 21 Nov

JUNIORS

Mark	Name		Nat	Born	Pos	Meet	Venue	Date	
9:51.02A	Fancy	Cherono	KEN	2.8.01	4	Keino	Nairobi	3	Oct
9:56.64	Claire	Palou	FRA	26.12.01	3=		Decines-Charpieu	29	Aug
9:57.95	Andrea	Engesæth	NOR	6.7.01	1	NC	Bergen (Fana)	19	Sep
10:04.4A	Dorothy	Kimutai	KEN	15.12.02	1		Nairobi	21	Nov
10:05.0A	Enda	Chepkemoi	KEN		2		Nairobi	21	Nov
10:08.64	Gréta	Varga	HUN-Y	19.12.03	1		Székesfehérvár	5	Sep
10:09.10		Qiao Yumeng	CHN	21.8.01	3	NC	Shaoxing	18	Sep
10:09.4A	Mekdes	Abebe	ETH	29.7.01	1		Addis Ababa	27	Dec
10:10.03	Andrea	Engesæth	NOR	6.7.01	4		Regensdorf	8	Aug
10:12.93	Oaula	Schneiders	GER	20.2.01	4	NC	Braunschweig	8	Aug

60 METRES HURDLES

Mark	Name		Nat	Born	Pos	Meet	Venue	Date	
7.80	Kendra	Harrison	USA	18.9.92	1		Clemson	14	Feb
7.81A		Harrison			1		Albuquerque	25	Jan
7.82	Christina	Clemons	USA	29.5.90	1		Madrid	21	Feb
7.84	Tobi	Amusan	NGR	23.4.97	1		Karlsruhe	31	Jan
7.85	Brianna	McNeal	USA	18.8.91	1		Houston	1	Feb
7.86	Tonea	Marshall	USA	17.10.98	1		Lubbock	18	Jan
7.86	Danielle	Williams	JAM	14.9.92	1		Columbia SC	7	Feb
7.87A		Amusan			2		Albuquerque	25	Jan
7.87	Alina	Talay	BLR	14.5.89	1		Torun	8	Feb
	(9/7)								
7.88	Nia	Ali	USA	23.10.88	1h2		Madrid	21	Feb
7.91	Grace	Stark	USA-J	6.5.01	2	SEC	College Station	29	Feb
7.92A	Gabriele	Cunningham	USA	22.2.98	1		Albuquerque	15	Feb
	(10)								
7.93	Tiara	McMinn	USA	23.2.99	1		Lubbock	1	Feb
7.94	Cindy	Roleder	GER	21.8.89	2		Düsseldorf	4	Feb

60 - 100 METRES HURDLES

Mark	Name		Nat	Born	Pos	Meet	Venue	Date	
7.94A	Payton	Chadwick	USA	29.11.95	2	NC	Albuquerque	15	Feb
7.95	Alia	Armstrong	USA	28.12.00	2		Fayetteville	14	Feb
7.96A	Tia	Jones	USA	8.9.00	1h1	NC	Albuquerque	15	Feb
7.96A	Tiffani	McReynolds	USA	4.12.91	3	NC	Albuquerque	15	Feb
7.97	Nooralotta	Neziri	FIN	9.11.92	4		Torun	8	Feb
7.97	Luca	Kozák	HUN	1.6.96	5		Torun	8	Feb
7.98	Cyrena	Samba-Mayela	FRA	31.10.00	1	NC-23	Saint-Brieuc	8	Feb
7.99	Reetta	Hurske	FIN	15.5.95	6		Torun	8	Feb
(20)									
8.00	Janeek	Brown	JAM	14.5.98	3		Boston (R)	25	Jan
8.00	Isabelle	Pedersen	NOR	27.1.92	3h2		Torun	8	Feb
8.00	Teresa	Errandonea	ESP	15.11.94	3		Madrid	21	Feb
8.01	Nadine	Visser	NED	9.2.95	3	ISTAF	Berlin	14	Feb
8.01	Anna	Cockrell	USA	28.8.97	2		Clemson	14	Feb
8.01	Mecca	McGlaston	USA	23.7.98	3		Clemson	14	Feb
8.01	Klaudia	Siciarz	POL	15.3.98	3h2		Liévin	19	Feb
8.02	Gabrielle	McDonald	JAM	14.3.98	2		Lubbock	18	Jan
8.02	Luminosa	Bogliolo	ITA	3.7.95	4		Karlsruhe	31	Jan
8.02	Evonne	Britton	USA	28.7.91	7		Torun	8	Feb
(30)									
8.02	Brittany	Anderson	JAM-J	31.1.01	4	Millrose	New York (A)	8	Feb
8.03	Matilda	Bogdanoff	FIN	8.10.90	1r2		Helsinki	19	Jan
8.03	Naomi	Taylor	USA	9.11.98	1		Birmingham AL	29	Feb
8.04	Pamela	Dutkiewicz	GER	28.9.91	3h1	ISTAF	Berlin	14	Feb
8.05	Pia	Skrzyszowska	POL	20.4.01	2		Łódź	11	Feb
8.05	Karolina	Koleczek	POL	15.1.93	5		Madrid	21	Feb
8.06	Kristi	Castlin	USA	7.7.88	2		Houston	1	Feb
8.07	Devynne	Charlton	BAH	26.11.95	1		Lexington	11	Jan
8.07	Jeanine	Williams	JAM	28.1.97	1		Clemson	11	Jan
8.07	Eline	Berings	BEL	28.5.86	1		Gent	26	Jan
(40)									
8.07	Emma	Nwofor	GBR	22.8.96	1	Big 10	Geneva OH	29	Feb
8.08	Taliyah	Brooks	USA	8.2.95	1h2		Iowa City	18	Jan
8.08	Madeleine	Akobundu	USA	24.4.98	1		Blacksburg	24	Jan
8.08	Paula	Salmon	USA	13.5.99	3		Fayetteville	11	Feb
8.09	Stanislava	Skvarková	SVK	20.4.96	1		Ostrava	5	Feb
8.09	Solène	Ndama	FRA	23.9.98	2		Eaubonne	17	Feb
8.09	Brittley	Humphrey	USA	6.3.98	2h2	SEC	College Station	28	Feb
8.09	Caridad	Jerez	ESP	23.1.91	2	NC	Ourense	1	Mar
8.10	Domonique	Turner	USA	9.10.97	2h1		Lubbock	1	Feb
8.10A	Cortney	Jones	USA	18.6.99	1	NC	Albuquerque	15	Feb
(50)									
8.10	Gréta	Kerekes	HUN	9.10.92	2	NC	Budapest	23	Feb
8.10	Alexis	Duncan	USA	16.8.98	3h2	SEC	College Station	28	Feb

8.11	Annimari	Korte	FIN	8.4.88	31 Jan	8.13	Ivana	Loncarek	CRO	8.4.91	15 Feb
8.11	Masumi	Aoki	JPN	16.4.94	1 Feb	8.14	Asuka	Terada	JPN	14.1.90	1 Feb
8.11	Laura	Valette	FRA	16.2.97	2 Feb	8.14	Lolo	Jones	USA	5.8.82	14 Feb
8.11	Masai	Russell	USA	17.6.00	14 Feb	8.14	Beate	Schrott	AUT	15.4.88	23 Feb
8.12	Anne	Zagré	BEL	13.3.90	25 Jan	8.15	Anamaria	Nesteriuc	ROU	29.11.93	1 Feb
8.12	Solenn	Compper	FRA	14.3.95	2 Feb	8.15	Hanna	Plotitsyna	UKR	1.1.87	4 Feb
8.12	Jasmine	Jones	USA-J	30.11.01	7 Feb	8.15	Elvira	German	BLR	9.1.97	14 Feb
8.12	Tejyrica	Robinson	USA	.98	29 Feb	8.15	Caroline	Klein	GER	4.3.96	22 Feb
8.13	Cindy	Ofili	GBR	5.8.94	31 Jan	8.15	Daszay	Freeman	JAM	25.1.00	29 Feb
8.13	Marthe Yasmine	Koala	BUR	8.3.94	9 Feb	8.15	Chanel	Brissett	USA	10.8.99	29 Feb
8.13A	Erica	Bougard	USA	26.7.93	15 Feb	8.15	Awa	Sène	FRA	24.7.94	1 Mar
						8.15	Michelle	Harrison	CAN	.92	6 Mar

Best at low altitude
7.99	Cunningham	1rB		Lubbock	1 Feb	8.00	Chadwick	3	Millrose	New York (A)	8 Feb
						8.02	McReynolds	2		MOndeville	1 Feb

100 METRES HURDLES

12.68	1.2	Nadine	Visser	NED	9.2.95	1	PNG	Turku	11	Aug
12.68	-0.2		Visser			1	Gyulai	Székesfehérvár	19	Aug
12.71	-0.2	Luca	Kozák	HUN	1.6.96	2	Gyulai	Székesfehérvár	19	Aug
12.72	0.1		Visser			1	GGala	Roma	17	Sep
12.73	0.5	Elvira	German	BLR	9.1.97	1		Minsk	25	Jun
12.73	1.5	Cyréna	Samba-Mayela	FRA	31.10.00	1	NC	Albi	12	Sep
		(6/4)								
12.76	0.7	Annimari	Korte	FIN	8.4.88	1		Jyväskylä	8	Jul
12.78	1.1	Payton	Chadwick	USA	29.11.95	1	DL	Doha	25	Sep
12.79	1.2	Luminosa	Bogliolo	ITA	3.7.95	2	PNG	Turku	11	Aug
12.82	1.3	Brittany	Anderson	JAM-J	31.1.01	1		Clermont	25	Jul
12.84	0.7	Nooralotta	Neziri	FIN	9.11.92	1h1		Jyväskylä	8	Jul

100 METRES HURDLES

Mark		Name		Nat	Born	Pos	Meet	Venue	Date	
12.86	1.1	Taliyah	Brooks	USA	8.2.95	2	DL	Doha	25	Sep
		(10)								
12.88	1.5	Cindy	Ofili	GBR	5.8.94	1		Marietta	1	Aug
12.90	1.5	Stanislava	Skvarková	SVK	20.4.96	1		Trnava	15	Aug
12.90	0.9	Tiffany	Porter	GBR	13.11.87	1r1		Des Moines	29	Aug
12.91	0.7	Reetta	Hurske	FIN	15.5.95	2		Jyväskylä	8	Jul
12.94	0.5	Elizabeth	Clay	AUS	9.5.95	1		Melbourne	6	Feb
12.96	0.9	Megan	Tapper	JAM	18.3.94	2r1		Des Moines	29	Aug
12.98	1.3	Karolina	Koleczek	POL	15.1.93	1	Szew	Bydgoszcz	19	Aug
13.01	1.3	Pia	Skrzyszowska	POL-J	20.4.01	1		Lódz	14	Sep
13.02	-0.1	Masumi	Aoki	JPN	16.4.94	1	NC	Niigata	3	Oct
13.03	0.3	Asuka	Terada	JPN	14.1.90	1		Tokyo	23	Aug
		(20)								
13.04	-0.3		Lin Shih-Ting	TPE	13.5.99	1		Kaohsiung	2	Nov
13.05	0.1	Elisa Maria	Di Lazzaro	ITA	5.6.98	6	GGala	Roma	17	Sep
13.06	1.1	Noemi	Zbären	SUI	12.3.94	1		Meilen	20	Jun
13.06	0.0	Beate	Schrott	AUT	15.4.88	1r1	NC	Südstadt	15	Aug
13.07	1.0	Lotta	Harala	FIN	26.3.92	2h1	NC	Turku	14	Aug
13.07	1.1	Ditaji	Kambundji	SUI-J	20.5.02	1		Basel	12	Sep
13.08	1.3	Klaudia	Wojtunik	POL	15.5.99	2		Lódz	14	Sep
13.09	0.5	Svetlana	Parakhonko	BLR	12.6.97	2		Minsk	25	Jun
13.09	-0.2	Sharika	Nelvis	USA	10.5.90	6	Gyulai	Székesfehérvár	19	Aug
13.09	-0.4		Wu Yanni	CHN	28.7.97	1	NC	Shaojing	15	Sep
		(30)								
13.11	1.3	Anne	Zagré	BEL	13.3.90	2	Szew	Bydgoszcz	19	Aug
13.11	0.6	Ketiley	Batista	BRA	13.7.99	1	NC-23	Bragança Paulista	17	Dec
13.12	1.3	Keily Linet	Pérez	CUB-J	26.4.01	1	NC	La Habana	20	Mar
13.12	0.5	Maria	Huntington	FIN	13.3.97	1H	NC	Turku	15	Aug
13.13	2.0	Chisato	Kiyoyama	JPN	24.7.91	18	Jul	13.22A	0.8	Sharona	Bakker	NED	12.4.90	10 Mar
13.13	1.4	Mette	Graversgaard	DEN	5.10.95	23 Aug	13.22	-0.4		Lin Yuwei	CHN	2.5.99	15 Sep
13.16	-0.4	Adriana	Rodríguez	CUB	12.7.99	20 Mar	13.23	0.0	Danielle	Williams	JAM	14.9.92	25 Jul
13.16	0.1	Gréta	Kerekes	HUN	9.10.92	8 Aug	13.23	0.7	Linda	Guizzetti	ITA	12.12.98	1 Aug
13.17	1.1	Ivana	Loncarek	CRO	8.4.91	6 Aug	13.23	1.0	Katerina	Cachová	CZE	26.2.90	8 Aug
13.17	0.9	Dawn	Harper-Nelson	USA	13.5.84	29 Aug	13.24	1.3	Giada	Carmassi	ITA	15.5.94	11 Jul
13.19	0.3	Ebony	Morrison	USA	28.12.94	22 Feb	13.24	0.5	Ricarda	Lobe	GER	13.4.94	8 Aug
13.19A	0.3	Rikenette	Steenkamp	RSA	16.10.92	7 Mar	13.24	1.1	Zoë	Sedney	NED-J	15.12.01	25 Sep
13.20	0.6	Celeste	Mucci	AUS	11.8.99	6 Feb	13.25	1.1	Ruslana	Rashkovan	BLR	18.3.97	25 Jun
13.20	0.3	Brianna	Beahan	AUS	1.11.91	22 Feb	13.25	0.7	Karin	Strametz	AUT	18.4.98	18 Jul
13.20	0.0	Greisys Lázaro	Roble	CUB	18.1.00	6 Mar	13.26	1.5	Ashley	Spencer	USA	8.6.93	1 Aug
13.20	-0.2	Evonne	Britton	USA	28.7.91	29 Aug	13.26	0.5	Markéta	Stolová	CZE	1.10.00	15 Aug
13.20	1.5	Lucy-Jane	Matthews	GBR-J	17.9.02	4 Sep	13.26	1.5	Nana	Fujimori	JPN	21.5.97	18 Oct
13.20	1.5	Solenn	Compper	FRA	14.3.95	12 Sep	13.27	0.3	Yumi	Tanaka	JPN	15.12.98	23 Aug
13.21	0.3	Abbie	Taddeo	AUS	8.2.94	22 Feb	13.27	1.7	Hitomi	Shimura	JPN	8.11.90	29 Aug
13.21	1.2	Solène	Ndama	FRA	2I3.9.98	11 Aug	13.30	0.9	Elena	Miteva	BUL	18.7.92	8 Aug
13.21	-0.5	Hanna	Plotitsyna	UKR	1.1.87	20 Sep	13.30	0.3	Miho	Suzuki	JPN	18.11.96	23 Aug

Wind assisted

12.71	3.0	Brittany	Anderson	JAM-J	31.1.01	1h		Clermont	25	Jul
12.74	3.0	Tiffany	Porter	GBR	13.11.87	2h		Clermont	25	Jul
12.87	2.1	Masumi	Aoki	JPN	16.4.94	1		Fukui	29	Aug
12.89	2.5	Elisa Maria	Di Lazzaro	ITA	5.6.98	2		Savona	16	Jul
12.92	2.3	Asuka	Terada	JPN	14.1.90	1h1		Fukui	29	Aug
13.03	3.7	Chisato	Kiyoyama	JPN	24.7.91	1h2		Fukui	29	Aug
13.04	2.6	Lotta	Harala	FIN	26.3.92	2		Espoo	5	Aug
13.05	3.9	Keily Linet	Pérez	CUB-J	26.4.01	1h	NC	La Habana	20	Mar
13.06	3.9	Greisys Lázaro	Roble	CUB	18.1.00	2h	NC	La Habana	20	Mar
13.07	3.3	Anne	Zagré	BEL	13.3.90	1	NC	Bruxelles	16	Aug
13.09	2.7	Brianna	Beahan	AUS	1.11.91	1		Perth	7	Mar
13.10	3.9	Ackera	Nugent	JAM-J	29.4.02	1		Kingston	8	Mar
13.12	2.1	Miho	Suzuki	JPN	18.11.96	4		Fukui	29	Aug
13.14	2.1	Hitomi	Shimura	JPN	8.11.90	29 Aug	13.29	3.7	Ayumi	Kobayashi	JPN-J	25.3.01	29 Aug
13.19	2.2	Laura	Valette	FRA	16.2.97	22 Aug	13.29	3.7	Mako	Fukube	JPN	28.10.95	29 Aug
13.26	2.9	Anais	Karayiánni	GRE	5.12.99	15 Jul	13.29	2.7	Andrea	Rooth	NOR-J	6.3.02	12 Sep
13.26	2.3	Hannah	Jones	AUS	5.10.95	19 Dec	13.30	3.9	Crystal	Morrison	JAM-J	6.2.02	8 Mar
13.29	4.4	Anni	Siirtola	FIN	12.9.98	14 Jun	13.30	3.7	Meg	Hemphill	JPN	23.5.96	29 Aug
							13.33	2.2	Nataliya	Yurchuk	UKR	28.5.96	15 Aug

Hand timed

13.0	2.0	Greisys Lázaro	Roble	CUB-J	18.1.00	22 Feb	13.1	0.9	Elena	Miteva	BUL	18.7.92	26 Jul
12.8w	2.3	Adriana	Rodríguez	CUB	12.7.99	1		La Habana	22	Feb

JUNIORS
4 juniors + 1wa in main list. 7 performances by 5 women to 13.15 inc. 3 wa). Additional juniors:

13.20	1.5	Lucy-Jane	Matthews	GBR	17.9.02	2	NC	Manchester (SC)	4	Sep
13.24	1.1	Zoë	Sedney	NED	15.12.01	5	DL	Doha	25	Sep
13.36	0.6	Mao	Shimano	JPN	2.10.01	1		Niigata	13	Sep

100 METRES HURDLES

Mark		Name		Nat	Born	Pos	Meet	Venue	Date	
Wind assisted		see main list for 3 juniors								
13.29	3.7	Ayumi	Kobayashi	JPN	25.3.01	2h2		Fukui	29	Aug
13.29	2.7	Andrea	Rooth	NOR	6.3.02	1H		Moss	12	Sep
13.30	3.9	Crystal	Morrison	JAM	6.2.02	2		Kingston	8	Mar

200 METRES HURDLES

Mark		Name		Nat	Born	Pos	Meet	Venue	Date	
26.10	-0.2	Jessica	Tappin	GBR	17.5.90	1		Bromley	11	Sep
26.11	-0.9	Line	Kloster	NOR	27.2.90	1		Oslo	11	Jun
26.65	-0.9	Nooralotta	Neziri	FIN	9.11.92	2		Oslo	11	Jun
26.70	-0.9	Annimari	Korte	FIN	8.4.88	3		Oslo	11	Jun
26.84	0.5	Andrea	Rooth	NOR-J	6.3.02	1		Oslo (L)	28	May
26.90	1.4	Linda	Olivieri	ITA	14.7.98	1		Formia	20	Jun
26.90		Heidi	Salminen	FIN-J	4.12.02	1		Jyväskylä	1	Sep
26.93	-0.2	Anastasia	Davies	GBR	9.4.99	2		Bromley	11	Sep

300 METRES HURDLES

Mark		Name		Nat	Born	Pos	Meet	Venue	Date	
38.55		Femke	Bol	NED	23.2.00	1	GS	Ostrava	6	Sep
38.97		Emma	Zapletalová	SVK	24.3.00	2	GS	Ostrava	6	Sep
39.08		Georhanne	Mline	USA	6.3.90	1		Walnut	9	Jul
39.25		Léa	Sprunger	SUI	5.3.90	1		Zürich	9	Jul
39.35		Jessie	Knight	GBR	15.6.94	3	GS	Ostrava	6	Sep
39.42		Sara	Slott Petersen	DEN	9.4.87	1		Oslo	11	Jun
39.44		Amalie Hammild	Iuel	NOR	17.4.94	2		Oslo	11	Jun
39.81		Leah	Nugent	JAM	23.11.92	1		Marietta	25	Jul

400 METRES HURDLES

Mark		Name		Nat	Born	Pos	Meet	Venue	Date	
53.79		Femke	Bol	NED	23.2.00	1		Papendal	18	Jul
53.90			Bol			1	GGala	Roma	17	Sep
54.33			Bol			1		Bellinzona	15	Sep
54.47			Bol			1		Papendal	4	Jul
54.54		Anna	Ryzhykova	UKR	24.11.89	2	GGala	Roma	17	Sep
54.67			Bol			1	Gyulai	Székesfehérvár	19	Aug
54.68			Bol			1	DL	Stockholm	23	Aug
54.93		Viktoriya	Tkachuk	UKR	8.11.94	3	GGala	Roma	17	Sep
54.98		Léa	Sprunger	SUI	5.3.90	2		Bellinzona	15	Sep
		(9/4)								
55.09		Sarah	Carli	AUS	5.9.94	1		Sydney	19	Dec
55.19		Emma	Zapletalová	SVK	24.3.00	1	NC	Trnava	30	Aug
55.20		Sara	Slott Petersen	DEN	9.4.87	4	GGala	Roma	17	Sep
55.27		Jessie	Knight	GBR	15.6.94	1		Bruxelles	9	Aug
55.27		Amalie Hammild	Iuel	NOR	17.4.94	5	GGala	Roma	17	Sep
55.40		Rhonda	Whyte	JAM	6.11.90	1		Kingston	18	Jul
		(10)								
55.40		Janieve	Russell	JAM	14.11.93	2		Kingston	18	Jul
55.40		Ayomide	Folorunso	ITA	17.10.96	1		Pavia	8	Aug
55.53		Jackie	Baumann	GER	24.8.95	2		Papendal	18	Jul
55.62		Line	Kloster	NOR	27.2.90	1		La Chaux-de-Fonds	15	Aug
55.70		Zuzana	Hejnová	CZE	19.12.86	1	NC	Plzen	9	Aug
55.77		Zurian	Hechavarría	CUB	10.8.95	1		Camagüey	7	Mar
55.89		Lauren	Boden	AUS	3.8.88	1		Canberra	24	Jan
55.89		Jessica	Turner	GBR	8.8.95	1		Poznan	11	Jul
55.90		Carolina	Krafzik	GER	27.3.95	1	NC	Braunschweig	9	Aug
55.98			Quach Thi Lan	VIE	18.10.95	1	NC	Hanoi	14	Nov
		(20)								
56.14		Paulien	Couckuyt	BEL	19.5.97	1	NC	Bruxelles	16	Aug
56.16		Joanna	Linkiewicz	POL	2.5.90	2	Maniak	Szczecin	16	Aug
56.29		Sage	Watson	CAN	20.6.94	3	Gyulai	Székesfehérvár	19	Aug
56.42		Yasmin	Giger	SUI	6.11.99	4		Bellinzona	15	Sep
56.49		Sara	Klein	AUS	19.5.94	3		Canberra	13	Feb
56.50		Ayesya	Ibrahim	JPN	16.1.98	1	NC	Niiigata	3	Oct
56.55		Portia	Bing	NZL	17.4.93	1		Wellington	28	Feb
56.58		Mariya	Mykolenko	UKR	4.4.94	1	NC	Lutsk	16	Aug
56.64		Djamila	Böhm	GER	15.7.94	2	NC	Braunschweig	9	Aug
56.77			Mo Jiadie	CHN	6.1.00	1	NC	Shaoxing	17	Sep
		(30)								
56.85		Noelle	Montcalm	CAN	3.4.88	1		Ottawa	15	Aug
56.94		Janka	Molnár	HUN-J	5.1.01	1	NC	Budapest	9	Aug
56.95		Andrea	Rooth	NOR-J	6.3.02	2	NC	Bergen (Fana)	20	Sep
56.96		Moeka	Sekimoto	JPN	23.2.00	1		Tokorozawa	26	Jul

400 METRES HURDLES - HIGH JUMP

Mark	Name		Nat	Born	Pos	Meet	Venue	Date
56.97	Sara	Gallego	ESP	11.10.00	1		Ciudad Real	19 Sep
56.98	Amanda	Holmberg	SWE	6.9.98	1	v FIN	Tampere	6 Sep
56.99	Lina	Nielsen	GBR	13.3.96	2	NC	Manchester (SC)	5 Sep
57.01	Vera	Rudakova/Chalaya	RUS	20.3.92	1	NC	Chelyabinsk	9 Sep
57.09	Eri	Utsunomiya	JPN	11.4.93	2	NC	Niigata	3 Oct
57.10	Nora Kollerød	Wold	NOR	21.6.97	3	NC	Bergen (Fana)	20 Sep
		(40)						
57.13	Sára	Mátó	HUN	23.12.00	5 Sep	57.65	Vera	Barbosa	POR	13.1.89	8 Aug
57.27	Lisa Sophie	Hartmann	GER	22.11.99	9 Aug	57.67	Modesta	Morauskaite	LTU	2.10.95	8 Aug
57.28		Lu Zhangwei	CHN-J	8.11.01	30 May	57.67	Eline	Claeys	BEL	4.6.00	9 Aug
57.33	Hanna	Palmqvist	SWE	20.1.96	16 Aug	57.70	Aneja	Simoncic	SLO	5.1.98	1 Aug
57.34	Akiko	Ito	JPN	25.5.95	3 Oct	57.70	Valentina	Cavalleri	ITA	8.12.95	6 Aug
57.35	Agata	Zupin	SLO	17.3.98	26 Jul	57.73	Mizuna	Ono	JPN-J	9.12.02	3 Nov
57.36	Lashanna	Graham	JAM	25.9.00	1 Feb	57.75	Hanna	Mikhaylova	BLR	25.3.98	2 Aug
57.36	Salma Celeste	Paralluelo	ESP-Y	13.11.03	19 Sep	57.76	Liliane	Fernandes	BRA	8.10.87	6 Dec
57.40	Natalia	Wosztyl	POL	28.8.99	29 Aug	57.76	Genevieve	Cowie	AUS	26.4.95	19 Dec
57.40	Bianca	dos Santos	BRA	1.1.91	6 Dec	57.81	Daniela	Roman	AUS	7.1.96	22 Feb
57.41		Huang Yan	CHN	12.1.96	30 May	57.82	Julia	Korzuch	POL	27.12.95	25 Aug
57.43	Ami	Yamamoto	JPN-J	19.4.02	3 Oct	57.83	Wanessa	Zavolski	BRA	6.3.89	18 Nov
57.44	Nikoleta	Jichová	CZE	29.8.00	4 Jul	57.85	Rui	Tsugawa	JPN-J	24.11.01	15 Aug
57.44	Eleonora	Marchiando	ITA	27.9.97	8 Aug	57.86	Nerea	Bermejo	ESP	20.12.88	13 Sep
57.44	Kane	Koyama	JPN	16.12.98	3 Oct	57.88A	Taylon	Bieldt	RSA	4.11.88	8 Feb
57.46	Daniela	Ledecká	SVK	4.11.96	25 Jul	57.88	Moa	Granat	SWE-Y	8.8.04	8 Aug
57.54		Nguyen Thi Huyen	VIE	19.5.93	14 Nov	57.89	Paulette Natacha Fernández	ESP	6.6.94	13 Sep
57.55	Nessa	Cooper Millet	IRL	5.12.94	11 Sep	57.91	Farah	Clerc	FRA	31.7.90	13 Sep
57.56	Annina	Fahr	SUI	6.4.93	8 Aug	57.92	Rebecca	Sartori	ITA	22.5.97	30 Aug
57.60	Shaquena	Foote	JAM-J	23.7.01	8 Mar	57.93	Oksana	Aeschbacher	SUI	25.6.98	8 Aug
57.60	Linda	Olivieri	ITA	14.7.98	30 Aug	57.93	Emilia	Ankiewicz	POL	22.11.90	13 Aug
57.61	Hayley	McLean	GBR	9.9.94	23 Aug	57.93	Shana	Grebo	FRA	9.11.00	19 Aug
57.62	Karolina	Pahlitzsch	GER	5.4.94	16 Aug	57.94	Izabela	Smolinska	POL	14.1.99	5 Sep

JUNIORS

2 juniors in main list. 2 performances by 2 women to 57.00. Additional marks and further juniors:

57.28		Lu Zhangwei	CHN	8.11.01	1		Nanjing	30 May
57.36	Salma Celeste	Paralluelo	ESP-Y	13.11.03	2		Ciudad Real	19 Sep
57.43	Ami	Yamamoto	JPN	19.4.02	4	NC	Niigata	3 Oct
57.60	Shaquena	Foote	JAM	23.7.01	1		Kingston	8 Mar
57.73	Mizuna	Ono	JPN	9.12.02	1		Niigata	3 Nov
57.85	Rui	Tsugawa	JPN	24.11.01	1		Tokorozawa	15 Aug
57.88	Moa	Granat	SWE-Y	8.8.04	1		Söderhamn	8 Aug

HIGH JUMP

2.05i	Mariya		Lasitskene	RUS	14.1.93	1		Moskva	9 Feb
			1.85/1 1.88/1 1.91/1 1.94/2 1.96/1 1.98/1 2.00/1 2.05/3 2.07/xxx
	2.04i	1	Moskva		1 Feb	1.85/1 1.90/1 1.93/1 1.96/1 2.00/1 2.04/1 2.07/xxx
	2.00i	1	Moskva		25 Feb	1.70/1 1.82/1 1.88/1 1.91/1 1.94/1 2.00/1 2.04/xxx
2.02i	Yaroslava		Mahuchikh	UKR-J	19.9.01	1		Karlsruhe	31 Jan
			1.85/1 1.89/1 1.93/2 1.96/1 1.99/1 2.02/1 2.04/xxx
	2.01i	1	Lviv		18 Jan	1.83/1 1.86/1 1.90/1 1.95/1 1.99/2 2.01/3
	2.01i	1 NC	Sumy		22 Feb	1.80/1 1.85/1 1.89/1 1.93/1 1.95/1 1.98/1 2.01/2
	2.00	1 DL	Stockholm		23 Aug	1.84/1 1.87/1 1.90/2 1.93/1 1.96/2 1.98/1 2.00/3 2.03/xxx
	1.98i	1	Cottbus		29 Jan	1.85/1.89/1 1.92/1 1.94/1 1.96/2 1.98/3 2.02/xxx
	1.98	1 Herc	Monaco		14 Aug	1.84/1 1.88/2 1.92/1 1.95/1 1.98/2 2.01/xxx
2.00i	Yuliya		Levchenko	UKR	28.11.97	1		Kyiv	11 Jan
			1.80/1 1.83/1 1.86/1 1.89/1 1.92/1 1.94/1 1.96/1 1.98/1 2.00/1 2.03/xxx
	2.00	1	Kyiv		23 Jul	
	2.00	1 Szew	Bydgoszcz		19 Aug	1.80/1 1.85/1 1.88/1 1.91/1 1.94/2 1.97/2 2.00/3 2.04/xxx
	1.99i	2	Karlsruhe		31 Jan	1.80/1 1.85/1 1.89/1 1.93/1 1.96/1 1.99/2 2.02/xxx
	1.98	2 Herc	Monaco		14 Aug	1.80/1 1.84/1 1.88/1 1.92/1 1.95/3 1.98/2 2.01/xxx
	1.98	2 DL	Stockholm		23 Aug	1.80/1 1.84/1 1.87/1 1.90/1 1.93/1 1.96/2 1.98/2.00/xxx
	1.98	1	GGala	Roma	17 Sep	
			1.80/1 1.84/1 1.88/1 1.92/1 1.95/1 1.98/1 2.01/xxx
1.99	Eleanor		Patterson	AUS	22.5.96	1		Wellington	28 Feb
			1.86/1 1.90/1 1.93/2 1.96/2 1.99/3 2.01/xxx
1.98	Nicola		McDermott	AUS	28.12.96	1		Sinn	29 Aug
	(18/5)					1.83/1 1.86/1 1.89/3 1.92/2 1.95/3 1.98/3 2.01/xx
1.97Ai	Vashti		Cunningham	USA	18.1.98	1	NC	Albuquerque	15 Feb
1.96i	Imke		Onnen	GER	17.8.94	3		Karlsruhe	31 Jan
1.96i	Anna		Chicherova	RUS	22.7.82	2		Moskva	9 Feb
1.96i	Elena		Vallortigara	ITA	21.9.91	1	NC	Ancona	23 Feb
1.95	Iryna		Herashchenko	UKR	10.3.95	2		Kyiv	23 Jul
	(10)							
1.95	Erika		Kinsey	SWE	10.3.88	1	NC	Uppsala	15 Aug
1.94i	Kamila		Licwinko	POL	22.3.86	3		Cottbus	29 Jan

… HIGH JUMP 353

Mark	Name		Nat	Born	Pos	Meet	Venue	Date	
1.94i	Salome	Lang	SUI	18.11.97	1	NC	St. Gallen	16	Feb
1.94	Erika	Furlani	ITA	2.1.96	1		Rieti	11	Jul
1.93i	Nikki	Manson	GBR	15.10.94	1		Hustopece	8	Feb
1.93i	Svetlana	Radzivil	UZB	17.1.87	1		Eaubonne	17	Feb
1.92i	Amina	Smith	USA	29.8.92	1		College Park	18	Jan
1.92i	Jeannelle	Scheper	LCA	21.11.94	1		Leverkusen	19	Jan
1.92i	Airine	Palsyte	LTU	13.7.92	5		Cottbus	29	Jan
1.92i	Yuliya (20)	Chumachenko	UKR	2.10.94	2		Trinec	2	Feb
1.92	Lija	Apostolovski	SLO	23.6.00	1		Slovenska Bistrica	13	Jun
1.92	Oksana	Okuneva	UKR	14.3.90	1	NC	Lutsk	30	Aug
1.91i	Bethan	Partridge	GBR	11.7.90	1		Nantes	25	Jan
1.91i	Kristina	Korolyova	RUS	6.11.90	3		Moskva	9	Feb
1.91i	Claire	Orcel	BEL	2.12.97	1	NC	Liévin	29	Feb
1.91i	Ellen	Ekholm	SWE	12.2.96	1	SEC	College Station	29	Feb
1.91	Bára	Sajdoková	CZE-J	5.10.01	1		Kladno	18	Jul
1.91	Ioánna	Zákka	GRE	28.5.96	1		Athína (AK)	19	Jul
1.91	Alina	Shukh	UKR	12.2.99	1		Lutsk	15	Aug
1.90Ai	Liz (30)	Patterson	USA	9.6.88	1		Air Force Academy	18	Jan
1.90i	Inika	McPherson	USA	29.9.86	1		Columbia SC	1	Feb
1.90i	Daniela	Stanciu	ROU	15.10.87	1		Bucuresti	1	Feb
1.90i	Tonje	Angelsen	NOR	17.1.90	1	NC	Rud	2	Feb
1.90i	Morgan	Lake	GBR	12.5.97	3		Hustopece	8	Feb
1.90i	Marusa	Cernjul	SLO	30.6.92	4		Banská Bystrica	11	Feb
1.90i	Nadezhda	Dubovitskaya	KAZ	12.3.98	1		Istanbul	16	Feb
1.90i	Alessia	Trost	ITA	8.3.93	2	NC	Ancona	23	Feb
1.90i	Idea	Pieroni	ITA-J	18.9.02	1	Jnr Int	Minsk	26	Feb
1.90	Ella	Junnila	FIN	6.12.98	1		Lahti	15	Jul
1.90	Christina (40)	Honsel	GER	7.7.97	1		Osterode	18	Jul
1.90	Mirela	Demireva	BUL	28.9.89	5	DL	Stockholm	23	Aug
1.90	Sofie	Skoog	SWE	7.6.90	1	v FIN	Tampere	6	Sep
1.90	Tatyana	Yermachenkova	RUS	9.9.98	3		Sochi	19	Sep
1.90	Safina	Sadullayeva	UZB	4.3.98	1	NC	Tashkent	25	Dec
1.89i	Priscilla	Frederick	ANT	14.2.89	2		Boston (R)	25	Jan
1.89i	Tynita	Butts-Townsend	USA	10.6.90	6		Karlsruhe	31	Jan
1.89i	Levern	Spencer	LCA	23.6.84	7		Karlsruhe	31	Jan
1.89i	Klára	Krejciríková	CZE-J	22.4.02	2		Ostrava	5	Feb
1.89i	Abigail	O'Donoghue	USA	21.5.99	1		Fayetteville	15	Feb
1.88i	Tatyana (50)	Odineva	RUS	25.5.83	1		Moskva	9	Jan
1.88i	Natalya	Aksenova	RUS	6.6.97	1		Irkutsk	11	Jan
1.88i	Darya	Slepova	RUS	10.4.00	2		Chelyabinsk	16	Jan
1.88i	Nadezhda	Andryukhina	RUS-J	3.7.01	3=		Chelyabinsk	16	Jan
1.88i	Barbara	Szabó	HUN	17.2.90	1		Nehvizdy	22	Jan
1.88i	Rachel	McCoy	USA	1.8.95	1		Lubbock	24	Jan
1.88i	Natalya	Spiridonova	RUS-J	31.7.02	1	NC-23	Sankt Peterburg	15	Feb
1.88i	Adelina	Khalikova	RUS-J	18.12.02	3	NC-23	Sankt Peterburg	15	Feb
1.88i	Marija	Vukovic	MNE	21.1.92	2	BalkC	Istanbul	15	Feb
1.88i	Serena	Capponcelli	ITA	24.1.89	4	NC	Ancona	23	Feb
1.88i	Britt (60)	Weerman	NED-Y	13.6.03	2	1 NC	Apeldoorn	23	Feb
1.88i	Kristina	Ovchinnikova	KAZ-J	21.3.01	2	Jnr Int	Minsk	26	Feb
1.88	Heta	Tuuri	FIN	14.1.95	2	vSWE	Tampere	6	Sep
1.87i	Jelena	Rowe	USA	1.8.99	2		Lubbock	1	Feb
1.87i	Bianca	Salming	SWE	22.11.98	1	NC	Växjö	23	Feb
1.87	Jessica	Kähärä	FIN-J	1.8.01	1		Jyväskylä	8	Jul
1.87	Teresa Maria	Rossi	ITA	12.4.92	1		Savona	16	Jul
1.87	Michaela	Hrubá	CZE	21.2.98	2		Kladno	18	Jul
1.87	Alexandra	Plaza	GER	10.8.94	2	NC	Braunschweig	8	Aug
1.87	Mariya	Zhodzik	BLR	19.1.97	1		Minsk	14	Aug
1.87	Sini (70)	Lällä	FIN	12.3.94	1		Jyväskylä	1	Sep
1.87	Cristina	Ferrando	ESP	12.1.92	1	NC	Alcobendas	12	Sep
1.87	Claudia	Conte	ESP	14.11.99	1H		Madrid (V)	12	Sep
1.87	Solène	Gicquel	FRA	1.12.94	1	NC	Albi	13	Sep
1.87	Alysha	Burnett	AUS	4.1.97	1		Sydney (Illawong)	28	Nov
1.86i	Polina	Parfenenko	RUS-Y 14.3.03	31 Jan	1.86i	Laura	Gröll	GER 11.4.98	23 Feb
1.86i	Ana	Simic	CRO 5.5.90	15 Feb	1.86i	Anabela	Neto	POR 25.3.91	29 Feb
1.86i	Urte	Baikstyte	LTU 8.5.99	15 Feb	1.86i	Tyra	Gittens	TTO 6.6.98	28 Feb
1.86i	Alisa	Presnyakova	RUS 7.3.98	17 Feb	1.86	Valdiléia	Martins	BRA 19.9.89	7 Mar

WOMEN 2020

354 HIGH JUMP - POLE VAULT

Mark	Name	Nat	Born	Pos	Meet	Venue	Date
1.86	Hu Linpeng	CHN	29.12.95	28	May		
1.86	Tatiána Goúsin	GRE	26.1.94	19	Jul		
1.85	Rose Yeboah	GHA-J	23.12.01	8	Jan		
1.85i	Nicole Greene	USA	2.5.97	25	Jan		
1.85i	Barbara Bitchoka	CAN	.96	25	Jan		
1.85i	Grete Udras	EST	11.3.88	26	Jan		
1.85i	Elisabeth Pihela	EST	15.3.04	15	Feb		
1.85i	Laura Rautanen	FIN	13.2.88	16	Feb		
1.85A	Ximena Esquivel	MEX	22.8.97	22	Feb		
1.85	Emily Whelan	AUS	10.1.00	29	Feb		
1.85	Alyssa Jones	USA-Y	6.2.04	29	Feb		
1.85	Lilian Turban	EST-J	25.9.01	4	Jul		
1.85	Maria Huntington	FIN	13.3.97	8	Jul		
1.85	Miia Sillman	FIN	3.6.95	8	Jul		
1.85	Panayióta Dósi	GRE-J	1.4.01	15	Jul		
1.85	Luca Renner	HUN	30.11.98	18	Jul		
1.85	Desirée Rossit	ITA	19.3.94	1	Aug		
1.85	Saleta Fernández	ESP	15.7.97	5	Aug		
1.85	Sommer Lecky	IRL	14.6.00	13	Aug		
1.85	Liliya Klintsova	UKR	12.7.97	16	Aug		
1.85	Paulina Borys	POL	14.5.98	15	Sep		
1.85	Marta Morara	ITA	26.12.99	18	Sep		
1.85	Shieriai Tsuda	JPN	9.9.96	20	Sep		
1.85	Keeley O'Hagan	NZL	11.3.94	21	Nov		
1.84i	Anna Hall	USA-J	23.3.01	25	Jan		
1.84i	Irina Iliyeva	RUS	22.12.95	28	Jan		
1.84i	Ligia-Damaris Bara	ROU	26.1.94	1	Feb		
1.84i	Lale Eden	GER	25.3.98	7	Feb		
1.84i	Pippa Rogan	IRL	4.2.94	8	Feb		
1.84i	Zarriea Willis	USA	14.11.96	21	Feb		
1.84i	Emily Borthwick	GBR	2.9.97	23	Feb		
1.84i	Wiktoria Miaso	POL-J	14.11.01	26	Feb		
1.84i	Leonie Cambours	FRA	31.7.00	1	Mar		
1.84	Adriana Rodríguez	CUB	12.7.99	20	Mar		
1.84	Danielle Frenkel	ISR	8.9.87	6	Aug		
1.84	Styliana Ioannidou	CYP-Y	17.12.03	17	Aug		
1.84	Lavinja Jürgens	GER	13.1.00	8	Aug		
1.84	Katarina Johnson-Thompson	GBR	9.1.93	14	Aug		
1.84	Merel Maes	BEL-Y	22.1.05	16	Aug		
1.84	Rebecca Pavan	ITA-J	31.5.01	25	Sep		

Best outdoors

1.97	Lasitskene	1		Sochi			19 Sep
1.90	Chicherova	1	NCp	Bryansk			29 Aug
1.89	Cernjul	2		Slovenska Bistrica			13 Jun
1.88	Spencer	4		Sollentuna			10 Aug
1.88	Scheper	3	Herc	Monaco			14 Aug
1.88	Licwinko	1	NC	Wloclawek			28 Aug
1.86	Chumachenko	30 Aug		1.85	Khalikova		29 Aug
1.86	Weerman	30 Aug		1.85	Andryukhina		29 Aug
1.88	Korolyova	2	NCp	Bryansk			29 Aug
1.88	Vallortigara	1	NC	Padova			30 Aug
1.88	Orcel	2		Heusden-Zolder			6 Sep
1.88	Lang	1	NC	Basel			12 Sep
1.88	Stanciu	1		Balk Ch Cluj-Napoca			20 Sep
1.87	Salming	3	NC	Uppsala			15 Aug
1.84	Pieroni	18	Jul	1.84	Vukovic		19 Jul
1.84	Trost	19	Jul	1.84	Szabó		8 Aug
				1.84	Spiridonova		15 Aug

JUNIORS
10 juniors in main list. 16 performances (inc. 8 indoor) by 3 women to 1.90. Additional marks and further juniors:

Mayuchikh	6+1.97		2	Szew Bydgoszcz	19 Aug	1.96	2	Dessau	8 Sep
	1.96i		1	Banská Bystrica	11 Feb	1.95	2	GGala Roma	17 Sep
	1.96i		1	Ulsteinvik	28 Feb	1.93i	1	Glasgow	15 Feb
Sajdoková	1.90		1	Ostrava	12 Jun	1.90	1	NC Plzen	9 Aug
1.86i		Polina Parfenenko	RUS-Y	14.3.03	1	NC-y	Novocheboksarsk	31 Jan
1.85		Rose Yeboah	GHA	23.12.01	1		Accra	8 Jan
1.85		Alyssa Jones	USA-Y	6.2.04	1		Miami Gardens	29 Feb
1.85		Lilian Turban	EST	25.9.01	1		Tallinn	4 Jul
1.85		Panayióta Dósi	GRE	1.4.01	2		Árgos Orestikó	15 Jul
1.84i		Anna Hall	USA	23.3.01	2		Clemson	25 Jan
1.84i		Wiktoria Miaso	POL	14.11.01	3	Jnr Int	Minsk	26 Feb
1.84		Styliana Ioannidou	CYP-Y	17.12.03	1	NC	Nicosia	17 Aug
1.84		Merel Maes	BEL-Y	22.1.05	1		Bruxelles	16 Aug
1.84		Rebecca Pavan (20)	ITA-J	31.5.01	1		Molfetta	25 Sep

Best outdoors

1.86	Weerman	1	NC	Utrecht	30 Aug	1.85	Andryukhina	4=	NCp	Bryansk	29 Aug
1.85	Khalikova	4=	NCp	Bryansk	29 Aug	1.84	Pieroni	1		Firenze	18 Jul

POLE VAULT

4.95i		Anzhelika	Sidorova	RUS	28.6.91	1		Moskva	29 Feb
					4.60/1	4.80/1	4.95/2	5.00/xxx	
	4.92i	1	NC	Moskva	25 Feb	4.60/1	4.75/1	4.92/3	
	4.86i	1		Moskva	9 Feb	4.55/1	4.70/1	4.86/3	4.92/xxx
	4.80i	1		Moskva	27 Jan	4.50/1	4.60/1	4.70/1	4.80/3 4.90/xxx
	4.80	1		Moskva	16 Aug	4.50/3	4.70/1	4.80/1	4.85/xxx
4.92		Katie	Nageotte	USA	13.6.91	1		Marietta	1 Aug
					4.60/1	4.83/1	4.92/2	5.01/xx	
	4.83	1		Marietta	18 Jul	4.45/2	4.55/1	4.70/2	4.83/2 4.92/xxx
	4.81	2		Piedmont	15 Jul	4.50/2	4.70/2	4.81/3	4.91/xxx
4.91i		Sandi	Morris	USA	8.7.92	1	Millrose	New York (A)	8 Feb
					4.50/1	4.65/2	4.75/1	4.81/2 4.91/1	5.04/xxx
	4.90Ai	1	NC	Albuquerque	15 Feb	4.50/1 4.60/1 4.70/1 4.75/3 4.80/1 4.85/1 4.90/3 5.00/xxx			
	4.83i	1		Liévin	19 Feb	4.53/1	4.63/2	4.73/1	4.78/3 4.83/2 5.03/xxx
	4.83	1		Piedmont	19 Sep				
	4.81	1		Piedmont	15 Jul	4.40/1	4.50/1	4.60/1	4.70/1 4.76/1 4.81/1 4.91/xxx
	4.80i	1		Clermont-Ferrand	23 Feb	4.56/1	4.66/1	4.74/1	4.80/3 4.93/xxx
4.85Ai		Jenn	Suhr	USA	5.2.82	2	NC	Albuquerque	15 Feb
					4.60/1	4.70/1	4.80/x	4.85/1 4.90/xxx	
4.83		Michaela	Meijer	SWE	30.7.93	1		Norrköping	1 Aug
					4.43/1	4.58/1	4.73/1	4.83/1 5.00/xxx	
4.78i		Robeilys	Peinado	VEN	26.11.97	2		Liévin	19 Feb
		(18/6)							

POLE VAULT

Mark	Name		Nat	Born	Pos	Meet	Venue	Date	
4.75	Tina	Sutej	SLO	7.11.88	1		Ljubljana	5	Jul
4.74i	Angelica	Bengtsson	SWE	8.7.93	1	NC	Växjö	22	Feb
4.74i	Yarisley	Silva	CUB	1.6.87	2		Clermont-Ferrand	23	Feb
4.73	Holly (10)	Bradshaw	GBR	2.11.91	1		Kuortane	1	Aug
4.72	Irina	Zhuk	BLR	26.1.93	1	NC	Minsk	20	Aug
4.72	Nina	Kennedy	AUS	5.4.97	1		Perth	16	Dec
4.70Ai	Olivia	Gruver	USA	29.7.97	3	NC	Albuquerque	15	Feb
4.70i	Morgann	LeLeux	USA	14.11.92	1		Baton Rouge	21	Feb
4.70	Eléni-Klaoúdia	Pólak	GRE	9.9.96	1		Athína (AK)	18	Jul
4.66i	Angelina	Krasnova	RUS	7.2.91	1		Chelyabinsk	16	Jan
4.66i	Ninon	Guillon-Romarin	FRA	15.4.95	1		Eaubonne	17	Feb
4.66	Angelica	Moser	SUI	9.10.97	1	NC	Basel	12	Sep
4.65i	Polina	Knoroz	RUS	20.7.99	2	NC	Moskva	25	Feb
4.63i	Alysha (20)	Newman	CAN	29.6.94	5		Liévin	19	Feb
4.63	Nikoléta	Kiriakopoúlou	GRE	21.3.86	1	PNG	Turku	11	Aug
4.61i	Bridget	Guy	USA	18.3.96	1		Blacksburg	22	Feb
4.60i	Wilma	Murto	FIN	11.6.98	1	v3N	Helsinki	9	Feb
4.60i		Xu Huiqin	CHN	4.9.93	2		Val-de-Reuil	14	Feb
4.60Ai	Megan	Clark	USA	10.6.94	4	NC	Albuquerque	15	Feb
4.60i	Irina	Ivanova	RUS	19.4.96	4		Moskva	29	Feb
4.60		Li Ling	CHN	6.7.89	1		Beijing	5	Jun
4.56Ai	Anicka	Newell	CAN	5.8.93	1		Albuquerque	14	Feb
4.55i	Yelizaveta	Bondarenko	RUS	1.7.99	3		Moskva	9	Feb
4.55i	Marion (30)	Lotout	FRA	19.11.89	3	NC	Liévin	29	Feb
4.55	Amálie	Svábíková	CZE	22.11.99	1		Kladno	18	Jul
4.53Ai	Rachel	Baxter	USA	5.4.99	1		Albuquerque	1	Feb
4.52i	Sophie	Gutermuth	USA	2.11.92	1		Hillsdale	7	Feb
4.52i	Romana	Malácová	CZE	15.5.87	4		Szczecin	25	Feb
4.52	Kortney	Ross	USA	26.7.92	1		Marietta	8	Aug
4.52	Alina	McDonald	USA	26.8.97	2		Marietta	8	Aug
4.51i	Lyudmila	Petrova	RUS	15.12.93	2		Chelyabinsk	16	Jan
4.51i	Lucy	Bryan	GBR	22.5.95	1		Akron	8	Feb
4.50i	Daylis	Caballero	USA	6.3.88	2		Belton	4	Jan
4.50Ai	Lisa (40)	Gunnarsson	SWE	20.8.99	1		Reno	17	Jan
4.50Ai	Lexi	Jacobus	USA	20.11.96	2		Reno	17	Jan
4.50i	Tuesdi	Tidwell	USA	20.9.98	1		College Station	25	Jan
4.50Ai	Kaylee	Bizzell	USA	/98	7	NC	Albuquerque	15	Feb
4.50Ai	Tori	Hoggard	USA	20.11.96	8	NC	Albuquerque	15	Feb
4.50Ai	Sydney	Walter	USA	15.11.93	9	NC	Albuquerque	15	Feb
4.50	Elizaveta	Parnova	AUS	9.5.94	1		Perth	22	Feb
4.50i	Sophie	Cook	GBR	12.9.94	1	NC	Glasgow	22	Feb
4.50	Elina	Lampela	FIN	18.2.98	2		Somero	19	Jun
4.50	Kristina	Kontsevenko	BLR-J	18.8.01	1	NCp	Brest	17	Jul
4.50	Aksana (50)	Gataullina	RUS	17.7.00	2		Moskva	16	Aug
4.50	Yana	Hladiychuk	UKR	21.5.93	1		Kyiv	19	Aug
4.50	Margot	Chevrier	FRA	21.12.99	1		Vénissieux	5	Sep
4.50	Imogen	Ayris	NZL	12.12.00	1		Auckland	21	Nov
4.50	Olivia	McTaggart	NZL	9.1.00	1		Auckland	5	Dec
4.47 unsanctioned meet: Leah		Pasqualetti	USA-J	25.8.01	1		Menifee	26	Jun
next best 4.34i					1		Houghton	1	Feb
4.46i	Stefanie	Dauber	GER	31.7.87	1		Chemnitz	7	Feb
4.46i	Julia	Fixsen	USA	13.11.00	2	SEC	College Station	29	Feb
4.46i	Bailee	McCorkle	USA	19.4.99	3	SEC	College Station	29	Feb
4.45i	Olga	Mullina	RUS	1.8.92	6		Moskva	9	Feb
4.45i	Lisa (60)	Ryzih	GER	27.9.88	1	NC	Leipzig	22	Feb
4.45i	Femke	Pluim	NED	10.5.94	1	NC	Apeldoorn	23	Feb
4.42	Paige	Sommers	USA-Y	20.5.03	1		Thousand Oaks	22	Feb
4.41Ai	Kelsie	Ahbe-Holahan	CAN	6.7.91	2		Albuquerque	14	Feb
4.40i	Annie	Johnigan	USA	13.5.95	3		Belton	4	Jan
4.40i	Malen Ruiz	de Azúa	ESP	17.11.95	1		San Sebastián	11	Jan
4.40i	Alyona	Lutkovskaya	RUS	15.3.96	5		Moskva	27	Jan
4.40i	Fanny	Smets	BEL	21.4.86	1	NC	Gent	16	Feb
4.40i	Gabriela	Leon	USA	17.6.99	2	ACC	Notre Dame	29	Feb
4.40	Ria	Möllers	GER	5.3.96	1=	NC	Braunschweig	8	Aug
4.40	Andrina (70)	Hodel	SUI	2.6.00	1	NC-23	Frauenfeld	22	Aug

POLE VAULT

Mark	Name		Nat	Born	Pos	Meet	Venue	Date	
4.40	Maryna	Kylypko	UKR	10.11.95	1	NC	Lutsk	29	Aug
4.38i	Lauren	Martinez	USA	16.10.96	1		Fayetteville	15	Feb
4.37i	Kayla	Smith	USA	6.5.97	1		Fayetteville	31	Jan
4.37i	Marissa	Kalsey	USA	23.3.94	3		Blacksburg	8	Feb
4.36 u	Amanda	Moll	USA-Y	31.1.05	1		Olympia WA	15	Jul
4.36i	Helen	Falda	ITA	13.2.96	1		Lincoln NB	1	Feb
4.35i	Hailey	Sweatman	USA	17.12.97	1		Columbia SC	7	Feb
4.35i	Caroline Bonde	Holm	DEN	19.7.90	4	v3N	Helsinki	9	Feb
4.35i	Chloe	Cunliffe	USA	10.5.00	1		Seattle	15	Feb
4.35Ai	Lauren (80)	Chorny	USA	22.6.93	13	NC	Albuquerque	15	Feb
4.35i	Chinne	Okoronkwo	USA	26.9.97	1	Big 12	Ames	28	Feb
4.35	Tatyana	Kalinina	RUS-J	3.8.01	3		Tver	30	Aug
4.35	Lea	Bachmann	SUI	25.6.96	3	NC	Basel	12	Sep
4.34Ai	Chloe	Wall	USA	10.3.99	3		Albuquerque	8	Feb
4.33i	Marta	Onofre	POR	28.1.91	3		Sätra	11	Feb
4.32i	Charlotte	Iva	FRA	11.2.99	11	Jan
4.32i	Miren	Bartolomé	ESP	2.1.98	29	Feb
4.32	Andrea	San José	ESP	4.10.97	13	Sep
4.31i	Elise	Romney	USA	23.3.96	8	Feb
4.31i	Katherine	Pitman	USA	21.11.94	16	Feb
4.31	Juliana	Campos	BRA	17.10.96	14	Mar
4.31	Mesure Tutku	Yilmaz	TUR	1.1.00	19	Aug
4.30i	Chloé	Henry	BEL	5.3.87	18	Jan
4.30i	Moana-Lou	Kleiner	GER-J	24.4.02	19	Jan
4.30i	Jessie	Johnson	USA	21.11.93	1	Feb
4.30i	Anna	Watson	USA	3.5.99	1	Feb
4.30i	Alice	Moindrot	FRA	20.8.99	8	Feb
4.30i	Pascale	Stöcklin	SUI	5.2.97	16	Feb
4.30Ai	Stephanie	Richartz (100)	USA	21.1.92	16	Feb
4.30i	Demet	Parlak	TUR	26.7.96	19	Feb
4.30i	Emily	Presley	USA	22.1.97	21	Feb
4.30i	Elisa	Molinarolo	ITA	29.1.94	22	Feb
4.30i	Hanga	Klekner	HUN	24.9.99	22	Feb
4.30i	Agnieszka	Kaszuba	POL	31.8.98	29	Feb
4.30i	Courtney	Smallacombe	AUS	18.1.91	29	Feb
4.30i	Buse	Arikazan	TUR	8.7.94	29	Feb
4.30	Jamie	Scroop	AUS	29,3.88	11	Mar
4.30	Megan	Zimlich	USA	30.4.93	3	Jun
4.30	Niu Chunge		CHN	14.2.00	5	Jun
4.30	Katharina	Bauer	GER	12.6.90	11	Jul
4.30	Natalie	Uy	PHI	6.9.94	15	Jul
4.30	Roberta	Bruni	ITA	8.3.94	23	Jul
4.30	Sonia	Malavisi	ITA	31.10.94	8	Aug
4.30		Song Tingting	CHN	8.10.93	15	Aug
4.30	Lene	Retzius	NOR	4.1.96	5	Sep
4.30i	Misaki	Morota	JPN	6.10.98	23	Aug
4.27i	Nati	Sheppard	USA	9.10.96	8	Feb
4.26i	Yekaterina	Bryanchina	RUS	11.11.98	16	Jan
4.26 u	Natassja	Campbell	USA	19.7.00	30	May
4.26	Ellen	Vekemans	BEL-J	30.4.01	18	Jul
4.25i	Janina	Pollatz	GER	24.12.94	19	Jan
4.25	Ayla	Silva	BRA	14.3.97	25	Jan
4.25i	Meagan	Gray	USA	15.8.97	8	Feb
4.25i	Na'ama	Bernstein	ISR	18.8.93	9	Feb
4.25A	Nicole	Hein	PER	14.2.96	22	Feb
4.25i	Killiana	Heymans	NED	24.1.97	23	Feb
4.25i	Anastasiya	Surova	RUS	26.9.96	25	Feb
4.25i	Katie	Jones	USA	13.7.99	28	Feb
4.25i	Hannah	Jefcoat	USA	17.2.99	29	Feb
4.25i	Olivia	Moore	USA	3.12.99	29	Feb
4.25	Ariádni	Adamapoúlou	GRE	19.12.00	8	Aug
4.25	Freya Leni	Wildgrube	GER-J	15.8.01	5	Sep
4.23i	Mackenzie	Hayward	USA	4.7.00	25	Jan
4.22i	Kamila	Przybyla	POL	3.5.96	5	Feb
4.21i	Landon	Kemp	USA	29.8.98	1	Feb
4.21Ai	Abby	Helminiak	USA		14	Feb
4.21i	Ana	Carrasco-J	ESP	12.5.01	22	Feb
4.21iA	Kaitlin	Heri	USA	.99	29	Feb
4.21	Ellianne (139)	Kimes	USA	22.10.98	29	Feb

Best outdoors
4.73	Bengtsson	1	vFIN	Tampere		6	Feb
4.60	Murto	1		Somero		19	Jun
4.55A	Newell	1		Ciudad de México		22	Feb
4.55	Lotout	1	NC	Albi		13	Sep
4.50	Ivanova	1		Tver		30	Aug
4.50	Clark	3		Piedmont		15	Jul
4.46	Malácová	1=	NC	Plzen		9	Aug
4.46	Gunnarsson	2	NC	Uppsala		15	Aug
4.45A	Caballero	2		Ciudad de México		22	Feb
4.45	Ryzih	1		Innsbruck		5	Sep
4.41	Pluim	1		Zoetemeer		6	Sep
4.40	Cook	2		Kuortane		1	Aug
4.40	Dauber	1=	NC	Braunschweig		8	Aug
4.40	Lutkovskaya	2		Moskva		23	Aug
4.40	Mullina	4	NC	Chelyabinsk		8	Sep
4.35	Jacobus	3		Ciudad de México		22	Feb
4.35	Gruver	3		Marietta		18	Jul
4.35	de Azúa	2		Madrid (V)		5	Sep
4.35	Peinado	3		Bellinzona		15	Sep

4.32	Smets		25	Jul	4.25	Kalsey	1 Aug
4.30	Stöcklin		16	Aug	4.25	Arikazan	28 Aug
4.25	Molinarolo		30	Aug	4.21	Morota	12 Sep
4.21	Holm		9	Jul			

JUNIORS
5 juniors in main list. 5 performances by 3 women to 4.38. Additional marks and further juniors:

Kontsevenko	4.45	1		Brest			8	Jul
4.40		2		NC	Minsk		2	Aug
4.30i	Moana-Lou	Kleiner	GER	24.4.02	1		Berlin	19 Jan
4.26	Ellen	Vekemans	BEL-	30.4.01	1		Amiens	18 Jul
4.25	Freya Leni	Wildgrube	GER	15.8.01	1	NC-j	Heilbronn	5 Sep
4.20i	Elina	Giallurachis (10)	FRA	29.5.01	1		Miramas	25 Jan
	4.20				2		Chateaudun	23 Aug
4.20i	Emma	Brentel	FRA	8.8.02	3		Rennes	15 Feb
4.20i	Marleen	Mülla	EST	28.6.01	2		Minsk	25 Feb
4.20	Ella	Buchner	GER	.01	1		Engen	18 Jul

Best outdoors
4.20	t	Moana-Lou	Kleiner	GER	24.4.02	2	NC-j	Heilbronn	5 Sep

+ intermediate time in longer race, A made at an altitude of 1000m or higher, D made in a decathlon, h made in a heat, qf quarter-final, sf semi-final, i indoors, Q qualifying round, r race number, -J juniors, -Y youths (b. 2003 or later)

LONG JUMP

Mark			Name		Nat	Born	Pos	Meet	Venue		Date	
7.07i			Malaika	Mihambo	GER	3.2.94	1	ISTAF	Berlin		14 Feb	
						6.68	6.67	6.41	6.84	6.73	7.07	
	7.03	0.8 1		Dessau		8 Sep	6.53	6.60	x	6.63	7.03	p
6.96i			Maryna	Bekh-Romanchuk	UKR	18.7.95	1		Torun		8 Feb	
						6.64	6.63	6.73	6.85	6.77	6.96	
	6.92i		1	Karlsruhe		31 Jan	x	x	6.92	x	x	x
	6.91	0.6 1	DL	Doha		25 Sep	6.55	x	6.67	6.79	6.91	
	6.90i		1 GP	Glasgow		15 Feb	x	6.81	6.90	6.83	6.90	x
	6.90i		1	Liévin		19 Feb	x	x	6.60	6.56	6.79	6.90
	6.87	-0.3 1	ISTAF	Berlin		13 Sep	6.44	6.62	6.87	6.70	x	6.77
	6.85	1.6 1	DL	Stockholm		23 Aug	6.53	x	6.71	x	x	6.85
	6.85	0.5 2		Dessau		8 Sep	6.68	6.60	x	6.47	6.85	6.76
6.94	1.0		Anastasiya	Mironchik-Ivanova	BLR	13.4.89	1		Innsbruck		8 Sep	
						6.75	6.83/0.4	6.94	x	x	x	
	6.93	0.2 1		Brest		17 Jul	6.45	6.72	x	x	6.77	6.93
6.92	0.2		Khaddi	Sagnia	SWE	20.4.94	1	Hanz	Zagreb		15 Sep	
						6.61	x	6.83/0.1	6.74	x	6.92	
	6.85	0.2 2	DL	Doha		25 Sep	x	6.85	6.73	x	6.74	6.55
			(14/4)									
6.82i			Ese	Brume	NGR	20.1.96	2		Liévin		19 Feb	
6.80			Ivana	Spanovic	SRB	10.5.90	1		Novi Sad		6 Jun	
6.80	0.7		Larissa	Iapichino	ITA-J	18.7.02	1		Savona		16 Jul	
6.79i			Nafissatou	Thiam	BEL	19.8.94	1	FRA Ch	Liévin		1 Mar	
6.76Ai			Quanesha	Burks	USA	15.3.95	1	NC	Albuquerque		15 Feb	
6.74i			Lorraine	Ugen	GBR	22.8.91	1		Clemson		17 Jan	
			(10)									
6.74			Chantel	Malone	IVB	2.12.91	1		Marietta		1 Aug	
6.71	0.4		Spiridoúla	Karídi	GRE-J	30.1.01	1	NC-J	Ioánnina		2 Aug	
6.71	1.4		Brooke	Stratton	AUS	12.7.93	1		Canberra		19 Dec	
6.69Ai			Kate	Hall	USA	12.1.97	2		Albuquerque		15 Feb	
6.69	0.5		Jazmin	Sawyers	GBR	21.5.94	1	NC	Manchester (SC)		4 Sep	
6.69	0.2		Alina	Rotaru	ROU	5.6.93	2	Hanz	Zagreb		15 Sep	
6.68	0.0		Keturah	Orji	USA	5.3.96	1		Marietta		25 Jul	
6.65i			Taishia	Pryce	JAM	14.7.97	1		Fayetteville		14 Feb	
6.64	0.4		Petra	Farkas	HUN	30.4.99	1		Tatabánya		18 Jul	
6.64	1.4		Evelise	Veiga	POR	3.3.96	1		Lisboa (U)		1 Aug	
			(20)									
6.63i			Yanis	David	FRA	12.12.97	1		Lubbock		1 Feb	
6.63	0.7			Xu Xiaoling	CHN	13.5.92	1	NC	Shaoxing		16 Sep	
6.62i			Éloyse	Lesueur-Aymonin	FRA	15.7.88	4		Karlsruhe		31 Jan	
6.62	0.4		Aries	Sánchez	VEN	1.3.96	1		Barquisimeto		10 Jan	
6.61Ai			Kendell	Williams	USA	14.6.95	3	NC	Albuquerque		15 Feb	
6.61	1.5		Erica	Jarder	SWE	2.4.86	1		Kil		14 Jun	
6.61	0.2		Anasztázia	Nguyen	HUN	9.1.93	2		Tatabánya		18 Jul	
6.61	1.1		Caterine	Ibargüen	COL	12.2.84	3	DL	Stockholm		23 Aug	
6.60i			Abigail	Irozuru	GBR	3.1.90	1	NC	Glasgow		23 Feb	
6.80	1.4		Tissanna	Hickling	JAM	7.1.98	1		Kingston		11 Jul	
			(30)									
6.60	1.2		Juliet	Itoya	ESP	17.8.86	1		Castellón		29 Jul	
6.60	0.7		Milica	Gardasevic	SRB	28.9.98	3	Hanz	Zagreb		15 Sep	
6.59i			Yulimar	Rojas	VEN	21.10.95	1		Valencia		1 Feb	
6.58i			Deborah	Acquah	GHA	23.5.96	2		Lubbock		1 Feb	
6.58	0.6		Lea-Jasmin	Riecke	GER	25.4.00	1		Berlin		28 Aug	
6.58	1.4		Olivia	Fotopoulou	CYP	20.12.96	1		Valencia		29 Aug	
6.58	1.4		Diána	Lesti	HUN	30.3.98	2		Székesfehérvár		6 Sep	
6.57Ai			Natalie	Aranda	PAN	22.2.95	1	SAm Ch	Cochabamba		1 Feb	
6.57Ai			Rhesa	Foster	USA	25.5.98	1		Albuquerque		13 Feb	
6.57i			Ruth	Usoro	NGR	8.10.97	1		Lubbock		14 Feb	
			(40)									
6.57Ai			Sarea	Alexander	USA	15.2.96	4	NC	Albuquerque		15 Feb	
6.57	0.6		Merle	Homeier	GER	27.8.99	1		Essen		12 Jul	
6.57	-0.2		Jogaile	Petrokaite	LTU	30.9.95	1	LAT Ch	Ogre		15 Aug	
6.57	0.5		Taliyah	Brooks	USA	8.2.95	2		Marseille		3 Sep	
6.57	1.5		Polina	Lukyanenkova	RUS	15.7.98	1	NC	Chelyabinsk		9 Sep	
6.56i			Fátima	Diame	ESP	22.9.96	2		Valencia		1 Feb	
6.56i			Violetta	Skvortsova	BLR	15.4.98	1		Tartu		4 Feb	
6.56	1.6		Neja	Filipic	SLO	22.4.95	1		Slovenska Bistrica		13 Jun	
6.56	1.5		Senni	Salminen	FIN	29.1.96	1	NC	Turku		14 Aug	
6.56	0.4		Annik	Kälin	SUI	27.4.00	1		Schaffhausen		15 Aug	
			(50)									

LONG JUMP

Mark	Wind	Name		Nat	Born	Pos	Meet	Venue	Date	
6.56	1.0	Tania	Vicenzino	ITA	1.4.86	2		Savona	16	Jul
6.54	1.9	Tähti	Alver	EST	4.12.94	1	NC	Tallinn	9	Aug
6.53i		Florentina	Iusco	ROU	8.4.96	1	BalkC	Istanbul	15	Feb
6.53	0.6		Guo Sijia	CHN	14.2.99	1		Chengdu	16	May
6.53	0.0	Maryse	Luzolo	GER	13.3.95	1		Weinheim	1	Aug
6.53	0.9	Ksenija	Balta	EST	1.11.86	2	NC	Tallinn	9	Aug
6.53	1.3	Tilde	Johansson	SWE-J	5.1.01	2	v FIN	Tampere	6	Sep
6.52i		Yuliana	Angúlo	ECU	6.7.94	1		Zaragoza	8	Feb
6.52i		Veronika	Semashko	RUS	17.10.90	1		Sankt Peterburg	17	Feb
6.52		Katarina (60)	Johnson-Thompson	GBR	9.1.93	5	DL	Stockholm	23	Aug
6.51	0.3	Maria	Huntington	FIN	13.3.97	1		Lahti	15	Jul
6.51	0.5	Rebecca	Chapman	GBR	27.9.92	1		Bournemouth	9	Aug
6.51	1.2	Yelena	Sokolova	RUS	23.7.86	2	NC	Chelyabinsk	9	Sep
6.50i		Milena	Mitkova	BUL	26.1.90	1	NC-i	Sofia	1	Feb
6.50A	1.7	Lynique	Beneke	RSA	30.3.91	1		Bloemfontein	26	Feb
6.50	0.9	Tamara	Myers	BAH	27.7.93	2		Kingston	29	Feb
6.50			Gong Luying	CHN	22.2.00	1		Zhejiang	1	Aug
6.50	-0.2		Lu Minjia	CHN	29.12.90	2	NC	Shaoxing	16	Sep
6.49	1.1	Eliane	Martins	BRA	26.5.86	1		Bragança Paulista	18	Nov
6.49	1.6	Annie (70)	McGuire	AUS-J	13.6.01	*		Brisbane (Nathan)	5	Dec
6.48i		Lucie	Kienast	GER-J	1.6.01	1		Halle	18	Jan
6.48i		Chanice	Porter	JAM	25.5.94	2		Clemson	25	Jan
6.47i		Jasmine	Moore	USA-J	1.5.01	2		Fayetteville	14	Feb
6.47	0.0	Tiffany	Flynn	USA	2.9.95	2		Marietta	12	Jul
6.47	0.8	Yuliya	Pidluzhnaya	RUS	1.10.88	3	NC	Chelyabinsk	9	Sep
6.47	0.3		Qin Huiling	CHN-Y	29.11.03	2	NC	Shaoxing	16	Sep

6.46i		Jada	Seaman	USA-J	18.7.01	28 Feb	6.40i		Nadia	Williams	USA	18.8.98	31 Jan
6.45i		Oksana	Martynova	UKR	11.9.96	31 Jan	6.40i		Aliyah	Whisby	USA	28.2.98	22 Feb
6.45i		Jasmyn	Steels	USA	8.4.99	31 Jan	6.40	-0.8	Hanne	Maudens	BEL	12.3.97	9 Aug
6.45i		Maelly	Dalmat	FRA-J	1.10.01	22 Feb	6.40	1.7	Kreete	Verlin	EST	14.2.97	9 Aug
6.45i		Karolina	Mlodawska	POL	4.10.96	1 Mar	6.39i		Christabel	Nettey	CAN	2.6.91	18 Jan
6.45	-1.6	Adriana	Rodríguez	CUB	12.7.89	21 Mar	6.39i		Irène	Pusterla	SUI	21.6.88	25 Jan
6.45	-0.3	Linda	Suchá	CZE-J	28.9.01	8 Aug	6.39	0.2	Joanna	Kurylo	POL	16.8.95	25 Aug
6.44	0.4	Génesis	Romero	VEN	6.11.95	10 Jan	6.39	1.5	Keila	Costa	BRA	6.2.83	13 Dec
6.44i		Lucia	Vadlejch	SVK	8.11.88	18 Jan	6.39	0.4	Letícia	Melo	BRA	5.10.97	13 Dec
6.44i		Mercy Uyoyo	Abire	NGR	20.7.97	18 Jan	6.39A	1.2	Macarena	Reyes	CHI	30.3.84	13 Dec
6.44i		Darrielle	McQueen	USA	29.5.96	1 Feb	6.38	1.5	Madsalena	Zebrowska	POL	29.6.96	8 Aug
6.44i		Monae'	Nichols	USA	.99	22 Feb	6.38	1.8	Marija	Stojadinovic	SRB	13.7.97	6 Sep
6.43i		Aet	Laurik	EST	13.3.95	4 Feb	6.37i		Fatim	Affessi	SUI	8.7.93	18 Jan
6.43	1.0	Kaiza	Karlén	SWE	4.12.98	14 Jun	6.37i		Mikaelle	Assani	GER-J	18.8.02	31 Jan
6.43	0.9	Efthimía	Kolokithá	GRE	9.7.87	15 Jul	6.37i		Hafdís	Sigurdardóttir	ISL	12.2.87	2 Feb
6.42i		Sarah	Abrams	GBR	11.1.93	25 Jan	6.37i		Darya	Reznichenko	UZB	3.4.91	15 Feb
6.42i		Akela	Jones	BAR	22.4.95	25 Jan	6.37	0.1	Sabina	Allen	JAM	27.12.94	25 Jul
6.42i		Tyra	Gittens	TTO	6.6.98	14 Feb	6.37	0.9	Jana	Novotná	CZE	26.1.99	8 Aug
6.42i		Laura	Strati	ITA	3.10.90	22 Feb	6.36	-1.7	Ancy	Sojan	IND-J	1.3.01	12 Jan
6.42	0.9	Jennifer	Montag	GER	11.2.98	25 Jul	6.36i		Noor	Vidts	BEL	30.5.96	2 Feb
6.41	1.5	Sha'Keela	Saunders	USA	18.12.93	23 Jul	6.36i		Hilary	Kpatcha	FRA	5.5.98	14 Feb
6.41	0.3		Liu Jiahui	CHN	21.4.98	1 Aug	6.36	-0.4	Michaela	Kuceruvá	CZE	1.8.92	31 Jul
6.41	0.9	Hrystyna	Hryshutyna	UKR	21.3.92	25 Aug	6.36	1.4	Oxána	Koréneva	GRE	29.9.92	9 Aug
6.41	0.4	Gabriela	Petrova	BUL	29.6.92	20 Sep	6.36	1.0		Chen Liwen	CHN	3.1.98	16 Sep
6.41A	-1.2	Natalia	Linares	COL-Y	3.1.03	13 Dec	6.35i		Yekaterina	Koneva	RUS	25.9.88	29 Jan
6.40i		Destiny	Longmire	USA	6.2.98	24 Jan	6.35		Shantae	Foreman	JAM-J	22.10.02	8 Feb
6.40i		Patrícia	Mamona	POR	21.11.88	25 Jan	6.35	0.8	Luka	Garsvaite	LTU-J	25.3.01	7 Aug

Wind assisted

Mark	Wind	Name		Nat	Born	Pos	Meet	Venue	Date	
6.78	2.9	Brooke	Stratton	AUS	12.7.93	1		Canberra	25	Jan
6.74	3.0	Jazmin	Sawyers	GBR	21.5.94	1	NC	Manchester (SC)	4	Sep
6.65	5.0	Diána	Lesti	HUN	30.3.98	3	Gyulai	Székesfehérvár	19	Aug
6.61	3.7	Olivia	Fotopoulou	CYP	20.12.96	1		Sagunto	17	Jul
6.54	2.8	Gabriela	Petrova	BUL	29.6.92	1		Athína (F)	11	Sep
6.52	2.5	Annie	McGuire	AUS-J	13.6.01	1		Brisbane (Nathan)	5	Dec
6.50	2.7	Sha'Keela	Saunders	USA	18.12.93	1		Fort Worth	20	Jul
6.44	2.6	Andrea	Thompson	AUS	2.10.98	25 Jun	6.38	2.1	Irati	Mitxelena	ESP	3.7.98	24 Aug
6.42	3.0	Eléni	Koutsaliári	GRE	27.6.98	9 Aug	6.37	2.2	Alosmaidy	Tamayo	CUB	23.6.98	21 Feb
6.42	2.5	Noor	Vidts	BEL	30.5.96	13 Sep	6.37	2.5	Luka	Garsvaite	LTU-J	25.3.01	21 Jul
6.41	3.4	Sarah	Abrams	GBR	11.1.93	2 Aug	6.35	2.4	Tereza	Sinova	CZE-J	17.8.01	18 Jul
6.41	2.5	Evelis	Aguilar	COL	3.1.93	13 Dec	6.35	2.2	Lishanna	Ilves	EST	295.00	9 Aug
6.39	2.2	Jana	Novotná	CZE	26.1.99	15 Aug	6.35	3.2	Lissandra	Campos	BRA-J	6.2.02	6 Nov
							6.35	2.5	Gabriele	dos Santos	BRA	23.2.95	13 Dec

Best outdoors

Mark	Wind	Name			Venue	Date	
6.71	-0.2	Brume	3	DL	Doha	25	Sep
6.57	1.3	Irozuru	5	DL	Stockholm	23	Aug
6.48	0.5	David	4		Marseille	3	Sep
		6.53w 2.7	3		Göteborg	29	Aug

6.44	1.2	Lesueur-Aymonin			12 Sep	6.37	0.4	Skvortsova	17 Jul
6.43	0.1	Iusco			23 Aug	6.35		Porter	15 Jul
6.39	1.2	Diame			29 Aug	6.41w 3.4	Abrams	2 Aug
6.38	0.0	Strati			11 Jul				
6.38	0.1	Kienast			1 Aug	6.35w 5.6	Affessi	11 Jul

LONG JUMP - TRIPLE JUMP

Mark	Wind	Name		Nat	Born	Pos	Meet	Venue	Date
Best at low altitude					6.55i		Williams 1	Clemson	25 Jan
6.73i		Burks	1	New York (A) 25 Jan	6.49i		Alexander 1	Lubbock	24 Jan

JUNIORS

7 juniors in main list. 8 performances by 5 women to 6.48. Additional marks and further juniors:

Iapichino	6.57	-0.3	1		Vittorio Veneto	4 Jul	6.48	0.1 *	NC-j Grosseto	19 Sep
Johansson	6.52	0.0	1		Stockholm	23 Aug				
6.46i		Jada		Seaman	USA	18.7.01	1	ACC	Notre Dame	28 Feb
6.45i		Maelly		Dalmat	FRA	1.10.01	1	NC-j	Miramas	22 Feb
6.45	-0.3	Linda		Suchá (10)	CZE	28.9.01	1	NC	Plzen	8 Aug
6.41A	-1.2	Natalia		Linares	COL-Y	3.1.03	1		Quito	13 Dec
6.37i		Mikaelle		Assani	GER	18.8.02	8		Karlsruhe	31 Jan
6.36	-1.7	Ancy		Sojan	IND	1.3.01	1		Guwahati	12 Jan
6.35		Shantae		Foreman	JAM	22.10.02	1		Kingston	8 Feb
6.35	0.8	Luka		Garsvaite	LTU	25.3.01	2	NC	Palanga	7 Aug
6.33		Alyssa		Jones	USA-Y	6.2.04	1		Miami	10 Mar
6.33	-1.3	Henriette		Jæger	NOR-Y	30.6.03	1H		Moss	13 Sep
Best out: 6.38	0.1			Kienast			3		Weinheim	1 Aug
Wind assisted		1 in main list			Iapichino	6.60	2.4	1 NC-j	Grosseto	19 Sep
6.37	2.5	Luka		Garsvaite	LTU	25.3.01	1		Vilnius	21 Jul
6.35	2.4	Tereza		Sinova	CZE	17.8.01	1		Kladno	18 Jul
6.35	3.2	Lissandra		Campos	BRA	6.2.02	1	NC-J	Bragança Paulista	6 Nov

TRIPLE JUMP

15.43i		Yulimar		Rojas	VEN	21.10.95	1		Madrid			21 Feb	
							x		14.65	x	15.29	x	15.43
	15.03i	1		Metz		9 Feb	x		14.94	14.91	x	x	15.03
	14.71	1		Castellón		5 Sep	x		14.47/0.3	14.42	13.62	x	14.71
14.64Ai		Tori		Franklin	USA	7.10.92	1	NC			Albuquerque		14 Feb
							x		14.04	14.15	14.46	x	14.64
14.60Ai		Keturah		Orji	USA	5.3.96	2	NC			Albuquerque		14 Feb
							14.26		14.60	x	x	x	14.40
14.56	1.9	Yekaterina		Koneva	RUS	25.9.88	1				Sochi		25 Sep
							14.56		14.28	p	14.50	p	p
14.55	1.6	Liadagmis		Povea	CUB	6.2.96	*				La Habana		8 Feb
							14.78w		12.85	x	14.55/1.6	12.79w	p
	14.52i	2		Madrid		21 Feb	14.08		14.13	14.36	14.52	x	x
	(8/5)												
14.43	1.2	Shanieka		Ricketts	JAM	2.2.92	1				Kingston		22 Aug
14.38	1.4	Gabriela		Petrova	BUL	29.6.92	1				Plovdiv		14 Jul
14.34	1.6	Davisleydi Lupes		Velazco	CUB	4.9.99	2	NC			La Habana		21 Mar
14.33i		Thea		LaFond	DMA	5.4.94	1				Staten Island		7 Feb
14.33i		Patrícia		Mamona	POR	21.11.88	3				Madrid		8 Feb
	(10)												
14.30	0.5	Kristiina		Mäkelä	FIN	20.11.92	*				Orimattila		21 Jul
14.28i		Violetta		Skvortsova	BLR	15.4.98	1				Minsk		22 Dec
14.24	0.3	Irina		Vaskovskaya	BLR	2.4.91	1	NC			Minsk		1 Aug
14.22	0.5	Neja		Filipic	SLO	22.4.95	1				Maribor		23 Jun
14.18	1.2	Dovile		Kilty	LTU	14.7.93	1	NC			Palanga		8 Aug
14.17i		Neele		Eckhardt	GER	2.7.92	1				Düsseldorf		4 Feb
14.17	1.1	Darya		Nidbaykina	RUS	26.12.94	*	NC			Chelyabinsk		11 Sep
14.17	-1.0	Gabriele		dos Santos	BRA	23.2.95	1	NC			São Paulo		11 Dec
14.16i		Natalya		Yevdokimova	RUS	7.9.93	1	NC			Moskva		27 Feb
14.15	0.7	Leyanis		Pérez	CUB-J	10.1.02	3	NC			La Habana		21 Mar
	(20)												
14.12i		Kimberly		Williams	JAM	3.11.88	1				Clemson		15 Feb
14.12	0.1	Spiridoúla		Karídi	GRE-J	30.1.01	1				Athína (K)		22 Jul
14.10	0.4			Yang Yang	CHN-J	23.8.01	1				Guangzhou		30 May
14.10	1.8	Susana		Costa	POR	22.9.84	3	NC			Lisboa (U)		8 Aug
14.10	-0.1			Zeng Rui	CHN	6.2.98	1				Nanjing		4 Sep
14.08i		Valentina		Kosolapova	RUS	11.7.97	1				Moskva		9 Feb
14.04	1.5	Senni		Salminen	FIN	29.1.96	1				Espoo		27 Jun
14.03i		Kristin		Gierisch	GER	20.8.90	2	NC			Leipzig		22 Feb
14.03A	-1.3	Zinzi		Chanbangu	RSA	28.9.96	1				Pretoria		7 Mar
14.02	1.3			Li Ying	CHN	29.3.94	1	NC			Shaoxing		18 Sep
	(30)												
13.99	0.8	Janne		Nielsen	DEN	8.6.93	1	FRA Ch			Albi		13 Sep
13.92	1.5	Keila		Costa	BRA	6.2.83	2	GP			São Paulo		6 Dec
13.90i		Jasmine		Moore	USA-J	1.5.01	1				Fayetteville		1 Feb
13.90i		Ana		Peleteiro	ESP	2.12.95	1	NC			Ourense		29 Feb
13.87i		Elena		Panturoiu	ROU	24.2.95	5				Madrid		21 Feb

TRIPLE JUMP

Mark	Wind	Name		Nat	Born	Pos	Meet	Venue	Date	
13.87	0.0		Tan Qiujiao	CHN	28.5.00	2	NC	Shaoxing	18	Sep
13.86	0.2		Rao Fan	CHN	1.1.96	2		Guangzhou	30	May
13.85i		Paraskeví	Papahrístou	GRE	17.4.89	5		Düsseldorf	4	Feb
13.85	2.0	Aleksandra	Krasina	RUS	12.9.98	3	NCp	Bryansk	30	Aug
13.84	0.9	Florentina	Iusco	ROU	8.4.96	1	NCp	Bucuresti	8	Aug
		(40)								
13.84	1.8	Veronica	Zanon	ITA-J	16.1.01	1	NC-j	Grosseto	20	Sep
13.84	1.4	Nubia	Soares	BRA	26.3.96	3	GP	São Paulo	6	Dec
13.83i		Naomi	Ogbeta	GBR	18.4.98	1	NC	Glasgow	23	Feb
13.83	1.1		Xu Ting	CHN	23.2.97	1		Fuzhou	24	May
13.82i		Fátima	Diame	ESP	22.9.96	1		Valencia	18	Jan
13.82	1.3	Ruta	Lasmane	LAT	17.12.00	1	NC	Jelgava	8	Aug
13.81	1.3	Tugba	Danismaz	TUR	1.9.99	1	NC	Istanbul	4	Sep
13.80Ai		Imani	Oliver	USA	7.3.93	3	NC	Albuquerque	14	Feb
13.78	1.6	Patricia	Sarrapio	ESP	16.11.82	1		Madrid	5	Sep
13.78	1.4	Viktoriya	Prokopenko	RUS	17.4.91	*	NC	Chelyabinsk	22	Sep
		(50)								
13.78A	1.0	Liuba M.	Zaldívar	ECU	5.4.93	1		Quito	13	Dec
13.77i		Deborah	Acquah	GHA	23.5.96	1		College Station	8	Feb
13.70	1.7	Eva	Pepelnak	SLO	4.10.00	2		Maribor	23	Jun
13.70		Sabina	Allen	JAM	27.12.94	2		Marietta	11	Jul
13.68i		Evelise	Veiga	POR	3.3.96	3	NC	Pombal	1	Mar
13.67	0.4	Maria	Purtsa	GER	18.8.95	1		Dresden	10	Jul
13.65	1.4	Linda	Suchá	CZE-J	28.9.01	1		Karpacz	20	Sep
13.64	0.3		Wu Mian	CHN	9.1.00	1		Chengdu	15	May
13.63	0.0	Parinya	Chuaimaroeng	THA	16.12.97	1		Bangkok	16	Jan
13.62		Sandisha	Antoine	LCA	5.11.91	1		Kingston	1	Feb
		(60)								
13.62	1.6	Emma	Pullola	FIN	18.12.96	2		Orimattila	21	Jul
13.62	0.6	Ottavia	Cestonaro	ITA	12.1.95	1		Vicenza	7	Aug
13.61	1.6	Paola	Borovic	CRO	26.6.95	1	NC	Zagreb	8	Aug
13.61	1.2	Diana	Zagainova	LTU	20.6.97	2	NC	Palanga	8	Aug
13.59	-0.7	Jeanine	Assani Issouf FRA		17.8.92	13	Sep			
13.58	0.5	Vaida	Padimanskaite	LTU	7.8.00	8	Aug			
13.58	1.0	Ana	Oliveira	POR	18.7.95	22	Aug			
13.58	0.8	Marija	Stojadinovic	SRB	13.7.97	22	Aug			
13.57i		Anne-Suzanna Fosther-Katta								
				FRA	13.11.98	29	Feb			
13.57	-0.2	Jessie	Maduka	GER	23.4.96	8	Aug			
13.56i		Lexi	Ellis	USA	15.10.99	1	Feb			
13.56	1.9	Rebecka	Abrahamsson	SWE	26.4.94	16	Aug			
13.56	-1.2	Dariya	Derkach	ITA	27.3.93	30	Aug			
13.55	-0.2	Karolina	Mlodzinska	POL	4.10.96	28	Aug			
13.55	1.3	Ilionis	Guillaume	FRA	13.1.98	13	Sep			
13.54i		Aleksandra	Malofeyeva	BLR	12.9.98	21	Feb			
13.52	-01.	Adrianna	Szóstak	POL	2.3.96	28	Aug			
13.51i		Cristina	Bujin	ROU	12.4.88	28	Feb			
13.51	-0.8	Mariya	Siney	UKR	29.3.97	20	Aug			
13.51	0.1		Wang Wupin	CHN	18.1.91	4	Sep			
13.50i		Yekaterina	Sariyeva	AZE	18.12.95	15	Feb			
13.50i		Oda Utsi	Onstad	NOR	12.5.90	16	Feb			
13.50A		Patience	Ntshingila	RSA	26.8.89	14	Mar			
13.49i		Ruth	Usoro	NGR	8.10.97	24	Jan			
13.49i		Ciynamon	Stevenson	USA	9.4.98	31	Jan			
13.48Ai		Charisma	Taylor	BAH	3.9.99	14	Feb			
13.47i		Alonie	Sutton	USA	19.12.97	28	Jan			
13.46		Aleksandra	Nacheva	BUL-J	20.8.01	1	Feb			
13.46	0.0		Chai Yuyue	CHN	20.10.99	30	May			
13.45Ai		Lynnika	Pitts	USA	19.5.92	14	Feb			
13.45Ai		Tiffany	Flynn	USA	2.9.95	14	Feb			
13.45	0.1	Agnieszka	Bednarek	POL	14.6.98	28	Aug			
13.44i		Zion	Lewis	USA	11.10.98	1	Mar			
13.44	0.9	Tugba	Aydin	TUR	25.8.94	29	Sep			
13.43			Li Xiaohong	CHN	8.1.95	24	May			
13.42i		Mariya	Ovchinnikova	KAZ	19.10.98	18	Jan			
13.42i		Bria	Matthews	USA	22.7.97	29	Feb			
13.42	1.1	Maja	Åskag	SWE-J	18.12.02	16	Aug			
13.41			Nguyen Thi Huong VIE-J		24.11.01	13	Nov			
13.40i			Mariya Privalova (100) RUS-J		25.12.01	8	Feb			
13.40	1.8	Irina	Pimenova	UKR	19.12.88	30	Aug			
13.40	1.4	Aleksandra	Skobel	RUS	27.2.99	11	Sep			
13.40	0.9	Tessy	Ebosele	NGR-J	28.7.02	4	Oct			
13.40			Vu Thi Ngoc Ha	VIE	21.5.00	13	Nov			
13.39	1.2	Tetyana	Ptashkina	UKR	29.3.97	30	Aug			
13.39	0.4	Diana	Ion	ROU	27.11.00	4	Sep			
13.39	-1.0	Irati	Mitxelena	ESP	3.7.98	27	Sep			
13.38i		Kala	Penn	IVB	31.7.98	1	Feb			
13.38	1.4	Dailin	Martínez	CUB	7.9.98	22	Feb			
13.37i		Essence	Thomas	USA	1.11.97	15	Feb			
13.37i		María	Vicente	ESP-J	28.3.01	21	Feb			
13.37	-0.3	Carolina	Joyeux	GER-J	26.3.01	8	Aug			
13.36	1.4	Esra	Yilmaz	TUR	5.1.00	4	Sep			
13.35	0.2		Chen Jie	CHN	2.3.98	18	Sep			
13.34i		Shardia	Lawrence	JAM	31.12.95	18	Jan			
13.34i		Alex	Madlock	USA	17.9.97	31	Jan			
13.34	1.7	Alna	Griksaite	LTU	23.11.94	6	Aug			
13.34	1.2	Sohane	Aucagos	FRA-Y	17.3.03	13	Sep			
13.33	0.8	Ailyah	Parker	AUS	16.12.96	26	Jan			
13.32i		Michelle	Fokam	USA	8.6.98	23	Feb			
13.32		Vinija	Vijayan	IND	11.10.96	4	Mar			
13.32	1.1	Merilyn	Uudmäe	EST	26.3.91	8	Aug			
13.32	1.5	Marija	Ivankovic	CRO	6.10.98	29	Aug			
13.31i		Titiana	Marsh	USA	13.12.99	1	Feb			
13.31i		Tamara	Myers	BAH	27.7.93	15	Feb			
13.31i		Ja'la	Henderson	USA	13.3.97	15	Feb			
13.31		Anastasia	Senchiv	MDA	2.1.98	26	Aug			
13.31	-0.5	Ingrid	Zanette	BRA	27.4.98	11	Dec			
13.30i		Michelle	Cobb	USA	9.8.99	31	Jan			
13.30i		Sasa	Babsek	SLO	27.3.92	22	Feb			
13.30i		Carmen	Toma	ROU	28.3.89	28	Feb			
13.30	2.0	Thalía de la C. Pedroso		CUB-J	27.12.01	22	Feb			
13.30	0.5		Chen Ting	CHN	28.8.97	16	Aug			
13.30	0.3	Beyza	Tilki	TUR	3.3.94	4	Sep			

Wind assisted

14.78	2.1		Povea	CUB		1		La Habana	8	Feb
14.75	2.3	Yekaterina	Koneva	RUS	25.9.88	1	NCp	Bryansk	30	Aug
					14.75w	p	p	12.34	p	p
	14.74	2.7 1 NC	Chelyabinsk		11 Sep	14.11w	14.17	x	13.91w 14.19/0.0	14.74w
14.33	3.1	Kristiina	Mäkelä	FIN	20.11.92	1		Orimattila	21	Jul
14.32	2.2	Neja	Filipic	SLO	22.4.95	1		Ljubljana	4	Jul
14.27	3.0	Darya	Nidbaykina	RUS	26.12.94	2	NC	Chelyabinsk	11	Sep

TRIPLE JUMP - SHOT

Mark	Wind	Name		Nat	Born	Pos	Meet	Venue		Date
14.16	3.2	Evelise	Veiga	POR	3.3.96	2	NC	Lisboa (U)		8 Aug
14.15	3.3	Viktoriya	Prokopenko	RUS	17.4.91	3	NC	Chelyabinsk		22 Sep
13.83	2.2	Tugba	Danismaz	TUR	1.9.99	1		Ankara		18 Jul
13.63	2.3	Tessy	Ebosele	NGR-J	28.7.02	1	ESP-J	Madrid (V)		4 Oct
13.56	2.2	Patience	Ntshingila	RSA	26.8.89	7 Mar	13.56	3.3 Thelma	Fuentes	GUA 20.8.92 28 Dec
13.56	3.2	Lucinda	Gomes	POR	16.4.95	8 Aug	13.47	2.9 Ailyah	Parker	AUS 16.12.96 26 Jan

Best outdoors

14.26	2.0	Mamona	1	NC	Lisboa (U)	8 Aug	13.74	1.6 Ogbeta	4	PNG Turku	11 Aug
14.17	-0.3	Skvortsova	1		Brest	16 Jul	13.73	0.6 Eckhardt	1	Essen	12 Jul
14.14	0.2	Orji	1		Marietta	25 Jul		13.80w 2.1	1	Osterode	18 Jul
13.53	0.8	Veiga		11 Aug	13.33		Malofeyeva	19 May			

Best at low altitude

13.74	1.3	Liuba M.	Zaldívar	ECU	5.4.93	4	GP	São Paulo	6 Dec

JUNIORS

6 juniors in main list. 10 performances (inc. 2 indoors) by 5 women to 13.74. Additional marks and further juniors:

Pérez		13.95	2.0	*	La Habana			8 Feb		
Yang Yang		13.93	1.1	2		Nanjing		4 Sep		
Karídi		13.91	-1.7	1	NC	Pátra	8 Aug	13.76	0.0 1	Ioánnina 17 Jul
Moore		13.74i	1		SEC	College Station	29 Feb			
13.46		Aleksandra	Nacheva	BUL	20.8.01	1		Parow		1 Feb
13.42	1.1	Maja	Åskag	SWE	18.12.02	2	NC	Uppsala		16 Aug
13.41			Nguyen Thi Huong	VIE	24.11.01	1	NC	Hanoi		13 Nov
13.40i		Mariya	Privalova (10)	RUS	25.12.01	1	NC-j	Volgograd		8 Feb
13.40	0.9	Tessy	Ebosele	NGR	28.7.02	*	ESP-J	Madrid (V)		4 Oct
13.37i		María	Vicente	ESP	28.3.01	8		Madrid		21 Feb
13.37	-0.3	Carolina	Joyeux	GER	26.3.01	3	NC	Braunschweig		8 Aug
13.34	1.2	Sohane	Aucagos	FRA-Y	17.3.03	3	NC	Albi		13 Sep
13.30	2.0	Thalía de la C	Pedroso	CUB	27.12.01	4		Camagüey		22 Feb

SHOT

19.70i			Gong Lijiao	CHN	24.1.89	1		Beijing		14 Mar
	19.53	1	Qinhuangdao	23 Aug	18.93	19.12	19.14	19.21	19.10	19.53
19.53		Auriol	Dongmo	POR	3.8.90	1	NC	Lisboa (U)		8 Aug
				x	18.90	18.80	18.85	x	19.53	
	19.27	1	Leiria	24 Jun	18.42	18.90	x	17.90	18.86	19.27
19.41		Chase	Ealey	USA	20.7.94	1		Rathdrum		1 Aug
					19.41	x	18.21	18.19	18.40	x
19.27		Alyona	Dubitskaya	BLR	25.1.90	1		Brest		17 Jul
					18.49	18.53	18.89	x	x	19.27
	19.19	1 NC	Minsk	28 Jul	18.76	19.19	x	18.72	18.50	18.29
19.18		Danniel	Thomas-Dodd	JAM	11.11.92	1		Marietta		15 Aug
		(9/5)								
18.95i		Jessica	Ramsey	USA	26.7.91	1		Nashville		18 Jan
18.88		Brittany	Crew	CAN	6.3.94	1		Christchurch		6 Mar
18.84		Sarah	Mitton	CAN	20.6.96	1		Auckland (Waitakere)		23 Feb
18.81		Valerie	Adams	NZL	6.10.84	1		Hamilton		15 Feb
18.80i		Maggie	Ewen	USA	23.9.94	2		New York (A)		25 Jan
		(10)								
18.77i		Anita	Márton	HUN	15.1.89	1		Budapest		8 Feb
18.77		Fanny	Roos	SWE	2.1.95	1		Helsingborg		21 Jun
18.50			Gao Yang	CHN	1.3.93	1		Bridgetown		25 Jan
18.50i		Dimitriana	Surdu	MDA	12.4.94	1	NC	Chisinau		1 Feb
18.44i		Rachel	Fatherly	USA	20.4.94	1		Iowa City		17 Jan
18.40i		Haley	Teel	USA	20.6.96	2	NC	Albuquerque		14 Feb
18.32		Markéta	Cervenková	CZE	20.8.91	2	Skol	Chorzów		6 Sep
18.28		Alena	Pasechnik	BLR	17.4.95	2		Brest		17 Jul
18.27		Jessica	Schilder	NED	19.3.99	1	NC	Utrecht		29 Aug
18.24i		Jeneva	Stevens	USA	28.10.89	2		Iowa City		17 Jan
		(20)								
18.20			Song Jiayuan	CHN	15.9.97	2		Shanghai		8 Aug
18.19i		Felisha	Johnson	USA	24.7.89	1		Indianapolis		18 Jan
18.17i		Samantha	Noennig	USA	28.7.98	1		Albuquerque		1 Feb
18.16		Sophie	McKinna	GBR	31.8.94	1		Chelmsford		29 Aug
18.14i		Alina	Kenzel	GER	10.8.97	1	NC	Leipzig		22 Feb
18.14		Julia	Ritter	GER	13.5.98	1		Osterode		18 Jul
18.09		Paulina	Guba	POL	14.5.91	1	NC	Wroclawek		30 Aug
18.08		Maddison-Lee	Wesche	NZL	13.6.99	1		Hamilton		11 Jan
18.02		Emel	Dereli	TUR	25.2.96	1		Izmir		12 Feb
17.99i		Jessica	Woodard	USA	4.2.95	1		Norman		8 Feb
		(30)								

WOMEN 2020

SHOT

Mark	Name	Nat	Born	Pos	Meet	Venue	Date
17.98i	Katharina Maisch	GER	12.6.97	2	NC	Leipzig	22 Feb
17.97i	Amelia Strickler	GBR	24.1.94	1	NC	Glasgow	23 Feb
17.96i	Laulauga Tausaga	USA	22.5.98	1		Notre Dame	8 Feb
17.84i	Raven Saunders	USA	15.5.96	1		Winston-Salem	8 Feb
17.82i	Adelaide Aquilla	USA	3.3.99	1	Big 10	Geneva OH	29 Feb
17.72i	Viktoryia Kolb ¶	BLR	26.10.93	1		Gomel	8 Feb
17.72i	Alena Abramchuk	BLR	14.2.88	3	NC	Mogilyov	21 Feb
17.72	Jorinde van Klinken	NED	2.2.00	2	NC	Utrecht	29 Aug
17.65	Klaudia Kardasz	POL	2.5.96	2		Poznan	11 Sep
17.63i	Michelle Carter (40)	USA	12.10.85	7	NC	Albuquerque	14 Feb
17.63	Jiang Yue	CHN	6.10.98	2	NC	Shaoxing	16 Sep
17.61i	Akealy Moton	USA	26.11.98	1		Fargo	8 Feb
17.61	Geisa Arcanjo	BRA	19.9.91	1		Bragança Paulista	14 Mar
17.58	Zhang Linru	CHN	23.9.99	1		Shijiazhuang	14 Apr
17.57i	Madison Pollard	USA	22.10.98	2		Bloomington	1 Feb
17.57i	Lloydricia Cameron	JAM	8.4.96	1		Clemson	15 Feb
17.56i	Khayla Dawson	USA	18.3.98	1		Notre Dame	22 Feb
17.55i	Alyona Gordeyeva	RUS	24.4.97	1		Moskva	26 Aug
17.55i	Melissa Boekelman	NED	11.5.89	1		Sittard	26 Jan
17.55i	Jessica Inchude (50)	GBS	25.3.96	1		Lisboa (Jamor)	29 Dec
17.50i	Anna Avdeyeva	RUS	6.4.85	1	NC	Moskva	26 Feb
17.50	Guo Tianqian	CHN	1.6.95	1		Shijiazhuang	29 May
17.49i	Latavia Maines	USA	.98	1		Clemson	14 Feb
17.49	Axelina Johansson	SWE	20.4.00	1		Falun	27 Jul
17.47	Cleopatra Borel	TTO	10.3.79	1		Port of Spain	11 Jan
17.43i	Alyssa Wilson	USA	20.2.99	1		Seattle	18 Jan
17.43i	Shelby Gunnells	USA	1.1.97	2		Fargo	8 Feb
17.40	Ahymara Espinoza	VEN	28.5.85	1		Ljubljana	16 Jul
17.39i	Eliana Bandeira	POR	1.7.96	2	NC	Pombal	29 Feb
17.39	Ivana Gallardo (60)	CHI	20.7.93	1		Santiago de Chile	19 Dec
17.36	Yemisi Ogunleye	GER	3.10.98	2		Halle	15 Aug
17.36	Frida Åkerström	SWE	29.11.90	2	vFIN	Tampere	5 Sep
17.29i	Olga Golodna	UKR	14.11.91	1	NC	Sumy	21 Feb
17.25i	Ieva Zarankaite	LTU	23.11.94	1		Kaunas	15 Feb
17.24i	Josephine Schaefer	USA	10.4.99	1		Ripon	8 Feb
17.24	Yevgeniya Solovyova	RUS	28.6.86	1		Adler	19 Sep
17.21i	María Belén Toimil	ESP	5.5.94	1		Valencia	1 Feb
17.20i	Chiara Rosa	ITA	28.1.83	1		Ancona	12 Jan
17.20	Yaniuvis López	CUB	1.2.86	1		Santiago de Cuba	29 Feb
17.19i	Francislaine Serra (70)	POR	10.1.94	3	NC	Pombal	29 Feb
17.08i	Claudine Vita	GER	19.9.96	6		Rochlitz	2 Feb
17.05i	Yuliya Leontyuk	BLR	31.1.84	3		Minsk	17 Jan
17.01	Senja Mäkitörmä	FIN	31.5.94	3	vSWE	Tampere	5 Sep
16.97	Keely Medeiros	BRA	30.4.87	1		Sao Bernardo do Campo	7 Mar
16.94	Lvia Avancini	BRA	8.5.92	2	NC	São Paulo	11 Dec
16.93i	Tarynn Sieg	USA	4.9.98	1	MWC	Albuquerque	29 Feb
16.90i	Sopo Shatirishvili	GEO	15.1.95	1	NC	Tbilisi	8 Feb

Mark	Name		Nat	Born			Mark	Name		Nat	Born		
16.87i	Devia	Brown	JAM	21.3.98	8	Feb	16.55	Violetta	Veiland	HUN	11.8.98	13	Jun
16.86i	Monique	Riddick	USA	8.11.89	25	Jan	16.52	Milena	Sens	BRA	23.7.99	11	Dec
16.85i	Lena	Giger	USA	7.6.96	18	Jan	16.51		Chen Xiarong	CHN	21.12.98	23	Aug
16.82i	Elena	Bruckner	USA	14.4.98	29	Feb	16.45i	Nora	Monie	USA	4.6.97	1	Feb
16.82	Natalya	Troneva	RUS	24.2.93	9	Sep	16.43		Geng Shuang	CHN	9.7.93	16	Sep
16.81i	Nayoka	Clunis	JAM	7.10.95	29	Feb	16.40i	Hannah	Hall	USA	30.9.00	29	Feb
16.80i	Debbie	Ajagbe	USA	2.11.98	29	Feb	16.39	Ischke	Senekal	RSA	8.1.93	13	Mar
16.80	Maja	Slepowronska	POL	2.12.98	30	Aug	16.39		Lee Su-kyung	KOR	15.2.93	25	Jun
16.76i	Kristina	Insingo	USA	10.1.97	8	Feb	16.38i	Snezhana	Trofimets	RUS	1.7.99	14	Feb
16.76	Sarah	Schmidt	GER	9.7.97	24	Jul	16.36i	Jessica	Cérival	FRA	20.1.82	29	Feb
16.75i	Lauren	Coleman	USA	18.2.97	14	Feb	16.36i	Mackenna	Howard	USA	25.1.96	29	Feb
16.75i	Benthe	König	NED	7.4.98	22	Feb	16.35	Eveliina	Rouvali	FIN	16.4.97	5	Sep
16.70i	Meia	Gordon	USA	12.3.98	25	Jan	16.33i	Pinar	Akyol	TUR-Y	2.10.03	9	Feb
16.70i	Hanna	Meinikmann	GER	28.3.99	22	Feb	16.33i	Annina	Brandenburg	GER	6.3.98	2	Mar
16.70		Sun Yue	CHN-J	19.6.01	23	Aug	16.33	Sara	Lennman	SWE	8.4.96	6	Aug
16.68i	Alexandra	Emilianov	MDA	19.9.99	29	Feb	16.31i	Nicole	Fautsch	USA	17.1.98	28	Feb
16.66i	Essence	Henderson	USA	11.3.99	29	Feb	16.30i	Michella	Obijiaku	ITA	6.11.97	14	Feb
16.60i	Tess	Keyzers	USA	31.7.98	17	Jan	16.30i	Payden	Montana	USA	26.11.99	5	Dec
16.59i	Samariae	Bonds	USA	.99	1	Feb	16.28i	Valeriya	Zyryanova	RUS	12.8.90	11	Jan
16.59	Úrsula	Ruiz	ESP	11.8.83	7	Mar	16.28i	Fiona	Richards	JAM	20.11.98	8	Feb
16.57	Maria Fernanda	Orozco	MEX	25.1.98	15	Dec	16.27i	Brittany	Jones	USA	15.5.99	1	Feb
16.55i	Nickolette	Dunbar	USA	5.4.98	8	Feb	16.24i	Maria	Muzzio	USA	20.1.98	29	Feb

SHOT - DISCUS

Mark	Name	Nat	Born	Pos	Meet	Venue	Date
16.23	Yekaterina Burmistrova	RUS	18.8.90	22	Aug		
16.19i	Erna Sóley Gunnarsdóttir	ISL	22.3.00	17	Jan		
16.19i	Patience Marshall	USA	23.9.00	1	Feb		
16.19i	Adele Nicoll	GBR	28.9.96	23	Feb		
16.18i	Ásdís Hjálmsdóttir Annerud	ISL	28.10.85	11	Feb		
16.17i	Cherisse Murray	TTO	13.9.93	29	Feb		
16.16	Maria Deaviz	USA-J	10.4.01	11	Jul		
16.16i	Faith Ette	USA	25.5.00	5	Dec		
16.15i	Aveun Moore	USA	16.11.98	21	Feb		
16.15i	Sherry Lubin	USA	1.4.98	29	Feb		
16.14i	Tedreauna Britt	USA	6.1.00	15	Feb		
16.14	Lin Chia-Ying	TPE	5.11.82	13	Mar		
16.13i	Gabrielle Bailey	JAM	19.10.98	24	Jan		
16.13i	Payton Roberts	USA	4.1.98	1	Mar		
16.12i	Tetyana Kravchenko	UKR	20.8.00	21	Feb		

Mark				Pos		Venue	Date
16.12i	Maia Campbell	USA				.98	23 Feb
16.10i	Veronica Fraley	USA				27.5.00	8 Feb
16.10i	Lindsey Baker	USA				10.4.99	29 Feb
16.10	Serena Vincent	GBR-J				5.12.01	13 Sep
16.10i	Emily Mikoud	USA				.98	5 Dec
16.08	Monia Cantarella	ITA				3.7.94	29 Jul
16.06i	Emily Stauffer	USA				29.1.98	15 Feb
16.04i	Grace Tennant	CAN				2.2.99	22 Feb
16.02i	Kayli Johnson	USA				.98	15 Feb
16.02i	Maia Garren	USA				9.9.98	15 Feb
16.02i	Rachel Tanczos	USA				27.9.99	29 Feb
16.01	Amanda Ngandu-Ntumba	FRA				24.6.00	12 Sep
16.00i	Zada Swoopes	USA				.99	1 Feb
16.00i	Trinity Tutti	CAN				3.5.00	8 Feb
16.00	Autavia Fluker	USA				6.6.97	8 Mar

Best outdoors

Mark	Name		Pos		Venue	Date
18.64	Ramsey	2			Marietta	29 Aug
17.96	Kenzel	1	NC		Braunschweig	8 Aug
17.61	Strickler	1			Loughborough	16 Aug
17.53	Boekelman	1			Lokeren	23 Aug
17.48	Abramchuk	3	NCp		Brest	17 Jul
17.42	Inchude	2	POR Ch		Lisboa (U)	8 Aug
17.40	Márton	1			Szeged	13 Jun
17.36	Bandeira	2			Lisboa (U)	1 Aug
17.14	Teel	1			Marietta	18 Jul
17.10	Serra	3	NC		Lisboa (U)	8 Aug
17.06	Rosa	1			Udine	8 Aug
17.02	Gordeyeva	1			Moskva	23 Aug
16.90	Toimil	1			León	16 Aug
16.80	Zarankaite			8 Aug	16.62 König	24 Jul
16.16	Meinikmann			13 Jun	16.02 Golodna	29 Aug

JUNIORS

Mark	Name		Nat	Born	Pos	Meet	Venue	Date
16.70		Sun Yue	CHN	19.6.01	2		Qinhuangdao	23 Aug
16.33i	Pınar	Akyol	TUR	2.10.03	1	Balk-J	Istanbul	9 Feb
	15.74				1	Balk-J	Istanbul	12 Sep
6.20i	Sina	Prüfer	GER	31.12.02	1	NC-j	Neubrandenburg	15 Feb
16.16	Maria	Deaviz	USA-	10.4.01	1		New Castle PA	11 Jul
16.10	Serena	Vincent	GBR	5.12.01	1		Portsmouth	13 Sep
15.98	Layselys	Jiménez	CUB	18.2.01	2		La Habana	13 Mar
15.90	Alina	van Daalen	NED	12.4.02	3		Leiden	19 Sep
15.88i	Mallory	Kauffman	USA	15.5.01	1		University Park	11 Dec
15.83		Meng Xiangyu	CHN	16.8.02	1		Zhengzhou	6 Aug
15.80		Yu Tianxiao	CHN	16.8.02	9	NC	Shaoxing	16 Sep

DISCUS

Mark	Name		Nat	Born	Pos	Meet	Venue	Date
70.15	Valarie	Allman	USA	23.2.95	1		Rathdrum	1 Aug
			70.15 x	x	65.86	66.03	62.09	
65.93	Sandra	Perkovic	CRO	21.6.90	1	NC-w	Split	7 Mar
			x	62.48	62.02	65.60	65.93 x	
65.58	Kristin	Pudenz	GER	9.2.93	1		Schönebeck	24 Jul
			64.53	64.95	64.15	65.58 x	63.23	
	64.92	1	Potsdam	19 Jun	63.21	64.92	62.56 64.56 63.78 x	
65.26		Chen Yang	CHN	10.7.91	1		Shijiazhuang	28 May
			62.46	60.62	65.26 x	62.20	x	
	64.88	1	Qinhuangdao	23 Aug	64.88	63.95	x x x	64.68
64.76	Yaimé	Pérez	CUB	29.5.91	1	NC	La Habana	20 Mar
	(7/5)			x	63.58	64.76	62.27 60.88	61.21
64.14	Mélina	Robert-Michon	FRA	18.7.79	1		Salon-de-Provence	16 Feb
64.09		Feng Bin	CHN	3.4.94	1		Beijing	7 Aug
64.03i	Shanice	Craft	GER	15.5.93	1		Berlin	14 Feb
63.90	Yekaterina	Strokova	RUS	17.12.89	1	NC	Chelyabinsk	8 Sep
63.71	Denia	Caballero	CUB	13.1.90	2		La Habana	8 Feb
	(10)							
63.21	Claudine	Vita	GER	19.9.96	1		Neubrandenburg	5 Aug
62.93	Irina	Rodrigues	POR	5.2.91	1		Leiria	27 Jun
62.37	Fernanda Raquel	Borges	BRA	26.7.88	1		São Bernardo do Campo	7 Mar
61.94		Su Xinyue	CHN	8.11.91	2		Shijiazhuang	28 May
61.91	Liliana	Cá	POR	5.11.86	1	GP	São Paulo	6 Dec
61.88	Ieva	Zarankaite	LTU	23.11.94	1		Vilnius	21 Jul
61.52	Natalya	Karpova	RUS	18.1.94	2	NC	Chelyabinsk	8 Sep
61.17	Julia	Harting	GER	1.4.90	3		Schönebeck	24 Jul
61.13	Yelena	Panova	RUS	2.3.87	2		Adler	18 Feb
60.84	Andressa	de Morais	BRA	21.12.90	2	GP	São Paulo	6 Dec
	(20)							
60.75	Marija	Tolj	CRO	29.11.99	2	NC-w	Split	7 Mar
60.64	Anastasiya	Vityugova	RUS	13.3.97	2		Adler	11 Feb
60.44i	Nadine	Müller	GER	21.11.85	2		Berlin	14 Feb
60.43	Kathrine	Bebe	DEN	27.1.91	1		Hvidovre	2 Aug
60.15	Izabela	da Silva	BRA	2.8.95	2		São Bernardo do Campo	7 Mar
60.01	Vanessa	Kamga	SWE	19.11.98	1		Södertälje	14 Jun

DISCUS - HAMMER

Mark	Name		Nat	Born	Pos	Meet	Venue	Date
59.99	Chioma	Onyekwere	NGR	28.6.94	1		Kutztown	24 Jul
59.98	Daisy	Osakue	ITA	16.1.96	1		Livorno	1 Aug
59.96	Hrisoúla	Anagnostopoúlou	GRE	27.8.91	1		Thessaloníki	8 Jul
59.75	Marike	Steinacker	GER	4.3.92	2		Neubrandenburg	27 May
	(30)							
59.64	Julia	Ritter	GER	13.5.98	1		Osterode	18 Jul
59.59	Jorinde	van Klinken	NED	2.2.00	1		Lisse	21 Aug
59.52	Salla	Sipponen	FIN	13.3.95	1		Espoo	5 Aug
59.40	Irene	Donzelot	FRA	8.12.88	2		Vénissieux	11 Jul
59.18A	Androniki	Lada	CYP	19.4.91	2		Potchefstroom	23 Feb
59.15	Alida	van Daalen	NED-J	12.4.02	1		Ede	1 Aug
59.12	Dragana	Tomasevic	SRB	4.6.82	5	Hanz	Zagreb	15 Sep
58.95	Jade	Lally	GBR	30.3.87	1		London (LV)	6 Sep
58.78	Daria	Zabawska	POL	16.4.95	1		Łódz	4 Jul
58.53A	Rachel	Andres	CAN	21.4.87	1		Calgary	27 Sep
	(40)							
58.50	Silinda Oneisi	Morales	CUB	30.8.00	3		La Habana	8 Feb
58.37	Subenrat	Insaeng	THA	10.2.94	1	NC	Bangkok	11 Dec
58.31	Eliska	Stanková	CZE	11.11.84	1		Praha	4 Jul
58.18	Emma	Ljungberg	SWE	23.1.94	1		Växjö	12 Sep
58.12	Zinaida	Sendriute	LTU	20.12.84	2	NCp	Ogre	14 Aug
58.09	Özlem	Becerek	TUR-J	22.4.02	1		Mersin	23 Feb
58.03	Lisa	Brix Pedersen	DEN	16.8.96	2		København	23 May
57.95	Kirsty	Law	GBR	11.10.86	1	NC	Manchester (SC)	4 Sep
57.94	Violetta	Ignatyeva	RUS-J	16.1.02	2		Adler	19 Sep
57.77	Taryn	Gollshewsky	AUS	18.5.93	1		Brisbane (Nathan)	25 Jan
	(50)							
57.35A	Riette	Heyns	RSA	26.2.97	1		Johannesburg	22 Feb
57.34		Xie Yuchen	CHN	12.5.96	1		Chengdu	15 May
57.32	Mariya	Ogritsko	RUS	1.3.94	4	NC	Chelyabinsk	8 Sep
57.19	Caisa-Marie	Lindfors	SWE	5.8.00	2		Norrköping	22 Aug
57.18	Anita	Márton	HUN	15.1.89	1		Szentes	20 Jun
57.17	Fanny	Roos	SWE	2.1.95	1		Växjö	26 Aug
57.08	Anna	Rüh	GER	17.6.93	3		Neubrandenburg	27 May
56.99	Karen	Gallardo	CHI	6.3.84	1		Santiago de Chile	14 Mar
56.95	Trinity	Tutti	CAN	3.5.00	1		Brampton	27 Sep
56.92	Melany del Pilar	Matheus	CUB-J	19.1.01	3		La Habana	14 Feb
	(60)							

56.45	Sanna	Kämäräinen	FIN	8.2.86	27 Jun	54.98	Estelle	Valeanu	ISR	1.8.99	15 Jun
56.20	Karolina	Urban	POL	20.10.98	3 Jul	54.92	Lotta-Kaisa	Eliander	FIN	25.1.85	13 Jun
55.86	Dóra	Kerekes	HUN	19.4.94	25 May	54.87	Yekaterina	Burmistrova	RUS	18.8.90	19 Sep
55.70	June	Kintana	ESP	12.4.95	29 Feb	54.82	Shadine	Duquemin	GBR	4.11.94	6 Sep
55.64	Nataliya	Semenova	UKR	7.7.82	16 Feb	54.71	Svetlana	Serova	BLR	21.8.86	19 Feb
55.61	Veronika	Domjan	SLO	3.9.96	30 Sep	54.61	Helena	Leveelahti	FIN	30.9.99	27 Jun
55.56	Lidiane	Cansian	BRA	8.1.92	12 Dec	54.56	Lauren	Bruce	NZL	23.3.97	8 Mar
55.53	Maki	Saito	JPN-J	13.2.01	25 Oct	54.55	Natalina	Capoferri	ITA	6.11.92	30 Aug
55.44	Nadezhda	Derkach	RUS	18.4.96	19 Sep	54.47	Alena	Belyakova	RUS	21.12.98	8 Sep
55.40	Samantha	Hall	JAM	19.4.93	11 Mar	54.29	Kimberley	Mulhall	AUS	9.1.91	7 Mar
55.37	Kätlin	Tõllasson	EST	4.6.93	17 Aug	54.09		Lu Xiaoxin	CHN	22.2.89	7 Aug
55.35	Te Rina	Keenan	NZL	29.9.90	8 Mar	54.08	Darya	Harkusha	UKR	20.4.00	16 Sep
55.18	Amanda	Ngandu-Ntumba	FRA	24.6.02	22 Aug	54.01		Yang Huanhuan	CHN	3.1.00	27 Mar
55.15	Djeneba	Touré	AUT	8.4.96	25 Jul	53.97	Paula	Ferrándiz	ESP	4.1.96	28 Aug
55.11	Antonia	Kinzel	GER	7.9.00	24 Jul	53.74	Rachel	Varner	USA	20.7.83	28 Feb
55.09	Yuliya	Maltseva	RUS	30.11.90	25 Feb			(91)			

JUNIORS
4 juniors in main list. 8 performances by 3 women to 57.00. Additional marks and further juniors:

van Daalen	59.08	1	NC-j	Amersfoort	12 Sep	58.17	1		Grootebroek	12 Jul
	58.28	1		Byuxelles	9 Aug	57.59	1	GS	Leiden	19 Sep
Becerek	57.09	1		Istanbul	4 Sep					
55.53	Maki		Saito	JPN-J	13.2.01	1		Kitakyushu	25 Oct
53.69	Kaia		Tupi-South	NZL	9.6.02	1		Christchurch	6 Mar
52.87			Sin Yu-jin	KOR	12.3.02	1		Yecheon	12 Jul

HAMMER

75.45		Hanna	Malyshik	BLR	4.2.94	1		Minsk		20 Feb
				72.71	75.45	x	74.72	75.05	73.29	
75.23		Alexandra	Tavernier	FRA	13.12.93	1		Kladno		16 Sep
				72.76	73.27	73.68	75.23	75.12	74.71	
	74.94	1		Vénissieux	11 Jul	73.60	74.94	x	72.54	73.46
	74.22	1		Barcelona (S)	22 Sep	74.22	74.02	42.98	x	71.84	x
	74.12	1	Skol	Chorzów	6 Sep	72.47	73.11	74.12	73.44	x	72.19
	73.09	1	Gyulai	Székesfehérvár	19 Aug	69.74	71.73	73.09	71.06	69.73	72.27

HAMMER

Mark	Name		Nat	Born	Pos	Meet	Venue	Date
74.18	Malwina	Kopron	POL	16.11.94	1		Spala	8 Aug
				72.12	72.60	72.15	73.50	74.18	72.62
	74.13	1	Puławy	20 Sep	x	72.10	70.44	73.27	70.72	74.13
	73.70	1	Lublin	26 Sep	x	68.50	x	71.49	70.96	73.70
73.61	Katarzyna	Furmanek	POL	19.2.96	1		Kielce	16 Aug
				70.60	68.33	72.90	71.97	71.96	73.61
73.55	Sofiya	Palkina	RUS	9.6.98	1		Zhukovskiy	11 Jun
	(11/5)			71.28	71.70	x	x	x	73.55
73.47	Lauren	Bruce	NZL	23.3.97	1		Hastings	20 Sep
73.01	Iryna	Klymets	UKR	4.10.94	1	NC	Lutsk	15 Aug
72.90	Zalina	Petrivskaya	MDA	5.2.88	1	NC-w	Chisinau	1 Feb
72.61	Iryna	Novozhylova	UKR	7.1.86	2	NC-w	Chisinau	1 Feb
72.35	Julia	Ratcliffe	NZL	14.7.93	1		Hamilton	15 Feb
	(10)							
72.18	Bianca	Ghelber	ROU	1.6.90	1	Balk Ch	Cluj-Napoca	20 Sep
72.12	Krista	Tervo	FIN	15.11.97	1		Somero	25 Jul
71.72	Anastasiya	Kolomoyets	BLR	15.7.94	1		Minsk	17 Jan
71.54	Rosa	Rodríguez	VEN	2.7.86	1		Celje	26 Jul
71.50	Kati	Ojaloo	EST	31.1.90	1		Pori	29 Aug
71.36		Wang Zheng	CHN	14.12.87	1		Huaian	7 Aug
71.34	Silja	Kosonen	FIN-J	16.12.02	2		Somero	26 Jul
70.99	Carolin	Paesler	GER	16.12.90	1	NC	Braunschweig	9 Aug
70.73	Sara	Fantini	ITA	16.9.97	1		Udine	8 Aug
70.71	Martina	Hrasnová	SVK	21.3.83	1	NC	Trnava	29 Aug
	(20)							
70.62	Alena	Soboleva	BLR	11.5.93	2		Minsk	20 Feb
70.55	Alex	Hulley	AUS	24.7.97	1		Sydney	22 Feb
70.50	Yelizaveta	Tsareva	RUS	26.3.93	2		Adler	25 Feb
70.46	Ida	Storm	SWE	26.12.91	1		Malmö	14 Jun
70.20	Réka	Gyurátz	HUN	31.5.96	1		Szombathely	6 Jun
70.15	Gwen	Berry	USA	29.6.89	2		Wellington	28 Feb
69.91	Vanessa	Sterckendries	BEL	5.5.89	1		Leverkusen	23 Aug
69.78	Beatrice Nedberge	Llano	NOR	14.12.97	1		Rygg	12 Jul
69.44i		Luo Na	CHN	8.10.93	1		Beijing	30 May
69.02	Laura	Redondo	ESP	3.7.88	1		Montijo	2 Sep
	(30)							
69.00	Samantha	Borutta	GER	7.8.00	1		Berlin	27 Jun
68.84	Anastasiya	Maslova	BLR	16.10.97	1		Minsk	14 Aug
68.45	Marina	Nikisenko	MDA	28.6.86	3	NC-w	Chisinau	1 Feb
68.26		Ji Li	CHN	14.12.00	2	NC	Shaoxing	17 Sep
68.25		Liu Tingting	CHN	29.1.90	2		Huaian	7 Aug
67.91	Tracey	Andersson	SWE	5.12.84	1		Bälsta	18 Jul
67.82	Ana	Stanciu	ROU	13.6.00	1		Bucuresti	24 Jul
67.81	Joanna	Fiodorow	POL	4.3.89	3	Kuso	Chorzów	25 Aug
67.69	Suvi	Koskinen	FIN	24.4.97	2		Kaustinen	1 Aug
67.57	Grete	Ahlberg	SWE	29.5.98	2		Bälsta	18 Jul
	(40)							
67.47	Aleksandra	Śmiech	POL	2.10.97	1		Warszawa	27 Jun
67.33	Berta	Castells	ESP	24.1.84	1		Barcelona (S)	16 Feb
67.26	Viktoriya	Khitko	RUS	3.8.99	1		Chelyabinsk	27 Aug
67.20		Zhao Fan	CHN	26.3.97	3		Huaian	7 Aug
67.17	Anastasiya	Borodulina	RUS	7.11.98	3		Adler	25 Feb
67.15	Kivilcim	Salman	TUR	27.3.92	1		Mersin	22 Feb
67.11	Nicole	Bradley	NZL	23.4.92	2		Hamilton	11 Jan
67.07	Tuğçe	Sahutoglu	TUR	1.5.88	2		Mersn	22 Feb
67.04	Alyona	Shamotina	UKR	27.12.95	2	NC	Lutsk	15 Aug
66.99	Marika	Kaczmarek	POL	25.4.96	2		Kielce	16 Aug
	(50)							
66.84		Xu Xinying	CHN	17.2.97	3	NC	Shaoxing	17 Sep
66.71	Barbara	Špiler	SLO	2.1.92	1	NC	Ptuj	7 Mar
66.54	Rose	Loga	FRA-J	27.7.02	1	NC-w	Salon-de-Provence	15 Feb
66.33	Mariana	García	CHI	19.3.99	1		Temuco	28 Dec
66.25		Yan Ni	CHN	7.2.93	5		Huaian	7 Aug
66.24	Anna Maria	Orel	EST	11.12.96	2		Randvere	18 Jul
66.05	Valeriya	Ivanenko	UKR-J	16.8.01	1	NC-J	Lutsk	12 Aug
65.75	Anamari	Kozul	CRO	20.1.96	1		Split	25 Jul
65.75		Huang Weilu	CHN	1.9.99	4	NC	Shaoxing	17 Sep
65.73	Yaritza de la Caridad	Martínez	CUB	3.2.00	1		Santiago de Cuba	1 Mar
	(60)							
65.61	Nicole	Zihlmann	SUI	30.7.86	1	NC	Basel	12 Sep
65.55	Helene	Ingvaldsen	NOR	22.6.96	1		Bergen (Fana)	5 Dec

WOMEN 2020

366 HAMMER - JAVELIN

Mark	Name		Nat	Born	Pos	Meet	Venue	Date	
65.48	Eleni	Larsson	SWE	9.2.93	1		Västerås	1	Aug
65.47	Jessica	Mayho	GBR	14.6.93	1	NC	Manchester (SC)	4	Sep
65.34	Natalya	Pospelova	RUS	28.6.96	4		Adler	25	Feb
65.32	Éva	Orbán	HUN	29.11.84	2	NC-w	Szombathley	7	Mar
65.32	Molli	Belanger	USA	15.1.96	1		Myrtle Beach	13	Mar
(70)									
65.22	Akane	Watanabe	JPN	13.8.91	20 Sep		63.73	Mariana Grasielly Marcelino	BRA	16.7.92	10 Dec
65.20	Alena	Lysenko	RUS	3.2.88	25 Feb		63.69	Bianca Lazar Fazecas (100)	ROU	24.2.93	1 Mar
65.19		Xue Yan	CHN	15.5.97	17 Sep		63.67dh	Meghan Serdock	USA		13 Sep
65.03	Rachele	Mori	ITA-Y	29.3.03	29 Aug		63.60	Alina Andritchi	MDA	16.1.99	1 Feb
64.93	Rawan	Barakat	EGY-J	17.7.01	20 Feb		63.44	Vigdis Jónsdóttir	ISL	11.2.96	27 Aug
64.77	Wendy	Koolhaas	NED	5.1.80	29 Aug		63.41	Liz Arleen Collia	CUB-J	26.7.01	13 Mar
64.70	Mayra	Gaviria	COL	21.5.97	29 Feb		63.38	Kinga Lepkowska	POL	30.4.97	23 Aug
64.65	Katerina	Safránková	CZE	8.6.89	30 May		63.32	Sara Killinen	FIN-J	9.4.01	2 Sep
64.60	Celine	Julin	DEN	12.8.94	21 May		63.22	Alegna Osoriu	CUB-J	5.2.02	13 Mar
64.57	Rigina	Adashboyeva	UZB-J	29.10.01	26 Nov		63.05	Wang Guanyi	CHN-J	25.4.01	16 May
64.54	Laëtitia	Bambara	BUR	30.3.84	15 Feb		63.04	Vânia Silva	POR	8.6.80	8 Feb
64.52	Jennifer	Dahlgren	ARG	21.4.84	21 Nov		62.99	Michelle Döpke	GER	21.7.97	8 Aug
64.42	Kiira	Väänänen	FIN	6.1.99	6 Jun		62.96	Anna Pronkina	RUS	7.9.96	29 Aug
64.40		Li Jiangyan	CHN	22.5.99	17 Sep		62.79	Aleksandra Nowaczewska	POL-J	31.10.02	20 Sep
64.35	Tereza	Králová	CZE	22.10.89	25 Aug		62.72	Marga Cumming	RSA	12.10.98	3 Nov
64.33	Cecilia	Desideri	ITA	23.5.99	16 Jan		62.70	Autavia Fluker	USA	6.6.97	6 Mar
64.32	Lorelei	Taillandier	FRA	8.8.91	13 Sep		62.62	Kseniya Isayeva	RUS	2.12.96	25 Feb
64.21	Osarumen	Odeh	ESP	15.11.95	19 Sep		62.55	Tiina Rinnekari	FIN	24.10.96	26 Aug
64.12	Aada	Koppeli	FIN-J	19.5.02	25 Jul		62.54	Stavroúla Kosmídou	GRE-J	14.9.01	8 Jul
64.12		Zhou Mengyuan	CHN	3.9.99	29 Sep		62.47	Hitomi Katsuyama	JPN	21.5.94	2 Oct
64.08dh	Alina	Duran	USA	28.3.90	13 Sep		62.46	Claudia Stravs	SLO	11.2.94	7 Mar
63.94	Iliána	Korosídou	GRE	14.1.95	9 Aug		62.24	Daniela Gómez	ARG	24.8.93	18 Dec
63.92	Charlotte	Payne	GBR-J	20.3.02	4 Sep		62.20	Sophie Gimmler	GER	18.3.96	8 Aug
63.90	Zsanett	Németh	HUN	19.12.00	6 Jun		62.20	Aleksandra Kokowska	POL	28.4.95	14 Aug
63.87	Zarina	Nosirzhoneva	UZB-J	23.3.02	26 Nov		62.10	Anisleydis Delmo	CUB	24.2.00	22 Mar
63.85	Maryola	Bukel	BLR-J	9.1.02	9 Jul		62.05	Alice Barnsdale	GBR	23.2.99	4 Sep
63.81	Ewa	Rozanska	POL	22.12.00	28 Aug		62.03	Natalia Sánchez	ESP	8.5.00	5 Sep
63.77	Tatyana	Romanovich	BLR	26.3.00	16 Jul		62.01	Jordana Badley-Costello	CAN	.93	1 Aug
							(126)				

JUNIORS
3 juniors in main list. 11 performances by 1 woman to 67.00. Additional marks and further juniors:

Kosonen	69.22	1	vSWE	Tampere	6 Sep	67.88	2		Vantaa	27 Jun
	68.70	2		Pori	29 Aug	67.39	1		Helsinki	27 Aug
	68.40	1	NC	Turku	14 Aug	67.35	3		Jyväskylä	8 Jul
	68.37	1		Somero	20 Sep	67.11	2		Kotka	16 Jul
	67.99	2		Somero	6 Jun	67.11	1		Turku	28 Jul
65.03	Rachele		Mori	ITA-Y	29.3.03	2	NC	Padova	29 Aug
64.93	Rawan		Barakat	EGY	17.7.01	1		Cairo	20 Feb
64.57	Rigina		Adashboyeva	UZB	29.10.01	1		Tashkent	26 Nov
64.12	Aada		Koppeli	FIN	19.5.02	3		Somero	25 Jul
63.92	Charlotte		Payne	GBR	20.3.02	2	NC	Manchester (SC)	4 Sep
63.87	Zarina		Nosirzhoneva	UZB	23.3.02	2		Tashkent	26 Nov
63.85	Maryola		Bukel (10)	BLR	9.1.02	1		Brest	9 Jul
63.41	Liz Arleen		Collia	CUB	26.7.01	2		La Habana	13 Mar
63.32	Sara		Killinen	FIN	9.4.01	1		Kauhajoki	2 Sep
63.22	Alegna		Osoriu	CUB	5.2.02	3		La Habana	13 Mar
63.05			Wang Guanyi	CHN	25.4.01	1		Chengdu	16 May
62.79	Aleksandra		Nowaczewska	POL	31.10.02	1	vCZE-J	Karpacz	20 Sep
62.54	Stavroúla		Kosmídou	GRE	14.9.01	1		Thessaloníki	8 Jul
61.58	Elisabet		Rúnarsdóttir	ISL	28.11.02	1		Reykvavik	24 Jun

JAVELIN

67.61			Lu Huihui	CHN	26.6.89	1		Beijing	30 Jun
				x	66.97	67.61	66.37	65.95	66.03
	66.27	1	Beijing	7 Aug	65.10	66.27	x	65.50	x	64.81
	65.70	2	NC	Shaoxing	15 Sep	61.06	62.71	64.98	x	65.70	63.18
67.29			Liu Shiying	CHN	24.9.93	1	NC	Shaoxing	15 Sep
				65.08	63.47	60.20	61.14	64.39	67.29
	66.14	1	Yantai	27 Jun	66.14	x	x	63.23	61.00	60.90
67.17	Tatyana		Kholodovich	BLR	21.6.91	1		Minsk	20 Feb
				65.65	62.48	63.00	63.81	67.17	64.73
	66.85	1	NC	Minsk	1 Aug	66.85	63.50	x	x	x
65.70	Maria		Andrejczyk	POL	9.3.96	1	Skol	Chorzów	6 Sep
				65.70	62.66	x	58.26	x	61.24
65.19	Barbora		Spotáková	CZE	30.6.81	1	GS	Ostrava	8 Sep
				65.19	x	x	x	55.37	60.81
64.44	Kara		Winger	USA	10.4.86	1		Rathdrum	1 Aug
	(10/6)			57.70	57.03	62.15	64.00	x	64.44

JAVELIN

Mark	Name		Nat	Born	Pos	Meet	Venue	Date	
64.22	Nikola	Ogrodníková	CZE	18.8.90	1	Odlozil	Praha	8	Jun
64.10	Christin	Hussong	GER	17.3.94	1		Luzern	3	Jul
63.96	Elína	Tzénggo	GRE-J	2.9.02	1	NC-J	Ioánnina	1	Aug
63.45	Haruka	Kitaguchi	JPN	16.3.98	1		Kumagaya	19	Sep
	(10)								
63.19	Lina	Muze	LAT	4.12.92	2	Skol	Chorzów	6	Sep
62.68	Sara	Kolak	CRO	22.6.95	1		Offenburg	29	Aug
62.56	Ásdís	Hjálmsdóttir Annerud	ISL	28.10.85	1		Bottharyd	28	Jun
62.45	Réka	Szilágyi	HUN	19.1.96	1		Székesfehérvár	5	Sep
62.04	Tori	Peeters	NZL	17.5.94	1		Sydney	22	Feb
61.87	Laila	Ferrer e Silva	BRA	30.7.82	1	NC	São Paulo	13	Dec
61.42	Mackenzie	Little	AUS	22.12.96	1		Sydney (Bankstown)	24	Oct
61.15A	Annu	Rani	IND	29.8.92	1		Potchefstroom	10	Mar
61.00A	Victoria	Hudson	AUT	28.5.96	1		Potchefstroom	3	Mar
60.89	Jucilene	de Lima	BRA	14.9.90	1	GP	São Paulo	6	Dec
	(20)								
60.69	Yuka	Sato	JPN	21.7.92	1		Osaka	24	Oct
60.45	Hanna	Hatsko	UKR	3.10.90	1		Mukachevo	15	Feb
60.43	Heidi	Nokelainen	FIN	30.9.90	1		Lahti	15	Jul
60.38	Eda	Tugsuz	TUR	27.3.97	1		Bursa	28	Aug
60.36	Mikhaela	Petkova	BUL	11.1.99	1		Balchik	2	Oct
60.28		Su Lingdan	CHN	12.1.97	2		Beijing	7	Aug
60.27	Liveta	Jasiunaite	LTU	26.7.94	1	NC	Palanga	8	Aug
60.20	Annika Marie	Fuchs	GER	29.4.97	1		Wetzlar	18	Jul
60.12	Vera	Markaryan (Rebrik)	RUS	25.2.89	1	NCp	Bryansk	30	Aug
60.00	Irena	Gillarová	CZE	19.1.92	1		Olomouc	27	Jun
	(30)								
60.00	Alexie	Alaïs	FRA	9.10.94	1		Toulon	5	Sep
59.88	Marcelina	Witek	POL	2.6.95	1		Kolobrzeg	4	Jul
59.82	Kathryn	Mitchell	AUS	10.7.82	1		Geelong	27	Jan
59.70	Christine	Winkler	GER	4.5.95	1		Jena	11	Jul
59.66	María Lucelly	Murillo	COL	5.5.91	2	GP	São Paulo	6	Dec
59.53	Lisanne	Schol	NED	22.6.91	1	NC	Utrecht	30	Aug
59.51	Anete	Kocina	LAT	5.2.96	1		Koknese	19	Sep
59.47		Ge Lijuan	CHN	17.7.97	3		Beijing	7	Aug
59.07	Mikako	Yamashita	JPN	3.5.97	2		Osaka	24	Oct
58.91	Svetlana	Pechnikova	RUS	6.9.94	2		Adler	17	Feb
	(40)								
58.91	Madara	Palameika	LAT	18.6.87	2		Ogre	14	Aug
58.64	Marina	Saito	JPN	15.10.95	2		Tokyo	23	Aug
58.44	Arantza	Moreno	ESP	16.1.95	1		Motril	7	Mar
58.42	Angéla	Moravcsik	HUN	13.5.96	1		Budapest	4	Jul
58.41	Luisa	Siniqaglia	ITA	27.9.97	1		Mariano Comense	15	Feb
58.30A	Sunette	Viljoen	RSA	6.1.83	1		Pretoria	13	Mar
58.25	Momone	Ueda	JPN	27.6.99	3		Niigata	1	Oct
58.03		Liu Lu	CHN	9.11.98	4	NC	Shaoxing	15	Sep
58.02	Melissa María	Hernández	CUB-J	16.3.01	1		La Habana	6	Mar
57.98	Ariana	Ince	USA	14.3.89	2		Rathdrau	1	Aug
	(50)								
57.91	Julia	Valtanen	FIN-J	6.5.01	1	vSWE	Tampere	5	Sep
57.90	Martina	Písová	CZE	20.7.94	2		Ústí nad Orlicí	29	Aug
57.78	Janette	Lepistö	FIN	20.10.93	1		Kuortane	13	Jun
57.67	Viktoriya	Yermakova	BLR	18.1.95	2	NC	Minsk	1	Aug
57.58		Yu Yuzhen	CHN	5.3.98	5	NC	Shaoxing	15	Sep
57.58		Sun Xiaomei	CHN	2.12.96	6	NC	Shaoxing	15	Sep
57.52	Jenni	Kangas	FIN	3.7.92	4		Kuortane	1	Aug
57.51	Risa	Miyashita	JPN	26.4.84	4		Tokyo	23	Aug
57.50	Leonie	Tröger	GER	22.12.00	1		Halle	15	Jul
57.48	Petra	Andrejsková	CZE	25.6.92	1		Ostrava	22	Aug
	(60)								
57.46	Yiselena	Ballar	CUB-Y	12.1.03	1		La Habana	13	Mar
57.46	Noémie	Pleimling	LUX	27.8.93	1	NC	Dudelange	6	Sep
57.43	Suvi	Kemppainen	FIN	25.1.98	1		Kuopio	9	Sep
57.43	Sae	Takemoto	JPN	23.11.99	2		Niigata	11	Sep
57.41	Adriana	Vilagos	SRB-Y	2.1.04	1		Novi Sad	22	Aug
57.38	Ashley	Pryke	CAN	7.7.97	1		Wellington	28	Feb
57.34	Yuliya	Makeyeva	BLR	5.11.00	1		Minsk	20	Feb
57.26	Mariya	Rybnikova	RUS	28.10.94	1		Adler	10	Feb
57.24	Nikol	Tabacková	CZE	24.1.98	2	Odlozil	Praha	8	Jun
57.15	Rafaela	Gonçalves	BRA	27.11.91	3	GP	São Paulo	6	Dec
	(60)								

368 JAVELIN - PENTATHLON

Mark	Name		Nat	Born	Pos	Meet	Venue		Date
57.04	Sanne	Erkkola	FIN	8.3.94	1	NC	Turku		15 Aug
57.03	Lea	Wipper	GER-J	14.10.01	3		Thum		22 Aug
56.98	Karyna	Butkevich	BLR-J	5.10.01	1	NC-j	Brest		8 Jul
56.96	Klaudia	Regin	POL	28.8.97	1		Slupsk		20 Sep
56.79	Mari	Klaup	EST	27.2.90	1		Göteborg		2 Sep
56.78	Carolina	Visca	ITA	31.5.00	1		Rieti		11 Jul
56.75	Pascaline	Adanhouegbe	BEN	19.10.95	2	Quercia	Rovereto		8 Sep
56.58	Mahiro	Osa	JPN	26.11.99	1		Tama		31 Oct
56.50	Jatta Mari	Jääskeläinen	FIN	27.2.94	2	NC	Turku		15 Aug
56.35		Li Yutong	CHN-J	19.5.01	7	NC	Shaoxing		15 Sep
	(70)								
56.28	Orie	Ushiro	JPN	24.8.90	3		Kumagaya		19 Sep
56.23A	Jo-Ané	van Dyk	RSA	3.10.97	1		Potchefstroom		14 Mar
56.10	Coralys	Ortiz	PUR	16.4.85	1		Gurabo		22 Feb
56.09	Jona	Aigouy	FRA	19.4.99	2	NC	Albi		12 Sep
55.93	Ane	Dahlen	NOR	6.6.94	30 Jun	54.72	Aoi	Murakami	JPN-Y 11.3.04	3 Nov
55.90	Esra	Türkmen	TUR-J	20.1.02	1 Sep	54.71	Lidia	Parada	ESP 11.6.93	15 Jul
55.89	Jelena	Jaakkola	FIN	7.3.89	15 Aug	54.70	Aleksandra	Ivanova	RUS 13.7.99	26 Aug
55.81	Gerli	Israel	EST	7.2.95	8 Aug	54.66	Claudia	Ferreira	POR 3.10.98	15 Aug
55.77	Sofía	Ifantídou	GRE	5.1.85	8 Aug	54.62	Münevver	Hanci	TUR-J 25.1.01	12 Sep
55.77	Saara	Lipsanen	FIN	13.9.95	15 Aug	54.59	Evelina	Mendes	FRA 2.1.98	22 Aug
55.77	Mirell	Luik	EST	3.1.77	18 Aug	54.55	Kathryn	Brooks	AUS 11.11.97	8 Mar
55.71	Stella	Weinberg	NOR	21.10.98	10 Sep	54.53	Roosa	Ylönen	FIN 29.4.99	27 Jul
55.63	Jana Marie	Lowka	GER	.00	15 Aug	54.50	Afroditi	Manioú	GRE 19.8.98	8 Aug
53.60	Andrea	Zelezná	CZE	4.7.93	1 Aug	54.47	Siiri	Elomaa	FIN-Y 19.9.03	15 Aug
55.59	Mirann	Naraoka	JPN-J	4.3.01	24 Jul	54.39	Polina	Losko	BLR 25.6.98	1 Aug
55.56		Jin Pingping	CHN	23.8.93	28 Jun	54.35	Tomoka	Kuwazoe	JPN 1.2.99	23 Jul
55.43	Julia	Ulbricht	GER	28.11.00	29 Aug	54.14		Kim Keong-ae	KOR 5.3.88	27 Jun
55.34	Aleksandra	Konshina	BLR-J	14.8.01	8 Jul	54.07	Stephanie	Wrathall	NZL 25.12.89	13 Feb
55.32	Veronika	Sokota	CRO-Y	9.3.04	9 Sep	54.06	Riko	Nishimura	JPN 1.11.93	1 Oct
55.31	Margaux	Nicollin	FRA	1.5.95	5 Aug	54.03		Liu Xinai	CHN 17.11.99	11 Apr
55.19		Chen Chen	CHN	19.1.96	15 Aug	53.97	Nadeeka	Lakmali	SRI 18.9.81	28 Dec
55.15	Dana	Bergrath	GER	24.4.94	8 Aug	53.96		Li Hui-Jun	TPE 15.12.99	1 Nov
55.14	Sara	Jemai	ITA	12.4.92	30 Aug	53.92	Viktoriya	Chervyakova	RUS-J 8.3.02	19 Sep
55.13	Sara	Zabarino	ITA	1.8.99	30 Aug	53.87	Shiori	Toma	JPN 7.2.96	19 Sep
55.12	Tetyana	Nychyporchuk	UKR	11.9.94	16 Aug	53.79	Margaryta	Dorozhon	ISR 4.9.87	30 Aug
55.10	Sofi	Flink	SWE	8.7.95	14 Aug	53.77	Hitomi	Sukenaga	JPN 4.5.88	23 Aug
55.05	Fanni	Kövér	HUN-Y	15.2.04	27 Jun	53.76		Chiu Yu-Ting	TPE 22.10.00	1 Nov
55.02	Indre	Jakubaityte	LTU	24.1.76	22 Aug	53.68	Natsumi	Terada	JPN-J 25.5.02	19 Jul
54.99		Suh Hae-an	KOR	1.7.85	26 Jul	53.64	Alina	Shukh	UKR 12.2.99	16 Aug
54.96	Federica	Botter	ITA-J	23.1.01	23 Feb	53.62	Anouk	Vetter	NED 4.2.93	30 Aug
54.90	Kiho	Kuze	JPN	28.3.95	24 Oct	53.61	Nuttha	Nacharn	THA 4.6.90	10 Dec
54.88	Alexia	Kogut Kubiak	FRA	22.1.88	15 Feb	53.55	Kaja	Petersen	NOR-J 6.11.01	17 Jun
54.83	Jariya	Wichaldt	THA	8.3.96	10 Dec	53.50	Vanja	Spajic	BIH 31.12.95	9 Aug
54.79	Nargiza	Kuchkarova	UZB	27.2.99	9 Oct	53.46	Matilda	Elfgaard	SWE 11.6.02	28 Jun
54.75		Ge Qiaohui	CHN	22.12.00	27 Jun	53.44	Kurumi	Nakano	JPN-J 20.10.02	24 Oct
54.74	Annabella	Bogdán	HUN	7.4.92	27 Sep	53.41	Karolina	Boldysz	POL 21.4.93	13 Aug

Online competition: Minsk (Staiki) 12 Jun: 1. 57.86 Karyna Butkevich BLR-J; 2. 54.42 Polina Losko BLR 25.6.98

JUNIORS
8 juniors in main list. 11 performances by 5 women to 57.10. Additional marks and further juniors:

Tzénggo	62.21	3	Kladno	16 Sep	61.53	1		Thessaloníki	8 Jul
	61.76	1	Pátra	8 Aug	60.80	1		Thessaloníki	19 Jul
Valtanen	57.84	1	Jyväskylä	21 Aug	57.66	1		Kemi	21 Aug
55.90	Esra	Türkmen	TUR	20.1.02	1	NC-J		Istanbul	1 Sep
55.59	Mirann	Naraoka (10)	JPN	4.3.01	2			Tokyo	24 Jul
55.34	Aleksandra	Konshina	BLR	14.8.01	2			Brest	8 Jul
55.32	Veronika	Sokota	CRO-Y	9.3.04	1			Karlovac	9 Sep
55.05	Fanni	Kövér	HUN-Y	15.2.04	1			Gödöllö	27 Jun
54.96	Federica	Botter	ITA	23.1.01	1			Udine	23 Feb
54.72	Aoi	Murakami	JPN-Y	11.3.04	1			Higashihiroshima	3 Nov
54.47	Siiri	Elomaa	FIN-Y	19.9.03	6	NC		Turku	15 Aug
53.92	Viktoriya	Chervyakova	RUS	8.3.02	2			Adleri	19 Sep
53.68	Natsumi	Terada	JPN	25.5.02	1			Isahara	19 Jul
53.55	Kaja	Petersen (20)	NOR	6.11.01	1			Larvik	17 Jun

INDOOR PENTATHLON

4629	Noor		Vidts		BEL	30.5.96	1	NC	
	8.31	1.79	13.55	6.36		2:16.07		Louvain-la-Neuve	2 Feb
4610	Annie		Kunz		USA	16.2.93	1	NC	
	8.16	1.82	14.97	5.95		2:20.17		Annapolis	7 Feb
4602	Alina		Shukh		UKR	12.2.99	1		
	8.86	1.88	14.29	6.13		2:15.92		Sumy	31 Jan
4518			Shukh				1		
	8.79	1.87	13.47	6.06		2:16.60		Tallinn	9 Feb

PENTATHLON - HEPTATHLON

Mark	Name	Nat	Born	Pos	Meet	Venue	Date
4503	Shukh			1	NC	Sumy	21 Feb
	8.88 1.90 13.65 5.91		2:16.69				
4488	Lucia Vadlejch	SVK	8.11.88	1		Ostrava	18 Jan
	8.54 1.81 11.32 6.44		2:15.56				
4451	Emilyn Dearman	USA	26.4.95	2	NC	Annapolis	7 Feb
	8.57 1.70 13.95 6.18		2:14.60		(7/5)		
4449	Hanna Kasyanova	UKR	24.4.83	2		Tallinn	9 Feb
	8.40 1.78 14.11 5.87		2:18.38				
4422	Bianca Salming	SWE	22.11.98	1	NC	Sollentuna	2 Feb
	8.93 1.86 13.89 5.75		2:15.75				
4393	Daryna Sloboda	UKR	19.6.95	2	NC	Sumy	21 Feb
	8.90 1.78 14.04 6.04		2:18.06				
4391	Tyra Gittens	TTO	6.6.98	1	SEC	College Station	29 Feb
	8.52 1.86 13.05 6.27		2:32.76				
4389	Annaëlle Nyabeu Djapa	FRA	15.9.92	1	NC	Liévin	1 Mar
	8.28 1.78 13.38 5.94		2:22.78				
	(10)						
4375	Shaina Burns	USA	21.3.96	3	NC	Annapolis	7 Feb
	8.67 1.79 13.74 5.85		2:18.19				
4373	Hanne Maudens	BEL	12.3.97	2	NC	Louvain-la-Neuve	2 Feb
	8.64 1.70 13.53 6.25		2:18.75				
4360	Rimma Buinenko	UKR	30.12.95	3		Tallinn	9 Feb
	8.34 1.78 13.13 6.19		2:28.58				
4359	Cassandre Aguessy Thomas	FRA	1.9.97	2	NC	Liévin	1 Mar
	8.40 1.75 12.44 6.22		2:22.03				
4353	Paulina Ligarska	POL	9.4.96	1	NC	Torun	29 Feb
	8.69 1.80 13.85 5.87		2:21.39				
4352	Lauren Taubert	USA	20.3.98	1		Fayetteville	31 Jan
	8.42 1.75 11.80 6.00		2:14.29				
4330	Esther Turpin	FRA	29.4.96	3	NC	Liévin	1 Mar
	8.35 1.69 13.56 5.95		2:18.87				
4318	Rita Nemes	HUN	30.11.89	1		Budapest	16 Feb
	8.70 1.73 13.58 5.93		2:17.42				
4309	Janina Lange	GER	23.11.97	1		Hamburg	9 Feb
	8.79 1.80 11.79 6.18		2:19.86				
4306	Emma Oosterwegel	NED	29.6.98	1	NC	Apeldoorn	9 Feb
	8.70 1.80 13.58 5.65		2:18.53				
	(20)						
4298	Caroline Agnou	SUI	26.5.96	2 Feb			
4291	Jan Novotná	CZE	26.1.99	18 Jan			
4277	Hope Bender	USA	2.1.97	7 Feb			
4274#	Madeline Holmberg	USA	26.10.96	28 Feb			
4269	Jenny Kimbro	USA	17.4.98	7 Feb			
4266	Iryna Rofe-Beketova	UKR	18.9.98	21 Feb			
4264	Marijke Esselink	NED	22.6.99	18 Jan			
4263	Vanessa Grimm	GER	22.4.97	2 Feb			
4261	Holly Mills	GBR	15.4.00	5 Jan			
4259	Aleksandra Butvina	RUS	14.2.86	16 Feb			
4258	Katie Stainton	GBR	8.1.95	9 Feb			
4250	Ashtin Zamzow-Mahler	USA	13.8.96	7 Feb			
4238	Jade O'Dowda	GBR	9.9.99	5 Jan			
4236	Yuliya Loban	UKR	7.8.00	31 Jan			
4221	Beatrice Puiu	ROU	1.1.86	8 Feb			
4216	Georgia Ellenwood	CAN	5.8.95	1 Feb			
4202	Anna Hall	USA-J	23.3.01	31 Jan			

4201	Marina Pshichkina	RUS	8.5.97	16 Feb
4190#	Hannah Rusnak	USA	.99	29 Feb
4189	Grace McKenzie	IRL	4.12.96	31 Jan
4186#	Erin Marsh	USA	12.7.99	29 Feb
4179	Leonie Cambours	FRA	31.7.00	11 Jan
4177	Tereza Elena Sínová	CZE-J	17.8.01	8 Feb
4169	Elizabeth Morland	IRL	3.3.98	9 Feb
4165	Yuliya Rout	BLR	22.1.95	6 Feb
4165	Kristine Blazevica	LAT-J	11.12.01	25 Feb
4157	Melissa de Haan	NED	15.8.97	9 Feb
4155#	Ayesha Champagnie	JAM	10.3.96	28 Feb
4154	Anne van de Wiel	NED	4.6.97	9 Feb
4150	Juanita Webster-Freeman	USA	13.11.96	7 Feb

HEPTATHLON

Mark	Name	Nat	Born	Pos	Meet	Venue	Date
6419	Ivona Dadic	AUT	29.12.93	1	NC	Götzis	30 Aug
	13.57/0.1 1.78 14.58 24.21/0.0		6.25/0.0		47.93	2:15.57	
6386	Alina Shukh	UKR	12.2.99	1		Lutsk	16 Aug
	14.11/1.7 1.91 13.94 26.62/-2.2		6.14/0.0		53.64	2:11.31	
6319	Carolin Schäfer	GER	5.12.91	1	NC	Vaterstetten	23 Aug
	13.40/0.7 1.80 13.25 24.12/-1.8		6.07/0.9		48.24	2:16.90)5	
6304	Adriana Rodríguez	CUB	12.7.99	1	NC	La Habana	21 Mar
	13.16/-0.4 1.84 12.83 23.59/0.8		6.45/-1.6		34.94	2:16.14	
6263	Xénia Krizsán	HUN	13.1.93	1	NC	Budapest	26 Jul
	13.68/-0.1 1.75 14.31 25.07/0.2		5.97/0.0		51.04	2:13.90	
6254	Evelis Aguilar	COL	3.1.93	1	ESP Ch	Madrid	13 Sep
	13.79/0.6 1.66 14.32 24.03/0.1		6.41w/2.5		47.00	2:16.85	
6235	Dadic			1		Amstetten	23 Jul
	13.64/0.2 1.80 14.84 24.32/-0.1		5.76/0.0		47.60	2:19.10	
6215	Shukh			1	NC	Lutsk	30 Aug
	14.57/-1.2 1.91 13.91 26.79/-1.1		6.19/0.8		49.77	2:13.37	

HEPTATHLON

Mark	Name		Nat	Born	Pos	Meet	Venue	Date
6192	Rita	Nemes	HUN	30.11.89	2	NC	Budapest	26 Jul
	13.77/-0.1	1.75 13.11	25.00/ 0.2	6.22/0.3		46.41	2:12.0	
6170	Annik	Kälin	SUI	27.4.00	1		Amriswil	19 Jul
	13.47/-0.9	1.74 13.19	24.86/-0.5	6.44/-0.7		47.31	2:23:54	
	(10/8)							
6167	Hanne	Maudens	BEL	12.3.97	1	NC	Bruxelles	16 Aug
	14.02/0.0	1.70 13.14	24.28/-0.7	6.32/ 0.3		40.51	2:06.31)	
6112	Anna	Maiwald (10)	GER	21.7.90	2	NC	Vaterstetten	23 Aug
	13.49/0.7	1.68 13.83	24.18/-1.8	5.88/-0.9		46.25	2:15.69	
6080(w)	Mari	Klaup	EST	27.2.90	1	NC	Tallinn	9 Aug
	13.69w/2.3	1.77 13.51	25.63w/2.5	5.76/1.4		53.54	2:23.36	
6074	Maria	Huntington	FIN	13.3.97	1	NC	Turku	16 Aug
	13.12/0.5	1.82 11.78	24.24/0.8	6.03/ 0.3		45.03	2:26.55	
6047	Vanessa	Grimm	GER	22.4.97	3	NC	Vaterstetten	23 Aug
	13.79/0.7	1.77 14.16	24.62/-1.8	5.96/0.1		42.06	2:19.77	
6042	Bianca	Salming	SWE	22.11.98	1	NC	Ljungberg	2 Aug
	14.76/-2.9	1.83 13.73	26.21/-0.8	5.86w/3.1		49.58	2:11.85	
6028	Tori	West	AUS	14.10.95	1	NC	Brisbane (Nathan)	16 Feb
	14.25/0.8	1.78 13.28	24.53/2.0	5.75/0.5		49.62	2:19.57	
6010	Sarah	Lagger	AUT	3.9.99	3		Saint Paul, Réunion	19 Dec
	14.37/0.6	1.77 14.11	25.54/1.3	5.90/-0.3		47.67	2:16.66	
6009	Lucie	Kienast	GER-J	1.6.01	1		Halle	19 Jul
	14.59/0.9	1.68 13.83	24.35/0.3	6.22/-1.9		47.30	2:19.83	
5978(w)	Katerina	Cachová	CZE	26.2.90	1		Plzen	21 Jun
& 5956	13.39/1.6	1.72 13.00	24.71/1.1	5.99w/3.6		42.33	2:19.25 & LJ 5.91w/2.6	
5962	Hanna	Kasyanova	UKR	24.4.83	2	NC	Lutsk	30 Aug
	13.59/-1.2	1.73 13.23	24.69/-1.1	5.91/1.7		40.32	2:15.87	
5937	Diana	Rabkova	BLR	14.6.98	1	NC	Minsk	2 Aug
	14.01/-1.9	1.78 14.37	25.44/-0.2	5.89/0.2		35.38	2:11.29	
	(20)							
5925	Anastasiya	Mokhnyuk	UKR	1.1.91	3	NC	Lutsk	30 Aug
	13.64/-1.2	1.70 13.91	25.43/-1.1	6.13/1.9		40.95	2:19.66	
5901	Adrianna	Sulek	POL	3.4.99	1		Warszawa	23 Aug
	14.12/-0.2	1.79 12.44	24.48/1.5	5.83/0.1		39.81	2:15.38	
5891	Claudia	Conte	ESP	14.11.99	2	1 NC	Madrid (V)	13 Sep
	14.18/0.6	1.87 11.95	26.04/0.1	5.96/1.0		42.92	2:17.41	
5878	Jana	Novotná	CZE	26.1.99	1	NC	Praha	26 Jul
	13.83/1.0	1.68 12.40	25.10/-1.1	6.31/-0.3		41.79	2:19.46	
5875	Henriette	Jæger	NOR-Y	30.6.03	1		Moss	5 Jul
	13.96w/2.4	1.73 12.30	23.84/0.1	6.01/0.0		34.31	2:13.67	
5870	Paulina	Ligarska	POL	9.4.96	2		Warszawa	23 Aug
	14.46/-0.2	1.79 13.40	24.73/1.5	5.66/-0.2		41.69	2:16.14	
5861	Saga	Vanninen	FIN-Y	4.5.03	2	NC	Turku	16 Aug
	13.81/0.5	1.79 14.32	24.87/0.8	5.76/-0.1		39.45	2:26.14	
5837	Noor	Vidts	BEL	30.5.96	1	NC	Deinze	27 Sep
	13.74/1.6	1.74 13.10	25.01/1.4	6.15/1.0		31.78	2:15.00	
5830	Janina	Lange	GER	23.11.97	1		Lübeck	19 Jul
	14.45/-2.0	1.78 12.00	25.01/-0.4	6.02/0.7		40.32	2:15.55	
5827	Iryna	Rofe-Beketova	UKR	18.9.98	4	NC	Lutsk	30 Aug
	14.37/-1.2	1.82 13.31	26.51/-1.1	6.00w/2.3		47.98	2:27.43	
	(30)							
5806	Celine	Albisser	SUI	5.5.96	2	NC	Langentahl	9 Aug
	13.75/0.1	1.69 12.25	24.16/-0.2	5.96/-0.9		35.73	2:15.634	
5804	Carmen	Ramos	ESP	18.6.98	3	NC	Madrid (V)	13 Sep
	14.02/0.6	1.72 12.75	25.38/0.1	5.70/-1.0		44.98	2:17/08	
5799	Yuki	Yamazaki	JPN	6.6.95	1	NC	Nagano	27 Sep
	13.95/0.1	1.58 12.13	24.81/1.1	6.05/1.6		47.60	2:18.11	
5779	Cassandre	Aguesy Thomas	FRA	1.9.97	5		Saint Paul, Réunion	19 Dec
	14.37/0.6	1.77 14.11	25.54/1.3	5.90/-0.3		47.67	2:16.66	
5772	Diane	Marie-Hardy	FRA	19.2.96	6		Saint Paul, Réunion	19 Dec
	14.37/0.6	1.77 14.11	25.54/1.3	5.90/-0.3		47.67	2:16.66	
5767	Marys Adela	Patterson	CUB-J	16.10.01	2	NC	La Habana	21 Mar
	14.53/-0.4	1.72 12.17	24.96/0.8	5.98/0.9		41.40	2:18.33	
5759	Raiane	Procópio	BRA	30.7.97	1	NC	São Paulo	11 Dec
	14.69/-0.9	1.76 12.84	25.60/-0.7	5.66/0.8		45.93	2:16:63	
5756	Anne	van de Wiel	NED	4.6.97	1	NC	Emmeloord	6 Sep
	13.45w/2.9	1.63 11.88	24.00/1.1	5.82/0.3		39.22	2:18.35	
5755	Sophie	Hamann	GER	12.8.96	4	NC	Vaterstetten	23 Aug
	13.48/0.7	1.74 11.15	24.95/-1.8	5.86/-0.8		37.13	2:15.61	
5746		Ren Shimei	CHN	26.5.96	1	NC	Shaoxing	16 Sep
	14.29/0.4	1.69 11.96	24.69/0.6	6.15/0.3		43.29	2:24.27	
	(40)							

HEPTATHLON - DECATHLON - RELAYS

Mark	Name		Nat	Born	Pos	Meet	Venue		Date
5741	Sveva	Gerevini	ITA	31.5.96	1	NC	Padova		30 Aug
	14.29/-2.2	1.62 12.14 23.86/-1.5		5.99/1.6	40.14		2:17.02		
5727 (w)	Katerna	Dvoráková	CZE	10.5.97	2		Plzen		21 Jun
	13.41/1.6	1.69 11.69 24.48/1.1		6.24w/4.0	34.35		2:19.99		
5715	Anna-Lena	Obermaier	GER	10.7.96	1		Regensburg		19 Jul
	14.33/0.2	1.80 12.06 26.12/0.4		5.65/-0.2	44.43		2:17.55		
5707	Yuliya	Rout	BLR	22.1.95	2	NC	Minsk		2 Aug
	13.97/-1.9	1.75 12.38 24.98/-0.2		5.92/1.0	39.36		2:25.28		
5699	Ellen	Barber	GBR	5.12.97	23 Aug	5526	Mareike	Rösing	GER	31.12.99 23 Aug
5690 (w)	Lovisa	Karlsson	SWE	15.1.00	15 Jun	5525		Zhou Jingjing	CHN	16.7.98 16 Sep
5687	Beatrice	Juskeviciute	LTU	10.1.00	8 Aug	5518	Denise	Majerová	CZE	27.10.97 26 Jul
5667	Dorota	Skrivanová	CZE	26.11.98	21 Jun	5502	Mathilde	Rey	SUI	29.3.00 9 Aug
5661	Michelle	Oud	NED	19.7.96	6 Sep	5495	Jessica	Rautelin	FIN	16.1.97 19 Jul
5660	Kristine	Blazevica	LAT-J	11.12.01	5 Aug	5490(w)	Melissa	de Haan	NED	15.8.97 6 Sep
5653	Sandra	Röthlin	SUI	2.1.99	9 Aug	5472	Vanesa	Spinola	BRA	5.3.90 11 Dec
5648w	Kristine	Siksaliete	LAT	31.10.98	5 Sep	5471	Rachel	Limburg	AUS	7.7.97 16 Feb
5646	Meg	Hemphill	JPN	23.5.96	26 Jul	5467	Amanda	Liljendal	FIN	16.1.97 16 Aug
5626	Annaëlle	Nyabeu Djapa	FRA	15.9.92	19 Dec	5459	Patricia	Ortega	ESP	18.4.94 13 Sep
5610	Aleksandra	Butvina	RUS	14.2.86	10 Sep	5445	Manon	Schoop	NED	7.8.99 6 Sep
5607	Alysha	Burnett	AUS	4.1.97	20 Dec	5442	Sandra	Böll	DEN	6.11.94 30 Aug
5574	Isabel	Mayer	GER	12.12.93	5 Jul	5433	Yuliya	Loban	UKR	7.8.00 30 Aug
5566	Célia	Perron	FRA	18.4.97	9 Aug	5433	Auriana	Lazraq	FRA	22.4.99 19 Sep
5538	Terza	Sinová	CZE-J	18.8.01	21 Jun	5430	Lilian	Tösmann	GER-J	.01 23 Aug
5545	Lara	Siemer	GER-J	13.8.02	23 Aug	5427	Sharlota	Paehlitse	BLR	20.11.98 2 Aug
5541	Karin	Odama	JPN	21.10.99	12 Sep	5416	Andrea	Rooth	NOR-J	6.3.02 5 Jul
5535		Jeong Yeon-jin	KOR	25.3.92	27 Jun	5410	Lydia	Boll	SUI	1.12.99 19 Jul
5532 (w)	Myke	van de Wiel	NED	4.6.97	6 Sep	5409	Jenifer	Norberto	BRA	4.10.96 11 Dec
5527	Barbora	Zatloukalová	CZE	3.6.97	26 Jul	**Best non wind-assisted**				
						5637	Katerina	Dvoráková	CZE	10.5.97 26 Jul

JUNIORS

4 juniors in main list. Further juniors:

5660	Kristine	Blazevica	LAT	11.12.01	1	NC-j	Ogre	5 Aug
	14.13/0.1	1.71 10.93 25.34/0.1		6.09/-1.35	59.22		2:17.53	
5538	Terza	Sinová	CZE	18.8.01	5		Plzen	21 Jun
	13.87/1.6	1.75 11.40 25.07/1.1		5.95w/2.6	28.82		2:22.42	
5545	Lara	Siemer	GER	13.8.02	1	NC-J	Vaterstetten	23 Aug
	14.23/-1.2	1.71 11.60 24.72/0.1		5.73/-1.2	39.42		2:24.75	
5430	Lilian	Tösmann	GER	.01	2	NC-J	Vaterstetten	23 Aug
	14.34/-0.9	1.59 12.47 25.93/-0.5		5.82/0.0	41.06		2:23.48	
5416	Andrea	Rooth	NOR	6.3.02	2		Moss	5 Jul
	13.66w/2.4	1.64 10.26 24.63/0.1		5.53/0.3	31.83		2:13.15	

DECATHLON

7627	Jordan	Gray	USA	28.12.95	1		Marble Falls	4 Oct
	12.45/1.1	6.19/1.9	12.70	1.67	58.46	14.80/1.0	38.09 3.60 37.74	5:27.35

4 X 100 METRES RELAY

43.47	JAM	Sportec		1		Kingston	29 Feb
43.80	JAM-J	Edwin Allen High U18		1		Spanish Town	19 Feb
44.00	JPN	Yuasa, Kodama, Saito, Tsuruta		1		Osaka	24 Oct
44.09	FIN	Francis. Mempinnen, Kortetmaa, Neziri		1	vSWE	Tampere	5 Sep
44.19	CZE	Seidlová, Pirková, Jiranová, Bendová		1		Tábor	14 Jul
44.20	NZL	Wilson, Hobbs, Hulls, Elliott		1		Canberra	13 Feb
44.22	AUS	Masters, Owusu-Afriyie, Day, Mucci		2		Canberra	13 Feb
44.28	BRA	EC Pinheiros Farias, R Santos, Krasucki, Rosa		1	NC	São Paulo	12 Dec
44.35	USA	Sheffield Elite		1		Long Beach	7 Mar
44.41 CHN 16 Sep	44.73 SUI 20 Sep	44.74 RUS 11 Sep	44.79 POL 29 Aug	44.84 CUB 22 Mar			
44.51 SWE 5 Sep							

4 X 400 METRES RELAY

3:29.60	CUB	Hechavarría 51.5, Almanza 52.5, Diago 54.0, Veitia 51.6	1	NC	La Habana	22 Mar
3:31.06	BLR	Luchsova, Mulyarchik, Kostsyuchkova, Kharashkevich	1		Brest	17 Jul
3:34.21 UKR 20Sep	3:35.42 JPN 18 Oct	3:37.6A KEN 6 Mar	3:38.29 USA 7 Mar	3:39.14 SWE 6Sep		
3:34.68 RUS 11Sep	3:35.58 JAM 8 Feb	3:37.70 POR 23 Sep	3:38.60 ROU 20Sep	3:39.75 FIN 6Sep		
3:34.80 ITA 30Aug	3:36.83 POL 30Aug	3:38.10 BRA 13Dec	3:38.66 CHN 18Sep			

Indoors

3:29.36i	Un. of Alabama USA T Roberson, D Baker, T Clark, N McDonald	1	SEC	College Station	29 Feb

4 X 1500 METRES RELAY

16:27.02	Nike Bowerman (USA)	1	Portland	31 Jul
	Quigley c.4:08, Cranny 4:09, Schweizer 4:06, Houlihan 4:04			

3000 - 5000 - 10,000 METRES WALK

Mark	Name	Nat	Born	Pos	Meet	Venue		Date
3000 METRES TRACK WALK								
12:35.03	Clémence Beretta	FRA	22.12.97	27 Sep		12:35.99 Mária Czaková	SVK	2.10.88 11 Sep
Indoors								
12:27.18	Antigóni Drisbióti	GRE	21.3.84	1		Pireás		9 Feb
12:30.52	Clémence Beretta	FRA	22.12.97	1	NC	Liévin		1 Mar
12:31.08	Meryem Bekmez	TUR	31.7.00	11 Jan		12:34.10 Ana Cabecinha	POR	29.4.84 29 Feb
12:32.65	Zivile Vaiciukeviciute	LTU	3.4.96	22 Feb		12:38.13 Émilie Menuet	FRA	27.11.91 1 Mar
5000 METRES TRACK WALK								
21:00.0	Antonella Palmisano	ITA	6.8.91	1		Tivoli		3 Oct
21:01.41	Viktória Madarász	HUN	12.5.85	1		Székesfehérvár		5 Sep
21:13.69	Katarzyna Zdziebło	POL	28.11.96	1	NC	Wlloclawek		29 Aug
21:17.82	Lyudmila Olyanovska	UKR	20.2.93	1	NC	Lutsk		15 Aug
21:20.54	Olena Sobchuk	UKR	23.11.95	2	NC	Lutsk		15 Aug
21:33.22	Kumiko Okada	JPN	17.10.91	25 Oct		21:45.84 Anna Terlyukevich	BLR	15.8.87 1 Aug
21:34.19	Jemima Montag	AUS	15.2.98	7 Mar		21:46.60 Masumi Fuchise	JPN	2.9.86 19 Sep
21:36.7	Yekaterina Petrova	RUS-Y	3.5.04	18 Feb		21:48.06mx Saskia Feige	GER	13.8.97 29 Aug
21:41.0	Mariavittoria Becchetti	ITA	12.12.94	3 Oct		21:52.12 Nicole Colombi	ITA	29.12.95 3 Oct
21:41.23	Kaori Kawazoe	JPN	30.5.95	19 Sep		21:53.86 Edna Barros	POR	18.12.96 18 Jan
Indoors						21:54.48 Ana Cabecinha	POR	29.4.84 18 Jan
20:04.4	Yelena Lashmanova	RUS	9.4.92	1		Saransk		27 Dec
20:21.5	Reykhan Kagramanova	RUS	1.6.97	2		Saransk		27 Dec
20:21.9	Elvira Khasanova	RUS	10.1.00	3		Saransk		27 Dec
20:55.80	Anna Terlyukevich	BLR	15.8.87	1	NC	Mogilyov		22 Feb
21:05.83	Darya Poluektova	BLR	4.3.93	2	NC	Mogilyov		22 Feb
21:06.92	Viktoriya Roshchupkina	BLR	23.5.95	3	NC	Mogilyov		22 Feb
21:14.6	Yuliya Turova	RUS	9.6.97	4		Saransk		27 Dec
21:19.5	Elmira Alembekova	RUS	30.6.90	5		Saransk		27 Dec
21:25.7	Darya Golubechkova	RUS	10.9.00	6		Saransk		27 Dec
21:29.3	Anastasiya Taushkanova	RUS	25.3.96	2		Chelyabinsk		6 Jan
10 KILOMETRES WALK				See also in 20k lists				
41:25		Yang Jiayu	CHN	18.2.96	1		Wenzhong	15 Dec
41:28	Antonella	Palmisano	ITA	6.8.91	1	NC	Modena	18 Oct
41:49+		Yang Jiayu			1	in 15k	Wenzhong	15 Dec
42:00.4At		Yang Jiayu			1		Huehot	8 May
42:09	Marina	Novikova	RUS	1.3.89	1		Voronovo	23 Aug
42:22+		Yang Jiayu			1	in 15k	Suqian	20 Dec
42:41		Qieyang Shenjie	CHN	11.11.90	2		Wenzhong	15 Dec
42:53+		Qieyang Shenjie				in 15k	Suqian	20 Dec
42:53+		Ma Zhenxia	CHN	1.8.98		in 15k	Suqian	20 Dec
43:00	Nadezhda	Sergeyeva	RUS	12.3.94	2		Voronovo	23 Aug
43:06+		Lu Xiuzhi	CHN	26.10.93		in 15k	Suqian	20 Dec
43:08		Lu Xiuzhi			3		Wenzhong	15 Dec
43:10+		Lu Xiuzhi				in 15k	Wenzhong	13 Dec
43:11+		Qieyang Shenjie				in 15k	Wenzhong	13 Dec
43:24+		Jiang Jinyan	CHN-Y	23.4.03		in 15k	Wenzhong	13 Dec
43:30+		Ma Zhenxia				in 15k	Wenzhong	13 Dec
43:37		Ma Zhenxia			4		Wenzhong	13 Dec
43:40	María	Pérez	ESP	29.4.96	1		Arahal	25 Jan
43:48+		Li Maocuo	CHN	20.10.92		in 15k	Wenzhong	15 Dec
43:55	Nicole (20/10)	Colombi	ITA	29.12.95	2	NC	Modena	18 Oct
43:57	Jemima	Montag	AUS	15.2.98	1		Melbourne	15 Nov
44:03	Mirna	Ortiz	GUA	28.2.87	2		Arahal	25 Jan
44:11.56t	Kumiko	Okada	JPN	17.10.91	1		Inzai	14 Nov
44:18.53t	Brigita	Virbalyte-Dimsiene	LTU	1.2.85	1		Birstonas	5 Sep
44:21.14t	Valentina	Trapletti	ITA	12.7.85	1		Bergamo	10 Sep
44:27	Yuliya	Khalilova	RUS-J	19.11.02	1	NC-wJ	Sochi	17 Feb
44:28.87t	Antigóni	Drisbióti	GRE	21.3.84	1		Thessaloníki	19 Jul
44:34+		Liang Rui	CHN	18.6.94		in 15k	Wenzhong	13 Dec
44:34.5t	Anezka	Drahotová	CZE	22.7.95	1		Melbourne	12 Jan
44:35+		Su Wenxiu	CHN	28.6.98		in 15k	Wenzhong	15 Dec
44:40	Mariavittoria	Becchetti	ITA	12.12.94	3	NC	Modena	18 Oct
44:43.31t	Anna	Terlyukevich	BLR	15.8.87	1		Minsk	31 Jul
44:43.85t	Evin	Demir	TUR-J	16.2.01	1		Istanbul	5 Sep
44:46	Kristina	Mavletova	RUS	28.9.98	3		Voronovo	23 Aug
44:48+		Niu Zhuomayingji	CHN-J	26.1.02		in 15k	Wenzhong	13 Dec
44:57.2t	Alana	Barber	NZL	8.7.87	2		Melbourne	12 Jan
45:05	Kaori	Kawazoe	JPN	30.5.95	1		Tokyo	1 Jan
45:07	Darya	Chernova	RUS-J	12.4.01	2	NC-wJ	Sochi	17 Feb

10 KM - 20 KILOMETRES WALK

Mark		Name		Nat	Born	Pos	Meet	Venue		Date
45:08		Zhang	Lingfen	CHN-J	22.10.01	2	NC-J	Taian		19 Sep
45:14	Heather		Lewis	GBR	25.10.93	1		Coventry		1 Mar
45:14.3t	Katie		Hayward	AUS	23.7.00	4		Melbourne		12 Jan
45:15		Xi	Ricuo	CHN-J	9.8.01	3	NC-J	Taian		19 Sep
45:16		Yan	Lamei	CHN-J	21.12.02	4	NC-J	Taian		19 Sep
45:21.21t	Darya	Poluektova		BLR	4.3.93	31 Jul				
45:27		Shi	Yuxia	CHN	28.1.99	15 Dec				
45:27.26t	Alegna	González		MEX	2.1.99	29 Dec				
45:28		Zhu	Kunyu	CHN	14.5.96	15 Dec				
45:35		Tang	Caihong	CHN	29.4.96	15 Dec				
45:35		Xiong	Cuihong	CHN	1.5.98	15 Dec				
45:35.94t	Rachelle	De Orbeta		PUR	27.3.00	7 Mar				
45:37		Wan	Jinyu	CHN-J	28.6.02	19 Sep				
45:38	Nami		Hayashi	JPN	11.8.99	1 Jan				
45:40		Liu	Roumei	CHN-J	10.12.02	19 Sep				
45:40		Cun	Hailu	CHN	15.8.97	15 Dec				
45:41							Duan Dandan	CHN	23,5,95	15 Dec
45:41							Sun Wenru	CHN	13.10.99	15 Dec
45:44.25t							Sun Qie	CHN-Y	9.1.03	8 May
45:45.50t	Beki						Smith	AUS	25.11.86	11 Jan
45:47							Yang Xinru	CHN-J	3.10.02	19 Sep
45:49							Jiao Shuangshuang	CHN-J	18.9.02	19 Sep
45:49.19t	Noelia	Vargas						CRC	17.4.00	29 Dec
45:50	Federica	Curiazzi						ITA	14.8.92	18 Oct
45:50.50t	Anastasiya	Rarovskaya						BLR	12.11.96	31 Jul
45:53	Jessica	Ching Siu Nga						HKG	11.2.87	1 Jan
45:59	Mar	Juárez						ESP	27.9.93	12 Jan
46:00	Lidia	Barcella						ITA	21.4.97	18 Oct

Best track times
44:24.0t	Lu Xiuzhi	1	Qinghuangdao	8 May						
44:24.1	Ma Zhenxia	2	Qinghuangdao	8 May		44:58.5t	Jemima Montag	1	Melbourne	25 Jan

Indoors
43:33.16	Anna		Terlyukevich	BLR	15.8.87	1	NC	Mogilyov	21 Feb
43:49.97	Viktoriya		Roshchupkina	BLR	23.5.95	2	NC	Mogilyov	21 Feb
44:03.97	Darya		Poluektova	BLR	4.3.93	3	NC	Mogilyov	21 Feb

JUNIORS
8 juniors in main list. 7 performances by 6 women to 45:10. Additional performances:

Niuzhuo Mayingji	44:55	1	NC-J	Taian	19 Sep				
45:37		Wan	Jinyu	CHN	28.6.02	5	NC-J	Taian	19 Sep
45:40		Liu	Roumei	CHN	10.12.02	6	NC-J	Taian	19 Sep
45:44.25t		Sun	Qie	CHN-Y	9.1.03	1		Changbaishan	8 May
45:47		Yang	Xinru	CHN	3.10.02	7	NC-J	Taian	19 Sep
45:49		Jiao	Shuangshuang	CHN	18.9.02	8	NC-J	Taian	19 Sep
46:04		Wang	Rentong	CHN	14.11.02	9	NC-J	Taian	19 Sep
46:05+		Li	Peng	CHN	27.8.02		in 15k	Wenzhong	13 Dec
46:06		Hu	Liyue	CHN	8.10.02	10	NC-J	Taian	19 Sep
46:10.77 t	Mimori	Yabuta		JPN	22.2.02	2		Otsu	13 Dec
46:21.46	Olga	Fiáska		GRE	9.11.01	1	NC-J	Ioánnina	2 Aug
46:29		Hu	Wenjing	CHN	16.9.02	11	NC-J	Taian	19 Sep

20 KILOMETRES WALK

WOMEN 2020

20k	10k									
1:26:43		Elvira	Khasanova	RUS	10.1.00	1	NC-w	Sochi		17 Feb
1:26:50		Reykhan	Kagramanova	RUS	1.6.97	2	NC-w	Sochi		17 Feb
1:27:25		Marina	Novikova	RUS	1.3.89	3	NC-w	Sochi		17 Feb
1:27:45			Khasanova			1	NC	Voronovskoye		6 Sep
1:27:48	44:17	Liu	Hong	CHN	12.5.87	1	NC	Taian		20 Sep
1:28:06	44:01	Yang	Jiayu	CHN	18.2.96	2	NC	Taian		20 Sep
1:28:27	44:42	Qieyang	Shenjie	CHN	11.11.90	3	NC	Taian		20 Sep
1:28:32			Kagramanova			2	NC	Voronovskoye		6 Sep
1:28:36		Yuliya	Turova	RUS	9.6.97	4	NC-w	Sochi		17 Feb
1:28:40	45:00	Antonella	Palmisano	ITA	6.8.91	3		Podebrady		10 Oct
1:28:43		Darya	Golubechkova	RUS	10.9.00	3	1 NC-23	Voronovskoye		6 Sep
1:29:12		Olena	Sobchuk (10)	UKR	23.11.95	1		Antalya		16 Feb
1:29:13		Lyudmila	Olyanovska	UKR	20.2.93	1	NC-w	Ivano-Frankivsk		14 Mar
1:29:14	45:01	Érica	de Sena	BRA	3.5.85	2		Podebrady		10 Oct
1:29:18			Olyanovska			1	NC	Ivano-Frankivsk		18 Oct
1:29:24		Meryem	Bekmez	TUR	31.7.00	2	1 NC	Antalya		16 Feb
1:29:31		Ayman	Ratova	KAZ	23.4.91	3		Antalya		16 Feb
1:29:32	45:00	Glenda	Morejón	ECU	30.5.00	3		Podebrady		10 Oct
1:29:35		Marila	Sakharuk	UKR	14.10.95	4		Antalya		16 Feb
1:29:36			Olyanovska			5		Antalya		16 Feb
1:29:43			Sakharuk			2	NC-w	Ivano-Frankivsk		14 Mar
1:29:54		Bhawana	Jat	IND	1.3.96	1		Ranchi		15 Feb
1:29:56	44:33	Kumiko	Okada	JPN	17.10.91	1	NC	Kobe		16 Feb
1:29:57		Nadoya	Borovska	UKR	25.2.81	6		Antalya		16 Feb
1:29:57			Turova			4	3 NC	Voronovskoye		6 Sep
1:29:59		Anna	Terlyukevich	BLR	15.8.87	7		Antalya		16 Feb
		(26/20)								
1:30:09		Nadezhda	Sergeyeva	RUS	12.3.94	5	4 NC	Voronovskoye		6 Sep
1:30:14		Elmira	Alembekova	RUS	30.6.90	6	NC	Voronovskoye		6 Sep
1:30:18		Ana	Cabecinha	POR	29.4.84	1	NC	Olhão		20 Dec
1:30:25	44:19	Antigóni	Drisbióti	GRE	21.3.84	4	2 Balk	Ivano-Frankivsk		14 Mar
1:30:39A		Karla	Jaramillo	ECU	21.1.97	1	NC	Macas		15 Feb

20 KILOMETRES WALK

Mark		Name		Nat	Born	Pos	Meet	Venue	Date	
1:30:41		Katarzyna	Zdzieblo	POL	28.11.96	1	NC	Warszawa	26 Sep	
1:30:54		Brigita	Virbalyte-Dimsiene	LTU	1.2.85	1	NC	Alytus	18 Sep	
1:30:56	46:02		Ni Yuanyuan	CHN	6.4.95	4	NC	Taian	20 Sep	
1:31:00	44:17		Yang Liujing	CHN	22.8.98	5	NC	Taian	20 Sep	
1:31:16		Olga	Shargina	RUS	24.7.96	8	NC	Voronovskoye	6 Sep	
										(30)
1:31:34A		Magaly	Bonilla	ECU	8.2.92	2	NC	Macas	15 Feb	
1:31:36		Priyanka	Goswami	IND	10.3.96	2	NC	Ranchi	15 Feb	
1:31:39	44:49	Panayióta	Tsinopoúlou	GRE	16.10.90	6	3 Balk	Ivano-Frankivsk	14 Mar	
1:31:46+		Yelena	Lashmanova	RUS	9.4.92	1	in 50k	Voronovskoye	5 Sep	
1:31:54		Maritza	Poncio	GUA	3.12.94	1		San Jeronimo	12 Dec	
1:31:55		Hanna	Shevchuk	UKR	18.7.96	5	NC	Ivano-Frankivsk	18 Oct	
1:32:02		Raquel	González	ESP	16.11.89	1		El Vendrell	26 Jan	
1:32:04A		Paola	Pérez	ECU	21.12.89	3	NC	Macas	15 Feb	
1:32:05		Valentina	Trapletti	ITA	12.7.85	1		Grosseto	28 Jan	
1:32:10		Johana	Ordóñez	ECU	12.12.87	2		San Jeronimo	12 Dec	
										(40)
1:32:12			Li Maocuo	CHN	20.10.92	1		Shilin	16 Jan	
1:32:25			Ma Zhenxia	CHN	1.8.98	2		Jinzhou	29 Jul	
1:32:31	45:02		Lu Xiuzhi	CHN	26.10.93	6	NC	Taian	20 Sep	
1:32:39		Anastasiya	Taushkanova	RUS	25.3.96	9	NC	Voronovskoye	6 Sep	
1:32:43		Mirna	Ortiz	GUA	28.2.87	1		Dublin	7 Mar	
1:32:47		María Luz	Andia	PER	9.11.00	1		Lima	1 Feb	
1:33:07		Sofiya	Timoshenko	RUS	5.1.98	8	2 NC-23	Voronovskoye	6 Sep	
1:33:08		Mayra Carolina	Herrera	GUA	20.12.88	3		San Jeronimo	12 Dec	
1:33:15		Jemima	Montag	AUS	15.2.98	1	Oce Ch	Adelaide	9 Feb	
1:33:15	45:33	Kaori	Kawazoe	JPN	30.5.95	2	NC	Kobe	16 Feb	
										(50)
1:33:15			Liang Rui	CHN	18.6.94	7	NC	Taian	20 Sep	
1:33:20		Nanako	Fujii	JPN	7.5.99	1		Nomi	15 Mar	
1:33:20			Bai Tiantian	CHN	14.8.98	8	NC	Taian	20 Sep	
1:33:26		Evin	Demir	TUR-J	16.2.01	8	2 NC	Antalya	16 Feb	
1:33:41		Karamjit	Kaur	IND	5.2.91	3	NC	Ranchi	15 Feb	
1:33:41		Masumi	Fuchise	JPN	2.9.86	2		Nomi	15 Mar	
1:33:41		Viktória	Madarász	HUN	12.5.85	2		Alytus	18 Sep	
1:33:46		Leyde	Guerra	PER	27.9.98	2		Lima	1 Feb	
1:33:48		Mária	Czaková	SVK	2.10.88	4		Podebrady	10 Oct	
1:33:54		Tereza	Durdiaková	CZE	20.2.91	5	1 NC	Podebrady	10 Oct	
										(60)
1:33:59		Anezka	Drahotová	CZE	22.7.95	6		Podebrady	10 Oct	
1:34:00		Katie	Hayward	AUS	23.7.00	2	Oce Ch	Adelaide	9 Feb	
1:34:03		Galina	Yakusheva	KAZ	14.7.88	16 Feb				
1:34:12			Ravina	IND	21.5.97	15 Feb				
1:34:13		Darya	Melenteva	RUS	7.4.98	17 Feb				
1:34:15+		Eleonora	Giorgi	ITA	14.9.89	26 Jan				
1:34:15		Sandra	Galvis (45:49)	COL	28.6.86	10 Oct				
1:34:20		Barbara	Kovács	HUN	26.7.93	27 Sep				
1:34:42A		Maritza	Guamán	ECU	17.1.88	15 Feb				
1:34:42		Viktoriya	Roshchupkina	BLR	23.5.95	3 Oct				
1:34:45			Su Wenxiu	CHN	28.6.98	20 Sep				
1:34:51			Ma Faying	CHN	30.8.93	16 Jan				
1:34:56		Yeseida	Carrillo	COL	22.10.93	10 Oct				
1:34:59			Cun Hailu	CHN	15.8.97	16 Jan				
1:34:59		Emilie	Menuet	FRA	27.11.91	10 Oct				
1:35:05+		Margarita	Nikiforova	RUS	19.8.98	5 Sep				
1:35:05		Lidia	Barcella	ITA	21.4.97	10 Oct				
1:35:06		Beki	Smith	AUS	25.11.86	9 Feb				
1:35:06			Gao Lan	CHN	18.1.00	20 Sep				
1:35:08		Kristina	Mavletova	RUS	28.9.98	17 Feb				
1:35:08		Mihaela	Acatrinei	ROU	26.2.96	22 Feb				
1:35:10		Nami	Hayashi	JPN	11.8.99	15 Mar				
1:35:20		Inês	Henriques	POR	1.5.80	5 Jan				
1:35:21		Serena	Sonoda	JPN	10.9.96	16 Feb				
1:35:21		Souad	Azzi	ALG	18.9.99	7 Mar				
1:35:33			Zhao Wenli	CHN	11.12.96	16 Jan				
1:35:38		Ana	Rodean	ROU	23.6.84	22 Feb				
1:35:45A		Maidy	Monge	GUA	12.9.00	2 Feb				
1:35:52		Alana	Barber	NZL	8.7.87	9 Feb				
1:35:55		Anastasiya	Yatsevich	BLR	18.1.85	16 Feb				
1:35:58		Violaime	Averous	FRA	15.3.85	10 Oct				
1:36:04			Xiao Xianghua	CHN	27.4.97	15 Jan				
1:36:08	(45:07)		Wu Quanming	CHN-J	16.11.01	20 Sep				
1:36:14			Bai Xueying	CHN-J	16.11.01	20 Sep				
1:36:25		Rachel	Seaman	CAN	14.1.86	25 Jan				
1:36:33		Hristína	Papadopoúou	GRE	5.9.96	14 Mar				
1:36:36		Ai	Michiguchi	JPN	3.6.88	16 Feb				
1:36:42		Clémence	Beretta	FRA	22.12.97	10 Oct				
1:36:49		Vivian	Castillo	MEX	10.6.98	9 Feb				
1:36:55		Yana	Smerdova (100)	RUS	7.2.98	17 Feb				
1:36:57			Shi Yuxia	CHN	28.1.99	20 Sep				
1:37:00A		Ángela	Castro	BOL	21.2.93	8 Feb				
1:37:02		Nadia	González	MEX	21.3.97	16 Feb				
1:37:07			Na Guo	CHN	22.6.99	20 Sep				
1:37:10		Anastasiya	Rarovskaya	BLR	12.11.96	3 Oct				
1:37:12			Xie Lijuan	CHN	14.5.93	16 Jan				
1:37:12		María	Peinado	GUA-J	12.11.01	12 Dec				
1:37:14			Zhao Xue	CHN	12.11.99	20 Sep				
1:37:19			Ji Haiying	CHN	25.2.00	16 Jan				
1:37:19		Mar	Juárez	ESP	27.9.93	26 Jan				
1:37:19.91		Viviane	Lyra	BRA	29.7.93	12 Dec				
1:37:21		Aleksandra	Simakova	RUS	6.1.99	17 Feb				
1:37:27		Sonal	Sukhwal	IND	28.1.98	15 Feb				
1:37:28A		Noelia	Vargas	CRC	17.4.00	1 Mar				
1:37:32		Simone	McInnes	AUS	27.11.91	9 Feb				
1:37:32A		Nathaly	León	ECU	3.6.98	15 Feb				
1:37:32		Nami	Kumagai	JPN	9.7.96	15 Mar				
1:37:33		Carolina	Costa	POR	12.3.98	26 Jan				
1:37:33			Yang Shuqing	CHN	30.8.96	20 Sep				
1:37:34			Tang Caihong	CHN	29.4.96	20 Sep				
1:37:38		Dímitra	Bohóri	GRE	17.6.98	9 Aug				
1:37:46		Mariya	Khadeyeva	RUS	9.3.99	6 Sep				
1:37:50		Khrystyna	Yudkina	UKR	4.12.84	16 Feb				
1:37:50		Ainhoa	Pinedo	ESP	17.2.83	18 Sep				
1:37:53			Yan Peirong	CHN	26.9.99	20 Sep				
						(125)				

Best track time: 1:37:19.91 Érica de Sena BRA 3.5.85 12 Dec

20 - 35 - 50 KILOMETRES WALK

Mark		Name		Nat	Born	Pos	Meet	Venue	Date	
				JUNIORS						
1:33:26		Evin	Demir	TUR	16.2.01	8	2 NC	Antalya	16	Feb
1:36:08	45:07		Wu Quanming	CHN	16.11.01	11	NC	Taian	20	Sep
1:36:14			Bai Xueying	CHN	16.11.01	12	NC	Taian	20	Sep
1:37:12		María	Peinado	GUA	12.11.01	5		San Jeronimo	12	Dec
1:38:17		Sara	Buglisi	ITA	11.2.01	1		Grosseto	26	Jan

30-35 KILOMETRES WALK

30k	35k									
2:17:28	2:40:22+	Yelena	Lashmanova	RUS	9.4.92	1	in 50k	Voronovskoye	5	Sep
2:21:09+	2:43:43	Eleonora	Giorgi	ITA	14.9.89	1	NC	Grosseto	26	Jan
	2:43:56	Vera	Sokolova	RUS	8.6.87	1	NC-w	Sochi	17	Feb
2:22:07	2:45:16+	Margarita	Nikiforova	RUS	19.8.98	2	in 50k	Voronovskoye	5	Sep
	2:48:52	Margarita	Nikiforova	RUS	19.8.98	2	NC-w	Sochi	17	Feb
	2:49:04	Anastasiya	Kalashnikova	RUS	29.6.97	3	NC-w	Sochi	17	Feb
	2:49:18	Kristina	Lyubushkina	RUS	19.9.95	4	NC-w	Sochi	17	Feb
	2:54:05	Aleksandra	Bushkova	RUS	13.1.97	5	NC-w	Sochi	17	Feb
	2:54:12	Nicole	Colombi	ITA	29.12.95	2	NC	Grosseto	26	Jan
	2:56:34	Valentyna	Myronchuk	UKR	10.8.94	1	NC-w	Ivano-Frankivsk	14	Mar
	2:58:37	Krisztina	Kudinova	RUS	25.10.98	6	NC-w	Sochi	17	Feb
	2:58:44	Lidia	Barcella	ITA	21.4.97	3		Grosseto	26	Jan
2:33:35	2:59:10+	Anastasiya	Kalashnikova	RUS	29.6.97	3	in 50k	Voronovskoye	5	Sep

50 KILOMETRES WALK

3:50:42	Yelena	Lashmanova	RUS	9.4.92	1	NC	Voronovskoye	5	Sep
3:59:56	Margarita	Nikiforova	RUS	19.8.98	2	NC	Voronovskoye	5	Sep
4:15:46	Mar	Juárez	ESP	27.9.93	1	NC	Torrevieja	16	Feb
4:18:26	Anastasiya	Kalashnikova	RUS	29.6.97	3	NC	Voronovskoye	5	Sep
4:22:24	Kristina	Lyubushkina	RUS	19.9.95	4	NC	Voronovskoye	5	Sep
4:25:32	Aleksandra	Bushkova	RUS	13.1.97	5	NC	Voronovskoye	5	Sep
4:32:11	Irina	Musikhina	RUS	7.6.88	6	NC	Voronovskoye	5	Sep
4:32:30	Khrystyna	Yudkina	UKR	4.12.84	1	NC	Ivano-Frankivsk	18	Oct
4:34:45	Krisztina	Kudinova	RUS	25.10.98	7	NC	Voronovskoye	5	Sep
4:37:33	Robyn	Stevens	USA	24.4.83	1	NC	Santee	26	Jan
4:38:38	Tamara	Havrylyuk	UKR	14.12.95	2	NC	Ivano-Frankivsk	18	Oct
4:38:44	Agnieszka	Ellward	POL	26.3.89	1	NC	Dudince	24	Oct
4:39:10	Aleksandra	Oksyannikova	RUS	16.6.93	8	NC	Voronovskoye	5	Sep
4:40:45	Ainhoa	Pinedo	ESP	17.2.83	2	NC	Torrevieja	16	Feb
4:41:07	Viviane	Lyra	BRA	29.7.93	1	S.Am Ch	Lima	7	Mar
4:41:16	Antonina	Lorek	POL	11.2.95	2	NC	Dudince	24	Oct
4:46:54	Stephanie	Casey	USA	1.8.83	2		Santee	25	Jan
4:47:02	Erin	Taylor Talcott	USA	21.5.78	3	2 NC	Santee	25	Jan
4:50:38	Oksana	Kulahina	UKR	1.4.87	3	NC	Ivano-Frankivsk	18	Oct
4:53:27	Kathleen	Burnett	USA	7.10.88	4	NC	Santee	25	Jan

LATE AMENDMENTS

Men
400mh: Best at low altitude: 49.82 Masaki Toyoda JPN 2 Tokyo 23 Aug
PV: 5.51 Daniel was in unsanctioned meeting, best then 5.50Ai 1c2 Reno 18 Jan; also u best out 5.61 Richartz

Women
5000m add to Juniors
15:34.47 Jenna Hutchins USA-Y 25.3.04 1 Columbia, SC 11 Dec
Half Marathon
69:55+	66:18	49:45	Sintayehu	Lewetegn	ETH	9.5.96	in Mar	Osaka	26	Jan
69:55+	66:18	49:45	Meskerem	Assefa	ETH	3.10.91	in Mar	Osaka	26	Jan
69:55+	66:18	49:44	Bornes	Kitur	KEN	23.11.86	in Mar	Osaka	26	Jan
70:04+	66:21	49:45	Kayoko	Fukushi	JPN	25.3.82	in Mar	Osaka	29	Jan

SP: add 16.07i Kiana Phelps USA 22.7.97 29 Feb
HT: 64.08 dh Dudan - best not downhill: 62.13 26 Jul

Drugs Bans
In 2021 it was announced that re-testing of Dilshod Nazarov's sample from the 2011 World Champs had proved positive and he received a 2-year ban with his hammer results annulled 29 Aug 2011 to 29 Aug 2013. Those included: 2011: World Ch 10th; 2012: 9th Olympic G; 2013: World Ch 5th & Asian Ch 1st.
He is also banned for 2 years from 24 Sep 2019.

Name		Nat	Born	Ht/Wt	Event	2020 Mark	Pre-2020 Best

MEN'S INDEX 2020

Athletes included are those ranked in the main lists (full details) at standard (World Championships) events. Those with detailed biographical profiles are indicated in first column by:
* in this year's Annual, ^ featured in a previous year's Annual. Final column indicates pb prior to 2020.

	Abdelrahman	Ihad	EGY	1.5.89 194/96	JT	80.64	89.21- 14
*	Abdi	Bashir	BEL	10.2.89 168/59	1Hr	21.332m	
					Mar	2:04:49	2:06:14- 19
	Abdi Ali	Mahadi	NED	8.11.95 183/64	1500	3:37.43	3:41.81- 19
	Abe	Takatoshi	JPN	12.11.91 192/81	400h	49.31	48.68- 18
	Abeykoon	K.M.Yupon	SRI	31.12.94 186/78	100	10.16	10.44- 19
	Abromavicius	Aleksas	LTU	6.12.84 197/115	DT	60.54	63.32- 10
^	Abshero	Ayele	ETH	28.12.90 167/52	Mar	2:08:20	2:04:23- 12
	Accetta	Edoardo	ITA	28.3.94 180/68	TJ	16.62i	16.28i, 16.28- 18
	Acet	Alperen	TUR	2.4.98 193/79	HJ	2.25	2.30- 18
	Aceti	Vladimir	ITA	16.10.98 181/73	400	45.65	45.92- 17
	Adane	Yihunilign	ETH	29.2.96 166/50	Mar	2:06:22	2:09:11- 19
*	Adola	Guye	ETH	20.10.90 175/54	HMar	60:50	59:06- 14
	Adugna	Olika	ETH	12.9.99 169/55	Mar	2:06:15	-0-
	Afonin	Maksim	RUS	6.1.92 184/115	SP	20.62i, 20.54	21.39i- 18, 21.07- 17
	Aghasyan	Levon	ARM	19.1.95 191/76	TJ	16.67	17.08- 19
	Agyekum	Emil	GER	22.5.99 188/75	400h	49.78	49.69- 19
*	Ahmed	Mohammed	CAN	5.1.91 175/61	1500	3:34.89	3:40.18- 15
	3000	7:46.64+	7:40.11i- 16, 7:40.49- 17		5000	12:47.20	12:58.16- 19
	Aikines-Aryeetey	Harry	GBR	29.8.88 180/87	100	10.12w	10.08- 13, 9.90w- 17
	Airiau	Gatien	FRA	9.6.93 172/62	3kSt	8:27.27	8:35.91- 19
	Aizawa	Akira	JPN	18.7.97 178/62	10000	27:18.75	28:17.81- 18
	Akalnew	Tesfahun	ETH	29.4.99 160/48	HMar	59:22	-0-
	Akamatsu	Ryoichi	JPN	2.5.95 183/60	HJ	2.28	2.25- 15
	Akcam	Berke	TUR-J	10.4.02 182/73	400h	49.78	52.78- 18
*	Akimenko	Mikhail	RUS	6.12.95 196/86	HJ	2.31i	2.35- 19
	Al-Gamal	Mostafa	EGY	1.10.88 191/105	HT	74.50	81.27- 14
	Al-Hizam	Hussain Asim	KSA	4.1.98 180/73	PV	5.61i	5.70i, 5.63- 18
	Al-Yoha	Yacoub Mohamed	KUW	31.1.93 185/70	110h	13.60	13.35- 19
	Alame	Haimro	ISR	8.6.90 175/55	Mar	2:07:45	2:11:03- 19
	Alemayehu	Belachew	ETH	26.10.85		Mar	2:07:55	2:09:49- 16
	Alexander	Colby	USA	13.6.91 183/64	1500	3:37.12	3:34.88- 16
	Alkana	Antonio	RSA	12.4.90 185/77	110h	13.40	13.11- 19
*	Allen	Devon	USA	12.12.94 183/82	110h	13.36	13.03- 16
*	Allen	Nathon	JAM	28.10.95 178/68	200	20.45	20.46, 20.39w- 18
	Almas	Deniz	GER	17.7.97 170/65	100	10.08	10.33- 17
	Almgren	Andreas	SWE	12.6.95 177/66	2000	5:00.23	-0-
	Alvarado	Abraham	USA	4.8.95 185/73	1500	3:36.82i	3:41.17- 18
	Amare	Girmaw	ISR	26.10.87 172/60	Mar	2:07:28	2:09:54- 19
*	Amb	Kim	SWE	31.7.90 180/85	JT	86.49	86.03- 19
	Ambesa	Tesfaye	ETH	0.97 170/59	Mar	2:06:18	2:10:49- 19
*	Amdouni	Mourad	FRA	21.1.88 175/60	HMar	59:40	-0-
	Amels	Douwe	NED	16.9.91 193/68	HJ	2.26	2.28- 13
	Anastasákis	Mihaíl	GRE	3.12.94 183/103	HT	75.85	77.72- 17
	Andraloits	Maksim	BLR	17.6.97 189/83	Dec	8100	7863- 18
	André	Thiago	BRA	4.8.95 177/62	800	1:46.33	1:44.81- 19
	Angela	Ramsey	NED	6.11.99 175/68	400h	49.60	50.10- 19
	Anishchenkov	Nikita	RUS	25.7.92 188/80	HJ	2.30i, 2.25	2.30- 11
	Aoki	Ryuma	JPN	16.6.97 166/56	3kSt	8:25.85	8:32.51- 19
	Aoki	Yuta	JPN	27.4.97 168/51	10000	27:58.63	28:50.98- 18
*	Apak	Esref	TUR	3.1.82 186/105	HT	77.56	81.45- 05
*	Arai	Hirooki	JPN	18.5.88 180/62	20kW	1:20:32	1:19:00- 19
^	Arai	Ryohei	JPN	23.6.91 183/94	JT	81.73	86.83- 14
	Arce	Daniel	ESP	22.4.92 190/72	3kSt	8:19.40	8:20.16- 19
*	Aregawi	Berihu	ETH-J	28.2.01 173/55	3000	7:35.78i	7:42.12- 18
					5000	13:08.91A	13:15.44- 18
	Armstrong	Angus	AUS	17.3.97 191/80	PV	5.65	5.52- 18
	Arnaudov	Tsanko	POR	14.3.92 192/118	SP	20.77	21.56- 17
*	Arop	Marco	CAN	20.9.98 194/82	800	1:44.14	1:44.25- 19
	Arrhenius	Leif	SWE	15.7.86 192/120	DT	62.88A	64.46- 11
	Arrhenius	Niklas	USA	10.9.82 192/125	DT	66.46A	66.22- 11
	Art	Arnaud	BEL	28.1.93 185/83	PV	5.54i	5.72, 5.74dh?- 17
	Asanov	Aleksandr	RUS	30.3.95 192/77	HJ	2.24	2.28i- 19, 2.26- 17
^	Ashmeade	Nickel	JAM	7.4.90 184/87	100	10.16	9.90- 13
					200	20.47	19.85- 12

INDEX 377

Name		Nat	Born	Ht/Wt	Event	2020 Mark	Pre-2020 Best
Atkin	Sam	GBR	14.3.93	186/70	5000	13:18.57	13:33.70, 13:33.51i- 19
					10000	27:26.58	29:44.33- 16
Atnafu	Yitayal	ETH	20.1.93	172/55	Mar	2:06:21	2:07:00- 18
Atsebha	Hailemariam	ETH	14.3.86		HMar	60:46	63:50- 19
^ Augustyn	Rafal	POL	14.5.84	178/71	50kW	3:47:42	3:43:22- 16
Auvinen	Roope	FIN	17.2.98	191/84	HT	71.18	70.76- 19
Avila	Eric	USA	3.10.89	176/64	5000	13:18.68	13:43.05- 14
Awotunde	Josh	USA	12.6.95	188/107	SP	20.45i	21.33i- 18, 21.13- 19
Ayenew	Mekuant	ETH	0.91		Mar	2:04:46	2:09:00- 17
Aysabakiyev	Aleksandr	RUS	10.12.89		50kW	4:02:55	4:12:04- 19
* Babayev	Nazim	AZE	8.10.97	185/70	TJ	17.15i	17.29i- 19, 17.18- 17
Bacha	Zelalem	BRN	10.1.88		Mar	2:07:09	2:09:16- 18
Bacon	Jaylen	USA	5.8.96	183/75	100	10.18	9.97- 18
Baden	Joel	AUS	1.2.96	190/70	HJ	2.24	2.30- 19
Bahník	Marek	CZE	10.5.99	192/69	HJ	2.25i	2.20i- 19
Baker	Johnathan	USA		188/77	LJ	7.99w	7.51, 7.57w- 19
* Baker	Ronnie	USA	15.10.93	178/80	100	10.00	9.87, 9.78w- 18
Ballantyne	Ryan	NZL	8.1.99	188/114	SP	19.85	19.12- 19
Baltaci	Izkan	TUR	13.2.94	187/111	HT	77.33	77.50- 19
Bando	Yuta	JPN	21.11.96	190/65	5000	13:18.49	13:26.70- 19
^ Baniótis	Konstadínos	GRE	6.11.86	202/80	HJ	2.27i	2.34- 13
Bantie	Aychew	ETH	12.9.95	164/50	Mar	2:06:23	2:06:23- 19
* Barega	Selemon	ETH	20.1.00	173/59	1500	3:32.97	-0-
3000	7:33.19i, 7:41.54		7:32.17- 19		5000	12:49.08	12:43.02- 18
Barkach	Alfred	KEN	2.3.97	167/52	HMar	59:49	59:46- 19
Barrondo	Bernardo Uriel	GUA	5.6.93	165/50	50kW	3:56:48	3:53:10- 18
^ Barrondo	Erick	GUA	16.9.96	172/60	20kW	1:22:12	1:18:15- 12
* Barsoton	Leonard	KEN	21.10.94	166/56	HMar	59:10	59:09- 19
Bárta	Dan	CZE	24.2.98		PV	5.52	5.32- 19
Bárta	Marek	CZE	8.12.92	197/111	DT	64.40	62.32- 19
Bashan	Nikolay	BLR	18.11.92	182/95	HT	75.00	75.00- 17
Bates	KeAndre	USA	24.5.96	181/75	LJ	7.98iA	8.11, 8.32w- 16
					TJ	17.00iA, 16.42i	17.16- 18
Baxter	Matt	NZL	6.8.94	175/59	3000	7:47.85i	8:10.28i-18, 8:14.73- 13
Bayer	Andrew	USA	3.2.90	180/60	5000	13:24.67i	13:32.74- 11
Bayer	Simon	GER	23.11.95	189/105	SP	20.01	20.26- 19
Beamish	George	NZL	24.10.96	185/64	3000	7:44.67i	8:23.15- 14
* Bednarek	Kenny	USA	14.10.98	185/84	100	10.09, 10.02w	10.42- 18, 10.22w- 19
					200	19.80	19.82A, 20.07, 19.49Aw- 19
Bednarek	Sylwester	POL	28.4.89	198/75	HJ	2.30i	2.33i- 17, 2.32- 09
* Bedrani	Djilali	FRA	1.10.93	179/59	1500	3:38.03	3:37.71- 19
3000	7:41.40i		7:50.84i- 19, 8:15.96- 18		3kSt	8:13.43	8:05.23- 19
Bekele	Gizaw	ETH	13.12.87		Mar	2:08:03	2:14:17- 18
* Bekele	Kenenisa	ETH	13.6.82	162/54	HMar	60:22	60:09- 13
Belhadj	Mehdi	FRA	10.6.95	183/72	3kSt	8:22.06	8:31.49- 19
* Belihu	Andamlak	ETH	20.11.98	181/62	HMar	58:54	59:10- 19
Bell	Connor	NZL-J	21.6.01	193/110	DT	63.25	56.41- 19
Bell	Dylan	USA	21.7.93	195/85	PV	5.61iA	5.70A, 5.60- 16
Belo	Francisco	POR	27.3.91	193/120	SP	20.94i	20.97i, 20.97- 19
* Bélocian	Wilhem	FRA	22.6.95	178/78	110h	13.18	13.25- 16, 13.14w- 19
Ben Daoud	Hamid	ESP	19.2.96		Mar	2:07:03	2:08:14- 19
* Benard	Chris	USA	4.4.90	190/79	TJ	17.02iA	17.48- 17
Bengtström	Carl	SWE	13.1.00	182/73	400h	49.69	50.20- 19
* Benjamin	Rai	USA	27.7.97	191/77	100	10.03	10.69-15, 10.40w- 19
Benkunskas	Edgaras	LTU	28.5.99		Dec	7643	7584- 19
Berglund	Kalle	SWE	11.3.96	179/62	1500	3:35.34	3:33.70- 19
					2000	4:59.71	5:36.5+- 19
Bertasius	Simas	LTU	31.10.93	173/61	1500	3:38.01	3:39.01- 18
* Bertemes	Bob	LUX	24.5.93	187/118	SP	21.21	22.22- 19
Bertolini	Roberto	ITA	9.10.85	187/100	JT	79.78	81.68- 17
Besson	Ludovic	FRA	27.1.98	195/88	Dec	7622	7792- 19
* Bett	Leonard	KEN	3.11.00	173/57	3kSt	8:08.78	8:08.61- 19
Bey	Augustin	FRA	6.6.95	180/63	LJ	8.13	7.90- 18, 8.08w- 19
Bibic	Elzan	SRB	8.1.99	197/72	1500	3:35.07	3:37.66- 19
3000	7:43.18		7:51.51- 18		5000	13:26.56	13:34.99- 19
* Bigot	Quentin	FRA	1.12.92	177/105	HT	76.42	78.58- 14
* Birgen	Bethwel	KEN	6.8.88	178/64	1500	3:36.22i, 3:36.67	3:30.77- 13
					3000	7:36.21i	7:32.48- 16
Birkinhead	Damien	AUS	8.4.93	190/130	SP	19.84	21.35- 19
Biya	Jarod	SUI	22.5.00	183/75	LJ	7.99i	7.78- 19
* Blake	Yohan	JAM	26.12.89	181/79	100	10.15, 10.07w	9.69- 12

Name		Nat	Born	Ht/Wt	Event	2020 Mark	Pre-2020 Best
Blankenship	Ben	USA	15.12.88	173/61	10000	28:08.20	-0-
* Blech	Torben	GER	12.2.95	192/87	PV	5.70i, 5.62	5.80- 19
Blignaut	Kyle	RSA	9.11.99	190/130	SP	20.75	20.03- 19
* Bloomfield	Akeem	JAM	10.11.97	188/77	400	45.07	43.94- 18
Bocchi	Tobia	ITA	7.4.97	187/80	TJ	16.62	16.73- 19
Bogutskiy	Yevgeniy	BLR	7.9.99	195/110	DT	60.77	61.51- 19
Boit	Solomon	KEN	1.10.99	170/55	10000	27:41.10	27:57.44- 18
Bol	Peter	AUS	22.2.94	168/57	800	1:44.96	1:44.56- 18
Bonvecchio	Norbert	ITA	14.8.85	181/80	JT	77.60	80.37- 14
Bor	Emmanuel	USA	14.4.88	167/52	5000	13:12.53i	13:10.23- 19
* Bor	Hillary	USA	22.11.89	168/57	5000	13:21.17i	13:14.96i- 19, 13:26.81- 18
3000	7:48.73i		8:14.60i- 09		10000	27:38.53	-0-
Bordier	Gabriel	FRA	8.10.97	183/70	20kW	1:20:19	1:21:43- 19
* Boreysha	Pavel	BLR	16.2.91	193/120	HT	76.41	78.60- 16
Borkowski	Mateusz	POL	2.4.97	189/76	800	1:46.28	1:45.42- 18
Bouqantar	Soufiyan	MAR	30.8.93	174/54	3000	7:46.32i	7:38.65- 17
Bradford	Zachery	USA	29.11.99	184/77	PV	5.80i	5.77- 19
Braido	William	BRA	18.3.92	186/95	SP	20.01	19.42- 18
Brandt	Robert	USA	2.11.96	183/64	10000	27:39.20	28:48.38- 17
Brandt	Torben	GER	19.5.95	190/105	DT	60.79	62.09- 17
Bray	Brandon	USA	24.4.97	180/65	PV	5.62i	5.70- 19
Bray	Ethan	USA	18.5.97	185/79	PV	5.51i	5.58- 18
* Braz da Silva	Thiago	BRA	16.12.93	193/84	PV	5.82	6.03- 16
* Brazier	Donavan	USA	15.4.97	188/73	800	1:43.15	1:42.34- 19
600	1:14.39i, 1:15.07		1:13.77i- 19		1500	3:35.85	3:37.18- 19
Brito	Jonathas	BRA	30.11.92	187/75	110h	13.57	13.50, 13.44w- 19
Broadbell	Rasheed	JAM	13.8.00	186/80	110h	13.47	-0-
* Broeders	Ben	BEL	21.6.95	178/75	PV	5.80i, 5.80	5.76- 19
* Bromell	Trayvon	USA	10.7.95	175/71	100	9.90, 9.87w	9.84, 9.76w- 15
* Brown	Aaron	CAN	27.5.92	185/79	100	10.15	9.96, 9.95w- 16
					200	20.24	19.95- 19
Brown	Clayton	JAM	8.12.96	184/77	HJ	2.25i	2.25i- 17, 2.25- 18
					TJ	16.50i	16.58i- 17, 16.42- 18
Browning	Rohan	AUS	31.12.97	179/73	100	10.16, 10.06w	10.08- 19
Bruintjies	Henricho	RSA	16.7.93	178/70	100	10.08A	9.97- 15, 9.89w- 16
Bubenik	Matús	SVK	14.11.89	197/78	HJ	2.24i	2.31i, 2.29- 15
Buchanan	Reid	USA	3.2.93	185/67	10000	28:07.62	27:58.67- 19
Budza	Serhiy	UKR	6.12.84	180/75	50kW	3:49:47	3:47:36- 13
Bühler	Matthias	GER	2.9.86	189/74	110h	13.60	13.34- 12, 13.20w- 14
* Bukowiecki	Konrad	POL	17.3.97	191/140	SP	21.88i, 20.88	22.25- 19
Bulakhov	Vladislav	BLR	23.1.99	187/72	LJ	8.10	7.85- 17, 7.88w- 19
Bunuka	James	KEN	1.11.97	165/52	10000	28:05.66	27:45.59- 19
					HMar	60:34	62:22- 19
Burgin	Max	GBR-J	20.5.02	181/61	800	1:44.75	1:45.36- 19
Burnet	Taymir	NED	1.10.92	184/73	200	20.76, 20.35w	20.34- 19
Bushendich	Mande	UGA	7.4.97	170/55	HMar	60:14	-0-
Bussotti Neves	João	ITA	10.5.93	180/62	1500	3:36.7+	3:37.12- 17
Bustos	David	ESP	25.8.90	182/65	1500	3:37.93	3:34.77- 12
Bychkov	Igor	ESP	7.3.87	189/80	PV	5.60i	5.70- 17
^ Cáceres	Eusebio	ESP	10.9.91	176/69	LJ	7.99i	8.37- 13
* Cai Zelin		CHN	11.4.91	172/55	20kW	1:22:03	1:18:47- 12
Caicedo	Juan José	ECU	20.7.92	185/105	DT	69.60	60.57- 18
* Cakss	Gatis	LAT	13.6.95	184/93	JT	84.56	83.89- 18
Calel	José Oswaldo	GUA	8.8.98		20kW	1:22:16	1:23:38- 19
Cambridge	Aska	JPN	31.5.93	180/77	100	10.03	10.08, 9.98w- 17
Campbell	Rajindra	JAM	29.2.96	183/102	SP	20.07i	18.43- 19
Campbell	Taylor	GBR	30.6.96	191/100	HT	74.98	74.63- 19
Campion	Kevin	FRA	23.5.88	183/63	20kW	1:21:35	1:20:28- 17
Carbin	Darius	USA	4.3.98	198/82	HJ	2.25i	2.26i- 19, 2.25- 16
Carlsson	Ragnar	SWE	16.11.00	180/84	HT	74.11	68.81- 18
Carmoy	Thomas	BEL	16.2.00	188/75	HJ	2.27	2.24- 19
* Carro	Fernando	ESP	1.4.92	175/67	1500	3:35.90	3:44.35i-18, 3:45.15- 17
5000	13:32.11		13:35.68- 19		3kSt	8:13.45	8:05.69- 19
* Carter	Chris	USA	11.3.89	186/80	TJ	16.65i	17.18- 16, 17.20Ai, 17.28w- 18
^ Carter	Nesta	JAM	11.10.85	178/70	100	10.18	9.78- 10
Carvalho	Florian	FRA	9.3.89	183/70	10000	28:04.05	28:06.78- 18
Carvalho	Lucas	BRA	16.7.93	183/73	200	20.40	20.81- 19
					400	45.53	45.37- 17
Castro	Luis Joel	PUR	28.1.91	195/72	HJ	2.24i	2.29- 16
* Ceh	Kristian	SLO	17.2.99	206/118	DT	68.75	63.82- 19
Ceko	Marko	CRO	3.8.00	192/82	LJ	8.04	7.78- 18

INDEX 379

Name		Nat	Born	Ht/Wt	Event	2020 Mark	Pre-2020 Best
Chakir	Ibrahim	ESP	4.9.94	178/62	3kSt	8:32.98	8:31.10- 17
Chalmers	Alastair	GBR	31.3.00	183/73	400h	49.66	50.07- 19
Chalu	Gelmisa	ETH		168/52	Mar	2:04:53	2:09:08- 19
Chalyy	Timofey	RUS	7.4.94	190/79	400h	49.77	48.57- 16
^ Chapelle	Axel	FRA	24.4.95	182/77	PV	5.53i	5.88i- 18, 5.72- 17
Chaussinand	Yann	FRA	11.5.98	196/94	HT	73.61	72.25- 19
* Chebet	Evans	KEN	10.11.88	170/54	Mar	2:03:00	2:05:00- 19
Chemjor	Vestus	KEN	0.87		HMar	60:47	62:48A-09
Chen Ding		CHN	5.8.92	180/62	20kW	1:22:12	1:17:40- 12
Chen Long		CHN-J	13.11.02		HJ	2.24	2.26- 19
* Cheng Chao-Tsun		TPE	17.10.93	182/88	JT	85.54	91.36- 17
* Cheparev	Dementiy	RUS	28.10.92		50kW	3:43:29	3:43:05- 17
* Cheptegei	Joshua	UGA	12.9.96	179/61	3000	7:35.14+	7:33.26- 19
5000	12:35.36 12:57.41- 19				10000	26:11.00	26:48.36- 19 HMar 59:21
Cherono	Alex	KEN	30.12.00		5000	13:25.28	13:30.56- 19
					10000	27:55.40	28:28.71- 19
* Cherono	Lawrence	KEN	7.8.88	178/61	Mar	2:03:04	2:04:06- 18
Cherry	Michael	USA	23.3.95	186/75	400	44.98	44.66- 17
* Cheruiyot	Evans Kipkorir	KEN	24.9.91	175/55	HMar	60:42	60:26- 18
* Cheruiyot	Ferguson Rotich	KEN	30.11.89	183/73	800	1:44.16	1:42.54- 19
* Cheruiyot	Timothy	KEN	20.11.95	178/64	1500	3:28.45	3:28.41- 18
* Cheserek	Edward	KEN	2.2.94	168/57	3000	7:46.74i	7:38.74i- 18, 7:43.47- 19
5000	13:09.05i, 13:21.78		13:04.44- 19		10000	27:23.58	28:30.18- 14
Chiaraviglio	German	ARG	16.4.87	192/77	PV	5.60	5.75- 15
Chiesa	Stefano	ITA	25.5.96	186/73	20kW	1:22:31	1:21:46- 18
Chila	Gabriele	ITA	17.9.97	177/64	LJ	8.00i	8.00- 19
^ Chizhikov	Dmitriy	RUS	6.12.93	194/85	TJ	16.91i	17.20- 15
Chmielak	Hubert	POL	19.6.89	188/88	JT	78.54	82.58- 14
^ Chocho	Andrés	ECU	4.11.83	167/67	50kW	3:48:57	3:42:57A- 16
Choi Byung-kwang		KOR	7.4.91	185/70	20kW	1:22:23	1:20:49- 19
* Chopra	Neeraj	IND	24.12.97	184/80	JT	87.86A	88.06- 19
Chumo	Victor	KEN	1.1.87	175/59	HMar	59:58	60:03- 18
Churylo	Andrey	BLR	19.5.93	190/72	HJ	2.24i, 2.22	2.30- 14
Ciattei	Vincent	USA	21.1.95	183/70	1500	3:36.35	3:39.60- 18
* Cienfuegos	Javier	ESP	15.7.90	193/134	HT	77.52	79.38- 19
Cissé	Arthur Gue	CIV	29.12.96	174/64	100	10.04	9.93- 19
					200	20.23	20.72- 16
Collet	Mathieu	FRA	15.3.95	180/72	PV	5.74i	5.55- 17
Collet	Thibaut	FRA	17.6.99	172/65	PV	5.62	5.62i, 5.61- 19
Comenentia	Denzel	NED	25.11.95	186/114	HT	74.42	76.80- 19
^ Compaoré	Benjamin	FRA	5.8.87	189/86	TJ	16.68	17.48- 14
Conceição	Paulo	POR	29.12.93	190/79	HJ	2.28i	2.24i, 2.23- 16
* Constantino	Gabriel	BRA	9.2.95	186/77	110h	13.60	13.18- 19
Copeland	Piers	GBR	26.11.98	188/70	800	1:46.24	1:48.03- 19
1500	3:35.32		3:39.50- 19		2000	4:57.61	-0-
* Copello	Alexis	AZE	12.8.85	185/80	TJ	16.92	17.68A- 11, 17.65, 17.69w- 09
* Copello	Yasmani	TUR	15.4.87	196/86	400h	49.04	47.81- 18
Coppell	Harry	GBR	11.7.96	175/73	PV	5.85	5.71- 19
Cormont	Ethan	FRA	29.9.00	178/62	PV	5.58	5.62i- 19, 5.42- 18
Coscoran	Andrew	IRL	18.6.96	186/72	1500	3:37.98i	3:40.79- 19
Coulon	Adam	USA	5.10.97	180/79	PV	5.65i	5.52i, 5.52- 19
Cowley	Joshua	AUS-J	13.3.01		LJ	7.74, 8.00w	7.83- 19
* Craddock	Omar	USA	26.4.91	178/79	TJ	17.14iA, 17.04	17.68- 19
Crawford	Graham	USA	29.12.92	180/64	1500	3:37.64	3:37.08- 16
					3000	7:46.30i, 7:52.45	7:49.12- 17
Cremona	Orazio	RSA	1.7.89	192/130	SP	20.22	21.51- 19
Crestan	Eliott	BEL	22.2.99	177/64	800	1:46.16	1:46.84- 18
* Crippa	Yemaneberhan	ITA	15.10.96	179/62	1500	3:35.26	3:37.81- 19
1M	3:52.08	-0-			3000	7:38.27	7:43.30- 18 5000 13:02.26 13:07.84+ 19
Crisp	Vincent	USA	17.8.97	175/64	800	1:46.29	1:46.31- 19
* Crittenden	Freddie	USA	3.8.94	183/73	110h	13.30	13.17- 19
* Crouser	Ryan	USA	18.12.92	201/135	SP	22.91	22.90- 19
Culver	Trey	USA	18.7.96	193/75	HJ	2.26i	2.33i, 2.28- 18
Cypres	Jules	FRA	9.8.97	175/63	PV	5.55i, 5.55	5.52- 18
Czykier	Damian	POL	10.8.92	186/73	110h	13.66	13.28- 17
Da'Vall Grice	Charlie	GBR	7.11.93	182/68	1500	3:34.63	3:30.62- 19
* Dacres	Fedrick	JAM	28.2.94	193/121	DT	69.67	70.78- 19
Dagher	Youssef Mohamed	KUW	15.7.93	180/75	400	45.25	44.84- 19
Dahm	Tobias	GER	23.5.87	203/117	SP	20.13i	20.56i, 20.42- 16
Dairokuno	Shuho	JPN	23.12.92	168/51	10000	28:01.29	27:46.55- 15
Dal Molin	Paolo	ITA	31.7.87	182/76	110h	13.61	13.40- 18

380　INDEX

Name		Nat	Born	Ht/Wt	Event	2020 Mark	Pre-2020 Best
Dallavalle	Andrea	ITA	31.10.99	183/73	TJ	16.79	16.95- 19
Dambile	Sinesipho	RSA-J	2.3.02	185/73	200	20.44A	20.32A- 19
Daniel	Keaton	USA-J	8.4.01	183/75	PV	5.51u, 5.50	5.00- 19
Davies	Jonathan	GBR	28.10.94	173/59	3000	7:45.75	7:50.18i- 18, 8:01.38- 16
Day	Tyler	USA	18.12.96	183/64	3000	7:45.70i	8:08.16i-18
					5000	13:16.95i	13:25.06- 19
de Arriba	Álvaro	ESP	2.6.94	180/65	800	1:45.60	1:44.99- 18
de Deus	Eduardo	BRA	8.10.95	187/82	110h	13.66	13.30- 19
* De Grasse	Andre	CAN	10.11.94	180/73	100	9.97	9.90- 19, 9.69w- 17
					200	20.24	19.80- 16, 19.58w- 15
de Oliveira	Paulo André	BRA	20.8.98	183/75	100	10.12	10.02- 18, 9.90w- 19
de Sa	Mateus Daniel	BRA	21.11.95	184/82	TJ	16.62iA	16.87- 17
de Vries	Ruan	RSA	1.2.86	187/88	110h	13.56Aw	13.45A, 13.42Aw- 19, 13.67- 13
Deadmon	Bryce	USA	26.3.97	188/82	400	45.51i	45.18- 19
Dean	Genki	JPN	30.12.91	182/88	JT	84.05	84.28- 17
Debjani	Ismael	BEL	25.9.90	174/60	1500	3:37.89	3:33.70- 17
Decroix Tetu	Enguerrand	FRA	1.1.97	184/95	HT	71.79	70.82- 19
Degirmenci	Unmet	TUR	23.7.98		JT	77.96	77.53- 19
del Real	Diego	MEX	6.3.94	185/103	HT	76.11	77.49- 16
^ Demps	Jeff	USA	8.1.90	175/77	100	10.09	10.01- 08, 9.90w- 17
Deng	Joseph	AUS	7.7.98	173/61	800	1:45.21A	1:44.21- 18
* Denny	Matthew	AUS	2.6.96	195/115	DT	65.47	65.43- 19
Derkach	Pavel	RUS	2.11.93		SP	20.47i, 19.92	19.56- 19
Desalu	Eseosa	ITA	19.2.94	179/69	200	20.35	20.13- 18
Dester	Dario	ITA	22.7.00		Dec	7655	-0-
Diakité	Malik	GER	13.3.00	184/79	Dec	7641	-0-
Diamond	Alec	AUS	9.8.97	190/82	Dec	7665	8229-- 18
* Diaz	Andy	CUB	25.12.95	191/68	TJ	17.30	17.40- 17, 17.41w- 19
* Díaz	Jordan	CUB-J	23.2.01	192/73	TJ	17.07i	17.49- 19
Díaz	Maximiliano	ARG	15.11.88	186/88	TJ	16.52iA, 16.70Aw, 16.44w	16.51, 16.77w- 11
Dickson	Michael	USA	25.1.97	188/75	110h	13.54	13.45- 19
Djouhan	Lolassonn	FRA	18.5.91	188/118	DT	63.04	65.10- 17
Dobber	Joachim	NED	8.7.97	184/79	400	45.64	46.45- 18
Dobrenhkiy	Aleksandr	RUS	11.3.94	195/110	DT	60.90	60.91- 18
Dobrynkin	Yevgeniy	RUS	19.7.97		20kW	1:22:38	-0-
Dobson	Charles	GBR	20.10.99	180/73	100	10.12w	10.40, 10.32w- 18
Dohmann	Carl	GER	18.5.90	182/62	20kW	1:22:41	1:21:26- 16
Dolezal	Riley	USA	16.11.85	188/100	JT	79.39	83.50- 13
Doroshchuk	Oleh	UKR-J	4.7.01	187/65	HJ	2.25i, 2.23	2.19- 19
Douvalídis	Konstadínos	GRE	10.3.87	184/78	110h	13.49, 13.46w	13.33- 15
Driouch	Hamza	QAT	16.11.94	180/67	1500	3:37.15	3:33.69- 12
* Dubler	Cedric	AUS	13.1.95	190/82	Dec	8367	8229-- 18
Dumecha	Lemi	ETH			Mar	2:07:43	2:10:06- 19
^ Dunfee	Evan	CAN	28.9.90	186/68	20kW	1:22:32	1:20:13- 14
* Duplantis	Armand	SWE	10.11.99	183/79	PV	6.18i, 6.15	6.00- 19
Eaddy	Maurice	USA	4.6.95	175/70	100	10.18	10.11- 15
* Echevarría	Juan Miguel	CUB	11.8.98	186/75	LJ	8.41i, 8.25	8.68- 18, 8.92w- 19
* Edris	Muktar	ETH	14.1.94	172/57	HMar	59:04	-0-
Edward	Alonso	PAN	8.12.89	183/73	200	20.45	19.81- 09
* Ehammer	Simon	SUI	7.2.00	183/78	110h	13.48	14.20- 19
	LJ	8.15				7.84- 19	
					Dec	8231	7735- 19
Ejima	Masaki	JPN	6.3.99	190/80	PV	5.52	5.71- 19
El Aaraby	Mohamed	MAR	12.11.89	164/52	HMar	60:17	60:38- 18
El Abbassi	El Hassan	BRN	13.4.84	171/54	Mar	2:06:22	2:04:43- 18
* El Bakkali	Soufiane	MAR	7.1.96	188/70	1500	3:33.45	3:45.36- 15
					3kSt	8:08.04	7:58.15- 18
El Goumri	Othmane	MAR	28.5.92	171/57	HMar	60:30	61:47- 18
El Otmani	Saïd	ITA	14.10.91	175/60	5000	13:24.13	13:19.30- 19
El-Ashry	Alaa El-Din	EGY	6.1.91	183/95	HT	73.40	75.41- 15
* El-Seify	Ashraf Amjad	QAT	20.2.95	183/100	HT	73.33	78.19- 16
Ellis	Branson	USA	19.7.00	185/77	PV	5.80iA	5.61- 19
Elmer	Tom	SUI	1.4.97	184/68	1500	3:37.84	3:41.42- 19
Endo	Hyuga	JPN	5.8.98	170/56	3000	7:47.99#i, 7:49.70	7:54.79- 17
					5000	13:18.99	13:27.81i, 13:38.82- 19
* Enekwechi	Chukwuebuka	NGR	28.1.93	181/107	SP	21.04i	21.80- 19
* Engels	Craig	USA	15.5.94	187/73	1500	3:35.42	3:34.04- 19
Entholzner	Maximilian	GER	18.8.94	182/79	LJ	7.97	7.92- 19
Estrada	Daniel	MEX	30.5.93		3000	7:44.31i	
* Etelätalo	Lassi	FIN	30.4.88	193/90	JT	82.20	84.98- 14
Eto	Takashi	JPN	5.2.91	183/68	HJ	2.27	2.30- 17
* Évora	Nelson	POR	20.4.84	181/70	TJ	16.51i	17.74- 07, 17.82w- 09

INDEX 381

	Name		Nat	Born	Ht/Wt	Event	2020 Mark	Pre-2020 Best
	Ewers	Andre	JAM	7.6.95	173/64	100	10.04	9.98- 18
	Ezzaydouni	Ibrahim	ESP	28.4.91	181/65	3kSt	8:32.10	8:14.49- 19
*	Fabbri	Leonardo	ITA	15.4.97	200/120	SP	21.99	20.99- 19
*	Fajdek	Pawel	POL	4.6.89	186/118	HT	79.81	83.93- 15
	Fall	Mouhamadou	FRA	25.2.92	192/87	100	10.16	10.12- 19
	Falloni	Simone	ITA	26.9.91	187/110	HT	74.13	75.73- 17
	Faloci	Giovanni	ITA	13.10.85	191/115	DT	61.87	65.30- 19
	Fang Yaoqing		CHN	20.4.96	182/70	TJ	17.13	17.17- 19
	Faniel	Eyob Ghebrehiwet	ITA	26.11.92	174/53	HMar	60:44	60:53- 19
						Mar	2:07:19	2:12:16- 17
*	Farah	Mohamed	GBR	23.3.83	171/58	1Hr	21,330m	
						HMar	60:27	59:32- 15, 59:07dh- 19
	Fedaczynski	Rafal	POL	3.12.80	168/61	50kW	3:56:31	3:46:05- 11
	Feletto	Leonardo	ITA	26.6.95		3kSt	8:28.33	8:34.17- 19
	Ferguson	Kord	USA	19.6.95	198/109	DT	63.37	63.25- 19
	Fernández	Jorge	CUB	2.10.87	190/100	DT	63.99	66.50- 14
	Fernández	Yasmani	CUB	7.4.95	180/85	HT	71.58	71.34- 18
	Ferreira	Fernando	BRA	13.12.94	188/57	HJ	2.26i, 2.26	2.30- 17
^	Filippídis	Konstadínos	GRE	26.11.86	188/73	PV	5.70i, 5.60	5.91- 15
	Fillery	Cameron	GBR	2.11.98	187/77	110h	13.55	13.54- 19
	Fink	Willy	USA	7.3.94	183/68	1500	3:37.16	3:40.31- 18
	3000	7:44.21i		7:53.35- 18		5000	13:17.15i	13:31.79- 19
*	Firfirica	Alin Alexandru	ROU	3.11.95	196/108	DT	66.22	67.32- 19
	Fisher	Grant	USA	22.4.97	178/61	1500	3:36.23	3:39.60- 19
	3000	7:39.99i, 7:46.10		7:42.62i- 19		5000	13:11.68	13:29.03- 19
	Flanagan	Ben	CAN	11.1.95	171/57	3000	7:47.37i	7:48.80i- 19
	Flanagan	Benjamin	CAN	11.1.95	171/57	10000	28:06.88	28:19.51- 19
	Fontes	Ignacio	ESP	22.6.98	172/61	1500	3:33.72	3:39.11- 19
	Foppen	Mike	NED	29.11.96	183/62	1500	3:36.01	3:38.95- 19
	2000	4:58.92		-0-		3000	7:39.75	7:52.21- 19
	5000	13:13.06		13:25.89- 19		10000	27:59.10	-0-
	Forte	Julian	JAM	7.1.93	186/73	100	10.03, 9.96w	9.91- 17
						200	20.39	19.97- 16
	Fortunato	Francesco	ITA	13.12.94	178/52	20kW	1:22:42	1:22:01- 17
	Foster	Brenton	AUS	26.2.98	191/75	HJ	2.26i	2.24i- 18, 2.23- 19
*	Frantzeskákis	Hrístos	GRE	26.4.00	186/86	HT	76.78	76.67- 19
	Fraresso	Mauro	ITA	13.1.93	195/92	JT	79.94	81.79- 19
	Freeman	Josh	USA	22.8.94	193/134	SP	20.56	20.91- 17
	Frere	Mehdi	FRA	27.7.96	183/66	10000	28:08.27	29:23.59- 19
	Fritsch	Clayton	USA	29.12.98	184/79	PV	5.55i	5.75- 19
^	Frydrych	Petr	CZE	13.1.88	198/99	JT	81.22	88.32- 17
	Fufa	Abdi	ETH	27.9.95		Mar	2:07:51	2:09:24- 18
	Fujii	Ryuta	JPN	29.7.96	180/65	110h	13.57	13.63- 19
	Fujikawa	Takuya	JPN	17.12.92	163/49	Mar	2:08:45	2:10:35- 19
	Fujimoto	Taku	JPN	11.9.99	166/54	5000	13:27.34	
						HMar	60:06	61:31- 15
	Fujisawa	Isamu	JPN	12.10.87	165/53	20kW	1:20:15	1:17:52- 19
	Fujita	Keitaro	JPN	2.10.97	187/65	HJ	2.28	2.25- 19
	Fukumoto	Masahiro	JPN	8.4.97	170/54	10000	28:07.89	28:58.42- 19
	Funatsu	Shoma	JPN	25.9.97	169/54	10000	28:06.56	28:35.07- 17
	Furtula	Danijel	MNE	31.7.92	195/115	DT	64.86	64.60- 13
	Furusawa	Kazuki	JPN-J	5.7.02	170/60	PV	5.51	5.30- 19
^	Fyodorov	Aleksey	RUS	25.5.91	184/73	TJ	16.83	17.42- 19
	Gado	Ruben	FRA	13.12.93	180/73	Dec	7738	8126(w)- 19
	Gaio	Finley	SUI	15.4.99		Dec	7668	7497- 19
*	Gale	Tom	GBR	18.12.98	197/82	HJ	2.33i	2.30- 17
	Garcia	Mariano	ESP	25.9.97	170/60	800	1:46.31i, 1:47.24	1:45.67- 19
	Gardenkrans	Jakob	SWE	15.8.97	207/110	DT	60.40	63.63- 18
*	Gardiner	Steven	BAH	12.9.95	195/82	200	19.96	19.75- 18
	Garin	Aleksandr	RUS	28.12.99		20kW	1:22:53	1:22:59- 19
	Gasch	Loïc	SUI	13.8.94	192/78	HJ	2.30	2.26- 19
	Gathimba	Samuel	KEN	26.10.87	165/52	20kW	1:22:56A	1:19:04A- 18
*	Gatlin	Justin	USA	10.2.82	185/79	100	10.07, 9.97w	9.74- 15
	Gavillon	Romain	FRA	4.11.98	174/70	PV	5.57i	5.45- 17
*	Gayle	Tajay	JAM	2.8.96	183/75	LJ	8.23, 8.52w	8.69- 19
	Gdula	Lukas	CZE	6.12.91	178/65	50kW	3:57:21.3	3:54:29- 16
	Geay	Gabriel	TAN	10.9.96	180/64	HMar	59:42	60:26- 19
*	Gebrselassie	Leul	ETH	20.9.93	170/55	HMar	59:45	59:18- 17
						Mar	2:05:29	2:04:02- 18
*	Geist	Jordan	USA	21.7.98	184/125	SP	20.91i, 20.91	21.59- 19
	Gemechu	Alemu	ETH	0.95		Mar	2:08:47	2:15:40- 18

INDEX

Name		Nat	Born	Ht/Wt	Event	2020 Mark		Pre-2020 Best
Gemeda	Dadi	ETH		0.82	Mar	2:07:40		2:11:39- 19
* Geremew	Mosinet	ETH	12.2.92	174/57	Mar	2:06:04		2:02:55- 19
Getahon	Tadesse	ISR	20.12.97	168/56	HMar	60:52		62:38- 19
Gezahegn	Kelkile	ETH	1.10.96	169/52	Mar	2:08:36		2:05:56- 18
Gilavert	Louis	FRA	1.1.98	181/62	3kSt	8:21.05		8:29.45- 19
* Giles	Elliot	GBR	26.5.94	173/64	800	1:44.56		1:44.99- 17
* Gill	Jacko	NZL	20.12.94	190/125	SP	21.07		21.47- 19
* Gillespie	Cravon	USA	31.7.96	175/66	100	10.09		9.93- 19
* Girma	Lamecha	ETH	26.11.00	186/65	1500	3:33.77		-0-
2000	4:57.87	-0-		3000	7:34.94i, 7:42.5+	-	3kSt	8:22.57	8:01.36- 19
Githae	Michael	KEN	26.8.94	Mar	168/54	2:08:17		2:09:21- 18
Giupponi	Matteo	ITA	8.10.88	190/70	20kW	1:19:58		1:20:27- 16
Givans	Senoj-Jay	JAM	30.12.93	178/73	100	10.11		9.96- 16, 9.90w- 14
Glebauskas	Adrijus	LTU	20.11.94	201/80	HJ	2.25i, 2.25		2.28- 19
Gletty	Makenson	FRA	2.4.99	186/82	Dec	7978		7747- 19
Godana	Abdela	ETH	11.9.92		Mar	2:08:06		2:08:32- 18
Gogois	Thomas	FRA	24.6.00	193/78	TJ	16.59w		15.88, 16.09w- 19
Golubovic	Dan	AUS	29.11.93	190/82	Dec	7651		7901- 19
Gómez	Jesús	ESP	24.4.91	182/70	1500	3:33.07		3:36.40- 19
Gómez	Joaquin	ARG	14.10.96	178/95	HT	71.32		75.96- 18
Gong Fanglong		CHN	12.7.98		50kW	3:59:01		4:00:48- 19
González	Alberto	ESP	1.6.98	195/110	HT	73.22		75.78- 19
Gorokhov	Georgiy	RUS	20.4.93	183/75	PV	5.60i, 5.55		5.70i- 16, 5.70- 18
Gregorek	Johnny	USA	7.12.91	178/61	1500	3:36.11		3:35.00- 17
Gregson	Ryan	AUS	26.4.90	184/68	1500	3:35.22		3:31.06- 10
1M	3:52.38		3:52.24- 10		5000	13:25.06		13:37.12- 13
Gressier	Jimmy	FRA	4.5.97	175/62	1500	3:36.04		3:37.83- 19
3000	7:48.54i	7:51.45i- 19, 7:53.81- 18		5000	13:15.77	13:23.04- 19	3kSt	8:24.72	-0-
Grey	Rayvon	USA	2.12.97	183/70	LJ	8.09i		8.06i, 7.89, 8.05w- 19
Grijalva	Luis	GUA	10.4.99	173/61	3000	7:43.73i		-0-
					5000	13:16.75		13:37.11- 19
Grimes	Isaac	USA	7.2.98	183/73	LJ	8.00i		7.95Ai- 18, 7.89, 8.08w- 19
Grimsey	William	GBR	14.12.96		HJ	2.24i		2.22- 19
^ Gripich	Aleksandr	RUS	21.9.86	190/80	PV	5.55i, 5.50		5.85i- 15, 5.75- 09
Griva	Janis Svens	LAT	23.4.93	185/90	JT	81.85		79.36- 16
Gudnason	Gudni Valur	ISL	11.10.95	198/115	DT	69.35		65.53- 18
* Gudzius	Andrius	LTU	14.2.91	200/130	DT	68.68		69.59- 18
Guerra	Javier	ESP	10.11.83	173/58	Mar	2:07:27		2:08:36- 18
Gulelauri	Lasha	GEO	26.5.93	174/65	TJ	17.16i	16.87A,16.62i- 16,16.58- 15,16.96dm?- 18
Guttormsen	Sondre	NOR	1.6.99	185/80	PV	5.65		5.80- 19
Habz	Azeddine	FRA	19.7.93	186/68	1500	3:35.87		3:38.11- 19
Hague	Adam	GBR	29.8.97	188/73	PV	5.60i, 5.41		5.65i, 5.65- 18
Hailu	Zewedu	ETH			Mar	2:06:31		
Hájek	Patrik	CZE	11.11.98	179/95	HT	72.02		67.05- 19
* Haile	Tilahun	ETH	13.5.99	171/55	3000	7:38.85i		7:38.55- 18
* Halasz	Bence	HUN	4.8.97	188/93	HT	79.88		79.57- 18
Hale	Jack	AUS	22.5.98	175/66	100	10.12, 10.10w		10.19, 10.12w- 19
Hall	Justin	USA	12.2.98	185/73	LJ	8.05i		8.05- 19
Hamza	Mohamed	EGY	30.8.96	189/115	SP	21.29		20.85- 19
Happio	Wilfried	FRA	22.9.98	185/71	400h	49.11		49.03- 19
* Haratyk	Michal	POL	10.4.92	194/136	SP	21.88		22.32- 19
Harris	Isaiah	USA	18.10.96	182/70	800	1:46.01i		1:44.42- 18
Harris	Micaiah	USA	19.12.98	185/77	200	20.49i		20.09- 19
Harrison [Blake]	Juvaughn	USA	30.4.99	196/75	HJ	2.28i		2.28i, 2.27- 19
					LJ	8.11i		8.20- 19
* Harting	Christoph	GER	10.4.90	207/120	DT	61.28i		68.87- 16
Hartmann	Joshua	GER	9.6.99	180/65	100	10.14		10.16- 19
Hasegawa	Kohei	JPN	1.1.90	184/102	JT	78.12		81.55- 16
Hasegawa	Naoto	JPN	15.11.96	177/66	HJ	2.25		2.25- 19
* Hashioka	Yuki	JPN	23.1.99	183/77	LJ	8.29		8.32- 19
Hassan	Mostafa Amr	EGY	16.12.95	193/118	SP	21.11		21.31- 17
Hassan	Suldan	SWE	1.4.98	179/59	5000	13:18.01		13:31.35- 19
Hassaous	Nassim	ESP	23.3.94	189/65	1500	3:36.95		3:38.43- 19
					3000	7:45.90		7:57.16i-18
Hattori	Yuma	JPN	13.11.93	176/63	10000	27:47.55		28:09.02- 15
Haugh	Daniel	USA	3.5.95	184/105	HT	76.22		76.44-19
Havrylyuk	Myhaylo	UKR	19.1.99	178/98	HT	71.30		72.58- 19
* Hawkins	Callum	GBR	22.6.92	179/62	HMar	60:01		60:00- 17
Hay	Hugo	FRA	28.3.97	182/59	5000	13:27.47		13:38.25- 19
He Yuhong		CHN-J	2.2.01	175/61	100	10.18		10.59- 19
Hechavarría	Andy Eugenio	CUB	14.9.00	192/75	TJ	16.78		16.98- 19

INDEX 383

Name		Nat	Born	Ht/Wt	Event	2020 Mark			Pre-2020 Best
Heil	Jander	EST	20.4.97		SP	19.81			19.10- 19
Hellström	Jesper	SWE	27.7.95		TJ	16.65			16.71- 19
Hendrix	Robin	BEL	14.1.95	176/60	2000	5:00.53			-0-
3000	7:51.29i	7:53.89i- 19, 7:56.74- 18			5000	13:25.52			13:19.50- 19
* Henriksen	Eivind	NOR	14.9.90	191/116	HT	76.40			78.25- 19
Herman	Timothy	BEL	19.10.90	179/75	JT	78.75			80.48- 19
* Hess	Max	GER	13.7.96	186/79	TJ	17.17		17.52i- 17,	17.20- 16, 17.24w-17
Hesselbjerg	Ole	DEN	23.4.90	183/70	3kSt	8:24.87			8:27.86- 17
^ Hill	Ryan	USA	31.1.90	176/60	1500	3:38.16			3:35.59- 16
3000	7:38.03i		7:30.93- 160		5000	13:05.69- 15			
Hlavac	Vit	CZE	26.2.97		50kW	3:56:28.4			4:30:46- 19
^ Hlavan	Ihor	UKR	25.9.90	168/61	20kW	1:22:29			1:19:59- 14
					50kW	3:47:31			3:40:39- 13
* Hoare	Oliver	AUS	29.1.97	188/73	1500	3:34.63			3:37.20- 19
1M	3:53.35	3:54.83i- 19, 3:59.70- 17			5000	13:28.33			14:47.97- 17
Hodbod	Lukas	CZE	2.3.96	181/69	800	1:46.26			1:46.50- 18
Hodebar	Enzo	FRA	17.5.99	186/79	TJ	16.72			16.60- 19
* Hofmann	Andreas	GER	16.12.91	195/108	JT	85.24			92.06- 18
Hogan	Victor	RSA	25.7.89	198/108	DT	60.01			65.33- 13, 67.62dq- 16
* Holloway	Grant	USA	19.11.97	190/86	110h	13.19			12.98- 19
Holttinen	Tommi	FIN	3.5.97	188/68	PV	5.52			5.55i, 5.51- 18
^ Holzdeppe	Raphael	GER	28.9.89	181/78	PV	5.76			5.94- 15
* Hoppel	Bryce	USA	5.9.97	179/68	800	1:43.23			1:44.25- 19
Horodyskyy	Bohdan-Ivan	UKR	18.5.94	178/62	HMar	60:40			64:43- 18
Hougardy	Benjamin	BEL	8.12.95		Dec	7761			7697- 19
Hough	Nick	AUS	20.10.93	191/86	110h	13.67, 13.46w			13.38- 18
Howard	Julian	GER	3.4.89	178/75	LJ	8.06			8.20- 18
Härstedt	Axel	SWE	28.2.87	197/130	DT	61.16			66.03- 16
Hu Yufei		CHN	9.11.93		Dec	7742			7664- 15
* Huang Changzhou		CHN	20.8.94	183/66	LJ	8.33			8.28- 17
Huang Shih-Feng		TPE	2.3.92	178/88	JT	78.73			86.64- 17
Hubert	Axel	FRA	16.2.96	185/91	Dec	8260			7810- 19
^ Hudson-Smith	Matthew	GBR	26.10.94	194/78	400	45.55			44.48- 16
* Hughes	Matt	CAN	3.8.89	180/64	1500	3:37.20			3:41.49- 15
5000	13:13.38i, 13:30.65		13:19.56- 15		3kSt	8:16.25			8:11.64- 13
Hunter	Charles	AUS	20.7.96	180/68	1M	3:55.41i			3:57.74i- 19, 4:06.5- 17
Hunter	Drew	USA	5.9.97	175/61	5000	13:17.55			13:21.18- 19
Hurisa	Derara	ETH	12.7.97	172/57	Mar	2:08:09			-0-
Hurt	Tripp	USA	30.10.92	190/73	1500	3:36.83			3:39.06- 19
Hurtado	David	ECU	21.4.99		20kW	1:22:52			1:22:03- 19
Huryn	Artyom	BLR	17.2.98		LJ	7.96w			7.89- 19
Huszák	Janos	HUN	5.2.92	197/118	DT	63.03			64.89- 16
Ibadin	Edose	NGR	27.2.93	172/64	800	1:44.81			1:45.60- 19
Ichida	Takashi	JPN	16.6.92	164/50	10000	27:52.35			27:53.59- 16
Iizuka	Shota	JPN	25.6.91	186/83	100	10.13			10.08- 17
					200	20.47			20.11- 16
* Ikeda	Koki	JPN	3.5.98	168/53	20kW	1:18:22			1:17:25- 19
Ikeda	Yohei	JPN	22.6.98	164/49	10000	27:58.52			28:47.05- 19
Ikehata	Hikaru	JPN	31.8.94	173/65	TJ	16.75			16.20, 16.31w- 15
İncel	Emin	TUR	1.5.97	186/100	JT	80.00			80.20- 17
* Ingebrigtsen	Filip	NOR	20.4.93	187/75	800	1:46.74			1:47.79- 16
1000	2:16.46	2:16.95- 1	1500	3:30.35		3:30.01- 18	2000	4:56.91	5:12.6+- 19
* Ingebrigtsen	Henrik	NOR	24.2.91	180/69	2000	4:53.72			5:09.5+- 19
					5000	13:19.65			13:15.38- 19
* Ingebrigtsen	Jakob	NOR	19.9.00	181/65	800	1:46.44			1:49.40- 17
1500	3:28.68	3:30.16- 19	2000	4:50.01		5:16.88+- 19	3000	7:27.05	7:51.20i- 19
Inoue	Hiroto	JPN	6.1.93	165/51	10000	27:59.40			27:56.27- 18
Iribarne	Roger Valentin	CUB	2.1.96	183/68	110h	13.55			13.39- 17
* Irwin	Andrew	USA	24.1.93	190/84	PV	5.80i			5.88i, 5.80- 19
Isachenkov	Yaroslav	UKR	2.3.95	179/86	LJ	7.97			7.91- 19
* Isene	Ola Stunes	NOR	29.1.95	194/107	DT	64.62			67.78- 19
Ishida	Higashi Tomasu	JPN	14.4.97	185/79	110h	13.61			13.45- 19
Ishida	Subaru	JPN	4.6.99		20kW	1:22:34			1:23:19- 19
Ishikawa	Shuhei	JPN	29.5.95	183/80	110h	13.39			13.49- 19
Isshiki	Tadashi	JPN	5.6.94	169/54	Mar	2:07:39			2:09:43- 18
Ito	Tatsuhiko	JPN	23.3.98	169/50	10000	27:25.73			28:26.50- 19
Ivanov	Tihomir	BUL	11.7.94	198/77	HJ	2.25i			2.31- 17
* Ivanyuk	Ilya	RUS	9.3.93	183/75	HJ	2.33i, 2.30			2.35- 19
Iwata	Yuji	JPN	9.7.87	170/54	Mar	2:08:45			2:09:30- 19
Izotov	Valeriy	BLR	12.4.97	186/86	JT	78.17			78.20- 18
Izumiya	Shunsuke	JPN	26.1.00	175/65	110h	13.45			13.36, 13.26w- 19

Name		Nat	Born	Ht/Wt	Event	2020 Mark	Pre-2020 Best
Jaakkola	Aleksi	FIN	17.11.97	192/117	HT	74.51	74.00- 19
* Jacobs	Lamont Marcell	ITA	26.9.94	188/79	100	10.10	10.03- 19
* Jager	Evan	USA	8.3.89	186/66	1500	3:36.31	3:32.97- 15
3000	7:38.25i, 7:46.31		7:35.16- 12		5000	13:12.12	13:02.40- 19
Jagers	Reggie	USA	13.8.94	188/118	DT	61.24	68.61- 18
Jainaga	Odel	ESP	14.10.97	193/86	JT	84.10	80.64- 18
Janssen	Henrik	GER	19.5.98	190/110	DT	61.16	58.87- 19
Jasinski	Daniel	GER	5.8.89	207/125	DT	61.68	67.16- 16
Jenkins	Eric	USA	24.11.91	170/61	3000	7:50.97	7:38.19- 18
5000	13:10.07i 13:07.33- 15, 13:05.85i- 17				10000	27:22.06	27:48.02- 16
Jerzy	Mateusz	POL	29.3.95	183/72	PV	5.61i	5.51- 19
Jeuschede	Jan Josef	GER	23.4.93	187/115	SP	19.90	20.06- 19
Jílek	Jaroslav	CZE	22.10.89	183/85	JT	78.99	83.19- 16
Jin Min-sub		KOR	2.9.92	185/77	PV	5.80	5.75- 19
Jocteur-Monrozier	Pierrik	FRA	23.3.98	163/53	1500	3:35.00	3:38.26- 19
Johnson	Cheswill	RSA	30.9.97	175/64	LJ	8.20A	8.12- 18, 8.25Aw- 19
Johnson	McKay	USA	15.4.98	180/105	SP	20.63i	20.47i- 19, 19.80- 18
Johnson	T'Mond	USA	29.7.97	181/136	SP	19.93	19.79- 18
Jones	Jonathan	USA	23.4.91	183/145	SP	20.14i	21.63- 19
Jones	Osian	GBR	23.6.93	185/102	HT	72.59	73.89- 19
Jónsson	Hilmar Örn	ISL	6.5.96	183/107	HT	77.10	75.26- 19
Joo Hyun-myung		KOR	31.5.97	172/64	20kW	1:22:12	1:22:34- 18
Jopek	Mateusz	POL	14.2.96	186/75	LJ	7.95	7.85- 19
Joseph	Jason	SUI	11.10.98	188/75	110h	13.29	13.39, 13.38w- 19
Jovancevic	Strahinja	SRB	28.2.93	187/75	LJ	8.05	8.03i- 19, 7.98- 18
Junghannss	Karl	GER	6.4.96	178/59	50kW	3:49:45	3:47:01- 17
Jusho	Hiroto	JPN	11.1.00		20kW	1:22:37	1:21:55- 19
Juska	Radek	CZE	8.3.93	195/82	LJ	8.10	8.31- 17
Kanai	Taio	JPN	28.9.95	179/65	110h	13.27	13.36- 18
Kandie	Cleophas	KEN	14.8.00	161/48	5000	13:27.37	13:30.80- 19
					10000	27:20.34	27:48.87- 19
Kandie	Felix	KEN	10.4.87	178/62	Mar	2:06:47	2:06:03- 17
* Kandie	Kibiwott	KEN	20.6.96	172/55	HMar	57:32	59:31- 19
* Kangas	Aaron	FIN	3.7.97	184/115	HT	79.05	74.40- 19
Karanja	Charles	KEN	5.8.97	178/60	5000	13:26.96	
					10000	28:03.56	
Karanja	Josephat	KEN	8.11.00		5000	13:26.96	14:04.36- 19
Kariuki	Simon	KEN	13.2.92	174/55	10000	28:00.29	27:53.50- 16
					Mar	2:07:56	2:09:41- 19
* Karlström	Perseus	SWE	2.5.90	184/73	20kW	1:19:34	1:18:07- 19
* Karoki	Bedan	KEN	21.8.90	169/53	10000	27:02.80	26:52.12- 17
					Mar	2:06:15	2:05:53- 19
Kashimura	Ryota	JPN	13.8.91	175/120	HT	71.03	71.36- 19
^ Kasyanov	Oleksiy	UKR	26.8.85	191/87	Dec	7716	8479- 09
Katayama	Kazuma	JPN	14.6.95		Dec	7603	7445- 17
Katir	Mohamed	ESP	17.2.98	180/65	1500	3:36.59	3:37.20- 19
					3000	7:44.13	7:53.81i- 19, 7:56.62- 18
Kawai	Daiji	JPN	22.9.91	176/54	10000	27:34.86	28:08.52- 18
Kawakami	Hideru	JPN	18.3.00	180/71	Dec	7653	7062- 19
Kawaou-Mathey	Justin	FRA	4.12.99	187/67	110h	13.61	13.79w- 19
Kaya	Aras	TUR	4.4.94	171/55	HMar	60:51	62:21- 19
Kbrom Mezngi	Zerei	NOR	12.1.86	183/65	10000	28:04.29	25:56.95- 17
Kebede	Abdi Asefa	ETH	11.9.97		Mar	2:07:58	2:10:23- 19
Keddar	Salim	ALG	23.11.93	176/65	1500	3:37.13	3:35.92- 15
Kehr	Gabriel Enrique	CHI	3.9.96	190/114	HT	76.61	76.42- 19
Keitany	Evans	KEN	27.11.99	184/64	5000	13:23.52	13:12.65- 19
					10000	27:36.08	27:40.69- 18
* Kejelcha	Yomif	ETH	1.8.97	186/58	1500	3:32.69	3:31.25i- 19, 3:32.59- 18
					5000	13:12.84	12:46.79- 18
Kekin	Stepan	RUS	13.11.00		Dec	7625	-0-
Kendagor	Jacob	KEN	24.8.84	158/50	Mar	2:07:16	2:07:33- 17
* Kendricks	Sam	USA	7.9.92	189/79	PV	6.02	6.06- 19
* Kendziera	David	USA	9.9.94	190/84	400h	49.35	48.42- 18
Kerio	Reuben	KEN	2.6.94	170/50	Mar	2:08:46	2:07:00- 19
Kerr	Hamish	NZL	17.8.96	197/80	HJ	2.27	2.30- 19
* Kerr	Josh	GBR	8.10.97	186/73	1500	3:34.53	3:32.52- 19
Keter	Vincent	KEN-J	11.3.02	172/57	1500	3:37.59A	3:36.27- 19
Khelaf	Yani	FRA	7.2.98	172/57	1500	3:37.70	3:41.07- 19
Khodjayev	Sukhrob	UZB	21.5.93	186/105	HT	71.05	78.22- 15
Kholmogorov	Konstantin	RUS	7.2.96	173/61	800	1:46.37	1:45.66- 19
Khorava	Bachana	GEO	15.3.93	172/67	LJ	8.08i	8.25i, 8.02- 16

Name		Nat	Born	Ht/Wt	Event	2020 Mark		Pre-2020 Best
Khudyakov	Aleksey	RUS	31.3.95	191/107	DT	62.86		64.96- 19
Kibet	Vincent	KEN	6.5.91	173/57	1500	3:38.27		3:31.96 -14
**Kibiwot	Abraham	KEN	6.4.96	175/55	3kSt	8:17.60A		8:05.72- 19
Kibrom	Oqbe	ERI	1.1.98		Mar	2:05:53		2:10:00- 19
Kidder	Brannon	USA	18.11.93	183/66	1500	3:36.51i		3:35.27- 19
Kikuchi	Masato	JPN	18.9.90	173/57	HMar	60:43		60:32- 15
					Mar	2:07:31		2:11:53- 19
Kikuchi	Shunya	JPN	26.7.98	167/53	10000	28:08.25		
Kimani	Bernard	KEN	10.9.93	172/54	HMar	60:00		60:05- 15
Kimeli	Benard	KEN	10.9.95	172/55	5000	13:16.61		13:17.65- 18
10000	28:19.38		27:36.60- 14		HMar	59:42		59:07- 19
Kimeli	Isaac	BEL	9.3.94	175/59	1500	3:37.60		3:36.51- 18
					3000	7:47.48		7:57.77- 15
Kimeli	Matthew	KEN	4.1.98	168/53	5000	13:24.54		13:33.7A- 17
Kimeli	Nicholas	KEN	29.9.98	170/55	5000	12:51.78		12:57.90- 19
					10000	26:58.97		29:52.15A-17
Kimura	Shin	JPN	8.2.94	171/53	Mar	2:07:20		2:12:12- 19
Kincaid	Woody	USA	21.9.92	173/55	1500	3:37.39		3:42.42- 19
					3000	7:47.04+		7:47.19i- 18
King	David	GBR	13.6.94	186/77	110h	13.51		13.48- 17, 13.4- 16
King	Devin	USA	12.3.96	185/75	PV	5.60i		5.80- 18
King	Kyree	USA	9.7.94	181/68	100	10.04		10.00, 9.98w- 17
Kingori	Silas	KEN	5.1.98	170/54	10000	27:49.38		
Kinnunen	Jami	FIN	31.3.95	185/90	JT	79.12		78.44- 18
*Kinyamal	Wycliffe	KEN	2.7.97	186/75	800	1:45.52A		1:43.12- 18
Kipchirchir	Shadrack	USA	22.2.89	175/60	5000	13:08.25i		13:18.52- 16
					10000	27:28.97		27:07.55- 17
*Kipchoge	Eliud	KEN	5.11.84	167/52	Mar	2:06:49		2:01:39- 18, 1:59:41irr- 17
Kipchumba	Abel	KEN	3.2.94	166/52	HMar	59:35		59:29- 18
*Kipchumba Torotich Vincent		KEN	3.8.90	178/61	Mar	2:05:42		2:05:09- 19
Kipkemboi	Geoffrey	KEN	.96		3kSt	8:27.58		8:43.8A- 19
Kipkemoi	Vincent	KEN	3.1.99	173/54	10000	28:03.30		27:52.00- 19
Kipkoech	Felix	KEN	1.2.98		HMar	60:40		60:12- 19
Kipkoech	Nicholas	KEN	22.10.92	168/57	800	1:46.38A		1:43.37A-16
Kiplangat	Dan	KEN	4.6.96	172/52	10000	27:59.95		28:23.64- 19
Kiplangat	Davis	KEN	10.7.98	167/52	3000	7:40.25i		7:38.33- 17
Kiplangat	Victor	UGA	19.11.99	170/50	HMar	59:26		60:16dh- 19
*Kiplimo	Jacob	UGA	14.11.00	170/55	2000	4:59.7+		-0-
3000	7:26.64	7:43.73- 17		5000	12:48.63		13:13.64- 17	HMar	57:37	61:53A-19
Kiplimo	Noah	KEN	22.11.00		HMar	60:23		-0-
Kiplimo	Philemon	KEN	10.10.98		HMar	58:11		59:57- 19
Kiprop	Jackson	UGA	20.10.86		Mar	2:08:41		2:09:32- 13
Kiprotich	Felix	KEN	7.12.88		Mar	2:08:48		2:05:33- 19
Kiprugut	Boaz	KEN	18.5.98	173/61	1500	3:36.97		3:36.47- 17
*Kipruto	Amos	KEN	16.9.92	165/50	Mar	2:03:30		2:05:43- 17
Kipruto	Benson	KEN	17.3.91	167/52	HMar	60:06		63:26+-18
					Mar	2:06:42		2:05:13- 19
Kipruto	Collins	KEN	12.4.94	175/59	800	1:45.26		1:44.42- 19
*Kipruto	Rhonex	KEN	12.10.99	172/57	HMar	57:49		-0-
Kipsang	Abel	KEN	12.3.93	176/59	1500	3:35.43A		
Kiptanui	Erick	KEN	19.4.90	173/62	Mar	2:06:17		-0-
Kiptoo	Bravin Kipkogei	KEN-J	26.2.01		HMar	59:37		-0-
Kiptoo	Wesley	KEN		174/62	10000	27:37.29		
Kiptum	Kelvin	KEN	2.12.99		HMar	58:42		59:53dh- 19
Kiptum	Barnabas	KEN	8.12.86	173/64	Mar	2:05:05		2:06:33- 19
Kipyego	Reuben Kiprop	KEN	21.8.96	170/50	Mar	2:04:12		2:04:40- 19
Kiros	Hailemariyam	ETH	5.2.97		HMar	60:01		61:08- 19
*Kirui	Abel	KEN	4.6.82	177/62	Mar	2:05:05		2:05:04- 09
Kiryu	Yoshihide	JPN	15.12.95	175/70	100	10.04A, 10.06		9.98- 17, 9.87w- 15
Kissa	Stephen	UGA	1.12.95	174/61	10000	27:34.48		27:47.66- 19
					HMar	58:56		-0-
*Kitata	Shura	ETH	9.6.96	165/50	HMar	59:47		59:17- 18
					Mar	2:05:41		2:04:49- 18
Klecker	Joe	USA	16.11.96	178/62	1500	3:37.55		3:41.69- 17
3000	7:47.57i	7:54.34i- 19		5000	13:28.98		13:30.39- 18	10000	27:35.57	-0-
Klimuk	Nikolay	BLR	20.12.96		JT	79.70		75.91- 19
Kloptsov	Yuriy	RUS	22.12.89	176/64	3kSt	8:27.60		8:28.03- 14
Knight	Corion	USA	18.8.96	193/84	LJ	7.96i		8.02i, 8.06w- 18, 7.93- 19
Knight	Justyn	CAN	19.7.96	171/59	1500	3:36.13i		3:36.07- 18
					3000	7:46.36i		7:45.86i- 18, 7:46.63+- 19
Knighton	Erriyon	USA-Y	29.1.04	191/77	200	20.33		21.15- 19

Name		Nat	Born	Ht/Wt	Event	2020 Mark	Pre-2020 Best
* Kobayashi	Kai	JPN	28.2.93	165/53	20kW	1:22:28	1:19:12- 15
Kobielski	Norbert	POL	28.1.97	202/80	HJ	2.29i, 2.28	2.27- 19
* Koech	Benard	KEN	25.11.99	159/42	5000	13:11.10	13:13.48- 19
					10000	27:02.39	27:26.11- 19
Koech	Geoffrey	KEN	28.8.93		HMar	59:36	59:50- 17
Koech	Moses	KEN	5.8.97	168/52	HMar	60:00	60:11dh- 19
Koga	Kiyoshi	JPN	30.4.96	168/51	HMar	60:49	63:33- 17
* Koga	Yutaro	JPN	15.7.99	177/58	20kW	1:18:42	1:20:24- 19
* Kokhan	Myhaylo	UKR-J	22.1.01	182/103	HT	77.78	77.39- 19
Kokoshko	Roman	UKR	16.8.96	194/107	SP	19.98	19.70- 19
* Kolasinac	Asmir	SRB	15.10.84	186/137	SP	21.01i	21.58- 15
Kolomoyets	Sergey	BLR	11.8.89	191/110	HT	72.84	78.13- 18
Kominami	Takuto	JPN	26.7.95	172/86	JT	80.55	81.73- 19
Komori	Kakeru	JPN	3.10.91		LJ	7.87, 7.96w	7.98- 19
Konle	Julian	AUS	4.6.97		TJ	16.66	16.20- 19
Kopecky	Ondrej	CZE	16.5.98		Dec	7575w	7627- 19
Köpp	Leo	GER	23.5.98		20kW	1:22:20	1:23:24- 19
Koppelaar	Rutger	NED	1.5.93	187/73	PV	5.75i	5.71- 19
Korir	Victor Kipkirui	KEN-J	21.3.02	180/64	5000	13:21.59	13:41.82- 19
					10000	27:52.89	28:05.14- 19
Korir Kimining	Shadrack	KEN	10.2.96	170/54	HMar	59:27	59:32- 19
Korkmaz	Salih	TUR	14.4.97		20kW	1:19:31	1:20:35- 19
Koroknai	Maté	HUN	13.1.93	191/79	400h	49.71	49.77- 18
Korst	Victor	POR	21.10.96	191/75	HJ	2.25	2.15- 19
Kosgei	Timothy	KEN	1.1.97		HMar	60:47	63:18- 19
Kosimbei	Nicholas	KEN	10.1.96	175/59	10000	27:48.64	27:02.59- 16
Kotkovets	Aleksey	BLR	7.6.98	186/85	JT	86.05	82.63- 19
* Kovacs	Joe	USA	28.6.89	181/132	SP	21.34i, 21.30	22.91- 19
Kovalenko	Kirill	RUS	20.1.94		TJ	16.48, 16.75w	16.50- 19
Kovalenko	Nazar	UKR	9.2.87	177/66	20kW	1:21:12	1:19:55- 19
Kovalyov	Andriy	UKR	11.6.92	198/78	HJ	2.27i	2.28i, 2.25- 15
Kozhevnikov	Sergey	RUS-J	9.5.01		20kW	1:22:02	-0-
Kozlowski	Aleksandr	BLR	6.2.95		JT	79.11	74.62- 19
* Kramer	Andreas	SWE	13.4.97	190/73	800	1:44.47	1:45.03- 18
Krasnov ¶	Maksim	RUS	10.2.96		20kW	1:22:46dq	1:23:45- 19
Kravchuk	Vadym	UKR	28.10.96	188/67	HJ	2.24i	2.23i- 19, 2.21- 17
* Krop	Jacob	KEN-J	4.6.01	169/55	5000	13:11.32	13:03.08- 19
* Krukowski	Marcin	POL	14.6.92	182/92	JT	87.07	88.09- 17
Krzewina	Jakub	POL	10.10.89	186/72	400	45.59	45.11- 14
* Kszczot	Adam	POL	2.9.89	178/64	800	1:45.64	1:43.30- 11
Kuali	Duke	RSA	26.5.98	172/64	200	20.0	21.11- 19
Kubota	Shinobu	JPN	12.12.91	167/53	10000	27:55.07	27:54.25- 14
Kuch	Andrzej	POL	27.10.91	176/70	LJ	7.95	7.76- 16
Kudashkin	Aleksey	RUS	1.2.97		20kW	1:21:02	1:20:46- 19
^ Kudlicka	Jan	CZE	29.4.88	184/76	PV	5.60i, 5.51	5.83- 16
Kujanpää	Urho	FIN	18.5.97	188/80	PV	5.51	5.56i- 19, 5.55- 18
Kunyuga	Michael	KEN	27.7.87		Mar	2:06:43	2:10:05- 19
^ Kupper	Martin	EST	31.5.89	195/108	DT	64.16	66.67- 15
Kurata	Shohei	JPN	5.8.92	173/54	Mar	2:08:44	2:13:16- 17
Kurbanov	Nikita	RUS	13.4.99		HJ	2.24i	2.23- 19
Kurgat	Amos	KEN	7.3.92	160/48	5000	13:21.39	13:27.16- 19
					HMar	60:20	59:37- 19
Kuriki	Anthony Tyrell	JPN	17.9.96	187/75	110h	13.64	13.59- 19, 13.57w- 18
Kurokawa	Kazuki	JPN-J	17.6.01	180/69	400h	49.19	51.06- 19
Kuruma	Koki	JPN	25.3.96	172/64	PV	5.60	5.55- 17
Kuster	David	FRA	25.3.99	169/59	50kW	4:01:24	4:19:44- 19
Kusu	Yasunari	JPN	21.8.93	170/60	3kSt	8:28.01	8:36.03- 19
Kusuro	Geoffrey	UGA	12.2.89	169/55	HMar	59:56	59:43- 15
Kuusela	Toni	FIN	21.1.94	183/82	JT	81.36	83.40- 19
Kwasniewski	Mateusz	POL	16.7.95	186/88	JT	80.15	79.76- 19
* Kwemoi	Ronald	KEN	19.9.95	180/60	5000	13:19.10	13:16.14- 15
* Kynard	Erik	USA	3.2.91	193/86	HJ	2.26iA, 2.21	2.37- 13
Lagat	Dominic	KEN	15.5.98	172/60	5000	13:22.42	13:20.25- 19
Laine	Topias	FIN-J	12.7.01	178/72	JT	78.42	76.98- 19
Laird	Terrance	USA	12.10.98	175/64	200	20.43i	20.41- 18, 19.64Aw- 19
Lambrughi	Mario	ITA	22.2.94	184/75	400h	49.83	48.99- 18
Lamdassem	Ayad	ESP	11.10.81	173/50	Mar	2:06:35	2:09:28- 13
Langat	Dominic	KEN	15.5.98	172/60	10000	27:50.93	27:44.27- 18
Langat	Leonard	KEN	7.8.90	170/55	HMar	60:03	59:18- 16
Langford	Kyle	GBR	2.2.96	183/66	800	1:44.83	1:44.97- 19
Laqouahi	Hicham	MAR	13.6.89		Mar	2:06:32	2:08:35- 19, 2:08:27sc- 18

Name		Nat	Born	Ht/Wt	Event	2020 Mark	Pre-2020 Best
Lara	Frank	USA	25.9.95	160/54	10000	27:44.65	28:47.89- 19
* Lavillenie	Renaud	FRA	18.9.86	177/71	PV	5.94i, 5.82	6.16i- 14, 6.05- 15
* Lavillenie	Valentin	FRA	16.7.91	170/66	PV	5.74i, 5.70	5.82- 19
Laviolette	Jeanice	FRA	25.1.00	186/82	110h	13.52	14.75- 16
Lawrence	Wayne	USA/JAM	21.11.98	192/79	400	45.56#i	45.33- 19
Lay	Joshua	GBR	11.4.00	188/73	1500	3:36.92	3:41.38- 19
Learmonth	Guy	GBR	20.4.92	184/73	800	1:45.57	1:44.73- 18
Lebioda	Piotr	POL	28.5.92	187/85	JT	78.58	78.56- 16
Ledama	Kisaisa	KEN	28.6.98	168/52	10000	27:47.49	27:43.52- 18
Ledama	Wesley	KEN	2.7.99	169/52	5000	13:21.22	13:19.12- 17
* Legese	Birhanu	ETH	11.9.94	168/55	Mar	2:03:16	2:02:48- 19
Lemeteki	Razini	KEN	21.12.98		HMar	60:13	61:23- 19
* Lemma	Sisay	ETH	12.12.90	170/57	Mar	2:04:51	2:03:36- 19
^ Lendore	Deon	TTO	28.10.92	179/75	400	45.65	44.36- 14
Lescay	Lester	CUB-J	15.10.01	182/68	LJ	8.28	8.07- 18
Lesnoy	Aleksandr	RUS	28.7.88	194/116	SP	21.04	21.40- 14
* Lewandowski	Marcin	POL	13.6.87	180/64	800	1:45.77	1:43.72- 15
1500	3:33.99		3:31.46- 19		2000	4:57.09	5:54.96- 02
Lewke	Dennis	GER	23.7.93	193/118	SP	20.03i	19.68- 17
Leyva	Isidro	ESP	25.4.99		PV	5.51	5.35i, 5.30- 19
Li Jialun		CHN	16.4.95		HJ	2.24	2.20- 18
Li Pangshuai		CHN	9.4.92		TJ	16.59	16.46- 19
Li Xiaobin		CHN	10.10.99		20kW	1:22:56	1:20:43- 19
* Lightfoot	K.C.	USA	11.11.99	188/75	PV	5.83i, 5.82	5.76- 19
Liipola	Henri	FIN	24.4.94	188/105	HT	74.92	75.47- 18
Lillefosse	Pål Haugen	NOR-J	4.6.01	179/61	PV	5.70i, 5.61	5.57i, 5.52- 19
Lillemets	Risto	EST	20.11.97	183/78	Dec	8133	7853- 19
Lin Yu-Tang		TPE	11.5.00		LJ	7.98, 8.07w	7.93- 19
Lincoln	Scott	GBR	7.5.93	184/114	SP	20.65	20.39- 19
^ Lingua	Marco	ITA	4.6.78	176/118	HT	72.37	79.97- 08
Lipsanen	Simo	FIN	13.9.95	191/72	TJ	16.59	17.14- 17
* Lisek	Piotr	POL	16.8.92	194/96	PV	5.90	6.02- 19
Liskowitz	Andrew	USA	22.5.97	188/120	SP	21.02i	21.15- 19
* Lita Baehre	Bo Kanda	GER	29.4.99	193/87	PV	5.81	5.72- 19
Litanyuk	Valeriy	UKR	2.4.94	175/75	50kW	3:52:58	3:51:27- 19
Liu Mingxuan		CHN	16.5.97		TJ	16.54	16.64- 17
Llopis	Enrique	ESP	15.10.00	186/77	110h	13.50	13.75- 19
Lobles	Djoão	NED-J	14.1.01	190/77	800	1:45.96	1:48.58-19
* Lomnicky	Marcel	SVK	6.7.87	177/106	HT	76.47	79.16- 14
* Lomong	Lopez	USA	1.1.85	178/67	3000	7:37.74i, 7:46.86+	7:39.81- 14
1500	3:39.98		3:32.20-10		5000	12:58.78	13:00.13- 19
López	Kevin	ESP	12.6.90	172/60	1500	3:35.98	3:34.83- 19
Lorot	Andrew	KEN	2.12.97	168/55	5000	13:25.76	13:26.40- 19
					10000	27:45.08	27:33.21- 19
Losev	Ivan	UKR	26.1.86	177/70	20kW	1:21:10	1:19:33- 14
* Ludwig	Matthew	USA	5.7.96	183/86	PV	5.90A	5.83i- 19, 5.71- 18
Lukyanenko	Artem	RUS	30.1.90	193/84	Dec	7637	8177- 13
Lukyanov	Denis	RUS	14.7.89	190/115	HT	76.12	79.61- 13
Lumb	Kieran	CAN	2.8.98	178/62	3000	7:45.50i	-0-
Luna	Jorge	MEX	8.6.96	175/68	PV	5.62A	5.60- 19
Lyadusov	Konstantin	RUS	2.3.88	190/125	SP	19.94	20.88i, 20.62- 16
Lyakhovich	Aleksandr	BLR	4.7.89	171/65	20kW	1:22:06	1:21:12- 17
Lyles	Josephus	USA	22.7.98	184/73	200	20.24	20.74- 15, 20.44w- 19
					400	45.40	45.71- 19
* Lyles	Noah	USA	18.7.97	180/70	100	10.04, 9.93w	9.88, 9.86w- 18
					200	19.76	19.50-19
Ma Qun		CHN	8.2.94	183/88	JT	81.13	82.46A- 18
Magakwe	Simon	RSA	25.5.85	177/73	100	10.17A	9.98A- 14, 10.06- 19
* Mägi	Rasmus	EST	4.5.92	188/74	400h	48.72	48.40- 16
Mahmoud	Hassan Mohamed	EGY	10.2.84	188/110	HT	73.23	78.39- 16
Mahoney	Travis	USA	25.7.90	175/61	3000	7:41.94i	7:47.66- 17
Maina	Anthony	KEN-Y	27.3.03	172/52	5000	13:22.40	13:28.94- 19
Mak	Léon	NED	5.9.00		Dec	7614	-0-
Mäkelä	Tino	FIN	31.7.99	179/88	JT	80.11	72.52- 19
Makhrosenko	Zakhar	BLR	10.10.91	182/105	HT	74.96	77.41- 16
* Malachowski	Piotr	POL	7.6.83	194/135	DT	64.87	71.84- 13
* Mallett	Aaron	USA	26.9.94	188/79	110h	13.15	13.37, 13.24w- 17
Mammedov	Mergen	TKM	24.12.90	187/108	HT	72.54	74.01- 13
Mande	Abdallah	UGA	10.5.95	166/52	HMar	60:35	60:14- 18
Mansilla	Humberto	CHI	22.5.96	180/100	HT	74.96	76.87- 18
Mantz	Conner	USA	8.12.96	172/54	10000	28:07.70	28:18.18- 19

Name		Nat	Born	Ht/Wt	Event	2020 Mark	Pre-2020 Best
Mapaya	Chengetayi	ZIM	19.12.98	178/64	TJ	16.48i	17.13- 19
Marchuk	Andriy	UKR	12.12.98	175/60	50kW	3:59:41	4:06:38- 19
Marcy	Tristan	FRA	5.1.00	192/75	Dec	7570	-0-
Mardal	Thomas	NOR	16.4.97	185/105	HT	74.28	73.10- 19
Mardare	Adrian	MDA	20.6.95	193/92	JT	84.41	84.43- 18
* Marghiev	Serghei	MDA	6.11.92	194/99	HT	75.70	78.72- 15
Markovic	Martin	CRO	13.1.96	190/110	DT	63.00	63.24- 18
* Marschall	Kurtis	AUS	25.4.97	188/78	PV	5.80	5.87i, 5.81- 19
* Martin	Álvaro	ESP	18.6.94	181/62	50kW	3:57:24	-0-
* Martínez	Lazaro	CUB	3.11.97	192/85	TJ	17.08	17.28- 18
Martínez	Lois Maikel	ESP	3.6.81	183/123	DT	64.66	67.98- 19
Martín	Pedro José	ESP	12.8.92	188/100	HT	71.94	74.63- 19
* Martinot Lagarde	Pascal	FRA	22.9.91	190/80	110h	13.63	12.95- 14
Martos	Sebastian	ESP	20.6.89	178/63	3kSt	8:30.54	8:18.31- 14
* Maruo	Satoshi	JPN	28.11.91	176/62	20kW	1:20:41	1:19:42- 15
Maruyama	Tatsuya	JPN	29.7.94	164/56	10000	27:52.27	28:31.87- 19
Masai	Samuel	KEN-J	20.3.01	178/60	5000	13:23.99	13:29.84- 19
					10000	27:36.37	
Mashele	Precious	RSA	13.10.90		HMar	60:24	60:28- 19
Masilo	Boitumelo	BOT	5.8.95	173/64	400	45.64A	45.69A- 17
* Massó	Maykel	CUB	8.5.99	178/69	LJ	8.26	8.33- 17
Mastianica	Artur	LTU	30.7.92	173/63	20kW	1:22:55	1:26:07- 19
Masuno	Genta	JPN	24.5.93	182/76	110h	13.59	13.40- 17
Maswanganye	Phatutshedzo	RSA-J	1.2.01	186/68	100	10.06A	10.25- 19
Mateo	Daniel	ESP	31.8.89		Mar	2:08:22	2:10:53- 19
Mathenge	Patrick	KEN	2.11.96	169/53	10000	27:56.81	27:44.22- 19
Matsueda	Hiroki	JPN	20.5.93	175/58	5000	13:24.29	13:28.61- 17
Mattis	Sam	USA	19.3.94	185/100	DT	62.46	67.45- 16
* Matusevicius	Edis	LTU	30.6.96	184/79	JT	81.38	89.17- 19
Maxwell	Joseph	CAN	3.4.98	183/107	SP	19.89i	19.50- 19
* Mayer	Kevin	FRA	10.2.92	186/77	110h	13.54	13.55, 13.49w- 19
					Dec	8552	9126- 18
Mayo	Carlos	ESP	18.9.95	179/65	HMar	60:06	-0-
McArthur	Daniel	USA	17.3.98	192/120	SP	20.35i	20.33i- 19, 19.11- 17
McCarter	Steffin	USA	19.1.97	176/73	LJ	8.02i	8.25- 19
McDonald	Morgan	AUS	23.4.96	183/66	1500	3:37.42	3:39.14- 18
McEntyre	Cameron	AUS	10.2.99	184/84	JT	81.51	74.70- 19
McEwen	Shelby	USA	6.4.96	190/77	HJ	2.26iA	2.31i, 2.30- 19
McGorty	Sean	USA	8.3.95	187/77	1500	3:37.12	3:36.61- 18
3000	7:46.48+	7:48.79i- 16, 8:03.92- 18			5000	13:11.22	13:21.35i- 19, 13:21.93- 18
McLeod	Carey	JAM	14.4.98	175/68	LJ	8.19i	7.79- 17
					TJ	16.68i	15.81- 17,16.09w- 16
McMillan	Connor	USA	15.11.95	180/59	10000	27:53.17	28:09.55- 18
* McSweyn	Stewart	AUS	1.6.95	188/68	1500	3:30.51	3:31.81- 19
1M	3:50.61		3:54.60- 18		2000	4:59.47+	-0-
3000	7:28.02		7:34.79- 18		5000	13:09.83	13:05.23- 18
McWhorter	Zach	USA	7.1.99	178/68	PV	5.61i	5.70i- 19
^ Mechaal	Adel	ESP	5.12.90	184/67	3000	7:45.08i	7:35.28- 17
Mecheso	Girma	USA	16.1.88	162/50	10000	27:49.53	27:52.38- 13
Mehrdelan	Shahin	IRI	21.6.95	188/135	SP	20.74i	19.95- 18
Mekonnen Lema	Alemayehu	ETH	12.10.82		Mar	2:07:23	2:14:54- 18
Meleshko	Pavel	BLR	24.11.92	187/90	JT	81.15	85.01- 17
Melly	Edwin	KEN	23.4.94	178/60	800	1:46.3A	1:43.81- 12
Melo	Alexsandro	BRA	29.9.95	179/56	LJ	8.16	8.19- 18
					TJ	17.10iA, 16.48	17.31A, 17.22- 19
Mena	Reynier	CUB	21.11.96	174/79	100	10.26, 10.02w	10.04, 9.99w- 19, 9.9- 17
					200	20.37	20.26, 19.9- 18, 20.05w- 19
* Mengistu	Asefa	ETH	18.1.85	166/52	Mar	2:06:23	2:04:06- 18
Mengistu	Gezahagn	ETH	0.93		Mar	2:08:48	2:25:42- 15
* Menkov	Aleksandr	RUS	7.12.90	178/74	LJ	8.06w	8.56- 19
Mesic	Kemal	BIH	4.8.85	196/110	SP	20.15i, 19.88	20.83- 19
* Mihaljevic	Filip	CRO	31.7.94	201/113	SP	21.84i/21.70	21.84- 19
Mikhan	Edward	BLR	7.6.89	194/85	Dec	7829	8152- 11
Mikkelsen	Emil	DEN	17.4.90	184/97	DT	59.99	59.37- 19
Milanov	Philip	BEL	6.7.91	191/118	DT	63.51	67.26- 16
Mileusnic	Dejan	BIH	16.11.91	183/84	JT	80.37	81.63- 16
Miller	Ashinia	JAM	6.6.93	189/100	SP	20.16	20.93- 18
Miller	Austin	USA	1.6.94	190/82	PV	5.73	5.66- 18
Mills	George	GBR	12.5.99	173/60	1500	3:36.72	3:40.32- 19
Mindaye	Regasa	ETH	20.4.80	165/50	Mar	2:06:24	2:09:38- 19

INDEX 389

Name		Nat	Born	Ht/Wt	Event	2020 Mark	Pre-2020 Best
Mischler	Baptiste	FRA	23.11.97	182/62	800	1:46.37	1:47.17- 16
					1500	3:36.39	3:37.17- 18
Miura	Ryuji	JPN-J	11.2.02	167/55	3kSt	8:19.37	8:39.37- 19
* Mizinov	Vasiliy	RUS	29.12.97	167/55	20kW	1:19:09	1:18:32- 19
Mizukubo	Soshi	JPN	1.3.99	174/69	100	10.14	10.36, 10.19w- 19
Mogeni	Benuel	KEN-J	11.3.01	170/52	5000	13:25.29	13:32.76- 19
Mogi	Keijiro	JPN	21.10.95	169/53	10000	27:57.36	28:06.51- 19
Mohumed	Mohamed	GER	24.3.99	173/57	5000	13:23.71	13:54.35- 19
* Mokoka	Stephen	RSA	31.1.85	156/50	HMar	59:36	59:51- 19
					Mar	2:08:05	2:07:40- 15
* Moloney	Ashley	AUS	13.3.00	187/79	Dec	8492	8103- 19
Montgomery	Kahmari	USA	16.8.97	184/72	400	45.50	44.23- 19
* Montler	Thobias	SWE	15.2.96	187/72	LJ	8.22i, 8.15	8.22, 8.43w- 19
* Morgunov	Timur	RUS	12.10.96	188/77	PV	5.86i	6.00- 18
Morrison	Willie	USA/PHI	23.11.96	184/120	SP	20.21i	20.40- 19
Moura	Thiago Julio	BRA	27.11.95		HJ	2.27	2.22- 19
^ Mrzygłód	Cyprian	POL	2.2.98	184/86	JT	79.45	84.97- 19
Muñoz	Uziel	MEX	8.9.95	179/110	SP	20.33	20.86- 19
Mudrov	Ilya	RUS	17.11.91	190/79	PV	5.55i	5.80- 16
Muema	Jackson Kavesa	KEN-J	3.9.01	172/54	5000	13:22.58	13:46.04A- 19
					10000	28:07.69	30:09.0 -17
Muiru	Muthoni	KEN	27.3.98	167/52	5000	13:26.70	13:32.42- 17
					10000	28:06.21	27:55.44- 19
Mujaridze	Giorgi	GEO	22.3.98	185/127	SP	21.21i	20.27- 19
Mulaudzi	Collen	RSA	8.4.91		HMar	60:51	62:02- 19
Muluwa	Philip	KEN-J	3.3.02	164/44	10000	27:50.43	28:38.32- 19
Mulwa	Boniface	KEN	16.4.00	181/52	10000	28:08.10	28:17.36- 19
* Munyai	Clarence	RSA	20.2.98	176/66	200	20.23A	19.69A- 18, 20.04- 19
Muratake	Rashid	JPN-J	6.2.02	179/60	110h	13.61	-0-
Murayama	Kenta	JPN	23.2.93	176/56	10000	27:50.09	27:39.95- 15
Murayama	Yutaro	JPN	29.9.98		20kW	1:20:49	1:21:30- 19
Murch	Craig	GBR	27.6.93	183/107	HT	73.24	73.64- 19
Musaab	Adam Ali	QAT	17.4.95	167/54	1500	3:35.60	3:36.67- 16
Musiyenko	Ihor	UKR	22.8.93	186/128	SP	20.00i, 19.48	20.14- 18
* Mutiso	Alexander	KEN	10.9.96	171/52	10000	27:30.81	27:36.84- 19
					HMar	57:59	60:11- 18
Mwangi	Joel	KEN	3.6.85		HMar	60:40	61:16- 14
Mwaura	Joel	KEN	20.1.99	168/50	10000	28:03.13	27:45.31- 18
					HMar	60:44	60:59- 17
Mwei	Robert	KEN	11.4.98	168/55	10000	27:51.27	27:57.14- 19
Myers	Charlie	GBR	12.6.97	188/79	PV	5.60i	5.71- 19
N'Ganga	Joseph Karanja	KEN	.89	171/55	HMar	60:13	66:33- 19
Nagato	Sho	JPN	13.1.97	163/49	10000	28:07.34	28:30.59- 17
Nageeye	Abdi	NED	2.3.89	165/54	Mar	2:07:09	2:06:17- 19
Nairn	Laquarn	BAH	31.7.96	178/64	LJ	8.02i	7.87i- 18, 7.83, 7.97w- 17
Nakamura	Akihiko	JPN	23.10.90	180/73	Dec	7739	8180- 16
Nakamura	Shin-ichiro	JPN	14.4.93	174/57	10000	28:06.91	28:37.05- 17
Nakamura	Taisei	JPN	5.10.97	177/55	10000	28:03.81	28:31.65- 19
Nakaya	Yuhi	JPN	11.6.99	169/57	10000	27:54.06	28:50.77- 19
* Nápoles	Cristian	CUB	27.11.98	181/80	TJ	17.18	17.38, 17.43w- 19
Napolitano	Rob	USA	3.11.94	175/60	1500	3:38.03i, 3:38.48	3:37.14i- 19, 3:38.03- 18
Narvi	Teemu	FIN	2.7.00	190/92	JT	77.56	75.90- 18
do Nascimento	Rodrigo	BRA	26.9.94	181/75	100	10.19, 10.13w	10.10- 19
* Ndiku	Jonathan	KEN	18.9.91	173/60	5000	13:10.64	13:11.99- 09
10000	27:01.95		27:11.23- 16		3kSt	8:24.38	8:07.75- 11
Ndikumwenayo	Thierry	BDI	26.3.97	163/50	5000	13:26.85	13:25.55- 19
Ndirangu	Joseph	KEN	9.9.94	168/49	10000	27:41.30	27:33.55- 18
Nebebew	Birhan	ETH	14.8.94	172/55	Mar	2:08:16	2:06:51- 19
* Nedosekov	Maksim	BLR	21.1.98	188/70	HJ	2.33	2.35- 19
^ Nedow	Tim	CAN	16.10.90	198/125	SP	20.90i	21.33i- 16, 21.18- 15
Negewo Degefa	Abebe	ETH	20.5.84		Mar	2:05:15	2:04:51- 19
Nesterenko	Maksim	BLR	1.9.92	193/82	TJ	16.70i	16.85- 16
Ngeno	Benard	KEN	10.8.96	175/55	HMar	59:26	59:07- 19
Nichipor	Aleksey	BLR	10.4.93	193/115	SP	20.52	20.52- 17
Niit	Pridu	EST	27.1.90	198/113	DT	59.88	60.69- 11
Nikitin	Dmytro	UKR	31.7.99	198/82	HJ	2.24i, 2.20	2.28- 17
Nikitin	Vladimir	RUS	5.8.92	168/60	3000	7:39.94i	7:42.82i- 18
5000	13:24.07i		13:22.72- 19		10000	28:16.44	28:16.43- 18
* Nilsen	Chris	USA	13.1.98	196/93	PV	5.93i, 5.70	5.95- 19
Nilsson	Marcus	SWE	3.5.91	185/90	Dec	7574	8120- 18
Ning Xiaohan		CHN	24.1.00	186/68	110h	13.60	14.07- 19

Name		Nat	Born	Ht/Wt	Event	2020 Mark	Pre-2020 Best
Nishiyama	Kazuya	JPN	5.11.98	167/53	10000	28:03.94	28:57.21- 19
Nishiyama	Yusuke	JPN	7.11.94	173/57	10000	27:56.78	28:16.41- 19
* Noda	Tomohiro	JPN	24.1.96	174/58	20kW	1:20:26	1:19:00- 19
Nomoto	Shusei	JPN	25.10.95	185/68	110h	13.45	13.62, 13.59w- 17
* Norman	Michael	USA	3.12.97	185/78	100	9.86	10.27- 16
Norman	Phil	GBR	20.10.89	180/66	3kSt	8:23.60	8:29.37- 19
Norris	Jake	GBR	30.6.99	186/102	HT	71.60	73.24- 19
Noskov	Ivan	RUS	16.7.88	177/62	50kW	3:51:17	3:37:41- 14
Novac	Alexandru	ROU	24.3.97	186/84	JT	79.04	86.37- 18
* Nowicki	Wojciech	POL	22.2.89	197/131	HT	80.28	81.85- 19
Nuguse	Yared	USA	1.6.99	183/63	1M	3:55.62#i	4:05.29i- 18, 4:07.28- 17
					3000	7:46.71#i	
O'Brien	Liam	AUS	13.4.96	186/90	JT	81.65	81.36- 19
O'Farrill	Yordan	CUB	9.2.93	183/72	110h	13.57	13.19, 12.9- 14
O'Hare	Chris	GBR	23.11.90	174/60	1500	3:36.40i	3:32.11- 18
					1M	3:55.61i	3:52.91i- 16, 3:53.34- 17
Oates	Tray	USA	14.3.95	186/79	PV	5.70	5.66- 18
Obasuyi	Michael	BEL	12.8.99	187/73	110h	13.57	13.54- 19
* Obiena	Ernest John	PHI	17.11.95	190/68	PV	5.80	5.81- 19
Obyortyshev	Denis	RUS	16.2.97		TJ	16.83	16.81- 18
Oda	Daiki	JPN	15.1.96	180/71	LJ	7.96, 8.04w	8.04- 17
Oda	Masaya	JPN	11.5.95	175/64	400h	49.79	49.42- 19
Oduduru	Divine	NGR	7.10.96	175/70	100	10.10	9.86- 19
					200	20.22	19.73- 19
Ogundeji	Ayomidotun	NGR	24.2.96	186/111	SP	19.85i	21.05- 19
Ogura	Yusuke	JPN	16.4.93	174/59	10000	28:03.33	28:08.80- 19
HMar	60:00				Mar	2:07:23	2:12:10- 19
			62:03- 15				
Oikawa	Fumitaka	JPN	5.4.95	168/54	20kW	1:22:04	1:19:17- 18
Oike	Tatsuya	JPN	18.5.90	173/55	10000	27:58.40	28:16.37- 19
Oishi	Minato	JPN	19.5.88	162/49	10000	28:04.56	27:48.56- 16
Okamoto	Naoki	JPN	26.5.84	176/57	Mar	2:08:37	2:11:29- 18
Okoro	Efekemo	GBR	21.2.92	187/77	400h	49.68	50.33- 19
* Okoye	Lawrence	GBR	6.10.91	198/137	DT	65.15	68.24- 12
Olivieri	Giorgio	ITA	5.11.00	182/94	HT	72.65	72.03- 19
Omwamba	Enoch	KEN	4.4.93	168/54	10000	28:02.29	27:47.36- 19
Opsal	Toralv	NOR	9.3.98	191/81	Dec	7694	-0-
Ordóñez	Saúl	ESP	10.4.94	178/63	800	1:45.71	1:43.65- 18
1000	2:18.81i		-0-		1500	3:34.98	3:39.40i- 19, 3:40.39- 17
Orlov	Nikolay	RUS	7.1.99	184/86	JT	82.70	77.62- 19
* Ortega	Mauricio	COL	4.8.94	184/102	DT	70.29	66.42- 19
* Ortega	Orlando	ESP	29.7.91	185/75	110h	13.11	12.94- 15
Ortiz	José	GUA	8.3.00		20kW	1:22:16	1:27:18- 19
* Osako	Suguru	JPN	23.5.91	170/52	10000	27:36.93	27:38.31- 13
					Mar	2:05:29	2:05:50- 18
Osman	Abrar	ERI	24.6.89	171/55	HMar	60:06	59:47- 19
Ota	Naoki	JPN	13.10.99	169/52	10000	27:55.59	28:48.69- 19
Otsuka	Shohei	JPN	13.8.94	170/55	Mar	2:07:38	2:10:12- 18
* Otterdahl	Payton	USA	2.4.96	193/125	SP	21.19	21.81i, 21.37- 19
Oukhefen	Abdessamad	ESP	18.12.98	177/62	3000	7:45.24	8:25.30i-17
					5000	13:17.95	13:39.27- 19
Oumaiz	Ouassim	ESP	30.3.99	173/60	3000	7:40.62	8:12.15- 18
					5000	13:13.14	14:56.19- 17
Outalha	Mouhcine	MAR	15.12.98	175/57	HMar	60:26	-0-
Paavola	Mikko	FIN	16.1.98	191/80	PV	5.54i, 5.46	5.36- 19
Pacho	José Rodolfo	ECU	30.1.96	171/68	PV	5.52A	5.52- 19
Pajuelo	Ivan	ESP	27.8.93	171/60	50kW	3:57:22	3:56:47- 19
Palcau	Fabien	FRA	22.6.97	172/55	10000	28:07.01	-0-
Panasenkov	Vladislav	RUS	22.5.96	190/95	JT	80.75	84.60- 19
Panning	Zachery	USA	29.3.95	172/59	10000	28:04.32	28:23.86- 19
Parakhonko	Vitaliy	BLR	18.8.93	190/78	110h	13.53	13.40- 18
Parkinson	Alexander	NZL	8.9.94		DT	60.86	58.32- 19
^ Pars	Krisztian	HUN	18.2.82	188/113	HT	74.89	82.69- 14
Pásztor	Bence	HUN	5.2.95	186/95	HT	71.51	75.74- 15
Pater	Kyle	USA	24.12.94	180/77	PV	5.82iA, 5.61A	5.73- 19
Patterson	Jacory	USA	2.2.00	183/73	400	45.66#i	45.46- 19
Paulson	William	CAN	17.11.94	183/70	1500	3:35.59	3:36.86- 19
Pavlov	Vitaliy	RUS	12.1.97	177/73	TJ	16.52	16.78i, 16.83w- 18, 16.61- 19
Peacock	Hamish	AUS	15.10.90	186/96	JT	80.21	84.39- 16
Percy	Nick	GBR	5.12.94	190/105	DT	63.02	64.47- 19
Pereira	Rafael	BRA	8.4.97	188/79	110h	13.64	13.76A- 18, 13.83- 17
Pereira	Tiago	POR	19.9.93	185/66	TJ	16.94	16.60, 16.75w- 19

Name		Nat	Born	Ht/Wt	Event	2020 Mark	Pre-2020 Best
Perevoznikov	Serhiy	UKR	7.4.95	184/120	HT	72.68	76.93- 19
Perinchief	Jah-Nhal	BER	31.12.97	190/68	TJ	16.64i	16.07A- 16, 16.75i- 19
Perini	Lorenzo	ITA	22.7.94	186/76	110h	13.53	13.46- 19
Peristéris	Aléxandros-Víktor	GRE	16.3.96	191/79	LJ	8.06	7.80- 19
Perlaza	Jhon	COL	26.8.94	180/60	400	45.56	44.86- 18
* Peters	Anderson	GRN	21.10.97	187/87	JT	80.50	87.31- 19
Petersen	Arthur Wiborg	DEN	18.8.99		JT	78.11	69.10- 19
Petersson	Wictor	SWE	1.5.98	197/115	SP	21.15i, 20.94	20.70- 19
Petros	Amanal	GER	17.5.95		Mar	2:07:18	2:10:29- 19
* Pettersson	Simon	SWE	3.1.94	198/105	DT	67.72	66.39- 19
Pezer	Mesud	BIH	27.8.94	198/120	SP	21.06i, 20.37	21.48- 19
Phelut	Alexis	FRA	31.3.98	180/63	3kSt	8:32.12	8:32.48- 19
Philibert-Thiboutot	Charles	CAN	31.12.90	178/62	5000	13:22.44	13:30.79i- 19, 13:33.25- 16
* Pichardo	Pedro Pablo	POR	30.6.93	185/71	TJ	17.28, 17.40w	18.08- 15
Pintado	Brian	ECU	29.7.95	168/57	20kW	1:21:53	1:20:44- 19
Piperi	Adrian	USA	20.1.99	188/130	SP	20.98i	21.11- 19
Pirjahan	Mehdi	IRI	23.9.99		400h	49.33A	49.33- 19
Piskunov	Hlib	UKR	25.11.98	182/96	HT	72.94	75.50- 18
Pittomvils	Niels	BEL	18.7.92	198/88	Dec	7516	8051- 16
Pless	David	USA	19.11.90	197/143	SP	20.04i	21.13- 19
Plokhotnikov	Konstantin	RUS	24.3.97	180/68	3kSt	8:20.56	8:24.14- 19
Pontvianne	Jean Marc	FRA	6.8.94	170/60	TJ	17.03	17.13- 17
* Ponzio	Nick	USA	5.1.95	183/132	SP	21.72	20.73- 19
Poska	Domantas	LTU	10.1.96	199/107	DT	60.66	62.47- 16
Potye	Tobias	GER	16.3.95	198/72	HJ	2.25	2.27- 18
* Pozzi	Andrew	GBR	15.5.92	186/79	110h	13.14	13.14, 13.13w- 17
Pradeep	Jay Shah	IND	11.10.97		TJ	16.53	16.36- 18
Prakel	Sam	USA	29.10.94	176/61	1500	3:36.54	3:35.66i- 19, 3:36.84- 18
Preis	Constantin	GER	16.5.98	181/73	400h	49.49	49.23- 19
Pretorius	Fredriech	RSA	4.8.95	187/84	Dec	7879A	8002A- 17, 7872- 19
Primak	Artyom	RUS	14.1.93	190/77	LJ	7.99	8.22- 17
Prince	Quamel	GUY	20.4.94	173/64	800	1:46.42	1:45.58- 19
* Pronkin	Valeriy	RUS	15.6.94	195/115	HT	76.50	79.32- 17
Proserpio	Giacomo	ITA	22.4.97	182/93	HT	71.06	71.33- 18
* Protsenko	Andriy	UKR	20.5.88	194/80	HJ	2.30	2.40- 14
Prüfer	Clemens	GER	13.8.97	198/113	DT	63.66	63.76- 19
Prüfer	Henning	GER	7.3.96	201/123	DT	62.65	63.52- 19
* Przybylko	Mateusz	GER	9.3.92	195/79	HJ	2.28	2.35- 17
Pullen	Clive	JAM	18.10.94	175/73	TJ	16.84i	17.19i- 17, 16.90- 16
Pulli	Kristian	FIN	2.9.94	189/71	LJ	8.27	8.07A- 17, 8.05, 8.10w- 19
Quijera	Manu	ESP	13.1.98	184/85	JT	79.70	81.31- 19
Quijera	Nicolas	ESP	24.6.96	188/85	JT	79.80	80.21- 18
Quinn	Devin	USA	8.6.96	183/75	100	10.12	10.01- 19
Raba	Daniel	HUN	24.4.98	184/105	HT	73.85	73.61- 19
Raap	Rafael	NED	18.3.99	195/85	Dec	7829	7702- 19
Rademeyer	Kyle	RSA-J	29.1.02	188/79	PV	5.55	5.30- 19
Radko	Anton	UKR	2.6.95	175/60	50kW	3:53:29	3:56:36- 19
Raess	Jonas	SUI	8.3.94	184/68	1500	3:37.46	3:40.52- 19
2000	5:00.47	-0-		3000	7:45.67i	7:59.82- 18	5000 13:20.08 13:37.98- 19
* Raffin	Melvin	FRA	9.8.98	186/66	TJ	17.07i	17.20i, 16.85- 17
Raimoi	Vincent	KEN	16.7.96	173/62	10000	27:39.80	28:03.74- 19
					HMar	59:51	60:10- 19
Raitanen	Topi	FIN	7.2.96	187/70	3kSt	8:16.57	8:21.47- 19
Rakov	Sergey	RUS	13.6.99		50kW	3:48:37	-0-
Ramsden	Matthew	AUS	23.7.97	190/75	1500	3:34.83	3:35.85- 19
1M	3:51.23	3:53.32- 19		2000	4:55.44	-0-	5000 13:16.63 14:01.89- 16
Randazzo	Filippo	ITA	27.4.96	188/70	LJ	8.12	8.07- 19
Rapinier	Yoann	FRA	29.9.89	182/70	TJ	16.52i	17.45- 13
Re	Davide	ITA	16.3.93	183/75	400	45.31	44.77- 19
Reals	William	SUI	4.5.99	180/73	200	20.24	20.85, 20.69w- 19
dos Reis	Douglas	BRA	9.12.95	188/98	DT	60.79	59.90- 17
Renner	Alex	USA	28.12.93	196/125	SP	20.06i	19.99- 19
Reuther	Marc	GER	23.6.96	193/77	800	1:44.93	1:45.22- 17
Riahi	Abdellah	FRA	13.10.9	189/72	3kSt	8:25.77	8:43.86- 19
Richards	Eric	USA	1.8.98	178/68	HJ	2.25i	2.24- 19
Richartz	Nate	USA	2.11.94	186/77	PV	5.65iA, 5.61	5.70- 18
Rivasz-Tóth	Norbert	HUN	6.5.96	182/86	JT	82.22	83.42- 19
^ Rivera	Edgar	MEX	13.2.91	191/80	HJ	2.28i, 2.25	2.30i, 2.29- 16
Rivero	Briander	CUB	23.4.91	189/91	Dec	7718	7858(w), 7836- 18
Roach	Jordan	USA	25.3.93	197/114	DT	60.18	60.47- 19
Robert	Benjamin	FRA	4.11.98	173/63	800	1:44.56	1:46.52- 19

Name		Nat	Born	Ht/Wt	Event	2020 Mark	Pre-2020 Best
Robertson	Andrew	GBR	17.12.90	174/72	100	10.26, 10.03w	10.10- 14, 10.03w- 19
Robertson	Jake	NZL	14.11.89	180/65	HMar	60:12	59:58- 18
Robinson	Brett	AUS	8.5.91	173/57	HMar	59:57	63:25+- 19
* Robinson	Jeron	USA	30.4.91	193/73	HJ	2.25i	2.31- 15
* Robinson	Justin	USA-J	30.3.02	180/73	400	44.91	44.84A, 45.07- 19
Robinson	Paul	IRL	24.5.91	175/64	1500	3:38.26	3:35.22- 13
* Rodgers	Michael	USA	24.4.85	178/73	100	10.12	9.85- 11, 9.80w- 14
Roe	Martin	NOR	1.4.92	187/86	Dec	7990	8228- 18
Rogestedt	Johan	SWE	27.1.93	196/82	1500	3:37.56	3:36.58- 16
Rogowski	Arkadiusz	POL	30.3.93	182/100	HT	71.78	73.10- 15
Rohila	Rahul	IND	5.7.96		20kW	1:21:59	1:24:31- 19
Rojas	Carlos	ESP	10.4.95	189/72	HJ	2.26	2.20- 18
* Romani	Darlan	BRA	9.4.91	188/140	SP	21.52	22.61- 19
Romanov	Andrey	RUS	19.9.94	180/90	HT	75.67	74.96- 19
Romero	Claudio	CHI	10.7.00	197/113	DT	64.24	58.94- 18
Rono	Philemon	KEN	8.2.91		Mar	2:05:37	2:05:00- 19
Ronoh	Henry	KEN	12.12.96		HMar	60:04	60:13- 19
Roper	Darcy	AUS	31.3.98	183/70	LJ	8.20	8.13, 8.32w- 19
Rose	Alex	SAM	7.11.91	188/127	DT	64.35	66.31- 19
Rosique	Henry Daniel	CUB	4.1.97	197/90	TJ	17.05	17.02- 18
Ross	Randolph	USA-J	1.1.01	185/75	400	45.44i	46.80- 19
Rotich	Lucas	KEN	16.4.90	171/57	Mar	2:07:26	2:07:17- 15
Rotich	Maxwell	UGA	5.8.98		HMar	60:20	61:11- 19
^ Roulhac	Brandon	USA	13.12.83	188/73	TJ	16.49iA	17.26, 17.44w- 09
* Rowden	Daniel	GBR	9.9.97	177/61	800	1:44.09	1:44.97- 18
Rozmys	Michal	POL	13.3.95	187/72	800	1:46.31	1:45.32- 18
1000	2:17.30	2:18.09- 18			1500	3:38.94	3:36.37- 17 2000 4:57.98 -0-
Rudnik	Matvey	RUS	8.6.99		HJ	2.24i	2.24i- 19
Ruhrmann	Jan	GER	14.7.97	193/90	Dec	7601	7834- 19
Ruiz	Marcos	ESP	10.3.95	183/69	TJ	16.60	16.81- 19
Rumbenieks	Arnis	LAT	4.4.88	173/63	50kW	3:55:27	3:57:09- 19
Rungaru	James	KEN	14.1.93	178/61	HMar	60:18	59:37- 18
* Rupp	Galen	USA	8.5.86	180/62	HMar	60:22	59:47- 18
Ruto	Philemon Kiplagat	KEN-J	20.9.01	187/68	5000	13:33.92	13:27.53- 19
10000	27:45.87				-0-	3kSt	8:19.60 8:21.30- 17
* Ruuskanen	Antti	FIN	21.2.84	189/86	JT	79.22	88.98- 15
Ryapolov	Anatoliy	RUS	31.1.97	183/65	LJ	8.01i	8.01- 19
Sable	Avinash	IND	13.9.94	171/60	HMar	60:30	63:58- 17
Sadakata	Toshiki	JPN	4.3.92	171/59	Mar	2:07:05	2:15:53- 19
Sagen	Kasper	NOR	19.4.99	194/97	JT	79.90	74.23- 19
Sahli	Hamza	MAR	10.5.93		HMar	60:04	62:45- 19
					Mar	2:08:01	2:10:19- 19
Saidimu	Simon	KEN	12.10.00	170/54	5000	13:26.92	13:25.07- 19
					10000	27:46.01	28:03.53- 19
Sakamoto	Tatsuya	JPN	4.5.96	188/91	JT	78.07	77.33- 18
Sakuda	Naoya	JPN	17.12.94	173/52	Mar	2:08:21	2:11:21- 19
* Samaai	Ruswahl	RSA	25.9.91	178/73	LJ	8.09	8.49A- 17, 8.45- 18
Samuelsson	Fredrik	SWE	16.2.95	187/83	Dec	7854	8172- 17
Sangwan	Sandeep Kumar	IND	1.5.86	183/68	20kW	1:21:34	1:20:44- 16
Santana	José Fernando	BRA	27.3.99		Dec	7753	7944- 19
* dos Santos	Almir	BRA	4.9.93	191/80	TJ	16.65	17.53- 18
* dos Santos	Felipe Barci	BRA	8.10.98	183/65	100	10.11, 10.03w	10.23- 19
dos Santos	Felipe Vinicius	BRA	30.7.94	181/80	Dec	8364	8019- 15
* Saruni	Michael	KEN	18.6.95	180/68	800	1:46.13	1:43.25- 19
Sasínek	Filip	CZE	8.1.96	181/62	800	1:46.24	1:46.42- 16
1500	3:35.02				3:36.32- 16	2000	4:57.60 -0-
Sasma	Ersu	TUR	30.9.99		PV	5.60i, 5.52	5.50- 19
Sato	Yuki	JPN	26.11.86	179/60	10000	27:41.84	27:38.25- 19
Sawe	Matthew	KEN	2.7.88	193/66	HJ	2.27i, 2.20	2.30A- 18, 2.28- 19
Schwandke	Tristan	GER	23.5.92	184/93	HT	73.23	74.03- 19
* Scott	Donald	USA	23.2.92	183/84	TJ	17.24iA	17.43, 17.74w- 19
Scott	Jordan	JAM	29.6.97	185/80	TJ	17.02	17.08, 17.37w- 19
* Scott	Marc	GBR	21.12.93	177/62	1500	3:35.93	3:42.39- 16
3000	7:43.48	7:43.37- 17			5000	13:08.87i, 13:32.92	13:21.97i- 19, 13:22.37- 19
					HMar	60:39	-0-
Scotti	Edoardo	ITA	9.5.00	186/65	400	45.21	45.84- 19
Sears	Earnie	USA	4.12.98	193/77	HJ	2.30i	2.27Ai, 2.27- 19
Seiler	Nathaniel	GER	6.4.96	175/65	50kW	3:57:34	3:54:08- 18
Seme	Abraham	ETH-J	7.11.01	181/64	3000	7:45.87i	
Sène	Alioune	FRA	3.2.96	186/78	PV	5.72i	5.72- 19
Senoduncu	Sahin	TUR	24.4.94		20kW	1:21:47	1:22:50- 19

INDEX 393

Name		Nat	Born	Ht/Wt	Event	2020 Mark	Pre-2020 Best
Seppänen	Tuomas	FIN	16.5.86	180/107	HT	73.05	76.20- 16
Seskin	Demyan	RUS	4.8.97		SP	19.97i	19.55- 18
Sevler	Mikdat	TUR	21.1.98	186/	110h	13.69, 13.55w	13.81- 19
Shankar	Tejaswin	IND	21.12.98	193/80	HJ	2.25i	2.29- 18
Shano	Hiribo	ETH	0.99	167/50	Mar	2:08:41	2:12:39- 18
Sharipov	Sergey	RUS	14.4.92		50kW	3:43:46	3:43:36- 19
Shaw	JeVaughn	JAM	2.1.94	188/116	DT	60.35	55.97- 15
Shayunov	Yuriy	BLR	22.10.87	189/120	HT	71.07	80.72- 09
Shigeno	Seiya	JPN	23.12.96	180/59	3kSt	8:31.88	8:37.63- 19
Shimanovich	Aleksandr	BLR	9.2.98	190/100	HT	75.07	73.00- 19
Shimoda	Yuta	JPN	31.3.96	168/53	Mar	2:07:27	2:11:34- 16
Shinno	Tomohiro	JPN	17.8.96	184/73	HJ	2.31	2.28- 19
* Shiroborokov	Sergey	RUS	16.2.99	168/57	20kW	1:19:34	1:17:25- 18
Shitara	Yuta	JPN	18.12.91	170/48	HMar	60:49	60:17- 17
					Mar	2:07:45	2:06:11- 18
* Shkurenyov	Ilya	RUS	11.1.91	191/82	Dec	8086	8601- 17
* Shubenkov	Sergey	RUS	4.10.90	190/75	110h	13.31	12.92- 18, 12.7- 16
Shumik	Viktor	UKR	21.5.98	180/70	20kW	1:21:35	1:22:24- 18
Siame	Sydney	ZAM	7.10.97	178/70	200	20.49A	20.16- 19
Sidorchenko	Gleb	RUS	15.5.86	197/110	DT	60.87	62.55- 13
^ Sidorov	Maksim	RUS	13.5.86	190/126	SP	20.27	21.51- 12
da Silva	Aldemir Gomes	BRA	8.6.92	191/84	200	20.41	20.15- 17, 20.13Aw- 19
da Silva	Altobeli	BRA	3.12.90	181/60	3kSt	8:32.71	8:23.67- 17
Silva	Derick	BRA	23.4.98	181/68	100	10.24, 10.11w	10.10- 18
* Simbine	Akani	RSA	21.9.93	176/74	100	9.91A, 9.96	9.89 -16
Sinancevic	Armin	SRB	14.8.96	192/130	SP	21.13i	21.51- 19
Singh	Mehakpreet	IND	26.3.95	180/73	LJ	7.96	7.76- 18
Singh	Shivpal	IND	6.7.95	181/90	JT	85.47A	86.23- 19
Singh	Vikash	IND	6.7.96		20kW	1:22:27	1:22:39- 18
Sitonik	Kiprono	KEN-J	10.11.01	167/52	10000	27:42.99	27:53.59- 18
Skagestad	Sven Martin	NOR	13.1.95	201/130	DT	63.35	65.20- 16
Skarvélis	Nikólaos	GRE	2.2.93	185/121	SP	21.05	20.61- 16
Skyers	Roberto	CUB	12.11.91	187/83	100	10.24, 10.07w, 9.9w	9.98- 19, 9.9- 17
Slavov	Mark	BUL	17.3.94	182/95	JT	83.40	74.76- 18
Slowikowski	Przemyslaw	POL	20.11.93	188/77	100	10.19, 10.05w	10.23- 18
Smaïli	Mostafa	MAR	9.1.97	172/61	800	1:46.38i	1:44.90- 18
Smidt	Nick	NED	15.5.97	184/79	400h	49.41	49.28- 19
* Smikle	Traves	JAM	7.5.92	193/126	DT	64.66	67.72- 18
Smith	David	GBR	14.7.91	188/77	HJ	2.24i	2.26i- 15, 2.26- 18
Smith	Henry	AUS	9.4.96	184/75	LJ	7.99	8.06- 19
Smith	Jake	GBR	19.5.98	170/52	HMar	60:31	62:03- 19
Smolonskis	Ruslans	LAT	15.12.96		50kW	3:56:02	-0-
Snyman	Wayne	RSA	8.3.85	177/64	20kW	1:22:16	1:20:46- 16
^ Sobera	Robert	POL	19.1.91	191/85	PV	5.64i, 5.60	5.81i- 15, 5.71- 19, 5.80ex- 14
Sobota	Josh	USA	23.6.00	184/100	SP	20.20i	19.33i, 18.60- 19
Sogawa	Kennosuke	JPN	12.7.94	178/79	JT	81.73	76.64- 17
Soget	Justus	KEN	22.10.99	178/61	3000	7:41.31i	7:39.09i- 18
5000	13:15.83				-0-		
					10000	27:35.57	-0-
Sokirskiy	Aleksey	RUS	16.3.85	185/108	HT	77.31	78.91- 12
Solomon	Steven	AUS	16.5.93	186/73	400	45.37	44.97- 12
Sotero	Yasiel	ESP-J	28.12.01	182/95	DT	60.02	59.23- 19
de Souza	Jordan	BRA	30.7.98		Dec	7545	7394- 19
^ Spank	Raul	GER	13.7.88	190/75	HJ	2.25	2.33- 09
Stój	Bartlomiej	POL	15.5.96	193/115	DT	63.94	64.64- 19
Stachnik	Oskar	POL	1.3.98	191/107	DT	61.46	60.61- 19
* Ståhl	Daniel	SWE	27.8.92	202/160	DT	71.37	71.86- 19
* Stanek	Tomas	CZE	13.6.91	190/127	SP	21.86i, 21.24	22.17i- 18, 22.01- 17
* Starc	Brandon	AUS	24.11.93	188/73	HJ	2.30	2.36- 18
Starkey	Garrett	USA	7.10.93	175/73	PV	5.62i	5.60Ai- 18, 5.50- 17
Stecchi	Claudio Michel	ITA	23.11.91	186/77	PV	5.82	5.80i, 5.75- 19
Steen	Roger	USA	17.5.92	185/118	SP	20.48i	20.36- 19
* Storl	David	GER	27.7.90	199/122	SP	21.20	22.20- 15
Su Wen		CHN	10.2.99		TJ	16.83	16.47- 19
Suárez	Leonel	CUB	1.9.87	181/76	Dec	7990	8654- 09
Sullivan	Darryl	USA	28.12.97	186/79	HJ	2.33i	2.26i- 19, 2.24- 16
Sundström	Simon	SWE	4.2.98	182/66	3kSt	8:25.35	8:41.39- 19
Suwa	Motofumi	JPN	22.10.99		20kW	1:20:49	1:22:08- 19
Suzuki	Hiroki	JPN	27.7.94	176/59	HMar	60:50	60:17- 17
Suzuki	Kengo	JPN	11.6.95	163/47	10000	27:49.16	28:30.16- 16
Suzuki	Yuki	JPN	1.11.95	167/53	10000	28:08.27	28:52.99- 16
* Suzuki	Yusuke	JPN	2.1.88	171/58	20kW	1:18:36	1:16:36- 15

Name		Nat	Born	Ht/Wt	Event	2020 Mark	Pre-2020 Best
Svela	Per	NOR	19.3.92	183/65	5000	13:23.97	13:35.09- 19
Svitlychnyy	Serhiy	UKR	13.7.94	171/58	20kW	1:21:36	1:22:53- 19
^ Svärd Jacobsson	Melker	SWE	8.1.94	188/78	PV	5.53	5.82i, 5.71- 19
Syrotchen	Josh	USA	19.4.94	188/107	DT	61.29	60.76- 18
Sysoyev	Aleksey	RUS	8.3.85	193/105	DT	60.61	59.72- 17
Szikszai	Róbert	HUN	30.9.94	200/118	DT	61.20	64.37- 18
Szücs	Valdó	HUN	29.6.95	190/82	110h	13.58	13.41- 19
Szyszkowski	Jakub	POL	21.8.91	193/145	SP	20.60	20.99- 19
Taam	Rik	NED	17.1.97	190/82	Dec	8031	7853- 18
Tada	Shuhei	JPN	24.6.96	176/66	100	10.18	10.07, 9.94w- 17
* Takahashi	Eiki	JPN	19.11.92	175/56	20kW	1:18:29	1:17:26- 18
Takahashi	Yusuke	JPN	5.7.96	185/74	110h	13.60, 13.54w	13.84- 19
Takaku	Ryu	JPN	18.2.93	169/52	Mar	2:06:45	2:10:03- 19
Takayama	Shun-ya	JPN	3.9.94	182/76	110h	13.34	13.25- 19
* Taki	Kumari	KEN	6.5.99	172/59	1500	3:34.14	3:34.57- 19
* Tamberi	Gianmarco	ITA	1.6.92	189/71	HJ	2.31i, 2.30	2.33- 18
* Tamire	Getaneh	ETH	10.1.94	171/55	Mar	2:08:12	2:03:34- 19
Tamura	Kazuki	JPN	16.7.95	162/52	10000	27:28.92	27:57.14- 19
Tanner	Samuel	NZL	24.8.00	178/64	1500	3:38.04	3:38.74- 19
* Tanui	Paul	KEN	22.12.90	172/54	5000	13:15.72i	12:58.69- 15
					10000	28:06.90A	26:50.60- 17
^ Tarabin	Dmitriy	RUS	29.10.91	176/85	JT	80.23	88.84- 13
Taue	Shun	JPN	30.5.97	181/66	Dec	7619	7546w- 17, 7475- 19
Tavernier	Hugo	FRA	1.12.99	192/108	HT	72.28	68.31- 19
* Taylor	Christian	USA	18.6.90	190/75	TJ	17.57	18.21- 15
Tazawa	Ren	JPN	11.11.00	180/61	10000	27:46.09	28:13.21- 19
Teare	Cooper	USA	18.8.99	183/64	1M	3:55.50i	4:00.16- 17
			3000	7:46.45#i		7:50.66i- 19	
					5000	13:17.13	13:32.73- 19
Tecueanu	Catalin	ROU	9.9.99	178/65	800	1:46.41	1:47.49- 19
Tefera	Samuel	ETH	23.10.99	171/52	1500	3:35.54i	3:31.04i, 3:31.39- 19
					1M	3:55.86i	3:49.45- 19
Teferi	Maru	ISR	17.2.92	164/52	Mar	2:07:20	2:08:09- 19
* Tentóglou	Miltiadis	GRE	18.3.98	187/70	LJ	8.26i	8.38i, 8.32- 19
Terada	Natsuki	JPN	30.8.91	174/54	Mar	2:08:03	2:10:55- 19
Terentyev	Aleksey	RUS	19.7.91		50kW	3:57:18	3:58:13- 19
Teshome	Birhanu	ETH	0.97		Mar	2:08:26	2:08:20- 19
Tharaldsen	Jonathan	USA	18.2.97	190/116	SP	20.50i	19.93- 19
Thiery	Baptiste	FRA-J	29.6.01	191/74	PV	5.51	5.32- 18
Thompson	Josh	USA	9.5.93	174/61	1500	3:34.77i	3:35.01- 19
Thompson	Shown-D	JAM	20.1.97		LJ	8.20	8.13, 8.17w- 19
Thomsen	Kristoffer	DEN	21.2.96	188/118	SP	20.33i	19.49- 19
Thomsen	Marcus	NOR	7.1.98	185/118	SP	21.03	20.59- 19
Tiernan	Patrick	AUS	11.9.94	183/68	10000	27:22.55	27:29.81- 19
Tikhonov	Nikolay	RUS	20.4.97		50kW	3:56:40	-0-
Timshin	Sergey	RUS	25.11.92	183/79	Dec	7609	7984- 15
Tiruneh	Workneh	ETH	30.9.84		Mar	2:06:27	2:08:51- 15
Tison	Quentin	FRA	16.4.96	177/62	1500	3:36.14	3:38.18- 19
Toader	Andrei	ROU	26.5.97	184/105	SP	20.79i, 19.71	20.60- 19
Tobalina	Carlos	ESP	2.8.85	187/127	SP	20.13i, 19.66	20.57- 17
* Tobe	Naoto	JPN	31.3.92	194/72	HJ	2.31i, 2.24	2.35i- 19, 2.32- 18
Tobin	Sean	IRL	20.7.94	173/62	3000	7:45.46	7:56.27i, 7:59.64- 19
* Tola	Tamirat	ETH	11.8.91	181/59	Mar	2:06:41	2:04:06- 18
Tomashevich	Oleg	BLR	31.5.00	192/115	SP	19.80	19.73i, 19.38- 19
Tontodonati	Federico	ITA	30.10.89	169/55	20kW	1:22:11	1:21:20- 19
* Torrijos	Pablo	ESP	12.5.92	187/78	TJ	17.18i, 17.09	17.04i- 15, 16.98, 17.23w- 18
Tortell	Marc	GER	26.12.97	183/64	1500	3:38.04	3:44.60- 17
Tortu	Filippo	ITA	15.6.98	187/75	100	10.07	9.99- 18, 9.97w- 19
* Tóth	Matej	SVK	10.2.83	185/72	50kW	3:41:15	3:34:38- 15
Toyoda	Masaki	JPN	17.1.98	180/72	400h	49.63A, 49.82	49.05- 19
Trio	Antonino	ITA	4.6.93	182/75	LJ	7.96	7.90- 19
Tsedat	Ayana	ETH	18.2.96	165/50	Mar	2:06:18	2:06:36- 19
Tsernjavski	Taavi	EST	4.3.95	196/86	Dec	8086	7873- 18
Tshite	Tshepo	RSA	15.1.97	165/55	800	1:46.23A	1:44.69A- 19
Tsuha	Hibiki	JPN	21.1.98	168/65	LJ	7.99	8.23, 8.26w- 19
Tsutsumi	Yuji	JPN	22.12.89	184/112	DT	62.59	61.64- 19
^ Tsyplakov	Daniyil	RUS	29.7.92	190/75	HJ	2.24i	2.34i, 2.33- 14
* Tuka	Amel	BIH	9.1.91	187/77	800	1:44.51	1:42.51- 15
Tura	Seifu	ETH	19.6.97	175/60	Mar	2:06:26	2:04:44- 19
Tuwei	Cornelius	KEN	24.5.93	179/64	800	1:45.68A	1:43.82- 18
Uekado	Daisuke	JPN	11.12.93	175/59	Mar	2:06:54	2:09:27- 17
^ Ujah	Chijindu	GBR	5.3.94	180/75	100	10.17	9.96- 14, 9.95w- 19

INDEX 395

Name		Nat	Born	Ht/Wt	Event	2020 Mark	Pre-2020 Best
Updike	Isaac	USA	21.3.92	180/64	3000	7:47.93i	7:56.63i- 19
Uradnik	Miroslav	SVK	24.3.96		20kW	1:22:30	1:23:46- 19
Urano	Yuhei	JPN	1.11.97	167/52	10000	28:05.37	28:25.45- 19
* Urbanek	Robert	POL	29.4.87	200/120	DT	65.99	66.93- 12
Ushiro	Keisuke	JPN	24.7.86	196/94	Dec	7684	8308- 14
* Vadlejch	Jakub	CZE	10.10.90	192/93	JT	84.31	89.73- 17
* Vaillant	Ludvy	FRA	15.3.95	180/64	400	45.46	45.25- 18
					400h	48.69	48.30- 19
Van De Velde	Tim	BEL	1.2.00	182/64	1500	3:38.15	3:41.10- 19
Van Der Plaetsen	Thomas	BEL	24.12.90	188/82	Dec	8027(w)	8332- 16
van Diepen	Tony	NED	17.4.96	183/68	800	1:44.82	1:46.90- 19
van Gool	Joris	NED	4.4.98	180/70	100	10.17	10.16- 19
* van Niekerk	Wayde	RSA	15.7.92	183/73	100	10.10A	9.94- 17
	200	20.31A		19.84- 17		400	45.58	43.03- 16
van Rensburg	Phil-Mar	RSA	23.6.89	188/92	JT	79.15A	80.49A- 17
van Rooyen	Jason	RSA	4.2.97	187/120	SP	20.70	19.66- 19
van Rooyen	Rocco	RSA	23.12.92	188/93	JT	85.50, 87.62u	85.39- 15
Varga	Balázs	HUN	30.1.98	188/116	HT	71.44	72.87- 19
Vasilchenko	Yuriy	BLR	4.1.94	194/115	HT	75.45	73.75- 19
* Vázquez	Wesley	PUR	27.3.94	184/73	800	1:45.18	1:43.83- 19
Vena	Nick	USA	16.4.93	194/120	SP	19.91	20.68i- 18, 20.60- 19
^ Vesely	Vitezslav	CZE	27.2.83	186/94	JT	83.03	88.34- 12
Vestlund	Oscar	SWE	27.4.93	189/110	HT	71.21	73.34- 17
Veszelka	Tomás	SVK	9.7.95	183/79	TJ	16.69	17.09- 19
* Vetter	Johannes	GER	26.3.93	188/105	JT	97.76	94.44- 17
Vindics	Balázs	HUN	28.3.94	178/64	800	1:46.18	1:46.63- 19
Visser	Werner	RSA	27.2.98		DT	60.97A	59.40- 19
* Vloon	Menno	NED	11.5.94	177/77	PV	5.76	5.85- 17
Vojta	Andreas	AUT	9.6.89	184/68	5000	13:24.03	13:38.03- 17
Volz	Drew	USA	20.11.92	181/75	PV	5.65i	5.62i- 16, 5.60- 18
Vonavka	Tomás	CZE	4.6.90	197/109	DT	60.28	63.53- 19
Vukicevic	Vladimir	NOR	6.5.91	193/83	110h	13.53, 13.48w	13.54- 16
Waithaka	Stanley	KEN	9.4.00	175/57	10000	27:48.27	27:13.01- 18
* Wale	Getnet	ETH	16.7.00	178/60	2000	4:58.26	-0-
	3000	7:32.80i		7:59.0+- 18		3kSt	8:35.85	8:05.21- 19
Walelegn	Amdework	ETH	11.3.99	167/52	HMar	58:53	59:22- 18
* Walsh	Cole	USA	14.6.95	190/80	PV	5.65, 5.80i dq	5.83- 19
* Walsh	Tom	NZL	1.3.92	186/123	SP	21.70	22.90- 19
Walton	Jamal	CAY	25.11.98	190/77	400	45.62i	44.99- 17
Wambua	Titus	KEN	14.8.97	166/52	5000	13:17.40	13:33.77- 19
					10000	27:39.50	28:12.16- 19
* Wanders	Julien	SUI	18.3.96	175/60	HMar	59:55	59:13- 19
* Wang Jianan		CHN	27.8.96	178/61	LJ	8.36	8.47A, 8.24- 18
* Wang Kaihua		CHN	16.2.94	180/65	20kW	1:19:46	1:17:54- 17
Wang Qi		CHN-J	10.2.01		HT	72.91	67.62- 18
Wang Rui		CHN	6.1.96	180/65	50kW	3:55:48	3:42:08- 19
Wang Shizhu		CHN	20.2.89	184/100	HT	71.89	76.12- 17
Wanjiku	Charles Kamau	KEN	16.5.00	178/60	5000	13:25.65	
					10000	27:30.09	-0-
Ward	Ja'Mari	USA	21.3.98	175/68	LJ	7.97i	8.13- 17
* Warholm	Karsten	NOR	28.2.96	187/78	400	45.05	44.87- 17
					400h	46.87	46.92- 19
Warren	John	USA	2.3.96	178/73	TJ	16.62iA	16.81i, 16.78- 19
Washington	Turner	USA	10.2.99	193/118	SP	20.43i	20.81- 19
* Wasihun	Mule	ETH	20.10.93	166/52	HMar	59:47	59:34- 19
					Mar	2:06:08	2:03:16- 19
Wasome	O'Brien	JAM	24.1.97	177/64	LJ	8.00i	7.82i- 18, 7.71-15
					TJ	16.56i	16.82i- 18, 16.40, 16.71w- 19
Waters	Carson	USA	5.6.96	188/79	PV	5.65iA	5.63- 19
Watson	Reese	USA	8.10.93	188/85	PV	5.75i	5.60- 15
Wegner	Dawid	POL	23.4.00	190/84	JT	78.90	71.80- 19
Weir	Zane	RSA/ITA	7.9.95	185/107	SP	20.70	19.09- 19
* Weisshaidinger	Lukas	AUT	20.2.92	196/136	DT	68.63	68.98- 18
West	James	GBR	30.1.96	172/59	1500	3:34.07	3:35.74- 19
	1M	3:57.43#i		3:56.79- 19		3000	7:43.79	7:51.18i- 19, 7:58.47- 16
Whiteaker	James	GBR	8.10.98	179/80	JT	77.81	77.03- 17
Wicki	Silvan	SUI	13.2.95	184/77	100	10.11	10.17- 18
					200	20.45	20.60- 18, 20.40w- 19
* Wierig	Martin	GER	10.6.87	202/127	DT	62.07i	68.33- 12
* Wightman	Jake	GBR	11.7.94	178/65	800	1:44.18	1:44.61- 19
	1000	2:17:51i		2:16.27- 18		1500	3:29.47	3:31.87- 19

Name		Nat	Born	Ht/Wt	Event	2020 Mark	Pre-2020 Best
Wilkinson	Callum	GBR	14.3.97	179/63	20kW	1:21:21	1:21:34- 19
Williams	Kendal	USA	23.9.95	180/73	100	10.14	9.99- 18, 9.98w- 15
Williams	Romario	JAM	17.11.95	178/73	200	20.46	20.47- 19
* Wilson	Jamal	BAH	1.9.88	188/68	HJ	2.33i, 2.30	2.31i, 2.30- 16
Wilson	Jonah	USA	2.2.99	186/114	SP	20.08i	19.69- 19
* Winkler	Rudy	USA	6.12.94	186/102	HT	80.70, 80.72dh	77.06- 19
* Wojciechowski	Pawel	POL	6.6.89	190/81	PV	5.70i, 5.62	5.93- 17
Wolde	Dawit	ETH	19.5.91	169/54	HMar	59:58	60:46- 12
Wolff	Jannis	GER	98	180/74	Dec	7670	7527- 19
Woo Sang-hyuk		KOR	23.4.96	187/66	HJ	2.30	2.30- 17
* Wooten	Jacob	USA	22.4.97	183/73	PV	5.90A	5.73i, 5.71- 19
Worknerh	Fikre	ETH	11.5.88		Mar	2:08:02	2:12:10- 17
Worku	Bazu	ETH	15.9.90	171/53	Mar	2:06:47	2:05:25- 10
Wright	Alex	IRL	19.12.90	173/64	50kW	3:56:17	3:48:31- 16
Wright	Chad	JAM	25.3.91	188/110	DT	66.54	65.47- 19
Wrobel	David	GER	13.2.91	195/125	DT	64.24	65.98- 18
Wrotynski	Marcin	POL	11.3.96	180/90	HT	71.65	69.85- 19
* Wu Ruiting		CHN	29.11.95	190/73	TJ	16.99i, 16.90	17.47- 19
Wyatt	Audie	USA	30.4.96	190/84	PV	5.82A	5.70- 17
* Xie Wenjun		CHN	11.7.90	188/77	110h	13.24, 13.20w	13.17- 19
* Xie Zhenye		CHN	17.8.93	185/80	100	10.13w	9.97- 18, 9.91w- 17
Yadav	Rohit	IND-J	6.6.01		JT	77.61A	78.98- 19
Yakovenko	Dmytro	UKR	17.9.92	191/72	HJ	2.26	2.30- 15
Yakushev	Maksim	RUS	15.3.92	173/61	3kSt	8:23.02	8:19.19- 17
Yamaguchi	Kosei	JPN	19.8.91	173/60	3kSt	8:24.19	8:30.98- 18
Yamamoto	Seito	JPN	11.3.92	181/70	PV	5.60	5.77Ai- 16, 5.75- 13
Yamamoto	Tatsuhiro	JPN	23.4.97	177/72	400h	49.12	49.69- 18
* Yamanishi	Toshikazu	JPN	15.2.96	164/54	20kW	1:17:36	1:17:15- 19
Yamauchi	Hiromu	JPN	24.8.99	178/71	400h	49.89	50.67- 19
Yang Chun-Han		TPE	1.1.97	176/65	100	10.11	10.11- 18
Yao Jie		CHN	21.9.90	188/85	PV	5.64i, 5.50	5.71- 19
* Yator	Richard Kimunyan	KEN	6.4.98	175/57	5000	13:18.76	12:59.44- 18
					10000	27:01.42	27:14.70- 18
Yee	Alexander	GBR	18.2.98	172/55	3000	7:45.81	8:00.1- 19
Yego	Evans	KEN	5.9.95	171/56	10000	27:53.95	28:00.56- 18
Yegon	Vincent	KEN	5.12.00	178/64	5000	13:20.39	13:28.17- 19
					10000	27:38.48	27:47.76- 19
* Yemataw	Birhanu	BRN	27.2.96	167/54	3000	7:34.58i	7:34.26- 18
Yerssie	Beshah	ETH	1.10.98	166/50	Mar	2:06:34	2:08:37- 19
Yevseyev	Igor	RUS	27.3.96		HT	71.26	72.29- 19
Yevstifeyev	Roma	RUS	19.9.92		20kW	1:21:38	1:20:21- 18
Yihunle	Balew	ETH	21.9.98	164/50	Mar	2:07:26	2:07:22- 19
* Yimer	Jemal	ETH	11.9.96	163/48	HMar	59:25	58:33- 18
Yin Jiaxing		CHN	16.3.94		20kW	1:22:54	1:20:41- 19
Yokochi	Hiromasa	JPN	1.10.00		110h	13.60	13.94- 19
Yorks	Izaic	USA	17.4.94	174/64	1500	3:37.81i	3:36.52- 19
Yoroizaka	Tetsuya	JPN	20.3.90	167/52	10000	27:36.29	27:29.74- 15
Yoshida	Hiromichi	JPN	8.8.99		LJ	7.86, 8.05w	7.88- 19
Yoshida	Kyohei	JPN	12.10.97	175/64	400h	49.40	50.16- 19
Yoshida	Yuya	JPN	23.4.97	164/48	Mar	2:07:05	-
Yoshii	Yamato	JPN-J	14.2.02	168/48	5000	13:25.87	14:08.12- 19
Young	Jordan	CAN	21.6.93	190/113	DT	61.05	62.76- 17
Yousif	Rabah	GBR	11.12.86	183/75	400	45.65	44.54- 15
Yurchenko	Aleksandr	RUS	30.7.92	182/73	TJ	16.64	17.15- 19
Zabuzhenko	Eduard	UKR	18.4.98	175/56	20kW	1:20:46	1:22:16- 19
* Zakalnytskyy	Maryan	UKR	19.8.94	175/56	20kW	1:21:56	1:30:44- 14
Zalewski	Karol	POL	7.8.93	189/86	400	45.47	45.11- 18
* Zango	Fabrice	BUR	25.6.93	180/75	TJ	17.77i/17.43	17.66- 19
* Zayas	Luis Enrique	CUB	7.6.97	194/79	HJ	2.33i, 2.20	2.30- 19
Zegeye	Feleke	ETH	0.88		Mar	2:07:32	
Zeng Jianhang		CHN	17.9.98	183/75	110h	13.47, 13.32w	13.45- 19
Zernikel	Oleg	GER	16.4.95	184/72	PV	5.60	5.51- 15
^ Zhang Guowei		CHN	4.6.91	200/77	HJ	2.28i	2.38- 15
Zhang Honglin		CHN	12.1.94	188/82	110h	13.66	13.53- 15
Zhang Jun		CHN	20.7.98		20kW	1:22:52	1:20:17- 19
Zhang Yaoguang		CHN	21.6.93	176/68	LJ	8.23	8.29A- 18, 8.25- 19
Zhaxi Yangben		CHN	15.4.96		50kW	3:52:19	3:49:43- 19
Zhelyabin	Dmitry	RUS	20.5.90	187/75	PV	5.61i	5.80i- 18, 5.65- 12
Zhu Yaming		CHN	4.5.94	187/74	TJ	16.91i, 16.86	17.40- 19
Zhuk	Vitaliy	BLR	10.9.96	187/86	Dec	8202	8290- 18
Zimmermann	Christian	GER	9.7.94	204/120	SP	20.09	19.91- 19
					DT	60.67	61.16- 19

Name		Nat	Born	Ht/Wt	Event	2020 Mark	Pre-2020 Best
Zoghlami	Ala	ITA	19.6.94	180/57	3kSt	8:26.22	8:26.18- 17
Zoghlami	Osama	ITA	19.6.94	182/58	3kSt	8:27.45	8:20.88- 19
Zótos	Kiriákos	GRE	17.1.96	187/100	SP	20.00	20.20i- 19, 19.47- 17

WOMEN'S INDEX 2020

Name		Nat	Born	Ht/Wt	Event	2020 Mark	Pre-2020 Best
Abayechew	Tigist	ETH	22.2.94	153/40	Mar	2:22:45	2:24:15- 19
Abramchuk	Alena	BLR	14.2.88	182/95	SP	17.72i, 17.48	19.24- 13
Acquah	Deborah	GHA	23.5.96	174/59	LJ	6.58i	6.63- 19
					TJ	13.77i	13.34- 18
* Adams	Valerie	NZL	6.10.84	193/123	SP	18.81	21.24- 11
Adanhouegbe	Pascaline	BEN	19.10.95		JT	56.75	54.88- 16
* Aga	Ruti	ETH	16.1.94	159/45	HMar	68:25	66:39- 18
					Mar	2:20:05	2:18:34- 18
Aguesy Thomas	Cassandre	FRA	1.9.97	175/64	Hep	5779	5837- 18
Aguilar	Evelis	COL	3.1.93	170/62	Hep	6254	6285- 18
Ahbe-Holahan	Kelsie	CAN	6.7.91	170/63	PV	4.41Ai	4.56i- 19, 4.55- 16
Ahlberg	Grete	SWE	29.5.98	176/79	HT	67.57	67.17- 18
Aigouy	Jona	FRA	19.4.99	175/70	JT	56.09	53.60- 19
* Aiyabei	Valary	KEN	8.6.91	156/42	HMar	69:06+	66:14- 19
Åkerström	Frida	SWE	29.11.90	172/88	SP	17.36	17.11- 18
Akins	Nia	USA	7.7.98	159/52	800	2:00.71i, 2:02.07	2:01.67- 19
Aksenova	Natalya	RUS	6.6.97	185/64	HJ	1.88i	1.92- 16
Aksyonova	Kseniya	RUS	14.1.88	177/60	400	51.71	49.92- 10
Alaïs	Alexie	FRA	9.10.94	168/68	JT	60.00	63.46- 19
Albisser	Celine	SUI	5.5.96		Hep	5806	5546(w)- 19
Aleksandrova	Dina	RUS	9.8.92	160/50	1500	4:08.24i	4:10.83- 16
Alembekova	Elmira	RUS	30.6.90		20kW	1:30:14	1:24:47- 15
* Alemu	Habitam	ETH	9.7.97	171/52	800	2:00.11	1:56.71- 18
					1500	4:08.23	4:01.41- 18
Alemu	Hawi	ETH	24.1.98		Mar	2:27:56	
Alexander	Sarea	USA	15.2.96	178/64	LJ	6.57Ai, 6.49i	6.60- 19
Alfred	Julien	LCA-J	10.6.01	170/52	200	22.99i	22.90- 19
Allen	Sabina	JAM	27.12.94		TJ	13.70	13.61i, 13.24- 18
* Allman	Valarie	USA	23.2.95	183/70	DT	70.15	67.15- 19
* Almanza	Rose Mary	CUB	13.7.92	166/53	800	1:58.92	1:57.70- 15
Alver	Tähti	EST	4.12.94	180/64	LJ	6.54	6.36i- 18
Anagnostopoúlou	Hrisoúla	GRE	27.8.91	176/79	DT	59.96	61.53- 17
Anais	Cynthia	FRA	18.1.88	158/48	800	2:00.76i, 2:01.77	2:00.60- 18
* Anderson	Brittany	JAM-J	31.1.01	165/60	100h	12.82, 12.71w	12.71- 19
Anderson	Doneisha	BAH	21.9.00	187/70	400	52.06i	52.15- 19
Anderson	Shae	USA	7.4.99	170/55	400	52.07Ai	51.99- 17
Andersson	Tracey	SWE	5.12.84	167/87	HT	67.91	70.99- 16
Andia	María Luz	PER	9.11.00		20kW	1:32:47	1:30:50- 19
Ando	Yuka	JPN	16.3.94	160/45	10000	31:37.71	31:58.71- 16
HMar 70:26			69:38- 19		Mar	2:22:41	2:21:36- 17
* Andrejczyk	Maria	POL	9.3.96	172/71	JT	65.70	67.11- 19
Andrejsková	Petra	CZE	25.6.92	176/64	JT	57.48	59.55- 19
Andres	Rachel	CAN	21.4.87		DT	58.53A	58.44- 19
Andryukhina	Nadezhda	RUS-J	3.7.01	173/57	HJ	1.88i	1.86- 19
^ Angelsen	Tonje	NOR	17.1.90	179/62	HJ	1.90i	1.97- 12
Angúlo	Yuliana	ECU	6.7.94	171/64	LJ	6.52i	6.60A- 19. 6.38- 15
Anmut	Atalel	ETH	.99		HMar	69:49	70:50- 19
Antoine	Sandisha	LCA	5.11.91	178/61	TJ	13.62	13.91- 18
Aoki	Masumi	JPN	16.4.94	167/62	100h	13.02, 12.87w	13.15, 13.11w- 19
Apostolovski	Lija	SLO-J	23.6.00		HJ	1.92	1.86- 19
Aquilla	Adelaide	USA	3.3.99	176/89	SP	17.82i	16.59- 19
Aranda	Natalie	PAN	22.2.95	175/85	LJ	6.57Ai	6.60A- 18. 6.55- 19
Arcanjo	Geisa	BRA	19.9.91	180/92	SP	17.61	19.02- 12
Aristarkhova	Natalya	RUS	31.10.89	163/46	3kSt	9:27.35	9:30.64- 13
Armino	Medina	ETH	22.10.97	160/46	Mar	2:26:12	2:27:25- 19
* Arrafi	Rababe	MAR	12.1.91	177/64	1500	4:02.46i	3:58.84- 19
Asefa	Sutume	ETH	11.12.94	153/42	HMar	69:17+	67:54- 18
					Mar	2:20:30	2:23:31- 19
* Assefa	Meskerem	ETH	3.10.91	155/43	HMar	69:55+	67:42- 17
					Mar	2:23:31	2:20:36- 19
Atatou	Wuided	FRA	15.7.99	170/58	100	11.26w	11.77, 11.66w- 19
Avancini	Lvia	BRA	8.5.92		SP	16.94	17.12- 17
Avdeyeva	Anna	RUS	6.4.85	171/100	SP	17.50	20.07- 09
Awoke	Asnakech	ETH	1.11.95	158/44	HMar	67:04	70:21- 19
Awuah	Kristal	GBR	7.8.99	166/55	100	11.27	11.16- 18

398 INDEX

Name		Nat	Born	Ht/Wt	Event	2020 Mark	Pre-2020 Best
^ Ayalew	Hiwot	ETH	6.3.90	173/51	Mar	2:26:54	2:26:40- 19
Ayele	Webalem	ETH	.89		Mar	2:27:39	2:34:11- 17
Ayris	Imogen	NZL	12.12.00		PV	4.50	4.20- 18
* Azimeraw	Degitu	ETH	24.1.99	165/48	HMar	67:02	66:07- 19
					Mar	2:19:56	2:19:26- 19
Bachmann	Lea	SUI	25.6.96		PV	4.35	4.35- 18
Bai Tiantian		CHN	14.8.98		20kW	1:33:20	1:35:59- 18
Baire	Cynthia	KEN-J	2.12.02	163/46	3000	8:53.04	8:49.72- 19
					5000	15:07.13	15:15.35- 18
Ballar	Yiselena	CUB-Y	12.1.03	183/72	JT	57.46	56.52- 19
^ Balta	Ksenija	EST	1.11.86	168/53	LJ	6.53	6.87i- 09, 6.87- 10
Bandeira	Eliana	POR	1.7.96		SP	17.39i, 17.36	16.95- 19
Barrie	Maggie	SLE	29.5.96	164/54	400	52.05#i	51.36- 18
Barsosio	Stella	KEN	12.3.93		HMar	69:54+	69:31- 17
Bates	Emma	USA	8.7.92	166/54	HMar	69:44	70:48- 19
					Mar	2:25:40	2:25:27- 19
Batista	Ketiley	BRA	13.7.99	168/57	100h	13.11	13.26- 19
Batt-Doyle	Isobel	AUS	14.9.95	160/50	10000	32:13.04	32:20.84- 19
Battle	Anavia	USA	28.3.99	171/57	200	22.66i	22.54- 19
Baumann	Jackie	GER	24.8.95	172/57	400h	55.53	55.72- 17
^ Baumgart-Witan	Iga	POL	11.4.89	178/55	400	52.04	51.02- 19
Baxter	Rachel	USA	5.4.99	163/52	PV	4.53Ai	4.50- 19
Bayartsogt	Munkhzaya	MGL	10.10.93	165/42	Mar	2:28:03	2:29:18- 19
Bayisa	Aysede	ETH	16.4.87	160/42	10000	32:15.69	
Bayoulgn	Selamawit	ISR	24.3.94	162/46	3000	8:48.85i	9:09.41- 19
Beahan	Brianna	AUS	1.11.91	168/57	100h	13.20, 13.09w	13.02- 18, 12.96w- 17
* Beard	Jessica	USA	8.1.89	168/57	400	51.71	50.08- 18
Bebe	Kathrine	DEN	27.1.91	182/	DT	60.43	56.21- 19
Becerek	Özlem	TUR-J	22.4.02		DT	58.09	57.50- 19
Beji	Bekelu	ETH	21.8/99		Mar	2:27:50	2:28:21- 19
* Bekere	Ashete	ETH	17.4.88	169/52	HMar	66:37	70:20- 19
					Mar	2:22:51	2:20:14- 19
* Bekh-Romanchuk	Maryna	UKR	18.7.95	172/63	LJ	6.96i, 6.91	6.93- 16
Bekmez	Meryem	TUR	31.7.00		20kW	1:29:24	1:29:36- 19
Belanger	Molli	USA			HT	65.32	
Belete	Meseret	ETH	16.9.99	173/55	Mar	2:24:54	2:26:56- 19
* Belete	Mimi	BRN	9.6.88	169/55	HMar	69:50	68:16- 19
					Mar	2:22:40	2:21:22- 19
Bell	Alexandra	GBR	4.11.92	166/55	800	2:00.28	1:59.82- 19
Bellò	Elena	ITA	18.1.97	164/52	800	2:01.34	2:02.28- 18
Beneke	Lyinque	RSA	30.3.91	165/54	LJ	6.50A	6.81- 13
* Bengtsson	Angelica	SWE	8.7.93	163/51	PV	4.74i, 4.73	4.81i, 4.80- 19
Beriso	Amane	ETH	13.10.91	165/52	Mar	2:24:51	2:20:48- 16
* Berry	Gwen	USA	29.6.89	178/88	HT	70.15	77.78- 18
Bing	Portia	NZL	17.4.93	179/65	400h	56.55	55.86, 55.49dq- 19
^ Bishop-Nriagu	Melissa	CAN	5.8.88	173/57	800	2:00.98i	1:57.01- 17
Bissett	Catriona	AUS	1.3.94	168/57	800	2:01.54	1:58.78- 19
Bizzell	Kaylee	USA	.98	171/60	PV	4.50Ai	4.26- 19
Blundell	Jenny	AUS	9.5.94	164/49	1500	4:05.35	4:04.62- 16
					5000	15:22.14	15:54.30- 19
Bobocea	Claudia	ROU	11.6.92	176/53	800	2:01.37	2:01.49- 16
	1500	4:01.31		4:02.27- 19	3000	8:51.06i	8:47.59i- 19, 8:55.34- 18
Boden	Lauren	AUS	3.8.88	179/86	400h	55.89	54.87- 19
Boekelman	Melissa	NED	11.5.89	177/66	SP	17.55i, 17.53	18.66- 17
Boffey	Isabelle	GBR	13.4.00	169/56	800	2:01.88	2:02.92- 19
* Bogliolo	Luminosa	ITA	3.7.95	170/60	100h	12.79	12.78- 19
Böhm	Djamila	GER	15.7.94	175/58	400h	56.64	56.54- 18
* Bol	Femke	NED	23.2.00	178/57	400	51.13	52.98- 19
					400h	53.79	55.32- 19
Bondarenko	Yelizaveta	RUS	1.7.99	170/57	PV	4.55i	4.51- 19
Bonilla	Magaly	ECU	8.2.92	152/54	20kW	1:31:34A	1:31:53- 19
Bontu	Gada	ETH		164/50	Mar	2:23:39	2:33:38- 19
^ Borel	Cleopatra	TTO	10.3.79	170/88	SP	17.47	19.48i- 04, 19.42- 11
* Borges	Fernanda Raquel	BRA	26.7.88	175/85	DT	62.37	64.66- 19
Borisevich	Darya	BLR	6.4.90	170/52	1500	4:06.77i	4:03.58- 19
Borodulina	Anastasiya	RUS	7.11.98		HT	67.17	65.05- 19
Borovic	Paola	CRO	26.6.95	175/61	TJ	13.61	13.55- 19
Borovska	Nadoya	UKR	25.2.81	163/50	20kW	1:29:57	1:29:22- 18
Borutta	Samantha	GER	7.8.00		HT	69.00	63.78- 19
Bouchard	Maité	CAN	24.8.95	174/60	800	2:00.93i, 2:01.92	2:01.25- 19
Bradley	Nicole	NZL	23.4.92	176/87	HT	67.11	66.07- 18

Name		Nat	Born	Ht/Wt	Event	2020 Mark	Pre-2020 Best
* Bradshaw	Holly	GBR	2.11.91	175/68	PV	4.73	4.87i- 12, 4.81- 17
Brix Pedersen	Lisa	DEN	16.8.96		DT	58.03	57.11- 19
Brooks	Taliyah	USA	8.2.95	176/60	100h	12.86	12.94, 12.82w- 18
					LJ	6.57	6.78- 18
Brown	Ce'Aira	USA	4.11.93	168/55	800	2:00.31	1:58.01- 18
Bruce	Lauren	NZL	23.3.97		HT	73.47	63.12- 19
Bruce	Stephanie	USA	14.1.84	165/49	5000	15:19.21	15:17.76- 19
					10000	31:24.47	31:59.88- 17
* Brume	Ese	NGR	20.1.96	167/58	LJ	6.82i, 6.71	7.05- 19
Bryan	Lucy	GBR	22.5.95	162/48	PV	4.51i	4.50- 19
Büchel (Rütz)	Selina	SUI	26.7.91	168/55	800	1:58.37	1:57.95- 15
					1000	2:35.58	
* Burka	Gelete	ETH	23.1.86	165/45	HMar	69:05	66:11- 18
Burkard	Elena	GER	10.2.92	167/52	1500	4:06.85	4:06.51- 18
3000	8:44.92		8:45.43- 182		3kSt	9:35.67	9:29.76- 18
* Burks	Quanesha	USA	15.3.95	160/55	LJ	6.76Ai, 6.73i	6.93A, 6.84, 6.91w- 15
Burnett	Alysha	AUS	4.1.97	182/68	HJ	1.87	1.91- 19
Bushkova	Aleksandra	RUS	13.1.97		50kW	4:25:32	4:22:36- 18
Butkevich	Karyna	BLR-J	5.10.01		JT	56.98	50.46- 19
Butterworth	Lindsey	CAN	27.9.92	175/60	800	2:01.01	2:00.31- 19
					1000	2:37.26	
Butts-Townsend	Tynita	USA	10.6.90	179/60	HJ	1.89i	1.93- 19
Cá	Liliana	POR	5.11.86	184/93	DT	61.91	61.02- 18
Caballero	Daylis	USA	6.3.88	166/59	PV	4.50i, 4.45A	4.60- 19
* Caballero	Denia	CUB	13.1.90	175/80	DT	63.71	70.65- 15
* Cabecinha	Ana	POR	29.4.84	168/52	20kW	1:30:18	1:27:46- 08
^ Cachová	Katerina	CZE	26.2.90	173/63	Hep	5978(w)	6400- 18
* Camacho-Quinn	Jasmine	PUR	21.8.96	180/73	100	11.22	11.61- 16
					200	22.45	22.69- 18
Cameron	Lloydricia	JAM	8.4.96	186/111	SP	17.57i	17.66- 18
Campbell	Paige	AUS	27.6.96	164/47	3kSt	9:44.00	9:44.80- 19
* Can	Yasemin	TUR	11.12.96	166/49	5000	14:40.70	14:36.82- 17
3000	8:57.64		8:36.24- 18		HMar	66:20	68:29- 19
Capponcelli	Serena	ITA	24.1.89	184/72	HJ	1.88i	1.90i- 18, 1.87- 08
Carli	Sarah	AUS	5.9.94	165/50	400h	55.09	55.43- 19
^ Carter	Michelle	USA	12.10.85	175/107	SP	17.63i	20.63- 16
Carvalho	Tabata	BRA	23.4.96	171/56	400	52.15	52.59- 16
Castells	Berta	ESP	24.1.84	174/79	HT	67.33	70.52- 16
Cernjul	Marusa	SLO	30.6.92	177/56	HJ	1.90i, 1.89	1.93- 16
Cervenková	Markéta	CZE	20.8.91	185/85	SP	18.32	17.70- 19
Cestonaro	Ottavia	ITA	12.1.95	176/68	TJ	13.62	14.18- 19
Chadwick	Payton	USA	29.11.95	174/73	100h	12.78	12.70- 19
Chanbangu	Zinzi	RSA	28.9.96	185/63	TJ	14.03A	13.65- 18
Changwony	Purity	KEN	.90	160/48	Mar	2:24:30	2:27:52- 16
Chapman	Rebecca	GBR	27.9.92	163/60	LJ	6.51	6.54- 17
Chebet	Beatrice	KEN	5.3.00	160/45	3000	8:50.40	8:48.8+- 19
* Chebet	Winny	KEN	20.12.90	165/50	1500	4:02.58	3:58.20- 19
Chekwel	Juliet	UGA	25.5.90	165/52	HMar	68:44	69:45- 18
					Mar	2:23:13	-0-
* Chelangat	Sarah	UGA-J	5.6.01	158/42	10000	31:06.46	-0-
Chelangat	Sheila	KEN	11.4.98	158/52	3000	8:54.83+	8:55.19- 18
5000	14:40.51		14:54.66- 17		10000	31:52.45+	
Chelimo	Edith	KEN	16.7.86	165/50	HMar	67:16	65:52- 17
Chelimo	Joan	KEN	10.11.90	168/50	HMar	66:16	65:04- 18
					Mar	2:20:57	2:26:24- 19
* Chemutai	Fancy	KEN	20.3.95	163/52	HMar	68:02	64:52- 18
					Mar	2:24:27	-0-
Chemutai	Joyline	KEN	31.12.94	165/50	HMar	69:44	71:20- 19
Chen Yang		CHN	10.7.91	180/97	DT	65.26	67.03- 18
Chepkemoi	Joan	KEN	24.11.93	163/48	5000	15:04.32	16:01.7A- 19
Chepkemoi Tele	Joyce	KEN	3.5.95		5000	15:19.79A	15:38.43A- 19
* Chepkirui	Sheila	KEN	27.12.90	172/52	HMar	65:39	71:51- 19
* Chepkoech	Beatrice	KEN	6.7.91	171/57	1500	4:02.09i	4:02.21i, 4:03.09- 18
2000	5:39.8+		5:44.0+- 197		3000	8:22.92	8:28.66- 17
5000	14:55.01		14:39.33- 17		3kSt	9:10.07	8:44.32- 18
Chepkurui	Mercy	KEN	16.9.00	163/45	3kSt	9:45.70	9:23.59- 19
Chepkurui	Vivian	KEN	.98	159/47	HMar	69:09	72:34- 19
Chepngetich	Roseline	KEN	17.6.97	166/55	3000	8:47.74i	-
					3kSt	9:46.14	9:08.23- 19
* Chepngetich	Ruth	KEN	8.8.94	161/44	HMar	65:06	65:29- 19
					Mar	2:22:05	2:17:08- 19

400   INDEX

Name		Nat	Born	Ht/Wt	Event	2020 Mark	Pre-2020 Best
Cheptai	Irene	KEN	4.2.92	160/45	HMar	66:43	67:39- 19
Chepyego	Selly	KEN	3.10.85	160/42	HMar	69:16+	67:52- 14
					Mar	2:21:42	2:21:06- 19
Cherono	Eva	KEN	15.8.96	163/48	HMar	67:18	-0-
Cherono	Fancy	KEN-J	2.8.01	165/45	3kSt	9:51.02A	9:23.92- 18
Cherono	Mercy	KEN	7.5.91	168/54	1500	4:06.79A	4:01.26- 15
Chevrier	Margot	FRA	21.12.99	162/52	PV	4.50	4.20- 19
* Chicherova	Anna	RUS	22.7.82	180/57	HJ	1.96i, 1.90	2.07- 11
Chiliquinga	Valeria	ECU	27.2.91	163/66	HT	65.53	67.32- 19
* Chirchir	Evaline	KEN	10.5.98	166/48	10000	31:08.09	32:06.74A- 19
					HMar	66:01	66:22- 19
Choi Kyung-sun		KOR	16.3.92	167/49	HMar	68:35	70:58- 19
Chorny	Lauren	USA	22.6.93		PV	4.35Ai	4.45i, 4.38- 19
Chuaimaroeng	Parinya	THA	16.12.97	165/50	TJ	13.63	14.17- 18
Chumachenko	Yuliya	UKR	2.10.94	185/65	HJ	1.92i, 1.86	1.94- 18
^ Cichocka	Angelika	POL	15.3.88	170/56	800	2:01.06	1:58.41- 17
Clark	Megan	USA	10.6.94	167/55	PV	4.60Ai, 4.50	4.63- 16
Clark	Tamara	USA	9.1.99	167/55	200	22.69i	22.53- 18
Clarke	Rosie	GBR	17.11.91	161/50	3000	8:49.49i	8:47.30i- 18. 8:51.02- 17
					3kSt	9:32.95	9:31.68- 19
Clay	Elizabeth	AUS	9.5.95	164/57	100h	12.94	13.36, 13.34w- 17
Cléirigh Büttner	Síofra	IRL	21.7.95	159/50	800	2:03.16i	2:01.67- 19
* Coburn	Emma	USA	19.10.90	173/55	800	2:01.10	2:09.81- 10
1500	4:03.82	4:04.40- 19		1M	4:23.65	4:29.86i- 13, 4:31.08- 18	2M	9:32.81i
Constantine	Kyra	CAN	1.8.98	167/53	400	52.14i	51.22- 19
Conte	Claudia	ESP	14.11.99	170/69	HJ	1.87	1.81i, 1.79- 19
					Hep	5891	5818- 18
Cook	Sophie	GBR	12.9.94	170/60	PV	4.50i, 4.40	4.40i, 4.36- 19
^ Costa	Keila	BRA	6.2.83	170/62	TJ	13.92	14.58- 13, 15.10w- 07
Costa	Susana	POR	22.9.84	178/65	TJ	14.10	14.43i- 19, 14.35- 17
Couckuyt	Paulien	BEL	19.5.97	173/59	400h	56.14	55.46- 19
* Courtney-Bryant	Melissa	GBR	30.8.93	170/54	1500	4:01.81	4:03.44- 18
3000	8:49.78i, 8:56.11		8:39.20- 18		5000	15:16.50	14:53.82- 19
* Craft	Shanice	GER	15.5.93	185/69	DT	64.03i	65.88- 14
Cranny	Elise	USA	8.5.96	161/48	1500	4:07.94	4:05.83- 19
3000	8:47.89+	8:58.88i- 15, 9:00.70- 19			5000	14:48.02	15:24.32i- 18, 15:25.66- 19
* Crew	Brittany	CAN	6.3.94	176/111	SP	18.88	19.28- 19
Cunliffe	Chloe	USA	10.5.00		PV	4.35i	4.50i, 4.47- 19
Cunliffe	Hannah	USA	9.1.96	169/55	100	11.14	10.99- 16
* Cunningham	Vashti	USA	18.1.98	185/66	HJ	1.97Ai	2.00- 19
Czaková	Mária	SVK	2.10.88	165/60	20kW	1:33:48	1:31:03- 18
D'Amato	Keira	USA	21.10.84	164/50	HMar	68:57	73:32- 19
10,000	32:33.44				Mar	2:22:56	2:34:55- 19
* Dadic	Ivona	AUT	29.12.93	179/65	Hep	6419	6552- 19
Danismaz	Tugba	TUR	1.9.99	173/61	TJ	13.81, 13.83w	13.85- 19
Dattke	Miriam	GER	24.6.98	163/50	HMar	69:42	71:56- 19
Dauber	Stefanie	GER	31.7.87	168/61	PV	4.46i, 4.40	4.46- 19
David	Yanis	FRA	12.12.97	169/58	LJ	6.63i, 6.48, 6.53w	6.84- 19
Davies	Thelma	USA	8.5.00	161/50	200	22.80i	22.95w- 19
Davis	Amy	USA	15.2.97	156/44	10000	32:13.54	33:12.26- 19
Davis	Kevona	JAM-J	20.12.01	170/60	200	22.86	22.72- 19
Davis	Stephanie	USA	7.2.99	167/52	400	52.15i	52.24- 18
Davis	Tamari	USA-Y	15.2.03	167/52	100	11.15	11.13- 18
Dawson	Khayla	USA	18.3.98		SP	17.56i	17.67- 19
de Azúa	Malen Ruiz	ESP	17.11.95	170/55	PV	4.40i, 4.35	4.38i- 19, 4.35- 18
de Lima	Jucilene	BRA	14.9.90	174/63	JT	60.89	62.89- 14
* de Morais	Andressa	BRA	21.12.90	178/100	DT	60.84	65.34, 65.98dq- 19
* de Sena	Érica	BRA	3.5.85	168/55	20kW	1:29:14	1:26:59- 17
de Witte	Lisanne	NED	10.9.92	175/65	400	51.90i	50.77- 18
Deba	Buzunesh	ETH	8.9.87	162/45	Mar	2:26:59	2:23:19- 19
Debebe	Zinash	ETH	12.10.96		Mar	2:27:41	2:27:15- 18
Debele	Birke	ETH	12.9.95	158/45	Mar	2:25:08	2:23:19- 19
* DeBues-Stafford	Gabriela	CAN	13.9.95	165/53	800	2:00.96i	2:02.48- 19
1500	4:00.80+i		3:56.12- 19		1M	4:19.73i	4:17.87- 19
Degefa	Beyenu	ETH	12.7.99		3000	8:44.10i	8:56.1A- 17
* Degefa	Worknesh	ETH	28.10.90	159/42	Mar	2:19:38	2:17:41- 19
* Del Ponte	Ajla	SUI	15.7.96	168/56	100	11.08	11.21- 18, 11.20w- 19
					200	23.02, 22.83w	23.07- 18
Demir	Evin	TUR-J	16.2.01		20kW	1:33:26	-0-
Demireva	Mirela	BUL	28.9.89	180/58	HJ	1.90	2.00- 19
* Demise	Shure	ETH	21.1.96	168/54	Mar	2:27:42	2:20:59- 15

INDEX   401

Name		Nat	Born	Ht/Wt	Event	2020 Mark	Pre-2020 Best
* Dereje	Roza	ETH	9.5.97	168/52	HMar	68:38	66:01- 19
Dereli	Emel	TUR	25.2.96	181/110	SP	18.02	18.57- 16
Detra	Brenna	USA	13.8.95		800	2:02.06i	2:03.95- 19
Di Lazzaro	Elisa Maria	ITA	5.6.98	177/59	100h	13.05, 12.89w	13.21- 18
Diago	Sahily	CUB	26.8.95	168/49	800	2:01.11	1:57.74- 14
Diame	Fátima	ESP	22.9.96	170/52	LJ	6.56i, 6.39	6.68- 17
					TJ	13.82i	14.03- 17
* Dibaba	Birhane	ETH	11.9.93	159/44	HMar	69:04+	65:57- 19
					Mar	2:18:35	2:18:46- 19
* Dibaba	Genzebe	ETH	8.2.91	168.52	HMar	65:18	-0-
* Dida	Dera	ETH	26.10.96	155/42	Mar	2:22:52	2:21:45- 18
Diver	Sinead	AUS	17.2.77	160/44	HMar	68:50	68:55- 19
					Mar	2:27:07	2:24:11- 19
Donaghu	Ella	USA	13.4.98		3000	8:54.72#i	-
* Dongmo	Auriol	POR	3.8.90	173/95	SP	19.53	18.37- 17
Donzelot	Irene	FRA	8.12.88	170/68	DT	59.40	57.66- 12
^ Drahotová	Anezka	CZE	22.7.95	183/63	20kW	1:33:59	1:26:53- 15
Drisbióti	Antigóni	GRE	21.3.84	162/52	20kW	1:30:25	1:30:56- 16
* Dubitskaya	Alyona	BLR	25.1.90	182/77	SP	19.27	19.21- 18
Dubovitskaya	Nadezhda	KAZ	12.3.98	177/56	HJ	1.90i	1.86- 19
Durdiaková	Tereza	CZE	20.2.91		20kW	1:33:54	-
Durgin	Emily	USA	15.5.94		10000	32:22.56	32:23.40- 19
Dvoráková	Katerina	CZE	10.5.97	166/56	Hep	5727(w), 5637	5671- 19
* Ealey	Chase	USA	20.7.94	178/84	SP	19.41	19.68- 19
Eccleston	Amanda	USA	18.6.90	160/50	1500	4:09.98i	4:03.25- 16
* Eckhardt	Neele	GER	2.7.92	168/52	TJ	14.17i, 13.73, 13.80w	14.35- 17
Edao	Bontu	BRN	12.12.97	164/50	HMar	69:47	
Edwards	Kaela	USA	8.12.93	165/52	800	2:00.39	2:01.97- 16
					1500	4:09.62	4:10.46- 17
Ekholm	Ellen	SWE	12.2.96	178/62	HJ	1.91i	1.83- 15
Ekidor	Margaret	KEN	26.6.00		3000	8:52.17	9:05.32- 19
					5000	15:10.10	-
Ellward	Agnieszka	POL	26.3.89	168/54	50kW	4:38:44	4:31:19- 19
Elmore	Malindi	CAN	13.3.80	168/53	Mar	2:24:50	2:32:15- 19
Embaye	Axumawit	ETH	18.10.94	160/50	1500	4:02.96i	3:59.02- 19
* Ennaoui	Sofia	POL	30.8.95	158/40	800	2:00.12	2:00.11- 15
1000	2:32.30		2:35.15- 16		1500	3:59.70	4:01.00- 16
Epis	Giovanna	ITA	11.10.88	164/46	Mar	2:28:03	2:29:11- 19
Erkkola	Sanne	FIN	8.3.94	170/63	JT	57.04	55.56- 19
^ Eshete	Shitaye	BRN	21.5.90	164/51	HMar	69:53+	68:25- 18
					Mar	2:27:34	2:21:33- 19
Eshetu	Biruktayit	ETH	29.9.90	157/40	Mar	2:24:47	2:22:40- 19
Espinoza	Ahymara	VEN	28.5.85	170/80	SP	17.40	18.19- 16
* Ewen	Maggie	USA	23.9.94	178/79	SP	18.80i	19.47- 19
Falda	Helen	ITA	13.2.96	162/52	PV	4.36i	4.40- 19
Fantini	Sara	ITA	16.9.97	170/72	HT	70.73	70.30- 19
Farkas	Petra	HUN	30.4.99	169/52	LJ	6.64	6.72- 19
Fatherly	Rachel	USA	20.4.94	180/86	SP	18.44i	18.48- 19
* Feng Bin		CHN	3.4.94	184/95	DT	64.09	65.45- 19
Ferrando	Cristina	ESP	12.1.92	175/59	HJ	1.87	1.88- 15
Ferrer e Silva	Laila	BRA	30.7.82	180/80	JT	61.87	62.52- 17
* Feysa	Hawi	ETH	1.2.99	160/45	Mar	2:23:36	-0-
Filipic	Neja	SLO	22.4.95	172/56	LJ	6.56	6.51- 16, 6.54w- 19
					TJ	14.22, 14.32w	13.91- 19
Finn	Michelle	IRL	16.12.89	160/52	3kSt	9:38.04	9:41.23- 19
Finot	Alice	FRA	9.2.91	172/58	3kSt	9:45.37	10:10.87- 19
* Fiodorow	Joanna	POL	4.3.89	169/89	HT	67.81	76.35- 19
Fixsen	Julia	USA	13.11.00	180/64	PV	4.46i	4.25- 18
Flanagan	Lindsay	USA	24.1.91	163/49	HMar	69:37	72:05- 16
Flannel	Kynnedy	USA	12.7.00	173/59	200	22.93i	22.71- 19
Flynn	Tiffany	USA	2.9.95	176/	LJ	6.47	6.23i, 5.97- 17
Folorunso	Ayomide	ITA	17.10.96	170/55	400H	55.40	54.75- 19
* Forbes	Shashalee	JAM	10.5.96	160/56	100	11.20, 11.05w	11.10- 17
Foster	Rhesa	USA	25.5.98		LJ	6.57Ai	6.43- 19
Fotopoulou	Olivia	CYP	20.12.96	162/53	LJ	6.58, 6.61w	6.35w- 19
* Franklin	Tori	USA	7.10.92	173/65	TJ	14.64Ai	14.84- 18
Fraser	Vanessa	USA	27.7.95	168/52	3000	8:51.39#i	8:54.58i, 9:02.34- 19
5000	14:48.51i		15:07.58- 19		10000	32:09.57	33:10.84- 18
* Fraser-Pryce	Shelly-Ann	JAM	27.12.86	160/52	100	10.86	10.70- 12
					200	22.57	22.09- 12
Frederick-Loomis	Priscilla	ANT	14.2.89	178/68	HJ	1.89i	1.91- 15

402 INDEX

Name		Nat	Born	Ht/Wt	Event	2020 Mark	Pre-2020 Best
* Frerichs	Courtney	USA	18.1.93	167/52	1500	4:07.39	4:11.05- 19
3000	8:47.31#i, 8:47.90		8:53.99- 17		5000	14:50.06	15:31.62i- 16, 16:22.98- 13
^ Fuchise	Masumi	JPN	2.9.86	161/51	20kW	1:33:41	1:28:03- 09
Fuchs	Annika Marie	GER	29.4.97	176/70	JT	60.20	63.68- 19
Fujii	Nanako	JPN	7.5.99	159/42	20kW	1:33:20	1:28:58- 19
Fukura	Ikumi	JPN	11.8.97	167/47	10000	32:10.29	32:36.90- 19
					HMar	69:58	72:24- 19
^ Fukushi	Kayoko	JPN	25.3.82	160/45	10000	32:17.65	30:51.81- 02
Fulton	Eleanor	USA	17.5.93	175/57	1500	4:08.92	4:08.42- 19
Furlani	Erika	ITA	2.1.96	175/53	HJ	1.94	1.92- 17
* Furmanek	Katarzyna	POL	19.2.96	174/76	HT	73.61	69.68- 19
Gaither	Tynia	BAH	16.3.93	158/50	100	11.25w	11.04- 19
Gajanová	Gabriela	SVK	12.10.99	167/52	800	2:01.26	2:00.58- 19
Gal ¶	Camelia	ROU	18.10.92	166/60	400	52.01	52.60- 17
Galimany	Marta	ESP	5.10.85	168/52	Mar	2:27:08	2:30:15- 19
Gallardo	Ivana	CHI	20.7.93	168/81	SP	17.39	17.25- 19
Gallardo	Karen	CHI	6.3.84	175/95	DT	56.99	61.10- 15
Gallego	Sara	ESP	11.10.00	164/51	400h	56.97	57.11- 18
Galván	Laura	MEX	5.10.91	162/48	3000	8:49.74i	9:33.06A- 10
5000	15:29.14		15:27.26- 19		10000	31:54.63	34:43.46- 15
Gao Yang		CHN	1.3.93	178/110	SP	18.50	19.20- 16
García	Mariana	CHI	19.3.99	167/73	HT	66.33	66.87- 19
Gardasevic	Milica	SRB	28.9.98	178/66	LJ	6.60	6.64- 18
Gataullina	Aksana	RUS	17.7.00	177/64	PV	4.50	4.55- 18
Ge Lijuan		CHN	17.7.97		JT	59.47	58.49- 19
Ge Manqi		CHN	13.10.97	160/54	200	22.69	23.15- 18
Gebre	Tsehay	ETH	11.9.92		Mar	2:27:22	2:28:06- 19
Gebrekidan	Berhane	ETH	13.3.99		Mar–	2:27:20	
Gebrekidan	Hiwot	ETH	11.5.95	156/44	Mar	2:24:30	2:23:50- 19
Gebreselama	Tsigie	ETH	30.9.00	160/47	3000	8:45.76i	8:53.98i- 19, 8:59.20- 18
					5000	15:13.38A	15:12.96- 19
Gebreselassie	Goytatom	ETH	15.1.95	152/42	HMar	68:19	68:58- 19
Gebru	Azmera	ETH	21.10.95	160/45	HMar	69:16+	70:40- 17
					Mar	2:22:58	2:20:48- 19
* Gega	Luiza	ALB	5.11.88	166/56	3000	8:44.46i, 9:04.22	8:52.53i- 17, 8:53.78- 16
Gemechu	Tsehay	ETH	12.12.98	160/52	2000	5:41.0+	
3000	8:33.42		8:45.35- 19		5000	14:54.03	14:29.60- 19
10000	30:57.73		30:53.11- 19		HMar	67:16	66:50- 18
George	Patience Okon	NGR	25.11.91	176/61	400	51.84	50.71- 15
Gerevini	Sveva	ITA	31.5.96	171/57	Hep	5741	5907- 19
* German	Elvira	BLR	9.1.97	168/54	100h	12.73	12.64- 18
* Ghelber	Bianca	ROU	1.6.90	170/70	HT	72.18	73.52- 10
Gicquel	Solène	FRA	1.12.94	186/60	HJ	1.87	1.88- 19
Gidey	Birho	ETH	.00		HMar	67:57	
* Gidey	Letesenbet	ETH	20.3.98	163/48	3000	8:31.9+	8:20.27- 19
					5000	14:06.62	14:23.14- 18
* Gierisch	Kristin	GER	20.8.90	178/69	TJ	14.03i	14.61- 19
Giger	Yasmin	SUI	6.11.99	180/60	400h	56.42	55.90- 17
Gillarová	Irena	CZE	19.1.92	173/70	JT	60.00	61.32- 19
Giordano	Dana	USA	30.12.93	174/57	1500	4:10.31i, 4:10.79	4:08.62- 18
3000	8:51.78i		8:55.14- 18		5000	15:18.06	15:53.96- 14
Girma	Tigist	ETH	12.7.93	168/52	HMar	69:05+	–
					Mar	2:19:56	2:19:52- 19
Gizaw	Melkaw	ETH	17.9.90	163/48	Mar	2:28:05	2:24:28- 16
Godfay	Afera	ETH	25.9.91	156/42	Mar	2:26:42	2:22:41- 19
Gola	Meseret	ETH	30.12.97	151/40	HMar	69:02	70:16- 18
Gollshewsky	Taryn	AUS	18.5.93	184/80	DT	57.77	60.27- 16
Golodna	Olga	UKR	14.11.91	183/95	SP	17.29i, 16.02	18.72- 13
Golubechkova	Darya	RUS	10.9.00		20kW	1:28:43	-0-
Gonçalves	Rafaela	BRA	27.11.91	168/70	JT	57.15	57.77- 17
* Gong Lijiao		CHN	24.1.89	174/110	SP	19.70i, 19.53	20.43- 16
Gong Luying		CHN	22.2.00		LJ	6.50	6.63- 19
González	Raquel	ESP	16.11.89	176/55	20kW	1:32:02	1:28:36- 14
Gordeyeva	Alyona	RUS	24.4.97	187/95	SP	17.55i, 17.02	18.52- 15
Goswami	Priyanka	IND	10.3.96		20kW	1:31:36	1:37:00.15t- 19
* Goule	Natoya	JAM	30.3.91	160/50	800	1:59.35i, 2:00.43	1:56.15- 18
* Grace	Kate	USA	24.10.88	173/55	1000	2:35.49i	2:36.97i- 17
2000	5:41.87+i				3000	8:46.86#i	8:47.26i- 17
Granz	Caterina	GER	14.3.94	173/53	1500	4:06.56mx irr, 4:11.19	4:05.60- 19
Gray	Jordan	USA	28.12.95	170/61	Dec	7627	7921- 19

INDEX 403

Name		Nat	Born	Ht/Wt	Event	2020 Mark			Pre-2020 Best
^ Green	Hanna	USA	16.10.94	168/59	1500	4:08.36i			4:06.66- 19
800	2:02.82Ai		1:58.19- 19		1M	4:28.06#i			4:32.50- 17
^ Gregson	Genevieve	AUS	4.8.89	168/54	1500	4:09.40			4:10.20- 16
5000	15:20.60		15:06.67- 16		3kSt	9:44.07			9:14.28- 16
Griffith	Georgia	AUS	5.12.96	163/50	800	2:00.88			2:00.13- 18
					1500	4:06.35			4:04.17- 18
Grimm	Vanessa	GER	22.4.97	175/64	Hep	6047			5929- 19
Grøvdal	Karoline Bjerkeli	NOR	14.6.90	167/52	5000	15:01.13			14:47.53- 16
Gruver	Olivia	USA	29.7.97	170/64	PV	4.70Ai, 4.35			4.73- 19
^ Guba	Paulina	POL	14.5.91	180/90	SP	18.09			19.38- 18
Gudeta	Bekelech	ETH	11.10.97	167/45	HMar	69:54			67:03- 18
* Gudeta	Netsanet	ETH	12.2.91	156/42	HMar	66:46			65:45- 19
Guerra	Leyde	PER	27.9.98		20kW	1:33:46			1:30:01A?, 1:33:39.2t- 19
Guerrero	Esther	ESP	7.2.90	160/57	800	1:59.22			2:00.77- 17
1000	2:35.64	2:37.85- 18		1500	4:03.13		4:05.70- 19	2000	5:41.30	-
* Guillon-Romarin	Ninon	FRA	15.4.95	163/53	PV	4.66i			4.75- 18
Gulyayeva	Aleksandra	RUS	30.4.94	173/59	800	2:00.07			1:58.34- 17
1000	2:37.17i		2:36.03i- 19		1500	4:05.69			4:04.49- 17
Gunnarsson	Lisa	SWE	20.8.99	171/62	PV	4.50Ai, 4.46			4.60- 18
Gunnells	Shelby	USA	1.1.97		SP	17.43i			16.90i, 16.33- 19
Guo Sijia		CHN	14.2.99		LJ	6.53			6.26- 19
Guo Tianqian		CHN	1.6.95	180/110	SP	17.50			18.59- 15
Gusarova	Inessa	RUS	29.10.95	162/52	800	2:01.00			2:02.86- 16
					1500	4:08.17			4:07.87- 18
Gutermuth	Sophie	USA	2.11.92	168/62	PV	4.52i			4.47- 17
Guy	Bridget	USA	18.3.96	165/57	PV	4.61i			4.50- 19
Gyurátz	Réka	HUN	31.5.96	175/70	HT	70.20			72.70- 19
Gyürkés (Wagner)	Viktória	HUN	15.10.92	172/61	3000	8:53.60			9:00.68- 19
Haase	Rebekka	GER	2.1.93	170/57	100	11.11			11.06, 10.94w- 17
Hagitani	Kaede	JPN	10.10.00	160/	3000	8:48.12			9:05.72- 19
1500	4:13.14		4:16.45- 19		5000	15:05.78			15:28.13- 19
Hagiwara	Ayumi	JPN	1.6.92	155/41	10000	31:36.04			31:41.80- 14
Hailu	Fireweyni	ETH-J	12.2.01	173/57	1500	4:05.91i			
* Hailu	Lemlem	ETH-J	21.5.01	162/52	1500	4:01.57i, 4:04.75			4:02.97- 19
2000	5:40.1+				3000	8:35.78			8:34.02- 19
Hall-Harnden	Kate	USA	12.1.97	173/64	LJ	6.69Ai			6.83- 15
* Hall	Linden	AUS	29.6.91	167/51	800	2:01.73			2:02.85- 16
1500	4:05.16	4:00.86- 18		3000	8:51.20		8:53.27- 18	5000	15:25.22	15:18.77- 19
Hall	Marielle	USA	28.1.92	160/52	3000	8:48.72			8:54.48- 14
1500	4:10.77		4:12.14- 17		5000	15:20.73i, 15:30.86			15:02.27- 19
* Hall	Sara	USA	15.4.83	163/51	HMar	68:18			69:27- 18
					Mar	2:20:32			2:22:16- 19
Hamann	Sophie	GER	12.8.96		Hep	5755			5726- 19
Harala	Lotta	FIN	26.3.92	170/56	100h	13.07, 13.04w			13.15- 18, 13.12w- 17
Harris	Jessica	USA	14.3.96	169/52	1500	4:08.81i			4:08.83- 19
^ Harting	Julia	GER	1.4.90	192/95	DT	61.17			68.49- 18
* Hassan	Sifan	NED	1.1.93	170/49	3000	8:49+ ?			8:18.49- 19
5000	14:37.85	14:22.12- 19		10000	29:36.67		30:17.62- 19	1Hr	18.930m	
Hatsko	Hanna	UKR	3.10.90	174/71	JT	60.45			67.29- 14
Havrylyuk	Tamara	UKR	14.12.95	163/53	50kW	4:38:38			-
* Hayes	Quenera	USA	7.3.92	172/59	200	22.80			22.55- 17
					400	52.07Ai			49.71- 17
Hayward	Katie	AUS	23.7.00		20kW	1:34:00			1:29:25- 19
Hechavarría	Zurian	CUB	10.8.95	164/58	400h	55.77			55.00- 19
* Hejnová	Zuzana	CZE	19.12.86	170/54	400h	55.70			52.83- 13
Hemida (Awad)	Basant	EGY	28.9.96	175/63	100	11.23			11.31, 11.27w- 19
					200	22.91			22.83- 19
Henes	Elly	USA	13.10.98	160/50	10000	32:12.06			-0-
* Herashchenko	Iryna	UKR	10.3.95	181/61	HJ	1.95			1.99- 19
Hering	Christina	GER	9.10.94	185/62	800	2:00.47			1:59.41- 19
					1500	4:08.30			-0-
Hermansson	Hanna	SWE	18.5.89	171/62	1500	4:07.07			4:07.16- 18
Hernández	Melissa María	CUB-J	16.3.01	173/64	JT	58.02			56.20- 19
Herrera	Mayra Carolina	GUA	20.12.88	163/54	20kW	1:33:08			1:30:41- 14
Heyns	Riette	RSA	26.2.97		DT	57.35A			57.25A- 19
Hickling	Tissanna	JAM	7.1.98	168/54	LJ	6.80			6.82- 19
Hiltz	Nikki	USA	23.10.94	162/52	1500	4:07.09+i			4:01.52- 19
					1M	4:24.45i			4:31.42i- 19
Hirai	Miki	JPN	12.2.96	162/50	10000	32:16.97			34:39.66- 19
Hironaka	Ririka	JPN	24.11.00	164/46	3000	8:52.80			8:56.29- 17
					5000	14:59.37			15:05.40- 19

INDEX

Name		Nat	Born	Ht/Wt	Event	2020 Mark		Pre-2020 Best
Hirpa	Bedatu	ETH	28.4.99	158/42	Mar	2:21:55		2:21:32- 19
Hjálmsdóttir Annerud	Ásdís	ISL	28.10.85	175/65	JT	62.56		63.43- 17
Hladiychuk	Yana	UKR	21.5.93	174/63	PV	4.50		4.40- 17
* Hobbs	Aleia	USA	24.2.96	172/59	100	11.12		10.85- 17, 10.83w- 19
Hodel	Andrina	SUI	2.6.00	163/54	PV	4.40		4.36- 19
* Hodgkinson	Keely	GBR-J	3.3.02	168/54	800	2:01.16i, 2:01.73		2:03.40- 19
Hoffmann	Lore	SUI	25.7.96	172/54	800	1:58.50		2:01.67- 18
Hoggard	Tori	USA	20.11.96	167/60	PV	4.50Ai		4.61i- 18, 4.57- 17
Holm	Caroline Bonde	DEN	19.7.90	178/68	PV	4.35i, 4.21		4.43i- 14, 4.36- 12
Holmberg	Amanda	SWE	6.9.98	170/57	400h	56.98		58.85- 15
Holmes	Alexis	USA	28.1.00	180/68	400	52.08i		51.21- 19
Holub-Kowalik	Malgorzata	POL	30.10.92	168/56	400	52.15		51.18- 18
Homeier	Merle	GER	27.8.99	177/60	LJ	6.57		6.45, 6.52w- 19
Honsel	Christina	GER	7.7.97	180/61	HJ	1.90		1.92- 19
Hosoda	Ai	JPN	27.11.95	154/	Mar	2:26:34		2:29:27- 19
* Houlihan	Shelby	USA	8.2.93	160/54	800	2:01.08		1:59.92- 19
1500	4:02.37	3:54.99- 19	1M	4:23.68#i	4:24.16i- 17, 4:31.79- 15		2000	5:40.33+i
3000	8:26.66i, 8:48.14	8:36.01i- 18, 8:37.40- 17			5000	14:23.92		14:34.45- 18
* Hrasnová	Martina	SVK	21.3.83	177/88	HT	70.71		76.90- 09
^ Hrubá	Michaela	CZE	21.2.98	182/62	HJ	1.87		1.95i- 16, 1.94- 17
Huang Weilu		CHN	1.9.99		HT	65.75		67.03- 19
* Huddle	Molly	USA	31.8.84	163/48	5000	15:20.80		14:42.64- 14
3000	8:59.82mx	8:42.99- 13	1Hr	17,930m			HMar	69:34	67:25- 18
Hudson	Victoria	AUT	28.5.96	169/64	JT	61.00A		59.98- 19
* Hull	Jessica	AUS	22.10.96	167/50	1500	4:00.42		4:01.80- 19
2000	5:40.6+		3000	8:36.03	8:53.91- 19, 9:08.85- 14		5000	14:43.80	15:00.32- 19
Hulley	Alex	AUS	24.7.97	171/90	HT	70.55		68.66- 17
Huntington	Maria	FIN	13.3.97	171/61	100h	13.12		13.09- 19
LJ	6.51		6.44, 6.56w- 19		Hep	6074		6339- 19
Hurske	Reetta	FIN	15.5.95	168/56	100h	12.91		12.78- 19
Husan	Zeyituna	ETH	12.1.99	152/38	5000	15:13.44		15:36.48- 19
10000	32:07.79			–	HMar	69:24		-0-
Hussen	Mesera	ETH	22.6.95	160/45	Mar	2:26:28		2:28:29- 19
* Hussong	Christin	GER	17.3.94	187/82	JT	64.10		67.90- 18
Hutchinson	Nicole	CAN	17.6.97	160/52	3000	8:48.92i		8:55.68i, 9:03.52- 19
* Hynne	Hedda	NOR	13.3.90	172/57	800	1:58.10		1:59.87- 19
* Iapichino	Larissa	ITA-J	18.7.02	171/56	LJ	6.80		6.64- 19
Ibargüen	Caterine	COL	12.2.84	185/70	LJ	6.61		6.93- 14
Ibrahim	Ayesya	JPN	16.1.98	173/55	400h	56.50		58.09- 19
Ichikawa	Juri	JPN	25.3.98	147/37	HMar	69:55		–
* Ichiyama	Mao	JPN	29.5.97	158/43	5000	15:06.66		15:41.22- 19
10000	31:11.56	31:34.56- 19	HMar	68:56		68:49- 19	Mar	2:20:29	2:24:33- 19
Ignatyeva	Violetta	RUS-J	16.1.02		DT	57.94		55.50- 10
Ikemitsu	Ayano	JPN	18.4.91	161/48	HMar	69:16		71:14- 17
Ince	Ariana	USA	14.3.89	180/75	JT	57.98		63.54- 19
Inchude	Jessica	GBS	25.3.96	175/81	SP	17.55i, 17.42		17.54- 19
Infeld	Emily	USA	21.3.90	163/48	3000	8:48.73#i		8:41.43- 13
					5000	14:51.91i		14:56.33- 17
Ingvaldsen	Helene	NOR	22.6.96		HT	65.55		64.77- 18
Inoue	Ayaka	JPN	19.6.91	164/46	Mar	2:27:54		2:30:43- 18
Insaeng	Subenrat	THA	10.2.94	183/105	DT	58.37		61.97- 15
* Irby	Lynna	USA	6.12.98	168/55	100	11.27		11.40 - 19
200	22.47		22.25, 22.06w- 18		400			49.80- 18
^ Irozuru	Abigail	GBR	3.1.90	170/61	LJ	6.60i, 6.57		6.86- 19
Ishizawa	Yukari	JPN	16.4.88	169/49	3kSt	9:48.76		9:53.22- 18
Itoya	Juliet	ESP	17.8.86	174/63	LJ	6.60		6.80, 6.88Aw- 19
Iuel	Amalie Hammill	NOR	17.4.94	180/59	400h	55.27		54.72- 19
^ Iusco	Florentina	ROU	8.4.96	178/60	LJ	6.53i, 6.43		6.92- 19
					TJ	13.84		13.81- 19
Ivanenko	Valeriya	UKR-J	16.8.01	172/65	HT	66.05		67.04- 19
Ivanova	Irina	RUS	19.4.96	169/60	PV	4.60i, 4.50		4.60- 19
Ivonina	Yekaterina	RUS	14.6.94	164/52	1500	4:10.00		4:12.53- 18
3000	8:55.56i	8:56.34i- 18, 9:04.90- 19			3kSt	9:16.84		9:16.68- 18
Izzo	Katie	USA	22.12.96	165/50	10000	32:28.89		-0-
Jääskeläinen	Jatta Mari	FIN	27.2.94	165/61	JT	56.50		57.47- 19
* Jackson	Shericka	JAM	16.7.94	173/60	200	22.70		22.05- 18
					400	51.76		49.83- 16
Jacobus	Lexi	USA	20.11.96	167/60	PV	4.50Ai, 4.35		4.70- 16
Jæger	Henriette	NOR-Y	30.6.03		Hep	5875		–
Jaramillo	Karla	ECU	21.1.97	160/58	20kW	1:30:39A		1:30:52.00t- 19
^ Jarder	Erica	SWE	2.4.86	173/59	LJ	6.61		6.71i- 13, 6.70- 15

INDEX 405

Name		Nat	Born	Ht/Wt	Event	2020 Mark	Pre-2020 Best
Jasiunaite	Liveta	LTU	26.7.94	174/68	JT	60.27	63.98- 19
Jat	Bhawana	IND	1.3.96		20kW	1:29:54	1:36:16.87t- 19
Jebitok	Edina	KEN-J	10.11.01	173/55	1500	4:07.24A	4:05.23- 19
* Jefferson	Kyra	USA	23.9.94	165/57	200	22.87, 22.69w	22.52- 15, 22.17w- 14
* Jepchirchir	Peres	KEN	27.9.93	153/40	HMar	65:16	65:06- 17
					Mar	2:17:16	2:23:50- 19
* Jepkemoi	Hyvin	KEN	13.1.92	156/45	2000	5:40.3+	5:43.2- 180
3000	8:25.13		8:30.51- 18		3kSt	9:06.14	9:00.01- 16
Jepkoech	Josephine	KEN	21.4.89	168/50	Mar	2:24:14	2:25:20- 19
* Jepkosgei	Joyciline	KEN	8.12.93	156/52	HMar	65:58	64:51- 17
					Mar	2:18:40	2:22:38- 19
^ Jepkosgei	Nelly	BRN	14.7.91	164/53	800	2:02.07A	1:58.96- 18
Jepleting	Brenda	KEN	2.12.99	163/48	HMar	67:07	-0-
Jepngetich	Judith	KEN-J	24.12.02		3000	8:54.57	9:26.24- 19
					5000	15:07.52	
Jermann	Katy	USA	20.4.92	168/52	HMar	69:35	70:27- 19
Jerotich	Winnie	KEN	27.11.99	160/49	5000	15:14.84	15:29.91- 19
Ji Li		CHN	14.12.00		HT	68.26	67.40- 19
Jiang Yue		CHN	6.10.98		SP	17.63	17.30- 19
Jing Mingming		CHN	10.12.96		Mar	2:27:08	2:33:21- 16
* Johannes	Helalia	NAM	13.8.80	165/48	HMar	68:10	70:30- 19
					Mar	2:19:52	2:22:25- 19
Johansson	Axelina	SWE	20.4.00		SP	17.49	15.44i, 15.18- 19
Johansson	Tilde	SWE-J	5.1.01	168/56	LJ	6.53	6.73- 19
Johaug	Therese	NOR	25.6.88	162/46	10000	31:40.67	32:20.86- 19
Johnigan	Annie	USA	13.5.95	173.64	PV	4.40i	4.65- 19
Johnson	Felisha	USA	24.7.89	185/105	SP	18.19i	19.26- 16
Johnson	Kortnei	USA	11.8.97	165/52	100	11.25, 11.15w	11.09- 17, 10.97w- 18
Johnson-Thompson	Katarina	GBR	9.1.93	183/70	LJ	6.52	6.93i- 15, 6.92- 14
* Jonathas	Wadeline	USA	19.2.98	178/58	400	51.23	49.60- 19
Jones	Danielle	USA	21.8.96	165/54	1500	4:05.03+	4:07.28- 19
1M	4:23.33		4:31.82i- 18, 4:39.88- 15		5000	15:17.11i	15:46.93- 19
Jorgensen	Gwen	USA	25.4.86	167/52	3000	8:48.48	9:20.42i- 19
5000	15:10.98i, 15:18.25		15:15.64i- 18, 15:52.19- 09		10000	32:12.22	31:55.68- 18
* Józwik	Joanna	POL	30.1.91	167/52	800	2:01.20mx. 2:01.26	1:57.37- 16
Juárez	Mar	ESP	27.9.93	156/47	50kW	4:15:46	4:28:58- 18
Judd	Jessica	GBR	7.1.95	178/60	1500	4:10.03	4:03.73- 17
* Junnila	Ella	FIN	6.12.98	183/60	HJ	1.90	1.95- 19
Kaczmarek	Marika	POL	25.4.96	170/75	HT	66.99	64.35- 17
* Kagramanova	Reykhan	RUS	1.6.97		20kW	1:26:50	1:29:50-18
Kähärä	Jessica	FIN-J	1.8.01	171/54	HJ	1.87	1.87- 18
Kalashnikova	Anastasiya	RUS	29.6.97		50kW	4:18:26	-
Kälin	Annik	SUI	27.4.00	168/57	LJ	6.56	6.39- 18
					Hep	6170	6132- 19
Kalinina	Tatyana	RUS-J	3.8.01		PV	4.35	4.00- 19
Kalsey	Marissa	USA	23.3.94		PV	4.37i, 4.25	4.30- 18
Kamau	Tabitha	KEN	3.7.00	155/40	5000	15:09.63	15:08.77- 19
					10000	31:45.83	31:28.45- 19
Kambundji	Ditaji	SUI-J	20.5.02	165/57	100h	13.07	13.92- 19
* Kambundji	Mujinga	SUI	17.6.92	168/59	100	11.21	10.95- 18
Kamga	Vanessa	SWE	19.11.98	177/90	DT	60.01	59.06- 19
* Kamulu	Pauline	KEN	30.12.94	154/45	5000	15:20.02	14:58.82- 17
Kanbouchia	Souad	MAR	12.8.82		Mar	2:28:07	2:28:56- 19
Kangas	Jenni	FIN	3.7.92	178/74	JT	57.52	60.98- 19
Kanuchová	Veronika	SVK	19.4.93	170/69	HT	65.53	69.48- 16
Kardasz	Klaudia	POL	2.5.96	179/82	SP	17.65	18.63i- 19, 18.48- 18
Karídi	Spiridoúla	GRE-J	30.1.01	163/54	LJ	6.71	6.46- 19
					TJ	14.12	14.00- 19
Karpova	Natalya	RUS	18.1.94	173/79	DT	61.52	62.88- 19
Kaseda	Rika	JPN	2.3.99	148/40	10000	31:39.86	32:29.92- 19
^ Kasyanova	Hanna	UKR	24.4.83	178/67	Hep	5962	6586- 13
Kato	Misaki	JPN	15.6.91	155/40	10000	32:13.23	31:59.02- 16
Kaur	Karamjit	IND	5.2.91		20kW	1:33:41	1:34:09- 18
Kawaguchi	Momoka	JPN	28.6.98	154/42	5000	15:24.24	15:51.60- 19
					10000	32:15.88	33:10.60- 19
Kawazoe	Kaori	JPN	30.5.95	158/48	20kW	1:33:15	1:31:10- 19
Kazimierska	Klaudia	POL-J	3.9.01	160/48	1500	4:07.47	4:15.60- 19
* Kejeta	Melat	GER	27.9.92	158/45	HMar	65:18	68:41- 18
Kelati	Weini	ERI	1.12.96	159/42	3000	8:54.66i	8:53.89- 19
					10000	31:10.08	32:09.10- 19
Kelly	Mariah	CAN	19.8.91	167/52	1500	4:10.01i	4:09.38- 17

INDEX

Name		Nat	Born	Ht/Wt	Event	2020 Mark	Pre-2020 Best
Kemp	Erika	USA	26.1.95	157/45	3000	8:53.06i	9:05.83i- 19
5000	15:14.76i		15:28.69- 19		10000	31:35.63	33:13.44- 15
Kemppainen	Suvi	FIN	25.1.98	165/61	JT	57.43	57.75- 18
Kennedy	Nina	AUS	5.4.97	166/57	PV	4.72	4.71- 18
Kenzel	Alina	GER	10.8.97	183/78	SP	18.14i, 17.96	18.21- 18
Ketema	Tigist	ETH	15.9.98	163/50	1500	4:07.40i	4:05.09- 19
Khalikova	Adelina	RUS-J	18.12.02	182/64	HJ	1.88i	1.90- 19
Khapilina	Viktoriya	UKR	23.4.92	164/50	Mar	2:27:57dq	2:28:03- 19
* Khasanova	Elvira	RUS	10.1.00		20kW	1:26:43	1:28:15- 19
Khitko	Viktoriya	RUS	3.8.99		HT	67.26	57.90- 19
* Kholodovich	Tatyana	BLR	21.6.91	181/83	JT	67.17	67.47- 18
Kienast	Lucie	GER-J	1.6.01	190/71	LJ	6.48i, 6.38	6.39- 19
					Hep	6009	5636- 19
Kilty	Dovile	LTU	14.7.93	168/58	TJ	14.18	14.28- 19
Kimais	Irene	KEN	10.10.98	163/52	HMar	69:01	69:51- 19
Kimeli	Dorcas	KEN	5.7.97	163/50	HMar	67:10	67:44- 19
* Kinsey	Erika	SWE	10.3.88	185/68	HJ	1.95	1.97- 15
* Kipkemboi	Margaret	KEN	9.2.93	162/45	2000	5:40.2+	
3000	8:24.76		8:30.11- 17		5000	15:11.11A	14:27.49- 19
Kipkemoi Rotich	Joan	KEN	27.11.93	160.45	HMar	69:28	-0-
Kipkirui	Caroline	KEN	26.5.94	162/47	HMar	68:13	65:44- 19
Kipkoech	Brillian	KEN	9.3.95	165/50	HMar	66:56	67:12- 19
Kiplagat	Vivian	KEN	9.11.91	160/48	HMar	66:38	66:55- 19
Kiplangat	Josephine	KEN	10.10.98	159/45	1500	4:08.68A	4:08.77- 18
Kiprop	Nancy	KEN	.79	164/48	HMar	69:32	67:22- 17
Kiprop	Quailyne	KEN	1.5.99	168/54	3000	8:39.88	–
* Kipyegon	Faith	KEN	10.1.94	157/42	800	1:57.68	1:58.02- 19
1000	2:29.15		2:37.44- 19		1500	3:59.05	3:54.22- 19
Kipyogei	Diana	KEN	5.5.94	160/54	Mar	2:22:06	2:22:07- 19
* Kiriakopoúlou	Nikoléta	GRE	21.3.86	167/56	PV	4.63	4.83- 15
Kitaguchi	Haruka	JPN	16.3.98	179/86	JT	63.45	66.00- 19
Kite	Gloria	KEN	29.12.98	170/52	3000	8:48.74i	8:29.91- 19
					10000	31:25.17	31:41.47- 18
Kitur	Bornes	KEN	23.11.86	157/42	HMar	69:55+	70:00- 16
					Mar	2:26:24	2:21:26- 19
Kiyoyama	Chisato	JPN	24.7.91	168/57	100h	13.03w, 13.13	13.20, 13.10w- 19
Klaup	Mari	EST	27.2.90	180/59	JT	56.79	55.23- 19
					Hep	6080(w)	6023(w)- 15
Klaver	Lieke	NED	20.8.98	178/63	200	22.66	23.35, 22.96w- 19
					400	50.98	53.18- 19
Klein	Hanna	GER	6.4.93	172/55	1500	4:04.90	4:04.15- 17
Klein	Sara	AUS	19.5.94	170/54	400h	56.49	56.07- 19
Kloster	Line	NOR	27.2.90	175/59	400h	55.62	55.49- 18
* Klosterhalfen	Konstanze	GER	18.2.97	174/48	1000	2:37.05	2:43.07i- 19
1500	3:59.87+i		3:58.92- 17		1M	4:17.26i	4:19.98i, 4:21.11- 19
3000	8:50.04+i		8:20.07- 19		5000	14:30.79i	14:26.76- 19
* Klymets	Iryna	UKR	4.10.94	169/71	HT	73.01	73.56- 19
Klymyuk	Kateryna	UKR	2.6.95	173/54	400	51.84	51.97- 19
Knight	Jessie	GBR	15.6.94	168/57	400	51.57i, 51.9mx, 52.42	53.16i- 19, 53.47- 17
					400h	55.27	56.04- 19
Knoroz	Polina	RUS	20.7.99	175/60	PV	4.65i	4.56- 19
Knott	Kristina	PHI	25.9.95	164/52	100	11.27	11.42- 19
Kobayashi	Narumi	JPN	17.4.00	155/41	10000	32:08.67	33:00.53- 19
Kocina	Anete	LAT	5.2.96	176/65	JT	59.51	64.47- 17
* Kolak	Sara	CRO	22.6.95	170/74	JT	62.68	68.43- 17
Kolb	Viktoriya	BLR	26.10.93	182/90	SP	17.72i	18.35- 18
Kolberg	Majtie	GER	5.12.99		800	2:02.77	2:05.41- 19
Koleczek	Karolina	POL	15.1.93	169/51	100h	12.98	12.75, 12.67w- 19
Kolomoyets	Anastasiya	BLR	15.7.94		HT	71.72	71.99- 19
* Koneva	Yekaterina	RUS	25.9.88	169/55	TJ	14.56, 14.75w	15.04- 15
Kontsevenko	Kristina	BLR-J	18.8.01	174/65	PV	4.50	4.30- 19
* Kopron	Malwina	POL	16.11.94	169/89	HT	74.18	76.85- 17
Korobkina	Yelena	RUS	25.11.90	163/47	1500	4:05.84i	4:04.90- 17
3000	8:50.99i, 8:52.22		8:47.61i- 15, 8:51.00- 14		10000	32:56.23	32:16.01-19
Korolyova	Kristina	RUS	6.11.90	183/68	HJ	1.91i, 1.88	1.92- 17
Korte	Annimari	FIN	8.4.88	164/52	100h	12.76	12.72- 19
* Kosgei	Brigid	KEN	20.2.94	161/46	1Hr	18.904 dq	
HMar	64:49		64:28dh- 19		Mar	2:18:58	2:14:04- 19
Koskinen	Suvi	FIN	24.4.97		HT	67.69	65.33- 19
Kosolapova	Valentina	RUS	11.7.97	168/52	TJ	14.08i	14.14- 18
Kosonen	Silja	FIN-J	16.12.02	170/84	HT	71.34	63.60- 19

INDEX 407

Name		Nat	Born	Ht/Wt	Event	2020 Mark	Pre-2020 Best
Koster	Maureen	NED	3.7.92	175/56	1500	4:09.82	3:59.79- 15
3000	8:43.08	8:43.12mx- 19, 8:44.63i- 17			5000	15:20.93	15:07.20- 16
* Kozák	Luca	HUN	1.6.96	166/55	100h	12.71	12.86- 18
Kozul	Anamari	CRO	20.1.96	178/76	HT	65.75	69.44- 19
Krafzik	Carolina	GER	27.3.95	165/52	400h	55.90	55.64- 19
Krasina	Aleksandra	RUS	12.9.98		TJ	13.85	13.29- 19
^ Krasnova	Angelina	RUS	7.2.91	168/55	PV	4.66i	4.70- 13
Krejciríková	Klára	CZE-J	22.4.02	188/61	HJ	1.89i	1.89i- 19
^ Krivoshapka	Antonina	RUS	21.7.87	168/60	400	52.02i	49.16- 12
* Krizsán	Xénia	HUN	13.1.93	171/62	Hep	6263	6619- 19
Kudinova	Krisztina	RUS	25.10.98		50kW	4:34:45	-
Kuivisto	Sara	FIN	18.8.91	175/55	800	2:01.60	2:01.85- 19
Kwayie	Lisa Marie	GER	27.10.96	173/55	100	11.19	11.22- 19
Kylypko	Maryna	UKR	10.11.95	165/58	PV	4.40	4.65- 16
Lada	Androniki	CYP	19.4.91	188/95	DT	59.18A	56.69- 14
LaFond	Thea	DMA	5.4.94	173/65	TJ	14.33i	14.38- 19
Lagat	Violah	KEN	13.3.89	165/49	HMar	66:47	0-
Lagger	Sarah	AUT	3.9.99	174/60	Hep	6010	6225- 19
Lahti	Sarah	SWE	18.2.95	177/57	HMar	69:52	69:58- 17
* Lake	Morgan	GBR	12.5.97	178/64	HJ	1.90i	1.97- 18
Lällä	Sini	FIN	12.3.94	168/56	HJ	1.87	1.84- 15
Lally	Jade	GBR	30.3.87	183/81	DT	58.95	65.10- 16
^ Lamote	Renelle	FRA	26.12.93	168/57	800	2:01.08	1:58.01- 16
Lampela	Elina	FIN	18.2.98	175/66	PV	4.50	4.32i- 15, 4.25- 18
Lang	Salome	SUI	18.11.97	178/64	HJ	1.94i, 1.88	1.91- 19
Lange	Janina	GER	23.11.97		Hep	5830	5586- 19
Lansiquot	Imani	GBR	17.12.97	170/59	100	11.16	11.09- 19
Larsson	Eleni	SWE	9.2.93	186/100	HT	65.48	68.76- 15
* Lashmanova	Yelena	RUS	9.4.92	170/48	20kW	1:31:46+	1:23:39- 18
					50kW	3:50:42	-0-
* Lasitskene	Mariya	RUS	14.1.93	182/60	HJ	2.05i, 1.97	2.06- 17
Lasmane	Ruta	LAT	17.12.00		TJ	13.82	13.59- 17
Lau	Jasmijn	NED	11.3.99	166/48	10000	32:20.75	33:30.97- 19
Law	Kirsty	GBR	11.10.86	177/80	DT	57.95	57.79- 12
Lear	Bailey	USA-J	17.3.01	165/52	400	51.60#i	52.07- 19
LeLeux	Morgann	USA	14.11.92	170/61	PV	4.70i	4.65- 17
Leon	Gabriela	USA	17.6.99		PV	4.40i	4.31i, 4.27- 19
^ Leontyuk	Yuliya	BLR	31.1.84	185/80	SP	17.05i	19.79- 08
Lepistö	Janette	FIN	20.10.93	171/62	JT	57.78	54.11A- 18
Lesti	Diána	HUN	30.3.98		LJ	6.58, 6.65w	6.38- 17
^ Lesueur-Aymonin	Éloyse	FRA	15.7.88	181/65	LJ	6.62i	6.92- 14, 7.04w- 12
* Levchenko	Yuliya	UKR	28.11.97	179/60	HJ	2.00i, 2.00	2.02- 19
Lewetegn	Sintayehu	ETH	9.5.96	161/48	HMar	69:55+	69:56- 16
					Mar	2:23:03	2:22:45- 18
Li Dan		CHN	1.5.95		Mar	2:26:59	2:29:20- 19
* Li Ling		CHN	6.7.89	180/65	PV	4.60	4.72- 19
* Li Maocuo		CHN	20.10.92		20kW	1:32:12	1:30:15- 18
Li Ying		CHN	29.3.94		TJ	14.02	13.82- 19
Li Yutong		CHN-J	19.5.01		JT	56.35	50.31- 19
Li Zhixuan		CHN	23.3.94	167/50	Mar	2:26:39	2:26:15- 19
* Liang Rui		CHN	18.6.94	159/48	20kW	1:33:15	1:28:43- 16
* Licwinko	Kamila	POL	22.3.86	184/66	HJ	1.94i, 1.88	2.02i- 15, 1.99- 13
Ligarska	Paulina	POL	9.4.96	184/64	Hep	5870	5845- 18
Lin Shih-Ting		TPE	13.5.99		100h	13.04	13.24- 19
Lindfors	Caisa-Marie	SWE	5.8.00		DT	57.19	55.98- 19
Linkiewicz	Joanna	POL	2.5.90	172/55	400h	56.16	55.25- 16
Lipari	Emily	USA	19.11.92	153/48	1500	4:06.49i, 4:08.66	4:05.68- 18
3000	8:54.43i		8:51.07i- 18		5000	15:07.44i, 15:17.72	15:33.99- 19
Little	Mackenzie	AUS	22.12.96	179/73	JT	61.42	60.36- 18
* Liu Hong		CHN	12.5.87	161/48	20kW	1:27:48	1:24:38- 15
Liu Lu		CHN	9.11.98		JT	58.03	52.81- 19
* Liu Shiying		CHN	24.9.93	179/76	JT	67.29	67.12- 18
Liu Tingting		CHN	29.1.90	178/87	HT	68.25	73.06- 14
Ljungberg	Emma	SWE	23.1.94		DT	58.18	55.15- 19
Llano	Beatrice Nedberge	NOR	14.12.97	169/90	HT	69.78	71.43- 19
Lobun	Helen Ekarare	KEN	18.3.99	170/46	1500	4:10.00	4:07.06- 17
3000	8:43.33		8:48.69- 18		5000	15:03.09	15:12.89- 16
Loga	Rose	FRA-J	27.7.02	177/72	HT	66.54	59.66- 19
Logue	Cailie	USA	4.1.99	164/50	10000	32:19.37	33:36.00- 19
Lokedi	Sharon	KEN	10.3.95	168/54	5000	15:13.04i, 15:18.03	15:15.47i, 15:27.09- 18
					10000	31:11.07	32:09.20- 18

Name		Nat	Born	Ht/Wt	Event	2020 Mark	Pre-2020 Best
López	Yaniuvis	CUB	1.2.86	180/71	SP	17.20	18.92- 17
Lorek	Antonina	POL	11.2.95	168/52	50kW	4:41:16	4:46:44- 19
Lotout	Marion	FRA	19.11.89	165/54	PV	4.55i, 4.55	4.60- 13
Lu Huihui		CHN	26.6.89	171/68	JT	67.61	67.98- 19
Lu Minjia		CHN	29.12.90	174/60	LJ	6.50	6.50- 18
Lu Xiuzhi		CHN	26.10.93	167/52	20kW	1:32:31	1:25:12- 15
Luchsova	Alina	BLR-J	30.8.01	163/52	400	51.84	52.94- 19
Lukyanenkova	Polina	RUS	15.7.98	172/62	LJ	6.57	6.64- 19
* Luo Na		CHN	8.10.93	173/75	HT	69.44i	75.02- 18
Lutkovskaya	Alyona	RUS	15.3.96	164/55	PV	4.40i, 4.40	4.61- 15
Luzolo	Maryse	GER	13.3.95	169/54	LJ	6.53	6.61- 17
Lyakhova	Olha	UKR	18.3.92	174/57	800	2:01.44	1:58.64- 15
Lyra	Viviane	BRA	29.7.93	172/55	50kW	4:41:07	4:22:46- 19
Lyubushkina	Kristina	RUS	19.9.95		50kW	4:22:24	4:28:52- 19
Ma Zhenxia		CHN	1.8.98		20kW	1:32:25	1:28:00- 19
Mackey	Katie	USA	12.11.87	165/53	1500	4:08.69i	4:03.81- 15
MacLean	Heather	USA	31.8.95	168/55	800	2:00.29	2:01.86- 19
1500	4:05.29i		4:05.27- 19		1M	4:25.98i	4:29.74i, 4:31.13- 19
Madarász	Viktória	HUN	12.5.85	153/46	20kW	1:33:41	1:30:05- 17
Maeda	Honami	JPN	17.7.96	166/43	10000	31:34.94	32:13.87- 18
* Mageean	Ciara	IRL	12.3.92	168/56	800	1:59.69	2:00.79- 16
1000	2:31.06	2:38.86- 19	1500	4:06.42i, 4:10.99	4:00.15- 19	3000	8:48.27i	8:55.09i- 15
* Mahuchikh	Yaroslava	UKR-J	19.9.01	181/55	HJ	2.02i, 2.00	2.04- 18
Maines	Latavia	USA	.98	178/105	SP	17.49i	16.46- 18
Maisch	Katharina	GER	12.6.97	177/78	SP	17.98i	17.46- 18
Maiwald	Anna	GER	21.7.90	176/62	Hep	6112	6174- 19
Mäkelä	Kristiina	FIN	20.11.92	185/67	TJ	14.30, 14.33w	14.38i- 19, 14.31- 18
Makeyeva	Yuliya	BLR	5.11.00		JT	57.34	57.12- 19
Mäki	Kristiina	CZE	22.9.91	170/50	1500	4:08.41i	4:06.61- 19
Mäkitörmä	Senja	FIN	31.5.94	180/82	SP	17.01	16.95- 18
Malácová	Romana	CZE	15.5.87	164/57	PV	4.52i, 4.46	4.62i- 16, 4.61- 17
Malíková	Barbora	CZE-J	30.12.01	179/64	400	51.65	52.37- 19
Malone	Chantel	IVB	2.12.91	175/62	LJ	6.74	6.90- 19
* Malyshik	Hanna	BLR	4.2.94	175/90	HT	75.45	76.26- 18
* Mamona	Patrícia	POR	21.11.88	168/53	TJ	14.33i, 14.26	14.65- 16
Manson	Nikki	GBR	15.10.94	174/65	HJ	1.93i	1.90i, 1.87- 19
Mansy	Megan	USA	27.3.94	168/52	1500	4:09.82	4:08.22- 19
					3000	8:54.40i	9:22.80i- 16
Marie-Hardy	Diane	FRA	19.2.96	166/59	Hep	5772	6015- 18
Markaryan (Rebrik)	Vera	RUS	25.2.89	175/62	JT	60.12	67.30- 16
Martinez	Lauren	USA	16.10.96	158/57	PV	4.38i	4.30i- 18, 4.20- 17
Martínez	Yaritza de la Caridad	CUB	3.2.00	171/73	HT	65.73	67.37- 19
Martins	Eliane	BRA	26.5.86	160/49	LJ	6.49	6.74- 19
* Márton	Anita	HUN	15.1.89	171/84	SP	18.77, 17.40i	19.87- 16
					DT	57.18	60.94- 16
* Masilingi	Beatrice	NAM-Y	10.4.03	172/66	200	22.94A, 22.71Aw	23.76- 19
					400	50.42A	52.33A, 52.39- 19
Maslova	Anastasiya	BLR	16.10.97	183/75	HT	68.84	69.48- 18
Mason	Symone	USA	31.8.99	161/55	200	22.76i	23.00- 17
Matheus	Melany del Pilar	CUB-J	19.1.01	172/73	DT	56.92	60.47- 19
Matsuda	Mizuki	JPN	31.5.95	159/46	10000	32:06.46	31:52.42- 19
HMar	69:54+		70:25- 16		Mar	2:21:47	2:22:23- 18
Matsushita	Natsumi	JPN	22.1.95	158/45	10000	32:15.10	32:27.58- 17
Mattuzzi	Isabel	ITA	23.4.95	163/47	3kSt	9:50.73	9:34.02- 18
Maudens	Hanne	BEL	12.3.97	178/64	Hep	6167	6252- 18
Mayho	Jessica	GBR	14.6.93	175/79	HT	65.47	66.44- 19
Mboma	Christine	NAM-Y	22.5.03	165/52	400	51.57A	
* McColgan	Eilish	GBR	25.11.90	176/59	1500	4:03.74	4:00.97- 19
3000	8:40.88		8:31.00- 17		5000	14:57.37	14:46.17- 19
McCorkle	Bailee	USA	19.4.99	163/55	PV	4.46i	4.07- 19
McCoy	Rachel	USA	1.8.95	180/70	HJ	1.88i	1.93- 16
* McDermott	Nicola	AUS	28.12.96	186/63	HJ	1.98	1.96- 19
McDonald	Alina	USA	26.8.97	168/57	PV	4.52	4.50- 17
McGee	Cory	USA	29.5.92	168/52	800	2:00.16	2:01.61- 18
1500	4:03.64		4:04.14- 19		1M	4:21.81	4:26.79i, 4:27.87- 19
McGuire	Annie	AUS-J	13.6.01		LJ	6.49, 6.52w	6.30- 19
McKinna	Sophie	GBR	31.8.94	172/95	SP	18.16	18.61- 19
McNeal	Brianna	USA	18.8.91	164/55	100	11.22w	11.20- 19
^ McPherson	Inika	USA	29.9.86	163/55	HJ	1.90i	1.96, 2.00dq- 14
* McPherson	Stephenie Ann	JAM	25.11.88	168/55	400	52.20	49.92- 13
McTaggart	Olivia	NZL-J	9.1.00	172/62	PV	4.50	4.46- 19

Name		Nat	Born	Ht/Wt	Event	2020 Mark	Pre-2020 Best
Medeiros	Keely	BRA	30.4.87	180/100	SP	16.97	17.58- 14
Megertu	Alemu	ETH	12.10.97	163/48	HMar	69:57+	66:43- 19
					Mar	2:24:23	2:21:10- 19
Mehra	Rebecca	USA	25.10.94	172/54	800	2:01.09	2:02.85- 19
					1500	4:08.45	4:08.14- 19
* Meijer	Michaela	SWE	30.7.93	172/63	PV	4.83	4.75i- 19, 4.71- 17
Melaku	Sifan	ETH	18.4.97	165/48	Mar	2:23:49	2:25:29- 19
^ Melese	Yebrgual	ETH	18.4.90	164/55	Mar	2:27:03	2:19:36- 18
Merachi	Askale	ETH	4.1.87	164/45	Mar	2:23:29	2:25:03- 19
Merlo	Martina	ITA	19.2.93	165/45	3kSt	9:48.62	9:41.05- 18
Mettler	Maria	USA	14.3.99	160/48	10000	32:09.37	
Mhlanga	Khahisa	GBR	26.12.99		800	2:01.91	2:04.34- 17
* Mihambo	Malaika	GER	3.2.94	170/56	LJ	7.07i, 7.03	7.30- 19
Miller	Polina	RUS	9.6.00	167/52	400	51.51	51.00- 19
* Miller-Uibo	Shaunae	BAH	15.4.94	185/69	100	10.98	11.19- 16
200	21.98		21.88, 21.76St- 17		400	50.52	48.37- 19
Minsewo	Aberash	ETH-J	22.2.01	168/52	3000	8:47.82i	8:51.93- 18
* Mironchik-Ivanova	Anastasiya	BLR	13.4.89	171/54	LJ	6.94	7.08, 7.22w- 12
Mismas-Zrimsek	Marusa	SLO	24.10.94	161/50	1500	4:03.05	4:06.64- 19
3000	8:46.44	9:02.91- 15		5000	15:38.33	16:19.04- 18 3kSt	9:20.68 9:20.97- 19
* Mitchell	Kathryn	AUS	10.7.82	168/72	JT	59.82	68.92- 18
Mitchell	Morgan	AUS	3.10.94	177/64	800	2:01.58	2:00.06- 19
Mitkova	Milena	BUL	26.1.90	168/60	LJ	6.50i	6.45- 15, 6.50W- 17
Mitton	Sarah	CAN	20.6.96	170/82	SP	18.84	18.52- 18
Miyashita	Risa	JPN	26.4.84	171/71	JT	57.51	60.86- 16
Mo Jiadie		CHN	6.1.00	162/50	400h	56.77	56.70- 19
Mokhnyuk	Anastasiya	UKR	1.1.91	175/67	Hep	5925	6359- 15
Moll	Amanda	USA-Y	31.1.05		PV	4.36u, 4.19	3.65- 19
* Møller	Anna Emilie	DEN	28.7.97	168/52	5000	15:21.0	15:07.70- 19
Möllers	Ria	GER	5.3.96	180/66	PV	4.40	4.31- 19
Molnár	Janka	HUN-J	5.1.01	172/57	400h	56.94	57.64- 19
Monson	Alicia	USA	13.5.98	168/52	3000	8:53.69i	8:45.97i- 19
5000	15:14.71	15:31.26i- 19. 15:38.32- 18			10000	31:10.84	33:02.91- 19
Montag	Jemima	AUS	15.2.98	159/50	20kW	1:33:15	1:30:51- 19
Montag	Jennifer	GER	11.2.98	164/48	100	11.23	11.36, 11.29w- 19
Montcalm	Noelle	CAN	3.4.88	166/53	400h	56.85	55.81- 14
Montoya	Maggie	USA	2.5.95	165/48	10000	32:06.87	33:40.85- 19
^ Montsho	Amantle	BOT	4.7.83	173/57	400	51.22A	49.33- 13
Moore	Jasmine	USA-J	1.5.01	175/61	LJ	6.47i	6.39, 6.41w- 18
					TJ	13.90i	13.86- 19, 13.83w- 18
Moraa	Mary	KEN	15.1.00	161/54	400	51.99A	51.75- 19
Morales	Silinda Oneisi	CUB	30.8.00	170/70	DT	58.50	59.07- 19
Moravcsik	Angéla	HUN	13.5.96	171/65	JT	58.42	59.64- 19
* Morejón	Glenda	ECU	30.5.00		20kW	1:29:32	1:25:29- 19
Moreno	Arantza	ESP	16.1.95	173/67	JT	58.44	59.69- 18
* Morris	Sandi	USA	8.7.92	172/65	PV	4.91i, 4.83	5.00- 16
^ Morrison	Natasha	JAM	17.11.92	170/57	100	11.25	10.96- 15
Moser	Angelica	SUI	9.10.97	168/63	PV	4.66	4.65i- 19, 4.61- 17
Moton	Akealy	USA	26.11.98		SP	17.61i	17.46- 19
Mpande	Felistus	ZAM	29.5.96	164/48	800	2:00.10A	
* Muir	Laura	GBR	9.5.93	162/54	800	1:58.44i, 1:58.84	1:58.42- 19
1000	2:30.82		2:31.93i- 17, 2:33.92- 18		1500	3:57.40	3:55.22- 16
* Müller	Nadine	GER	21.11.85	192/95	DT	60.44I	68.89- 12
Mullina	Olga	RUS	1.8.92	166/60	PV	4.45i, 4.40	4.67- 19
Murillo	María Lucelly	COL	5.5.91	170/62	JT	59.66	61.46A- 19
Murto	Wilma	FIN	11.6.98	182/68	PV	4.60i, 4.60	4.71i- 16, 4.60- 18
Musikhina	Irina	RUS	7.6.88		50kW	4:32:11	-
* Muze	Lina	LAT	4.12.92	182/75	JT	63.19	64.87- 19
Mwangi	Rebecca	KEN-J	15.6.01	148/36	5000	14:55.32	15:32.64- 19
Mwikali	Agnes Mukari	KEN-J	15.12.02	152/44	3000	8:52.22	8:54.71- 18
					5000	15:09.32	
Myers	Tamara	BAH	27.7.93	173/55	LJ	6.50	6.51, 6.61w- 17
Mykhaylova	Darya	UKR	29.4.89	182/60	Mar	2:27:29	2:28:15- 19
Mykolenko	Mariya	UKR	4.4.94	170/58	400h	56.58	56.25- 18
Nabeshima	Rina	JPN	16.12.93	160/45	10000	31:31.52	31:28.81- 17
* Nageotte	Katie	USA	13.6.91	168/59	PV	4.92	4.91Ai- 18, 4.82- 19
* Nakaayi	Halimah	UGA	16.10.94	160/66	800	2:01.96i	1:58.39- 18
					1000	2:32.12	2:34.88- 19
* Nanyondo	Winnie	UGA	23.8.93	164/48	800	2:00.49	1:58.63- 14
1000	2:36.54+		2:36.13- 18		1500	4:06.13i, 4:07.94	3:59.56- 19
Neale (- Markovc)	Amy-Eloise	GBR	5.8.95	176/57	1500	4:09.44	4:09.31- 19

INDEX

Name		Nat	Born	Ht/Wt	Event	2020 Mark		Pre-2020 Best	
Nelson	Karisa	USA	12.6.96	173/54	1500	4:08.48		4:06.14-	10
* Nelvis	Sharika	USA	10.5.90	178/64	110h	13.09		12.34-	15
Nemes	Rita	HUN	30.11.89	178/65	Hep	6192		5960-	19
Newell	Anicka	CAN	5.8.93	175/64	PV	4.56Ai, 4.55A		4.65-	17
* Newman	Alysha	CAN	29.6.94	172/67	PV	4.63i		4.82-	19
Neziri	Nooralotta	FIN	9.11.92	174/60	100h	12.84		12.81-	16
Ngarambe	Yolanda	SWE	14.9.91	166/54	1500	4:08.81		4:03.43-	19
Ngige Wanjuhi	Monicah	KEN	7.11.93	172/52	HMar	69:29		67:29-	19
Nguyen	Anasztázia	HUN	9.1.93	160/52	LJ	6.61		6.43-	18
Ni Yuanyuan		CHN	6.4.95		20kW	1:30:56		1:29:01-	19
* Nidbaykina	Darya	RUS	26.12.94	168/57	TJ	14.17, 14.27w		14.64-	19
Nielsen	Janne	DEN	8.6.93	173/63	TJ	13.99		13.74, 13.83w-	19
Nielsen	Laviai	GBR	13.3.96	168/54	400	51.70		50.83-	19
Nielsen	Lina	GBR	13.3.96	168/54	400h	56.99		56.67-	19
* Niiya	Hitomi	JPN	26.2.88	166/43	5000	14:55.83		15:10.20-	12
10000	30:20.44				30:56.70- 19	HMar	66:38		71:41-	08
* Nikiforova	Margarita	RUS	19.8.98		50kW	3:59:56		4:05:58-	19
Nikisenko	Marina	MDA	28.6.86	185/85	HT	68.45		72.53-	15
Nishida	Misaki	JPN	7.8.91	146/36	10000	32:09.91		32:22.29-	19
Nishihara	Kasumi	JPN	1.3.89	162/	5000	15:23.88		15:20.20-	15
Njobwu	Rhodah	ZAM	29.1.94	176/56	100	11.20A			?
Noennig	Samantha	USA	28.7.98	180/85	SP	18.17i		18.14-	19
Nokelainen	Heidi	FIN	30.9.90	170/68	JT	60.43		62.13-	16
* Novikova	Marina	RUS	1.3.89		20kW	1:27:25		1:25:03-	15
Novotná	Jana	CZE	26.1.99	175/65	Hep	5878		5905-	19
Novozhylova	Iryna	UKR	7.1.86	175/90	HT	72.61		74.10-	12
Nugent	Ackera	JAM-J	29.4.02	168/57	100h	13.10w		13.24-	19
O'Donoghue	Abigail	USA	21.5.99	178/60	HJ	1.89i		1.82i, 1.81-	19
O'Keeffe	Fiona	USA	24.5.98	159/50	10000	32:12.28		33:36.25-	18
Obermaier	Anna-Lena	GER	10.7.96		Hep	5715		5535-	19
* Obiri	Hellen	KEN	13.12.89	160/50	2000	5:39.70+		5:34.83-	17
1500	4:10.53	3:57.05- 14		3000	8:22.54		8:20.88- 14	5000	14:22.12	14:18.37- 17
Oboya	Bendere	AUS	17.4.00	165/44	400	52.06		51.21-	19
Odineva	Tatyana	RUS	25.5.83	181/64	HJ	1.88i		1.91-	19
* Ofili	Cindy	GBR	5.8.94	172/60	100h	12.88		12.60-	15
Ogasawara	Shuri	JPN	3.10.00	161/42	10000	32:10.69		32:23.88-	19
Ogbeta	Naomi	GBR	18.4.98	180/64	TJ	13.83i, 13.74		14.15-	18
Ogritsko	Mariya	RUS	1.3.94	179/84	DT	57.32		58.69-	19
* Ogrodníková	Nikola	CZE	18.8.90	175/73	JT	64.22		67.40-	19
Ogunleye	Yemisi	GER	3.10.98	183/67	SP	17.36		17.36-	19
Ohara	Rei	JPN	10.8.90	165/47	Mar	2:28:12		2:23:20-	16
Ojaloo	Kati	EST	31.1.90	165/72	HT	71.50		68.16-	19
* Okada	Kumiko	JPN	17.10.91	158/47	20kW	1:29:56		1:27:41-	19
* Okolo	Courtney	USA	15.3.94	168/54	400	51.52		49.71-	16
Okoronkwo	Chinne	USA	26.9.97	168/	PV	4.35i		4.33i, 4.32-	19
Oksyannikova	Aleksandra	RUS	16.6.93		50kW	4:39:10		4:40:00-	18
Okuneva	Oksana	UKR	14.3.90	175/62	HJ	1.92		1.98-	14
Oliver	Imani	USA	7.3.93	165/59	TJ	13.80Ai		14.02- 16, 14.22w-	18
* Oliver	Javianne	USA	26.12.94	155/57	100	11.44, 11.27w		11.10, 11.04w-	18
* Olyanovska	Lyudmila	UKR	20.2.93	172/57	20kW	1:29:13		1:27:09-	15
Onishi	Hikari	JPN	26.4.00	158/44	10000	32:10.56		32:35.64-	19
Onnen	Imke	GER	17.8.94	190/66	HJ	1.96i		1.96i, 1.94-	19
Onyekwere	Chioma	NGR	28.6.94	180/100	DT	59.99		61.38-	19
Orbán	Éva	HUN	29.11.84	173/75	HT	65.32		73.44-	13
Orcel	Claire	BEL	2.12.97	191/68	HJ	1.91i, 1.88		1.94-	19
Ordóñez	Johana	ECU	12.12.87	166/52	20kW	1:32:10		1:31:36-	19
Orel	Anna Maria	EST	11.12.96	171/70	HT	66.24		69.85-	19
* Orji	Keturah	USA	5.3.96	166/61	LJ	6.68		6.81-	18
					TJ	14.60Ai, 14.14		14.72-	19
Ortiz	Coralys	PUR	16.4.85	178/61	JT	56.10		60.37-	16
Ortiz	Mirna	GUA	28.2.87	158/44	20kW	1:32:43		1:28:32-	13
Orton	Whittni	USA		165/50	1M	4:29.76i		4:35.44i-	18
1500	4:12.34i				4:13.58- 19	3000	8:49.63#i			
Osa	Mahiro	JPN	26.11.99	173/65	JT	56.58		56.48-	16
Osakue	Daisy	ITA	16.1.96	181/74	DT	59.98		61.69-	19
Osika	Shannon	USA	15.6.93	161/48	800	2:02.11i		2:02.36-	17
1500	4:09.32Ai	4:01.80- 19		1M	4:28.79i		4:25.47- 18	3000	9:00.42i	8:56.52i- 17
^ Oskan-Clarke	Shelayna	GBR	20.1.90	167/54	800	2:02.22		1:58.86-	15
Ostrander	Allie	USA	24.12.96	158/45	3000	8:48.94i		8:54.27i-	16
					5000	15:19.71i		15:16.38i- 18, 15:24.74-	16
Ovchinnikova	Kristina	KAZ-J	21.3.01	183/62	HJ	1.88i		1.80-	19

Name		Nat	Born	Ht/Wt	Event	2020 Mark	Pre-2020 Best
Paesler	Carolin	GER	16.12.90	167/72	HT	70.99	70.76- 14
Pahlitzsch	Karolina	GER	5.4.94	174/61	400	51.88	52.60- 19
* Palameika	Madara	LAT	18.6.87	184/76	JT	58.91	66.18- 16
Palkina	Sofiya	RUS	9.6.98	174/70	HT	73.55	72.18- 19
Palmer	Samantha	USA	17.6.91	158/46	10000	32:11.92	33:00.59- 18
Palmisano	Antonella	ITA	6.8.91	166/49	20kW	1:28:40	1:26:36- 17
* Palsyte	Airine	LTU	13.7.92	186/62	HJ	1.92i	2.01i- 17, 1.98- 14
Panova	Yelena	RUS	2.3.87	185/95	DT	61.13	63.92- 18
* Panturoiu	Elena	ROU	24.2.95	170/57	TJ	13.87i	14.47- 18
* Papahrístou	Paraskeví	GRE	17.4.89	170/53	TJ	13.85i	14.73- 16, 14.77w- 12
Paquette	Lauren	USA	27.6.86	163/45	5000	15:10.01	15:14.45- 16
					10000	31:53.72mx, 32:01.25	-0-
Parakhonko	Svetlana	BLR	12.6.97	166/54	100h	13.09	13.18- 19
Parnova	Elizaveta	AUS	9.5.94	175/57	PV	4.50	4.60- 19
Partridge	Bethan	GBR	11.7.90	178/60	HJ	1.91i	1.89i- 17, 1.87- 15
Pasechnik	Alena	BLR	17.4.95		SP	18.28	18.15i, 18.01- 19
Pasqualetti	Leah	USA-J	25.8.01	158/47	PV	4.47u, 4.34i	4.03i, 4.00- 19
* Patterson	Eleanor	AUS	22.5.96	182/66	HJ	1.99	1.96- 13
Patterson	Liz	USA	9.6.88	183/65	HJ	1.90Ai	1.94- 17
Patterson	Marys Adela	CUB-J	16.10.01	173/60	Hep	5767	5630- 19
Paulino	Marileidy	DOM	25.10.96	172/58	400	51.88	56.30- 17?
Pechnikova	Svetlana	RUS	6.9.94		JT	58.91	59.32- 18
Peeters	Tori	NZL	17.5.94	174/67	JT	62.04	57.00- 18
^ Peinado	Robeilys	VEN	26.11.97	168/62	PV	4.78i, 4.35	4.70A- 19
* Peleteiro	Ana	ESP	2.12.95	171/52	TJ	13.90i	14.73i, 14.59- 19
Pen	Marta	POR	31.7.93	163/46	1500	4:06.91	4:03.99- 18
Pepelnak	Eva	SLO	4.10.00		TJ	13.70	13.68- 18
Pérez	Keily Linet	CUB-J	26.4.01	160/50	100h	13.12, 13.05w	13.31, 13.27w- 19, 13.2- 18
Pérez	Leyanis	CUB-J	10.1.02	182/67	TJ	14.15	14.13- 19
Pérez	Marta	ESP	19.4.93	169/53	1500	4:07.37i	4:04.88- 18
Pérez	Paola	ECU	21.12.89	148/55	20kW	1:32:04A	1:29:06- 17
* Pérez	Yaimé	CUB	29.5.91	172/80	DT	64.76	69.39- 19
* Perkovic	Sandra	CRO	21.6.90	183/80	DT	65.93	71.41- 17
Petersen	Laura	DEN	28.12.00	168/53	5000	15:21.44	16:10.44- 19
					10000	32:19.65mx	35:24.83mx- 18
Petkova	Mikhaela	BUL	11.1.99		JT	60.36	50.71- 19
* Petrivskaya	Zalina	MDA	5.2.88	174/90	HT	72.90	74.70- 19
Petrokaite	Jogaile	LTU	30.9.95		LJ	6.57	6.50, 6.52w- 16
* Petrova	Gabriela	BUL	29.6.92	167.61	LJ	6.41, 6.54w	6.62- 19
					TJ	14.38	14.66, 14.85w- 15
Petrova	Lyudmila	RUS	15.12.93	168/58	PV	4.51i	4.45i, 4.35- 19
Pidluzhnaya	Yuliya	RUS	1.10.88	180/63	LJ	6.47	6.87- 15
Pieroni	Idea	ITA-J	18.9.02	182/66	HJ	1.90i	1.85- 19
Pinedo	Ainhoa	ESP	17.2.83	171/60	50kW	4:40:45	4:18:56- 18
Pinto	Tatjana	GER	2.7.92	170/56	100	11.21	11.00, 10.96w- 17
Písová	Martina	CZE	20.7.94		JT	57.90	56.37- 19
Plaza	Alexandra	GER	10.8.94	176/58	HJ	1.87	1.88- 12
Pleimling	Noémie	LUX	27.8.93		JT	57.46	54.25- 19
Pluim	Femke	NED	10.5.94	180/62	PV	4.45i, 4.41	4.55- 15
Pólak	Eléni-Klaoúdia	GRE	9.9.96	174/61	PV	4.70	4.50i- 10, 4.46- 18
Pollard	Madison	USA	22.10.98		SP	17.57i	16.94- 19
Poncio	Maritza	GUA	3.12.94	158/41	20kW	1:31:54	1:30:52- 16
Porter	Chanice	JAM	25.5.94	170/57	LJ	6.48i, 6.35	6.75- 18
* Porter	Tiffany	GBR	13.11.87	172/62	100h	12.90, 12.74w	12.51- 14, 12.47w- 12
Pospelova	Natalya	RUS	28.6.96		HT	65.34	65.81- 18
* Povea	Liadagmis	CUB	6.2.96	166/52	TJ	14.55	14.77- 19
Power	Nadia	IRL	11.1.98	157/46	800	2:01.01	2:02.39- 19
Pratt	Aimee	GBR	3.10.97	171/57	3kSt	9:30.73	9:38.91- 19
Pratt	Olivia	USA	21.1.94		10000	31:48.72	33:08.31- 16
Price	Chanelle	USA	22.8.90	166/53	800	2:00.12mx, 2:01.47	1:59.10- 15
Procópio	Raiane	BRA	30.7.97		Hep	5759	5342- 18
Prokopenko	Viktoriya	RUS	17.4.91	174/60	TJ	13.78, 14.15w	14.44i- 18, 14.28- 16
Pryce	Taishia	JAM	14.7.97	170/54	LJ	6.65i	6.45- 18, 6.60w- 19
Pryke	Ashley	CAN	7.7.97	167/73	JT	57.38	57.47- 19
* Pudenz	Kristin	GER	9.2.93	180/92	DT	65.58	64.36- 19 17
Pullola	Emma	FIN	18.12.96	180/65	TJ	13.62	6.48, 6.35- 19
Purdue	Charlotte	GBR	10.6.91	155/47	HMar	68:23	68:10dh, 68:45- 19
* Purrier	Elinor	USA	20.2.95	160/50	800	2:00.70	2:03.55- 19
1500	4:00.77, 4:00.20i		4:02.34- 19		1M	4:16.85i	4:24.88i, 4:30.30- 19
3000	8:56.54i		8:46.43- 18		2M	9:29.17i	9:31.38i- 19
Purtsa	Maria	GER	18.8.95	176/65	TJ	13.67	13.46i, 13.43- 19

Name		Nat	Born	Ht/Wt	Event	2020 Mark	Pre-2020 Best
* Qieyang Shenjie		CHN	11.11.90	160/50	20kW	1:28:27	1:25:16- 12
Qin Huiling		CHN-J	29.11.03		LJ	6.47	
Quach Thi Lan		VIE	18.10.95	173/54	400h	55.98	55.30- 18
* Quigley	Colleen	USA	20.11.92	173/59	1500	4:03.98	4:03.02- 18
2000	5:40.9+i		3000	8:28.71i, 8:48.93		9:13.79i- 13	5000	15:10.42	15:58.90- 13
Quirk	Amelia	GBR	18.12.99	156/45	3000	8:54.09	9:11.20- 18
Rabkova	Diana	BLR	14.6.98		Hep	5937	5372- 19
* Radzivil	Svetlana	UZB	17.1.87	184/61	HJ	1.93i	1.97- 12
Ramírez	Andrea	MEX	5.12.92	164/48	Mar	2:26:34	2:57:47- 18
Ramos	Carmen	ESP	18.6.98	167/60	Hep	5804	5905A- 18, 5643- 19
^ Ramsey	Jessica	USA	26.7.91	165/85	SP	18.95i, 18.64	19.23- 18
Rani	Annu	IND	29.8.92	165/63	JT	61.15A	62.43- 19
Rao Fan		CHN	1.1.96	170/59	TJ	13.86	13.93i- 17, 13.56- 15
Ratcliffe	Julia	NZL	14.7.93	171/66	HT	72.35	71.39- 19
Ratova	Ayman	KAZ	23.4.91		20kW	1:29:31	1:35:00- 18
Redondo	Laura	ESP	3.7.88	165/80	HT	69.02	69.59- 13
* Reekie	Jemma	GBR	6.3.98	164/50	800	1:57.91i, 1:58.63	2:01.45- 19
1000	2:31.11	2:36.79- 18	1500	4:00.52+i, 4:02.20		4:02.09- 19	1M	4:17.88i	4:27.00- 19
Regin	Klaudia	POL	28.8.97	179/76	JT	56.96	57.59- 16
Reh	Alina	GER	23.5.97	174/52	3000	8:51.36	8:39.45- 19, 9:05.07- 14
Ren Shimei		CHN	26.5.96		Hep	5746	5228- 19
* Richardson	Sha'Carri	USA	25.3.00	168/52	100	10.95, 10.79w	10.75- 19
					200	22.00	22.17- 19
* Ricketts	Shanieka	JAM	2.2.92	162/66	TJ	14.43	14.93- 19
Riecke	Lea-Jasmin	GER	25.4.00	182/65	LJ	6.58	6.51- 18
Rionoripo	Purity	KEN	10.6.93	165/48	Mar	2:22:56	2:20:39- 19
Ritter	Julia	GER	13.5.98	180/95	SP	18.14	17.63- 19
					DT	59.64	58.19- 18
* Robert-Michon	Mélina	FRA	18.7.79	180/85	DT	64.14	66.73- 16
Roberts	Kaelin	USA	6.1.99	168/55	400	52.06#i	51.25- 19
Robinson	Na'Asha	USA	23.1.97	168/54	400	51.98Ai	52.00- 17
Roble	Greisys Lázaro	CUB	18.1.00	170/60	100h	13.06w	13.24, 13.01w, 13.0w- 19
Rodrigues	Irina	POR	5.2.91	181/81	DT	62.93	63.96- 16
* Rodríguez	Adriana	CUB	12.7.99	172/62	Hep	6304	6293w, 6113- 19
^ Rodríguez	Rosa	VEN	2.7.86	180/85	HT	71.54	73.64- 13
Rofe-Beketova	Iryna	UKR	18.9.98	180/68	Hep	5827	5705- 19
Rogers	Natosha	USA	7.5.91	164/48	10000	31:12.28	31:54.62- 17
* Rogers	Raevyn	USA	7.9.96	171/64	800	2:01.02	1:57.69- 19
400	52.50			52.06- 18	1000	2:37.10	
* Rojas	Yulimar	VEN	21.10.95	189/75	LJ	6.59i	6.57- 15, 6.79w- 19
					TJ	15.43i, 14.71	15.41- 19
* Roos	Fanny	SWE	2.1.95	173/79	SP	18.77	19.06- 19
					DT	57.17	56.89- 19
Rooth	Andrea	NOR-J	6.3.02	164/50	400h	56.95	58.83- 19
^ Rosa	Chiara	ITA	28.1.83	178/95	SP	17.20i, 17.06	19.15- 07
Ross	Kortney	USA	26.7.92	180/64	PV	4.52	4.63Ai- 19, 4.55- 17
Rossi	Teresa Maria	ITA	12.4.92	181/53	HJ	1.87	1.85- 18
^ Rotaru	Alina	ROU	5.6.93	175/54	LJ	6.69	6.91- 19
Rotich	Caroline	KEN	13.5.84	161/45	HMar	68:53	68:52- 11
Rotich	Naomi	KEN	5.4.94		Mar	2:27:57	2:47:00A- 19
Rout	Yuliya	BLR	22.1.95		Hep	5707	5762- 19
* Rowbury	Shannon	USA	19.9.84	165/52	1500	4:02.56	3:56.29- 15
3000	8:40.26			8:29.39- 14	5000	14:45.11	14:38.92- 16
Rowe	Jelena	USA	1.8.99	193/68	HJ	1.87i	1.90- 19
Rudakova/Chalaya Vera		RUS	20.3.92	175/57	400h	57.01	54.48- 19
^ Rüh	Anna	GER	17.6.93	184/74	DT	57.08	66.14- 15
* Russell	Janieve	JAM	14.11.93	175/63	400	51.67	51.17- 19
					400h	55.40	53.46- 18
Rutto	Stella	KEN	12.12.96	163/50	5000	15:18.82	15:53.25- 19
					3kSt	9:32.90	9:44.07- 19
Ryan	Lauren	AUS	15.3.98	159/46	3000	8:54.54	9:21.21- 16
Rybnikova	Mariya	RUS	28.10.94		JT	57.26	58.80- 18
* Ryzhykova	Anna	UKR	24.11.89	177/67	400	51.70	52.11- 14
					400h	54.54	54.35- 12
^ Ryzih	Lisa	GER	27.9.88	179/60	PV	4.45i, 4.45	4.75i- 17, 4.73- 16
Sabat	Anna	POL	9.11.93	168/53	800	2:00.61	2:00.32- 18
Sado	Fatuma	ETH	11.10.91	165/48	HMar	69:54+	69:02- 11
					Mar	2:27:17	2:24:16- 15
Sadullayeva	Safina	UZB	4.3.98	180/57	HJ	1.90	1.92i, 1.87- 19
Sæten	Amalie	NOR	1.12.97	177/62	1500	4:09.78	4:16.43- 19
* Sagnia	Khaddi	SWE	20.4.94	173/63	LJ	6.92	6.92i- 18, 6.78- 15

Name		Nat	Born	Ht/Wt	Event	2020 Mark	Pre-2020 Best
Sahutoglu	Tugçe	TUR	1.5.88	180/120	HT	67.07	74.17- 12
Saito	Marina	JPN	15.10.95	164/64	JT	58.64	62.37- 17
Sajdoková	Bára	CZE-J	5.10.01	170/48	HJ	1.91	1.86- 19
Sakharuk	Marila	UKR	14.10.95	164/49	20kW	1:29;35	1:33:34- 18
Salman	Kivilcim	TUR	27.3.92	167/80	HT	67.15	72.55- 12
Salminen	Senni	FIN	29.1.96	175/58	LJ	6.56	6.12- 18
					TJ	14.04	13.85- 19
Salming	Bianca	SWE	22.11.98	178/67	HJ	1.87i, 1.87	1.92- 19
					Hep	6042	5985- 18
* Salpeter	Lonah Chemtai	ISR	12.12.88	165/52	1Hr	18,571	
HMar	68:31		66:09- 19		Mar	2:17:45	2:19:46- 19
Samba-Mayela	Cyréna	FRA	31.10.00	166.57	100h	12.73	13.00- 18
Sánchez	Aries	VEN	1.3.96	170/59	LJ	6.62	6.54- 18
Sánchez-Escribano	Irene	ESP	25.9.92	173/57	3kSt	9:48.57	9:31.84- 18
dos Santos	Gabriele	BRA	23.2.95	175/63	TJ	14.17	14.03. 14.06w- 19
Sarna	Angelika	POL	1.10.97	178/55	800	2:00.89	2:02.53- 18
Sarrapio	Patricia	ESP	16.11.82	168/58	TJ	13.78	14.27- 19, 14.30w- 12
Sato	Sayaka	JPN	27.5.94	156/41	5000	15:16.52	15:27.47- 19
10000	31:30.19		31:59.64- 19		Mar	2:23:27	-
Sato	Yuka	JPN	21.7.92	162/63	JT	60.69	59.22- 12
* Saunders	Raven	USA	15.5.96	165/125	SP	17.84i	19.76- 17
* Saunders	Sha'Keela	USA	18.12.93	168/59	LJ	6.50w, 6.41	6.90i, 6.92w- 17, 6.89- 16
^ Sawyers	Jazmin	GBR	21.5.94	167/52	LJ	6.69, 6.74w	6.86- 18
Schaefer	Josephine	USA	10.4.99		SP	17.24i	15.56i, 15.51- 19
* Schäfer	Carolin	GER	5.12.91	176/66	Hep	6319	6836- 17
Scheper	Jeannelle	LCA	21.11.94	175/60	HJ	1.92i, 1.88	1.96- 15
Scherrer	Chiara	SUI	24.1.96	163/45	3kSt	9:51.27	9:44.59- 18
Schilder	Jessica	NED	19.3.99	177/82	SP	18.27	17.50- 19
* Schippers	Dafne	NED	15.6.92	179/68	100	11.26	10.81- 15
					200	22.94	21.63- 15
Schlachtenhaufen	Helen	USA	14.3.95	163/47	1500	4:08.30	4:03.59- 19
Schlumpf	Fabienne	SUI	17.11.90	183/62	5000	15:10.31	15:23.44- 18
10000	32:16.37		-0-		HMar	68:38	70:17- 17
Schneider	Rachel	USA	18.7.91	168/52	10000	31:09.79	-0-
Schol	Lisanne	NED	22.6.91	176/63	JT	59.53	60.92- 19
Schöneborn	Deborah	GER	13.3.94	176/57	Mar	2:26:55	2:31:18- 19
^ Schrott	Beate	AUT	15.4.88	177/68	100h	13.06	12.82- 12
Schwab	Corinna	GER	5.4.99	174/61	400	51.73	53.09- 17
Schweizer	Karissa	USA	4.5.96	164/50	1500	4:00.02	4:06.77- 18
1M	4:24.32#i		4:27.54i- 18		2000	5:40.6+i	
3000	8:25.70i, 8:48.37		8:41.60i- 18, 8:43.15- 19		5000	14:26.34	14:45.18- 19
Sclabas	Delia	SUI	8.11.00	161/47	800	2:01.93i	2:01.29- 18
Scott	Dominique	RSA	24.6.92	160/50	2M	9:31.98i	
1500	4:11.83		4:07.20- 18		5000	15:20.84i, 15:28.51	14:59.08- 19
Seccafien	Andrea	CAN	27.8.90	152/44	HMar	69:38	73:19- 18
See	Heidi	AUS	9.8.89	168/52	3000	8:52.94i	8:54.13- 17
Segrave	Hannah	GBR	14.4.95	165/53	800	2:01.89	2:00.18- 19
Seidel	Molly	USA	12.7.94	163/48	HMar	69:35	70:27- 1
					Mar	2:25:13	-0-
Sekgodiso	Prudence	RSA-J	5.1.02		800	2:02.16A	2:03.98A- 19
Sekimoto	Moeka	JPN	23.2.00	168/52	400h	56.96	57.73- 19
Semashko	Veronika	RUS	17.10.90	172/57	LJ	6.52i	6.79- 13
^ Sendriute	Zinaida	LTU	20.12.84	188/89	DT	58.12	65.97- 13
Sergeyeva	Nadezhda	RUS	12.3.94		20kW	1:30:09	1:29:43- 19
Serksniené	Agné	LTU	18.2.88	173/60	400	51.80	50.99- 18
Serra	Francislaine	POR	1.10.94		SP	17.19i, 17.10	15.72- 18
* Seyaum	Dawit	ETH	27.7.96	158/45	1500	4:04.24i	3:58.09- 16
Seymour	Ka'tia	USA	3.10.97	164/50	200	22.82#i	22.55- 19
Shamotina	Alyona	UKR	27.12.95	178/96	HT	67.04	72.37- 17
Shanahan	Danielle	USA	13.8.94	164/48	10000	31:22.86	32:22.59- 19
Shargina	Olga	RUS	24.7.96		20kW	1:31:16	1:29:56- 17
Shatirishvili	Sopo	GEO	15.1.95	180/130	SP	16.90i	15.58- 18
Shauri	Magdalena	TAN	25.2.96	163/48	HMar	66:37	74:57- 14
Shchagina	Anna	RUS	7.12.91	166/54	1500	4:07.51i	4:01.46- 15
					3000	8:52.53i	9:05.35- 16
Shevchuk	Hanna	UKR	18.7.96	165/55	20kW	1:31:55	1:35:18- 19
Shone	Guteni	ETH	17.11.91	166/50	Mar	2:20:11	2:23:32- 16
* Shukh	Alina	UKR	12.2.99	175/60	HJ	1.91	1.92- 16
				0	Hep	6386	6381- 17
* Sidorova	Anzhelika	RUS	28.6.91	166/52	PV	4.95i, 4.80	4.95- 19
Sieg	Tarynn	USA	4.9.98		SP	16.93i	17.44- 19

Name		Nat	Born	Ht/Wt	Event	2020 Mark	Pre-2020 Best
da Silva	Izabela	BRA	2.8.95	178/95	DT	60.15	58.85- 18
* Silva	Yarisley	CUB	1.6.87	169/68	PV	4.74i	4.91- 15
Simon	Kennedy	USA	12.2.00	168/54	400	51.81#i	52.28- 19
* Simpson	Jenny	USA	23.8.86	165/50	3000	8:51.49i	8:29.58- 14
					5000	14:58.67i	14:56.26- 13
Sinigaglia	Luisa	ITA	27.9.97		JT	58.41	52.84- 19
Sipponen	Salla	FIN	13.3.95	178/80	DT	59.52	58.36- 18
* Sisson	Emily	USA	12.10.91	165/47	HMar	67:26	67:30- 19
^ Skoog	Sofie	SWE	7.6.90	181/65	HJ	1.90	1.94- 16
Skrzyszowska	Pia	POL-J	20.4.01	168/51	100h	13.01	13.35- 19
Skvarková	Stanislava	SVK	20.4.96	165/52	100h	12.90	13.08- 19
* Skvortsova	Violetta	BLR	15.4.98	178/58	LJ	6.56i	6.45- 15
					TJ	14.28i, 14.17	13.95- 18, 14.21w- 17
Slepova	Darya	RUS	10.4.00	174/60	HJ	1.88i	1.86- 19
Sloot	Bregje	NED	28.1.00		800	2:01.53	2:07.86- 19
* Slott Petersen	Sara	DEN	9.4.87	171/57	400h	55.20	53.55- 16
Smets	Fanny	BEL	21.4.86	173/58	PV	4.40i, 4.32	4.51- 19
Smiech	Aleksandra	POL	2.10.97	170/70	HT	67.47	68.96- 19
Smith	Amina	USA	29.8.92	175/59	HJ	1.92i	1.91- 16
Smith	Jaci	USA	5.1.97	161/48	10000	32:10.31	32:28.15- 18
Smith	Kayla	USA	6.5.97	173/59	PV	4.37i	4.31- 19
Snowden	Katie	GBR	9.3.94	171/55	800	2:01.91mx, 2:02.40	2:00.92mx-17, 2:01.75- 18
					1500	4:09.63	4:05.29- 17
Soares	Nubia	BRA	26.3.96	176/52	TJ	13.84	14.69- 18
Sobchuk	Olena	UKR	23.11.95	172/53	20kW	1:29:12	1:33:25- 16
Soboleva	Alena	BLR	11.5.93	180/96	HT	70.62	72.86- 15
Söderholm	Linn	SWE	5.5.96	173/58	3kSt	9:50.17	10:03.09- 19
* Sokolova	Yelena	RUS	23.7.86	170/61	LJ	6.51	7.07- 12
Solovyova	Yevgeniya	RUS	28.6.86	185/90	SP	17.24	18.71i- 12, 18.50- 16
Sommers	Paige	USA-Y	20.5.03	172/62	PV	4.42	4.11- 19
Song Jiayuan		CHN	15.9.97	179/90	SP	18.20	18.32- 19
* Spanovic	Ivana	SRB	10.5.90	176/65	LJ	6.80	7.24i- 17, 7.10- 16
Spelmeyer	Ruth Sophia	GER	19.9.90	174/61	400	52.15	51.43- 16
* Spencer	Levern	LCA	23.6.84	180/54	HJ	1.89i, 1.88	1.98- 10
Spiler	Barbara	SLO	2.1.92	184/79	HT	66.71	71.25- 12
Spill	Tanja	GER	16.12.95	167/52	800	2:02.07	2:10.63- 16
Spiridonova	Natalya	RUS-J	31.7.02	179/60	HJ	1.88i, 1.84	1.91-19
* Spotáková	Barbora	CZE	30.6.81	182/80	JT	65.19	72.28- 08
* Sprunger	Léa	SUI	5.3.90	183/69	400	51.93i, 52.51	50.52- 18
	200 23.08				22.38- 16	400h	54.98	54.06- 19
Staehli	Julie-Anne	CAN	21.12.93	159/48	3000	8:47.97i	9:01.27- 19
Stafford	Lucia	CAN	17.8.98	162/52	800	2:02.07	2:02.94- 19
Stanciu	Ana	ROU	13.6.00		HT	67.82	66.24- 19
Stanciu	Daniela	ROU	15.10.87	175/57	HJ	1.90i, 1.88	1.96- 19
Stanková	Eliska	CZE	11.11.84	181/82	DT	58.31	60.48- 16
Steinacker	Marike	GER	4.3.92	184/80	DT	59.75	63.24- 19
Steiner	Abby	USA	24.11.99	168/55	200	22.57i	22.59- 19
Sterckendries	Vanessa	BEL	5.5.89		HT	69.91	67.78- 19
^ Stevens	Jeneva	USA	28.10.89	178/102	SP	18.24i	19.11- 16
Stevens	Robyn	USA	24.4.83	155/45	50kW	4:37:33	4:34:24- 19
Steyn	Gerda	RSA	3.3.90		Mar	2:26:51	2:27:48- 19
Stoner	Paige	USA	31.1.96	160/60	10000	32:30.13	32:07.36- 19
Storm	Ida	SWE	26.12.91	190/95	HT	70.46	71.52- 17
Strachan	Anthonique	BAH	22.8.93	168/57	200	22.67	22.32- 13
* Stratton	Brooke	AUS	12.7.93	168/58	LJ	6.71, 6.78w	7.05- 16
Strebkova	Nataliya	UKR	6.3.95	167/50	3kSt	9:41.38	9:37.28- 18
Strickler	Amelia	GBR	24.1.94	171/100	SP	17.97i, 17.61	17.83- 19
* Strokova	Yekaterina	RUS	17.12.89	184/80	DT	63.90	65.78- 14
Su Lingdan		CHN	12.1.97	175/59	JT	60.28	62.59- 19
Su Xinyue		CHN	8.11.91	179/70	DT	61.94	65.25- 19
Suárez	Gabriela Anahí	ECU-J	2.2.01	165/52	100	11.16A	11.40A- 19, 11.29w- 18
Suchá	Linda	CZE-J	28.9.01	175/60	TJ	13.65	11.72- 19
* Suhr	Jenn	USA	5.2.82	180/64	PV	4.85Ai	5.03i- 16, 4.93- 18
Sulek	Adrianna	POL	3.4.99	173/62	Hep	5901	6171- 19
Sun Xiaomei		CHN	2.12.96		JT	57.58	55.84- 19
Surdu	Dimitriana	MDA	12.4.94	174/95	SP	18.50i	18.83- 11
* Sutej	Tina	SLO	7.11.88	173/59	PV	4.75	4.73- 19
Suzuki	Miho	JPN	18.11.96	162/48	100h	13.39, 13.12w	13.21A, 13.26- 19
Suzuki	Yuka	JPN	14.9.99	159/48	10000	32:11.66	31:37.88- 19
Sváblková	Amálie	CZE	22.11.99	181/64	PV	4.55	4.51- 18
Sweatman	Hailey	USA	17.12.97		PV	4.35i	4.20- 18

INDEX

Name		Nat	Born	Ht/Wt	Event	2020 Mark	Pre-2020 Best
* Swiety-Ersetic	Justyna	POL	3.12.92	167/57	400	51.33	50.41- 18
* Swoboda	Ewa	POL	26.7.97	167/62	100	11.24	11.07- 19
Szabó	Barbara	HUN	17.2.90	175/59	HJ	1.88i, 1.84	1.94- 15
Szilágyi	Réka	HUN	19.1.96	173/65	JT	62.45	60.44- 19
* Ta Lou	Marie Josée	CIV	18.11.88	159/57	100	11.14	10.85, 10.7mx- 18
Tabacková	Nikol	CZE	24.1.98	164/61	JT	57.24	57.50- 19
Tabb	Elaina	USA	17.12.91	173/55	10000	31:45.27	31:55.72- 19
Takemoto	Sae	JPN	23.11.99	160/59	JT	57.43	55.01- 17
Takeyama	Kaena	JPN	30.10.95	163/	HMar	69:12	72:58- 19
Tan Qiujiao		CHN	28.5.00		TJ	13.87	13.77- 19
Tanaka	Hanae	JPN	12.2.90	160/48	Mar	2:27:51	2:26:19- 17
Tanaka	Nozomi	JPN	4.9.99	153/41	1500	4:05.27	4:11.50- 19
3000	8:41.35		8:45.38- 19		5000	15:02.62	15:00.01- 19
Tanui	Rodah	KEN	25.4.91	160/44	Mar	2:27:14	2:25:46- 19
* Tapper	Megan	JAM	18.3.94	169/48	100h	12.96	12.61- 19
Tausaga	Laulauga	USA	22.5.98	188/105	SP	17.96i	18.02- 19
Taushkanova	Anastasiya	RUS	25.3.96		20kW	1:32:35	1:31:33- 19
* Tavernier	Alexandra	FRA	13.12.93	170/82	HT	75.23	74.84- 19
Taylor	Kellyn	USA	22.7.86	167/52	5000	15:11.50	15:19.23- 19
10000	31:07.60		31:40.70- 18		Mar	2:25:22	2:24:29- 18
Tazaki	Yuri	JPN-J	13.2.01	158/43	5000	15:24.61	15:48.95- 19
Teel	Haley	USA	20.6.96	171/88	SP	18.40i, 17.14	17.25- 19
* Teferi	Senbere	ETH	3.5.95	159.45	HMar	65:51	65:32- 19
					Mar	2:25:22	2:24:11- 18
Tejeda	Gladys	PER	30.9.85	162/46	Mar	2:27:07	2:28:12- 15
Terada	Asuka	JPN	14.1.90	166/54	100h	13.03, 12.92w	12.97A, 13.00- 19
Terlyukevich	Anna	BLR	15.8.87		20kW	1:29:59	1:29:39- 14
Tervo	Krista	FIN	15.11.97	165/78	HT	72.12	70.18- 19
Tesfay	Haftamnesh	ETH	28.4.94	162/48	HMar	69:54+	69:02- 18
					Mar	2:27:50	2:20:13- 18
Teshome	Tadu	ETH-J	9.6.01	159/44	HMar	69:57	70:21- 19
* Thiam	Nafissatou	BEL	19.8.94	184/69	LJ	6.79i	6.86- 19
* Thomas	Gabrielle	USA	7.12.96	170/57	200	22.63	22.19, 22.13w- 18
* Thomas-Dodd	Danniel	JAM	11.11.92	168/91	SP	19.18	19.55- 19
* Thompson-Herah	Elaine	JAM	28.6.92	169/57	100	10.85, 10.73w	10.70- 16
					200	22.19	21.66- 15
Tibebu	Hirut	ETH	13.12.94	153/40	Mar	2:23:17	2:23:35-17
Tidwell	Tuesdi	USA	20.9.98	168/57	PV	4.50i	4.33i, 4.32- 19
Tighe	Chloe	AUS	28.9.90	173/54	3000	8:54.9	9:09.82- 18
Timoshenko	Sofiya	RUS	5.1.98		20kW	1:33:07	1:36:42- 19
* Tirop	Agnes	KEN	23.10.95	159/44	2000	5:39.9+	5:42.67- 19
3000	8.22.92		8:27.51- 19		5000	15:06.71A	14:20.68- 19
Tkachuk	Viktoriya	UKR	8.11.94	178/69	400	51.85	52.58- 16
					400h	54.93	55.28- 18
Toimil	María Belén	ESP	5.5.94	175/89	SP	17.21i, 16.90	17.38- 17
Tola	Helen	ETH	21.11.94	166/50	10000	32:12.49	-0-
1Hr	17,974m				Mar	2:23:52	2:21:11- 19
Tolj	Marija	CRO	29.11.99	184/85	DT	60.75	62.76- 19
^ Tomasevic	Dragana	SRB	4.6.82	175/80	DT	59.12	63.63- 06
Tonn	Jessica	USA	15.2.92	164/48	3000	8:54.19#i	9:01.84i- 15, 9:22.32- 14
					5000	15:12.33i	15:18.85- 15
Tracey	Adelle	GBR	27.5.93	164/50	800	1:59.87	1:59.86- 18
1000	2:37.95i		2:34.59- 18		1500	4:07.47	4:10.03mx- 19, 4:10.30- 17
Trapletti	Valentina	ITA	12.7.85	173/53	20kW	1:32:05	1:29:57- 19
Trofimova	Sardana	RUS	28.3.88	164/50	Mar	2:27:08	2:24:38- 15
Tröger	Leonie	GER	22.12.00		JT	57.29	55.72- 19
Tropina	Anna	RUS	3.11.98	161/44	3kSt	9:28.12	9:31.86- 19
* Trost	Alessia	ITA	8.3.93	188/68	HJ	1.90i	2.00i, 1.98- 13
Trost	Katharina	GER	28.6.95	164/47	800	2:00.82	2:00.36- 19
1000	2:37.96i	2:40.29- 19	1500	4:09.43		4:10.71- 18	1M	4:29.35
Tsareva	Yelizaveta	RUS	26.3.93	177/82	HT	70.50	73.22- 18
* Tsegay	Gudaf	ETH	23.1.97	159/45	1500	4:00.09i	3:54.38- 19
2000	5:40.4+ 5:43.6+- 15		3000	8:25.23		8:30.65- 19	5000	14:46.22 14:51.30- 19
Tsinopoúlou	Panayióta	GRE	16.10.90	164/53	20kW	1:31:39	1:33:47- 16
Tsutsui	Sakiho	JPN	19.1.96	154/38	10000	31:36.19	32:02.36- 19
5000	15:32.96		15:36.61- 19		HMar	69:14	70:55- 17
* Tugsuz	Eda	TUR	27.3.97	171/68	JT	60.88	67.21- 17
Tuitoek	Dorcas	KEN	31.1.96	159/45	HMar	67:18	66:33- 19
Tuliamuk/Bolton	Aliphine	USA	5.4.89	163/50	HMar	69:49	69:16- 13
					Mar	2:27:23	2:26:50- 19
Turner	Jessica	GBR	8.8.95	180/60	400h	55.89	55.72- 19

INDEX

Name		Nat	Born	Ht/Wt	Event	2020 Mark	Pre-2020 Best
Turova	Yuliya	RUS	9.6.97		20kW	1:28:36	1:31:59- 19
Tutti	Trinity	CAN	3.5.00		DT	56.95	56.95- 19
Tuuri	Heta	FIN	14.1.95	185/65	HJ	1.88	1.88- 19
^ Twell	Stephanie	GBR	17.8.89	168/54	HMar	68:55	70:52dh. 71:33- 19
* Tzénggo	Elína	GRE-J	2.9.02	172/72	JT	63.96	61.48- 19
Ueda	Momone	JPN	27.6.99	160/61	JT	58.25	57.02- 19
* Ugen	Lorraine	GBR	22.8.91	178/64	LJ	6.74i	7.05- 18
Uloga	Svetlana	RUS	23.11.86	162/55	800	2:01.30	1:59.20- 17
Ummels	Bo	NED	24.8.93	171/50	10000	32:25.41	33:42.60- 19
Ushiro	Orie	JPN	24.8.90	174/68	JT	56.28	59.16- 19
Usoro	Ruth	NGR	8.10.97	161/52	LJ	6.57i	6.61Aw- 19. 6.19- 18
Utsunomiya	Eri	JPN	11.4.93	166/54	400h	57.09	56.84- 18
Valesová	Lenka	CZE	11.8.85	180/80	HT	65.50	70.51- 09
* Vallortigara	Elena	ITA	21.9.91	184/66	HJ	1.96i, 1.88	2.02- 18
Valtanen	Julia	FIN-J	6.5.01	169/67	JT	57.91	54.78- 19
van Daalen	Alida	NED-J	12.4.02		DT	59.15	58.28- 19
van de Wiel	Anne	NED	4.6.97		Hep	5756	5712- 19
van der Reijken	Irene	NED	13.8.93	158/47	3kSt	9:34.80	9:43.76- 19
van Dyk	Jo-Ané	RSA	3.10.97	171/63	JT	56.23A	57.36- 19
van Es	Diane	NED	22.3.99	170/54	3000	8:53.46	9:10.83- 19
van Hunenstijn	Marije	NED	2.3.95	174/61	200	22.91	23.25- 19
van Klinken	Jorinde	NED	2.2.00	180/85	SP	17.72	17.76- 19
					DT	59.59	61.33- 19
Vanderelst	Elise	BEL	27.1.88	172/57	1000	2:37.86	2:42.54- 19
				7	1500	4:05.76	4:05.75- 18
Vandi	Eleonora	ITA	15.3.96	181/58	800	2:01.83	2:00.88- 19
Vanninen	Saga	FIN-Y	4.5.03	172/	Hep	5861	5449- 19
Vaskovskaya	Irina	BLR	2.4.91	179/65	TJ	14.24	14.30i- 18, 14.19- 16
Veiga	Evelise	POR	3.3.96	168/55	LJ	6.64	6.62- 18
					TJ	13.68i, 13.53, 14.16w	14.32- 19
Velazco	Davisleydi Lupes	CUB	4.9.99	170/60	TJ	14.34	14.08- 16, 14.11w- 19
Verdon	Carrie	USA	8.3.94	158/48	10000	32:09.82	33:42.02- 14
Vicenzino	Tania	ITA	1.4.86	167/64	LJ	6.56	6.68i- 19, 6.65- 14
* Vidts	Noor	BEL	30.5.96	177/70	Hep	5837	6194- 19
Vilagos	Adriana	SRB-Y	2.1.04	176/71	JT	57.41	-0-
Viljoen	Sunette	RSA	6.1.83	168/64	JT	58.30A	69.35- 12
* Virbalyte-Dimsiene	Brigita	LTU	1.2.85	165/50	20kW	1:30:54	1:27:59- 18
Visca	Carolina	ITA	31.5.00	169/65	JT	56.78	58.47- 19
* Visser	Nadine	NED	9.2.95	175/63	100	11.25	11.34- 19
					100h	12.68	12.62- 19, 12.57w- 17
* Vita	Claudine	GER	19.9.96	179/81	SP	17.08i	18.09i- 17,17.90- 16
					DT	63.21	65.16- 18
Vityugova	Anastasiya	RUS	13.3.97	184/85	DT	60.64	58.57- 19
Vondrová	Lada	CZE	6.9.99	163/61	400	51.35	51.71- 19
Vovk	Olga	RUS	13.2.93	163/50	3kSt	9:23.86	9:33.70- 16
Vrzalová	Simona	CZE	7.4.88	168/52	1500	4:07.30	4:04.80- 18
Vukovic	Marija	MNE	21.1.92	194/69	HJ	1.88i, 1.84	1.95- 16
Wade	Becky	USA	9.2.89	153/42	HMar	69:40	71:15- 18
Walter	Sydney	USA	15.11.93	170/58	PV	4.50Ai	4.55- 17
Wambui	Esther	KEN-Y	8.5.03	167/49	5000	15:18.56	
* Wang Zheng		CHN	14.12.87	174/108	HT	71.36	77.68- 14
* Wanjiru	Rosemary	KEN	9.12.94	159/44	5000	15:03.49	15:08.61- 18
10000	30:38.18		30:35.75- 19		HMar	65:34	-0-
* Watson	Sage	CAN	20.6.94	175/62	400h	56.29	54.32- 19
Watychowicz	Jessica	USA	27.1.91	161/48	10000	32:11.93	33:19.89- 19
Weerman	Britt	NED-Y	13.6.03	178/62	HJ	1.88i, 1.86	1.85- 19
Weigel	Maya	USA	1.7.95	160/48	10000	32:14.23	-0-
Weightman	Laura	GBR	1.7.91	172/58	1500	4:00.09	4:00.17- 14
2000	5:40.5+	5:44.22- 13	3000	8:26.31		8:26.07- 19 5000	14:35.44 14:44.57- 19
* Weightman	Lisa	AUS	16.1.79	157/44	Mar	2:26:02	2:25:15- 17
Weldu	Nazret	ERI	1.1.90	169/52	HMar	69:47	70:51- 14
Werner	Taylor	USA	1.5.98	165/52	3000	8:51.91i	8:56.97i- 19, 9:16.12- 19
Wesche	Maddison-Lee	NZL	13.6.99	179/85	SP	18.08	18.32- 19
West	Tori	AUS	14.10.95	179/65	Hep	6028	5793- 19
White	Kayla	USA	24.9.96	165/52	100	11.18	10.95- 19
^ Whitney	Kaylin	USA	9.3.98	167/57	400	51.99	52.02- 19
Whyte	Natalliah	JAM	9.8.97	170/55	100	11.15	11.04- 18
Whyte	Rhonda	JAM	6.11.90	170/55	400h	55.40	54.29- 19
Wikström	Carolina	SWE	4.9.93	175/57	Mar	2:26:42	2:33:49- 19
* Williams	Kendell	USA	14.6.95	173/64	LJ	6.61iA, 6.55i	6.71- 19, 6.91w- 18
* Williams	Kimberly	JAM	3.11.88	169/66	TJ	14.12i	14.64- 18, 14.78w- 13

	Name		Nat	Born	Ht/Wt	Event	2020 Mark	Pre-2020 Best
*	Wilson	Ajee'	USA	8.5.94	169/55	800	1:58.29i	1:55.61- 17
	Wilson	Alyssa	USA	20.2.99	178/91	SP	17.43i	18.02- 19
*	Wimbley	Shakima	USA	23.4.95	187/61	200	22.88	22.34- 18
*	Winger	Kara	USA	10.4.86	183/86	JT	64.44	66.67- 19
	Winkler	Christine	GER	4.5.95	178/70	JT	59.70	58.18- 17
	Wipper	Lea	GER-J	14.10.01		JT	57.03	54.08- 19
	Witek	Marcelina	POL	2.6.95	174/67	JT	59.88	66.53- 18
	Wodak	Natasha	CAN	17.12.81	160/45	HMar	69:41	70:33- 19
						Mar	2:26:19	2:35:16- 13
	Wojtunik	Klaudia	POL	15.5.99	167/58	100h	13.08	13.21- 19
	Wold	Nora Kollerød	NOR	21.6.97	163/50	400h	57.10	58.58- 18
	Woodard	Jessica	USA	4.2.95	178/86	SP	17.99i	18.68- 18
*	Worku	Fantu	ETH	29.3.99	162/46	1500	4:06.39i	4:05.81- 17
						3000	8:37.58i	8:32.10- 19
	Wu Mian		CHN	9.1.00		TJ	13.64	13.08- 17
	Wu Yanni		CHN	28.7.97	169/55	100h	13.09	13.17- 18
	Xaba	Glenrose	RSA	31.12.94	155/44	HMar	69:26	69:46- 19
	Xie Yuchen		CHN	12.5.96	197/79	DT	57.34	58.30- 16
	Xu Huiqin		CHN	4.9.93	184/65	PV	4.60i	4.70- 19
	Xu Ting		CHN	23.2.97		TJ	13.83	13.95- 19
	Xu Xiaoling		CHN	13.5.92	175.64	LJ	6.63	6.66i- 16, 6.64A- 18, 6.63- 12
	Xu Xinying		CHN	17.2.97		HT	66.84	65.35- 18
	Yabuta	Yui	JPN	4.3.96	168/46	3kSt	9:52.19	9:58.89- 18
	Yada	Mikuni	JPN	29.10.99	159/42	5000	15:19.67	15:25.87- 16
						10000	31:34.39	33:27.83- 19
	Yamaguchi	Haruka	JPN	7.7.87		10000	32:28.90	33:46.23- 19
						Mar	2:26:35	2:27:39- 19
	Yamanaka	Yuno	JPN	25.12.00	153/43	3kSt	9:50.45	10:06.33-- 19
	Yamashita	Mikako	JPN	3.5.97	168/75	JT	59.07	59.94- 17
	Yamazaki	Yuki	JPN	6.6.95	165/58	Hep	5799	5873- 18
	Yan Ni		CHN	7.2.93	176.62	HT	66.25	68.56- 16
*	Yang Jiayu		CHN	18.2.96	163/48	20kW	1:28:06	1:25:34- 19
*	Yang Liujing		CHN	22.8.98		20kW	1:31:00	1:27:15- 19
	Yang Yang		CHN-J	23.8.01		TJ	14.10	13.97- 19
	Yano	Shiori	JPN	11.2.95	151/39	10000	31:46.84	31:44.13- 18
	Yarigo	Noélie	BEN	26.12.85	165/52	800	2:00.11	1:59.12- 16
*	Yavi	Winfred	BRN	31.12.99	157/48	3000	8:39.64i	9:10.5A- 16
						3kSt	9:52.99A	9:05.68- 19
*	Yehualaw	Yalemzerf	ETH	3.8.99	158/45	HMar	64:46	66:01- 19
	Yermachenkova	Tatyana	RUS	9.9.98	174/55	HJ	1.90	1.90i- 19, 1.89- 18
	Yermakova	Viktoriya	BLR	18.1.95		JT	57.67	59.35- 17
*	Yeshaneh	Ababel	ETH	22.7.91	158/42	HMar	64:31	65:46- 18
	Yevdokimova	Natalya	RUS	7.9.93	164/50	TJ	14.16i	14.02i- 18, 14.00- 19
*	Yimer	Zeineba	ETH	17.6.98	162/48	HMar	65:39	65:46- 19
						Mar	2:19:54	-0-
	Yoshimura	Reimi	JPN	22.4.00	160/47	3kSt	9:49.45	9:49.30- 19
	Yu Yuzhen		CHN	5.3.98		JT	57.58	62.30- 19
	Yudkina	Khrystyna	UKR	4.12.84	167/58	50kW	4:32:30	4:19:57- 19
	Zabawska	Daria	POL	16.4.95	185/92	DT	58.78	62.36- 19
	Zagainova	Diana	LTU	20.6.97	179/62	TJ	13.61	14.43- 19
	Zagré	Anne	BEL	13.3.90	176/69	100h	13.11, 13.07w	12.71- 15
	Zahi	Carolle	FRA	12.6.94	170/66	200	22.98	22.85, 22.78w- 19
	Zákka	Ioánna	GRE	28.5.96	180/57	HJ	1.91	1.84- 19
	Zaldívar	Liuba M.	ECU	5.4.93	161/54	TJ	13.78A, 13.74	14.51A- 16, 14.20- 13
	Zanon	Veronica	ITA-J	16.1.01		TJ	13.84	13.15- 19
	Zapletalová	Emma	SVK	24.3.00	178/61	400h	55.19	57.22- 18
	Zarankaite	Ieva	LTU	23.11.94	176/80	SP	17.25i, 16.80	16.58- 19
						DT	61.88	58.37- 19
	Zbären	Noemi	SUI	12.3.94	177/65	100h	13.06	12.71- 15
	Zdzieblo	Katarzyna	POL	28.11.96	162/52	20kW	1:30:41	1:32:03- 19
	Zeng Rui		CHN	6.2.98		TJ	14.10	13.81- 19
	Zerfe	Wondemagegn	ETH-J	26.10.02	161/50	3000	8:45.84i	-
	Zhang Linru		CHN	23.9.99	176/82	SP	17.58	18.05- 19
	Zhao Fan		CHN	26.3.97		HT	67.20	63.27- 16
	Zhodzik	Mariya	BLR	19.1.97		HJ	1.87	1.89i, 1.86- 17
	Zhuk	Irina	BLR	26.1.93	166/60	PV	4.72	4.67- 18
	Zihlmann	Nicole	SUI	30.7.86		HT	65.61	67.42- 18

WORLD INDOOR LISTS 2021 – MEN

Note: including some marks from December 2020 (*),   # Oversized track (over 200m)

60 METRES
6.47	Lamont Marcell	Jacobs	ITA	26.9.94	1	EI	Toruń		6 Mar
6.48	Trayvon	Bromell	USA	10.7.95	1	ATL	Fayetteville		24 Jan
6.49A	Micah	Williams	USA	12.11.01	1		Air Force Academy		27 Feb
6.49		Su Bingtian	CHN	29.8.89	1		Chengdu		12 Mar
6.52	Mike	Rodgers	USA	24.4.85	1		Łódź		12 Feb
6.52	Kevin	Kranz	GER	20.6.98	1	NC	Dortmund		20 Feb
6.53	Arthur Gue	Cissé	CIV	29.12.96	1		Berlin		5 Feb
6.53	Ronnie	Baker	USA	15.10.93	1		Fayetteville		7 Feb
6.54	Devin	Quinn	USA	8.6.96	1		Metz		6 Feb
6.54A	Hassan	Taftian	IRI	4.5.93	1		Tehran		28 Feb
6.54	Raymond	Ekevwo	NGR	23.3.99	2	NCAA	Fayetteville		13 Mar
6.55	Rikkoi	Brathwaite	IVB	13.2.99	1	Big 10	Geneva		27 Feb
6.56	Tavarius	Wright	USA	.98	2h1	NCAA	Fayetteville		12 Mar
6.56	Shuhei	Tada	JPN	24.6.96	1	NC	Osaka		18 Mar
6.57	Igor	Obraztsov	RUS	21.10.95	1		Yekaterinburg		7 Jan
6.57	Kasaun	James	USA	22.12.97	1		Columbia SC		16 Jan
6.57	Ján	Volko	SVK	2.11.96	1s3	EI	Toruń		6 Mar
6.58	Joris	van Gool	NED	4.4.98	1		Dortmund		7 Feb
6.58	Brendon	Stewart	USA	29.7.00	1		Lubbock		12 Feb
6.58	Zachary	Jewell	USA	.98	1		Fayetteville		21 Feb
6.58	Shaun Phatutshedzo	Maswanganyi	RSA	1.2.01	1		Houston		28 Feb
6.58	Cameron	Burrell	USA	11.9.94	2		Houston		28 Feb
6.59	Courtney	Lindsey	USA	18.11.98	1		Lubbock		16 Jan
6.59	Mudiyanselage	Abeykoon	SRI	31.12.94	1h1		Ancona		24 Jan
6.59	Benjamin	Azamati-Kwaku	GHA	14.1.98	1		Topeka		29 Jan
6.59	Julian	Wagner	GER	18.3.98	2	NC	Dortmund		20 Feb
6.59	Silvan	Wicki	SUI	13.2.95	1	NC	Magglingen		20 Feb
6.59	Remigiusz	Olszewski	POL	20.9.92	1	NC	Toruń		20 Feb
6.59	Jackson	Webb	USA	27.2.97	2		Fayetteville		21 Feb
6.59	Andrew	Robertson	GBR	17.12.90	1s1	EI	Toruń		6 Mar

6.60	Michael	Pohl		GER	18.11.89	20 Feb	6.62	Philipp	Corucle	GER	18.7.97	20 Feb
6.60	Mouhamadou	Fall		FRA	25.2.92	24 Feb	6.62	Bence	Boros	HUN	24.12.96	20 Feb
6.61	Andrew	Hudson		USA	14.12.96	7 Feb	6.62	Jarrion	Lawson	USA	6.5.94	21 Feb
6.61	Joseph	Amoah		GHA	12.1.97	12 Feb	6.62	Dante	Brown	USA	16.5.00	26 Feb
6.61	Kojo	Musah		DEN	15.4.96	20 Feb	6.62	Terrance	Ware	USA	.98	28 Feb
6.61A	Gaston	Bouchereau		USA	.98	27 Feb	6.62	Karl Erik	Nazarov	EST	17.3.99	6 Mar
6.61	Travis	Collins		USA	26.2.96	28 Feb	6.62	Carlos	Nascimento	POR	12.10.94	6 Mar
6.62	Amaury	Golitin		FRA	28.1.97	6 Feb	6.62	Sterling	Warner-Savage	USA	7.1.00	12 Mar

Best at low altitude
6.49	Micah	Williams	USA	12.11.01	1	NCAA	Fayetteville		13 Mar
6.62	Hassan	Taftian	IRI	4.5.93	1	FRA Ch	Miramas		20 Feb

200 METRES
20.19	Matthew	Boling	USA	20.6.00	1	NCAA	Fayetteville		13 Mar
20.20	Terrance	Laird	USA	12.10.98	2	NCAA	Fayetteville		13 Mar
20.32	Joe	Fahnbulleh	USA	11.9.01	1rB	SEC	Fayetteville		27 Feb
20.38	Micaiah	Harris	USA	19.12.98	1	Big 12	Lubbock		27 Feb
20.39	Javonte	Harding	USA	29.8.01	3	NCAA	Fayetteville		13 Mar
20.45	Courtney	Lindsey	USA	18.11.98	1		Lubbock		16 Jan
20.48	Trevor	Bassitt	USA	26.2.98	1	NCAA-II	Birmingham AL		13 Mar
20.50	Randolph	Ross	USA	1.1.01	1		Clemson		13 Feb
20.60	Karayme	Bartley	JAM	.97	1		Lubbock		13 Feb

20.62	Jaylen	Slade	USA-J	27.10.03	21 Feb	20.70	Zach	Shinnick	USA	8.2.98	13 Feb
20.62	Jacory	Patterson	USA	2.2.00	27 Feb	20.71	Steven	Gardiner	BAH	12.9.95	6 Feb
20.68	Kasaun	James	USA	22.12.97	13 Feb	20.72	JoVaughn	Martin	USA	15.7.99	25 Feb
						20.72	Tyler	Davis	USA	22.11.00	12 Mar

Oversized track
20.40	Trevor	Bassitt	USA	26.2.98	1		Saginaw	28 Feb

300 METRES
32.47	Karsten	Warholm	NOR	28.2.96	1		Bærum	28 Feb
32.61	Jacory	Patterson	USA	2.2.00	1		Blacksburg	15 Jan

32.70	Steven	Gardiner	BAH	12.9.95	15 Jan	32.77	Jaylen	Slade	USA-J	27.10.03	16 Jan
32.71	Jereem	Richards	TTO	13.1.94	13 Feb	32.80	Christopher	Taylor	JAM	1.10.99	13 Feb
32.73	Bryce	Deadmon	USA	26.3.97	23 Jan	32.82	Pavel	Maslák	CZE	21.2.91	14 Feb

400 METRES
44.71	Noah	Williams	USA	1.1.99	1	NCAA	Fayetteville		13 Mar
44.99	Randolph	Ross	USA	1.1.01	1rB	NCAA	Fayetteville		13 Mar
45.03	Fred	Kerley	USA	7.5.95	1	ATL	Fayetteville		24 Jan
45.14	Jacory	Patterson	USA	2.2.00	2rB	NCAA	Fayetteville		13 Mar
45.22	Bryce	Deadmon	USA	26.3.97	1		Fayetteville		12 Feb

WORLD INDOOR LISTS 2021   419

45.24	Michael	Cherry	USA	23.3.95	1		Fayetteville		7 Feb
45.27	Trevor	Bassitt	USA	26.2.98	1rB		Fayetteville		7 Feb
45.34	Michael	Norman	USA	3.12.97	1	WIT	New York (SI)		13 Feb
45.37	Elija	Godwin	USA	1.7.99	2	SEC	Fayetteville		27 Feb
45.39	Rai	Benjamin	USA	27.7.97	2	WIT	New York (SI)		13 Feb
45.40	Ryan	Willie	USA-J	24.6.02	2	NCAA	Fayetteville		13 Mar
45.51	Matthew	Boling	USA	20.6.01	1		Columbia SC		23 Jan
45.55	Trevor	Stewart	USA	20.5.97	3		Clemson		12 Feb
45.57	Sean	Burrell	USA-J	23.2.02	2		College Station		6 Feb
45.64	Dwight	St. Hillare	TTO	5.12.97	1rB		Clemson		12 Feb
45.73	Christopher	Taylor	JAM	1.10.99	2	ATL	Fayetteville		24 Jan
45.79	Champion	Allison	USA	5.11.98	3rB	NCAA	Fayetteville		13 Mar

45.92	Kyron	McMaster	IVB	3.1.97	12 Feb	46.02	Ashton	Hicks	USA	16.2.99	27 Feb
45.97	Isaiah	Palmer	USA	17.7.98	27 Feb	46.06	Tony	van Diepen	NED	17.4.96	5 Mar
45.99	Liemarvin	Bonevacia	NED	5.4.89	21 Feb	46.08	Deon	Lendore	TTO	28.10.92	7 Feb
45.99	Leander	Forbes	USA	6.6.98	27 Feb	46.12	Pavel	Maslák	CZE	21.2.91	24 Feb

Oversized track

45.07	Tyler	Johnson	USA	11.2.98	1	Big 10	Geneva		27 Feb
45.40	Wayne	Lawrence	JAM	21.11.98	1rB	Big 10	Geneva		27 Feb
45.82	Taj	Burgess	USA	15.4.99	2	Big 10	Geneva		27 Feb
45.87	Brian	Faust	USA	12.1.99	2rB	Big 10	Geneva		27 Feb

500 Metres: 1:00.66 Alejandro Perlaza COL 26.8.94 1 Lynchburg 23 Jan

600 METRES

1:16.16	Kameron	Jones	USA	12.11.97	1		Clemson	9 Jan
1:16.47	Vincent	Crisp	USA	17.8.97	1		Virginia Beach	30 Jan

800 METRES

1:43.63	Elliot	Giles	GBR	26.5.94	1	WIT	Torun		17 Feb
1:44.21	Donavan	Brazier	USA	15.4.97	1	WIT	New York (SI)		13 Feb
1:44.37	Bryce	Hoppel	USA	5.9.97	1		Fayetteville		31 Jan
1:44.54	Jamie	Webb	GBR	1.6.92	2	WIT	Torun		17 Feb
1:45.09	Andreas	Kramer	SWE	13.4.97	3	WIT	Torun		17 Feb
1:45.22	Adam	Kszczot	POL	2.9.89	4	WIT	Torun		17 Feb
1:45.34	Michael	Saruni	KEN	18.6.95	1		Fayetteville		21 Feb
1:45.59	Charles	Hunter	AUS	20.7.96	1		Fayetteville		13 Feb
1:45.62	Charlie	Da'Vall Grice	GBR	7.11.93	2		Fayetteville		31 Jan
1:45.66	Mariano	Garcia	ESP	25.9.97	1	WIT	Madrid		24 Feb
1:45.69	Erik	Sowinski	USA	21.12.89	3		Fayetteville		31 Jan
1:45.79	Mateusz	Borkowski	POL	2.4.97	1s2	EI	Torun		6 Mar
1:45.91	Finley	McLear	GBR	25.5.00	2	NCAA	Fayetteville		13 Mar
1:45.95	Amel	Tuka	BIH	9.1.91	2	WIT	Madrid		24 Feb
1:45.95	Pierre-Ambroise	Bosse	FRA	11.5.92	3	WIT	Madrid		24 Feb
1:45.98	Takieddine	Hedeilli	ALG	6.6.96	1		Lubbock		16 Jan
1:46.06	Benjamin	Robert	FRA	4.1.98	1	NC	Miramas		20 Feb
1:46.10	Craig	Engels	USA	1.5.94	4		Fayetteville		31 Jan
1:46.10	Mark	English	IRL	18.3.93	1		Dublin		20 Feb
1:46.13	Cian	McPhillips	IRL-J	7.6.02	2		Dublin		20 Feb
1:46.21	Marc	Reuther	GER	23.6.96	1		Erfurt		2 Feb
1:46.23	Kameron	Jones	USA	12.11.97	2		Fayetteville		21 Feb
1:46.40	Eliott	Crestan	BEL	22.2.99	1		Metz		6 Feb
1:46.51	Baptiste	Mischler	FRA	23.11.97	4		Karlsruhe		29 Jan

1:46.61	Collins	Kipruto	KEN	12.4.94	17 Feb	1:46.97	Tony	van Diepen	NED	17.4.96	17 Feb
1:46.63	Filip	Snejdr	CZE	16.4.95	3 Feb	1:46.99	Marius	Probst	GER	20.8.95	2 Feb
1:46.65	Djoao	Lobles	NED	14.1.01	21 Feb	1:47.02#	Jason	Gomez	USA	8.8.00	23 Jan
1:46.73	Guy	Learmonth	GBR	20.4.92	30 Jan	1:47.09	Marvin	Heinrich	GER	29.1.97	14 Feb
1:46.81	Patryk	Dobek	POL	13.2.94	7 Mar	1:47.14	Christoph	Kessler	GER	28.4.95	29 Jan
1:46.86	Balázs	Vindics	HUN	28.3.94	21 Feb	1:47.24	Neil	Gourley	GBR	7.2.95	30 Jan
1:46.88	Cornelius	Tuwei	KEN	24.4593	9 Feb	1:47.28	Nasredine	Khatir	FRA	30.1.95	7 Feb
1:46.88	Adrian	Ben	ESP	4.8.98	24 Feb	1:47.30	Pablo	Sánchez-Valladares	ESP	12.11.97	29 Jan
1:46.91	Thijmen	Kupers	NED	4.10.91	10 Feb	1:47.33	Karl	Bebendorf	GER	7.5.96	2 Feb
1:46.93	Lukáš	Hodbod	CZE	2.3.96	3 Feb	1:47.35	Jan	Fris	CZE	19.12.95	30 Jan
1:46.93	Álvaro	de Arriba	ESP	2.6.94	24 Feb						

1000 METRES

2:16.27	Bryce	Hoppel	USA	5.9.97	1	WIT	New York (SI)		13 Feb
2:17.10	Marco	Arop	CAN	20.9.98	2	WIT	New York (SI)		13 Feb
2:17.20	Charlie	Da'Vall Grice	GBR	7.11.93	3	WIT	New York (SI)		13 Feb
2:18.68	Neil	Gourley	GBR	7.2.95	1		Blacksburg		22 Jan

2:18.98#	Festus	Lagat	KEN	10.10.96	12 Feb	2:19.45	Lukáš	Hodbod	CZE	2.3.96	23 Jan
2:19.11#	Jason	Gomez	USA	8.8.00	12 Feb	2:19.62	Filip	Sasínek	CZE	8.1.96	23 Jan
2:19.13#	Roshon	Roomes	USA	19.11.96	12 Feb	2:19.69	Diego	Zarate	USA	3.9.97	22 Jan

1500 METRES

3:31.80	Jakob	Ingebrigtsen	NOR	19.9.00	1	WIT	Liévin		9 Feb
3:32.35	Oliver	Hoare	AUS	29.1.97	1	WIT	New York (SI)		13 Feb

3:32.97	Selemon	Barega	ETH	20.1.00	1	WIT	Torun		17 Feb
3:34.48	Jake	Wightman	GBR	11.7.94	2	WIT	New York (SI)		13 Feb
3:34.67	Bethwel	Birgen	KEN	6.8.88	2		Metz		6 Feb
3:34.72	Samuel	Tanner	NZL	24.8.00	3	WIT	New York (SI)		13 Feb
3:35.46+	Cooper	Teare	USA	18.8.99	1	in 1M	Fayetteville		12 Feb
3:35.54	Getnet	Wale	ETH	16.7.00	1		Val-de-Reuil		14 Feb
3:35.60	Lamecha	Girma	ETH	26.11.00	2		Val-de-Reuil		14 Feb
3:35.63+	Cole	Hocker	USA	6.6.01	2	in 1M	Fayetteville		12 Feb
3:35.71	Marcin	Lewandowski	POL	13.6.87	2	WIT	Torun		17 Feb
3:35.79	Neil	Gourley	GBR	7.2.95	3	WIT	Torun		17 Feb
3:36.10	Michał	Rozmys	POL	13.3.95	4	WIT	Torun		17 Feb
3:36.32	Jesús	Gómez	ESP	24.4.91	2	WIT	Madrid		24 Feb
3:36.36	Sam	Prakel	USA	29.10.94	4	WIT	New York (SI)		13 Feb
3:36.49	Craig	Engels	USA	1.5.94	5	WIT	New York (SI)		13 Feb
3:36.53	Filip	Sasínek	CZE	8.1.96	5	WIT	Torun		17 Feb
3:36.89	Mohamed	Katir	ESP	17.2.98	3	WIT	Liévin		9 Feb
3:36.89	Ignacio	Fontes	ESP	22.6.98	4	WIT	Liévin		9 Feb
3:36.90	Elliot	Giles	GBR	26.5.94	3		Val-de-Reuil		14 Feb
3:36.94+	Charles	Hunter	AUS	20.7.96	3	in 1M	Fayetteville		12 Feb
3:37.20	Andrew	Coscoran	IRL	18.6.96	5	WIT	Liévin		9 Feb
3:37.22	Johnny	Gregorek	USA	7.12.91	6	WIT	New York (SI)		13 Feb
3:37.28	Kumari	Taki	KEN	6.5.99	7	WIT	Torun		17 Feb
3:37.53	Nick	Willis	NZL	25.4.83	7	WIT	New York (SI)		13 Feb
3:37.55	István	Szögi	HUN	12.9.95	1		Wien		30 Jan
3:38.03	Jimmy	Gressier	FRA	4.5.97	7	WIT	Liévin		9 Feb
3:38.16	Amos	Bartelsmeyer	GER	25.7.94	8	WIT	New York (SI)		13 Feb
3:38.23	Simon	Denissel	FRA	22.5.90	8	WIT	Liévin		9 Feb
3:38.55	Piers	Copeland	GBR	26.11.98	13 Feb	3:39.04	Bram	Anderiessen	NED 1.8.99 10 Feb
3:38.65	Charles	Grethen	LUX	2.6.92	13 Feb	3:39.09	Sergio	Paniagua	ESP 26.10.95 24 Feb
3:38.85	Baptiste	Mischler	FRA	23.11.97	14 Feb	3:39.27	Samuel	Tefera	ETH 23.10.99 9 Feb
3:38.91	Cornelius	Tuwei	KEN	24.5.93	13 Feb	3:39.36	Paul	Robinson	IRL 24.5.91 14 Feb
3:39.04	Quentin	Tison	FRA	16.4.96	9 Feb	3:39.41*	Homiyu	Tesfaye	GER 23.6.93 19 Dec

ONE MILE

3:50.39	Cooper	Teare	USA	18.8.99	1		Fayetteville		12 Feb
3:50.55	Cole	Hocker	USA	6.6.01	2		Fayetteville		12 Feb
3:53.49	Charles	Hunter	AUS	20.7.96	3		Fayetteville		12 Feb
3:55.23#	Samuel	Tanner	NZL	24.8.00	1		Seattle		27 Feb
3:55.45#	Lucas	Bons	USA	9.10.99	2		Seattle		27 Feb
3:55.60#	Waleed	Suliman	USA	22.9.99	1		Nashville		12 Feb
3:55.93	Eliud	Kipsang	KEN	9.9.96	2	NCAA	Fayetteville		13 Mar
3:56.46#	Mario	García	ESP	29.6.99	12 Feb	3:56.82	Nick	Willis	NZL 25.4.83 7 Feb
3:56.61	Reed	Brown	USA	6.8.98	30 Jan	3:56.82#	Patrick	Tiernan	AUS 11.9.94 13 Feb
3:56.79	Takieddine	Hedeili	ALG	6.6.96	7 Feb	3:57.00	Tom	Dodd	GBR 2.10.98 12 Mar

2000 METRES

5:01.11+	Vincent	Keter	KEN-J	11.3.02	1	in 3000	Liévin		9 Feb
5:01.3+	Lamecha	Girma	ETH	26.11.00	9 Feb	5:01.7+	Selemon	Barega	ETH 20.1.00 9 Feb
5:01.5+	Getnet	Wale	ETH	16.7.00	9 Feb	5:02.0+	Berihu	Aregawi	ETH 28.2.01 9 Feb

3000 METRES

7:24.98	Getnet	Wale	ETH	16.7.00	1	WIT	Liévin	9 Feb
7:26.10	Selemon	Barega	ETH	20.1.00	2	WIT	Liévin	9 Feb
7:27.98	Lamecha	Girma	ETH	26.11.00	3	WIT	Liévin	9 Feb
7:29.24	Berihu	Aregawi	ETH	28.2.01	4	WIT	Liévin	9 Feb
7:34.12	Bethwel	Birgen	KEN	6.8.88	1		Karlsruhe	29 Jan
7:35.29	Mohamed	Katir	ESP	17.2.98	2		Karlsruhe	29 Jan
7:37.99	Birhanu	Yemataw	BRN	27.2.96	5	WIT	Liévin	9 Feb
7:39.70	Jimmy	Gressier	FRA	4.5.97	3		Karlsruhe	29 Jan
7:40.85	Andrew	Butchart	GBR	14.10.91	4		Karlsruhe	29 Jan
7:41.06	Tadese	Worku	ETH-J	20.1.02	6	WIT	Liévin	9 Feb
7:41.6	Andreas	Almgren	SWE	12.6.95	1		Sollentuna	30 Jan
7:42.55	Mike	Foppen	NED	29.11.96	7	WIT	Liévin	9 Feb
7:42.71	Abdelaati	Iguider	MAR	25.3.87	5		Karlsruhe	29 Jan
7:44.17	Isaac	Kimeli	BEL	9.3.94	1		Gent	13 Feb
7:44.60+	Morgan	McDonald	AUS	23.4.96	1	in 2M	New York (SI)	13 Feb
7:44.61+	Justyn	Knight	CAN	19.7.96	2	in 2M	New York (SI)	13 Feb
7:44.91+	Joe	Klecker	USA	16.11.96	3	in 2M	New York (SI)	13 Feb
7:45.54	Carlos	Mayo	ESP	18.9.95	1		Barcelona	8 Feb
7:46.10	Cooper	Teare	USA	18.8.99	1		Fayetteville	30 Jan
7:46.14+	Eric	Jenkins	USA	24.11.91	4	in 2M	New York (SI)	13 Feb
7:46.15	Cole	Hocker	USA	6.6.01	1	NCAA	Fayetteville	13 Mar
7:46.26+	Kieran	Lumb	CAN	2.8.98	5	in 2M	New York (SI)	13 Feb
7:46.38+	Maximilian	Thorwirth	GER	9.1.95	6	in 2M	New York (SI)	13 Feb
7:46.52	Djilali	Bedrani	FRA	1.10.93	8	WIT	Liévin	9 Feb

WORLD INDOOR LISTS 2021   421

7:46.52	Adel	Mechaal		ESP	5.12.90	2h2	El	Toruń		6 Mar
7:46.76	Robin	Hendrix		BEL	14.1.95	3h2	El	Toruń		6 Mar
7:47.30	Hugo	Hay	FRA	28.3.97	6 Mar	7:48.36	Wesley	Kiptoo	KEN	30 Jan
7:47.50	Jonas	Raess	SUI	8.3.94	9 Feb	7:48.40	Mario	García	ESP 29.6.99	30 Jan
7:47.71	Seán	Tobin	IRL	20.7.94	6 Mar	7:48.63+	Paul	Chelimo	USA 27.10.90	4 Mar
7:47.74+	Emmanuel	Bor	USA	14.4.88	4 Mar	7:49.27	Yann	Schrub	FRA 20.3.96	6 Feb
7:47.94+	Willy	Fink	USA	7.3.94	4 Mar	7:49.27	Davis	Kiplangat	KEN 10.7.98	9 Feb
7:47.98	Yassin	Bouih	ITA	24.11.96	9 Feb	7:49.74	Louis	Gilavert	FRA 1.1.98	6 Feb
7:48.06	Marcel	Fehr	GER	20.6.92	6 Mar	7:49.82	Charles	Philibert-Thiboutot CAN 31.12.90		29 Jan
7:48.20	Jakob	Ingebrigtsen	NOR	19.9.00	7 Mar					

TWO MILES

8:13.92	Justyn	Knight	CAN	19.7.96	1	WIT	New York (SI)	13 Feb
8:14.20	Joe	Klecker	USA	16.11.96	2	WIT	New York (SI)	13 Feb
8:14.92	Morgan	McDonald	AUS	23.4.96	3	WIT	New York (SI)	13 Feb
8:17.78	Maximilian	Thorwirth	GER	9.1.95	4	WIT	New York (SI)	13 Feb
8:19.54	Eric	Jenkins	USA	24.11.91	5	WIT	New York (SI)	13 Feb
8:22.03	Kieran	Lumb	CAN	2.8.98	6	WIT	New York (SI)	13 Feb

5000 METRES

13:05.60	Emmanuel	Bor		USA	14.4.88	1		Virginia Beach		4 Mar
13:09.90	Paul	Chelimo		USA	27.10.90	1		Virginia Beach		18 Mar
13:23.77	Wesley	Kiptoo		KEN		1	NCAA	Fayetteville		12 Mar
13:28.00#	Connor	Mantz	USA	8.12.96	12 Feb	13:29.96	Morgan	Beadlescomb USA	1.6.98	12 Mar
13:28.79#	Casey	Clinger	USA	9.10.98	12 Feb	13:30.55	Adrian	Wildschutt RSA	3.5.98	12 Mar
13:29.16#	Brandon	Garnica	USA	14.11.99	12 Feb	13:31.45	Aaron	Bienenfeld GER	25.9.97	12 Mar
13:29.60	Eric	Hamer	USA	23.3.97	12 Mar					

60 METRES HURDLES

7.29	Grant	Holloway		USA	19.11.97	1	WIT	Madrid		24 Feb
7.42	Wilhem	Bélocian		FRA	22.6.95	1	El	Toruń		7 Mar
7.43	Andy	Pozzi		GBR	15.5.92	2	El	Toruń		7 Mar
7.50	Shunsuke	Izumiya		JPN	26.1.00	1		Osaka		17 Mar
7.51	Jarret	Eaton		USA	24.6.89	1		Łódź		12 Feb
7.51	Damion	Thomas		JAM	29.6.99	1	NCAA	Fayetteville		13 Mar
7.52	Jamal	Britt		USA	28.12.98	2	NCAA	Fayetteville		13 Mar
7.53	Omar	McLeod		JAM	25.4.94	1		Fayetteville		7 Mar
7.53	Michael	Dickson		USA	25.1.97	1h1		Fayetteville		21 Feb
7.53	Trey	Cunningham		USA	26.8.98	3	NCAA	Fayetteville		13 Mar
7.54	Pascal	Martinot-Lagarde		FRA	22.9.91	1		Miramas		22 Jan
7.54	Phillip	Lemonious		JAM	12.12.98	4	NCAA	Fayetteville		13 Mar
7.55	Paolo	Dal Molin		ITA	31.7.87	3	WIT	Liévin		9 Feb
7.55		Zeng Jianhang		CHN	17.9.98	1		Chengdu		13 Mar
7.56	Taio	Kanai		JPN	28.9.95	2h1		Osaka		17 Mar
7.57	Aaron	Mallett		USA	26.9.94	4	WIT	Liévin		9 Feb
7.57	Damian	Czykier		POL	10.8.92	1h3	El	Toruń		6 Mar
7.57	Shuhei	Ishikawa		JPN	29.5.95	2		Osaka		17 Mar
7.58	Aurel	Manga		FRA	24.7.92	2	NC	Miramas		21 Feb
7.58	Eric	Edwards Jr.		USA	3.1.00	5	NCAA	Fayetteville		13 Mar
7.59A	Jamar	Marshall		USA	18.12.01	1		Air Force Academy		27 Feb
7.60	Asier	Martínez		ESP	22.4.00	4	El	Toruń		7 Mar
7.61*	Jaylan	McConico		USA	17.8.98	1		Iowa City		11 Dec
7.61	Artem	Makarenko		RUS	23.4.97	1		Moskva		7 Feb
7.62	Yaqoub	Al-Yoha	KUW	31.1.93	17 Feb	7.65	David	Efremov KAZ	15.1.99	20 Feb
7.62	Shun-ya	Takayama	JPN	3.9.94	18 Mar	7.65	Koen	Smet NED	9.8.92	21 Feb
7.63	Jason	Joseph	SUI	11.10.98	7 Feb	7.65	Krzysztof	Kiljan POL	30.12.99	21 Feb
7.63	Elmo	Lakka	FIN	10.4.93	21 Feb	7.66A	Kentre	Patterson USA	20.6.99	27 Feb
7.64	Artur	Noga	POL	2.5.88	23 Jan	7.66	Jesse	Henderson USA	22.12.99	12 Mar
7.64	Orlando	Ortega	ESP	29.7.91	5 Feb	7.67	Michael	Obasuyi BEL	12.8.99	9 Feb
7.65	Ruebin	Walters	TTO	2.4.95	24 Jan	7.67	Konstadínos	Douvalídis GRE	10.3.87	13 Feb
7.65	Gabriel	Constantino	BRA	9.2.95	14 Feb	7.67	Trevor	Bassitt USA	26.2.98	28 Feb

HIGH JUMP

2.37	Maksim	Nedosekov		BLR	21.1.98	1	El	Toruń	7 Mar
2.35	Gianmarco	Tamberi		ITA	1.6.92	1	NC	Ancona	21 Feb
2.34	Andrii	Protsenko		UKR	20.5.88	2	WIT	Toruń	17 Feb
2.33	Trey	Culver		USA	18.7.96	1	WIT	New York (SI)	13 Feb
2.31	Mikhail	Akimenko		RUS	6.12.95	1		Moskva	24 Jan
2.31	Luis	Zayas		CUB	7.6.97	2		Banská Bystrica	2 Feb
2.30	JuVaughn	Harrison		USA	30.4.99	1	NCAA	Fayetteville	12 Mar
2.29	Daniyil	Tsyplakov		RUS	29.7.92	2		Moskva	24 Jan
2.28	Mateusz	Przybylko		GER	9.3.92	4		Banská Bystrica	2 Feb
2.28	Dmytro	Nikitin		UKR	31.7.99	1		Kyiv	5 Feb
2.28	Oleh	Doroshchuk		UKR	4.7.01	2	NC	Sumy	11 Feb
2.28	Thomas	Carmoy		BEL	16.2.00	1		Luxembourg	13 Feb
2.28	Jonas	Wagner		GER	29.5.97	1	NC	Dortmund	21 Feb
2.28		Wang Yu		CHN	18.8.91	1		Jinan	18 Mar

2.27		Adrijus	Glebauskas	LTU	20.11.94	1			Kladno		8 Feb
2.26	Ilya		Ivanyuk	RUS	9.3.93	24 Jan	2.25	Tihomir	Ivanov	BUL	11.7.94	16 Jan
2.26	Earnie		Sears	USA	4.12.98	29 Jan	2.25	Falk	Wendrich	GER	12.6.95	23 Jan
2.26	Tobias		Potye	GER	16.3.95	30 Jan	2.25	Tejaswin	Shankar	IND	21.12.98	29 Jan
2.26	Nikita		Kurbanov	RUS	13.4.99	24 Feb	2.25	Jeron	Robinson	USA	30.4.91	13 Feb
2.26	Ushan		Perera	SRI	22.1.98	12 Mar						

POLE VAULT

6.10		Armand	Duplantis	SWE	10.11.99	1		Beograd	24 Feb
6.06		Renaud	Lavillenie	FRA	18.9.86	1		Aubière	27 Feb
6.00		KC	Lightfoot	USA	11.11.99	1		Lubbock	13 Feb
5.96		Menno	Vloon	NED	11.5.94	2		Aubière	27 Feb
5.93		Chris	Nilsen	USA	13.1.98	2=		Rouen	6 Feb
5.86		Torben	Blech	GER	12.2.95	2	ISTAF	Düsseldorf	31 Jan
5.86		Sam	Kendricks	USA	7.9.92	1		Lódz	12 Feb
5.86		Ernest John	Obiena	PHI	17.11.95	2		Lódz	12 Feb
5.80		Matt	Ludwig	USA	5.7.96	2		Karlsruhe	29 Jan
5.80		Thiago	Braz da Silva	BRA	16.12.93	3		Lódz	12 Feb
5.80		Piotr	Lisek	POL	16.8.92	2	WIT	Torun	17 Feb
5.80		Ethan	Cormont	FRA	29.9.00	4		Aubière	27 Feb
5.80		Valentin	Lavillenie	FRA	16.7.91	5		Aubière	27 Feb
5.80		Zach	McWhorter	USA	7.1.99	2	NCAA	Fayetteville	13 Mar
5.75		Jacob	Wooten	USA	22.4.97	1		Belton	2 Jan
5.75		Nate	Richartz	USA	2.11.94	2		Belton	2 Jan
5.75		Scott	Houston	USA	11.6.90	1		Lynchburg	23 Jan
5.75		Zachary	Bradford	USA	29.11.99	2		Lubbock	30 Jan
5.74		Sondre	Guttormsen	NOR	1.6.99	1		Kalmar	6 Feb
5.73		Cole	Walsh	USA	14.6.95	7		Rouen	6 Feb
5.72		Viktor	Pintusov	RUS	7.2.00	1		Chelyabinsk	19 Jan
5.72		Bo Kanda	Lita Baehre	GER	29.4.99	5	ISTAF	Düsseldorf	31 Jan
5.72		Oleg	Zernikel	GER	16.4.95	3		Berlin	5 Feb
5.72		Ersu	Sasma	TUR	30.9.99	1	NC	Istanbul	7 Feb
5.70		Andrew	Irwin	USA	24.1.93	1		Fayetteville	21 Feb
5.70			Ding Bangchao	CHN	11.10.96	1		Jinan	18 Mar
5.70		Takuma	Ishikawa	JPN	7.11.97	1	NC	Osaka	18 Mar
5.70		Seito	Yamamoto	JPN	11.3.92	2	NC	Osaka	18 Mar
5.66		Urho	Kujanpää	FIN	18.5.97	1	NC	Jyväskylä	21 Feb
5.65			Yao Jie	CHN	21.9.90	1		Xi'an	1 Feb
5.65		Charlie	Myers	GBR	12.6.97	1		Loughborough	14 Feb
5.65		Ethan	Bray	USA	18.5.97	1		Brookings	20 Feb
5.65		Timur	Morgunov	RUS	12.10.96	1		Moskva	21 Feb
5.62		Raphael	Holzdeppe	GER	28.9.89	6		Karlsruhe	29 Jan
5.62		Robert	Sobera	POL	19.1.91	4		Berlin	5 Feb
5.60	Tray	Oates	USA-Y	14.3.95	2 Jan	5.60	Ivan	Horvat	CRO	17.8.93	24 Feb
5.60	Carson	Waters	USA	5.6.96	2 Jan	5.60	Thibaut	Collet	FRA	17.6.99	27 Feb
5.60	Mathieu	Collet	FRA	15.3.95	6 Feb	5.60	Eerik	Haamer	EST	6.1.01	13 Mar
5.60	Matvey	Volkov	BLR-Y	13.3.04	12 Feb	5.56A	Kyle	Pater	USA	24.12.94	23 Jan
5.60	Austin	Miller	USA	1.6.94	21 Feb	5.55	eight men				

LONG JUMP

8.45		JuVaughn	Harrison	USA	30.4.99	1	NCAA	Fayetteville	12 Mar
8.35		Miltiádis	Tentóglou	GRE	18.3.98	1	EI	Torun	5 Mar
8.35		Isaac	Grimes	USA	7.2.98	2	NCAA	Fayetteville	12 Mar
8.31		Thobias	Montler	SWE	15.2.96	2	EI	Torun	5 Mar
8.26		Carey	McLeod	JAM	14.4.98	3	NCAA	Fayetteville	12 Mar
8.25		Juan Miguel	Echevarría	CUB	11.8.98	1	WIT	Liévin	9 Feb
8.24		Kristian	Pulli	FIN	2.9.94	3	EI	Torun	5 Mar
8.21		Marquis	Dendy	USA	17.11.92	1		Fayetteville	7 Feb
8.19		Yuki	Hashioka	JPN	23.1.99	1	NC	Osaka	18 Mar
8.16		Laquarn	Nairn	BAH	31.7.96	2		Fayetteville	7 Feb
8.14		Gabriel	Bitan	ROU	23.7.98	1	NC	Bucuresti	6 Feb
8.14		Vladyslav	Mazur	UKR	21.11.96	4	EI	Torun	5 Mar
8.12		Ryan	Brown	JAM	10.11.98	3	SEC	Fayetteville	26 Feb
8.12			Huang Changzhou	CHN	20.8.94	1		Chengdu	12 Mar
8.11		Ja'Mari	Ward	USA	21.3.98	4	NCAA	Fayetteville	12 Mar
8.08		Maykel D.	Massó	CUB	8.5.99	2		Karlsruhe	29 Jan
8.08		Jacob	Fincham-Dukes	GBR	12.1.97	1		London (LV)	20 Feb
8.07		Matthew	Boling	USA	20.6.00	4	SEC	Fayetteville	26 Feb
8.01		Justin	Hall	USA	12.2.98	1		Lubbock	16 Jan
8.01		Serhiy	Nykyforov	UKR	6.2.94	1		Istanbul	23 Jan
7.99		Jeremiah	Davis	USA	31.8.01	2		Clemson	29 Jan
7.97		Maximilian	Entholzner	GER	18.8.94	1		Barcelona	6 Feb
7.97		Radek	Juska	CZE	8.3.93	1		Praha	14 Feb
7.97		Sebastian Ree	Pedersen	DEN	13.7.97	1		Aarhus	23 Feb

WORLD INDOOR LISTS 2021   423

7.96	Daniyil	Chechela	RUS	30.3.00	1	NC	Moskva		16 Feb
7.96	Vladislav	Kuznetsov	RUS	27.2.97	2	NC	Moskva		16 Feb
7.95	PJ	Austin	USA	19.9.00	26 Feb	7.91	Izmir	Smajlaj	ALB	29.3.93	20 Feb
7.94	Jean-Pierre	Bertrand	FRA	5.11.92	16 Jan	7.91	Eusebio	Cáceres	ESP	10.9.91	21 Feb
7.94	Fabian	Heinle	GER	14.5.94	17 Jan	7.91	Lazar	Anic	SRB	14.12.91	24 Feb
7.94	Antonino	Trio	ITA	4.6.93	20 Feb	7.90	Aleksandr	Menkov	RUS	7.12.90	16 Jan
7.94		Wang Jianan	CHN	27.8.96	12 Mar					

TRIPLE JUMP

18.07	Fabrice	Zango	BUR	25.6.93	1		Aubière	16 Jan
17.36	Pedro Pablo	Pichardo	POR	30.6.93	1	NC	Braga	13 Feb
17.32		Zhu Yaming	CHN	4.5.94	1		Chengdu	13 Mar
17.26	Emmanuel	Ihemeje	ITA	9.10.98	1	NCAA	Fayetteville	13 Mar
17.20		Wu Ruiting	CHN	29.11.95	2		Chengdu	13 Mar
17.17	Carey	McLeod	JAM	14.4.98	1	SEC	Fayetteville	27 Feb
17.15		Fang Yaoqing	CHN	20.4.96	3		Chengdu	13 Mar
17.09	Melvin	Raffin	FRA	9.8.98	2	NC	Miramas	20 Feb
17.06	Andy	Díaz	CUB	25.12.95	1		Metz	6 Feb
17.04	Alexis	Copello	AZE	12.8.85	2	EI	Torun	7 Mar
17.01	Max	Hess	GER	13.7.96	3	EI	Torun	7 Mar
16.95	Chengetayi	Mapaya	ZIM	19.12.98	2	NCAA	Fayetteville	13 Mar
16.94	Donald	Scott	USA	23.2.92	2		Val-de-Reuil	14 Feb
16.92	Maksim	Nestserenko	BLR	1.9.92	1		Gomel	29 Jan
16.89	Tobia	Bocchi	ITA	7.4.97	4	WIT	Liévin	9 Feb
16.82	Lasha	Gulelauri	GEO	26.5.93	1	NC	Tbilisi	19 Feb
16.80	Dmitriy	Chizhikov	RUS	6.12.93	1	NC	Moskva	17 Feb
16.70		Xu Xiaolong	CHN	20.12.92	4		Chengdu	13 Mar
16.69	Jesper	Hellström	SWE	27.7.95	1	NC	Malmö/A	20 Feb
16.67	Adrian	Swiderski	POL	27.9.86	1		Ostrava	3 Feb
16.66	Enzo	Hodebar	FRA	17.5.99	3	NC	Miramas	20 Feb
16.65	Tiago	Pereira	POR	19.9.93	1		Lisboa (Jamor)	10 Jan
16.64	Chris	Edwards	USA	23.3.99	27 Feb	16.53	Owayne	Owens	JAM	8.3.00	13 Mar
16.59	Sean	Dixon-Bodie	USA-J	17.3.02	13 Mar	16.50	Vitaliy	Pavlov	RUS	12.1.97	17 Feb
16.57	Nazim	Babayev	AZE	8.10.97	20 Feb	16.49	Jean-Marc	Pontvianne	FRA	6.8.94	14 Feb
16.55	Levon	Aghasyan	ARM	19.1.95	7 Mar	16.49	Aleksey	Fyodorov	RUS	25.5.91	17 Feb
16.54	Alphonso	Jordan	USA	1.11.87	13 Feb						

SHOT

22.82	Ryan	Crouser	USA	18.12.92	1	ATL	Fayetteville	24 Jan
22.05	Joe	Kovacs	USA	28.6.89	1		Geneva	13 Feb
21.85	Turner	Washington	USA	10.2.99	1		Lubbock	13 Feb
21.83	Michał	Haratyk	POL	10.4.92	1		Łódz	12 Feb
21.74	Adrian	Piperi	USA	20.1.99	1		College Station	6 Feb
21.62	Tomás	Stanek	CZE	13.6.91	1	EI	Torun	5 Mar
21.54	Payton	Otterdahl	USA	2.4.96	1		Fargo	6 Feb
21.45	McKay	Johnson	USA	15.4.98	2		Lubbock	13 Feb
21.31	Filip	Mihaljevic	CRO	31.7.94	3	EI	Torun	5 Mar
21.28	Francisco	Belo	POR	27.3.91	4	EI	Torun	5 Mar
21.27	Josh	Awotunde	USA	12.6.95	3		Fayetteville	21 Feb
21.25	Armin	Sinancevic	SRB	14.8.96	1		Beograd	24 Feb
21.13	Aleksandr	Lesnoy	RUS	28.7.88	1		Slavyansk-na-Kubani	31 Jan
21.13	Wictor	Petersson	SWE	1.5.98	1	NC	Malmö/A	19 Feb
21.10	Abdelrahman	Mahmoud	BRN	1.1.01	1		Gomel	29 Jan
21.09	Marcus	Thomsen	NOR	7.1.98	1		Växjö	1 Feb
20.93	Mostafa Amr	Hassan	EGY	16.12.95	2		Nehvizdy	5 Feb
20.83	David	Storl	GER	27.7.90	1	NC	Dortmund	20 Feb
20.78	Mesud	Pezer	BIH	27.8.94	2		Beograd	24 Feb
20.69	Daniel	McArthur	USA	17.3.98	1	ACC	Clemson	27 Feb
20.68	Nick	Ponzio	USA	4.1.95	4		Fayetteville	21 Feb
20.65	Chukwuebuka	Enekwechi	NGR	28.1.93	2	ATL	Fayetteville	24 Jan
20.65	Bob	Bertemes	LUX	24.5.93	1		Luxembourg	13 Feb
20.54	Alex	Talley	USA	.98	1		Grand Forks	30 Jan
20.54	Konrad	Bukowiecki	POL	17.3.97	4	WIT	Torun	17 Feb
20.54	Burger	Lambrechts	RSA	6.8.98	1	Big 10	Geneva	27 Feb
20.53*	Asmir	Kolasinac	SRB	15.10.84	1		Beograd	26 Dec
	20.52				3		Beograd	24 Feb
20.50	Isaac	Odugbesan	NGR	22.4.98	1	SEC	Fayetteville	27 Feb
20.46	Leonardo	Fabbri	ITA	15.4.97	1		Padova	28 Feb
20.45	Maksim	Afonin	RUS	6.1.92	2		Moskva	7 Feb
20.45	Jakub	Szyszkowski	POL	21.8.91	2	NC	Torun	21 Feb
20.43	Shahin	Mehrdelan	IRI	21.6.95	1		Tehran	1 Mar
20.38	Andrei	Toader	ROU	26.5.97	1		Bucuresti	22 Jan
20.37	Jordan	Geist	USA	21.7.98	3		Lubbock	13 Feb
20.21	Tim	Nedow	CAN	16.10.90	1		Toronto	19 Mar
20.20	Tsanko	Arnaudov	POR	14.3.92	2		Lisboa (Jamor)	16 Jan

WORLD INDOOR LISTS 2021

20.20	Giorgi	Mujaridze	GEO	22.3.98	1	NC	Tbilisi			19 Feb
20.19	Pavel	Derkach	RUS	2.11.93	3		Moskva			7 Feb
20.13	Dmitriy	Karpuk	BLR	5.11.99	1	NC	Mogilyov			12 Feb
20.12	Simon	Bayer	GER	23.11.95	1		Sindelfingen			24 Jan
20.11	Konstantin	Lyadusov	RUS	2.3.88	2		Slavyansk-na-Kubani			31 Jan
20.09	Christian	Zimmermann	GER	9.7.94	2	NC	Dortmund			20 Feb
20.06	Darius	King	USA	1.9.99	1		Cedar Falls			22 Jan
20.06	Scott	Lincoln	GBR	7.5.93	1		Loughborough			14 Feb
20.01	Garrett	Appier	USA	15.10.92	1		Maryville			6 Feb
19.98	Jordan	West	USA	27.6.99	27 Feb	19.74	Odisséas	Mouzenidis	GRE	30.6.99	12 Feb
19.94	Dennis	Lewke	GER	23.7.93	5 Feb	19.70	Maksim	Sidorov	RUS	13.5.86	7 Feb
19.90	John	Meyer	USA	1.12.99	27 Feb	19.69	Franck	Elemba	CGO	21.7.90	13 Feb
19.88	Ihor	Musiyenko	UKR	22.8.93	10 Feb	19.68	Eric	Favors	IRL	16.11.96	6 Feb
19.87	Kiriákos	Zótos	GRE	17.1.96	6 Feb	19.67	Carlos	Tobalina	ESP	2.8.85	20 Feb
19.81	Ayomidotun	Ogundeji	NGR	24.2.96	26 Feb	19.66	Maxwell	Otterdahl	USA	31.5.01	20 Feb
19.80	Roger	Steen	USA	17.5.92	31 Jan	19.63	Ashinia	Miller	JAM	6.6.93	5 Feb
19.75	Liu Yang		CHN	29.10.86	12 Mar	19.61	Oleg	Tomashevich	BLR	31.5.00	12 Feb

DISCUS

66.32	Simon	Pettersson	SWE	3.1.94	1	Växjö		13 Feb
61.20	Jakob	Gardenkrans	SWE	15.8.97	2	Växjö		7 Feb

WEIGHT (35 LB)

24.82	Gleb	Dudarev	BLR	17.10.96	1		Lawrence	22 Jan
24.46	Thomas	Mardal	NOR	16.4.97	1	NCAA	Fayetteville	11 Mar
24.25	Denzel	Comenentia	NED	25.11.95	1		Blacksburg	19 Feb
24.21	Daniel	Haugh	USA	3.5.95	2		Blacksburg	19 Feb
23.79	Israel	Oloyede	USA	.98	2	NCAA	Fayetteville	11 Mar
23.52	Ragnar	Carlsson	SWE	16.11.00	1		Falun	18 Jan
22.90*	Alex	Talley	USA	.98	4 Dec	22.54	Bobby	Colantonio	USA	18.5.98	12 Feb
22.73	Manning	Plater	USA	12.6.97	11 Mar	22.53	Daniel	Roberts	USA	11.12.94	13 Feb
22.55	Tanner	Berg	USA	26.7.99	20 Feb	22.47	Jake	Wickey	USA	6.8.98	26 Feb

HEPTATHLON

6392	Kevin	Mayer	FRA	10.2.92	1	EI	Torun		7 Mar
	6.86	7.47 16.32	2.04	7.78		5.20	2:45.72		
6269	Ilya	Shkurenyov	RUS	11.1.91	1	NC	Smolensk		19 Feb
	6.99	7.46 14.29	2.11	7.97		5.40	2:48.48		
6264	Karel	Tilga	EST	5.2.98	1	NCAA	Fayetteville		12 Mar
	7.09	7.62 16.04	2.06	8.24		4.96	2:36.32		
6200	Kyle	Garland	USA	28.5.00	2	NCAA	Fayetteville		12 Mar
	7.06	7.50 15.41	2.15	8.07		4.86	2:45.53		
6158	Jorge	Ureña	ESP	8.10.93	2	EI	Torun		7 Mar
	7.03	7.33 14.57	2.10	7.87		4.90	2:43.16		
6133	Paweł	Wiesiołek	POL	13.8.91	3	EI	Torun		7 Mar
	6.95	7.31 15.27	2.01	8.27		5.20	2:43.13		
6111	Rik	Taam	NED	17.1.97	4	EI	Torun		7 Mar
	6.94	7.29 14.52	2.04	8.13		4.80	2:35.35		
6092	Simon	Ehammer	SUI	7.2.00	1		Frankfurt-am-Main		14 Feb
	6.82	7.73 14.78	1.95	7.83		4.80	2:51.93		
6089	Risto	Lillemets	EST	20.11.97	1		Tallinn		7 Feb
	6.97	7.28 14.14	2.07	8.14		5.01	2:42.15		
6076	Dario	Dester	ITA	22.7.00	1	NC	Ancona		21 Feb
	7.02	7.66 14.03	2.01	8.13		5.00	2:44.53		
6057	Maksim	Andraloits	BLR	17.6.97	1	NC	Gomel		28 Jan
	7.09	7.49 15.11	2.12	8.02		4.80	2:55.17		
6057	Andreas	Bechmann	GER	28.9.99	2		Frankfurt-am-Main		14 Feb
	7.02	7.41 14.08	2.10	8.62		5.20	2:43.38		
6036	Darko	Pesic	MNE	30.11.92	1	SRB Ch	Beograd		7 Feb
	7.19	7.24 16.69	2.08	8.12		4.60	2:43.45		
6010	Vitaliy	Zhuk	BLR	10.9.96	2		Tallinn		7 Feb
	7.04	7.01 16.51	2.01	8.16		4.91	2:46.27		
5995	Ayden	Owens	PUR	28.5.00	3	NCAA	Fayetteville		12 Mar
	6.82	7.36 14.07	1.94	7.87		4.56	2:40.07		
5986	Simone	Cairoli	ITA	12.9.90	2	NC	Ancona		21 Feb
	7.00	7.73 13.42	2.04	8.33		4.80	2:43.94		
5960	Leo	Neugebauer	GER	19.6.00	1		Lubbock		30 Jan
	7.05	7.57 15.94	2.06	8.37		5.00	3:03.00		
5950	Yuriy	Yeremich	BLR	24.10.95	2	NC	Gomel		28 Jan
	7.01	7.68 13.51	2.03	8.07		5.00	2:57.64		
5940	Andri	Oberholzer	SUI	24.7.96	1		Magglingen		7 Feb
	7.14	7.34 14.75	1.99	8.30		5.20	2:50.20		
5931	Fredrik	Samuelsson	SWE	16.2.95	1		Växjö		14 Feb
	7.15	7.41 14.80	2.04	8.20		4.84	2:48.89		

5913	Adam Sebastian	Helcelet		CZE	27.10.91	1		Praha	14 Feb
	7.10	7.30	15.64	1.95	7.98		4.90	2:53.83	
5907	Felix	Wolter		GER	4.10.97	4	NCAA	Fayetteville	12 Mar
	7.04	7.58	14.13	1.97	8.32		4.86	2:46.66	

5898	Markus	Ballengee	USA	8.1.98	26 Feb	5813	Sun	Qihao	CHN	18.2.00	13 Mar
5863	Jérémy	Lelièvre	FRA	8.2.91	20 Feb	5805	Romain	Martin	FRA	12.7.88	20 Feb
5863	Aléxandros	Spiridonídis	GRE	12.3.98	12 Mar	5800	Rody	de Wolff	NED	9.4.97	14 Feb

5000 Metres Walk: 18:33.6 Vasiliy Mizinov RUS 29.12.97 1 Chelyabinsk 6 Jan
10,000 Metres Walk: 40:27.86 Aleksandr Lyakhovich BLR 4.7.89 1 NC Mogilyov 12 Feb

WORLD INDOOR LISTS 2021 – WOMEN

60 METRES

7.03	Ajla	Del Ponte		SUI	15.7.96	1	EI	Toruń	7 Mar
7.05	Kemba	Nelson		JAM	23.2.00	1	NCAA	Fayetteville	13 Mar
7.08	Dina	Asher-Smith		GBR	4.12.95	1		Karlsruhe	29 Jan
7.08	Javianne	Oliver		USA	26.12.94	1	WIT	Toruń	17 Feb
7.09	TeeTee	Terry		USA	24.1.99	1h2	NCAA	Fayetteville	12 Mar
7.10	Blessing	Okagbare		NGR	9.10.88	1		Fayetteville	7 Feb
7.10	Aleia	Hobbs		USA	24.2.96	1	WIT	New York (SI)	13 Feb
7.10	Ewa	Swoboda		POL	26.7.97	1	NC	Toruń	20 Feb
7.11	Kiara	Grant		JAM	8.10.00	1h1	NCAA	Fayetteville	12 Mar
7.12	Amelie-Sophie	Lederer		GER	22.4.94	1	NC	Dortmund	20 Feb
7.14	Mikiah	Brisco		USA	14.7.96	1		Baton Rouge	16 Jan
7.14	Christania	Williams		JAM	17.10.94	2		Fayetteville	7 Feb
7.15	Julien	Alfred		LCA	10.6.01	1h2		College Station	6 Feb
7.15	Kayla	White		USA	24.9.96	1	WIT	New York (SI)	13 Feb
7.15	Joella	Lloyd		ANT-J	4.12.02	1	SEC	Fayetteville	27 Feb
7.15	Jada	Baylark		USA	17.10.97	3h2	NCAA	Fayetteville	12 Mar
7.16	Orlann	Ombissa-Dzangue	FRA	26.5.91	2		Karlsruhe	29 Jan
7.16	Candace	Hill		USA	11.2.99	1	WIT	New York (SI)	13 Feb
7.16	Lotta	Kemppinen		FIN	1.4.98	1	NC	Jyväskylä	20 Feb
7.17	Teahna	Daniels		USA	27.3.97	3		Fayetteville	7 Feb
7.17	Rosângela	Santos		BRA	20.12.90	2	WIT	Liévin	9 Feb
7.17	Hannah	Cunliffe		USA	9.1.96	2	WIT	New York (SI)	13 Feb
7.17	Kristina	Makarenko		RUS	28.2.97	1	NC	Moskva	15 Feb
7.18	Tatjana	Pinto		GER	2.7.92	1r1		Leverkusen	23 Jan
7.18	Tamari	Davis		USA-J	15.2.03	1		Virginia Beach	6 Feb
7.18	Tamara	Clark		USA	9.1.99	3h1	NCAA	Fayetteville	12 Mar
7.19	Carolle	Zahi		FRA	12.6.94	1		Miramas	22 Jan
7.19	Dezerea	Bryant		USA	27.4.93	3		Metz	6 Feb
7.19	Jenna	Prandini		USA	20.11.92	4	WIT	New York (SI)	13 Feb
7.19	Jennifer	Montag		GER	11.2.98	2	NC	Dortmund	20 Feb
7.19	Yasmin	Kwadwo		GER	9.11.90	3	NC	Dortmund	20 Feb

7.20	Morolake	Akinosun	USA	17.5.94	24 Jan	7.22	Jamile	Samuel	NED	24.4.92	7 Mar
7.20	Rebekka	Haase	GER	2.1.93	20 Feb	7.22	Alfreda	Steele	USA	19.12.97	13 Mar
7.20A	Brianna	Duncan	USA	6.10.98	27 Feb	7.23	Maja	Mihalinec	SLO	17.12.89	30 Jan
7.21	Gabby	Thomas	USA	7.12.96	24 Jan	7.23	Kynnedy	Flannel	USA	12.7.00	6 Feb
7.21	Lisa	Mayer	GER	2.5.96	29 Jan	7.23	Rafailía Spanoudáki-Hatzirígа	GRE	7.6.94	12 Feb
7.21	Anna	Kiełbasińska	POL	26.6.90	30 Jan	7.23	Jayla	Kirkland	USA	13.2.99	21 Feb
7.21	Daryll	Neita	GBR	29.8.96	7 Feb	7.23	Halle	Hazzard	GRN	4.2.99	12 Mar
7.21	Abby	Steiner	USA	24.11.99	12 Feb	7.24	Pia	Skrzyszowska	POL	20.4.01	23 Jan
7.21	Semira	Killebrew	USA	30.3.01	27 Feb	7.24	Shawnti	Jackson	USA-Y	2.5.05	7 Feb
7.22	Asha	Philip	GBR	25.10.90	29 Jan	7.24	Alexandra	Burghardt	GER	28.4.94	20 Feb
7.22	Briana	Williams	JAM-J	21.3.02	13 Feb	7.24	Cynthia	Leduc	FRA	16.2.97	14 Feb

200 METRES

22.38	Abby	Steiner	USA	24.11.99	1	NCAA	Fayetteville	13 Mar
22.40	Shaunae	Miller-Uibo	BAH	15.4.94	1		Fayetteville	31 Jan
22.45	Tamara	Clark	USA	9.1.99	2	NCAA	Fayetteville	13 Mar
22.55	Jenna	Prandini	USA	20.11.92	1		Fayetteville	7 Feb
22.55	Kynnedy	Flannel	USA	12.7.00	1	Big 12	Lubbock	27 Feb
22.59	Allyson	Felix	USA	18.11.85	1		Fayetteville	21 Feb
22.70	Quanera	Hayes	USA	7.3.92	2		Fayetteville	7 Feb
22.75	Favour	Ofili	NGR-J	31.12.02	1rB	SEC	Fayetteville	27 Feb
22.75	TeeTee	Terry	USA	24.1.99	2rB	NCAA	Fayetteville	13 Mar
22.76	Anavia	Battle	USA	28.3.99	3rB	NCAA	Fayetteville	13 Mar
22.83	Rebekka	Haase	GER	2.1.93	1r1		Leipzig	12 Feb
22.87	Kevona	Davis	JAM	20.12.01	2	Big 12	Lubbock	27 Feb
22.91	Jasmine	Camacho-Quinn	PUR	21.8.96	2		Fayetteville	21 Feb
22.94	Talitha	Diggs	USA-J	22.8.02	1rB		Fayetteville	13 Mar
22.94	Delecia	McDuffie	USA		3h1	NCAA	Fayetteville	12 Mar
23.00	Corinna	Schwab	GER	5.4.99	2r2		Leipzig	12 Feb

23.01	Blessing	Okagbare	NGR	9.10.88	7 Feb	23.16	Dajour	Miles	USA	25.7.01	27 Feb
23.03	Arria	Minor	USA	9.2.01	27 Feb	23.16	Amira	Young	USA	15.6.00	12 Mar
23.07	Jessica-Bianca	Wessolly	GER	11.12.96	30 Jan	23.17	Jania	Martin	USA	9.5.00	26 Feb
23.09	Jada	Baylark	USA	17.10.97	26 Feb	23.23	Shawnti	Jackson	USA-Y	2.5.05	27 Feb
23.10	Lieke	Klaver	NED	20.8.98	6 Mar	23.23	Tiana	Wilson	USA	19.7.00	26 Feb
23.12	Trishauna	Hemmings	JAM	17.11.97	27 Feb						

300 METRES

35.73	Gabby	Thomas		USA	7.12.96	1			New York (SI)		13 Feb
35.99	Lynne	Irby		USA	6.12.98	2			New York (SI)		13 Feb
36.68	Jenna	Prandini		USA	20.11.92	1B	ATL		Fayetteville		24 Jan
36.69	Kendall	Ellis		USA	8.3.96	3			New York (SI)		13 Feb
36.69+	Femke	Bol		NED	23.2.00	1	in 400		Torun		6 Mar
36.78	Shakima	Wimbley	USA	23.4.95	24 Jan	36.95+	Justyna	Swiety-Eresticl	POL	3.12.92	6 Mar
36.83	Kendra	Harrison	USA	18.9.92	24 Jan	36.97	Kyra	Jefferson	USA	23.9.94	24 Jan
36.93+	Lieke	Klaver	NED	20.8.98	6 Mar	37.10	Brittany	Aveni	USA	18.1.98	22 Jan
36.95	Ashley	Henderson	USA	4.12.95	24 Jan	37.10+	Jodie	Williams	GBR	28.9.93	6 Mar

400 METRES

50.21	Shaunae	Miller-Uibo		BAH	15.4.94	1	WIT	New York (SI)	13 Feb
50.52	Athing	Mu		USA-J	8.6.02	1		College Station	6 Feb
50.57	Shamier	Little		USA	20.3.95	1		Fayetteville	21 Feb
50.63	Femke	Bol		NED	23.2.00	1	EI	Torun	6 Mar
50.84	Kaelin	Roberts		USA	6.1.99	1	NCAA	Fayetteville	13 Mar
51.14	Talitha	Diggs		USA-J	22.8.02	1	SEC	Fayetteville	27 Feb
51.21	Lieke	Klaver		NED	20.8.98	2	NC	Apeldoorn	21 Feb
51.34	Justyna	Swiety-Eresticl		POL	3.12.92	1s2	EI	Torun	5 Mar
51.41	Charokee	Young		JAM	21.8.00	3	NCAA	Fayetteville	13 Mar
51.60	Stacey-Ann	Williams		JAM	8.3.99	1	Big 12	Lubbock	27 Feb
51.73	Jodie	Williams		GBR	28.9.93	3	EI	Torun	6 Mar
51.76	Quanera	Hayes		USA	7.3.92	1	ATL	Fayetteville	24 Jan
51.82	Taylor	Manson		USA	29.9.99	2	SEC	Fayetteville	27 Feb
51.82	Rosaline	Effiong		USA	8.5.01	3h3	NCAA	Fayetteville	12 Mar
51.83	Amber	Anning		GBR	18.11.00	4	NCAA	Fayetteville	13 Mar
51.92	Wadeline	Jonathas		USA	19.2.98	1		Columbia SC	6 Feb
51.92	Andrea	Miklos		ROU	17.4.99	1	Balk Ch	Istanbul	20 Feb
51.94	Bailey	Lear		USA	17.3.01	1		Lubbock	12 Feb
51.94	Phil	Healy		IRL	19.11.94	4	EI	Torun	6 Mar
52.01	Corinna	Schwab		GER	5.4.99	1	NC	Dortmund	21 Feb
52.02	Tiana	Wilson		USA	19.7.00	2rB	NCAA	Fayetteville	13 Mar
52.03	Zoey	Clark		GBR	25.10.94	1		Glasgow	6 Feb
52.04	Yekaterina	Renzhina		RUS	18.10.94	1	NC	Moskva	16 Feb
52.06	Chrisann	Gordon		JAM	18.9.94	2		Fayetteville	21 Feb
52.10	Morgan	Burks-Magee		USA	6.3.99	1rB	SEC	Fayetteville	27 Feb
52.11	Anna	Ryzhykova		UKR	24.11.89	3s2	EI	Torun	5 Mar
52.12	Shakima	Wimbley		USA	23.4.95	1rB		Fayetteville	7 Feb
52.12	Agne	Serksniene		LTU	18.2.88	1		Magglingen	13 Feb
52.12	Polina	Miller		RUS	9.6.00	2	NC	Moskva	16 Feb
52.14	Amandine	Brossier		FRA	15.8.95	1rC		Metz	6 Feb
52.14	Kennedy	Simon		USA	12.2.00	4h3	NCAA	Fayetteville	12 Mar
52.17	Jessie	Knight		GBR	15.6.94	2h3	EI	Torun	5 Mar
52.20	Lada	Vondrová		CZE	6.9.99	1	NC	Ostrava	21 Feb
52.22	Léa	Sprunger		SUI	5.3.90	2rC		Metz	6 Feb
52.27	Paris	Peoples		USA	27.5.00	1h2	SEC	Fayetteville	26 Feb
52.27	Honour	Finley		USA	11.8.99	1rB	Big 12	Lubbock	27 Feb
52.27	Cynthia	Bolingo Mbongo		BEL	12.1.93	3h3	EI	Torun	5 Mar
52.28	Aliyah	Abrams		GUY	3.4.97	2		Columbia SC	6 Feb
52.32	Megan	Moss	BAH-J	22.3.02	27 Feb	52.52	Modesta	Morauskaite	LTU	2.10.95	5 Mar
52.35	Brittany	Aveni	USA	18.1.98	12 Feb	52.54	Amarachi	Pipi	GBR	26.11.95	5 Mar
52.39	Hanna	Mikhailova	BLR	29.3.98	12 Feb	52.56	Kornelia	Lesiewicz	POL-J	14.8.03	21 Feb
52.40	Nicole	Yeargin	GBR	11.8.97	12 Feb	52.60	Jessica	Beard	USA	8.1.89	13 Feb
52.51	Syaira	Richardson	USA	29.10.98	12 Feb	52.60	Laura	Müller	GER	11.12.95	21 Feb
52.51	Shafiqua	Maloney	VIN	27.2.99	12 Feb	Oversized track					
						52.55	Ziyah	Holman	USA-J	1.3.02	26 Feb

600 METRES

1:25.80	Athing	Mu		USA-J	8.6.02	1			College Station		23 Jan
1:25.85	Natoya	Goule		JAM	30.3.91	1			Clemson		15 Jan
1:27.02	Sophia	Gorriaran	USA-Y	20.6.05	30 Jan	1:27.20	Roisin	Willis	USA-Y	6.8.04	30 Jan

800 METRES

1:57.52	Gudaf	Tsegay		ETH	23.1.97	1		Val-de-Reuil	14 Feb
1:58.19	Habitam	Alemu		ETH	9.7.97	1	WIT	Torun	17 Feb
1:58.40	Athing	Mu		USA-J	8.6.02	1	SEC	Fayetteville	27 Feb
1:59.03	Keely	Hodgkinson		GBR-J	3.3.02	1		Wien	30 Jan
1:59.90	Aleksandra	Gulyayeva		RUS	30.4.94	1	NC	Moskva	16 Feb
2:00.42	Joanna	Józwik		POL	30.1.91	2	WIT	Torun	17 Feb

2:00.53	Heather	MacLean	USA	31.8.95	1			Fayetteville		21 Feb
2:00.58	Síofra	Cléirigh Büttner	IRL	21.7.95	2			Fayetteville		21 Feb
2:00.64	Jemma	Reekie	GBR	6.3.98	1	WIT		Liévin		9 Feb
2:00.69	Aaliyah	Miller	USA	28.8.98	1	NCAA		Fayetteville		13 Mar
2:00.92	Hedda	Hynne	NOR	13.3.90	3	WIT		Liévin		9 Feb
2:00.98	Nadia	Power	IRL	11.1.98	3	WIT		Torun		17 Feb
2:01.01	Noélie	Yarigo	BEN	26.12.85	4	WIT		Torun		17 Feb
2:01.07	Angelika	Cichocka	POL	15.3.88	5	WIT		Torun		17 Feb
2:01.08	Natoya	Goule	JAM	30.3.91	1			Clemson		30 Jan
2:01.13	Esther	Guerrero	ESP	7.2.90	2	WIT		Madrid		24 Feb
2:01.14#	Hanna	Green	USA	16.10.94	1			Seattle		27 Feb
2:01.21	Laurie	Barton	USA	13.2.98	2	NCAA		Fayetteville		13 Mar
2:01.22	Shafiqua	Maloney	VIN	27.2.99	3	NCAA		Fayetteville		13 Mar
2:01.44	Adelle	Tracey	GBR	27.5.93	3			Fayetteville		21 Feb
2:01.48	Georgie	Hartigan	IRL	1.3.96	1			Dublin (Abbotstown)		21 Feb
2:01.65	Marusa	Mismas-Zrimsek	SLO	24.10.94	1	NC		Novo Mesto		13 Feb
2:01.67	Louise	Shanahan	IRL	26.1.97	2			Dublin (Abbotstown)		21 Feb
2:01.79	Ajee'	Wilson	USA	8.5.94	1	WIT		New York (SI)		13 Feb
2:01.85	Britt	Ummels	NED	24.8.93	1			Apeldoorn		10 Feb
2:01.96	Lindsey	Butler	USA	26.8.00	1	ACC		Clemson		27 Feb
2:01.99	Lore	Hoffmann	SUI	25.7.96	2			Metz		6 Feb

2:02.07	Juliette	Whittaker	USA-J	1.12.03	16	Jan	2:02.48	Bregje	Sloot	NED	28.1.00	10 Feb
2:02.07	Bianka	Bartha-Kéri	HUN	19.4.94	13	Feb	2:02.50	Elise	Vanderelst	BEL	27.1.98	20 Feb
2:02.17	Kaela	Edwards	USA	8.12.93	13	Feb	2:02.51	Nikki	Hiltz	USA	23.10.94	7 Feb
2:02.20#	Claire	Seymour	USA	.99	27	Feb	2:02.54	Sage	Hurta	USA	23.6.98	30 Jan
	2:02.25				13	Mar	2:02.57	Lovisa	Lindh	SWE	9.7.91	6 Feb
2:02.24	Renée	Eykens	BEL	8.6.96	20	Feb	2:02.71	Irene	Baldessari	ITA	21.1.93	30 Jan
2:02.29	Iseult	O'Donnell	IRL	20.7.93	21	Feb	2:02.73	Ellie	Baker	GBR	3.6.98	13 Feb
2:02.33	Cynthia	Anais	FRA	18.1.88	13	Feb	2:02.79	Suzanne	Voorrips	NED	11.10.93	10 Feb
2:02.40	Dana	Mecke	USA	20.9.87	21	Feb	2:02.79	Anna	Wielgosz	POL	9.11.93	5 Mar
2:02.44	Sophia	Gorriaran	USA-Y	20.6.05	7	Feb	2:02.81	Amber	Tanner	USA	24.1.98	13 Feb
2:02.45	Isabelle	Boffey	GBR	13.4.00	13	Feb	2:02.85	Gabrielle	Wilkinson	USA	10.6.99	27 Feb
2:02.45	Lena	Kandissounon	FRA	26.11.98	14	Feb	2:02.88	Kelsey	Harris	USA	29.5.97	6 Feb

1000 METRES

2:37.35	Aleksandra	Gulyayeva	RUS	30.4.94	1			Yekaterinburg		7 Jan
2:37.36+	Gudaf	Tsegay	ETH	23.1.97	1	in 1500		Liévin		9 Feb
2:37.73	Lucia	Stafford	CAN	17.8.98	5 Feb	2:41.0+	Laura	Muir	GBR	9.5.93	9 Feb

1500 METRES

3:53.09	Gudaf	Tsegay	ETH	23.1.97	1	WIT		Liévin		9 Feb
3:59.58	Laura	Muir	GBR	9.5.93	2	WIT		Liévin		9 Feb
4:04.79	Melissa	Courtney-Bryant	GBR	30.8.93	3	WIT		Liévin		9 Feb
4:05.70	Lucia	Stafford	CAN	17.8.98	1			Toronto		29 Jan
4:05.71	Elise	Vanderelst	BEL	27.1.98	4	WIT		Liévin		9 Feb
4:06.32	Heather	MacLean	USA	31.8.95	1	WIT		New York (SI)		13 Feb
4:06.86	Hanna	Klein	GER	6.4.93	5	WIT		Liévin		9 Feb
4:07.21	Cory	McGee	USA	29.5.92	2	WIT		New York (SI)		13 Feb
4:07.48	Esther	Guerrero	ESP	7.2.90	1	NC		Madrid		21 Feb
4:08.46	Yelena	Korobkina	RUS	25.11.90	1			Moskva		7 Feb

4:09.40	Josephine	Chelangat	KEN	10.10.98	13	Feb	4:10.33	Caterina	Granz	GER	14.3.94	7 Feb
4:09.42	Hirut	Meshesha	ETH	20.1.01	24	Feb	4:10.43	Katie	Snowden	GBR	9.3.94	13 Feb
4:09.43	Marusa	Mismas-Zrimsek	SLO	24.10.94	20	Feb	4:10.56	Katharina	Trost	GER	28.6.95	7 Feb
4:09.44	Marta	Pérez	ESP	19.4.93	21	Feb	4:10.77	Millie	Paladino	USA	18.10.95	13 Feb
4:09.46	Edina	Jebitok	KEN	10.11.01	13	Feb	4:10.84	Mariah	Kelly	CAN	19.8.91	13 Feb
4:09.67	Síofra	Cléirigh Büttner	IRL	21.7.95	13	Feb	4:11.11	Elena	Burkard	GER	10.2.92	7 Feb
4:09.77	Holly	Archer	GBR	7.11.93	5	Mar	4:11.26	Alexa	Efraimson	USA	20.2.97	13 Feb
4:09.82	Nikki	Hiltz	USA	23.10.94	13	Feb	4:11.42	Sara	Kuivisto	FIN	17.8.91	20 Feb
4:09.92	Gesa-Felicitas	Krause	GER	3.8.92	5	Mar	4:11.48	Diana	Mezuliániková	CZE	10.4.92	5 Ma
4:09.94	Agueda	Muñoz	ESP	19.3.99	5	Mar	4:11.55	Martyna	Galant	POL	26.1.95	13 Feb

ONE MILE

4:27.54	Heather	MacLean	USA	31.8.95	1			Fayetteville		31 Jan
4:27.68	Aleksandra	Gulyayeva	RUS	30.4.94	1			Orenburg		30 Jan
4:29.08#	Hanna	Green	USA	16.10.94	1			Seattle		13 Feb

4:30.47#	Courtney	Wayment	USA	.98	26	Feb	4:31.06#	Rebecca	Mehra	USA	25.10.94	26 Feb
4:30.54	Rachel	Schneider	USA	18.7.91	20	Feb	4:31.21#	Allie	Schadler	USA	7.7.99	26 Feb
4:30.56	Danielle	Jones	USA	21.8.96	31	Jan	4:31.39	Josette	Norris	USA	15.12.95	1 Feb
4:30.58	Sage	Hurta	USA	23.6.98	13	Mar	4:31.73#	Olivia	Hoj	USA	.98	26 Feb
4:30.65#	Angel	Piccirillo	USA	8.1.94	26	Feb	4:31.83	Kristlin	Gear	USA	20.7.99	13 Feb
4:30.67#	Alli	Cash	USA	1.11.94	13	Feb						

2000 METRES

5:37.2+	Gudaf	Tsegay	ETH	23.1.97	1	in 3000		Madrid		24 Feb
5:37.5+	Lemlem	Hailu	ETH	21.5.01	2	in 3000		Madrid		24 Feb
5:43.32	Yelena	Korobkina	RUS	25.11.90	1			Yekaterinburg		7 Jan
5:44.54	Anna	Tropina	RUS	3.11.98	2			Yekaterinburg		7 Jan

3000 METRES

8:22.65	Gudaf	Tsegay	ETH	23.1.97	1	WIT	Madrid		24 Feb
8:29.28	Lemlem	Hailu	ETH	21.5.01	2	WIT	Madrid		24 Feb
8:31.72	Beatrice	Chepkoech	KEN	6.7.91	2	WIT	Torun		17 Feb
8:33.62	Sifan	Hassan	NED	1.1.93	2	WIT	Liévin		9 Feb
8:36.41+	Elle	Purrier	USA	20.2.95	1	in 2M	New York (SI)		13 Feb
8:37.06	Beatrice	Chebet	KEN	5.3.00	3	WIT	Madrid		24 Feb
8:37.84	Fantu	Worku	ETH	29.3.99	4	WIT	Liévin		9 Feb
8:38.20	Tsige	Gebreselama	ETH	30.9.00	5	WIT	Liévin		9 Feb
8:39.19+	Emma	Coburn	USA	19.10.90	2	in 2M	New York (SI)		13 Feb
8:42.41	Melissa	Courtney-Bryant	GBR	30.8.93	3		Karlsruhe		29 Jan
8:44.43	Gloria	Kite	KEN	29.12.98	4		Karlsruhe		29 Jan
8:45.66	Svetlana	Aplachkina	RUS	28.11.92	1	NC	Moskva		15 Feb
8:46.03	Yelena	Korobkina	RUS	25.11.90	2	NC	Moskva		15 Feb
8:46.43	Amy-Eloise	Markovc	GBR	5.8.95	1	EI	Torun		5 Mar
8:46.54	Alice	Finot	FRA	9.2.91	2	EI	Torun		5 Mar
8:46.60	Verity	Ockenden	GBR	31.8.91	3	EI	Torun		5 Mar
8:47.73+	Julie-Anne	Staehli	CAN	21.12.93	3	in 2M	New York (SI)		13 Feb
8:48.78	Meraf	Bahta	SWE	24.6.89	4	EI	Torun		5 Mar
8:48.82	Marusa	Mismas-Zrimsek	SLO	24.10.94	5		Karlsruhe		29 Jan
8:48.82	Amelia	Quirk	GBR	18.12.99	5	EI	Torun		5 Mar
8:49.13	Selamawit	Bayoulgn	ISR	24.3.94	6	EI	Torun		5 Mar
8:49.63	Maureen	Koster	NED	3.7.92	8	WIT	Liévin		9 Feb
8:51.09	Elena	Burkard	GER	10.2.92	5 Mar	8:54.18	Nataliya	Strebkova	UKR	6.3.95	5 Mar
8:51.43+	Katrina	Coogan	USA	15.11.93	13 Feb	8:54.37	Hanna	Klein	GER	6.4.93	21 Feb
8:51.66+	Emily	Lipari	USA	19.11.92	13 Feb	8:54.66	Ciara	Mageean	IRL	12.3.92	2 Jan
8:52.75#	Anna	Camp	USA	9.4.98	12 Feb	8:54.90#	Courtney	Wayment	USA	.98	12 Feb
8:52.76	Jip	Vastenburg	NED	21.3.94	29 Jan	8:55.19#	Eleanor	Fulton	USA	17.5.93	12 Feb
8:53.39+	Helen	Schlachtenhaufen	USA	14.3.95	13 Feb	8:55.25	Gesa-Felicitas	Krause	GER	3.8.92	9 Feb
8:53.52#	Alli	Cash	USA	1.11.94	12 Feb	8:55.45	Viktória	Wagner-Gyürkes	HUN	15.10.92	17 Feb
8:53.90	Lucía	Rodríguez	ESP	26.7.98	5 Mar	8:56.02	Joyce	Kimeli	KEN	9.5.97	27 Feb

TWO MILES

9:10.28	Elle	Purrier	USA	20.2.95	1	WIT	New York (SI)		13 Feb
9:15.71	Emma	Coburn	USA	19.10.90	2	WIT	New York (SI)		13 Feb
9:22.66	Julie-Anne	Staehli	CAN	21.12.93	3	WIT	New York (SI)		13 Feb
9:26.87	Emily	Lipari	USA	19.11.92	4	WIT	New York (SI)		13 Feb
9:26.95	Helen	Schlachtenhaufen	USA	14.3.95	5	WIT	New York (SI)		13 Feb
9:27.45	Katrina	Coogan	USA	15.11.93	6	WIT	New York (SI)		13 Feb
9:30.69	Amy-Eloise	Markovc	GBR	5.8.95	7	WIT	New York (SI)		13 Feb

5000 Metres: 15:26.54 Ednah Kurgat USA 15.6.91 1   Virginia Beach   4 Mar

60 METRES HURDLES

7.77	Nadine	Visser	NED	9.2.95	1	EI	Torun		7 Mar
7.81	Christina	Clemons	USA	29.5.90	1	WIT	Torun		17 Feb
7.82	Kendra	Harrison	USA	18.9.92	1	WIT	New York (SI)		13 Feb
7.86	Tonea	Marshall	USA	17.10.98	1	ATL	Fayetteville		24 Jan
7.86	Danielle	Williams	JAM	14.9.92	1		Fayetteville		21 Feb
7.88	Pia	Skrzyszowska	POL	20.4.01	1s3	EI	Torun		7 Mar
7.89	Tiffany	Porter	GBR	13.11.87	3	ATL	Fayetteville		24 Jan
7.89	Gabriele	Cunningham	USA	22.2.93	3	WIT	New York (SI)		13 Feb
7.89	Chanel	Brissett	USA	18.8.99	1	Big 12	Lubbock		27 Feb
7.89	Cindy	Sember	GBR	5.8.94	2s2	EI	Torun		7 Mar
7.91	Nooralotta	Neziri	FIN	9.11.92	3r2		Berlin		5 Feb
7.91	Elvira	German	BLR	9.1.97	1	NC	Mogilyov		12 Feb
7.91	Ackera	Nugent	JAM-J	29.4.02	1h2	Big 12	Lubbock		26 Feb
7.93	Laeticia	Bapte	FRA	8.2.99	1	NC	Miramas		20 Feb
7.94	Tobi	Amusan	NGR	23.4.97	2		Karlsruhe		29 Jan
7.94	Cyrena	Samba-Mayela	FRA	31.10.00	2	NC	Miramas		20 Feb
7.96	Brittany	Anderson	JAM	31.1.01	2h1		Fayetteville		7 Feb
7.96	Grace	Stark	USA	6.5.01	1		Fayetteville		12 Feb
7.96	Karolina	Kołeczek	POL	15.1.93	1	NC	Torun		20 Feb
7.98	Jasmine	Jones	USA	30.11.01	1		Lubbock		12 Feb
7.98	Zoë	Sedney	NED	15.12.01	2	NC	Apeldoorn		21 Feb
7.98	Luca	Kozák	HUN	6.1.96	3s2	EI	Torun		7 Mar
7.99	Luminosa	Bogliolo	ITA	3.7.95	2s3	EI	Torun		7 Mar
7.99	Daszay	Freeman	JAM	25.1.00	2	NCAA	Fayetteville		13 Mar
8.00	Tiara	McMinn	USA	23.2.99	1	ACC	Clemson		27 Feb
8.01	Alina	Talay	BLR	14.5.89	31 Jan	8.04	Masumi	Aoki	JPN	16.4.94	17 Feb
8.02A	Emily	Sloan	USA	26.5.00	27 Feb	8.05	Anne	Zagré	BEL	13.3.90	5 Feb
8.03	Svetlana	Parakhonko	BLR	12.6.97	12 Feb	8.05	Ruslana	Rashkovan	BLR	18.3.97	12 Feb
8.03	Taliyah	Brooks	USA	8.2.95	21 Feb	8.05	Kseniya	Labygina	RUS	20.2.00	23 Feb
8.03	Milan	Young	USA	22.6.99	27 Feb	8.05	Emelia	Chatfield	USA	23.11.01	27 Feb
8.04	Reetta	Hurske	FIN	15.5.95	29 Jan	8.05	Ditaji	Kambundji	SUI-J	20.5.02	6 Mar

WORLD INDOOR LISTS 2021   429

8.06	Imani	Carothers	USA	21.10.99	30 Jan	8.07	Mecca	McGlaston	USA	23.7.98	13 Mar
8.06	Teresa	Errandonea	ESP	15.11.94	24 Feb	8.08	Evonne	Britton	USA	28.7.91	14 Feb
8.06	Erin	Marsh	USA	12.7.99	27 Feb	8.09	Vitoria	Alves	BRA	11.3.98	26 Feb
8.06	Sarah	Lavin	IRL	28.5.94	6 Mar	8.09	Trishauna	Hemmings	JAM	17.11.97	27 Feb
8.07	Fanny	Quénot	FRA	2.10.90	20 Feb						

HIGH JUMP

2.06	Yaroslava	Mahuchikh	UKR	19.9.01	1			Banská Bystrica	2 Feb
2.00	Mariya	Lasitskene	RUS	14.1.93	1			Moskva	24 Jan
2.00	Vashti	Cunningham	USA	18.1.98	1			Fayetteville	7 Feb
1.98	Iryna	Herashchenko	UKR	10.3.95	2	EI		Toruń	7 Mar
1.96	Yuliya	Levchenko	UKR	28.11.97	2			Banská Bystrica	2 Feb
1.96	Morgan	Lake	GBR	12.5.97	1			Beograd	24 Feb
1.96	Ella	Junnila	FIN	6.12.98	3	EI		Toruń	7 Mar
1.94	Karina	Demidik	BLR	10.2.99	1	NC		Mogilyov	12 Feb
1.94	Alessia	Trost	ITA	8.3.93	1			Łódź	12 Feb
1.94	Mariya	Kochanova	RUS-J	30.5.02	1	NC-23		Kirov	25 Feb
1.93	Kristina	Korolyova	RUS	6.11.90	2			Moskva	24 Jan
1.93	Kristina	Ovchinnikova	KAZ	21.3.01	1			Ust-Kamenogorsk	30 Jan
1.93	Elena	Vallortigara	ITA	21.9.91	4			Banská Bystrica	2 Feb
1.93	Marija	Vukovic	MNE	21.1.92	1	SRB Ch		Beograd	7 Feb
1.93	Tyra	Gittens	TTO	6.6.98	1P	NCAA		Fayetteville	11 Mar
1.93 ?	Jelena	Rowe	USA	1.8.99	1			Louisville	7 Mar
1.92	Nadezhda	Dubovitskaya	KAZ	12.3.98	1	NC		Ust-Kamenogorsk	19 Feb
1.92	Nadezhda	Andryukhina	RUS	3.7.01	2	NC-23		Kirov	25 Feb
1.92	Daniela	Stanciu	ROU	15.10.87	5	EI		Toruń	7 Mar
1.91	Tatyana	Yermachenkova	RUS	9.9.98	2			Slavyansk-na-Kubani	31 Jan
1.91	Darya	Slepova	RUS	10.4.00	3			Moskva	7 Feb
1.91	Merel	Maes	BEL-Y	22.1.05	1	NC		Louvain-la-Neuve	20 Feb
1.91	Maja	Nilsson	SWE	8.12.99	1	NC		Malmö/A	21 Feb
1.91	Emily	Borthwick	GBR	2.9.97	Q	EI		Toruń	5 Mar
1.90	Anna	Chicherova	RUS	22.7.82	4			Moskva	24 Jan
1.90	Salomé	Lang	SUI	18.11.97	1			Magglingen	31 Jan
1.90	Claire	Orcel	BEL	2.12.97	7			Banská Bystrica	2 Feb
1.90	Yuliya	Chumachenko	UKR	2.10.94	4	NC		Sumy	11 Feb

1.89	Abigail	O'Donoghue	USA	21.5.99	22 Jan	1.89	Nafissatou	Thiam	BEL	19.8.94	5 Mar
1.89	Oksana	Okuneva	UKR	14.3.90	30 Jan	1.88	Christina	Honsel	GER	7.7.97	2 Feb
1.89	Anna	Hall	USA	23.3.01	25 Feb	1.88	Jeannelle	Scheper	LCA	21.11.94	21 Feb

POLE VAULT

4.90	Anzhelika	Sidorova	RUS	28.6.91	1			Moskva	21 Feb
4.88	Sandi	Morris	USA	8.7.92	1			Fayetteville	7 Feb
4.85	Holly	Bradshaw	GBR	2.11.91	1			Rouen	6 Feb
4.78	Olivia	Gruver	USA	29.7.97	2			Fayetteville	7 Feb
4.75	Angelica	Moser	SUI	9.10.97	1	EI		Toruń	6 Mar
4.73	Irina	Zhuk	BLR	26.1.93	2			Aubière	27 Feb
4.71	Eléni-Klaoúdia	Pólak	GRE	9.9.96	1			Pireás	13 Feb
4.70	Anicka	Newell	CAN	5.8.93	1			Belton	2 Jan
4.70	Tina	Sutej	SLO	7.11.88	1			Ostrava	3 Feb
4.70	Bridget	Guy	USA	18.3.96	1			Blacksburg	6 Feb
4.70	Aksana	Gataullina	RUS	17.7.00	2			Moskva	7 Feb
4.70	Polina	Knoroz	RUS	20.7.99	2			Moskva	21 Feb
4.70	Irina	Ivanova	RUS	19.4.96	3			Moskva	21 Feb
4.65	Alysha	Newman	CAN	29.6.94	2			Belton	2 Jan
4.63	Ekateríni	Stefanídi	GRE	4.2.90	2	WIT		Liévin	9 Feb
4.61	Yana	Hladiychuk	UKR	21.5.93	1	NC		Sumy	10 Feb
4.60		Li Ling	CHN	6.7.89	1			Chengdu	12 Mar
4.58	Megan	Clark	USA	10.6.94	3			Fayetteville	7 Feb
4.56	Lisa	Gunnarsson	SWE	20.8.99	1	NCAA		Fayetteville	12 Mar
4.55	Olga	Mullina	RUS	1.8.92	3	NC		Moskva	15 Feb
4.55	Wilma	Murto	FIN	11.6.98	6	EI		Toruń	6 Mar
4.53		Xu Huiqin	CHN	4.9.93	1			Xi'an	1 Feb
4.53	Fanny	Smets	BEL	21.4.86	1	NC		Louvain-la-Neuve	20 Feb
4.52	Femke	Pluim	NED	10.5.94	2			Tourcoing	31 Jan
4.52	Kristen	Leland	USA	1.7.92	1			Allendale	13 Feb
4.51	Kortney	Oates	USA	26.7.92	1			Seattle	26 Feb
4.50	Katie	Nageotte	USA	13.6.91	2	ATL		Fayetteville	24 Jan
4.50	Alyona	Lutkovskaya	RUS	15.3.96	3	NC		Moskva	27 Jan
4.50	Maryna	Kylypko	UKR	10.11.95	2	Balk Ch		Istanbul	20 Feb

4.47	Michaela	Meijer	SWE	30.7.93	20 Feb	4.43	Malen Ruiz	de Azúa	ESP	17.11.95	21 Feb
4.46	Tuesdi	Tidwell	USA	20.9.98	29 Jan	4.42	Lisa	Ryzih	GER	27.9.88	31 Jan
4.45	Sonia	Malavisi	ITA	31.10.94	17 Jan	4.42	Andrea	San José	ESP	4.10.97	6 Feb
4.44	Rachel	Baxter	USA	5.4.99	6 Feb	4.41	Alina	McDonald	USA	26.8.97	6 Feb
4.44	Margot	Chevrier	FRA	21.12.99	13 Feb	4.41	Elina	Giallurachis	FRA	29.5.01	20 Feb
4.43	Romana	Malácová	CZE	15.5.87	3 Feb	4.41	Roberta	Bruni	ITA	8.3.94	21 Feb

4.41	Mesure Tutku	Yılmaz	TUR	1.1.00	23 Feb	4.40	Diamara	Planell	PUR	16.2.93	12 Feb
4.41	Kayla	Smith	USA	6.5.97	12 Mar	4.40	Julia	Fixsen	USA	13.11.00	26 Feb
4.41	Sydney	Horn	USA-J	26.7.02	12 Mar	4.40		Chen Qiaoling	CHN	22.11.99	12 Mar
4.40	Yelizaveta	Bondarenko	RUS	1.7.99	27 Jan	4.40		Song Tingting	CHN	8.10.93	12 Mar
4.40	Stefanie	Berndorfer	GER	31.7.87	2 Feb	4.38	Miren	Bartolome	ESP	2.1.98	21 Feb

LONG JUMP

6.93	Tara	Davis	USA	20.5.99	1	NCAA	Fayetteville			12 Mar
6.92	Maryna	Bekh-Romanchuk	UKR	18.7.95	1	EI	Torun			6 Mar
6.91	Larissa	Iapichino	ITA-J	18.7.02	1	NC	Ancona			20 Feb
6.88	Malaika	Mihambo	GER	3.2.94	2	EI	Torun			6 Mar
6.82	Khaddi	Sagnia	SWE	20.4.94	1		Dortmund			7 Feb
6.82	Ruth	Usoro	NGR	8.10.97	1	Big 12	Lubbock			26 Feb
6.75	Monae'	Nichols	USA	.99	1		Lubbock			23 Jan
6.75	Ivana	Spanovic	SRB	10.5.90	1	Balk Ch	Istanbul			20 Feb
6.73	Anastasiya	Mironchik-Ivanova	BLR	13.4.89	1	NC	Mogilyov			13 Feb
6.70	Yelena	Sokolova	RUS	23.7.86	1	NC	Moskva			16 Feb
6.70	Claire	Bryant	USA	25.8.01	2	NCAA	Fayetteville			12 Mar
6.68	Agate	De Sousa	STP	5.6.00	1		Lisboa (Jamor)			10 Jan
6.68	Tyra	Gittens	TTO	6.6.98	3	NCAA	Fayetteville			12 Mar
6.66	Laura	Strati	ITA	3.10.90	1		Ancona			24 Jan
6.66	Aliyah	Whisby	USA	28.2.98	4	NCAA	Fayetteville			12 Mar
6.65	Deborah	Acquah	GHA	23.5.96	1		College Station			23 Jan
6.62	Fatima	Diame	ESP	22.9.96	Q	EI	Torun			5 Mar
6.60	Kendell	Williams	USA	14.6.95	1		Fayetteville			31 Jan
6.60	Nafissatou	Thiam	BEL	19.8.94	1P	EI	Torun			5 Mar
6.58	Hilary	Kpatcha	FRA	5.5.98	1		Aubière			16 Jan
6.57	Florentina	Iusco	ROU	8.4.96	Q	EI	Torun			5 Mar
6.55	María	Vicente	ESP	28.3.01	1		Valencia			14 Feb
6.55	Merle	Homeier	GER	27.8.99	2	NC	Dortmund			21 Feb
6.53	Maryse	Luzolo	GER	15.3.95	1P		Frankfurt-am-Main			13 Feb
6.53	Filippa	Fotopoulou	CYP	20.12.96	2	Balk Ch	Istanbul			20 Feb
6.53	Jogaile	Petrokaite	LTU	30.9.95	9q	EI	Torun			5 Mar
6.53	Alina	Rotaru-Kottmann	ROU	5.6.93	10q	EI	Torun			5 Mar
6.53		Tan Mengyi	CHN-J	5.9.02	1		Chengdu			12 Mar
6.52	Chanice	Porter	JAM	25.5.94	2		Fayetteville			31 Jan
6.50	Jazmin	Sawyers	GBR	21.5.94	24 Feb	6.47	Rougui	Sow	FRA	7.6.95	16 Jan
6.49	Taliyah	Brooks	USA	8.2.95	5 Feb	6.47	Annik	Kälin	SUI	27.4.00	7 Feb
6.49	Senni	Salminen	FIN	29.1.96	20 Feb	6.47	Noor	Vidts	BEL	30.5.96	5 Feb
6.48	Polina	Lukyanenkova	RUS	15.7.98	7 Feb	6.46	Yuliana	Angúlo	ECU	6.7.94	6 Feb
6.48	Diána	Lesti	HUN	30.3.98	14 Feb	6.46	Taika	Koilahti	FIN	4.12.98	7 Feb
6.48	Taishia	Pryce	JAM	14.7.97	12 Mar	6.46	Avery	Lewis	USA-Y	21.12.05	27 Feb

TRIPLE JUMP

14.60	Paraskeví	Papahrístou	GRE	17.4.89	1	WIT	Torun			17 Feb
14.54	Liadagmis	Povea	CUB	6.2.96	1		Karlsruhe			29 Jan
14.54	Thea	LaFond	DMA	5.4.94	1		Virginia Beach			6 Feb
14.53	Patrícia	Mamona	POR	21.11.88	1	EI	Torun			7 Mar
14.52	Ana	Peleteiro	ESP	2.12.95	2	EI	Torun			7 Mar
14.52	Neele	Eckhardt	GER	2.7.92	3	EI	Torun			7 Mar
14.39	Violetta	Skvortsova	BLR	15.4.98	2	WIT	Torun			17 Feb
14.36	Ruth	Usoro	NGR	8.10.97	1	Big 12	Lubbock			27 Feb
14.27	Deborah	Acquah	GHA	23.5.96	2	NCAA	Fayetteville			13 Mar
14.23	Kristiina	Mäkelä	FIN	20.11.92	6	EI	Torun			7 Mar
14.22	Tori	Franklin	USA	7.10.92	1	WIT	Madrid			24 Feb
14.22	Senni	Salminen	FIN	29.1.96	Q	EI	Torun			6 Mar
14.15	Ruta	Lasmane	LAT	17.12.00	3	NCAA	Fayetteville			13 Mar
14.09	Neja	Filipic	SLO	22.4.95	Q	EI	Torun			6 Mar
14.05	Darya	Nidbaykina	RUS	26.12.94	1		Moskva			7 Feb
14.05		Yang Yang	CHN	23.8.01	1		Chengdu			13 Mar
14.00	Rouguy	Diallo	FRA	5.2.95	1		Amiens			6 Feb
13.97	Tugba	Danismaz	TUR	1.9.99	1	Balk Ch	Istanbul			20 Feb
13.97	Jasmine	Moore	USA	1.5.01	1	SEC	Fayetteville			27 Feb
13.90	Mariya	Ovchinnikova	KAZ	19.10.98	1	NC	Ust-Kamenogorsk			19 Feb
13.90	Ottavia	Cestonaro	ITA	12.1.95	9q	EI	Torun			6 Mar
13.87	Florentina	Iusco	ROU	8.4.96	1		Bucuresti			22 Jan
13.84	Irina	Vaskovskaya	BLR	2.4.91	12 Feb	13.68	Diana	Ion	ROU	27.11.00	5 Feb
13.82	Dariya	Derkach	ITA	27.3.93	21 Feb	13.68	Diana	Zagainova	LTU	20.6.97	21 Feb
13.79	Jessie	Maduka	GER	23.4.96	29 Jan	13.67	Dovile	Kilty	LTU	14.7.93	30 Jan
13.77	Susana	Costa	POR	22.9.84	30 Jan	13.67	Maria	Purtsa	GER	18.8.95	20 Feb
13.77	Patricia	Sarrapio	ESP	16.11.82	20 Feb	13.67	Maja	Åskag	SWE-J	18.12.02	21 Feb
13.73	Jeanine	Assani Issouf	FRA	17.8.92	21 Feb	13.61	Anigbata	Chinonyelum	USA	16.9.98	5 Feb
13.73	Hanna	Minenko	ISR	25.9.89	6 Mar	13.61	Charisma	Taylor	BAH	3.9.99	13 Mar
13.72	Spiridoúla	Karidi	GRE	30.1.01	12 Feb	13.60	Chantoba	Bright	GUY	4.4.00	27 Feb
13.69	Olga	Rypakova	KAZ	30.11.84	30 Jan						

WORLD INDOOR LISTS 2021   431

SHOT

19.65		Auriol	Dongmo	POR	3.8.90	1		Karlsruhe	29 Jan
19.57		Raven	Saunders	USA	15.5.96	1		Fayetteville	21 Feb
19.54		Maggie	Ewen	USA	23.9.94	2		Fayetteville	21 Feb
19.50		Jessica	Ramsey	USA	26.7.91	3		Fayetteville	21 Feb
19.45			Gong Lijiao	CHN	24.1.89	1		Jinan	17 Mar
19.29		Fanny	Roos	SWE	2.1.95	2	EI	Torun	5 Mar
19.11		Christina	Schwanitz	GER	24.12.85	1		Chemnitz	24 Jan
18.86		Alyona	Dubitskaya	BLR	25.1.90	4	EI	Torun	5 Mar
18.69		Jessica	Schilder	NED	19.3.99	5	EI	Torun	5 Mar
18.66			Gao Yang	CHN	1.3.93	1		Chengdu	13 Mar
18.76		Sarah	Mitton	CAN	20.6.96	1		St. Catherine's	21 Mar
18.64		María Belén	Toimil	ESP	5.5.94	Q	EI	Torun	4 Mar
18.59		Danniel	Thomas-Dodd	JAM	11.11.92	1		Blacksburg	23 Jan
18.57		Klaudia	Kardasz	POL	2.5.96	1	NC	Torun	20 Feb
18.54		Sophie	McKinna	GBR	31.8.94	1		Loughborough	21 Feb
18.43		Sara	Gambetta	GER	18.2.93	Q	EI	Torun	4 Mar
18.41		Felisha	Johnson	USA	24.7.89	1		Indianapolis	20 Feb
18.34		Chase	Ealey	USA	20.7.94	4		Karlsruhe	29 Jan
18.26*		Alena	Pasechnik	BLR	17.4.95	1		Minsk	23 Dec
17.75						1		Minsk	16 Jan
18.25		Samantha	Noennig	USA	28.7.98	1		Lubbock	13 Feb
18.21		Khayla	Dawson	USA	18.3.98	1		Bloomington IN	6 Feb
18.18		Laulauga	Tausaga	USA	22.5.98	1		Iowa City	13 Feb
18.16		Markéta	Cervenková	CZE	20.8.91	Q	EI	Torun	4 Mar
18.13		Jessica	Inchude	GBS	25.3.96	2	POR Ch	Braga	13 Feb
18.13		Emel	Dereli	TUR	25.2.96	1	Balk Ch	Istanbul	20 Feb
18.12		Katharina	Maisch	GER	12.6.97	3		Chemnitz	24 Jan
18.12		Adelaide	Aquilla	USA	3.3.99	1	NCAA	Fayetteville	12 Mar
18.10		Sopo	Shatirishvili	GEO	15.1.95	1	NC	Tbilisi	19 Feb
18.09		Josephine	Schaefer	USA	10.4.99	1		Madison	16 Jan
18.06		Akealy	Moton	USA	26.11.98	1		Ames	13 Feb
17.94		Brittany	Crew	CAN	6.3.94	2		Toronto	13 Mar
17.81		Latavia	Maines	USA	.98	1	SEC	Fayetteville	27 Feb
17.76	Jorinde	van Klinken	NED	2.2.00	27 Feb	17.53	Portious	Warren	TTO	2.3.96	21 Feb
17.66	Shelby	Gunnells	USA	1.1.97	13 Feb	17.48	Zada	Swoopes	USA	.99	12 Mar
17.62	Alyona	Gordeyeva	RUS	24.4.97	7 Feb	17.41	Sara	Lennman	SWE	8.4.96	1 Mar
17.59		Jiang Yue	CHN	6.10.98	17 Mar	17.40	Chiara	Rosa	ITA	28.1.83	21 Feb
17.58	Haley	Teel	USA	20.6.96	30 Jan	17.39	Francislaine	Serra	POR	10.1.94	13 Feb

Discus: 59.70 Salla Sipponen FIN 13.3.95 1   Tampere 24 Feb

WEIGHT

24.93		Erin	Reese	USA	14.1.85	1		Terre Haute	13 Feb
24.04		DeAnna	Price	USA	8.6.93	1		Carbondale	5 Feb
23.50		Maddy	Nilles	USA	3.3.97	1		Grand Forks	30 Jan
23.42		Ida	Storm	SWE	11.10.91	1	NC	Malmö/A	20 Feb
23.40		Sade	Olatoye	NGR	25.1.97	1		Geneva	12 Feb
23.26		Makenli	Forrest	USA	2.12.99	1	NCAA	Fayetteville	11 Mar
23.24		Jasmine	Mitchell	USA	1.5.00	1	SEC	Fayetteville	25 Feb
23.24		Rachel	Tanczos	USA	27.9.99	2	NCAA	Fayetteville	11 Mar
23.04		Shey	Taiwo	USA	10.11.99	2	SEC	Fayetteville	25 Feb
22.89	Madi	Malone	USA	31.5.99	25 Feb	22.72	Shauniece	O'Neal	USA	5.8.99	26 Feb
22.77	Deenia	McMiller	USA	15.2.98	12 Feb	22.33	Lara	Boman	USA	16.2.96	16 Jan

PENTATHLON

4904	Nafissatou	Thiam		BEL	19.8.94	1	EI	Torun	5 Mar
	8.31	1.89	15.16	6.60	2:18.80				
4791	Noor	Vidts		BEL	30.5.96	2	EI	Torun	5 Mar
	8.27	1.83	13.83	6.47	2:12.59				
4746	Tyra	Gittens		TTO	6.6.98	1	NCAA	Fayetteville	11 Mar
	8.27	1.93	13.86	6.58	2:28.22				
4664	Xénia	Krizsán		HUN	13.1.93	3	EI	Torun	5 Mar
	8.27	1.77	14.48	6.10	2:12.49				
4614#	Annie	Kunz		USA	16.2.93	1		Seattle	26 Feb
	8.17	1.81	15.59	5.97	2:22.37				
4590	Anna	Hall		USA	23.3.01	1		Fayetteville	29 Jan
	8.48	1.86	12.26	5.99	2:08.19				
4587	Ivona	Dadic		AUT	29.12.93	4	EI	Torun	5 Mar
	8.38	1.77	13.67	6.30	2:15.41				
4557	Holly	Mills		GBR	15.4.00	1		Manchester	21 Feb
	8.22	1.73	14.03	6.02	2:12.07				
4532	Rita	Nemes		HUN	30.11.89	2	NC	Budapest	14 Feb
	8.50	1.73	13.41	6.29	2:12.48				

4514	Nadine	Broersen	NED	29.4.90	1		Apeldoorn		14 Feb
	8.46	1.82	14.35	6.02	2:20.86				
4507	Annik	Kälin	SUI	27.4.00	1	SUI Ch	Magglingen		7 Feb
	8.14	1.75	13.14	6.47	2:24.80				
4501	María	Vicente	ESP	28.3.01	1	NC	Madrid		19 Feb
	8.25	1.75	12.25	6.49	2:19.51				
4484	Paulina	Ligarska	POL	9.4.96	7	EI	Torun		5 Mar
	8.67	1.80	13.59	6.14	2:16.88				
4471	Henriette	Jæger	NOR-J	30.6.03	1	NC	Bærum		21 Feb
	8.39	1.76	12.44	6.02	2:10.60				
4461	Odile	Ahouanwanou	BEN	5.1.91	2		Aubière		24 Jan
	8.30	1.73	15.10	6.09	2:24.42				
4442	Adrianna	Sułek	POL	3.4.99	1		Tallinn		7 Feb
	8.51	1.83	12.35	6.04	2:16.97				
4434	Hanna	Kasyanova	UKR	24.4.83	1	NC	Sumy		11 Feb
	8.33	1.74	13.88	6.00	2:18.82				
4434	Célia	Perron	FRA	18.4.97	1	NC	Miramas		19 Feb
	8.36	1.78	11.77	5.99	2:11.65				
4415	Vanessa	Grimm	GER	22.4.97	1		Frankfurt-am-Main		13 Feb
	8.61	1.74	14.75	6.19	2:24.20				
4412	Alina	Shukh	UKR	12.2.99	2	NC	Sumy		11 Feb
	9.01	1.83	14.28	5.94	2:18.53				
4393	Anastasiya	Mokhnyuk	UKR	1.1.91	2		Tallinn		7 Feb
	8.23	1.74	13.78	6.09	2:24.98				
4380	Diane	Marie-Hardy	FRA	19.2.96	2	NC	Miramas		19 Feb
	8.57	1.69	13.77	5.96	2:13.09				
4361	Claudia	Conte	ESP	14.11.99	2	NC	Madrid		19 Feb
	8.63	1.81	11.86	6.02	2:16.41				
4344	Erin	Marsh	USA	12.7.99	3	NCAA	Fayetteville		11 Mar
	8.13	1.72	11.95	6.00	2:17.53				
4337	Anaelle	Nyabeu Djapa	FRA	15.9.92	3	NC	Miramas		19 Feb
	8.35	1.69	13.71	5.95	2:19.07				
4325	Aleksandra	Butvina	RUS	14.2.86	18 Feb	4258	Yuliya	Loban	UKR	7.8.00	11 Feb
4301	Solène	Ndama	FRA	23.9.98	24 Jan	4244	Yana	Maksimova	BLR	9.1.89	27 Jan
4296	Jadin	O'Brien	USA-J	8.5.02	11 Mar	4238	Dorota	Skrivanová	CZE	26.11.98	13 Feb
4262	Jade	O'Dowda	GBR	9.9.99	21 Feb	4232	Melissa	de Haan	NED	15.8.97	14 Feb
4259	Caroline	Agnou	SUI	26.5.96	7 Feb	4230	Lauren	Taubert	USA	20.3.98	29 Jan

3000 METRES WALK

12:14.95	Brigita	Virbalyte-Dimsiene	LTU	1.2.85	1	NC	Klaipeda	20 Feb
12:21.43	Antigóni	Drisbióti	GRE	21.3.84	1		Pireás	12 Feb
12:30.25	Hristína	Papadopoúlou	GRE	5.9.96	2		Pireás	12 Feb

5000 METRES WALK

and see 2020 lists for marks at Saransk 27 Dec 2020

20:59.1	Lyudmyla	Olyanovska	UKR	20.2.93	1		Kyiv	9 Jan
21:00.97	Ayse	Tekdal	TUR	28.10.99	1		Istanbul	17 Jan
21:05.56	Meryem	Bekmez	TUR	31.7.00	2		Istanbul	17 Jan

4 X 400 METRES – MEN

3:03.16	North Carolina A&T (USA)		1	NCAA	Fayetteville 13 Mar
	Ross 45.68, Stokes 46.04, E Young 46.78, T Stewart 44.67				
3:03.61	Un. Kentucky		2	NCAA	Fayetteville 13 Mar
	J Smith 46.79, Lang 44.93, K Williams 46.61, St. Hilaire TTO 45.28				
3:04.08	Un. Tennessee		1	SEC	Fayetteville 27 Feb
	S Cooper 47.72, C Bailey JAM 44.79, Bynum 45.79, Sacoor BEL 45.80				
Nations					
3:06.06	NED	Dobber 46.68, Bonevacia 46.64, Angela 46.49, van Diepen 46.25	1	EI	Torun 7 Mar
3:06.54	CZE	Müller 47.08, Maslák 46.24, Desensky 46.93, Sorm 46.29	2	EI	Torun 7 Mar
3:06.70	GBR	Brier 47.43, O Smith 47.05 J Williams 46.09, Thompson 46.13	3	EI	Torun 7 Mar
3:06.96	BEL	Doom 47.45, J Borlée 47.44, D Borlée 46.38, K Borlée 45.69	4	EI	Torun 7 Mar
3:07.37	ITA	Scotti 47.05, Grant 47.73, Lopez 46.53, Aceti 46.06	5	EI	Torun 7 Mar

4 X 400 METRES – WOMEN

3:26.27	Texas A&M (USA/JAM)		1		Fayetteville 13 Feb
	J Martin 53.04, C Young JAM 51.86, S Richardson 51.12, Mu 50.27				
3:27.15	NED	Klaver 51.67, Dopheide 53.18, L de Witte 51.31, Bol 49.99	1	EI	Torun 7 Mar
3:27.91	USC	Lear 52.75, Ford 51.92, Yweargin GBR 52.08, K Roberts 51.16	2	NCAA	Fayetteville 13 Mar
3:28.07	Un. Arkansas (USA/VIN)		3	NCAA	Fayetteville 13 Mar
	Peoples 52.83, Burks Magee 52.17, T Wilson 52.24, Maloney VIN 50.83				
3:28.20	GBR	Clark 51.83, J Williams 52.17, Pipi 52.62, Knight 51.58	2	EI	Torun 7 Mar
3:29.94	POL		3	EI	Torun 7 Mar
	Kaczmarek 52.55, Holub-Kowalik 51.45, Lesiewicz 53.35, Gaworska 52.59				
3:30.32	ITA	Borga 53.54, Mangione 52.01, Marchiando 52.55, Coiro 52.22	4	EI	Torun 7 Mar
3:30.38	UKR	Tkachuk 53.41, Bryzhina 52.58, Klymyuk 52.40, Ryzhykova 51.99	5	EI	Torun 7 Mar